1 MONTH OF
FREE
READING

at

www.ForgottenBooks.com

By purchasing this book you are eligible for one month membership to ForgottenBooks.com, giving you unlimited access to our entire collection of over 1,000,000 titles via our web site and mobile apps.

To claim your free month visit:
www.forgottenbooks.com/free925882

ISBN 978-0-260-07192-7
PIBN 10925882

Y 4. J 59/2: H 34/pt. 2

COMPETITION IN THE HEALTH SERVICES MARKET

HEARINGS

BEFORE THE

SUBCOMMITTEE ON ANTITRUST AND MONOPOLY

OF THE

COMMITTEE ON THE JUDICIARY

UNITED STATES SENATE

NINETY-THIRD CONGRESS

SECOND SESSION

Part 2

MAY 17, 1974

Printed for the use of the Committee on the Judiciary

(Pursuant to S. Res. 255, sec. 4)

COMPETITION IN THE HEALTH SERVICES MARKET

HEARINGS

BEFORE THE

SUBCOMMITTEE ON ANTITRUST AND MONOPOLY

OF THE

COMMITTEE ON THE JUDICIARY UNITED STATES SENATE

NINETY-THIRD CONGRESS

SECOND SESSION

Part 2

MAY 17, 1974

Printed for the use of the Committee on the Judiciary

(Pursuant to S. Res. 255, sec. 4)

U.S. GOVERNMENT PRINTING OFFICE

35–554 O WASHINGTON : 1974

For sale by the Superintendent of Documents, U.S. Government Printing Office
Washington, D.C. 20402 - Price $6.45
Stock Number 5270–02602

(II)

CONTENTS

MATERIAL RECEIVED FOR THE RECORD

Bernal, Joe, former State senator, executive director, Commission for Mexican-American Affairs, San Antonio, Tex.; Jackee Cox, consumer advocate writer on health care matters, Austin, Tex.; Dr. Walter Faggett, chairman of the board, Bexar County Anemia Association, Inc., San Antonio, Tex.; Mickey Leland, State representative, Houston, Tex.; Michael Mendelson, attorney, Mexican-American Legal Defense and Educational Fund; and Dr. F. Carter Pannill, vice president, health sciences, University of New York, Buffalo, N.Y., former dean, University of Texas Medical School, San Antonio, Tex.; material relating to the testimony of:

APPENDIX

COMPETITION IN THE HEALTH SERVICES MARKET

FRIDAY, MAY 17, 1974

U.S. Senate,
Subcommittee on Antitrust and Monopoly
of the Committee on the Judiciary,
Washington, D.C.

The subcommittee met at 9:30 a.m., in room 4200, Dirksen Office Building, Senator Philip A. Hart (chairman of the subcommittee) presiding.

Present: Senator Hart and Senator Hruska.

Staff present: Howard E. O'Leary, Jr., chief counsel; Dean E. Sharp, assistant counsel; Patricia Y. Bario, editorial director; Janice Williams, chief clerk; Peter N. Chumbris, minority chief counsel; and Michael Granfield, minority economist.

Also present: Philip Caper, M.D., staff member, Subcommittee on Health, Senate Committee on Labor and Public Welfare.

Senator Hart. The subcommittee will be in order.

In welcoming our first witness, I should note for the record that Senator Hruska is involved in other committee assignments and has asked us to proceed.

We will soon be joined by Mr. Chumbris, in his stead.

The first witness is Dr. Daniel S. Blumenthal. Doctor, we will provide for the record a biographical summary so those following this hearing will know the basis on which to evaluate this testimony.

[The biography referred to appears as exhibit 1 at the end of Dr. Blumenthal's oral testimony.]

STATEMENT OF DANIEL S. BLUMENTHAL, M.D., FORMER VISTA VOLUNTEER, ATLANTA, GA.

Dr. Blumenthal. Thank you, Senator.

I appreciate very much the opportunity to be here today. My name is Daniel S. Blumenthal. I am a doctor of medicine, and I am currently a commissioned officer in the U.S. Public Health Service.

However, I would like to emphasize that I am not representing the Public Health Service in my appearance here, and my remarks do not reflect any position or opinion of the U.S. Public Health Service.

I am on annual leave today and am not appearing in any official capacity as a commissioned officer.

I have three episodes to relate in which I was involved either personally or in a consultant capacity, and I have documentation of these episodes, which I would like to offer into the record.

Senator HART. We will receive them.

[See exhibits 2–4 at the end of Dr. Blumenthal's oral testimony.]

Dr. BLUMENTHAL. All three, I believe, illustrate ways in which groups of physicians—particularly medical societies—can act in concert to prevent the development of new and innovative modes of health care delivery, especially as these arise to serve the poor.

The first incident concerns my personal experiences as a VISTA volunteer physician in Lee County, Ark. in 1969–70.

Lee County was—and still is—one of the poorest counties in the country. Seventy-two percent of the population had incomes below the poverty level, and about one-third of the population had yearly incomes of less than $1,000; 83 percent of the housing was substandard or without plumbing. About 60 percent of the county's residents were black.

When I arrived in 1969, there were four doctors in Lee County to serve a population of 20,000 persons. Two of these doctors were over 65 years old. All were dedicated and hard working, yet were unable by themselves to provide adequate health care for the county's population, particularly the poor.

This is reflected in the infant mortality rates in Lee County for that year. For the poor, there were 57 infant deaths per 1,000 live births; for those above poverty level, there were 35 per 1,000; for the Nation as a whole, the infant mortality rate was 22 per 1,000.

The poverty community, with the assistance of the six VISTA volunteers who were assigned to Lee County at that time, organized around the issue of health care and was able to obtain a small grant from OEO to establish a community-controlled clinic, which was known as the Lee County Cooperative Clinic.

I served as the physician in that clinic. However, my efforts at delivering medical care were greatly hampered by the county medical society, which was composed of the four local doctors.

The major action by the medical society in this regard was to refuse me membership in that society. Since medical society membership was a prerequisite to obtaining staff privileges at the county's only hospital, the result of the society's action was to deny me access to the hospital.

This action was reaffirmed when the members of the society, acting, in their role as hospital staff, voted expressly not to recommend me for admitting privileges at the hospital.

The medical society made it clear that its objections were not to me, personally, nor to my capabilities as a physician. Rather, I was denied medical society membership and hospital staff privileges because I represented an alternative mode of health care delivery. I was providing free care to poor people; I was part of a Federal Government program; I was not in private practice.

This was expressly stated by the president of the county medical society in an interview with the local paper.

He said:

The private physicians in Marianna [the Lee County seat] have no argument with Dr. Blumenthal as an individual doctor.

We do object to a group [VISTA] financed by the Federal Government coming into the community and, in effect, practicing medicine as a group.

We have, on several occasions, told Dr. Blumenthal that we would welcome him into the community and the local medical society if he would leave the VISTA program and function as a private physician.

It became necessary to sue the Lee Memorial Hospital to gain hospital privileges for physicians working at the Lee County Cooperative Clinic.

The case was settled out of court in the summer of 1971, a year after I had left the county; the settlement provides that clinic physicians shall have hospital privileges.

All roadblocks erected by the county medical society have not been removed, however. Under pressure from the society, the National Health Service Corps has agreed not to assign a physician to the clinic, although the hospital has been approved as a National Health Services Corps site.

The Corps a year ago specifically refused to assign me to Lee County for fear of antagonizing the local physicians.

Nonetheless, the clinic has continued to grow, and today offers a greatly expanded program of medical, dental, and environmental services to the people of Lee County.

Moreover, control of the clinic has remained in the hands of the people it serves through an elected board of directors.

The second episode I have to relate concerns a seasonal farmworker population in rural Louisiana. Again, these people are poor and black, and many live in substandard houses which lack plumbing.

Again, they have not in the past received adequate health care. Screening examinations on 107 of these farmworkers in March 1971 revealed the following: Of 37 adults, 29 were found to be in need of immediate medical care; only 12 were under the care of a doctor.

Only 16 of the 70 children were completely healthy; of 30 examined for worms, 28 were found to be infected with roundworm, whipworm, or both.

It must be pointed out that this did not represent a random sample of the population; nonetheless, it gives some indication of the outstanding health care needs in the area.

In 1971 I served as a consultant—and I would like to say that I was only a consultant and was not intimately involved in this project— to a community oriented group which was attempting to obtain funding for a clinic to serve this population. The parish—that is, county—medical society opposed the establishment of this clinic; because of this the clinic was also opposed by the area health planning council.

Despite this opposition the clinic was awarded a grant by the Department of Health, Education, and Welfare. The parish medical society, however, refused to give the approval required to enable the clinic to be authorized as a National Health Service Corps site.

Hence, the clinic was unable to obtain a National Health Service Corps physician. Now, 3 years later, the clinic still does not have a full-time doctor.

A truce with the local medical society has been established, however, and prospects for obtaining such a doctor have improved greatly.

It does appear that one of the local doctors is going to become a full-time clinic physician at that clinic.

Senator HART. What is available, given the recital of opposition of the four local physicians in that first clinic you described? You say the clinic continued to grow. I am talking about the one——

Dr. BLUMENTHAL. In Lee County, Ark?

Senator HART. Yes.

Dr. BLUMENTHAL. The first year of that clinic, or the first 6 months that that clinic was in existence, I served as the physician. I then recruited another physician who followed me to that clinic. His name was Ralph Wolf, and he served also as a VISTA volunteer physician for a year.

He recruited two physicians to follow him, one of whom was a VISTA volunteer. One of them served 1 year and the other 2 years.

There are currently four physicians serving at that clinic. It has a substantial grant from Health, Education, and Welfare, and approximately 60 employees that are doing a number of, I think, very important things in the county.

The third incident concerns the Black Belt Family Health Center in Epes, Ala. This clinic has never become operational. It was awarded a planning grant through the Federation of Southern Cooperatives by the HEW family health center program for fiscal year 1972-73.

The clinic would have provided medical care for poor and near poor persons—mostly black—living in Sumter County and parts of Pickens, Greene, Marengo, and Choctaw Counties.

I was asked to serve on the technical advisory council for this clinic. The population which was to be served by this clinic lives in environmental circumstances similar to those described in the previous two episodes, and health care is for these people equally difficult to obtain.

Sumter County, where the clinic would have been located, has five physicians to serve its 17,000 citizens; the average age of these physicians is approximately 59.

My conversations last year with two of these physicians and with the hospital administrator confirmed that there was a felt need on their part for additional physician manpower in the county.

Nonetheless, in February 1973 the Medical Association of the State of Alabama, at the urging of some of the physicians in Sumter County, expressed public opposition to the continued funding of the Black Belt Family Health Center and asked Alabama's Representatives in Congress to seek revocation of the center's grant.

When the center's planning grant expired in June 1973, HEW refused to provide operating funds and the clinic has not been able to open its doors.

One of the reasons cited by HEW in its rejection of the clinic's request was the failure of the program to gain the cooperation of the State and county medical societies. In the documentation I have offered, the letters from HEW refer to these as "organized provider groups," or words to that effect, which indicate medical societies.

The clinic is currently struggling to develop a program without Federal money.

A common theme runs through all three of these cases. In each instance community groups in rural poverty areas have attempted to improve their own health care and have been opposed by the local and/or State medical societies.

In each instance the proposed facility was controlled by a group other than doctors; each was offering free or low-cost medical care to the poor; each was set up to provide care outside of the traditional fee-for-service, private practice mechanism; and Government funds were involved.

In each case the medical society was acting to preserve the delivery system as it existed despite the fact that the existing system had failed to provide adequate care to the local population.

In no case was it alleged that additional health services were not needed in the area in question; yet inadequate services were considered by the doctors to be preferable to allowing an alternative delivery mechanism provide additional health care.

I would submit that these are not isolated incidents; in fact, similar episodes have occurred elsewhere in the country.

These incidents in many ways represent microcosms of the national health care picture. On the national scene, organized medicine has staunchly defended the traditional and existing mechanisms of health care delivery, regardless of their performance.

The American Medical Association and its component State and local societies represent a great deal of power in influencing the ways in which health care is delivered in this country.

Unfortunately, this power has not always been used to promote the best interests of the consumer of medical care, particularly if that consumer is poor, or black, or brown.

In the absence of a countervailing power protecting the interests of these consumers, it would appear to fall to Government to assume this function.

At best, however, the performance of the Government in this role could be said to be spotty; at times, the Government and the physician organizations appear to be working together to the detriment of the consumer.

I would like to examine the overall situation briefly from the point of view of the poverty-level consumer of health care.

A patient who cannot afford to purchase private medical care is usually faced with what might be viewed as a monopoly situation.

Unlike the private patient, who may at least change doctors if he is dissatisfied with his care, the poor person can turn only to whichever institution within the public sector is responsible for providing the particular health service he is seeking.

The public hospital, the city or county health department, the public family planning clinic, and other local or State governmental institutions all provide different health care services for the "medically indigent."

In the interest of economy there is usually no "duplication of services." The patient often has no choice of physician, and may see a different physician at each visit. Services may be highly fragmented.

Since the poverty-level consumer of health care has no choice of providers, but is locked in to a group of public institutions, it would seem imperative that he have a voice in the way these institutions are run.

Unfortunately this is not usually the case. Public health-care facilities are governed by health departments and by city or county hospital boards, and the consumer is generally without representation.

Because this mode of health care delivery essentially represents charity medicine provided by State and local governments, and because it is a noncompetitive situation, care and facilities for indigent patients often do not measure up to that provided by the private sector.

This has resulted in what is often known as a two-class system of health-care delivery: One class for paying patients, another class for the poor.

Health centers such as the three I have described represent one alternative to this situation. Although they are intended to provide care primarily for poor people, they differ from most public health care institutions in that they are community controlled, or provide for a substantial consumer voice in their operation.

This is one of the most important ways in which they differ from most institutions providing health care for the poor.

They differ, too, in the comprehensiveness of their services and the way in which they deliver these services.

It is precisely because these clinics offer an alternative mode of health care delivery that they have been opposed by the medical societies. It is unfortunate that, despite the clear need for alternatives such as these, organized medicine has often been successful in hampering their operations or in preventing their existence completely.

The Nation is beginning to face the fact that millions of its citizens who live in poverty, particularly in rural areas, are the recipients of inadequate health care.

Even for the middle-class patient, the health care situation is far from ideal. It is clear that alternatives are going to have to be developed. I can only hope that these alternatives will be developed despite the resistance of organized medicine.

Thank you.

Senator HART. Thank you, Doctor, for testimony which, though brief, is explicit and graphic, based on those three experiences of yours.

What was the civil action which was brought, to open things up in Lee County, Ark?

Dr. BLUMENTHAL. The relevant papers have been filed, including the complaint and the answer and the settlement.

Senator HART. Do you know specifically whether it was an antitrust action?

Dr. BLUMENTHAL. It was a class-action suit filed on behalf of the VISTA physicians and other qualified physicians working at the Lee County Cooperative Clinic, and on behalf of the class of patients at the Lee County Cooperative Clinic, represented by four patients who had had problems as a result of my inability to use the hospital.

It was filed also on behalf of the clinic. I'm not sure how that meshes with the other——

Senator HART. I guess we will look at the pleadings and see what the basis was. Were the four physicians in practice in Lee County named as the defendants?

Dr. BLUMENTHAL. The defendants were actually the hospital board of directors. The way the requirements were set up was that a physician applying for hospital staff membership had to first receive the recommendation of the hospital staff.

The hospital staff, of course, was one and the same as the medical society. One of the requirements for membership on the hospital staff was membership in the medical society.

The board of governors, though, legally had the right to affirm or deny hospital staff membership. The medical staff, according to the letter of the law, must abide by their ruling.

In fact, the board of directors did exactly what the medical staff requested them to do. It adhered exactly to the medical staff recommendations, so that the hospital board of directors was the defendant in the suit.

The suit, I think, was based on the 14th amendment rights of due process and the first amendment rights of association. It was eventually settled out of court, after it had strung on for about a year, and the settlement does provide that clinic physicians shall have the right to use the hospital.

It was not an ideal settlement from my point of view in that it really specifies only clinic physicians, and I think it should have specified any qualified physician who wishes to use the hospital, whether he is on the clinic staff or not.

Senator HART. We would all agree that there should be an assurance to the user of a hospital that the professionals who treat them are qualified. You are suggesting in that answer that anyone who passes the State board should be——

Dr. BLUMENTHAL. Right. I think that the State board of medical examiners is the body that legally establishes assurance that physicians practicing in the State are competent.

And, as I said, the reason that I was rejected for membership was not any allegation that I was incompetent. It referred to the way I was practicing medicine; the way I was delivering health care.

Senator HART. In your testimony you acknowledged that the four physicians in practice in Lee County themselves were dedicated and hard working. I take it the conclusion is that the whole argument is over whether a different system of delivery should be permitted or not permitted?

Dr. BLUMENTHAL. Right. They were certainly hard working physicians. I think any solo general practitioner in a rural area is bound to find himself working hard, and these four physicians certainly did.

One of these doctors was 85 years old and still getting up in the middle of the night to deliver babies and really providing the model of an old country doctor. But they felt very strongly that the only proper way to practice medicine was private practice, preferably solo practice, and felt that they needed to do whatever they could to prevent Government programs providing free medical care, utilizing para-professionals, doing the various unusual things—unusual in their eyes—that we were doing which needed to be opposed, and they opposed them.

Senator HART. I was struck by the fact that you say that the National Health Service Corps still hasn't assigned a physician to this clinic.

Do you know whether local medical societies have the power under the law to keep the physician from being assigned to a clinic?

Dr. BLUMENTHAL. Under the original law, the local medical society had to sign off before a physician could be assigned to the county.

That law has now been changed, I believe, to give the Director of the National Health Service Corps the power to override the local medical society if he desires to do so.

I don't know if that power has ever been used or how frequently it has been used. I know that this clinic in Lee County is one clinic which is unable to obtain a National Health Service Corps physician because of that requirement. Although there is an approved site in the county: The hospital was approved as a National Health Service Corps sponsor, and I believe that they are going to be getting a physician through the program.

The clinic in Louisiana is another one which has not received a physician, and I don't believe they have reapplied since the law was changed; I'm not sure about that. But at any rate, one of the reasons they do not have a physician today is because of that law.

There are other clinics I know of which have had this problem. There is a clinic in Lexington, Miss. which has been unable to obtain a National Health Service Corps physician because of the requirement that the medical society sign off first.

Senator HART. As I understand it, the Congress has indicated that while it would ask the National Health Service Corps to consult the local medical society, it was intended to eliminate any veto by a local medical society.

Dr. BLUMENTHAL. Well, as I said, as I understand the law the medical society has the power to veto. The Director of the National Health Service Corps has the power to override that veto if he wishes.

In practice, certainly, if the Corps wants to assign a physician to a particular area it tries to reach some kind of an understanding with the medical society. I don't know if, when it fails to reach such an understanding, the Director of the National Health Service Corps ever has used his power to override the veto. I don't know the answer to that.

Senator HART. I am sure we will attempt to determine whether in fact the local societies have ever been overridden by the Director.

In the case of that Black Belt Family Health Center, are we to understand that the HEW grant is discontinued as a result of the State medical society's opposition, not from the local society.

Dr. BLUMENTHAL. The formal opposition came from the State medical society; that is correct.

Senator HART. But their reason for opposition?

Dr. BLUMENTHAL. Many of the local doctors asked the State medical society—the Medical Association of the State of Alabama—to intercede with their Congressional Representatives and ask that this grant be revoked or at least not renewed.

The reasons expressed by the local medical society are included in some of the documentation that I have submitted.

If I can locate that, I think at least some of that would be worth repeating out loud here, because I think it is very revealing. I wish I had it right on top.

I have a copy of the minutes of the Sumter County Board of Censors, which is the county medical society in Alabama, and they express several reasons for which they are opposed to it. They think that the clinic should be located next to the hospital rather than away from the hospital.

They feel that the clinic should locate a medical director who would also practice private medicine as well as participating in the activities of the Black Belt Family Health Center.

And one of the reasons which they state is:

> The Sumter County Board of Directors is opposed to this and any scheme which offers a threat to the free choice of a physician and other providers of health delivery and care which are, after all, threats to free enterprise.

And I think that this pretty much summarizes their viewpoint. They are afraid that this is an encroachment on the free enterprise system of practicing medicine, the way that they have traditionally practiced medicine, and for that reason are opposed to it.

The reasons cited for opposing the clinic involve a number of financial things, things relating to the location of the clinic, to the way in which they practice medicine, and so on, but I think that this is the crux of the matter; the fact that it is a different mode of health care delivery.

It is something that they see as a threat to free enterprise.

The Alabama State Medical Society said publicly that it was a waste of tax money, or a generality to that effect.

I am not sure if that answers the question adequately.

[For further information on the above subject see exhibit 4 at the end of Dr. Blumenthal's oral testimony.]

Senator HART. I think it gives us an understanding of the difference in philosophy that the organized societies have and the philosophy that you have.

One can add in whatever he wants as to the economics and self-interests points of view.

Mr. Sharp?

Mr. SHARP. No questions.

Senator HART. Mr. Chumbris?

Mr. CHUMBRIS. Thank you, Mr. Chairman.

I have no specific questions on the paper. I was wondering if in the States where you have participated in your program, how much of the health care costs were taken care of by the welfare laws of the State.

For example, wasn't it the District of Columbia where the welfare pays $38 for the welfare patient for the hospital use? Do you have a similar situation in those States?

Dr. BLUMENTHAL. I couldn't give you the exact concurrent figures, and I'm not sure whether your question refers to the percentage of the people that are covered under welfare or the——

Mr. CHUMBRIS. How many of the poor people in the States that you are familiar with get hospital care and the State will pay a certain amount. In the District of Columbia they pay $38 for the welfare patient.

Dr. BLUMENTHAL. In Lee County, where approximately 70 percent of the people were below the poverty level, something on the order of 16 percent of the people were on welfare.

The only people that were covered by medicaid were people who were on welfare. Medicaid at that time, or welfare, would pay for 12 outpatient doctor visits a year—1 a month—although they could be used at any time.

I am not sure what fraction of hospitalization or laboratory studies would be paid for by medicaid. I do know from my experience not only in these three clinics, but from my experience working at a public hospital in New Orleans, La., and from observing the situation in different places throughout the country, that medicaid has had a not very large impact on the way that people receive medical care in this country.

At Charity Hospital in New Orleans the impact of medicaid simply has been to allow the public hospital to gain a large part of its financing through the Federal Government rather than from the State government, as it previously did. People who cannot afford private care still come to the public hospital. They still go to the parish health unit for their family planning information or for their immunizations.

If medicaid was intended to enable poor people to obtain private medical care I think it has by and large failed.

Certainly in my experience poor people are still getting medical care the same way they have always gotten medical care.

Mr. CHUMBRIS. Thank you very much.

Senator HART. You mentioned the suggestion made by the Alabama State Medical Society that the delivery system that the clinic would provide was harmful to free enterprise. I am reminded of the first public employment that I ever had, as commissioner of corporations in the State of Michigan.

Under our law, that office, the commission passed upon issues of licenses to engage in real estate, brokerage and sales, and I would often go to meetings of a county real estate board or State real estate board and frequently the principal speaker was inveighing against the State intrusion private enterprise.

And, as I would leave—this happened more than once—the president of the local real estate board or the director of the State association of realities, after thanking me for coming, would express regret that I was issuing so many licenses. It seemed they always listened to the speaker and applauded him; they never noted the inconsistency, and I never argued with them.

But I have never forgotten the way that operated; the economic interest got hung up.

For Senator Kennedy, Dr. Caper?

Dr. CAPER. I have no questions.

Senator HART. Doctor, thank you very much.

Dr. BLUMENTHAL. Thank you very much.

[The following was received for the record. Testimony resumes on p. 999.]

MATERIAL RELATING TO THE TESTIMONY OF DR. DANIEL S. BLUMENTHAL

Exhibit 1.—*Curriculum Vitae of Dr. Blumenthal*

CURRICULUM VITAE OF DANIEL SENDER BLUMENTHAL

Date and place of birth: May 26, 1942, St. Louis, Mo.

Education: Oberlin College, B.S., 1964 (Cum Laude with high honors in biology); Major: biology. University of Chicago, M.D., 1968.

Professional experience: Epidemic Intelligence Service, U.S. Public Health Service; assigned as medical epidemiologist, Parasitic Diseases Branch, Center for Disease Control, Atlanta, Ga. Major duties involve epidemiologic investigations of parasitic diseases in the United States. 7/73–present.

Visiting instructor in pediatrics, Emory University, Atlanta, Georgia. 11/72–present.

Epidemic Intelligence Service, U.S. Public Health Service; assigned as medical officer, Nutrition Program, Center for Disease Control, Atlanta, Ga. Major duties included participation in the design and implementation of nutrition surveys among low-income groups in various areas of the U.S. 7/72–7/73.

Resident in Pediatrics, Charity Hospital of Louisiana, Tulane Division, New Orleans, La. 7/70–6/72.

VISTA (Volunteers in Service to America) volunteer, Marianna, Arkansas. Was instrumental in planning and establishing the Lee County Cooperative Clinic. Participated in community organizing, served as medical director of the clinic, and engaged in general practice. 7/69–6/70.

Intern (rotating), Charity Hospital of Louisiana, Tulane Division, New Orleans, La. 7/68–6/69.

Student Health Project, Chicago, Illinois. Activities included community organizing and a survey of health-care facilities and needs of a ghetto community. Was instrumental in establishing the Community Health Center of Englewood, Chicago's first free clinic. 6/67–8/67.

Louisiana State University Fellow in Tropical Medicine, Gorgas Memorial Laboratory, Panama City, Panama. Participated in laboratory and field studies of endemic tropical diseases. 10/66–12/66.

Licensure and certification: Georgia, medical license, 1972-present; Louisiana, medical license, 1970-present; Arkansas, medical license, 1969-present; National Board of Medical Examiners diplomate, 1969; American Board of Pediatrics, board qualified, 1972.

Honors and professional organizations: Sigma Xi, American Public Health Association (Secretary, Medical Care Section, Southern Branch, 1970–71; Vice-Chairman, 1971–72); Outstanding Intern, Charity Hospital, 1968–69; Board of Directors, New Orleans Sickle Cell Anemia Foundation, 1971–72; Medical Committee for Human Rights; Chairman, New Orleans Chapter, 1970–72.

Publications: Mohammed M. Sayeed, Daniel S. Blumenthal, and Herman T. Blumenthal: Effect of Cortisone and Growth Hormones on Cellular Proliferation During Early Embryogenesis. Proceedings of the Society for Experimental Biology and Medicine, 109: 261-264, 1962.

Daniel S. Blumenthal, Aline W. Berns, and Herman T. Blumenthal: Anti-Insulin Serum Effects on Islets of Langerhans of Chick Embryo. Archives of Pathology, 77: 107-112, 1964.

Daniel S. Blumenthal: Lead Ingestion in New Orleans Children. Southern Medical Journal, 64: 364-365, 1971.

———

Exhibit 2.—*Material Submitted Re Lee County (Ark.) Medical Society Refusal of Membership to Dr. Blumenthal*

[Marianna Courier-Index, Nov. 20, 1969]

MEDICAL SOCIETY REFUSES MEMBERSHIP TO VISTA DOCTOR

Dr. Blumenthal, VISTA doctor working in Lee County, has been denied membership in the Lee County Medical Society.

The denial does not affect Dr. Blumenthall's ability to function as a physician however it does deny him the right to use the facilities at Lee Memorial Hospital. It also prevents his membership in the Arkansas Medical Society.

Dr. Blumenthall's application for membership in the local society was rejected by a vote of three to one by the four member physicians.

"I will continue to carry on the medical work as best I can under the circumstance," Dr. Blumenthall said today. "We are still working on facilities for a clinic and hopefully will receive federal funds to finance the clinic. However, patients that need hospital care and facilities will have to be sent to Little Rock or Memphis."

"The private physicians in Marianna have no argument with Dr. Blumenthall as an individual doctor," Dr. Dwight Gray, president of the Medical society said. "We do object to a group (VISTA) financed by the federal government coming into the community and, in effect, practicing medicine as a group.

"We have, on several occasions, told Dr. Blumenthall that we would welcome him into the community and the local medical society if he would leave the VISTA program and function as a private physician.

"The local private physicians a have been giving their services and utilizing the charity hospitals of Memphis and Little Rock throughout their practice of medicine. We believe that we understand the problems of this community and that continued progress can be made best without a federally controlled agency such as VISTA dominating a program.

The present physicians recognize the dire need for additional doctors in our community and we would welcome Dr. Blumenthall into our ranks on that basis."

The story was picked up by two state papers and given widespread publicity. Both Dr. Gray and Dr. Blumenthall expressed the opinion today that the story had been blown out of all proportion to its importance by the state papers.

The VISTA doctor, categorically denied that he is here to "stir up trouble" and agitate racial differences.

"Nothing could be further from the truth," the doctor said. "I just can't imagine where they got some of the statements and actions attributed to me."

Hon. JOHN L. McCLELLAN,
U. S. Senate,
Washington, D.C.

SIR: In behalf of the local Physicians, Pharmacists, and many concerned taxpayers of Lee County, we would like to enlighten you, as our Senator, as to some of the happenings in our county due to the government's Vista program.

We have been invaded by a group called "Vista", which is composed of seven workers, of which one is a Medical Doctor. We will make no statement against this group without evidence to confirm our grievances.

One newspaper published an article which states that this *group has attended the Negro churches, urging them to fight for what is theirs, another group was told of government funds to be had, but that they would have to fight to get them.* We feel that this would only agitate more dissension among the races.

Our Local newspaper carried an article in the October 23, 1969 edition, and a member of the group was on our local radio station soliciting donations for the program until their $20,000 grant is received. This grant is supposed to be used for the purpose of establishing a clinic and dispensing drugs on the "ability to pay basis". We feel that our county has no need for this, and it will jeopardize our local Pharmacists, or put them completely out of business.

Who knows the amount of money received through their soliciting funds, and who will control these funds, and funds received on the "ability to pay basis"? Who will supervise the financial management of this program? We quote from Dr. Ralph Phelps, former president of Ouachita Baptist University, will it be the "grossly incompetent" or those who were "highly allergic to work"?

As Physicians, Pharmacists, and taxpayers, we feel no need for such a program in our county, and find this very appalling to many.

If the young Physician with this group would be willing to do days work without greed, graft, and have the interest of the people at heart, we would be happy to have him, otherwise we do not need or want their assistance, as we have to the best of our knowledge, and abilities cared for our people who are truly needy.

Sir, any consideration that you may give us in this matter will greately appreciated.

Very truly yours,

————— ——————,

(Numerous Signatures.)

APRIL 7, 1970.

BOARD OF GOVERNORS,
Lee Memorial Hospital,
Marianna, Ark.

GENTLEMEN: You have requested of our Society a written statement relative Dr. Dan Blumenthal's application for staff membership at Lee Memorial Hospital.

Our Society has always welcomed to its memberhips, and endorsed for membership to the staff of your hospital, any qualified, licensed, private practitioner engaged in the general practice of medicine in Lee County, Arkansas. If and when Dr. Blumenthal meets these requirements, as well as the conditions of membership as prescribed by Article II, Section I of the By-Laws of the Medical Staff of Lee Memorial Hospital, he should be admitted to your staff, but not before.

————— ——————,

Chief of Staff.

————— ——————,

Secretary.

————— ——————,

Member.

————— ——————,

Member.

LEE MEMORIAL HOSPITAL,
Marianna, Ark., April 23, 1970.

Dr. DANIEL BLUMENTHAL,
30 East Mississippi St.,
Marianna, Ark.

DEAR DR. BLUMENTHAL: This will acknowledge receipt of your letter under date of March 26, 1970 in which you gave me one week in which to answer your letter. I apologize for not complying with the one week time frame which you allowed me in your letter.

I would like to clear up what is apparently a gross misrepresentation of the remarks and dicussion that took place during the meeting between myself, Judge Haskell Adams and the Committee to Open Lee Memorial Hospital to Patients of Dr. Dan Blumenthal—T. Ishmael, Chairman. I assure you, Dr. Blumenthal. that neither Judge Adams or myself made the statement that you would not be allowed to have staff privileges at the hospital. In fact neither of us have the authority to make such a statement. The only way I could make such a statement would be based on instructions from the Board of Governors. I am sorry that the remarks made at the time of the meeting were misunderstood.

Our files reflect the fact that we have corresponded several times in regard to your application for staff privileges, and each time your letters were answered explaining the position of the Board of Governors to you. If you will review your file I think you will find this to be true.

I am sure that you understand that the Board of Governors could take no action on your application until we received the recommendation of the Medical Staff. When we received your application in the proper form it was submitted to the Credentials Committee of the Staff, and a request for a recommendation was made. The recommendation was received at the hospital on April 7, 1970, and I enclose a copy herewith.

In view of the fact that in the opinion of the Medical Staff you do not meet the requirements for membership the Board of Governors has no alternative but to deny your application for staff privileges.

I would like to take the opportunity, Dr. Blumenthal, to join the Doctors in expressing their desire to have you enter the private practice of medicine in Lee County. Speaking for myself I can assure you that the denial of your request for staff privileges has nothing to do with your professional qualifications nor is it intended to reflect thereon. Please understand that we have a set of rules as set forth in the Constitution and By Laws of the Lee Memorial Hospital, and we are bound to abide by them.

If you would like to meet with me personally to discuss this matter further I will be happy to meet with you at your convenience.

Yours very truly,

PAUL B. BENHAM, JR.

———

[Arkansas Gazette, Nov. 16, 1969]

FOUR-MEMBER MEDICAL SOCIETY BLOCKS VISTA DOCTOR

(By Wayne Jordan of the Gazette Staff)

MARIANNA.—Dr. Dan Blumenthal, 28, who has been rejected for membership in the four-member Lee County Medical Society, is the first doctor in the nation to work in a pilot project for the government-sponsored Volunteers in Service to America.

Dr. Blumenthal was sent here to help care for the 73 per cent of the county's 21,000 people classified as living in poverty, his wife, Janet, said last week.

Mrs. Blumenthal also is a VISTA worker, who shortly will be writing her thesis for a doctor's degree in child psychology from the University of Chicago.

The Blumenthals are paid $170 a month each by Vista.

(Dr. Blumenthal was named the most outstanding intern out of 60 interns "either a year ago or the year before," at Tulane University's Charity Hospital at New Orleans, Dr. George Cook, the Hospital's assistant clinical director, said in a telephone interview Saturday. Dr. Cook called the young doctor "very knowledgeable.")

Dr. Blumenthal, a native of St. Louis has been here since August, trying to find a suitable building to serve as a community clinic to provide health services to the poor. These services would be provided at a minimum fee—or free—depending on person's ability to pay, Dr. Blumenthal said. Patients also would get free medicine if they had no money.

"It's not the doctor they're fighting," said Dr. Elizabeth C. Fields, president of the County Medical Society. "They're fighting VISTA."

The government's entry into the treatment of patients on a local level has irritated the doctors here, Dr. Blumenthal says.

"The hospital [Lee County Memorial Hospital] exists on Medicare and welfare [patients]," he said.

If he's not a member of the county Medical Society, he cannot use the 27-bed county hospital here or any of its equipment, such as X-ray machines and laboratory facilities. Moreover, without being a member of the county society, he cannot join the state organization.

Dr. Blumenthal has written a letter to the hospital administrator R. Bryon Payne asking for permission to practice in the hospital. If he cannot practice there, the letters asked that Payne state the reasons.

Dr. Payne couldn't be reached for comment.

Since Dr. Blumenthal cannot send patients to the hospital here or use its laboratory and X-ray facilities, he said that he probably would send them to either the University of Arkansas Medical Center at Little Rock or a Memphis hospital.

He said that he hadn't any thought to seeking legal recourse to be admitted to the county Society.

HOW THEY VOTE NOBODY'S BUSINESS'

Dr. Fields was the only one of the four doctors to approve Dr. Blumenthal's entry into the Medical Society, but she said the reason she voted that way isn't "anybody's business but my own."

Dr. Blumenthal said that Dr. Fields probably treats more poor persons than the other three doctors.

Drs. Mac McLendon, Dwight W. Gray and Floyd Dozier voted against Dr. Blumenthal.

Asked last week why he led the fight to exclude Dr. Blumenthal from the Society, Dr. Gray said as he wagged his finger, "It's none of the Gazette's business—it's none of their Goddamn business. You can quote that."

Dr. Gray's waiting rooms are segregated.

He was asked if the Society had some medical diagnosis against Dr. Blumenthal. Dr. Gray answered, "It's medical stuff."

That "stuff," according to Dr. Blumenthal, was a non-fatal diagnosis that he had made on a woman recently.

"It was a mistake," he said. "But all physicians make mistakes.

Without mentioning this particular diagnosis, Dr. Fields said, "He's already made one big mistake. * * * They were looking for that.

Marianna has a population of almost 6,000, and like the county, much of the population is black. It's a farming county, where cotton nudges fences around cemeteries and where a statue of Confederate hero Gen. Robert E. Lee looks down on Marianna's old brick pavement around the city square.

In an interview with the Memphis Commercial Appeal, Dr. McLendon, who has been a physician here many years, gave his reasons for disapproving Dr. Blumenthal's application.

Dr. McLendon said that part of the reason was that Dr. Blumenthal had "agitated" local Negroes to demand more rights.

The Commercial Appeal quoted Dr. McLendon: "He's going to the churches and telling Negroes all they have to do to get what they want is to rear up. That's enough for me."

When the newspaper's John Bennett tried to question Dr. Dozier about the situation, the doctor hung up the telephone on him.

The Blumenthals said that they had been invited to speak at two Negro churches. Dr. Blumenthal said that he gave talks about the VISTA programs and told the congregations how to get aid through other government programs.

He said that Dr. McLendon probably received his information through an ultra-conservative newspaper called the Daily Record, which is published at Little Rock. Dr. Blumenthal said that he had been quoted, correctly, in one issue as saying blacks should "rise up on their hind legs and demand their rights."

He said that "One doctor expressed the opinion that the organization [VISTA] was spying on the Society. * * * It's suspicion. That's one of the frustrating things about being here. I haven't been able to do anything here."

The Blumenthals added that with the exception of the Medical Society and a local pharmacist, who has complained to the state pharmacists' association about the doctor giving free medicine to the poor, the "rest of the people have been friendly and helpful."

"I just want to stay here," Mrs. Blumenthal said.

"Only two doctors have expressed any hostility to me," said Dr. Blumenthal, who now is in a jam as to where to hospitalize patients and set up a practice. His rented house near the downtown business district here is a storehouse for his meager supply of medicine, which is mostly samples donated by drug companies.

Although the drug companies have given him supplies, he said they might refrain from continuing if they get pressure from the state pharmacists' association.

Dr. Fields said that a local pharmacist had "a hissy" about Dr. Blumenthal's supplies.

Dr. Blumenthal's laboratory work is done by his father in St. Louis who is a pathologist and who also supplies his son with some of his medicines.

The Blumenthals have been negotiating with the Missouri Pacific Lines to rent the railroad company's abandoned depot here. They plan to set up the community clinic in the old brick building.

Three weeks ago, Mrs. Blumenthal said, a railroad official at Little Rock said that it was "90 per cent sure" that the VISTA workers could rent the building. The railroad, at first, wanted $150 rent, but when the VISTA workers told it they could'nt afford to pay that amount, the company reduced it to $50 a month.

Then Friday, after Dr. Blumenthal's plight with the Society was published in the Commercial Appeal, the railroad telephoned the Blumenthals and told them that they had chosen to rent the building to a grain elevator operator who was going to build a grain elevator across the tracks from the old depot and wanted to use the depot as an office.

The MoPac official denied knowing of the doctor's situation with the medical society.

The Blumenthals said that as they understood it, the railroad received a better business deal from the businessman.

When questioned Friday night, another MoPac official, George Graham, the railroad's traffic manager at Little Rock, said that negotiations were continuing and that "nothing definite" had occurred.

THIS PROGRAM SPECIAL PROJECT

The Blumenthals arrived here in August with 33 other VISTA workers. They said this VISTA program was a special pilot project because all of the workers were specialists. Six of them are nurses, others are sanitation experts, housing specialists and so on.

Officials in Washington told them that "everything was set up" for the doctor and the others to start working when they arrived here. The Blumenthals didn't bring a car because the government said they would provide transportation. There were no facilities available for Dr. Blumenthal to set up practice and the government hadn't provided any supplies or medical equipment.

"We expected help from Washngton, but we haven't gotten it," Dr. Blumenthal said. Since arriving, the doctor has had to get to his patients in the county by whatever transportation he could find.

Commenting on VISTA officials from Washington, Dr. Blumenthal said, "If we just had the money they've spent flying down here, we could have supplied our clinic."

However, he said, with the help of Governor Rockefeller who went to Washington recently for help, the VISTA program in six counties in Eastern Arkansas will get $50,000. He said that $20,000 of this is earmarked for setting up his community clinic.

The Blumenthals emphasized that they, weren't being critical of VISTA's purpose, which is to help poor white and black people help themselves.

"We're trying to let them determine their own destiny," Dr. Blumenthal said. That is, he said, to help "poor people to work in concert" to solve their problems.

IF HE QUITS VISTA, MAY GET ACCEPTED

Dr. Fields said that the other doctors "probably would have welcomed him with open arms" if he hadn't been a VISTA doctor and probably still would accept him if he would resign and set up a private practice.

She also said that VISTA workers don't "understand the psychology of the population." She said the workers sometimes are misled by their good intentions. If the VISTA workers do come to an understanding of Lee County, Dr. Fields said, "They could be of great value to the county."

Asked why he signed up with VISTA, Dr. Blumenthal, a graduate of the University of Chicago Medical School, "They didn't recruit me. I just applied."

"I was concerned * * * with the status of American health care," he said. Throughout the medical profession, he said, the emphasis is on the treatment of disease rather than treating people.

"I just didn't want to treat that cardiac arrest in bed number two," the doctor said. "I wanted to get away from that for awhile to treat people rather than a disease."

He added that medicine's philosophy is to treat the whole of a person, spiritually as well as physically.

Mrs. Blumenthal, a native of Boston, said that Negro churches and individuals had gathered "$25 there and $35 here" to help establish the clinic.

"We like the people here," she said. "There's so much to do and we want to complete this job."

[Memphis Commercial-Appeal, Nov. 14, 1969]

MEDICAL SOCIETY LOCKS OUT PHYSICIAN TO POOR

By John Bennett, From The Commercial Appeal Little Rock Bureau)

LITTLE ROCK, Nov. 13.—Dr. Dan Blumenthal, 27, the only medical doctor with Volunteers in Service to America, has been excluded from the Lee County Medical Society.

The society voted three-to-one to exclude the young VISTA doctor who came to Marianna last August under a special government-financed plan to attack health problems in Eastern Arkansas.

Unless Dr. Blumenthal is admitted to the local medical society, he cannot send patients to the 27-bed Lee County Memorial Hospital or use its facilities.

And unless he bacomes a member of the county society he cannot become a member of the state medical society.

R. B. Payne, administrator of the Lee County hospital, said Thursday the society has advised the hospital of its vote to exclude Dr. Blumenthal.

He said the only vote in favor of Dr. Blumenthal was cast by Dr. Elizabeth C. Fields, president of the local society.

Dr. Blumenthal presently practices at his rented frame home in Marianna and is seeking to convert an old railroad depot in Marianna to a community clinic.

"But I will still need to use the hospital for patients, X-rays and laboratory work," he said Thursday.

Dr. Blumenthal wrote Mr. Payne Thursday for permission to practice at the hospital. He also requested written reasons why he might be refused.

Lee County has four practicing doctors for 21,000 people. Nearly a third of its citizens earn annual incomes less than $1,000. Many of the poor in Lee County travel to Memphis for treatment at John Gaston Hospital or to the University of Arkansas Medical Center in Little Rock.

Dr. Mac McLendon, a Marianna physician, said Thursday the medical society refused Dr. Blumenthal admittance partly because he had "agitated" local Negroes to demand more rights.

"He's going to the churches and telling Negroes all they have to do to get what they want is to rare up," Dr. McClendon said. "That's enough for me."

Dr. Floyd Dozier of Marianna, another member of the Lee County Medical Society, said Thursday he knew nothing about Dr. Blumenthal's application to the society.

Asked if he had voted on the admittance, Dr. Dozier hung up the telephone receiver.

Mrs. Janet Blumenthal, also a VISTA worker, said she and her husband have sought to organize poor citizens of Lee County into a community clinic managed by the involved citizens. She denied, however, that she and her husband had attended Negro churches to "agitate" Negroes.

[Memphis Commercial-Appeal, July 4, 1970]

LEE COUNTY VISTA DOCTOR TO CHALLENGE HOSPITAL SNUB

(By John Bennett, From The Commercial Appeal Little Rock Bureau)

MARIANNA, June 3.—A young doctor who treats Lee County poor free of charge, Thursday will challenge a local hospital's refusal to admit his patients.

Little Rock attorney Jack Levy is expected to file a lawsuit in federal court here Thursday challenging the hospital on constitutional grounds.

The lawsuit will name the Lee County Memorial Hospital as defendant in behalf of Dr. Dan Blumenthal, the only practicing physician with Volunteers In Service to America (VISTA).

The 25-bed Lee County hospital has refused to treat Dr. Blumenthal's patients since the VISTA doctor came here a year ago.

The Lee County Medical Society has also refused to admit the young doctor.

Local physicians, pharmacists and politicians have also opposed giving free medical aid to the hundreds of county poor.

Dr. Blumenthal, who heads the Lee County Cooperative Clinic, Inc., in Marianna, will be leaving the clinic at the end of this month.

The lawsuit is expected to break ground for his successor.

The lawsuit, testing the right of the hospital to deny Dr. Blumenthal admittance and the use of laboratory facilities, has "precedent." Dr. Blumenthal said.

"We simply feel they (the hospital) don't have a legitimate reason for denying us hospital priciliges," Dr. Blumenthal said recently. "There are court precedents that they don't have grounds."

Dr. Blumenthal has tried twice to be admitted to the hospital and the medical association. He has twice been rejected.

He said he wants to insure his successor will have access to the hospital.
Groundwork for his replacement has already been laid, he added.
"The clinic will definitely go on when I am gone," he said. "It looks very good."

The reason it will go on is not because of VISTA, Dr. Blumenthal said, but because of his own efforts. He waged a personal nationwide mail campaign to recruit a replacement.

"We had little or no help from VISTA," he said.

Dr. Blumenthal, sent to Marianna by VISTA, has taken some pretty acid potshots at the federal agency. He believes it sent him here not knowing why.

The indigent sick come daily to the little frame home clinic in Marianna operated chiefly by the patients themselves.

Despite opposition, the clinic has grown. In less than three months about 1,100 indigents have been treated there.

"The rate is now about 40 a day," Dr. Blumenthal said.

One VISTA opponent is County Judge Haskell Adams who recently signed approval for OEO operations in Lee County after a one-year delay.

Judge Adams joined with other local doctors, pharmacists and politicians in writing Senator John L. McClellan (D.-Ark.) to ask that he help eject VISTA from Lee County.

"Like all of the poverty programs, a lot of whites resent it and the blacks are all for it," Judge Adams said. "We've got 66 per cent black population and so I guess you can say the majority is for it."

He said he first opposed VISTA to keep the peace between whites and blacks.

"I thought it was better for the county if the whole VISTA program pulled out," the judge said. "I was just trying to keep down the friction between the races. I let that rule me rather than what good, if any, they did."

Dr. Blumenthal believes much local opposition to his clinic has eased in recent months.

"But the medical association is even more opposed than ever," he said.

Olly Neal, clinic administrator, believes opposition will finally die down, if not go away.

"It is my opinion as we show our worth that some of the opposition will ease off."

The federal lawsuit, to be filed with the aid of the National Association for the Advancement of Colored People Legal Defense Fund, is to go to federal court Thursday afternoon, Mr. Lavey said.

[VISTA Magazine, June 1971]

VISTA MEDICS BRING CARE TO ISOLATED POOR

America's rural poor are often virtually invisible. They live on out-of-the-way roads in rundown houses or shacks, which are often inhabited by women who already have several small children. The children are frequently ill or hungry.

In Lee County, Arkansas, the poor are mostly out of sight but they can be found up rutted county roads. Surveys have shown that 75 per cent of these people are indigent and of most of these families live on less than $2,000 a year.

Dr. Ralph (Robbi) Wolfe is the second VISTA doctor to work in the area as a physician for the Lee County Cooperative Health Clinic, which opened in March 1970. He said, "When people began to trust me and started asking me to come to their homes, I found out that families live in two rooms, have no plumbing, and minimum electricity. About half have refrigerators, a few have washing machines, but usually the only furniture is one or two chairs, and beds."

There are 19,000 people in the county, of which 14,000 are indigent, with 45 percent of these under 18 years of age.

Poverty has long been a way of life for people in many parts of the rural South and Lee County is no exception. Because of a lack of industry, it is getting worse in some areas. The ablest young men and women go to the already crowded cities, leaving behind the old and the very young, the overburdened and the apathetic. "A lot of people see no hope of improving," Dr. Wolfe said.

Changing this attitude of hopelessness is the long range purpose of the Lee County Cooperative Health Clinic. It was organized by local low-income people whose roots are in Lee County and who are determined to uplift living conditions in the county. Through the clinic, the people are getting needed medical assistance while building community awareness on how to use all available resources for economic improvement upon which good health ultimately depends.

Funded with grants from the Office of Economic Opportunity's Emergency Food and Medical Services Division through a multi-county Community Action Program, the clinic has an administrative staff of local people plus six health aides, a driver and 10 VISTA Volunteers. Eight of the VISTAS are professional health people, including a physician, three nurses, a dentist, a lab technician, a sanitarian, and two local Community Volunteers who serve as liaison between the clinic and the communities.

Organized so that anyone can be a member for a dollar a year, the clinic offers free services to all people whose family income falls below federal poverty guidelines. Low-income people are sought for jobs created by the clinic which offers opportunities for job-training and career advancement.

During the first year of operation, the clinic treated 4,000 cases.

Two more VISTA doctors are expected to arrive this summer, one a pediatrician. (Dr. Wolfe will complete his year of service.)

Thirty-five to forty patients a day come to the clinic, and Dr. Wolfe and three nurses see others on home visits. For patients who need hospitalization or to see specialists, a clinic van carries up to fifteen people on trips to Little Rock or Helena, Arkansas three days a week. A community clinic has been established in the Haynes community, which is a long drive from the main clinic, and three other small clinics are being set up in three other sections of the county. These will be visited once a week by a mobile health unit donated to the Cooperative by the United Auto Workers. Dr. Ben Hubby, a young physician associated with the Tufts Medical Center in Mississippi, volunteers a day a week to the clinic.

The clinic is a hub of activity—no one except the patients in the waiting room seems to sit still for more than a moment. Everyone's actions and words —whether it is the receptionist, an apprentice lab technician, or a health aide—emanates a sense of purpose, and it is catching.

Dr. Thomas Sweigart, the dentist, at first was dismayed when he arrived in early April to find no equipment for dentistry, and no space. "They told me to relax, keep cool," he said, "So I am trying." He is sending out letters to procure the equipment he needs as donations or at low cost. "I will have to locate it myself, because as a dentist I know what avenues you have to take," he said. An experienced dentist, Dr. Sweigart joined VISTA instead of retiring. But no one ever asked him to scare up dental equipment out of the blue before. He has been there long enough, however, to realize that the clinic itself would never have gotten started if people had not been willing to start with practically nothing.

The clinic grew out of the Health Advocates program which was operating in 1969 in a five-county area of eastern Arkansas under the auspices of the East Central Arkansas Economic Opportunity Corporation. Funds came from the Emergency Food and Medical Services division of the Office of Economic Opportunity. VISTA Volunteers were recruited to coordinate federal and local government efforts to reach the people who don't know about existing programs. One of their jobs was to help organize Neighborhood Action Councils to locate and inform the scattered poor families about existing health and food programs, such as Food stamps, and how to make use of them.

The VISTAs learned that many people were not getting food and health services because they lived long distances from distribution points and had no transportation. They found too that many homes lacked knowledge of basic nutrition and sanitation and that there was a desperate need for doctors and nurses. In Lee County there are only six doctors, one of whom is 74, another 82.

The Neigrborhood Action Councils in Lee County decided that their most urgent need was for medical service. Mildred Broadway, local Lee County woman who was trained for a job at the clinic as a counsellor and dietician, said: "The program came from the people, not from the professionals."

The NACs in the county held a fund-raising drive to start the clinic before government funding was available, and raised more than $1,000 in contributions, half of it from local people. The Board of Directors of the Councils then drew up bylaws for the clinic and wrote a proposal for a cooperative health clinic that required participation of the low-income people in the county, which they submitted to the Office of Economic Opportunity's Emergency Food and Medical Services. Helping prepare the proposal were the VISTA Health Advocates, especially Jan Wrede, who according to Mrs. Broadway, "was responsible for getting the clinic underway."

The primary professional voice in the proposal was that of Dr. Dan Blumenthal, a VISTA doctor who Miss Wrede had persuaded to come to Lee County. Blumenthal, who completed his residency at Charity Hospital in New Orleans in 1969, arrived in the county in August 1969 and with nurse Corrine Cass, one of the VISTA Health Advocates, began to treat indigent sick people and to help organize the clinic.

One of the biggest problems was gaining acceptance of the idea of a cooperative clinic by the white, more affluent people in the county. Black people outnumber white people two to one, and 80 percent of the patients are black people. Also there is a long standing distrust in the area of government programs that provide free services to the poor. Some of the doctors in the county opposed the clinic, saying it was socialistic.

Finding a building for the clinic was also a major problem until Lacy J. Kennedy, black funeral home director, rented them a house on Liberty Street next to his business establishment. But attitudes have changed over time. Olly Neal, a tall, lanky black community leader who typifies the spirit of the clinic, has won recognition as an influential community voice, and was recently appointed by the Governor of Arkansas to the State Health Planning Council. Neal said: "Our two major contributors in the beginning were Mr. Kennedy (the funeral director) and the United Auto Workers. When nobody else had a good word for us, they came out publicly in our support. At first we were totally rejected by other health agencies, except for the University of Arkansas Medical Center, but now other health institutions are helping us."

An important part of the VISTA health professionals' job is to establish relationships with other institutions or agencies and they are increasingly successful. For example, St. Jude's Childrens' Hospital in Memphis provided a free training course for the clinic's Health Aides and after correspondence with VISTA pharmacist Michael McCarthy, the Veterans Hospital in Arkansas started providing low cost drugs to the clinic. "Formerly all we had were sample drugs," McCarthy said. VISTA nurse Sue Christman serves as official liaison between the clinic and the County Public Health Department, so that the clinic refers patients to the health department for family planning and other health information, and county case workers refer cases to the clinic.

The busiest and most vital person to the clinic is the physician. Dr. Blumenthal stayed in Lee County for two years, and was replaced by Dr. Wolfe in July 1970. A resident intern at the same hospital as his predecessor, Dr. Wolfe responded to Blumenthal's recruitment efforts. He had visited the clinic a few times, and decided to spend a year there as a VISTA Volunteer.

"Dr. Wolfe works 14 or 15 hours a day six days a week, and 8 hours on the seventh day," said Neal. "We don't expect to find another Robbi Wolfe."

The apparent inertia of so many of the poor in the county and the non-poor are depressing to any outsider who comes to help. and Dr. Wolfe admits the emotional rewards have not been what he thought they would be. But sometimes an expression of gratitude offers a quick uplift. "This is the only place where you can get paid with a side of bacon," Dr. Wolfe said. "That's beautiful."

The worst medical problems, according to Dr. Wolfe, are infections and subtle malnutrition, evident in abnormally low height and weight of children for their age. "It's devastating if a child doesn't get proper nutrition in his first year of life," Dr. Wolfe said. "It stunts the mental as well as the physical growth."

"The fetal mortality rate is twice the national average in the county," he said. He attributes this to lack of prenatal care and the widespread use of midwives and "grannies" to deliver babies.

Since the clinic opened. some serious child health cases have been discovered. "One woman brought in her baby because he kept spitting up his food." VISTA nurse Anna Chapman said. "It was discovered that a sphincter muscle was not letting food into his stomach. He was taken to St. Jude's Children's Hospital where it was found that he also had a bone deformity and a heart problem." The child was operated on and seems to be getting along all right. He is now home with his mother and five brothers and sisters where Miss Chapman visits them periodically to check up on the baby.

Some of the people live in adequate homes, but do not have enough money to pay for medical services. One such case is a childless old couple. The man had a stroke which partially paralyzed one side of his body. VISTA Nurse Chapman visits him regularly to exercise his hand, arm and foot to keep up the circulation in them. "His wife is not strong enough to help him much, but I think we can get some neighbors to learn how," she said.

Training of local people for jobs in the clinic and encouraging people to go into health careers is a major part of the clinic program. Many of the services that the nurses perform can be done by paraprofessional people, and the VISTA nurses transfer as many duties as possible to the Health Aides. The aides do most of the follow-up calls to patients' homes.

The VISTA nurses also periodically teach classes in first aid and basic human anatomy. The first such classes were for the Health Aides, but now the Neighborhood Action Councils are selecting members of their communities to take the course. Two of the Health Aides also are enrolled in nursing school in a local community college.

Another VISTA, John Rose, is the lab technician for the clinic. He was a chemistry major in college, and spent two years in the Peace Corps teaching in the Philippines. Rose has been training Allen Noah, a local man, to take his place when Rose leaves VISTA.

VISTA Harry Conard serves as an advisor to communities on environmental sanitation problems, showing people how to build sanitary outhouses and promoting basic health education. He learned about excavating from his father and how to build outhouses while in VISTA training at the Tufts Delta Health Center in Mississippi.

"Lack of well-built, properly placed outhouses is one reason why so many children in the county have worms," he said. They get both ringworm, which enters through the feet, and roundworms which get into the children's bodies when they touch the ground and then put their hands in their mouths, or when they eat food that flies have infested.

"Many people think that having worms is a natural part of growing up," Conard said. "They are learning that doesn't have to be."

Another project Conard worked on was starting food buying cooperatives. He has taken groups of people to visit existing cooperatives formed by low income people to see how they work.

Helping overcome the problem of distrust of outsiders. and white people by low-income black people are the local community VISTAs, Mrs. Mary Carlock and Mrs. Rosetta Williams. They serve as outreach workers for the clinic. Highly respected low-income people who know many of the residents in Lee County, they help inform people about the clinic and inspire community involvement. For many people, the association of Mrs. Williams and Mrs. Carlock with the clinic makes it acceptable. In emergencies, Mrs. Carlock and Mrs. Williams take people to Little Rock to the hospital. And they are now organizing car pools in different communities to take people places when emergencies or special needs arise.

In November 1970, the clinic held a membership meeting in which 500 people elected a board of directors. Some of the people on the board have always worked for community improvement, and two-thirds of the board members are low-income people.

On the advisory board are such people as "Big John" Wilson, a black leader in the Haynes community in Lee County, who is organizing a rabbit-raising cooperative in his area.

But community involvement is a new and difficult thing for most of the poor people in the area. A lot depends on a few dynamic leaders. Olly Neal keeps driving home the point: "Health is not just a medical problem. Economic development will have to come before there can be real change. There has been only one business brought into the county in ten years." He does not foresee any change in the local employment situation in the near future. although the clinic is doing what it can to promote the idea of getting industry into the county. Getting industry will require the combined effort of the influential members of the communities, black and white. Neal feels that the major challenge to the clinic is the awakening of the social consciousness of the people. It has started. "The community will never be the same," he said. "And the changes are for the better. Expectations have been raised—that is the important thing."

United States District Court, Eastern District of Arkansas, Eastern Division

Civil Action No. —

DANIEL S. BLUMENTHAL; RALPH WOLF; LEE COUNTY COOPERATIVE CLINIC; GINNIE B. GAY; MAURICE JOHNSON, A MINOR, BY HIS MOTHER AND NEXT FRIEND JO ANN JOHNSON; LEILA BARNETT; AND MILDRED BROADWAY, PLAINTIFFS

v.

LEE MEMORIAL HOSPITAL; R. B. PAYNE, INDIVIDUALLY AND AS ADMINISTRATOR OF LEE MEMORIAL HOSPITAL; PAUL B. BENHAM, JR., INDIVIDUALLY AND AS CHAIRMAN OF THE BOARD OF GOVERNORS OF LEE MEMORIAL HOSPITAL; JOHN F. MILLER, INDIVIDUALLY AND AS SECRETARY OF THE BOARD OF GOVERNORS OF LEE MEMORIAL HOSPITAL; ED CONNER, SR., INDIVIDUALLY AND AS A MEMBER OF THE BOARD OF GOVERNORS OF LEE MEMORIAL ,HOSPITAL; GEORGE L. CHRISTENSON, INDIVIDUALLY AND AS A MEMBER OF THE BOARD OF GOVERNORS OF LEE MEMORIAL HOSPITAL; C. W. HARRINGTON, SR., INDIVIDUALLY AND AS A MEMBER OF THE BOARD OF GOVERNORS OF LEE MEMORIAL HOSPITAL; C. R. WEST, INDIVIDUALLY AND AS A MEMBER OF THE BOARD OF GOVERNORS OF LEE MEMORIAL HOSPITAL; J. P. DOZIER, INDIVIDUALLY AND AS A MEMBER OF THE BOARD OF GOVERNORS OF LEE MEMORIAL HOSPITAL; AND COUNTY JUDGE HASKELL A. ADAMS, SR., INDIVIDUALLY AND AS AN EX-OFFICIO MEMBER OF THE BOARD OF GOVERNORS OF LEE MEMORIAL HOSPITAL, DEFENDANTS

COMPLAINT

1. The jurisdiction of this Court is invoked pursuant to 28 U.S.C. §1343(3) and (4). This is an action in equity authorized by 42 U.S.C. §§1981 and 1983 seeking to secure rights, privileges and immunities guaranteed by the due process and equal protection clauses of the Fourteenth Amendment to the Constitution of the United States, and the right of association guaranteed by he First Amendment to the Constitution of the United States.

2. This is a proceeding for a declaratory judgment pursuant to the provisions of 28 U.S.C. §§2201 and 2202 to determine the legal rights and relations of and between the respective parties.

3. This is an action for injunctive relief to secure for qualified Volunteers In Service To America, hereinafter called VISTA, doctors staff privileges at the Lee Memorial Hospital, hereinafter called the Hospital, which are being denied to them for arbitrary and invidious reasons in violation of the due process and equal protection clauses of the Fourteenth Amendment to the Constitution of the United States.

4. This is an action for injunctive relief to secure for the indigent citizens of Lee County, Arkansas, in need of medical assistance, the right to be treated at the Hospital by a qualified doctor of their choice, which is being denied to them for arbitrary and invidious reasons in violation of the due process and equal protection clauses of the Fourteenth Amendment to the Constitution of the United States, and in violation of their right of association guaranteed by the First Amendment to the Constitution of the United States.

5. This is an action for injunctive relief to secure for the indigent patients of the Lee County Cooperative Clinic, hereinafter called the Clinic, the right to be treated at the Hospital by a qualified VISTA doctor or any other qualified doctor of their choice. which is being denied to them for arbitrary and in_ vidious reasons in violation of the due process and equal protection clauses of the Fourteenth Amendment to the Constitution of the United States, and in violation of their right of association guaranteed by the First Amendment to the Constitution of the United States.

6. (a) Daniel S. Blumenthal is a resident of Marianna, Lee County, Arkansas, and a citizen of the United States. He is a VISTA medical doctor who is

licensed to practice medicine in the State of Arkansas, and is currently employed as a VISTA doctor by the Clinic. He is to cease functioning as a VISTA doctor for the Clinic on June 30, 1970. VISTA (Domestic Peace Corps) is an agency of the U.S. Government and it consists of volunteers who donate a year of their life to work in poverty areas to assist poor people and subsist on income commensurate with the poverty income in the area.

(b) Ralph Wolf is currently a resident of New Orleans, Louisiana, and a citizen of the United States. He is a medical doctor, and, as of July 1, 1970, will succeed Daniel S. Blumenthal as the VISTA doctor for Lee County, Arkansas. On July 1, 1970, he will commence wosking for the Clinic as a VISTA doctor.

(c) The Clinic is a nonprofit charitable corporation duly organized pursuant to the. laws of the State of Arkansas for the purpose of promoting, in a charitable manner, the medical health and welfare of all of the indigent inhabitants of Lee County, Arkansas. Its principal office and place of business is located at 35 Liberty Street, Marianna, Arkansas 72360.

(d) Ginnie B. Gay is a black citizen of Brickeys, Lee County, Arkansas, and a citizen of the United States. At all times material herein, she has been a patient of Daniel S. Blumenthal, who treated her in his capacity as the Clinic's VISTA doctor.

(e) Maurice Johnson, a minor, is a black citizen of Rondo, Lee County, Arkansas, and a citizen of the United States. At all times material herein, he has been a patient of Daniel S. Blumenthal, who treated him in his capacity as the Clinic's VISTA doctor.

(f) Leila Barnett is a black citizen of Marianna, Lee County, Arkansas, and a citizen of the United States. At all times material herein, she has been a patient of Daniel S. Blumenthal, who treated her in his capacity as the Clinic's VISTA doctor.

(g) Mildred Broadway is a black citizen of Mora, Lee County, Arkansas, and a citizen of the United States. At all times material herein, she has been a patient of Daniel S. Blumenthal, who treated her in his capacity as the Clinic's VISTA doctor.

7. Plaintiffs, Daniel S. Blumenthal and Ralph Wolf, bring this action on behalf of themselves and all other duly qualified VISTA doctors, who may be assigned to Lee County, Arkansas, and seek staff privileges at the Hospital pursuant to Rule 23(a) and (b)(2) of the Federal Rules of Civil Procedure. There are common questions of law and fact applicable to the class and a common injunctive relief is sought. The members of the class are so numerous as to make it impractical to bring them all before this Court. The interests of this class are adequately represented by plaintiffs.

8. Plaintiffs, Ginnie B. Gay, Maurice Johnson, Leila Barnett, and Mildred Broadway, bring this action on behalf of themselves and all other indigent citizens of Lee County, Arkansas, in need of medical assistance, who want to be treated at the Hospital by a qualified doctor of their choice pursuant to Rule 23(a) and (b)(2) of the Federal Rules of Civil Procedure. There are common questions of law and fact applicable to the class and a common injunctive relief is sought. The members of the class are so numerous as to make it impractical to bring them all before this Court. The interests of this class are adequately represented by plaintiffs.

9. Plaintiff Clinic brings this action on its own behalf and on behalf of all of its indigent patients, who desire treatment at the Hospital by a qualified VISTA doctor or any other qualified doctor of their choice pursuant to Rule 23(a) and (b)(2) of the Federal Rules of Civil Procedure. There are common questions of law and fact applicable to the class and a common injunctive relief is sought. The members of the class are so numerous as to make it impractical to bring them all before this Court. The interests of this class are adequately represented by plaintiff Clinic.

10. Lee County, Arkansas, is a political subdivision of the State of Arkansas, and it owns and ultimately operates the Hospital, which is the only hospital in Lee County, Arkansas.

11. The Hospital is a nonprofit corporation duly organized pursuant to the laws of the State of Arkansas for the purpose of affording medical and surgical aid and for nursing sick and disabled inhabitants of Lee County, Arkansas.

12. The business of the Hospital is managed, controlled and operated by its Board of Governors which ultimately derives its authority to do so from the

Hospital's Constitution and ARK. STAT. ANN. §§17–1501, 17–1502, 17–1503 and 17–1504 (Repl. 1968).

13. At all times material herein, the following named individuals occupied the positions on the Hospital's Board of Governors set forth opposite their respective names: Paul B. Benham, Jr., Chairman; John F. Miller, Secretary; Ed Conner, Sr., Member; George L. Christenson, Member; C. W. Harrington, Sr., Member; C. R. West, Member; J. P. Dozier, Member; County Judge Haskell A. Adams, Sr., Ex-Officio Member.

14. The Hospital's chief executive and administrative officer is its administrator, who is employed by the Hospital's Board of Governors and acts as the Board's agent. The Hospital's administrator is responsible for its management, and, at all times material herein, R. B. Payne has been the Hospital's administrator.

15. The Hospital was constructed pursuant to federal grants to the State of Arkansas under the Hill-Burton Act, 42 U.S.C. §291, et seq. The Hospital's construction was completed in 1958, and the total cost of construction was $337,881.06. Of this total, the federal grant and share was $218,587.37, and the local share was $119,293.69.

16. Under Health Insurance for the Aged (Medicare), 42 U.S.C. §1395 et seq., the Hospital received $78,419.74 for its fiscal year ending June 30, 1967; $104,192.57 for its fiscal year ending June 30, 1968; and tentatively $126,811.75 for its fiscal year ending June 30, 1969. From July 1, 1969, through May 15, 1970, the Hospital has received $98,918.70 pursuant to Medicare.

17. The Hospital is participating in Grants to States for Medical Assistance programs (Medicaid), 42 U.S.C. §1396, et seq. From January 1, 1970, to May 18, 1970, the Hospital has received $9,286.00 pursuant to its participation in the State of Arkansas' Medicaid Program.

18. Pursuant to its power to do so, the Hospital's Board of Governors adopted a Constitution for the Hospital on May 21, 1966, which remains in full force and effect. Pursuant to this same authority, the Hospital's Board of Governors adopted By-laws, Rules and Regulations of the Medical Staff on May 21, 1966. The Hospital's Board amended the aforementioned By-laws, Rules and Regulations of the Medical Staff on December 9, 1969. As amended, the By-Laws, Rules and Regulations of the Medical Staff remain in full force and effect.

19. Article XIV, Section A of the Hospital's Constitution provides in pertinent part: The applicant for membership on the Medical Staff shall be a graduate of an approved or recognized Medical School legally licensed to practice in the State of Arkansas and professionally qualified for membership in the local Medical Society.

20. Article II, Section 1 of the Hospital's By-laws, Rules and Regulations of the Medical Staff states: The application for membership to the active medical staff shall be a graduate of a recognized medical school, legally licensed to practice in the State of Arkansas, engaged in the private practice of medicine in the County of Lee, a member of the Lee County Medical Society.

21. Article XIV, Section D of the Hospital's Constitution and Article II, Section 5 of the Hospital's By-laws, Rules and Regulations of the Medical Staff enumerate the procedures an applicant for staff membership at the Hospital must follow. Daniel S. Blumenthal, in applying for staff membership at the Hospital, followed the aforementioned procedures.

22. By letter dated April 23, 1970, addressed to Daniel S. Blumenthal, the Hospital's Board of Governors denied staff membership and privileges to Daniel S. Blumenthal because he was not engaged in the general private practice of medicine in Lee County, Arkansas, and was not a member of the Lee County Medical Society. See Exhibit 1 attached.

23. Because Daniel S. Blumenthal has been denied staff membership and privileges at the Hospital, he cannot use the Hospital's facilities and equipment and he cannot treat his patients there.

24. To become a member of the Lee County Medical Society, an applying doctor, such as Daniel S. Blumenthal, must, among other qualifications, be a resident of Lee County, Arkansas, and be engaged in the private practice of medicine in Lee County, Arkansas.

25. Article XIV, Section A of the Hospital's Constitution and Article II, Section 1 of the Hospital's By-laws, Rules and Regulations of the Medical Staff, as applied to Daniel S. Blumenthal and the class of VISTA doctors he

represents, are unconstitutional, because their eligibility criteria for staff membership and privileges at the Hospital are predicated upon illegal, arbitrary and invidious classifications which have no rational relationship to the Hospital's purposes described above in paragraph 11 and violate the due process and equal protection clauses of the Fourteenth Amendment to the Constitution of the United States and 42 U.S.C. §§1981 and 1983.

26. Because the Hospital has illegally denied staff privileges and membership to Daniel S. Blumenthal and the class of VISTA doctors he represents for the reasons described above in paragraph 25 based on an application of Article XIV, Section A of the Hospital's Constitution and Article II, Section 1 of its By-laws, Rules and Regulations of the Medical Staff, all of the Clinic's indigent patients such as, for example, Ginnie B. Gay, Maurice Johnson, Leila Barnett and Mildred Broadway, are being denied their right to a healthful life in violation of the due process and equal protection clauses of the Fourteenth Amendment to the Constitution of the United States and to their right of association guaranteed by the First Amendment to the Constitution of the United States and 42 U.S.C. §§1981 and 1983.

27. Article XIV, Section A of the Hospital's Constitution and Article II, Section 1 of the Hospital's By-laws, Rules, Regulations of the Medical Staff deny Plaintiffs Ginnie B. Gay, Maurice Johnson, Leila Barnett and Mildred Broadway and the class of indigent citizens of Lee County, Arkansas, they represent of their right to a healthful life, because the aforementioned Hospital regulations are based on illegal, arbitrary and invidious criteria which have no rational relationship to the Hospital's purposes described above in paragraph 11 and violate the due process and equal protection clauses of the Fourteenth Amendment to the Constitution of the United States and their right of association guaranteed by the First Amendment to the Constitution of the United States and 42 U.S.C. §§1981 and 1983.

Accordingly, plaintiffs urge the Court to grant the following relief:

A. That a temporary restraining order, preliminary and permanent injunction issue, enjoining and restraining the defendants, their successors, officers, agents and employees and all persons acting in concert or in participation with any of them from enforcing Article XIV, Section A of the Hospital's Constitution and Article II, Section 1 of the Hospital's By-laws, Rules and Regulations of the Medical Staff against Daniel S. Blumenthal and the class of VISTA doctors he represents or any other qualified doctor who may not be a resident of Lee County, Arkansas; may not be a member of the Lee County Medical Society; and who may not be engaged in the general private practice of medicine in Lee County, Arkansas. from denying all inhabitants of Lee County, Arkansas, the right to be treated at the Hospital by any qualified doctor of their choice; and from denying all patients of the Clinic the right to be treated at the Hospital by any qualified Clinic doctor or any other qualified doctor they may choose.

B. That a temporary restraining order, preliminary and permanent injunction issue affirmatively ordering defendants, their successors, officers, agents and employees and all persons acting in concert or in participation with any of them to expunge Section A from Article XIV of the Hospital's Constitution; to expunge Section 1 of Article II from the Hospital's By-laws, Rules and Regulations of the Medical Staff; to grant Daniel S. Blumenthal and all other qualified VISTA doctors and all other qualified doctors staff privileges at the Hospital regardless of whether they are residents of Lee County, Arkansas, members of the Lee County Medical Society, and engaged in the general private practice of medicine in Lee County, Arkansas; to grant all inhabitants of Lee County, Arkansas, the right to be treated at the Hospital by any qualified doctor of their choice; and to grant all patients of the Clinic the right to be treated at the Hospital by any qualified Clinic doctor or any other qualified doctor they may choose.

C. That a declaratory judgment issue declaring that the due process and equal protection clauses of the Fourteenth Amendment to the Constitution of the United States and the right of association guaranteed by the First Amendment to the Constitution of the United States prohibit defendants from enforcing Article XIV, Section A of the Hospital's Constitution and Article II, Section 1 of the Hospital's By-laws. Rules and Regulations of the Medical Staff against Daniel S. Blumenthal and the class of VISTA doctors he represents; prohibit defendants from denying staff privileges at the Hospital to any qualified doctor; prohibit defendants from refusing to allow the Clinic's patients to be treated by a qualified doctor of their choice; and prohibit defendants from refusing to allow the inhabitants of Lee County, Arkansas, to be treated at the Hospital by a qualified doctor of their choice.

D. Plaintiffs further pray that the Court grant them their costs herein, reasonable attorney's fees, and such further, other or additional relief as is just and equitable under the facts developed.

Respectfully submitted,

WALKER, ROTENBERRY, KAPLAN, LAVEY & HOLLINGSWORTH,
1820 West 13th Street,
Little Rock, Arkansas 72202.
By JOHN W. WALKER,
By JOHN T. LAVEY,
JACK GREENBERG,
JAMES M. NABRIT, III,
MICHAEL MELTSNER,
10 Columbus Circle,
New York, New York 10019,
Attorneys for Plaintiffs.

In the United States District Court for the Eastern District of Arkansas
Eastern Division
Civil Action No. H 70 C–5

DANIEL S. BLUMENTHAL, ET AL. PLAINTIFFS
vs.
LEE MEMORIAL HOSPITAL, ET AL. DEFENDANTS

ANSWER

For their Answer to the plaintiffs' Complaint, as amended, defendants state:

1. The allegations of paragraph 1 are jurisdictional and as such, require no answer. However, to the extent that such allegations imply that defendants have deprived plaintiffs of, or infringed upon, their constitutional rights, they are denied.

2. The allegations of paragraphs 2 through 5 are merely descriptive of the relief sought by the plaintiffs and to that extent, require no answer. However, to the extent that these paragraphs expressly allege or imply that defendants have deprived plaintiffs of, or infringed upon, their constitutional right, the allegations thereof are denied.

3. Defendants are without information sufficient to form a belief as to the truth or falsity of the allegations of paragraph 6, sub-paragraphs (a) through (g), and therefore deny such allegations.

4. The first sentence of paragraph 7 attempts to define the class or sub-class which Daniel F. Blumenthal and Ralph Wolf seek to represent and to that extent requires no answer. However, defendants deny that the issues asserted by Plaintiffs Blumenthal and Wolf may be appropriately maintained by them as a class action, assert that Plaintiff Blumenthal is not an appropriate representative of the class or sub-class defined in paragraph 7 since he is not a member of such class or sub-class, deny that these plaintiffs have standing to raise the issues asserted, and deny the remaining allegations of paragraph 7.

5. The first sentence of paragraph 8 attempts to define the class or sub-class which Plaintiffs Gay, Johnson, Barnett and Broadway seek to represent, and to that extent requires no anwser. However, defendants deny that the issues asserted by these plaintiffs may be appropriately maintained by them as a class action, deny that they have standing to raise the issues asserted and deny the remaining allegations of paragraph 8.

6. The first sentence of paragraph 9 attempts to define the class or sub-class which the Plaintiff Clinic seeks to represent and to that extent requires no answer. However, defendants deny that the issues asserted by Plaintiff Clinic may be appropriately maintained by it as a class action, asserts that Plaintiff Clinic is not an appropriate representative of the class or sub-class defined in paragraph 9 since it is not a member of such class or sub-class, deny that it has standing to raise the issues asserted and deny the remaining allegations of paragraph 9.

7. In response to the allegations of paragraph 10, defendants admit that Lee County, Arkansas is a political subdivision of the State of Arkansas and admit that Lee Memorial Hospital is the only hospital situated in Lee County, Arkansas.

8. In response to the allegations of paragraph 11, defendants admit that the Hospital is a nonprofit corporation duly organized pursuant to the laws of the State of Arkansas and state that its principal object is to afford medical and surgical aid for nursing the sick and disabled persons of every creed, nationality and condition.

9. Defendants admit that the Hospital's Board of Governors, along with its Administrator, manages, controls and operates the business of the Hospital and admit that the Board of Governors derives authority from the Hospital Constitution and the laws of the State of Arkansas.

10. Defendants admit the allegations of paragraph 13, as amended.

11. Defendants admit the allegations of paragraph 14.

12. Defendants admit the allegations of paragraphs 15, 16 and 17 and admit that the figures stated therein are approximately correct.

13. Defendants admit the allegations of paragraphs 18, 19, 20 and 21.

14. Responding to the allegations of paragraph 22, defendants admit that by letter dated April 23, 1970, addressed to Plaintiff Blumenthal, the Hospital Board of Governors denied staff membership and privileges to Plaintiff Blumenthal principally because he was not engaged in the general private practice of medicine in Lee County, Arkansas and admit that Plaintiff Blumenthal was further advised that to become eligible for staff membership he must meet all conditions prescribed for eligibility by Article II, Section 1 of the By-laws, rules and regulations of the medical staff, the provisions of which include a requirement that an applicant for staff privileges by a member of the Lee County Medical Society.

15. Defendants admit the allegations of paragraph 23.

16. Defendants deny the allegations of paragraph 24, 25, 26 and 27.

17. Defendants deny each and every material allegation of the Complaint which is not specifically admitted herein.

18. The Complaint fails to state a claim for which relief may be granted.

WHEREFORE, defendants pray that the Complaint be dismissed, for their costs herein expended and all other proper relief.

DAGGETT & DAGGETT,
Suite 1,
8 South Poplar Street,
Marianna, Arkansas 72360.
SMITH, WILLIAMS, FRIDAY & BOWEN,
1100 Boyle Building,
Little Rock, Arkansas 72201,
Attorneys for Defendants.
By G. ROSS SMITH.

CERTIFICATE OF SERVICE

I certify that on July 17, 1970, I mailed a copy of the foregoing Answer to Mr. John T. Lavey, 1820 West 13th Street, Little Rock, Arkansas, 72201, postage prepaid.

G. ROSS SMITH.

———

United States District Court, Eastern District of Arkansas, Western Division
Civil Action No. H–70–C–5

DANIEL S. BLUMENTHAL, ET AL. PLAINTIFFS
v.
LEE MEMORIAL HOSPITAL, ET AL., DEFENDANTS

CONSENT DECREE

1. On June 4, 1970, plaintiffs filed a Complaint with this Court alleging that defendants denied medical staff privileges at the Lee Memorial Hospital in Lee County, Arkansas to Daniel S. Blumenthal and Ralph Wolf and the class of qualified VISTA doctors they purport to represent in violation of the due process and equal protection clauses of the Fourteenth Amendment to the Constitution of the United States; denied the indigent patients of the Lee

County Cooperative Clinic and the class they purport to represent the right to be treated at the Lee Memorial Hospital by a qualified VISTA doctor or any other qualified doctor of their choice in violation of the due process and equal protection clauses of the Fourteenth Amendment to the Constitution of the United States, and in violation of their right of association guaranteed by the First Amendment to the Constitution of the United States; and denied the indigent citizens of Lee County and the class they purport to represent the right to be treated at Lee Memorial Hospital by a qualified doctor of their choice in violation of the due process and equal protection clauses of the Fourteenth Amendment to the Constitution of the United States, and in violation of their right of association guaranteed by the First Amendment to the Constitution of the United States.

2. Defendants have admitted that Daniel S. Blumenthal was denied staff privileges at the Lee Memorial Hospital, principally because he was not engaged in the private practice of medicine in Lee County, Arkansas and have contended that such status is a necessary prerequisite for eligibility for staff privileges pursuant to Hospital regulations; have denied that Plaintiff Blumenthal was by such action deprived of any constitutional or statutory rights; have denied that the regulations of the Hospital and those of the Lee County Medical Society are unconstitutional or unlawful in any manner; have denied that the constitutional or statutory rights of any of the plaintiffs or members of the respective classes they purport to represent have in any way been infringed by the defendants; have asserted that the issues alleged may not appropriately be maintained as a class action and have asserted that the Complaint fails to state a claim for which relief may be granted.

3. Plaintiffs do not admit that the defendants' contentions are true or correct in any respect. Defendants do not admit that the plaintiffs' contentions are true or correct in any respect. However, in order to amicably settle disputed issues of fact and law to the advantage of all concerned, the plaintiffs on their own behalf and on behalf of the respective classes they purport to represent, and the defendants have agreed to the entry of a decree by this Court if such decree receives the Court's approval.

4. Whereas it appears to the Court that the agreement reached between the plaintiffs and the defendants is reasonable and advantageous to the defendants and to the plaintiffs and the members of the respective classes they purport to represent, the Court finds that such agreement should be approved and a Consent Decree entered.

It is, therefore, considered ordered, adjudged and decreed that the plaintiffs and the defendants and their respective successors, agents, officers and employees, and all persons acting in concert or in participation with any of them, including the members of the various classes sought to be represented by the plaintiffs, shall abide by and perform the conditions prescribed in the Order hereinafter set forth.

ORDER

1. Defendants shall, subject to the terms and conditions contained herein, grant Daniel S. Blumenthal, Ralph R. Wolf and all other doctors associated with the Lee County Cooperative Clinic (hereinafter "the Clinic") active medical staff privileges at the Lee Memorial Hospital (hereinafter "the Hospital") equal to the active medical staff privileges accorded to other doctors on the Hospital's active medical staff, provided that the doctors associated with the Clinic are graduates of a recognized medical school, are qualified and are properly licensed to practice medicine in Arkansas.

2. The doctors associated with the Clinic shall seek to have admitted to the Hospital only those patients of the Clinic who are eligible under the guidelines provided by the Office of Economic Opportunity (hereinafter "OEO") for the determination of eligibility of low income individuals for OEO sponsored medical serivces, or for medical services sponsored by organizations or entities affiliated with OEO. If a patient is admitted to the Hospital by a doctor associated with the Clinic and is subsequently determined to be ineligible for the receipt of medical services under such guidelines, the doctor associated with the Clinic shall withdraw from the case and will be succeeded by any doctor engaged in the private practice of medicine in Lee County, Arkansas who is voluntarily chosen by the patient. In the event the OEO rescinds or otherwise fails to provide guidelines pertaining to the eligibility of indigents for the receipt of

medical services, the parties hereto agree to meet and negotiate in good faith for the purpose of establishing standards to be used to determine eligibility of the Clinic's patients for admittance to the Hospital under the terms hereof.

3. Patients admitted to the Hospital by doctors associated with the Clinic will be billed directly, in the same manner as are the patients of the other doctors comprising the Hospital's active medical staff; provided however, that if such a patient does not have means to pay reasonable charges incurred because of the utilization by such patients, or by a doctor on his behalf, of the services or facilities of the Hospital, the Clinic shall be responsible for paying to the Hospital the amount of such reasonable charges.

4. Patients of the doctors associated with the Clinic shall be admitted to the Hospital in the same manner as are the patients of the other doctors of the Hospital's active medical staff. Beds shall be allocated to the doctors associated with the Clinic on an equal basis with other staff doctors at the Hospital.

5. Within two weeks after this Consent Decree is entered by the Court, the Board of Governors of the Hospital and the Hospital's active medical staff and administrator shall meet with the Board of Directors and the administrator of the Clinic and Dr. Ralph R. Wolf at a time and place to be designated by agreement of the Chairman of the Board of Governors of the Hospital and the Chairman of the Board of Directors of the Clinic.

6. The costs of this action are hereby taxed against the defendants.

7. The plaintiffs contend that the defendants are legally obligated to pay to John T. Lavey, their attorney, a reasonable attorney fee for his legal services rendered. Defendants deny that they are so obligated. This issue is therefore reserved for decision and counsel for the respective parties are hereby directed to submit memoranda in support of their positions.

8. The Court hereby retains jurisdiction in this cause for a period of one year from the date of entry of this Consent Decree for such further proceedings as may be necessary or appropriate.

Dated this 6th day of August, 1971.

OREN HARRIS,
United States District Judge.

Approved:
WALKER, KAPLAN, LAVEY & MAYS,
Attorneys for Plaintiffs,
1820 West Thirteenth Street,
Little Rock, Arkansas 72202.
By JOHN T. LAVEY,
DAGGETT & DAGGETT,
Suite 1, 8 South Poplar Street,
Marianna, Arkansas 72360
SMITH, WILLIAMS, FRIDAY & BOWEN,
1100 Boyle Building,
Little Rock, Arkansas 72201,
Attorneys for Defendants.
By J. ROSS SMITH,
G. Ross Smith,
1100 Boyle Building,
Little Rock, Arkansas 72281.

In the United States District Court Eastern District of Arkansas
Eastern Division
No. H 70–C–5

DANIEL S. BLUMENTHAL, ET AL., PLAINTIFFS
v.
LEE MEMORIAL HOSPITAL, ET AL., DEFENDANTS

OPINION AND SUPPLEMENTAL DECREE

The plaintiffs filed this action against the defendants on on June 4, 1970. Jurisdiction is alleged pursuant to 28 U.S.C.A. §1343(3) and (4). Equity jurisdiction is alleged pursuant to 42 U.S.C.A. §§1981 and 1983, seeking rights, privileges and immunities guaranteed by the due process and equal protection clauses of the Fourteenth Amendment to the Constitution of the United States.

and the right of association guaranteed by the First Amendment to the Constitution of the United States.

The plaintiffs seek declaratory judgment under the provisions of 28 U.S.C.A. §§2201 and 2202 to determine the legal rights and relations of and between the respective parties, together with injunctive relief for qualified Volunteers In Service To America, called VISTA, staff privileges for doctors at Lee Memorial Hospital and for indigent citizens of Lee County, Arkansas, in need of medical assistance which was denied to them for arbitrary and invidious reasons in violation of the due process and equal protection clauses of the Fourteenth Amendment to the Constitution of the United States. Further, injunctive relief is sought to secure for indigent patients of the Lee County Cooperative Clinic the right to be treated at the hospital by qualified VISTA doctors, or other qualified doctors of their choice.

Pursuant to joint motion for entry of Consent Decree by the parties, the Court entered an Order on July 7, 1971, treating the proceeding as a class action applicable to all parties, plaintiffs and defendants and their respective successors, agents, officers or employees, and all persons acting in concert or in participation with any of them and to the effect they shall abide by and perform the conditions prescribed in the Order of the Court as a part of the Consent Decree. The effect of the Order is to grant relief sought by the plaintiffs subject to the conditions and requirements described therein.

All questions were resolved with the exception of:

1. Whether the plaintiffs are entitled to reasonable attorney's fee for the legal services rendered by the Honorable John T. Lavey, as a part of the costs taxable to the defendants, and

2. The time by which the Court retains jurisdiction in the cause for further proceedings as may be necessary and appropriate.

Section 6 of the Order as part of the Consent Decree provides: "The costs of this action are hereby taxed against the defendants."

Although the defendants deny certain of the allegations of the complaint of the plaintiffs, it is admitted that Daniel S. Blumenthal, a VISTA doctor, was denied staff privileges at the Lee Memorial Hospital. It follows that the indigent patients generally of the black race within the area and the members of their respective class have likewise been denied privileges at the hospital. Consequently, for the purposes of concluding the questions at issue in this action, the Court finds from the record and the provisions of the Consent Decree and Order applicable to all parties, including their respective classes, and inferences that the allegation of the complaint as to discriminatory practices as established facts.

The Court further concludes that jurisdiction is established, 28 U.S.C.A. §§143(3) and (4); 42 U.S.C.A. §§1981, 1983,2000a–6.

While it is admitted by the parties that the issues involved in this case are "novel and difficult," the Court cannot agree that the law in this area is unsettled. Although no cases are cited applicable to VISTA, an agency of the government to assist poor people in poverty areas operating in behalf of indigent patients of the Lee County Cooperative Clinic, a non-profit charitable corporation organized under the laws of the State of Arkansas, and similar programs pursuant to the Economic opportunity Program established by Congress (42 U.S.C.A. §2701, et seq.), it is well established that a hospital supported by federal funds under federal programs are subject to federal law. While 42 U.S.C.A. §2000a(b)(4) has in most instances been applied to confer derivative coverage on recreational facilities, the legislative history makes it clear that retail stores with lunch counters and "medical facilities" were also intended to be covered. *United States* v. *Medical Society of South Carolina*, 298 F. Supp. 145, 152. In that case the Court stated:

"The right of Negroes to admission to Roper Hospital as patients and to equal employment opportunities is protected by 42 U.S.C. Sections 1981, 1982. See Jones v. Alfred H. Mayer Co., 392 U.S. 409, 88 S.Ct. 2186, 20 L.Ed.2d 1189 (1968); United States v. Beach Associates, Inc, 286 F.Supp. 801, 808 (D.Md. 1968); Dobbins v. Local 212, International Bro. of Elec. Wkrs., 292 F. Supp 413 (S.D.Ohio 1968).

"Since Roper Hospital has approximately 523 employees, it is an employer within the meaning of 42 U.S.C. §2000e(b). Its operation affects commerce within the meaning of 42 U.S.C. §2000e(h).

"A man is presumed to intend the probable consequences of his conduct. Radio Officers' Union etc. v. National Labor Relations Board, 347 U.S. 17, 74 S.Ct. 323, 98 L.Ed. 455, 41 A.L.R.2d 621 (1954). Where, as here, the defendants' course of conduct has predictably resulted in practically no Negroes being patients at Roper Hospital, this is sufficient to meet the requirements of 42 U.S.C.A. §2000a-5(a).

"In cases of racial discrimination, this Court has not only the power but the duty both to enjoin future discrimination, and so far as possible, to eliminate the Louisiana v. United States, 380 U.S. 145, 154, 85 S.Ct. 817, 13 L.Ed.2d 709 (1965); Quarles v. Philip Morris, Incorporated, 279 F.Supp. 505 (E.D.Va. 1968); United Paperworkers, 282 F.Supp. 39 (E.D.La. 1968). In order to assure equal employment opportunities for all employees and applicants for employment in the future and the correction of past discrimination, the plaintiff is entitled to the relief provided for herein. See United States v. Southern Weaving Co., No. 68-10 (D.S.C. June 24, 1968)."

While in the instant case there is no issue with reference to "equal employment opportunities" for employees and applicants for employment, the use of Lee Memorial Hospital for the purposes alleged in the action are reached within the framework of the civil rights act, including the Civil Rights Act of 1964. This has reference to the use of the hospital facilities by voluntary workers under voluntary programs with qualified doctors and the admission of patients under the program for treatment and use of the facilities established largely through federal funds.

This proceeding, therefore, coming within the framework of the Civil Rights Act of 1964, 42 U.S.C.A. §2000a(3)(b), is applicable and authorized that reasonable attorney's fee in the discretion of the Court may be allowed to the prevailing party, other than the United States.[1]

Pursuant to the foregoing findings of fact and conclusions of law, the Court is of the opinion that the plaintiffs are entitled to a reasonable attorney's fee for the services of Honorable John T. Lavey, their attorney, to be taxed as costs against the defendants.

In support of the request, Mr. Lavey has filed by letter a log of services, itemizing the services performed, including the dates and hours, which total the sum of $1,550. Although counsel for the defendants object on the basis: First, that the defendants should not be penalized by assessment of attorney's fee, and, second, the itemized sum requested appears to be excessive, it is noted, however, that no item of the itemized services is specifically challenged.

Both parties have submitted the issues to the court for the determination on the record. The Court is of the opinion that the amount contained in the itemized statement of services is reasonable and should be approved.

It is, therefore, considered, ordered and adjudged that the plaintiffs have judgment against the defendants in the sum of $1,550 as reasonable attorney's fee to be taxed as costs in this proceeding.

IT IS FURTHER ORDERED that jurisdiction of the Court be continued for a period of one year.

In all other respects and conclusions, the Consent Decree pursuant to the joint motion of the parties is reaffirmed.

Dated: August 6, 1971.

OREN HARRIS,

————————,

United States District Judge.

---

[1] 42 U.S.C.A. §2000a-3. (b): (b) In any action commenced pursuant to this subchapter, the court, in its discretion, may allow the prevailing party, other than the United States, a reasonable attorney's fee as part of the costs, and the United States shall be liable for costs the same as a private person.

In The United States District Court For The Eastern District Of Arkansas
Eastern Division
Civil Action No. H–70–C–5

DANIEL S. BLUMENTHAL ET AL. PLAINTIFFS
v.
LEE MEMORIAL HOSPITAL ET AL. DEFENDANTS

MOTION FOR LEAVE TO FILE BRIEF IN SUPPORT OF PLAINTIFFS AS AMICUS CURIAE

The National Legal Program on Health Problems of the Poor respectfully moves this Court for leave to file a Brief in support of the Plaintiffs in this case. We have attached to this Motion copies of the Brief which we ask leave to file.

The National Legal Program on Health Problems of the Poor is a law reform center sponsored and funded by the U.S. Office of Economic Opportunity to provide support for Legal Services and other OEO programs across the country in cases involving health problems of the poor and to provide, through education, research, and legal representation, assistance in the preparation and development of important litigation in health law. The Program is based at the University of California, Los Angeles, School of Law, and has available to it a full staff of attorneys and the resources of the University in support of its work.

The Lee County Cooperative Clinic, one of the Plaintiffs in the instant proceeding, was established under an OEO grant, for the purpose of providing health, nutritional, and medical care to the poor of Lee County. A copy of the original grant application is attached to this Motion and marked Appendix A. The National Legal Program on Health Problems of the Poor considers this Clinic, and the program under which is was established, to be of critical importance to the development of health delivery services to the poor, especially the rural poor, for whom access into the regular health channels has been traditionally limited because of socio-economic reasons.

In addition, the Lee Memorial Hospital is a publicly-owned hospital which was constructed with federal funds under the Hill-Burton Program. Challenges have been brought in other Circuits concerning the obligations of such hospitals to admit physicians to staff privileges without discrimination and without restriction for arbitrary and invidious reasons, as well as the obligations of these hospitals to serve the poor. The Program staff has done extensive research into these issues, is participating in some of the current challenges, and believes that its observations and arguments set forth in the attached brief will be useful to the Court in considering this case.

This brief will concentrate on the issues of: (1) The constitutionality of the hospital's constitution and bylaws with respect to staff privileges under the 14th Amendment of the U.S. Constitution; and (2) the standing of the Plaintiffs.

Respectfully submitted,

Marilyn G. Rose,
MARILYN G. ROSE,

Senior Staff Attorney, National Legal Program on Health Problems of the Poor, Room 2477, School of Law, University of California at Los Angeles, Los Angeles, California 90024.

HIGHLIGHT MEMORANDUM

APPENDIX A

SECTION I. IDENTIFICATION OF COMMUNITY ACTION AGENCY

NAME OF CAA	ORGANIZATION NO.
East-Central Arkansas Economic Opportunity Corporation	

ADDRESS

NO. AND STREET	CITY	STATE	ZIP CODE
P.O. Box 709	Forrest City	Arkansas	72335

EXECUTIVE DIRECTOR

John B. Clark

COUNTIES SERVED

Lee County

CONGRESSMEN

William V. Alexander

CONGRESSIONAL DISTRICTS

First

SECTION II. FUNDING SUMMARY

TYPE OF GRANT ACTION

a. [X] INITIAL   b. [ ] INITIAL PROGRAM YEAR   c. [ ] OTHER (Specify)

PROGRAM YEAR/GRANT ACTION NO.	EOA SECTION(S)
A/0	222 (a) (5)

PROGRAM YEAR		TOTAL FEDERAL SHARE PREVIOUS PROGRAM YEAR	
FROM	TO	AMOUNT	NO. OF MONTHS
January 1, 1970	August 31, 1970	$	

RECOMMENDED THIS GRANT ACTION

FEDERAL SHARE	NON-FEDERAL SHARE	TOTAL COSTS
$39,875	$19,480	$59,355

NEW FEDERAL FUNDS	CASH	ACTUAL PERCENTAGE OF NFS THIS ACTION
39,875	$1,000	33 %

CARRY-OVER FUNDS	IN-KIND	
- 0 -	18,480	

TOTAL FEDERAL SHARE APPROVED FOR PROGRAM YEAR TO DATE	PERCENTAGE OF NON-FEDERAL SHARE FOR PROGRAM YEAR TO DATE
--	-- %

SECTION III. HISTORICAL INFORMATION

DATE OF INITIAL OEO/CAP FUNDING	CUMULATIVE TOTAL FEDERAL NOA FUNDS AWARDED
NA	NA

DATE AND DESCRIPTION OF MERGERS

NA

CAP FORM 10   (REV. AUG 68)

Page 2 of ___

HIGHLIGHT MEMORANDUM

SECTION VI.	SUMMARY OF PROGRAM ACCOUNT		
NAME OF CAA			GRANT NO.
East Central Arkansas Economic Opportunity Corp.			CG-9862
PROGRAM ACCOUNT TITLE			PROGRAM ACCOUNT NO.
Emergency Food and Medical Services			55
ADMINISTERING AGENCY (Use continuation sheet if necessary)		FEDERAL SHARE	NON-FEDERAL SHARE
Lee County Co-operative Clinic		$39,875	$19,480

TOTAL NO. PROFESSIONAL EMPLOYEES	TOTAL NO. NONPROFESSIONAL EMPLOYEES	TOTAL NO. VOLUNTEERS
1	4	3

TOTAL NO. OF PARTICIPANTS	AGE GROUP SERVED	COST PER PARTICIPANT
1200	ALL	$33

NO. OF MONTHS	NO. OF LOCATIONS	NO. OF CLASSES	HOURS
8			

Do you recommend that this program account be funded?

☐ YES, AS REQUESTED

☒ YES, WITH BUDGET AND WORK PROGRAM CHANGES OR CONDITIONS NOTED UNDER COMMENTS

☐ NO (Explanation included in comments)

SUMMARY OF WORK PROGRAM:

Attach a brief descriptive summary of the following topics from the program account work program. Use additional sheets as necessary.

1. Problems Addressed, Objectives and Expected Benefits
2. Activities
3. Resident Participation
4. Training and Technical Assistance Needs
5. Coordination
6. Evaluation
7. Comments

If the program account has been operated previously, give a brief assessment of its strengths and weaknesses.

PURPOSE OF THE GRANT

The purpose of this grant is to establish a community owned cooperative nutrition clinic in Lee County, Arkansas; which will operate with the assistance of VISTA volunteers.

ACTIVITIES OF THE PROGRAM

Concentrating on a focus of identifying and treating nutritional problems the clinic activities will include the following:

(1) Evaluation of the nutritional status of all patients and appropriate treatment of nutritional problems.

(2) Training and employment of two health/nutrition aides drawn from the target population.

(3) Provision of health & nutrition education, home followup, and case finding by the two health aides.

(4) Referral to the food stamp program and the Emergency Food and Medical Services program of all patients needing food.

(5) Referral of patients, when appropriate, to VISTA volunteers trained in housing, sanitation, & economic development, for assistance in dealing with the environmental causes of health and nutrition problems.

(6) Provision of related medical care by a volunteer physician provided by VISTA.

(7) Transportation of patients to the clinic.

(8) Direct involvement of the patients with the clinic as owners and policy-makers.

ORGANIZATION OF THE PROBLEM

(1) The grantee will delegate administration of the program to the Lee County Co-operative Clinic.

(2) The clinic will be operated as a co-operative with a Board of Directors elected by the co-op members.

(3) An advisory board of professions will make recommendations but will not have decision making authority.

(4) Staff will consit of: a. A physician, recruited by VISTA. b. A licensed practical nurse, recruited by VISTA. c. A child psychologist, recruited by VISTA. d. A business administrator to manage the clinic. e. Two health/nutrition aides. f. A secretary. g. A bus driver.

(5) Most laboratory work and drugs are being donated to the clinic by private concerns.

(6) Program activities will be coordinated with the local welfare department, Emergency Food and Medical Services project of the CAA, University of Arkansas Medical Center, state and county extension services nutritionists, and other appropriate agencies.

(7) A commitment has been received from VISTA to recruit another physician to replace the one presently assigned to Lee County.

DEMONSTRATION FEATURES

This grant will demonstrate the following:

(1) The extent of the problem of malnutrition and its health consequences in a rural community.

(2) Methods of treating and solving the health problems of malnutrition in a rural community.

(3) Methods of operation of a clinic which focuses on nutrition. Nutritional problems will be the channel through which patients are contacted and treated.

(4) Involvement of VISTA in assisting in the development of health care for the poor.

(5) Cooperative ownership of a clinic by the low-income population being served.

In the United States District Court for the Eastern District of Arkansas
Eastern Division
Civil Action No. H–70–C–5

DANIEL S. BLUEMENTHAL ET AL. PLAINTIFFS
v.
LEE MEMORIAL HOSPITAL ET AL DEFENDANTS

BRIEF OF THE NATIONAL LEGAL PROGRAM ON HEALTH PROBLEMS OF THE POOR
AS AMICUS CURIAE IN SUPPORT OF ALL PLAINTIFFS

MARILYN G. ROSE,
Senior Staff Attorney, National Legal Program on Health Problems of the Poor, Room 2477, School of Law, University of California at Los Angeles, Los Angeles, California 90024.

QUESTIONS PRESENTED

(1) Whether the provision of the defendant hospital's constitution requiring that an applicant for staff privileges be professionally qualified for membership in the local medical society violates the equal protection clauses of the 14th Amendment of the U.S. Constitution.

(2) Whether the provision of the defendant hospital's by-laws requiring that an applicant for staff privileges be engaged in the private practice of medicine in the county of Lee and a member of the Lee County Medical Society violates the equal protection of the U.S. Constitution.

(3) Whether the plaintiffs have standing to bring this action.

INTRODUCTION AND STATEMENT OF THE CASE

This action was brought by two fully licensed, professionally qualified physicians who were recruited and assigned by VISTA (Volunteers in Service to America), an office of the U.S. Office of Economic Opportunity, to serve successively as staff physician for the Lee County Cooperative Clinic, by four patients of the two physicians, and by the Clinic. As set forth in the Motion for Leave to File Brief in Support of Plaintiffs as Amicus Curiae, the Lee County Cooperative Clinic was established under an OEO grant for the purpose of providing health, nutritional, and medical care to the poor of Lee County, Arkansas. One of the demonstration features of the project is described as "Involvement of VISTA in assisting in the development of health care for the poor" (See Application attached to Motion as Appendix A). The initial funds were approximately $59,355, some $39,875 of which were awarded as the federal share. The non-federal share was $19,480, of which $18,480 was designed to be met by in-kind volunteer service. The application specifically states that the staff would include a physician, recruited by VISTA, and that VISTA would recruit another physician to replace the physician presently assigned. These two physicians are Plaintiffs Blumenthal and Wolf.

The context in which the VISTA project was established, i.e. the poverty and health problems of the poor in Lee County, can be documented by statistics recorded by the U.S. Census Bureau. (Although the official figures given herein are those of the 1960 census, they have not vastly improved in the ensuing decade). Thus, the median family income for Lee County in 1960 was $1,710, the second lowest in the State (U.S. Population Census, General Social and Economic Characteristics, Arkansas, 1960, p. 5–134). The Arkansas State-wide figure was $3,184 (Ibid). Lee County also has the lowest figure in the State in terms of median school years completed (Ibid). While the statistics for the State of Arkansas did not compare too unfavorably with the infant death rates in the nation in 1960 (the statistic which is characteristically used as a sensitive indicator of health status), Lee County compared quite unfavorably, especially for non-white infant deaths. Thus, a computation from the 1960 U.S. Census and the 1960 vital health statics shows : [1]

	Fetal death rate [1]		Infant mortality rate [2]		Neonatal mortality rate [3]	
	White	Nonwhite	White	Nonwhite	White	Nonwhite
Lee County.............	19. 2	36. 2	19. 2	65. 2	19. 2	21. 7
State of Arkansas.......	12. 6	25. 2	22. 4	38. 2	16. 5	20. 2
United States...........	14. 1	26. 8	22. 9	43. 2	17. 2	26. 9

[1] Fetal Deaths per 1,000 live births (i.e. still births).
[2] Infant Deaths per 1,000 live births (i.e. deaths under 1 year).
[3] Neonatal Deaths per 1,000 live births (i.e. deaths under 28 days).

The Defendants are Lee Memorial Hospital, its Administrator, and the members of its Board of Governors. The gravamen of the Action involves the provisions of the Constitution and by-laws of the Hospital which operate to deny State of Arkansas and *professionally qualified for membership in the local* services to the poor of Lee County, thereby precluding the patients of these physicians from admission into the Lee Memorial Hospital.

As alleged in the Complaint (Complaint, para. 19 and 20) and admitted in the Answer (Answer, para. 12), the Constitution and by-laws of the Hospital provide as follows:

"The applicant for membership on the Medical Staff shall be a graduate of an approved or recognized Medical School legally licensed to practice in the

---

[1] The figures for the United States were obtained from the census reports. The figures for Arkansas and for Lee County were computed from an extraction of figures from *Vital Statistics of U.S.*, Vol. II, Part B (Mortality) projected per 1000 live births from *Vital Statistics, 1960*, Vol. I (Natality).

State of Arkansas and *professionalyl qualified for membership in the local Medical Society.*" Article XIV, Section A of the Constitution (emphasis supplied).

"The application for membership to the active medical staff shall be a graduate of a recognized medical school, legally licensed to practice in the State of Arkansas, *engaged in the private practice of medicine in the County of Lee, a member of the Lee County Medical Society.*" Article II, Section 1, of the By-Laws (emphasis supplied).

Further, the Defendants admit in their Answer (Answer, para. 14) that,

". . . the Hospital Board of Governors denied staff membership and privileges to Plaintiff Blumenthal principally because he was not engaged in the general practice of medicine in Lee County, Arkansas and admit that Plaintiff Blumenthal was further advised that to become eligible for staff membership he must meet all conditions prescribed for eligibility by Article II, Section 1 of the By-laws, rules and regulations of the medical staff, the provisions of which include a requirement that an applicant for staff privileges be a member of the Lee County Medical Society."

In said letter of April 23, 1970, a copy of which is attached to the Complaint and marked Exhibit I, Defendants also clearly informed Plaintiff Blumenthal "that the denial of your request for staff privileges has nothing to with your professional qualifications nor is it intended to reflect thereon."

The Plaintiffs challenge the constitutionality of these provisions of the Hospital's constitution and by-laws.

ARGUMENT

I. THE PROVISIONS IN DEFENDANT HOSPITAL'S CONSTITUTION AND BY-LAWS REQUIRING (1) THAT AN APPLICANT FOR STAFF PRIVILEGES BE PROFESSIONALLY QUALIFIED FOR MEMBERSHIP IN THE LOCAL MEDICAL SOCIETY, (2) THAT AN APPLICANT FOR STAFF PRIVILEGES BE ENGAGED IN THE PRIVATE PRACTICE OF MEDICINE IN THE COUNTY OF LEE, AND (3) THAT AN APPLICANT FOR STAFF PRIVILEGES BE A MEMBER OF THE LEE COUNTY MEDICAL SOCIETY, ARE UNCONSTITUTIONAL UNDER THE DUE PROCESS AND EQUAL PROTECTION CLAUSES OF THE 14TH AMENDMENT OF THE U.S. CONSTITUTION.

A. The hospital is publicly-owned and is otherwise engaged in "state-action"

In order to violate the 14th Amendment Defendant Hospital must be either an entity of the State and the other Defendants must be State officials or Defendants must be engaged in "state-action." Defendants qualify under both conditions, as the institution is publicly-owned, by the County of Lee, and it was constructed with federal funds pursuant to the Hospital Survey and Construction Act of 1946 (42 U.S.C. 291 et seq.).

With respect to its ownership, while the Answer admits the allegations of the Complaint that the Hospital is the only one situated in Lee County, Arkansas and that Lee County is a political sub-division of the State of Arkansas, it does not respond to that portion of the allegation that the Defendant Hospital is owned by the County (Complaint, para. 10; Answer, para. 7). Under the Federal Rules averments in a pleading to which a responsive pleading is required are admitted when not denied (Fed. Rules of Civil Procedure, Rule 8(d)). However, one need not reply upon the technical application of the rules of procedure, as the Hospital is officially reported to be a county-owned hospital in the records of the Arkansas Department of Health, Division of Hospitals and Nursing Homes, and the U.S. Department of Health, Education and Welfare. Public Health Service, Health Facilities Planning and Construction Services, which respectively administer the State of Arkansas and Federal aspects of the Hill-Burton program.

The Lee Memorial Hospital is reported by the federal agency as county-owned, constructed as a new facility to supply 27 beds under a Hill-Burton award initially approved in April, 1956; the total cost of such construction is reported to have been $337,881 and the federal share is reported to have been $218,587 (Hill-Burton Project Register, July 1, 1947-June 30, 1969, p. 50).[2] The federal participation and the monetary figures are admitted as substantially accurate by the Answer (Complaint, para. 15; Answer, para. 12). Two Circuits

---

[2] With respect to ownership, the code letter "3" under the "control" column is explained on p. iv of the same document as signifying "county."

have specifically held that participation by an otherwise private, non-profit hospital in the Hill-Burton program rendered the action of the hospital "state-action" for 14th Amendment purposes (*Simkins* v. *Moses Cone Memorial Hospital*, 323 F.2d 959, C.A. 4, 1963, cert. den. 376 U.S. 938; *Sams* v. *Ohio Valley General Hospital*, 413 F.2d 826, C.A.4, 1969; *Meredith* v. *Allen County War Memorial Hospital*, 397 F.2d 33, C.A. 6, 1968).[3]

The active participation of both State and Federal governments in hospital planning and construction as well as the sheer volume of money involved was considered significant by the Fourth Circuit in *Simkins* v. *Moses Cone, supra.* In this regard it should be noted that in the first twenty years the program was in operation the program produced over 424,000 in-patient hospital beds in the United States, some 312,000 of which were in general hospitals (the category in which Defendant Lee Memorial Hospital falls),[4] or 35% of the general hospital beds in the United States.[5] With respect to the State of Arkansas, the records of the Arkansas State Department of Hospitals and Nursing Homes, the designated State Agency, indicate that since the first award was made under the program in Arkansas in 1947, some 37 private, non-profit and 85 publicly-owned general hospitals have been awarded Hill-Burton moneys. In accordance with the federal Statute (42 U.S.C. 291d), the State agency annually submits a state plan, detailing hospital needs, practices, and future plans to the Surgeon General, U.S. Public Health Service. Awards of Hill-Burton moneys are made in accordance with the Plan. The activities of the State agency in planning and participating in the programming of these facilities as well as the enormous amount of federal funds involved renders the action of the Hospital "state-action" for 14th Amendment purposes apart from any doubt that still might exist as to its ownership.

B. The provisions of the constitution and bylaws of the hospital are arbitrary and capricious, and a denial of equal protection of the laws within the meaning of the 14th amendment

As admitted by Defendants, the constitution and bylaws of the Lee Memorial Hospital require an applicant for staff privileges to satisfy the following three requirements: (1) he must be "professionally qualified for membership in the local medical society"; (2) he must be engaged in the private practice of medicine in Lee County; and (3) he must be a member of the Lee County Medical Society. Dr. Blumenthal was specifically informed that he was rejected because he did not satisfy these requirements and that the rejection in no way reflected upon his professional qualifications.[6] Dr. Wolf, who replaced Dr. Blumenthal as the VISTA physician at the Lee County Cooperative Clinic, also does not meet the three qualifications. Indeed no VISTA physician at the Clinic, by the very nature of his position, can meet the qualifications of being engaged in the private practice of medicine. The Answer specifically admits that this is the principal reason for the rejection of Dr. Blumenthal (Answer, para. 14). Under both State Law and the 14th Amendment, these qualifications constitute invidious discrimination.

With respect to qualification (3), i.e. membership in the County Medical Society, both State and Federal Courts (including the Supreme Court of Arkansas) which have considered the issue have held consistently that the requirement that a physician be a member of the medical association or that he

---

[3] In the only case in which the Eighth Circuit considered the implications of Hill-Burton participation upon the "state-action" doctrine, the Court specifically refrained from deciding the question, accepting it for that case and deciding the case on grounds that the Plaintiff has failed to show "unreasonable, arbitrary, or invidious discrimination." *Stanturf* v. *Sipes*. 335 F.2d 224, 226, 229 (C.A. 8, 1964). The case involved claims brought against a Hill-Burton funded hospital arising from a denial of admission to a man lacking means to pay a deposit. That Court did note that *Simkins* dealt with the special situation of racial discrimination and a provision of the Hill-Burton Act which unconstitutionally permitted "separate-but-equal" facilities. Since the 8th Circuit considered the issue, both the 4th Circuit in *Sams, supra,* and the 6th Circut in *Meredith, supra,* have applied the doctrine to the area of staff privileges in a non-racial context.

[4] Facts about the Hill-Burton Program, July 1, 1947-December 31, 1968, U.S. Department of Health, Education and Welfare. Public Health Service, p. 5.

[5] Hospitals, Journal of the American Hospital Association. August 1, 1969, Part Two, p. 476, lists 5880 general, short term hospitals in the United States in 1958, with 894,416 beds.

[6] Dr. Blumenthal, in the year prior to his service at the Lee Cooperative Clinic, was selected as the outstanding intern of the year at Charity Hospital of New Orleans, a matter which we believe that the Court can officially take notice.

be approved by the medical society as a condition to staff privileges at a publicly-owned hospital is arbitrary, invidious discrimination. *Hamilton County Hospital* v. *Andrews*, 227 Ind.217, 84 NE2d 469(1949), reh. den. 227 Ind. 228, 85 NE 2d 365, cert. den. 338 U.S. 831; *Ware* v. *Benedikt*, 280 SW 2d 234 (Ark. 1955); *Foster* v. *Mobile County Hospital Board*, 398 F2d 227 (C.A. 5, 1968). See also Farbo, *Legal Relationship of Physician to Hospital*, 43 Conn. Bar Journal 418 (1968).

The *Hamilton* case involved bylaws which required the recommendation by the staff and membership in the county medical society as conditions precedent to receiving staff privileges. The Indiana Court set the tenor of subsequent decisions throughout the country on the issue by finding that such rules amounted to an unconstitutional delegation of the powers of the hospital. That court stated, "It will be further noted that by the involved rules, appellee's right to practice in the hospital is not only conditioned on his being a member of the staff, but also on his being a member of the Hamilton County Medical Society. [cites] Whether he could ever become a member depends upon conditions beyond his control. By this rule the hospital again delegates its powers to determine what physicians may use its facilities. It amounts to a preference in favor of the society and a discrimination against the physicians who by choice or otherwise, are not members of same." (84 NE2d at 472).

In *Ware* v. *Benedikt*, the Arkansas Supreme Court cited *Hamilton* with approval, finding that the original bylaw requiring membership in the medical society and the amended bylaw requiring the approval of the medical society were both unreasonable and discriminatory at defendant public hospital. The Fifth Circuit similarly agreed in *Foster* v. *Mobile County Hospital Board, supra.*

With respect to the requirement relating to the private practice of medicine, Courts have struck down requirements that impose the concepts of the local medical society upon the grant of staff privileges at a public hospital (*Group Health Corporation* v. *King County Medical Society*, 39 Wash. 2d 386, 237 P2d 737, 781 (1951)) or at one affected with a public interest (*Greisman* v. *Newcomb Hospital*, 40 N.J. 389, 192 A2d 817 (1963). Thus in the *Group Health* case the Washington Supreme Court found that the exclusion of physicians from the staff of a public hospital because they practiced contract medicine to be "unreasonable, arbitrary, capricious, and discriminatory."

The decision of the New Jersey Supreme Court in *Greisman* is particularly appropriate to the consideration of the facts herein. That hospital was a private hospital, but the only one in the County. The physician had been denied staff privileges because he was a doctor of osteopathy and had not been admitted for that reason to the County Medical Society. In an earlier case the New Jersey Supreme Court had rejected that as a basis for denial of membership in the County Medical Society, in view of the fact that the State of New Jersey fully licensed doctors of osteopathy.[7] In *Greisman* the Court said "The Newcomb Hospital is the only hospital in the Vineland metropolitan area and it is publicly dedicated primarily to the care of the sick and injred of Vineland and its vicinity and, thereafter to the care of such other persons as may be accommodated. Doctors need hospital facilities and a physician practicing in the metropolitan Vineland area will understandably seek them at the Newcomb Hospital. Furthermore, every patient of his will want the Newcomb Hospital facilities to be readily available. It hardly suffices to say that the patients could enter the hospital under the care of a member of the existing staff, for his personal physician would have no opportunity of participating in his treatment; nor does it suffice to say that there are other hospitals outside the metropolitan Vineland area, for they may be too distant or unsuitable to his needs and desires. All this indicates very pointedly that, while the managing officials may have discretionary powers in the selection of the medical staff, those powers are deeply imbedded in public aspects, and are rightly viewed, for policy reasons entirely comparable to those expressed in Falcone, as fiduciary powers to be exercised reasonably and for the public good." (192 A2d at 824).

The qualification relating to being "professionally qualified for membership in the local medical society" carries the odious traits rejected in both lines of cases. It delegates to a private body, the medical society, the determination of what qualifications are professionally necessary for admission to staff privileges at a public hospital, constructed with federal funds, albeit the appli-

---

[7] *Falcone* v. *Middlesex County Medical Society*, 34 N.J. 582, 170 A2d 791.

cant is fully licensed to practice in the State of Arkansas, and it enforces the concepts of the private group upon the method of practice *albeit* lawful in the State of Arkansas.

All three requirements constitute the type of discrimination condemned by the 14th Amendment. In *Foster* v. *Mobile Medical Society, supra,* the Fifth Circuit found that the bylaws of the hospital which required membership in the Mobile Medical Society thus discriminated between members and non-members, a distinction not related to the express purpose for the formation of the medical staff, nor resting on any reasonable basis which may be constitutionally applied in determining the class of people who are eligible to practice at a public hospital. Similarly in *Sams* v. *Ohio Valley General Hospital,* 413 F2d 826, the Fourth Circut found that a residence requirement for staff privileges was one without rationality, constitutionally frigolous, and may not be used to bar physicians from the grant of staff privileges at a privately-owned hospital constructed with Hill-Burton moneys.[8]

II. The Plaintiffs have Standing To Bring This Action

Plaintiffs in this Action fit into three basic categories. The first category is that of VISTA physician. Daniel Blumenthal was the VISTA physician assigned to the Lee County Cooperative Clinic at the time the Action commenced, and as Defendants admit was denied staff privileges at the only hospital in the County principally because he was not engaged in the private practice of medicine in the County, but also because he did not meet the by-law requirement of being a member of the County Medical Society, both requirements which we have shown above are unlawful. Ralph Wolf is the VISTA physician assigned to replace Dan Blumenthal on July 1, 1970; he also fails to meet the hospital's unlawful by-law requirements. They bring the Action on their own behalf and on behalf of all other duly qualified VISTA physicians who may be assigned to Lee County to serve as staff physician at the Lee County Cooperative Clinic.

The second category of plaintiffs is represented by Ginnie Gay, Maurice Johnson, Leila Barnett and Mildred Broadway, who are citizens and residents of Lee County, and patients of the VISTA physician at the Lee County Cooperative Clinic. They sue on their own behalf and on behalf of all other indigent persons similarly situated who are citizens and residents of Lee County who want to be hospitalized at the Lee Memorial Hospital and desire to have the choice of their own physician.

The third category of plaintiffs is the Clinic which brought the action on its own behalf and on behalf of all of its indigent patients who want to be hospitalized at the Lee Memorial Hospital and desire to be treated by a qualified physician of their own choice.

Defendants deny the standing of each of the Plantiffs to bring the Action. Their position not only thus denies standing to every party who could possibly have an interest to bring the lawsuit, but also completely ignores the present status of the doctrine of standing to sue as it has developed in recent years in the U.S. Courts of Appeals and Supreme Court.

There are two basic predicates to the concept of standing: (1) that the plaintiffs have the personal stake in the outcome necessary to satisfy the case or controversy requirements of Article III of the Constitution; (2) that the plaintiffs are asserting rights within the "zone of interests" of the Statute or Constitutional provision asserted. Interwoven into the consideration of these predicates is the further concept that when the rights are asserted by one as a representative of a class, the case is not mooted by the possible mooting of the relief sought for the individual plantiff, so long as the interests asserted for other members of the class persist.

A. The plaintiffs have the necessary adverseness to satisfy case or controversy requirements

The first basic predicate is a requirement that plaintiffs possess the personal stake and interest in the outcome of the action that import the concrete adverseness required by Article III. E.g. *Barlow* v. *Collins,* 397 U.S. 159;

---

[8] *Sams* appears to have followed *Shapiro* v. *Thompson,* 394 U.S. 618, wherein residence as a basis of benefits conferred by a State was struck down as constitutionally infirm.

Data Processing Service v. *Camp*, 397 U.S. 150; *Flast* v. *Cohen*, 392 U.S. 83. The Supreme Court articulated the concept thus in *Flast*:

"The fundamental aspect of standing is that it focuses on the party seeking to get his complain before a federal court and not on the issues he wishes to have ajudicated. The 'gist of the question' is whether the party seeking relief has alleged such a personal stake in the outcome of the controversy as to assure that concrete adverseness which sharpens the presentation of issues upon which the court so largely depends for illumination of difficult constitutional questions.'" (At 99)

". . . in ruling on standing, it is both appropriate and necessary to look to the substantive issues for another purpose, namely to determine whether there is a logical nexus between the status asserted and the claim sought to be adjudicated." (At 102)

In *Flast* the Supreme Court held that federal taxpayers had standing to challenge a federal spending program on the grounds it constituted a violation of the establishment and free exercise of religion clauses of the First Amendment. A taxpayer thus has status to challenge the expenditure of his moneys, no matter how small a part of the whole, in the fulfillment of a purpose clearly interdicted by the Constitution.

In the instant case the rights asserted are those of physicians denied staff privileges and consequently the means and facilities to treat their patients at a public hospital, those patients of those physicians who are denied the choice of their physician by rules which are demonstrably unlawful, and those of a publicly-funded Clinic to fulfill the purpose for which it was funded by being able to have its patients admitted to the local hospital when necessary. The rights of all three categories are indeed personal and the stake of all three categories is clear.

Cases considered by the various Courts of Appeals support this obvious conclusion that the rights of all three categories are personal and the stake of each is clear. In *Cypress* v. *Newport News General Hospital*, 375 F.2d 648 (G.A. 4, 1967) the Fourth Circuit held that two physicians who were denied staff privileges on the basis of race may bring an action on their own behalf, on behalf of all Negro physicians practicing in Neport News, and on behalf of *"those Negro physicians who are not now members of the community because of discriminatory practises of hospitals there."* (At 653 fn9). The fact that Dr. Cypress was given staff privileges did not moot the matter, although individual relief as to him was no longer necessary; he still could represent the rights of the class denied privileges which were denied to him at the commencement of the litigation for discriminatory reasons. Dan Blumenthal stands in the same position; he represents all physicians whom the Clinic would employ, as none by virtue of such employment can qualify as being engaged in the private practice of medicine. The Hospital Board has clearly admitted in the Answer that such "failure" precludes the grant of staff privileges. So too did the Fifth Circuit hold in *Otis* v. *Crown Zellerbach*, 398 F.2d 496 (1968) in which the named plaintiff had voluntarily moved from the public housing from which she was allegedly being discriminatorily evicted. In this regard see also *McSwain* v. *Board of Education*, 138 F. Supp. 570 (E.D. Tenn. 1956), where all the children named as plaintiffs in a school desegregation case had graduated; *Rackley* v. *Board of Trustees of Orangeburg Hospital*, 238 F. Supp. 512 (E.D. S.C., 1965) where the named Plaintiffs were not then living in the State; and *Gaddis* v. *Wyman*, 304 F. Supp. 713 (1969) where the named Plaintiffs had all been put on welfare rolls. The interest of the class, *qua* class persists.

To the extent that Ralph Wolf stands in a slightly different position from Dan Blumenthal, it is that of the new physician who has not been specifically turned down for staff privilieges. But, as recognized by the Fifth Circuit in *Oatis*, with respect to the class for which Oatis claimed relief, none of whom had followed the required statutory procedure of filing charges with the E.E.O.C., "Moreover, it does not appear that to allow a class action, within proper confines, would in any way frustrate the purposes of the Act that the settlement of grievances be first attempted through the office of the EEOC. It would be wasteful, if not vain, for numerous employees, all with the same grievance, to have to process many identical complaints with the E.E.O.C." (At 498).

In this case the Board of the Hospital has made it clear in its Answer that the private practice requirement will be followed. It would be vain to require each physician at the Clinic to go through the procedure of applying, awaiting disposition, and being finally turned down, maybe after several of his patients have suffered irreparable harm or death. After all, we are talking about admission to a hospital!

Patients of these Clinic physicians also clearly have the personal stake and interest required by the Court. As recognized in *Cypress*, patients of physicians denied staff privileges ". . . are unreasonably forced to a hard choice. They must elect either to forgo treatment at that hospital or relinquish their personal physicians, since patients can be admitted to Riverside only on referral by members of the staff." (At 653).

See also *Griswold v. Connecticut*, 381 U.S. 479 (1965). Further, Lee Memorial Hospital is publicly-owned and the only hospital in the county, and denial of admission at that hospital, especially to indigent persons, effectively means no hospitalization for such persons.

The Clinic also possesses the personal interest and stake in the outcome, for one of the basic purposes for which it was formed was to promote the health of the indigent of Lee County and to bring health services to them by employing a qualified physician. If that physician can not obtain staff privileges at the hospital, then this health services purpose is diminished if not destroyed. Further, the Clinic may represent in interests of all indigent persons in the County who need hospitalization, as service to these persons and the effectuation of this need comes within the purpose of the Clinic's organization. The Eighth Circuit has recognized that an organization may be a proper party in a lawsuit in which its members are a class of persons claiming to have been denied equal protection. See *Smith v. Board of Education of Morrilton*, 365 F. 2d 770 (1965). The Court of Appeals for the District of Columbia has held that the President of a labor union is a proper party to assert rights of the individual members of the union against action of the government which could cost them jobs, *Curran v. Laird* (420 F.2d 122 (1969)). And in *Data Processing Services v. Camp*, 397 U.S. 160, Plaintiff was an association suing on behalf of its members.

Individually and collectively plaintiffs herein have the personal stake and concrete adverseness necessary to satisfy the constitutional predicate for standing.

B. The rights of plaintiffs are within the "zone of interests" of their constitutional and statutory claims

Most of the discussion under the "zone of interests" aspect is already incorporated into the prior discussion, both as to the illegality of the three requirements in issue and as to the necessary stake in the outcome aspect of this part. Thus, in *Foster v. Mobile County Hospital Board*, 398 F.2d 227-230, the requirement that a physician be a member of the County Medical society as a condition for staff privileges operates as a denial of equal protection of the laws with respect to such nonmembers. Such a requirement was characterized as "unreasonable, arbitrary, capricious or discriminatory" by the Arkansas Supreme Court in *Ware v. Benedikt*, 280 S.W.2d 234, 236; those characterizations are the elements of which a denial of due process or equal protection are made. The claims of the physicians are clearly within the zone of interests of the 14th Amendment protection. So too are the rights of the patients of these physicians, to be treated by physicians of their choice, (e.g. *Cypress v. Newport News General Hospital*, 375 F.2d at 653) and the Clinic on behalf of all such indigent persons.

In addition to the constitutional "zone of interests" consideration, there is a statutory claim, flowing from the Hill-Burton nature of this hospital. As discussed earlier, this hospital was constructed pursuant to the federal-state hospital construction program. In order to be awarded funds it had to satisfy priorities set by the State in a Federally-approved State Plan; in fact it received ⅔ of its construction money under that grant. Certain subprovisions of the Hill-Burton Act have particular reference to the instant case. Thus, Lee Memorial Hospital was given a statutory priority as a facility serving a rural community [9] and the facility will provide a reasonable volume of free patient care." [10] The State must also provide in its plan for adequate hospitals for persons unable to pay. [11]

The Hill-Burton Act was born of a crisis, that of the dire shortage of hospitals in the United States in 1946. During the course of hearings on the Hill-Burton bill the needs of poor, rural communities were reiterated. [12]

The four citizen-resident plaintiffs, patients of the physicians at the Lee County Cooperative Clinic, and others in the class of indigent citizens and residents of Lee County, are by their very description beneficiaries of all three provisions of the Hill-Burton Act and the contractual commitment made by the hospital. As such they have standing to bring a claim of abridgment of their rights under that Statute. As stated by the Fifth Circuit with respect to the claims of Negro school children against a school district which received Federal financial assistance under a commitment not to discriminate as set forth in Title VI of the Civil Rights Act of 1964, "In the absence of a procedure through which the individuals protected by section 601's prohibition may assert their rights under it, violations of the law are cognizable by the courts. [cites] The Bossier Parish School Board accepted federal financial assistance in November 1964, and thereby brought its school system within the class of programs subject to the section 601 rights." *Bossier Parish School Board* v. *Lemon*, 370 F.2d 847, 851 (C.A. 5, 1967).

The denial of staff privileges to their physicians in a very real sense operates as a denial of admission for services to them as patients by the hospital. As stated by the Fourth Circuit in this regard: ". . . the plaintiffs [physicians] are forced to place their Ohio County patients in hospitals situated out of the vicinage of the ill persons. Thus, not alone appellant doctors, but as well the inhabitants of Ohio County are disserved by this rule. This thought discloses an especially nocuous aspect: hospitals sponsored by the Federal and State government for the public generally have voluntarily curtailed the fulfillment

---

[9] For twenty-four years, i.e. from the beginning of the program until June 30, 1970, the Act provided that by general regulations the Surgeon General prescribe the manner in which the State Agency determines priorities, "giving special consideration——' (1) in the case of projects for the construction of hospitals to facilities serving rural communities and areas with relatively small financial resources.'" Section 603, Title VI of the Public Health Service Act, Pub. Law 88–443. See U.S. Code Congressional and Administrative News, Hospital and Medical Facilities Amendments of 1964, pp. 518 et seq, pp 2800 et seq. The earlier version, containing the same words, may be found at U.S. Code Congressional Service, 79th Cong., 2nd Sess. (1946) Pub. Law 725, p. 1007, 1109, sec. 622(e). In the 1970 version of the Act, the mandatory nature of the rural priority was deleted, and Section 603 now gives priority to "areas with relatively small financial resources and, at the option of the State, rural communities." PL–91–296, on HR 11102, June 30, 1970.

[10] The official records of both the State agency and the U.S. Department of Health, Education, and Welfare contain the application for the grant. The language quoted above is the exact language in the application, which was the standard form then used by the Hill-Burton program (Budget Bureau No. 68.R309.5). The authorization for the provision was then, and is now, found in the Statute and the Hill-Burton regulation. Specifically, section 622(f) provided that the Surgeon General may issue a regulation to provide that before an application by approved by the State agency, the individual applicant give assurance that "there will be made available in each such hospital or addition to a hospital a reasonable volume of hospital services to persons unable to pay therefor, but an exception shall be made if such a requirement is not feasible from a financial standpoint." See U.S. Code Congressional Service, 79th Cong., 2nd Sess. (1964) Pub. Law 725, at p. 1009. The Regulation issued thereunder contained such a provision. (12 Fed. Reg. 6176; 1947 Supp. CFR, Part 53, Section 53.63). The 1964 and 1970 versions of the Statute also contain the provision, as does the existing Regulation (42 U.S.C. 291c(e); 42 CFR 53.111).

[11] The same section of the statute, referred to in footnote 10, contains a requirement that "the State plan shall provide for adequate hospital facilities for the people residing in a State . . . and shall provide for adequate hospital facilities for persons unable to pay therefor."

[12] As stated by the then Surgeon General of the Public Health Service: "Of the more than 3,000 counties in the Nation, approximately 40 percent have no registered hospitals. While not every one of these counties may need a separate hospital, many unquestionably need some type of health facility. Thes inadequacies are not due to a lack of interest or initiative. They are caused primarily by a lack of economic means by which hospital and health facilities are acquired. Hospitals are expensive to build and require a high concentration of skills for their operation. It is in the wealthier States and metropolitan areas that the best and most abundant of our hospital facilities are concentrated." Hearings before a Subcommittee of the Committee on Interstate and Foreign Commerce, 79th Cong., 2nd Sess., on S191, (Surgeon General Thomas Parran) p. 16.

of this goal . . ." *Sams* v. *Ohio Valley General Hospital*, 413 F.2d 826, 829 (C.A. 4, 1969).

The certainly come within the "zone of interest" of the Statute as recently ennunciated by the Supreme Court in *Data Processing* v. *Camp*, 397 U.S. 180, and *Barlow* v. *Collins*, 397 U.S. 159.

CONCLUSION

For the foregoing reasons, and on the record as it stands, the Court may and should grant the relief sought by the Plaintiffs in this matter.

Dated: August 26, 1970

Respectfully submitted,

Marilyn G. Rose,
MARILYN G. ROSE,
Senior Staff Attorney, National Legal Program on Health Problems of the Poor, UCLA School of Law, Los Angeles, California 90024.

DECLARATION OF SERVICE

I hereby certify that I have served copies of the attached Motion for Leave to File Brief Amicus Curiae and copies of the Brief Amicus Curiae on all plaintiffs and defendants in the action by placing copies of same in the United States mail at Los Angeles, California, on the date below indicated, addressed as follows:

JOHN T. LAVEY AND JOHN W. WALKER,
WALKER, ROTENBERRY, KAPLAN, LAVEY & HOLLINSWORTH,
1820 West 13th Street,
Little Rock, Arkansas 72202.

JACK GREENBERG, JAMES M. NABRIT III, AND MICHAEL MELTSNER,
10 Columbus Circle,
New York, New York.
Attorneys for Plaintiffs.

DAGGETT & DAGGETT,
Suite 1,
8 South Popular Street,
Marianna, Arkansas 72360.
G. ROSS SMITH,
SMITH, WILLIAMS, FRIDAY & BOWEN,
1100 Boyle Building,
Little Rock, Arkansas 72201,
Attorneys for Defendants.

Dated: August 26, 1970.

MARILYN G. ROSE,
Senior Staff Attorney, National Legal Program on Health Problems of the Poor, UCLA School of Law, Los Angeles, California 90024.

———

Exhibit 3.—*Material Submitted Re "Black Belt Community Health Center" Application*

DEPARTMENT OF HEALTH, EDUCATION, AND WELFARE,
REGION IV,
Atlanta, Ga., 30323 December 11, 1973.

Miss MELBAH J. McAFEE,
Acting Project Director,
Black Belt Community Health Center,
P.O. Box 95,
Epes, Ala.

Re Project Application No. 04–H–000816–01.

DEAR MISS McAFEE: Your application entitled "Black Belt Community Health Center" has been reviewed by the Regional Office according to 314(e) policies and program guidelines governing neighborhood health center projects. I regret to inform you that your application was disapproved.

In reviewing your application, reviewers noted that total community support failed to be demonstrated and endorsements from organized health planning and medical agencies were not evident. It was further noted that the plan failed to provide for dental services, and pharmaceutical services, as described, were inadequate. It was also noted that administrative control elements (measurable objectives) were not evident in the plan.

If you have any questions concerning this action, please contact Dr. Herbert A. Hudgins, Associate Regional Health Director for Health Services Delivery, telephone (494) 526-5561.

Sincerely yours,

EDDIE J. SESSIONS,
Acting Regional Health Administrator, H.

DEPARTMENT OF HEALTH, EDUCATION, AND WELFARE,
REGION IV,
Atlanta, Ga., 30323 June 11, 1973.

Miss MELBAH J. MCAFEE,
Project Administrator,
Black Belt Family Health Care Center,
P.O. Box 95
Epes, Ala.
Re: Project No. 04-H-000658-02-0.

DEAR MISS MCAFEE: Your continuation application entitled "Black Belt Family Health Care Center," has been reviewed in accordance with current review procedures and priorities governing Family Health Center project grants. We regret to inform you that your continuation application was not approved.

In reviewing your application, it was noted that you were awarded a grant last year in which to develop an operational Family Health Center. However, your continuation application, as submitted, did not meet the refunding criteria. For example; (1)* there is no evidence of provider support, (2) no formal commitments from hospital, specialists, or third party payors, and (3) inadequate capitation premium rates.

We are aware of the need for health services in this area. However, we cannot support this program under Family Health Center Legislation. In line with this, we would consider a phase out period up to three months not to exceed $50,000 of anticipated lapsing funds. It will be necessary for you to submit a budget and a time frame for phasing out this federally supported project as described above. This budget should be received by this office no later than July 1, 1973.

For further information concerning this action, please contact your project officer.

Sincerely yours,

EDDIE J. SESSIONS,
Interim Regional Health Director.

HOME OF LIVINGSTON UNIVERSITY,
Livingston, Ala., April 26, 1973.

Hon. JACK EDWARDS,
Congressman of Alabama,
Sam Rayburn Building,

DEAR CONGRESSMAN EDWARDS: I enclose the Minutes of a meeting of the Sumter County Board of Census which was held for the purpose of discussing the Federation of Southern Cooperative HEW grant.

The Federation and Black Belt Family Health Care Center have applied for the second year of grant money in the approximate amount of $500,000.00. This organization points out in the application that they have been unable to find a physician in their first year of operation, after expenditure of almost $230,000.00. They state that they have some prospects for locating a physician. During the same period of time, without the help of Federal monies, the City of Livingston, its hospital board and staff, have brought in a doctor from Keywest, Florida, who is a general practitioner; has obtained the agreement of a graduate from the University of Alabama to locate in Livingston in

July of 1973, (a clinic is presently under construction for him) and it has obtained the consent of an outstanding pathologist who will handle the pathological work for West Alabama area. This will increase the medical team in Sumter County to six general practitioners, a Board certified general surgeon, and a qualified pathologist. (Compared to three general practitioners in 1969) We have working with us through the West Alabama Mental Health Department, an active Mental Health Organization and have reached a tentative agreement with Livingston University whereby two unused dormitories will be made available for minimum security mental care patients. We obtained a license and authority from the State of Alabama Board of Health, Board of Census, and nursing department to establish a nursing school at Livingston University, a school to train laboratory technicians. We are nearing completion of a forty-bed addition to the Sumter Memorial Hospital to make this hospital an eighty-bed hospital with intensive care, cardiac units, two emergency rooms, pathological lab and radiological laboratory.

The application by the Federation shows that no means of transportation have been devised whereby the needy could be transported to health care facilities, but we have, in conjunction with West Alabama Mental Health Department, begun a study for a program to provide transportation for those in need of health care. Negotiations are only in the preliminary stages, but stand a much more reasonable chance of success than the undefined and untried transportation described in the application of the Federation only as a need.

The aggregate amount of all funds applied for by this organization would more than pay for the construction of all of the hospitals and doctors' clinics in Sumter County, and yet they have no doctor to utilize the clinic, and they do not have adequate health manpower. The facilities which we are preparing, however, will not only provide facilities for the treatment of the sick in the entire West Alabama area, but also provide facilities for the training of health manpower in a regional medical facility. This regional medical facility complex conforms to the method which was recommended by the Alabama Regional Medical Program for solving the health care needs for the people in rural areas.

The application points out that this organization proposes to solicit from a membership of 2,000 families a contribution based on the income of the family. If the organization operates at its maximum output on an expenditure of 1.5 million as shown by its third year budget figure, then those families, after the discontinuation of Federal Grants, will have to contribute $750.00 for each family to maintain the program. This is a pretty stiff to pay, especially in an area where the average family income is less tht $3,500.00. It would appear that at the end of the five-year Federal participation period, HEW, the Federation, and the Black Belt Care Center will pick up their skirts and skedaddle and leave us with 2,000 families who expect medical miracles to be accomplished by local officials.

For the good of all concerned, except those who are receiving the salaries paid by the Federal Grants, this project should be discontinued. We solicit your help.

Sincerely,

DRAYTON PRUITT, JR.

THE SUMTER COUNTY BOARD OF CENSORS

The Sumter County Board of Censors met on call of the chairman, H. C. Hunt, M.D., at the Sumter Memorial Hospital. In addition to Dr. Hunt, who presided, all the Censors were present; namely, Drs. F. M. Crenshaw, D. P. Hightower, J. R. Walton (who is also chief of the Hill Hospital of York), Sidney J. Williams, Dr. E. L. Gegan, Chief of staff of the Sumter Memorial Hospital, attended.

Others present were Aubrey D. Green, Chairman of Hill Hospital Board, J. L. Sims, Administrator of The Hill Hospital of York, W. T. Steele, Administrator of The Sumter Memorial Hospital, Livingston Mayor Drayton Pruitt, Jr., (York Mayor W. C. Grant was unable to attend as was Mack Binion of Medical Association of the State of Alabama because of unresolvable conflicts), Charles Stewart, representing Preston Blanks, Acting Director of the

State Office of Comprehensive Health Planning and Pete Bailey, representing Dr. Elizabeth Cleino, Director of the West Alabama Comprehensive Health Planning Council.

This meeeting had been called for a full and frank discussion the The Black Belt Family Health Center, at Epes sponsored by the Federation of Southern Cooperatives.

PREFACE

The history of fruitless efforts on the part of local people representing health and government, the Comprehensive Health Planning "A" and "B" Agencies meeting with representatives of the Federation of Southern Cooperatives and on at least two occasions with representatives of HEW Atlanta people, to bring about a meeting of minds on cooperation. In each of these meetings expressions of consideration (agreement?) were voiced by The Federation of Southern Cooperative people, but were never implemented by that group.

A case in point! On June 10, 1972 Dr. John Packard, Director of Alabama Regional Medical Program, Mr. M. D. Plowden also of ARMP, Dr. Williams (representing public health and Mayor Pruitt) met with representatives of The Federation of Southern Cooperatives, and after discussion made certain concrete recommendations; namely, (1) That any center built be immediately adjacent to a hospital; (2) That a medical director—a qualified physician— be recruited who would not limit his practice to Federation of Southern Cooperatives clients and who could qualify as a member of the hospital's medical staff and practices in conformity with the hospital staff's rules and regulations (to this end those present offered support), (3) That The Federation Southern Cooperatives seek ways to assists its clientele in purchasing low cost hospital (health) insurance, perhaps using the plan enacted by the 1971 legislature; (4) That a joint effort be made toward these ends.

Subsequently and without further consultation with local government and health leaders on the part of the Federation, we learned that an application for funding had been made directly to the Department of HEW in Washington. Although, all State of Alabama planning agencies, and even the HEW Regional Office in Atlanta were bypassed, a grant of over $200,000.00 was made to the Federation.

Other conferences including local, county, and state leaders, and on at least two occasions, representatives from The HEW Regional office in Atlanta, were held, trying to find a workable solution were to no avail.

After failure of these local efforts, and, upon request from The State Board of Censors upon a request to the entire Alabama congressional delegation to intercede in the matter. This The State Board of Censors did. Subsequently a conference was held in the office of Congressman Walter Flowers on January 17, 1973. At this conference were Mr. Flowers, staff members of the other Representatives and Senators, Mayor Pruitt, Dr. Williams, Dr. Paul B. Batalden and a member of his staff.

It was very carefully pointed out at this meeting that local and state leaders had tried to cooperate with the Federation of Southern Cooperatives, but had been completely ignored in every instance.

At hand for our consideration was a discussion of the Continuing Grant Application for the Black Belt Family Health Care Center for the second year.

The following are matters of record :

1. Mr. Stewart presented the critical analysis by the Comprehensive Health Planning Agency. (attached)

2. Mayor Pruitt discussed past difficulties and made cogent observations as to fiscal matters pertaining to The Federation of Southern Cooperative's Black Belt Family Health Center. (attached)

3. The members of the Sumter County Board of Censors and the others present living in Sumter County were unanimous in willingness to work with the Federation of Southern Cooperatives in efforts to improve the health and health care delivery to all of our citizens.

4. The Sumter County Board of Censors is opposed to this and any scheme which offers a threat to the free choice of physician and other providers of health delivery and care, which are after all, threats to free enterprise.

5. Three badly needed providers of health care, one a physician and the others dentists, lost interest in locating here after learning of the Federation of Southern Cooperatives activities.

6. The application lists endorsements from local (Sumter County) persons engaged in health delivery which endorsements do not exist or which have been repudiated, because these statements were made as results of information supplied staff members (or a staff member) of the Federation of Southern Cooperatives to certain people which were, to say the least, half truths. These facts lead to incredibility of the stated Southern Federation of Cooperatives objectives.

Whereas, all of the above items and statements have been heard and freely discussed,

Be it resolved that The Sumter County Board of Censors, with the unanimous endorsement of all present, takes the following actions:

1. The Sumter County Board of Censors concurs with the evaluation that the Alabama Comprehensive Health Planning Agency has made of the application and includes additions as well be noted below.

2. The activities of the Federation of Southern Cooperatives are deterrents to our efforts to recruit primary providers of health deliver.

3. That racist attitudes on the part of some Federation of Southern Cooperatives staff members is evidenced by this statement of page 1 of the "Introduction" in the application; "An agriculturally based economy, years of neglect and discrimination practiced against the area's majority Black population."

4. Building a health facility in such an isolated place is impractical and a waste of money, both public and private.

[American Medical News, Feb. 19, 1973]

MDs Ask Revocation of Federal Grant

Officials of the Medical Assn. of the State of Alabama (MASA) have asked Alabama's representatives in Congress to seek revocation of a federal grant made last year for development of a family health care center in the west-central part of the state.

The proposed center, a project of the Atlanta-based Federation of Southern Cooperatives, was approved last July for a one-year developmental grant of $201,000 through an agency of the U.S. Dept. of Health, Education, and Welfare.

If and when the center becomes operational, it will serve several thousand persons—mostly poor and near-poor blacks—in part of Sumter, Greene, Pickens, Choctaw, and Marengo counties, according to organizers.

MASA's request for a halt in funding was approved by the association's board of censors, or directors, at the urging of the Sumter County Medical Society. The society had charged that state planning agencies and other concerned organizations were bypassed when organizers of the family health care center applied for federal money—an apparent violation of federal regulations. Sumter County officials also had voiced concern that the center might duplicate existing health care services.

In requesting the revocation of funding MASA's Board of Censors characterized the grant as an "ill-conceived and wasteful" use of tax money. Under an arrangement unique to Alabama, the board of censors also serves as the state board of health. A MASA spokesman emphasized, however, that the board was not acting in a governmental capacity when it called for revocation.

Melba McAfee, project director for the proposed family health care center, admitted that the grant application was not forwarded through the usual channels. But said it was only one week before the application deadline that project organizers learned of the availability of funding.

However, she added, attempts were made to notify all appropriate agencies that a grant application was being prepared. And after the grant was awarded, meetings were held with regional, state, county, and local officials in an effort to develop working relationships, she said.

As a result of those contacts, Miss McAfee said representatives of both the state and local comprehensive health planning agencies are serving in a direct advisory capacity on the health center project.

As currently planned, the center will not duplicate any of the services now provided by the county health department, according to Miss McAfee. To do otherwise, she indicated, would unnecessarily increase the center's projected operating costs.

If funding continues beyond the developmental stage, the center is slated to become self-supporting within three years. Located in Epes, Ala., the center is expected to operate on a prepaid basis.

———

DEPARTMENT OF HEALTH, EDUCATION, AND WELFARE,
PUBLIC HEALTH SERVICE,
HEALTH SERVICES AND MENTAL HEALTH ADMINISTRATION,
Rockville, Md., Sep. 17, 1973.

DANIEL S. BLUMENTHAL, M.D.
EIS Officer, CDC,
Atlanta, Ga.

DEAR DR. BLUMENTHAL: Thank you for your letter of September 7 about the Black Belt Family Health Center in Epes, Alabama. We appreciate your interest in the project and its efforts to improve health services in the five-county area of Alabama.

It is important to understand that the Family Health Center program was designed to meet specific objectives and has certain goals which must be met by all projects receiving such grants. These concepts were incorporated in the Family Health Center regulations and were applied in the initial Family Health Center funding last year, as well as in the review cycle carried out for the second year funding process completed in June of this year. The Black Belt Family Health Center was not approved for refunding because it was unable to meet these objectives in carrying out its first year grant.

A meeting was held in my office on July 13 between representatives of the Black Belt Family Health Center and members of my staff. The discussion included the criteria against which the project was measured in considering continued funding for the Health Center, the unquestioned need for improved health services by the target populations, the limitations of a family health center structure in developing rural health services, and a commitment to look into Federal support to meet the health needs in the area, perhaps using a more suitable delivery mechanism. It is our hope that some assistance can be located so that improved health services can be made more accessible to the residents of Epes and the surrounding area.

Sincerely yours,

PAUL B. BATALDEN, M.D.
Assistant Surgeon General,
Acting Director, Bureau of Community Health Services.

———

JUNE 17, 1974.

Ms. ELIZABETH CLEINO,
Director,
West Alabama Comprehensive Health Planning Council,
P.O. Box 1488,
Tuscaloosa, Ala.

DEAR Ms. CLEINO: Thank you for your letter concerning the testimony of Dr. Daniel Blumenthal and the Black Belt Family Health Center.

We certainly are interested in obtaining the full story concerning the Federation of Southern Cooperatives and its Black Belt Family Health Center. To this end we are enclosing Dr. Blumenthal's prepared statement and the documents submitted for the hearing record concerning the Center.

In your letter you noted that the Center after a year of operation under a $210,000 HEW grant "could show no tangible results." Could you please supply for the record documentation supporting this conclusion?

We note from the HEW letter of June 11, 1973 (copy enclosed) that two of the reasons for the denial of the continuation application of the Center was "there is no evidence of provider support," and "no formal commitments from hospital, specialists, or third party payors." In HEW's letter of December 11, 1973, (copy enclosed) reaffirming the denial of the Black Belt Family

Health Center's continuation application, the following statement was made: "... endorsements from organized health planning and medical agencies were not evident." The document, "The Sumter County Board of Censors," April 20, 1973, on page 2, states that the local people representing health and government made a concrete recommendation "that a medical doctor—a qualified physician—be recruited, *who would not limit his practice to Federation of Southern Cooperatives' clients* and who could qualify as a member of the hospital's medcal staff and practice in conformity with the hospital staff's rules and regulations (to this end those present offered support)." (Emphasis added). Further, at the bottom of page 3, the following appears: "4. The Sumter County Board of Censors is opposed to this and any scheme which offers a threat to the free choice of physician and other providers of health delivery and care, which are after all, threats to free enterprise."

The HEW letters and the Sumter County Board of Censors document seem to indicate that the Foundation of Southern Cooperatives wanted to operate the Center as a closed-panel health care plan, as opposed to a fee-for-service type plan. Is West Alabama Clinic Services, Inc. a closed or open panel plan? We would appreciate it if you would send us the West Alabama Health Services, Inc.'s charter of incorporation, by-laws, and any other relevant documents indicating its mode and method of operation, including agreements or contracts with local physicians, dentists and hospitals. We also would like to know the names and occupations of the "six other persons representing consumer interests."

Please submit copies of all correspondence between and among your organization, HEW, West Alabama Health Services, Inc., physicians, dentists, hospitals and any other health care providers, pertaning to the Federation of Southern Cooperatives, and the Black Belt Family Health Center. We would welcome any other documentation which you would care to submit.

As soon as our hearing record is printed, we will send it to you. We would appreciate receiving the material within the next two weeks in order that we may publish the record as soon as possible. Please send it directly to Mr. Dean E. Sharp, Senate Antitrust and Monopoly Subcommittee, A517 Senate Office Building, Washington, D.C. 20510. Mr. Sharp is the staff counsel who is handling the Subcommittee investigation.

Sincerely,

PHILIP A. HART, *Chairman.*

Enclosures.

———

COMPREHENSIVE HEALTH PLANNING COUNCIL,
Tuscaloosa, Ala., June 4, 1974.

Hon. PHILIP HART,
Senate Office Building,
Washington, D. C.

DEAR SENATOR HART: Recent columns by Jack Anderson discuss hearings of the Senate Anti-Trust Subcommittee related to medical society intervention in the creation of low-cost health care centers.

Cited in columns is the story of Dr. Daniel Blumenthal who was evidently associated with antipoverty clinics in Louisiana, Arkansas and Alabama. According to Jack Anderson's report of the Senate investigation. "* * * Blumenthal served as consultant for another poverty clinic but was stymied by the Alabama State Medical Society. In this case, the Hart documents show, The U.S. Health, Education and Welfare Department refused funds to the clinic".

The "poverty clinic" referenced above is actually a proposed health center described in an application for Federal assistance under Section 314(e) of P.L. 89-749 submitted by the Federation of Southern Cooperatives through a subsidiary organization known as the Black Belt Family Health Center. This application was denied by DHEW for a variety of reasons. Most important was the fact that the Federation of Southern Cooperatives had received a $210,000 grant in the preceeding fiscal year to develop this clinic but could show no tangible results.

A desperate need remained for additional health care resources to serve the area's indigent residents. Judge William M. Branch, Chief Executive of Greene County, led the formation of a new organization to develop a proposal for establishing a community health care center. He was elected President of "West Alabama Health Services, Incorporated" and was joined on the Board of Directors by three area physicians, the Chief Executive of adjacent Sumter County, and six other persons representing consumer interests. This Board is majority Black, majority Consumer, and united in its desire to provide high quality primary care to all those area residents in need of such services. It has received active support from the Sixth District Dental Society, the West Alabama Hospital Council, and numerous other organizations, and approval of the State Comprehensive Health Planning Agency and the State Board of Health (Alabama State Medical Society). On April 24, 1974, the Department of Health, Education and Welfare approved a grant of $251,000 to fund first-year activity.

The West Alabama Comprehensive Health Planning Council has been active in this project since its inception. In fact, the Council first became associated with the project in the Spring of 1972 when the Federation of Southern Co-peratives requested assistance in obtaining Federal funding for health services development. During the Summer of 1973, when it became evident that the Federation would not be funded for the second year of the proposed Black Belt Family Health Center, Congressman Walter Flowers asked the Council to work with all relevant local organizations in developing a workable program. We have an extensive file of material concerning this entire project, dating from early 1972 and would be happy to make this information available to your staff.

The Jack Anderson column refers to the "Hart documents." We assume these are reports of the Antitrust Subcommittee Hearings. We would very much appreciate your providing us with copies of the hearings and any documentary material submitted as evidence that relate to activity in the State of Alabama. One of the functions of a Comprehensive Health Planning Council is the identification of health problems and needs in its region. If health problems in Alabama have been brought to the attention of the United States Senate, it would certainly be helpful to those of us charged with their solution if these findings were made known to us.

Thank you very much for your assistance. Please feel free to call on us if we may assist you in any way.

Sincerely,

ELIZABETH W. CLEINO, Ph.D.,
Director.

Exhibit 4—Letter From Elizabeth Cleino to Dean Sharp Re Information Relating to the Federation of Southern Cooperatives, Black Belt Family Health Center, and West Alabama Health Services, Inc.

WEST ALABAMA COMPREHENSIVE HEALTH PLANNING COUNCIL,
Tuscaloosa, Ala., June 27, 1974.

Mr. DEAN E. SHARP,
Senate Antitrust and Monopoly Subcommittee,
Senate Office Building, Washington, D.C.

DEAR MR. SHARP: Senator Hart, in his letter of June 17, 1974 has asked that we provide you with information relating to the Federation of Southern Cooperatives, the Black Belt Family Health Center, and West Alabama Health Services, Inc.

Senator Hart asked that we supply for the record, documentation supporting our conclusion that the Federation could show no tangible results after a year of operation under a $210,000 grant from HEW. This would require a comparison of objectives stated in the original grant application with actual results achieved. Despite requirements for review and comment by 314(a) and 314(b) agencies, neither the West Alabama Comprehensive Health Planning Council nor the Alabama Comprehensive Health Planning Administration were provided with copies of the proposal. Furthermore, neither agency was aware of the application until it had been funded. We suggest that the appropriate DHEW officials be requested to document the nature and extent of tangible results in the first year of operation.

Local opposition to this project was initially based on two factors:

1. The proposed clinic site in a remote corner of Sumter County (six miles from Epes, Alabama).

2. The "closed-panel" structure of the BBFHC which would require membership in the Federation in order to obtain health care services.

Let us examine both of these factors in more detail.

PROPOSED CLINIC SITE

The location of the clinic was opposed for the following reasons:

1. It would preclude development of a multi-purpose transportation system which could improve the accessibility of many other social services now available in Livingston, the county seat. These would include the Department of Pensions and Security (Food Stamps, AFDC, ADC, other welfare services); Alabama Employment Service (job training and placement); Public Health Department (immunization, maternal and child health, specialty clinics); Social Security Administration (Medicare, SSI benefits); and several other agencies.

2. The BBFHC and the local hospitals would be unable to share services such as laboratory and radiology. This would result in either a duplication of services (at an additional cost to the taxpayers because of Federal third-party reimbursement) or a lack of such vital services to BBFHC patients.

3. Local physicians would be essentially prevented from providing coverage of the BBFHC clinic when the regular staff physician was off duty or out of town. This is because the existing physicians must be available to their own patients, to persons in the hospital, and to cover the emergency room.

CLOSED-PANEL STRUCTURE

There is an acknowledged need for additional primary health care in Sumter County. This is due, not to a critical shortage of physicians, but to a lack of a transportation mechanism, the existence of a very large indigent population, and an absence of after care and preventive health education. The closed-panel structure proposed by the Federation would essentially deny health care to those who did not wish to associate themselves with the Federation. Based on our interview with several leaders of the Black community, the Federation is by no means representative of the local population.

This agency was requested to review and comment on the "Continuing Grant Application for the Black Belt Family Health Care Center" and we are thus in a position to comment on certain statements made in the Progress Report (pages 13–13e) of this document:

Page 13b, para. 3: The Federation states that local hospital administrators had expressed their willingness to support BBFHC clinical services. Based on our discussions with Mr. Sims and Mr. Steele, the hospital administrators, this statement was indeed true *provided* that the clinic was located in proximity to the hospital and organized so as to function within and support the existing health delivery system. Furthermore, any arrangement would require a contractual arrangement satisfactory to both parties.

Page 13c, para. 4: The clinic was to have been constructed during the first year (see page 13) yet, as acknowledged by the Federation, this was not accomplished. The BBFHC, as described in the proposal, would have been ineligible for a HUD loan guarantee under the "Group Practice Medical Facilities Program".

Page 13d, para. 4: Dr. Gaugh was engaged by the Federation as a physician yet, to the best of our knowledge, was not licensed to practice in either Mississippi or Alabama.

Senator Hart also requested that the nature of West Alabama Health Services, Inc. be more fully described. We enclose the project proposal submitted to DHEW which includes the charter of incorporation, by-laws, supporting letters, and a description of the proposed plan of operation. Present plans call for a fee-for-service structure with a liberal write-off policy so that health care is available to all in need, regardless of financial status. This system was selected because the client population is expected to include two main categories of individuals: those covered by third party insurance such as Medicare or Medicaid and medically indigent persons without third-party coverage. At the present time an HMO-type structure, in this particular setting, is impractical. As to the medically indigent population, the question of fee-for-service versus capitation is meaningless. However, we do not rule out future transition to an HMO structure. In fact, a comment of HEW officials who reviewed our proposal was that they envisioned a smooth transition to an HMO because there would be a large group of potential enrollees and adequate cost data would have been accumulated.

Included with this letter, you will find the following materials:

1. *Log on the Development of the West Alabama Health Service Project*

This log was maintained by the Director of the Council and the staff member responsible for the project. Such a log is not normal procedure for this organization but, from the outset, it was evident that all action needed to be documented.

2. *Minutes of Meetings of the Executive Committee, West Alabama Comprehensive Health Planning Council*

The Council staff is directly responsible to an Executive Committee and regular reports were made at monthly meetings describing relations with the Federation and development of the West Alabama Health Services Project.

3. *Correspondence and Other Materials from the WACHPC Files*

The Council initially became aware of the BBFHC project in June, 1972 when the Medical Association of the State of Alabama forwarded a copy of a letter they had received outlining Federation plans for health delivery.

4. *Minutes of Meetings Describing the Evolution of the West Alabama Health Services Project*

Included are meetings with the Federation, HEW officials, community representatives and the WAHS, Inc. Board of Directors.

5. *Application for 501(c)(3) Status Filed by West Alabama Health Services Inc.*

This photostatic copy of the forms SS-4 and 1023 provide additional information concerning the organization and purposes of the West Alabama Health Services project.

6. *Grant Application Submitted to U.S. PHS/DHEW by West Alabama Health Services, Inc.*

This is a copy of the proposal which was submitted to DHEW in support of a request for Section 314(e) funding.

We are also including a copy of an article which appeared in *Southern Voices* magazine which is published by the Southern Regional Council. This may assist you in understanding the importance of the West Alabama Health Services project within the context of the area in which it is being developed. The article should give you some insight into the character of Judge Branch, a remarkable man who is the President of West Alabama Health Services, Inc.

We sincerely hope that this material will assist you in your investigation. If this should raise additional questions, please do not hesitate to ask us for further assistance.

Sincerely,

ELIZABETH W. CLEINO, *Ph. D., Director.*

Enclosures: (5).

Enclosure 1

[From Southern Voices, vol. 1, No. 1, Mar.-Apr., 1974]

SLUMBERING GREENE COUNTY, A REMOTE SLIVER OF ALABAMA, WHERE BLACKS AND WHITES MAY REALIZE THE HIGHEST HOPE FOR THE SOUTH AND AMERICA

(By Joseph B. Cumming)

When black people took political control, they did not close the door to whites—though the threat of racial antagonism in politics remains. And whites, though they haven't yet been able to accept fully an equal, open society, have not sullenly abandoned the government. The hope of the future is there, fragile, tender, perishable. But perhaps on the golf course, maybe at the PTA. . .

To the white people of Greene County, Alabama—where blacks outnumber whites three to one—the idea of blacks taking over the county government was simply an idea that could not be taken seriously. It was a non-idea. In 1956 when a white businessman named Eugene Johnston warned white leaders that the Supreme Court would one day order complete integration of the Greene County public schools he was considered a bit kooky or at least out of line with a tasteless joke. And Eugene Johnston got little support for his plan to start a private school for whites. For anyone to have further suggested that one day blacks might vote themselves into dominant political power would have been to murder sleep, to stir the slumbering rape fantasy and the waking nightmare of social chaos and political anarchy. It was unthinkable.

Five years later the unthinkable had happened. Today black men occupy all five positions on the school board, all four seats on the county commission. The school superintendent is a black educator named Robert Brown and about 97 per cent of the public school students are black. (Whites eventually gave full, frantic support to the private school started by Eugene Johnston.) More important, the probate judge, the most powerful elected official in the county, is a 56-year-old black preacher and one-time teacher in the county school system, William McKinley Branch. And one of Branch's former pupils is the sheriff. His name is Thomas Earl Gilmore. He is tall, cool, dapper and, at age 33, often singled out by those who follow civil rights in the nation as a model of the best of the kind of black man who came out of the movement and ended up in politics. Sheriff Gilmore is a native of Greene County. Years earlier he had been pushed by his anger to California and into the black militant organization SNCC.

As a Southern reports for *Newsweek* magazine for 17 years, have covered the major events of the civil rights struggle in the South from the federal bayonets at Little Rock in 1957 through the assassination of Martin Luther King in 1968. I was in Birmingham in 1963 when Police Commissioner Eugene "Bull" Connor used police dogs and fire hoses against demonstrating blacks. I followed the series of killings of civil rights workers in Alabama in 1965 (Jimmie Lee Jackson in Marion, the Rev. James Reeb in Selma) and beatings (Sheriff Jim Clark's mounted posse at the Edmund Pettus Bridge) that culminated in the Selma march which I was on. There were two more civil rights killings in that general area of Alabama that year: Mrs. Viola Liuzzo, Detroit housewife, and Jonathan M. Daniels, Episcopal seminary student from New Hampshire—both in the South to work for black civil rights.

All of these events took place in what is called the black belt of Alabama. Greene County is at the northwest end of the black belt and had the vague reputation among us reporters of being rough. By the time I made my first—and very brief—visit there is 1965 there were stories of how the sheriff, Big Bill Lee, a former All-American football player, had brought his heavy cattle stick down on the head of young black "agitator" Tom Gilmore. But, as a native Southerner, I am also plugged into that white South that is one big small town and I discovered I had gone to college with a couple of the scions of the Banks family, the leading dynasty in Greene County. It was my old college chum Ralph Banks who later told me the story of how Sheriff Bill Lee had broken up a Klan rally one night by kicking over the cross and otherwise making the hooded ones feel unwelcomed. I also realized from Ralph Banks that there is a spirit of noblesse oblige in Greene County left over from the cotton plantation culture that existed there in the 1840s and 1850s. The Ku Klux Klan mentality never set the tone in Greene County. For one thing, the Banks family would never allow it.

Even so, that black ascendency was an outright political miracle. It took five years of exhausting, complex and bitter struggle. Even now both blacks and whites seem too stunned from the historic event to quite know what to do with it. A few whites, like the former probate judge, Dennis Herndon, left town to make their careers elsewhere. But most still seem too exhausted from the years of struggle to take decisive action toward the future. I went down from Atlanta to live in Greene County in the early spring of 1973. For a month I stayed, as an outsider, and saw what few who live there can see: There is a hushed quality of possibility in the air. Something important seems to be taking place in Greene County. In small, slow ways a few people are beginning to stir with life in the context of a new, enlarged reality. In the end it may be too few, too small, and too slow. But, for the moment, there is the fascinating chance that something important could take place in Greene County in the next five years that America could do well to notice.

To some it is miracle enough that there is surface peace between the races. Judge William Branch and Sheriff Thomas Gilmore, the two top political leaders of the blacks as well as the highest elected county officials, are both preachers and disciples of Marin Luther King's teachings of love. After their victory in November 1970, they made it a point to meet hostile glowers with unangry neutrality if not overtures of friendship. They wanted to show that they were as interested in cooperating with whites as they were in helping the impoverished blacks who put them in office. Since that time whites have generally settled into a noncommittal attitude with public appearances of calm and courtesy.

"We're getting along just fine," they studiously say to outsiders, which is something, even if it is said more for the sake of decorum than deep decency.

But, of course, it is not enough. Already a faction of more militant blacks is challenging the lack of substance in this strained, brittle politeness. Soon, in the city of Eutaw, black voters may outnumber whites, as they now do in the county, through annexation of black housing projects on the city limits. This could bring to an end the white control of the city of Eutaw, and the last enclave of white dominance. The idea of coalition politics would be the only hope for whites. People like Judge Branch and Tom Gilmore are always open to coalition whites but they are also under pressure from black militants who seem to be rallying around the emerging leadership of School Superintendent Robert Brown. In the next five years the initiative will be with the whites. Their own self-interest will demand something very interesting and unaccustomed of them : that they enlarge the frame of reference in which they live and perceive their values. Because of a century of rigid defensiveness it will take many whites some effort to understand and help define the larger psychic horizon for coalition politics to work.

They will have have to change so much, but they will have to grow considerably. In a way, the people of Greene County seem to stand at the classic dividing point between decadence and renewal, at that provocative Toynbeesque moment in their history when a culture either responds to the new challenge or is trapped forever in the backwaters. From what I saw in the after-image of my visit there, Greene County stands fair to round out an epoch of its history by producing a miracle : a situation of self-confidence and creative stability. However, this is a fragile image. Things could almost as easily go the other way. If not enough people— white and black—expand their perspective, Greene County could be doomed to a sour, mean and altogether typical small-town obscurity.

The first five years of this epoch of the miracle belonged to the blacks. From 1965 to 1970 they were in resonance with the civil rights movement as it swept across rural Alabama like a gust like a ghost cloud filled with the sounds of battle, like an Old Testament epic. In the early days of this movement the very act of registering to vote was a personal act of courage for blacks in the movement.

And, with the election of black officials the black citizens of Greene County took on that restlessness called hope. In the phrase of Jack Burden in *All the King's Men* they moved out of history, into history and the awful responsibility of time.

The next five years whites will have to make their own existential choice. "We are proud of our Greek revival and our white survival," an elegant lady whispered playfully. (The hilltops of the county brood with ante-bellum homes with classic-columned porticoes.) But the expansive spirit that built and dwelt in those mansions seems to have shriveled in the descendants. And whites will not "survive" if survival is the limit of their striving.

When I checked into the old white brick Hotel Eutaw on the corner of the courthouse square for my month-long visit many people received me warmly and were friendly and helpful. But I was fairly overwhelmed by the tightness and fear I found among a great many others. It was much more suffocating than the caution and restraint I have learned to expect of people in small towns toward reporters.

"I heard you were in town," said a throaty female voice to me in an anonymous call to the hotel one night near midnight. "I've heard people say they're not going to tell you the truth. They tell you everybody's getting along fine but they're really suffering on the inside. You'll never know."

The caller was willing to talk further if I signed a paper swearing I would not use her name. That was hardly necessary. I had already been refused interviews by four people, including the chairman of the membership committee of the Chamber of Commerce. There were others who met me with wintry monosyllables. The effect was that of people caught behind that thick and heatless bullet-proof glass used in drive-in windows in suburban banks. One leading white citizen who knows the town well put it this way : "This town is paranoid."

That's a fun thing to say, of course, but it has no real meaning. More specifically it could be said that Greene County needs new industry. It needs political stability. And its citizens are in search of a richer meaning to their lives (A sense of pervasive boredom emanates from the therapy sessions recently begun by the State Mental Health Department, held twice a week at the county health building in Eutaw. A notable number of white middle class folk consume too much alcohol desperately, as if life held no other serious choices. The suicide rate in Greene County is the highest in the State.) These three specific needs—new industry, political stability, a deeper meaning to life—are closely inter-related. And they stand unfulfilled from nothing more substantial than a lack of imagination.

There is a strange, lingering fear—not of members of one race of the other—but a fear of seeming to be too helpful and cooperative across racial lines. Whites, for example, have never taken the least interest in Tom Gilmore's noble dream of boys' ranch for the under-privileged for his Junior Deputy Program to inspire and teach the idle and mischievous-inclined black youth. On the other hand, Sheriff Gilmore can be a bit cautious, too. He once declined an invitation to attend a white church service when his presence on the occasion might have been helpful.

But who knows? I mean, it could happen on the golf course. Back in 1968 when whites controlled the county they began construction of a nine-hole golf course two miles outside of Eutaw. Then, under the black regime, the golf course was completed. It is now owned and operated by the black county govern-ment, but it is used much more by whites. Indeed, it is an important amenity in the lives of many whites: housewives, retired executives and military folk who have found Greene County a good home. Former Sheriff Bill Lee plays every day in a foursome. My friend Ralph Banks gets away from his law office three or four times a week to play. Listening to the way people talked about that golf course, the devotion and interest they had for the course and the game, made me realize it is an overwhelming symbol of the hope of Greene County.

While it has been a white man's game, blacks are coming to use the course more and are showing a competence that demands respect. A kind of suspension of disbelief takes place on the links that makes golf a working metaphor for the larger games. It is possible that the Greene County Golf Course will provide a stage on which blacks and whites can act out their relationships under the forgiving spaciousness of the sky, within the wider horizons of the land. For all the overtones of elitist power structure deals made among the neat, stick-clicking cliques out there on the fairway, there is a ruthless accountability in the game that humbles and, for an instant, tends to make folk equal.

Greene County lies 40 miles west of the steel-mill smoke of Birmingham, 32 miles south of Tuscaloosa, home of the University of Alabama, and past two brick silos painted like Schlitz beer cans. Some call it the middle of nowhere. The Greene County Chamber of Commerce, back when it had self-confidence, called it "the cross roads to everywhere."

Driving south out of the neon-gaudy highways around Tuscaloosa into lonely and uncluttered Greene County is like going from Technicolor into black and white. The town of Eutaw, with its Victorian and ante-bellum houses, has the effect of faded dignity like some grainy newsreel of visiting European royalty before World War I. Before the Civil War the county was rich with thriving fields of cotton and planters living in hilltop mansions. Today, most of the land has an idle look as it grows up in timber, or its hilly fields graze cattle. Little towns like Forkland and Boligee lie in weeds, half blind with memories, their empty brick stores baked in a Hopper light in the late day's sun. The flaking mansions that loom in silhouette are mostly unoccupied now. They are preserved as grand architectural examples of the culture that existed over a century ago when cotton was king. With names like Rosemount, Thornhill, Kirkwood, they are still honored by local ladies' societies and their Carrara marble mantels and walnut balustrades still bring soft in-takes of breath from tourists on the spring Pilgrimage of homes.

Since the beginning of the 20th century Greene County has lived with a sense of slow doom, of time running out. In 1900 the population of the county was 20.000. It decreased every census and today is stable at 10,000. In slavery times it was the largest county in Alabama in population. Today it is the small-est in population and land area (it was divided up) and the second poorest in per capita income. A few industries have come in successfully in the past decade but others have failed. A group of Midwest farm entrepreneurs went broke in the 1960s trying to turn the gumbo soil of Greene County into a major soybean producer.

Yet, for those who read signs, there were also hints that Greene County might be preparing for some new destiny. One of these came out of a great personal tragedy in the early 1960s when Jamie O. Banks lost his wife in a fire that also destroyed their home. For a while there was talk that Jamie Banks might leave the country. If he did the county would suffer from the neglect of absentee ownership because Jamie Banks, now in his early 40s, owns more land and has more economic power than any other one individual in the county. He is head of Banks and Co., the family business established in 1889, and he is chairman of the board of the Merchants and Farmers Bank, the only bank in town. Jamie Banks is a hearty, bluff, likable man who works hard, dresses sharp and likes to travel about the world when he takes time off. As a child he showed a sharp trading instinct to the delight of his grandfather J. O. Banks, Jr., after whom he is named. Jamie Banks decided not to move and, eventually, he married again and built a new home.

"I know a lot of people around here were reassured when Jamie built his house back," said an older man who moved to Greene County in the 1920s in search of opportunity. "They felt like if Jamie Banks stays it means he is committed to the future of the county."

But, it happens, there are a number of men in the community who feel Jamie is also very unprogressive. "He can always figure out why not to do something," one of them said.

Jamie is the key man people look to for leadership in getting new industry. He insists he tries but he seems to come up way short on imagination.

"We just don't know what else to do," he shrugs.

Once he and Judge Branch made a trip to Birmingham on an industry-seeking trip which, like others, turned out to be too little and too late. Driving home along the miles of unproductive land, Judge Branch asked casually:

"Who you reckon owns this land along here?"

"This?" replied Jamie. "This along here . . . I own it."

They drove a few miles and Branch again wondered aloud who owned the land they were now passing.

"Well, that's some of mine too," said Jamie. "Yessir . . ."

And, once more, after a long silence and many miles of unused land Branch inquired and Jamie nodded it was his.

"Jamie," said Judge Branch, his voice rising in that singy, disarming way he uses with whites (citicized by some blacks as Uncle Tomish), "you better change your ways or you gonna burn in hell. "When you die the Lord's gonna say 'I was hungry and you fed me not. I needed shelter and you left me out!'"

Judge Branch was not dismayed by the amount of land owned by one man; it was that the land was idle when he knew there were thousands of unemployed blacks who might work the land.

To some young business-minded men in town Jamie is only one of a whole class of old family people who are holding back progress. "They've got their land and they've got their money and they've got their way of life and they're not interested in anything else."

For the handful of families at the top of the caste system, names like the Banks or the Rogers, this way of life would appear to be remarkably agreeable. They dwell in cool, tasteful and fiercely symmetrical homes set back in pine shade and well-tended gardens. The social ceremonials have not been touched by the new black political order. These people stay enormously busy with business, committee meetings, suppers, Heart Fund drives, bridge games, Army Reserve drills. The men come home in mid-day for "dinner" with their wives. ("Supper" is the evening meal.) The ladies take to heart what they learn in church study groups and are equally attentive to their appointments at the beauty parlor and dates for golf. In due season the men take off to hunt and fish. Trips to Tuscaloosa or Birmingham to shop or for a movie and a meal at a good restaurant come more frequently than the special vacation trips to New Orleans or New York or Europe. Football weekends and lavish expeditions to watch Bear Bryant's Crimson Tide play the inevitable bowl games are high points on the calendar. Christmas holidays are shiny with sacred services and the secular clinking of cocktails.

Now-a-days, a quiet tension runs through much of the social ceremonial. That old sense of the slow tolling of a bell marking the last days has given way to a confusion with the arrival of a new order that cannot be absorbed. The most diligent attention to social ritual cannot always obliterate the anguish. Indeed, at times it almost seems that some insist on celebrating the negative.

A 9 o'clock every weekday morning, promptly and unfailingly, Jamie Banks and his brother Phil, a quiet, decent, perpetually vexed man, walk down the wooden floored aisle of Banks and Co., their footsteps muffled by the thick racks of soft-goods merchandise, out the front door and down the square to Jimmy's Restaurant where they are joined for coffee by friends varying in number up to eight. Bradly Brown, manager of the Cotton Patch Restaurant—a famous evening eating place outside town—is usually there. And Peter McLean, a huge, shrewd-eyed dairy farmer. McLean has a regular thing of his own, too, a Thursday afternoon dice game out at his farm. It was robbed two years ago by masked bandits who went off with several thousand dollars.

The main function of this 9 o'clock coffee session seems to be for these white men to reassure each other that things *are* going to the dogs. Out of the specific topics such as land prices, beef market, government programs, and sorry labor come generalizations on the decline of values, the breakdown of discipline and the work ethic and, in general, despair over forces seeking to corrupt the cherished way. "Nigras" or, sometimes "niggers" come out to be a major cause and symbol of their woes.

Ralph Banks never joins his two younger brothers at Jimmy's Restaurant for 9 o'clock coffee. At that hour he is checking the morning mail at his cluttered office across the street from the courthouse, or whipping across the street to the sheriff's office, or lining up appointments with county committees, talking to Judge Branch. Ralph Banks, it turns out, is county attorney and deputy circuit solicitor which means he has constant business with Judge Branch and Sheriff Gilmore. Around 10 o'clock Ralph usually goes across the hall from the sheriff's office on the ground floor of the courthouse, to join him for a cup of coffee, usually over in Ralph's office, Breck Rogers, to join him for a cup of coffee, usually over in Ralph's office. Breckenridge A. B. Rogers is 37, white, and, like Ralph, a certified aristocrat from one of the top county families. He has a wife and kids, a clean college face and a sense of whimsy which he hides behind serious-rimmed glasses and an unconvincing, arms-length, innocent politeness. That Breck and Ralph have daily coffee together, usually alone, and have become friends has a symbolic significance neither of them would like to admit. For, as fellow conservative white Southerners, they would not like the idea that they are carriers of the hope of some kind of coalition politics between white and black in Greene County.

They both came to this uneasy position accidentally. Breck Rogers was securely ensconced as tax assessor during the time blacks were developing their political power and their political party—called National Democratic Party of Alabama. Then, in 1972, after blacks had clearly shown their power at the polls, it came time for Breck to run for re-election. Blacks came to him and asked him to run on their NDPA ticket. Breck agreed to do so, knowing they would run a candidate against him if he did not, but also knowing that he risked scorn from his fellow whites if he did. NDPA was still—and is still—anathema to most whites. There really wasn't much choice since Breck wanted the job. But there was *some* choice and the decision he made could end up being significant when the history of these times are written. The only thing that would keep it from being very significant is the fact that Ralph Banks had already opened up that territory to tolerance two years before.

Ralph Roundtree Banks Jr. is the oldest son of Miss Sarah (Mrs. Ralph) Banks, the grand dame of the Banks family and of Eutaw. (Her husband, father of Ralph, Phil and Jamie, died in 1959.) Ralph, now 49, is a high-strung, chain-smoking, spare man with a quick wit and a quick temper. He is an intellectual and an aristocrat and, in the tradition of both these types, has the dowdy sartorial instincts of a ferry boat captain or a police reporter. He is a hurrying, scurrying, restless man who is totally at peace with his chosen profession, the law. He is a loner, but one who loves the comradeship of a friend with a bottle after hours. He has a mean streak, but is also a compassionate man and as relentlessly fairminded as a Roman when it comes to the law.

"It's the Law," he will insist in an argument, his voice rising on the word "law" like an exegete trying to convince the world of the ultimate answer.

If Ralph Banks had been called to the stage instead of the bar he could have won parts playing the role of President Andrew Jackson, a man Ralph hates because of Jackson's inhumane treatment of the Indians. Ralph has the same long jaw, high forehead, ruddy cheeks and intensity of expression with its flickering hints of storm. He talks with rapid-fire logic, his mind clicking like pool balls searching for pockets after the break. His eyes dart to the side as if to check something that just flashed across his peripheral vision. He moves about the county offices, seeming to pass through walls and closed doors. His advice is needed at all times and in all places in the county government and he gives it, quickly and surely, out of a profound knowledge of the law and the lore of the county.

Blacks in general, do not trust Ralph Banks. He does not go out of his way to inspire their confidence. Neither his pronunciation nor his inflection in pronouncing "Negro" nor his sparing use of courtesy titles reflect any change in attitude toward blacks from days before the civil rights movement. But then, he is a bit like Henry Higgins. He treats everybody alike. He has the same harsh exactitude toward whites, especially in matters of law.

But there is a special significance about Ralph Banks that no one in Greene County seems to realize. Including Ralph Banks. For years he was the chief strategist of resistance to black political ascendency. It was his high dedication to prevent William Branch and Tom Gilmore from winning power over whites. Through those years of conflict he developed a genuine hostility toward them and felt the same from them toward him. Then, after the final black victory in November, 1970, Judge Branch asked Ralph to become county attorney, a position he had held off and on over the years. Ralph blinked in astonishment.

"Are you out of your mind?" he scowled at the new black judge. "I have fought you tooth and nail for five years . . ."

"Indeed so," said Judge Branch who is also a preacher and a man who can cast a conflict in large, forgiving tones. "But I would like you to consider staying as part of the county government . . ."

Ralph tried the idea out with a number of key whites whose opinion he respected and they almost agreed it would be a helpful thing, not only to the inexperienced blacks but helpful for whites to have one of their own in there watching after their interests. So Ralph stayed with the county—both as county attorney and deputy circuit solicitor.

It was not particularly heroic of Ralph to accept these county jobs. He would draw a health salary from the positions—around $600 a month—with a generous retirement from the state for a few more years of county service. He would be doing what he loved and did well. He was independent enough and socially secure enough to ignore the criticisms that did come from some whites who preferred the strategy of "let 'em mess up and we'll take back over." But because Ralph Banks stayed and worked with the black administration, the possibility was opened for future cooperation by other whites, making it somehow acceptable. Breck Rogers' decision to run on the NDPA ticket was much easier to make because of Ralph Banks. And when white-black political coalitions begin, it will be because Ralph Banks was there, keeping the lines open.

(As a matter of fact, Ralph Banks recognized the need for coalition politics even when fighting Branch and Gilmore. He helped invent the Spotted Horse Party in 1970 so blacks could vote for white candidates without having to pull the regular Democratic Party handle that had George Wallace, then running for Governor, at the head of the ticket.)

Now, after more than two years as county attorney under Probate Judge Branch, Ralph Banks says, "Judge Branch is the least vindictive man I have ever known."

His feelings about Tom Gilmore go deeper than that. Through many long hours of association with the sheriff, working together on county cases, in court, and in many long, after-hours bull sessions, Ralph has come to admire Gilmore as a man of honor and imagination. They have a relationship that approaches a man-to-man friendship, transcending the traditional, structured racial friendships in the South. When Gilmore asked Ralph if he would support him when he ran for re-election as sheriff, Ralph said, "Hell, Tom I'll be your campaign manager."

Ralph has not really had to "change" to come to this relationship. He is still a conservative, an orthodox member of the social structure, husband and father of two (both off at college, one married). And it might sound equally static and circumscribed that the institution that means the most to Ralph Banks is the Episcopal Church. But therein is one of the surprises I found.

St. Stephen's Episcopal Church is a modest stone structure two blocks from the square, spaciously surrounded by some of the loveliest of the old white wood homes. Its congregation is a remarkable concentration of secular power. Most of the members have claim to prominence, wealth or influence. The leading families in the county—the Banks, the Rogers—are the controlling voices of St. Stephen's.

On Dec. 9, 1970, a month after the traumatic election of Gilmore and Branch which completed the black takeover, an historic meeting was held in the parish house of the church. The 20-member vestry—the ruling body—was there along with a representative teenager, Lucile Banks, the lively daughter of Phil Banks who was himself present. The main point of the meeting was to discuss the kind of new minister they would like to replace their beloved Rev. Ralph Kendall who was retiring the next spring. To help direct the discussion, the bishop in Birmingham had sent over a young clergyman named Bob Ross who was experienced in group dynamics and sensitivity techniques.

"I didn't want to go," Ross recalled later. "I figured it would be a conservative group that wouldn't want to change anything. But when I walked in that meeting I caught something. And they caught something."

It became apparent immediately, to the surprise of everyone, that they were all hungry for new dynamic leadership and ideas. They were led by Ross to speak openly of their feelings of fear from the black take-over and, in general, the sense of decline and dying in the country. As Ross later wrote in his report to the bishop, he found "a general feeling of malaise connected with dwindling population, lack of vigorous people in their 20s and 30s, and boredom." He discerned "a general wish for excitement and hope."

With great skill Ross was able to summon up the hope, deep-buried though it was, and marshal it as antidote to the fear. He invited them to fantasize the kind of parish they would most want and when "Cile" Banks brought up the idea of having a folk mass and said, "But y'all won't let us do that," Bob Ross, who had been listening to the unspoken mood, addressed "Cile": "Honey, it sounds to me like they're saying they will let you . . . if you'll listen."

And, in ways some of the members still remember and remark, they did listen to each other that afternoon. From that meeting they agreed on the kind of new minister they wanted. And, to a stunning degree, they got exactly such a man in David Veal, a plump, pleasant, brilliant, 35-year-old man who was just finishing up theological seminary at Sewanee, Tenn.

David Veal gives a first impression of a man mild and smiling. But he is also deep and his smile is seen as what Sir Kenneth Clark called on Voltaire "the smile of reason." Except David Veal's heart is less with the 18th century enlightenment than it is with the cavalier spirit of the Stuart kings in 17th century England. He still hates Cromwell. He loves that Divine Right tradition of the Episcopal church and fights to recover some of its grandeur from the dry and pinching puritanism that has come to dominate in the South. For something more important than shock value, David Veal will make a strong case for pornography in the company of important and highly shockable parishioners. He does it jokingly, of course. Yet they thought he must be joking when he said he voted for McGovern.

From the start everyone loved David. They didn't mind his being an admitted integrationist because he obviously did not have that bony sainthood, feverish quality that is the giveaway of an activist. In his plump and sure-footed way he broke through one sacred barrier after another. A few months after arriving he was host to Bishop Alphaeus Hamilton Zulu, black, English-educated, conservative cleric from South Africa. It was almost exclusively members of St. Stephen's who made up the 20 or so whites in the audience for Bishop Zulu's public address at the courthouse.

Three months later, at ordination services when David Veal officially became a priest, he directly disobeyed the wishes of his senior warden by inviting the Rev. Branch and the Rev. Gilmore to participate. Only Branch showed up, looking impressive in his scarlet-trimmed robes. The senior warden made a special point of welcoming Judge Branch and kneeling next to him during communion.

Somehow, because he is at once firm and unthreatening, David Veal came to be a source of strength for a number of people in Eutaw who felt the need to break out of the tight and orthodox expectancies. One young white family with enough money to send their children to the private school elected to send them to the public school and David Veal, in a quiet way, gave crucial, if silent, support to them in this lonely decision. And, because David Veal was there, I think, it gave courage to Eugene Johnston to push forward on his perilous course of being a Christian. (Veal left for a church in Texas in 1973. After months of searching, the vestry found a new man in January 1974.)

Eugene Johnston is the man who was so disturbed about the possibility of integration in 1965 that he started the move that led to the establishment of the Warrior Academy, the all-white private school. I noticed him my first night in Eutaw. He and his wife came to the hotel restaurant to try the boiled shrimp that was the Tuesday night special. I noticed them because, of the hundreds of married couples I see in restaurants as I have traveled about the South, they were one of those few who seemed to be truly alive to each other. There was also a vunerable quality about them: she with her fragile, wispy sincerity, he with boyish blue eyes, chubby, sun-tanned face. I got to know Eugene best out of all the people in Greene County. He was least afraid of what I was about. But his openness came more from the fact that he was probably the only man there with any real, existential courage. He is the manager of the Greene County Golf Course and always seems involved in some elaborate scheme, the ultimate point of which is to "increase communications between people." Some regard him as a wacky sort of busybody. He doesn't mind.

"I have a gimmick," he explained, looking out of his wide-set eyes with a curiously innocent intensity. "I have been without a job. Do you understand?"

He was out of a job for two-and-a-half years and received a lot of criticism. He also went through a conversion experience and, as he puts it, "made the decision to take the Lord's Prayer seriously."

Eugene Johnston, 42, was raised in Selma, Ala., in the upper-middle class, enjoyed the typical warm but hierarchial relationship with Negroes. He went to the U.S. Naval Academy, married Mary Lou Off, a graduate of Goucher, received a medical discharge from the Navy and ended up back in Alabama in 1960. He showed himself to be a kind of natural engineering genius by designing and supervising the building of a soybean and fertilizer plant for a farm cooperative called Centrala in the south part of Greene County. The growing civil rights movement stirred labor troubles at his plant and, for a while, Eugene kept a pistol on the seat of his car. He was plant manager of Centrala when the question came up of whether Negro farmers should be allowed to be members of the co-op. At first Eugene was neutral on the question. The co-op president pointed out to Eugene that a Negro in the membership could, at least theoretically, mean his having a black boss. With that news, Eugene firmly opposed black membership. The idea of a black boss was unacceptable. Eugene became concerned about the threat of blacks to all areas of life. That's when he organized the effort to start a private school.

Then he lost his job. During the next few years he attended several communications conferences put on by the Episcopal church where full-scale sensitivity training techniques were used—the touching and shouting and weeping and growing.

"They were strong medicine," he says. He began to open up in ways he had never dared to before.

He began to rethink his traditional attitude on race. When the job of golf course manager opened, he had reached the point where he could go to Judge Branch and the black county commission and ask them for the job. Black men would be his bosses.

"All at once the roles were reversed," he explained. "All my life I had looked down on the black man. Now I consider him at least an equal. You can't look down on somebody you're asking for a job."

He remembers well the day he started walking from his home toward the town square to ask for the job. A friend pulled up in a car.

"Where are you going?" the friend called out.

"Well, would believe I'm going up here and ask Judge Branch to give me that job out at the golf course?"

"Eugene! You're kidding."

"I am not. I need the job. How about giving me a ride."

"Hell no," said the friend in genuine anger. "And I hope you don't get the job."

Eugene got the job; he learned to play the game, and he set about to get blacks and whites involved and in communication. He is still trying. He feels his job depends on it, for one thing. Whites make up nearly 90 percent of the habitual users of the golf course, but blacks in effect, own and operate it. More important is the rightness for enlarging communications. He put together a greens committee, a semiformal advisory body to help him in setting up programs and running the golf course. This is perilous work and it has been very tricky just getting whites and blacks to agree to serve on the committee. (The percentage of each race, for example, required elaborate diplomacy and negotiation.)

On the night of Feb. 27, 1973, the greens committee met in the brightly lit, sterile conference room in city hall. Six whites, three blacks. Eugene sat at the head of the long table with a yellow pad full of notes. The friendly informality was a bit restrained. As the meeting went on, phrases like "we seem to be divided" and occasional brief flare-ups kept a quality of animosity in the air.

Eugene, going down his list, told of taking a group of high school golfers from Warrior Academy up to Tuscaloosa to meet the golf coaches at the university to work up a summer golf clinic for students.

"That's very nice," said E. W. Underwood, a fretful, reserved black man at the far end of the table. "But it sound's like you're kind of one-sided. How come you just took the white up there? Why didn't you take some black?"

"Because they didn't ask!" the sharp voice came from J. E. Gay, tired manager of the local Alabama Power office.

"I'd like him to answer the question," Underwood replied and the air bristled.

Eugene came forward in his chair, his face calm, alert. He planted his elbow far out on the table, pointed an open palm at the whole group, fingers extended like a hypnotist. Slowly the atmosphere calmed and the attention swung to Eugene.

He couldn't have asked for a better opening to describe his elaborate plans for a golf program in the public schools as well as the white private academy. And it also gave him a chance to air his own frustration in dealing with the black school superintendent, Robert Brown. Eugene revealed his annoyance at not being able to get an appointment with Brown inside of a week, with the failure of Brown to get the school coaches together as he had promised. Gay was not really listening. He was still smarting from what he considered a rudeness by Underwood.

The blacks on the greens committee, especially Underwood, approved of Eugene's efforts to start a program in the public schools. And, no doubt, they understood more of the political dynamics motivating Robert Brown than Eugene did. For it had been coming clear for some time to blacks that Superintendent Brown was emerging as a political force that might, in time, challenge Sheriff Gilmore Branch by developing black vs. white strategies. Brown had already shown himself willing to use his power as school superintendent in traditional political ways, like ordering the milk contract to be switched to a company represented by a political crony, or asking teachers for contributions for political campaigns and keeping a list of who gives and who does not.

Gay, uninterested in all this, brooded for days over Underwood's remark at the meeting. "I'm just not going to put up with that kind of thing," he told his golf buddies out at the pro shop.

Eugene may not have understood Robert Brown. But Brown was a challenge to Eugene. From his encounters with the superintendent, Eugene saw Brown as a man uptight. This was something Eugene did understand. He made a special appointment to talk to Brown with the idea of offering to help with some advice about management techniques. Eugene has a master's degree in industrial management. He wanted to show Brown how helpful it is in management to deal more openly with problems. Eugene finally got his interview with Brown but he received only a polite, passive listening.

Robert Brown is clearly interested in politics. Politics and sensitivity training don't mix. They are involved with different goals. Political power requires an intense concentration and carefulness. Sensitivity work encourages a spontaneity and an honesty of feeling that are exceedingly dangerous in politics. There are times when Robert Brown's political strategies appear to damage examples of rare and beautiful biracial harmony.

The PTA of the Middle Grade School in Eutaw, for example, has produced a model of biracial cooperation. Yet because the president of the PTA, a mild-mannered black man named David Spencer, appears to be a potential political threat, groups of blacks who are political associates of Robert Brown began showing up at the PTA meetings, challenging Spencer's authority, creating divisions and factionalism.

There is a new, hopeful element present in that PTA that is likely to survive. It is a fresh, strong, unselfconscious spirit together outside the ken of Ralph Banks or Breck Rogers or even Eugene Johnston. It is the open and fiesty involvement of a few working-class whites, traditionally the bitterest foes of blacks, with the black parents at Middle Grade. Greene County does not have many working-class whites and most of those managed to get their kids into the

Warrior Academy. So those four or five poor white families who have their kids at the predominantly black school are not typical. But neither are they passive, forlorn victims. They are vigorous, scrappy participants, wholly inspired by the native leadership of one of their group named Betty Jones, a truck driver's wife with three beautiful children at Middle Grade. At first she and her husband Sparky tried to get their kids in Warrior Academy. They didn't have the money so they tried for a scholarship which is usually available to keep working-class whites from breaking caste. But, in the process Sparky and Betty Jones felt they were being snooted.

"He jes' turned away and wouldn't sign the paper," Betty related of the time they tried to get the final signature for the scholarship. "So we jes' said, well, to hell with you, and we come over here and put 'em in Middle Grade."

Betty Jones is a salty, angular country-twangy, hotdiggity-dog kind of woman with endless energy and a Chaucerian breadth of spirit. Her eyes glitter in tight new, moons of merriment when she tells the saga of "them lockers."

"Well, we seen there weren't no way for them kids to leave their books and coats and things at school. They'd have to drag 'em all home ever' day. So we said, OK, we going to get us some lockers . . ."

And for 18 months, white and black parents assaulted the problem of raising money for lockers. They put on cake bakes and attic sales and advertised each event as widely as possible.

"I even went to Birmingham to get Country Boy Eddie to talk about our cake bake on his radio program. Well, this man heard Country Boy Eddie talking about us needing lockers and he called up and offered us some second-hand. They'd been used in the dressing room of coal miners."

Even this good luck presented problems which led to Steinbeckian trips to Birmingham in battered, bluesmoking cars to tie the huge metal lockers precariously into the car trunks.

The final and successful conclusion of this project took place while I was in the county. And my last full day in town coincided with the PTA meeting at which Betty Jones and her committee were to proudly present the lockers. There was some uneasiness that something could happen to spoil the occasion. Only a few days before, Superintendent Brown had tossed in some arbitrary ruling that, if allowed to stand, would have delayed the presentation. That was worked out but there were fears the group challenging David Spencer might show up and disrupt the triumphant moment.

This last full day for me in Greene County was Ash Wednesday. It was one of God's most beautiful days. The sky was open and soft blue and everywhere were blooming golden jonquils, redbud, flowering quince and narcissus with hints of azalea and dogwood to come soon. The golf greens winked like jewels. Eugene Johnson, on this day, was able to persuade Sheriff Gilmore to come out to the golf course for the first time. The sheriff swore he had never before swung at a golf ball as he stepped up and clicked off a fine drive after brief instructions from Eugene. Unfortunately, the moment was marred when Eugene used his traditional pronunciation of "nigra" and the sheriff called him down about it and Eugene insisted on his right to his natural pronunciation instead of an awkward "Kneegrow." They agreed "black" would suffice but the two men did not make progress toward the larger perspective.

I had a brief, pleasant interview with Mrs. Sarah Banks over tea and cheese wafers in her cool, elegant living room with its large portraits, Williamsburg hurricane lamp and delicate porcelain figurines.

"Yes, people were afraid," she said of those times before the unthinkable had come to pass. "They thought the bottom was going to drop out, that it would be like living through Reconstruction again."

But we did not talk much of the present or the future. Conversation flowed more easily on talk of travel and family history.

That evening I attended a meeting of the Greene County Chamber of Commerce. It had not meet for four months and was coming together to decide if the organization should continue. The industrial development picture was still dismal. But there was the feeling that the effort had to continue.

"I just don't understand where we're missing," Breck Rogers exploded after half an hour of the group spitting out the butt ends of many industrial prospects that had come to nothing. "We've got the transportation, and water. We have an industrial park, an airport. Interstate 59 connects us to everything. We must be doing something wrong. You drive up through Tennessee and every little town has industry with grounds just manicured to a tee. . . . I just don't understand."

"What we need," said Haynie Williams, present manager of the Alabama Power Co., "is some new ideas."

"Why don't we find somebody who can tell us the kind of things we need to do," offered Oscar Williams, a black man with long sideburns. There was a silence. If Jamie Banks had, at that moment, remembered the experience of St. Stephen's when Bob Ross came in and helped them understand their needs and express them, it might have saved Greene County years of unnecessary struggle. There are men only 32 miles away in Tuscaloosa at the University of Alabama who could do for the Chamber of Commerce what Bob Ross did for St. Stephen's. But Jamies Banks, the key leader in any such effort, was not thinking in those terms. Instead, he thought it might be time for his old joke about Levi Morrow's one-time bootlegging. Morrow is black, an elected member of the county commissioners, and he was present as a member of the chamber.

"Maybe we can find some way to legalize old Levi," said Jamie, chuckling.

"Ah, now . . .," Levi muttered, having long since wearied of the joke about this part of his past.

While this meeting was going on, so was the one of the PTA at Middle Grade school. To the relief of those present, the faction of dissidents, for some reason, did not show up. So, in flowing good will, the group congratulated themselves on the successful conclusion of the monumental locker project—they had some of the lockers on display in the meeting room—and talked of holding a dance or a tea. O. B. Harris, a round and pleasant black businessman who had come to the rescue at the last minute with some needed money to finish the locker payments, asked for the floor. (Harris, years ago, had instituted a voter-registration drive among blacks before the movement ever existed, and he was dubbed an Uncle Tom by the movement when he opposed its coming into Greene. He says he is going to write a book someday called Uncle Tom Speaks Out.) At the PTA meeting he rose to make his contribution to the interpretation of the problem in Greene County and its possible solution by reading a poem by Edwin Markham:

> He drew a circle that shut me out
> Heretic, rebel, a thing to flout.
> But love and I had the wit to win:
> We drew a circle that took him in.

When the meeting was over, O. B. Harris drove by the concrete-block church where the movement had begun in 1965. The lights were on and the sounds of a meeting came out as Harris parked and went in. Here were the people who had not come to challenge the PTA meeting. They were meeting in the church to organize a new local chapter of SCLC. Harris spoke to the meeting, trying to cool the idea of such a new organization, feeling that it meant a new effort to stir the spirit of antipathy between black and white.

"I was too late," he said later. "They were already talking about boycotts and legal defense funds."

Greene County, and especially its center, the town of Eutaw, is facing one of the most interesting futures in America. The myth of the small town as a place for the good life has never been wholly true. Provincial attitudes have always inhibited the larger scope of thought and action, whether in New England, the Midwest or the Texas Panhandle. But in Greene County, unlike most other places in the South where blacks have taken political power (Hancock County, Ga.; Fayette, Miss., etc.), the blacks have made it possible for whites to cooperate, and whites have not officially withdrawn behind a line of perpetual hostility. The forces of self-interest seem to be working toward a broader view.

Tom Gilmore left Alabama when he was a young man and went to California where he found racism as bad if not worse than he had known in Alabama. He told his wife, "If it's this way all over we just as well go home. A man's got to have a home and, hell, we know what it's like there."

Another time he said, half to himself, half to me, "People are always in search of some mystical place. . . ."

His tone suggested that the mystical place does not exist. But it was also saying maybe . . . And Tom Gilmore has done his part to make Greene County some such land. He waits, and hopes.

The Rev. Bob Ross, a man who has a grasp of how the inner force in people can shape the outer space, said recently, "If racial accord ever occurs in the United States, Greene County will be the first place . . ."

Enclosure 2

LOG ON THE DEVELOPMENT OF THE
WEST ALABAMA HEALTH SERVICES PROJECT

Maintained by the Staff of the
West Alabama Comprehensive Health
Planning Council—July 31, 1973-March 14, 1974

1973

July 31   Mr. Andrew Dearman, representative of Congressman Walter
                 Flowers, conferred with West Alabama Comprehensive Health
                 Planning Council Director. He stated that the Black Belt
                 Family Health Center project was not approved for continuation
                 grant with all congressmen and senators from Alabama concur-
                 ring with "a" and "b" agencies. Since that time, pressure
                 tactics had convinced some HEW officials of need for ambulatory
                 health care in the West Alabama area. Asked HPC to work with
                 Federation and help to find a way to get services to people in
                 the area and make recommendations to Congressman Flowers.

August 9   Conference with Federation representatives: Melba McAfee and
                 John Zippert and WACHPC staff representatives: Pete Bailey
                 and Elizabeth Cleino.

                 Discussed ways to get health services to people organized by
                 Black Belt Family Health Center. Recommended that present
                 physician get licensed and go ahead and offer service at Epes
                 in temporary quarters to test whether people will come - can
                 they get transportation and what will be volume of response.

August 17   Presented planned suggestions to Executive Committee before
                 sending to Congressman Flowers. Left for Dr. Williams to
                 approve. He did not approve - letter not sent.

August 29   Jim West, HEW Regional Office, called to make appointment to
                 come to Tuscaloosa to discuss feasibility of WACHPC develop-
                 ing plan for Neighborhood Health Center grant.

                 Talked to Dr. Packard, University of Alabama, about College
                 of Community Health Sciences being applicant. University
                 could not be applicant but would cooperate.

September 19   Sketch of plan for Hale and Greene Counties developed.

September 20   Jim West and Pete Yarnell met with Executive Committee and
                 presented plan. Executive Committee asked staff to work on
                 this project with all parties to participate. Want Sumter and
                 Greene Counties included.

                 Called Melba McAfee. Asked her to come up to discuss this
                 with Regional Office representatives.

September 21   Conference with Federation representatives: Melba McAfee, John Zippert and Lewis Black; Regional Office representatives: Pete Yarnell and Jim West; and WACHPC staff: Greg de Lissovoy, Pete Bailey, Albert Metts, Mary Jo Looser and Elizabeth Cleino.

Called Mayor Pruitt, Judge Branch and Dr. Williams to tell them we would work on grant.

Dr. Williams arranged for Sumter County group to meet.

September 24   Prepared summary of provisions of grant and possible Board structure for preliminary meetings in Greene and Sumter Counties.

Reported to Congressman Flowers' office events of past several days.

Called Melba McAfee. Asked what Federation had decided. Said they had not caucused yet. Indicated she might be interested in a job with the project.

September 26   Dr. Cleino and Mr. Bailey met with Sumter County Medical Society - Doctors Hunt, Gegan, Crenshaw, Hightower and Williams - Mayor Ira Pruitt from Sumter County and Mr. Coleman from Greene County Commission to explain elements of project and determine their willingness to participate in the project.

Sumter County Medical Society voted to endorse project and two members, Dr. Gegan and Dr. Crenshaw, agreed to assist on a part-time basis.

Attended Sumter County Memorial Hospital Staff Meeting and received their endorsement.

Mayor Pruitt was aware of pressures from Washington, as he had recently returned from a conference there.

Members present suggested that the Federation should have two, not four, members but agreed to go along at this time.

September 28   Conference with Greene County Medical Society, Dentist, Hospital Administrator, Judge and Dr. Cleino. Endorsements received and pledge to participate from three physicians and cooperation from hospital administration and support from Judge. Felt Federation had too many representatives but would go along.

October 1	Telephone conference with Melba McAfee. Said they had caucused and would go along. Felt four members of Board was generous.
October 18	Sent out draft of Project Proposal and notice of meeting.
October 22	Tried to call Melba McAfee to discuss proposal - Holiday - no answer.
October 23	Tried to call Melba McAfee - no answer.
	Meeting with all factions (7:30-10:30 p.m.) Greene County Health Department. <u>Present</u>: Drs. Williams, Gegan, Crenshaw, Frederick, Staggers, and Smith; Mr. Patton; Mr. Lockard; Mrs. Melba McAfee; Mr. Spivey Gordon; Mr. John Zippert; Mr. Ayers; Dr. Cleino; Mr. Bailey and Mr. de Lissovoy; State - Mr. Max Benson, MASA; and Mr. Charlie Stewart, CHP (a).
	Budget presented at meeting.
	Project proposal suggestions made - main hangup was composition of Board. Federation would not approve. Demanded all consumer representatives, Black Project Director, Center at Epes, etc. Meeting ended with no concensus. Federation hurled charges at others for lack of care, etc.
October 24	Judge Branch conference in office of the WACHPC. Will go along with the project proposal. Will appoint three members truly representative of people.
October 25	Called Melba. Asked for final decision. Said they would not go along; also threatened to go to Washington and see to it no money was given to our project. Asked if interested in services to people or money to Federation? Said would have written reply by Friday, October 26.
October 29	Talked with Congressman Flowers about this project and events.
October 31	Conference with Dr. Hudgins, Mr. West and Dr. Cleino in Regional Office in Atlanta. Relayed events. Suggested proceed with all haste with those who want to participate.
November 1	Called Dr. Williams to notify people from Sumter County to meet on November 7 to make final plans for West Alabama Health Services Project.

November 2	Received call from Dr. Hudgins and Mr. West. Had received BBFHC Project with three-page cover letter. Advised to proceed with plans and get incorporated and endorsement letters.
November 2	Sent letters to Planning Committee omitting Federation. Sent progress report and suggested Articles of Incorporation and by-Laws. Asked help with endorsement letters.
November 2	Sent seven copies of official proposal to Dr. Hudgins. Sent two copies to CHP (a) Agency for review and concurrent.
November 4	Dr. Cleino talked with Sumter County Commission . . Sumter County OEO Director and D.P.S. and Mayor Prui . All agreed to write endorsement letters.
	Dr. Cleino went to Greene County to explain project and get endorsement letters from Chamber of Commerce, OEO, Extension Division and D.P.S.
November 7	Report to Congressman Flowers' office.
	Meeting held at Greene County Hospital of new Board members, plus Planning Committee. Approved project proposal as revised. Board approved By-Laws and signed Articles of Incorporation.
	Letter from CHP (a) approving presented by Mr. Stewart.
November 8	All new documents sent to Regional Office - Articles of Incorporation, By-Laws, Letters of Endorsement, and Job Descriptions.
November 9	Took Articles of Incorporation with all signatures to Judge Branch. Got incorporated at Greene County Courthouse.
November 15	Gave final copies to Executive Committee. Review and comment on Federation's application. Non-concurred.
November 16	Duplicated final copy of Project Proposal and sent copies to all Board members, Planning Committee and endorsers.
November 19	Received copy of CHP (a) Review and Comment on BBFHC Proposal - Non-concurrence.

November 21	Call from Regional Office saying site visit would be held November 28. Asked to change to 27th - did so.
	Contacted Judge Branch. Asked to see site visitors. He has appointment with Governor - will change if necessary.
	Called Dr. Williams and asked him to arrange for the meeting in Sumter County.
November 26	Call to Regional Office confirmed site team: Mr. Ted Griffith, Mr. Al Baldwin, Mr. Pete Yarnell. Will arrivee Tuscaloosa 8:30 p.m. Monday. Arrangements made to see providers, consumers and politicians in Greene and Sumter Counties, Tuesday, November 27.
November 26	Met Mr. Yarnell and Mr. Griffith at airport. Dr. Packard talked with them at the hotel.
November 27	Mr. Yarnell, Mr. Griffith, Mr. de Lissovoy and Dr. Cleino (later joined by Mr. Baldwin) met with people in Greene and Sumter Counties for site visit.
November 29	Called by Judge Branch to come to Greene County to meet with Federation representatives Mr. Zippert, Miss McAfee, and Mr. Ayers. Also present at the meeting were Mr. Jones, Mr. de Lissovoy, and Dr. Cleino. Purpose was to compromise but same demands were made. Asked grant to be rewritten with Epes as site, 3 counties, Board to include Federation representatives in Sumter and Marengo Counties. Dr. Cleino did not agree to rewrite. Reminded all present that Federation was offered more than half consumer representatives.

December 21	Called Al Baldwin (Grants Management, DHEW) to discuss proposal review. His comments were:

> Budget to high-reduce to $250,000
> Too much money in administrative overhead
> Salaries a little high
> 8 Clinic design could eventually be converted to HMO--this is good.
> o Looks like a paper plan--need to detail scope of services, linkages.

1974

January 2	Dr. Willard called to say Dr. Packard has learned of a husband-wife team of medical missionaries (Drs. Brown) possibly interested in relocating in this area.
January 7	Al Baldwin (DHEW) called to discuss criticisms of proposal, per our request. Previous points were confirmed (re Dec. 21). Suggested MASA be asked for help in specifiying medical equipment. Most prices were reasonable but quantities should be reduced.

Greg de Lissovoy spent all day in Greene and Sumter counties discusssing DHEW proposal review with board members, other interested parties. Persons contacted included:

- o   Mayor Pruitt (Livingston)
- o   C. T. Lockard, Jr. (Vice pres.WAHS)
- o   Dr. Edward P. Gegan(board, WAHS)
- o   Mr. Leo Fields   (Sumter Co. OEO)
- o   Mr. James Colemand (Greene Co. Commision)
- o   Mr. Charles Jones   (Greene Co. OEO)
- o   Mr. John Modley   (Board, WAHS)
- o   Mr. Dave Patton   (Greene Co. Hospital)

January 8	Meeting of Board of Directors and other inetersted parties of WAHS Project at 7:00 PM, Sumter County Public Health Dept.

14   Called Don Scheer (National Health Service Corps) re potential staffing. He says very difficult to get an MD but possibility of dentsists is very good. Urged that we apply as soon as possible.

14   Called HEW Regional Office to confirm meeting for January 21st in Eutaw. Pete Yarnell said that another meeting needed to be held with Federation to seek compromise proposal. Gave detailed instructions for negotiations. Implied that no grant unless compromise achieved.

14   Called Dr. Hudgins and Jim West at Regional Office.' They confirmed Pete's instructions but also indicated that reason for change was political pressure. Read us letters to Undersecretary Edwards (HEW) from Alabama congressmen. All congressmen rescinded June 6th letter.

15   Called Senator Sparkman's office to determine reason for change in position re June 6th letter. Rob Lockland said because of "congressional courtsey"to Walter Flowers. Said that Sparkman would follow Flower's lead so we needed to talk to him.

16   Went to Greene County. Met with following members of WAHS Board: Judge Branch, John Modley, Willie Hill, Rucker Staggers. Also spoke with Charles Jones, Jim Coleman, Bill Fredricks, Dave Patton, Explained to each the current situation. Feeling was that compromise should be attempted if needed to insure grant. However, should not give our project away. Let them compromise with us.

17   Melbah McAfee called to propose joint meeting of the two Boards. We asked for points that needed to be resolved. She had John Zippert pick up the phone. We suggested key points were: (1) Board composition, (2) Project Director, (3) Epes clinic site. Melbah said their Board might be willing to add "a couple" of our members; we said that this would probably be unacceptable to our board, they would be willing to add several BBCHS members. Zippert mentioned service area to include Marengo County; we said budget only allowed two counties but expansion could be considered in second year. Melbah said Jim West was talking out of two sides of his mouth. She would call him to get points straight and call us back.

17   Melbah called back to say Jim West was out; she would try to reach him and call us back,

January 17, 1974,

(Compromise discussed with Branch, Pruitt, Lockard, Flowers)

[Tentative-for submission to WAHS Board]

WEST ALABAMA HEALTH SERVICES, INC.

PROPOSED BOARD OF DIRECTORS

NAME OF BOARD MEMBER AND COUNTY OR AREA REPRESENTED	GROUP REPRESENTED		RACE	
	CONSUMER	PROVIDER	BLACK	WHITE
Greene County				
Judge William Branch		X	X	
*Sheriff Thomas Gilmore		X	X	
*Mr. Marcus Kirksey	X		X	
Dr. Rucker Staggers		X		
Mr. Willie Hill	X		X	
*Mr. Louis Barnett	X		X	
*Mr. Eddie Ayers	X		X	
	4	3	6	1
Sumter County				
Mr. C.T. Lockard, Jr.		X		X
Dr. Edward Gegan		X		X
*Dr. T.C. Looney		X		X
Mrs. Zora Gibbs	X		..	..
Mr. Edward Ozment	X			
Mr. Robert Cook	X		X	
*Rev. J. Hoard	X		X	
	4	3	3	4
West Alabama Region				
Dr. John Packard		X		
	......	......	......	......
	8	7	9	6
BOARD OF DIRECTORS COMPOSITION	8	7	9	6

*New Members of the Board of Directors (Proposed)

January 17	Called Judge Branch to discuss possible compromise. Board of WAHS could expand itself at next meeting to include several members of Federation/BBCHS board and also other community persons who needed to be represented. Names were discussed. He agreed.
January 17	Called Mayor Pruitt's office to discuss board expansion and new members suggested. He was in conference; gave list of names to his secretary with instructions for him to call back if any problems.
January 17	Called Mr. Lockard in Meridian, Mississippi to discuss Board expansion. He gave OK. He noted that York area needs to be considered in development of proposal. We said that we are available to meet there and had discussed this with Cmdr Simms.
January 17	Met with Walter Flowers and Andrew Dearman re status of project. Reviewed events since Dearman contacted this office. Stressed need for unified effort. He said he would discuss project with Judge Branch.
January 18	Melbah called to say she had spoken with Pete Yarnell at the Rgional Office. HEW plans to meet with WAHS board at 3:00 PM January 21st and at 7:00 PM (???) with BBFHS Board--this time to be confirmed. HEW will have written policy statement so that each board understands its position.
January 18	Spoke with Dr. Hiram Johnson regarding dental services. Project to be discussed at District meeting on Jan. 26. He suggests that all mention of project be restricted to Greene and Sumter to avoid controversy. He estimates $50,000 for three chair operatory and supplies for one year. Figure does not include salaries.

January 21 WAHS,Inc. Board of Directors met with Pete Yarnell and Al Baldwin (Region IV-CHS) to learn of HEW's position. See minutes of meeting.

January 23 Called Sheriff Gilmore to see if he went to BBFHC Board meeting. He did not. He has accepted WAHS invitation to serve on Board.

January 24 Dr. Williams called to say Mr. Lockard was calling a meeting in Livingston at 5:00 PM January 25 to discuss project with York representatives. He asked if we would attend. Told him that WACHP is trying to minimize influence in project; we are glad to discuss grant guidelines and restrictions but feel WAHS Board should be represnted. He asked us to notify Dr. Staggers.

January 24 Called Dr. Konigsberg to relay this latest development.

January 24 Called Andrew Dearman and discussed meeting of WAHS Board with HEW representatives. Emphasized need for Congressman Flowers to make his position clear via letter to Eddie Ayers. Told Dearman we would send him copy of minutes of meeting and HEW position statement.

January 24 Called Dr. Staggers and advised him of Dr. William's phone call. Will call him back if meeting is definite for Livingston.

January 24 Called Dr. Williams to advise that Dr. Cleino will be unavailable Friday PM--he will call Friday morning to arrange a time for meeting next week.

January 25 Dr. Williams called to say meeting with York group scheduled for 5:00 PM January 30 at Sumter County Health Dept.

January 25   Judge Branch called to say he had met with
              Eddie Ayers. Preliminary position of BBFHC
              Board is that they want:

              • Dissolution of present WAHS Board

              • Melbah McAfee to be Project Director

              • Dr. Gough to be physician

              • Eliminate present black board members
                from Sumter County.

              Suggested to Judge Branch that he document
              this meeting in a letter to Jim West or Pete
              Yarnell (CHS-Region IV) with copies to
              Walter Flowers and us.

January 30   Meeting at Sumter Co. Health Dept. called by
              Mr. Lockard. Mayor Pruitt stayed briefly.
              Mostly York people including Mayor Grant,
              Mr. Green, Dr. Gilbert, Dr. Walton. All members
              of Hill Hospital Board were present. General
              opposition to project. Felt medical services
              not needed because Drs. Walton & Gilbert not
              busy. Do see need for dental care, ancillary
              services such as PT, OT. See need for trans-
              portation. Oppose "socialism."

January 31   Called Judge Branch to hear progress of nego-
              tiations. He has seen Eddie Ayers twice more
              but no change in position. Urged that Judge
              write letter to HEW immediately to document
              status of negotiations.

February 4   Met with Dr. William Cole and Dr. Hiram Johnson
              (Sixth District Dental Society) to receive a
              proposed contract for the development and manage-
              ment of a dental services program component.

February 6   Called Pete Yarnell at Regional Office to discuss project status. Told him we are sending the proposed Dental Society contract to him at the request of Judge Branch. He said we need to submit a revised proposal by first week in March because of pressure to release funds to another area.

February 7   Contacted Richard Taylor at Medicare in Atlanta. He will send applications and instructions for reimbursement and a letter confirming that we have made contact.

February 7   Called Dr. Williams in Livingston to check developments in Sumter County. No meetings have been held but Medical Society meeting is planned. He suggested we call Aubrey Green and Thurman Lockard to discuss project.

February 8   Called Livingston University, spoke to Comptroller regarding data processing capability. Need to talk to them in person as capacity is limited.

February 8   Called Aubrey Green and discussed project. Told him Sumter County would not be committed to anything except a study to determine needs in that area--local people need to make decisions affecting them. He requested we call John Sims.

February 8   Called Jim Hamilton (Dist. 6 Health Planner) to check on developments. He asked for letter outlining current thinking on proposal so he could discuss this with York people.

February 11   Discussed various aspects of project with
following persons in Eutaw:

Dave Patton: contracting lab work with hospital;
he is opposed because they are not
equipped in terms of personnel.

Dr. Staggers; staff for clinic; Dental Society
contract.

Judge Branch: Negotiations with BBFHSC Board;
Dental Society contract.

Charles Jones: Dr. Maddox' role; transportation.

Also talked to Sheriff Gilmore. Met local
pharmacists.

Feb. 12   Spoke with Nolan (?) VP for Business at Livingtson
University re project, especially data processing needs.
He wants to set up meeting with his staff and us.
Said he had been contacted by Fred Brodt regarding
Livingston U. donating office space for project. What is
Brodt's status with project. Told him that he is an
interested person who is volunteering time and expertise
but is not acting in an official capacity.

Feb. 13	Met with Drs. Keoenemann and Shields (Druid City pathologists) re design of clinical lab for WAHS. Discussed various types of equipment, staffing and training, and screening strategies.
Feb. 15	Discussed new project objectives with Mayor Grant of York, especially Obj. #2 relating to Sumter Co.
Feb. 20	Discussed project status with Dr. Williams. He says York people are evidently satisfied with new aproach.
March 1	Asked Jim Coleman ; to arrange for us to visit potential clinic sites.
March 4	Inspected several potential sites in Eutaw.
March 11	Met with Sixth District dental society re their propesed agreement. Showed them letter from Dr. Hudgins saying that project could not be "contracted out". Went over text of new proposal. They are evidently satisfied.
March 12	Regional office asked that proposal be completed and submitted immediatly.
March 13	Called following persons to explain this new situation and ask if they felt a Board meeting was needed before submitting proposal:
	Judge Branch Sheriff Gilmore Mr. Lockard Dr. Williams Jim Hamilton (couldn't be reached)
	All agreed:complete proposal and send it on; they were satisfied with major thrust and trusted us with details.
March 14	Proposal hand carried to Atlanta.

Minutes of Meetings of the Executive Committee
West Alabama Comprehensive Health Planning Council
Which Included Discussion of the Following:

Federation of Southern Cooperatives
Black Belt Family Health Center

West Alabama Health Services Project

WEST ALABAMA COMPREHENSIVE HEALTH PLANNING COUNCIL
EXECUTIVE COMMITTEE MEETING
September 28, 1972

MINUTES

PRESENT

Dr. Everett Hale, Chairman
Dr. Howard B. Gundy
Reverend James M. Lilly
Mr. D. O. McClusky, Jr.
Mrs. Marjorie Meredith
Judge John M. Puryear
Dr. Sidney J. Williams

ABSENT

Mr. Norman C. Cephus
Mr. Robert Boone
Dr. R. O. Rutland, Jr.
Judge Robert Kirksey

STAFF

Dr. Elizabeth W. Cleino, Director
Mr. Pete Bailey, Health Planner
Mr. Sonny Metts, Environmental Health Planner
Miss Carole Warren, Administrative Resident
Mrs. Peggy Hooks, Administrative Assistant
Mrs. Marty Armistead, Secretary

The Executive Committee of the West Alabama Comprehensive Health
Planning Council met September 28, 1972, in the office of the Council. Dr.
Everett Hale, Chairman, called the meeting to order at 12:30 p.m.

Dr. Cleino introduced the new Staff members, Miss Carole Warren and
Mr. Albert Metts. Miss Warren is an Administrative Resident completing require-
ments for a Master's Degree in Health Care Administration at the University of
Alabama at Birmingham. Mr. Metts is filling the position of Environmental
Health Planner.

The minutes of the August 31, 1972, meeting were approved as distributed.
The financial statement was also reviewed and approved.

As a follow-up to the minutes, Dr. Cleino reported that she had received
a call from Mr. Ed Robertson, of the Northport Hospital Board, requesting assistance
from the Council in planning for the Northport Hospital.

Dr. Cleino also reported that she had suggested that the University might
secure an Emergency Medical Services helicopter from Craig AFB for the University
football games. This would be a voluntary effort on the part of Craig AFB. With
the heavy traffic following the football games, land transportation for emergencies
is virtually impossible.

Contract with V.A. Hospital for Manpower and Education Program

Dr. Hale circulated copies of the contract that was signed between the Council and the Tuscaloosa Veterans Administration Hospital for up to $50,000 to provide for a manpower and education specialist and support services for this program. This person will provide the Staff assistance for the Manpower and Education Committee of the Council.

Dr. Charles Joiner has been selected for the position and offered a salary of $21,996. He has requested to remain under the benefit program of the UAB. Arrangements have been made with the Alabama Regional Medical Program to handle this. Dr. Joiner has also requested to continue to serve on the faculty in the Health Administration Program.

After considerable discussion on whether these activities would interfere with his full-time employment here, it was decided to get more definite information on his prior commitments before making a decision.

Request for Funds

Dr. Cleino stated that while attending the CHP Conference in Nashville, she talked with representatives from ARC and CHP concerning the WACHPC Continuation Grant for next year. The application should be submitted by January, 1973. The representatives suggested that the same grant request be sent simultaneously to CHP and ARC indicating in the Budget the amount of funds being requested from each agency. To receive funding from ARC for five counties would have the advantage of requiring less matching funds.

Federation of Southern Cooperatives

Mr. Bailey reported that on request of Dr. John Packard, Director of the Alabama Regional Medical Program, he attended a meeting of representatives of the Federation of Southern Cooperatives in Atlanta ten days ago. The purpose of the meeting was to set up an Advisory Committee to the Black Belt Family Health Care Center, located in Epes, Alabama. No Advisory Committee was set up because of poor attendance at the meeting. The Center expects to offer complete health care to those who are enrolled in the program, similar to an HMO.

Miss Melbah Jean McAfee, Administrator of the Family Health Care Center, had made contact with the National Health Service Corps in hopes of getting a qualified physician and other health personnel for the Center. A meeting of local, areawide, State, and Regional Office personnel will be held on October 4 in Livingston to further discuss this program.

Combined Boards of Health meeting, September 12

Dr. Hale reported that a meeting was held on September 12 of the County Boards of Health to discuss the possibility of developing a District Health Department. Dr. George Hardy from the Jefferson County Health Department and

Dr. W. J. Donald from the Bureau of County Health Services of the State Health Department were consultants.

The idea was well received and a Committee was formed to further consider the development of a District Health Department. This Committee will be chaired by Dr. John Shamblin and co-chaired by Dr. Sidney Williams. The Committee will be made up of the Chairmen of the County Boards of Health and the Probate Judges.

Dr. Williams stated that as a first step, the appointed Committee should map out the goals and objectives of a District Health Department, consider pooling of funds that could provide the participating counties with increased services to the public.

Dr. Hale stated that he thought a Regional Health Director with a specialty in Public Health could be secured if a decent salary were offered and if the person is given an opportunity to develop new programs in community medicine and community health.

Dr. Williams further stated that a compilation of the existing funds and names of personnel should be made before the next meeting.

CHP Conference in Nashville

Time did not permit a detailed report of the Region IV Conference, but Dr. Cleino reported that there was a great deal of discussion about the physical planning agencies wishing to absorb CHP areawide agencies. This is not a problem in this area. The trend toward assignment of health related planning to the Council of Governments is illustrated by the Alabama Committee on Aging allocating planning money for Aging to the Planning and Development Councils throughout this State.

National Health Service Corps

Dr. Cleino reported that two applications for NHSC personnel had been completed and submitted to the Regional Office. They included one from Bibb County requesting two nurses and two doctors, and one from Lamar County requesting one dentist. A meeting had been held in Pickens County with the Hospital Board and County Medical Society concerning the possibility of applying for a physician for Pickens County; but they decided not to apply. The Lamar County application requires the endorsement of the Sixth District Dental Society. Dr. Cleino spoke to this group and received a mixed response. The final decision was to write a letter of endorsement only if (1) the Dentist in Lamar County endorsed the project, (2) the NHSC Dentist be licensed in Alabama, and (3) he spend 50 percent of his time in caring for indigent people.

New Doctors for Tuscaloosa.

Dr. Hale reported that due to the recruitment efforts of the Tuscaloosa County Medical Society, an Ear, Nose, and Throat specialist will be moving to Tuscaloosa in November and at least one Pediatrician is expected in July.

New Business

Emergency Medical Technician Training Program

Miss Warren reported that an application for funding for EMT training programs had been written and submitted to the State Division of EMS by the Emergency Medical Services Committee. The University of Alabama, through the Division of Continuing Education, has agreed to provide the administrative support for the two training programs. Miss Jeanette Latham will serve as Clinical Coordinator and liason with Druid City Hospital. The WACHPC will handle the funds for the program.

Plans are to offer two 81-hour Dunlap Courses with an enrollment of 30 students each. The courses will begin November 2, 1972, and March 1, 1973.

Health Facilities Committee

In the absence of the Chairman, Judge Kirksey, Mr. Bailey presented the recommendations of the Health Facilities Committee on the Alabama Master Hospital Plan for 1973.

The recommendations were discussed. Dr. Williams moved that the recommendations be approved by the Executive Committee. The motion was seconded and carried.

Certificate of Need Legislation

Dr. Cleino reported that according to a publication of August, 1971, there were 14 states who had adopted Certificate of Need Legislation, and 10 others with legislation pending. Subsequently, those states which have not enacted such legislation are seeing increased activity by national hospital corporations and for-profit hospital firms that wish to build hospitals. The many problems that are associated with overbuilding of hospitals were discussed.

The Health Facilities Committee, at the meeting on September 25, went on record as approving the concept of Certificate of Need by taking the following position:

> "Recognizing that underutilization of Health Facilities increases cost and overbuilding compounds problems in the utilization of health manpower and also contributes to increased costs, the Committee wishes to go on record as endorsing the principal of Certificate of Need Legislation for all non-federal nursing homes and hospitals. Certification will be granted by a State Agency on advice and consent of the areawide health planning agency."

Mr. McClusky moved that the Executive Committee approve this action of the Health Facilities Committee. The motion was seconded and carried.

Feasibility Grant for a Baccalaureate Program in Nursing

Dr. Cleino reported that the University of Alabama is preparing a grant request for a feasibility study for a Baccalaureate Program in Nursing. She has been working with Dr. Willard and Dr. Moore in preparing the grant request.

Mr. McClusky moved that the Council endorse the Feasibility Study for the Nursing Program. The motion carried unanimously.

Review and Comment

The proposal from the Town of Sulligent for $1,297,000 for a Waste and Water System was thoroughly reviewed by Mr. Metts. He pointed out the area to be served, and recommended approval with the following recommendations:

(1) that the water system be flouridated
(2) that the raw water supply meet acceptable biological and chemical standards.

The Review and Comment on the Alabama Regional Medical Program annual grant request would have to be postponed until the next meeting as the final copy has not yet been received.

There being no further business, the Executive Committee adjourned at 2:30 p.m.

WEST ALABAMA COMPREHENSIVE HEALTH PLANNING COUNCIL
EXECUTIVE COMMITTEE MEETING
April 26, 1973

MINUTES

PRESENT	ABSENT
Dr. Galen Drewry	Dr. Everett Hale
Mrs. Cynthia Lanford	Mr. Norman Cephus
Mr. James Lilly	Judge Robert Kirksey
Mr. D. O. McClusky, Jr.	Judge John M. Puryear
Dr. R. O. Rutland, Jr.	Mr. Robert H. Boone
Dr. Sidney J. Williams	

STAFF PRESENT

Dr. Elizabeth W. Cleino, Director
Mr. Pete Bailey, Health Planner
Mr. Albert Metts, Environmentalist
Mr. Bill Hunter, Assistant to Dr. Williams
Mrs. Marty Armistead, Secretary

The Executive Committee of the West Alabama Comprehensive Health Planning
Council met on April 26, 1973, at 12:00 noon in the conference room of the
Council. Mr. James Lilly, presided in the absence of the Chairman. The
meeting was called to order at 12:20 p.m.

Minutes

The minutes of the March 22, 1973, meeting were approved as distributed.

Financial Report

Expenditures for March were approved under the ARC and ARMP grants.
Approval was given for the purchase of the four folding conference tables.
Dr. Cleino reported that Mr. Robert McWhirter had been engaged to audit the
WACHPC books at a cost of $750.

ARMP Grant-Dr. Cleino reported that the grant from ARMP for the development of the Regional Health Department had been used to employ Mr. Bill
Hunter, engage Dr. W. J. Donald as a consultant, and pay for office rent,
telephone expense, and supplies. Mr. Hunter will be placed on the Health
Department staff soon. The expenses for the Regional Health Department were
approved as distributed.

OLD BUSINESS

Equipment and Furniture Purchased under ARMP Grant

Office furniture and other equipment purchased by the Council under the ARMP grant is currently assigned to the University of Alabama in Birmingham. As the ARMP is being phased out, a request was made to have the responsibility for this equipment reassigned to the WACHPC.

Report on Sickle Cell Program

Through the coordinating effort of the staff, 14 groups and agencies in Tuscaloosa have provided a sickle cell program. Approximately 2,000 people were tested for sickle cell anemia. The results have been received from the State Health Laboratory and counselors have been trained to talk with those who have traits or the disease. Volunteers are taking the information from the Lab reports and making a card with the results for each person tested.

Report on the Initial Meeting of the Ad Hoc Committee for Hale Memorial Hospital and Follow-up Report

Dr. Cleino explained that the Ad Hoc Committee for Hale Memorial met and was presented an agenda with possible uses for the hospital. Those present were convinced that if they made alternative suggestions for Hale Memorial before the State Board of Health considered the tuberculosis hospital situation, this might be detrimental to Hale Memorial. The Committee agreed to support the continued use of Hale Memorial Hospital for tuberculosis care and an effort to make it the last tuberculosis hospital in the State to be closed. In the meantime, the State Board of Health met and voted to allow three hospitals, (Decatur, Gadsden, and Tuscaloosa) to remain open with support for 50 beds each. By 1974, all tuberculosis hospitals will be closed.

Dr. Cleino stated that the Appalachian Regional Commission is concerned about the high incidence of tuberculosis in our area; and Mr. Robert McDonald has initiated action that may get us some help with this problem.

Recommendations from the Health Facilities Committee

Mr. Bailey presented the recommendations from the Health Facilities Committee as submitted from the March 8 and April 24 meetings. Members at the March 8 meeting voted to (1) approve the addition of 104 beds to Druid City Hospital. Dr. Drewry moved the approval of the recommendations; Dr. Williams seconded; and the motion carried. The Health Facilities Committee had requested that the Executive Committee review and comment on Addendum II of the Community Mental Health Facilities Plan. The decision was that this cannot be done without further information.

The Health Facilities Committee meeting April 24 recommended:

1. That the Master Hospital Plan be revised utilizing the actual bed complement as opposed to bed capacity. The Executive Committee approved this recommendation.

2. Approval of the application from Park Manor Nursing Home for 150 nursing home beds to be divided between skilled and ICF.

3. Approval of the application from Glen Haven Nursing Home for 100 ICF beds. Since the Health Facilities Committee meeting, a clarification from Mr. Dean's office on the available nursing home beds determined that the extended care beds were available for distribution. Since the two applications had been approved by the Health Facilities Committee, the Executive Committee recommended that the Committee meet again and make the final decision on allocation of beds.

4. Request again that the Master Hospital Plan be revised to include a new Pickens County Hospital at Carrollton. This recommendation was approved as presented.

5. Request a 60-day extension of the deadline date for review and recommendation on the Aliceville and Gordo Nursing Home applications and request clarification of the two proposed nursing homes in Pickens County, whether they are consistent with the Master Hospital Plan. This recommendation was approved as presented.

6. That the staff develop an areawide Health Facilities Plan for West Alabama. This recommendation was approved as presented.

Recommendations from the Emergency Medical Services Committee

Dr. Cleino reported that $15 million would be available from the Robert Wood Johnson Foundation for 50 EMS grants. The State of Alabama could submit a single grant for all areawide plans, but the EMS Committee felt that our area would benefit more if a West Alabama grant were submitted independently. Therefore, the former EMS grant proposal will be revised to include communications, extra training for hospital personnel and EMT's, and radio equipment for hospitals and ambulances. Dr. Rutland moved that a new proposal be submitted, Dr. Williams seconded the motion, and the motion carried.

Dr. Rutland stressed the need for a good ambulance service in any County. This has been exemplified by the closing of one ambulance company in Fayette and the opening of another which is not yet licensed. He stated that Fayette has had an epidemic of wrecks since March and this may be attributed to the high instance of drunken driving. The physicians of Fayette County have taken action by writing letters to judges who are in a position to sentence the drunken driver, and urging other physicians in emergency rooms to record information stating whether a driver has been drinking at the time of an accident.

Dr. Drewry suggested that the Council urge the law enforcement officers to report correct information and give the breath alizer test when possible.

Report on Regional Health Department Development

Dr. Cleino reported that an applicant for the position of Regional Health Director, Dr. C.M.G. Buttery, was to meet with the Search Committee in Tuscaloosa, May 13-14. Dr. Buttery is board certified in Preventive Medicine and has had experience in both private practice and in public health. Ads have been placed in the Army, Navy and Air Force Times and Stars and Stripes hoping to attract M.D.'s, Dentists, and R.N.'s to the area.

Report from Environmental Health Committee

Mr. Metts reported that the Environmental Health Committee met April 17 and is in the process of documenting need and identifying problem areas so that proper recommendations can be made to the Council. Mr. Metts is serving as the coordinator in an effort to get standards written for residential sub-divisions.

Status of NHSC Application for Bibb County

Even though approval was granted for a physician under the National Health Service Corps program for Bibb County, all efforts to recruit a physician for the position so far have failed.

Publicity

Newsletter-Dr. Cleino stated that the first edition of the Council's newsletter was in the mail. Hopefully, an issue will be published each month.

Careers Fair-There will be a health careers fair in McFarland Mall May 10-12. The Council will be participating in the fair by having a booth and presenting brochures explaining the work of the Council.

Both the Newsletter and the Health Careers Fair will help educate the public on the work of the Council.

Health Advisory Board, Tuscaloosa County

Dr. Cleino reported that the official designation of the Tuscaloosa County Health Advisory Board would be delayed until after the coming city elections.

NEW BUSINESS

Proposed West Alabama Medical Care Study by Dr. Irving Webber

Dr. Cleino reported that the contract with Swinea and Associates had been cancelled, leaving extra funds in the Consultant category. With the approval of the Executive Committee at the March meeting, arrangements were made with Dr. Irving Webber, a Medical Sociologist at the University, to conduct a study of the health care needs and health delivery system in the West Alabama area. Dr. Drewry moved the approval of the proposed study as presented to the Executive Committee. Dr. Rutland seconded the motion, and the motion carried. Dr. Cleino stated that a request had been made to the Reional Office to allow the use of year-end funds for this project.

Review and Comment

Black Belt Family Health Care Center, Epes, Alabama-requesting $473,389 in HEW funds, with $53,883 in local funds and returning $16,719 for a total of $527,272. Comments from the Executive Committee members:

Mr. McClusky stated that the Center was established by breaking the pattern of the health planning system which our Council has worked so hard to set up. Dr. Williams stated that Hospital Administrators and health officials in the Black Belt area had suggested that a health facility be constructed adjacent to the established hospital allowing the medical director and hospital administrator to operate in conformity to the hospital rules and also allowing the Center to be covered under lower health insurance rates.

Dr. Cleino stated that there is a definite need to provide improved health care to the people in the area not normally able to get it. She stated that she was concerned about how the project would be continued when HEW discontinues its funding since the project is built outside the usual health care system.

Dr. Williams moved that the Executive Committee give non-concurrence to the application for the above-named reasons. Mr. McClusky seconded the motion, and it carried. The Executive Committee recommended that the money applied for in the grant be rechanneled through the proper health agencies.

There being no futher business, the Executive Committee adjourned at 2:35 p.m.

WEST ALABAMA COMPREHENSIVE HEALTH PLANNING COUNCIL
EXECUTIVE COMMITTEE MEETING
August 16, 1973

MINUTES

PRESENT	ABSENT
Dr. Everett Hale	Judge John Puryear
Mr. D. O. McClusky, Jr.	Dr. Galen Drewry
Dr. Sidney Williams	Mr. Norman C. Cephus
Dr. R. O. Rutland, Jr.	Rev. James M. Lilly
Mr. Robert Boone	
Mrs. Cynthia Lanford	
Judge Robert Kirksey	

STAFF PRESENT

Dr. Elizabeth Cleino, Director
Mr. Walter P. Bailey, Health Planner
Mrs. Mary Jo Looser, Information Specialist
Mrs. Marty Armistead, Secretary
Mr. Greg deLissovoy, Health Planner

The Executive Committee of the Comprehensive Health Planning Council met on Thursday, August 16, 1973, at 12:00 noon in the conference room of the Council. Judge Robert Kirksey presided until Dr. Everett Hale, Chairman, arrived. The minutes of the previous meeting were approved as previously distributed on a motion by Mr. Boone and a second by Dr. Rutland.

Financial Affairs

A. Monthly Expenditures: The monthly financial statement was presented. Mr. Boone moved that the expenditures be approved as presented. Motion was seconded and carried.

B. Budget Needs: Dr. Cleino reported that the Council's budget for the year is about $8,000.00 short. She stated that all requests from the governing bodies had been paid, except Greene and Hale Counties, and the City of Tuscaloosa. Only Hale County has not voted the funds as requested. Other sources of funds were discussed.

1. Insurance Companies: On a request from Dr. Hale, a check for $2,073 was received from Blue Cross-Blue Shield. Another possible source is the Health Insurance Association of America. They have set aside $500,000 nationally for funding of B agencies, according to correspondence from the A agency. Mr. Boone moved that the Council follow up on this proposal and take whatever steps are necessary to apply. Dr. Rutland seconded and the motion carried.

2. Contract: Dr. Cleino proposed that the Council offer to contract with the University of Alabama College of Community Health Sciences to conduct a study of nursing manpower.

3. Request from Hospitals: A third proposal for securing additional funds was to ask each hospital to provide $2.00 per bed for the Council's support.

Dr. Cleino was authorized to proceed with these requests for assistance.

C. Funds Transfer: On a motion by Dr. Williams, Dr. Cleino was authorized to transfer funds at First Federal Savings and Loan to a 90-Day Certificate of Deposit account. Dr. Hale seconded the motion and it carried.

D. State Audit: The State Auditors have completed their investigation of the Council's books for the last grat year (August 1, 1972 - May 1, 1973). Although the final report has not yet been received, the auditor suggested that those who handle the money should be bonded. Mr. Boone moved that the staff investigate a blanket bond or a position bond and secure whichever appears best suited to the Council's needs. Dr. Williams seconded the motion, which was approved.

E. Fringe Benefit: Dr. Cleino reported that the staff is waiting for a recommendation from Mr. Joe Lane on the fringe benefit program for employees. She said that a bank plan and several insurance company plans are under consideration. Dr. Williams suggested the state employee retirement system might be investigated. Following further discussion, Dr. Williams moved that the matter be referred to the personnel committee for a decision. Motion carried.

Council Membership

The resignation of Mr. John Faust as Administrator of the Pickens County Hospital created the need for a replacement from the West Alabama Hospital Council to serve on the WACHPC. Mr. Frank Bynum was selected by the Hospital Council as its representative. Dr. Williams moved, motion was seconded and approved that Mr. Bynum be approved for membership to fill Mr. Faust's unexpired term.

The committee discussed ways of increasing attendance at the quarterly meetings. Dr. Rutland suggested that county organizations would provide great incentive in this area. Judge Kirksey expressed the view that an attendance chairman in each county could be designated to remind council members of the meetings and to urge attendance. A record of attendance of each council member was presented to the ccommittee, and it was pointed out that two consecutive inexcused absences were considered grounds for naming a replacement. Dr. Rutland suggested that a letter be written to be members who had been absent reminding them of the importance of their attendance and also asking for their resignations if they could not attend. Mr. Boone suggested that this record of attendance be sent along with the letter.

Dr. Rutland stated that he would have to resign from the Executive Committee due to increasing responsibilities at the University of Alabama College of Community Health Sciences. Dr. Hale expressed the appreciation of the Council to Dr. Rutland for his fine contributions and loyal attendance at the meetings. Dr. Rutland agreed to remain a member of the Council.

Appointment to Focus Board

Mr. Don Morton was nominated by Judge Kirksey to continue to represent the Council on the Focus Board for a three-year term. Mrs. Lanford seconded the nomination and Mr. Morton was unanimously elected.

Condition to Grant

Dr. Cleino brought to the attention of the committee a condition to the ARC Grant, which states: "within ninety days of funding date the applicant submit to the Regional Office of Comprehensive Health Planning revised criteria for selection of Council membership and the time frame for implementation." The revised Comprehensive Health Law lists consumers, providers, and elected officials as members to be included on health planning councils. General Council has issued an opinion that elected officials could not be called consumers. Since there can be no more than 49 per cent providers, this seems to indicate that elected officials are to be considered with the provider quota. General Council's ruling can be challenged.

Dr. Williams moved that the WACHPC notify the regional office that we will meet the condition of the grant as members' terms expire, to begin with the annual meeting and that we write General Council for clarification. Mr. Boone seconded this motion and it passed.

Report from Committees

A. Family Planning Committee: Dr. Williams reported that the first monthly meeting of the new Family Planning Committee met in the conference room of the Council on August 9, 1973. The new budget has not been finalized. All county units were reported to be progressing well, as the project begins its second year.

B. Health Facilities Committee: Judge Kirksey presented the report of the Health Facilities Committee. The Health Facilities Committee made the following recommendations: 140 ICF beds for Bryce Nursing Home; 72 beds for the Sick and Shut-In Nursing Home; 54 beds for the Bibb County Nursing Home; a road and parking system for Druid City Hospital; the Alabama Master Hospital Plan, FY 1973, for Bibb and Tuscaloosa County; a statement that the beds to be used by Druid City Hospital at Hale Memorial Hospital be considered temporary and not counted against their bed allotment on a long-term basis; and that the Tuscaloosa County Health Department be enlarged. These recommendations were approved on a motion by Mr. Boone, seconded by Judge Kirksey.

C. Emergency Medical Services Committee: Dr. Cleino reported that the Governor had set aside $400,000 in Revenue Sharing funds for the installment of radio equipment in the public hospitals of the state. The staff is coordinating the project in this district.

The Robert Wood Johnson Grant, which had been sent to the Executive Committee members by mail, was reviewed and formally approved. Dr. Hale commended the staff on the proposal.

Conference Attendance

Approval was granted to Dr. Cleino and Mr. Bailey to attend two conferences: Region IV CHP Conference, August 21-23, in St. Petersburg, Florida, and Region IV and VI Certificate of Need Conference, September 5-7, in New Orleans, Louisiana.

Health Legislation

Two bills now pending in the legislature to provide $250,000 for District Health Departments were brought to the attention of the Executive Committee. Judge Kirksey moved that the Council write letters to all area legislators under the signature of Dr. Hale urging their support of legislative bills to fund District Health Departments. Mr. Boone seconded this motion. Motion carried.

Black Belt Family Health Care Center Project

Congressman Flowers' office had requested that the WACHPC work with the Black Belt Family Health Care Center Project and suggest ways in which this project could provide needed services in the area in a manner acceptable to the on-going health care system. The staff had discussed several alternatives with representatives of the center project and recommended that the health team give services on a "fee for service" basis to people in the area and evaluate the effectiveness of this approach before applying for federal funds for support.

After a lengthy discussion of the many aspects of this project, Dr. Cleino was instructed to write a letter to Congressman Flowers suggesting that since there is a need, that the physician be licensed in Alabama and then offer services so people will have an additional choice for health care.

There was an agreement among all the members, except Dr. Williams, that this was an acceptable alternative. Since this is a very sensitive area, Dr. Hale was asked to approve the letter. Also, since Dr. Williams had been involved with this project from its beginning, the Executive Committee asked him to look over the letter before it was mailed.

Other Business

Dr. Williams announced that Dr. Kornigsberg is interested in the District Health Officer Position, and he will be invited for an interview soon. He has the M.P.H. and is 32 years old.

There being no further business, the meeting was adjourned at 3:15 p.m.

WEST ALABAMA COMPREHENSIVE HEALTH PLANNING COUNCIL
EXECUTIVE COMMITTEE MEETING
September 20, 1973

MINUTES

PRESENT

Dr. Everett Hale, Chairman
Mr. D. O. McClusky, Jr.
Dr. Sidney Williams
Mr. Robert Boone
Mrs. Cynthia Lanford
Judge Robert Kirksey
Judge John Puryear
Dr. Galen Drewry
Mr. Norman C. Cephus
Rev. James M. Lilly

GUESTS

Mr. Jim West
  Regional Office HEW
Mr. Pete Yarnell
  Regional Office HEW
Dr. John Packard

STAFF PRESENT

Dr. Elizabeth Cleino, Director
Mr. Walter P. Bailey, Health Planner
Mr. Walter Metts, Health Planner
Mr. Greg de Lissovoy, Health Planner
Mrs. Mary Jo Looser, Information Specialist
Mrs. Anna Adkins, Secretary

The Executive Committee of the Comprehensive Health Planning Council met on Thursday, September 20, 1973, at 12:00 noon in the conference room of the Council with Dr. Everett Hale, Chairman, presiding. The minutes of the previous meeting were approved as distributed on a motion by Judge Puryear and a second by Judge Kirksey.

Financial Affairs

A. Monthly Expenditures: Copies of the August expenditure report were presented. Dr. Hale moved the expenditures be approved as presented. Mr. Lilly seconded the motion and it carried unanimously.

B. Funds Received: Dr. Hale explained that the Council had requested $2.00 per bed from each hospital in the area. Checks were received from Pickens County, Lamar County, Druid City and Greene County Hospitals.

The Council received a check in the amount of $1,800 from Dr. William Willard for the contract with the University of Alabama for the nursing manpower study.

Dr. Cleino reported that the V.A. Hospital had received tentative approval from the regional office to give "in-kind" services, since it could not make a cash contribution. They have been asked to print the Council's newsletter and other materials which would amount to approximately $100.00 per month in service. A letter requesting "in-kind" service from Bryce Hospital had also been written.

ARMP Representatives

The Alabama Regional Medical Program has requested that two representatives of the WACHPC (one consumer and one provider) be appointed to serve on their Regional Advisory Council. Dr. Howard Gundy and Judge Kirksey were the representatives last year. Judge Kirksey requested that someone else be given the opportunity to serve in his place. Dr. Galen Drewry was appointed to serve in Dr. Gundy's place, and Mr. D. O. McClusky was appointed as the provider representative. The RAC meeting was scheduled for September 25.

Report from Committees

A. Health Facilities Committee: Judge Kirksey reported that the Health Facilities Committee had received an application from the Riverside Medical Center to build a nursing home in Tuscaloosa County. Long-range plans had been developed for this facility two years ago as a part of the total center. Judge Kirksey noted, however, that there were no more beds to be allocated right now. The Health Facilities Committee was impressed with the thoroughness of the plan and the design of the total center; but since there was no bed need, could not grant approval to the project. The Committee recommended a 30-day extension in order to give the applicant time for further study of the situation.

There was considerable discussion in the group about the quality of care in nursing homes. There seems to be a wide variance from one nursing home to another. The difficulty of measuring quality care was also discussed.

It was also pointed out that there was a need for a new formula in forecasting beds needed in order to predict more accurately the actual need.

Approval of the Fayette County Nursing Home's grant request for Hill-Burton and ARC funding was recommended by the Health Facilities Committee. Judge Kirksey moved approval of the Executive Committee; Judge Puryear seconded and the motion passed unanimously with Mr. Boone, the administrator, abstaining.

The recommendations of the Health Facilities Committee on the Master Hospital Plan were presented:

Fayette County: The population projections were based on extrapolations of one year estimates which resulted in a decrease in bed need. Plans are being formulated to add 25 beds to the Fayette County Hospital based on current occupancy rates and anticipated growth in the county.

Pickens County: The Committee again recommended that the Plan be amended to include a replacement hospital in Carrollton.

Hale County: The number of beds should be increased to coincide with the recommendation of Mr. Dean earlier in the year.

Dr. Williams stated there was a need for construction of a health center that would in general house the personnel of the District Health Office and provide facilities for the Tuscaloosa County Health Department. Dr. Cleino noted that the recommendation had already been made to change the Master Hospital Plan to accommodate this need.

Judge Kirksey moved acceptance of the Master Hospital Plan with these recommendations. Mr. Lilly seconded and the motion carried.

Mr. Lilly reminded the Committee of the need for a retirement home. Dr. Cleino said she understood Glen Haven would build 50 such beds in their new addition.

B. Environmental Health Committee: Mr. Lilly reported that during the month of July the EHC sponsored an all day meeting with the National Sanitation Foundation, inviting personnel from all over the state interested in setting standards. Attendance was very good.

Mr. Lilly also stated that he had submitted his resignation as chairman of the Committee, effective September 30. Dr. Hale commended Mr. Lilly for the excellent work he had done as chairman. Mr. Metts also extended his appreciation to Mr. Lilly for help given to the Environmental Committee.

Emergency Medical Technician Training Program

The University of Alabama Division of Continuing Education will offer three EMT courses during the year, Dr. Cleino stated. A request for Manpower Development Training Act funds of $3,500 per course is now in the regional office for final approval. Enrollment for the sessions is especially high with some students having to be turned away from the first session, Dr. Cleino said.

Emergency Medical Services

Dr. Cleino reported to the Committee that the Tuscaloosa Emergency Medical Service was much improved. Four ambulances are now equipped and operating with mostly trained Emergency Medical Technicians. The bill authorizing cities and counties to pay for these services did not pass the Senate. The local legislators have been contacted to prepare a local bill in case there is a special session.

Mr. Boone noted the critical situation in Fayette County. Lack of stable personnel to run the ambulance service is causing a major problem.

Dr. Webber's Study

Work is underway on the study of health care delivery to be conducted by Dr. Irving Webber, medical sociologist at the University of Alabama. Mr. Ferris Richey, a third year graduate student, will be the project assistant and employ field workers to conduct the study in Fayette and Hale Counties. Interviewing will begin the middle of October.

CHP Conferences

Dr. Cleino and Mr. Bailey attended the Region IV CHP Conference, August 21-23, in St. Petersburg, Florida. Dr. Cleino reported that they were given the latest information out of Washington. Grants programs have been greatly simplified by streamlining many of the requirements. Previously every grant had its own rules, forms, etc. Now one set of rules will be followed for applications, reporting, audits, etc.

Dr. Cleino said they also learned that it is expected that CHP will be given increased responsibility, certainly no less, and may possibly be given regulatory powers. CHP agencies will be assessed and if they are considered effective will be given help to further strengthen the agency. New B agencies will not be funded, but Mr. Gene Rubel, head of CHP, said that we will not be considered a new agency because we have been approved by HEW regardless of the funding source.

Membership Attendance

In order to increase participation of Council members, Dr. Cleino proposed that two or three members of the Council be invited to attend each Executive Committee meeting. Dr. Hale suggested this proposal be implemented at the next meeting. All agreed. Since the Executive Committee is short a member, Dr. Hale suggested that we seek a practicing doctor from a rural county to replace Dr. Rutland, perhaps Dr. Rucker Staggers or Dr. Chester Singleton.

Report on Nursing Manpower Study

Dr. Cleino reported that work has begun on the nursing manpower study and that Greg de Lissovoy is working on the project. He has discovered that he can do a statewide study by region as easily as just a regional study and plans to do this utilizing computer information and getting assistance from several sources. Completion date is projected for December 1.

Ambulatory Health Care Service Project

Mr. Jim West and Mr. Pete Yarnell from the Regional Office of HEW were present at the meeting to discuss the development of a Neighborhood Health Center Project. Dr. John Packard from the University of Alabama College of Community Health Sciences was also present. Mr. West stated that last year the Black Belt Family Health Center was funded, but in the estimation of the regional office, it did not reach its objectives and would not be funded for a second year.

Funding is available for new Neighborhood Health Centers Projects under 314 (e) funds for a five-year period, providing yearly objectives are met. Twenty-eight are now operational in the eight states. They are designed to provide individual health care on an outpatient basis to both the non-paying and the paying patient. Drugs, dental and medical care and transportation can be funded; but no training funds will be included. No construction funds are available but lease money and renovation can be included. No matching funds are required, but some input from the communities served is expected. The Board would have to have 51 percent consumer members (those who use the center); the "start up" area should not be more than two counties; and the project would not need to be self supporting.

Mr. West stated there was no question of the need for health services in the area, but the project must be designed to produce the maximum impact and must bring together all factions in the area. He said HEW was not interested in funding any one agency in the area, but HEW would be responsive to a proposal bringing together the Federation, the community and the political structure.

Dr. Packard said that the University could not be the applicant, but they would cooperate particularly by assisting in recruiting MDs, providing continuing education and training allied health workers. He also urged the use of nurse practitioners and technicians in the project and referred the group to the Lawrence County Project.

The Executive Committee gave approval to the staff to develop a proposal to submit to HEW.

Regional Health Department

     Dr. Williams reviewed a written progress report on the developing District Health Department. He stated that County Health Departments would receive $2,000,000 from the legislature with $100,000 being set aside for District Health Departments ($25,000 for this District). Each county will receive $16,000, plus 60¢ per capita. This will give the region $4.28 per capita.

     Interim District personnel will serve pending the procurement of a District Health Office. These are Dr. Williams, Marie Cox and Bill Hunter.

     He stated that one candidate for the District Health Officer position had been interviewed and another one was being investigated.

     Dr. Williams stated his dissatisfaction with the involvement of the Council staff in the development of the District Health Department and asked that the Council staff act only in an advisory capacity on request.

     There was considerable discussion on the role of the Council in the District Health Department development. It was the concensus that the Board of the West Alabama District Health Department was now organized and could provide for itself. The larger issue of the role of a health planning agency was not discussed.

     There being no further business, the meeting was adjourned at 3:30 p.m.

WEST ALABAMA COMPREHENSIVE HEALTH PLANNING COUNCIL
EXECUTIVE COMMITTEE MEETING
October 18, 1973

MINUTES

MEMBERS PRESENT

Dr. Everett Hale, Chairman
Judge Robert Kirksey
Mr. D. O. McClusky, Jr.
Rev. James M. Lilly
Dr. Galen Drewry

STAFF PRESENT

Dr. Elizabeth Cleino, Director
Mr. Walter P. Bailey, Health Planner
Mr. Walter Metts, Health Planner
Mr. Greg de Lissovoy, Health Planner
Mrs. Mary Jo Looser, Information Specialist
Mrs. Anna Adkins, Secretary

OTHER COUNCIL MEMBERS PRESENT

The Rev. James P. Woodson
Mr. A. C. Mullins
Mr. Paul Jackson

MEMBERS ABSENT

Dr. Sidney Williams
Mr. Robert Boone
Mrs. Cynthia Lanford
Judge John Puryear
Mr. Norman C. Cephus

The Executive Committee of the West Alabama Comprehensive Health Planning Council met on Thursday, October 18, 1973, at 12:00 noon in the conference room of the Council with Dr. Everett Hale, Chairman, presiding. The minutes of the previous meeting were approved as distributed on a motion by Mr. Lilly and a second by Mr. McClusky.

Financial Report

A. Monthly Expenditures: Copies of the September financial report were distributed to the Committee. Mr. Lilly moved the expenditures be approved, and Judge Kirksey seconded. Motion carried unanimously.

B. Funds Received: Dr. Hale reported that a total of $2,993.25 had been received during the month of September. The Council has received the funds requested from all counties, except Greene. Five hospitals have contributed to the Council's support, leaving two outstanding requests. Dr. Hale reported that he had talked with Mayor Snow Hinton about the City of Tuscaloosa's contribution and was assured that $6,000 had been set aside for the Council's support.

Emergency Medical Technician Training Funds

Dr. Cleino reported that $3,500 in MDTA funds had been secured by the Council to support the fall Emergency Medical Technician Training Course at the University of Alabama. Additional support will be sought to continue the course. There were still 34 people in this class.

Hale County Emergency Medical Services

Dr. Cleino reported that the funeral home in Greensboro had given up its ambulance service leaving Hale County without emergency medical services. Judge Avery requested the Council's assistance in setting up an emergency medical services program. Key people in Hale County met in Judge Avery's office on October 5 and decided to call a public meeting to make plans for provisions for emergency medical care. Approximately 70 people attended the public meeting on October 15. Ambulance Service Company provided a new ambulance and an EMT to demonstrate the latest equipment and procedures. Jeanette Latham and Dr. Cleino provided the program. Mr. Walter Owens, Judge, Avery, and Mr. Norman Cephus also participated. A rescue squad is being organized. A grant for an ambulance had been prepared by Dr. Cleino. Until other arrangements could be made, Tuscaloosa Ambulance Service offered to provide one ambulance with EMTs for the county, to be stationed in Greensboro.

Quarterly Council Meeting Report

The quarterly meeting of the membership of the Council was held October 10, 1973, at the University of Alabama Continuing Education Center. Dr. Cleino reported that the attendance was much improved and expressed her thanks to the Executive Committee members who took responsibility for reminding the local people. The next meeting will also be held at the Center on January 17, 1974.

Ambulatory Health Care Project

The proposal for the Ambulatory Health Care Project for Sumter and Greene Counties was presented to the Executive Committee by Mr. de Lissovoy. Two clinic sites are proposed - one to become operational in the 7th month, the other the 12th month. Medical and dental services will be offered. Drugs may be supplied and reimbursements offered for transportation. A sliding scale of fees will be established.

The Board will be composed of 11 members: 2 county commissions, 2 physicians, 1 representative of the WACHPC and 6 consumer members. It is proposed that 2 of the consumer members be appointed by the county commissions (one each county) and the Federation appoint 2 in each county.

Meetings have been held with representatives of Sumter County, Greene County and the Federation of Southern Cooperatives. Each group has tentatively agreed to the main points of the proposal. A joint meeting of all interested parties has been scheduled for October 23 at the Greene County Health Department.

Considerable discussion was held on the proposal. Dr. John Packard was nominated by Judge Kirksey as the representative for the Council. Mr. Lilly seconded and the motion carried unanimously.

Judge Kirksey suggested that Greene County be required to pay the annual assessment before implementation of the project.

Dr. Drewry moved that the project as proposed be approved by the Executive Committee with the understanding that if any major change had to be made following the Planning Committee meeting, Dr. Cleino and Dr. Hale would confer and decide if the Executive Committee needed to be consulted again. Mr. McClusky seconded the motion and it carried unanimously.

The official concurrence of the WACHPC will be sent with the project proposal to the Regional Office.

Application for ARMP Grants

Dr. Drewry reported that at the recent Regional Advisory Council meeting, it was announced that ARMP would receive $700,000 this year in funds. Applications are being requested for projects to be completed in six months.

Since there was a limited amount of time, Dr. Cleino stated that the staff had decided to prepare a proposal for the consortium of hospitals project. A summary of the proposed project was presented for review. Mr. McClusky suggested changing the wording of the primary objective. Dr. Drewry moved that the proposal as amended be approved and Mr. Lilly seconded. The motion carried unanimously.

Approval was given for the staff to develop another proposal if time permitted.

Selection of Fair Hearing Officers for West Alabama

In a letter from Mr. Clay Dean, each "B" Agency has been requested to suggest someone from each county who could act as a "fair hearing" officer for the Section 1122 of the Social Security Act. Mr. Dean stipulated that the person should not have ties with either (a) or (b) agency.

Dr. Hale suggested that the individual be a lawyer or judge from the area. Several names were suggested. Dr. Cleino was instructed to contact a key Council member from Lamar, Hale, Greene and Bibb Counties for suggestions for these counties.

Residential Environmental Report

Mr. Metts presented the Residential Environmental Task Force report to the Executive Committee. Dr. Hay Black had served as the Chairman of the

Task Force. The Environmental Health Committee had approved the report. Mr. Metts stated that the reported included information from the West Alabama Planning and Development Office and complemented the work Mr. McCray and his organization had done.

In a discussion of land use planning, Mr. Mullins stated that on the county level, regulations were being prepared to be submitted to the County Board of Health for approval that would require that proper water facilities be available before any living structure could be built.

Mr. McClusky moved that the report be approved and Mr. Lilly seconded. Referring to page 35 of the report, Mr. Mullins pointed out that East Tuscaloosa cannot have a sewer system, since drainage into the Warrior River at that point is prohibited. Only septic tanks can be used in that section of the county.

The regular meeting was adjourned at 2:30 p.m.

Mr. McClusky invited the other Council members to remain and participate with the Personnel Committee members in a discussion of a matter of concern to a member of the staff, Mr. Pete Bailey.

WEST ALABAMA COMPREHENSIVE HEALTH PLANNING COUNCIL
EXECUTIVE COMMITTEE MEETING

November 15, 1973

MINUTES

OTHER COUNCIL
MEMBERS PRESENT

MEMBERS PRESENT

Dr. Everett Hale, Chairman
Mr. D. O. McClusky, Jr.
Mr. Robert H. Boone
Mrs. Cynthia Lanford
Dr. Sidney J. Williams
Dr. Galen Drewry
Rev. James M. Lilly
Judge John Puryear

Dr. William Frederick

MEMBERS ABSENT

Judge Robert H. Kirksey
Mr. Norman C. Cephus

STAFF PRESENT

Dr. Elizabeth Cleino, Director
Mr. Albert Metts, Health Planner
Mr. Greg de Lissovoy, Health Planner
Mrs. Mary Jo Looser, Information Specialist
Mrs. Anna Adkins, Secretary

GUESTS PRESENT

Mr. Noel Hart, Administrative
Resident, Druid City Hospital

The Executive Committee of the West Alabama Comprehensive Health Planning Council met on Thursday, November 15, 1973, at 12:00 noon in the conference room of the Council with Dr. Everett Hale, Chairman, presiding. The minutes of the previous meeting were approved as distributed on a motion by Mr. Lilly and a second by Mr. Boone.

Financial Report

A. Monthly Expenditures: Copies of the October financial report were distributed to the Committee. Judge Puryear moved that the expenditures be approved, and Mr. Lilly seconded. Motion carried unanimously.

B. Funds Received: Dr. Cleino reported that the Council had received a total of $2,693.53 in funds during the month of October. Although Greene County's contribution had not been received, Dr. Cleino reported that Judge Branch told her in a telephone conversation that the check would be in the mail that same day. It was also reported that the Council had not received the contribution from the City of Tuscaloosa.

Change of Meeting Date to Tuesdays

Mr. Boone reported Dr. Jon Sanford could accept an appointment to the Executive Committee to replace Dr. Rutland, if meetings were held on Tuesdays rather than Thursdays. All members, except Mrs. Lanford, stated that they could attend as well on Tuesdays. Since she had some problems on any date, she asked that the Committee change the date so Dr. Sanford could attend. The Committee voted unanimously to appoint Dr. Sanford and change the date to the the third Tuesdays.

Report on ARMP Meeting

Dr. Drewry and Mr. McClusky reported on the meeting of the Alabama Regional Medical Program held on November 8. Mr. McClusky reported that grant applications had been screened by the staff, Project Committee and Executive Board before being presented to the Regional Advisory Council. The proceedings of the meeting were explained. The project proposals which were tabled can be approved by the Executive Board at a later date if more funds become available.

Two proposals submitted to ARMP by WACHPC were disapproved, and one was tabled.

Dr. Hale expressed the Council's appreciation to Dr. Drewry and Mr. McClusky for attending the meeting and representing the Council's interests.

Report on Regional Health Department

Dr. Williams reported that Dr. Charles Konigsberg, Jr. has accepted the position of Director, District Health Department and is expected to assume his duties about January 2, 1974. He is in the process of getting his Alabama license. Dr. Williams has promised to assist Dr. Konigsberg at least for a few months.

Dr. Hale expressed the Council's appreciation to Dr. Williams for his leadership in developing the District Health Department.

Emergency Medical Services Grant from ARMP

The Council was notified that the Emergency Medical Service grant proposal approved by ARMP last year has been funded for $20,450. Since the original request was for $140,000, major changes in the work program had to be made. Dr. Cleino proposed to ARMP that training of Emergency Medical Technicians, R.N.'s and other health professions and development of EMS systems be given first priority. Mrs. Pat Bradford has been employed as Secretary/Administrative Assistant for the EMS project. Interviews are in progress for a coordinator for the project. The EMS Committee will meet on Wednesday, November 22, to go over the plans.

The budget was submitted to the Executive Committee for approval. Dr. Drewry moved that the budget be approved as presented. Mr. McClusky seconded and the motion carried.

A general discussion of the Emergency Medical Technician Training Program followed. MTDA funds have been requested for a second course this year. Also, funds from Mr. Dean's office will be requested.

Mr. Boone told the group of a new program at the UAB for preparation of Multiple Competency Clinical Technicians. Mr. Dennis Adams, Coordinator, had described the program as including the EMT training program. Mr. Boone stated that it was an impressive program and could be a big help to small hospitals.

West Alabama Health Services Project

Mr. McClusky reviewed last month's Executive Committee meeting minutes regarding the West Alabama Health Services Project.

Mr. de Lissovoy brought the Executive Committee up to date on the events associated with this proposal. He reported that at the planning meeting held on October 23 at the Greene County Health Department, despite agreements from all parties before the meeting on the Board composition, the Federation of Southern Cooperatives representatives demanded that all the consumer members be black, that the project director be black, that the clinic be at Epes and other demands totally unacceptable to the other groups represented at the meeting. Later, the Federation formally withdrew from the project and submitted a competing application. Miss McAfee from the Federation threatened to go to Washington and see to it that the proposal prepared by WACHPC would not get funded.

Dr. Cleino reported on her meeting with Dr. Hudgins and Mr. West of the Regional Office. They told her to proceed with the project without the Federation if all attempts to include them had failed. The project proposal was then rewritten excluding the Federation.

Another planning meeting was held on November 7 at the Greene County Hospital. Attending the meeting were two consumers from Greene County, one consumer from Sumter County, representatives of the two medical societies, couunty commissions, one hospital administrator, and the WACHPC staff. The Board for the West Alabama Health Services Project was formally organized at this meeting. Officers elected to the Board were as follow: Judge William McKinley Branch, President; Mr. W. T. Lockard, Vice President; Dr. Rucker L. Staggers, Treasurer; and Mrs. Zora C. Gibbs, Secretary.

Since a quorum was present, the Board was convened and accomplished the following: (1) adoped Articles of Incorporation to be incorporated in Greene County with Judge Branch to act as registrar and (2) approved the proposal as revised. (Project proposal was submitted to Regional Office November 3, 1973.)

At the last meeting of the Executive Committee, the draft proposal had been approved. A copy of the revised West Alabama Health Services Project Application was approved on a motion by Dr. Drewry and a second by Judge Puryear. The motion carried.

Review and Comment

Black Belt Family Health Center Grant Application: Mr. de Lissovoy presented a resume of the proposal. After discussion, Mr. Lilly moved that the project proposal be disapproved. Judge Puryear seconded the motion. Motion carried unanimously. Dr. Cleino was instructed to prepare a letter for the Federation regarding disapproval of the project proposal. Dr. Drewry suggested that the letter include the following reasons for disapproval: (1) Organizations were not widely representative of the people in the counties. (2) Proposal omitted longstanding providers and agencies. (3) The site location at Epes was not accessible to the people of the two counties.

Health Facilities Committee Report

A. Riverside Nursing Home Application: Mr. de Lissovoy reported that the Health Facilities Committee recommended that a letter be sent to Mr. Dean recommending that the Riverside Nursing Home application be given high priority in the event the beds become available. Dr. Cleino stated that 269 nursing home beds have been approved and 542 beds are now in use.

B. Guidelines for Section 1122 for Alabama: Guidelines for the State of Alabama have been prepared by Mr. Dean's office. Following a meeting of (b) agency directors, several changes have been agreed upon. The recommendations of the Health Facilities Committee were presented. Mr. McClusky moved that the review and comments be approved and Judge Puryear seconded. Motion carried unanimously.

Personnel Committee Report

The WACHPC Personnel Committee was called to meet immediately following the Executive Committee meeting. Members of the Executive Committee agreed to concur with decisions made by the Personnel Committee, barring unusual circumstances.

WACHPC Planning Grant Application

Dr. Cleino reported that she recently visited the Regional Office in Atlanta to get instruction for the preparation of a five-year planning grant. Even though WACHPC is considered an old agency and hence subject to funding by HEW, no new monies will be available for the beginning of our grant year in May. ARC has been asked to fund our organization another year.

A continuation grant is due into ARC by January 4 to cover funding beginning May 1, 1974. Dr. Cleino stated she had requested a budget of $85,000 for next year. Matching funds should total $26,000. It was the general concensus of the Committee that $85,000 should be requested for the Council's continued operation.

Dr. Hale commended Dr. Cleino for her management of the funds for the Council.

There being no further business, the meeting adjourned at 2:30 p.m.

WEST ALABAMA COMPREHENSIVE HEALTH PLANNING COUNCIL
EXECUTIVE COMMITTEE MEETING
December 18, 1973

MINUTES

MEMBERS PRESENT

Dr. E. Everett Hale, Chairman
Mr. Robert H. Boone
The Rev. James M. Lilly
Dr. Jon Sanford
Dr. Sidney J. Williams
Judge Robert H. Kirksey

STAFF PRESENT

Dr. Elizabeth W. Cleino, Director
Mr. Gerald A. Buckingham, Health Planner
Mr. Gregory V. de Lissovoy, Health Planner
Mrs. Mary Jo Looser, Information Specialist
Mrs. Anna L. Adkins, Secretary

OTHER COUNCIL
MEMBERS PRESENT

Mrs. Betty Burell

MEMBERS ABSENT

Mr. Norman Cephus
Dr. Galen Drewry
Mr. D. O. McClusky, Jr.
Judge John Puryear

The Executive Committee of the West Alabama Comprehensive Health Planning Council met on Tuesday, December 18, 1973, at 12:00 noon in the conference room of the Council with Dr. Everett Hale, Chairman, presiding. The minutes of the previous meeting were approved as distributed on a motion by Mr. Lilly and a second by Judge Kirksey.

Dr. Hale welcomed Mrs. Burell to the meeting and introduced the new staff member, Mr. Gerald Buckingham. Mr. Buckingham will be in charge of the Health Facilities Committee and will assist with the administration of the Council.

Financial Report

A. Monthly Expenditures: Copies of the November financial report were distributed to the Committee. Mr. Lilly moved that the expenditures for November be approved as published and Judge Kirksey seconded. Motion carried.

B. Funds Received: Dr. Cleino noted that $1,500 was received from Greene County in November. She also noted that the Council had not received a check from the City of Tuscaloosa.

C. Investment of Funds: Dr. Cleino requested approval for the transfer of Council funds from the savings account at the City National Bank to First Federal Savings and Loan Association of Tuscaloosa. She stated that First Federal offered a better interest plan. They recommended two accounts: a Business and Professional Account for the employee retirement funds and a regular 90-day account for the matching funds. Mr. Lilly moved that the transfer of funds be approved and Mr. Boone seconded. Motion carried.

D. Report of State Audit: Dr. Cleino reported that the official report from the State Auditors had been received. The only recommendation was that the individuals handling funds should be bonded. The WACHPC books were found to be in good order.

Personnel Committee Report

Dr. Cleino reported that the Personnel Committee had approved the employment of Gerald Buckingham as Health Planner I. The Committee also approved the employment of Mrs. Jean Henderson as EMS Coordinator and Mrs. Pat Bradford as Administrative Assistant to the Emergency Medical Services Project. Raises were approved for the Council secretaries and personnel policies were changed to accommodate eight set holidays (George Washington's Birthday, 4th of July, Labor Day, Thanksgiving Day, day following Thanksgiving, Christmas Eve, Christmas Day and New Years Day). The mileage reimbursement was increased to 12¢ a mile.

Report on West Alabama Health Services Project

Dr. Cleino reported to the Committee that in a telephone conversation Mr. Jim West stated that a decision had been made regarding the project application and that a letter was in the mail notifying the Council of the Regional Office decision. A general discussion followed. The consensus of the Committee was that the Council should continue to support the project.

Dr. Williams moved that Dr. Cleino be authorized to write such correspondence to the Alabama delegation and State Senators as necessary and appropriate in support of the project. Mr. Lilly seconded and the motion carried unanimously.

Dr. Cleino stated that she had written a letter to Mayor Pruitt asking him to request an audit of the Epes project.

Emergency Medical Services Project Report

Dr. Cleino reported that Mrs. Jean Henderson attended the Region IV Conference on Emergency Medical Services held in Atlanta, Georgia.

She also reported that 29 Emergency Medical Technicians graduated from the EMT Training Program December 13. Another class will begin January 22, 1974. Mr. Peter Balsamo has replaced Mr. Ron Sorrells as Coordinator of Continuing Education, and Mrs. Jane Townsend has replaced Mrs. Jeanette Latham as the EMT Coordinator.

Alabama Regional Medical Program Grant Requests

The Alabama Regional Medical Program has announced that money has been released for grants. Dr. Cleino stated that the WACHPC would rewrite the grant applications previously submitted to ARMP but not funded.

Report on Health Facilities Committee

A. Greensboro Nursing Home: Mr. Buckingham told the Committee that a mail ballot had been taken regarding the Greensboro Nursing Home request for a 20-bed ICF addition. The results, with a 75 per cent response, was to approve the application. No negative votes were received. Judge Kirksey moved that the recommendation be approved and Mr. Lilly seconded. Motion carried unanimously.

B. Pickens County Hospital: Dr. Cleino stated that a group in Aliceville had proposed that a new hospital be built in Aliceville for Pickens County. Their proposal is in conflict with plans for the new hospital proposed for Carrollton. Mr. Clay Dean has not yet approved plans for the hospital in Carrollton. Dr. Cleino stated that Mr. Buckingham would be working with the Pickens County people regarding this situation.

Judge Kirksey stated that he had learned that funds might be available through the 1972 Rural Development Act. He suggested that Mr. Garrett, State Home Administrator, be contacted regarding obtaining these funds if possible.

Family Planning Areawide Project (Request for Change of Lead Agency)

Dr. Cleino told the Committee that she had a letter from the District Board of Health requesting that they be named lead agency for the Family Planning Project for FY 75. In a conversation with Mrs. Wanda Paul, she learned that Planned Parenthood Association of Tuscaloosa County is planning to serve as lead agency another year. Mr. Lilly, speaking as first Vice President of Planned Parenthood, presented the position of Planned Parenthood stating that the state agencies had requested that they continue to serve as lead agency.

Dr. Cleino traced the history of the project from the time the first grant was written in the Council office to the request she made to Planned Parenthood to be the applicant agency. The second year, Planned Parenthood was requested again to serve as lead agency until such time the District Health Department could be organized to assume responsibility for the project. She stated that the

District Health Department has now been organized and is ready to take over responsibility for the project at the end of this grant year, July 1, 1974. The Family Planning Committee set up to advise the Council and the project has not met for the past two months.

Mr. Lilly provided copies of letters recommending that Planned Parenthood be the leady agency for FY 75 from Dr. Chism, Mr. Pratt and Mrs. Mitchell. He said since the project is providing good services, no change in leady agency is indicated. Planned Parenthood believes they are in a better position to handle the grant than the District Health Department now.

A lengthy discussion followed concerning the merits of the two agencies as leady agency for the Family Planning Project for District II. A vote was called for regarding the position of the Executive Committee on the issue. Dr. Williams moved that the issue be tabled until after the January 14 meeting of the Family Planning Advisory Committee. Mr. Boone seconded. After much discussion, the motion carried.

West Alabama Comprehensive Health Planning Council Five-Year Planning Grant Application

Copies of the WACHPC Five-Year Planning Grant Application were distributed to all the Committee members present. No changes or recommendations were made. Judge Kirksey moved that the grant application be approved as published and Mr. Boone seconded. Motion carried.

Other Business

For the month of January only, the meeting date for the Executive Committee was changed to Thursday, January 17, 1974, at 4:00 P.M. The Executive Committee will meet prior to the WACHPC quarterly meeting being held at 6:00 P.M. at the Continuing Education Center. Dr. Cleino suggested that Dr. Charles Konigsberg, Jr., District Health Officer, be invited to attend the Executive Committee meeting.

Report on Need for Renal Dialysis Unit

The unit in Birmingham is presently serving the needs of the Tuscaloosa are adequately. No patients from District II are presently on dialysis at the Medical Center and there are only two patients in West Alabama on home dialysis. It was the opinion of the Committee that a renal dialysis unit was not needed in West Alabama at this time.

There being no further business, the meeting adjourned at 2:15 P.M.

WEST ALABAMA COMPREHENSIVE HEALTH PLANNING COUNCIL
EXECUTIVE COMMITTEE MEETING
January 17, 1974

MINUTES

MEMBERS PRESENT

Dr. Everett Hale, Chairman
Mr. Robert Boone
Dr. Galen Drewry
Judge Robert Kirksey
The Rev. James L. Lilly
Mr. D. O. McClusky, Jr.
Judge John Puryear
Dr. Sidney Williams
Dr. Charles Konigsberg

MEMBERS ABSENT

Mr. Norman Cephus
Dr. Jon Sanford (excused)

STAFF PRESENT

Dr. Elizabeth W. Cleino
Mr. Gerald A. Buckingham
Mr. Albert Metts
Mrs. Mary Jo Looser
Mr. Greg de Lissovoy
Mrs. Anna Adkins

A meeting of the Executive Committee was held in the offices of the West Alabama
Comprehensive Health Planning Council on Thursday, January 17, 1974, at 4:00 P.M.
Judge Kirksey presided over the meeting until Dr. Hale's arrival. The minutes of the
previous meeting were approved as distributed on a motion by Dr. Drewry and a
second by Mr. Lilly. Motion carried.

Financial Report

A. Monthly Expenditures: Copies of the December financial report were distributed to the Committee. Judge Puryear moved that the expenditures for December be
approved as published and Dr. Williams seconded. Motion carried.

B. Funds Received: Dr. Cleino pointed out that a check in the amount of $100
had been received from the IBM Corporation. She also noted that interest on the matching funds deposited in City National Bank amounted to $70.56.

Review of Agenda for WACHPC Quarterly Meeting

Copies of the agenda for the WACHPC Quarterly Meeting were distributed to the
Committee. Important items to be discussed were reviewed briefly.

Family Planning Committee Report

Mr. Lilly reported to the Committee that the Family Planning Advisory Committee had met on January 14 to discuss the lead agency for 1974-1975. He stated that a general agreement was made between Planned Parenthood Association of Tuscaloosa County and the District Health Department. It was decided that the District Health Department should assume responsibility as lead agency for the family planning project at the appropriate time to be decided by representatives of Planned Parenthood and Dr. Konigsberg.

Dr. Hale stated that the recommendation of the Executive Committee, therefore, was that Planned Parenthood Association of Tuscaloosa County and the District Health Department should work together to determine the change-over date. The deadline for submission of the application is March 30, 1974, and the Executive Committee will have an opportunity to review and comment.

District Health Department Report

Dr. Cleino reported that Dr. Betty Vaughn had an appointment to ask the Governor to release th $100,000 in revenue sharing funds which were requested for the district health departments. Dr. Cleino stated that she had written a letter to Representative Bert Bank requesting his assistance in obtaining the funds.

Dr. Hale expressed appreciation to Dr. Williams for his work in developing the District Health Department.

Emergency Medical Services Report

A. Tuscaloosa County Council: Dr. Cleino reported that she had just left a meeting of the Emergency Medical Services Council of Tuscaloosa County. She said that Mayor Hinton had called her and requested that an emergency medical services council be developed. Representatives were chosen and a meeting called for 2:00 P.M. January 17, 1974.

Mr. Harlan Meredith was elected chairman. Dr. Cleino will serve as ex-officio secretary to the EMS Council. Dr. Cleino recommended that a Council member be appointed to represent WACHPC. Judge Puryear moved that Mr. Paul Jackson be appointed to represent WACHPC and Mr. McClusky seconded. Motion carried. Mr. McClusky commended Dr. Cleino on setting the EMS Council up in such a short time.

Mr. McClusky reported that Hank's Ambulance Company was going to take over the ambulance service for Tuscaloosa County and operate it in the same manner as Ambulance Service Company.

B. Changes in EMS Grant Personnel: Dr. Cleino reported that Pat Bradford had resigned as Administrative Assistant and Secretary to the program and another secretary is being sought.

C. Activities Report: Dr. Cleino reported to the Committee that Jean Henderson, EMS Coordinator, had been to several counties to give assistance to hospitals regarding their emergency procedures. Mrs. Henderson is planning a workshop for M.D.s and R.N.s and advanced training for EMTs. The workshop will bring the medical personnel up to date on procedures in emergency care.

D. Emergency Medical Technician Training Program: Dr. Cleino told the Committee that the next class of EMT students would begin Tuesday, January 22. Over 60 applications have been received for the course and only 38 can be accepted. New College has agreed to give college credit to those who enroll in it as a proper course of study.

Dr. Cleino also reported that MDTA funds had been promised for two more courses. Due to the overwhelming acceptance of the course and large number of applications, the Committee discussed several possibilities in handling the increased number of applicants, including offering this in other counties.

Changes in Membership

Dr. Cleino reported that there are several slots vacant on the WACHP Council. Dr. Hale told the Committee that Dr. Williams had submitted his letter of resignation and had recommended that Dr. Charles Konigsberg, Jr. be elected to serve the balance of his term on the Council and the Executive Committee. Mr. McClusky moved that Dr. Williams' letter of resignation be accepted with regret and expressed the Committee's appreciation to Dr. Williams for his loyal service to the Council. Mr. Lilly seconded and the motion carried. Dr. williams will continue in an advisory capacity to the Executive Committee and Council.

Dr. Cleino informed the Committee that Anne Plott had agreed to serve the remaining term for Paul Davis on the Council. Judge Puryear moved that Mrs. Plott's appointment be approved and Mr. Lilly seconded. Motion carried.

Cynthia Lanford has had to resign from the Council due to difficulty in attending meetings.

Dr. Cleino also told the Committee that Mr. Mason will remain in his position of Director at the Veterans Administration Hospital. Mr. Mason has expressed a desire to reassume his position on the Council. Dr. Lewis plans to resign in order for Mr. Mason to retain Council membership. Judge Kirksey moved that Mr. Mason be renamed to the Council and Mr. Lilly seconded. Motion carried.

Druid City Hospital Nursing Study

Mr. McClusky informed the Committee that he had assigned Druid City Hospital's Administration Resident the task of preparing a nursing manpower availability study. Although statistics indicate that West Alabama is in pretty good shape, job availability and the nurse/bed ratio contradict this. Mr. McClusky stated that Druid City Hospital has a critical shortage of nursing manpower and has asked Congressman to declare West Alabama a disaster areas as far as recruiting nursing manpower is concerned. He has also asked that the Federal Government be restrained from recruiting nurses in this area. Mr. McClusky said that he would distribute a copy of the nursing survey to each Committee member upon its completion.

Selection of Nominating Committee

The following were selected to serve on the Nominating Committee:

> Paul Jackson, Chairman
> Betty Burell
> Ray Austell
> Robert Boone

Nominations will be presented at the April meeting of the WACHPC. Dr. Cleino also explained that at that time members formerly designated as elected officials will have to be counted as providers.

WACHPC Fice-Year Planning Grant Application

Dr. Cleino stated that parts of the original application had been rewritten. New copies have been distributed to Council members. She also told the Committee that the application had been reviewed by the CHP Review Committee and had been approved. The application will be reviewed by the State CHP Advisory Council on January 25.

ARMP Grant Submission

Dr. Cleino asked if the Committee would recommend applying to ARMP for an extension of the Emergency Medical Services grant. Dr. Drewry stated that as a RAC member he had received a letter stating that they will receive additional money for funding the projects already approved. The letter indicated that ARMP also expected to receive additional monies for other projects. Mr. McClusky recommended that Dr. Cleino contact the chairman of RAC for clarification.

The Committee recommended that previous grant applications submitted to ARMP be rewritten and resubmitted for approval. Also recommended was the submission of a grant request for continuation of the Emergency Medical Services Program.

Health Facilities Committee Report

Spearman Nursing Home Application: Judge Kirksey reported that the Health Facilities Committee had received an application for an Assurance of Need from Spearman Nursing Home requesting eight additional ICF beds. This request would supplement previous request for 46 beds already approved. A mail ballot was taken and the Health Facilities Committee recommended approval unanimously. Judge Kirksey moved that the Executive Committee concur in this recommendation, Mr. McClusky seconded and the motion carried.

Report on West Alabama Health Services Project

Dr. Cleino reported to the Committee that the Regional Office had informed the Council that it was to try to work out a compromise with the Epes people. Representatives of the Regional Office are to meet with the Project Board Monday and Tuesday, January 21 and 22. Dr. Cleino said that she called Dr. Hudgins and Mr. West. She was informed that letters had been received from Senator Sparkman, Tom Bevill, Bob Jones, and Congressman Flowers in support of the Epes Project. Dr. Cleino said she had met with Congressman Flowers in an effort to clarify the situation. Judge Branch also spoke to Congressman Flowers reaffirming his support of the WAHS Project.

Mr. Boone recommended that the Council obtain a letter from Congressman Flowers endorsing the WAHS Project. This letter then could be quoted to others.

Dr. Williams moved that the following resolution be made by the Council:

"This Council reaffirms its previous endorsement of the WAHS Project as proposed. In light of the confusion of the congressmen regarding which project is which, the Council asks the congressmen to reaffirm their support of this project."

Mr. Lilly seconded the motion and all approved.

There being no further business, the meeting adjourned at 5:45 P.M.

716

WEST ALABAMA COMPREHENSIVE HEALTH PLANNING COUNCIL
EXECUTIVE COMMITTEE MEETING
February 19, 1974

MINUTES

MEMBERS PRESENT	MEMBERS ABSENT
Dr. E. Everett Hale, Chairman	Dr. Galen Drewry
Mr. Robert Boone	
Mr. Norman Cephus	STAFF PRESENT
Judge Robert Kirksey	
The Rev. James Lilly	Dr. Elizabeth Cleino, Director
Mr. D. O. McClusky, Jr.	Mr. Gerald Buckingham
Judge John Puryear	Mr. Greg de Lissovoy
Dr. Jon Sanford	Mrs. Mary Jo Looser
Dr. Charles Konigsberg	Mrs. Anna Adkins

A meeting of the Executive Committee was held in the offices of the West Alabama Comprehensive Health Planning Council on Tuesday, February 19, 1974, at 12:00 P.M., with Dr. Hale presiding.

Correction of Minutes

Family Planning Committee Report: Mr. Lilly asked that the minutes pertaining to the recommendations of the Advisory Committee on the Family Planning Grant be corrected to state that the Advisory Committee recommended unanimously that Planned Parenthood Association of Tuscaloosa County be named lead agency for FY 75. Mr. Lilly told the Committee that Planned Parenthood would work toward turning over the project to the District Health Department at the appropriate time. The correction was approved. There being no further changes, the minutes stood approved as corrected.

Financial Report

A. Monthly Expenditures: Copies of the January financial report were distributed to the Committee. Mr. Lilly moved that the expenditures for January be approved and Judge Puryear seconded. The motion carried.

B. Funds Received: Dr. Cleino reported to the Committee that the Council had received the last of the requested matching funds for this grant year - a check for $6,000 from the City of Tuscaloosa. She also pointed out that all of the ARC funds, except about $500, had been used and the Council was at this time operating on matching funds.

C. Position Schedule Bond: Dr. Cleino told the Committee that the Position Schedule Bond had been received in compliance with recommendations made by the state auditors. Those covered by the bond are Dr. Cleino, Mrs. Waldrep and Mrs. Adkins.

WACHPC Five-Year Planning Grant

Mr. Blue Barber, Assistant Director of the Alabama Development Office who is responsible for the Appalachian Regional Commission funds, visited the West Alabama Comprehensive Health Planning Council in January, and the WACHPC staff met with him to discuss the five-year planning grant application under consideration for FY 75. At that time, Dr. Cleino discussed the WACHPC financing with Mr. Barber. He recommended that the Council apply for an extension of the grant year to July 1 to use the $14,000 returned last year. The Committee concurred with this recommendation and instructed Dr. Cleino to write a letter requesting approval.

Since Mr. Barber's visit, Dr. Cleino said she had learned that Mr. Red Bamberg, Director of the Alabama Development Office, would be making the decision regarding allocation of ARC funds. She told the Committee that Mr. Bamberg had stated that he would not fund our Council (or the Gadsden Council) for the full amount requested. Considerable discussion followed with various suggestions being made.

Dr. Hale suggested that members of the Council should write to Mr. Bamberg. Judge Kirksey recommended a follow-up visit. He also suggested asking the Industrial Development Boards to help us. Dr. Sanford suggested that his brother might be able to help. Dr. Cleino stated that if funding could be obtained from ARC this year, funds might be more available from HEW next year.

Report on District Health Department

Dr. Konigsberg stated that the District Health Department's main problem was obtaining funds for developmental purposes, since the $100,000 Revenue Sharing monies requested for the district health departments still has not been released. He asked for suggestions. Judge Puryear suggested that Governor Wallace be approached through local contacts. He also suggested that a good public relations program would benefit the health department. Judge Kirksey asked the Council staff to assist Dr. Konigsberg in an effective public relations program. Mrs. Looser agreed to assist. Judge Puryear also stated that the District Health Department should concentrate on the county commissions for support.

Dr. Konigsberg reported to the Committee that on February 25, 1974, the District Helath Department would initiate its first separate Family Planning Clinic at the offices of Planned Parenthood Association.

Report on RAC Meeting of ARMP

Mr. McClusky reported on the meeting of the Regional Advisory Council of the Alabama Regional Medical Program held in Birmingham on February 13. Mr. McClusky reported that the WACHPC projects previously tabled were disapproved at this meeting. Dr. Hale stated that the Council needed to get more people from the area appointed to the RAC.

Health Facilities Report

Judge Kirksey referring to the printed report summarized business of the Health Facilities Committee. He pointed out that an Assurance of Need had been issued to Spearman Nursing Home for the additional eight beds and Druid City Hospital had received a six-months extension. Applications were received from the Moundville Nursing Home for an additional three beds, from Mr. W. A. Keelon for a 79-bed nursing home in Fayette and from the Fayette County Nursing Home for the same 79 beds. The Hale Memorial Hospital application for change of service was returned for additional financial information. These applications will be considered by the Health Facilities Committee before the next Executive Committee Meeting. The Procedures Manual for Assurance of Need has been revised and the Health Facilities Committee will make appropriate modifications in procedures.

The crowded conditions of the Health Department building in Tuscaloosa were discussed. The possibility of applying for Hill Burton funds was suggested. Mr. McClusky and Dr. Konigsberg will discuss further future plans for the facility.

Mr. Boone expressed concern over the news release from Clay Dean's office regarding the Keelon Nursing Home application and stated that it would be in order for the Council to contact Mr. Dean officially concerning procedures to be established in using the Council's name in news releases in the future. He suggested that the releases should come from the areawide office.

Personnel Report

Mr. Buckingham summarized briefly the proposed retirement program for the WACHPC employees. A tax sheltered annuity program with the Standard Life Insurance Company has been selected from a number of policies as being the best for this organization. Mr. Joe Lane has worked with the staff. Dr. Hale referred the proposed plan to the Personnel Committee for further study before approval is given by the Executive Committee.

Mr. Buckingham stated that the Council is now on Social Security and all new employees since October 1, 1973, will be covered. The WACHPC employees who had paid into the system prior to July 1, 1973, have been refunded what was sent in 1972. The first two quarters for 1973 have not yet been received from IRS but will also be refunded.

The WACHPC payroll has been processed through the First National Bank's computer system. However, this system has not proved to be flexible enough to meet the needs of the Council and it was suggested that, beginning with the February payroll, the Council handle its own payroll accounting. All members agreed.

Emergency Medical Services Report

Dr. Cleino and Mrs. Henderson attended a meeting on Emergency Medical Services Care in Charleston, South Carolina, on February 12-13 to learn about the provisions of the new EMS Systems Act. Dr. Cleino stated that April 15, 1974, is the deadline for applications to be submitted to DHEW. Under this act, grant requests for planning and feasibility and for training may be submitted for 100 per cent Federal funding. Implementation requests will be on a 50-50 basis and must contain 15 elements. She suggested that the proposal from the Council be for planning at this time.

An emergency medical care symposium sponsored by the WACHPC under the ARMP grant will be held at the Druid City Hospital School of Nursing Auditorium on February 28 and March 1. The symposium is to update physicians and nurses in procedures of emergency medical care.

Mr. McClusky reported that the Emergency Medical Services Council of Tuscaloosa County had approved the provisions of a contract between Mr. Everett Gilliland, owner of City Ambulance Company in Montgomery, and Druid City Hospital Board to be signed this week. He stated that this Council had served effectively to solve a problem in Tuscaloosa County, and he thanked the staff for their assistance.

Report on West Alabama Health Services Project

Mr. de Lissovoy reported that on January 21, 1974, Mr. Al Baldwin and Mr. Pete Yarnell met with the West Alabama Health Services Board of Directors and later with the Black Belt Board of Directors. At that time, Mr. Baldwin distributed copies of the policy statement issued by the Regional Office. The Regional Office states that it recognizes the WAHS Board as the official negotiating board. Judge Branch, President of the Board, met with representatives of the Federation in an attempt to compromise with the Black Belt Board of Directors. However, the Federation has not changed its demands and a compromise is not possible. Mr. de Lissovoy stated that the proposal is in the process of being rewritten and will be submitted to the Regional Office the first of March.

Review and Comment

A. Family Planning Grant: Mr. Lilly reported that the Planned Parenthood Association of Tuscaloosa County had to submit its financial budget application as soon as possible and needed a letter from this Council stating its approval of Planned

720

Parenthood being named lead agency for FY 75. Considerable discussion followed concerning Planned Parenthood vs. District Health Department as the lead agency. A copy of the budget was circulated to members of the Committee for their review. Concern was expressed that some of the salaries proposed in this budget may complicate the eventual change over to the District Health Department. Mr. Boone moved that the Executive Committee concur with the proposal with the recommendation that administrative salary increases be restricted in order not to create a greater problem when the program is transferred to the District Health Department and the merit system. Dr. Sanford seconded and motion passed. Dr. Konigsberg recommended that the Family Planning Project be transferred to the District Health Dept. no later than July 1, 1975. All members agreed.

B. Nutrition Project with V.A. Hospital: Dr. Cleino reported that the Department of Nutrition at the University of Alabama had prepared a proposal for additional teaching faculty and a learning program at the V.A. Hospital to be submitted for special funds. A copy of the proposed project was circulated among the Committee members. Mr. McClusky moved that the Executive Committee approve the proposal and Mr. Lilly seconded. Motion carried.

C. Middle Management Training Program with V.A. Hospital: The Department of Health Care Management of the University of Alabama is planning to submit a proposal to train middle management people in the V.A. Hospitals and community hospitals in the same cities. The University of Alabama has requested the Council's concurrence of this project. In the absence of a written proposal, no action was taken.

D. Aid - West Alabama: Dr. Cleino reported that Aid-West Alabama was requesting $166,000 in funding for general operations and had requested concurrence for funding. Mr. Boone moved that the Committee concur in this request and Dr. Konigsberg seconded. Motion carried.

E. Pickens County Community Action Committee: Judge Kirksey reported that the Pickens County Community Action Committee had provided needed services, and particularly commended the Head Start Program. He recommended that the Council concur. Mr. Lilly seconded the motion and it carried.

There being no further business, the meeting adjourned at 3:15 P.M.

WEST ALABAMA COMPREHENSIVE HEALTH PLANNING COUNCIL
EXECUTIVE COMMITTEE
MEETING
March 19, 1974

MINUTES

MEMBERS PRESENT

Dr. Everett Hale, Chairman
Mr. Robert Boone
Rev. James M. Lilly
Mr. D. O. McClusky, Jr.
Judge John Puryear
Dr. Jon Sanford
Dr. Charles Konigsberg
Dr. Galen Drewry

GUEST PRESENT

Mr. Jim Ford

MEMBERS ABSENT

Mr. Norman Cephus
Judge Robert Kirksey

STAFF PRESENT

Dr. Elizabeth Cleino, Director
Mr. Gerald Buckingham
Mr. Greg de Lissovoy
Mr. Albert Metts
Mrs. Mary Jo Looser
Mrs. Jean Henderson
Mr. Joe Gribbin, Student Planner

The Executive Committee of the West Alabama Comprehensive Health Planning Council met on Tuesday, March 19, 1974, at 12 noon in the conference room of the Council with Dr. Everett Hale, Chairman, presiding.

Minutes

The minutes of the February 19, meeting were approved as distributed on a motion by Mr. McClusky and a second by Dr. Sanford.

Financial Report

Copies of the February financial report were distributed to the Committee. Mr. Lilly moved that the expenditures for February be approved and Judge Puryear seconded. The motion carried.

West Alabama Health Services Project

Mr. de Lissovoy reported that the WAHS project has been revised and copies were taken to the Regional Office last week. He commended the dentists for their services in developing the dental component. A meeting of the Board and other interested citizens is set for March 21, to go over the final proposal. July 1, is proposed as the beginning date for the project.

Dr. Sanford asked to have this project explained in more detail. After considerable discussion, Dr. Hale expressed appreciation to the staff for the development of this project.

National Health Service Corps

Joe Gribbin reported that on March 4, a meeting was held with Greene County community leaders in Eutaw to discuss a possible application to the National Health Service Corps for a dentist and two nurses for the County. The Committee agreed to look into the resources they might be able to provide in order to meet requirements of the NHSC program. Dr. Cleino stated that Bibb County had an approved application for a physician but no one has been found to take the appointment.

Five Year Planning Grant

Dr. Cleino brought members of the Committee up to date on various efforts that had been made to secure funding for WACH PC. She stated that one person had asked Mr. Bamburg not to fund the Council while many had requested funding. Considerable discussion followed with various suggestions being made. The concensus was that contacts need to be made with probate judges in the counties outside Tuscaloosa and they be asked to call Mr. Bamberg in support of the Council's funding. It was decided to ask members of the legislative delegations to give support to the Council.

"A" Council Membership

Dr. Cleino stated that she would be completing her second term as an A Council member as of January 1, 1975 and asked for suggestions of a consumer who could represent this district. Dr. Hale suggested that it would be helpful to have a probate judge serve on this Council. Judge Puryear and Judge Kirksey were both suggested. Judge Puryear will discuss this with Judge Kirksey and they will decide which one would agree to serve (if elected) on the "A" Council.

ARMP will have a meeting of the RAC on April 26 and 27 at Gulf Shores. Since Mr. McClusky has a conflict and will be unable to attend, Dr. Hale agreed to serve as his alternate.

Health Facilities Committee Report

In the absence of the chairman, Judge Kirksey, Mr. Buckingham reported the recommendations from the Health Facility Committee meeting of March 18. The Health Facilities Committee reviewed two applications for nursing home beds from Fayette County. They recommended approval of the application of Fayette County Nursing Home for a 76 bed addition and recommended disapproval of the application from Mr. W. A. Keelon to build a 79 bed nursing home in Fayette County. Mr. McClusky moved that they Council approve the committee's recommendation for the Fayette County Nursing Home application. Judge Puryear seconded and the motion carried with Mr. Boone abstaining.

The Health Facilities Committee recommended approval of Hale Memorial Hospital's request for a change of service to 105 long term care beds. Since there were questions about the effect these beds would have on area hospitals, the rates to be charged, and the type of licensure, Dr. Drewry moved that action be deferred to seek clarification of these questions. Dr. Sanford seconded and the motion carried.

The request by Moundville Nursing Home for a 3-bed addition was recommended by the Health Facilities Committee. Mr. McClusky moved that the Executive Committee approve; Dr. Drewry seconded and the motion carried.

<u>Planned Parenthood Request for United Fund Support</u>

Dr. Drewry, who serves as chairman of the Review Council of the United Fund, asked for the advise of the Executive Committee on an application from Planned Parenthood Association of Tuscaloosa County for future funding through the United Fund. Planned Parenthood is seeking United Fund support to begin when the Health Department assumes the role of lead agency for the family planning grant on July 1, 1975 and will take over the responsibility for clinical services in 7 counties. Dr. Konigsberg stated that he would support the request for funds for Planned Parenthood as a vital community agency for education for family planning. After discussion, the members agreed to give support to Planned Parenthood's request for funding for 1975.

<u>Personnel Committee Report</u>

Mr. McClusky stated that the personnel committee had met and reviewed in detail the proposed tax sheltered annuity program with Standard Life Insurance Company. They recommended that the Executive Committee approve this plan with the suggestion that each employee sign an agreement form on enrolling. Mr. McClusky moved approval of the plan. Dr. Sanford seconded, the motion carried.

<u>EMS Report</u>

Mrs. Henderson, EMS Coordinator, stated that inservice training has been provided 180 persons involved in hospital emergency care. Approximately 300 nurses and doctors attended the Emergency Care Symposium at Druid City Hospital on February 28 and March 1. Evaluation forms are being sent out to those who attended. Dr. Konigsberg stated that he felt the symposium was very worthwhile and that more continuing education programs should be presented. Mrs. Henderson also reported that the City of Aliceville has applied for an ambulance grant and that she has done some basic first aid training for the attendants there. She also reported that the 99 EMT graduates are being mailed questionnaires to determine how they are utilizing their training. A new EMT course will get underway on May 7. Ambulance design was discussed. It was pointed out that there is no good standard interior design.

Environmental Health Committee

Mr. Albert Metts reported that the Environmental Health Committee studied water supplies at the February 21 meeting with emphasis given to Greene and Fayette counties.

It was recommended by the Environmental Health Committee that the appropriate officials in each county undertake a survey and testing program of private wells to determine their chemical and bacteriological quality and that special emphasis be given to educating the public on the virtues of safe drinking water.

Mr. Metts reported that the Council has received National Climatic Center wind data for a four year period for this area. With the data, wind roses will be constructed. This includes information on prevailing winds, speed of winds, etc. At the next meeting the subjects will be air pollution and food protection.

District Health Department

Dr. Konigsberg reported that on March 12, the Executive Committee of the Board of Health met with excellent attendance. Since funding is the great need of the moment, efforts are being made to secure the revenue sharing funds. A letter was sent to the Governor asking for the $100,000 for the District. Development of a staff is essential so that crossing county lines with special services will be possible. An Environmental Health Director, a Nursing Director and support personnel are needed for the District.

The Health Department is working with the Mental Health Board in Greene County for a Children's Service Program. There is a need to establish a pre-natal clinic in Bibb County. At the present time the only physician clinic offered in Bibb County is the family planning clinic.

The Dental Health project, supported by state funds and Junior Welfare Associations, needs expanding.

Funds for a Tuberculosis control nurse will be made available to the District. Health Department sponsored Family Planning Clinics have been held in conjunction with Planned Parenthood Association. Dr. Konigsberg serves as the clinician.

Members of the Executive Committee commented on the good job Dr. Konigsberg was doing with the District Health Department and offered their support.

Nursing Manpower Study

Dr. Cleino stated that the nursing manpower study which the UA College of Community Health Sciences contracted with WACHPC to produce is nearly completed. Excerpts from the study were supplied to the UA Committee on Nursing and members of the Executive Committee. Dr. Cleino said this will be used in connection with a study underway to determine the offering in nursing education at the University.

Review and Comment

Mr. Buckingham gave a brief review of the application submitted to HEW for a staffing grant for the Mental Health Board of Bibb, Pickens and Tuscaloosa Counties. A total budget of $741,375 was submitted. Of that amount $495,248 in federal funds was requested from HEW and the remaining $246,127 represents state and local funds. Several comments were made on the large number of professionals and questions were raised about the inpatient care arrangements. On a motion by Mr. McClusky and a second by Mr. Boone, the Committee voted to endorse the application and work out details later. Judge Puryear stated that the Mental Health Board has made tremendous contributions to this area and that the Council should continue to offer its support to the Board.

A letter from Dr. Williard asked for the support of the Council for a research grant application to the National Institutes of Health for "The Design of Computer Systems to Improve Health Care" in the amount of $154,687 for the first year and $824,934 for 5 years.

Request for review of 4 projects submitted by the University of Alabama for funds under VA Allied Health Training Act were received after the last meeting. The summaries were mailed. There was general concurrence.

1. Coordinated Undergraduate Program in Dietetics, University of Alabama and VA Hospital. $36,687 first year, total $294,430. Approved at last meeting.

2. Certificate Program in Public Sector Management – Public Administration using conference telephone capability. $50,840 first year, total $99,788.

3. Grant to assist in the education and training of student in clinical laboratory sciences in microbiology. $75,203 first year, total $796,457.

4. Allied Health Management Project in Speech Pathology and Audiology. $34,301 first year, total $273,565.

5. Training for Gerantology and Health Care Services in Social Work. First year $90,103, total $744,936.

Council Meeting

In planning for the Council meeting on April 17, Dr. Hale asked to have written reports so more time will be available for Council member's participation. Congressman Walter Flowers will be asked to give a report on health legislation pending in Congress.

There being no further business, the meeting adjourned at 3:15 p.m.

Enclosure 3
CORRESPONDENCE AND OTHER MATERIALS FROM THE FILES OF THE
WEST ALABAMA COMPREHENSIVE HEALTH PLANNING COUNCIL

RELATED TO THE FEDERATION OF SOUTHERN COOPERATIVES,
BLACK BELT FAMILY HEALTH CENTER, AND
WEST ALABAMA HEALTH SERVICES PROJECT

Federation of Southern Cooperatives

10 Marietta Street, N.W. /Suite 1200/ Atlanta, Georgia 30303/Phone (404) 524-1266

June 20, 1972

Alabama Medical Association
19 South Jackson Street
Montgomery, Alabama 36104

M.A.S.A.

Dear Sir:

This letter is to inform you of recent progress we have made in
an effort to develop a medical component within our program of assistance
for low-income cooperatives, and to seek your advice and assistance in the
continued development and implementation of that program.

The enclosed brochure details the nature and operation of the Federation of Southern Cooperatives. In Alabama, we are assisting many cooperatives and in Epes, Alabama (Sumter County) we have recently constructed a
modern Training and Research Center and demonstration farm to further serve
the member cooperatives of this organization. The Training Center is also
detailed in the brochure.

The medical program we have developed will be located at the Training Center. It will be a demonstration project in providing comprehensive ambulatory care and preventive medical practices, on a pre-paid basis, to a primarily low-income consumer population. This project has the support of the
Family Health Care Centers Branch of the Health Services and Mental Health
Administration, and representatives of the local government and health bodies
in Sumter County.

This project, as it is presently designed, includes a staff physician,
2 nurses, 7 outreach workers and several administrative personnel. It has been
designed to develop over a four year period into a comprehensive program, progressing from a first year that will largely be devoted to the development of
the delivery system for care, enrollment of consumers, and structuring the
data, record keeping and cost-accounting systems.

At the present time, we are beginning the process of locating
a physician for the project. According to the design, a family practitioner
or pediatrician would be most desirable. Obtaining the services of a
qualified physician will be of paramount importance to the overall success
of the program, and this is one area in which we are in great need of your
expertise.

Several alternatives may be open to us in regard to obtaining a
physician. If possible, we would like to hire a physician to work and live
full time in the area. The possibility of contracting with a physician
currently in the area to provide a specified amount of time at the clinic is
also available.

I would like to have the chance to discuss this at more length
with you, and to receive your advice in the development of this program. I
can provide more information if you feel that would be valuable or you could
contact our Alabama representative, Mr. John Zippert, at the following
address:

> Federation of Southern Cooperatives
> Training and Research Center
> P. O. Box 95
> Epes, Alabama   35460

I am looking forward to hearing from you and working with you closely in this
project. Thank you for your time.

Cooperatively yours,

Donald Speicher
Research and Resource Department

DS/cj

Federation of Southern Cooperatives
Training and Research Center
P. O. Box 95/Epes, Alabama 35460/Phone (205) 652-7406

BLACK BELT FAMILY HEALTH CARE CENTER   August 29, 1972

Dr. Elizabeth Cleino, Director
West Alabama Comprehensive Health Planning
P. O. Box 1488
Tuscaloosa, Alabama

Dear Dr. Cleino:

This letter is to inform you of recent grant funds received to
develop a Family Health Care Center in Epes, Alabama (Sumter County)
that will provide medical services to Five county area (Marengo,
Choctow, Greene, Pickens, and Sumter).

This Family Health Care Center is now being called The Black Belt
Family Health Care Center, which will be a demonstration project providing
comprehensive ambulatory care and preventive medical practices, on a prepaid basis, to a primarily low-income consumer population.

The project includes a Project Administrator, Medical Director
(physician), Registered Nurse, two (2) Para-medical aids, five (5)
Community Health Workers and several clerical personnel. It has been
designed to develop over a four year period into a comprehensive program,
progressing from a first year that will largely be devoted to the hiring
and training of staff, developing care delivery systems, orgainzing,
training and making functional a consumer board, negotiating third party
reimbursements, along with Back-up and Referral Services, and enrolling
of consumers.

At the present we are in the process of securing, a physician and
back-up and referral services which will be of paramount importance to
the overall success of the program.

I would like to have the chance to discuss our program at more
length with you and to receive your advice in the development of this
program.

I am looking forward to hearing from you and working with you closely in this project.

Sincerely,

Melbah Jean McAfee,
Project Administrator

P.S. May I have a copy of the Community Resources Directory - 1972?

MJM/fjj

West Alabama

Comprehensive Health Planning Council

P O BOX 1488 — TUSCALOOSA, ALABAMA 35401 — TELEPHONE (205) 345-9918

Everett Hale, M.D.
Chairman

Elizabeth Cleino, R.N., Ph.D.
Director

September 1, 1972

Miss Melbah Jean McAfee
Project Administrator
Black Belt Family Health Care Center
P. O. Box 95
Epes, Alabama   35460

Dear Miss McAfee:

Thank you for your letter of August 29 explaining the Family Health Care Center Project. Since our Council is concerned with two of the counties which will be covered by this Project, we will, of course, expect to assist in the overall planning and coordination.

Dr. Sidney Williams, Health Officer in several of these counties, was here at a meeting yesterday and told me of a meeting which you and he were to set up to discuss the Project. I would like very much to attend this meeting.

In order to assist you in becoming familiar with the community service agencies in Pickens and Greene County, I am sending to you under separate cover a copy of the Directory of Community Services published by our Organization, complements of Dr. Williams and the Greene County Health Department.

Our office will be pleased to work with you in this project and do whatever we can to assist.

Sincerely,

Elizabeth W. Cleino

Elizabeth W. Cleino, Ph.D.
Director

EWC:mka

CC: Dr. Sidney Williams
    Mr. Ira Pruitt
BCC: Dr. John M. Packard
    Mr. C. Preston Blanks, Jr.

SEP 7 1972

ALABAMA ADVISORY COUNCIL FOR
COMPREHENSIVE HEALTH PLANNING

Mailing Address:
State Office Building
Montgomery, Alabama 36104
Telephone (205) 269-6376

CHAIRMAN
Ira L. Myers, M.D.

MEMBERS

Mrs Coleman Beale
    Elmore
Elizabeth W. Cleino, Ph.D.
    Tuscaloosa
Mrs Robert M. Combs
    Montgomery
E. E. Eddleman, Jr., M.D
    Birmingham
Mrs Elizabeth T. Edwards
    Wetumpka
Henry W Foster, M D
    Tuskegee
Robert E Fay, Jr., M D
    Enterprise
James Friend
    Huntsville
Roy W. Gilbert
    Birmingham
Lillian H. Harvey, Ed D.
    Tuskegee
S. Richardson Hill, Jr., M.D.
    Birmingham
George Hutchinson
    Montgomery
William E. Jennings, D V.M.
    Auburn
John LeFlore
    Mobile
Mrs. Lillian G. Meade
    Homewood
Mrs Majorie M. Meredith
    Tuscaloosa
Mrs. Agnes R. Mills
    Montgomery
Miss Mary Proctor
    Montgomery
W. H Russell, D D S.
    Chickasaw
Sen. A C. Shelton
    Jacksonville
Barrett C. Shelton
    Decatur
Stonewall B. Stickney, M D.
    Montgomery
Lester Thagard, Jr.
    Birmingham
James V. Walters, Ph.D.
    Tuscaloosa
Mrs. Ernest Warren
    Montgomery
W. C. Williamson
    Montgomery
O. F. Wise, L.H.D.
    Montgomery
Rev. James P. Woodson
    Auburn
R. Floyd Yarbough
    Birmingham

September 1, 1972

Dr. Sidney J. Williams
Health Officer
Sumter County Health Department
Drawer 340
Livingston, Alabama 35470

Dear Sidney,

Attached is a copy of a letter from me to Mr. Busby and
from Mr. Busby to me concerning a meeting in Atlanta on
September 16, which we shall be unable to attend.

I understand that HEW plans another site visit in Sumter
County beginning September 11 for several days. We would
be glad to have someone from this office participate in
that meeting if you are agreeable. Please let us know.

With best regards,

Yours sincerely,

C. Preston Blanks, Jr.
Health Planning Administrator

CPB/ec

Federation of Southern Cooperatives
40 Marietta Street, N.W./Suite 1209/Atlanta, Georgia, 30303/Phone (404) 524-4266

August 30, 1972

Mr. Preston Blanks
Acting Director
State Department of Health
State Office Building
Montgomery, Alabama. 36104

Dear Mr. Blanks:

The Federation of Southern Cooperatives has been awarded a grant for
the planning and development of a Family Health Care Center by the
Department of Health, Education and Welfare - Public Health Services
Division - Region IV - Atlanta, Georgia. The location of the center,
to be.constructed later this year, will be in Epes, Alabama. This area
has been declared a medically scarcity area by Federal Health Officials.

In an effort to assure that the recipients of services of the "Black
Belt Family Health Care Center" receive the best.possible care, we
have so structured the orgainzation to include a Technical Advisory
Board made up of experts and practioners in health and related fields.
It is for this reason that we are contacting you as a prospective
member of this board. However, at this time, we feel it premature to
ask.for a commitment on your part until you have more exposure to the
project. Consequently, we are planning a program for this purpose,
and invite you to attend. For the convenience of everyone, particularly the flight accomodations, this initial meeting is planned for
Atlanta, Georgia, on Saturday, September 16, 1972 at 10:30 A.M., at the
Atlanta American Motor Hotel - 160 Spring Street and Carnegie Way.
The phone number is (404) 688-8600. We are taking the liberty of
making reservations for you on the night of Friday, September 15th
if you wish to come the night before.

We will assume the expenses of your trip, limited to food, travel, and
lodging accomodations, and shall be re-imburseable upon presentation

of receipts. Taxi fare and tips shall not require documentation be-
youn your word. If you desire a pre-paid air ticket, please com-
municate with my Secretary Ms. Sonia Weathers, at the phone number
on the letterhead . We also request that you advise us no later
than Friday, September 8, 1972, if your schedule will permit you to
attend.

In closing, we wish you continued good health, and we look forward to
your attendance.

Sincerely,

Wm. H. Busby
Administrative Assistant

WHB/saw

State of Alabama
Department of Public Health
State Office Building
Montgomery, Alabama 36104

IRA L. MYERS, M. D.
STATE HEALTH OFFICER

September 1, 1972

Mr. William H. Busby
Administrative Assistant
Federation of Southern Cooperatives
40 Marietta Street, N.W.
Suite 1200
Atlanta, Georgia 30303

Dear Mr. Busby:

Thank you for your invitation to attend a meeting on September 16, 1972 in Atlanta. Unfortunately, my schedule will not permit my being present at that meeting; however, we shall be glad to meet with you at some later date. Possibly, a meeting at the project site would be beneficial to all parties concerned. Please let me hear from you concerning this.

Yours sincerely,

C. Preston Blanks, Jr.
Health Planning Administrator

cc: Dr. Sidney Williams

CPB/ec

SEP 7 1972

Sumter County

Department of Public Health

Livingston, Alabama

September 6, 1972

Dr. Elizabeth W. Cleino, Director
West Alabama Comprehensive Health Planning Council
P. O. Box 1488
Tuscaloosa, Alabama   35401

Re: Federation of Southern Cooperatives

Dear Bettie:

Since I have not been contacted by the director of the health project,
please write her at the earliest possible moment and urge her
to write me requesting the proposed conference.

Thanking you, I am

Sincerely yours,

Sidney J. Williams, M. D.
County Health Officer

SJW:ech

cc: The Honorable Drayton Pruitt, Jr.
     Mayor
     Livingston, Alabama

armp

September 11, 1972

Dr. Elizabeth W. Cleino, Director
West Alabama CHP Council
P. O. Box 1488
Tuscaloosa, Alabama 35401

Dear Betty:

At our meeting on June 10th with the representatives
of the Family Health Center in Epes, Alabama, it was
our understanding that the Center would treat members
of the Cooperatives, which extend from Louisiana to
North Carolina, while they were in Epes attending
the training courses. It was only at the meeting of
August 28th that it became clear that Pickens and
Greene Counties were to be involved. I am glad that
you have made direct contact with Miss McAfee and
hope that you will be included in any future meetings.

Attached is a letter to me from Mr. Busby inviting me
to attend a meeting in Atlanta on September 16th.
Since I cannot go, I hope that Pete Bailey might be
able to represent both ARMP and the West Alabama
Comprehensive Health Planning Council at this meeting.
Because time is short, I will try to check by phone
on Monday with both you, Pete, and Mr. Busby.

Sincerely,

John M. Packard, M.D.
Director

JMP:ms

cc: Dr. S. J. Williams

Sumter County
Department of Public Health
Livingston, Alabama

SEP 1 8 1972

September 15, 1972

Dr. Elizabeth Cleino, Director
West Alabama Comprehensive Health Planning Council
P. O. Box 1488
Tuscaloosa, Alabama   35401

Dear Dr. Cleino:

Re: Black Belt Family Health Care Center
(Federation of Southern Cooperatives)

Acting upon your offer to Miss Melbah Jean McAfee, and upon
Miss McAfee's request that a conference of parties concerned with
the working out of plans which will offer the most workable ones
to insure the success of the above captioned project in the best
interests of the health of all of the people in the area, such a
conference has been arranged. We hope that out of such a conference concrete steps will have been taken toward a long range
solution of all of our health and health related problems.

I have accepted the offer of Dr. Ralph M. Lyon, President of
Livingston University that we hold the conference at 1:00 P. M.
Wednesday, October 4, 1972, in his office.

After not being able to contact Miss McAfee before she left for a
conference in Atlanta to be held tomorrow, I requested Mr. Bailey,
as ARMP representative to that conference, to advise Miss AcAfee
and Mr. James W. West of the plans. (As I told you by telephone
this afternoon, Mr. West had requested that he be advised of the
conference and that such be arranged for a time the first week
in October).

Thanking you for your offer to assist us, and again inviting you to
this conference, I am

Sincerely yours,

Sidney J. Williams, M.D.
County Health Officer

SJW:ech

cc: Miss Melbah Jean McAfee   Blind cc: Dr. John Packard
     Mr. James W. West   Mr. Preston Blanks
     Dr. Ralph Lyon   Dr. Edward L. Gegan
                                                 Mr. Will Baker
                                                 Honorable Drayton Pruitt

West Alabama

Comprehensive Health Planning Council

P. O. BOX 1488 — TUSCALOOSA, ALABAMA 35401 — TELEPHONE (205) 345-4916

Everett Hale, M.D.
Chairman

Elizabeth Cleino, R.N., Ph.D.
Director

September 26, 1972

Dr. Sidney J. Williams
P. O. Drawer 340
Livingston, Alabama   35470

Dear Dr. Williams:

This is to confirm the attendance of Mr. Pete Bailey and myself at the meeting
on October 4, 1972, at 1:00 p.m. at Livingston University to discuss the
Black Belt Family Health Care Center.

Mr. James West and Dr. Tom Kaselieus (sp?) will also attend the meeting
as representatives of the Regional Office.

Sincerely,

Elizabeth W. Cleino
Elizabeth W. Cleino, Ph.D.
Director

EWC:mka

cc: Miss Melbah Jean McAfee

I am looking forward to meeting with you and working out plans for increased
health services in the two counties, Greene and Pickens, which overlap the
Black Belt Family Health Care Center territory.

West Alabama

Comprehensive Health Planning Council

P O. BOX 1488 — TUSCALOOSA, ALABAMA 35401 — TELEPHONE (205) 345,4916

Everett Hale, M D.
Chairman

Elizabeth Cleino, R N., Ph D.
Director

September 26, 1972

Dr. Tomas A. Kisielius and
  Mr. James West
Community Health Services
Department of Health, Education & Welfare
50 7th Street, N. E.
Atlanta, Georgia 30323

Dear Dr. Kisielius and Mr. West:

We are looking forward to your visit to West Alabama on October 4, 1972.
Pete Bailey and I will meet you at the airport at 10:00 a.m., and we will
drive directly to Livingston.

There are a few people in the area I would like you to have an opportunity
to meet before the conference at 1:00 p.m.

We will return to Tuscaloosa after the meeting is over and after seeing
Epes if you so desire. Please let me know if you would like for me to
make reservations for you at a local motel.

Sincerely,

Elizabeth Cleino

Elizabeth W. Cleino, Ph.D.
Director

EWC:mka

NOV 13 1972

ALABAMA ADVISORY COUNCIL FOR COMPREHENSIVE HEALTH PLANNING

Mailing Address:
State Office Building
Montgomery, Alabama 36104
Telephone (205) 269-6376

October 30, 1972

Mrs. Dwight J. Miller
Project Administrator
Black Belt Family Health Care Center
P. O. Box 15
Pyne, Alabama 35460

Dear Mrs. Miller:

With reference to your letter of October 10, 1972, we have reviewed the information transmitted with your letter. The limitation of information in the materials naturally deficits our review capability. However, the following comments are indicated:

1. Staffing does not include a registered nurse(s), a key position in developing and in launching a primary health care program.

2. There is no indication of linkages (relationships with other health service resources connected to the project, e.g. hospital services, specialized or sub-specialized services, dental services, or to health-related organizations.)

3. Prehospital services are not referred to in the budget. These services are considered essential in primary health care.

4. The material does not identify where the primary professional health manpower will be obtained.

5. Although the material indicates project evaluation is a basic component of the program, there is no reference to qualitative evaluation of services rendered.

6. It is our understanding that the project will not provide (comprehensive) care to the clients. The 1,500 enrolled clients indicates approximately 65 - 80 percent of complete health care being provided in the environs served by the clinic to the time on available resources. We do not believe that any prospective clients will obtain or be able to obtain the anticipated clinic.

We appreciate the opportunity to discuss the project with you.

Sincerely yours,

C. Preston Blanks, Jr.
Health Planning Administrator

cc: Dr. Sydney Williams, Health Officer
Sumter County Health Department

Dr. John Packard, Director
Alabama Regional Medical Program

Dr. Herbert Hudgins
Health Services, Mental Health Administration

CPB/mm/ec

BLACK BELT FAMILY HEALTH CARE CENTER
POST OFFICE BOX 95   EPES, ALA. 35460
Telephone: 205/652-7406

MELBAH MC AFEE
Project Administrator

November 16, 1972

CHARLES O. PREJEAN
Executive Director/FSC

Dr. Elizabeth W. Cleino, R.N., Ph.D.
West Alabama Comprehensive Health
Planning Council, Inc.
Cotton States Building
P. O. Box 1488
Tuscaloosa, Alabama 35401

Dear Dr. Cleino:

We are now in the process of finalizing the membership list for the Technical Advisory Committee of the Black Belt Family Health Care Center and would like very much to have you serve on the committee.

The purpose of the committee is to provide technical assistance in an advisory capacity to a Health Board comprised of consumers. Each person of the committee will be expected to lend his expertise and knowledge as a resource to the consumer Board and Project Administrator.

A second meeting of the advisory committee will be held, hopefully, within the next two weeks at our Epes office. I do hope you will be able to attend. I will notify you of this date.

Good Health,

Melbah J. McAfee

MJM/fjj

West Alabama

Comprehensive Health Planning Council

P. O. BOX 1488   —   TUSCALOOSA, ALABAMA 35401   —   TELEPHONE (205) 345-4916

Everett Hale, M.D.
Chairman

Elizabeth Cleino, R.N., Ph.D.
Director

November 22, 1972

Miss Melbah J. McAfee
Project Administrator
Black Belt Family Health Care Center
P. O. Box 95
Epes, Alabama   35460

Dear Miss McAfee:

Thank you very much for your invitation to serve as a member of the
Technical Advisory Committee of the Black Belt Family Health Care
Center. I will be very pleased to serve on this Committee. Anytime
when I will not be able to attend the meeting, Mr. Pete Bailey from our
office will attend for me if this is satisfactory.

I am sorry I was not able to reach you the other day when you called,
but I understand you were interested in perhaps applying to the National
Health Service Corps for a physician. I believe, if you study the guidelines, you will see that this program does not really fit into your needs,
as the NHSC insists that their physician be assigned to work with the
total population, as a private practitioner would and not for any special
group or any special project. However, we are planning to run some
ads in national publications to recruit physicians for this area. If we
have any leads of interest for your program, we will certainly refer them
to you.

Sincerely,

Elizabeth W. Cleino, Ph.D.
Director

EWC:mka

DEC 6 1972

BLACK BELT FAMILY HEALTH CARE CENTER
POST OFFICE BOX 95   EPES, ALA. 35460
Telephone: 205/652-7406

MELBAH MC AFEE
Project Administrator   December 5, 1972   CHARLES O. PREJEAN
                                                          Executive Director/FSC

Dr. Elizabeth W. Cleino, R.N., Ph.D.
West Alabama Comprehensive Health
Planning Council, Inc.
Cotton States Building
P. O. Box 1488
Tuscaloosa, Alabama 35401

Dear Dr. Cleino:

    The second meeting of the Technical Advisory Committee will
be held on December 16, 1972 at 10:00 A.M. in Epes, Alabama at
the Rural Research and Training Center.

    The purpose of this meeting is to become organized as a committee,
elect officers, and to define and develop the relationship and responsibilities of this committee to the Consumer Board and Administrator.

    Accommodations will be made for you at the Training Center if you
wish to come the night before.

    I do hope you will be able to attend. If for some reason you
cannot come, please call me at 205-652-7406.

Good Health,

Melbah J. McAfee

MJM/fjj

West Alabama

Comprehensive Health Planning Council

P. O. BOX 1488 — TUSCALOOSA, ALABAMA 35401 — TELEPHONE (205) 345-4916

Everett Hale, M D.
Chairman

Elizabeth Cleino, R.N., Ph.D.
Director

December 12, 1972

Miss Melbah Jean McAfee
Project Administrator
Black Belt Family Health Care Center
P. O. Box 95
Epes, Alabama   35460

Dear Miss McAfee:

I am very sorry that I will be unable to attend the second meeting of the
Technical Advisory Committee on December 16. However, Mr. Pete
Bailey, from our Staff, will attend to represent the Council. He will
drive down the morning of the meeting.

Sincerely,

Elizabeth W. Cleino, Ph.D.
Director

EWC:mka

FEB 6 1973

BLACK BELT FAMILY HEALTH CARE CENTER
POST OFFICE BOX 95   EPES, ALA.35460
Telephone: 205/652-7406

MELBAH MC AFEE   CHARLES O. PREJEAN
Project Administrator   February 5, 1973   Executive Director/FSC

Dr. Elizabeth W. Cleino, R.N., Ph.D.
West Alabama Comprehensive Health
Planning Council, Inc.
Cotton States Building
P. O. Box 1488
Tuscaloosa, Alabama 35401

Dear Dr. Cleino:

We are now moving into the final phase of planning for our Black
Belt Family Health Care Program, prior to the implementation-operational
period, slated to begin on July 1, 1973. Our community health workers,
in all areas to be served by the program, are being warmly received at
community meetings by even larger audiences as they explain the details
and benefits of the program. Our "consumer-community health councils"
are in various stages of formation and development throughout the Black
Belt Family Health Care Center service area.

As you know our program is set up to serve the residents of the
"medical scarcity area" including all of Sumter County and parts of
Greene, Pickens, Marengo, and Choctaw Counties within a twenty-five
mile radius of our Epes medical center and Rural Research and Training
Center. We plan to provide ambulatory medical care and preventive
health program for about 2,500 or more families. We anticipate that
fifteen to twenty percent (15%-20%) of our enrollment will come from
the southern portion of Pickens county which is part of our service
area.

We understand that the Appalachian Regional Commission has a
special program, to provide funds and assistance to rural health
demonstration projects, within counties designated as part of the
Appalachian area. Since Pickens county, which we will be serving, is
part of the Appalachian Regional Area, we feel the Black Belt Family
Health Care Program is elligible for some of this special assistance.

We are planning to construct a $140,000 medical center facility; provide a transportation system to bring indigent people to our service facilities, referral and specialist services, and ancillary social service agencies they may need; insure certain other specialized medical attention and in-hospital care for those too poor to afford it on their own; develop a cadre of trained community and paraprofessional health workers. These aspects of the program may not be completely funded by the Community Health Service/HSMHA/HEW for our members, so we are seeking other funds to fulfill these needs.

For these reasons, we are requesting that you forward to us any information, guidelines, and application forms, for securing assistance through the Appalachian Regional Program. Please send us this data and materials as soon as possible, so we can proceed rapidly to include this in our planning-implementation process. If you feel it would be helpful for us to meet with you to discuss our plans in relation to assistance available through ARC, we would be glad to get together with you.

Thank you for your kind interest and concern for our project.

Cooperatively yours,

Melbah J. McAfee

cc: Alabama Development Office
   Dr. John Packard, ARMP
   Mr. James West
   Dr. Hazel Swann
   Mr. Meredith Richardson, FSC

MJM/fjj

FEB 14 1973

BLACK BELT FAMILY HEALTH CARE CENTER
POST OFFICE BOX 95   EPES, ALA.35460
Telephone: 205/652-7406

LBAH MC AFEE
oJect Administrator   February 9, 1973

CHARLES O. PREJEAN
Executive Director/FSC

Dr. Elizabeth Cleino, Director
West Alabama Comprehensive Health
Planning Council-Cotton States Bldg.
P. O. Box 1488
Tuscaloosa, Alabama

Dear Dr. Cleino;

The Black Belt Family Health Care Center invites you to take an active
part in our Conference entitled, "HEALTH DELIVERY IN RURAL AREAS", on
April 4th, 5th, and 6th, 1973 (Wednesday, Thursday, and Friday).

Most rural areas in the United States, as well as in our region of
Alabama, are highly characterized by poor people. There is a severe lack
of vital essentials, such as inadequate housings, insufficient medical
personnel and resources, among other major deficiencies. These circumstances were the basis for which we planned this Conference.

Specifically, our objectives are:

1. To provide and promote efficient Health Care.

2. To bring together Rural Health Care Repre-
    sentatives to solve problems that exist in all
    areas.

3. To establish good sound working relation-
    ships with all local forces for better commun-
    al development and services.

4. To secure funds and methods of funding for
    continuation of health facilities.

We need your participation and cooperation to make this Conference a success and to aid in the establishment and continuation of all Rural Health Centers. Thus, explains our motive for soliciting funds and participation from you.

Attached, please find Conference Attendance Form for your completion and return to our office so that the necessary materials may be sent to you in time for the Conference.

We look forward to your response to our request.

Sincerely yours,

Linda E. Roland, A.R.T.
Black Belt Family Health
Care Center

Encl.

West Alabama

Comprehensive Health Planning Council

P. O. BOX 1488   —   TUSCALOOSA, ALABAMA 35401   —   TELEPHONE (205) 345-4916

Everett Hale, M.D.
Chairman

Elizabeth Cleino, R N., Ph D.
Director

February 14, 1973

Miss Melbah J. McAfee
Project Administrator
Black Belt Family Health Care Center
P. O. Box 95
Epes, Alabama   35460

Dear Miss McAfee:

Thank you for your letter of February 5 inquiring about the possibility
of using Appalachian Regional Commission funds to support the Black
Belt Family Health Care Center. As you realize, the only county involved
in your program which is also in the Appalachian Regional Commission program
district is Pickens County. The Appalachian Regional Commission program,
quite different from many Federal programs, is designed to improve both
the economic and living conditions of the people in a 13-state area of
Appalachia. In each state, a health demonstration area was established
and funds were made available to those demonstration areas exclusively
until last year. Funds are now available for other areas in the Appalachian
district.

We applied for and received $85,472 in Appalachian Regional Commission
funds for our present grant year for Health Planning. Because ARC funds
are so limited, our second year grant will be cut approximately in half.
None of the projects which we proposed for the West Alabama area are being
considered by the Appalachian Regional Commission for funding. Of course,
you are at liberty to prepare a project proposal for assistance from the ARC;
but since the major thrust of your program is outside the Appalachian district
and because the funds have been limited, I do not think that this is a very
likely source for support.

Enclosed is a copy of the application form and guidelines for the development of a project proposal to the Appalachian Regional Commission. All
projects in this area from this source must have the approval of the West
Alabama Comprehensive Health Planning Council.

I have heard lately of several projects which have been funded through the NAACP. I do not know if you would be interested in pursuing this, but apparently at least in the recent past, they have had funds for worthy projects.

I am sorry that we will be unable to attend fully the conference on Health Delivery in Rural Areas in April. The Alabama Public Health Association meeting will be held on April 3 and 4, and our Council is scheduled to meet on April 5. Perhaps we will be able to attend part of the meeting on the 6th.

We will be very happy to discuss any of these items with you if you so desire.

Sincerely,

Elizabeth W. Cleino, Ph.D.
Director

EWC:mka

Enclosures: application form
guidelines

BLACK BELT FAMILY HEALTH CARE CENTER
POST OFFICE BOX 95 EPES, ALA. 35460
Telephone: 205/652-7406

MELBAH MC AFEE
Project Administrator

February 21, 1973

CHARLES O. PREJEAN
Executive Director/FSC

ANNOUNCEMENT TO TECHNICAL ADVISORY BOARD MEMBERS
BLACK BELT FAMILY HEALTH CARE CENTER
FEDERATION OF SOUTHERN COOPERATIVES, GRANTEE

SPECIAL MEETING MARCH 10, 1973

Dr. Elizabeth W. Cleino, R.N., Ph.D.
West Alabama Comprehensive Health
Planning Council, Inc.
Cotton States Building
P. O. Box 1488
Tuscaloosa, Alabama 35401

Dear Dr. Cleino:

The Black Belt Family Health Care Center has reached a pivotal point
in its first year's development.

Several staff members, including a consulting physician have been
acquired. A health Packaging firm is becoming instrumental in setting
up the various mechanisms for a successful benefit package system;
community councils are being elected from the impact area and training
for the councilmen will commence shortly. Plans for the July 1, 1973,
delivery of medical services to the consumer community are operating
at full blast with an all out recruitment program for physicians.

A national conference on Rural Health Delivery entitled; "Health
Delivery Realization of Ruralization" is planned for April 4, 5, and 6,
at the home of the Black Belt Family Health Care Center. Representatives
of a variety of factors related to this delivery are being contacted.
The staff looks forward to the imput and participation of the Advisory
Board in the development and implementation of this first conference.

It is vitally necessary to rally all conceivable support from
every resource to insure continuation of the project. We have called
for this special meeting to bring everyone up to date on the progress
of the project. Final plans for the conference will be made at this
meeting.

One of the lagging efforts has been the development of a functioning advisory system. The initial stage of development was a burden shouldered by staff and grantee.

The Community Consumer Board will be formed prior to the March 10 meeting. And will afford the opportunity for advisors and implementors to come together and discuss strategies productive to the overall goals of the project.

The Technical Advisory Board has yet to elect its officers and develop a working perspective for operations. We plan to finalize the board at this meeting and will have to count our board among the March 10, participants.

On behalf of Miss McAfee and staff, I ask that you adjust your schedule if at all possible to attend this meeting. Looking forward to a productive and enjoyable session.

Cooperatively Yours,

Steve Wilson, Project Evaluator

cc: Melbah J. McAfee

SW/fjj

West Alabama

Comprehensive Health Planning Council

P O BOX 1488 — TUSCALOOSA, ALABAMA 35401 — TELEPHONE (205) 345,4916

Everett Hale, M D.
Chairman

Elizabeth Cleino, R N , Ph.D.
Director

February 27, 1973

Mr. Steve Wilson, Project Evaluator
Black Belt Family Health Care Center
P. O. Box 95
Epes, Alabama   35460

Dear Mr. Wilson:

I am sorry that I will not be able to attend the meeting on March 10. As I have indicated previously, meetings on Saturday are very difficult to attend since many of us have outside responsibilities on the weekend which cannot be broken. On the weekend of March 10, we are having out-of-town guests and I will be unable to attend the meeting on that date.

I am very interested in your program progress and will be glad to assist in any way I can but I would ask that the meetings be scheduled for some other date than on the weekend.

Sincerely,

Elizabeth W. Cleino, Ph.D.
Director

EWC: mka

CC: Miss Melbah J. McAfee

BLACK BELT FAMILY HEALTH CARE CENTER
POST OFFICE BOX 95   EPES, ALA.35460
Telephone: 205/652-7406

MELBAH MC AFEE
Project Administrator   March 19, 1973

Meredith Richardson
Executive Director/FSC

Dr. Sidney J. Williams
County Health Officer
Sumter County Health Department
Livingston, Alabama 35470

Dear Dr. Williams:

We are now at the point in our program where we've determined the
scope of benefits (services) that will be provided by the program.

We certainly do not want to duplicate those services being
provided presently by the Health Department and we too, understand your
problem with the shortage of manpower and funds. Therefore, after careful
consideration as to how we could assist each other, I was able to come
up with what I thought, a very good, sound working relationship.

Thus:

We (or you) employ a public Health nurse being paid by
our program, stationed in your department, providing all
services to our enrollees on a scheduled basis.

I surely would like to discuss this relationship with you further
as soon as possible.

A similar contract has been drawn by one of the other funded centers.
For further information contact:

Director
Wake County Family Health Center
P. O. Box 25431
Raleigh, N.C. 27611
Phone: (919) 834-7250

Cooperatively,

Melbah J. McAfee

MJM/fjj

Sumter County
Department of Public Health
Livingston, Alabama

March 25, 1973

Dr. M. B. Bethel, Health Officer
Wake County Health Department
Raleigh, North Carolina   27602

Dear Dr. Bethel:

I am advised that The Wake County Family Health Center
has contracted with your agency to provide certain services.

I shall appreciate very much your furnishing me with a
copy of the contract and such other information as you
think would be helpful to us.

Thanking you, I am

Sincerely yours,

Sidney J. Williams, M. D.
County Health Officer

SJW:ech

APR 6 1973

WAKE COUNTY HEALTH DEPARTMENT

P O Box 949, RALEIGH, NORTH CAROLINA 27602

TELEPHONE
755-6107
AREA 919

April 2, 1973

Sidney J. Williams M.D.
County Health Officer
Department of Public Health
Livingston, Alabama

Dear Dr. Williams:

We have not as yet reached the contract stage with Wake Health Services, Inc. We have committed our support. It will be mostly in communicable disease control, child health services, family planning and home health care.

Most sincerely,

M. B. Bethel

Millard B. Bethel, M.D., M.P.H.
Director

MBB/gi

West Alabama

Comprehensive Health Planning Council

P. O. BOX 1488   —   TUSCALOOSA, ALABAMA 35401   —   TELEPHONE (205) 345-4916

Everett Hale, M.D.
Chairman

Elizabeth Cleino, R.N., Ph.D.
Director

April 30, 1973

Dr. Herbert Hudgins
Department of Health, Education and Welfare
50 Seventh Street, N. E.
Atlanta, Georgia   30323

Dear Dr. Hudgins:

The West Alabama Comprehensive Health Planning Council has reviewed
the continuation application from the Federation of Southern Cooperatives
concerning the Black Belt Family Health Care Center. The application
is very detailed and shows that much work has gone into its formation.
The need to improve ambulatory health care services for the people in
West Alabama has been documented in the past by existing agencies and
has been well identified by the Center. Nevertheless, the application
as planned is outside of and lacks the support of the regular health care
giving system.

It is the opinion of the Council that for the sake of permanence, for better
use of scarce health manpower, for sounder fiscal management, coupled
with greater expectations for doing the most good for the clientele of
the Federation of Southern Cooperatives and the area as a whole, that
we do not concur with the application as proposed.

We would give positive consideration to a proposal where services could
be provided on a more cooperative basis with the existing health care
system. We would also like to see a system developed where health
care could be taken to the people from a central location in a recognized
center. A further consideration should be given to the practical solution
of how these services will be continued after HEW support has ended.

It is the Council's recommendation that consideration be given to revising
the proposal to overcome the objectives as stated above.

Sincerely,

E. Everett Hale, M.D.
Chairman

EEH:EWC:mka

CC: Mr. C. Preston Blanks, Jr.
      Miss Melbah J. McAfee

AUG 15 1973

THE FEDERATION OF SOUTHERN COOPERATIVES

Rural Training and Research Center

P O. Box 95 / Epes, Alabama 35460 / Phone (205) 652 5181

ames O. Jones
Executive Director

652 - 2453 - residence home

August 14, 1973

Field Offices

208 ath Jefferson
Albany Georgia 31705
912 436-4832

P C ox 1128
Aut Alabama 36830
205 887-6566

P O Box 117
For Mississippi 39074
601 469 1591

500 hater Street
Hattiesburg Mississippi
601 483-3515

P C ox 390
Kingtree South Carolina 29556
803 354-6123

P C ox 184
Lex on Mississippi 39095
601 134 5515

P O Box 1009
Marianna, Florida 32446
90 A2 7011

P.O. ox 1146
Palmetto Florida 33561
813 j 52

27H anklin Street
Selr Alabama 36701
205 475 2181

P O Box 455
Tall on, Georgia 31827
404 65 3381

P. O Box 148
Tallulah Louisiana 71282
318 474 1622

610 dereau Street
Whb gton North Carolina
919 763 2480

Dr. Elizabeth Cleino, Director
West Alabama Comprehensive Health Planning Council
Cotton States Building
P. O. Box # 1488
Tuscaloosa, Alabama

Dear Dr. Cleino;

My appreciation to you and Mr. Pete Bailey for meeting with
Mr. John Zippert and I on last Thursday.

The meeting, I feel proved to be very fruitful and I am looking
forward to continuing our discussion as soon as possible at your
conVenience.

My schedule for the remainder of this week is somewhat tied
up due to our Annual meeting, but any day during the week of
August 20-24th will be fine with me.

May I hear from you concerning a possible time??

Sincerely,

Melbah J. McAfee,
Project Administrator

MJM/ler

Comprehensive Health Planning Council

P. O. BOX 1488   —   TUSCALOOSA, ALABAMA 35401   —   TELEPHONE (205) 345.4916

Everett Hale, M.D.
Chairman

Elizabeth Cleino, R.N., Ph.D.
Director

August 15, 1973

Miss Melbah J. McAfee
Project Administrator
Black Belt Family Health Care Center
P. O. Box 95
Epes, Alabama 35460

Dear Miss McAfee:

After our meeting with you and Mr. Zippert last Thursday, Mr. Bailey and I have continued our discussions with the entire staff; and we will also discuss this with our Executive Committee this week.

Next week Mr. Bailey and I will be attending the Regional Comprehensive Health Planning Conference in Florida and will not be available for a conference next week. We would be free from 1:00 to 4:00 p.m. on Thursday, August 30, if this would be convenient for you.

Sincerely,

Elizabeth W. Cleino, Ph.D.
Director

EWC:mka

BCC: Mr. Andrew Dearman
      Dr. Sidney Williams

West Alabama

Comprehensive Health Planning Council

P.O BOX 1488   —   TUSCALOOSA, ALABAMA 35401   —   TELEPHONE (205) 345-4916

Everett Hale, M.D.
Chairman

Elizabeth Cleino, R N., Ph D.
Director

August 17, 1973

Congressman Walter Flowers
1118 Greensboro Avenue
Tuscaloosa, Alabama 35401

Dear Congressman Flowers:

Mr. Bailey and I met with Miss McAffee and Mr. Zippert of the Black Belt Family Health Care Center on August 9 for the purpose of determining in what ways the plans of the Black Belt Family Health Care Center could be integrated with the plans of the region for improving health service to the citizens. Although we will continue discussion on August 30, preliminary discussions have led the staff to recommend a course of action which we believe would be advantageous to the people to be served and fit in with the ongoing health care system in the area.

This plan is basically that the Health Care Center offer to the people of the area a way of obtaining primary health care such as one would obtain from any other doctor's office except that these services would be provided by a team of people whose purpose would be not only to meet the immediate need but to provide extended education about health matters.

Since most rural physicians are able to make a living while carrying a rather large load of patients who do not pay, it would seem reasonable for the Black Belt Family Health Care Center to be able to operate on a fee-for-service basis and still absorb some patients who would be unable to pay. In the original proposal for HEW funding, it is stated that approximately 65 per cent of the population surveyed had some form of public assistance which would indicate that approximately this number would be covered by Medicaid, Medicare or Veterans Benefits and certainly some of the other 35 per cent would be able to pay for services rendered.

This would give the people of the area an additional opportunity to receive health care through a team effort located at the headquarters of the Federation of Southern Cooperatives since this is primarily the target population but also give a choice to others who live in the area to receive health care from this group.

In addition, it was suggested that services might be rendered in other parts of the area simply by utilizing community facilities such as churches for certain types of health services as examinations, treatments, and education. If the project were conducted in this manner, it would not need Federal funds.

All of this is based on the assumption that the physician will be duly licensed to practice medicine in Alabama and the necessary support personnel will be recruited.

These suggestions were discussed by the Executive Committee of the West Alabama Comprehensive Health Planning Council on August 16. We will be glad to discuss this further with you at any time.

Sincerely,

Elizabeth W. Cleino, Ph.D.
Director

EWC:mka

Tuscaloosa County

Health Department

TUSCALOOSA, ALA.

August 23, 1973

607 - 10TH ST., EAST

Mrs. Elizabeth Cleino , Ph. D.
West Alabama Comprehensive Health Planning Council
P. O. Box 1488
Tuscaloosa, Alabama

Dear Bettie:

Since our most recent executive committee meeting there
have been some developments in Sumter County which have
drastically changed the picture as to availability of medical
care.

One additional physician has just opened his office
in York, one other has come into Livingston and a third has
evidenced his intention to move to livingston, this to the
extent of enrolling his children in the Sumter Academy and
seeking living quarters. All of these are primary providers
(general practitioners) and this will raise the number of
primary providers in Sumter County from four to seven.
This pulls the rug as to the cry of medical scarcity and
negates the position that has been taken by some as the
justification for supporting the Federation of Southern
Cooperatives as a primary provider of health and medical
care.

Sincerely yours,

Sidney J. Williams, M. D.,
Health Officer

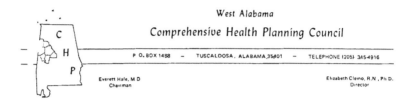

West Alabama

Comprehensive Health Planning Council

P.O. BOX 1488 — TUSCALOOSA, ALABAMA, 35401 — TELEPHONE (205) 345-4916

Everett Hale, M.D.
Chairman

Elizabeth Cleino, R.N., Ph.D.
Director

October 16, 1973

TO: Those Involved in Developing the Ambulatory Health Care Project
          for Greene and Sumter Counties

FROM: Elizabeth W. Cleino, Ph.D.

SUBJECT: Meeting to Discuss the Proposal

On Tuesday, October 23, 1973, the group involved in developing the Ambulatory
Health Care Project in Greene and Sumter Counties will meet at the Greene County
Health Department at 7:30 p.m.

The first draft of the proposal is scheduled to be mailed to you tomorrow,
October 17. Please be ready with your comments so there can be an agreement
(if at all possible) on the proposal at the meeting on the 23rd.

If you have any questions you wish to discuss before the meeting, please do not
hesitate to call me.

EWC/ala

Distribution:

1. Greene County Medical Society
2. Sumter County Medical Society
3. Health Officer Sumter & Greene Counties
4. Greene & Sumter County Dentists
5. Federation of Southern Cooperatives
6. Chairman of County Commissioners - Greene County
·7. Chairman of County Commissioners - Sumter County
8. Mayor, City of Livingston
9. Mayor, City of Eutaw
10. University of Alabama College of Community Health Sciences
11. CHP (a) Office

October 31, 1973

Dr. Elizabeth Cleino, Director
West Alabama Comprehensive
Health Planning Council
P. O. Box 1488
Tuscaloosa, Alabama

Dear Dr. Cleino;

Due to the insensitivity and intransigent attitudes exhibi
in the meeting held on last Tuesday, October 23, 1973, it is
imperative that we take the independent course of developing t
enclosed "Black Belt Community Health Center" Proposal.

We cannot accept and ascribe to a "new program" that was
merely formed "to get Federal Funds", but will represent no chan
or improvement over the existing inadequate health care system i
the area.

The Black Belt Community Health Center, an outgrowth of the
Black Belt Family Health Care Center, is an independent applican
with status as a separate non-profit legal entity, in the proces
of now being incorporated.

We would like during your review and comment to keep in min
that the ability of this Program is to rely on the planning and
development activities already begun by the Black Belt Family
Health Care Center and the support our Program has among the
community people who need the services.

Please forward copies of all comments to the Dept. of H.E.W
Region IV.

Your immediate consideration is appreciated.

Sincerely,

Eddie W. Ayers

Eddie W. Ayers, Presiden
Black Belt Community
Health Center

Enclosure

cc: Mr. C. Preston Blanks, Jr.
Health Planning Administrator

MEMORANDUM   NOV 2 1973

ate: November 1, 1973

o: Those in Sumter County involved   Re: Ambulatory Health Services Project

ro : Sidney J. Williams, M. D.

Dr. Elizabeth Cleino has informed me that it is quite urgent that we have a meeting to discuss the latest developments in the above captioned project.

The Federation of Southern Cooperatives will not be represented at this meeting which is to be held at the Greene County Hospital Wednesday November 7 at 6:00 P. M. unless you are advised to the contrary as to place and time of meeting.

Please let me know whether or not you can attend this meeting.

West Alabama Comprehensive
Health Planning Council

November 2, 1973

TO: Planning Committee for West Alabama Health Services Project

FROM: Elizabeth W. Cleino, Ph.D. *Ewc*

SUBJECT: Progress report and next meeting

After our meeting on October 23, I'm sure no one had any question as to the position of the Federation group. In a conversation with Melba McAfee on the 25th, she indicated that the Federation would reject any offer of the committee short of meeting their demands. She also threatened to "go to Washington" and stop the money for our project. I asked her to let me have their decision in writing.

I went to the Regional Office of HEW on Wednesday, October 31, and discussed the developments with their top staff. They indicated that if we had made every effort to include the Federation and they had rejected our offer then we were free to omit them as a partner in the project.

On Thursday, November 1, the enclosed letter came from the Epes group along with a competing project proposal. The West Alabama Comprehensive Health Planning Council will review this on November 15. Meanwhile, we need to finish our proposal and get this in to HEW with all haste.

A meeting of the planning group will be held on Wednesday, November 7, at 6:00 p.m. for a light supper at the Greene County Hospital. We need your approval of the Articles of Incorporation and By-laws and the members of the Board of Directors. Hereafter, the Board will meet and make its own decisions.

Those invited to the Wednesday meeting are:

> Dr. Williams; Mr. Lockard; Dr. Gegan; Dr. Grenshaw and any
> others from Sumter County Medical Society; Judge Branch;
> Dr. Staggers; Dr. Smith; Dr. Frederick; Mr. Patton, our
> host; and Dr. Packard; and Mayor Ira Pruitt, Jr.

Your proposal, omitting the Federation as a participant, is being mailed to the Regional Office and to the State CHP Office today (November 2).

We need endorsement letters from the following:

> Greene County Medical Society
> Sumter County Medical Society
> Two County Health Departments
> County agents--DPS - Extension Service, etc.
> Sumter County Commission
> Greene County Commission (already promised)
> Mayors
> Dentists
> Anyone else you want to ask

Please help me get these letters!

If you have any questions about this, please call me collect or ask Dr. Williams.

EWC/ala

Enclosures: (1) Articles of Incorporation
          (2) By-laws
          (3) Letter from Mr. Ayers

West Alabama Comprehensive
Health Planning Council

TO: Dr. Cleino   DATE: November 6, 1973

FROM: Greg de Lissovoy

RE: Conversation with Ms. Melbah McAfee

Following your instructions, I prepared a brief summary of the
"Black Belt Community Health Center Program" proposal to
facilitate review and comment by the WACHPC Executive Committee.

I noted what appeared to be a discrepancy in the Summary Budget
(page 4, HSM-550-1). "Total Direct Costs" under the column
"Requested from HSMA" were listed as $432,252 while the amount
listed under "Financial Assistance--Cash Award" was listed as
$326,933.

I then telephoned Ms. McAfee and requested clarification. This
conversation took place at aproximately 1:30 PM on Monday,
November 5.

She stated that $326,933 figure was correct. In the lower
section of the Summary Budget (Sources of Funds--Applicant and
Other) the sum of $105,298 had been listed as "Payment for
Services Provided By Project." This represented patient fees
and third-party reimbursement. Due to clerical error, this
amount had not been included in the column labeled "Source of
Funds--Applicant and Other" in the upper portion of the Summary
Budget.

Ms. McAfee said that a revised budget would be submitted to
DHEW. I offered to clarify this error during the Executive
Committee's review and comment, should I have the opportunity.

The conversation terminated on a friendly note with both of us
expressing the feeling "may the best man win."

West Alabama

Comprehensive Health Planning Council

P O BOX 1488 — TUSCALOOSA, ALABAMA 35401 — TELEPHONE (205) 345-4916

Everett Hale, M D
Chairman

Elizabeth Cleino, R N., Ph D.
Director

November 8, 1973

Dr. Herbert Hudgins
50 Seventh Street, N.E.
Atlanta, Georgia   30304

Dear Dr. Hudgins:

Enclosed please find the Articles of Incorporation, By-Laws, letters of endorsement, and job descriptions for the Project Director and physicians. We request that these be added to the application for the West Alabama Health Services Project.

The first meeting of the Board was held on November 7 at which time the Articles of Incorporation were signed and the By-Laws approved. Officers were elected with Judge Branch as chairman.

If there is additional information we need to send, please advise.

Sincerely,

Elizabeth W. Cleino, Ph.D.
Director

EWC/ala

Enclosures

West Alabama

Comprehensive Health Planning Council

P. O. BOX 1485 · TUSCALOOSA, ALABAMA 35401 · TELEPHONE 205-758-7051

Everett Hale, M D
Chairman

Elizabeth Cleino, R N , Ph D.
Director

November 14, 1973

Mr James West
Department of Health, Education & Welfare
Public Health Service - Region IV
50 Seventh Street, N.E.
Atlanta, Georgia   30303

Dear Mr. West:

Enclosed are letters of endorsement from Sumter Memorial Hospital and
Hill Hospital of York. Please include these two additional letters in the
West Alabama Health Services Project proposal.

Sincerely,

Bettie Ann

Elizabeth W. Cleino, Ph.D.
Director

EWC/ala

Enclosures

NOV 3 0 1973

Division of Nursing
Livingston University
Livingston, Alabama 35470
November 28, 1973

Dr. Elizabeth Cleino, Director
West Alabama Comprehensive Health Planning Council
P. O. Box 1488
Tuscaloosa, Alabama 35401

Dear Dr. Cleino:

It was indeed a pleasure to meet you yesterday in addition to attend
the Site Visit meeting of the West Alabama Health Services Project. You
and your associates are to be commended for the development and cogent
writing of this project proposal. I certainly do hope it gets funded.
If we can be of any further assistance in the project, please let us know.

You inquired about the availability of my husband, Mr. Frederick Brodt,
to assist with this project, indicating that Mayor Pruitt suggested he be
contacted regarding it. Because of these references, I have taken the liberty
to enclose his resume.

Fred's resume only touches on his considerable contact with doctors,
nurses, and medical technologists. These contacts spanned seven years and
were national in scope. These health care personnel are part of the 59 Red
Cross blood program. Additional details can be provided for the asking.
Fred could come to Tuscaloosa any time to discuss the project with you and/or
others.

Since Fred retired from the Red Cross to permit me to lend my efforts to
establish the Livingston University nursing program and thus improve health
care in West Alabama, I feel very responsible to secure for him a position which
will use his vast administrative and technical experience and education. The
procurement of a suitable position for him will directly affect the length of
time I will be able to remain in West Alabama and thus success of the Livingston
University nursing program. Any assistance which you can offer toward the solution
of this problem will be greatly appreciated.

In addition, I am enclosing a few faculty recruitment flyers. Should you know
of any one personally in any part of the country who qualifies and may be interested,
a direct contact to that person by you would be very much appreciated. In order for
the Livingston Nursing Program to become a reality we must have qualified faculty.
Furthermore, the provision of names and addresses of prospective candidates for
faculty positions will enable me to contact them directly.

Again, let me reiterate how much I am pleased to have met you and to know you as a colleague for improved health care in West Alabama. I am scheduled for the initial State Board Review on December 13. When I have the materials for that review assembled I shall share a copy with you. Your comments and suggestions will be solicited. Since I have been here I do miss the opportunity to share my thinking with nursing colleagues.

Best wishes and much success in all of your efforts.

Sincerely,

Dagmar E. Brodt, Ph.D., R. N.
Chairman

DEB:gf

enclosures

Dec 3
~~NOV 3 0~~ 1973

State of Alabama
Department of Public Health
State Office Building
Montgomery, Alabama 36104

November 29, 1973

IRA L. MYERS, M. D.
STATE HEALTH OFFICER

M E M O R A N D U M

TO: Dr. Elizabeth W. Cleino, Director
West Alabama Comprehensive Health
   Planning Council
P. O. Box 1488
Tuscaloosa, Alabama

FROM: C. Preston Blanks Jr.,
Health Planning Administrator

SUBJECT: Attached Memorandum from Director,
Bureau of Dental Health,
State Health Department

    Attached is copy of memorandum received concerning the application for
West Alabama Health Services Project. The memorandum should be considered
in any revision of the application.

CPBJr:pt

ATTACHMENT: as stated

cc: Dr. Naseeb L. Shory
     Mr. Charlie Stewart

Department of Public Health
State Office Building
Montgomery, Alabama 36104

November 27, 1973

IRA L. MYERS, M. D.
STATE HEALTH OFFICER

NOV 2 0 1973

COMPREHEN... .....LTH
PLANNING

M E M O R A N D U M

TO   : Mr. C. Preston Blanks, Director
            Comprehensive Health Planning
            10 High Building
            Montgomery, Alabama

FROM : Naseeb L. Shory, D. D. S.
            Director
            Bureau of Dental Health

SUBJECT: West Alabama Health Services Project Application

        I have received a copy of the West Alabama Health Services
Project Application.

        In reading it over, I notice that in the listing "Relations With
Other Organizations" dentistry is not represented by the District Dental
Society. I would like to suggest that the Sixth District Dental Society
should be a full participant in the same manner as the Greene County
and Sumter County Medical Societies. Also I note that, although a rather
sizable portion of the care budget will be used for dentistry, there is no
dentist designated as a member of the Board of Directors.

        Also, the reference to "dental technicians" and their use as
"extenders" in providing services could cause considerable concern and
confusion.

        As we discussed in our telephone conversation today, it is my
understanding that you agree that it will be appropriate for me to discuss
this application with the Council on Dental Health of the Alabama Dental
Association at their meeting later this week on November 29, 1973.

NLS:rk

West Alabama

Comprehensive Health Planning Council

P O BOX 1488 — TUSCALOOSA, ALABAMA 35401 — TELEPHONE (205) 345-4916

Everett Hale, M D.
Chairman

Elizabeth Cleino, R N., Ph D.
Director

November 29, 1973

Mr. W. T. Lockard
P. O. Box 216
York, Alabama 36925

Dear Mr. Lockard:

We missed you at the meeting on Tuesday to discuss the West Alabama Health Services Project with the site visitors.

I believe that they were impressed with the sincerity of the local people to operate this program. From all indications, I believe we will soon be meeting to make definitive plans to go ahead.

Enclosed are copies of our last meeting minutes which include minutes of the initial meeting of your Board.

Sincerely,

Elizabeth W. Cleino, Ph.D.
Director

EWC/ala

Enclosure

West Alabama
Comprehensive Health Planning Council

P. O. BOX 1488 — TUSCALOOSA, ALABAMA 35401 — TELEPHONE (205) 345-4916

Everett Hale, M.D.
Chairman

Elizabeth Cleino, R.N., Ph D.
Director

November 29, 1973

Mr. Charles Stewart
Comprehensive Health Planning
State Office Building
Montgomery, Alabama 36104

Dear Charlie:

Enclosed is a copy of the minutes of the Planning Committee meeting
for the West Alabama Health Services Project and the initial meeting
of the Board. I thought you might like this for your files.

Sincerely,

Bettie Anne

Elizabeth W. Cleino, Ph.D.
Director

EWC/ala

Enclosure

West Alabama

Comprehensive Health Planning Council

P. O. BOX 1488   —   TUSCALOOSA, ALABAMA 35401   —   TELEPHONE (205) 345-4916

Everett Hale, M.D.
Chairman

Elizabeth Cleino, R N., Ph.D.
Director

November 30, 1973

Mr. James West
Department of Health, Education & Welfare
Public Health Service - Region IV
50 Seventh Street, N.E.
Atlanta, Georgia   30303

Dear Mr. West:

Enclosed are two copies of the final document for the West Alabama Health Services Project Application. The application has been retyped, making several minor changes. These documents also include all the letters of endorsement, Articles of Incorporation, By-Laws, etc. that have been sent to you piecemeal. We gave a copy to Ted Griffith when he was here.

I thought you would like these two copies for your files. If you require any additional copies or information, please let me know.

Sincerely,

Elizabeth W Cleino

Elizabeth W. Cleino, Ph.D.
Director

EWC/ala

Enclosures

DEC 7 1973

HILL HOSPITAL OF YORK
York, Alabama
December 3, 1973

Dr. Herbert Huggins
Department of Health, Education and Welfare
57th Street N.E. Region 4
Atlanta, Georgia 303303

Dear Dr. Huggins:

I am writing to you concerning the West Alabama Health Services Project application forwarded to your office on 31 October 1973 by Dr. Elizabeth Cleino, R.N., Ph.D., Director of West Alabama Health Planning Council, Tuscaloosa, Alabama.

The comments and opinions as expressed herein are offered from the position of Administrator, Hill Hospital of York and as a private tax payer. The opinions do not reflect the sentiment of the Hospital Governing Authority of the City of York inasmuch as that authority has not met in formal session since the project proposal was provided to me for review. I hasten to point out that by letter of 13 November 1973 and by verbal expressions at a meeting held in the County Public Health Office, Livingston, Alabama on 27 November 1973, I expressed concurrence and support of the project. I have since that date had second thoughts and wish to express them by this letter.

At first blush, the project appears to warrant approval without further delay. The proposal does point out a need for a project along this line. However, the bureaucracy and unnecessary expenses associated with the project seem to be grossly disproportionate to the benefits to be derived, that is, the establishment of a management office together with two primary care clinic sites would appear unnecessary when in fact concerted coordination with existing practicing physicians and hospitals, would serve to provide the same service. There are physicians offices geographically located on a continuum from Eutaw in Green County to York in Sumter County. Most of these offices are within walking distance of the hospitals which could provide ancillary supportive service to the practicing physician to whom the patient population might be referred by a field or social worker. As was pointed out at the meeting of 27 November 1973 and agreed to by those present, the two greatest problems in the area as related to the delivery of health care in this area are (1) making the population to be served aware of an assistance program of this nature and (2) the transporting of the served group to the delivery site. Both of these could be accomplished without the establishment of new physical facilities for delivery of the care. Moreover, while some of the physicians in either county might not be able to donate time or provide time on a reimbursement basis at the delivery sites without taking away from other segments of the population, I cannot conceive of any of them denying care to those transported to their existing office facilities. Unless there is unanimous participation by the physicians, I can readily see how discontentment can develop among the practicing physicians as a result of clinic referrals to other than specialists. Since all but two of the practicing physicians in Sumter County are general practitioners, a division of effort direction and cooperative spirit is likely to occur immediately. In this connection, the project proposal alludes to complete agreement by all physicians; it is my understanding that at least one of the physicians in Sumter County was not actively or aggressively approached so that she might be enlightened on the proposal.

As a final note of concern, the selection of a proposed site of clinic #1 as referred to at the meeting of 27 November 1973 by Dr. Cleino, does not appear to represent a sound management decision. Livingston, Alabama has a population of 2,358 versus York at 3,044. The Livingston population when the University enrollees are included is approximately 7,358. (Data from project application statement) But, the point to be made is that the 5,000 students are not the population towards which the project is directed. Therefore, it would seem that the site, if a new facility is to be established, should be one nearest the largest segment of population to be served. This should not be construed as recommending that one be located in York for surely I cannot see a need for additional physical plant facilities in view of the existing ones, i.e. practicing physicians offices, county public health office and three community hospitals.

I do not wish to appear negative in every sense. There is a need for a project which would incorporate portions of the proposal such as a small management staff working to coordinate the referral efforts of field social workers and a transportation system supported by Department of Health, Education and Welfare funds so as to make available to the underprivileged a system of ambulatory health care delivery. The project, however, as written is extravagant.

If I can answer any questions, or if I have been ambiguous in any way, please do not hesitate to contact me.

I thank you for your indulgence and remain,

Sincerely,

HILL HOSPITAL OF YORK

John L. Sims,
Administrator

JLS/jkl
Attached list of copy to

Copies

Dr. S. J. Williams, Sumter County Health Officer
Dr. F. N. Crenshaw, Chairman Sumter County Medical Society
Dr. Elizabeth Cleino, R.N., Ph.D., Director of West Alabama Health
Planning Council
Mayor Ira Pruitt
Dr. Johnye R. Walton, Chief of Staff, Hill Hospital of York

DEC 7 1973

State of Alabama
Department of Public Health
State Office Building
Montgomery, Alabama 36104

IRA L. MYERS, M. D.
STATE HEALTH OFFICER

December 5, 1973

Rev. Lawrence F. Haygood
P. O. Box 688
Tuskegee, Alabama

Dear Rev. Haygood:

Governor George C. Wallace has requested this office to provide you with information in response to your telegram dated November 20, 1973 in which you recommended approval of a project proposal to the U. S. Department of Health, Education, and Welfare entitled, "The Black Belt Family Health Care Center of Epes, Alabama".

An application for this endeavor has been under consideration for about a year. Approval was granted for one year by the U. S. Department of Health, Education, and Welfare to see if the program as then proposed could attain the objectives as stated in the proposal. The first year's trial was a failure, as the applicant did not reach his stated goal. The U. S. Department of Health, Education, and Welfare for that reason and, also, for the additional reason that the applicant could not assure attainment of goals during a second year, did not approve continuation of the program beyond the first year, and suspended additional funding. I should also point out that the office of Comprehensive Health Planning recognized the weaknesses in this application from the beginning and did not approve the first year's approval and did not recommend continued funding for the second year. The program was poorly planned and poorly conceived from the beginning. Attainment of stated objectives could never be reached based on the procedures stated in the project proposals and in the methods attempted during the first year of trial.

At the present time two new applications have been prepared and submitted to local groups in that area and to this office for consideration. The two applications clearly reflect a division between two opposite groups in the area with different conceptions of how such a program should be conducted. We have studied both of these new proposals, and based upon the merits thereof, we have recommended approval of one and disapproval of the other. The one for which we have recommended approval is entitled, "West Alabama Health Services Project". The one for which we have recommended disapproval is entitled, "Black Belt Community Health Center".

As you realize, no matter how noble a goal may be, unless the means for reaching it are well planned, all efforts and resources are expended in vain and the goal remains as distant as ever.

Yours sincerely,

C. Preston Blanks, Jr.
Health Planning Administrator

CPB/ec

cc: Honorable George C. Wallace
    Attn: Jesse Gann
    (Correspondence No. 23355)

   Dr. Elizabeth Cleino

GREENE COUNTY COMMISSION

COMMISSIONERS
VASSIE KNOTT - Dist. #1
HARRY C MEANS - Dist #2
LEVI MORROW - Dist. #3
FRENCHIE BURTON - Dist #4

TELEPHONE 372 3349

P. O BOX 347

EUTAW, ALABAMA 35462

CHAIRMAN
WILLIAM McKINLEY BRANCH
PROBATE OFFICE
TELEPHONE 372 3349

ADMINISTRATIVE ASSISTANT
CHARLES JONES

December 5, 1973

Mr. Pete Yarnell
Department of Health, Education & Welfare
Public Health Services – Region IV
50 Seventh Street, N.E.
Atlanta, Georgia 30303

Dear Mr. Yarnell:

The Board of Directors of the West Alabama Health Services Project wishes to express its appreciation to you and your colleagues for visiting Greene and Sumter Counties on November 27.

As you observed, this project is advocated by a broad range of organizations and individuals who are concerned with the health of people in our two counties. Medical and dental services are the heart of the program; but in addition, it will greatly strengthen existing programs of outreach, transportation, education and social services. This program is intended to contribute to a united effort of many agencies to provide a full range of human services.

If we can provide any additional information concerning our proposal, please feel free to contact me. Once again, thank you for your consideration.

Sincerely,

William McKinley Branch
President
West Alabama Health Services, Inc.

/ala

DEC 13 1973

Sumter County

Department of Public Health

Livingston, Alabama

December 12, 1973

Dr. Elizabeth Cleino, Director
West Alabama Comprehensive Health
Planning Council
P. O. Box 1488
Tuscaloosa, Alabama 35401

Re: West Alabama
Health Services Project

Dear Bettie:

Being a member of the Medical-Dental staff of the Hill Hospital
of York, I attended the regular monthly meeting last night.

Mr. John Sims, Hospital Administrator, reported his change in
position as to the above captioned project, which statement was
as set forth in his recent letter. This report was received in
dead silence. There was evidenced no opposition to the project;
in fact, after the meeting in private conversation with some of
the physicians it was apparent that there is no opposition within
the medical community.

Mr. Sims also publicly announced his resignation as administrator,
giving the reason as difficulties pertaining to problems which
he is encountering in administration and which in no way relate
to the proposed project.

In fairness to all, it should be stated that we all realize, which
realization was enforced last night, that Mr. Sims was stating his
own personal opinion without support of the hospital board and
obviously without the support of the Medical-Dental staff. Candidly,
we feel that this opposition should have been stated when he attended our last conference held here in my office.

We hope that we will receive speedy approval of the project as
submitted by you.

Sincerely yours,

Sidney J. Williams, M. D.
County Health Officer

SJW:ech

cc: Mr. James West

West Alabama

Comprehensive Health Planning Council

P O BOX 1488 — TUSCALOOSA, ALABAMA 35401 — TELEPHONE (205) 315-010

Everett Hale, M.D.
Chairman

Elizabeth Cleino, R N., Ph.D.
Director

December 12, 1973

The Honorable Ira D. Pruitt, Jr.
Mayor of Livingston
P. O. Drawer W
Livingston, Alabama 35470

Dear Mayor Pruitt,

During our conversations with people in Sumter and Greene Counties concerning the development of the West Alabama Health Services Project, we were asked repeatedly to account for the funds which were granted to the Federation of Southern Cooperatives for the Black Belt Family Health Center project which ended, I believe, October 31, 1973. The Project Identification Number was 04-H-00658-01-0.

Mr. Al Baldwin, one of the site visitors, is with Grants Management in the Regional Office. He indicated to me that any public official could request an audit of the funds appropriated through HEW. Usually, projects are given 90 days in which to account to HEW for funds they have spent, and within 3 years, one could expect a Federal audit of these funds. I believe that a request from you for an earlier audit would bring results.

Our Council could ask for this information; but since there is only one county included in our area which was covered by this project, it might be better for someone in the headquarters county to request this information.

Enclosed are some pages from the continuation application from the Black Belt Family Health Care Center. This application was turned down at the Regional Office level, but it includes some figures on the budget, actual expenditures and a progress report on last year's grant.

If there is additional information which I can supply, please let me know.

Sincerely,

Elizabeth W. Cleino, Ph.D.
Director

EWC/ala

DEPARTMENT OF HEALTH, EDUCATION, AND WELFARE
REGION IV
50 7TH STREET N E
ATLANTA, GEORGIA 30323

DEC 2 0 1973

Office of Grants Management
Room 866

PUBLIC HEALTH SERVICE
HEALTH SERVICES AND MENTAL HEALTH
ADMINISTRATION

December 18, 1973

Dr. Elizabeth W. Cleino, Director
West Alabama Comprehensive Health Planning Council
P. O. Box 1488
Tuscaloosa, Alabama 35401

Re: Project Grant Application No. 04-H-000815-01-0

Dear Dr. Cleino:

Your application entitled "West Alabama Health Services, Inc." has been
reviewed by the Regional Office in accordance with 314(e) policies and
program guidelines governing neighborhood health centers. At this time,
final action on your application has been deferred pending clarification
and additional information regarding program operations.

Specifically, it was felt that the budget was not sufficiently justified
and that certain categories, such as equipment, were unrealistic. In
addition, the overall budget request should be reduced during the initial
year of the proposal.

The staff of the Community Health Service Program will be contacting you
regarding further details to be addressed in your application.

Sincerely yours,

Eddie J. Sessions
Acting Regional Health Administrator, H

DEC 26 1973

THE CITY OF LIVINGSTON ALABAMA

TELEPHONE 205/652-2505 • POST OFFICE DRAWER W • LIVINGSTON, ALABAMA 35470

December 21, 1973

Dr. Elizabeth W. Cleino, Director
West Alabama Comprehensive Health Planning Council
P.O. Box 1488
Tuscaloosa, Alabama 35401

Dear Bettie:

INRE: Black Belt Family Health Center
project no. 04-H-00658-01-0

I have your letter of December 12, advising that an audit of this project would be helpful.

Let me bring you up to date on our situation concerning the West Alabama Health Services application. We are in a position to provide space for the West Alabama Health Services Project in our hospital, in addition we have a doctor who would be agreeable to managing the project. I have not yet requested the audit of Black Belt Family Health Center, as I felt that to convince the senators who are supporting them that our application is a steady one would be the best approach. For this reason I am taking the liberty of contacting Senator Sparkman and asking him to confer with the supporters of the opposing project to attempt to realign their thinking and support.

Thereafter I will request the audit, I will inform Senator Sparkman that I propose to request an audit also.

Sincerely,

Ira Q. Pruitt, Jr.

IDPjr/rbc

West Alabama Comprehensive
Health Planning Council

TO: Bettie   January 13, 1974

FROM: Greg

SUBJECT: Telephone conversation with Pete Yarnell (CHS/Region IV/HEW)

I telephoned Pete to confirm the meeting scheduled for January 21.
He stated that plans are now in abeyance pending a compromise
between the boards of West Alabama Health Services and the Black Belt
Family Health Center.

His instructions for attempting to arrive at a compromise were very
specific.

A preliminary meeting should be held as soon as possible which will
include key members of each board and their advisors (WACHP and FSC).
Minutes of this meeting should be carefully maintained. The minutes
should document the following:

1. Key issues in which both Boards can <u>agree</u>

2. Key issues in which agreement <u>is not</u> achieved

3. An agenda of three (3) to five (5) key items which
    will be discussed with HEW representatives. These
    should be the points of contention. (We must adhere
    to this agenda at the meeting on Monday.)

4. A list of persons who will be invited to the meeting
    on Monday. This should include adequate representation
    from each Board so that firm decisions can be made.

We need to advise the WAHS officials of this situation. I have called
Judge Branch. Melbah McAffee is to call us by Wednesday afternoon so
that a time and place for the meeting can be decided. If we do not
hear from her, we need to make contact but should also advise Jim
West or Pete Yarnell that she did not call. Melbah is supposed to
call Jim sometime late Wednesday to confirm the meeting arrangements.

HEW will not come unless this meeting is held. They should be supplied
with minutes of the Monday meeting, an agenda, and
a list of participants prior to Monday. If this is not possible, they
should at least be told by phone what the agenda is and who will come.

Pete said that HEW will not be caught in the middle on this project.
Either an agreement is reached or else no funds will be awarded.

Pete also said that FSC is not receiving any money from HEW, so far
as he can determine. Possibly, they are still spending their
90 day continuation funds.

VANCE R. KANE, D. M. D.
401 SOUTH CEDAR STREET
DEMOPOLIS, ALABAMA 36732

TELEPHONE 1206
289?

JAN 18 1974

January 17, 1974

Dr. Elizabeth W. Cleino
West Alabama
Comprehensive Health Planning Council
P. O. Box 1488
Tuscaloosa, Al. 35401

Dear Dr. Cleino:

Thank you for the minutes of the January 8th meeting.

Dr. Cole and I met January 12th and did the preliminary planning on the budget requirements and the proposed participation
of the 6th District Dental Society.

I am very pleased about the reception this program has received
from the District to date. This is a new roll for us. The District leadership appears ready to accept the responsibility to
establish a quality dental program for these counties.

I know we will be meeting again about this in the near future.
I would appreciate your correcting my title as shown below and
my complete address is above.

Sincerely,

Dr. Vance R. Kane
Chairman, Council on Dental Health
Alabama Dental Association

VRK/sc

West Alabama

Comprehensive Health Planning Council

P O. BOX 1488 — TUSCALOOSA, ALABAMA 35401 — TELEPHONE (205) 345-4910

Everett Hale, M.D.
Chairman

Elizabeth Cleino, R N., Ph.D.
Director

February 6, 1974

Mr. Pete Yarnell
Department of Health, Education
and Welfare
Public Health Service, Region IV
50 Seventh Street, N.E.
Atlanta, Georgia 30303

Dear Pete:

Following our telephone conversation of February 6, I am enclosing a proposed contract between West Alabama Health Services, Inc. and the Sixth District Dental Society.

The Sixth District appointed a special committee to study the WAHS project and determine a manner in which they could aid in the development and management of an effective program of dental services. The committee spent several hours drafting a proposal and this was presented to a regular meeting of the Sixth District Dental Society. The District in turn devoted several hours to analysis and revision of this proposal.

Dr. Cleino and I met with Dr. William Cole (President, Sixth District) and Dr. Hiram Johnson (Sixth District representative to West Alabama CHP) Monday. We briefly discussed the proposal and agreed to present it to the Board of Directors of West Alabama Health Services.

I have discussed this with Judge Branch and he asked that you review the proposed contract to determine any possible conflict with either the grant guidelines or DHEW policy. Your written comments would be most helpful when the WAHS, Inc. Board meets to discuss the contract.

Please address your comments directly to Judge Branch.

Thank you for your assistance.

Sincerely,

Greg de Lissovoy
Health Planner

GD/ala

SIXTH DISTRICT DENTAL SOCIETY
Tuscaloosa, Alabama

Feb. 4, 1974

THE DENTAL PROGRAM OF THE WEST ALABAMA HEALTH SERVICES PROJECT

The Sixth District Dental Society in cooperation with the
Alabama Dental Association and the Alabama Bureau of Dental Health
accepts the responsibility to assist in this project to provide
health services to the residents of Greene and Sumter Counties.
This proposal for Dental Services does not imply or infer approval
or endorsement by the Sixth District Dental Society to any other
Health Programs that may be planned or started in any other county
or counties by the West Alabama Health Services Project Incorporated.
The Dental Health Program will include dental health education, all
known preventive dental health procedures and dental health care.
Strong emphasis will be placed on prevention of oral disease.

Dental caries, or decay, affects 95% of our population. Periodontal disease affects 50% of all 6-12 year old school children.
These are two preventable diseases. Primary efforts will be directed
toward a prevention and education program.

In order to initiate this program, cooperation, communication,
and coordination between State, County, and Local Health Departments,
dentists, educators, Livingston University, University of Alabama
School of Dentistry, county and city governing bodies, and the professional health societies must be established.

Goals of the Dental Program of the West Alabama Health Services
Project are:

1. To increase and to enhance the public attainment of good dental health through an effective education and preventive oral health program.

2. To provide dental services for financially indigent children who would not otherwise receive dental care.

3. To provide services to other residents who are unable to obtain services from the private sector.

4. To provide an emergency service for the treatment of dental pain for patients who are unable to obtain service from the private sector.

Administration

The responsibility for administration and control of the dental services, its employees, and consultants will be vested in a board called the Dental Advisory Board (DAB). This board will provide the leadership necessary to insure a high quality dental service for the residents treated from Greene and Sumter Counties. The board will be composed of the following members:

1. A local dentist in either Greene, Sumter or a neighboring county appointed by the Sixth District Dental Society.

2. The Director of the Alabama Bureau of Dental Health or his representative.

3. An elected member of the Sixth District Dental Society.

4. Any other person deemed necessary and appointed by the Dental Advisory Board.

The DAB will elect a chairman from this group and will be free to establish whatever organizational structure as may be required to conduct its business. The Sixth District Dental Society will reserve the right to appoint and/or approve members of the DAB when replacements are necessary and to investigate any and/or all activities of the DAB and, if necessary, make any changes in the DAB that a majority of the membership may feel necessary to improve the administration or function of the DAB and the dental program. The Sixth District Dental Society will advise the Board of Directors of the West Alabama Health Services Project Incorporated of its decisions. The DAB will be responsive to the Project Director and to the Board of Directors of the West Alabama Health Services Project Incorporated. The DAB may be overruled on matters, except in aspects of clinical services where a dentist's professional judgment must be exercised, by a unanimous vote of all the Board of Directors of the West Alabama Health Services Project Incorporated. The members of the DAB will be compensated for their participation in official called meetings by its elected chairman in the same amount as dental consultants.

Final approval of this proposed dental program by the Sixth District Dental Society will be contingent on:

1. Written acceptance and approval of this dental program by the Board of Directors of the West Alabama Health Services Project Incorporated.

2. The Sixth District's review and acceptance of the grant, as it pertains to the dental program, that is submitted to the Department of Health, Education, and Welfare by the West Alabama Health Services Project Incorporated.

Any proposed changes or deletion to this proposed dental program as set forth in this proposal will be coordinated and approved by the

Sixth District Dental Society or its appointed representatives.

Dental Clinic Location, Equipment and Facilities – OK

It is understood and agreed that, initially, one clinic will
be located and operated in one location in Greene or Sumter County.
This location will be approved by the DAB. The West Alabama Health
Services Project agrees to provide suitable space for the clinical
installation. The space should be lighted in accordance with at
least minimum ADA lighting specifications, have toilet facilities
for clinic personnel only, in accordance with ADA specifications,
have sinks in each operatory, and be equipped with equipment, or
the approved equal, listed in the Appendix of this proposal. Space
requirements will be equal to the space requirements listed in the
Appendix of this proposal. Install adequate heating and air conditioning.

Personnel

All Dental Personnel and Consultants will conform to the Alabama
Dental Practice Law Act 100 and to the rules of the Alabama Board of
Dental Examiners. The DAB will appoint a Director of Dental Services
and delegate to the Director whatever authority and responsibility is
necessary to carry out a successful dental program. Only the DAB or
the Director of Dental Services may employ or relieve dental employees.
The DAB may not employ more than the number of employees listed in the
grant without written approval from the Project Director.

Dentists who are approved by the DAB or Director of Dental Services may participate in the dental program by rendering dental
services on an hourly basis. A minimum participation is two hours per
day and a maximum is eight hours per day. The recommended policy is
for the total participation not exceed eight hours per week, unless

approved by the Dental Director and DAB. A recommended minimum
consultation fee of $25 per hour is proposed and travel to and from
the site of consultation will be at the same rate as other travel
paid by the project.

Each dentist may utilize the auxiliaries employed by the dental
program, but may bring their own auxiliaries with the written approval
of the Director of Dental Services and the Project Director of the
West Alabama Health Services Project. The dentist will take full
responsibility for the safety and reimbursement of his auxiliaries.
Professional employees will be individually responsible for providing
their own Professional Liability Insurance to protect them while
working in this project. It is recommended that all regular employees
of the Dental Clinic work 40 hours per week. Holidays and vacation
time will be computed on the same basis as other employees of the
project. Additional hours or days of operation of the clinic and
compensation for same may be arranged with the approval of the Project
Director, the DAB, and the Director of Dental Services.

Clinical Services

Priorities for clinical dental services must be established
since the proposed clinical facility and staff cannot provide unlimited
dental services to all residents of Greene and Sumter Counties.

The priorities for dental treatment will be as follows, but may
be changed or further defined by unanimous approval of the DAB and the
Director of Dental Services. The Director of Dental Services, with
concurrence of the DAB, is responsible for determining each patient's
priority and sequence of treatment.

Priority I

Financially indigent children less than 21 years of age who would not otherwise receive care.

Priority II

a. Handicapped residents who are indigent and the medical-dental team have judged that dental treatment would significantly reduce the handicapping condition or improve the resident's chances for rehabilitation.

b. Indigent prenatal patients.

Priority III

Any indigent resident of Greene or Sumter County.

Patients in pain who are unable to receive treatment through private sources will be treated promptly with full consideration for conservation of oral structures.

The amount and type of dental services provided to any patient will depend on patient need and the ability of the dental staff to deliver the service.

No clinical services will be provided to any member of the clinical staff, employees of the West Alabama Health Services Project, its directors, or to the immediate families of such clinic staff members, employees or directors unless they qualify. If they qualify, no special treatment consideration will be given that is not given to any other patient.

Children, once admitted to the Dental Clinic for clinical services, should be scheduled to return weekly, or as often as practical, until all services are completed. Those completed should be recalled not less than once-a-year for periodic checkups and needed maintenance care. They may be recalled at any time up to a year.

Teeth should be extracted only after all other treatment methods have been attempted or considered.

No patient will be treated without a medical history.

Preventive Services OV-

All dental employees will be engaged to some extent in the delivery of preventive services, but the dental hygienist and dental assistant will be primarily engaged in this service. They will instruct patients individually and in groups, in proper oral care for prevention of dental disease. They may visit schools, churches, or other organizations to instruct in proper oral care. Dietary consultation with school officials shall be conducted. Day care centers, kindergartens, nurseries, schools, and new mothers shall receive information and instruction on preventing oral disease.

Clerical Services, Records, and Reports

Adequate clerical services will be provided by the West Alabama Health Services Project to the Dental Service. This will include secretarial services, typing, reception room activities, and record keeping. Individual patient dental records will be maintained as part of the medical record. Dental clinic employees will furnish patient treatment information to the clerical services and this information will be entered by the clerical services on the patient's record.

All patients or their parent or guardian will be required to sign an authorization for dental treatment.

Reports will be submitted to the Project Director and to the DAB on a regular basis. The frequency and content of these reports

will be jointly determined by the Project Director, DAB and Director
of Dental Services.

Referrals

Patients should be referred for dental care regardless of the
status of their oral health. Treatment will be provided as outlined
in this proposal. Preventive services should receive top priority
in the treatment plan.

Peer Review

The Dental Advisory Board will establish a peer review committee
for the Dental Program. The committee will be compensated in the
same manner as dentists.

Budget

The budget as set forth in this proposal allows for payment
of personnel and equipment as listed in Appendix I for the first
year of operation. These estimates are based on prices as of
January 1, 1974. Purchases after that date may be somewhat higher.
Supplies and equipment needed for the second thru fifth years will
be determined by the DAB and Director of Dental Services. Adequate
funds must be forthcoming to conitnue quality dental services.

Disposition of Equipment and Supplies

If, at any time after dental equipment and supplies are purchased for this project, the dental facilities are closed or ceases
to serve the residents of Greene and Sumter County as set forth in
this proposal, the DAB will dispose of the said dental equipment
and supplies through whatever process that will produce the best
price for the items. The net proceeds from the sale will be returned
to the proper government agency.

APPENDIX I

Personnel Salaries

Director	$25,000	-	$28,000	per yr.	Hire 1
Hygienist	6,000	-	8,000	per yr.	Hire 1
Dental Assistant	4,000	-	5,500	per yr.	Hire 2
	$39,000		$47,000		

Dental Supplies (ordered as required by the Director of Dental Service)

First year - up to $10,000

Dental Equipment (detailed list to be attached)

First year - up to $40,000

Space Requirements

	Size (minimum)
3 operating rooms	8' x 10' per room
1 x-ray room	8' x 10'
1 laboratory	8' x 10'
1 consultation--Dr.'s office	8' x 10'
1 preventive room	16' x 12'
1 storage and supply room	8' x 10'
1 dark room	6' x 4'
9 total rooms + toilet	

FEB 8 1974

West Alabama Health Service Project
P. O. Box 347
Eutaw, Alabama 35462
February 7, 1974

Dr. Herbert Hudgins
50 Seventh Street, N. E.
Atlanta, Georgia 30304

Dear Dr. Hudgins:

We are responding in part to the position taken by the Regional Grant Office
on the West Alabama Health Service Project for Greene and Sumter Counties.

Several meetings and telephone conversations have been held between representatives of the West Alabama Health Service Board and the Black Belt
Community Health Center Board.

The position of the Black Belt Community Health Center "Board" has not
changed. Its position contain the following:

1. That it will appoint a majority of the Board members.
2. That the Health Center will be stationed at the Federation which is
   located in Epes and under the direction of the Federation.
3. That the West Alabama Health Service Board be dissolved.
4. That the physcan recruited by the Federation of Southern Cooperatives
   will be hired as the resident physican.

The position of the West Alabama Health Service Board has been as follows:

Response to #1
    This Board has always offered positions on the Board to this group.
    However, the Articles of Incorporation will not allow any organization
    to gain control. Our position is that no group or organization
    should have such control if it is the "intent" of the group to provide
    services.

Reponse to #2
    Transportation was a serious problem prior to the enegy crisis and does
    not make sense to place a clinic in an isolated area some ten miles from
    the target populous.

Response to #3

Initial efforts were made to include all pertinent groups in Greene and Sumter Counties. Several meetings were held prior to the formulation of any specific plan so that all would have input. The Black Belt Community Center Board (Federation) was offered representation on the West Alabama Health Service Board, however, such offer was refused.

Response to #4

This Board does not object to hiring any qualified physican who agrees to work with the scope of the approved project and meets those conditions as prescribed. Again, all qualified applications will be considered.

Another meeting has been scheduled and you will be informed about the results as well as a full response to the position taken by the Regional Office on Grant approval.

Sincerely,

William M. Branch, Chairman
West Alabama Health Service Board

WMB/ldc

DEPARTMENT OF HEALTH, EDUCATION, AND WELFARE
REGION IV
50 7TH STREET N.E
ATLANTA, GEORGIA 30323

PUBLIC HEALTH SERVICE

February 19, 1974

Judge William M. Branch
President
West Alabama Comprehensive Health Planning Council
P.O. Box 1488
Tuscaloosa, Alabama 35401

Project # 04-H-000815-01-0

Dear Judge Branch:

In order to keep you informed and thus promote the full involvement
of your Board of Directors in the revision of your grant application,
I would like to share with you the reasons the review committee
recommended deferral of your grant application.

The application was found to have the following weaknesses and
omissions:

1. Lack of a financial plan in accordance with Grants
   Management requirements:

2. Total cost was in excess of grant funds available.

3. Excesses in budget for administrative cost, especially
   equipment:

4. Lack of plan for coordination and liaison with third
   party reimbursement agencies; and

5. Weak in operational detail, narrative needs to be
   expanded to provide more specifics on where, who, what
   and how.

Judge William M. Branch, February 19, 1974   Page 2

These points have previously been discussed in detail with
your planning staff. Subsequently, we have received a preliminary
proposal you requested from the Sixth District Dental Society
for a Dental Program.

It will be excellent to develop a dental program with the close
cooperation and participation of the Dental Society. However,
any such cooperative Agreements must be consistent with our
regulations which require maintaining administration and control
directly under the Project Director and your board, plus
consistent with your by-laws and policies.

We are interested to see the future developments of this dental
program.agreement and anticipate the resubmission of your
application in the near future.

                              Sincerely yours,

                              Herbert A. Hudgins, M.D.
                              Acting Chief, Division of Health Services

By: Pete Yarnell
     Project Officer

FEB 26 1974

West Alabama Health Service Board
Post Office Box 347
Eutaw, Alabama 35462
February 22, 1974

Dr. Herbert Hudgins
50 Seventh Street, N. E.
Atlanta, Georgia 30304

Dear Dr. Hudgins:

Reference is made to our letter to you of February 7 and
several phone conversations with members of your staff relative
to the Ambulatory Health Care proposal for Greene and Sumter
Counties.

It is our sincere effort to clear up this entire matter so that
this much needed project can be funded

Enclosed please find a copy of the minutes of the last conference
with the Black Belt Community Health Center Board and our supplemental response to the conditions proposed by your staff in a
January 21, 1974 conference.

Accept our sincere thanks for your very kind consideration.

Sincerely Yours,

William M. Branch

William M. Branch, Chairman
West Alabama Health Service Board

WMB/enb

POSITION OF THE REGIONAL OFFICE ON GRANT APPROVAL FOR SUMTER
AND GREENE COUNTIES, ALABAMA

(January 21, 1974 Confernece)

1. There can be only one grant award for community health
   services made to one project administered by one Board
   of the target counties.

   | RESPONSE: West Alabama Health Service Board Concur.

2. Composition is that Board of Directors must be representative of all pertinent components and groups in the target
   counties.

   RESPONSE: The present board could be tentative until such time
             as the consumer group participants are actual users
             of the services provided by the project. However,
             the present board does have representation from
             all pertinent components and groups within the
             target counties desiring to have representation.

3. Membership of the Board should have a majority consumer
   representation and a racial ratio similar to that of the
   total population in the target counties.

   RESPONSE: Serious consideration must be given to expanding
             board membership from eleven to thirteen with the
             added members being consumers and of the majority
             racial groups.

4. The Board of Directors must be prepared to assume administrative independence from the West Alabama Comprehensive Health
   Council and the Black Belt Federation as soon as possible.

   RESPONSE: The West Alabama Health Service Board chairman
             has assumed the administrative responsibility of
             the project.

5. Association with these two above named groups, and other
   groups in the target counties and the State, must be on a
   technical assistance basis by request of the board.

   RESPONSE: Contracts for technical assistance are being
             formulated for your approval prior to the
             final approval of the Board.

A

6. *The Regional Office recognizes:*

The West Alabama Health Service Board as a viable grant applicant whose application has been deferred until organizational conditions (Nos. 2, 3 and 4 above) plus modifications in objectives, budget, etc., can be resolved.

RESPONSE: *Conditions 2, 3 and 4 are enclosed herein. Modifications in objectives, budget, etc. should be completed by March 4, 1974.*

7. *|The Regional Office recognizes:*

The Black Belt Community Health Center Board as an applicant whose grant has been denied. This is based on incomplete community and existing organized health services representation, plus the other criteria as stated in the Regional Health Administrator's letter dated December 11, 1973.

RESPONSE: N/A

RECOMMENDATION (MADE BY REGIONAL STAFF):

That a small representative committee from each of the above Boards (3-4each) meet to determine how a single board can be composed that will represent the Health Service Consumers and providers (not represent existing political entities).

RESPONSE: *Minutes of the February 12, 1974 meeting.*

6:30 P M
PLACE: *York, Alabama*

This is a meeting which had been agreed upon by members of the Black Belt Community Health Center Board and the West Alabama Health Service Board.

Black Belt Community Health Center Board member present:

Mr. Eddie Ayers, Chairman
Mr. Lucius Black, Member
Mr. William May, Member
Mr. Elma Howkins, Secretary

ℬ

West Alabama Health Service Board members present:

Judge William M. Branch, Chairman
Mr. Willie Hill, Member
Mr. Allen Turner, Member
Mr. John Modley, Jr., Member

Judge Branch serve as chairman of the conference. He made it clear that the representative of the West Alabama Health Service Board could not make a decision on any proposal presented but would discuss the matter in question and make a full report to his Board and the Regional office of H E W.

The Representatives of the Black Belt Community Health Center Board again made their demands as follow:

1. That they would name eight consumer to the Board governing the project.

2. That the West Alabama Health Service Board be dissolved.

3. That the physician recruit by the Federation of Southern Cooperative will be hired as the resident physician for this project.

4. That the project director used by the Federation last year by named project director of this project.

5. That they were first to get a health care program and should be allowed control of the project.

6. That they did not wish to have representation on the project Board unless they are allowed to appoint a "Controlling" majority.

After considerable discussion of the demands, the meeting was adjourned.

William M. Branch
Judge Branch

March 4, 1974

Judge Willie . . Branch, Chairman
West Alabama . . alth Services Board
P.O. Box 347
Eutaw, Alaba . . 35462

Dear Judge Branch:

Thank you for your February 22, 1974 letter, your response to our
enumerated p . . tion on a grant for Greene and Sumpter Counties, . . .
the minutes of your February 12 meeting with representatives of the
Black Belt C. . unity Health Services Board.

It is recom . . . d that you proceed with the present board
composition . . resubmit your project proposal as soon as
feasible with . he programmatic and budget modifications
previously s . . cted in my February 19, letter.

I anticipate receiving your proposal in the near future and assure
you it will . . live our immediate attention.

Sincerely yours,

/S/

Herbert A. Hudgins, M.D.
Acting Chief, Division of Health
Services

By: Pete Ye . . 11
Project . . ficer

cc: Dr. Clei . o . .
OG M
Pete

PY:lk 3/5/74

West Alabama Comprehensive
Health Planning Council

TO: Dr. Cleino   April 17, 1974

FROM: Greg de Lissovoy

SUBJECT: Conversation with Pete Yarnell, Region IV HEW

Pete called to say that HEW/Atlanta has just received a
petition stating:'

> "We demand that the Department of Health, Education and
> Welfare withold Federal money from the West Alabama
> Health Services project because all community groups were
> not included in planning."

A cover letter was addressed to Dr. Patauldin and Dr. Hudgins
and signed by Mrs. Rosie L. Carpenter.

Persons signing the petition were:

Peter J. Kirksey	Robert Hines
Dorsey Chambers	John Head
Ezekiel Harrison	Dr. Robert Brown
Reverend Palmer	Russell Carpenter
Dora Rumley	Oscar Williams
Herbert Sapp	Jaanita Pellington
Robert Young	Booker Forte
Sarah Eatman	Joseph Wilson
J.J. Purter	Spiver Gordon
Leona Morrow	Eunice Outland
Rev. Harold Milton	Rev. W.D. Lewis
William Underwood, II	Louis Barnett
Harry Means	Vassie Knott
Martin Goodson	Wadine Williams
Robert Cook	

Most of these people are closely associated with the county
school system as members of the Board of Education, the central
office staff, principles, etc. Two county commissioners are listed
as is the county coroner, tax collecter, clerk of court, and various
program coordinators.

I have discussed this with Andrew Dearman and Judge Branch at a
meeting in Walter Flower's office at 11:30 this morning. HEW
suggests that the news releases concerning grant award stress
early action in Sumter County (i.e. Federation territory).

This petition does not affect the status of the project since
the Notice of Grant Award has now been signed.

western union **Mailgram** U.S. MAIL

```
          
L-0013J&LIUS  04/15/74
ICC IFDSPG7 CSP
  C      196  WUH TDRM LIVINGSTON AL 166  04-15  0151/  EST
ZIP  35462
```

WILLIAM H BRANCH
PRESIDENT BOARD OF DIRECTORS WEST ALABAMA HEALTH PROJECT OFFICE
OF PRODATE JUDGE
EUTAW AL 35460

COPIES OF THIS MESSAGE SENT TO THE FOLLOWING CALDER WEL BRANCH
SECRETARY DEPT HEALTH EDUCATION AND WELFARE DOCTOR ALBERT J
HODGINS DHEW REGION 4   HAROLD RUSSELLDIRECTOR HEALTH SERVICES
ADMINISTRATION HOWARD MOORE ATTORNEY DHCHC
  DEAR SIR STOP FUNDING OR TRANSIT OF FUNDS TO THE WEST ALABAMA
HEALTH PROJECT PURSUANT TO DIRECTION OF NEW REGION 4 ON JANUARY
21 1974. THE WEST ALABAMA HEALTH PROJECT HAS FAILED TO WORK
IN GOOD FAITH WITH THE BLACK BELT COMMUNITY HEALTH CENTER TO
REACH A COMPROMISE ON BOARD COMPOSITION, FUNDS, PROGRAMS AND
 OPERATIONS OF A RURAL HEALTH CENTER IN WEST ALABAMA.
 TO FUND THE WEST ALABAMA HEALTH PROJECT AND NOT THE BLACK BELT
COMMUNITY HEALTH CENTER WOULD BE DISCRIMINATORY, ARBITRARY,
UNREASONABLE AND ABSOLUTELY NOT IN GOOD FAITH
THE BLACK BELT COMMUNITY HEALTH CENTER IS READY , WILLING AND
ABLE TO MEET UNDER THE AGENCY OF DHEW, TO RESOLVE DIFFERENCES
DHEW WEST ALABAMA HEALTH PROJECT AND BLACK BELT COMMUNITY HEALTH
CENTER
PLEASE NOTIFY US BY RETURN WIRE OF YOUR RESPONSE TO THIS TELEGRAM
 EDDIE W AYERS PRESIDENT BOARD OF DIRECTORS BLACK BELT COMMUNITY
HEALTH CENTER

0144 EDT

COMBHMC BHM

● Thursday, April 18, 1974 THE TUSCALOOSA NEWS

Funds delayed for area project

By ANNE PLOTT
News Staff Writer

Seventh District U S Rep. Walter Flowers predicted some "good news" on funding for an ambulatory health care project for Greene and Sumter counties Wednesday at a meeting of the West Alabama Comprehensive Health Planning Council

It had been anticipated that Flowers might announce that the $264,000 in Health Education and Welfare money requested for the project had been authorized.

But apparently the funding has been delayed

"I'm proud to announce that there has been a whole lot of progress on this," Flowers did tell members of the health planning agency.

'I'm very confident some good news will be coming in the very near future," the congressman said

Probate Judge William Branch of Greene County is chairman of the West Alabama Health Services, Inc. a non-profit corporation created to administer the hoped-for program

During the first year, the funds would be used to create a community health center in Greene County where residents could secure medical and dental services either free or for fees based on their ability to pay, Judge Branch said

"The project will be a landmark in the history of medical science," he said. "It will help people who are otherwise unable to get medical care "

During the second year, another center would be opened in Sumter County, Flowers said.

Judge Branch said that the plans for the program call for just over $1 million spread over a five year period.

Flowers, who was trailed by a camera crew from a national television network all day Wednesday, did not discuss his role as a member of the House Judiciary Committee.

That house body is to consider evidence in connection with a possible recommendation that President Nixon be impeached.

Instead, Flowers outlined the various pieces of health legislation now pending in Congress He outlined the different and competing versions of national health insurance now under consideration.

"There is a complicated and comprehensive battle brewing in the Congress over national health insurance," Flowers said "Most of us, I know I am, are interested in getting some type of national health insurance going."

But what form the final bill takes, if and when it passes, is still up in the air.

According to Dr. Charles Konigsberg, district health officer, his "good news" has already come. Konigsberg informed the council as a whole that Gov. George C Wallace has released $100,000 in revenue sharing funds requested to fund the West Alabama District Health Department

The money will enable the new regional department to add needed personnel too Dr Konigsberg said

"There's a lot more to a district health department than having a district health officer," he said

A lack of funding had so far prevented beefing up the staff to the point where the regional concept could be implemented fully.

Californian gives Nixon $10,000

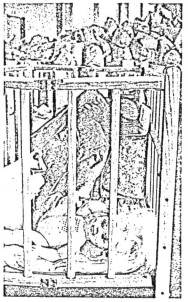

Bound for flooded area

Bedding, clothes and toys collected by the Tuscaloosa Salvation Army Corps was sorted by Civil Defense volunteers and loaded this morning onto a huge truck for transfer to the Hattiesburg, Miss., area, where it will be distributed among persons affected by extensive flooding. The goods, which had been stored at Fort Brandon Armory after being originally collected for victims of tornadoes in north Alabama, were transported on a truck provided by Bama Feed Center.

Tracks here checked out

A professional appraiser was in Tuscaloosa today to make a survey of the value of the tracks located in 25th Avenue for the state Highway Department

The tracks, a spur line from the Illinois Central-Gulf line, are located in the middle of the street which is a main approach to the Hugh Thomas Bridge.

Bobby Joe Kemp, division highway engineer, said the new appraisal was required by the

removing the rail line.

Kemp said an agreement had been reached on the track between the state Highway Department and the railroad, but a new appraisal was requested by the Atlanta office of the federal road agency.

Following completion of the agreement by the Highway Department for purchase of the tracks, 45 days would be

DEPARTMENT OF HEALTH, EDUCATION, AND WELFARE

APR 2 2 1974

Office of Management Support
Room 849

Mr. William M. Branch, President
West Alabama Health Services, Inc.
Box 347
Eutaw, AL 35462

Reference: Health Services Development Grant No. 04-H-000815-01-0

Dear Mr. Branch:

The attached Notice of Award approves your application for the
"Neighborhood Health Center" and provides financial assistance of
$251,243 for the first year budget 7/1/74 through 6/30/75.

Your financial officer is being advised of this action and provided
the appropriate forms for submission of the expenditure report. Funds
are to be requested on a monthly cash request basis from the National
Institutes of Health Payment Center. Your Public Health Service
Account Number is 41D835 for requesting payments. Correspondence
and documents to the Regional Office should always reference the
subject project number.

Also enclosed is an application to be used in requesting future support.
The continuation application should be submitted to the Regional Office
prior to 4/1/75.

If we may assist you in any way, please do not hesitate to call.

Sincerely yours,

G. A. Reich, M. D., M. P. H.
Regional Health Administrator

Enclosures

cc: Financial Officer (Ltr, Award)
Hq CHS (Ltr, Award)
Reg. IV CHS (Award, Ltr, A. L., Summary)
State Health Planning (Award)
GDS (Award)
Orgn (Award)
RFMO - Records (Award, 2 A. L.)
        Payment Station (Award, 2 A. L.)

EVon Glahn:vr 4/18/74

DEPARTMENT OF
HEALTH, EDUCATION, AND WELFARE
PUBLIC HEALTH SERVICE

NOTICE OF GRANT AWARD
REGION IV, 50 7th St., NE
ATLANTA, GA. 30323
Under Authority of Federal Statutes and Regulations, and
Policy Standards Applicable to the Following Grant Program.

HEALTH SERVICES DEVELOPMENT

8 TITLE OF PROJECT (OR PROGRAM) (Limit to 56 spaces)

Neighborhood Health Center

9 GRANTEE (Name and Address)
a NAME West Alabama Health Services, Inc.

b NAME
c STREET Post Office Box 347
d CITY Eutaw
e STATE Alabama
f ZIP CODE 35462   g FOREIGN COUNTRY

11 APPROVED BUDGET FOR PHS FUNDS

BUDGET CATEGORIES For items identified by Asterisk*, see remarks	FINANCIAL ASSISTANCE A	DIRECT ASSISTANCE B
a PERSONAL SERVICES	$ 133,855	$ -0-
b PATIENT CARE	25,543	
c EQUIPMENT	38,455	
d CONSTRUCTION		
OTHER Lease	15,000	
specify Supplies	1,000	
Travel	2,250	
Data Processing	5,000	
Equip. Main. & Rental	6,350	
Auditing & Legal Fees	1,300	
ALL OTHER *	22,490	
f TRAINEE COSTS		
TOTAL APPROVED BUDGET	g. $ 251,243	h. $ -0-

REMARKS

Utilities, Insurance, Communications $ 5,300
T.A. & Related Contracts   17,190

See page 2 for Special Conditions.
Report of Expenditures to be submitted on or
before October 1, 1975.

FINANCIAL MANAGEMENT OFFICIAL (Title & Address)

Treasurer (Zora C. Gibbs)
Post Office Box 141
Livingston, Alabama 35470

1. DATE ISSUED Mo./Day/Yr.	4/24/74	2. CATALOG OF FED. DOM ASSIST. NO.	13.224

3. SUPERSEDES AWARD NOTICE dated N/A
except that any conditions or restrictions previously imposed remain in
effect unless specifically rescinded.

4. PROJECT IDENTIFICATION NO.	5. ADMINISTRATIVE CODE
04-H-000815-01-0 Formerly:	CS-H27

6. PROJECT PERIOD Mo./Day/Yr.		Mo./Day/Yr.
From 7/1/74	Through	6/30/75

7. BUDGET PERIOD Mo./Day/Yr.		Mo./Day/Yr.
From 7/1/74	Through	6/30/75

10. DIRECTOR OF PROJECT (PROGRAM OR CENTER DIRECTOR,
COORDINATOR OR PRINCIPAL INVESTIGATOR

NAME Branch   William   M.
        LAST   FIRST   INITIAL

ADDRESS: Same as item 9.   (President)

12 SOURCE OF FINANCIAL ASSISTANCE

a APPROVED BUDGET (11 g Col A)		$ 251,243
b. INDIRECT COSTS N/A		
(RATE ___ %)		$ -0-
Base: S&W — TADC of $_____)		
c TOTAL		$ 251,243
d LESS UNOBLIGATED BALANCE FROM PRIOR BUDGET PERIOD(S)		$ -0-
e. LESS CUMULATIVE PRIOR AWARD(S) THIS BUDGET PERIOD		$ -0-
f. AMOUNT OF THIS ACTION		$ 251,243

13. REQUIRED GRANTEE PARTICIPATION

☐ INSTITUTIONAL COST SHARING AGREEMENT
   EFFECTIVE DATE _____

☐ INDIVIDUAL GRANT AGREEMENT _____ %
☐ MATCHING AGREEMENT _____ %
☒ OTHER $ 13,687   ☐ NONE REQUIRED

15. RECOMMENDED FUTURE SUPPORT (Subject to availability of funds)

	BUDGET YEAR	FISCAL YEAR	TOTAL DIRECT COSTS	BUDGET PERIOD
a.				
b.				
c.				

16. ACCOUNTABILITY FOR EQUIPMENT

☐ CONDITIONALLY WAIVED ☒ NOT WAIVED ☐ NOT APPLICABLE

18. AGENCY OFFICIAL (Signature, Name and Title)

G. A. Reich, M.D., M.P.H.
Regional Health Administrator

a. PHS LIST NO.	b. PAYMENT SYSTEM	c. ENTITY CODE	VENDOR CODE	d. ORGANIZATION DESCRIPTORS
F NIH-346-74	☒ NIH ☐ R.O. ☐ OTHER	1-63-0662922-A1	41E836	39-240

	APPROPRIATION	CAN #	OBJECT CLASS	TRANSACTION NO.	FY	SECONDARY ADM. CODE	AMT. ACTION FIN. ASST.	AMT. ACTION DIR. ASST.
20.	a. 7540350	b. 3048050	c. 41.51	d. 01-0-M5299	e. 4	f. N/A	g. N/A	h. N/A
21.	a.	b.	c.	d.	e.	f.	g.	h.
22.	a.	b.	c.	d.	e.	f.	g.	h.

Conditions of Grant Award

SOUTHWEST ALABAMA HEALTH SERVICES, INC., EUTAW, ALABAMA
PROJECT NO 04-H-000815-01-0

1. No funds are to be expended for building lease until documentation
   is submitted for approval by the Regional Office identifying specific
   site, appraisals from at least two realtors on cost per square
   foot, as well as renovation and/or construction involvement by
   the county commission.

2. All contracts to be entered into by Grantee must have prior
   approval of the Regional Office.

3. Before a full time Project Director can be employed a biographical
   sketch on the prospect will be submitted to the Regional
   Office for concurrence.

4. Prior to finalizing any equipment lease-purchase agreement,
   the agreement and a justification substantiating it as "more
   advantageous to the government" will be submitted to the
   Regional Office for Review.

5. Before dispensing any pharmaceuticals, submit a plan for in-house
   pharmacy services which involves participation by a registered
   pharmacist who will provide properly labelled, prepackaged
   units in commonly used amounts to insure control and ease of
   dispensing by designated, qualified health center staff.

Within sixty(60) days of the Grant Award the grantee will submit to
the Regional Office:

6. A complete description of the existing transportation system including
   total budget, utilization by classification of passengers, scheduling,
   area served and administration of system. Describe integration
   of Health Center Transportation services into the existing system
   to include training of outreach workers for Health Services,
   anticipated patient utilization and method employed to determine
   Health Center Cost participation.

7. Job descriptions for all budgeted positions not previously
   submitted.

817

Conditions of Grant Award (continued)
SOUTHWEST ALABAMA HEALTH SERVICES, INC.,EUTAW, ALABAMA
PROJECT NO 04-H-000815-01-0

8. Document the person or position immediately responsible for "thorough analysis of health needs and resources of Sumter County".

9. Develope a clinic schedule with explanation of allowable adjustments for evening hours and arrangements for coverage of emergencies, after hours, and weekends.

Within 90 days of the Grant Award the Grantee will submit for Regional Office Concurrence:

10. A personnel and procurement policy manual.

11. Policies, developed within the framework of the by-laws, delineating responsibilities of the Board of Directors from responsibilities of the Project Director for administration and management of the Health Center.

MAY 24 1974

THOMAS H. HOOKS D D S, PRES.
115 FOREST ROAD
HUEYTOWN ALA 35020

JOHN D. DAVIS, D M D., VICE PRES.
209 W. TROY
DOTHAN, ALA. 36301

EUGENE J. CHENAULT D D S
1115 SOMERVILLE RD, SE
DECATUR, ALA 35601

EDWARD M. LINDSEY D D I
313 SOUTH 5TH STREET
GADSDEN, ALA 35901

BOARD OF DENTAL EXAMINERS OF ALABAMA

LEONARD MICHELSON D D S, SEC Y-TREAS.
240 SOUTH RIPLEY STREET
MONTGOMERY ALA 36104

May 24, 1974

Judge William M. Branch, Board of Directors, West Ala. Health Project
P. O. Box 347
Eutaw, Alabama 35462

Dear Judge Branch:

The Board of Dental Examiners of Alabama has been approached by the President of
the Sixth District Dental Society concerning the dental aspect of the development
of a health services project, West Alabama Health Services Project, Inc., in
Sumter and Greene Counties.

Two basic questions were posed to the Board by Dr. W. C. Cole, President of the
Dental Society, in a letter of February 13, 1974. They were:

1. Will the West Alabama Health Service Project, a corporation, be
in violation of Act 100, Alabama Dental Practice Act, Sec. 13 -
Proprietor Defined - by employing an Alabama Licensed Dentist to
provide dental services as outlined in the Sixth District proposal?

2. Can the Sixth District Dental Society ethically and legally
participate in this project as set forth in the Grant application
and as outlined in our proposed dental program?

Section 13 of the Alabama Dental Practice Act provides as follows:

Section 13. Proprietor defined; revocation of license, when - The term
"proprietor" as used in this act shall not in any way pertain to state
institutions and shall be deemed to include any person who employs one
or more dentists and dental hygienists in the operation of a dental
office; or places in possession of a dentist, dental hygienist, may
be necessary for the management of a dental office on the basis of a
lease or any other agreement for compensation for the use of such
material, equipment or offices; or retains the ownership or control
of dental equipment, material, or office and makes the same available in any manner for the use by a dentist, dental hygienist, or
other agent; provided, however, that nothing in this act shall
apply to bona fide sales of dental equipment or material secured
by a chattel mortgage or retention title agreement, and, provided
further, that this section shall not prohibit or restrict persons,
firms, corporations from employing or retaining licensed dentists

THOMAS H. HOORJ D.D.S., PRES.
118 FOREST ROAD
HUEYTOWN, ALA 35020

JOHN D. DAVIS, D.M.D., VICE PRES
209 W. TROY
DOTHAN, ALA. 36301

EUGENE J. CHENAULT, D.D.S
1118 SOMERVILLE RD., SE
DECATUR ALA 35601

EDWARD H. LINDSEY D.D.S.,
313 SOUTH 5TH STREET
GADSDEN, ALA. 35901

BOARD OF DENTAL EXAMINERS OF ALABAMA

LEONARD MICHELSON, D.D.S., SEC'Y-TREAS.
240 SOUTH RIPLEY STREET
MONTGOMERY, ALA. 36104

Page Two letter to Judge Branch

to furnish dental treatment for their employees or dependents of
their employees. A licensed dentist or dental hygienist who enters
into any of the above described arrangements with an unlicensed
proprietor may have his license and license certificate suspended
or revoked by the Board.

The Board suggests that it might be appropriate if you and your principles could
meet with us sometimes during the month of July to analyze and try to find an
amicable solution to the situation which we are all confronted with. A week-end
meeting would be best for our group since we each maintain private practices and
are from different cities around the state. Since my office is in Montgomery, the
Board finds it convenient to function in the Capital City; however, we can meet at
your convenience.

We are looking forward to a meeting with you and a resolution to this question, and
we will anticipate a reply from you.

Sincerely,

Leonard Michelson, D.D.S.

LM:nhm

cc: All Board Members
     Mr. Maury Smith
     Mr. Marty Van Tassel
     Dr. William Cole
     Dr. Vance R. Kane
     Dr. Elizabeth Cleino

comma and the word "in" following the word 'engineer," deleted the
former second proviso relative to

contractors previously licensed, and
added the last two exemptions.

§ 79. Copy of law to be included in plans of architects and engineers.—All architects and engineers preparing plans and specifications
for work to be contracted in the state of Alabama shall include in their in-
vitations to bidders and their specifications a copy of this chapter or such
portions thereof as are deemed necessary to convey to the invited bidder
whether he be a resident or non-resident of this state and whether a license has been issued to him or not the information that it will be necessary for him to show evidence of license before his bid is considered. (1935,
p. 721; 1959, p. 1429, appvd. Nov. 19, 1959.)

Note. — The 1959 amendment deleted
the former second sentence relative to
the monthly report of the secretary
of the board.

§ 80. Regulations as to issue of building permits.—Any person,
firm or corporation, upon making application to the building inspector or
such other authority of any incorporated city, town or village in Alabama
charged with ~~the duty of issuing~~ building or other permits for the construction of a   , grading or any improvement or
structure whe   twenty thousand ($20,000.) dol-
lars, or more   l to the issuance of such permits,
furnish satisf   :tor or authority that he is duly
licensed unde   and it shall be unlawful for such
building insp   ssue or allow the issuance of such
building pern   licant has furnished evidence that
he is either e   of this chapter or is duly licensed
under this ch   intend the work for which permit
has been app   :ctor, or other such authority, violating the ter   guilty of a misdemeanor and subject to a fine   '.00) dollars. (1935, p. 721; 1947,
p. 293, appvi   429, appvd. Nov. 19, 1959.)

Note.   section related to the limitations upon
   The 1959   awarding authorities and their con-
   section. Prii   formity with this section.

§ 81. Ir   -In all prosecutions for the violation of the f   his title, for engaging in the business of gene   ertificate of authority, it shall be
sufficient to   ffidavit or complaint that "A. B.
unlawfully e   ieral contractor, without authority
from the lic   i so to do." (1935, p. 721; 1959,
p. 1429, app

Note.—The 1
   this section

CODE OF ALABAMA (Recompiled 1971)
See 120(13) and 120(14)

§ 82. Appeal.—Any party aggrieved by any decision of the state licensing board, either in denying an application for license as a general contractor or in revoking a license, may appeal to the circuit court of Montgomery county, in equity, by filing a bond with the clerk of said court,
conditioned to pay all costs of the appeal. Upon notice of said appeal
being served upon the licensing board, an issue shall be made up by the court
between the appellant and the licensing board, in which appellant shall al-

ʰɢe in what respect the action of the licensing board was erroneous and prejudicial to him; whereupon the court shall hear the evidence and without regard to the decision of the licensing board, shall render such decision as the court is of the opinion the licensing board should have rendered in the first instance. (1935, p. 721, 1959, p. 1429, appvd. Nov. 19, 1959.)

Note.—The 1959 amendment re-enacted this section without change.

CHAPTER 5.

DENTISTS AND DENTAL HYGIENISTS.

a state or the District of Columbia of the United States and furnishes such other evidence as to his qualifications and lawful practice as the board may deem necessary. No license shall be issued under this section unless the state from which the applicant comes (or the District of Columbia) shall accord equal rights to licensed dentists of this state. The fee for issuing such reciprocal license shall be not less than fifty dollars ($50.00) nor more than one hundred dollars ($100.00), to be determined by the board. (1959, p. 576, § 14, appvd June 24, 1959.)

§ 120(15). Examination of applicants; issuance of licenses. —When application and accompanying proof as are required herein are found satisfactory, the board shall notify the applicant to appear before it for examination at a time and place to be fixed by the board and each applicant shall be examined and graded by number in lieu of name. All examinations provided for in this chapter shall be conducted by the board and shall be of such type and character as to test the qualifications of the applicant to practice dentistry. In conducting examinations, each member of the board shall submit his questions to the other board members and the entire board shall decide whether or not each proposed question is fair and practical. It is provided, however, that the board may recognize any written parts of an examination given by the national board of dental examiners in lieu of such examinations or subject to such examinations as the board may require. All examination papers, including questions and answers, with a separate list of those taking each examination and the numbers under which the examination was taken shall be filed by the secretary-treasurer of the board with the Alabama state department of archives and history within thirty (30) days after the examination has been completed, to be kept for a period of not less than three (3) years. Those found qualified by the board shall be granted a license and a license certificate which shall bear a serial number, the full name of the licensee, the date of issuance, and the seal of the board, and shall be signed by each member of the board. (1959, p. 577, § 15, appvd. June 24, 1959.)

§ 120(16). Recording of license certificate. — Every person granted a license to practice dentistry or dental hygiene in this state by the board of dental examiners of Alabama, as herein provided, shall cause his license certificate to be recorded in the office of the judge of probate of the county in which he desires to practice before beginning the practice of dentistry or dental hygiene in said county. Any person receiving a license from the board, whether or not intending to immediately engage in the practice of dentistry or dental hygiene in this state, shall cause his license certificate to be recorded in the office of the judge of probate in one of the counties of this state within sixty (60) days of the issuance of the license certificate. (1959, p. 577, § 16, appvd. June 24, 1959.)

§ 120(17). License and registration certificates to be kept in office of practitioner. —Every practitioner of dentistry and dental hygiene within the meaning of this chapter shall have in his possession a license certificate and an annual registration certificate in the office wherein he practices. (1959, p. 578, § 17, appvd. June 24, 1959.)

§ 120(18). Change of address. —Every licensed dentist and dental hygienist upon changing his place of practice, whether from one building, city, street address, or county, to another, shall within thirty (30) days thereafter furnish the secretary-treasurer of the board with the new address. The secretary-treasurer shall acknowledge receipt of change of address within thirty (30) days. (1959, p. 578, § 18, appvd. June 24, 1959.)

§ 120(19). **Annual registration; suspension of license for failure to renew registration; waiver of fees.**—No person shall practice dentistry in the state of Alabama unless licensed by the board and registered annually as required by this chapter. The secretary-treasurer of the board shall mail to each such licensee an initial registration form which shall contain space for the insertion of his name, address, date and number of his license certificate, and such other information as the board shall deem necessary. The licensee shall sign and verify the accuracy of his registration before a notary public after which he shall forward said registration to the secretary-treasurer of the board together with a fee established by the board not to exceed ten dollars ($10.00). Each subsequent registration shall be made upon the form as above prescribed except that it need not be verified. On or before the first day of October of each year, every dentist licensed to practice dentistry in the state shall transmit to the secretary-treasurer of the board the completed form prescribed by the board, together with a fee established by the board not to exceed ten dollars ($10.00), and receive therefor the current annual registration certificate authorizing him to continue the practice of dentistry in the state for a period of one year. Any license and license certificate previously granted under the authority of this or any prior dental practice act shall automatically be suspended if the holder thereof fails to secure the annual registration certificate herein provided for before the first day of January each year. Any dentist whose license shall be automatically suspended by reason of failure, neglect, or refusal to secure the annual registration certificate shall be reinstated by the board upon payment of the penalty fee of twenty-five dollars ($25.00) plus all accrued annual registration fees up to a maximum of five (5) years, accompanied with the prescribed form for annual registration of such license. Upon failure of any licensee to file application for the annual registration certificate and pay the annual registration fee on or before the 30th day of November each year, the board shall notify such licensee by certified mail addressed to his last address of record that such application and fee have not been received and that unless such application and fee are received on or before the first day of January his license and license certificate shall be automatically suspended. The board shall notify such licensee by certified mail addressed to his last address of record the effective date of his automatic suspension and the provisions for registration of such license. The board shall waive the annual payment of fees herein provided for and issue a current annual registration certificate to any licensee who, because of age or physical disability, has retired from the practice of dentistry or who is suffering a malady of a lingering or permanent nature. The board by rule shall waive annual registration and the payment of fees while any licensee is on temporary active duty with any of the armed forces of the United States. The waiver of fees herein provided shall be effective so long as said retirement because of age or physical disability or temporary active duty continues. (1959, p. 578, § 19, appvd. June 24, 1959; 1965, 3rd Ex. Sess., p. 232, appvd. Oct. 29, 1965.)

Note.—The 1965 amendment substituted "a fee established by the board not to exceed ten dollars ($10.00)" for "a fee of four dollars ($4.00)" at the end

1. To the practice of his profession by a physician or surgeon holding a certificate or qualification as a medical doctor and licensed as such under the laws of this state, provided he shall not practice dentistry as a specialty.

2. The practice of dentistry in the discharge of their official duties by graduate dentists or dental surgeons in the United States army, navy, air force, or other armed services, public health service, coast guard, or veterans' administration; or

3. The practice of dentistry by a licensed dentist of other states or countries at meetings of the Alabama dental association or components thereof, or other like dental organizations approved by the board, while appearing as clinicians, or when appearing in emergency cases upon the specific call of dentists duly licensed under the provisions of this chapter; or

4. To the filling of prescriptions of a licensed and registered dentist, as hereinafter provided, by any person or persons, association, corporation, or other entity, for the construction, reproduction, or repair of prosthetic dentures, bridges, plates, or appliances on a model made by or from impressions taken by a licensed and currently registered dentist, to be used or worn as a substitute for natural teeth, provided that such person or persons, association, corporation, or other entity, shall not solicit or advertise, directly or indirectly by mail, card, newspaper, pamphlet, radio, television, or otherwise, to the general public to construct, reproduce, or repair prosthetic dentures, bridges, plates, or other appliances to be used or worn as substitutes for natural teeth; or

5. To the use of roentgen machines or other rays for making radiograms or similar records, of dental or oral tissues under the supervision of a licensed dentist or physician; provided, however, that such services shall not be advertised by any name whatever as an aid or inducement to secure dental patronage, and no person shall advertise that he has, leases, owns or operates a roentgen machine for the purpose of making dental radiograms of the human teeth or tissues or the oral cavity, or administering treatments thereto for any disease thereof.

6. To the giving of a general anesthetic by a nurse anesthetist who administers a general anesthetic under the direct supervision of a duly licensed dentist to a patient who is undergoing dental treatment rendered by said dentist.

7. To the use of a nurse in the practice of professional or practical nursing as defined in Act #867, regular session 1965 [sections 189(33) to 189-(47) of this title], by a dentist. (1959, p. 574, § 1, appvd. June 24, 1959; 1967, p. 1564, appvd. Sept. 8, 1967.)

Note. — The 1967 amendment added paragraphs 6 and 7.

§ 120(12). Teaching permits. — The board shall issue teaching permits to persons who hold a dental degree where such persons are not licensed and registered to practice dentistry or dental hygiene in this state. The dean of a dental college located in this state shall be required to annually certify to the board the members of the school's clinical faculty who are not licensed and registered to practice dentistry or dental hygiene in the state and shall be required to promptly notify the board of any change in personnel on the clinical faculty. The board shall be required to issue teaching permits to applicants upon the certification of the dean of a dental college located in this state setting forth that such applicant is a bona fide member of the clinical faculty of such college. Such teaching permit shall be valid so long as the holder thereof remains a member of the clinical faculty of such dental college. The holder of a teaching permit shall be subject to all provisions of this chapter regulating the practice of dentistry and dental hygiene in this state and shall be entitled to perform all clinical operations which a person licensed to practice dentistry or dental hygiene in this state would be entitled to perform but only within the facilities of the dental college and as an adjunct to his teaching functions in such college. A fee of five dollars ($5.00) shall be paid to the board on the issuance of a teaching permit. (1959, p. 575, § 12, appvd. June 24, 1959.)

§ 120(13). "Proprietor" defined; arrangements with unlicensed proprietor grounds for suspension or revocation of license. —The term "proprietor" as used in this chapter shall not in any way pertain to state institutions and shall be deemed to include any person who employs one or more dentists and dental hygienists in the operation of a dental office; or places in possession of a dentist, dental hygienist, or other agent, such dental material equipment as may be necessary for the management of a dental office on the basis of a lease or any other agreement for compensation for the use of such material, equipment or offices; or retains the ownership or control of dental equipment, material, or office and makes the same available in any manner for the use by a dentist, dental hygienist, or other agent; provided, however, that nothing in this chapter shall apply to bona fide sales of dental equipment or material secured by a chattel mortgage or retention title agreement, and, provided further, that this section shall not prohibit or restrict persons, firms, or corporations from employing or retaining licensed dentists to furnish dental treatment for their employees or dependents of their employees. A licensed dentist or dental hygienist who enters into any of the above described arrangements with an unlicensed proprietor may have his license and license certificate suspended or revoked by the board. (1959, p. 576, § 13, appvd. June 24, 1959.)

§ 120(14). Application for license; qualifications of applicants; licensing of persons licensed in other states; fees. — Every person who desires to practice dentistry within the state of Alabama shall file with the secretary-treasurer of the board his written application for a license, and furnish satisfactory proof that he is twenty-one (21) years of age, of good moral character, a citizen of the United States, and that he is a graduate of a dental school or college approved by the board. Such application must be upon the form prescribed and furnished by the board and verified by the oath of the applicant, accompanied by a fee to be determined by the board, but said fee shall not be less than twenty-five dollars ($25.00) nor more than fifty dollars ($50.00), and such application must contain a recent unmounted autographed photograph of the applicant. The board may issue a license without examination other than clinical to an applicant who is a citizen of the United States and who furnishes satisfactory proof that he is a graduate of a dental school approved by the board if such applicant holds a license under equal requirements to those of this state, and has for five (5) consecutive years immediately prior to the filing of his application been engaged in the legal and ethical practice of dentistry in

Enclosure 4

MINUTES OF MEETINGS DESCRIBING THE EVOLUTION OF THE
WEST ALABAMA HEALTH SERVICES PROJECT.

APPLICATION FOR 501(C)(3) STATUS
FILED WITH INTERNAL REVENUE SERVICE
BY
WEST ALABAMA HEALTH SERVICES, INC.

MEETING ON AMBULATORY HEALTH CARE PLAN

September 21, 1973

MINUTES

PRESENT

Mr. James West	Regional Office, Dept. of HEW
Mr. Pete Yarnell	Regional Office, Dept. of HEW
Miss Melba McAfee	Federation of Southern Cooperatives
Mr. John Zippert	Federation of Southern Cooperatives
Mr. Lewis Brown	Federation of Southern Cooperatives
Mr. Pete Bailey	Staff, WACHPC
Mr. Greg de Lissovoy	Staff, WACHPC
Mrs. Mary Jo Looser	Staff, WACHPC
Dr. Elizabeth Cleino	Director, WACHPC

Dr. Cleino opened the meeting at 9:15 a.m. in the conference room of the West Alabama Comprehensive Health Planning Council (WACHPC). Representatives of the Federation of Southern Cooperatives had been invited to meet with the staff of the WACHPC and two representatives of the Regional Office of the Department of Health, Education and Welfare to discuss a new proposal for an ambulatory health care project for the area.

Dr. Cleino thanked the representatives from the Federation for coming and gave a brief resume of the discussion which had been held with the Executive Committee of the WACHPC and the Regional Office representatives the previous day. She pointed out that the WACHPC had been asked to assist in developing a proposal which would meet the needs for ambulatory health care and have the approval of the major factions in the area. She stated that she had talked with Dr. Packard about the possibility of the University of Alabama College of Community Health Sciences sponsoring such a project, but they were not now in a position to do this. In order to qualify, there will need to be a separate Corporate Board to operate the project.

When Mr. West and Mr. Yarnell joined the group, Mr. West explained that there was a good chance of a proposal being funded for this area. He stated that they preferred one application which would be developed cooperatively by those in the area.

Since there are limited funds, this project should be confined to two counties, at least to start with.

Dr. Cleino asked if these could be Greene and Hale - both counties in need but within the 314(b) agency jurisdiction.

Mr. West stated that Sumter County should be one of the counties with probably Greene the other.

Mr. West asked Miss McAfee how she felt about this proposition. She stated that she felt the Federation had worked hard and put alot of pressure on people to get this money. She did not think it was fair to go to someone else to develop another application.

Mr. West stated that HEW would fund a project to alleviate the health problems in the area, but this project needs to be a cooperative one.

Mr. Zippert stated that the Federation would develop a program for the people in the area to be controlled by the poor people, who will be consuming the services.

Mr. West explained the provisions of the grant:

1. It should encompass probably two counties.

2. A budget of $200,000 - $300,000 - to give the most for the dollars spent.

3. Would be a joint effort of the political structure, medical society, federation and community.

4. Will provide expert care by regular practitioners, not a career ladder program or way to employ people who might be interested in a health career.

5. Can include cost of drugs, reimbursement for transportation, incidentals.

6. Services open to all ages, races, and income groups.

7. Sliding scale of fees to be charged with collections to be returned to project budget.

8. Medicare reimbursement scale will be determined by a representative from the Regional Office.

9. Up to $7,500 may be spent for renovation but no construction funds available.

10. If objectives are met in first year, there is a moral obligation to fund
for four more years, providing project is progressing.

11. Since the project director is the key to success, the Regional Office
of HEW will have final approving authority on recommendations from
the Board.

12. The Board of the Corporation should be composed of 51 percent consumers and the others representative of the community. A Board of
11 members was proposed to be composed of 6 consumers (3 from each
county) and 5 community representatives (1 member of the Medical
Society of each county and 1 member of the County Commission). The
other representative would not be a resident of either county but would
represent the WACHPC.

Mr. West stated that the pressure is to relieve the health needs of the area,
not to fund the Federation or the City of Livingston or any separate group; but the
project to be funded will be the one to get the most mileage out of the Federal dollars.

Mr. Zippert stated that his people believe that health care is a right of all
people and the U.S. can afford the best quality.

Mr. West again asked that all groups cooperate in developing one project
proposal.

A break was taken, as Mr. West and Mr. Yarnell had to catch a plane.

The meeting reconvened at 1:30 p.m. with the following present: Mr. Brown,
Mr. Zippert, Miss McAfee, Dr. Cleino, Mr. Bailey and Mr. de Lissovoy.

The Board composition was discussed at length.

The Federation representatives stated that the Federation would not participate unless there was a majority of blacks on the Board. They also stated that
there would have to be a black project director.

Miss McAfee questioned the right of the (b) agency to be involved in the
development of this project. She stated that she put pressure on people in
Washington and got this money, and now we say we should all get together.

Dr. Cleino explained that (b) agencies were set up by the Federal government for the purpose of planning and developing programs to meet health needs.
One of the roles is to get various factions together, so the program can operate
cooperatively. She explained that she understood that the Federation's proposal
would not be funded, but a cooperative proposal would have a good chance.

4

There was lengthy expression of the Federation's view that the physicians, health department and other agencies were not providing needed care, and only their group could provide such care. A decision was reached for the Federation representatives to go back to their groups and get their decision. The representatives stated that they could not make decisions for the Federation but would "caucus" and let Dr. Cleino know what they planned to do.

The meeting was adjourned at 3:45 p.m.

MEETING OF THE SUMTER COUNTY MEDICAL SOCIETY AND WACHPC STAFF
LIVINGSTON, ALABAMA
September 26, 1973

MINUTES

MEDICAL SOCIETY MEMBERS PRESENT

Dr. Sidney Williams
Dr. Horace Hunt
Dr. Peter Hightower
Dr. Edward Gegan
Dr. Francis Crenshaw

ABSENT

Dr. Jonnie Ruth Walton

OTHERS PRESENT

Mayor Ira D. Pruitt, Jr.
Mr. James Coleman - Greene
    County Comm. Representative
Mr. Pete Bailey - WACHPC Staff
Dr. Elizabeth Cleino
    Director of WACHPC

The meeting was opened at 5:00 p.m. by Dr. Williams. He explained that the purpose of this meeting was to discuss with the Sumter County Medical Society and Mayor Pruitt the possibility of developing a cooperative neighborhood health services project to include Sumter County.

Dr. Cleino distributed a summary of the major provisions for this particular Federal program and explained the events of the past week in the development of this project.

Mayor Pruitt stated that he had just returned from Washington and knew of the pressure to fund a health care project in the area.

The proposed Board membership was explained with 11 members, 2 M.D.'s 2 representatives of county commissions, one representative of the WACHPC, and 6 consumers; 4 to be appointed by the Federation and 2 by the county governing bodies. Dr. Cleino stated that she hoped all physicians in Sumter and Greene counties would participate in the project, either by giving some time to the clinic or at least by giving the clinic their support. Drs. Gegan and Crenshaw stated that they would provide some time at the clinic, if possible. Cooperative arrangements with the local hospitals was discussed.

Even though the number of consumer members of the Board would heavily favor the Federation under the present proposal, the group agreed to these plans.

The members of the Medical Society voted to endorse the project.

The meeting adjourned at 6:00 p.m.

Later a meeting of the Sumter County Hospital Staff was held at the Sumter County Memorial Hospital in Livingston at which meeting the group endorsed the proposed project.

MEETING WITH ALL PARTIES TO APPROVE PROJECT PROPOSAL
FOR
WEST ALABAMA HEALTH SERVICES PROJECT

GREENE COUNTY HEALTH DEPARTMENT - EUTAW, ALABAMA

October 23, 1973

MINUTES

MEMBERS PRESENT

(Sumter County)
Dr. Sidney Williams
Dr. Edward Gegan
Dr. Francis Crenshaw
Mr. W. T. Lockard

(Greene County)
Dr. William Frederick
Dr. Rucker Staggers
Dr. Joe P. Smith
Mr. David Patton

(Federation of Southern Cooperatives)
Miss Melba McAfee
Mr. John Zippert
Mr. Lewis Black
Mr. Spivey Gordon
Mr. Eddie Ayers

(WACHPC Staff)
Dr. Elizabeth Cleino
Mr. Pete Bailey
Mr. Greg de Lissovoy

(Others Present)
Mr. Max Benson   Representative State Medical Association
Mr. Charlie Stewart   Representative CHP (a) Office

The meeting was called to order at 7:45 p.m. by Dr. Elizabeth Cleino.
Proposals had been mailed to those invited to attend, but the full budget was given out
at the meeting.

Dr. Gegan expressed concern over being able to secure dentists to help with
the project, since none of the three practicing dentists can give any time to the project.
It was agreed that dental services would have to be recruited from outside the two
counties.

Some physicians in the area will assist, but a full-time M.D. will be required.
The clinic sites will have to be leased space. Dr. Gegan offered his office and stated
he would build a new office. Miss McAfee stated they would like to offer their building
as the clinic site. Dr. Cleino stated this would be decided by the Board.

Dr. Clieno announced that Dr. John Packard has agreed to serve on the Board, representing the WACHPC and also the University of Alabama College of Community Health Sciences.

Dr. Cleino asked if there were comments about the proposal. She asked to discuss Mr. Stewart's comments with him later. She stated that each of the three main groups had agreed separately to the essentials contained in the proposal, and this meeting was for the purpose of giving final approval after agreeing on minor revisions.

Mr. Zippert asked Dr. Cleino to explain what the others had been told. She explained the essentials, Board structure, two clinic sites, medical and dental care, etc.

Mr. Zippert and others from the Federation began a lengthy attack on the medical professions and health care giving institutions. He stated that the poor blacks had been deprived of health care and denied services. Both Mr. Lockard, a member of the Hill Hospital Board, and Dr. Gegan denied that anyone had been denied care. They stated that all emergencies are seen, and no patients are turned away from the physician's office.

Mr. Zippert stated that requests have been submitted to 50 foundations for this need, and already some response has been made.

Dr. Frederick remarked that it seemed to him that right now the Federation was "out of funds and out of favor", at least as far as HEW was concerned.

Mr. Zippert was asked to state what the Federation wanted, in order to coop-erate with this project. He stated: All consumer members appointed by Black Belt Family Health Center, black project director, and site of clinics to be Federation's building to be built on Gainsville Road.

After considerable discussion, Dr. Cleino asked first for a vote, and later amended to ask for a talley of how each person present felt about the Board structure as proposed.

Drs. Gegan, Crenshaw, Frederick, Staggers and Smith voted for the Board as proposed. Dr. Williams and Mr. Lockard wanted further consideration, and all the Federation representatives voted against 4 of 6 consumer members. Being appointed by the Federation, Miss McAfee suggested waiting until after services were rendered to appoint consumer members.

The meeting was adjourned at 10:15 p.m. with no ~~argument~~ *agreement* about the Board composition.

WEST ALABAMA HEALTH SERVICES PROJECT APPLICATION
DR. CLEINO'S VISIT TO REGIONAL OFFICE

October 31, 1973

Dr. Cleino met in Atlanta with Dr. Herbert Hudgins and Mr. James West in Mr. West's office. Dr. Cleino brought the others up to date on events which had occurred during the developmental phase of the health services project. She presented a copy of the proposal at this meeting.

She reported that conferences had been held with the Greene County representatives, Sumter County representatives, and the Federation of Southern Cooperatives and that each separately had agreed with the major provisions which are included in the grant proposal.

She described the meeting of October 23 and stated that she felt that the Federation now had no intention of cooperating with the rest of the community leaders in Greene and Sumter Counties.

Dr. Hudgins advised that the group complete its planning for this project and provide a copy of the Articles of Incorporation, letters of endorsement and a final copy of the grant application as soon as possible.

The meeting ended at 12:00 noon.

MEETING OF THE
WEST ALABAMA HEALTH SERVICES PROJECT PLANNING COMMITTEE
EUTAW, ALABAMA

November 7, 1973

MINUTES

MEMBERS PRESENT

Judge William Branch	Greene County Commission
Mr. David Patton	Greene County Hospital
Dr. Joe P. Smith	Greene County Medical Society
Dr. Rucker Staggers	Greene County Medical Society
Dr. William Frederick	Greene County Medical Society
Mr. William Hill	Greene County Consumer
Mr. Joe Modley	Greene County Consumer
Mr. C. T. Lockard, Jr.	Sumter County Commission
Mayor Ira D. Pruitt, Jr.	Town of Livingston (Sumter County)
Dr. Edward Gagen	Sumter County Medical Society
Mrs. Zora C. Gibbs	Sumter County Consumer
Dr. Sidney Williams	Greene-Sumter Counties Public Health Officer

STAFF PRESENT

Dr. Elizabeth Cleino	West Alabama Comprehensive Health Planning Council
Mr. Greg de Lissovoy	West Alabama Comprehensive Health Planning Council
Mr. Charles Stewart	Alabama Comprehensive Health Planning Council

---

The meeting of the West Alabama Health Services Project Planning Committee was convened at the Greene County Hospital by Dr. Cleino at 6:45 p.m. Copies of the project proposal were distributed to members of the group and changes from the previous version were noted. These mainly involved the addition of letters of endorsement from various organizations and the deletion of the Federation of Southern Cooperatives as a partner in the project.

Dr. Cleino summarized the last meeting of the Planning Committee at which Federation representatives had presented certain demands which were unacceptable to other community members. She added that the Federation had officially withdrawn from the planning group and had submitted its own application to HEW for a similar project.

2

Copies of the proposed Articles of Incorporation and By-Laws of the West Alabama Health Services Project were distributed to those persons who had not previously received them by mail. Mayor Pruitt stated that, from a legal standpoint, the Articles of Incorporation were in good order. Dr. Gagen noted that the By-laws could be amended at a later time, should this prove desirable.

Dr. Cleino announced that she had that day received a letter from Dr. John Packard stating that he would be unable to serve on the Board of Directors as a representative of the West Alabama Comprehensive Health Planning Council. Several members suggested that Dr. Packard be asked to reconsider this decision. There was a general consensus that he would have much to offer the project by serving as a Director.

Mr. Lockard announced that the Sumter County Commission had appointed Mrs. Zora C. Gibbs and Mr. Robert Cook as consumer representatives. Selection of the third representative would be completed by the end of the week. He explained that Mr. Cook was unable to attend this meeting because of another engagement.

Judge Branch stated that the Greene County Commission had appointed Mr. Willie Hill, Mr. Joe Modley, and Mr. Allen Turner as consumer representatives. He added that Mr. Turner was not able to attend this meeting because of a previous commitment.

Mr. Lockard said that he planned to discuss the project with Mr. Warren C. Grant, the mayor of York, Alabama. Judge Branch said that he would contact Mr. Burton Payne, Mayor of Boligee, and discuss the project with him.

Dr. Cleino suggested that a decision be made as to the county where the West Alabama Health Services Project (WAHSP) would be incorporated. There was a general discussion concerning the relative merits of Greene and Sumter Counties. A consensus soon developed in favor or Greene County.

The Board of Directors of the WAHSP was then called into session. Members of the Board who were present were identified as follows:

Judge William Branch	Greene County
Dr. Rucker Staggers	Greene County
Mr. Willie Hill	Greene County
Mr. C. T. Lockard, Jr.	Sumter County
Dr. Edward Gagen	Sumter County
Mrs. Zora C. Gibbs	Sumter County

3

Members of the Board who were absent were identified as follows:

Mr. Joe Modley	Greene County
Mr. Allen Turner	Greene County
Mr. Robert Cook	Sumter County
(Not Selected)	Sumter County
Dr. John Packard	West Alabama Comprehensive Health Planning Council

It was determined that a quorum was present.

Decisions Made by the WAHS Project Board of Directors

Dr. Staggers moved that the West Alabama Health Services Project be incorporated in Greene County. This was seconded by Dr. Gagen. The motion carried unanimously.

Judge Branch was nominated to serve as President of the Board by Dr. Staggers and the motion was seconded by Dr. Gagen. The motion carried unanimously.

At this time, a seventh member of the Board arrived, Mr. Joe Modley of Greene County.

Dr. Gagen nominated Mr. Lockard to serve as Vice-President of the Board of Directors. Judge Branch seconded the motion and it was unanimously approved.

Mr. Lockard nominated Mrs. Gibbs to serve as Treasurer of the corporation. Judge Branch seconded the motion and it carried unanimously.

Judge Branch offered to serve as Registered Agent of the Corporation and suggested the Greene County Courthouse as the Registered Office. All members of the Board agreed.

The members of the Board then proceeded to sign the Articles of Incorporation of the West Alabama Health Services Project.

Dr. Staggers moved that the West Alabama Comprehensive Health Planning Council complete the application for funding and submit it to the Department of Health, Education and Welfare as expediently as possible. Judge Branch seconded the motion and it carried unanimously.

Mr. Charlie Stewart from the State Comprehensive Health Planning Office presented a letter of concurrence for the project.

There being no further business, Dr. Gagen moved to adjourn the meeting and Judge Branch seconded. The motion carried unanimously.

The meeting adjourned at 7:40 p.m.

WEST ALABAMA HEALTH SERVICES PROJECT
SITE VISIT

November 26 and 27, 1973

November 26

Dr. Cleino met Mr. Pete Yarnell and Mr. Ted Griffith at the airport and took them to the hotel where Dr. John Packard joined the group to discuss the West Alabama Health Services Project. Dr. Packard discussed the University's role in the project and stated that as soon as residents where available in larger numbers the University intended to use the ambulatory health care project for experience for some of the residents. Dr. Packard confirmed for the site visitors that he would participate on the Board.

November 27

Mr. Pete Yarnell, Mr. Ted Griffith, Mr. Greg de Lissovoy and Dr. Elizabeth Cleino drove to Greene County to meet with the medical staff and hospital administrator at the Greene County Hospital. Dr. Rucker Staggers, Mr. David Patton, and Dr. William Frederick met with the group to discuss the project.

The physicians indicated that this project would not interfere with their private practices, since all the physicians in the county had more patients than they could comfortably see now. The two physicians did indicate their willingness to participate in the clinic, and Dr. Staggers indicated that he had agreed to serve on the Board. Mr. Patton indicated his willingness to give support and assistance to the project.

The site visitors then went to the Greene County Courthouse to meet with representatives of the county governing body and other agencies in Greene County Present at this meeting were Judge William Branch; Mr. Charles Earl Jones, Coordinator, Federal Programs; Mr. John Modley, member of the Board; Mr. P. J. Kirksey, representing the Urban League; Mr. James Coleman, assistant to Judge Branch; and Mrs. Branch and Mrs. Rumney, representing the county school system. Mr. Al Baldwin, site visitor from the Regional Office, joined the group during the meeting.

Mr. Jones stated that the OEO grant, which had been operational for two years, had used outreach workers to assist people in seeking medical care before they were acutely ill and had also provided a physician on a one-day-a-week basis. He stated that he would like to see the essence of this program assumed by the West Alabama Health Services Project.

Mr. Griffith asked how this project would help the citizens of Greene County. Judge Branch stated that many of the people in his county needed services, and he believed that a good program of ambulatory health care would help to supplement the services now being given. Mr. Coleman stated that as a former principal of a school he had conducted a study which showed that more than 50 percent of the students had not had any medical service. He also stated that there was a large need for general services. He stated that if a person wishes to see a physician in Eutaw he has to pay approximately $4.00 for transportation, must wait from 3 to 8 hours and pay a doctor bill with drugs amounting to approximately $7.00.

Mr. Griffith asked how this project would fit into the existing system. Mr. Jones said that it would provide a service center which could act as an extension to the OEO Program already in action and could also fit in with the long-range plans of the county for improving all types of service to poor people. The Judge spoke of the development of a community center to house the food stamps program, employment service, legal aid, medical service, etc. Transportation costs can be partially born by this project to assist patients to get to the center to meet a variety of needs.

Mr. Coleman stressed that any Federal program should provide maximum service for the people and must not be disruptive but must work within the ongoing organization of the community.

Mrs. Branch asked about the selection of the Board members. Mr. Hill and Mr. Modley were identified to the group as consumer representatives of the Board who had been appointed by the Greene County Commission. Mrs. Branch had a number of questions about the ongoing program under OEO, as well as the proposed project. She asked about the Federation's involvement in this project. Dr. Cleino explained the history and the development of this grant, from the time the Federation was first given money to develop the Family Health Center until the present site visit. She explained that the Federation had been invited to participate as a full partner and had elected to develop a competing application.

The difference in developing a prepaid group versus opening a clinic which services could be used by anyone in the county was pointed out. Mrs. Branch was surprised to find that a sliding scale of fees had been established for Dr. Maddox's services, as she was under the impression that these services were free.

Mr. Kirksey stated that he felt this project would be helpful to Greene County, would not take away from any program and would help to expand the program now operated by OEO. He stated that he would assist in helping people find transportation to the clinic site.

Mrs. Branch asked what this project would do in Epes. Dr. Cleino explained that the clinic sites would probably be located in Eutaw and Livingston.

Mr. Yarnell explained to the group that the Regional Office reserved the right to approve the project director, since this was a crucial position in the effectiveness of an ambulatory health care center.

The meeting adjourned at 12:00 noon.

November 27

A meeting was held with the Sumter County representatives in Dr. Williams' office at 1:30 p.m. Present at the meeting were Dr. Sidney Williams, Health Officer; Mr. W. T. Steele, Administrator of Sumter Memorial Hospital; Mr. John L. Sims, Administrator of Hill Hospital of York; Dr. Dagmar Brodt, head of the nursing program at Livingston University; Mr. Drayton Pruitt, Mayor City of Livingston; Dr. Will Baker, Director of West Alabama Mental Health Center; Drs. Edward Gegan, Francis Crenshaw, and Horace Hunt, private practitioners; Mr. Leo Fields, Director OEO Program; Mrs. Zora Gibbs, consumer member of the Board; Mr. Greg de Lissovoy and Dr. Elizabeth Cleino, WACHPC; and Regional Office representatives Mr. Al Baldwin and Mr. Ted Griffith. Mr. Pete Yarnell was ill.

Dr. Williams opened the meeting by introducing all present. Dr. Cleino welcomed all those present, explaining to the group assembled that the purpose of this visit was for the Regional Office personnel to determine from a first hand visit the desires of the people concerning the grant proposal.

Dr. Williams explained the College of Community Health Sciences' tie to the project and desire to work closely with this program.

Transportation was notably a problem in Sumter County, but plans are being developed for a new public system.

Dr. Gegan stated that the project would be an asset, and some of the physicians would be able to volunteer some time each week and felt that it would not hurt their practice. Other providers present stated that they were fully supportive of the project.

Mr. Baldwin asked what the consumers thought of the project. Mr. Fields stated that this would work in very nicely with ongoing programs of the OEO and that he would be glad to work through his committees in his organization to cooperate in every way with this project. Mrs. Gibbs stated that the biggest problem in Sumter County would probably be dental care, and she would be pleased to find a way to provide this needed care.

4

Dr. Will Baker stated that the mental health system was one of the newest systems to be developed and that he had found the political structure and the providers to be extremely supportive of the new service.

Mayor Pruitt requested that in making a decision concerning the two grant applicantions now before the site visitors that the history of the accomplishments of the applicants be considered. There was evidence presented that the county had supported improvements of health services and facilities and would continue to support the proposed project.

After a very pleasant discussion with the two site visitors, the meeting was adjourned at approximately 4: 00 p.m.

MEETING WITH FEDERATION OF SOUTHERN COOPERATIVES
EUTAW, ALABAMA

November 29, 1973

MINUTES

PRESENT

Judge William M. Branch	Chairman, West Alabama Health Services Project
Mr. Charles Earl Jones	Coordinator, Federal Programs - Greene County
Miss Melba McAfee	Federation of Southern Cooperatives
Mr. John Zippert	Federation of Southern Cooperatives
Mr. Eddie Ayers	Federation of Southern Cooperatives
Dr. Elizabeth W. Cleino	Director, WACHPC
Mr. Greg de Lissovoy	WACHPC Staff

At 3:15 p.m. in Eutaw, the above named met at the request of Judge Branch to discuss a possible compromise on the proposal prepared by the WACHPC on behalf of the West Alabama Health Service Project, Inc.

Earlier in the day, a group had assembled to prepare recommendations to be presented to the planning group for the WAHS Project.

Miss McAfee stated that they were surprised to find out on Monday that Judge Branch was the Chairman. A group of concerned citizens had gone to Judge Branch's house on Wednesday night to ask that he resign from the Board of the WAHS Project, because they did not wish to see blacks in opposition to each other. The morning meeting was attended by the following: Judge Branch, Mr. Jones, Mr. Coleman, Rev. Lines, Mr. Pentor, Mr. Chambers and Mrs. Annie Brown (precinct chairman) interested citizens and Sheriff Gilmore.

This group recommended that the Board composition be changed to a 13-member Board with the following representation:

7 Consumer Members (54%)	3 Greene Co.	Appointed by Commission
	2 Sumter Co.	Appointed by Federation
	2 Marengo Co.	Appointed by Federation
6 Provider Members	2 Greene Co.	1 - Co. Commissioner
		1 - Medical
	2 Sumter Co.	1 - Co. Commissioner
		1 - Medical
	2 Marengo Co.	1 - Co. Commissioner
		1 - Medical

Miss McAfee explained that the Board of the Black Belt Community Health Center was now composed of 18 members (11 former Board members of the BBFHC) and that members include Judge Sammie Daniels and Dr. Fitzgerald from Marengo County. The other 5 had not been selected, but they would represent the medical profession and county governing bodies. This Board has not been incorporated, but the BBFHC Board is incorporated in Sumter Counyy.

Mr. Zippert stated that he wanted us to agree to take♦ the best of the two proposals with essentials to include three counties, black control and a black project director.

Miss McAfee stated, "We see in the long run that the quality and extent of services will be the same services not received from the physicians in the counties now." She stated that physicians had separate waiting rooms, and with pressure they would knock out the receptionist space to make them one. She stated that after awhile "we will have zero people who don't want this program", and "it will be like so many Federal programs that have come into communities and not been used." Criticism was also laid on health department programs, local M.D.'s and WACHPC.

Mr. Zippert and Miss McAfee criticized the staff of the WACHPC as not being competent to write such a proposal, because no black staff member was employed and no concern for blacks.

Dr. Clieno reminded the group that she had helped write the first grant proposal for the OEO Emergency Food and Medical Services Grant to Greene County; and the Council worked equally for all 207,000 people in West Alabama without regard to color, race, age or county of residence. She reminded the group that the Greene County Commission was represented on the Council by Judge Branch.

Judge Branch indicated that in the morning meeting the group asked him to resign from the Board of the WAHS Project, but he didn't feel he should, since he was a member of the WACHP Council and felt he had an obligation to assist with projects supported by this group.

Mr. Jones further explained that while the situation was not the same in Sumter County, in Greene County there is black leadership. Judge Branch is Chairman of the County Commissioners and, as such, a leader of the people of Greene County (both black and white). Judge Branch is not "copping out" on anyone but wishes to avoid the hurt and confusion that can occur - wants to work for reconciliation. Judge Branch suggested a joint meeting of the Boards.

Dr. Cleino asked Mr. Ayers what he was unhappy about. He stated that he did not like the way it was handled from the beginning - we said project wasn't needed. Dr. Cleino reminded him that the WACHPC said there was a need.

3

Miss McAfee stated she had hoped our project wouldn't come up.

Dr. Cleino asked if the group wished to withdraw the two proposals and prepare a third to include Marengo County and the new proposed Board. She reminded the group that this would take another two months to go through the whole process of development, (a) and (b) agency review, etc. She stated that the Federation had been offered four of the six consumer representatives originally, and the other members of the Board would be the same and the Federation had rejected.

Mr. Zippert stated that nothing could be worked out; so, he, Mr. Ayers and Miss McAfee prepared to leave. They stated that if the Judge's Board is awarded the grant, they will organize 3,000 people to march in protest.

After the Federation representatives left, the others discussed possible repercussions and agreed that the group would continue to work with the regular agencies in the county and hope to work with all the citizens - those who belong to the Federation and those who don't.

The meeting adjourned at 4: 45 p.m.

Meeting of the
WEST ALABAMA HEALTH SERVICES PROJECT BOARD OF DIRECTORS

Livingston, Alabama
January 8, 1974

MINUTES

BOARD MEMBERS PRESENT

Judge William Branch	Greene County Commission
Mr. Robert Cook	Sumter County Commission
Dr. Edward Gegan	Greene County Commission
Mr. Willie Hill	Sumter County Consumer
Mr. W. T. Lockard	Sumter County Commission
Mr. John Modley	Greene County Consumer
Mr. Edward Ozment	Sumter County Consumer
Dr. John Packard	West Alabama Comprehensive Health Planning Council
Dr. Rucker Staggers	Greene County Medical Society

BOARD MEMBERS ABSENT

Mrs. Zora C. Gibbs	Sumter County Consumer
Mr. Allen Turner	Greene County Consumer

ADVISORS AND GUESTS PRESENT

Dr. Dagmar Brodt	Nursing Program, Livingston University
Mr. Frederick Brodt	Guest
Dr. Vance R. Kane	Chairman, Council on Dental Health Alabama Dental Association
Dr. William Cole	President, Sixth District Dental Society
Mrs. William Cole	Guest
Mr. James Coleman	Federal Programs Coordinator, Greene Co.
Mr. Leo Fields	Director, Sumter Co. Head Start Program
Mr. Frank Hinckley	Professor, Health Care Management, U. of A.
Dr. Hiram Johnson	Sixth District Dental Society Representative to West Alabama CHP Council
Dr. T. C. Looney	Sumter County Dentist

STAFF PRESENT

Dr. Elizabeth W. Cleino	Director, West Alabama Comprehensive Health Planning Council
Mr. Greg de Lissovoy	West Alabama Comprehensive Health Planning Council

2

The meeting was called to order by Judge Branch at 7:15 P.M. in the auditorium of the Sumter County Health Department. Judge Branch welcomed members and guests. He explained that minutes from the previous meeting were available and would be distributed with those of the present meeting. Judge Branch then asked Dr. Cleino to review events since the last formal meeting which was held on November 7, 1973.

Dr. Cleino stated that, in accordance with the resolution passed by the Board, the project proposal had been submitted to the Department of Health, Education and Welfare by the West Alabama Comprehensive Health Planning Council staff.

HEW representatives made a site visit to Greene and Sumter Counties on November 27 and 28. They toured local health facilities and met with community representatives from each county. HEW has just advised the WAHS Board that, while they viewed the project favorably, the proposal needed to be revised. Required changes involve a reduction of the budget to $250,000 and preparation of a more detailed plan of action.

Judge Branch asked Mr. de Lissovoy to discuss changes in the proposal which needed to be made. Mr. de Lissovoy stated that, in the weeks since the proposal was submitted to HEW, he had met with individual members of the Board and other interested community representatives from both counties to receive suggestions for possible modifications in the original proposal. The Department of Health, Education and Welfare's request for a revised project description has now created an opportunity to incorporate the many suggested changes.

Mr. de Lissovoy noted that the project had three major components:

1. The health care clinics

2. A system for providing and coordinating transportation and communication

3. A management and administrative structure

He stated that community representatives generally believed that the budget for the coordination and management components should be greatly reduced while giving the clinic services high priority. As the need arose, the administrative component could be expanded. Transportation and communication could be provided by existing organizations in each county; this could also be expanded if necessary.

Mr. de Lissovoy stated that the Board needs to decide if the project should begin with a small partially-staffed clinic in each county or organize a fully-staffed clinic in one county and, as soon as possible, organize a second fully-staffed clinic in the other county.

A prolonged discussion followed in which the merits of the two alternatives were discussed. Representatives of the Sixth District Dental Society stressed the heavy capital investment in dental facilities and the need to insure full utilization of this equipment. The possibility of a mobile dental unit was raised but eventually ruled out because of the great expense and low productivity.

A consensus developed favoring the idea of a single fully-staffed clinic, to be followed by a second facility as the resources became available.

Dr. Packard moved that one fully operational clinic be developed first, to be followed by a second clinic as soon as feasible. The motion was seconded by Dr. Gegan and carried unanimously.

Mr. de Lissovoy asked the group to decide which county should have the first clinic. Mr. Lockard stated that the Livingston Development Corporation might be able to buy a modular clinic and lease it to the project. Judge Branch stated that Greene County could provide a similar facility. Judge Branch suggested that the two county officials, and such advisors they might select, meet and resolve the issue.

Dr. Cleino asked the physicians and dentists present if they would propose the facilities and staff needed to operate the health care clinic. The discussion that followed raised many critical issues concerning the recruitment of health manpower, the organization and staffing patterns of such a clinic, and the need for a carefully engineered building.

Speaking on behalf of the Sixth District Dental Society, Dr. Cole offered to meet with project representatives to specify the staff, supplies, and equipment needed for dental care. Dr. Gegan, Dr. Staggers and Dr. Packard offered their assistance in the specification of medical facilities.

Dr. Staggers moved that the WAHS Project apply for eligibility to receive Federal surplus property. Mr. Hill seconded the motion and it carried unanimously. Judge Branch asked Dr. Cleino if the West Alabama Comprehensive Health Planning Council would arrange this.

Mr. de Lissovoy stated that the "outreach" system which would bring patients to the clinic needed to be defined. Judge Branch explained Greene County's outreach program which is based on private cars and reimbursement for mileage. Mr. Fields said that Sumter County is now offering bus transportation for senior citizens on a limited basis but capable of expansion. Dr. Cain stated that, from his experience, an effective transportation system linked to scheduled appointments with patients is vital to clinic productivity. Limited funds could be provided from the project budget for transportation.

4

Judge Branch noted that many areas of the project needed refinement. He reminded the group that representatives from the Department of Health, Education and Welfare were coming on January 21, 1974, to discuss the revised proposal with members of the Board. He suggested that the West Alabama Comprehensive Health Planning Council be requested to prepare a revised proposal in outline form that could be made available to community representatives prior to January 21. He suggested that each county appoint one person to work closely with the Council staff in preparing this revision; he appointed Mr. Coleman as the Greene County liaison.

Judge Branch thanked all participants for coming and invited the guests to attend the meeting with HEW representatives.

There being no further business, the meeting was adjourned at 9:40 P.M.

Meeting of
WEST ALABAMA HEALTH SERVICES, INC. BOARD OF DIRECTORS
Eutaw, Alabama
January 21, 1974

MINUTES

BOARD MEMBERS PRESENT

Judge William Branch	Greene County Commission
Mr. Robert Cook	Sumter County Consumer
Dr. Edward Gegan	Sumter County Medical Society
Mrs. Zora Gibbs	Sumter County Consumer
Mr. Edward Ozment	Sumter County Consumer
Dr. John Packard	West Alabama Comprehensive Health Planning Council
Dr. Rucker Staggers	Greene County Medical Society

BOARD MEMBERS ABSENT

Mr. Willie Hill	Greene County Consumer
Mr. W. T. Lockard	Sumter County Commission
Mr. John Modley	Greene County Consumer
Mr. Allen Turner	Greene County Consumer

GUESTS PRESENT

Mr. Al Baldwin	Department of Health, Education and Welfare, Region IV
Dr. Charles Konigsberg, Jr.	District Health Officer
Dr. Sidney Williams	Deputy District Health Officer
Mr. Pete Yarnell	Department of Health, Education and Welfare, Region IV

STAFF PRESENT

Dr. Elizabeth Cleino	West Alabama Comprehensive Health Planning Council
Mr. Greg de Lissovoy	West Alabama Comprehensive Health Planning Council

The meeting was called to order at 3:20 P.M. at the Greene County Health Department by Judge William Branch, President of the Board of Directors. The representatives from the Department of Health, Education and Welfare, Mr. Al Baldwin and Mr. Pete Yarnell, were introduced to all present.

At Judge Branch's request, Dr. Cleino gave a brief review of the project to date. She then stated that the original purpose of this meeting was to discuss modifications to the original proposal and details of the project plan of action. However, Regional Office representatives had requested that another attempt be made to seek the cooperation of the Federation of Southern Cooperatives in the project.

Dr. Cleino stated that the letter from Eddie Sessions deferring action on the WAHS proposal made no mention of the need for more joint meetings. Only recently had the staff learned about the letters from the congressmen supporting the Black Belt Family Health Center project. It was determined that the first letter in support of the project was written because the congressman was assured that all groups in the community were working on a single project. The Federation used his letter to obtain similar letters from other congressmen. This has now been straightened out.

Dr. Cleino asked Mr. Pete Yarnell of Community Health Services (Department of HEW, Region IV) to explain the position of the Regional Office. Mr. Yarnell explained that the Department of HEW had a responsibility to award the grant where both the need and ability to manage the project existed. The primary purpose of this visit to Alabama was to discuss the position of the Regional Office with the Board of the West Alabama Health Services Project and the Board of the Black Belt Family Health Center. Then a combined meeting of the two Boards is requested to work out a compromise, if possible.

Mr. Yarnell distributed copies of the position statement prepared by the staff of the Community Health Services Division of Region IV (copy attached).

Item 1   Only one grant can be made to the area.

Item 2-3   Stated that the composition of the Board of Directors must be representative of all pertinent components and groups in the target counties and that the Board must assume administrative independence from the WACHPC and the Federation.

There was considerable discussion on these points.

Judge Branch explained that the consumer representatives from Greene County were selected by the 13 precinct leaders. He emphasized that consumer representatives were selected by the people and appointed by the County Commission, not by the WACHPC staff.

Mr. Lockard also pointed out that consumer members were selected by the Sumter County Commissioners. Members of the medical society were selected by their own groups.

Dr. Cleino said that the Board members were selected to represent groups already identified and approved by the Regional Office. She stated again that the Federation, only one of many groups and organizations in the area, had been offered a larger percentage of the consumer members than other groups but had refused to select any consumer members.

Mr. Ozment suggested that there was considerable overlapping among the membership of various community groups. Over time the composition of the Board will change and nobody will be left out.

Judge Branch stated that the Federation should negotiate through established channels to obtain Board representation. If they wished representatives from Sumter County, they should approach the Sumter County Commission.

On the matter of the WAHS Board independence from the WACHPC, Dr. Cleino noted that WACHPC has devoted considerable time to this project at the expense of other projects. The Council is eager to withdraw as soon as possible but recognized that considerable staff support is still required to get the project underway. The staff's role is to provide technical assistance, not to dominate.

Mr. Baldwin stated that the West Alabama Comprehensive Health Planning Council had done an excellent job in assisting the project reach the present stage of development. The proposal now needs to be more detailed and specific and the budget needs to be reduced.

The recommendation of the Regional Office position paper that a small representative committee from each Board meet to determine how a single Board can be composed that will represent both consumers and providers was discussed. Mr. Yarnell was asked to explain why this recommendation was made.

Mr. Yarnell stated that a delegation from the Federation of Southern Cooperatives, including Ms. McAfee, Mr. Zippert and Mr. Prejean, met with HEW representatives in Atlanta on Monday, January 14, to protest the rejection of the BBFHC proposal. They asked for a meeting of the Boards in order to work out a compromise. He stated that the WAHS Board and the BBFHC Board needed to resolve their differences independently of the Federation and the West Alabama Comprehensive Health Planning Council in a joint meeting.

Dr. Packard moved that the elected officers of the WAHS Board be delegated the responsibility of negotiating with the Black Belt Board. This would include the following persons:

Judge William Branch	President
Mr. W. T. Lockard	Vice-President
Mrs. Zora Gibbs	Treasurer
Dr. Rucker Staggers	Secretary

Dr. Staggers seconded and the motion carried unanimously.

4

Dr. Staggers stated that a representative from HEW should be present as an observer when the two Board representatives meet.

Mr. Ozment asked what compromise was the Federation suggesting.

Mr. Yarnell replied that the Federation people were essentially bargaining for everything they could get. They might change after tonight's meeting once their position with the Regional Office had been clarified, as they are no longer considered an applicant for the project. They may well claim that they are not represented in the WAHS project. The Regional Office is merely trying to clarify the problem, but local people must justify any position taken.

He said he sensed that the group was very open to discussion and that this was a very good sign.

Mr. Ozment noted that several informal subcommittees had been formed to work on detailed aspects of the project design. Should this be curtailed until negotiations with the Black Belt Board had been completed?

Mr. Yarnell said that this work should continue and that a compromise with the Black Belt Board was only one aspect of the proposal.

Dr. Staggers noted that Mr. Turner, consumer representative from Greene County, has missed three consecutive meetings of the Board and under the provisions of the By-Laws, has forfeited his membership. Dr. Staggers moved that Sheriff Gilmore be appointed to replace Mr. Turner. The motion was seconded by Dr. Gegan and carried unanimously. Judge Branch asked the secretary to discuss the matter with Sheriff Gilmore.

Judge Branch asked if there were any other matters that need to be discussed.

Mr. de Lissovoy stated that representatives from the Sixth District Dental Society had met to discuss requirements for a dental services program. They had made a preliminary estimate of $50,000 for dental supplies and equipment at one site. Mr. de Lissovoy said that he was to have met with Dr. Staggers and Dr. Gegan concerning the medical services plan, but the events of last week forced cancellation of this meeting.

Dr. Williams reported that he and Mr. Fred Brodt had met with York (Sumter County) representatives to discuss the proposal. They felt that Eutaw should be the initial site.

Dr. Williams said that a dental chair now at the Sumter County Health Department could be used very satisfactorily for the dental hygenist.

Dr. Williams added that consideration has been given to expansion of the Greene County Health Department to include a waiting room-meeting room, dental services wing, and demonstration kitchen, which might be used by the project.

Mr. Baldwin said that there is a fine line between construction and renovation. The Bord should consider various alternatives when locating a suitable facility and should investigage modular units or trailers.

Dr. Williams asked if patients enrolled at the project clinic could see both health center physicians and private physicians. Mr. Baldwin said that they could, but all concerned should be careful to avoid potential conflicts of interest.

Judge Branch stated that he would convene a meeting of the Board once negotiations with the Black Belt Board had been attempted.

There being no further business, the meeting was adjourned at 5:15 P.M.

POSITION OF THE REGIONAL OFFICE ON GRANT
APPROVAL FOR SUMTER AND GREENE COUNTIES,
ALABAMA

1. There can. be only one grant award for community health
   services made to one project administered by one Board
   of Directors for the target counties.

2. Composition is that Board of Directors must be representative of all pertinent components and groups in the target
   counties.

3. Membership of the Board should have a majority consumer
   representation and a racial ratio similar to that of the
   total population in the target counties.

4. The Board of Directors must be prepared to assume administrative independence from the West Alabama Comprehensive Health
   Council and the ~~Black Belt~~ Federation/as soon as possible.
   of Southern Cooperative

5. Association with these two above named groups, and other
   groups in the target counties and the State, must be on
   a technical assistance basis by request of the board.

6. The Regional Office recognizes:

   The West Alabama Health Services Board as a viable
   grant applicant whose application has been deferred
   until organizational conditions (Nos. 2, 3 and 4 above)
   plus modifications in objectives, budget, etc., can
   be resolved.

7. The Regional Office recognizes:

   The Black Belt Community Health Center Board as an applicant
   whose grant has been denied. This is based on incomplete
   community and existing organized health services representation, plus the other criteria as stated in the Regional Health
   Administrator's letter dated December 11, 1973.

RECOMMENDATION:

That a small representative committee from each of the above
Boards (3-4 each) meet to determine how a single board can be
composed that will represent the Health Service Consumers and
providers (not represent existing political entities).

Meeting Concerning
WEST ALABAMA HEALTH SERVICES PROJECT
Livingston, Alabama
January 30, 1974

.   MINUTES

INDIVIDUALS PRESENT

Mr. Marion Brown	Sumter County Commission
Mr. Henry Lawrence Cobb	Pharmacist, York AL
Mr. Johnnie Bell	Pharmacist, York AL
Mayor Warren Grant	Mayor, York AL
Mr. W. T. Lockard	Chairman, Sumter County Commission
Mr. Aubrey Green	Chairman, Hill Hospital Board of Trustees
The Rev. C. M. Roberts	Minister, York AL
Mr. John Sims	Administrator, Hill Hospital
Mr. Robert Cook	Member, Board of Directors - West Alabama Health Services Project '
Dr. Johnnie Ruth Walton	Physician, York AL
Dr. Wendall Gilbert	Physician, York AL
Mrs. Mamie J. Marbley	Board Member, Hill Hospital
Dr. Sidney J. Williams	Health Officer, Sumter County
Mayor Drayton Pruitt	Mayor, Livingston AL
Mr. James G. Hamilton	Health Planner, District VI
(Unidentified)	Sumter County Nursing Home
Dr. Elizabeth W. Cleino	Director, West Alabama Comprehensive Health Planning Council, District II
Mr. Greg de Lissovoy	Health Planner, West Alabama Comprehensive Health Planning Council, District II

Dr. Cleino opened the meeting at 5:10 P.M. at the Sumter County Health Department in Livingston, Alabama. She explained that the purpose of comprehensive health planning was to improve health services, manpower and facilities. Dr. Cleino explained that Sumter County is in District VI, although it was once in District II; and the West Alabama Comprehensive Health Planning Council was working in this area at the request of Congressman Walter Flowers with the cooperation of Sumter County officials, because District VI did not have a health planning council. Mr. James Hamilton has recently been appointed as the District Health Planner.

Mr. Hamilton then discussed his role as District VI Health Planner. He stated that his first responsibility relates to the organization of a health planning council.

The main thrust of the meeting was to question the need for the West Alabama Health Services Project as proposed for Sumter County.

2

Drs. Hunt, Gilbert and Walton stated that they could see many more patients and stated that they would like to see a way to pay the transportation for patients to come to their offices, a way to pay drug bills and also a way to pay indigent patients' bills.

The need for dental services was acknowledged. Mr. Sims also stated that there was a need for a physical therapist and occupational therapist at York, so the physicians could make referrals and also a need for a dentist.

Data on the number of people in the medically indigent group as taken from census data was disputed by Mr. Sims. The group generally supported Mr. Sims' contention that there were not many medically indigent people in Sumter County. The need for the project to serve those not now being served was established originally by the Federation of Southern Cooperatives and supported by the Regional Office of the Department of Health, Education and Welfare.

The question of need for "a socialized health service" was debated with the York based physicians stating that they were not very busy now.

The group agreed that Greene County should establish the first clinic and then the Sumter County people could get a better idea of the operation. Data will be gathered on the clinic's operation and its affect on the local doctors' private practices.

Drs. Williams and Gegan spoke in favor of the project and endorsed the plan for the beginning clinic in Eutaw.

Drs. Gilbert and Walton spoke in opposition to the project on the grounds that it would decrease their private practices.

Dr. Cleino reminded the group that one-half of the representatives on the Board are from Sumter County, and the expectation is that they would want to establish a clinic in Sumter County at the end of the first year. She suggested that the people of Sumter County, Livingston and York, get together and work out what they wish to do. She stated that it was her opinion that the Federation would be given money to serve the underserved in Sumter County, if this project cannot do it.

Dr. Williams proposed another meeting of the medical society for further discussion of the project.

The meeting concluded at 9:15 P.M.

Meeting of
WEST ALABAMA HEALTH SERVICES, INC. BOARD OF DIRECTORS
Livingston, Alabama
March 21, 1974

MINUTES

BOARD MEMBERS PRESENT

Judge William M. Branch	Greene County Commission
Mr. Robert Cook	Sumter County Consumer
Sheriff Thomas Gilmore	Greene County Consumer
Mrs. Zora Gibbs	Sumter County Consumer
Mr. Willie Hill	Greene County Consumer
Mr. John Modley	Greene County Consumer
Mr. W. T. Lockard	Sumter County Commission
Mr. Edward Ozment	Sumter County Consumer
Dr. Rucker Staggers	Greene County Medical Society

BOARD MEMBERS ABSENT

Dr. Edward Gegan	Sumter County Medical Society
Dr. John Packard	West Alabama Comprehensive Health Planning Council

OTHERS PRESENT

Dr. Roland Ficken	Representing Dr. John Packard - College of Community Health Sciences
Mrs. Mamie Marbley	Hill Hospital of York Board
Mr. Jim Coleman	Greene County Commission Staff
Mr. Andrew Dearman	Representing Congressman Walter Flowers
Mr. M. E. Brown	Sumter County Commission
Mr. Harold Pittman	Administrator, Sumter Memorial Hospital
Mr. John Sims	Administrator, Hill Hospital of York
Dr. Vance R. Kane	Sixth District Dental Society
Mr. Aubrey Green	Chairman, Hill Hospital Board of Trustees
Mr. Henry L. Cobb	Pharmacist, York AL
Mr. Jim Hamilton	Health Planner, District VI
The Rev. Nixon	Ministry
The Rev. Hoard	Ministry
Dr. Elizabeth Cleino	West Alabama Comprehensive Health Planning Council - District II
Mr. Gerald Buckingham	West Alabama Comprehensive Health Planning Council - District II
Mr. Greg de Lissovoy	West Alabama Comprehensive Health Planning Council - District II

The meeting was called to order at 7:15 P.M. at the Sumter County Health Department in Livingston, Alabama, by Judge William Branch, President of the Board of Directors. Dr. Staggers read the minutes of the meeting held January 21. Copies of the minutes had been previously mailed to the Board members. There being no additions or corrections, the minutes stood approved as published.

Report of Events Since January 21

Dr. Cleino reported to the Board that two meetings had been held with the Federation of Southern Cooperatives since the last meeting on January 21. The meetings were held in an attempt to reach a compromise with the Federation, but the Federation remained firm in its demands. She also stated that the Regional Office had stated that it was satisfied every effort had been made to reach a fair compromise between the two Boards. The Regional Office representatives recommended that the revised proposal be completed and forwarded to their office as soon as possible.

A meeting was held with representatives of the York area and resulted in many new ideas. A meeting was also held with the Sixth District Dental Society to help develop a detailed plan for dental services. Dr. Cleino stated that the grant budget request was reduced by $125,000. Upon completion, Dr. Cleino hand-carried the revised project proposal to the Regional Office on March 13. The Department of Health, Education and Welfare will hold its final review of the grant application March 28, 1974.

Presentation of Revised Grant Application

Mr. de Lissovoy distributed copies of the final proposal to the representatives of organizations present at the meeting. He noted that each copy cost approximately $5.00, so there are a limited number of copies.

The objectives of the project were discussed and the contributions of the many people who helped develop the plans were acknowledged. The budget was discussed at length and it was pointed out that a large amount was set aside for health service personnel while the administrative costs had been reduced.

Nomination of Chairman, Professional Advisory Committee

Judge Branch stessed the need for a Professional Advisory Committee and explained how helpful the area health professionals had been in developing the project proposal. He emphasized the need for continued cooperation and assistance

3

from those persons who live and work in the health services professions. Details of the Committee were discussed at length. Finally, it was decided that the Professional Advisory Committee would include the following:

Hospital Administration	3
Pharmacy	2
Dental Society	3
Nurses' Association	2
Physician	1
Total	11

Dr. Staggers moved that Mr Sims be appointed Chairman of the Professional Advisory Committee and Mr. Ozment seconded. The motion carried and Judge Branch asked Mr. Sims to accept the appointment of committee chairman and to present a list of prospective members for the Committee to the Board. Mr. Sims then expressed his appreciation to the Board for this expression of confidence and said that he would make every effort to maintain the spirit of cooperation that had developed during the planning phase of this project.

Appointment of Committee Memberships

Judge Branch appointed members of committees who would be responsible for recruiting potential candidates for the key staff positions of Project Director, Physician and Dentist. Those appointed to the committees were as follow:

Project Director Search Committee:

Judge William Branch (Chairman)
Mr. W. T. Lockard
Sheriff Thomas Gilmore

Physician Search Committee:

Dr. John Packard (Chairman)
Dr. Edward Gegan
Dr. Rucker Staggers

Dentist Search Committee:

Dr. T. C. Looney (Chairman)
Dr. William Cole
Dr. J. S. Morris

Other Business

Mr. Andrew Dearman, representing Congressman Walter Flowers, addressed the meeting. He stated that Congressman Flowers is most gratified to see so many people of the two counties working together to develop a project to improve health care in the area. He stated that he had called Dr. Hudgins at the Regional Office to determine the status of the grant but was informed that Dr. Hudgins was out of town. Another HEW official told him that final action on the project would be taken March 28. Mr. Dearman said that he would call DHEW on Monday to see if there have been any new developments. He said that they are confident that the grant will be awarded shortly, and Congressman Flowers encourages the people to continue their development of the project.

Dr. Kane stated that he was certain that the Board was aware that a corporation may not legally employ a dentist in Alabama. Judge Branch replied that the Board had not been previously informed of such a law, where upon, Dr. Kane produced a copy of the Code of Alabama and began reading provisions of the law to the group. Since this was very technical and lengthy, he said that anyone who wished to examine this copy is free to do so. There was some discussion of this matter. Finally, Judge Branch said that he would refer this matter to the firm of Pruitt and Pruitt, who are serving as counsel to the WAHS Project.

Mr. Green, representing Mayor Grant of the Town of York, asked Dr. Cleino to explain aspects of the project affecting Sumter County. Dr. Cleino stated that in a meeting with various members of the communities in Greene and Sumter Counties a concensus developed that the project should begin in Greene County. A meeting had been held with representatives from the York area and they expressed a need to make a detailed study of health problems in Sumter County before preparing a detailed plan for activities in that county. This is reflected in the objectives which are stated in the revised application, which has been submitted to DHEW.

Rev. Nixon noted that the salaries and other cost had been spelled out in detail in the proposal but wondered what provisions had been made for charging patients for care. Mr. de Lissovoy referred the group to page 35 of the grant application, and the fee system was discussed. He stressed the importance of generating as much revenue as possible through clinical services in order to reduce the need of Federal subsidy and increase the amount of services provided to the people in the area. However, this is not a money making project and the major concern is for the people's health and no one will be denied treatment because he cannot afford to pay.

Judge Branch expressed his appreciation to the West Alabama Comprehensive Health Planning Council on behalf of the Board of Directors for all the work that the Council has done in helping to develop this project. Several other persons present also expressed appreciation to the Council.

There being no further business, the meeting was adjourned at 8:35 P.M.

MEETING OF THE BOARD OF DIRECTORS
WEST ALABAMA HEALTH SERVICES, INC.
Eutaw, Alabama
May 22, 1974

MINUTES

BOARD MEMBERS PRESENT

Judge William M. Branch	Greene County Commission
Mr. Robert Cook	Sumter County Consumers
Mrs. Zora Gibbs	Sumter County Consumers
Dr. Edward Gegan	Sumter County Medical Society
Mr. Willie Hill	Greene County Consumer
Mr. W. T. Lockard	Sumter County Commission
Mr. John Modley	Greene County Consumer
Mr. Edward Ozment	Sumter County Consumer
Dr. John Packard	West Alabama Comprehensive Health Planning Council
Dr. Rucker Staggers	Greene County Medical Society

BOARD MEMBERS ABSENT

Sheriff Thomas E. Gilmore	Greene County Consumers

OTHERS PRESENT

Mr. Marvin Barton	Greene County Hospital
Dr. Elizabeth Cleino	West Alabama CHP Council
Mr. James Coleman	Greene County Finance Officer
Mr. Greg deLissovoy	West Alabama CHP Council
Ms. Jane deLissovoy	Guest
Dr. T. C. Looney	Sixth District Dental Society
Rev. Nixon	Guest
Mr. David Patton	Greene County Hospital
Mr. John Sims	Professional Advisory Committee
Mrs. John Sims	Guest
Mayor William Tuck	Town of Eutaw

The meeting was called to order at 7:40 p.m. at the Greene County
Health Department in Eutaw, Alabama, by Judge William M. Branch, President
of the Board of Directors. Dr. Staggers presented the minutes of the meeting of
March 21, 1974. It was moved by Dr. Gegan and seconded by Dr. Packard that
the minutes be adopted as published. The motion was approved.

Announcement of Grant Award

Judge Branch announced that the Department of Health, Education and Welfare had approved the West Alabama Health Services project proposal and awarded a grant of $251,243 for the period July 1, 1974 through June 30, 1975. He reminded the Board that local organizations have pledged $13,687 as "in-kind" contributions. Copies of the Notice of Grant Award had been mailed to members of the Board on May 8, 1974.

Terms and Conditions of the Grant Award

Judge Branch asked Mr. deLissovoy to review the Terms and Conditions of the Grant Award. Mr. deLissovoy reminded the Board that they were entering into a contract with the Federal Government and that the Terms and Conditions were a part of this contract.

Dr. Staggers told the Board that he had been contacted by a representative of the Internal Revenue Service in Atlanta in regard to the request of the West Alabama Health Services to become a tax exempt organization. IRS suggested that it might be necessary for the Board to amend the By-Laws of the Corporation to state that it would not enter into competition with local profit-making organizations in areas unrelated to the project objectives.

Discussion of the Terms and Conditions

1. Building Lease

   Mr. Ozment suggested that planning for the clinic building be undertaken immediately since this could delay the project. Mr. Coleman stated that Greene County was prepared to construct a clinic building to the Board's specifications and lease it to West Alabama Health Services at a fair and reasonable rate, as determined by independent appraisal. The Board authorized Mr. Coleman to prepare preliminary plans and cost estimates for a clinic building.

2. DHEW Approval of Contracts

   Members of the Board agreed that DHEW's review and approval of all contracts would provide an additional safeguard for the project.

3. Project Director

   Judge Branch stated that the Search Committee for a Project Director would prepare an abstract of the Job Description which could be utilized in advertising the position vacancy. He asked Dr. Cleino for assistance in the placement of advertisements. The Board agreed that the selection of a Project Director must be given immediate priority.

Dr. Packard suggested that the Physician and Dentist positions also be advertised and that the West Alabama Comprehensive Health Planning Council be requested to assist in the preparation and placement of announcements. Judge Branch stated that advertisements should be placed in local newspapers in Greene and Sumter County and in the Birmingham and Montgomery papers as a minimum. Dr. Looney said that the Journal of the Americal Dental Association would be appropriate for recruitment of the Dentist. Dr. Cleino suggested the American Public Health Association Journal would reach all types of health professionals.

4. Lease or Lease-Purchase of Equipment

Dr. Looney questioned whether a vendor would be willing to lease equipment to an organization which was guaranteed funding for only one year. He stated that leasing is advantageous for a private practice dentist or physician because it conserves capital and has tax advantages. He believes that the dental section could be adequately equipped for about $30,000 as opposed to the original estimate of $50,000. Mr. Sims estimated that leased equipment would cost approximately $600 per month for each $10,000 of equipment--roughly $7,200 a year. Dr. Looney said that he would investigate dental equipment for the clinic and Dr. Staggers offered to do the same for medical equipment.

5. Pharmaceutical Services

The Board decided to investigate this question at a later date since there were other matters which now have a higher priority.

6. Transportation and Outreach

Mr. Cook offered to help develop the description of this component as it concerned Sumter County. Mr. Lockard offered to arrange a meeting with Mr. Leo Fields, Sumter County Head Start Director since that project has a transportation component. Judge Branch stated that he would arrange a meeting with Mr. Charles Jones, Director of Greene County's outreach system. The Board requested that the West Alabama Comprehensive Health Planning Council coordinate the response to this particular Condition of Grant Award.

-4-

7. Job Descriptions

The Board requested that the WACHPC prepare the necessary job
descriptions patterning these after job descriptions from similar
clinics. The Board and the Professional Advisory Committee will
then review these for use by West Alabama Health Services.

8. Responsibility for Sumter County Health Plan

Mr. deLissovoy read Objective No. 2 in the Project Proposal which
stated that:

"Within nine (9) months from the date of grant award, West
Alabama Health Services, Inc. shall have developed a detailed
plan for the provision of primary care in Sumter County. This
shall be performed with the cooperation and assistance of concerned private and public organizations as well as the District
VI Health Planning Council."

Mr. Lockard said he was sure that organizations in Sumter County
would provide extensive support in the development of this plan.
Dr. Looney suggested that the Project Director be given ultimate
responsibility for this task, subject to final approval of the plan
by the Board of Directors. Dr. Staggers moved that the Project
Director be responsible for development of the Sumter County plan
as specified in Objective No. 2. This was seconded by Mr. Ozment
and approved unanimously.

9. Clinic Schedule and Provision for Emergency Services

Dr. Staggers and Dr. Gegan volunteered to prepare a tentative
clinic schedule and plan for emergency services for review by
the full Board of Directors.

10. Personnel and Procurement Policies

The Board requested that the West Alabama Comprehensive Health
Planning Council prepare personnel policy statements patterned
after similar community clinics. These could then be reviewed
and modified as necessary by the Board of Directors.

11. Delineation of the Project Director-Board of Director Responsibilities

The Board requested that the WACHPC staff provide the Board with samples of policy statements developed by other clinics which delineate the role of the Project Director and the responsibility of the Board for review by the Board.

Presentation of Contract for Technical Assistance

Dr. Cleino presented the draft of a contract for technical assistance to West Alabama Health Services, Inc. to be provided by West Alabama Comprehensive Health Planning Council. She explained that the type of assistance the Council has provided to West Alabama Health Services during the past few months, and the assistance which will be required during the initial stages of project implementation, is far beyond the normal activity of Health Planning Councils. The Council is willing to continue its assistance to West Alabama Health Services, Inc. provided that it is reimbursed for expenses incurred in this activity.

Dr. Staggers moved that West Alabama Health Services enter into the contract submitted by the West Alabama Comprehensive Health Planning Council, subject to approval by the Department of Health, Education and Welfare. The motion was seconded by Dr. Gegan and carried unanimously. The Board directed Judge Branch to sign the agreement on behalf of WAHS and forward a copy to Atlanta for concurrence.

Remarks Concerning West Alabama Comprehensive Health Planning Council

Mr. Patton noted the Health Planning Council has been deeply involved in the WAHS project since July, 1973. He commended the Council staff for the excellent job in helping to develop the project. Several other persons present expressed similar views.

Other Business

Mr. deLissovoy announced that he would be visiting Health Services, Inc. on May 22. This is a community clinic in Montgomery which is also funded by 314 (e) funds, and is regarded by HEW officials as the most successful project in the region. Mr. James Coleman will accompany Mr. deLissovoy as a representative of Judge Branch and the Board of Directors. Others present were invited to participate.

After some discussion, members of the Board decided to hold the next meeting on Wednesday, June 5th, at 7:30 p.m. at the Sumter County Health Department in Livingston.

There being no further business, the meeting adjourned at 9:35 p.m.

WEST ALABAMA HEALTH SERVICES, INC.
Livingston, Alabama
Meeting of the Board of Directors
June 5, 1974

MINUTES

BOARD MEMBERS PRESENT

Judge William M. Branch
Mr. Robert Cook
Dr. Edward Gegan
Mrs. Zora Gibbs
Mr. W. T. Lockard
Mr. John Modley

BOARD MEMBERS ABSENT

Sheriff Thomas Gilmore
Mr. Willie Hill
Mr. Edward Ozment
Dr. John Packard
Dr. Rucker Staggers

OTHERS PRESENT

Mr. Malcolm Branch
Mr. Thaddeus Branch
Mr. William Branch, II
Ms. Jane de Lissovoy
Mr. Leo Fields

The meeting was called to order at 7:45 p.m. at the Sumter County Health Department in Livingston, Alabama by Judge William M. Branch, President of the Board of Directors. In the absence of Dr. Staggers, Judge Branch called the roll. A quorum was present. The Board noted that Sheriff Gilmore had now missed two consecutive meetings. Mr. Lockard read the minutes of the meeting of May 22, 1974.

Mr. Cook offered a correction to the Minutes to the effect that Reverand Gibbs had been erroneously identified as Reverand Nixon. It was moved by Dr. Gegan and seconded by Mr. Lockard that the minutes be adopted as published, with the change suggested by Mr. Cook. The motion was approved.

Mr. Lockard referred the group to page 2 of the May 22 minutes and the statement that "local organizations have pledged $13,687 in matching funds". Mr. de Lissovoy explained that one of HEW's criteria for evaluating proposals is the extent of local support. This support can usually be provided as "in-kind" services.

866

OLD BUSINESS

Recruitment of a Project Director

Judge Branch reported that advertisements had been placed in the Greene County
Democrat and the Sumter County Home Record to announce the availability of the
Project Director position. Mr. Lockard stated that a similar advertisement should
be placed in the Sumter County Journal. The Board directed the WACHPC to place
additional advertisements in the Tuscaloosa and Birmingham newspapers. There
are presently six candidates for the position.

Clinic Schedule and Emergency Coverage

Dr. Gegan introduced a letter from Dr. Staggers, speaking on behalf of the Greene
County Medical Society. The Society will provide physician coverage of the WAHS
clinic five days per week, four hours per day, until a full-time physician has been
engaged. The Board members present felt that this is an exceptionally generous
offer and commended the Greene County Medical Society for its dedication to the
health needs of local people. Once a physician has been recruited, they will provide
emergency and weekend coverage at the Greene County Hospital emergency room,
but only for true emergencies. There was some discussion of the definition of a
"true emergency".

Lease/Purchase of Clinical Equipment

Mr. de Lissovoy reported that he had discussed the project with one of the
Nation's largest leasing firms, a subsidiary of City National Bank of New York.
They have no interest in a project like West Alabama Health Services.
However, another company contacted, the CMS Division of Coulter Electronics,
has worked with many Federal programs and would be interested in exploring
the possibility of equipment financing. Dr. Gegan questioned the need for
sophisticated equipment, such a comprehensive clinical laboratory, during the
early life of the WAHS Project. He said that sophisticated procedures can be
performed in Selma and Tuscaloosa at reasonable cost and that the State Laboratory
will provide many services at no charge.

Job Description for Clinic Staff

Mr. deLissovoy introduced draft job descriptions for positions in the clinic which
were not fully described in the proposal. These were adapted from job descriptions
developed by Health Services, Inc. in Montgomery. The Board decided to review
these in detail at the next meeting. Members of the Professional Advisory Committee
will be asked for assistance in defining job requirements.

NEW BUSINESS

Visit to Health Services, Inc. (Montgomery)

Judge Branch asked Mr. de Lissovoy to report on a visit to Health Services,
Inc. in Montgomery. This is a community health center funded under Section

314 (e), like West Alabama Health Services. Mr. de Lissovoy said that he and Mr. Coleman spent most of an entire day meeting with members of the HSI staff and observing clinic operation. Mr. de Lissovoy described the procedures used to speed the flow of patients in some detail. Dr. Gegan stated that all this sounded very impersonal and that the doctor-patient relationship was lost. Other members of the Board agreed that when a person goes to the doctor, he wants to see the physician or dentist personally.

Summer Youth Employment Program

Judge Branch discussed Greene County's Summer employment program and the possibility of obtaining temporary clerical support for the WAHS project at no cost. The Board responded favorably to this suggestion and left this to Judge Branch's discretion.

Review of a Text on Design of Community Health Centers

Mr. de Lissovoy read a review of Planning for the Organization and Delivery of Community Health Centers by Byron A. McDonald which appeared in the ARC Journal, an official government publication. The price of this five column work is $50.00. The Board authorized WACHPC to order it on approval for review by the Board.

Agenda for Next Meeting

Mr. Lockard suggested that the Board meet again in two weeks and that the primary item of business be the review of applications for Project Director. There was some discussion concerning legal requirements for advertising the position availability. Mr. Fields stated that, to the best of his knowledge, HEW guidelines required a minimum of ten (10) business days or two calendar weeks of public announcement. The Board requested that WACHPC prepare an adver- tisement for the Tuscaloosa and Birmingham papers which would state that the deadline for receipt of applications was June 21. The Board decided to hold its next meeting on June 24 at 7:30 p.m. to review applications for Project Director. The Screening Committee will meet at 7:00 to review the applications and screen out any obviously unsuitable candidates. The screening committee is composed of:

> Judge Branch
> Mr. Lockard
> Sheriff Gilmore

Dr. Gegan suggested that Mr. Patton, Greene County Hospital Administrator, be asked to participate in the review of candidates. Mr. Lockard stated that all three hospital administrators should participate (Mr. Sims, Mr. Pittman and Mr. Patton). After some discussion, the Board agreed to invite all interested physicians and dentist, as well.

-4-

Mr. Lockard moved that the meeting be adjourned. The motion was seconded by Mrs. Gibbs and approved. The meeting adjourned at 9:17 p.m.

NEXT MEETING OF THE BOARD OF DIRECTORS:

Sumter County Health Department (Livingston)
Monday, June 24, 1974
7:30 P.M.

PROJECT DIRECTOR SCREENING COMMITTEE

Meet at 7:00 P.M.

Special Meeting
WEST ALABAMA HEALTH SERVICES
Livingston, Alabama
June 15, 1974

SUMMARY

Participants

Judge William Branch   Greene County Commission
Mr. W. T. Lockard   Sumter County Commission
Mr. Greg de Lissovoy   West Alabama Health
                                        Planning Council

The meeting convened at the Sumter County Courthouse at 10:00 AM, Saturday, June 15, 1974.

The purpose of this meeting was to discuss tentative criteria for review of applicants for the position of Project Director.

Response to Advertisement

Advertisements for the Project Director position have been placed in newspapers in Greene and Sumter Counties as well as Tuscaloosa and Birmingham. Only a few applications were expected but more than a dozen have been received and others are arriving daily. They are coming from across the United States, not just from within Alabama.

This surprising response was the reason for today's meeting. The Board expected to receive only a few applications and this would make screening relatively easy. Now it was obvious that some criteria were required.

Criteria for Applicant Review

It was first suggested that identifying information should be removed from applications presented to the Board to facilitate objective review of candidates. Once the field had been narrowed down, the individuals would be identified.

- 2 -

Everyone present agreed that the first consideration in selecting a Project Director must be proven ability to get the job done. The Project Director must be a highly capable individual if the project is to be successful and receive full five year funding.

The second consideration must be evidence of the applicant's probable commitment to the project. The Board must be careful of the "job hoppers" who go from one Federal project to another. This consideration would tend to favor persons having ties to the region.

Finally, it was agreed that all due consideration should be given to the opinions of the Greene County board members. Similar consideration will be given to the Sumter County board members when the time comes to select a Site Manager for the Sumter County activity.

Judge Branch is providing copies of the applications received to Mr. Lockard and Mr. de Lissovoy.

OTHER MATTERS DISCUSSED

Dental Services

The WAHS planning staff received substantial support from the Sixth District Dental Society in development of the dental services program outlined in the Proposal submitted to HEW (see page 34). Studies have shown that increased dental care for children is one of Greene County's most important health needs.

At the March 21, 1974 meeting of the WAHS Board of Directors, Dr. Vance Kane raised the possibility of legal difficulties in the provision of dental care. The Board referred this matter to the Sixth District Dental Society for furthur study.

It was agreed today that the time has come for beginning recruitment of a dentist and detailed planning of the dental services. It was decided that Mr. de Lissovoy would contact Dr. Hiram Johnson, President of the Sixth District Dental Society, to request furthur assistance in this regard.

Planning for Sumter County Activity

The proposal for the second year of West Alabama Health Services will be due in Atlanta during March, 1975. This is only nine (9) months away. The study of Sumter County health needs and resources must begin early in the Fall so that the first draft of the proposal can be completed in December.

It was agreed that the Board should give serious consideration to contracting for technical support in performing this study. The Board could engage a person who is a resident of Sumter County and experienced in health services. However, it may be difficult to find someone who has the required experience and is available on a part-time consulting basis. It was suggested that this individual might be able to provide valuable assistance to the Project Director in specific areas, depending on background and experience. Furthurmore, this person would be a logical candidate for the position of Site Manager for Sumter County Operations in the second year of the project.

APPLICATION FOR STATUS AS A 501(C) (3) CORPORATION
FILED WITH THE INTERNAL REVENUE SERVICE BY
WEST ALABAMA HEALTH SERVICES, INC.

WEST ALABAMA HEALTH SERVICES, INC.
P.O. Box 347
Eutaw, Alabama 35462

District Director   April 3, 1974
Internal Revenue Service
P.O. Box 737
Atlanta, Ga. 30301

Att: Determination Section

Gentlemen:

Enclosed please find Form 1023 with attached Schedule D submitted in the
name of West Alabama Health Services, Inc..

This organization was created to apply for a Federal grant from the Department of Health, Education and Welfare to provide ambulatory health care in
Greene and Sumter Counties (Alabama).

Since the grant has not yet been awarded the corporation has no funds.
Consequently, the financial statements in Form 1023 are left blank.

Attached to the required forms are copies of the Project Summary and
Budget Summary as submitted in the proposal to DHEW. These describe
the project and its estimated budget and may assist you in making your
determination.

The grant cannot be awarded until a ruling is received from IRS. Thus,
we would greatly appreciate your attention to this matter.

Thank you for your assistance.

                              Sincerely,

                              William M. Branch, President
                              West Alabama Health Services, Inc.
Encl.
cc: Dept. of HEW, Region IV

WMB/gdl

☆ U S GOVERNMENT PRINTING OFFICE 1973 —492 · 951

FOR CLEAR COPY ON ALL PARTS TYPEWRITE OR PRINT WITH BALL-POINT PEN—PRESS FIRMLY
(See Instructions on Reverse)

FORM SS-4 (7-69)
PART 1 U S, TREASURY DEPARTMENT—INTERNAL REVENUE SERVICE
APPLICATION FOR EMPLOYER IDENTIFICATION NUMBER

1. NAME (TRUE name as distinguished from TRADE name.)
West Alabama Health Services, Incorporated

2. TRADE NAME, IF ANY (Enter name under which business is operated, if different from item 1.)
None

3. ADDRESS OF PRINCIPAL PLACE OF BUSINESS (No. and Street, City, State, Zip Code)
P.O. Box 347 Eutaw, Alabama 35462

4. COUNTY OF BUSINESS LOCATION
Greene

5. ORGANIZATION Check Type
☐ Individual ☐ Partnership ☐ Corporation ☐ Other (specify e.g. estate, trust, etc.)
☐ Governmental ☒ Nonprofit Organization
☐ (See Instr. 5) ☐ (See Instr. 5)

6. Ending Month of Accounting year
June

7. REASON FOR APPLYING (If "other" specify such as "Corporate structure change," "Acquired by gift or trust," etc.)
☒ Started new business ☐ Purchased going business ☐ Other

8. Date you acquired or started business (Mo. day, year)
9 Nov. 1973

9. First date you paid or will pay wages (Mo. day, year)
1 July 1974

10. NATURE OF BUSINESS (See Instructions)
Ambulatory Health Services

11. NUMBER OF EMPLOYEES IF "NONE" ENTER "0"
Non-agricultural **0** | Agricultural

12. If nature of business is MANUFACTURING, list in order of their importance the principal products manufactured and the estimated percentage of the total value of all products which each represents.
A _____ %
B _____ % C _____ %

PLEASE LEAVE BLANK
R | DO | TA
FR | FRC

13. Do you operate more than one place of business? ☐ Yes ☒ No
If "Yes," attach a list showing for each separate establishment.
a. Name and address b. Nature of business c. Number of employees.

14. To whom do you sell most of your products or services?
☐ Business establishments ☒ General public ☐ Other (Specify)

PLEASE LEAVE BLANK →
Geo. | Ind. | Class | Size | Reas. for Appl. | Bus. Bir. Date

FORM SS-4 (3-69)
PART 2
DO NOT DETACH ANY PART
OF THIS FORM SEND ALL COPIES TO
INTERNAL REVENUE SERVICE

PLEASE LEAVE BLANK

NAME AND COMPLETE ADDRESS

1. Name (TRUE name as distinguished from TRADE name.)
West Alabama Health Services, Incorporated

2. TRADE NAME, IF ANY (Enter name under which business is operated, if different from item 1.)
None

3. ADDRESS OF PRINCIPAL PLACE OF BUSINESS (No. and Street)
P.O. Box 347

(City, State, Zip Code)
Eutaw, Alabama 35462

4. COUNTY OF BUSINESS LOCATION
Greene

5. ORGANIZATION Check Type
☐ Individual ☐ Partnership ☐ Corporation ☐ Other (specify e.g. estate, trust, etc.)
☐ Governmental ☒ Nonprofit Organization
☐ (See Instr. 5) ☐ (See Instr. 5)

6. Ending Month of Accounting year
June

7. REASON FOR APPLYING (If "other" specify such as "Corporate structure change," "Acquired by gift or trust," etc.)
☒ Started new business ☐ Purchased going business ☐ Other

8. Date you acquired or started business (Mo. day, year)
9 Nov. 1973

9. First date you paid or will pay wages (Mo. day, year)
1 July 1974

10. NATURE OF BUSINESS (See Instructions)
Ambulatory Health Services

11. NUMBER OF EMPLOYEES IF "NONE" ENTER "0"
Non-agricultural **0** | Agricultural

12. Have you ever applied for an identification number for this or any other business? ☒ No ☐ Yes
If "Yes," enter name and trade name (if any). Also enter the approximate date, city, and state where you first applied and previous number if known. ➝

DATE
April 3, 1974

SIGNATURE

TITLE
President

Form **1023** (Rev. November 1972) Department of the Treasury Internal Revenue Service	**Application for Recognition of Exemption** Under Section 501(c)(3) of the Internal Revenue Code	To be filed in the District in which the organization has its principal office or place of business.

This application, when properly completed, shall constitute the notice required under section 508(a) of the Internal Revenue Code in order that organizations may be treated as described in section 501(c)(3) of the code, and the notice under section 508(b) appropriate to those organizations claiming not to be private foundations within the meaning of section 509(a).

Part I.—Identification (See instructions)

1 Full name of organization	2 Employer identification number (If none, attach Form SS-4)
West Alabama Health Services, Inc.	None

3(a) Address (number and street)

P.O. Box 347

3(b) City or town, State and ZIP code	4 Name and phone number of person to be contacted
Eutaw, Alabama 35462	Judge William M. Branch (205)372-33

5 Month the annual accounting period ends December	6 Date incorporated or formed November 9, 1973	7 Activity Codes (see instructions) 155 165 179

Part II.—Organizational Documents (See instructions)

1 Attach a conformed copy of the organization's creating instruments (articles of incorporation, constitution, articles of association, deed of trust, etc.).

2 Attach a conformed copy of the organization's by-laws or other rules for its operation.

3 If the organization does not have a creating instrument, check here (See instructions) . . . . ☐

Part III.—Activities and Operational Information (See instructions)

1 What are or will be the organization's sources of financial support? List in order of magnitude. If a portion of the receipts is or will be derived from the earnings of patents, copyrights, or other assets (excluding stock, bonds, etc.), identify such item as a separate source of receipt. Attach representative copies of solicitations for financial support.

(a) Grant from Dept. of Health Education and Welfare (PL 91-515, Section 314(e) "Neighborhood Health Centers").

(b) Reimbursement for clinical services (MEDICARE, MEDICAID, private insurors).

(c) Community fund raising (Bazaars, Fairs, Benefit Concerts, Banquet

(d) Gifts from organizations and individuals.

(e) Patient fees for clinical services.

2 Describe the organization's fund-raising program and explain to what extent it has been put into effect. (Include details of fund-raising activities such as selective mailings, formation of fund raising committees, use of professional fund raisers, etc.)

Sole activity to date is submission of grant application to the Department of Health, Education and Welfare.

I declare under the penalties of perjury that I am authorized to sign this application on behalf of the above organization and I have examined this application, including the accompanying statements, and to the best of my knowledge it is true, correct and complete

---   --   ---------------------------
      (Signature)   (Title or authority of signer)   (Date)

Part III.—Activities and Operational Information (Continued)

3 Give a narrative description of the activities presently carried on by the organization, and also those that will be carried on. If the organization is not fully operational, explain what stage of development its activities have reached, what further steps remain for the organization to become fully operational, and when such further steps will take place. The narrative should specifically identify the services performed or to be performed by the organization (Do not state the purposes of the organization in general terms or repeat the language of the organizational documents.) If the organization is a school, hospital, or medical research organization, include sufficient information in your description to clearly show that the organization meets the definition of that particular activity that is contained in the instructions for Part VII–A on page 3 of the instructions.

West Alabama Health Services, Inc. will eventually provide a full range of ambulatory health care services, beginning with the following:

- Routine physical and dental examination and treatment
- Diagnostic tests and procedures
- Provision of drugs and other health care supplies as prescribed by staff professionals
- Patient education in preventive health care
- Counseling and social services

Since the date of incorporation (9 November 1973), the organization's sole activity has been the development of a grant application for submission to the Dept. of Health Education and Welfare.

At the present time, this application has been submitted to DHEW and is under study. To become operational, the organization must receive tax exempt status from Internal Revenue and funding approval from DHEW. Approval from DHEW awaits IRS certification.

Once the organization is funded, key staff members (Project Director, physician, dentist, etc.) will be engaged, a clinic site selected, equipment purchased, and services as described above will be rendered. This phase should begin in July, 1974, if the grant is approved by DHEW.

Although the purpose of West Alabama Health Services, Inc. is the direct provision of medical care, the organization may offer its clinic for use as a training site in the various health professions in conjunction with programs of study offered by neighboring universities, technical schools, etc. This would be accomplished by creating "work-study" programs whereby students would be employed in the clinic and assist in the provision of health care under the supervision of experienced professionals.

Form 1023 (Rev. 11-72)   Page **3**

Part III.—Activities and Operational Information (Continued)

4 The membership of the organization's governing body is:

(a) Names, addresses, and duties of officers, directors, trustees, etc.	(b) Specialized knowledge, training, expertise, or particular qualifications
SEE ATTACHED LIST	SEE ATTACHED LIST

(c) Do any of the above persons serve as members of the governing body by reason of being public officials or being appointed by public officials? . . . . ☒ Yes ☐ No
If "Yes," please name such persons and explain the basis of their selection or appointment.

SEE ATTACHED LIST

(d) Are any members of the organization's governing body "disqualified persons" with respect to the organization (other than by reason of being a member of the governing body) or do any of the members have either a business or family relationship with "disqualified persons"? (See specific instructions 4(d).) . . ☐ Yes ☒ No
If "Yes," please explain.

5 Does the organization control or is it controlled by any other organization? . . . . ☐ Yes ☒ No
Is the organization the outgrowth of another organization, or does it have a special relationship to another organization by reason of interlocking directorates or other factors? . . . . ☐ Yes ☒ No
If either of these questions is answered "Yes," please explain.

6 Is the organization financially accountable to any other organization? . . . . ☒ Yes ☐ No
If "Yes," please explain and identify the other organization. Include details concerning accountability or attach copies of reports if any have been rendered.

Accountable to Dept. of Health, Education and Welfare under regulations prescribed by OMB for grants under P.L. 91-515 Sect. 314(e)

7 What assets does the organization have that are used in the performance of its exempt function? (Do not include income producing property.) If any assets are not fully operational, explain what stage of completion has been reached, what additional steps remain to be completed, and when such final steps will be taken.

NONE. Grant from DHEW is anticipated pending IRS tax-exemption letter and funding approval. Final approval anticipated by 1 May 1974

AT~~HMENT TO FORM 1023---WEST ALABAMA HEALTH ~~RVICES, INCORPORATED--P.O. BOX 347, EUTAW, ~

Part III   No. 4:   (a)   Membership of the Organization Governing Body   (Board of Directors)

NAME	ADDRESS	DUTIES
Judge William M. Branch	P.O. Box 347, Eutaw, Alabama 35462	President, Board of Directors
Thomas E. Gilmore	P.O. Box 347, Eutaw, Alabama 35462	Member, " " "
Willie Hill	Route 3, Box 145, Eutaw, Alabama 35462	Member " " "
John H. Modley	Route 1, Box 90, Forkland, Alabama 36740	Member " " "
Dr. Rucker Staggers	202 Pickens St., Eutaw, Alabama 35462	Secretary " " "
Robert Cook	York, Alabama 36925	Member " " "
Dr. Edward Gegan	Box 781, Livingston, Alabama 35470	Member " " "
Zora C. Gibbs	Box 141, Livngston, Alabama 35470	Treasurer " " "
W. T. Lockard	Box 216, York, Alabama 36925	Vice-president " " "
Edward Ozment	Sumterville, Alabama 35485	Member " " "
Dr. John Packard	Box 6291, University, Alabama 35486	Member " " "

NOTE: The Board of Directors is the final authority for all aspects of the West Alabama
Health Services, Inc. project management. The Board exercises fiscal control,
establishes policy, selects key staff and monitors project operation.

ATTACHMENT TO FORM 1023---WEST ALABAMA HEALTH SERVICES, INCORPORATED -- P.O. BOX 347, EUTAW, AL.

Part III   No. 4:   (b)   Specialized Knowledge or Training of Members of the Board of Directors

NAME	ADDRESS	SPECIALIZED KNOWLEDGE
Judge William M. Branch	P.O. Box 347, Eutaw, Alabama 35462	Community Organization; Human Services
Thomas E. Gilmore	P.O. Box 347, Eutaw, Alabama 35462	Community Organization; Human Services
Willie Hill	Route 3, Box 145, Eutaw, Alabama 35462	Environmental Health; Transportation management
John H. Modley	Route 1, Box 90, Forkland, Alabama 36740	Social Services Outreach Program Management
Dr. Rucker Staggers	202 Pickens St., Eutaw, Alabama 35462	Medical Care; Clinical Management
Robert Cook	York, Alabama 36925	Community Organization; Human Services
Dr. Edward Gegan	Box 781, Livingston, Alabama 35470	Medical Care; Clinical Management
Zora C. Gibbs	Box 141, Livingston, Alabama 35470	Public Health
W. T. Lockard	Box 216, York, Alabama 36925	Public Administration; Financial Management
Edward Ozment	Sumterville, Alabama 35485	Public Administration; Construction
Dr. John Packard	Box 6291, University, Alabama 35486	Medical Care; Professional Education

NAME	ADDRESS	BASIS OF SELECTION
Judge William M. Branch	P.O. Box 347, Eutaw, Alabama 35462	Chairman of Greene County Commission
Thomas E. Gilmore	P.O. Box 347, Eutaw, Alabama 35462	Greene County Consumer Representative*
Willie Hill	Route 3, Box 145, Eutaw, Alabama 35462	Greene County Consumer Representative*
John H. Modley	Route 1, Box 90, Forkland, Alabama 36740	Greene County Consumer Representative*
Dr. Rucker Staggers	202 Pickens St., Eutaw, Alabama 35462	Appointed by Greene Co. Medical Society
Robert Cook	York, Alabama 36925	Sumter Co. Consumer Representative*
Dr. Edward Gegan	Box 781, Livingston, Alabama 35470	Appointed by Sumter Co. Medical Society
Zora C. Gibbs	Box 141, Livingston, Alabama 35470	Sumter Co. Consumer Representative*
W. T. Lockard	Box 216, York, Alabama 36925	Chairman of Sumter County Commission
Edward Ozment	Sumterville, Alabama 35485	Sumter County Consumer Representative*
Dr. John Packard	Box 6291, University, Alabama 35486	Appointed by West Alabama Comprehensive Health Planning Council

*NOTE: Consumer representatives were selected by the Greene and Sumter County Commission to represent a broad cross section of persons who may be expected to utilize the services to be provided by the Corporation.

Part III.—Activities and Operational Information (Continued)

8 (a) What benefits, services, or products will the organization provide with respect to its exempt function?

Ambulatory Health Care to include:

      Routine medical and dental examination and treatment
      Diagnostic tests and procedures
      Provision of therapeutic drugs or other supplies
      Patient education in preventive health care

(b) Have the recipients been required or will they be required to pay for the organization's benefits, services, or products? . . . . ☒ **Yes** ☐ **No**

If "Yes," please explain and show how the charges are determined.

Patients will be charged a fee based on minimum prevaliling rates established by local practitioners'. Other patients will be eligible for coverage under Medicare or Medicaid. No patient will be refused treatment because of inability to pay; many will be charity patients.

9 Does or will the organization limit its benefits, services or products to specific classes of individuals? . . . ☐ Yes ☒ No

If "Yes," please explain how the recipients or beneficiaries are or will be selected.

Preference will be given to low-income families

10 Is the organization a membership organization? . . . . ☐ Yes ☒ No

If "Yes," complete the following:

(a) Please describe the organization's membership requirements and attach a schedule of membership fees and dues.

(b) Are benefits limited to members? . . . . ☐ Yes ☐ No

If "No," please explain.

(c) Attach a copy of the descriptive literature or promotional material used to attract members to the organization.

11 Does or will the organization engage in activities tending to influence legislation or intervene in any way in political campaigns? . . . . ☐ Yes ☒ No

If "Yes," please explain.

Part IV.—Statement as to Private Foundation Status (See instructions)

1 Is the organization a private foundation? . . . . ☐ Yes ☒ No

2 If question 1 is answered "No," indicate the type of ruling being requested as to the organization's status under section 509 by checking the applicable box below:

  ☐ Definitive ruling under section 509(a)(1), (2), (3), or (4) — complete Part VII.

  ☒ Advance or extended advance ruling under section 509(a)(1) or (2) — See instructions.

3 If question 1 is an answered "Yes," and the organization claims to be a private operating foundation, check here ☐ and complete Part VIII.

Form 1023 (Rev. 11-72)   NO RECEIPTS OR EXPENSES.   APPLICATION FOR FUNDING   Page 5

Part V.—Financial Data (See instructions) PENDING WITH DEPT. OF HEW UNDER PL 91-515 Sect 314

Statement of Receipts and Expenditures, for period ending ...., 19........

Receipts

1 Gross contributions, gifts, grants and similar amounts received . . . .

2 Gross dues and assessments of members . . . .

3 Gross amounts derived from activities related to organization's exempt purpose

    Less cost of sales . . . .

4 Gross amounts from unrelated business activities . . . .

    Less cost of sales . . . .

5 Gross amount received from sale of assets, excluding inventory items (attach schedule) . . . .

    Less cost or other basis and sales expense of assets sold . . . . . .

6 Interest, dividends, rents and royalties . . . .

7   Total receipts . . . .

Expenditures

8 Contributions, gifts, grants, and similar amounts paid (attach schedule) . . . .

9 Disbursements to or for benefit of members (attach schedule) . . . .

10 Compensation of officers, directors, and trustees (attach schedule) . . . .

11 Other salaries and wages . . . .

12 Interest . . . .

13 Rent . . . .

14 Depreciation and depletion . . . .

15 Other (attach schedule) . . . .

16   Total expenditures . . . .

17 Excess of receipts over expenditures (line 7 less line 16) . . . .

Balance Sheets	Enter dates ▶	Beginning date	Ending date
Assets			
18 Cash (a) interest bearing accounts			
(b) Other			
19 Accounts receivable, net			
20 Inventories			
21 Bonds and notes (attach schedule)			
22 Corporate stocks (attach schedule)			
23 Mortgage loans (attach schedule)			
24 Other investments (attach schedule)			
25 Depreciable and depletable assets (attach schedule)			
26 Land			
27 Other assets (attach schedule)			
28 Total assets			
Liabilities			
29 Accounts payable			
30 Contributions, gifts, grants, etc., payable			
31 Mortgages and notes payable (attach schedule)			
32 Other liabilities (attach schedule)			
33 Total liabilities			
Fund Balance or Net Worth			
34 Total fund balance or net worth			
35 Total liabilities and fund balance or net worth (line 33 plus line 34) . . .			

Part VI.—Required Schedules for Special Activities (See instructions)	If "Yes," check here;	And, complete schedule—
1 Is the organization, or any part of it, a school?		A
2 Does the organization provide or administer any scholarship benefits, student aid, etc.?		B.
3 Has the organization taken over, or will it take over, the facilities of a "for profit" institution? . . .		C
4 Is the organization, or any part of it, a hospital?		D
5 Is the organization, or any part of it, a home for the aged?		E
6 Is the organization, or any part of it, a litigating organization (public interest law firm or similar organization)?		F

Form 1023 (Rev 11–72)   Page 6

Part VII.—Non-Private Foundation Status (Definitive ruling only)

A.—Basis for Non-Private Foundation Status

The organization is not a private foundation because it qualifies as:

	✓	Kind of organization	Within the meaning of	Complete
1		a church	Sections 509(a)(1) and 170(b)(1)(A)(i)	
2		a school	Sections 509(a)(1) and 170(b)(1)(A)(ii)	
3	X	a hospital	Sections 509(a)(1) and 170(b)(1)(A)(iii)	
4		a medical research organization operated in conjunction with a hospital	Sections 509(a)(1) and 170(b)(1)(A)(iii)	
5		being organized and operated exclusively for testing for public safety	Section 509(a)(4)	
6		being operated for the benefit of a college or university which is owned or operated by a governmental unit	Sections 509(a)(1) and 170(b)(1)(A)(iv)	Part VII.–B
7		normally receiving a substantial part of its support from a governmental unit or from the general public	Sections 509(a)(1) and 170(b)(1)(A)(vi)	Part VII.–B
8		normally receiving not more than one-third of its support from gross investment income and more than one-third of its support from contributions, membership fees, and gross receipts from activities related to its exempt functions (subject to certain exceptions)	Section 509(a)(2)	Part VII.–B
9		being operated solely for the benefit of or in connection with one or more of the organizations described in 1 through 4, or 6, 7 and 8, above	Section 509(a)(3)	Part VII –C

B.—Analysis of Financial Support

NO REVENUE OR EXPENSE TO DATE: APPLICATION PENDING WITH DHEW FOR GRANT AWARD

		(a) Most recent taxable year 19	(Years next preceding most recent taxable year)			(e) Total
			(b) 19......	(c) 19......	(d) 19.	
1	Gifts, grants, and contributions received					
2	Membership fees received .					
3	Gross receipts from admissions, sales of merchandise or services, or furnishing of facilities in any activity which is not an unrelated business within the meaning of section 513					
4	Gross income from interest, dividends, rents and royalties					
5	Net income from organization's unrelated business activities					
6	Tax revenues levied for and either paid to or expended on behalf of the organization .					
7	Value of services or facilities furnished by a governmental unit to the organization without charge (not including the value of services or facilities generally furnished the public without charge)					
8	Other income (not including gain or loss from sale of capital assets)—attach schedule.					
9	Total of lines 1 through 8 .					
10	Line 9 less line 3					
11	Enter 2% of line 10, column (e) only					

12 If the organization has received any unusual grants during any of the above taxable years, attach a list for each year showing the name of the contributor, the date and amount of grant, and a brief description of the nature of such grant Do not include such grants in line 1 above. (See instructions)

883

Organization is an Ambulatory Care (Outpatient) Clinic; will not provide inpatient care.

Form 1023 (Rev 11-72)

Page 11

SCHEDULE D.—Hospitals (See instructions)

1 (a) How many doctors are on the hospital's courtesy staff?. . . . . **NONE**

(b) Do such doctors include all the doctors in the community? . . . . ☐ Yes ☐ No

If "No," please give the reasons why and explain how the courtesy staff is selected.

Organization is not operational; grant application pending with DHEW under PL 91-515 Sect. 314(e).

2 Composition of board of directors or trustees. (If more space is needed, attach schedule.)

Name and address	Occupation
SEE ATTACHED SCHEDULE	

3 (a) Does the hospital maintain a full-time emergency room? . . . . ☐ Yes ☒ No

(b) What is the hospital's policy as to administering emergency services to persons without apparent means to pay?

Health services will be provided without regard to ability to pay.

(c) Does the hospital have any arrangements with police, fire, and voluntary ambulance services as to the delivery or admission of emergency cases? . . . . ☐ Yes ☐ No

Please explain.

Organization is not yet operational and no arrangements have been made with local organizations.

4 Does or will the hospital require a deposit or otherwise discriminate against persons covered by Medicare or Medicaid in its admission practices? . . . . ☐ Yes ☒ No

If "Yes," please explain.

5 Does or will the hospital provide for a portion of its services and facilities to be used for charity patients? ☒ Yes ☐ No

Please explain (include data as to the hospital's past experience in admitting charity patients and arrangements it may have with municipal or governmental agencies for absorbing the cost of such care).

Organization will be funded by DHEW primarily because of numerous low-income persons in target area requiring ambulatory health services. Such costs will be absorbed under budget requested from DHEW

6 Does or will the hospital carry on a formal program of medical training and research? . . . . ☐ Yes ☒ No

If "Yes," please describe.

7 Does the hospital provide office space to physicians carrying on a medical practice? . . . . ☐ Yes ☒ No

If "Yes," attach a list setting forth the name of each physician, the amount of space provided, the annual rent (if any), and the expiration of the current lease.

NAME	ADDRESS	OCCUPATION
Judge William M. Branch	P.O. Box 347, Eutaw, Alabama 35462	Minister; Elected Official (Probate Judge)
Thomas E. Gilmore	P.O. Box 347, Eutaw, Alabama 35462	Minister; Elected Official (Sheriff)
Willie Hill	Route 3, Box 145, Eutaw, Alabama 35462	Supervisor, County Solid Waste Dept.
John H. Modley	Route 1, Box 90, Forkland, Alabama 36740	Outreach Worker; Greene County Opportunity
Dr. Rucker Staggers	202 Pickens St., Eutaw, Alabama 35462	Physician in private practice
Robert Cook	York, Alabama 36925	Laborer
Dr. Edward Gegan	Box 781, Livingston, Alabama 35470	Physician in private practice
Zora C. Gibbs	Box 141, Livngston, Alabama 35470	Retired public health nurse
W. T. Lockard	Box 216, York, Alabama 36925	Farm Equipment and Supplies Dealer; Elected Official (County Commission Chairman)
Edward Ozment	Sumterville, Alabama 35485	Supervisor, Construction and Maintenance,
Dr. John Packard	Box 6291, University, Alabama 35486	Associate Dean, University of Alabama College of Community Health Sciences

SHORT SUMMARY OF PROJECT	PROJECT IDENTIFICATION NO.

E OF PROJECT

WEST ALABAMA HEALTH SERVICES, INC.

M) Y STATEMENT *(Not to exceed 200 words)*

Greene and Sumter Counties, initial focus of the West Alabama Health Services Project, exemplify areas of the rural South where the inaccessibility of adequate health care is a major detriment to economic and social progress.

Project goal is development of a comprehensive primary care system to serve target area residents. This will be achieved through the cooperative and coordinated efforts of the private and public sectors and will entail mobilization of existing resources coupled with the identification and acquisition of new health delivery facilities where required.

During the first budget year, a community health center will be established in Greene County to provide ambulatory medical and dental services for residents of the target area. Emphasizing a team approach to primary care, the clinic will feature a sophisticated management system designed to ease the administrative tasks of health care providers and to facilitate continuous process evaluation.

A second objective is development of an action plan for activity during the second project year. Building on the Greene County clinic, new program components will include satellite health centers, multiphasic screening, an expanded dental care program, and intensified consumer health education.

Th project has received the endorsement of local health providers, as well as many other organizations. The Board of Directors represents a broad cross section of the local community.

AME (PROJECT DIRECTOR

Judge William M. Branch
(Acting Project Director)

NAME AND ADDRESS OF APPLICANT

West Alabama Health Services, Inc.
P. O. Box 347
Eutaw, Alabama 35462

SM-550-1 (PAGE 11)   (FOR NEW APPLICATIONS ONLY)

APPLICANT WEST ALABAMA HEALTH SERVICES, INC.		PROJECT IDENTIFICATION NO.		
SUMMARY BUDGET FOR THIS PERIOD			SOURCE OF FUNDS	
FROM 1 July 1974	THROUGH 30 June 1974	TOTAL AMOUNT REQUIRED	APPLICANT AND OTHER	REQUES FROM HSMH.
1. PERSONAL SERVICES		133,855	–	133,85
2. PATIENT CARE		33,930	8,387	25,54
3. EQUIPMENT		39,455	1,000	38,45
4. CONSTRUCTION		–	– –	–
5. OTHER		57,090	3,700	53,39
6. TRAINEE COSTS		600	600	
7. TOTAL DIRECT COSTS		$ 264,930	$ 13,687	$ 251,2
8. REQUESTED FROM HSMHA	A. FINANCIAL ASSISTANCE (Cash Award) $ 251,243			
	B. DIRECT ASSISTANCE $			
9. INDIRECT COST ALLOWANCE (Leave Blank)				
10. TOTAL COSTS (Leave Blank)		$	$	$

11. SOURCES OF FUNDS - APPLICANT & OTHER	(F)(S)(L)(O)	MATCHING OR COST PARTICIPATION REQUIREMENTS	OTHE
A. Applicant's Funds	I	$	$
B. Other Sources (Identify Each Source Separately)			
Greene Co. Chamber of Commerce	O		1,0
University of Alabama	o		1,0
Livingston University	O		2,0
Tuscaloosa Pathology Associates	O		6
Pruitt & Pruitt, Attorneys-At-Law	O		2
Huntsville Hospital (Huntsville, Alabama)	O		5
Greene County Medical Society	O		1,5
C. Payment for Services Provided by Project (fees, collections, etc.)			
(1) Title XIX (Medicaid)	F		1,7
(2) Other Medicare (Part B)	F		5
Fee-for-Service	O		4,7
TOTAL		$	$ 13,6

| 12. INDIRECT COST (See Instructions) | _____ % S & W* _____ % TADC* *IF THIS IS SPECIAL RATE (e.g. off-site), SO INDICATE | DATE OF DHEW AGREEMENT: | ☐ REQUESTED ☐ WAIVED ☐ UNDER NEGOTIATION WIT |

Enclosure 5

WEST ALABAMA HEALTH SERVICES PROJECT

GRANT APPLICATION SUBMITTED TO
U.S.P.H.S., DEPT. OF HEALTH, EDUCATION & WELFARE
MARCH 11, 1974

MAR 1 3 1974

JUDGE WILLIAM MCKINLEY BRANCH, CHAIRMAN

WEST ALABAMA HEALTH SERVICE, INCORPROATED

P. O. Box 347
Eutaw, Alabama 35462

March 11, 1974

Dr. Herbert Hudgins
50 Seventh Street, N. E.
Atlanta, Georgia 30304

Dear Mr. Hudgins:

The enclosed project proposal for the West Alabama Health
Services Project has been developed by our planning staff with
consultation from governmental and medical leaders in Greene
and Sumter Counties. Our planning staff included the West
Alabama Comprehensive Health Planning Council.

This project will serve to provide needed health care to the
citizens of Greene and Sumter Counties within the regular structure of health care and county governing activities. The approval of your office will be greatly appreciated.

Sincerely,

William M. Branch, Chairman

WMB/enb

Enclosure

888

West Alabama

Comprehensive Health Planning Council

P O BOX 1488 — TUSCALOOSA, ALABAMA 35401 — TELEPHONE (205) 345-4916

Everett Hale, M.D.
Chairman

Elizabeth Cleino, R N., Ph D.
Director

March 12, 1974

Dr. Herbert Hudgins, Acting Chief
Division of Health Services
Department of Health, Education & Welfare
50 Seventh Street, N.E.
Atlanta, Georgia 30304

Dear Dr. Hudgins:

The West Alabama Comprehensive Health Planning Council has reviewed
the revised application for the West Alabama Health Services Project for
Greene and Sumter Counties.

During the past several months, the staff has worked with a variety of
consumers and providers in these counties to develop a project which
will meet the needs of the citizens for health services. We believe that
this will be a very worthwhile addition to health services in these two
counties. We pledge our continued support to this project and urge that
it be funded as soon as possible.

Sincerely,

E. Everett Hale, M.D.
Chairman

EWC/EEH/ala

MAR 1 4 1974

ALABAMA ADVISORY COUNCIL FOR
COMPREHENSIVE HEALTH PLANNING

Mailing Address:
State Office Building
Montgomery, Alabama 36104
Telephone (205) 269—6376

CHAIRMAN
Ira L. Myers, M.D.

MEMBERS

Mrs. Coleman Beale
Elmore
Elizabeth W. Cleino, Ph.D.
Tuscaloosa
Mrs. Robert H. Combs
Montgomery
E. E. Eddleman, Jr., M.D.
Birmingham
Mrs. Elizabeth T. Edwards
Wetumpka
Henry W. Foster, M.D.
Tuskegee
James Friend
Huntsville
Ted Gerber
Florence
Roy W. Gilbert
Birmingham
Lillian H. Harvey, Ed.D.
Tuskegee
S. Richardson Hill, Jr., M.D.
Birmingham
George Hutchinson
Montgomery
John LeFlore
Mobile
Mrs. L. Ellen G. Meade
Homewood
Mrs. Agnes R. Mills
Montgomery
U. H. Pritchett
Gadsden
Miss Mary Proctor
Montgomery
W. H. Russell, D.D.S.
Chickasaw
Paul R. Schnurrenberger, D.V.M.
Auburn
Sen. A. C. Shelton
Jacksonville
Barton C. Shelton
Decatur
Lester Thagard, Jr.
Birmingham
Mrs. Frances Todd
Montgomery
James V. Walters, Ph.D.
Tuscaloosa
Mrs. Ernest Waron
Montgomery
O. F. Wise, L.H.D.
Montgomery
Rev. James P. Woodson
Auburn
R. Floyd Yarbrough
Birmingham
Ex-Officio
John M. Packard, M.D.
Birmingham
Clyde Cox
Birmingham

March 12, 1974

Dr. Herbert Hudgins
DHEW-Region IV
50 Seventh Street, N.E.
Atlanta, Georgia 30304

Re: West Alabama Health Services Project
Application - Greene & Sumter Counties,
Alabama

Dear Dr. Hudgins:

The project proposal for the West Alabama Health Services Project,
as amended, has been thoroughly evaluated by this office. We find it
to be feasible and recommend approval without reservation.

It is unique in it's systematic approach to the delivery of primary care in basically a rural area encompassing two counties.

The total support of the existing health professionals, health
institutions, elected officials, and consumer citizens, attests to
the validity and the dire need for this project.

This office accepts the responsibility of lending full support
to the project.

Sincerely yours,

C. Preston Blanks, Jr.
Health Planning Administrator

CPBJr:CES:pt

cc: Dr. Elizabeth Cleino, Director
West Alabama CHP Council

WEST ALABAMA HEALTH SERVICES PROJECT
APPLICATION

TABLE OF CONTENTS

TABLES AND GRAPHS

DEPARTMENT OF
HEALTH, EDUCATION, AND WELFARE
PUBLIC HEALTH SERVICE
HEALTH SERVICES AND MENTAL HEALTH ADMINISTRATION

LEAVE BLANK - For HSMHA Use Only

GRANT APPLICATION FOR HEALTH SERVICES

PROJECT IDENTIFICATION NUMBER

Administering Component | Major Program Categories | Serial Number | Type of Support | Supplement Number

PROGRAM (Identify program support requested)

ADMINISTRATIVE CODES   **PROGRAM DATA**

HSMHA Programs | Type of Program | Type of Application | Residential

P. O. 91-515
"Neighborhood Health Centers"

TYPE OF APPLICATION

- [X] New
- [ ] Renewal
- [ ] Continuation
- [ ] Supplement
- [ ] Revision

1. TITLE OF PROJECT (OR PROGRAM) (Limit to 53 spaces)

WEST ALABAMA HEALTH SERVICES, INC.

2. NAME AND ADDRESS OF APPLICANT (Street Number, Street Name, City, County, State or Country, ZIP Code, and Congressional District)	5. PROGRAM/PROJECT PERIOD	
	FROM (Mo., Day, Yr.)	THROUGH (Mo., Day, Yr.)
West Alabama Health Services, Inc. P. O. Box 347 Eutaw, Alabama 35462	July 1, 1974	June 30, 1979

	6. BUDGET PERIOD	
	FROM (Mo., Day, Yr.)	THROUGH (Mo., Day, Yr.)
CONG. DISTRICT 7	July 1, 1974	June 30, 1975

3. EMPLOYER'S IDENTIFICATION NUMBER

7. AMOUNT REQUESTED FOR (Direct costs only)

a. Budget Period: 7/1/74 - 6/30/75 $ 251,243

b. Program/Project Period 7/1/74 - 6/30/79 $ 1,790,043

4. DIRECTOR OF PROJECT (Program or Center Director, Coordinator or Principal Investigator)

- [ ] Mr.   NAME (Last, First, Middle Initial)
- [ ] Miss
- [ ] Mrs.
- [X] Judge   Branch, William M. (Acting)
- (Specify)

TITLE   President
West Alabama Health Services, Inc.

DEGREE   SOCIAL SECURITY NO.

ADDRESS (Street Number (or Box Number), Street Name, City, State (or Country), Zip Code)

Greene County Courthouse
P. O. Box 347
Eutaw, Alabama 35462

8. FINANCIAL MANAGEMENT OFFICIAL

- [ ] Mr.   NAME (Last, First, Middle Initial)
- [ ] Miss
- [X] Mrs.   Gibbs, Zora C. R.N.
- (Specify)

TITLE   Treasurer
West Alabama Health Services, Inc.

ADDRESS (Street Number (or Box Number), Street Name, City, State (or Country), Zip Code)

P. O. Box 141
Livingston, Alabama 35470

OFFICE TELEPHONE (Area Code, Tel. No. Extension)
(205) 372-3349

OFFICE TELEPHONE (Area Code, Tel. No., Extension)
(205) 652-7420

HSM-550-1 (PAGE 1)
REV. 1-72

FORM APPROVED
O.M.B. NUMBER 68-R 1221

PROJECT IDENTIFICATION NO.

ASSURANCES AND CERTIFICATIONS BY APPLICANT

The following assurances and certifications are part of the project grant application and must be signed by an official duly authorized to commit and assure that the applicant will comply with the provisions of the applicable laws, regulations, and policies relating to the project

The applicant assures and certifies that he has read and will comply with the following:

Title VI—Civil Rights Act of 1964 (PL 88-352) and Part 80 of Title 45, Code of Federal Regulations, so that no person will be excluded from participation in, be denied the benefits of, or be otherwise subjected to discrimination on the grounds of race, color, or national origin.

Patents and inventions (Current PHS Policy Statement) under which all inventions made in the course of or under any grant shall be promptly and fully reported to HEW

Specific assurances, policies, guidelines, regulations and requirements in effect at the time the grant award is made and applicable to this project (including the making of reports as required and the maintenance of necessary records and accounts, which will be made available to the Department of HEW for audit purposes) which are contained and listed in the grant application package and made a part hereof.

SIGNATURES — Use ink. Autographic signature of Official authorized to sign for applicant and Project Director or other person(s) authorized to sign in their behalf.

APPLICANT NO 1 *(Name only)*

WEST ALABAMA HEALTH SERVICES, INC.

DIRECTOR OF PROJECT	*(Signature only)* William M. Branch	DATE *(Mo., day, yr.)*
	SIGNATURE	DATE *(Mo., day, yr.)*
OFFICIAL AUTHORIZED TO SIGN FOR APPLICANT.	(Acting)	March 11, 1974
	☐ MR. NAME *(First, middle initial, last)* AND TITLE ☐ MRS. ☐ MISS ☒ Judge Branch, William M. , President *(Specify)* West Alabama Health Services, Inc.	DEGREE
COMPLETE FOR RMPS ONLY	SIGNATURE OF CHAIRMAN OF ADVISORY GROUP	DATE *(Mo., day, Yr.)*

APPLICANT NO. 2 *(Name only) (Use only for joint applications)*

DIRECTOR OF PROJECT	*(Signature only)*	DATE *(Mo., day, yr.)*
	SIGNATURE	DATE *(Mo., day, yr.)*
OFFICIAL AUTHORIZED TO SIGN FOR APPLICANT.	☐ MR. NAME *(First, middle initial, last)* AND TITLE ☐ MRS. ☐ MISS ☐ ____ *(Specify)*	DEGREE

HSM-550-1 (PAGE 2)

ORGANIZATION AND PERFORMANCE SITE DATA	For HSMHA Use Only

1. APPLICANT *(Name only)*

ORGANIZATIONAL LEVEL - 1
West Alabama Health Services, Inc.

ORGANIZATIONAL LEVEL - 2
N/A

ORGANIZATIONAL LEVEL - 3
N/A

ORGANIZATIONAL LEVEL - 4
N/A

ORGANIZATIONAL LEVEL - 5
N/A

2. OFFICIAL TO WHOM CHECKS ARE TO BE MAILED *(If different from Financial Management Official)*

☐ MR.   NAME *(Last, First, Middle Initial)*
☐ MISS
☐ MRS.
☐ (Specify)

TITLE

ADDRESS *(Number, Street Name, City, State or County, ZIP Code)*

4. MODEL CITY INVOLVEMENT N/A %

5. INVENTIONS *(Complete for continuation and renewal applications only)*

A. ☒ No
B. ☐ Yes – Not previously reported
C. ☐ Yes – Previously reported

6. HUMAN SUBJECTS AT RISK ☐ Yes ☒ No *(see instructions)*

CERTIFICATION ☐ Yes – Approved *(Date)* _____
☐ Yes – Pending Review *(Date)* _____

SPECIAL ASSURANCE CERTIFICATION ☐ *(attached)*

PROJECT IDENTIFICATION NO.

7. ARE FEDERAL FACILITIES TO BE USED FOR THIS PROJECT?

☐ NO   ☐ YES   _____ % OF TIME

8. ORGANIZATION DESCRIPTORS

A. TYPE

(1) PUBLIC
☐ Federal   ☐ County
☐ State   ☐ City
☐ Interstate ☐ School District
☐ Metropolitan ☐ Special Unit
☐ Other (specify) _____

(2) PUBLIC SPONSORED
☐ Community Action
☒ Sponsored Organization
☐ Other (specify)

(3) PRIVATE NONPROFIT

Indicate the type of proof of NON-PROFIT STATUS furnished:

(a) IRS Cumulative List Reference: _____

	COPY ATTACHED	PREVIOUSLY SUBMITTED*
(b) IRS Tax Exemption Certificate	☐	☐
(c) State Certification Statement	☐	☐
(d) Certificate of Incorporation	☒	☐
(e) Statement of Affiliation With Parent Organization	☐	☐

*Indicate the Place and Date filed: _____

B. FUNCTION

☐ EDUCATIONAL ☐ PLANNING ☐ OTHER (specify)
☐ HOSPITAL   ☒ SERVICE

9. GEOGRAPHIC SCOPE OF PROJECT

☐ NATIONAL ☐ STATEWIDE ☐ LOCAL
☐ REGIONAL ☒ AREAWIDE   ☐ OTHER (specify)

10. PERFORMANCE SITE(S) The places where the project will be conducted:

A ☐ AT APPLICANT ADDRESS ONLY   B ☐ AT APPLICANT ADDRESS AND OTHER SITE(S)   C ☐ AT OTHER SITE(S) ONLY

If B or C identify other sites below

SITE NO. 1 *(Name)*
Greene County Clinic
ADDRESS *(Street Number, Street Name, City, County, State or Country)*
Eutaw, Alabama
CONG. DISTRICT 7

SITE NO. 3 *(Name)*
York Health Center
ADDRESS *(Street Number, Street Name, County, State or Country)*
c/o Hill Hospital of York
York, Alabama
CONG. DISTRICT 7

SITE NO. 2 *(Name)*
Livingston Health Center
ADDRESS *(Street Number, Street Name, City, County, State or Country)*
c/o Sumter Memorial Hospital
Livingston, Alabama
CONG. DISTRICT 7

SITE NO. _____ *(Name)*
ADDRESS *(Street Number, Street Name, City, County, State or Country)*
CONG. DISTRICT

HSM-550-1 (PAGE 3A)
REV 1-72
If more than 4 sites use page 3B.

APPLICANT WEST ALABAMA HEALTH SERVICES, INC.	PROJECT IDENTIFICATION NO.		

SUMMARY BUDGET FOR THIS PERIOD		TOTAL AMOUNT REQUIRED	SOURCE OF FUNDS	
			APPLICANT AND OTHER	REQUESTED FROM HSMHA
FROM 1 July 1974	THROUGH 30 June 1974			
1. PERSONAL SERVICES		133,855	–	133,855
2. PATIENT CARE		33,930	8,387	25,543
3. EQUIPMENT		39,455	1,000	38,455
4. CONSTRUCTION		–	--	–
5. OTHER		57,090	3,700	53,390
6. TRAINEE COSTS		600	600	
7. TOTAL DIRECT COSTS		$264,930	$13,687	$251,243
8. REQUESTED FROM HSMHA	A. FINANCIAL ASSISTANCE (Cash Award) $251,243			
	B. DIRECT ASSISTANCE $_____			
9. INDIRECT COST ALLOWANCE (Leave Blank)				
10. TOTAL COSTS (Leave Blank)		$	$	$

11. SOURCES OF FUNDS - APPLICANT & OTHER	(F)(S)(L)(O)	MATCHING OR COST PARTICIPATION REQUIREMENTS	OTHER
A. Applicant's Funds		$	$
B. Other Sources (Identify Each Source Separately)			
Greene Co. Chamber of Commerce	O		1,000
University of Alabama	O		1,000
Livingston University	O		2,000
Tuscaloosa Pathology Associates	O		600
Pruitt & Pruitt, Attorneys-At-Law	O		200
Huntsville Hospital (Huntsville, Alabama)	O		500
Greene County Medical Society	O		1,900
C. Payment for Services Provided by Project (fees, collections, etc.)			
(1) Title XIX (Medicaid)	F		1,297
(2) Other Medicare (Part B)	F		973
Fee-for-Service	O		4,217
TOTAL		$	$ 13,687

12. INDIRECT COST (See Instructions)	_____ % S & W* _____ % TADC* *IF THIS IS SPECIAL RATE (e.g. off-site), SO INDICATE	DATE OF DHEW AGREEMENT:	☐ REQUESTED ☐ WAIVED ☐ UNDER NEGOTIATION WITH:

HSM-550-1 (PAGE 4)
REV. 1-72

DEPARTMENT OF
HEALTH, EDUCATION, AND WELFARE
HEALTH SERVICES AND MENTAL HEALTH ADMINISTRATION

PROJECT IDENT. NO.(B)
(Grant or Contract)

FINANCIAL PLAN—SUMMARY SHEET

NAME OF INSTITUTION: WEST ALABAMA HEALTH SERVICES, INC.

PROJECT TITLE: WEST ALABAMA HEALTH SERVICES, INC.

I. INCOME	ACTUAL PREVIOUS BUDGET PERIOD (YEAR)			ESTIMATED THIS BUDGET PERIOD (YEAR)			ESTIMATED NEXT BUDGET PERIOD (YEAR)		
	PREPAYMENT 1	FEE-FOR-SERVICE 2	TOTAL 3	PREPAYMENT 4	FEE-FOR-SERVICE 5	TOTAL 6	PREPAYMENT 7	FEE-FOR-SERVICE 8	TOTAL 9
A. FEDERAL SUPPORT - THIS GRANT/CONTRACT						251,243			359,600
B. STATE AND LOCAL GOVERNMENT						—			—
1. STATE									20,000
2. LOCAL									
C. THIRD PARTY PAYORS:									
1. MEDICARE					973	973		12,540	12,540
2. MEDICAID					1,297	1,297		50,160	50,160
3. OTHER (Specify)									
a.									
b.									
c.									
d.									
e.									
4. TOTAL - SECTION C					2,270	2,270		62,700	62,700
D. DIRECT PATIENT PAYMENTS					4,217	4,217		20,900	20,900
E. TOTAL PAYMENTS FOR SERVICES (C4 + D)					6,487	6,487		83,600	83,600
F. FOUNDATIONS, ENDOWMENTS, AND OTHER PRIVATE SOURCES						—			—
G. LOANS						—			—
H. OTHER (Specify)									
1. Local In-Kind						7,200			14,000
2.									
3.									
4.									
5.									
I. TOTAL INCOME (A thru H)						264,930			477,200
II. EXPENDITURES						264,930			477,200
III. BALANCE (Difference between I & II) A. NET						-0-			-0-
B. CUMULATIVE						-0-			-0-

HSM-735 (PAGE 1)
4-73

APPLICANT WEST ALABAMA HEALTH SERVICES, INC.				PROJECT IDENTIFICATION NO.		
DETAILED BUDGET FOR THIS PERIOD (DIRECT COSTS ONLY)	ANNUAL SALARY RATE	NO. MOS. BUDG.	% TIME	TOTAL AMOUNT REQUIRED	SOURCE OF FUNDS	
					APPLICANT AND OTHER	REQUESTED FROM HSMHA
	(1)	(2)	(3)	(4)	(5)	(6)
1. PERSONAL SERVICES						
Project Director	15,000	12	100	15,000	–	15,000
Physician	35,000	10	100	29,170	–	29,170
Registered Nurse	10,000	9	100	7,497	–	7,497
Registered Nurse	10,000	8	100	6,664	–	6,664
Nurse's Aide	4,200	7	100	2,450	–	2,450
Nurse's Aide	4,200	6	100	2,100	–	2,100
Laboratory Assistant	4,200	10	100	3,500	–	3,500
Dentist	28,000	10	100	23,330	–	23,330
Dental Hygenist	7,800	9	100	5,850	–	5,850
Dental Assistant	4,200	8	100	2,800	–	2,800
Dental Assistant	4,200	7	100	2,450	–	2,450
Intake Interviewer/LPN Nurse	5,100	9	100	3,825	–	3,825
Office Mgr./Bookkeeper	6,000	11	100	5,500	–	5,500
Secretary	5,000	10	100	4,160	–	4,160
Clerk-Typist	4,200	6	100	2,100	–	2,100
Sub-Total				116,396	–	116,396
Fringe Benefits 15%				17,459	–	27,459
GRAND TOTAL				133,855	–	133,855
FRINGE BENEFITS (Rate ____)						
		CATEGORY TOTAL		$	$	$

HSM-550-1 (PAGE 5)
7-71

APPLICANT WEST ALABAMA HEALTH SERVICES, INC.	PROJECT IDENTIFICATION NO.		
DETAILED BUDGET FOR THIS PERIOD (Continued)	TOTAL AMOUNT REQUIRED	SOURCE OF FUNDS	
		APPLICANT AND OTHER	REQUESTED FROM HSMHA
	(4)	(5)	(6)
2. PATIENT CARE			
Medical Record Sets ($1 x 2,232)	2,232	–	2,232
Medical Supplies (drapes, swabs, disposables, etc.) ($1 x 2,232 encounters)	2,232	–	2,232
Dental Supplies (X-ray film, developer, amalgam, xylocaine, etc.) ($4 x 1,452 encounters)	5,808	–	5,808
Laboratory Supplies ($1 x 3,348 procedures)	3,348	1,127	2,221
Prescription Drugs ($4 x 1,500 Rx's)	6,000	3,000	3,000
Clinical Laboratory Referrals (SMA-12, Pap Tests, bacteriology, etc.) ($6 x 700 procedures)	4,200	–	4,200
Radiology Referrals ($10 x 300)	3,000	1,500	1,500
Professional Medical and Dental Services (On-Site at WAHS Clinic) ($25 x 250 hours)	6,250	1,900	4,350
Patient Education ($5 x 1720 hours)	860	860	–
CATEGORY TOTAL	$ 33,930	$ 8,387	$ 25,543
3. EQUIPMENT SEE ATTACHED LIST			
CATEGORY TOTAL	$	$	$
4. CONSTRUCTION NONE			
CATEGORY TOTAL	$	$	$

EQUIPMENT	Total Amount Required	SOURCE OF FUNDS	
		Applicant & Other	Requested from HSMA
Medical Equipment			
Equipment for Examining Rooms (4): Examining Table, High Intensity Lamp, Instrument Cabinet, Selected Instruments, Baumanometer, Otoscope, Digital Thermometer, etc.			
Total Cost Per Room = $1,300	5,200	–	5,200
Electrocardiograph with stand and initial supply of chart paper	1,200	–	1,200
Platform Scales ($110 ea. x 2)	220	–	220
Audiometer	350	–	350
Wheelchair, folding ($120 ea. x 2)	240	–	240
Medical Laboratory			
Coulter Blood Cell Counting System Clinicard Blood Chemistry System			
LEASE/PURCHASE $500 per month x 10	5,000	–	5,000
Refrigerator	500	–	500
Autoclave	400	–	400
Centrifuge	300	–	300
Microscope	1,200	–	1,200
Glassware and Miscellaneous	500	–	500
Dental Equipment			
Dental Operatory (Four-Hand) (Fully-Equipped) Dental Hygenist Station Dental Laboratory X-ray Unit and Developing Unit			
LEASE/PURCHASE $2,000 per month x 9	18,000	–	18,000

EQUIPMENT (Continued)	Total Amount Required	SOURCE OF FUNDS	
		Applicant & Other	Requested from HSMA
Office Equipment			
Typewriters ($600ea. x 3)	1,800	–	1,800
Desks ($150ea. x 3)	450	–	450
Chairs for Desks ($75ea. x 3)	225	–	225
Calculator, Printing	250	–	250
Calculator, Non-Print ($60ea. x 2)	120	–	120
File Cabinet, Vertical ($150ea. x 3)	450	–	450
Rolodex Card Files ($50ea. x 4)	200	–	200
Lateral Shelving (Medical Records) ($300ea. x 4 Units)	1,200	–	1,200
Casette Tape Recorder Dictation System	150	–	150
Waiting Room Furniture	1,000	1,000	–
Miscellaneous Small Equipment: Staplers, Paper Punch, Pencil Sharpener, Paper Cutter, Calendars, etc.	500	–	500
SUMMARY TOTALS			
Medical Equipment	7,210	–	7,210
Medical Laboratory	7,900	–	7,900
Dental Equipment	18,000	–	18,000
Office Equipment	6,345	1,000	5,345
GRAND TOTAL - EQUIPMENT	39,455	1,000	38,455

APPLICANT WEST ALABAMA HEALTH SERVICES, INC.	PROJECT IDENTIFICATION NO.		
DETAILED BUDGET FOR THIS PERIOD (Continued)	TOTAL AMOUNT REQUIRED	SOURCE OF FUNDS	
		APPLICANT AND OTHER	REQUESTED FROM HSMHA
	(4)	(5)	(6)
5 OTHER			
Building Lease (3,000 ft.^{2} x $5/year)	15,000	–	15,000
Electricity, Gas, Water	800	–	800
Insurance (Building, Contents, Liability, Blanket Malpractice)	1,600	–	1,600
Telephone (3 trunk/5 extension)	800	–	800
Equipment Maintenance	350	–	350
Auditing and Legal Fees	1,500	200	1,300
Copy Machine Rental	750	–	750
Office Supplies	1,000	–	1,000
Data Processing (Accounts Receivable, Medical Records, Payroll, Statistical Reports, etc.)	7,000	2,000	5,000
Printing and Publishing (publicity, patient education, forms, etc.)	600	–	600
Professional Reference Material (Physician's Desk Reference, Current Therapy)	500	–	500
Clinical Accounting System Software (IBM Corp. Field Developed Program)	3,500	–	3,500
Staff Travel (16,250 miles x $0.12)	2,250	–	2,250
Linen Rental ($100/mo. x 8 mos.)	800	–	800
Technical Assistance and Related Contracts			
Huntsville Hospital (Modification of IBM Corp. Software; Installation and User Training)	1,000	500	500
Greene County Commission (Partial Funding of Patient Transportation System)	5,200	–	5,200
West Alabama Comprehensive Health Planning Council (Technical Assistance for Board of Directors and Project Director)	8,490	–	8,490
University of Alabama (Impact Evaluation Survey and Analysis)	4,000	1,000	3,000
CATEGORY TOTAL	$ 57,090	$ 3,700	$ 53,390
6 TRAINEE COSTS			
Clinical Laboratory Assistant Training (Druid City Hospital, Tuscaloosa, Alabama)	600	600	
CATEGORY TOTAL	$ 600	$ 600	$

HSM-550-1 (PAGE 7)
REV 1-72

APPLICANT WEST ALABAMA HEALTH SERVICES, INC. | PROJECT IDENTIFICATION NO.

BUDGET JUSTIFICATION

INSTRUCTIONS: Show justification for specific items or categories listed in the detailed budget for which the need is not self-evident. Justifications should clearly indicate that the items being requested are essential to the achievement of the stated project objectives and the conduct of the proposed procedures.

1. Personal Services

The positions described are considered the minimum required staff for the provision of high quality primary care in an ambulatory clinic. Salaries are comparable to existing levels within the target area. The staff will be phased-in over a seven month period to permit adequate orientation of each new employee and insure that each individual is productively occupied in the performance of defined tasks once employed.

2. Patient Care

Medical Record Sets: Represents the one-time expense of establishing a medical records jacket for each new patient. Includes cost of a patient history such as the Roche "Review of Systems".

Medical Supplies: Cost of incidental and disposable items associated with treatment.

Dental Supplies: Cost of incidental and disposable items associated with treatment.

Laboratory Supplies: Cost of reagents and pre-packaged test kits.

Prescription Drugs Cost of pharmaceuticals obtained through a referral pharmacy.

Clinical Laboratory Referrals Only basic procedures will be performed at the clinic. Complex procedures, cytology and bacteriology will be performed by a referral laboratory.

Radiology Referrals All radiology will be referred to a local health facility on a contractual basis.

Professional Medical and Dental Services: Services provided by the staff physician and dentist will be supplemented by area physicians and dentists to permit maximum clinic utilization. Services will be provided within the clinic on a negotiated hourly or per diem rate to the extent that additional services are needed, funding is adequate, and local practitioners are able to participate.

BUDGET JUSTIFICATION
(Continued)

Patient Education: Counseling in nutrition, home sanitation, and family preventive health care will be provided to patients in need of these services. Counseling will be provided by public health nurses, teachers from the local school system, and graduate students in the University of Alabama nutritional sciences curriculum.

3. Equipment

Medical Equipment: Cost of fully equipping four examining rooms based on the recent experience of the University of Alabama Family Practice Clinic. Each room shall be equipped for gynecological and obstetrical examinations.

The electrocardiograph will be installed in a special room equipped with examining table and doubling as a treatment room when required.

The audiometer will be used in screening and initial health examinations.

Wheelchairs are needed because of the numerous elderly and infirm persons expected to be treated in the clinic.

Medical Laboratory: The major equipment (Coulter and Clinicard) is required for blood chemistry and cell counting and will enable the clinic to perform a large volume of procedures using semi-skilled personnel. Equipment will be lease-purchased because of funding uncertainties and rapid obsolescence.

The refrigerator is required for storage of reagents.

The autoclave is required for sterilization of instruments.

The centrifuge will be used in blood chemistry and urinalysis.

The microscope will be available for use by the physician when needed.

Glassware and miscellaneous includes automatic pipettes, beakers, test tubes, slides, etc.

Dental Equipment: Equipment listed is sufficient to provide two "four-handed" dental operatories, a hygienist's treatment room, and an X-ray room. A small dental laboratory will also be provided. The equipment will be lease-purchased because of funding uncertainties and rapid obsolescence. Costs are based on recent experience of the Jefferson County Health Department in equipping their neighborhood health center in Ensley, Alabama (suburb of Birmingham).

BUDGET JUSTIFICATION
(Continued)

Office Equipment:

Typewriters are for use by the Office Manager/Bookkeeper, the clerk-typist, and the secretary. Prices are based on costs of IBM Selectric.

Desks and chairs are for the Project Director, physician and dentist. Other required desks and chairs will be obtained through federal surplus property.

A printing calculator is required for preparation of batch proof totals, bank deposits, and other procedures where a permanent tape is needed. Two non-printing calculators are provided -- one for the Project Director and the other for the clerk-typist.

Vertical file cabinets are for storage of administrative records. One is provided for each of the following: Board of Directors, Project Administration, Medical Administration, and Dental Administration.

Rolodex card files will provide an index to medical records. Two files will be sorted alphabetically on patient name, the other two will be sorted numerically on patient record number. A file set will be placed at the intake station and the other set will be in the administrative office for use by the clerical staff.

Lateral shelving will be used to store medical records.

Casette tape recorder dictation system will use inexpensive units for dictation of project correspondence, medical records, etc.

Waiting room furniture will be obtained through local sources.

Miscellaneous equipment includes numerous small items such as desk lamps, paper cutters, punches, in-out baskets, etc.

4. Other

Building Lease: Estimated cost of reimbursing Greene County for extensive renovation of clinic facility.

Electricity, Gas, Water: Based on experience of local practitioners.

Insurance: Estimate provided by Duckworth-Morris Agency (Tuscaloosa) based on preliminary review of project needs.

BUDGET JUSTIFICATION
(Continued)

Auditing and Legal Fees: Includes one-time set up charge for developing chart of accounts and financial controls, training of administrative
staff in proper procedures, periodic inspection, and first-year audit.
All to be performed by Certified Public Accountant. Legal costs include
preparation and filing of incorporation papers and application for
501 (c) 3 status.

Data Processing: Includes patient billing system and accounts receivable
processing, clinical activity analysis, statistical studies. Costs include
keypunching, forms, machine time.

Printing and Publishing: Cost of preparing special forms for medical
records and data processing system, public relations materials, patient
education materials, newsletters, periodic mailings to friends of West
Alabama Health Services.

Clinical Accounting System: Includes source program listing, installation, debugging and training for an IBM developed clinical accounting
package which will prove vital in project management and financial
control.

Staff Travel: Includes cost of transporting specimens to referral laboratory, transporting patients to referral agencies (i.e , radiology),
reimbursement of Board of Directors for travel to meetings, consultation
with State officials (Montgomery), HEW officials (Atlanta), medical and
dental schools (Tuscaloosa, Birmingham).

Linen Rental: Cost of uniforms provided to non-professional employees.

5. Technical Assistance and Related Contracts

Huntsville Hospital: Data Processing Department of this hospital adapted
the IBM software for use by the Family Practice Clinic operated by the
University of Alabama in Huntsville. Cost of performing modifications
exceeded $5,000. Total amount of this contract ($1,000) includes partial
reimbursement for modification costs; this is being donated by Huntsville
Hospital. Additional $500 is cost of travel, personnel and computer time
for transferring this sytem to West Alabama Health Services.

BUDGET JUSTIFICATION
(Continued)

Greene County Commission: Greene County now operates a small community transportation and outreach system which brings clients to local social service and community action programs. Contract for $5,200 will permit expansion of operation to provide transportation to patients of West Alabama Health Services.

West Alabama Comprehensive Health Planning Council: Council will assist in negotiation with potential contractors; provide liaison with area health providers; staff support to Board of Directors; expertise in clinic administration, fiscal management, epidemiology, data processing. Costs include staff time, travel, administrative expenses.

University of Alabama: Department of Medical Sociology will perform survey of Greene County health needs and services prior to project implementation and at close of project year. Costs include development of methodology, validation, computer programming. University will donate $1,000 of $4,000 cost.

6. Trainee Costs

Clinical laboratory assistants will be trained at the Druid City Hospital School of Medical Technology in Tuscaloosa at no cost to West Alabama Health Services.

AF .LICANT					PROJECT IDENTIFICATION NUMBER		

WEST ALABAMA HEALTH SERVICES, INC.

ESTIMATES OF PROJECT COSTS AND SOURCES OF FUNDS

A. PROJECT COSTS BY BUDGET CATEGORY	(DOLLAR AMOUNTS IN HUNDREDS ONLY)						
	2ND BUDGET YEAR	3RD BUDGET YEAR	4TH BUDGET YEAR	5TH BUDGET YEAR	6TH BUDGET YEAR	7TH BUDGET YEAR	8TH BUDGET YEAR
1. PERSONAL SERVICES	$ 2300	$ 3050	$ 3900	$ 4250	$	$	$
2. PATIENT CARE	900	1400	2150	2750			
3. EQUIPMENT	800	900	1400	1600			
4. CONSTRUCTION	-	-	-	-			
5. OTHER	760	1170	1630	1850			
6. TRAINEE COSTS	12	12	14	16			
7. TOTAL DIRECT COSTS	$ 4772	$ 6532	$ 9094	$ 10466	$	$	$
B. SOURCES OF FUNDS							
1. SMHA	3596	3802	4244	3746			
2. APPLICANT	200	400	700	1000			
3. OTHER	140	230	350	420			
4. PAYMENT FOR SERVICES	836	2100	3800	5300			
5. TOTAL FUNDS AVAILABLE	$ 4772	$ 6532	$ 9094	$ 10466	$	$	$

JUSTIFICATION

During the second beduget year, two health centers will be established in Sumter County. Health services will be provided in Hale County during the third budget year and in Marengo County during the fourth budget year. Allowances have been made for annual salary increases, equipment replacement, and training of non-professional staff. Local financial support is expected to increase as economic benefits accrue to the target area.

908

SHORT SUMMARY OF PROJECT	PROJECT IDENTIFICATION NO.

TITLE OF PROJECT

WEST ALABAMA HEALTH SERVICES, INC.

SUMMARY STATEMENT *(Not to exceed 200 words)*

Greene and Sumter Counties, initial focus of the West Alabama Health Services Project, exemplify areas of the rural South where the inaccessibility of adequate health care is a major detriment to economic and social progress.

Project goal is development of a comprehensive primary care system to serve target area residents. This will be achieved through the cooperative and coordinated efforts of the private and public sectors and will entail mobilization of existing resources coupled with the identification and acquisition of new health delivery facilities where required.

During the first budget year, a community health center will be established in Greene County to provide ambulatory medical and dental services for residents of the target area. Emphasizing a team approach to primary care, the clinic will feature a sophisticated management system designed to ease the administrative tasks of health care providers and to facilitate continuous process evaluation.

A second objective is development of an action plan for activity during the second project year. Building on the Greene County clinic, new program components will include satellite health centers, multiphasic screening, an expanded dental care program, and intensified consumer health education.

Th project has received the endorsement of local health providers, as well as many other organizations. The Board of Directors represents a broad cross section of the local community.

NAME OF PROJECT DIRECTOR	NAME AND ADDRESS OF APPLICANT
Judge William M. Branch (Acting Project Director)	West Alabama Health Services, Inc. P. O. Box 347 Eutaw, Alabama 35462

HSM-550-1 (PAGE 11)
7-71

(FOR NEW APPLICATIONS ONLY)

NEED FOR THE PROJECT

The inaccessibility of adequate health care is a major problem in many areas of the United States. Because of its enormous cost in economic productivity and detrimental effect on the quality of life, additional primary health care facilities are vitally needed in West Alabama.

This great need has stimulated efforts to develop the West Alabama Health Services Project, an ambulatory health care program which will initially focus on Greene and Sumter Counties. Both fall within the Alabama "Black Belt" Region, a term denoting the rich soil, and are important producers of beef cattle, cotton, soy beans, and timber. The area is strikingly beautiful because of its large plantations, secluded hunting lodges and gently rolling hills. Efforts to attract industry are beginning to succeed and development of the Tombigbee River System, which bisects the two counties, should stimulate long-term economic growth.

For all its beauty and potential for development, Greene and Sumter Counties are still a generally impoverished area where many residents do not share the advantages enjoyed by most Americans. Table I illustrates significant characteristics of the area compared with Alabama and the United States.

TABLE I

Population Characteristics

CHARACTERISTIC	GREENE COUNTY	SUMTER COUNTY	ALABAMA	UNITED STATES
Persons per Square Mile (Pop. Density)	17	19	68	57
Median Age	24.7	22.9	27.1	28.3
Median School Years Completed	8.3	8.8	10.8	12.1
Median Family Income	$3,032	$3,937	$7,263	$9,586
Percent White Resident	24%	33%	73%	87%
Percent Non-White Resident	76%	67%	27%	13%

Source: U. S. Bureau of the Census, County and City Data Book

Greene and Sumter Counties have been selected as the initial focus of the West Alabama Health Services Project because they exemplify problems facing the area which new ambulatory care resources can help alleviate. These problems include the following:

1. Mortality rates significantly greater than State or National averages

2. Critical shortage of key health providers

3. Economic barriers to obtaining existing health services

Mortality Rate Analysis

Selected mortality rates are shown in Table II for Greene and Sumter Counties compared with State and National averages. Morbidity data is unavailable since only communicable disease is reported; but limited Medicaid screening programs show a high incidence of anemia, impetigo, parasitism, dermatitis and multiple dental caries.

TABLE II

Selected Mortality Rates

MORTALITY RATE	GREENE COUNTY	SUMTER COUNTY	ALABAMA	UNITED STATES
Infant Death Rate (1) per 1,000 live births	38.1	36.4	25.4	20.8
Maternal Death Rate per 10,000 live births	9.5	16.8	4.6	2.5
Age Adjusted Mortality Rate, Age 55-Above (2)	28.0	27.3	21.4	21.1

(1) Infant and Maternal Death Rates represent a five-year average for the period 1967-1971.

(2) Based on a three-year average for the period 1969-1971.

Source: Alabama Department of Health, Bureau of Vital Statistics

Critical Shortage of Health Providers

Routine diagnosis and treatment is not readily available to many area residents because of an extreme shortage of health manpower. As an indication, some twenty percent of babies born in Greene and Sumter Counties during 1971 were delivered by midwives, compared to less than five percent statewide and under one percent nationally. The availability of key health providers is illustrated in Table III.

TABLE III

Target Area Health Manpower Analysis

MANPOWER CATEGORY (Actual Practice)	GREENE COUNTY	SUMTER COUNTY	ALABAMA	UNITED STATES
	(1)	(1)	(2)	(3)
Physicians in County	4	6	N/A	N/A
Population Per Physician	2,663	2,829	1,258	585
Dentists in County	1	2	N/A	N/A
Population Per Dentist	10,650	8,487	2,975	2,127
Registered Nurses In County	7	16	N/A	N/A
Population Per Registered Nurse	1,521	1,063	478	319

Source: (1) West Alabama Comprehensive Health Planning Council
        (2) Alabama State Office of Comprehensive Health Planning
        (3) U.S. Bureau of the Census, Statistical Abstract of the United States

Both Greene and Sumter Counties are served by public health departments, but limited funding precludes the delivery of services adequate to meet the needs of the population. Medical clinics are notably absent from health department operations. Table IV lists the staff and services of the Greene and Sumter County Public Health Departments.

TABLE IV

Public Health Department Staff and Services Offered

JOB TITLE or SERVICE OFFERED	GREENE COUNTY	SUMTER COUNTY
Health Officer (M.D.)	0.2 FTE	0.2 FTE
Public Health Nurse	1.5 FTE	3.0 FTE
Sanitarian	0.2 FTE	0.8 FTE
Immunization Clinic	Yes	Yes
Maternal and Child Health Clinic	Yes	Yes
TB Clinic	Yes	Yes
Family Planning Program	Yes	Yes
Home Health Service	No	No
Dental Clinic	No	No
Medicaid Screening	Yes	Yes

Source: Greene and Sumter County Health Department

Economic Barriers to Health Care

Despite the enactment of Medicare and Medicaid legislation, poverty is
still a major barrier to adequate health care. The "medically indigent"
can be conservatively described as those persons whose incomes are
less than 125% of poverty level. In Greene County 7,274 persons fall in
this category which is some 68% of the total population. Sumter County
has 10,322 persons in this category or 61% of the total population. Many
of these persons are eligible for health care under Medicare and Medicaid
but a substantial number are not, generally because their incomes exceed
applicable guidelines. An analysis of the "medically indigent" population
of Greene and Sumter Counties, together with the State of Alabama is
presented in Table V.

TABLE V

Analysis of the Medically Indigent Population

POPULATION CATEGORY	GREENE COUNTY		SUMTER COUNTY		ALABAMA	
	NUMBER	PCT	NUMBER	PCT	NUMBER	PCT
Total Medically Indigent (1)	7,274	100%	10,322	100%	1,094,871	100%
LESS:						
Persons Certified for Medicaid (2)	2,783	38%	3,550	34%	306,664	28%
Persons Eligible for Medicare (3)	1,018	14%	1,548	15%	172,990	16%
DIFFERENCE:						
Medically Indigent Without Medicare or Medicaid	3,473	48%	5,224	51%	615,217	56%

Source: (1) Persons with Income Below 125% of Poverty Level; U.S. Bureau
            of the Census, General Social and Economic Characteristics
        (2) Alabama Department of Pensions and Security
        (3) Persons Aged 65 Years and Over with Income Below 125% of
            Poverty Level; U. S. Bureau of the Census, General Social
            and Economic Characteristics

Even for those persons receiving public assistance and eligible for health services under Medicaid, economic barriers to adequate medical care are substantial. Many households in Greene and Sumter Counties lack a telephone and are thus unable to schedule appointments with physicians or secure advice concerning minor ailments. Automobiles are not available to many families and they must depend on friends or neighbors for transportation to health facilities. This also discourages medical treatment, except in emergency. The shortage of telephones and automobiles in Greene and Sumter Counties is demonstrated in Table VI.

TABLE VI

Communication and Transportation

HOUSEHOLDS LACKING:	GREENE COUNTY	SUMTER COUNTY	ALABAMA	UNITED STATES
Telephone	55%	47%	22%	8%
Automobile	35%	32%	19%	20%

Source: U. S. Bureau of the Census, County and City Data Book

PROJECT OBJECTIVES

Objective 1

Within one (1) year from the date of grant award, West Alabama Health Services, Inc. shall have established a primary care clinic in Greene County and delivered a minimum of 2,200 medical encounters and 1,200 dental encounters. These encounters will include one or more of the following health services:

- o   Routine Physical and Dental Examination and Treatment   ·

- o   Diagnostic Tests and Procedures

- o   Provision of Drugs and Other Health Supplies Prescribed by Staff Practitioners

- o   Client Education in Preventive Health Care

- o   Client Referral to Other Agencies for Specialist or Ancillary Services

Objective 2

Within nine (9) months from the date of grant award, West Alabama Health Services, Inc. shall have developed a detailed plan for the provision of primary care in Sumter County. This shall be performed with the cooperation and assistance of concerned private and public organizations as well as the District VI (Alabama-Tombigbee) Health Planning Council.

RESULTS AND BENEFITS EXPECTED

The West Alabama Health Services Project should offer a significant improvement in the quality of life for residents of Greene and Sumter Counties. Among benefits anticipated are the following:

Increased Availability of Ambulatory Health Care

Many residents are under-served by presently available medical and dental services because of both a critical shortage of health providers and a substantial number of medically indigent persons.

Improvement in the Quality of Available Health Care

Because of the manpower shortage, most local practitioners carry extremely heavy case loads and are unable to spend as much time with individual patients as they would like. The creation of additional primary care facilities will permit the health team to devote more time to preventive care and patient education.

Continued Cooperation Among Community Groups

The present need for health services existing in this area of West Alabama has united various segments of the community in search of a solution to common problems. Hopefully, the spirit of cooperation accompanying development of the West Alabama Health Services Proposal can be further developed through this program.

Improved Health Care for the West Alabama Region

Experience gained in development of the West Alabama Health Services Project will benefit the establishment of similar facilities in the region. As a model family practice clinic, it will serve as a training site for students of the health sciences in area educational institutions, many of whom may be attracted to the area.

Economic Benefits for the Target Area

The project will substantially benefit the target area, especially Greene County, during the first project year. Benefits will accrue both directly, through employment of local residents, and indirectly, through the multiplier effect. Improved health of local residents should also increase job productivity and reduce absenteeism.

APPROACH

Introduction

Two major objectives have been established for the initial project year:

1. Development of an operational clinic in Greene County

2. Preparation of a detailed plan of action for activity in Sumter County

Early in the planning process it became evident that the West Alabama Health Services Project is a large and complex undertaking, and the cost of establishing and operating a primary care clinic is much greather than had been anticipated. It was decided that chances of success would be much greater if all efforts were initially concentrated in a limited area. After careful analysis, Greene County was selected as the site of an initial clinic.

While the Greene County clinic is being implemented, a thorough analysis of the health needs and resources in Sumter County will be performed. Local organizations and the areawide health planning agency will assist the Board of Directors in designing a program that makes the best use of new and existing resources. This strategy will permit building on the experience gained in Greene County and insures the most effective use of Federal funds.

Project Strategy

West Alabama Health Services will be a catalyst for eventual development of a comprehensive primary care system serving the people of Greene and Sumter Counties. Primary care is the point of initial contact between people who need health care and the health delivery system. It has three major goals:

1. Treating common acute illness and injury before serious problems develop

2. Providing continuing care of common chronic illness so that the affected person can remain productive

3. Teaching preventive health care so that healthy people can remain in good health

A primary care clinic has several important features which distinguish it from the traditional outpatient clinic. Among the most important characteristics are:

o   Health services are provided by teams which may include physicians, dentists, nurses, social workers, home health aides, and others.

o   There is a concern for the needs of the individual and an awareness of social and economic problems which indirectly affect physical and mental health.

o   The primary care center builds strong linkages with other community agencies to facilitate referrals between human service organizations.

Three concepts were stressed in planning for the West Alabama Health Services Project:

1.   Building on the existing health delivery system

2.   Strengthening community resources

3.   Continuous planning and evaluation

Existing Health Delivery System

West Alabama Health Services is designed to supplement and complement existing resources in Greene and Sumter Counties. The area now has a limited number of dedicated health providers, some of whom were practicing long before the advent of Medicare and Medicaid. Their participation in this project indicates the desire to provide the type of health care which is not feasible using private resources alone.

Three local hospitals (one in Greene County, two in Sumter County) will accept referrals for inpatient care with other services such as radiology and certain laboratory procedures available on an outpatient basis.

Public health departments in both counties offer programs of family planning, communicable disease control and maternal and child health. The health officers have been active participants in the development of this project and pledge continuing support.

Greene County has sponsored a limited ambulatory care program for the past two years. Originally funded under an Office of Economic Opportunity (OEO) emergency medical services grant, the effort serves mostly indigent persons who are not covered by third-party insurance. Services are offered only one day per week through an arrangement with a physician who is in full-time private practice in Selma, Alabama. OEO support has ended and Greene County is anxious to maintain program continuity by transitioning the practitioner and patients into the West Alabama Health Services Project. This existing client group and the goodwill which has developed will be a valuable asset in promoting acceptance of the Greene County Clinic described in this proposal.

Strengthening Community Resources

West Alabama Health Services will actively seek partnership agreements with local organizations which will both aid overall community development and further project objectives. Some examples of planned activity include the following:

o   A transportation system for clients of the primary care
     clinic is required because of the shortage of private
     vehicles and the disastrous effect of the energy crisis
     on low income families. However, a similar transporta-
     tion need exists for other social services, for employment
     and for shopping. A multi-purpose transportation system
     would be more beneficial than one designed only to serve
     clinic users.

     Both County Commissions have agreed to lend their full
     support to developing a multi-purpose transportation
     system. Other agencies and the local Chambers of
     Commerce will be asked to participate.

o   Livingston University (Sumter County) is developing an
     associate degree nursing program which is scheduled to
     admit students in September, 1974. The program is
     expected to emphasize the problems of rural health care.
     The director has been an active participant in planning
     for the West Alabama Health Services Project.

     Nursing students will gain an important phase of their
     clinical experience in the Primary Care Clinic and, hope-
     fully, many will choose to remain in the area. The clinic
     will utilize these students to extend its services and to
     increase the availability of health care at minimum cost.

. o   Rural hospitals, such as those in Greene and Sumter
Counties, are in an increasingly precarious financial
position. One reason for this is the burden of expensive equipment such as X-ray machines which are
generally under-utilized.

West Alabama Health Services will generate frequent
referrals for special procedures such as radiology.
This should improve the cash flow of hospitals providing
the service; of course, any such arrangement must be
mutually beneficial and cost-effective.

Continuous Planning and Evaluation

Planning for the West Alabama Health Services Project began during the
summer of 1973 and has remained vigorous since that time. This proposal
represents a cash outlay of nearly $8,000 and is the culmination of dozens of
meetings and many hundreds of man-hours. Among the participants have
been nearly every organized group in Greene and Sumter Counties, local and
state medical and dental societies, two areawide health planning agencies,
elected officials at the local, state and national level, and the Department of
Health, Education and Welfare.

Each participant in this long and often difficult initial planning has contributed
to what we believe is a realistic yet challenging program. As the project is
implemented, performance will be closely monitored by the Project Director,
Board of Directors and technicial consultants. Tasks will be revised as necessary to insure the accomplishment of project objectives.

Project Organization and Staffing

Project Organization. The organization of West Alabama Health Services
reflects the two major activities specified in the project objectives:

1.   Implementation of the Greene County clinic

2.   Development of the Sumter County plan of
action

Organizational components include the following groups:

1.   Board of Directors

2.   Professional Advisory Committee

The Board of Directors is the final authority for all aspects of the West Alabama Health Services Project, subject to legal and ethical constraints regarding the delivery of professional health services. The Board delegates operational authority to the Project Director.

The Professional Advisory Committee provides consultation and assistance to the Project Director and Board of Directors. Membership includes representatives of the health care professions: medicine, dentistry, nursing and pharmacy. Function of this organization will include assistance in recruitment and selection of potential staff members and professional service review. This group has rendered invaluable assistance during the initial project planning.

Project Staffing. During the initial project year, the staff will consist entirely of personnel involved in the delivery of health services at the Greene County Clinic. One exception to this is the Project Director.

The Project Director will be responsible for implementation of the West Alabama Health Services program as described in this proposal and will report directly to the Board of Directors. He will be responsible for establishment and maintenance of relationships with other organizations and the dissemination of information concerning the project. The Project Director will be responsible for implementing an effective system of financial management and control so that quality health care can be rendered at the lowest possible cost. The Project Director will be responsible for recruitment, consulting with members of the staff as appropriate.

The rendering of medical and dental services will be under professional supervision of the physician and dentist. They hold ultimate responsibility for the quality of care and exercise of professional judgment in clinical matters. Their areas of concern include:

      o   Formulation of clinical protocols and
            procedures and treatment

      o   Diagnosis of health disorders

      o   Supervision of appropriate clinical
            personnel

COMPOSITION OF THE BOARD OF DIRECTORS		
NAME OF MEMBER AND GEOGRAPHIC AREA REPRESENTED	REPRESENTING	
	CONS.	PROV.
Greene County		
Judge William M. Branch (President)		X
Sheriff Thomas E. Gilmore	X	
Mr. Willie Hill	X	
Mr. John Modley	X	
Dr. Rucker Staggers (Secretary)		X
Sumter County		
Mr. Robert Cook	X	
Dr. Edward L. Gegan .		X
Mrs. Zora C. Gibbs (Treasurer)	X	
Mr. W. T. Lockard (Vice-President)		X
Mr. Edward Ozment	X	
West Alabama Comprehensive Health Planning Council		
Dr. John Packard		X
TOTALS	6	5

Two Registered Nurses will play a key role in maximizing clinic productivity by relieving the physician of many of the more routine aspects of medical practice. Among their duties will be the following:

o   In-service training of non-professional staff

o   Supervision of the clinical laboratory

o   Health maintenance of chronic patients

o   Health education

A Practical Nurse will function as an Intake Interviewer. Depending on the protocols established for the clinic, the interviewer can substantially contribute to productivity by recognizing and recording sigificant symptoms or complaints. Specific functions may include the following:

o   Initial history taking

o   Determining and recording client-reported changes or incidents since the last clinic visit

o   Placing clients at ease by explaining clinic procedures or answering specific questions

For an organization as complex as a primary care clinic, a strong administrative component is mandatory for efficiency and fiscal integrity. The Office Manager will function as an administrative aide to the Project Director by assuming the following duties:

o   Accounting and bookkeeping

o   Supervision of clerical personnel

Other members of the clinic staff, listed by job title, include the following:

o   Dental Hygienist
o   Dental Assistants (2)
o   Laboratory Assistant
o   Nurse's Aides (2)
o   Secretary
o   Clerk-Typist

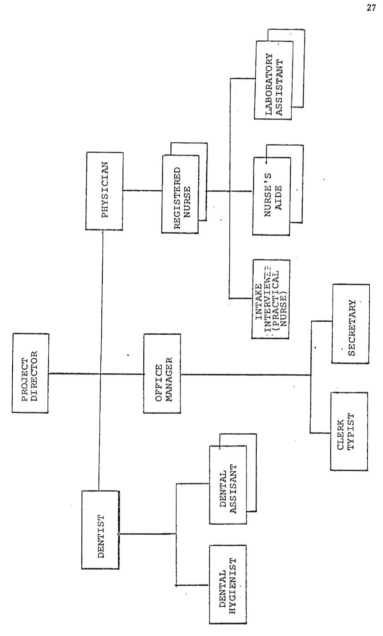

In planning the clinic staff, both the needs of the health services program and the availability of personnel have been considered. West Alabama is a health manpower scarcity area and the types of personnel that might be optimum are not readily available. It might be possible to attract sophisticated personnel through premium salaries but this would disrupt existing health care facilities in Greene and Sumter Counties. The solution which has been adopted is to begin with a core staff of experienced professionals and supplement them with local personnel who can be trained to perform defined tasks. With strong ties to the local area, they will be stable employees and can promote acceptance and utilization of the clinic among their friends and neighbors. Because unemployment is high in Greene County, West Alabama Health Services can draw on a large pool of high school graduates as potential staff members.

Project Implementation

Two objectives for the first project year have been established: implementation of the Greene County health care center and development of the Sumter County plan of action. This discussion will focus on the Greene County health care center and is divided in two sections. First, the health center and its activities as they should exist at the completion of the project year will be discussed. Second, a task analysis and implementation schedule will be provided.

Description of the Health Center

Physical Facilities. Two sites which are suitable for use as a health center have been identified. Both are County property, in good condition, and located within the city limits of Eutaw, which is the county seat and trade center of Greene County.

Site #1 is a two-story masonary structure less than one hundred (100) yards from the town square and adjacent to the county health department. The hospital and offices of local physicians are within a five minute walk. Presently the building is fully occupied by various State and Federal agencies. The Department of Pensions and Security occupies the entire second floor. Advantages of this site are its central location and proximity to the health department. The major disadvantage is that it is fully occupied by agencies who have been in the same location for several years and would object to relocation.

Site #2 is a single-story brick building within a quarter mile of the town square. A fifty-unit low income housing project is located six (6) blocks from the site and another two hundred (200) units are under construction. County officials estimate that some 2,000 low-income persons live within a half-mile radius of this site. A county school (grades 1-12) is within two

CLINIC SITE 1

STRUCTURE VIEWED RIGHT-FRONT

STRUCTURE VIEWED LEFT-FRONT

Clinic Site 1

(GROUND FLOOR)

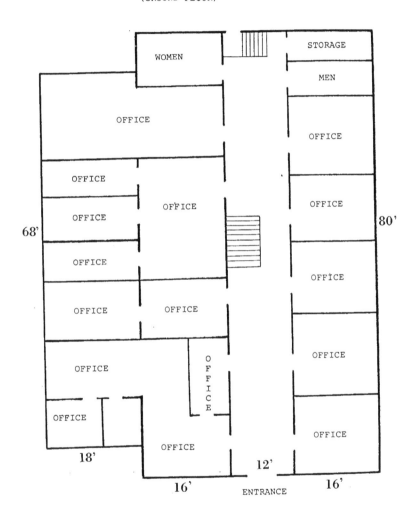

CLINIC SITE 2

STRUCTURE VIEWED
RIGHT-FRONT

STRUCTURE VIEWED
RIGHT-REAR

STRUCTURE VIEWED REAR
SHOWING EXPANSION AREA

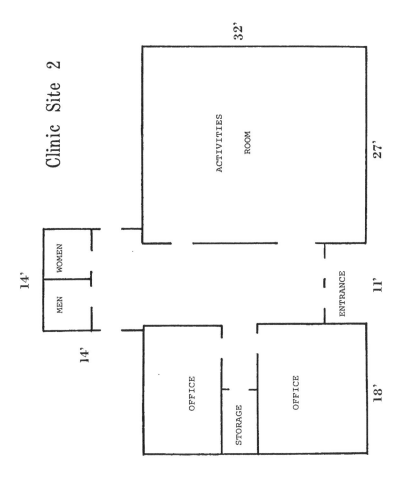

Clinic Site 2

ACTIVITIES ROOM

32'

27'

WOMEN

MEN

14'

14'

ENTRANCE

11'

OFFICE

STORAGE

OFFICE

18'

hundred (200) yards. The building presently serves as a community center and site of weekly congregate meals for the elderly. The advantage of this site is its proximity to a large potential client group (students and housing project residents). The disadvantage is its relatively small size which would necessitate construction of a new wing.

The County Commission has agreed to undertake required construction or renovation. West Alabama Health Services will enter into a lease agreement with the County which will provide for reimbursement of costs incurred and a reasonable additional amount for maintenance. This lease agreement shall be submitted to the Department of Health, Education and Welfare for approval.

Internal design of the clinic facility must await selection of the site. It would be desirable to include the physician and dentist in the design process so that the arrangement is one in which they feel comfortable and can work effectively. An esthetic goal is to avoid any suggestion of a "poverty" clinic by creating a clean, comfortable and cheery atmosphere.

Clinical Procedures. The key to efficient delivery of quality primary care lies in development of protocols for management of patient care. Protocols are decision rules which guide members of the health care team in collecting, recording and acting upon data describing the status of individual clients. The goal of this strategy is rapid diagnosis and a planned program of health maintenance for each client. Costs are minimized by using non-professional workers who perform specific tasks under the supervision of professional providers. Efficiency and accuracy are achieved by collecting data at each level of decision-making which facilitates decision-making at the next higher level.

Development of these protocols will be the responsibility of the professional staff. Many factors will influence this task including:

o   Personal preferences and "style" of the
     physician and dentist

o   Clinic floor plan and equipment complement

o   Skills and abilities of supporting staff

o   Characteristics of the client population

o   Operational experience

The health care center will include a small but efficient clinical laboratory designed to process a high volume of routine "stat" procedures. On-site capability for basic biochemical screening is needed because it is both difficult and expensive to arrange follow-up visits for patients. Tests performed at the clinic will be of the "go, no-go" variety; if abnormality is detected additional specimens are taken and transmitted to a referral laboratory for further analysis. The most important laboratory equipment will be a small Coulter blood cell counter (or equivalent) and a Clinicard blood chemistry system (or equivalent). Both of these machines are rugged, easily mastered, and produce consistently reliable results. This is an important consideration in an area such as Greene County. A low priced blood analysis system was investigated but it evidently requires constant maintenance and produces sometimes erratic results. The laboratory will be staffed by a laboratory assistant, a relatively low-skilled person who can be recruited locally and trained to perform a limited number of procedures with a high degree of accuracy; this is made possible through the use of semi-automated equipment. This person will be trained by consulting pathologists at no cost to West Alabama Health Services. Preliminary negotiations with the anticipated referral laboratory indicates that the clinic will receive very favorable prices for procedures such as SMA-12 blood chemistry, exfoliative cytology, etc.

Routine radiological procedures will be performed at Greene County Hospital and the Public Health Department. The hospital is well equipped for all common procedures while the health department has a small portable X-ray unit.

Prescription drugs will be issued through an arrangement with local pharmacists. Drugs will be specified by generic name whenever possible. Those most frequently dispensed will be purchased in bulk and dispensed at the health care center by staff practitioners. In other cases, the patient will be given a prescription which also serves as a payment voucher.

The dental program will stress preventive oral health and strongly emphasize pediatric care. Adults who are in pain and unable to receive treatment through private sources will be treated promptly with full consideration for conservation of oral structures. Children, once admitted, will be scheduled to return weekly, or as often as practical until all services are completed. Those completed will be recalled not less than once a year for periodic checkups and needed maintenance. Teeth will be extracted only after all other treatment methods have been attempted or considered. No patient will be treated without an initial medical history and physical examination.

Because of the great demand for dental services in the target area, it will be necessary to develop priorities for treating various categories of patients. These priorities will be formulated by the dentist with consultation from the Professional Advisory Committee and approved by the Project Director and Board of Directors.

Administrative Procedures. Efficient administrative procedures are one of the keys to clinic productivity. Goals are to free the providers from as much paperwork as possible so that their time can be devoted to patient care services, while speeding the flow of information required for decision making at all levels. The medical records system will use a problem-oriented record and will minimize writing through use of pre-printed forms adapted to particular classes of patients. Multi-part forms will permit capture of selected data at the source and will provide inputs to the accounting system.

Most of the project accounting is related to management of accounts receivable, that is, preparation of statements for individuals and third-parties. Purchase of an existing data processing package is anticipated and its effectiveness has been demonstrated by the Family Practice Clinic operated by the University of Alabama in Huntsville.

Payment for clinical services will come from the following sources:

1. Medicaid
2. Medicare
3. Self-coverage
4. Private insurance plans

The project has been discussed with appropriate officials of the Medicare and Medicaid agencies (See Appendix), and no difficulty is anticipated in obtaining status as an authorized provider. Reimbursement rates will be negotiated as prescribed by current guidelines.

For those clients not covered by third-parties, a fee schedule based on minimum prevailing rates in the local area will be established. Every patient will be billed a standard amount depending on services received. Adjustments will be made to individual accounts from time to time, depending on individual family circumstances. This technique is superior to use of a sliding scale fee schedule because every patient is made aware of the value of services which have been rendered. Every patient is treated with equal dignity and the humiliating financial investigation and frequent recertification required for a sliding scale is eliminated. Administrative procedures are considerably simplified. Some clients may feel uneasy when they receive a substantial billing; the solution to this problem is careful training of intake interviewers and other members of the clinic staff so that they may explain the billing procedure and help clients to understand that there is more concern for the state of their health than the state of their finances. Naturally, this system is subject to abuse, but one advantage of a rural area such as Greene County is that most everyone knows his neighbor's financial resources.

Third-party payers will be billed in accordance with the prevailing schedule of fees or a negotiated rate as appropriate. The clinic may enter into agreements with area employers for regular physical examinations of their workers. This may involve the development of special package rates.

Transportation and Outreach. West Alabama Health Services will contract with the Greene County Commision for the provision of transportation for health center clients. The County has conducted a highly successful community outreach program for more than two years which is designed to locate isolated persons in need of social services and assure that they receive appropriate and available assistance. Existing outreach workers, whose salaries are paid by Greene County, will receive training in health care from the clinic staff.

The present outreach system is based on the outreach worker's use of his private vehicle. Ideally, larger vehicles such as "mini-buses" will eventually be obtained because of the lower passenger-mile cost. However, a problem in Greene County is that the population is thinly scattered over a large area; a larger vehicle would thus be only partially filled. During the project year, we will study this problem and, together with the Greene County Commission and other local agencies, attempt to develop some type of optimum mix of transportation services.

Outreach will also be conducted through other organizations. Several local churches have expressed an interest in the program and see the potential benefit for their members. The county school system is eager to improve the health of students and has been affected in this regard by the loss of Title I funding. As previously noted, the public health officer is an active participant in current West Alabama Health Services planning and full cooperation can be expected from this agency.

Implementation Schedule

The Greene County Clinic will be phased in over approximately a twelve-month period with limited clinical services scheduled to begin during the fifth month from date of grant award. An as overview of first-year activity, there are three major phases of implementation, each with certain broad objectives:

> Phase I: Mobilization of Resources
>
> Tasks: 1. Select and Orient Key Personnel
>
>   2. Define Policies and Draft Procedures
>
>   3. Obtain Building and Major Equipment
>
>   4. Negotiate Key Contracts
>
> Phase II: Deployment of Resources
>
> Tasks: 1. Select and Orient Support Personnel
>
>   2. Finalize Procedures and Draft Protocols
>
>   3. Obtain Minor Equipment and Supplies
>
>   4. Finalize Key Contracts and Negotiate Secondary Contracts
>
> Phase III: Application of Resources
>
> Tasks: 1. Select and Orient Support Personnel
>
>   2. Adopt Interim Protocols
>
>   3. Finalize Secondary Contracts
>
>   4. Evaluate Project Activity

In general, Phase I is preliminary to the delivery of health services; Phase II is a trial period during which concepts are tested and modified as necessary, while Phase III marks the beginning of full-scale operations. Clinical services

935

WEST ALABAMA HEALTH SERVICES PROJECT: SUMMARY SCHEDULE
Implementation of Greene County Clinic

PROJECTED ENCOUNTERS

38

PHASE III

PHASE II

PHASE I

900
900
750
520
330
192
60
32

PROJECTED ENCOUNTERS

will begin during the fifth month on a limited scale. Patients will be carefully selected from defined groups so that various categories of persons
(i.e. children, adults, elderly) can be seen under controlled conditions.
Early in Phase III the clinic will be fully staffed and the number of encounters
should increase progressively as a team spirit develops among the clinic
staff.

Tasks involved in attaining project objectives during the first year can be
analyzed in terms of four categories:

1. Staff recruitment and orientation

2. Development of policies, procedures
   and protocols

3. Selection and acquisition of facilities,
   equipment and supplies

4. Formalization of agreements with
   external organizations

Staff Recruitment and Orientation. The staffing strategy is designed to
achieve optimum utilization of human and financial resources. Personnel will
be added gradually, beginning with key staff members, so that each supervisor can play a major role in defining duties of subordinates and in their
selection and orientation to the program. This will insure that each individual
can be productively occupied as soon as possible.

The project director will be responsible for recruitment of the physician and
dentist with review of candidates and final selection performed by the Board
of Directors. For other employees, the Project Director, in consultation with
the physician and dentist where appropriate, will submit names of potential
employees to the Board for confirmation.

Development of Policies, Procedures, and Protocols. Policies are broad
statements of project goals and objectives which provide the basis for creation
and maintenance of the desired organizational environment. Policy will be
developed by the Board of Directors with the aid of the Project Director,
physician and dentist. Examples of areas in which policy decisions are
required include the following:

o Personnel Policy
o Client Service Policy (priorities)
o Fee Schedule and Fee Collection Policy
o Evaluation Criteria

PROJECT STAFFING SCHEDULE

POSITION TITLE	MONTHS FROM DATE OF GRANT AWARD											
	1	2	3	4	5	6	7	8	9	10	11	12
Project Director												
Physician												
Registered Nurse												
Registered Nurse												
Intake Interviewer (Practical Nurse)												
Nurse's Aide												
Nurse's Aide												
Laboratory Assistant												
Dentist												
Dental Hygienist												
Dental Assistant												
Dental Assistant												
Office Manager/Book.												
Clerk Typist												
Secretary												

LEGEND

RECRUITMENT   ORIENTATION &   PRODUCTIVE
TRAINING   ACTIVITY

Procedures are the means by which policy is implemented and relate to
project operation on a daily basis. These will be determined by the Project
Director and staff and discussed with the Board of Directors. Examples of
procedures would include the following:

o   Maintenance of medical records

o   Appointment Scheduling System

o   Preparation of monthly reports

o   Safeguarding cash receipts

o   Interface with the data processing
    facility

Protocols define specific action taken during particular encounter situations.
These will be defined by the Project Director, physician and dentist with the
assistance of their key subordinates, although they may decide to apply some
of the numerous protocols which has been published. Sample protocols
which will be applicable in the Greene County Clinic include the following:

o   Taking the health history of a new client

o   Measuring vital signs

o   Performing an electrocardiogram

o   Counseling the hypertensive patient

Protocols will be subject to continuous modification as the clinic gains operational experience. The data processing system will prove enormously
beneficial to protocol development by generating frequency distributions
for diagnoses and procedures.

Selection and Acquisition of Facilities, Equipment, and Supplies. Final
choice of a clinic site will be made as soon as possible after announcement of
the grant award. It is realized that completion of any required renovation
imposes a time constraint on other activities. Renovation to be performed will
be determined by the Board of Directors, based on recommendations submitted
by the Project Director, Technical Advisory Committee, and the consulting
architect retained by Greene County.

Specifications for major clinical equipment such as examining tables, laboratory equipment, and the dental operatory will be prepared by the Project
Director with the assistance of the Technical Advisory Committee. It would
be desirable to have the physician and dentist participate in equipment
selection, but the long lead time between order and delivery of most health
care equipment may prevent this.

Clinical supplies will be selected by the physician and dentist; this includes small instruments. Purchasing procedures will be evaluated so as to obtain the best possible prices through bulk purchases, "generic" name items, and cooperative buying with local health organizations.

West Alabama Health Services, Inc. is eligible to purchase surplus Federal property at nominal cost. The State Agency for Surplus Property has been contacted and advised that items such as desks, filing cabinets, lamps, and chairs are available although mostly in somewhat battered condition. Clinical equipment is not available.

Formalization of Agreements. West Alabama Health Services will need to establish formal relationships with many agencies in order to achieve project objectives. These arrangements will fall in three categories:

1. Clinical Services

    o   Contracts with other health providers for
        referral of diagnostic procedures such as
        radiology, hematology, etc.

    o   Contract with local pharmacies for provision
        of prescription drugs

    o   Contract with local physicians and dentists
        for services rendered within the clinic

2. Ancillary Services

    o   Contract with County Commission for
        establishment of a patient transportation
        system

    o   Agreement with Public Health Department
        regarding referrals between the organizations

    o   Agreement with County Board of Education
        regarding school health and dental hygiene
        program

3. Third-Party Reimbursement

    o   Agreement with State Medicaid Agency regard-
ing reimbursement for services provided to
eligible clients

    o   Agreement with Social Security Administration
regarding reimbursement for services provided
to eligible clients

    o   Agreement with Blue Cross and other private
insurers regarding reimbursement for services
provided to policyholders.

This is only a sample listing of agreements with other organizations.

Possible Delays in Project Implementation. Planned Activity associated with
project implementation could be delayed for many reasons. These can be
analyzed in terms of the four major areas of project implementation:

    1.   Staffing

    2.   Development of Policy, Procedures,
Protocols

    3.   Facilities, Equipment, Supplies

    4.   Formalization of Agreements

Staffing. Although several prospective physicians and dentists have contacted
project planners, difficulty may arise in obtaining qualified professionals
within the time period indicated on the staffing schedule. This also applies to
some of the other staff professionals. Some of those persons recruited locally
and trained within the clinic may not prove satisfactory and result in personnel
turnover.

Policy, Procedures, Protocols. Procedures and protocols must be defined
with reference to defined equipment and staff. Delays in these areas would
impact the task of procedure and protocol definition.

Facilities, Equipment, Supplies. The extent of renovation required to make
the building suitable for use as a clinic will determine the time required for
task completion. Delivery of equipment could be delayed, preventing completion of staff orientation and the delivery of health services. Supplies are not
likely to present a problem but various shortages and disruptions of the
national economy could easily affect delivery times and quantities available.

<u>Formalization of Agreements</u>. Every agreement will be preceeded by a period of negotiation. Even agencies pursuing similar objectives frequently discover points of disagreement once a verbal understanding is translated into a written agreement. The time invested in negotiation and preparation of written agreements will be a good investment in that possible future misunderstanding may be avoided.

DATA COLLECTION AND EVALUATION

The collection and analysis of data generated in the course of clinic operations is a necessary evil. On one hand, it represents a fairly substantial expense which the Board would prefer spending on patient care. On the other hand, it indicates performance in comparison with objectives and can indicate possible avenues of improvement. Before collecting data one should know why it is collected, in other words, how it is to be evaluated.

Data Evaluation

Evaluation can be viewed from two perspectives:

Process Evaluation (accomplishment of objectives)

Impact Evaluation (achievement of objectives)

The short-run objective, for purposes of process evaluation, could be stated as:

"Increase clinic productivity so as to provide highest quality health care at the least possible cost to project clients and the Federal Government."

The long-run objective, which could serve as the basis for impact evaluation, might be stated as:

"Reduce the relative incidence of disease and disability so as to minimize the total cost to society."

Process Evaluation. Evaluation will be performed on a monthly cycle. Should undesirable conditions develop the frequency may be increased so that evaluation reports are generated every two weeks. The following four reports form the basis of process evaluation:

1. Monthly financial analysis

2. Monthly utilization analysis

3. Monthly epidemiological analysis

4. Monthly client attitude survey

The financial analysis summarizes revenue and expense on a monthly and year-to-date basis and indicates deviation from the project budget. Cost-per-treatment will be calculated for various types of encounter.

The utilization analysis will compare the numbers and types of clients receiving services with predicted levels. Use of the transportation system and the number and types of referrals to other agencies will also be indicated.

The epidemiological analysis will list medical and dental problems diagnosed by the staff professionals and the frequency each problem was detected on a monthly and year-to-date basis. Therapeutic procedures performed by the clinic staff will be similarly listed.

The client attitude survey will measure attitudes towards the staff and services of the health care center as expressed by clients. This will be performed on a sampling basis.

In conducting the monthly evaluation, all of these reports must be considered together. For example, the utilization analysis may show that the clinic is operating well below expected capacity indicating a need to expand outreach efforts; however, the financial analysis could show that increased volume would peril financial stability. If volume were increased, a later client attitude survey might show that clients sense that they are being rushed through the clinic.

Increased productivity will be obtained after study of the epidemiological analysis. The frequency distribution of problems and procedures will indicate the most common encounter situations. Protocols can then be developed and refined for common procedures so as to help eliminate wasted time by facilitating decision making at the lowest possible level in the organization. Used in conjunction with the financial analysis, the epidemiological analysis can guide decisions concerning facilities and staff modification or the need for automated equipment.

Conduct of monthly process evaluation is the responsibility of the Project Director with assistance from the physician and dentist. They will review operating reports, draw tentative conclusions and determine alternative courses of action. The Project Director will make a monthly report to a meeting of the Board of Directors where the alternatives and recommended course of action will be discussed.

Impact Evaluation. Impact evaluation will determine the effect of the West Alabama Health Services Project in comparison to the results and benefits expected.

The most important result anticipated is a reduction in the incidence in disease and disability. One of the major problems of health planning for rural areas is the lack of morbidity data and this especially applies to Greene and Sumter Counties. It will thus be impossible to quantatively measure the clinic's effect on morbidity during the initial project year. However, the epidemiological analysis will indicate the area's most frequent health problems and this should serve as the basis for a coordinated program of preventive health under the auspices of West Alabama Health Services, the Public Health Department, the Board of Education and the county and city governments.

The principal measure of impact during the first project year will stem from a study of attitudes toward health care in general and the health care center in particular. One barrier to good health which has been detected in the target area is that many persons do not perceive a need for regular health care. The existence of West Alabama Health Services will modify this situation by creating an interest and awareness of health. The attitudinal study will be performed by the University of Alabama Department of Medical Sociology using a methodology validated in a survey performed in two adjacent counties. Based on interviews conducted among randomly selected rural households, the study is designed to determine both the incidence of disease and attitudes towards the availability of health services. The target area will be surveyed both prior to implementation of the clinic and at the close of the project year so that baseline data is available for comparative purposes.

It will also be desirable to document the economic impact of the West Alabama Health Services Project on the Greene County area; the impact is expected to be substantial. One technique which has been discussed is to track retail sales in the City of Eutaw. A baseline would be established for each participating merchant by averaging monthly sales over a three-year period. Monthly sales during the project year would be converted to the baseline index and correlated with the number of clients receiving treatment at the health center. This would demonstrate that a community health center is a welcome addition to a rural area and thereby justify increased local support.

Data Collection

The heart of the data collection system is the clinical accounting system. Current plans call for the purchase of software developed by IBM Corporation and extensively modified by Huntsville (Alabama) Hospital for use by the Family Practice Clinic sponsored by the University of Alabama (Huntsville) School of Primary Care. Basically an accounts receivable system, it is capable of generating the following reports:

1. Private patient statement

2. Medicare statement

3. Medicaid statement

4. Miscellaneous insurance company statement

5. Summary of diagnoses, by frequency of occurrence

6. Summary of procedures, by frequency of occurrence

7. Summary of encounters, by patient category

8. Aged listing of accounts receivable

9. Trial balance

Additional reports are also produced for use in batch verification and file updating. Input forms include a Family Registration Form, which assigns patient numbers and creates master file records, and various Encounter Forms which record diagnoses and procedures. The system is currently operating on a System 3 Model 10. Adequate data processing facilities are available at Livingston University (Sumter County).

SAMPLE STATEMENTS GENERATED BY

ANTICIPATED CLINICAL DATA PROCESSING SYSTEM

1.   Private Patient (Self-Coverage)

2.   Insurance Company Statement

3.   Blue Cross-Blue Shield Statement

4.   Medicaid Statement (Blue Cross)

Note the detail of information shown on these statements.
Summarization and analysis of these data will be used to
continually improve productivity fo the clinic.

50

FAMILY PRACTICE CENTER

810 FRANKLIN ST.   HUNTSVILLE, ALA 35801

PHONE 539-0474

	ACCOUNT NUMBER	DATE
~~SANDERSON GLENN~~	800492-1	12/31/73
~~RIVERSIDE~~ AVENUE		
HUNTSVILLE, ALA	ALL PAYMENTS AND CHARGES AFTER THE ABOVE DATE WILL APPEAR ON NEXT STATEMENT	

DETACH AND RETURN THIS STUB WITH REMITTANCE

PATIENT	DESCRIPTION	DOCTOR	DATE	AMOUNT
	BALANCE FORWARD			250.00
PAYMENT.	CASH		12/12/73	12.00
DEBBIE	LAB, GC CULTURE	RAB	12/20/73	3.00
PAYMENT.	CASH		12/18/73	25.00
DEBBIE	ROUTINE OFFICE VISIT, ADU	HTS	12/12/73	7.00
DEBBIE	DRUGS, OTHER	HTS	12/12/73	5.00
MEDICAID HAS BEEN FILED			12/31/73	

800492-1	OVER 30 DAYS .00	OVER 60 DAYS 213.00	OVER 90 DAYS .00	DATE 12/18/	AMOUNT 25.00	228.00
ACCOUNT NUMBER	OUTSTANDING ACCOUNTS RECEIVABLE			LAST PAYMENT		BALANCE DUE

PAY THIS AMOUNT
TO
FAMILY PRACTICE CENTER

TERMS CASH ON RECEIPT OF STATEMENT

948

FAMILY PRACTICE CENTER   51
810 FRANKLIN STREET   HUNTSVILLE, ALABAMA 35801
PHONE 539-0474

ATTENDING PHYSICIANS STATEMENT

INSURANCE COMPANY	INS. CO.	POLICY NUMBER	MEMBER'S NAME
MISC INS CO	099		
		RELATION TO MEMBER	PATIENT'S NAME
		SELF SPOUSE CHILD ☐ ☐ ☐	

CAUSE OF TREATMENT	CAUSE OF TREATMENT	CAUSE OF TREATMENT
ILLNESS ☐ DATE OF FIRST SYMPTOMS	INJURY ☐ DATE OF INJURY	MATERNITY ☐ DATE OF CONCEPTION

AS PATIENT HAD SIMILAR CONDITION BEFORE? YES ☐ NO ☐ DATE | WAS CONDITION RELATED TO EMPLOYMENT? YES ☐ NO ☐ DATE OF 1ST CONSULTATION | CAN PATIENT RETURN TO WORK? YES ☐ NO ☐ DATE

DOES PATIENT HAVE OTHER GROUP INSURANCE OR MEDICAL COVERAGE? YES ☐ NO ☐ NAME OF COMPANY OR PLAN | POLICY NUMBER

DATES OF DISABILITY FROM TO	PATIENT'S ACCOUNT NUMBER	DATES OF SERVICES FROM TO
	800332-9 02	11/01/73 12/31/73

DIAGNOSIS   401.0   HYPERTENSION

DATE OF SERVICE	PATIENT NAME	LOCATION	DESCRIPTION OF SERVICE	PRIMARY ICDA	SECONDARY ICDA	AMOUNT
11/20/73	EILEEN	O	ROUTINE OFFICE VISIT, ADU			7.00
11/20/73	EILEEN	O	LAB, URINALYSIS			3.00
11/20/73	EILEEN	O	LAB, RA			5.00
11/20/73	EILEEN	O	DRUGS, DEPOMEDROL			5.00
11/01/73	EILEEN	O	ROUTINE OFFICE VISIT, ADU			7.00
11/01/73	EILEEN	O	DRUGS, OTHER			5.00
12/31/73	EILEEN	O	OV OTHER	401.0		3.00
12/31/73	EILEEN	O	DRUGS, OTHER	401.0		5.00
12/11/73	EILEEN	O	ROUTINE OFFICE VISIT, ADU			7.00
12/11/73	EILEEN	O	LAB, URINALYSIS			4.00
12/11/73	EILEEN	O	DRUGS, OTHER			5.00

LOCATION CODES:
O—DOCTORS OFFICE
(—PATIENTS HOME
IH—INPATIENT HOSPITAL
OH—OUTPATIENT HOSPITAL
NH—NURSING HOME
IL—INDEPENDENT LAB
ECF—EXTENDED CARE FACIL.
OL—OTHER LOCATIONS

REMARKS:

TOTAL CHARGES $ 56.00

PLEASE MAKE CHECKS PAYABLE TO
FAMILY PRACTICE CENTER

R A BROWN   M.D.   DATE

52

DOCTOR'S SERVICE REPORT

BLUE CROSS—BLUE SHIELD OF ALABAMA

930 South 20th Street • Birmingham, Alabama 35298 • Phone 251.4233

SECTION 1 — TO BE COMPLETED FOR ALL CLAIMS

CASE PRINT OR TYPE			CONTRACT NUMBER	PATIENT BIRTHDATE			DOCTOR CASE NUMBER
PATIENTS LAST NAME	FIRST NAME	INITIAL	PREFIX NUMBER	MO.	DAY	YR	
C̶ ̶ ̶ ̶ ̶ ̶ ̶ ̶			R00788179	10	02	13	8010563

SUBSCRIBERS LAST NAME	FIRST NAME	INITIAL
CARROLL	TROY	M

IF INJURY, GIVE DATE OF ACCIDENT

MO.	DAY	YEAR

DOES THIS PATIENT HAVE OTHER GROUP HEALTH INSURANCE OR HEALTH PLAN COVERAGE?

STREET ADDRESS OR P.O. BOX

HUNTSVILLE, AL

DID ACCIDENT OCCUR DURING THE COURSE OF EMPLOYMENT? YES ☐ NO ☒

YES ___ NO ___ IF YES, LIST NAME OF CARRIER

RELATIONSHIP OF PATIENT TO SUBSCRIBER

SELF ☐ SPOUSE ☒ SON ☐ DAUGHTER ☐ OTHER ☐

IF PREGNANCY GIVE THE NORMAL EXPECTED DELIVERY DATE

MO.	DAY	YEAR

DID ANY OTHER PHYSICIAN PARTICIPATE IN THE CARE? YES ☐ NO ☐

IF YES, LIST PHYSICIAN'S NAME AND TYPE SERVICE

HOSPITAL IN-PATIENT ☐ HOSPITAL OUT-PATIENT ☐ OFFICE ☒

IF HOSPITAL IN-PATIENT OR OUT-PATIENT, GIVE NAME OF HOSPITAL

SECTION 2—IN-HOSPITAL MEDICAL VISITS DIAG 713.0 ARTHRITIS

DATE ADMITTED			DATE DISCHARGED		
MON	DAY	YR	MON	DAY	YR

INDICATE ALL VISITS	1	2	3	4	5	6	7	8	9	10	11	12	13	14	15	16	17	18	19	20	21	22	23	24	25	26	27	28	29	30	31
MONTH																															
INTH																															
INTH																															

SECTION 3—SURGERY, ANESTHESIOLOGY, OBSTETRICS, RADIOLOGY, OR PATHOLOGY FOR BC-BS USE ONLY

	LIST SERVICES RENDERED: GIVE DATE AND CHARGE FOR EACH PROCEDURE	DATE OF SERVICE	DOCTOR'S CHARGE	RIDER	PAID AMOUNT	MAJ/ MINOR	PLOR TR.	STAT CODE
1	AB, GLUCOSE TOLER	1212 73	25.00					
2	OV OTHER	1212 73	.00					
	ROUTINE OFFICE VISIT, ADU	1217 73	7.00					
3	LAB, URINALYSIS	1207 73	4.00					
	LAB, HGB & HCT	1207 73	5.00					
4	INITIAL OFFICE VISIT, ADU	1207 73	10.00					
	LAB, SMA 12/60	1207 73	10.00					
05	ELECTROCARDIOGRAM	1207 73	15.00					
6								
7								
08								
9								
10								

GENERAL ANESTHESIA: YES ☐ NO ☐ LOCAL ANESTHESIA: YES ☐ NO ☐

DOCTOR'S NAME (PLEASE PRINT)

RICHARD A. BROWN MD

TOTAL DOCTOR CHARGE	TYPE PROV	SER. BENEFIT	SEX REL.	DISF
76.00	1	1		1

STREET ADDRESS

810 FRANKLIN   HUNTSVILLE AL 35801

TYPE CLAIM	CONF. CODE	OVERRIDE	HOSPITAL CODE
	0		

DOCTOR CODE

PAYMENT OF BENEFITS SHOULD BE MADE TO: THE SUBSCRIBER ☐ ME ☒

I CERTIFY THAT I PERFORMED THE SERVICES ENUMERATED ABOVE.

GOVT AGENCY	FEE TYPE	MED. TYPE	DOCTOR NAME

SIGNED ___ M.D. ___ NO. ___

GROUP	DIVISION	PAYMENT DATE

HERBERT T. SMITH MD
FAMILY PRACTICE CENTER
810 FRANKLIN STREET

DEBR NR.	CLAIM NUMBER

BLUE SHIELD
OF ALABAMA

53.

REQUEST FOR MEDICAID BENEFITS
ALABAMA MEDICAL ASSISTANCE PLAN – TITLE XIX

PATIENT'S NAME (Last Name, First, Middle Initial)	2. MEDICAID IDENTIFICATION NO.
SHERRY S	3 4 5 0 0 3 7 9 3 6 0 2 2

a. PATIENT'S ADDRESS (Street Number, City, State, Zip Code)	4. DATE OF BIRTH	5. SEX	6. TELEPHONE NUMBER
AVENUE HUNTSVILLE, ALA	MO 04 DAY 22 YR 47 □ M ☒ F		533-4668

MUST BE COMPLETED IN ALL CASES

7. a. Are you covered under any other health and/or accident insurance plan? Yes_____ No _____
If yes, give name, address of insurance company, and policy or medical assistance number:

b. Is your condition due to an accident? Yes _____ No_____ If yes, give complete details on the reverse side.

I authorize any holder of medical or other information about me to release any information needed for this or any related Medicaid Claim to Blue Cross-Blue Shield of Alabama and the Alabama State Board of Health and I authorize the further release of any such information to any other parties who may be liable for any of my medical expenses. I hereby assign to the Alabama State Board of Health all claims against third parties who may be liable for any of my medical expenses to the extent that such expenses are paid by Medicaid. I permit a copy of this authorization to be used in place of the original.
I understand that obtaining anything of value to which any person is not entitled under Medicaid laws and regulations is unlawful and such person is subject to arrest and trial under State and/or Federal law.

SIGNATURE OF PATIENT OR REPRESENTATIVE (Please identify if other than recipient)	DATE SIGNED
BLANKET SIGNATURE	10/31/73

EXAMINATION AND TREATMENT RECORD

A. Date of each service	B. Place of service (See Codes below)	C. Fully describe surgical or medical procedures and other services or supplies furnished for each date given	D. DIAGNOSIS—Nature of illness or injury requiring services or supplies	E. Charges (If related to unusual circumstances explain in 9 C.)	Leave Blank
11/15	O	ROUTINE OFFICE VISIT, ADU		7.00	
11/15	O	LAB, URINALYSIS		3.00	
11/15	O	LAB, SMEAR HANGING DROP		2.00	

10. Name and address of physician or supplier (Number and street, city, State, Zip code)	Telephone No.	11. Total Charges
RICHARD A. BROWN MD	539-0474	12.00
FAMILY PRACTICE CLINIC		12. Amount paid or payable by Third Party
310 FRANKLIN STREET	Physician/supplier code	
HUNTSVILLE, ALA 35810	0776	13. Any unpaid balance due 12.00

14. Show name and facility where services were performed (If other than home or office visits)	15. Laboratory work performed in your office?
FAMILY PRACTICE CENTER	□ No (If No, enter name and address of Lab.) ☒ Yes

16. Was this patient referred from the diagnostic and screening program? If yes, give name and address of referring agency. □ Yes x ☒ No	17. If the service of another physician was necessary, advise full name.

I hereby certify that the above claim for services is true, accurate, and complete, that the amount is due, that the amount received (as determined by the Single State Agency within limits defined by State and Federal laws) will be accepted as full payment for all services rendered the patient as set forth herein; that no unlisted payment is due or has been received, and that no third party payments will be accepted in excess of the determined usual and customary charges for services rendered under the Medicaid—Title XIX Program. I certify that this claim for payment under Medicaid—Title XIX Program is for services rendered to an individual with proper papers to establish eligibility and that the services were personally rendered or directed by me, and hereby agree to keep such records as are necessary to support this claim for a period of five years from date of service and consent to furnish information and allow the inspection of said records by authorized representatives of the State Agency. The State Agency operates under the provisions of Title VI of the Civil Rights Act of 1964. Under the provisions of this Act, any provider of services receiving Federal funds must comply with the intent of this Act and this means there shall be no discrimination because of race, color or national origin. This Title also provides for a strict compliance and complaint procedure.

I understand that payment and satisfaction of this claim will be from Federal and State funds, and that any false claims, statements, or documents, or Concealment of a material fact, may be prosecuted under applicable Federal or State laws.

18 SIGNATURE OF PHYSICIAN OR SUPPLIER	□ M.D. □ D.O. □ O.O. DATE SIGNED
	OTHER DEGREE

*O—Doctor's Office   H—Patient's Home (If portable X-ray services, identify the supplier)   ECF—Extended Care Facility OL—Other Locations

Other components of the clinical accounting system such as accounts payable, payroll, etc. can be adequately maintained through a pegboard system.

The medical records system will use a problem-oriented record. A specific system has not been selected because the physician and dentist should have a voice in this decision. It would also be desirable to maintain compatibility with the system used by the Family Practice Clinic at the University of Alabama in Tuscaloosa. Several commercially available systems are under study.

A brief client attitude survey form will be developed once the factors which are important in measuring the attitudes of clinic users is more fully understood. This survey will be administered by the scheduling clerk who is the last health center staff member encountered by each patient.

RELATIONSHIPS WITH OTHER ORGANIZATIONS

The shortage of primary care facilities in West Alabama is a major concern
for many area organizations, both public and private. Their encouragement of this project and promises of support will help insure effective health
services delivery which includes more than just treatment in a clinic.
Participating organizations and their anticipated contributions are listed
below.

ORGANIZATION AND LOCATION	ANTICIPATED CONTRIBUTION
Greene Co. Medical Society (Eutaw) Sumter Co. Medical Society (Livingston) Greene Co. Dentists Sumter Co. Dentists	Assistance in Clinical Services Planning and Evaluation; Clinical staffing as feasible
Greene Co. Public Health Dept. (Eutaw) Sumter Co. Public Health Dept. (Livingston)	Maternal and Child Health Clinics; Communicable Disease Clinics; Family Planning; Home Health Services (Sumter Co. Only); Environmental Sanitation
Greene Co. Hospital and Nursing Home (Eutaw) Sumter Memorial Hospital (Livingston) Hill Hospital (York)	Inpatient care; Emergency Services; X-ray and Laboratory Services; Skilled Nursing Care
Druid City Hospital (Tuscaloosa)	Regional Hospital Center; Special Diagnostic Procedures and Treatments; Referral Center for Inpatient Care
Vocational Rehabilitation Service (Tuscaloosa)	Physical Therapy; Speech and Hearing Therapy; Counseling and Training of Handicapped and Retarded persons
West Alabama Mental Health Board (Eutaw, Livingston, additional "outreach" clinics)	Full Mental Health Services; Diagnosis and Treatment of Emotionally Disturbed Persons; Inpatient and Outpatient Care
Greene Co. Dept. of Pensions and Security (Eutaw) Sumter Co. Dept. of Pensions and Security (Livingston)	Social Services; Financial Assistance; Food Stamps; Medicaid Certification

ORGANIZATION AND LOCATION	ANTICIPATED CONTRIBUTION
Federation of Southern Cooperatives (Epes)	Outreach; Consumer Health Education; Social Services; Transportation
Social Security Administration (Tuscaloosa)	Medicare Certification; Financial Assistance
West Alabama Planning and Development Council (Tuscaloosa - Greene Co.) Tombigbee Planning and Development Commission (Camden-Dumter Co.)	Environmental Analysis and Planning Socioeconomic Studies
West Alabama Project on Aging Tuscaloosa) Tombigbee Project on Aging (Sumter)	Congregate Meals; Home Visitation; Counseling
University of Alabama College of Community Health Sciences (Tuscaloosa)	Services Planning and Evaluation; Staff Training; Consultation Concerning Medical Records Systems, Fiscal Management
West Alabama Comprehensive Health Planning Council (Tuscaloosa)	Formal Liason to Other Area Health Providers and Consumers; Planning and Evaluation; Initial Project Management and Administrative Support

GEOGRAPHIC LOCATION

The West Alabama Health Services Project will initially focus on Greene and Sumter Counties. Both counties fall within the Alabama "Black Belt" Region, a name reflecting the rich soil, and are characterized by gently rolling hills, dense forests, and large open pastures. The Tombigbee River bisects the two counties and will eventually link Gulf Coast ports to the extensive inland water system. Interstate Highway I-59 cuts through both counties and, when completed, will be a major artery between Atlanta and New Orleans.

Greene County has a land area of 627 square miles and a population density of 17 persons per square mile. As a unit of Alabama Planning District II, it is served by the West Alabama Planning and Development Council. Eutaw, the county seat and central city, has a population of 2,805 according to the 1970 Census. It is located 35 miles from Tuscaloosa, which serves as Greene County's principle trade and medical referral center.

Sunter County has an area of 915 square miles and a population density of 19 persons per square mile. It falls within Alabama Planning District VI and is a member of the Alabama-Tombigbee Planning and Development Commission. Livingston is the county seat and has a population of 2,358. York, with a population of 3,044, is the other major city. One of the county's important resources is Livingston University, a former state teacher's college, which has an enrollment of some 5,000 students. Meridian, Mississippi, is the county's primary trade and medical referral area and is located about 24 miles from York and 38 miles from Livingston.

A map of the State of Alabama is shown on the following page and illustrates Greene and Sumter Counties in relationship to the State as a whole. On the page following is a more detailed map of the target area with major cities and highways indicated.

WEST ALABAMA HEALTH SERVICES PROJECT

TARGET AREA

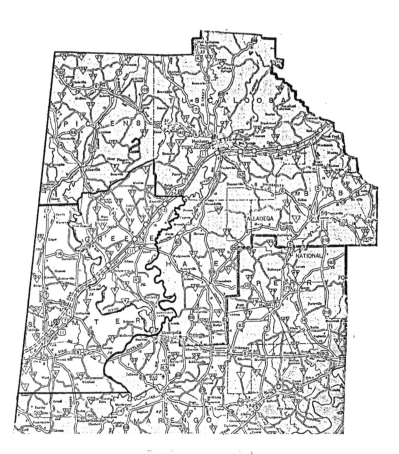

WEST ALABAMA

HEALTH SERVICES PROJECT

TARGET AREA

RELATIONSHIP TO OTHER PROJECTS

West Alabama Health Services will develop important working relationships with four major health-related programs in the area:

    o   University of Alabama

    o   Livingston University

    o   West Alabama Mental Health Center

    o   West Alabama Comprehensive Health Planning Council

University of Alabama

The University of Alabama College of Community Health Sciences is developing a residency program in Family Practice. Undergraduate clerkships give medical students experience in family practice, pediatrics, psychiatry, and other aspects of primary care. A nursing porgram is now under development. The University also offers degree programs in nutrition and dietetics, laboratory technology and social work. A new program in health care administration will focus on management of health facilities. A strong reciprocal arrangement between West Alabama Health Services and the University is contemplated.

Livingston University

Livingston University is developing an associate degree nursing curriculum and the West Alabama Health Services Clinic will serve as a training site for student nurses. The University's Commerce and Business Administration Department will provide assistance in project management. Data processing for the clinic will be performed by Livingston University. Plans are being made for paramedical training programs to help meet the area's critical need for health technicians; here again, mutual benefit is anticipated.

West Alabama Mental Health Center

The Mental Health Center, headquartered in Demopolis (15 miles from Eutaw),
serves both Greene and Sumter Counties with a full range of inpatient and outpatient services. The inpatient clinic is located in Sumter Memorial Hospital
in Livingston. Services include diagnostic testing, pre- and post-hospitalization
counseling and therapy, and child care. The program is federally funded and
has a budget of roughly $465,000. Close cooperation between the West Alabama
Health Services Clinic and the mental health program will insure coordinated
care in both mental and physical health.

West Alabama Comprehensive Health Planning Council

The Council is the designated 314(b) Agency serving seven counties in West
Alabama. It played a major role in the initial development of the West Alabama
Health Services Project and will provide continuing support as the project
develops. The staff offers a broad range of expertise relevant to the successful
development, management and evaluation of community health services.

A P P E N D I X

ARTICLES OF INCORPORATION

OF THE

WEST ALABAMA HEALTH SERVICES PROJECT

We, the undersigned natural persons of the age of 21 years, or more, acting as incorporators of the corporation under the Alabama Non-Profit Corporation Act, adopt the following articles of incorporation for such corporation, and do sign, verify, and file the same with the Judge of Probate of Greene County, Alabama, the County in which the principal office of the Corporation is established.

ARTICLE I

The name of the corporation is: West Alabama Health Services Project.

ARTICLE II

The purpose of the corporation is to provide health services in Greene and Sumter Counties Alabama and such other counties as may be selected by the Corporation and to engage in related activities and business as may be determined by the Corporation.

ARTICLE III

The duration of the corporation is indefinite.

ARTICLE IV

The Corporation shall have no members.

ARTICLE V

There shall be a Board of Directors selected to represent the interest of both consumers and providers of Health Services and to geographically represent the counties served by the Corporation. Members of the Board shall be selected as described in the By-laws of the Corporation. This Board constitutes the legal authority of the Corporation.

ARTICLE VI

The President of the Board of Directors shall be the principal executive officer of the Corporation and, subject to control of the Board of Directors, shall in general be responsible for the affairs of the Corporation and may sign with other officers, any deeds or contracts which the Corporation is authorized to execute.

ARTICLE VII

In the event of dissolution, the residual assets of the organization will be turned over to one or more organizations which themselves are exempt as as organizations described in Section 501 (c) (3) and 170 (c) of the Internal Revenue Code of 1954 or corresponding sections of any prior or future Internal Revenue Code, or to the Federal, State or Local government for exclusive public purpose.

ARTICLE VIII

The Corporation is not organized for pecuniary profit nor shall it have any power to issue certificates of stock or to declare dividends. No pecuniary gain or profit to the directors thereof or any private person, firm or corporation shall ever occur and no part of its net earnings shall inure to the benefit of any director or individual or any private person, firm or corporation, except that the Corporation shall be authorized and implemented to pay reasonable compensation for services rendered and to make payments and distributions in furtherance of the purposes set forth in Article III thereof.

ARTICLE IX

The address of the initial registered office of the Corporation is:

P. O. Box 347, Greene County Commissioner, Eutaw, Alabama   and the name of the initial registered agent at such address is: Judge William McKinley Branch.

ARTICLE X

Tne initial Board of Directors is made up of eleven (11) persons. The names and addresses of the persons who are to serve as initial members of the Board of Directors and also as incorporators are as follows:

Allen Turner, Route 1, Boligee, Alabama

Willie Hill, Route 3, Box 145, Eutaw, Alabama

Rucker L. Staggers, M.D., 202 Pickens Street, Eutaw, Alabama

Edward L. Gegan, M.D., Box 781, Livingston, Alabama

Judge William M. Branch, P. O. Box 347, Eutaw, Alabama

W. T. Lockard, 505 Broad Street, P. O. Box 216, York, Alabama

John H. Modley, Jr., Route 1, Box 900, Forkland, Alabama

Zora C. Gibbs, P. O. Box 141, Livingston, Alabama

Edward Ozment, Sumterville, Alabama

Robert Cook, York, Alabama

John M. Packard, M.D., Associate Dean, College of Community Health Sciences, P. O. Box 6291, University, Alabama

The initial officer of the said Corporation who shall serve until their successors are elected and take office are:

William M. Branch	President
W. J. Lockard	Vice President
Rucker Lewis Staggers	Secretary
Cora C. Gibbs	Treasurer

IN WITNESS WHEREOF, we, and each of us, have hereunto set our hands and have sworn to and subscribed to these articles of incorporation and do depose and say that the statements contained therein are true before the respective undersigned authorities on this the ninth day

of November , 1973.

William M. Branch

W. J. Lockard

Rucker Staggers

Edward L. Degar, MD

Cora C. Gibbs

Willie Hill

John H. Medley, Jr

John M. Lockard, M.D.

Robert Cook, Jr.*

Edward Ozment*

Allen Turner*

Sworn to and subscribed before me by the above named officers of the Corporation.

Bettie Jean Knott
Notary Public in and for Greene County, Alabama

Prepared by Pruitt and Pruitt

*Signatures on record at Greene County Courthouse, page 283 and 283

The initial officer of the said Corporation who shall serve until their successors are elected and take office are:

_____	President
_____	Vice President
_____	Secretary
_____	Treasurer

IN WITNESS WHEREOF, we, and each of us, have hereunto set our hands and have sworn to and subscribed to these articles of incorporation and do depose and say that the statements contained therein are true before the respective undersigned authorities on this_____ *8th* *Day*

_____*November*_____, 1973.

✓ _____*Robert Cook, Jr.*_____

✓ _____*Edward Emest*_____

_____

_____

_____

_____

_____

_____

_____

Sworn to and subscribed before me by the above named officers of the Corporation.

_____*Caulton E. Vaughan*_____

Notary Public in and for ~~Greene~~ County, Alabama *Sumter*

The initial officer of the said Corporation who shall serve until their successors are elected and take office are:

_William M. Branch_____ President
_____ Vice President
_____ Secretary
_____ Treasurer

IN WITNESS WHEREOF, we, and each of us, have hereunto set our hands and have sworn to and subscribed to these articles of incorporation and do depose and say that the statements contained therein are true before the respective undersigned authorities on this _8th_ day _of November_____, 1973.

_Allen Turner_____

Sworn to and subscribed before me by the above named officers of the Corporation.

_Earlean M Isaac_____
Notary Public in and for Greene County,
Alabama

WEST ALABAMA HEALTH SERVICES PROJECT

BY-LAWS

ARTICLE I

Name

The name of the incorporated body is the West Alabama Health Services Project.

ARTICLE II

Articles of Incorporation

The West Alabama Health Services Project is a non-profit corporation organized under the laws of the State of Alabama and the Internal Revenue Code.

ARTICLE III

Purpose

The purpose of the West Alabama Health Services Project is to provide ambulatory health care for citizens of Greene and Sumter Counties. Other counties may be included at a later time.

ARTICLE IV

Objectives

The objectives of the West Alabama Health Services Project shall be the provision of medical and dental services for residents of Greene and Sumter Counties and such other counties as may later be included in the service area. The Board of Directors shall from time to time evaluate and modify the services offered in accordance with the needs of the people to be served. The West Alabama Health Services Project shall participate in educational programs for health care providers as may be appropriate.

ARTICLE V

Board of Directors

Section 1

The Board of Directors shall initially be composed of eleven (11) members. Fifty-one percent of the membership shall be composed of consumers who receive services from the West Alabama Health Services Project and shall be representative of the total population of the counties served. The County Commissioners of Greene County shall appoint three consumer members from Greene County, and the Sumter County Board of Commissioners shall appoint three consumer members from Sumter County to the Board of Directors.

Section 2

The five (5) community representatives shall be selected as follows: One (1) representative of the Greene County Medical Society appointed by that body; one (1) representative of the Sumter County Medical Society appointed by that body; one (1) representative of the Greene County Commission; one (1) representative of the Sumter County Commission; one (1) representative of the West Alabama Comprehensive Health Planning Council who is not a resident of either Greene or Sumter County.

ARTICLE VI

Meetings of the Board of Directors

Section 1

The Board shall hold a regular meeting once a month at a time and place convenient to the members. Special meetings may be called at any time by the Chairman of the Board with the consent of two other members. One meeting each year shall be designated the annual meeting.

Section 2

A quorum shall consist of a majority of the membership.

Section 3

Only members of the Board of Directors shall be entitled to vote. A member of the Board may send an alternate to a meeting but the alternate will have no voting rights.

Section 4

A member who is absent from three consecutive regular meetings will be replaced by the original appointing authority.

ARTICLE VII

Officers

Officers of the Board of Directors shall consist of a President, Vice-Preisdent, Secretary, and Treasurer. They shall serve for a period of one year and may succeed themselves.

Officers shall be selected at the annual meeting.

An unexpired term of any officer shall be filled by means of a special election.

ARTICLE VIII

Duties of Officers

Section 1

The President shall be the principal officer of the corporation and subject to the control of the Board of Directors, shall in general supervise and control all the business and affairs of the corporation. He may sign, with the secretary or other proper officer of the corporation thereto authorized by the Board of Directors, any deeds or other instruments which the Board of Directors has authorized to be executed and, in general, shall perform all the duties incident to the office of President and such other duties as may be prescribed by the Board of Directors.

Section 2

The Vice President shall act as an assistant to the President and shall perform the duties of the President in the absence or disability of the President.

Section 3

The Secretary shall keep a record of all the affairs of the corporation and of all the proceedings, accounts, funds and securities of the corporation and shall keep a record of the minutes of the meetings of the Board of Directors.

Section 4

The Treasurer shall be custodian of the corporation's funds; he shall accept and deposit in accounts in banks established for that purpose all incoming monies in the name of the corporation; he shall issue checks for payment of any approved indebtedness of the corporation. The Treasurer shall maintain a set of books showing all receipts of money, all disbursements and shall make proper accounting to the Board of Directors. These duties may, at the discretion of the Board of Directors, be delegated to a staff member.

ARTICLE IX

Standing and Special Committees

Section 1

The Board of Directors may create such standing and special committees as it may deem necessary to carry out he purpose of the Corporation. Persons may be appointed to special committees or task forces who are not members of the Board.

Section 2

Each committee shall work under the guidance of the Board of Directors. Recommendations will be made to the Board of Directors for final decision.

Section 3

The President and project director shall serve as ex-officio members of these committees.

ARTICLE X

The agency shall not be bound by nor assume responsibility for the independent actions of any of its members.

ARTICLE XI

Fiscal

The Board shall seek, accept and deposit to its accounts funds for the operation of the Board's business.

ARTICLE XII

Parliamentary Authority

Robert Rules of Order Revised shall govern the Board in all cases where applicable.

ARTICLE XIII

Amendments

The By-Laws may be amended at any regular meeting of the Board by a two-thirds (2/3) vote of the members present and voting.

APPENDIX C-1

JOB DESCRIPTION

Job Title: Dentist

Qualifications

EDUCATION   D.D.S. or D.M.D. degree from a recognized school of
                 dentistry and licensed or eligible for license to practice
                 dentistry in the State of Alabama.

EXPERIENCE   At least two years of experience in the delivery of dental
                 care, either in private practice or in an institutional
                 setting, is desirable.

OTHER   Must be sensitive to the problems and needs of persons
                 from widely divergent cultural backgrounds. Desire
                 to develop a team approach to comprehensive primary care.

Responsibilities and Duties

RESPONSIBILITY   Directly responsible to the Project Director, except in
                 the real of a dentist's professional judgment.

DUTIES   1.   Shall establish clinical standards for the rendering
                      of quality dental care.

                 2.   Shall provide a full range of dental care including
                      diagnosis and treatment, counseling and referral
                      as necessary. Specific tasks may be delegated to
                      other members of the dental staff, consonant with
                      legal restrictions and quality care.

                 3.   In conjunction with the Board of Directors and Project
                      Director, shall develop policies and procedures for
                      the delivery of ambulatory care.

                 4.   Shall supervise the daily activities of the dental
                      staff, delegating this reponsibility where appropriate.

                 5.   Shall assist the Project Director in the preparation of
                      morbidity studies required for project planning and
                      evaluation.

APPENDIX C-2

JOB DESCRIPTION

Job Title: Physician

Qualifications

EDUCATION   M.D. Degree from a recognized medical school and
               licensed or eligible for license to practice medicine in
               Alabama.

EXPERIENCE   Shall have completed one year of an approved internship.
               Completion of a residency in Family Practice, Internal
               Medicine or Pediatrics is desirable. At least one year of
               experience in the provision of ambulatory health care.

OTHER   Must be sensitive to the problems and needs of persons
               from widely divergent cultural backgrounds. Desire to
               develop a team approach to comprehensive primary care.

Responsibilities and Duties

RESPONSIBILITY Directly responsible to the Project Director, except in the
                realm of a physician's professional judgment.

DUTIES   1.   Shall establish clinical standards for the rendering
                of quality medical care.

           2.   Shall provide a full range of ambulatory medical care
                including diagnosis and treatment, counseling and
                referral as necessary. Specific tasks may be delegated
                to other members of the staff, consonant with legal
                restrictions and quality care.

           3.   In conjunction with the Board of Directors and Project
                Director, shall develop policies and procedures for
                the deliveyr of ambulatory care.

           4.   Shall supervise the daily activities of the medical
                staff, delegating this responsibility where appropriate.

           5.   Shall assist the Project Director in the preparation of
                morbidity studies required for project planning and
                evaluation.

APPENDIX C-3

JOB DESCRIPTION

Job Title: Project Director

Qualifications

EDUCATION   Bachelor's Degree from an accredited college or university. Graduate study in some field of administration or public health is desirable.

EXPERIENCE   Progressively responsible administrative experience. Managerial experience within the framework of a non-profit health care, educational, social services, or similar organization is desirable.

OTHER   Must have a thorough knowledge of the problems and techniques of human services delivery in a rural area. Must be capable of dealing with persons of diverse educational and cultural backgrounds.

Responsibility and Duties

RESPONSIBILITY   Directly responsible to the Board of Directors for all aspects of project organization and management, except in aspects of clinical services where the judgment of a licensed health provider must be exercised.

DUTIES

1. Prepares job descriptions, recruits potential staff members and orients new employees, in accordance with personnel policies established by the Board of Directors.

2. Supervises all employees of the project, delegating this responsibility where appropriate.

3. With consultation from the Professional Advisory Committee, selects project sites and supervises required construction or renovation.

4. Develops and implements administrative systems in the areas of financial management, medical records, patient scheduling, transportation, inter-agency referral, and other aspects of project management, delegating specific tasks to members of the staff where appropriate.

APPENDIX C-3a

5. Selects and purchases equipment and supplies,
    seeking guidance from members of the staff or
    Professional Advisory Committee where appropriate.

6. Prepares monthly reports to the Board of Directors
    summarizing clinic activity, financial status of the
    project, morbidity characteristics and trends of the
    client population, and other aspects of project
    operations. Reports will include comments and
    recommendations as to the need for policy and pro-
    cedural modifications.

7. Performs other duties which may be assigned by the
    Board of Directors.

MAR 12 1974

SUMTER COUNTY MEDICAL SOCIETY
LIVINGSTON, ALABAMA

March 11, 1974

Dr. Elizabeth Cleino, Director
West Alabama Comprehensive Health
Planning Council
P. O. Box 1488
Tuscaloosa, Alabama   35401

                              Re: West Alabama Health Services Project
                                   Revised

Dear Dr. Cleino:

This is to certify that The Sumter County Medical Society has
endorsed the above captioned project.

This carries with it the endorsement of the Medical-Dental
staffs of the Sumter County Hospitals.

                              Sincerely yours,

                              Sidney J. Williams, M. D.
                              Secretary
                              Sumter County Medical Society

sjw:ech

STATE OF ALABAMA

State Agency for Surplus Property

DEC 12 1973

D E P A R T M E N T   O F   E D U C A T I O N   ★   ★   ★

P. O. Box 1100
GADSDEN, ALABAMA 35902
PHONE 492-6711

P. O. Box 5317
MOBILE, ALABAMA 36605
PHONE 438-1289

December 10, 1973

Mr. Greg Delessovay
West Alabama Comprehensive Health
  Planning Agency
P. O. Box 1488
Tuscaloosa, Alabama

Dear Mr. Delessovay:

Pursuant to your telephone request, we are enclosing the following
self-explanatory forms:

1. Application for Eligibility To Participate
   In The Federal Surplus Property Utilization
   Program - Public Health Institution

2. Authorized Representative Certification

3. HEW Form No. 441

You may have these forms executed in the interest of the medical clinic
the West Alabama Comprehensive Health Planning Agency plans to establish
and returned to this office for an eligibility determination.

Sincerely,

N. J. Kitchens, Manager

NJK/bw
Enc:

State of Alabama
Department of Public Health

February 25, 1974

IRA L. MYERS, M.D
STATE HEALTH OFFICER

PAUL I. ROBINSON, M.D.
DIRECTOR, MEDICAL SERVICES ADMINISTRATION

ADDRESS REPLY TO:
MEDICAL SERVICES ADMINISTRATION
304 DEXTER AVENUE
MONTGOMERY, ALABAMA 36104

Judge William Branch, Chairman
West Alabama Health Services, Inc.
P. O. Box 347
Eutaw, Alabama   35462

Dear Judge Branch:

In reply to your letter of February 21, 1974, this letter will confirm
Mr. Lewis' statements by telephone. The Medicaid program does not pay
for clinic services; we pay for physician service, laboratory and x-ray
on the basis of the cost to the clinics.

Our intermediary for these services is Blue-Cross and Blue Shield of
Alabama, and it will be necessary for you to discuss payment procedures
with that organization before starting to submit claims.

Sincerely,

Paul I. Robinson, M. D., Director
Medical Services Administration

PIR:gw

cc: Greg de Lissovoy
     Health Planner

DEPARTMENT OF HEALTH, EDUCATION, AND WELFARE
SOCIAL SECURITY ADMINISTRATION
REGION IV
50 7th Street, N. E., Room 250
Atlanta, Georgia 30323

FEB 26 1974

February 21, 1974

Bureau of Health Insurance

Refer to:
CO:RT

Judge William M. Branch
President of Board of Directors
West Alabama Health Services, Inc.
Eutaw, Alabama 35462

Dear Judge Branch:

We have been informed by Greg DeLissovoy that you are in the process of forming a comprehensive health center in Eutaw, Alabama, which will be funded by a grant under section 314(e) of the Public Health Service Act. Physician-directed, free-standing, federally-funded comprehensive health centers are entitled to receive reimbursement for services rendered to Medicare patients on a cost-related-to-charge basis. We are enclosing a copy of the instructional material which explains Medicare reimbursement rate and billing procedures. Please advise us when the grant has been approved by the Public Health Service so that arrangements can be made to meet with you and appropriate members of your staff to set up the procedures for Medicare reimbursement. You may contact Richard Taylor of my staff at (404)526-3686. He will be glad to make arrangements for this meeting.

Sincerely yours,

Richard L. Morris
Program Officer
Contractors

Enclosure

11/5/73

The Greene County Medical Society
Eutaw, Alabama

TO WHOM IT MAY CONCERN:

The Greene County Medical Society is pleased to endorse the
West Alabama Health Services Program and will assist in every
way possible to assure its success.

Sincerely,

Joe P. Smith, MD
President

MAR 12 1974

Sumter County
Department of Public Health
Livingston, Alabama

March 11, 1974

Dr. Elizabeth Cleino, Director
West Alabama Comprehensive Health
Planning Council
P.O. Box 1488
Tuscaloosa, Alabama   35401

                    Re: West Alabama Health
                         Services Project Revised

Dear Dr. Cleino:

This is to advise you that the above captioned project
is endorsed by the Greene County and Sumter County Boards
of Health and the health departments of these counties.

I request that you proceed as rapidly as possible toward
the ultimate implementation of this project.

Thanking you, I am

                    Sincerely yours,

                    Sidney J. Williams, M.D.
                    Health Officer
                    Greene and Sumter Counties

SJW: bi

J. S. MORRIS, D.D.S.
EUTAW, ALABAMA 35462

Nov. 8, 1973

To Whom it may concern:

I have seen, for a number of years, the need for an additional dentist in this county and am only too happy to endorse and support the plan of the West Alabama Health Services Project in its effort to bring much needed health services to the people of our community.

J. S. Morris D.D.S.

THE UNIVERSITY OF ALABAMA
POST OFFICE BOX 6291
UNIVERSITY, ALABAMA 35486

OF COMMUNITY HEALTH SCIENCES   November 7, 1973   TELEPI

Dr. Betty Ann Cleino
Director
West Alabama Comprehensive Health
  Planning Council
P. O. Box 1488
Tuscaloosa, Alabama 35401

Dear Dr. Cleino:

This letter is to express the endorsement of the West Alabama Health Services project by the College of Community Health Sciences. We recognize the urgent need for more primary care in the area which will be served by this project if it is approved. The College will be glad to cooperate with the project to the extent that our resources permit.

I trust that this project will receive favorable consideration by the reviewing authorities who must approve it for funding.

Yours sincerely,

William R. Willard, M.D.
Dean

WRW:cw

GREENE COUNTY HOSPITAL AND NURSING HO

509 WILSON AVENUE EUTAW, ALABAMA 35462

D.B. PATTON, JR., ADMINISTRATOR

11/7/73

TO WHOM IT MAY CONCERN:

The Greene County Hospital is pleased to endorse the
West Alabama Health Service Program and will assist in every
way possible to assure its success.

Sincerely,

D.B.Patton Jr.
Administrator

SUMTER

NOV 14 1973

MEMORIAL HOSPITAL
LIVINGSTON, ALABAMA 35470

November 13, 1973

Dr. Betty Cleino
Director of West Alabama Health Services Project
P.O. Box 1488
Tuscaloosa, Alabama

Dear Betty:

In an effort to upgrade the level of patient care here in this area, efforts are being made to provide additional facilities through the West Alabama Health Care Project in rendering such care. We who are presently engaged in the delivery of medical care here are perhaps more keenly aware of this need than anyone else. Therefore we urge you to use your best efforts toward getting this project established here. Likewise we pledge to you and to those who shall be working with you in this project, our wholehearted cooperation.

You may be assured of my own personal interest and of my desire to be of assistance.

Sincerely,

SUMTER MEMORIAL HOSPITAL

W. T. Steele
Administrator

WTS/rt

cc: Mr. Winton Wise
    Dr. Sidney J. Williams
    Dr. Edward L. Gegan

GREENE COUNTY
DEPARTMENT OF PENSIONS AND SECURITY
EUTAW, ALABAMA 35462

November 8, 1973

Dr. Elizabeth Cleino, Director
West Alabama Comprehensive Health Planning Council
P. O. Box 1488
Tuscaloosa, Alabama 35401

Dear Dr. Cleino:

There is a great need for ambulatory health care in Greene County.
We will be glad to cooperate with the West Alabama Health Services Project.

Sincerely,

Martha H. Echols

Mrs. Joe Echols
Casework Reviewer
In Charge

ME/cs

SUMTER COUNTY
DEPARTMENT OF PENSIONS AND SECURITY
LIVINGSTON, ALABAMA 35470

November 7, 1973

Dr. Elizabeth W. Cleino, Director
West Alabama
Comprehensive Health and Planning Council
 Box 1488
Tuscaloosa, Alabama 35401

Dear Dr. Cleino:

I believe that the West Alabama Health Services Project is a very
needed service to this county.

The Sumter County Department of Pensions and Security will be glad
to assist and co-operate with you in any way possible.

Sincerely yours,

(Mrs.) Frances Rumley
Director

FLR/pw

STATE OF ALABAMA
DEPARTMENT OF EDUCATION
REHABILITATION AND CRIPPLED CHILDREN SERVICE
1107 SIXTH AVENUE EAST
TELEPHONE: 759-5711
TUSCALOOSA, ALABAMA 35401

November 7, 1973

Dr. Elizabeth Cleino, Director
West Alabama Comprehensive
Health Planning Council
P.O. Box 1488
Tuscaloosa, Alabama 35401   RE: West Alabama Health
                                          Services Project
Dear Dr. Cleino:

The proposal describing a West Alabama Health Services
Project, an ambulatory clinic for the medical treatment
of rural people, is commendable and a very interesting
method for treating citizens of rural areas, especially
the poor. This should provide a very workable plan to
insure that all persons in sparsely populated areas receive adequate medical care. The proposed project is
organizationally sound and its structure provides the
vehicle to deliver services to the people needing them.

Once such a project is implemented, it appears certain
that many of its patients could need services provided
by the State Agency Program of Vocational Rehabilitation
Services for Adults and Crippled Children.

With this in mind, I have alerted our Crippled Children
and Rehabilitation workers to be ready to join hands with
this organization to accept referrals and provide services
to such patients as are deemed feasible and meet the criteria
for eligibility of Rehabilitation and Crippled Children
Services.

Please rest assured that we stand ready to assist in any way
we can in meeting the needs of persons who are disabled.

Please keep us informed on the progress of this project in
order that we can participate at the appropriate time.

                          Sincerely yours,

                          Paul Jackson, Area Supervisor
                          Rehabilitation Service

PJ/lb

987

Planned Parenthood Association of Tuscaloosa County

916-18 5th Ave., E. — P. O. Box 2311 — Telephone 758-9066
TUSCALOOSA, ALABAMA 35401

Executive Director
MRS. WANDA PAUL

November 6, 1973

Dr. Elizabeth Cleino
West Alabama Comprehensive Health Planning Council
P.O. Box 1488
Tuscaloosa, Alabama 35401

Dear Dr. Cleino,

The West Alabama Family Planning Project enthusiastically endorses
the West Alabama Health Services Project.

If at any time we can be of assistance please call on us. I pledge
to you our fullest cooperation.

Sincerely,

(Mrs.) Wanda Paul
Executive Director

blb

AGRICULTURE • HOME DEMONSTRATION • 4-H CLUBS

AUBURN UNIVERSITY | COOPERATIVE EXTENSION SERVICE

AUBURN UNIVERSITY, UNITED STATES DEPARTMENT OF AGRICULTURE AND
GREENE COUNTY COMMISSIONERS COURT COOPERATING

POST OFFICE, EUTAW, ALABAMA 35462 • TEL. 372-3401

November 7, 1973

Dr. Elizabeth W. Cleino, Director
West Alabama Comprehensive Health
Planning Council
P. O. Box 1488
Tuscaloosa, Alabama   35401

Dear Dr. Cleino:

The Cooperative Extension Service wish to endorse the West Alabama
Health Service Project, which will provide ambulatory health care
services for the people of Greene County. This medical service
project will tie in with a joint Health Education Program of the
Cooperative Extension Service.

Miss Linda W. Goodson, Health Education Specialist have been assigned
to this area. Through project HELP those in need can be identified
and referred to the project for treatment.

We would like to commend your group for the leadership in developing
this ambulatory health care project. We believe that this will
greatly improve the health service available to the people in Greene
County. We are happy to pledge our full support.

Sincerely,

Charles S. Foreman
County Extension Chairman

CSF/mrm

COUNCILMEN
HENRY W. ROBINSON
JOE L. SANDERS
MELVIN K. DURRETT
J. E. TRENTHAM
PAUL STOKES

CITY OF EUTAW

EUTAW ALABAMA 35462

TELEPHONE 372-4212

AREA CODE 205

WILLIAM H TUCK, MAYOR

MAR·

November 16, 1973

The City of Eutaw is pleased to endorse the West Alabama Health Service Program and will assist as much as possible in assuring a successful endeavor.

Sincerely yours,

William H. Tuck

Mayor William H. Tuck

THE CITY OF LIVINGSTON ALABAMA

TELEPHONE 205/652-2505 • POST OFFICE DRAWER W • LIVINGSTON, ALABAMA 35470

November 5, 1973

Dr. Elizabeth W. Cleino, Director
West Alabama Comprehensive Health
    Planning Council
P. O. Box 1488
Tuscaloosa, Alabama 35401

Dear Dr. Cleino:

    I have been informed that an application is being submitted to the Department of Health, Education and Welfare for funds which will be used to provide ambulatory health care services for the people of Livingston, Sumter and Greene Counties, Alabama.

    I understand that a non-profit corporation, known as West Alabama Health Services, has submitted the application. This corporation is composed of consumers, professionals and representatives of the county governing bodies. I endorse this effort. If there are services which can be provided by the Town of Livingston, please advise us as we will be happy to cooperate in this endeavor.

Sincerely,

Ira D. Pruitt, Jr.
Mayor

IDPjr/sej

BOARD OF COMMISSIONERS
SUMTER COUNTY
LIVINGSTON, ALABAMA 35470

November 4, 1973

Dr. Elizabeth W. Cleino, Director
West Alabama Comprehensive Health
   Planning Council
P. O. Box 1488
Tuscaloosa, Alabama 35401

Dear Dr. Cleino:

The Sumter County Commissioners wish to endorse the West Alabama Health Services Project, which will provide ambulatory health care services for the people of Sumter County

I will serve as a member of the Board, representing the Sumter County Commission. In addition, the Commission will appoint three citizen representatives to serve as consumer members to represent the people of Sumter County.

We would like to commend your group for the leadership in developing this ambulatory health care project. We believe that this will greatly improve the health services available to the people in Sumter County. We pledge you our full support in this project.

Sincerely,

W. T. Lockard
Chairman

GREENE COUNTY CHAMBER OF COMMERCE

P. O. BOX 70

EUTAW, ALABAMA 35462

Dr. Elizabeth Cleino, Director
West Alabama Comprehensive Health Planning Council
% Greene County Hospital
Eutaw, Alabama 35462

Dear Dr. Cleino:

It was a pleasure discussing with you the Health Care
Program. The Greene County Chamber of Commerce wishes
to endorse this program and to assure you of the
Chamber's full support.

When the Chamber can be of further assistance to you
and your Health Care Program please don't hesitate to
contact us.

Very truly yours,

Greene County Chamber of Commerce

Robert C. Farnham
President

$\mathfrak{S}$ $\mathfrak{C}$ $\mathfrak{O}$ Sumter County Opportunity, Inc.

Phones — 652.5011 & 5021

Leo Fields, Director   Mary Beeks, Fiscal Officer

P. O. Drawer 908 • Washington Street Bank Building • Livingston, Alabama 35470

November 6, 1973

Dr. Elizabeth W. Cleino, Director
West Alabama Comprehensive
Health Planning Council
Box 1488
Tuscaloosa, Alabama 35401

Dear Dr. Cleino:

It is my understanding that a Neighborhood Health Center is being
planned for Sumter County Alabama through which medical services are
available for all residents. The fees for these services will be based
upon the ability of the recipients to pay.

I feel that a program of this nature will prove very beneficial to the
residents of Sumter County and I am sure that some of the medical services will prove beneficial to our Head Start Program.

Sincerely,

Leo Fields, Director

bh

November 8, 1973

Dr. Elizabeth W. Cleino, Director
West Alabama Comprehensive Health
 Planning Council
P.O. Box 1488
Tuscaloosa, Alabama 35401

Dear Dr. Cleino:

The Sumter County NAACP wishes to endorse the West Alabama Health
Services Project, which will provide ambulatory health care services
for the people of Sumter County.

We would like to commend your group for the leadership in developing this
ambulatory health care project. We believe that this will greatly improve
the health services available to the people in Sumter County. We pledge you
our full support in this project.

Sincerely,

Robert Cook Jr. Sec'y N.A.A.C.P

SUMTER COUNTY
DEPARTMENT OF PENSIONS AND SECURITY
LIVINGSTON, ALABAMA 35470
March 12, 1974

Dr. Elizabeth Cleino, Director
West Alabama Comprehensive Health
Planning Council
P. O. Box 1488
Tuscaloosa, Alabama 35401

Re: West Alabama Health
     Services Project Revised

Dear Dr. Cleino:

This is to advise you that the above-mentioned project is e
by the Sumter County Department of Pensions and Security.

Our department will be glad to assist and co-operate in any
possible, according to agency policies.

Sincerely yours,

(Mrs.) Frances L. Rumley,
    Director

FLR
jld

Exhibit 5.—*Statement of Jeff S. Gordon Re Health Status of Sugar Cane Workers in Louisiana*

STATEMENT OF JEFF S. GORDON, CONCERN ON SUGAR CANE WAGES

(Presented to Department of Agriculture, July 9, 1971)

Good day Gentlemen, my name is Jeff Gordon. I am a senior student at Tulane Medical School, and what I have to present to you today is a preliminary survey of the health status of an average group of southern Louisiana sugar workers and their families. My intention today is to give you a physician's eye view of the health and well-being of sugar workers with the hope that your influence on sugar worker wages benefits will include some provision for their health.

This preliminary health study and medical service project was organized and implemented by Dr. Max Van Gilder, Joe Licata, an Antioch student on field placement with Southern Mutual Help Association, and myself. The study was designed to ascertain the health needs of the sugar workers on an absolute medical basis, and to provide medical care for each of the problems diagnosed.

To do this, we asked a group of physicians to perform general medical examinations on each of the 107 people included in this study. We also performed a group of routine diagnostic studies which included complete blood counts, urinalysis, and the SMA-12 battery of blood chemistries on the adults, and hematocrit, blood smears, urinalysis, and stool studies for intestinal parasites on the children.

Highest priority was given to providing medical care to the people involved in the study, and, as an internal control, the physicians were not informed about our interest in ascertaining the health status of this group. They were only asked to exam the sugar workers as regular patients, evaluate the clinical and laboratory findings, make the diagnoses, and provide therapy or refer the patients to generalists or specialists who could provide the proper management of the patient problems.

It should be stressed then that the results included herein are the clinical diagnoses by physicians, not the academic assessments of health often generated by some studies that only involve questionnaires and laboratory studies, and not the direct examination of patients by physicians.

The patients chosen for the health assessment were the total resident population of two sugar plantations in southern Louisiana. They were chosen because it was felt their living conditions, dietary habits, and ability to obtain medical care was about average, being neither the worst nor the best in any of these categories.

The examinations were performed over a two week period in March, 1971. Most of the minor or chronic problems uncovered were referred to local physicians, who cooperated fully with the patient care. The serious problems requiring diagnostic, therapeutic, or surgical follow-up were referred to the Tulane services at Charity Hospital of New Orleans. In all, 42 people were felt to have serious enough medical problems to be referred.

I invite you now to exam the results of our medical examinations included in the lists and medical diagnoses following this text. In summary, 37 adults and 700 children under 14 years of age were examined. Of the 37 adults, only two were found to be medically normal, and only eight were *not* in need of immediate medical care. (Obesity and asymtomatic multiple dental caries being excluded as reasons for immediate medical attention). A total of 102 pathological diagnoses were made and only 12 medical problems were currently under the care of a physician. The most serious, life threatening problems discovered include two cases of previously undiagnosed congestive heart failure, and two cases of undiagnosed valvular heart disease. Problems demanding immediate aggressive medical therapy included two cases of uncontrolled diabetes, and three cases of uncontrolled hypertension. Both disorders often predispose patients to other rapidly fatal problems.

As you might expect, the children proved to be somewhat more healthy than the adults, but even among this group the results were incredible. Only 16 out of 70 children were completely healthy. The most devastating finding was the high incidence of gross developmental and mental retardation—five children out of 70 are grossly retarded and condemned to subnormality for life. Another seven children were retarded by growth, a finding that often correlates with mental subnormality in later life. The most common medical problem among this population is intestinal parasites; we found 20 cases of the roundworm Ascaris, four cases of the roundworm Trichuris, and four cases of combined Ascaris and Trichuris infestation. I should point out that these findings are somewhat misleading. These diagnoses are made from clinical signs plus stool exams and we were only able to obtain stool samples from 30 of the children—28 were infected. Again, the most significant medical problems were cardiac—two cases of probable heart disease were discovered and referred to specialists.

Before commenting on these results, I should point out that our diagnoses probably tend to be somewhat conservative. As I have stressed, this was a preliminary survey to get a rough approximation of the health and well-being of this population. Many problems such as dental disorders, visual disorders, and hearing disorders were not checked by objective dental, visual or hearing exams, and only show here if they were overt clinical disorders.

In conclusion, these preliminary studies indicate that this sugar worker population has significant unmet medical and health needs. Their current state of health is the result of the combination of 1) inadequate housing, 2) inadequate diet, 3) inadequate sanitation, 4) inadequate education, 5) inability to afford medical care, and 6) the lack of available physicians and other health services. It should be pointed out that arrangements now exist where the employers of sugar workers pay the first five dollars ($5.00) of their medical care for each illness. But looking at the enclosed diagnoses, it is obvious these problems will easily require more than five dollars, and more than one visit. Moreover, local physicians, by their own choice, do not participate in medicare or vendor payment medical benefit programs, so patients are aware they have to pay or accept a physician's charity to get medical care. The usual situation is something like this for the sugar worker: He goes to a physician only when his children are sick with fever or pain, or when he or his wife have obvious pain. They usually go knowing they cannot afford the medical care and usually incur a bill with the physician that they cannot pay. But the simple fact that they haven't paid their bill makes them feel guilty about going back to the physician.

The physician, on the other hand, has a full medical practice that demands long hours seeing his regular paying patients. He has little time to see non-paying "charity" patients, but he will usually squeeze them in if he can. With little available time he usually directs his attention to the immediate complaint, often overlooking underlying chronic problems like diabetes, hypertension, or even mild congestive heart failure. The result is usually poor medical care, but the best both patient and doctor can do under prevailing social and economic conditions.

The solution to this problem will not be simple. On the national level, the answer we will ultimately seek will probably involve a form of national health insurance and increased production of physicians and para medical personnel. But this group of sugar workers has far greater medical and health needs than the average population in this country. And they need the best possible solution we can provide now. Given the medical care situation as it now exists, probably the best immediate health benefit that you can specify for the sugar worker and his family would be a total health insurance that provides payment for preventative services including yearly physical exams, outpatient care, hospital services, psychiatric services, dental care, and drugs. The goal of this insurance would be to at least make the sugar worker and his family an equal competitor for the medical and health services that now exist in the area.

Health insurance is the minimum benefit that might help the sugar worker obtain better health care. But his increased degree of medical needs merits the attention of a full-time health system actively working to improve his health. What these people require to bring them back into the mainstream of health is a program that addresses itself toward improving their income, housing, nutrition, education, and sanitation as well as their medical and dental care. Anything less will continue to leave these people in a medically underdeveloped country.

ADULT DIAGNOSES

Number of patients	Age	Sex	Clinical diagnoses
2 to 5	61	M	Hypertension; Congestive heart failure; Alcoholism; Osteoarthritis; Pharyngitis; Anemia; Obesity.
10 to 85	60±	F	Arterioscleroitic heart disease; Hypertension; Osteoarthritis.
9 to 87	59	M	Hypertrophic prostatism; Congestive heart failure; Cerevellar dysfunction; Alcoholic gastritis; Peptic ulcer disease; Anemia.
5 to 14	53	M	Valvular heart, disease—Aortic stenosis; Emphysema; Blindness—Left eye; Hypertrophic prostatism; Hypertension; Anemia; Obesity.
3 to 60	50	F	Hypertension; Angina; Upper GI bleeding; Rheumatoid arthritis; Obesity.
4 to 71	46	F	Hypertension; Arteriosclerotic heart disease; Diabetes; Obesity.
8 to 51	45	M	Arteriosclerotic heart disease; Emphysema; Lipoma—Right temporal area; Multiple dental caries.
3 to 52	40	F	Diabetes; Arteriosclerotic heart disease; Anemia; Obesity.
3 to 54	40	F	Normal.
8 to 44	39	F	Valvular heart disease—Miltral insufficiency; Obesity.
13 to 31	36	M	Obesity.
1 to 105	35	F	Hypertension; Congestive heart failure; Obesity.
1 to 99	34	F	Psychiatric disorder; Anemia.
2 to 88	33	F	Asthma; Congestive heart failure; Obesity.
6 to 26	33	M	Anemia; Obesity.
2 to 89	30	M	Hypertension; Urinary tract infection.
3 to 6	29	F	Migraine headaches; Multiple caries; Obesity.
4 to 61	26	F	Urinary tract infection.
4 to 10	26	F	Urinary tract infection; Obesity.
6 to 21	25	F	Strabismus; Pelvic inflammatory disease; Kidney infection; Multyple caries.
1 to 28	25	F	Pyelonephritis; Migraine headaches; Gastritis; Anemia; Obesity.
7 to 33	25	F	Pregnancy at 4 months; Vaginal discharge; Uterine fibroids; Anemia.
5 to 12	24	F	Hypertension; Congestive heart failure; Urinary tract infection; Pregnancy at 3 months; Severe anemia; Obesity.
5 to 11	22	F	Lymphadenopathy.
3 to 15	21	F	Arthritis; Anemia; Obesity.
3 to 8	19	F	Multiple caries; Obesity.
3 to 9	19	F	Pregnant at 3 months; Anemia; Obesity.
3 to 32	18	F	Obesity.
8 to 40	18	F	Anemia.
8 to 41	17	F	Multiple caries.
4 to 77	17	F	Urinary tract infection; Anemia; Breast mass.
8 to 42	15	F	Normal.
11 to 84	15	F	Urinary tract infection; Anemia.
8 to 43	14	F	Multiple dental caries.
3 to 53	14	F	Obesity.
4 to 73	14	M	Umbilical hernia.
8 to 110		F	Pharyngitis; Multiple caries.

PEDIATRIC DIAGNOSES

Number of patients	Age	Sex	Clinical diagnoses
3 to 60	13	F	Normal.
4 to 45	12	M	Umbilical hernia; Urinary tract infection.
4 to 72	12	F	Cardiac enlargement.
2 to 98	12	F	Normal.
2 to 97	11	M	Post-irradiation epiderma; Carcinoma of the forehaed.
12 to 106	11	M	Normal.
8 to 107	11	F	Do.
3 to 3	11	M	Systolic heart murmur; Recurrent epistaxis; Asthma; Impetigo.
4 to 70	11	M	Umbilical hernia.
3 to 55	11	M	Normal.
8 to 46	11	M	Mental retardation.
4 to 68	10	F	Congenital heart disease—Ventral septal defect.
4 to 69	10	F	Normal.
3 to 7	10	M	Growth retardation; Behavior problem.
3 to 27	10	F	Multiple caries.
2 to 96	9	F	Pica.
1 to 102	9	M	Mental retardation; Growth retardation; Diastasis recti; Ascariasis.
3 to 4	9	F	Multiple caries; Asthma; Ascariasis.
7 to 38	9	F	Urinary tract infection.
8 to 49	9	F	Normal.
4 to 67	9	F	Do.
8 to 47	9	M	Do.
2 to 95	8	F	Ascariasis; Trichuriasis.
2 to 94	8	M	Ascariasis.
7 to 37	8	M	Rickets.
1 to 29A	8	M	Normal.
8 to 48	8	F	Upper respiratory infection.
4 to 80	8	M	Normal.
1 to 104	7	M	Do.
3 to 56	7	F	Ascariasis.
3 to 16	7	M	Multiple caries; Ascariasis.

PEDIATRIC DIAGNOSES—Continued

Number of patients	Age	Sex	Clinical diagnoses
4 to 66	7	M	Ascariasis.
1 to 101	6	M	Do.
2 to 93	6	M	Do.
8 to 109	6	F	Urinary tract infection; Enuresis; Ascariasis; Trichuriasis.
7 to 39	6	M	Mentally retarded; Speech defect; Trichuriasis.
8 to 49	6	M	Normal.
6 to 111	6	F	Seizure disorder.
3 to 17	6	F	Multiple caries; Ascariasis.
4 to 81	6	M	Normal.
3 to 57	5	F	Ascariasis.
6 to 23	5	F	Growth retardation; Urinary tract infection.
3 to 18	5	M	Urinary tract infection; Ascariasis; Multiple caries.
4 to 82	5	F	Growth retardation.
8 to 108	4	F	Febrile upper respiratory infection; Ascariasis; Trichuriasis.
7 to 35	4	F	Upper respiratory infection; Trichuriasis.
1 to 30	4	F	Ringworm.
3 to 58	4	M	Urinary tract infection; Ascariasis.
6 to 24	4	F	Developmental retardation; Urinary tract infection.
4 to 65	4	M	Normal.
2 to 92	3	M	Asthma; Trichuriasis; Ascariasis.
7 to 34	3	F	Trichuriasis.
6 to 25	3	M	Growth retardation; Multiple caries.
8 to 50	3	M	Upper respiratory infection.
3 to 19	3	M	Developmental retardation; Growth retardation; Incontinence of urine and feces; Ascariasis.
3 to 59	2	F	Ascariasis.
3 to 13	2	F	Upper respiratory infection.
4 to 64	2	M	Ascariasis.
4 to 83	2	F	Anemia.
4 to 79	2	F	Ascariasis.
4 to 63	¹ 22	M	Growth retardation; Ascariasis.
4 to 62	¹ 22	M	Growth retardation; Ascariasis.
7 to 36	¹ 18	M	Upper respiratory infection; Trichuriasis.
2 to 91	¹ 18	M	Ascariasis.
1 to 100	¹ 12	F	Upper respiratory infection; Growth retardation.
1 to 29B	¹ 12	M	Otitis media.
3 to 20	¹ 12	F	Ascariasis.
4 to 78	¹ 11	M	Normal.
1 to 86	¹ 7	M	Asthma.
2 to 90		M	Upper respiratory infection.

¹ Months.

Senator HART. Our next witness is Mr. Charles W. Rawlings, former director, Center for Health Consumer Affairs, Case Western Reserve University, Cleveland, Ohio.

Mr. Rawlings, you may proceed.

STATEMENT OF CHARLES W. RAWLINGS, FORMER DIRECTOR, CENTER FOR HEALTH CONSUMER AFFAIRS, CASE WESTERN RESERVE UNIVERSITY, CLEVELAND, OHIO

Mr. RAWLINGS. Thank you, Mr. Chairman.

My name is Charles W. Rawlings. I am a resident of Shaker Heights, Ohio, a suburb of Cleveland. I am presently editor and publisher of a semimonthly newsletter called Telos.

Until June 1973 I had been director of the Center for Health Consumer Affairs at Case Western Reserve University in Cleveland.

I am an ordained minister in the United Presbyterian Church, although I am presently inactive. Over the past 15 years I have worked on a variety of urban problems related to the issues of race and poverty as an ecumenical church executive and as an administrator of university programs in continuing education aimed at such urban problems.

I would like to address my testimony today to attempt to identify the dominant direction and thrust of our present health care system as I have come to see it through a consumer perspective. Whatever I say today is not intended to defame or cast doubt on the many persons who work hard in our country to deliver good health care.

It is, rather, my intention to show how the broad and fundamental direction of the health system confounds the many personally commendable efforts by health professionals and ultimately frustrates their own high goals.

In the summer of 1972 one of Cleveland's larger general hospitals, St. Luke's announced that due to the rising cost of unreimbursed indigent care they were closing their ambulatory, outpatient clinic to any new patients.

A cry of outrage arose, especially from the black community, but other hospitals joined St. Luke's in maintaining that hospitals faced bankruptcy if more adequate State reimbursement were not forthcoming.

After weeks of furor the matter was defused by an emergency allocation by the State of Ohio for increased and retroactive reimbursement.

St. Luke's rescinded its announced intention to bar further new patients from receiving care. Less than a month later, St. Luke's announced a $17.5 million capital expansion program.

According to the figures of the Ohio Department of Health, St. Luke's faced an indigent care loss of only $753,737 when it decided to close its doors to the poor.

Clearly, it was simultaneously planning to use its extensive financial capacity to launch a major building program, had in fact already launched it.

This is not an isolated example of where our priority dollars go in health care today. St. Vincent's is underway with a $13.5 million expansion, Fairview General is spending $4.5 million, Cleveland Clinic is spending somewhere near $35 million not counting its new luxury hotel which is said to cost $10 million.

My own count, hastily made, adds up to more than $75 million in hospital construction underway in Cleveland.

The estimated loss from indigent care was reported by the Ohio Department of Health to be about $13 million in 1972 in Cleveland area hospitals.

Admittedly, this reflects something seriously wrong with the way health care is financed for the poor in Ohio and in the country in general.

Yet it has not deterred the hospitals from a $75 million expenditure—and I suspect the real figure is much higher than that—for their own institutional expansion.

I would like to direct your attention to the details of one hospital's expansion by way of further illustration.

In the telling I think you will be able to see how the private sector insurance industry and the private, supposedly nonprofit hospitals, make health policy and set priorities; how areawide comprehensive health planning agencies function as handmaidens to such power apparatus.

Cleveland Clinic is one of the finest health facilities in the country. Yet it is located in the heart of the black community at the edge of the Hough and Central Districts which surround it on the north and south.

Unfortunately, one of its black neighbors, stricken before its very door cannot receive emergency treatment in this citadel of health care, but must await an ambulance for transport to some other hosptial.

Since 1968 the clinic has gradually consumed several blocks of land which contained moderately priced housing. Because it has been criticized for failure to offer health care to the community around it the clinic announced that as part of their multimillion dollar program they would work with the city "to provide medical services to the area."

That was in 1968. In January 1971 the clinic signed a formal agreement with the areawide health planning agency known as the Metropolitan Health Planning Corp.—which I will subsequently refer to as MHPC—in which it received approval for its construction program including a shelled-in area that would not be finished provided it "would proceed with the development of the primary-care program."

The quotations are from the minutes of Metropolitan Health Planning Corp. The letter of agreement said in part:

The corporation—MHPC—also has received assurance from you that the additional facilities being requested will provide sufficient and suitable in-hospital facilities for patients who will be cared for in the primary-care program now being planned by the Cleveland Clinic.

When the clinic announced its $10 million hotel in 1972 it also made much of the fact that it would soon offer a prepaid, HMO-style, primary-care service to the Greater Cleveland residents.

The announcement said nothing about the fact that such a program would be too expensive for most of the improverished neighbors who live around the clinic.

Yet it was said that other developments and subsidy programs might overcome that problem.

By 1973 it became known that the clinic did not, after all, intend to offer a program of primary care to the neighborhood around it.

On May 9, 1974, I spoke with an official of the clinic who told me there were no definite plans and anything of the sort was at least several years away.

After 6 years of promises to the neighborhood and somewhere between $30 and $40 million in expansion there is still no health care for the needy folks of Hough and central areas at Cleveland Clinic.

How these things happen is very illuminating. For example, it was not until a consumer group in Cleveland discovered the clinic had converted a motel it built in 1965 to use for acute and convalescent care last year that MHPC finally took the matter into "retrospective review."

It then developed that the chairman of this areawide health planning corporation was none other than the president of Blue Cross of Northeast Ohio.

Further, that it was this Blue Cross executive who was leading the way in defense of the practice of retrospective review; that is, reviewing the suitability of hospital construction after the fact of their construction.

MHPC had been keeping the fact of Cleveland Clinic's unapproved conversion of motel beds in committee for 6 months. More, Blue Cross was reimbursing the clinic for these beds even though its own regulations expressly forbid reimbursement for interest or capital depreciation on such construction if the areawide health planning group has not approved it.

Even though these matters were publicly aired in the press and the Blue Cross executive castigated for his obvious conflict of interest, he not only continued in both positions but in the same month—even within an 8-day period—Cleveland Clinic notified MHPC—although this was at the time not known to the public—that it now intended to complete the 152 beds in the shelled-in area even though it had no intention of operating primary-care service on which those beds were contingent.

Very strangely, the staff of MHPC took no action and neither did the board. In August 1973, Cleveland Clinic notified MHPC that it was nearing completion of this new 152-bed area.

It was not until October 1973, long after the horse was gone from the barn, that MHPC took action disapproving these beds.

It is true that as a result Cleveland Clinic cannot receive that portion of the reimbursement formula that covers interest or capital depreciation reimbursement.

It is also true that this is a relatively small amount of money. It is further true that a huge hospital added a total of 272 unapproved beds without much pain at all.

Finally, it is true that Cleveland Clinic is now operating these beds in direct and open defiance of a letter of agreement signed by its officers in which it promised to operate such beds only in conjunction with the offering of primary care service to the community around it. The point, clearly, is that it is the common, average people who end up in pain in situations like this.

The large institutions violate both letter and spirit of regulations and do so with virtual impunity. They make a mockery of any pretense that the Comprehensive Health Planning Act has brought rationality to our health care problems.

I must add one footnote to my story of Cleveland Clinic. The clinic announced grandly in September 1973, that they would join with the county hospital system in aiding an outpatient center to be constructed an esthetic 12 blocks away from the clinic and out of sight.

Primary care that was supposed to be given from Cleveland Clinic's facilities will now require the county to spend $3.5 million on another facility.

The clinic's contribution is to be a gift of $200,000 toward capital needs and an agreement to share up to $200,000 each year in unreimbursed deficits of the center's patient-care costs.

This is not in my prepared text but that amounts to about 5 percent of what the larger hospitals in Cleveland carry by way of unreimbursed patient-care costs.

Oh yes, they will also help the largest teaching hospital in Ohio recruit doctors for the center. Will the doctors be appointed to Cleveland Clinic staff duties as well as the county center?

No, according to a county hospital official. Will patients needing hospital care who have come to the county center be taken to Cleveland Clinic for care? No.

This scandalous story is, I believe, not the exception but the rule of how health care policy is formulated in urban communities today. While urban communities like Cleveland have some 200,000 medically indigent persons, the bulk of health care dollars goes to institutional expansion without primary care.

The director of the Cleveland Department of Health promised Cleveland residents that if they trusted him he would develop a $20 million network of satellite clinics to serve everyone who needed care.

That was 2 years ago. He not only does not have even one satellite clinic, but cannot find funds to staff fully his already meager three health centers.

The hospital establishment turned their back on the city health director when he asked their help in implementing his plan. Reams have been written about the need for dental care in Cleveland but most of the recommendations are for education and the formation of more committees, what people need is someone who will fix their teeth, not education or committees.

When a task force created by the State of Ohio sought to draw up legislation for hospital licensure and certification of need, the membership was dominated by the medical, hospital, and insurance interests.

It delayed its work until it was past the deadline for submission for action in the current legislative year. Moreover, the vocal consumer on the task force saw every one of her resolutions calling for public disclosure, abolition of conflicts of interest, and public hearings before issuance of a license, voted down by these health providers.

A new task force created by the Governor has been bogged down all winter in internal strife over what to recommend.

What happens when critical voices are raised about these matters? The experience at the center for health consumer affairs where I worked until a year ago is instructive.

No one paid a minute's attention to this consumer center until some questions were raised by it in connection with the issues surrounding Cleveland Clinic and Blue Cross; until it produced an amateurish slide show that said in essence, there is too much profit-making in the present operation of the health care system.

These moves produced a national attack by the American Medical Association on Case Western Reserve University for housing the center.

A campaign threatening contributions to the medical school was conducted. Representations were made by the Cleveland Academy of Medicine and Blue Cross objecting to the program.

The university responded by imposing censorship on the program and by refusing to approve its routine reapplication for refunding for another year.

On June 30, 1973, a small program whose total budget hardly exceeded the median income of a single American physician was silenced.

I conclude my testimony with the wish that the health care powers that be could have spent as much energy and efficiency reshaping our ineffective but lucrative health care system to meet the public's needs.

Our tiny voice of criticism was apparently a threat to institutional interests. If that is so, then perhaps institutions were justified in defending themselves.

Yet the whole point is that the function of health care today should be for the public good, not for institutional self-serving.

It is exactly that public good that is least served today by the sectors of private, self-interest that dominate medical and health care policymaking today.

In closing, Mr. Chairman, I have documentation of the moves made by the American Medical Association concerning our center and I would suggest that they be placed in the record.

Senator HART. They will be, with staff checking to see the appropriateness and relevance.

[See exhibit 2 at the end of Mr. Rawlings' oral testimony.]

Senator HART. Yours is a pretty tough bite, spoken with spirit I should add, and an enormously discouraging one.

Who funded the consumer program that was responsible for the slide show?

Mr. RAWLINGS. It was funded under the B-agency program of the, Comprehensive Health Planning Act by the Public Health Service.

Senator HART. Federal money was involved?

Mr. RAWLINGS. Yes, it was a Federal grant.

Senator HART. For the record and for those of us here, add a fuller explanation of what the program did; what kind of personnel did it involve; how long was its life?

Mr. RAWLINGS. The history of the program lies in some grants that were given in a scattered fashion across the country, beginning around 1968, under the Conprehensive Health Planning Act, to train consumers to be knowledgeable participants in the health planning process; meaning that it was intended that universities and other institutions that received such grants would train consumers, usually inner city consumers.

It was anticipated that these consumers would end up on the boards of hospitals and areawide health planning agencies, playing a knowledgeable consumer role in the planning process.

In Cleveland it soon became evident that few of those boards wanted such persons among their membership and we submitted in 1970 and 1971 a proposal for the training of consumers to simply be knowledgeable advocates in their own self-interest about obtaining better health care and improvements in the health care system, and our dream, as expressed in the grant was that Case Western Reserve University, where there is a huge medical complex and center of medical education, would now begin to lend its resources to the consumer as well as the professional. The university at first approved that idea and it was funded in that sense.

It was to have an advisory committee composed of consumers. It was also to have a second advisory committee composed of professionals and hospital representatives and the idea was to build some bridges between these estranged groups and to get the consumer knowledgeably into the health decisionmaking process.

The staff consisted of a director, two research persons with bachelor's degree education, and two paraprofessional people from the neighborhood who were to help in outreach and making sure that the program actually reached the people of the community.

Senator HART. How long a period? You say it began in 1971?

Mr. RAWLINGS. Case Western Reserve University received grants under the original concept of consumer training that I mentioned beginning in 1968.

In 1971, on the basis of the experience that these people who were being trained didn't end up on the boards, we remodeled the proposal and were funded beginning July 1, 1972, to be a center for health consumer affairs.

In essence, a center for information for the consumer, and within the first 4 months we fell under heavy fire and the univeristy, in effect, said you won't be around next year.

As a matter of fact, they didn't say it in effect. They said it very explicitly and in writing.

Senator HART. And their prediction was correct?

Mr. RAWLINGS. Well, they exerted their authority by refusing to sign off on the routine grant application to HEW for refunding.

In the fall of 1972 the American Medical Association wrote a scathing editorial attack aimed not so much at us as at the university for daring to sponsor this program.

The consequence of that was that we were asked to submit to the governance of the advisory committee composed of doctors and hospital administrators and we were asked to alter the shape of the programs so that those persons would now decide what would now be suitable in a consumer program.

As director of the staff I talked with the staff and we collectively decided that we would not do that, that that was inappropriate for a consumer program.

We then designed a refunding application which was due in late November and when it went through the routine process of the university we suddenly were informed on the final date for submission by the vice president of the university that the university would not sign or approve this grant, that it involved something that was inappropriate for a university.

Senator HART. As a result of that where does it stand now?

Mr. RAWLINGS. It completed its funding year, which was 1972, 1973, and expired on June 30, 1973.

Senator HART. What formal group remains in Cleveland that speaks to consumers about the medical delivery problems, and for consumers to the providers?

Mr. RAWLINGS. There are one or two small, free clinics that operate in the inner city of Cleveland which frequently articulate some of these problems and raise these kinds of issues.

However, they are primarily preoccupied with trying to deliver health care itself so, to the best of my knowledge, I think the answer is there is no consumer-oriented agency now.

The areawide health planning agencies say that they are representatives of the consumer, but I don't think their record, particularly as I have outlined it here, would support that kind of claim.

Senator HART. I can understand why—you know, we can personalize it—it is uncomfortable to bring into the establishment people who have never been part of the establishment; and that is true whether you are organizing a political campaign or running a hospital, practicing law or selling real estate. The problem is that we tend to assume we know best and the poor unfortunate on the outside is lucky that we are at work, but don't let him come in and help us.

It is a perfectly understandable human characteristic and in those cases, in the 1960's, community participation was a reality.

It ruffled an awful lot of feathers and created an awful lot of waves, but it was good and we should at least protest the elimination.

I figure that yours was that kind of situation.

Mr. Sharp?

Mr. SHARP. Thank you, Senator.

Mr. Rawlings, was the basis for the attack by the Blue Cross and the Cleveland Clinic of Medicine simply that portion of the slide show that alleged that there was too much profitmaking in the system, or was there some other reason?

Mr. RAWLINGS. I am very sorry; I couldn't hear the first part of your quesiton.

Mr. SHARP. Was the basis for the attack by Blue Cross and the Cleveland Clinic of Medicine simply that portion of the slide show which alleged that there was too much profitmaking in the present system, or was there some other reason advanced?

Mr. RAWLINGS. They were disturbed about several things, and if you will give me a minute I will make reference to that.

In the letter by the local Cleveland Academy of Medicine they refer to the slide program as obviously a piece of propaganda designed to whip up enthusiasm for this consumer training group's own preferred program, and they objected to the use of Federal money for that purpose.

In the editorial which appeared in the American Medical News of October 2, 1972, they objected to several things we said, and described them as either false, exaggerated, misleading, or defamatory.

One of them we have already alluded to: It was the statement that private doctors work separately with their own patients; that private doctors have left the inner city and rural areas where people do not have as much money to pay them. Making a large amount of money is often a major consideration for many private physicians.

In addition to that, we indicated that public health programs have become a stopgap measure to fill the more dangerous holes of the private health system, usually when those gaps begin to endanger the health, safety, or profits of the wealthier community.

Public health programs carefully avoid competing with private institutions by only serving people who cannot afford private care for illnesses and usually by offering inadequate service.

We made other comments about the fact that there was a difference between the ideal of comprehensive health care and the kind of fragmented health system that we have today that lacks continuity.

We referred to the critical shortage of doctors and to the historic role of the American Medical Association in limiting the number of medical schools in the country.

We referred to the general system of financing of health care today as connected with profit. And it was statements of that kind in the health care slide show that the AMA said were the basis for their attack.

Mr. SHARP. Thank you. I assume that both the Cleveland Clinic and the Ohio Blue Cross are not profitmaking operations. What was there in your slide show other than profitmaking which aroused their opposition?

Mr. RAWLINGS. Well, we referred to some of the basic material that I have presented to you today about the history of Cleveland Clinic, gobbling up lots of inner-city property where people lived, announcing major capital expansion programs, and simultaneously promising that they would soon give health care to the poor in the community around them.

I was called into the office of the vice president of Case Western Reserve University in the spring of 1972 and asked if we had prepared a research paper on Cleveland Clinic.

I said we had, and he asked that we not publish it. I thought it was an interesting request since he hadn't seen the paper. Sight unseen, it had come to his attention on the grapevine that this was happening.

He said he had had a few calls from the Cleveland Clinic staff and officials and he thought it would be better for the university if we didn't put out this kind of information.

Mr. SHARP. I would like to get your reaction, Mr. Rawlings, to statements made earlier in these hearings by Dr. Jesse Steinfeld, the former Surgeon General of the United States.

Dr. Steinfeld repeatedly made the point that if we are going to have a pluralistic approach to the problems of health care delivery in this country, if we are going to operate in a free market economy for health care, one of the traditional assumptions is that we have well-informed consumers so that they can make an adequate choice; be educated enough to make choices as to various programs.

I would like to get your reaction to one of the statements that Dr. Steinfeld made. He said that in the field of health education for citizens, there is normally no competition; there is apathy.

He went on, of course, to point out that competition would be valuable, particularly if we could and would evaluate the results of our attempts at health education for our citizens.

He stated that he began a 4-year campaign for more health education for our citizens after he became Surgeon General in 1969, but the results were very, very slow in developing.

Now, what is your feeling? Do you think it was organized medicine's idea—at least in Cleveland—to kill your effort that you made to bring some health education to the very people in that area who needed it the most? Do you feel that we can have a pluralistic system if we have these attitudes on the part of local medical societies? Do you think it is realistic to hope for a free market in the health care field?

Mr. RAWLINGS. Well, Mr. Sharp, first of all, I don't think that it is fair to say that the consumer is apathetic. Every group of consumers we talked with, without exception, produced vigorous complaints about their experience in getting health care. And I am talking not simply about the low-income consumer, I am talking about a virtually across-the-board cross-section of income levels.

The problem is that they are powerless; they are not apathetic, but they are powerless. And I think this points to the limitation that exists in the whole concept of consumerism.

First of all, I have come to the conclusion after trafficking in the idea of consumerism for some years that it is something of a denigration of the stature of citizenship of people in our country.

People are more than consumers. They are citizens. They are part of a whole society. They are contributers. They pay for that society.

I think that the solution to the kinds of problems we are talking about with regard to the consumer is not to put more consumers on boards or to make sure that a certain percentage of consumers are on boards—because as long as the decisionmaking power is tied to those people who control millions of dollars, those consumers never really counterbalance that. I think the solution lies rather in giving teeth to legislation that says the purpose of these health care dollars will be to provide these kinds of services to the whole public—to everyone—on an equal basis.

The reason why areawide health planning agencies are—I want to choose my words carefully; I don't want to be too harsh on them because I think they try very hard—so helpless is because they have no real enforcement power, and so the drift of their policymaking is guided by the large institutions, regardless of how many consumers, so-called, are on the board.

That is because we don't have any public policy that says that the purpose of our health care dollars shall be channeled into these prior ity areas.

And that is where we clearly have to move. We have to develop public policy that says that, you can't spend $75 million on institutional expansion at a time when people need to have their teeth fixed, need to be able to take their babies someplace to be treated, need to be able to take care of their own health care problems.

We have to have legislation, I think, that begins to spell that out: That you can't spend the money here until it is spent there.

Mr. SHARP. Well, perhaps what you are suggesting is that, after all, the comprehensive health planning agencies are nothing but a form of regulation attempting to regulate the planning and allocation of resources; is that true?

Mr. RAWLINGS. Well, yes; I will buy that paraphrase.

Mr. SHARP. Well, if that is true, then the opposite of that is a free market economy doing the allocating. Is it consumers purchasing service through which his dollars are allocating resources? Obviously, it hasn't worked, because we have comprehensive planning.

Mr. RAWLINGS. I hesitated when you asked me if I agreed with your characterization of the areawide health planning agency, and I am glad I hesitated because I think what you said next made me want to hesitate even more.

I think that they constantly suggest to the community that we have a way to engage in rational planning, when in fact we don't.

The Metropolitan Health Planning Corp. in Cleveland is clearly guided by the dominant presence of Blue Cross and the hospitals on the governing board.

I think that there is supposed to be planning integrated with the free market economy that you are talking about, and I don't think it is either. I don't think it is either a free market economy, and I don't think it is planned.

Mr. SHARP. So nothing has happened from the consumer's point of view or from the patient's point of view, at least for the people in the area you are speaking of. There is no access to the system.

Mr. RAWLINGS. Citizens do not have equal access to the health care system. They also do not have any measure of substantial public control over that system—over its quality, over the distribution of its services.

Mr. SHARP. Where is the accountability to the public that you are speaking of? Whose dollars are paying for all of this?

Mr. RAWLINGS. Well, I don't want to be glib in discussing what is obviously a complex subject. But I think that the way the areawide health planning agency is organized in Cleveland, you could make an argument that it involves accountability.

It has the medical providers on its board. It has representatives of all levels of government. And in those terms you could say it has accountability; what it doesn't have is a clear mandate as to what the priorities are in health planning.

So they are tough on the small health provider, the little suburban hospital; and the large hospitals do whatever they damned please.

Mr. SHARP. But assume for the moment Congress and the State gave teeth or enforcement sanctions to the planning agencies. There would then be a regulated public utility type of system, as opposed to a free market system.

Would that be a preferred system?

Mr. RAWLINGS. The direction of my thinking is that with the inequality in buying power of our public, a free market system is not a realistic way to get equal access to health care for all of our citizens, and that some form of regulation of that system, some very emphatic form, is the only solution.

Mr. SHARP. But we have had regulation for many years at the State level through certificate of need and licensure, and now the Federal Government under this cooperative program with health providers and insurance companies have engaged since the late 1960's in this planned organization through areawide health planning agencies.

And what you are suggesting isn't working.

Mr. RAWLINGS. I am suggesting that the crux of my testimony is that if that is regulation, it stretches the word pretty far.

Mr. SHARP. What kind of regulation, then, would you suggest?

Mr. RAWLINGS. Well, I believe very frankly we need a national health system in this country; that every time we increase the flow of public dollars into the privately controlled system it simply ends up in institutional expansion.

It ends up in a more profitable health system for those who are on the provider end of it. It doesn't redistribute services. It doesn't create any equitability in the system, and I think only by connecting very strong with-teeth regulation to the Federal dollars do we have any hope of really beginning to solve our problems.

Mr. SHARP. What you are really saying is that if we are going to put more dollars into health care we are going to have to do some serious restructuring of the supply end of the equation, as Dr. Steinfeld suggested?

Mr. RAWLINGS. Yes; I am definitely saying that.

Mr. SHARP. Thank you, Mr. Rawlings.

Senator HART. Mr. Chumbris?

Mr. CHUMBRIS. Thank you, Mr. Chairman.

I am not so sure how we ended up on the colloquy that you had with Mr. Sharp. I think what Mr. Sharp was trying to get you to say, but what you didn't follow up on, was that we shouldn't have a continuation of the approach that we are now having.

Some people say the national health insurance plan would just add to the woes as more billions of dollars are poured into the system.

Dr. Steinfeld's statement does go along with that, as I heard his testimony. He also pointed out that you have to have a little bit of both—more of the competitive—but there has to be a certain amount of Government activity in the area.

The question is, where do you draw the line on a situation like that. Is that getting closer to your position?

Mr. RAWLINGS. Well, I am at a bit of a disadvantage, since I haven't seen Dr. Steinfeld's testimony and I don't know what he said in detail.

I wouldn't want to put myself among the utopians who simply announce, "What we need is a national health system, and we will go out and nationalize everything tomorrow, and then we will have solved our problems."

I very firmly believe that the distribution of health care services must be regulated by the Federal Government according to certain priorities that serve the public good; that any steps in that direction would involve much more regulation in the health care system than we now have.

And yet, I am convinced on the basis of what I have seen firsthand, my own study of the literature, that we have to move in that direction; that we are in danger of a very bad move governmentally in the proposals for national health insurance that are now pending because they open the possibility for a repeat of the medicare experience, which is simply an inflationary impact upon a system without any real reordering of the priorities.

Mr. CHUMBRIS. Have you had the opportunity to read the hearings of this particular subcommittee, the ones that we had in 1970, on high hospital cost; in 1971 dealing with Blue Cross, primarily; and in 1972 with the private insurers. Have you had a chance to review those?

Mr. RAWLINGS I have. I wouldn't want to be tested on it today.

Mr. CHUMBRIS. Well, I am not bringing that up to test you on it. There has been testimony in those three sets of hearings that I am referring to that brings some competition into play.

For example, we had a witness from Fort Myers, Fla., I believe, who was complaining that his hospital had 70 percent filled beds and 30 percent empty beds, and he was complaining that proprietary hospital corporations were planning to come into Fort Meyers even though they contended that they wouldn't move in where there were unfilled beds in the hospitals in the particular area. That is competition of a sort, another hospital coming in to compete with a nonprivate hospital.

And we have had illustrations now, with HMO's coming into certain areas. For example, in Washington, D.C., the metropolitan area has a great number of Government employees who selected the HMO plan over the private insurer and over Blue Cross. Some are from here on the Hill, and I imagine in the agencies downtown, also.

Now, the point the people have raised is that hasn't spread far enough, and there should be more of that. So there is competition there. But at the same time, I think the witnesses indicate that the Government still has to look into the problem of how far they should go in regulating the health care services.

So a little of that is already in the record, and I would like you to comment at this point before moving on to another question.

Mr. RAWLINGS. I have some difficulty relating to the concept of competition because I always feel like that is a rubric that produces winners and losers.

And, in health care, we really can't afford to have losers, because that is what happens to the patients; they become losers, sometimes they fall in between the gaps.

Well, you know, the Cleveland Clinic story involves an element of competition. Cleveland Clinic competes with other health providers for the more complex and expensive forms of health care.

Although they call themselves a tertiary facility, a very large part of their care is routine general hospital care, because their doctors are all private practitioners, as well as part of the medical group.

So they are competing constantly. To give you one case example which I think illustrates the problem: 2 years ago the heart unit at Cleveland Clinic had a substantial backlog of cases. The heart unit at University Hospital was underutilized. Instead of referring the overload from Cleveland Clinic to University Hospital, Cleveland Clinic trained a new heart team unit and arranged for it to be set up at a West Side hospital.

You know, that is all competition. You might say it is healthy in terms of competition, but actually it just drains more and more dollars and more and more medical expertise into a very narrow channel where there continues to be evidence of underutilization.

I would have preferred to see an absence of the rubric of competition and instead promotion of a public policy that said where we need now to distribute our health care resources is to take care of the people in this improverished neighborhood around us who have no real access to health care.

But there was no one to say that, and there was no law to lay down that kind of enforcement; and I don't see any form of competition as really relieving that problem.

Senator HART. Are you saying with respect to the heart care facility that somebody should have the authority to prevent, in this case, Cleveland Clinic from establishing an additional service and requiring those in need of the service to go to University Hospital?

Mr. RAWLINGS Yes; that the existing facility for heart care, for heart surgery, should be utilized to the fullest before any expansion is undertaken.

Mr. CHUMBRIS. Have you had an opportunity to read "Regulating Health Facilities Construction," a conference held by the American Enterprise Institute and Duke University?

Professor Havighurst, our next witness, was the editor of the booklet. It is a rather significant one, in which many ideas were thrown into the discussion.

As Professor Havighurst stated, there was a lot of debate but there were no conclusions reached in the discussion; where some people espoused more competition, others espoused more Government regulation; others saying that taking a look at this history so far shows that we have had problems and that no definite conclusion was reached.

Have you had an opportunity to see this?

Mr. RAWLINGS. I am sorry to say I have not.

Mr. CHUMBRIS. Recently, we were luckly enough to receive copies of it and there were some very, very interesting and thought-provoking ideas in it. I don't know how the readers of it will resolve the net result of the statements, but the book is for this type of a discussion, which brings me to my next point.

Have you been following the activity in the Senate and in the House on new legislation? For example, there have been some discussions on the fact that some Members of Congress as well as the administration feel that the Hill-Burton hospital construction bill, which will expire, I think, at the end of June, is something that should not continue in the vein that the law was first initiated; that there is constant regulation of hospital construction, or unless you get approval, you won't get money from the act's program to build those hospitals. That may be what curtailed, you were saying earlier, community hospitals in getting into a certain area.

There would be some unfilled beds, and it could cause loss to the community.

Mr. RAWLINGS. Of course, the hospitals in the Cleveland area—the larger ones—have learned increasingly not to rely on Hill-Burton kinds of money, so that that kind of provision doesn't restrict them very much.

Mr. CHUMBRIS. And the other point that legislators are considering, is either revising or doing away with the regional medical program; and the third is the Comprehensive Health Planning Act of 1966, which indicates that the Government so far in this plan is not too happy, and the legislators feel that some serious study should be made in either implementing, amending them, or just starting with something new completely.

How do you view that?

Mr. RAWLINGS. Well, I think some of those things I have said already touch upon.

Mr. CHUMBRIS. Briefly, so you won't have to repeat what you said.

Mr. RAWLINGS. I believe that a stronger legislative approach is needed. I can't say whether it should be amendment of the existing acts. I am not a technician of legislation.

I think a stronger, perhaps new, legislative approach is needed that gives planning agencies enforcement power. You know, all these hospitals, according to the book, have to go through these planning agencies for permission and so forth. but if they disobey the ruling of the agency there is very little punishment. There is very little consequence.

So it is a process that for the large health provider institutions has little meaning.

Mr. CHUMBRIS. We have been listening to testimony over the past 3 years.

We have been through so much of it we catch ourselves coming and going, and we are trying to reach a conclusion as to the best methods of reducing health care costs while maintaining good services. Then, someone will come in and say, "Competition is good," and another one will come along and say, "Competition is good up to a certain point, but you still need Government intervention in the marketplace," and someone will come along and go a little further.

And each of the witnesses document their thinking pretty well. Professor Havighurst, for example, could sell you the Brooklyn Bridge he is so effective in his presentation.

Mr. RAWLINGS. I can't afford to buy the Brooklyn Bridge.

Mr. CHUMBRIS. I don't say that facetiously. I am just trying to make a point that the gentlemen who have come before us have not been light in their approach. They come in and give some pretty good reasons, so that the judges will have to stop and think very carefully in making their decision.

The Senate and the House are the judges in this instance and are trying to come up with some conclusions. So, here you have Congress reviewing action that they have already completed. Now, here is a bill, H.R. 12053; have you had an opportunity to see that bill?

Mr. RAWLINGS. Can you identify it with something besides the number?

Mr. CHUMBRIS. That is Congressman Rogers' bill to amend the Public Service Act to ensure the health units of a national health policy, and of effective State health regulatory programs, and area health planning programs, for other purposes, which is exactly what we are talking about here.

Mr. RAWLINGS. No, I haven't seen the bill.

Mr. CHUMBRIS. It might be well for you to get a copy of this bill, and also Senator Kennedy's bill.

Dr. CAPER. S. 2994.

Mr. CHUMBRIS. S. 2994, and the administration's bill.

Dr. CAPER. S. 3166.

Mr. CHUMBRIS. S. 3166. Those three bills are under serious consideration at this time. In fact, Congressman Rogers' bill and the House bill are under hearings this week; they started on April 30, and they had the first day last Tuesday. But you might want to look at that because you seemed to put a lot of thought into this subject, and it might be to your benefit to read and maybe express an opinion to Rogers' committee, to Senator Kennedy's committee and also send us a copy so we will have the benefit of your thinking.

Mr. RAWLINGS I appreciate the reference.

Mr. CHUMBRIS. Now, there was one other thought that I had, and I would like to have your reaction to it; maybe you are aware of it, since you have been in Cleveland.

Several years ago there was a very serious study made by a consultant on the health care program in Detroit, Mich. with Blue Cross, United Auto Workers, and almost evry facet of the community dealing with health and hospital services and construction.

They ran into some problems. There were State laws that prohibited certain things, and there were certain Federal laws that caused impediments and so forth.

Are you aware of that study in Detroit?

Mr. RAWLINGS. Yes; I am.

Mr. CHUMBRIS. Do you see any similarity between what went on in Detroit and what is trying to be done in other cities such as you talked about in Cleveland. How do you compare the kind in Detroit with the one you have in Cleveland?

Mr. RAWLINGS. Well, Mr. Chumbris, I am simply not prepared to make such a comparison on an off-the-cuff basis——

Mr. CHUMBRIS. Well, if you wish, when you get back, the record will be open for you to file a response. If you wish to comment on that, it would be greatly appreciated.

Mr. Chairman, I think I could ask this witness questions for another half an hour, but our time is running late. We do have Professor Havighurst; Dr. Caper and Dr. Granfield may have some questions they would like to ask, so I will yield.

Mr. SHARP. Mr. Chairman?

Senator HART. Mr. Sharp.

Mr. SHARP. I would just like to make the record straight on one point. I think there was a misrepresentation by my learned friend on the other side of the table in that he thought he was proposing that national health insurance was going to be the panacea to solve the problem. Quite to the contrary, I was trying to make the point simply, in your own words, that we must reorder the priorities. We must do some serious reordering of the structure of the supply end of the equation. And that, even if we remove finance as a barrier to care and create more demand dollars in the market, the question will be, will there be adequate supply to handle the increased demand without having run-away inflation? That was my sole point.

Mr. CHUMBRIS. Mr. Chairman, just one point, with the witness. How did you arrive at the name Telos, which means "the end?"

Mr. RAWLINGS. I am interested in writing about the issues of the day in terms of assessing those issues in terms of their ultimate objective, or the end toward which they move. It is an historic, philosophic concept.

Senator HART. Dr. Caper?

Dr. CAPER. Thank you, Senator Hart. A few questions.

The hospitals you described and the Cleveland Clinic, I assume, are tax-exempt hospitals; are they not?

Mr. RAWLINGS. Yes.

Dr. CAPER. What is the basis of that tax exemption?

Mr. RAWLINGS. Well, Cleveland Clinic and other hospitals like it in Cleveland—you are leading me into an area where I lack technical expertise—but these are nonprofit corporations and, as I understand that, that is that they are incorporated in such a manner that no moneys are distributed to shareholders or stockholders, and that they therefore also, in the case of the hospitals, are engaged in some sort of public service, which leads to their tax exemption.

However, as I said, that is an area in which I have little expertise.

Dr. CAPER. I wonder if you would mind, when you get back to Cleveland, looking into that and supplying an answer for the record with respect to the reasons for that tax exemption; whether, for example, the concept of being a charitable institution or providing public service, has anything to do with the reasons for a tax exemption.

In the cases that have received in the past Hill-Burton funds, according to your earlier testimony, is there a requirement for public service or so-called nonreimbursable services associated with the possibility of Hill-Burton funds?

Mr. RAWLINGS. First of all, there may be a misunderstanding. Cleveland Clinic, I think in the expansion program that began in 1968, did not use Hill-Burton money.

[For information requested see exhibits 3 and 3a.]

Dr. CAPER. The Health Subcommitte does have a number of proposals with respect to intentions for modification of the Comprehensive Health Planning Act, before us at the present time, as Mr. Chumbris pointed out, and with respect to the regional medical programs and the Hill-Burton program.

These are extremely complex issues, and ones which present very many problems in terms of effective mechanisms for improving the equity within the health care system, for improving the distribution of health care services and resources.

And perhaps, based upon testimony I heard here so far this week, upon reallocation of some of the power relationships within the health care system. I know that Senator Kennedy, who is very sorry he cannot be here today, would welcome any suggestions or comments you have with respect to specific measures and specific steps which could be taken by the Federal Government to improve some of the weaknesses you perceive, and have testified to today, with respect to these programs.

That is all I have, Mr. Chairman.

Senator HART. Thank you.

Mr. Granfield?

Mr. GRANFIELD. No.

Senator HART. As you sense from the requests that have been made of you, we enjoyed and appreciated very much the contribution you have made to this record.

Mr. RAWLINGS. It is a pleasure to be here. Thank you.

[The following was received for the record. Testimony resumes on p. 1036.]

MATERIAL RELATING TO THE TESTIMONY OF CHARLES W. RAWLINGS FOLLOWS

Mr. Rawlings is a native of West Virginia, born in Wheeling on February 10, 1931 and raised in near-by Parkersburg where he attended public schools. He is married and the father of three children age 18, 16 and 12.

Mr. Rawlings received the B.A. degree from Marietta College in 1952 and graduated from Union Theological Seminary, New York City in 1955 with a Master of Divinity Degree. He is an ordained minister in the United Presbyterian Church, although presently inactive. His first parish was in Eastern Pennsylvania at Lehighton and Jim Thorpe.

In 1959 Mr. Rawlings came to Cleveland where he was director of an inner city settlement house for four years. In 1963 he was appointed Director of the Office of Religion and Race jointly sponsored by five protestant denominations. He served on the Vice-President's Northern Cities Task Force for the U.S. Community Relations Service in the Summer of 1965. He was appointed Executive Director of the Commission on Metropolitan Affairs of the Greater Cleveland Council of Churches in 1965 where he served for the following three years. In 1968 he joined the division of adult and continuing education at Case Western Reserve University where he administered programs in juvenile delinquency, housing, leadership training and consumer health. From 1970 to 1973 he was the chief administrator of the Center For Health Consumer Affairs at the University.

Mr. Rawlings is the author of many articles on urban problems. He is currently editor and publisher of TELOS, a semi-monthly newsletter discussing issues of the day from the perspective of our historical and religious roots.

———

Exhibit 2.—*Documentation of Organized Medicine's Actions Re Center for Health Consumer Affairs, Case Western Reserve University*

ACADEMY OF MEDICINE OF CLEVELAND,
Cleveland, Ohio, August 8, 1972.

JESSE L. STEINFELD, M.D.,
Surgeon General, USPHS,
Department HEW,
Washington, D.C.

DEAR DR. STEINFELD: I am enclosing a copy of an outline review of a slide program entitled, "Search for Health Care" which was developed by the Consumer Training Program for Health Planning of Case Western Reserve University. It was funded by a United States Public Health Service grant. I am amazed that either the University or the USPHS could allow their monies and name to be used in connection with such a biased enterprise. If this is to be a Consumer Training Program, then it should be accurate and informative rather than defamatory. This is obviously a piece of propaganda designed to whip up enthusiasm for this Consumer Training group's own preferred program

I have no objection to any group exploring various methods of delivery of health care. In fact, the Academy of Medicine itself has been much involved in this process. However I do strenuously object to the use of government funds and a University appointment to provide a platform for attacking the entire medical profession as well as community leaders who do happen to be poor.

I would much appreciate your comments concerning this program.

Sincerely yours,

ROBERT A. LANG,
Executive Secretary.

AUGUST 21, 1972.

ROBERT A. LANG, Ph. D.,
Executive Secretary,
Academy of Medicine of Cleveland,
Cleveland, Ohio.

DEAR MR. LANG: The Surgeon General has asked me to respond to your letter of August 8, expressing concern about the outline for a slide program developed for the consumer training program for health planning at Case Western Reserve University.

Although the outline notes some statements that I realize are objectionable to you, it reflects widely held opinions, and was prepared, I am sure, as a basis for discussion.

If you feel that the medical profession is being defamed, I suggest that you request the opportunity for representatives of the Academy to participate in some of the program's sessions. Te program director is Mr. Charles W. Rawlings, and his telephone number is 216-368-2111.

Sincerely yours,

ROBERT P. JONES,
Director, Comprehensive Health Planning Service.

[From the American Medical News, Sept. 25, 1972]

Use of a U.S. Public Health Service-financed slide presentation that is highly derogatory of the nation's health care system and health professions in general has been protested by the AMA. Presentation was prepared by the Consumer Training Program for Health Planning at Case Western Reserve U., Cleveland, Ohio, and funded by a PHS grant.

In a letter to Vernon H. Wilson, MD, administrator for HEW's Health Services and Mental Health Administration, the AMA urged that the program not be distributed and asked that HSMHA give serious consideration to withdrawing support to the grantee.

The AMA said the program, *Search for Health Care,* represented one of the "worst attacks" made on health professionals in recent memory. The Academy of Medicine of Cleveland earlier had presented similar complaints to the dean of the university. It expressed amazement that either the institution or the PHS would allow their funds and names to be linked "with such a biased enterprise." It objected to use of government funds and a university appointment "to provide a platform for attacking the entire medical profession as well as community leaders. . . ."

The slide presentation calls for establishment of a "People's Health Plan" funded entirely by the federal government.

[From the American Medical News, Oct. 2, 1972]

AN UNWARRANTED PROPAGANDA ATTACK

Under the guise of consumer education, a program prepared by a branch of the Case Western Reserve U.. School of Medicine in Cleveland has perpetrated one of the worst attacks in some time on the medical profession and other health workers.

The attack is contained in a slide program, "Search for Health Care," developed by the Cleveland school's Consumer Training Program for Health Planning. and funded by a U.S. Public Health Service grant.

An outline review of the program includes these examples of false, exaggerated, misleading, and defamatory statements:

"Private doctors work separately with their own patients, who pay their doctor directly for each visit or service. Private doctors have left the inner city and rural areas where people do not have as much money to pay them. Making large amounts of money is often a major consideration for many private physicians."

"Public health programs have become stop-gap measures to fill the more dangerous holes of the private health system—usually when those gaps begin to endanger the health, safety, or profits of the wealthier communities. . . .

Public health programs carefully avoid competing with private institutions by only serving people who cannot afford private care for illnesses and usually by offering inadequate service."

"Comprehensive health care is a system in which all of a patient's health needs are met in a well-ordered and easy way by a team of doctors, nurses, dentists, and other health workers. Comprehensive care would make available: complete screening and testing facilities to diagnose diseases; complete treatment facilities; complete follow-up care; and preventive care for physical, mental, dental, and environmental health problems."

"There is a critical shortage of doctors in the U.S. because limits are put on the number of students who may be accepted into medical schools each year. Policies of the American Medical Association and the medical schools in limiting the supply of doctors has (sic) resulted in the high price of the few remaining doctors."

"The financing of health care is based on profits, not on meeting a need. Public health budgets are funded from taxes which are collected in greater amounts from lower income working people than from wealthy people or corporations. Insurance policy costs are increasing beyond the means of many people. The median physician's salary was over $38,000 in 1969. Pharmaceutical companies had over one billion dollars in profits in 1971. Many people cannot afford the cost of health care and must do without care except in emergencies."

"Decisions about the health care system have been made by the medical schools, large hospitals, the American Medical Association, pharmaceutical companies, hospital supply companies, and health insurance companies and their governmental representatives. These people are usually quite wealthy and do not use the stop-gap public health facilities that are available to the lower income people. They can well afford the outrageous cost of private medical care which has left many middle income and lower income families in financial ruin. They make decisions about health care which will bring greater profits, prestige, and influence to their institutions. They maintain a physician and cooperation partnership that controls health care for the people of this country."

After this series of propaganda statements, the program goes on to call for establishment of a "People's Health Plan," featuring neighborhood health centers and hospitals and larger regional hospitals, governed by neighborhood health council and financed by: "Total federal funding . . . based on a truly progressive tax structure which means that higher income individuals and powerful corporations will pay a much larger share of the cost than the average or low income family. Except for a fair share of tax payments, people would receive their health care with no additional charges. Health care will then become a right instead of a privilege that only serves those who can afford it."

Innovation and exploration of ways to improve the health care system are laudable goals and medicine, including the AMA, has an honorable record in this area; so is consumer education. But cloaking an unfactual, sinisterly biased, and emotional attack on the medical profession and our current health system with the costume of consumerism reflects poorly on all of those involved in the Cleveland program. It is incredible that university and PHS funds with their implied endorsements could be used in such an obvious propaganda attack.

Exhibit 3.—*Letter of C. W. Rawlings Re Reasons for Tax-Exempt Status of Cleveland Clinic*

JUNE 3, 1974.

MR. ROBERT J. DATH
District Director,
Internal Revenue Service,
Cleveland, Ohio

DEAR MR. DATH: I am writing for the purpose of requesting the opportunity to examine Form 990 filed by the Cleveland Clinic Foundation for the years 1971 and 1972. My reason for examining these forms is in order to respond to a request made by the United States Senate Subcommittee On

Monopoly and Antitrust in the course of my testimony before it on May 17th of this year. I was testifying on the subject of the failure of Cleveland Clinic Foundation to offer health care services to the impoverished neighborhood around it in spite of a $35 million dollar expansion program. The hearings on the 17th were chaired by Senator Philip Hart. In the course of questioning I was asked by the Subcommittee to explore the nature of the tax exemption of the Cleveland Clinic Foundation in relation to their income and expenditures and to report concerning this to the Subcommittee in order that my answer could be entered in the record of the hearings.

In a conversation with members of your staff in the Collection Division last Friday I was told that a response to my request would require ten weeks. I have subsequently informed Mr. Dean Sharp, Counsel to the Senate Subcommittee On Monopoly and Antitrust of the anticipated delay. He has indicated to me that I should request a very early and expeditious handling of this request in light of the fact that the Senate Hearing Record can only be held open a short while for entry of this requested information.

Herewith is my request for the opportunity to examine these Form 990s of the Cleveland Clinic Foundation at the earliest possible moment.

I would like to state, for the record, that my interest in the subject of the suitability of the Cleveland Clinic Foundation's Tax Exempt status extends beyond my role as a witness before the Senate Subcommittee. I would, therefor, expect to make use of the information in the 990s for the purposes of my own citizen interest in this subject as well as for the purpose of response to the Senate Subcommittee.

Thanking you in advance for your cooperation am

Very truly yours,

CHARLES W. RAWLINGS.

Exhibit 3a.—*Memorandum From Mr. Rawlings Re Tax-Exempt Status of Cleveland Clinic Foundation*

JUNE 29, 1974.

To: Dean Sharp, Counsel, U.S. Senate Subcommittee on Monopoly and Antitrust.
From: Charles W. Rawlings.
Re: Response to question from Dr. Phillip Caper during my testimony before the Subcommittee May 17, 1974.

PREFACE

During the question period following my prepared statement before the U.S. Senate Subcommittee on Monopoly and Antitrust May 17, 1974, I was asked by Dr. Caper to look at the tax exempt status of the Cleveland Clinic Foundation in relation to its financial operations and to report my findings to the Subcommittee for their inclusion in the hearing record. What follows is my response to Dr. Caper's question.

Mr. Chairman, responding to Dr. Caper's question concerning the tax-exempt status of the Cleveland Clinic Foundation in relation to its financial operations I am able to report the following:

1. According to information supplied by the Internal Revenue Service the Cleveland Clinic Foundation is a tax exempt public foundation under the provisions of Internal Revenue Code 501(c)(3). The letter of exemption was issued by IRS on October 25, 1938.

2. Details of the basis on which this exemption was granted are not available in IRS files dating back to that period. According to the Office of Public Information of the District Director of IRS in Cleveland, files of that period have been destroyed by Congressional act.

3. Rulings issued from time to time concerning the Cleveland Clinic Foundation by the Internal Revenue Service are not permitted to be released to the public according to the District Director's Office of Public Information in Cleveland.

4. The District Director did make available to me copies of the 990 forms filed by the Cleveland Clinic Foundation entitled "Return of Organization Exempt from Income Tax" for the years 1971 and 1972. I was not given copies but could inspect them at IRS offices. The forms show that in 1971 the Clinic shows

an excess of receipts over disbursements and expenses of $9,717,259 and an increase in net worth from $48,210,365 at the beginning of that year to $57,663,623 at the end of the year. For 1972 the forms show the Clinic received an excess of receipts over disbursements and expenses of $8,665,227 with an increase of net worth from $57,663,263 at the beginning of the year to $66,373,850 at the end of the year.

5. In addition, I have also examined a copy of a 1967 Form 990 on Cleveland Clinic in the files of the Cleveland Foundation library. For that year, and with a different form, the Clinic had Gross sales of $27,062,126 and expenses of $16,406,733 thus showing an excess of receipts of $10,655,399.

IRS rules permit only an examination of two years for an organization.

6. In 1971 the Clinic reported new construction of $9,394,334 according to the 990 form. In 1972 they reported new construction of $21,403,375.

7. The percentage of profit shown in the Clinic's operations compares favorably with some of the largest for-profit business enterprises in the country. While the comparisons are not exact because of certain elements of the calculations that are different, they are in general comparable. The Clinic shows a percentage increase in revenues over expenses of more than 17 percent in 1971 and more than 15 percent in 1972. Compare with Standard Oil of New Jersey (now Exxon) in 1972 with an operating profit margin of some 14 percent; of General Electric at some 7 percent; or General Motors at nearly 13 percent. (Corporate margins quoted from "Moody's Handbook of Common Stocks, Fourth Quarter, 1972.")

8. It is apparent that the total real worth of the Clinic cannot be seen in the figures of their 990 forms. Their accounting procedures involve extensive depreciation of their assets which results in a carrying value far below actual market value. This is why net worth is not much larger on the 990 forms given an apparent annual increase of $8 to $11 million dollars in accumulations beyond expenses.

9. A further examination of Internal Revenue Standards for exempt organizations casts serious doubt on the legitimacy of their tax exempt status. According to the "Exempt Organization's Handbook," (11)671–56 dated April 9, 1972 the Clinic appears to violate many of the criteria listed in section 743.5 where exemption is described as depending on evidence that "use and control of a particular hospital are for the benefit of the public." This includes:

"a. The control . . . rests in a board . . . of civic leaders who have no direct economic interest in the hospital."

In fact Cleveland Clinic has dual controls: a Board of civic leaders and a Board of Governors composed of medical staff personnel.

"b. The hospital maintains an open medical staff, with privileges available to all qualified physicians . . ."

In fact, the Clinic medical staff is closed.

"d. The hospital operates an active emergency room and/or outpatient department accessible to the general public."

The Clinic, in fact, operates no public emergency room whatsoever. They have also declined to open an out-patient primary care program after promising to do so for six years.

"f. the hospital is involved in various projects and programs to improve the health of the community."

In an application for federal money in 1970 the Clinic referred to "90,000 people with substandard incomes in the general area who need primary care." In 1973 the Metropolitan Health Planning Corporation disapproved a total of 272 new beds at the Clinic because of their failure to provide a promised primary care program that was part of the original proposal approved by the planning agency. The Clinic still refuses to begin the promised service.

Negative conditions indicating a lack of exemption status listed in the IRS Handbook include:

"a. The hospital is controlled by members of the medical staff . . ."

At the least the function of the Board of Governors requires clarification if this does not in fact amount to such control.

"d. The hospital attempts to limit the use of its emergency room to patients of its medical staff, rather than making its facilities freely available to the public."

Police ambulances are under instruction not to take accident or emergency illness cases to Cleveland Clinic.

"f. The hospital has a record of negligible uncollectible accounts and charity cases;"

According to State records quoted by the Ohio Department of Insurance, the Clinic had only 42 Medicare patients in 1973.

Section 753.1 of the Handbook dealing with "Relief of the Distressed" states "In the case of a nonprofit hospital, the operation of an emergency room open to all persons and the provisions of hospital care to all persons in the community able to pay the cost thereof, either directly or through third-party reimbursement, is evidence that a hospital is promoting the health of a class of persons that is broad enough to benefit the community."

In conclusion I believe serious doubt exists as to the legitimacy of the tax exempt status of the Cleveland Clinic foundation. Yet the role of such institutions in affecting the supply of health care resources goes even beyond the question of tax status to the question of who lives and who dies if resources are maldistributed. The Clinic serves the paying patient. It does not serve the impoverished who surround it to any appreciable degree. In 1973 the Clinic hired twenty-five (25) new physicians. In the near-by Glenville area of nearly 90,000 persons there is a severe health care shortage. Only five physicians are full time in practice in that area. Next year a special community-medical school program will deploy the grand total of two (2) more physicians in that community.

Thank you Mr. Chairman, for the opportunity to amplify the record in response to Dr. Caper's question.

Exhibit 4.—*Final Staff Report on the Center for Health Consumer Affairs, Case Western Reserve University, June 29, 1973*

A project supported by grant number 000048 from section 314(c) of the Public Health Service Act as amended, for the period of July 1, 1972 to June 30, 1973

Charles W. Rawlings, Project Director; Myrtle Dennis, Outreach Coordinator; Elizabeth Cagan, Education Coordinator; Linda Watkins, Research Coordinator.

FINAL STAFF REPORT ON THE CENTER FOR HEALTH CONSUMER AFFAIRS

INTRODUCTION

Many people ask why the Center For Health Consumer Affairs has been discontinued. In answer, it can be reported that the Center suffered a sudden reversal of fortune following criticism of its views by the American Medical Association. The reader alone can decide the legitimacy of the change in position taken by Case Western Reserve University. In the Spring and Fall of 1972 the University had supported the Center. Later it contended that the Center involved "advocacy" not appropriate to a University setting. Even later it indicated it found the staff to lack competence.

It is interesting to note that the remedy chosen by the Administration was to bring consumer health planning education to an end. It did not opt to replace a staff it found wanting in ability. Nor did it entertain any negotiations concerning adjustments in the Center's advocacy role. In fairness it must be said that an alternative course was offered by the Administration. That course was to subject the work of the Center to the review and approval of an advisory committee composed of Health Science Faculty and hospital representatives.

This alternative, rejected by the staff of the Center, may be what the hue and cry over the Center really has been about. That is, the Center developed perspectives on health problems, compiled information on health systems, and spoke of these perspectives without reference to whether such views were acceptable to the prominent and large forces that control the shape of health care in the United States.

The University demanded the Center's work on behalf of consumers be subject to the very providers with whom there was conflict. The reader may find it curious that a small project whose combined staff salaries barely exceeded the median income of a single physician required preemptory administrative action to terminate it. Curious also is the sequence of University censorship that became standard operating procedure in the wake of representations made to the Administration by Blue Cross of Northeast Ohio. Cleveland Clinic, the Cleveland Academy of Medicine and School of Medicine alumni. This censorship, shocking in an academic community, seemed readily acceptable to much of that community when it involved the Center. It began with a request that the Center not publish its paper on the role of Cleveland Clinic in meeting the health care needs of the neighborhood in which it is located. The request was made although no one in the administration had even seen the paper. Then followed the demand in the Fall of 1972 that the slide show "In Search of Health Care" be withdrawn from circulation or revised. The request was made following AMA criticism which came after a member of the administration had already viewed the show without complaint. This censorship reached its height in February 1973 when the Administration phoned a printer and ordered a stop placed on printing a brochure of the Center's dealing with the subject of National Health Insurance. Over a period of six weeks that followed the Administration styled itself as an expert on the subject. Drafts with their marginal comments are available for examination. In this instance the censorship produced an unofficial senior faculty delegation which confronted the administration on two grounds. First on the principle of censorship itself, second on the point that the administration's substantive objections were in point of fact incorrect. These had been with specific reference to inaccessibility of health care, discrimination in health care, profiteering in health care and the impact of Medicare which authorities have identified as regularly providing handouts to providers without altering, in the long run, the amount of out of pocket expense the elderly face in seeking health care today.[1] The University Administration contended that these views were substantively incorrect. The faculty committee corrected that situation and the pamphlet was printed. But the faculty committee could not correct the Administration's decision to silence this voice of dissent on its campus. That decision came in the form of University refusal to permit submission of the Center's refunding application to HEW. It was pre-emptive in the fact that it came, without warning or evaluation, one day before the deadline for submission.

In the following pages of this report the reader will find further evidence of the voice of the Center in the form of a summary of the major concerns which the Center came to believe were of first importance to the consumer of health care. Readers can judge for themselves not only the legitimacy of the Center but the role they themselves will play with regard to these issues that will not dissappear with the demise of the Center.

The Economic Picture

During a seventeen year period ending in 1969 the Blue Cross rates in Northeast Ohio rose 512 percent while the cost of living measured by the consumer price index was increasing only 40 percent.[2] This and many other indications of runaway inflation and profiteering present a clue to the unusual aspects of what is an $80 billion dollar health care industry.[3] Unusual because it is a tightly controlled economic system based on consumer dollars while simultaneously barring the consumer from any role in setting policy about how those dollars are spent. Over a thirty year period Blue Cross was controlled by the hospitals so that rate negotiations were, in effect, the hospitals negotiating with themselves.[4] The consumer voice was virtually non-existent. Physicians, who through the American Medical Association have opposed most progressive social legislation since World War I on the grounds of free enterprise, strictly bar such free enterprise when it is not to their personal advantage. The Center has examined many books and essays documenting the steady opposition by the AMA until the late 1960s to increasing the supply of doctors.[5] It was straight market manipulation. When the supply is scarce

---

[1] Address by Dr. Lester Breslow, Dean of the School of Public Health Service, UCLA, at Health Security Action Council Health Care Conference, Washington, D.C., March 17, 1972.
[2] Figures supplied by Ohio Department of Insurance and U.S. Department of Commerce, Consumer Price Index.
[3] *Chart Book, 1972*, by U.S. Department of Health, Education and Welfare, Social Security Administration, Office of Research and Statistics.
[4] Blue Cross of Northeast Ohio's Regulations until passage of Senate Bill 80 in 1971 required that a majority of its Board be members of Boards of Trustees or Advisory committees of hospitals. (Article II, Section 1)
[5] Stevens, Rosemary, *American Medicine and the Public Interest*, Yale University Press, 1971, p. 307.
Friedson, Eliot, *The Profession of Medicine*, Dodd, Mead, 1970. p. 31.
Somers, Anne, *Health Care In Transition*, Princeton University, 1971, p. 8.
Harris, Richard, *A Sacred Trust: The Story of Organized Medicine's Multi-million Dollar Fight Against Public Health Legislation*, New American Library, 1966.

the price rises. The median income of physicians stands today at over $40,000 annually. Dr. John Knowles, former general director of Massachusetts General Hospital, estimates that 30 to 40 percent of the nation's doctors are "making a killing." "Some doctor's incomes . . . have become exhorbitant" Dr. Knowles said, "I mean $120,000-$150,000-$160,000 annually." [6]

The economic forces that interplay in the health system control, to a dominant degree, how that system functions. For example, economic conditions for decades have encouraged over-utilization of hospitals because the insurance system made hospitalization an easy route to physician fee collection. For the hospital it has often been an economic necessity that beds be kept full. Three hospitals studied by the Center this past year showed that women without hospital insurance stayed an average 1.7 days less than women with insurance coverage in the Obstetric divisions.[7]

At Metropolitan General Hospital lower revenues in 1972 were the consequence of medical efficiency in the hospital. Because the hospital last year served more patients for fewer average days of stay the total patient days dropped. The Hospital's administrators promptly urged the medical staff to increase patient stays in order to increase revenues. Of course one consequence of that would be service to fewer patients.[8]

The critical point for the consumer is that when he used to stay longer in hospitals it was not necessarily in the interests of his health. Today, he may stay a shorter time, but again, not necessarily in the name of his health. The new provider emphasis is now on control of utilization because of runaway inflation.[9] The Consumer cannot be sure when he is encountering new scientific advances and medical efficiency or when he is encoutering the hospital defecit. Because of hospital and Blue Cross secrecy the consumer today cannot know for sure what are the true facts.

But the consumer can know the impact of health care economics on his own pocketbook. When Blue Cross began around 1940 it paid for about one-fourth of the average person's health care costs. Today, thirty years later it still pays only about one-fourth.[10] The average per admission cost has jumped from $130 dollars in 1950 to $671 dollars in 1970. When Medicare was enacted into law in 1965 it quickly evolved, as Rosemary Stevens of Yale University has pointed out, "into an amorphous network of handouts to medical providers". Out-of-pocket payments for health care by the elderly today are equal to or greater than the amount before Medicare was passed into law.[11]

Perhaps the most telling research on hospital costs has been done by Anderson and May in the *Annals of the American Academy of Political and Social Science*, January 1972. Identifying a $7.5 billion dollar hospital cost increase from 1965 to 1970 they showed that only 12 percent of that increase amounted to increased use of health facilities by consumers. The rest is expensive new facilities and staff, equipment, inflation and rising wages and salaries. In noting this the reader should know that salaries and wages as a percentage of total hospital costs have decreased in recent years in Greater Cleveland. Furthermore, much of the expansion of technical capabilities of hospitals is based on unnecessary duplication of infrequently used, expensive equipment.[12]

A look around Cleveland confirms the study. Cleveland Clinic is expanding to the tune of over $30 million dollars with no increase of service to the community in which it is located. In fact only 11 percent of its patients come from Cleveland, less than a third come from Cuyahoga County.[13] St. Luke's Hospital is replacing old facilities, building new doctor's offices, parking garages and out-patient facilities while threatening to close their facilities

[6] Quoted in *The Plain Dealer*, Cleveland. Ohio, January 1, 1971.
[7] Rowland, Ann, *A Survey of Maternity Care For Lakewood Residents*, Center For Health Consumer Affairs, April 16. 1973, p. 11.
[8] Information supplied in confidence by member of the Medical Staff.
[9] *Hospital Utilization and Costs In Northeast Ohio*, Published by the Metropolitan Health Planning Corporation, Cleveland, Ohio, 1970.
[10] Stevens. Rosemary, op. cit. p. 187.
[11] Sylvia Porter quoted in the Plain Dealer, Cleveland, Ohio, June 27, 1973 ". . . the amount of money today's average elderly must pay in direct, out-of-pocket costs for medical care actually is more than in fiscal '66 . . . $404 or $95 MORE than in 1966."
[12] See *Hospital Utilization and Costs In Northeast Ohio*, published by the Metropolitan Health Planning Corporation, Cleveland. Ohio, 1970.
[13] Interview by Center staff person with Dan Moose, Staff member, Metropolitan Health Planning Corporation, April 1972.

to new outpatients.[14] Their price tag is $17.5 million. St. Vincent Charity hospital is into a similar program.

When Cleveland Clinic in 1971 quietly began to use their motel for additional hospital beds (thus, according to economists, threatening to make all hospital beds more costly by creating a bed surplus) they asked the Metropolitan Health Planning Corporation for approval after the fact. Blue Cross, which was reimbursing for these beds continued to do so although its own regulations stipulate that lack of MHPC approval required that they not give such reimbursement. After a public exposure in the Cleveland Press Blue Cross switched positions and MHPC disapproved the motel beds. *But* with Blue Cross and MHPC possessing the same leadership in Vernon Burt, MHPC voted to permit "retroactive" approval of other hospital expansion.[15] Thus did economic and institutional power make a mockery of the concept of rational planning of health facilities.

In all these matters, the issue for the consumer is how he/she can influence the health care system and control the private sector forces that turn the system constantly to serve it own profit-making and institutional purposes. It is clear the consumer supplies the fuel but someone else drives the car in their own direction. In a later section of this report the question of public regulation of the health system is discussed in some detail.

Professionalism and Quality Control

In recent years hospitals and doctors have become alarmed over the financial threat of increasing numbers of medical malpractice suits. Accordingly, a Secretary's Commission on Medical Malpractice was created by the then Secretary of HEW, Elliott Richardson. Instead of a picture of costly nuisance suits in the rare instance of damage to patients, the study produced an astounding picture of damage to patients far beyond that reflected in the number of malpractice complaints.

The Commission report issued in May 1973 includes a study by Pocinki, Dogger and Schwartz entitled "The Incidence of Iatrogenic Injuries." (The word iatrogenic means sickness or illness caused by treatment.) Briefly, the research had focused on careful examination by expert medical and legal panels of random samples of the medical discharge records of two large hospitals. To measure the expert's ability to identify instances of damage, known cases of damage to patients were identified and those files were mixed with the random sample without the expert's knowledge. They identified only 60 percent of the already identified cases of damage to patients. Even with this indication that their findings are on the low side of the range of accuracy, here is what the projections from the random sample suggest:

Out of 23,750 discharges from the two hospitals there were 1780 iatrogenic injuries to patients. 517 of these injuries could be attributed to negligence by the hospital or staff. *But*, there were only 31 claims filed by the consumer-patients. If this situation prevails in other hospitals it means that negligence to patients occurs sixteen times more than the number of patient complaints.

The Center for Health Consumer Affairs found other indications that the quality of medical care is highly questionable. The sheer volume of complaints coming into the Center and they were not solicited since the Center had no means to achieve redress for consumers—was one clue. For example, on the ocassion of the much publicised incident where an Academy of Medicine physician refused to treat a patient during a house call because she lacked $30.00 cash, the Center received complaints from six persons in the same building where it is located of similar experiences with Academy physicians. Other persons called the Center with complaints of a similar nature from other locations in the City. During the recent series of public hearings on health care held by three different groups there was an almost unending series of citizen complaints about the health care system and the people who deliver

---

[14] In July 1972 St. Luke's announced intentions to close its doors to new outpatients because of inadequate state reimbursement for indigent care. They waved the flag of bankruptcy. Six weeks later they announced a $17.5 million dollar capital expansion program on which they had embarked months earlier.

[15] See Minutes of the Metropolitan Health Planning Corporation October 10, 1972, December 12, 1972 and February 13, 1972. See also Exhibit X, Amended Articles of Regulation, Blue Cross of Northeast Ohio, 1971.

care.[16] A few examples of the problems of care may help the reader to add his or her own.

One of the frequent claims of the private physician, fee-for-service, is the freedom of choice to which the patient is entitled. Through the AMA, physicians have fought social reform for fifty years on the grounds that such reforms are socialistic.[17] Yet here is what consumers told the Center. In the case of three different families with serious illness requiring a specialist, when dissatisfaction developed on the family's part and they sought treatment from another specialist, they ran into collusion between specialists and were forced to remain with the first specialist because the other one would not take them on the grounds that the other doctor "is a friend of mine", or because it was held to be "unethical".

There is also the documented story involving one of the biggest providers of health care in Cleveland—and stories of complaint about them are of avalanche proportions—about the woman who entered the hospital for surgery. She was to have two minor problems taken care of surgically at the same time a more urgent surgical procedure was performed. Two different specialists would be involved. The woman had been forced to make these arrangements through her doctor's secretary-nurse and was anxious that there be no misunderstanding since she had never reviewed the entire procedure with her doctor personally. Repeated requests the night before surgery produced no conference with her doctor. As a last resort she asked her husband to make sure, in the morning, that he talked with the doctor before surgery. As she was lying in the operating room being prepared for surgery she heard one nurse in the background say sarcastically to the other "There is some man downstairs at the desk who insists he must talk with Dr.——— about his precious wife." Those were virtually the last words she heard before receiving the anesthetic.[18] Not only does this reflect gross insensitivity by the medical staff, but it also illustrates the lack of control over vital procedures that consumers feel largely because of physician shortages and specialization. Disasterous errors have occurred precisely because of such lack of communication.

It has been the Center's experience that the notion of shared responsibility between professionals and consumers for quality control in health care is, again, faced with the barriers of tradition and professional prerogative. But the Center asks this question: If the only criticism a doctor hears is from his peers can it really be expected that complaints of the kind mentioned above will subside? In the future, the Center believes that patient committees for grievance as well as planning purposes must be accepted as part of the policy-formulation of health providers. In the Center's experience the professionalism in medical care stands as a barrier to such consumer in-put. More often than not consumer participation in Greater Cleveland health matters is little more than public relations window dressing.

The Center has come to believe that the only answer to the need to make health systems accountable to a consumer public is a national health system that can planfully distribute health care resources in an equitable way to the entire population of this city and this country. It is the private and profit-making aspects of the system that make it both inequitable and with accountability not to its patients but to its private interests.

An important corrolary to this view is the hard political reality that consumers must face. It is that most of the resources of the $80 billion dollar health care industry in this country will be turned in coming months to preventing just this from happening. The present health care system is heavily invested in perpetuating health care inequality. Its profits, its suburban affluence, its vast institutions, and not least, its business partners in the equipment, construction, and insurance industries cannot prosper early so well if health care is publicly regulated and a right, without financial barrier, for every citizen of the United State.

---

[16] Public Hearings, State Task Force On Hospital Licensure and Certification of Need, Cleveland, Ohio, March 12, 1973.
Public Hearings, Governor's Task Force on the Cost of Health Care, Cleveland, Ohio, May 3, 4, 1973.
Public Hearings, Cuyahoga County Health Coalition, Cleveland, Ohio, April 24–25, 1973.
[17] See references in footnote number five.
[18] Confidential patient report to staff member of the Center For Health Consumer Affairs. Period of hospitalization, surgical procedures, attending physicians and surgeons, and husbands corroboration verified.

The consumer should be on guard for many gayly dressed packages offering panaceas in health care in future months and years. Most of these will be clothing on the body of a private health care system oriented to profiteering and inequality as a matter of policy.

Relationships Between Providers and Consumers

There are not many market enterprises that affect so fundamentally the life and death of the buyer. This no doubt accounts for much of the consumer mystification that has characterized relationships with health care providers in modern time. The consumer usually approaches health providers in a time of serious need. He is dependant in the relationship. Added to that is the tradition of professionalism that surrounds the doctor. In his book *The Profession of Medicine*, Eliot Friedson discusses the term "profession" as an activity which is able to define both the problem and the solution and control the delivery of that solution. In the instance of Medicine, the professional doctor defines both sickness and wellness and has nearly absolute control over prescription for the solution. This mystification about health care has been extended in the twentieth century to include the technical and organizational complexities of large hospitals, complicated treatments, and complicated formulas for reimbursement by insurance companies. Decisions about facilities for health care, manpower for health care, and financing systems for health care, have become feats of technical wizardry, far beyond the layman's ability to understand. Or so it is said by the planners and hospital administrators.

It is an understatement to say that there is a serious gap between the consumer and the health provider. It may be more proper to describe the gap as true alianation. The consumer, in need of health care, places himself in the trust of a physician whom he has been trained to view as larger than life. The same consumer must view the provider of his health care as a virtual last court of appeal. He must gain satisfaction here or the consequences could mean his death. By the same token he must find the means to pay for this desperately important service. When he pays it is often exhorbitant and it is to a health care system too complicated, too large, too technically beyond him to permit challenge or question. Perhaps this is why the Medical Malpractice Commission found only 31 complaints of negligence filed in two hospitals with an estimated 517 patient injuries due to negligence.

The point is that special steps must be taken if the gap between consumer and provider is to be closed. Here are some of the steps that may be necessary to begin the closing of that gap:

1. The policies of secrecy that govern private business have been applied also to the realm of non-profit health care institutions and insurance programs. It is impossible to know what the questions are in particular provider policies if consumers do not have access to accurate information. When they have no such access they are then branded by providers as incompetent to make weighty decisions. But consumers have begun to realize from various recent revelations that the policy of secrecy really means there is something to hide.. When a Center research project showed evidence of over-crowding at Fairview General Hospital's Obstetrics Ward the hospital refused to release their day-to-day utilization statistics. Instead it impugned student involvement in the research. When news investigators uncovered financial transactions of some hospitals in the Cleveland area and in Washington, D.C. they discovered hospital assets being used for a bank's benefit, some of whose officers were also on the hospital board. (See especially the Washington Post series of October 29, 1972.) Consumers must demand full disclosure of those institutions that have non-profit purposes and depend on both consumer dollars and government dollars for their existence. Until that disclosure comes the gap of suspicion will widen in an unlimited way.

2. Consumers, for their part must begin to understand that the operation of health care systems and services cannot be left simply to those with a professional or economic interest in that system. The chaotic condition of health care and its economics is the result of such consumer absence from the policy-making tables. Consumer participation may be significant in small ways through substantial membership in boards and policy committees of local clinics and health centers. However, the consumer must beware of the token game. Unless his role means a vote on policy questions he is probably being used to create the illusion of consumer participation for the sake of the provider's

public image. Moreover, unless there is a consumer constituency with real political clout even a consumer votes on a board dominated by ownership class business and professional men will still only be tokenism. The Center staff seriously doubts that a few consumers can effect change in large provider institutions, although it may be tactically necessary for consumers to seek such board roles.[19] For the longrange, the consumer must see government regulation of the health care system as the only political means truly available to him for basic health systems change and improvement. The economic inequities that prevail today can only be cured through equitable distribution of scarce health care resources to all citizens. The government is the only vehicle with the power and susbtance to make such changes. When the consumer is able to move the action from the private to the public sector he has moved it to an arena where he is potentially more powerful.

3. The self image of physicians may have to undergo sympathetic but thorough alterations. At the Center we often heard that we had reduced all health care problems to "the good guys versus the bad guys". The Center staff does not hold such a view of the problems of health care. However, it may be more than chance that such a metaphor was repeatedly used by medical critics of the Center. The choice of a vocation so enshrined in reputational virtue as Medicine may be a result of many motivies, one of which may be to identify one's self as good. It is an old puritan ethic that moves such an impulse and manifests itself in an extremely hard-working profession where virtue is so solidly installed. The re-identification of the physician to himself as not specially virtuous because of his profession and not necessarily good because of his work may help align him with the rest of the human race so that dialogue of a kind seldom encountered during the Center's work will begin to happen between provider and consumer.

Postcript

The health care system in this country is financially enormous and scientifically complex. It is over-layed with professionalism and large sectors of private self-interest. It is like the person one cannot get along without and cannot get along with. The Center for Health Consumer Affairs was one effort to move the consumer closer to the system through education, access to resources at the University, and perspectives developed from consumer points of view rather than those of providers. The staff of the Center had many failings. Others must judge concerning the shortcomings of substance and tactics. However, the staff is convinced that the problems in health care are real, that it would have been far better for a university to have strengthened such a program rather than demand either its obeisance to medical professional domination or its demise. As with so many areas in recent years, this University has dropped yet another initiative for service to the public. Perhaps this is not so serious as the broader trend of events in which the simple human instincts and perceptions of men and women, their ideas about responsibility to each other, and their integrity to principle are gradually eroded with the new vision of loyalty to institutions and the status institutions confer.

Exhibit 5.—*Excerpts From Minutes of Metropolitan Health Planning Corp. Board of Trustees Meetings, 1972–74, Re Cleveland Clinic, October 10, 1972*

⁂

IX. REPORT OF HEALTH FACILITIES ADVISORY COMMITTEE

Mr. Johnstone presented the report of the Health Facilities Advisory Committee. At its meeting on October 3. 1972, the HFAC considered two proposals: one from the Cleveland Clinic pertaining to the operation of a 121 bed inpatient unit in the Clinic Inn for convalescent care and one from Huron Hospital for

---

[19] For a thorough discussion of the issues in consumer participation see the paper by Edward V. Sparer. *On the Matter of "Community Relations": The Consumer Movement In Health Care and The Albert Einstein Medical Center* for presentation at the Long Range Planning Seminar, Saturday, June 12, 1971 of the Albert Einstein Medical Center.

the operation of a 23 bed minimal care program. The Committee questioned the utilization of inpatient facilities for the provision of convalescent care and minimal care. Mr. Johnstone also reported that as both of these programs had been implemented, they were reviewed retrospectively.

Because of the issues raised by each proposal, the Committee made the following recommendations: (1) that the Corporation establish a policy that proposals involving the construction or modification of health care facilities not be endorsed retrospectively; (2) that the Corporation establish a policy that special care units, other than acute care units, will be endorsed by the Corporation only if the demand for such units is clearly demonstrated and if the institution proposing the unit has demonstrated that the care provided in the special care unit could not be provided on an outpatient basis; and (3) that staff be advised to notify Cleveland Clinic and Huron Road Hospital of these policies if they are adopted and to request each of those institutions to submit appropriate justification for the review of its proposal.

In the course of reviewing the Cleveland Clinic proposal, the Committee also reviewed the progress made by the Cleveland Clinic in developing its primary care program for neighborhood residents. The Committee recommended that the Cleveland Clinic be notified that the Corporation had understood that the Clinic's primary care program would be developed simultaneously with the construction of the additional inpatient facilities endorsed in February, 1972. Therefore, the Cleveland Clinic should be urged to proceed as rapidly as possible with the development of a primary care program serving neighborhood residents.

During discussion of the Committee's report, Mr. Burt indicated that there were many considerations involved in the Committee's recommendation involving retrospective review and approval. As such, he suggested that the Board separate the Committee's recommendations into two parts, referring the part on retrospective review to the Executive Committee. He added that the recommendation to request a report from Cleveland Clinic seemed appropriate and desirable, and urged that it be affirmed.

Mr. Lewine pointed out the recommendation dealing with minimal care units and suggested that it be affirmed along with the recommendation regarding the Cleveland Clinic's primary care program.

' A motion was made to refer the Committee's recommendation on retrospective review to the Executive Committee. The motion was seconded and passed unanimously.

It then was moved to accept the Committee's recommendations relative to minimal care units and the Cleveland Clinic. The motion was seconded and carried unanimously.

X. HEALTH SERVICES ADVISORY COMMITTEE REPORT

As the HSAC Chairman was not in attendance, Dr. Stein was asked to present the Committee's report:

A. *Renal Dialysis*

In response to a request from the Kidney Foundation of Northeast Ohio after a preliminary staff meeting with physicians involved in renal dialysis in the area, the Committee decided to form a subcommittee to establish community guidelines for renal dialysis and to work in this regard with the Northeast Ohio Regional Medical Program.

B. *Emergency Medical Services*

It was reported that the Committee heard a report on emergency medical services planning, including an account of State and local activity. The Ohio Department of Health is in the process of organizing an Emergency Medical Services Coordinating Committee to determine avenues for greater coordination in statewide emergency medical services. Dr. Cashman, Director of the Ohio Department of Health, also recently has asked for areawide agency review of applications for highway safety fund monies for the purchase of ambulance and rescue equipment. This procedure has necessitated increased planning activity by Corporation staff. The Committee voted to establish a subcommittee to facilitate community-wide emergency medical care planning in cooperation with medical societies, the Hospital Association and other groups involved in emergency medical care in our area.

DECEMBER 12, 1972

C. Retrospective Reviews

The Board was reminded that it had referred a recommendation by the HFAC relative to prohibiting retrospective reviews to the Executive Committee. Mr. Burt reported that the Executive Committee discussed the issue in detail and had agreed that the Corporation should not prohibit retrospective reviews but should continue its practice of examining each project on its own merit. However, the Committee also agreed that all institutions should be advised that the Corporation continues to expect them to obtain prior approval for any modification, expansion or construction and that if a hospital proceeds without prior approval, it does so at its own risk.

*   *   *   *   *   *   *

B. Ambulatory Care Program—Cleveland Clinic

At its October 10 meeting, the Board adopted a recommendation of the Committee that the Corporation notify the Cleveland Clinic that its February, 1971 endorsement of the 330-bed addition to inpatient facilities was made with the understanding that the primary care program for neighborhood residents would be developed simultaneously with new inpatient facilities and that the Cleveland Clinic be urged to proceed as rapidly as possible with the development of a primary care program serving neighborhood residents.

Subsequently, a letter was sent to the Cleveland Clinic reporting this action and asking for a progress report on the status of the ambulatory care program. The Committee found the Clinic's response unacceptable in terms of the institution's lack of commitment to the provision of ambulatory care services to all residents of the area.

After discussing Cleveland Clinic's current plans for its ambulatory care program t,he Committee made the following recommendations to the Board: "That the Corporation request the Cleveland Clinic to proceed immediately to expand its present emergency room facilities commensurate with existing facilities in area hospitals of a similar size, and to provide a full program of emergency care services to residents of the area. This initial step in expanding both facilities and service should be integrated into the primary care program when it is developed."

Mr. Burt suggested that the Committee's recommendation be referred to the Ambulatory Care Committee as it was established to address the kind of issues raised by the Cleveland Clinic program.

Dr. Huggins objected to the recommendation being referred to the Ambulatory Care Committee and spoke in support of the Board's reaffirming its position on Cleveland Clinic's program.

After considerable discussion ,it was moved and seconded that the Committee's recommendation be accepted. A motion carried, with one negative vote being recorded.

FEBRUARY 13, 1973

XI. OTHER BUSINESS

A. Cleveland Clinic

It was asked whether the Corporation had received a reply to a letter which the Board previously had requested be sent to the Cleveland Clinic. Mr. Burt reported that the Corporation had not as yet received a reply to the letter regarding the Clinic's ambulatory care program. It was agreed that the staff would report to the Board on this matter after the receipt of a response from the Cleveland Clinic.

B. Community Committee on Black Physicians

It was urged that the Activities of the Committee on Black Physicians proceed as expeditiously as possible. It was reported that there are approximately 50 black physicians still practicing in the central city and concern was expressed at their rapidly decreasing numbers.

APRIL 10, 1973

A. *Cleveland Clinic*

The Cleveland Clinic had requested endorsement for the use of two floors of the Clinic Inn, a hotel owned by a subsidiary of the Cleveland Clinic Foundation, for 121 inpatient convalescent care beds. Cleveland Clinic has utilized these beds since 1971 on the assumption that the Corporation's February 1971 endorsement of a 330-bed addition could be interpreted to cover the interim use of beds in the Clinic Inn until the new addition is opened.

It was the Committee's recommendation that the use of the Clinic Inn for inpatient services not be endorsed for the following reasons: 1) the February 1971 endorsement could not be interpreted to include the temporary use of hotel rooms for inpatient care; and 2) the February 1971 endorsement was for additional acute care beds—convalescent care beds were not included in the proposal nor in the endorsed expansion.

After a thorough discussion of the proposal and the recommendation, it was moved, seconded and unanimously adopted that the Committee's recommendation be accepted.

CLEVELAND CLINIC HOSPITAL SUMMARY OF PROPOSAL AND RECOMMENDATION OF THE HEALTH FACILITIES ADVISORY COMMITTEE

I. SUMMARY

Since 1971, the Cleveland Clinic has utilized two floors of the Clinic Inn, a hotel owned by a subsidiary of the Cleveland Clinic Foundation, for inpatient convalescent care. According to the Cleveland Clinic, this unit, which has a total of 121 inpatient care beds, was opened in order to reduce the backlog of patients waiting for admission. One of the Clinic Inn floors is used almost exclusively in conjunction with cardiac surgery and cardiac catheterization. Other service categories include dermatology, liver and kidney biopsy, and minor surgery.

The Cleveland Clinic has utilized these beds on the assumption that the Corporation's February, 1971 endorsement of a 330 bed addition could be interpreted to cover the interim use of beds in the Clinic Inn until the new addition is operational in late 1974. However, when the Corporation became aware of the use of the Clinic Inn for convalescent care in April, 1972, the Cleveland Clinic was notified that the Corporation's 1971 endorsement did not address the use of the Clinic Inn for inpatient services and that a separate review of the Clinic Inn program would be required.

The Health Facilities Advisory Committee as well as a Site Committee have reviewed the Clinic Inn program. The reviews of both of these Committees have included meetings and discussions with representatives of Cleveland Clinic.

II. RECOMMENDATION

The Health Facilities Advisory Committee recommends to the Board of Trustees that the Clinic Inn proposal of Cleveland Clinic should not be endorsed for the following reasons

1. In February, 1971 the Corporation endorsed facilities for 330 additional *acute* care beds. Convalescent care beds were not included in the proposed or endorsed expansion. The term convalescent care, which has been used by the Cleveland Clinic to describe the Clinic Inn program, indicates that the Clinic Inn is not used to provide acute care services.

2. The February, 1971 endorsement cannot be interpreted to include the temporary use of hotel rooms for inpatient acute care or convalescent care services.

———

OCTOBER 9, 1973

A. *Construction at Cleveland Clinic*

Mr. Burt referred the Trustees to that section of the Executive Committee minutes which relates to the construction at the Cleveland Clinic Hospital and to Mr. Podolin's memorandum on the subject which is attached to those minutes. That memorandum is attached also to these minutes as Exhibit C.

Mr. Burt presented a review of the situation. He pointed out that in 1971, after many meetings and considerable deliberation by the Health Facilities Advisory Committee and the Board, the Corporation had endorsed a major construction program at the Cleveland Clinic Hospital which included the construction of shelled-in space for 1052 beds. The endorsement of the shelled-in space was made with the expressed condition that the space would not be completed without the prior approval of MHPC. That condition had been acknowledged and agreed to in writing by the Clinic.

Mr. Burt pointed out that in April of this year, the Cleveland Clinic wrote to MHPC that it intended to complete the shelled-in space, pointing out that the demands for beds from its physicians warranted such action. This letter had been acknowledged by Mr. Podolin who had pointed out that in accordance with the 1971 endorsement, such action would require MHPC's prior approval. Unfortunately, due to the press of other activities, there was no follow up on this by MHPC staff during the spring and summer. In the latter part of August, the Clinic advised Mr. Podolin that its construction program—including the completion of the 152 beds in the shelled-in space and the orders to move ahead on this work must have been given at or about the same time that MHPC was first notified of the Clinic's "intent" in April.

Mr. Burt pointed out that although there was no follow up by MHPC staff after April, there was also no follow up by the Clinic until late August when it advised MHPC that the work was nearing completion.

Mr. Burt pointed out that the matter had been brought to the Executive Committee rather than to the Health Facilities Advisory Committee because it appeared that the issue involved was not so much the "need" for the construction but rather whether or not the Clinic had acted properly in completing the space in violation of its written agreement with MHPC that such completion would not be undertaken without prior approval.

Mr. Burt reported that the Executive Committee had discussed the issue at length and in detail and had concluded that the completion of the shelled-in space should not be approved. He pointed out that what was at stake so far as the Clinic was concerned was the interest and depreciation costs associated with the completion of the space. He indicated that he felt motion votes not to endorse the completion of the 152 bed shell by the Cleveland Clinic." The motion carried with sixteen voting for and five against. With the Chair's permission, Mr. Calgie who had voted against the motion explained that he had voted against it because he felt it was not strong enough and that he believed the motion should have used the word "disapprove" rather than "not endorse."

SEPTEMBER 12, 1973.

Memorandum To: Members of the Executive Committee.

From: Lee J. Podolin.

Subject: Cleveland Clinic Foundation.

In July 1970, the Cleveland Clinic Foundation (the "Clinic") submitted a construction program to MHPC for review and endorsement. The program proposed the construction of 178 acute care beds, shelled space for 152 additional beds and the expansion of space for radiology, laboratory, electrocardiography, cardiac catheterization, central supply, pharmacy, surgery and certain other administrative and service departments. The estimated cost of the proposed project was $25,000,000 which was to be financed by loans.

This proposal was reviewed by staff, a subcommittee of the Health Facilities Advisory Committee and by the Health Facilities Advisory Committee. Included in the review process were meetings with representatives of the Clinic, not only to discuss the proposed construction program but also the Clinic's proposed primary care program. During the course of these discussions, MHPC was informed that the Clinic would proceed with the development of the primary care program. This was a key factor leading to the decision of MHPC's Board of Trustees on January 20, 1971 to endorse the construction program. The endorsement was given with certain conditions, including the following: (1) "that the Cleveland Clinic Foundation will obtain the approval of the Corporation prior to the completion of the space for the 152 beds which is planned to be shelled in at this time" and (2) "that at the completion of this construction program, the Hospital's bed complement, including the potential 152 beds in shelled space, will not exceed 924." Also included in its letter of endorsement was the following statement: "The Corporation also has received assurance from you that the additional facilities being requested will provide sufficient and suitable in-hospital facilities for patients who will be cared for in the primary care program now being planned by the Cleveland Clinic Foundation."

The Clinic accepted MHPC's endorsement and agreed to abide by the stipulated conditions. This agreement was signed by Mr. James G. Harding who was then the Administrator of the Cleveland Clinic Hospital.

In April 1972, Dr. Carl E. Wasmuth, Chairman of the Clinic's Board of Governors, informed MHPC that it was the Clinic's intent to gradually convert the Clinic Inn to a medical facility. The purpose given for this conversion was to implement the first phase of the primary care program and to explore the feasibility of establishing a "surgicenter." Dr. Wasmuth further noted that the wing then under construction would not be completed and ready for occupancy until the latter part of 1974. However, in order to meet an increasing demand for inpatient services, the Clinic felt that it had to utilize available resources. Accordingly, one floor of the Clinic Inn (60 beds) had been converted to inpatient convalescent care and the Clinic planned to convert an additional floor (same capacity) for the same purpose. The Clinic believed that these conversions were covered by the Corporation's endorsement of the construction of 178 new acute care beds.

An extensive review of the Clinic's use of the Clinic Inn for inpatient services wa conducted and in April of 1973, MHPC's Board of Trustees voted not to endorse the use of the space in the Clinic Inn for inpatient services. MHPC pointed out that the use of that space was not included in the program which had been endorsed in 1971 and that the endorsement could not be interpreted to cover the temporary use of hotel rooms for acute or convalescent inpatient services. The Clinic was advised of this action on April 11, 1973.

On April 3, 1973, Dr. Wasmuth, in a letter to Mr. Burt, stated that demand for inpatient facilities at the Clinic had increased significantly and that the Clinic intended to complete the shelled-in space. He pointed out that requests from physicians who refer patients to the Clinic for specialized medical treatment continued at an unprecedented rate.

Because of this, he stated, the factors which led to the development of this initial program had changed and to avoid jeopardizing the trust placed in the Clinic by its referring physicians and patients, it needed additional beds at once.

In response to this letter, Dr. Wasmuth was informed by Mr. Podolin (on April 10, 1973) that such action required the prior approval of MHPC and that his letter would be considered a request for endorsement of the completion of the space and that it would be processed routinely. There was no follow up of this matter by MHPC staff during the spring and summer.

In August (August 29), the Clinic advised Mr. Podolin that the total hospital construction program, including the completion of the two floor, 152-bed shelled-in area, was near completion. This matter was subsequently discussed in detail at a meeting between Mr. Lees, an official of the Clinic, and Mr. Johnstone on September 6. The following is a summary of that meeting.

The construction contractor was authorized in April to complete the shelled-in area and the entire new facility is scheduled to be opened on October 1, 1973. The total bed complement at that time will be 1043 beds, including the 120 beds now in operation in the Clinic Inn. No determination has been made as to the future use of the beds in the Clinic Inn, but there is a possibility that they will remain in operation. One of the primary reasons for the increased demand for inpatient services is the addition of 25 physicians to the medical staff over the past eight months. Mr. Lees was not clear regarding the Clinic's commitment to the development of the primary care center. He noted that Phase One, a health care program for employees and their families, was in operation. However, he could not indicate a schedule for implementation of Phases Two and Three. Mr. Lees stated that the Board of Trustees of the Clinic, at a meeting held on September 5, 1973, had agreed to participate in the ambulatory care program being developed by the Cuyahoga County Hospital to be located on Cleveland's east side. This participation would include the assignment of physicians and other Clinic personnel to the Ambulatory Care Center. The Clinic would also financially participate in the development of the Center. However, all patients seen in the Center who needed hospitalization would be admitted to Metropolitan General Hospital. Mr. Lees left the impression that he felt that MHPC would not endorse the completion of the 152 bed shelled-in area. Because of this, he requested that MHPC delay any action on this matter until the Clinic and Cuyahoga County Hospital had time to publicly announce its joint venture in the east side ambulatory care center.

As things now stand, assuming the accuracy of Mr. Lees' statements and assuming that the Clinic maintains in operation the 120 beds in the Clinic Inn, the Clinic will have, on October 1, 272 beds which have not been endorsed by MHPC. Of these, 120 (the Clinic Inn) were disapproved. The remainder, the 152 beds in the shelled-in area, have not received MHPC approval but have not been disapproved either. It is these beds that represent the issue before MHPC at this time.

It would appear that the primary question is not the need for the construction of these 152 beds but rather the Clinic's violation of its agreement made in February of 1971 not to proceed with the completion of the shelled space without MHPC's endorsement.

The Clinic was aware that MHPC's endorsement was necessary and had, in 1971, agreed in writing that that was indeed the case. The Clinic did advise MHPC in April of 1973 of its desire to proceed with the completion of this space. MHPC was, without a doubt, remiss in not vigorously following up this matter after acknowledging the receipt of the Clinic's letter. Nonetheless, it is also a fact that the Clinic itself never followed up to determine the status of its proposal until August 29. It appears that the decision to complete the shelled space was made and the order given to the contractor at approximately the same time that the Clinic notified MHPC. The Clinic's actions suggest that from the time it decided to go forward with the completion of this shelled space, it did not care much whether or not it received MHPC's endorsement.

It is recommended that the completion of the shelled space not be endorsed on the following grounds:

(1) The Clinic violated its written agreement with MHPC not to complete the space until it had received MHPC's endorsement.

(2) Quite apart from the Clinic's agreement, the Clinic is aware that MHPC endorsement is needed for major capital construction programs. Notwithstanding this, the Clinic proceeded without such endorsement.

FEBRUARY 12, 1974

II. REPORT OF AD HOC COMMITTEE WHICH MET WITH THE CLEVELAND CLINIC

Mr. Ginn pointed out that Mr. deConingh, who had been Chairman of MHPC's Ad Hoc Committee, was absent and asked Dr. Robertson to give the report of the Committee's meeting with the Cleveland Clinic committee.

Dr. Robertson reported that the meeting had taken place on January 15 at the Cleveland Clinic Inn. Representing MHPC were Mr. deConingh, Committee Chairman; Mr. Collens; Mr. Calgie; Dr. Walzer; Mr. Podolin and himself. Neither Mr. Ginn nor Mr. Lewin were able to make the meeting. Representing the Cleveland Clinic were Mr. Holden, Chairman of the Board of Trustees; Mr. deWindt and Mr. Hughes, Trustees; Dr. Wasmuth and Dr. Kiser of the Clinic's Board of Governors; Mr. Auble, Secretary of the Cleveland Clinic Foundation and Mr. Lees, Executive Secretary of the Board of Governors.

Mr. Holden had opened the meeting by briefly recounting the history of the Clinic and the nature of its activities as an international teaching, research and tertiary referral center. He highlighted the Clinic's major expansion program now underway and pointed out that to finance it the Clinic had had to borrow $25 million. This large debt, combined with their primary mission of teaching, research and tertiary referral, precluded the Clinic's doing very much in the way of direct primary care. He did discuss the Clinic's efforts in

Collinwood, including the fact that their physicians voluntarily work in that clinic. The Clinic representatives also discussed the program of comprehensive care for their employees and employees' families as well as their plans for cooperative efforts with Metropolitan General Hospital regarding the proposed east side clinic.

Mr. Podolin had given a brief review of MHPC's development, organization and activities and stressed that planning was no longer solely a voluntary matter but was now mandated both through Federal legislation and through specific contractual requirements of Blue Cross. The broad community nature of MHPC and its Board of Trustees was stressed.

Dr. Robertson reported that he and Mr. Calgie expressed clearly to the Clinic how important it was that it be responsive to the needs of the people within the community and that it share the responsibility for meeing the health needs of those people, including primary and emergency health needs. Mr. Calgie stressed the fact that the Clinic had displaced a number of people in its expansion program and that those people expected something in return.

Dr. Robertson indicated that although these remarks were emphatically made, and although there was general discussion on a number of subjects, no specific responses had been received to his or Mr. Calgie's specific suggestions. He reported that no plans had been made for future meetings but that it was his hope that MHPC would contact the Clinic again for another meeting. Dr. Walzer suggested that if there is another meeting that it not be held at the Clinic.

During the discussion of the Committee's report, Councilman Bell referred to discussions the City had had several years ago with the Clinic during which it had indicated plans to provide large-scale outpatient services. It was Councilman Bell's opinion that MHPC should vigorously pursue this matter through another meeting with the Clinic.

It was also pointed out during discussion that patients from the Collinwood clinic who needed hospitalization were referred to hospitals other than the Cleveland Clinic. Questions were raised whether this would not also be the case with respect to Metro's east side clinic.

Mr. Ginn thanked Dr. Robertson for the report and indicated that while the meeting was in no way conclusive, it did apparently represent the beginning of a dialogue which he hoped would continue. He asked Mr. Podolin to contact the Clinic to arrange for a second meeting.

———

Exhibit 6.—*Various Newspaper Articles Re Cleveland Clinic and Center for Health Consumer Affairs*

[From the Cleveland (Ohio) Plain Dealer, May 18, 1974]

CLEVELAND CLINIC NEGLECTS POOR, FORMER CWRU AIDE TELLS PANEL

(By Robert J. Havel)

WASHINGTON—A former program administrator at Case Western Reserve University told a Senate subcommittee yesterday that Cleveland Clinic has reneged on promises to provide health care for the poor. He charged that the areawide health planning agency is a "handmaiden" of the "power apparatus" in Cleveland.

"While urban communities like Cleveland have some 200,000 medically indigent persons, the bulk of health-care dollars goes to institutional expansion without primary care," Charles W. Rawlings told the antitrust and monopoly committee.

The panel is examining the planning, organization, delivery and financing of health care to determine if increased competition might lower costs and improve quality.

Until a year ago, Rawlings headed the Center for Health Consumer Affairs at CWRU. The university refused to approve his application for continued federal aid for the center under pressure from organized medicine, Rawlings told the panel.

The refusal came after the center had raised questions about Cleveland Clinic and Blue Cross of Northeast Ohio and had produced "an amateurish slide show" that said there is too much profit making in the present operation of the health-care system, he said.

Despite promises in 1968 and 1971 by Cleveland Clinic to the Metropolitan Health Planning Corp. to provide medical services for residents in the clinic area, nothing has been done, Rawlings said.

"After six years of promises to the neighborhood and somewhere between $30 million and $40 million in expansion, there is still no health care for the needy folks of the Hough and Central areas at Cleveland Clinic," he added.

Rawlings also charged that Cleveland Clinic is operating beds "in direct and open defiance" of an agreement with the planning agency, headed by the president of Blue Cross.

The private-sector insurance industry and the private, "supposedly non-profit" hospitals make health policy and set priorities, he said, and "area-wide comprehensive health-planning agencies function as handmaidens to such power apparatus," he said.

Rawlings told the committee he was skeptical about the merit of competition in health care.

"Competition produces winners and losers, and the patients would fall in the gaps," he said. "We can't afford to have losers in health care."

He would prefer, he said, a public policy aimed at distributing resources to take care of the impoverished. Planning agencies, he added, need enforcement powers.

Rawlings said that these agencies have "no clear mandate as to what the priorities are."

"They can be tough on the small hospitals," he said, "while the big ones do as they please."

[From the Cleveland (Ohio) Press, May 20, 1974]

ACADEMY OF MEDICINE SAYS ANDERSON ERRED

Anyone who happened to read Jack Anderson's column in The Press on May 13 may have gotten the impression that the Academy of Medcine had "halted low-cost clinics" in this area.

The fact is that the Acedemy helped start the Hough-Norwood Neighborhood Clinic, one of the most successful in the nation in providing health care for the poor. The Academy also approved the University Free Clinic to provide free care to patients in that area and helped find physicians to donate free time to work in the clinic.

Anderson equated Academy opposition to an "innocuous little presentation" by Charles Rawlings, director of the now defunct Consumer Training Program for Health Planning at Case Western Reserve University, with opposition to low-cost health care centers for the poor.

The fact is, Rawlings' program had nothing to do with health care centers. CWRU dropped the program because the academic quality of the program didn't "meet the standards of other university programs . . ." in the words of CWRU Associate Vice-President Donald R. Whitman. Funds for the center were cut off by the Federal Government as a result of overall cut-backs in Public Health Service grants.

The Academy objected to the slide program because it was based on inaccurate, misleading or false information, and presented only Rawlings' personal bias on the matter of health care. It suggested a quite unworkable reorganization of the entire medical care system and offered not one word of advice on how people might take advantage of existing medical services in this area.

The real danger in Anderson's column is his claim that all this was "discovered" by the Senate Antitrust Subcommittee chaired by Sen. Phillip Hart (D-Mich.). He thus tries to lend plausibility to his false charges and erroneous conclusions.

Robert A. Lang, executive director, Academy of Medicine of Cleveland, 10525 Carnegie Ave.

[From the Cleveland (Ohio) Press, May 25, 1974]

RAWLINGS BACKS UP ANDERSON COLUMN

Press readers may be helped by some factual underlining of the issues related to the Jack Anderson column of May 13 about the pressure which caused Case Western Reserve University to close the Center for Health Consumer Affairs.

In his reply to Anderson on May 20, Robert Lang of the Cleveland Academy of Medicine took credit for opposing the consumer center's existence but also claimed federal funds "were cut off . . . as a result of over-all cutbacks." That is factually incorrect. Organized medicine gets all the credit.

Press readers should note that the remedy CWRU officials chose for the alleged academic deficiencies did not consist of securing more competent personnel. Instead, the university eliminated the consumer program altogether.

The Anderson column correctly reported to readers the familiar pattern of American Medical Assn. power exerted to suppress information to the public and block programs which seek innovative changes in the delivery of health care. In this case the Federal Government stood its ground against these pressures and did not cut off or deny funds to the consumer program. The university capitulated under pressure.

Readers of The Press may well ask what it was about a five-person staff that posed so great a threat to the $90 billion dollar health establishment? Consider that the aggregate salaries of the consumer staff barely exceeded the median income of a single physician. ($43,000 annually).

What do health professionals seek to keep the public in the dark about? Mainly the consumer program based its thought on evidence that profit-seeking in health care has caused poor distribution of services to the public and this will be corrected only when public regulation and control of the health industry are asserted.

Charles W. Rawlings, former director, Center For Health Consumer Affairs, Case Western Reserve University.

Senator HART. Our concluding witness for today, to whom reference several times has been made, is Prof. Clark Havighurst of Duke Law School. The professor has written in this area over a long term, and from a point of view that isn't often expressed.

We are especially grateful that you could come.

Mr. CHUMBRIS. Professor, I hope I didn't hurt you with that characterization that you could sell somebody the Brooklyn Bridge, but you did have a very well-written statement.

STATEMENT OF CLARK C. HAVIGHURST, PROFESSOR OF LAW, DUKE UNIVERSITY SCROOL OF LAW, DURHAM, N.C.

Mr. HAVIGHURST. Thank you, Mr. Chairman; and thank you, Mr. Chumbris—I think. Obviously, I have been trying to sell something, but my success has not been as great as I might hope. For example, I have been trying to sell Dr. Caper in particular for a long time. Due to a problem of consumer ignorance, however, I have not yet succeeded, but the educational process continues.

Dr. CAPER. I would like to point out, just for the record, that I am a provider, not a consumer, so I don't know whom you are referring to Mr. Havighurst.

Mr. HAVIGHURST. Mr. Chairman, I am going to summarize the long prepared statement.

Senator HART. The prepared statement will be printed in full in the record.

[The statement referred to appears as exhibit 1 at the end of Mr. Havighurst's oral testimony.]

Mr. HAVIGHURST. As you have indicated, Mr. Chairman, I am a professor of law at Duke University, where I teach courses in the fields of antitrust and regulated industries. I think this subcommittee is in a better position than most people to understand what it is about the health care system which attracts the interests of an academic lawyer with a background in those fields. Indeed, these hearings seem to open up all of the issues concerning health services which I have found to be the most interesting; namely, those which determine whether the competitive market can be relied upon as the primary instrument of social control. Having examined in my published writings both the prospects for a competitive health care system and the implications of adopting various regulatory approaches used in public utility and .common carrier regulation, I have come to the conclusion that market-oriented solutions to the health care industry's problem are preferable to the others which have been attempted or suggested, but that they are in grave danger of being either neglected or rejected too quickly.

It seems to me that the many past failures of the health care system have been unfairly regarded as market failures, and that, in fact, the market has been systematically prevented from serving consumers' interests when it was capable of doing so. Moreover, I have found that legislators' sense of urgency about the need to do something about the many existing problems frequently leads them to intrude even further on the market's ability to function. Even the best-intentioned legislators, it appears to me, frequently exhibit a bias in favor of direct regulatory approaches over approaches which involve improving market performance, since the latter seem less direct—a less direct means of achieving the desired ends—and do not satisfy the politician's predilection for "programs" and regulatory machinery at which he can point with pride.

Having this perception of the policy debate, I have become something of a self-appointed advocate for market-oriented solutions, and I fear that as a result I have been typed as an idealogue, a sort of unreconstructed "free marketeer." My own view, Mr. Chairman, is that the posture in which I find myself results from leaning into a very strong wind. I certainly have never meant to deny Government's responsibility in this field, and I recognize the need for intervention at numerous points to assure the quality of care, accessibility of care, and the market's good performance.

In these remarks, as in my prepared statement, I will try to summarize my reasons for believing that competition can be made to work tolerably well to organize and motivate the health care system—not perfectly, of course, but better than the alternative of a regulated or centrally controlled system. I shall thus be examining only one side of the policy dilemma, since I shall not address myself to the shortcomings of regulation. I believe that this is outside of the immediate scope of these hearings, and I have addressed myself to those matters in some detail in a recent article in the Virginia Law Review. Although I fully recognize the attractiveness of regulatory solutions and cannot pretend to have demonstrated conclusively that they will always fail or be less effective than the market might be, I believe there is one powerful argument why a market-oriented system should nevertheless be given priority in public policy at this time. The argument is simply that the market system can always be scrapped if it fails to perform acceptably after a fair trial, but there is no way of going back to a market system once we have embarked on the course of regulation and ever-increasing central control. Thus, I would submit that Congress bears a very great responsibility if it should commit us to an uncertain but irrevocable course toward greater Government control of the health care system. I regard this subcommittee as the one most capable of illuminating the market alternative and at least seeing that it receives a fair hearing in these halls.

Incidentally, with respect to the regulatory solution, Mr. Rawlings' description of the performance of the planning agencies in Cleveland confirms the predictions of agency behavior that I made in the Virginia Law Review article.

[The articles referred to appear as exhibits 2 and 3 at the end of Mr. Havighurst oral testimony.]

Mr. HAVIGHURST. And that history—as I think your record shows—has been repeated again and again, confirming that the regulatory health planning process tends to be dominated by the regulated interests themselves. Influential parties tend to win, and people who are not so influential tend usually to lose.

Senator HART. Professor, I agree with that, but it need not be that way; or is that being too idealistic.

Mr. HAVIGHURST. As I have said, Senator, one cannot conclude that such regulation could never work, and, in some places and at some times, planning agencies have done some good things. But to take health care and convert it into a politicized enterprise, which is what this involves, is to invite this kind of pressure and this kind of behavior. One is never free from the threat of it.

We know from the experience of other regulatory agencies in other industries that, while there are occasions when the agencies will perform well, there are more occasions when they don't seem to. The general trend over the years has been toward inefficiency and excessive recognition of provider interests.

Although I find it regrettable, as do you, regulation has a high probability of poor performance. Thus, one problem in health care is to weight one imperfect solution—regulation—against another—the market. Of course, reasonable minds can differ about which is least imperfect. And I think that is the issue that you are trying to explore.

Senator HART. My question implied that—I thought or I had the feeling—that our experience with regulation was encouraging.

Now, that is not my feeling—I share your feeling that the track record—whether it is with railroads or real estate—the ideal has not been achieved.

Mr. HAVIGHURST. Of course, that is my impression, too. My Virginia Law Review article does attempt to examine that experience and to see whether or not there is any reason to hope that the regulators of the health care system will perform better than other have done. And I find many reasons for not being hopeful. But, of course, one cannot be certain.

Mr. Chairman, my prepared statement is something of a brief for the market solution, the other side of the policy coin which is being tossed. The statement may appear to be excessively tendentious at a number of points. This results in part from my characterizing aspects of the health system in the language of antitrust, including references to monopoly, cartels, market division, entry barriers, and so on. Fortunately, this subcommittee can understand this language as more than mere rhetoric and may feel as I do that it provides both a useful means of conceptualizing the problems and a needed antidote to the euphemisms which the health world uses to obscure the ways in which beneficial market forces have been systematically repressed. The rest of my oral remarks will employ this language, hopefully in a way which you will find enlightening.

I think it is useful to conceptualize each physician's ability to dominate the physician-patient relationship as being essentially monopolistic. The consumer's ignorance and dependency and his willingness to pay for the things the doctor says he needs tend to make the provider rather than the consumer sovereign in this field. Of course, the individual practitioner's monopoly is a "natural" one, flowing from the nature of the service and the market, and it is not a matter for antitrust action. However, the combination of doctors in professional societies to preserve and strengthen their individual monopoly power is indeed a cause for public concern. Unfortunately, when the medical profession exalts and righteously defends the so-called doctor-patient relationship, its primary concern may be not so much ethical as economic, flowing from the natural desire of monopolists to protect their relationship with the consumers they exploit. While I, too, value the doctor-patient relationship, I am also aware of criticism that the doctors have made it too one-sided, not only as a matter of economics but also in human terms.

Consumer ignorance is, of course, a major feature of the health services marketplace, but I do not believe that it precludes a market-oriented solution, as many seem to assert. For one thing, consumers can determine many of the things which matter in health care, and I would therefore be reluctant to limit their opportunities for choice too sharply. Beyond this, there are numerous ways in which the market can generate corrections for the problem of consumer ignorance on technical matters. This is not the only area where consumers are at a substantial disadvantage in assessing the quality of goods and services, and I do not regard this market as unique.

My prepared statement briefly examines some of the ways in which advertising, brand names, dealer reputation, and certification programs are used to give consumers either useful information or assurances which adequately substitute for it. It also examines the possibilities for giving the consumer direct purchasing assistance through various organizational adjustments. Finally, it observes the appropriateness of Government intervention in the furnishing of information to consumers.

The problem of third-party payment is, to my mind, a somewhat more serious one than consumer ignorance, but here again the market is capable of generating solutions. One set of solutions would get competing health insurers more deeply involved in the controlling of provider decisionmaking with a view to reducing costs and thereby increasing the marketability of their respective insurance plans. I speculate in the prepared statement about how the market would look if insurers were able to compete actively in cost control.

This subcommittee has itself investigated problems which insurers confront in attempting to control costs incurred by fee-for-service providers. My statement mentions these problems, but concentrates on the experience in Oregon in the 1940's, which is reflected in the trial record in the case of *United States* v. *Oregon State Medical Society*, 343 U.S. 326 (1952). In that case, it appears that the medical society there established a Blue Shield plan and allowed it to engage in disciplinary pricing as a means of bringing other insurers, which had actively engaged in cost control, around to the medical society's way of thinking about the inappropriateness of second-guessing physicians' decisions.

Although the Government lost the Oregon case, it is my view that the concerted establishment of a Blue Shield plan for the purpose of strengthening the monopoly power of individual physicians should have been found unlawful under both sections 1 and 2 of the Sherman Act.

The other way in which the market can respond to the distortions which third-party payment necessarily create is, of course, through the HMO device.

Because HMO's are paid in advance rather than retrospectively, they have an incentive to conserve their resources and to seek efficiency in providing needed treatment. Precisely because the prepayment feature of HMO's leads them to conserve resources, their presence in the marketplace is felt by the fee-for-service sector as a pressure to reduce costs. This subcommittee has already heard testimony regarding the report prepared under the auspices of the Institute of Medicine of the National Academy of Sciences entitled, "Health Maintenance Organizations: Toward a Fair Market Test."

This statement rather dramatically illuminates the possibility that HMO's will spring up spontaneously in a market where obstacles to their creation have been removed. Precisely to the extent that the fee-for-service system, as currently financed and organized, contains substantial "fat," a market opportunity for HMO's exists. Given a chance, they should be able to offer consumers an adequate service at a rate which substantially undercuts health insurance premiums.

The simplest conceptualization of HMO's and their potential market impact is as a close substitute for the services sold by the fee-for-service monopoly. Because of the immense practical difficulty of altering the numerous economic and political conditions which foster the monopoly power of individual fee-for-service providers—namely, consumer ignorance, provider control of demand, third-party payment, inhibitions on insurer competition based on cost control, and so on—creation of opportunities for independent marketing of a substitute service is probably the best policy alternative currently available. In technical terms, introduction of such a substitute tends to flatten the demand curve for the monopolized service, lowering the monopolist's profit-maximizing price. If consumers find the two services reasonably interchangeable, "cross elasticity of demand" is high, and the monopoly of one service is of lessened, or no, consequence. Here I cite the *Dupont Cellophane* case.

The so-called HMO strategy, best articulated in the Institute of Medicine report, is designed precisely to make it possible for HMO developers to outflank the fee-for-service system, marketing independently a proven method of health care delivery which should prove an attractive alternative to the existing system. Advocacy of a "fair market test" for HMO's means simply that the market should be given a chance to solve the problems which past restraints on the market's operation have created. While the Institute of Medicine report's agenda of needed policy initiatives to make the market viable is a lengthy one, this course toward major improvements in the health care system can be charted with greater confidence than any other which has yet been proposed.

My prepared statement does not attempt to retrace the ground covered in the Institute of Medicine report, but I recommend that report to the subcommittee as presenting the conceptual framework in which HMO's can best be understood and as identifying the problem areas which must be addressed in legislation at either the State or Federal level. I should perhaps mention that I was a member of the Committee which produced that document.

The prepared statement contains a rather lengthy critique of the HMO Act of 1973, which I regard as a "white elephant," likely to spawn HMO's which are themselves white elephants, beautiful perhaps to look at but oversized and essentially clumsy when it comes to delivering the kind of care which people want. My criticism is that while the legislation attempts to create an ideal type of HMO, which may or may not be viable in the marketplace, it at the same time creates or perpetuates obstacles to the creation of HMO's of other types, which in my view, would prove more viable and more competitive in the long run. In each of its numerous restrictive provisions, the HMO Act of 1973 appears to opt for increasing the likelihood of monopoly in health care delivery by guaranteeing that HMO's will be of very large size. The subcommittee will appreciate that legislation dictating market concentration is unlikely to generate active competition.

The prepared statement also addresses the subject of foundations for medical care as another obstacle to HMO development. The discussion focuses specifically on how the antitrust laws would affect foundations, applying Sherman Act principles to determine whether the collective establishment by medical societies of prepayment plans can be justified as anything more than a further defensive activity of the medical cartel, as in the *Oregon Medical Society* case. The argument gets quite technical and tightly reasoned and the conclusion remains uncertain. On the one hand, foundations' opportunities for foreclosing HMO development by raising entry barriers are very great, and it is far from clear that it would not be better to encourage insurers to compete independently in cost control rather than allowing cost control efforts in the fee-for-service sector to be monopolized by the foundations. On the other hand, in some limited circumstances, foundations seem to me to be possibly justified as a market response to HMO competition, one which confirms my argument that HMO competition will induce responsive change in the fee-for-service sector.

The prepared statement, operating on the assumption that the foundation operates in a market where independent HMO's have gotten a competitive toehold and that insurers have been found a weak and inadequate mechanisms for bringing cost and utilization controls to bear on the fee-for-service sector, provides some guidelines for judging the foundations under the Sherman Act. The subcommittee will find that the line I have drawn for foundations to walk is a very narrow one. It seems probable, however, that the blessing which the foundations have received in the HMO Act of 1973 will permit them wider scope than I believe should be tolerated.

The prepared statement also addresses the subject of PSRO's which are another cartellike approach to solving the health care industry's problems. The PSRO, like the foundation, is a device for in effect monopolizing fee-for-service care, allowing standards to be set in such a way that the welfare of the cartel members is maximized within the constraint that greater governmental intervention will attend efforts to extract too much profit from the cartel. Putting these issues aside, however, the statement addresses the serious problem which attends giving PSRO's jurisdiction over HMO's.

Believing as I do in the need for competition between HMO's and the fee-for-service sector, I can hardly be enthusiastic about letting PSRO's regulate the quality of care and utilization in HMO's. The Institute of Medicine Committee took something of a "wait and see" position on this point, and I wrote a separate statement because I could see no basis at all for doubting that one of two equally pernicious outcomes would occur.

The most obvious possibility is the PSRO's will regulate HMO's in the interest of minimizing their competitive impact. This means imposing in the name of quality, standards which are so high that HMO's costs would be well above what they would otherwise be.

The other possibility, and probably the greater likelihood, is that HMO representatives will participate in PSRO standard setting and will be able to prevent the worst excesses of anti-HMO regulation. But this is no answer to the problem at all, for it will lead to conspiracies in restraint of the very competition which should be preserved against all of the threats which can be mounted against it. Gentlemen's agreements not to compete, to divide markets and to restrict fledgling HMO's, or those which threaten to compete too hard, are perfectly predictable by reference to a law of human nature first announced by Adam Smith.

I see no way that Federal oversight or anything else can change the essential outcome of putting competitors together to negotiate their differences, with governmental sanctions to enforce the agreements reached. I do not, of course, deny that HMO's need to be watched to assure the quality of care delivered. But surely there are better ways of assuring quality than delivering HMO's into the hands of their competitors.

The final point addressed in the statement regarding HMO's prospects has to do with their treatment under so-called certificate-of-need laws. These laws present special problems for HMO's and I would favor a total exemption for them, or at least an exemption from certification requirements for their outpatient facilities. I discussed this problem at length in the Virginia Law Review article. One reason for my concern is that the planners who must pass on HMO developments are likely to have the same preferences as the draftsmen of the HMO Act of 1973 for one big HMO under safe management over a variety of competing HMO's of different shapes, sizes, and sponsorship. A competitive market is impossible if entry is regulated by people who think that something called "pluralism" is all we need. While many people confuse pluralism with competition, I think that this subcommittee will recognize that they are not necessarily even remotely similar. Perhaps it's enough simply to point out that even the AMA professes to believe in pluralism.

In conclusion, Mr. Chairman, let me say I have not brought with me a legislative blueprint, other than a few isolated suggestions and the agenda contained in or suggested by the Institute of Medicine report on HMO's.

More importantly, I have emphasized the need for Congress to attach a high level of commitment to competition in health services. Promotion of competition must be an explicit, high-priority objective, and every piece of health legislation should be subjected to careful evaluation in light of this goal. Whatever form national health insurance may take, it should be tailored to maximize competition, rather than allowed to foreclose it further.

Because compromise with a policy of competition can be costly it should not be permitted to occur. Unfortunately, such compromises are occurring all of the time in this industry. While paying lip-service to pluralism, health planners and legislators are stifling competition in the belief that retention of limited consumer choice is all that is required. The result is a pallid and inadequate substitute for a dynamic, competitive market which can adjust quickly to new circumstances and correct its own faults.

This subcommittee has a peculiar responsibility as a watchdog of competition in the economy and I hope it will expressly assume this role with respect to the market for health services.

Thank you.

Senator HART. Professor, thank you. I am committing to you that I shall read, much more carefully than I was able to, your full text.

I profess that I am only up to page 14 and that was a leaf reading, but it is the first time I have seen what you would call traditional antitrust ideas applied to the problem of health care delivery, and it is very interesting.

Mr. HAVIGHURST. Antitrust is a powerful too, as you know.

Senator HART. It is. But I have a hangup to discuss, then I will turn you over to the staff. I have a hangup when you talk about antitrust being a powerful tool against a piece of the economy which is largely in the hands of professionals and professions.

Maybe the antitrust tool is powerful against foundries or boiler-makers. Traditionally it has been held to be not available when we are talking of lawyers or doctors.

I guess in both cases they are beginning to show signs of life, but, aren't medical services local and involve personal services of the medical profession?

Wouldn't you as a general rule say that antitrust is not available?

Mr. HAVIGHURST. Senator, what you say is true. There are significant doubts that one can advance about whether antitrust is available because of problems in meeting the jurisdictional requirements of the Sherman Act. For example, there has been a sort of informal exception carved out for the learned professions, courts being more or less unwilling to plunge deeply into treating a professional as just another tradesman. I think historically, at common law, doctors were treated like everybody else engaged in trade, and the law of restraints of trade was applied to physicians. There is nothing in the Sherman Act that says that should not still be so.

I am attended by language of the district judge in Virginia who held that a minimum fee schedule of lawyers was a violation of the antitrust laws. He said that setting minimum fees was "the least learned part of the profession," and I take it that that points us in the right direction; namely, that we ought to consider wnere the activities of professions are legitimate and where they begin to encroach on economic performance. Unfortunately, that decision was recently reversed in a 2-1 decision which gave more substance to the "learned profession" exemption than it had ever had before.

Nevertheless, the possibility is still present for judges and the antitrust division to look with considerably more skepticism than in the past on activities of professions. Certainly the evidence which you have begun to collect in this hearing adds to the record of information that leads us to recognize that medical societies have engaged very substantially in anticompetitive practices over a period of time.

They have often attempted to justify their anticompetitive practices in terms of ethics. Well, we have heard that before. Many other industries have talked of ethics and have attempted to enforce ethical behavior among their members, but when one looks at it carefully—and fortunately in these other areas the courts have been persuaded to do so—one finds that they are simply restraining trade. I think we are now in a position where we can use economic analysis to separate out those things that professionalism may, in fact, provide a defense for, and yet recognize that it doesn't provide a defense for everything that might be done under its name.

Senator HART. Let me interrupt you there. You may not have read the testimony that this subcommiteee received a few days ago describing certain practices in the State of Texas.

The allegation is that the State medical society had a foundation for medical care to sort of torpedo the HMO, and doctors were intimidated, as the allegation went, to participate in certain health delivery plans that offended the traditional physician.

Now, I know it won't be off the top of your head. I know you have thought about it a long time. To what extent, if those allegations were true, can existing antitrust law guard against them?

Mr. HAVIGHURST. There are lots of problems, Senators, as you recognize. Let me tick off a few. I've looked quickly at the evidence, the allegations as to the situation in Texas. I'm not sure I've been able to digest it all and I don't want to really speak specifically about the Texas situation. But I think I can speak about the class of cases in which that case might fall.

The great problem, of course, is that as government involves itself more and more deeply in the decisionmaking in this field, and takes over more and more of the control of the system, antitrust becomes less and less a viable device. We've got—in this field, particularly—the McCarran-Ferguson Act, which says that the States control in the area of insurance. We also have the doctrine of *Parker* v. *Brown*, which says that States have a certain, not very well-defined, power to exempt activity from the antitrust laws through legislation.

We have the *Noerr* case, which suggests that political activity by trade associations is protected against antitrust scrutiny by essentially, the first amendment. And when you add that all up, it sounds like it would be very hard to attack a medical monopoly which was based in part on the political power of a medical society exercised through the State legislature through the State board of medical examiners, and through other State entities.

Nevertheless, there are some possibilities, I think that we might entertain. If the situation in Texas or in any State was a serious one—allegations are that in Texas it is serious—one might begin to devise a theory based on section 2 of the Sherman Act. I guess I would treat it as a conspiracy to monopolize; that is, I would regard the matter as one of collective activity by the medical society dedicated to the strengthening and preservation of individual monopolies enjoyed by fee-for-service practitioners in the State.

One could, I think, begin to accumulate a long list of exclusionary practices which the society had engaged in in pursuit of monopolistic end. For example, there were allegations about violations of State law in Texas, both by the medical society and by the agencies they allegedly dominate politically, and I believe that all of that illegal activity could be treated as an exclusionary practice for purposes of section 2. The exclusion of HMO's also seems to me to be easily includable as an exclusionary practice, and any activity which had that effect or which seemed to have been undertaken with that intent would place the medical society in a position of considerable jeopardy.

The alleged attempts to monopolize the peer review process, the PSRO mechanism, on a statewide basis would seem to me to contribute to monopoly as well, because it is a way of making sure that the PSRO mechanism will not substantially interfere with the monopolistic practices of individual practioners. Intimidation and harassment of doctors who deviate in any way from the kind of medical care delivery that the society approves would seem to me to add to the weight of evidence in this area. Domination of Blue Cross and Blue Shield would also, I suppose, have some effect as well, since those plans effectively preclude other methods of cost control particularly those introduced by insurers, as in Oregon in the 1940's. Finally, I suppose the activities of the foundation plans, which are sponsored by medical societies, would also add to the record that one would want to make.

I have a sense, Mr. Chairman, that in areas of this kind, where trade associations are engaged in activities that come close to the line, if you will, the court should shift the burden of proof from the plaintiff—the government or some private plaintiff—so as to require that the reasonableness of the activity be established by the defendant. For some inexplicable reason, the courts in the past have said that if it's not a per se offense then the plaintiff bears the burden of establishing the unreasonableness of whatever activity the defendant was engaged in. It seems to me that the policy of the Sherman Act is altogether the other way—that collective activity of competitors is inherently suspect—and that the burden of proof is a convenient way of giving effect to that basic policy. I would therefore hope that the medical society would have to justify what it was doing rather than that the Government would have to establish in each case that somehow the proffered justifications were not legitimate and that the ethical considerations advanced weren't the true reasons or weren't adequate to justify what was being done. The burden of proof has a great deal to do with the outcome of cases of this kind, as I think you would agree, because the judge will often find himself in a position of having to balance conflicting values and may feel that the government has to carry the weight, the substantial burden, of establishing that the reasons advanced—the professions of the profession, if you will—are not in fact the real motives.

In short, I would like to see it tried. I think a substantial antitrust victory against the medical profession would be one of the most fortunate developments that could occur in trying to get the health services marketplace in order.

Senator HART. Thank you for making that point for the record.

Mr. HAVIGHURST. Senator, there was a small technical point that I might mention. I think you referred to it, but I didn't touch on it in my response. This is the interstate commerce issue.

For many years there have been cases that seem to say that, when medical services are involved, the antitrust laws don't apply because the case involves only a local market and there is no interstate impact.

In the case of *Burke* v. *Ford*, the Supreme Court more or less established that it's not important that the activities be in interstate commerce. It's enough that they have a substantial impact on interstate commerce. That principle was only recently applied in the health field in a case in the third circuit, *Doctors, Inc.* v. *Blue Cross*. The fourth circuit has been much harder to convince, I regret to say.

The impact test seems rather easily satisfied to my mind. Certainly the substantial flow of medical supplies and drugs in this industry is a persuasive circumstance. Perhaps even more important is the impact on the cost of health insurance.

Insurance, as we know from the care, Southeastern Underwriters is interstate commerce, and clearly the restraints of trade which we are talking about here do affect the cost of health insurance. It seems to me that the case is not even a hard one.

Even so, there may be a few restraints which the antitrust laws couldn't reach. I think if a single doctor is denied staff privileges at a single hospital, and it's not part of a scheme to keep HMO's out of the market or something else, it might be hard to use *Silver* v. *New York Stock Exchange* as a basis for, say, giving procedural rights to the doctor in that case. Obviously, the *Associated Press* case would also have a certain bearing since the need for access to the hospital is very great. If a physician can't get into a hospital he has a hard time practicing medicine. The *Associated Press* case calls for opening up monopolies of that kind more widely. Nevertheless, the interstate commerce issue seems to me to be present in that case, and it might be one area that one couldn't eventually reach by using the antitrust laws.

Senator HART. Whatever may happen in connection with antitrust action against organizations of lawyers or the bar, even if ultimately it is held that those are beyond the reach of the antitrust law, it doesn't necessarily affect the activities of the medical profession because of that flow of dollars and the insurance, that you just were talking about, across the State lines.

Mr. HAVIGHURST. That's entirely correct. I certainly agree.

Senator Hart. Well, before I ask the staff to develop their questions, I think it would be useful, almost in your own defense, if I read two passages which I noted in my hurried reading of your first 14 pages.

On page 5—and this is from your Virginia Law Review article— which before we forget, we should put it into the record, following your statement.

Mr. GRANFIELD. Yes, Mr. Chairman. He has an article that appeared in the Duke University Law Contemporary Problems Series.

Senator HART. Both of those articles should be printed following your testimony.

[See exhibits 2 and 3 at the end of Mr. Havighurst's oral testimony.]

Senator HART. At page 5, in a passage from the Virginia Law Review article, you say:

It is not inaccurate to view the fundamental health policy choice as being between a system controlled directly or indirectly by essentially well-meaning providers who accommodate their public responsibilities with their own self-interest and a system of social control by impersonal market forces allowing consumers a larger impact and assigning Government the less intrusive roles of promoter of the competition and referee.

And then on page 10 you say:

It is certainly true that as long as fee-for-service medicine with extensive third-party payment is the exclusive mode of health care delivery, the market cannot work efficiently.

Now, then, skipping to page 11:

Without Government involvement and the Blues' dominance in the insurance industry the market would have behaved quite differently.

Now, the question is how effective can HMO's be, and how disciplined can the marketplace be?

Senator HART. Mr. Sharp?

Mr. SHARP. Thank you, Senator.

Professor Havighurst, you say in your prepared statement that the free market can do the job of regulating the cost and quality of medical care, despite widespread consumer ignorance.

Do you believe that this is realistic today?

Mr. HAVIGHURST. Mr. Sharp, I think consumers are ignorant about most things they do, but it's obvious, I guess, that consumer ignorance is particularly important here since mistakes can be serious. If a consumer buys the wrong thing in this market, the consequences can be, in fact, fatal. That's true in some other markets, but perhaps one is more conscious of it here.

This circumstance justifies some kind of regulation—to guarantee that minimum quality standards are, in fact, adhered to. Licensure of physicians, for example, I've never chosen to dispute, though I think we could improve the way the licensure system works in order to make it a better, quality-assurance mechanism.

I believe rather strongly that to protect consumers further we need a better system of compensating patients who are, in fact, injured in the system. The medical malpractice system seems to me to be seriously defective and I have prepared in another article a no-fault approach to the problem of medical malpractice. It borrows the workmen's compensation model, using experience-rated insurance as a way of keeping providers attentive to the quality of the outcomes they're getting in treating their patients. That conception is still a long way from being embodied in law, of course.

Senator HART. That would be slow, I'm sure.

Mr. HAVIGHURST. Nevertheless, I would hope we could in time develop such a mechanism of quality control to protect the consumer against the consequences of bad choices by improving incentives for providers to perform well, and putting out of business, in fact, those that perform badly.

In spite of these problems, anyone who would use consumer ignorance as an excuse for doing away with the market altogether is, in fact, dedicated to doing away with the market not to evaluating the evidence. There are lots of ways that markets, can in fact, give people either information they can use or assurances which substitute adequately for information; my statement talks about some of those ways, although it's not meant to be a thorough examination of all of the possibilities. But the main thing to observe is that consumer ignorance is, to a large extent, the product of the medical conspiracy. It is a result of repression of advertising and of those modes of practice which may give consumers something more to rely on than just the individual doctor and his seeming reputation.

Given a chance to get established in the marketplace, HMO's would earn over time—and maybe not quickly—a reputation for doing well or not so well, and consumers would be able to rely on that reputation and on their own experiences in repeated dealings with that particular provider. So ignorance should not be disabling. My conclusion is that the issue has been exaggerated by people who don't want a market system for reasons of their own. Careful analysis doesn't lead to that conclusion.

Mr. SHARP. You mentioned medical malpractice and I just would like to introduce into the record at this point a report prepared for the HEW Secretary's Commission on Medical Malpractice dealing with the incidence of iatrogenic injuries—injuries that occur because of the treatment.

And I will just read into the record one portion of it. This bears exactly on your points concerning consumer ignorance and medical malpractice.

It says here:

Finally, making use of the available data, projections for both hospitals were made for the estimated 23,750 patients discharged during 1972.

The projections indicated that 1,780 patient injuries occurred; 517 of the injuries were due to negligence, but only 31 claims were filed against the hospital or medical staff on behalf of patients discharged during that year.

Senator HART. It will be received.

[The document referred to appears as exhibit 4 at the end of Mr. Havighurst's oral testimony.]

Mr. SHARP. Mr. Havighurst, as long as insurance companies and Government pay 64 percent of the personal medical care bill in this country today, neither patients nor providers have any incentive to control cost.

My first question is: How can a relatively uncontrolled market function in that setting?

Mr. HAVIGHURST. The insurance system, third-party payment, in effect externalizes costs. And it externalizes them to a degree that is quite serious. It creates, for example, the problem of hospitals overexpanding. We've heard testimony this morning about how proprietary hospitals tend to enter the market and expand excessively. Other hospitals do as well. The Cleveland Clinic, I guess, is a good example. That problem results from the fact that unlike other industries, in this industry we have pretty much given a guarantee that if you can get a patient into the bed the price that you'll get for selling that service will be compensatory; cost reimbursement by insurance companies and other third-party payers provides that guarantee. In other industries you don't have that guarantee, and if you decide to build a facility and thereby create excess capacity all you do is lower prices to the point where nobody makes any money. Therefore, you have a disincentive to build the facility in the first place—unless you have some reason to think you're going to be more efficient than the other firms in the industry and will be able to outlast them—in which case, I take it, we should encourage growth in that industry.

Well, the same problem exists with respect to any medical decision— that is, the tendency not to count the true cost. And, therefore, if insured fee for service is the exclusive means whereby health services are provided and paid for, one can't rely on the market.

What is proposed, then, is several things. First of all I discuss the possibility that insurers in a market of that kind would recognize that they're paying more for services than they probably ought to have to pay. They would also recognize that if they would intervene in some fashion to control costs by controlling what the doctors do, by controlling what hospitals they'll do business with, by restricting what they'll pay for a day in the hospital, and by a variety of other things, they might be able to provide the same service or at least nearly the same service, a very adequate service, for less money, thereby attracting more customers and thereby generating, in fact, a competitive influence on all other insurers to do the same thing. In time one would find that insurers competing in this way would be able to bring costs down substantially. In other words, the third-party-payment system has within it the potential, at least, for introducing controls that would be useful in the consumer's interest.

That's what happened in Oregon in the 1940's and that's what the medical profession stamped out by starting their own Blue Shield plan. Now, a lot of problems can be raised with that particular approach. One might be troubled, for example, by the possibility of lay interference in medical decisionmaking. I have no opinion on that. I don't know how serious a problem it might be. I could imagine, however, that it could be done in a way that would not be dangerous. I suggest, in passing, that maybe a piece of legislation that regulated the extent to which insurers engaged in this practice, or the manner in which they engaged in it, would be useful. Such a law would also have the effect of legitimizing insurance company to second-guessing of provider decisions in a way that is not legitimate today.

Perhaps a more valuable mechanism for dealing with this issue, though, is the HMO, which has incentives which are altogether the opposite of fee-for-service providers. Because HMO's have an incentive to conserve in the use of resources, once they're present in the market, the insured fee-for-service system, would also have to take costs into account. Each insurance company, or the fee-for-service system as a whole as monopolized through PSRO's or foundations for medical care, would have to control costs within itself. And that's where I expect the HMO to ultimately have the greatest impact. That's not our typical model of a perfect marketplace, of course, but it might be that if people could choose between the heavily cost controlled plans and ones that were not so cost-controlled they would express their preferences as they do in all other areas, for Cadillacs or Volkswagens or Pintos. One way or another consumer preferences for cost and other things would sort themselves out. And it seems to me that's where the decisions ought to be made.

Nevertheless, I think this is the area that creates the greatest problems and I certainly must admit that we do not yet have clear evidence that the market will solve it completely. But we've certainly not given it a chance to be tested.

Mr. SHARP. After the subcommittee's commercial health insurance hearings in 1972, the American Medical Association had its meeting, I believe, on the west coast, and the Aetna Life & Casualty Insurance Co. went out to the west coast and said, "All right. We now want to work with the doctors and work up some methodology for controlling provider costs."

And the American Medical Association, as reported in the paper, slapped the wrists of the Aetna Life & Casualty Co. and other insurance companies who would dare interfere in attempting cost control.

Well, if you get concerted action such as by organized medicine, how, then, can you get the insurers free to do what you are suggesting?

Mr. HAVIGHURST. I regard that kind of collective professional activity as monopolistic. The Oregon situation seems to me to be as clear a case as one could have to reveal the way in which the collective power of the profession can be used to stop this kind of control being exerted on the physician-monopolist. I would hope we could find a way to use the antitrust laws to deal directly with that problem. It seems to me that it's one that could be dealt with directly, although there may be some State laws which would make it difficult to——

Mr. SHARP. There is another practical problem. There is a practical problem involved in that the commercial health insurance company policy runs to the policyholder—it does not run to the provider, for example, as does the Blue Cross.

Their contracts run with the hospital. The Blue Shield's service contracts run with the doctors. Therefore, with Blue Shield you could have some hope of societal pressure to negotiate the contract between Blue Shield and doctors; likewise with the Blue Cross and the hospitals.

But with the commercial health insurance companies, they are merely fiscal intermediaries and how are we to go about this as a practical matter, with the hundreds of thousands of hospitals and as many doctors in this country, and a thousand commercial health insurance companies?

How do you have this policing of cost by these commercial companies where there is really no nexus of jurisdiction?

Mr. HAVIGHURST. I recognize that problem. The first step, of course, is to deal with the Blue Shield plans. One wonders who is being "shielded" from what, and my sense is that they, in fact, shield the profession from the kinds of cost controls that they find unacceptable. It would be strong medicine, I suppose, to even suggest that the Blues ought to be removed from their preferred position, but I think that would probably be necessary if one were going to rely on insurers to, in fact, provide the cost controls we need.

Beyond that, one would have, I think, to contemplate the ways in which the insurers could establish more direct relations with providers. I would predict that they would do so by approaching providers and saying, "Will you or won't you cooperate with our cost control program? If you will, we will then pay for the care rendered by you to our insureds. If you won't, we won't. Or else we will only do so if we agree with what you're doing and will advise our insureds accordingly." Now, that is not the world we've lived in; it's not a world we've ever seen, except maybe in Oregon in the 1940's; and I'd like to know more about that world and may do some more research to find out what it was like. But it's not an impossibility, it seems to me, and I would like to see a market where it was tried.

Mr. SHARP. Unless there is this kind of control over costs you are speaking of, we do increase the amount of the insurance company and Government payout of dollars for personal health care services, would we not have increased inflation?

Mr. HAVIGHURST. I, of course, would fear that. I might not oppose national health insurance on that basis, but I would hope that it would be done in such a way that competitive opportunities would be opened up, not foreclosed. I would hope that consumers would have some reason for choosing one provider, or insurance, or HMO over another on the basis of cost. If he doesn't get some kind of a rebate from the purchase price he should get at least more benefits one place than another so that he has an incentive to shop on that basis. If one makes the basic benefit package too large, maybe one loses the opportunity to make that a useful form of competition. I'm not sure.

But certainly I subscribe to the general proposition that restructuring of the health care delivery system is a desirable thing, and I regard it as a problem of eliminating monopoly in the purest sense.

Mr. SHARP. But we do need to have realistic cost control some place along the line, or rationing of the service, or absolute price control. Is that fair?

Mr. HAVIGHURST. One could go further, I think, and say that even if one wants to go with the market system, there is a serious transitional problem presented. If one is going to rely on the antitrust laws, it takes years to litigate a case and get things changed in some substantial way. Moreover, the HMO movement will not work overnight. HMO's will not spring up and suddenly be embraced by consumers because they've been waiting for one to happen. In fact, it's a new mechanism, one they don't easily understand; it's not an area where people are likely to leap into the unknown too quickly.

And, consequently, the HMO movement may take some time to get started.

Incidentally, we don't know how effective HMO's will be in competing. It could be that there's a lot less fat in this market than we think there is, in which case HMO's will not be as obvious a success as many of us think they will be. But it seems to me that if HMO's do have the opportunity to enter the market, and if the restraints on their activities are removed, one could then say that at least their potential competition operates to restrain the excesses of the fee-for-service system, that consumers have, in effect, made their choice, that they prefer fee-for-service in large numbers, and that they're willing to pay the cost.

I would suppose, though, that some kind of transitional regulation of, say, the growth of hospitals, of hospital charges, maybe physician as well, would be acceptable. I would hope this could be done in a temporary way, perhaps establishing price ceilings so that competition can go on under those ceilings and can encourage HMO growth, so that in due course we can reexamine the situation and see if, in fact, competition has taken hold. In view of the need to move ahead in the area of national health insurance, perhaps we ought to consider ways of doing the temporizing thing—encouraging this transition to occur and addressing the problem frankly in those terms, instead of setting a regulatory mechanism in place and saying, "That solves the problem for all time." That's where I begin to have great difficulties.

Mr. SHARP. In your Duke Law Review article in 1971, you indicated that doctor controlled foundations for medical care are per se violations of the Sherman Act.

Would you explain your reasoning for this view? And do you still hold this view today?

Mr. HAVIGHURST. That was a fairly academic view, I think. It's an extremely interesting academic question whether or not a trade association that gets together to curb abuses wihin its ranks—and to do nothing else, we'll assume—and thus lowers the prices of the services its members provide, is doing anything illegal under the Sherman Act. Now, their purpose may be to discourage new entry—HMO entry in the foundation case—by making market opportunities less attractive. As far as I know, such entry-limiting behavior in and of itself has never been treated as an antitrust violation. For example, we've never treated it as an exclusionary practice for a monopolist to set a lower price than he might otherwise set as a way of discouraging entry into his business which would erode his monopoly in time. It would be interesting to argue that we should; it's an intriguing academic question which one can play within the classroom, at least.

It seemed to me that the foundation for medical care is a little of that kind. If one accepts the foundation movement at face value, all they are setting out to do is, in fact, to eliminae the worst abuses in the fee-for-service sector. The people bhind the foundation movement are, I think, generally wll-motivatd medical people who are, in fact, concerned about abuses that occur and recognize the need to do something about them. I'm afraid that the way the foundation is sold to the profession as a whole however, is as a protection against HMO entry and against worst kinds of intervention by the Government. And then the foundation movement becomes less attractive, it seems to me. At any rate, I conclude that the foundation for medical care is a rather nicely balanced issue.

I thing ultimately the antitrust issue depends on whether or not you want to see cost control in the fee-for-service sector undertaken by one entity—the foundation or a PSRO—or by a number of entities; namely, the competing insurers, who would each establish their own cost control mechanisms. That's a choice that I think involves great difficulty and I'm not quite prepared to make it myself. I would think this committee, having examined the prospects for more competition in the insurance industry might be in a position to make a judgment about whether that's a viable option. If it is not, then the foundation may be the best way eventually to get some kind of cost control in the fee-for-service sector. It's monopolistic cost control, but at least it's cost control, and if it's a competitive response to actual HMO entry, then it seems to me that maybe we ought to permit it to occur. Indeed, I would probably have the matter turn ultimately on whether we have an actively competitive set of HMO's in the market. If so, foundations seem to be an acceptable means of self-defense for the profession to use.

Mr. SHARP. We had testimony, of course, from the Texas witnesses here Wednesday, that in the Bexar County Medical Foundation situation, the Bexar County Medical Society made no bones about it. They set up the foundation to preempt market and preclude a consumer-oriented HMO. I would take it that this kind of activity is exclusionary, the very type of activity you would be opposed to.

Mr. HAVIGHURST. I regard that as monopolistic behavior. Any attempt to preempt the market, to save it for fee for service, should, I think, be treated as monopolizing conduct.

Mr. SHARP. Do you believe that there is justification—and you have touched upon this briefly—for the Institute of Medicine's statement: "The PSRO provides a mechanism for regulating HMO's and thereby weakening their competitive impact on the market."

Mr. HAVIGHURST. As I think I mentioned, I went somewhat further than the Institute of Medicine report did on that subject, though I notice that Paul Ward's testimony was rather explicit on the point.

I do find it seriously troublesome that PSRO's should be given the job of regulating quality in HMO's. That job should be done by any other entity it seems to me.

Mr. SHARP. Well, in line with this, Mr. Chairman, the subcommittee received from the Louisiana State Medical Society a series of pamphlets requesting the doctors in Louisiana to write their Congressman to repeal PSRO. I wish at this point to introduce into the record this literature from the Louisiana State Medical Society protesting the PSRO's.

Senator HART. It will be received.

[The documents referred to appear as exhibit 5 at the end of Mr. Havighurst's oral testimony.]

Mr. SHARP. Do you feel we can have a consumer-oriented competitive market when free entry allows proprietary for-profit hospitals to provide only profitable services, leaving the community hospitals to provide the unprofitable services?

What is your reaction to this?

Mr. HAVIGHURST. Your question goes to the issue that is usually denominated by the term "cream-skimming." What you're describing is the process whereby certain hospitals—it's usually said to be proprietary hospitals, but they are not exclusively at fault—enter a market and provide only those services which are traditionally the profitable ones in the hospital. This, of course, greatly troubles the existing hospitals which have to compete with them, because they lose the opportunity to overcharge some patients for the purpose of providing services to other patients.

The issue is thus really a financing question: How are we going to finance health care in this country? What is suggested is that it is altogether appropriate for some patients to pay monopoly prices in order to provide other services in the hospital. This process is called "internal subsidization," and we find it in other regulated industries. Indeed it is, in fact, a major feature of all comprehensively regulated industries.

One way that I find it helpful to describe what's being done is to say that regulation is being used to impose a tax. The paying sick are taxed for the purpose of providing services to other sick people who either cannot pay or whose services aren't priced at a level reflecting the costs of providing them. And that tax strikes me as, not the most equitable way of raising money to finance the health care system. Moreover, it is deceptive in that nobody is ever in a position to count the costs of the services that are being subsidized. We don't know if there are some services that are badly needed and really deserving of a public subsidy or not. That seems to have been left pretty much to the hospital administrator to determine.

So I see it as a financing question. I think national health insurance should remove the need to use the hospital as a device for providing these internal subsidies, making some things cheaper and other things more expensive. In my view, the hospital ought not to be a revenue-raising device, providing the financing for the health care system, except insofar as it obtains a payment which is commensurate with the cost of the services provided.

More serious I think, is the problem of what to do once you've decided to finance health care by franchising hospitals to engage in internal subsidization, to impose these hidden taxes and allocate the revenue to uses which they determine are appropriate. That decision requires that we limit entry into the business and it seems to me that creates serious side effects. Indeed, limiting entry tends to remove the very force, potential competition, which I think we should be relying on to keep the system efficient and to provide opportunities for new forms of delivery to enter the marketplace.

Now, having said that, I guess I have to say that as long as third-party payment guarantees that those new hospitals will obtain adequate revenue for the services they provide, we do have a distortion since—and I went through this argument earlier—we've externalized the risk of creating excess capacity in the hospital industry. To the extent we've done that, it seems to me, we have a problem that has to be controlled by the public. Whether certificate-of-need laws are an adequate way of doing that, I'm not sure. My sense is that some kind of moratorium might be appropriate. I see it as a transitional matter, designed to hold the line until we have reached the point where we can rely on the market more actively to control the growth of the system and to allocate resources to it.

Mr. SHARP. Thank you, Doctor.

Senator HART. Mr. Chumbris?

Mr. CHUMBRIS. Thank you, Mr. Chairman.

I am not going to ask the professor any questions. I'm going to leave that to Dr. Granfield. I just wanted to get a little bit of background as to how much time you have spent in relating your thoughts to the health committees of the Senate and the House—the Senate Finance Committee and the House Ways and Means Committee—as to the national health insurance bill and these other bills that I was discussing earlier with the two other witnesses.

Mr. HAVIGHURST. Mr. Chumbris, I haven't worked very hard at communicating my views directly. My thought has been that, having published them, I have at least made them available. Some time ago I testified on H.R. 1, and had an argument with Senator Bennett about whether PSRO's ought to cover the HMO, an argument which I obviously lost. I have also testified on HMO's before the Ways and Means Committee.

I have thought, I guess, that it's more incumbent on them to invite me. I may be wrong in that feeling, but I appreciate the invitation here today particularly. In general, I sense that the staff people may not be very interested in hearing these views, and, therefore, I have not intruded myself.

Nevertheless, I'm available to attempt to illuminate some of these questions for the benefit of those who are working on them.

I know that the legislation you referred to earlier is in the works. My recent writing bears very directly on the proposals that are being entertained. I don't have a great deal more to add to the article that

I wrote in the Virginia Law Review at this time, and I know that they are at least aware of that article and that line of thinking. Perhaps they will take it into account in some fashion.

Mr. CHUMBRIS. Well, I gathered when I talked with Dr. Caper, and the colloquy that you had with him this morning, that at least you two have been doing business in this area.

And I understand that he has some questions that he may ask.

Mr. HAVIGHURST. We have gotten together on a few occasions, but not, I would say, extensively.

Mr. CHUMBRIS. I understand that he probably has some questions that he would like to ask you, so I yield to either Dr. Granfield or Dr. Caper.

Senator HART. Dr. Granfield?

Mr. GRANFIELD. Thank you, Mr. Chairman. Let me first extend a very warm welcome to you, Professor. Being an alumnus of Duke University, it is with great pride that I view your appearance here this morning before the committee.

Let me say it is with greater pride that I view your testimony, viewing problems of the health care industry—and I don't say I endorse all of your policy recommendations—

As a problem of competition, antitrurst, and so forth, in which you take the view of an economist-lawyer in the field of antitrust.

In so doing, you inform us, at least from your point of view, that we ought not to view this industry as unique, or its problems as unique, but rather as simply a generic problem in understanding competition and how to improve competition for consumers.

That, to me, is extremely gratifying because economists at least pretend that with their analytics they can generalize problems and see similar problems in many areas.

Let's deal with, I think, part of the problem of regulation which oftentimes is not brought out. Specifically, I am referring to the problem of regulation; where we have too much regulation.

You have indicated, and Senator Hart has expressed his deep concern, that when we have too little regulation and we set up a regulatory system, either a commission or some other device, the regulated industry gets control of such a device and uses it for cartel purposes.

I think that regulation has before it even a greater challenge, or at least equal challenges, as when we have too much regulation. I specifically refer to, as an example, the Federal Power Commission regulation of natural gas.

Would you care to comment on this? I mean, is it really symmetric, because it's a fine road regulation must travel to produce the kind of results we want for consumers.

Mr. HAVIGHURST. I usually conceptualize the matter as being a rather pure choice between regulation and competition. I guess the choice really is, "Which is to be the primary controlling mechanism?" At some point one passes the point of no return, where the market become impossible, untenable. I hope we wouldn't pass that point and that we would use regulation to improve the market and address it expressly to that purpose, perhaps by setting some minimum standards to protect consumers against their ignorance. I hope we will not allow regulation to replace the market or to prevent the market from functioning in areas where it might well be useful.

The literature on regulation often refers to the so-called tar baby effect. This results from starting down the road to regulate in a small way and when one finds that that doesn't work, regulating a little more. Pretty soon one finds that he can't stop, that he is entangled completely in a regulatory system, and that there is no road going back from it.

We have get to deregulate anything in this country. Indeed, in the wide world, one finds almost no examples of deregulation, though I have heard that in Sweden they've deregulated motor carriers.

Mr. GRANFIELD. Would you agree that at times we impose regulations with the idea of punishing industry for abuses which we perceive or——

Mr. HAVIGHURST. I think the political process lends itself to that kind of response. When an issue is presented, a great deal of vindictiveness can be generated; and the result is a somewhat punitive approach to regulation. I would agree with that.

Mr. GRANFIELD. Would you say that the worst punishment we can condone in any industry is increased competition?

Mr. HAVIGHURST. One finds that they fight awfully hard if one proposes that. Regulatory solutions, on the other hand, often meet considerably less resistance from the industries affected.

Mr. GRANFIELD. You indicated that you would prefer competition to solve some of the problems you perceive in the medical industry.

You have also indicated that you think it would be possible to set up a system where private insurers would impose, through competition for the consumer, some kinds of monitoring device and cost controls in the health industry.

Could you indicate what you think currently? I know you have been over this, but what are the major road blocks occurring now; are they legal, or institutional, or what?

Mr. HAVIGHURST. I am really not familiar with all the legal limitations on insurers' powers. I think some States have laws that would make it very hard for the insurer to ask a question of the doctor.

I think the Blues are a problem because they have, as Mr. Sharp's earlier question indicated, a preferred position in the industry. They tend to be, to a large degree, responsive to industry interests. They are playing more and more a political role, and they are gradually being pressured into doing a little more than they used to do. But I don't find it attractive or hopeful to rely solely on our ability to force the Blues to exercise their monopsony power over the medical profession or the hospitals as a way of solving the problem.

I would be troubled by monopsony as much as, on the part of the insurers nearly as much as I am by monopoly on the part of providers. I think that's partly what the doctors fear, and I think that some kind of regulation of insurers' practices in this area would be justified, in part on that basis and in part to protect the patient against overzealous cost controls by insurers.

Mr. GRANFIELD. Based on our experience with medicare or medicaid, would you be any way apprehensive about seeing the Government as major insurance agent for the national health insurance system?

Mr. HAVIGHURST. That's a hard question. I have not studied either the administration proposal or Mills-Kennedy to the degree that I should have, but I have this impression which I offer in a very tentative way. That the distinction in the roles accorded private health insurance companies in those two programs is not very important.

I don't see that the administration has given the insurers anything very useful to do. They have relied upon PSRO's as the primary cost-control device and I'm virtually certain that they do not contemplate that the insurers, themselves, will engage in cost control. If that's the case, I don't see what useful function competition among insurers is going to perform, and I would not be, I think, any less troubled than by going the Mills-Kennedy route. But it's a tentative impression, and I haven't really examined it in detail.

Mr. GRANFIELD. It's my understanding that at least one of the motivations for PSRO's is the kind of alleged cost excesses that occur as a result of medicare and medicaid, yet you indicate PSRO's at least have a distinct potential; if I may quote:

> The PSRO's would then function as a cartel, allocating markets, defining modes of competition, and denying competitive opportunities to new HMO entrants which might be inclined to offer a different cost-quality mix than was convenient from the standpoint of the providers controlling the PSRO. Established HMO's would be equally anxious to pressure their market opportunities against the threat of such competitive entry.

Also we've received in testimony evidence that PSRO's may be used to extend the alleged cartel or to strengthen it.

Is this your impression: That this is the more likely result of PSRO

Mr. HAVIGHURST. I'm not an all-out opponent of the PSRO idea. I think it turns ultimately on the question of whether insurer-initiated controls would work. And I have indicated I'm not sure about that. Acceptance of the PSRO idea implies that monopolization of the fee-for-service sector is okay, and I could accept this as long as we have a competitive alternative; namely, the HMO.

But, as I've indicated, the problem that I see is in giving the PSRO jurisdiction over HMO's. That is where I begin to have very great trouble. But, that problem aside, PSRO's would behave like a cartel in the fee-for-service sector. It is in their interest to do so, and there is not enough control over their behavior in the law to guarantee that they will not. I see no way that they will not maximize provider incomes, maybe curbing the fringe abuses—the outliers on a bell-shaped curve, if you will—and the things that everyone agrees are terrible but not making much of a dent in the general tendency of the fee-for-service sector to overuse resources.

Now, that means that fee-for-service medicine will probably in the long run be quite expensive. The insurance policy you buy which gives you access to fee-for-service providers will cost a lot. HMO's, if they are available—and I would insist that they be available— would be a good deal cheaper, and I suppose on that basis would attract more consumers. What that suggests is that the market share of fee for service will in fact be smaller under PSRO's or under foundation plans than it would be if you had insurer-initiated cost controls, which would be more effective in keeping the price down and would allow more fee-for-service care to be provided.

Thus, those who say that PSRO's and foundation are the saviour of fee-for-service medicine are, I think, wrong—there will probably be a lot less of it rendered if it's monopolized than if it's not. That's familiar antitrust analysis, I take it.

In any event, I would not favor that kind of cost control over the fee-for-service sector as a whole unless the HMO option is freely available and active competition really occurs.

Mr. GRANFIELD. Let me paint a scenario of what my impression has been of the medical industry in the last 10 years—that's the only period I'm very much familiar with—and see what your comments are.

We perceived the problem back in the early sixties and even before that, but it received a lot more political support that certain portions of our population—the aged, the poor, sometimes both together—were not receiving adequate medical care.

We instituted a system—medicare or medicaid—to hence "solve the problem' by pumping more money into the system.

This money was then used, allegedly, by hospitals to increase their capacity—in many instances their capacity to perform certain, what we call, "Cadillac industry procedures" and exotic techniques to solve this problem.

Some people alleged that medicare and medicaid were not accomplishing their goals. To rectify that we decided that in order to deal with this problem of excess capacity in certain areas, we would set up comprehensive health planning agencies which would prevent such excesses.

You have indicated that one of the roles of comprehensive health planning agencies has been to prevent competition in the industry.

So to solve one problem we impose a form of regulation which increases the monopoly abuses which are already occurring.

Then in order to monitor physicians so that they don't take excessive advantage of this incredible amount of money being pumped into the system, we have PSRO's.

But, of course, to have a successful PSRO, one must have peer review and these, you alleged, may be used as cartelizing devices.

A second layer of regulation once again enhances the potential for regulation. Mr. Sharp indicates, "Let's go one step further. Let's add explicit price controls on doctors."

Now, it seems to me that in the service industry, price controls are about as meaningful as the white elephant you discussed in your paper, because it's so easy to rectify the quantity-quality factors to get the feed you want anyway.

I suspect that after you impose price controls in a frustrated area we will go on from there and socialize medicine to even a greater degree, adding one more layer of monopoly.

What will be the end of the scenario? What is your comment on what would be the most reasonable alternative procedure, to pursue to really get out of this mode where we add monopoly upon monopoly to cure monopolies?

Dr. HAVIGHURST. I have to, I think, accept your description of the situation. Obviously, it is a simplification, but it sketches rather accurately, I believe, the way we're going.

I keep coming back to the HMO as my only hope; and whether it's a realistic hope, of course, one can always dispute. But it seems to me that when you add up the list of things that one would have to do to make it work, you have a really quite powerful argument for giving it a chance. There is also reason to believe that it could be understood and sold in a political marketplace, even where providers have a good deal of power. And I have urged for some time that people accept it as a competitive answer and not merely as a nice way to deliver medical care. I fear that too many people see it simply as a nice thing which we ought to have more of, but don't see it as making the market work in a way that is effective and efficient. Until we embrace the thing fully as a competitive response, I don't think it will ever be as effective as we would want it to be.

Mr. GRANFIELD. My final set of questions deals with this whole issue of HMO's. You've indicated that you were very apprehensive about salutory aspects of HMO's if we subsidize them.

Because if, indeed, they are the response that you've indicated they are, if we subsidize them they become too large—they become comprehensive carriers themselves.

They, too, become yet another threat of monopoly abuse of the market. So I gather from this that you are not in favor of subsidizing HMO's or promoting large comprehensive HMO's to the exclusion of more limited HMO's.

Mr. HAVIGHURST. Yes. I think a subsidy could be justified on a few grounds, though perhaps not large subsidies. One would be that we have a heritage of past restraints of trade. We have consumers who don't yet understand what an HMO is. We have a system in which there are a large number of barriers to HMO entry which are not a product of anything except that we haven't had them in the past. Now, I think subsidies could be used to speed up the process of overcoming that inertia which the system presents. Although I'm not enough of an economist to address this directly, I think there is a kind of infant industry argument that might be advanced. Maybe that's not a respectable line of argument in some circles, but it has certainly been used in the past.

I would, however, say that I don't approve of subsidies simply because HMO's are nice things to have. I think consumers could make those choices themselves and ought to be given the chance to do so. Subsidies simply bias the probable outcome of those choices by making the HMO more attractive pricewise than it would otherwise be.

One could also argue of course, that the fee-for-service system has had its own share of subsidies in the past and that this is an equalizing measure. How much subsidy is appropriate on those principles is, I think, impossible to determine. I would think that some subsidies, but probably not lavish ones, would be justified.

Mr. GRANFIELD. Well, you would agree, though, that it would be a better world if we had a lot of HMO's competing with each other, as well as competing against what you regard as a fee-for-service situation?

Mr. HAVIGHURST. Yes. I, of course, tend to agree that subsidies ought to run to consumers and not to providers in a market of this kind. That's where the subsidies really belong, with those people who can't afford to buy care that we think they ought to have. And I would hope that that would be the direction we would go.

Mr. GRANFIELD. Thank you very much, Mr. Chairman.

Senator HART. Dr. Caper?

Dr. CAPER. Thank you, Mr. Chairman.

Professor Havighurst, I'd like to say first of all that I am delighted to see that the committee accepted my recommendation that you be invited to testify.

I think that you have an interesting point of view and you certainly have spent a good deal of time thinking about these issues.

I still believe, however, that there are some grounds for questioning some of your basic assumptions. Perhaps my point of view comes from my background as much as yours does from your background.

I am not an attorney; I am a physician and I have had, I suppose, a little bit different perspective over the years in forming my views, in forming some of the questions I have about the applicability of marketplace economics to the health care field.

I think that as you point out, in the area of medical services the stakes are often very high. The complexity of the services involved, the jargon, the technical language involved in the health field makes it, I think, more difficult than in some other fields to objectively evaluate the quality and the value of the services the consumer purchases.

In addition, I think that a patient purchasing services which he hopes will cure a disease he has, or improve his health in some way, or perhaps save his life, is not in a position at that time to make an objective, detached judgment concerning the nature of the services he is receiving.

Finally, it seems to me that there is an ethical consideration here. It is a question which has been debated extensively and is still being debated. That is whether as a society the provision of "Cadillac health care" for one person and "Volkswagen health care" for another person is acceptable.

I'm not talking about amenities, whether somebody has French wine put on his hospital menu, but whether discrimination based upon ability to pay is an appropriate marketplace force in the health care industry.

I think Senator Kennedy has made it clear that he thinks it isn't; although some still, I think, believe that it is.

I don't think you share that viewpoint. I don't think you think it is an appropriate marketplace barrier; but some, people, I think, do.

To set the stage for some of my questions I think it is important to examine the HMO Act, which you criticize in your paper, for what it is and what it was intended to be, at least according to my understanding of the committee's intentions.

I think it is plain and simple. It is an attempt to provide Federal assistance in three ways to entities desiring to become HMO's.

It was not in anyway coercive. If an applicant did not wish to comply with the application requirements, or does not wish to comply with the application requirements, there is nothing in the act that says he must change the way he does business.

It is simply a device to try to stimulate what I think has ended up to be very modest degree of change in the health care industry. I assume that you would approve of that type of activity.

Where you criticize the legislation is the extent to which it sets standards which may differ from standards prevalent in the remainder of the health care industry.

The question there supposedly is whether the requirements for qualifying for assistance under the Federal act are stringent enough to discourage applicants from taking advantage of the incentives provided under the act, which I think, even though the amount of dollars in the act are limited—I believe there are other strong incentives within the act to make HMO more attractive for them to attempt to qualify for that assistance, specifically, I think that the mandated multiple choice provision is perhaps the most potent provision of the act. It stipulates that any HMO complying with the definitional requirements of the act must be offered as an option by any employer covered under the Fair Labor Standards Act as long as the cost to the employer is no greater than his existing health plan.

The intent of that, obviously, is to greatly increase the market demand for the services of HMO's that meet the definitional requirements of the act. Of course, there is a provision that would supersede certain restrictive statutes such as ones we heard described earlier this week. The legislation which was finally enacted in December 1973 underwent the most extensive debate of any legislation I have ever seen come out of that committee since I have been on the staff—which has been 3 years—and, I am told, was the most controversial legislation ever to come out of that particular committee.

And I think it is probably because it addressed the issue of the nature of the health care delivery system in Federal law for the first time. Legislation previously passed by the Congress and existing Federal law—almost without exception—does not address the issue of the nature of the delivery system and the set of incentives existing in the delivery system.

So, I believe that that was one of the reasons it generated so much controversy. As you know, the legislation was 2 years in the making from the time our sub-committee began working on it until the time it was finally enacted. It passed the Senate twice. It passed the House and was signed by the President, finally, last December.

I think there is one more question concerning whether the standards described in the legislation will discourage the entrance of HMO's into the marketplace. I think that question is still an open one and won't be decided for some time. I think there is apprehension not only on the part of the fee-for-service sector about the HMO legislation because it is a challenge to the patterns of practice which have been prevalent in this country for many years but also to the HMO's, themselves, because it requires many of them to do things that they are not now doing.

As I said earlier, whether the requirements are too stringent or not remains to be seen. I think from what I have heard the committee is going to be watching these developments closely, and if the requirements turn out to be too stringent they will be reexamined.

Mr. HAVIGHURST. What would the test be to determine whether they were too stringent?

Dr. CAPER. I think one of the important tests will be in seeing how the program is implemented—how rapidly.

Mr. HAVIGHURST. Whether there are HMO's that meet those requirements and that can actually be sold?

Dr. CAPER. That is right. Whether HMO's come forward to take advantage of the assistance under the act.

Mr. HAVIGHURST. Of course, I would apply a different test; namely, whether consumers would choose all of those things that you require if they had a choice of a different package or a different provider. Whether it is the most efficient way to run a health care system can't be determined by subsidizing one class of HMO's and not another.

Dr. CAPER. Well, I think those are questions that have to be considered, but I don't want you to go away with the impression that the issues weren't examined and weren't considered fully, because I am sure that the Senate and the House very carefully scrutinized every provision in that act, and people who were representing all points of view came forward and made their stand. Some were persuasive and others weren't.

I think whether or not the legislation will be successful in achieving its goals remains to be seen. Now there are several, as you call them, subsidies, I would like to think of them as forms of assistance. The HMO Act is intended to capitalize the cost of organizing health services, and to help the HMO defray some of its cost of initial operations prior to the time it can become self-sufficient. In other words, the purpose of the act, as I understand it, is to infuse capital into the health system to induce change to occur. The HMO's are on their own after 3 years—and if they can make it, fine; if they can't then they won't continue to exist unless they can find other forms of subsidy.

Mr. HAVIGHURST. But the subsidy continues, in effect, because you have provided free capital in a sense, so that they have been lower costs through the long pull. I do, however, agree that one ought to stop giving the money after a fairly reasonable period of time.

Dr. CAPER. Well, you are a member of the Institute of Medicine Committee which published a report that Paul Ward described to us earlier this week. How does the subsidy in the HMO Act differ from the form of subsidy recommended by that committee?

Mr. HAVIGHURST. I am not prepared to say. It's not very different, I would have to say, as I recall now. That was written, of course, before the act became law. I was not altogether happy with the discussion of the subsidies, and, had I chosen to dissent on another issue, I think it might have been on that one. I might have said that I thought the subsidies provided for were perhaps too lavish, or at least I might have suggested some principles on which one could base an estimate as to what an appropriate subsidy was, something along the lines of my earlier conversation with Mr. Granfield. But my recollection is that the act and the statement are not far apart on the subsidy question.

Dr. CAPER. That is correct. In fact, I am reading from the Institute of Medicine report and it says:

However, the Committee believes that the Federal assistance to HMO capital needs is justified for several reasons which are consistent with the objective of a fair market.

In any event, the Institute of Medicine Committee which studied this does think that the Federal Government is justified in providing at least the currently authorized capital system for HMO's.

Mr. HAVIGHURST. I think one could get into a debate as to whether or not, in a fair market test, subsidies for one class of providers are justified. I was surprised, in fact, that no one did dissent on that question. I considered it and rejected it, partly because I don't think it is really a terribly important issue. But I know that the AMA has long said that it's not fair to subsidize one class of providers and not another. And I have some sympathy for that point of view; I think that is a serious question, and I would not have been as anxious to subsidize HMO's as the Congress apparently was.

Dr. CAPER. In any event, there is some disagreement on that issue. The Institute of Medicine also testified before us on Tuesday that their concept of a fair market for HMO's would encompass profit as well as nonprofit HMO's. Do you agree that profit ought to be a motivating force; and if so, how are we to insure the consumer high-quality services?

Mr. HAVIGHURST. I think that is an extremely important question. I have written something about it, as you know, and I worry about it a good deal. There are several answers. Perhaps the easiest one, the one that really begs the question and is something of a cop-out, is that it is awfully hard to tell a profitmaking enterprise from a nonprofit enterprise. Many organizations organized as nonprofit firms are, in fact, run for the profit of the people who draw salaries from it or otherwise benefit through contracts, leases, and so on. To sort out all those matters is very difficult.

Clearly, profits still motivate people in this world. I thought some of Mr. Rawlings earlier remarks indicated a desire on his part to repeal self-interest in the world—which I am afraid we are not going to be able to do. Self-interest operates in nonprofit enterprises as it does in any other, and the behavior of nonprofit enterprises is not very different from that of for-profit enterprises—particularly professionally managed for-profit enterprises.

Therefore, the chief difficulty may be that we can't adequately guarantee that an enterprise is nonprofit in fact in order to decide that it should be treated specially. But that's the easy way out. The real question is whether profits ought to motivate people in this industry. My sense is that profits will attract capital, managerial talent, and innovative ideas and will cause new entry to occur where it would not occur if one had to limit oneself to waiting until someone decided that he was called to start a nonprofit enterprise—one that would not reward him much, but one that he thought the world needed.

In other words, we need incentives for change and innovation in this industry. Indeed, we talk about restructuring, and yet we will seem unwilling to provide what it takes to encourage people to go into the business of restructuring. Thus, although I am a bit apologetic about saying it, I think the profit motive has a place. Although I think that it probably has done some harm in this industry and that one will have to watch it with great care, nevertheless I think maybe that is the more productive route to go.

I thought that the Institute of Medicine report's recommendations on the quality issue were quite good. I don't purport to be an expert on regulation of the quality care, and I know that it is extremely difficult to regulate in that area. I also know that regulation can be carried to extremes and that we can regulate the wrong things; we frequently regulate appearances and not reality. We can't regulate outcomes very easily; so we regulate inputs instead, thinking that somehow we can identify proxies for better outcomes.

When you add all that up, I still think that regulation may be adequate to deal with this main quality concern, and I would certainly favor active and careful regulation—not simply comprehensive regulation, because that tends to be too restrictive.

Let me also say something about the ethic that is involved here, since I think I share the concern about relying on profit motives and not solely on people's general desire to do good. Certainly one could have greater confidence that somebody motivated by a humanitarian impulse would do the kind of job you wanted to see done. But it is hard, you know, to come up with many of those people. Some people have that impulse for a few years and then find that it doesn't sustain them for an entire lifetime, and it is more important to provide a college education for their children and so on. Therefore I guess I just find it an inadequate way to organize very large areas of activity, though one would certainly want to preserve outlets in a society for those impulses and to encourage them.

But in the health world, the established ethic against profitmaking enterprise seems to me to have generated in part what is now perceived to be the problem. This is because the ethic involves a self-fulfilling prophecy. As the more ethically inclined people accept this notion that it is wrong to perform health services for profit, they tend to hang back, creating opportunities for the more commercial types, if you will, to enter certain phases of the business. What you get then is a certain selected class of people providing care in proprietary settings, and when you then look at the industry you find that the nice guys are over here and the bad guys are over there. Well, that is because the nice guys selected themselves out and failed to enter certain phases of the industry where the lure was money and not something else.

I don't think that we are right in being too critical of those who do enter, or in judging the results of proprietary impulses, because, in fact, our ethic has worked to exclude the more ethically conscious people from the proprietary end of the industry.

What I am saying is that if one could get more general acceptance of profitmaking as a legitimate way of doing business in this field, one would then not be so troubled by the kind of people who were engaged in it, and we would then have less reason then to be ethically concerned about it. In other words, we rely on profits as a motivating force elsewhere, and we don't have this ethic that seems to get in our way in this industry. Whether we can change people's perceptions, of course, is far from clear. But my sense is that one ought not to accept that self-fulfilling prophecy as a basis for future policymaking. That is a complicated argument. I am sorry to take up so much time with it.

Dr. CAPER. Well, I think the act as it was finally passed recognizes that position, because assistance in the form of the employee health benefits plans and superceding of some restrictive State laws applies not only to nonprofit, as you know, but to for-profit HMO's as well—but the overriding concern about our ability to assess the quality of medical services—and I think that our committee's concern about the absence of any standards of quality, in terms of the outcome, the impact of medical services upon the health of the people being served, is reflected in many of the act's provisions. This has been demonstrated by the repeated references to quality in the act. I suppose that perhaps you could consider that some of the provisions of the act—some of what you referred to as restrictive provisions—to have had their genesis in that concern, and to be intended as a proxy for quality assurance in the absence of any more satisfactory way to measure quality.

I don't think that it is an accident that that act contains a provision which directs the Secretary of HEW to fund a substantial study to look into those very kinds of question: How do we measure quality? What is quality? And again to explore what has, until the present time, been a totally unexplored area.

There is a great deal of debate, as you know, among perfectly credible physicians concerning the efficacy of very expensive procedures. And these things need to be looked at, and to be tested in an objective way—and they haven't been.

I agree with you. I think that your comments are certainly well put, but that we have to be very careful about what we are willing to endorse in the absence of an adequate ability to assess the quality of the services that we are receiving. I am sure you are aware of the experience in many prepaid health plans in California where HMO's were given government sanction by the State government and were allowed to participate in the State medicaid program in the absence of any quality standards. Such programs have produced many, many problems. The same is true in Florida as well.

I think that some of what you characterized as restrictive provisions of the act may be explainable in terms of a concern on the part of the committee that both the House and Senate committees had in terms of the assurance of quality. I think that is an undefined issue and a problem that has to be dealt with before a really free market-place economy in the health care field can operate.

Mr. HAVIGHURST. Well, I think you are giving up a great deal on the basis of an uncertainty, which we may all share, and I see a very substantial sacrifice involved in your reticence. The problem seems to me to be that the Government feels that if they subsidize these things, then they are somehow responsible for every bad thing that might occur. This is one of the problems with getting Government into the health business. The dynamic of Government concern is that life and death is at stake here; it will cause them to spend lots of money; it will cause them to be very restrictive; it will cause inflation because of the sense that they don't want to get anywhere near that point where somebody might get hurt. For this reason I can't share your unwillingness to face the thing a bit more forthrightly at this time, although I certainly understand it.

Dr. CAPER. Well, I think the Government whether some people are happy about it or not, is involved to the tune of about $30 billion a year, and up to this point has been involved without any attempt to intervene in the nature of the way services are delivered. I think we are exploring in a relatively new territory with this legislation. Undoubtedly, mistakes will be made; I don't know if any have been made specifically with respect to the HMO Act; I think the jury is still very much out on that issue, but I think there are enough questions from both sides. And it certainly bears very careful watching, and I am sure it will be carefully monitored.

In your testimony I think that in some ways you have interpreted the language of the statute to be much narrower than it actually is. I think there is room for a great deal more flexibility than you seem to imply.

Mr. HAVIGHURST. I would be quite encouraged if my reading is, indeed, too narrow.

Mr. SHARP. I have one brief question.

Mr. Havighurst, since the courts are not holding the Federal antitrust laws applicable to the medical profession, do you recommend this subcommittee to put in draft form a bill applying the Federal antitrust laws to the medical profession.

Mr. HAVIGHURST. I would think that it might be appropriate, at some point in a legislative way, perhaps as legislative history underlying some of the national health insurance legislation or something else, to indicate the degree to which Congress, in fact, contemplates the policing of this industry by antitrust. Conceivably, a section could be added to such a law that would state explicitly the understanding of Congress that the antitrust laws do apply in this industry. I would, I think, favor that if you could find the appropriate place and time to introduce it. It doesn't seem to me that a separate act of Congress, a little Sherman Act for this industry alone, would be possible or in the correct proportion. But it could be done together with the other steps which need to be taken to improve the prospect for competition in this industry. Perhaps a better place to introduce it would be in a new and more procompetitive HMO law.

Senator HART. Mr. Granfield.

Mr. GRANFIELD. I have no further questions except to add that sometimes when there are subsidies, this encourages eccentricity. Eccentricity means industry comes to Congress looking for redress of the issue of a regulation. I would just like to point out that this is an area that we have to be very careful of, even an area where it looks like you have sufficient entry to some parties.

I just wanted to make that one statement. Thank you again for coming, and I would hope that your reticence to come before a committee is dissipating and the reticence of colleagues like yourself.

I think it is unfortunate that academia has developed an attitude—and I am very familiar with that, having been in academia for 5 years—that we are not worthy of their attention; that they are the theologians and we are the practitioners; and that somehow what we do here is below them.

I would like to see us go back to the concept, not economics and not science, of the political commune where economics got its real start in the latter part of the 18th and the early part of the 19th centuries, where economists attempting to help the Government were trying to make better policies.

I really think that that is the role of the university. But if you don't come to us, you can't expect us to read the journal because I am forbidden to read the journals so that I don't become a theologian again.

Thank you again.

Senator HART. I want to close, as I opened this morning, by thanking all of the witnesses: Dr. Blumenthal, Mr. Rawlings, and Professor Havighurst, for an interesting and useful addition to this record.

Perhaps the quality today was unusually high. Of course, today we are not faced with the Senate over there sitting, and people breathing on us. I think it was very unusual.

Thank you Professor.

Mr. HAVIGHURST. Thank you, sir.

Senator HART. We are adjourning to resume on May 29. The balance of the hearings will be chaired by a member of the subcommittee, Senator Kennedy, who by reason of the chairmanship of the Health Subcommittee will bring an unusually well-informed background.

Thank you very much.

[Whereupon, at 1:25 p.m., the subcommittee was adjourned, to reconvene on May 29, 1974, at 12:30 p.m., in room 1202, Dirksen Senate Office Building.]

[The following was received for the record. Testimony resumes on p. 1421, pt. 3.]

MATERIAL RELATING TO THE TESTIMONY OF
CLARK C. HAVIGHURST

Exhibit 1.—*Prepared Statement*

PREPARED STATEMENT OF CLARK C. HAVIGHURST, PROFESSOR OF LAW, DUKE UNIVERSITY

Mr. Chairman, my active interest in the health care system dates from about 1969, when my instincts first told me that an academic lawyer with an interest in antitrust, public regulation of business, and economics might have something useful to say about the directions in which health policy was taking us. My professional work since then has caused me to become one of those queer people who believes that a market-oriented solution to the so-called health care crisis is possible—indeed, not only possible but preferable to all of the other possibilities being tried or considered. In 1971, I discussed the prospects for a competitive health care system in an article entitled "Health Maintenance

Organizations and the Market for Health Services" in the juornal *Law & Contemporary Problems* (vol. 35, p. 716), and this past Fall I examined the implications of adopting variations of public-utility regulation for the health care system in an article in the *Virginia Law Review* (vol. 59, p. 1143) entitled "Regulation of Health Facilities and Services by 'Certificate of Needs.'" In these and other writings I have canvassed both sides of the central health policy issue—namely the choice between a competitive market and comprehensive regulation as the primary mechanism of social control. In these remarks I will try to summarize my reasons for believing a competitive system can be made to work tolerably well—not perfectly, of course, but better than the alternative of a fully regulated or centrally controlled system.

I shall not examine the shortcomings of regulation for dealing with the problems, however, as the *Virginia Law Review* article is sufficiently up to date on that issue. I should point out, however, that these hearings are likely to add some new evidence to support my judgment that health planning is unavoidably too political, too prone to subversion by vested interests, to be relied upon to do the long-run job of controlling the nature and extent of the delivery system's development. It is my opinion, Mr. Chairman, that special interests in the health world. will find it easier to pervert regulatory processes to their private advantage, than to prevent the market, once it is properly ordered and policed, from serving the interests of consumers. But before the market can be depended on, certain factors which currently restrain its operation must be eliminated by, or from, legislation and by intelligent application of antitrust principles to the health care system. I shall discuss many of these matters in these remarks.

The choice between a market-oriented health care system and a regulated one is difficult, depending to a considerable degree on judgments about the probable behavior of numerous actors in the system under the particular constraints and incentives which each possible "solution" and all its possible variations would generate. Value judgments are also prominent, and people differ widely in their view of markets. I, for example, regard them as our most democratic institutions, allowing individual consumer sovereignty, calling forth resources to serve minority tastes, and avoiding the baneful impact of majority rule which our political institutions cannot escape. Others of course see markets primarily as an arena for exploitation and would regard with distaste a health system which relied on competition for the consumer's dollar as a central control mechanism. I have great respect for the antimarket point of view but have found it unable to generate a workable alternative which is not fraught with elitism, special privilege, and high costs, features which our health system already exhibits too plainly. Although the dilemma is undeniable, there is one simple but powerful reason why the market-oriented system should nevertheless be given priority in public policy at this time—namely that the market can always be scrapped if it fails to perform acceptably, but there is "no way"—as the current expression goes—of going back to a market system once we have elected the regulatory route. Thus, Congress would bear a great responsibility if it should commit us to an uncertain but irrevocable course, and I regard this subcommittee as the one most capable of illuminating an alternative which is much misunderstood and therefore in grave danger of being neglected.

I. The problems of the health care industry are essentially problems of monopoly and restraints of trade, fostered both by anticompetitive public policies and by private action. Many proposed solutions to the industry's problems would perpetuate and strengthen cartel influence, neglecting the possibilities for establishing a competitive regime.

It is useful to conceptualize the health care system's problems in antitrust terms. Characterizing features of the system in the language of antitrust—including references to "monopoly," "cartels," "market division," "price fixing," "entry barriers," and so forth—may seem unnecessarily inflammatory, but I regard it as a needed antidote to the euphemisms which the health world uses to obscure the ways in which beneficial market forces have been systematically repressed.

Let me quote some of my own writing which introduces antitrust concepts in an effort to clarify the behavior of the health care system and improve understanding of its problem. The first reference (35 *Law & Contemp. Prob.* at 298–99) describes the fee-for-service "monopoly" and illuminates the role of organized medicine:

"Each fee-for-service has a substantial amount of monopoly power over her individual patients as a result of their medical ignorance and dependency and their willingness to pay. Medical societies can thus be viewed as coalitions of monopolists whose purpose in coming together include protection and strengthening of their individual market power. This view explains why the medical societies behave somewhat differently than do classical cartels, not bothering to fix prices or to make overt anticompetitive agreements; not facing intense competition to begin with, they have no need to collude to eliminate it and can be content merely to preserve the status quo. In a sense, of course, the societies engage in market division—a common cartel practice— by enforcement of ethical undertakings not to advertise their services or to criticize their competitors, in effect recognizing each doctor's 'sphere of influence' over his particular patients. A further parallel to the activities of other cartels is reflected in the societies' commitment to preservation of a particular, higher discriminatory [151] pricing system—fee-for-service." [152]

"The power of a coalition of lawful monopolies may be greater than the sum of its parts.[153] Thus a medical society can preserve and strengthen the market power of each physician-monopolist by enforcing mutual recognition of spheres of influence, by collective maintenance of the conditions giving rise to such power—such as consumer ignorance and inability to combine for bargaining effectiveness—, by influencing legislation, by collective opposition to forms of health care financing and delivery that would weaken individual monopolies, and perhaps even by controlling members' exploitation of their individual monopolies so as to reduce the likelihood of government intervention or new entry."

Note that the fee-for-service doctor's "monopoly" is to a large extent a "natural" one, flowing from consumer ignorance and third-party payment. What is unnatural is the combination of doctors to preserve and strengthen their indivdual monopolies. Seen in this light, the medical profession's exaltation and defense of the "doctor-patient relationship" seem to spring not so much from ethical impulses as from the natural desire of a monopolist to protect his "relationship" with the consumers he exploits. The sacred aspect of the doctor-patient relationship cannot of course be denied, but doctors have been much criticized for making it too one-sided, not only as a matter of economics but also in human terms.

The second reference which I want to quote (59 *Va. L. Rev.* at 1149–50) looks at "health planning's" somewhat jaundiced eye:

"In helping communities to identify their most urgent health needs and to meet them by cooperative and consensual development, health planning

---

[151] Price discrimination in medicine involves charging different prices for the same service, usually on the basis of ability to pay. *See generally* Kessel, *supra* note 70. *See also* notes 84 *supra* & 159 *infra*. The presence of such discrimination proves the absence of effective competition since competing providers would drive each other to price uniformly in accordance with cost or the physician's supply function. Health insurance and prepaid group practice reduce the discrimination possibilities and have thus been opposed by the profession except as a means of providing for low-income persons, whom they make better able to pay. *See* Kessel, *supra.* The popular justification for such price discrimination was that it permitted free care for the indigent and made care available irrespective of wealth. As health insurance covers more people and as government pays more and more of the cost of care for the elderly and the poor, this justification, whatever it was once worth, fades. *But see* note 84 *supra.*

[152] Maintenance of a particular pricing system seems often to characterize the stabler form of cartel. For helpful comparisons, see FTV v. Cement Institute, 333 U.S. 683 (1948) ("basing-point" pricing, which produced complete price uniformity, irrespective of freight differentials, from all sellers to each buyer, making shopping and bargaining unproductive); United States v. Paramount Pictures, Inc., 334 U.S. 131 (1948) (motion picture distributors' efforts to preserve a particular system of "runs and clearances"); Securities Exchange Act Release No. 8239 (1968) (describing the New York Stock Exchange's long battle to repress cost-justified quantity discounts and "give-ups" on brokerage services).

[153] In United States v. Grinnell Corp., 384 U.S. 563 (1966), it was held to be monopolization to join together firms controlling 87% of "accredited central station protective service," a business having distinct natural monopoly characteristics at the local level. The Supreme Court's analysis was not satisfying, but the result is easily defensible by observing that the local monopolies were greatly strengthened by eliminating competition along the margin of market areas and the threat of new entry in expanding markets.

agencies have also served to simpify the hospitals' problems by curbing competitive excesses. Indeed, many of the activities undertaken in the name of planning were indistinguishable from such typical cartel practices os output restriction (collective determination of the bed supply) and market division (allocation of areas of responsibility both geographically and by activity).[22] The cartel characterization need not be read pejoratively, however, since agreements among competitors can, in some industry settings, be quite useful in preventing unnecessary duplication of facilities and other wasteful side effects of competition.[23] Even though cartels have been outlawed in other industries, special considerations, such as the impact of third-party payment and the prevalence of nonprofit firms, might dictate dispensation for cartel-like behavior in the hospital industry.

"Voluntary health planning failed to achieve its promise for the same reason that cartels usually founder—that is, the self-interest of the participants tended to take precedence whenever an opportunity for institutional aggrandizement present itself . . . . [Therefore,] logic appeared to point to the conclusion that, because neither pure voluntarism nor partial control over the various purse strings resulted in adequate effectuation of the planners' directives, "teeth" were essential to make health facilities planning effective. The pattern was similar to that in any cartel, where sanctions against uncooperative members, preferably governmentally imposed, are esssential if the plan is not to break down."

These references set the tone of my analysis of the health care system's current problems. Morever, I have tended to see most of the proposed "solutions" to these problems as also featuring cartel characteristics, and I believe this characterization is helpful in getting a balanced view of what is likely to occur. For example, in my article on certificate-of-need laws, I conclude, on the basis of experience in other regulated industries, that state agencies charged with regulating entry are likely to behave very much as a hospital cartel would behave. As the following quotation (59 *Va. L. Rev.* 1216–17) reveals, however, this conceptualization does not conclude the argument, for a strengthened cartel may in fact improve existing conditions somewhat, thus presenting the central dilemma facing health policymakers today:

"Characterizing agency performance as at best cartel-like should not obscure the possibile desirability of whatever reduction they do achieve in the supply of hospital beds and services. However, the dilemma of whether to accept substantially less than total relief is a real one. It is similar to the choice presented by other cartel-like solutions to the health care industry's problems. For example, PSROs and the so-called foundations for medical care may also be analyzed as cartels which, though dedicated to improving existing conditions in real and important ways, will ultimately stop well short of delivering to the public all of the benefits which a well-organized competitive market would

---

[22] D. Brown, *The Process of Areawide Health Planning: Model for the Future?*, 11 MED. CARE 1, 3 (1973), describes areawide hospital planning as "a process of blended provider interests," implying its desirability. For a scathing analysis consistent with the cartel characterization, see HEALTH POLICY ADVISORY CENTER (HEALTH-PAC), THE AMERICAN HEALTH EMPIRE: POWER, PROFITS AND POLITICS 191–231 (1971).

[23] P. AREEDA, ANTITRUST ANALYSIS 186–92 (1967). The nonprofit character of most hospitals may make the cartel characterization of their concerted action seem inappropriate. Nevertheless, nonprofit enterprises probably do not differ greatly in their behavior from professionally managed for-profit firms, both seeking growth as the primary source of managerial gratification. Under conditions of reasonably prosperity, management of either type of organization is constrained only partially by the need to show an acceptable relation between costs and revenues. *Compare generally* W. NISKANEN, BUREAUCRACY AND REPRESENTATIVE GOVERNMENT (1971) (treating nonprofit organizations as "bureaus"), *with* R. MARRIS, THE ECONOMIC THEORY OF MANAGERIAL CAPITALISM (1964). Nonprofit hospitals sometimes "distribute" profits in the form of perquisites to—or lucrative business contracts with enterprises controlled by—trustees, managers, or controlling physicians. *See, e.g.*, Kessler, *The Hospital Business*, Washington Post, Oct. 29-Nov. 3, 1972, at 1 each day, *reprinted in* 119 CONG. REC. H188-H204 (daily ed. Jan. 11, 1973). *See also* Sonora Community Hosp., 46 T.C. 519 (1966), *aff'd per curiam*, 397 F.2d 814 (9th Cir. 1968). Moreover, it has been shown that, under the demand conditions of a seller's market, hospitals' costs tend to rise so that their prices seem to behave not too differently from those of for-profit firms. Feldstein, *Hospital Cost Inflation: A Study of Nonprofit Price Dynamics*, 61 AM. ECON. REV. 853 (1971). If the excess earnings of nonprofit hospitals are used to supply more or better services and are not wasted in overpayments or invested improperly, there is no reason to object to them, on distributive grounds, as monopoly profits and perhaps no reason to condemn cartel practices which produce them.

yield.[234] Indeed, it is not inaccurate to view the fundamental health policy choice as being between a system controlled directly or indirectly by essentially well-meaning providers who accommodate their public reponsibilities with their own self-interest and a system of social control by impersonal market forces allowing consumers a larger impact and assigning government the less intrusive roles of promoter of the competition and referee."

My own conclusion is that a competitive system supplemented by and integrated with a carefully designed system of health insurance for those unable to pay holds out greater hope for satisfying results than does any other program I have heard about. I do not of course deny the necessity for some regulatory controls to assure that competitive efforts are appropriately channelled and that consumers are fairly treated. But maintenance of a competitive market should not be jeopardized by short-sighted policies, by compromises with special interests, or by excessive paternalism. Unfortunately, competition is all too often sacrificed by legislation simply because its preservation is not made an explicit first priority.

II. Competition *can* work effectively for the general welfare even in a market where consumer ignorance and uncertainty prevail, where providers dictate the need for service, and where payment is made in large measure through third parties.

1. *The Problem of Consumer Ignorance*

Students of the health care system all too frequently dismiss the case for a market-oriented solution to the system's problems by simply observing that consumers do not understand medical care and are essentially unable to make intelligent choices concerning the need for particular treatments or the proficiency of particular providers. I have had this simple fact pointed out to me with great solemnity on many occasions by people who apparently feel that they have thereby demolished the case which I have painstakingly tried to make for not giving up on market-oriented solutions too quickly. They imply that I have obtusely failed to observe this important feature in the landscape and that all my arguments are therefore built on sand. I would suppose, however, that intellectual honesty would lead these people at least to consider the possibility that I, too, have observed the difficulties which consumers confront in this particular market but have not regarded this this undeniable circumstances as destroying the case for using the market as the primary mechanism of social control.

To a small extent, my argument rests on the perception that consumers do have the ability to perceive many important things about health care providers and the care they as patients are receiving. Medical care is not purely a technical business, as doctors are quick to remind us. As I have stated elsewhere (35 *Law & Contemp. Prob.* at 753-54).

"Consumer preferences for such things as convenience, personalized care, and certain amenities are entitled to expression, and indeed irrational factors have an important place in medical care, suggesting that consumers' wishes ought not to be too regularly second-guessed. Moreover, the consumer's highly valued right to take his business elsewhere should not be curtailed without good reasons, particularly in a field, unlike telephone service, where personal rapport with and confidence in the provider of the service are so important."

Consumer preferences aside, however, the case for a market-oriented system rests on the demarkable capacity of markets to generate corrections for their own imperfections, particularly the problem of consumer ignorance. Health care is not the only area where consumers are at a substantial disadvantage in assessing the quality of goods purveyed and services rendered. Indeed, not only is the problem not unique, it is not even unusual, for all markets depart in some respects from the economist's model of perfect competition and yet serve the public quite well. One response to consumer ignorance is advertising which seeks to educate consumers on relevant matters within their understanding. But many other matters are beyond the consumers capacity to understand.

---

[234] Both devices have as a goal the reduction of costs by policing physician behavior, but in each case the cartel orientation is clear. Indeed, to ask the question whether physician-dominated agencies such as these will be dedicated primarily to reducing health care costs to the level dictated by the public interest—*i.e.*, that which an ideal competitive market would yield—is to answer it negatively.

and, in these cases, the market has found substitutes for actual understanding of qualitative details. Thus, brand names serve as proxies for quality information, identifying products which have established themselves in the market and earned a following. Similarly, retailers frequently put their own reputations, as established local businessmen, as reputable department stores, or as nationally known chains or mail order houses, behind particular products which they sell. Moreover, manufacturers' warranties are used to provide assurance of the quality of the merchandise sold (e.g., American Motors' "Buyer Protection Plan," a sort of automotive HMO). Independent quality-certification programs are another market-inspired device.

In all these ways, consumers are given either useful information or assurances which adequately substitute for information and thereby help to solve the problem of consumer ignorance. Because firms compete primarily for regional customers, the quantity of information needed to induce striving after quality is not high. Thus, markets can perform acceptably where only a minority of consumers are reasonably well informed; the ignorant benefit from competitors' efforts to woo the knowledgeable. Moreover, behind this market mechanism stands the law of products liability, which assures consumers of protection against injuries caused by defective products, and creates incentives for manufacturers to avoid producing goods which do harm. Thus, consumer ignorance does not prevent the market from functioning in vast areas of the American economy, and the burden of establishing that consumer ignorance somehow sets the medical world apart should be on those who represent this to be the case.

What does set the medical world apart is the extent to which the market has been prevented from generating responses to the ignorance problem, rendering it more serious than it would otherwise be. Thus, the health care marketplace has been systematically prevented from providing consumers with information which would be helpful to them in assessing the quality of care they are receiving or can expect to receive. The medical profession, because of the monopoly position which its members enjoy with respect to their individual patients, has systematically prevented information from reaching consumers, either in the form of advertising or by private criticism of fellow practitioners. Surely the medical profession's economic stake in perpetuating consumer ignorance should be recognized, and what passes for fastidiousness about commercialization should be seen as making a conspiracy to deny the public access to information which would make the medical profession substantially more accountable to consumer preferences. One does not have to advocate total commercialization of the business of rendering medical care in order to favor substantially greater disclosure, including advertising at least of objective facts relating to the cost and quality of care available. It should be noted in passing that the recent HMO Act of 1973 largely accedes to the medical profession's preference that information as to the quality of medical care should not be given to the public.

The health care marketplace could assist the consumer to overcome the problem of ignorance in many other ways. Institutionalization of care by HMOs and group practices is a possible means whereby this could occur. HMOs would have to survive on the basis of a reputation established in a community, where derogatory word-of-mouth and repeated bad experiences would quickly result in the HMO's disappearance from the market—as long as alternatives were available. Like the department store, the HMO or other group practice would cultivate its reputation and be extremely careful about jeopardizing it through poor-quality service. Indeed, Milton Friedman has argued convincingly the case for such "department stores of medicine," M. Friedman, *Capitalism & Freedom* 159 (1962), stressing both their importance in overcoming consumer ignorance and the profession's consequent resistance to them on "ethical" grounds.

In other markets where consumer ignorance is a problem, middlemen have stepped in, as brokers or in other capacities, to perform the function of collecting and translating information in the consumer's interest. In different market context, a physician could easily become a sort of middleman, acting in part as a fiduciary for the patient and advising him as to where to obtain needed care and how much to pay for it. Small-scale HMOs could also serve in such a middleman a role, providing some basic care in-house but referring the patient to specific providers in the fee-for-service sector for needed specialist attention. Such an HMO would be precisely the informed purchaser which the critics of the system say we can never have because of consumer ignorance.

My point here is simply that those who think that consumer ignorance makes a workable health care marketplace impossible have vastly underestimated the market's ability to cope with the difficulties which the state of the world presents to consumers. While regulation may be need to prevent exploitation of consumer ignorance, this can be accomplished without denying the public the right to obtain both information and purchasing assistance in a market where the individual has a great deal to gain as well as to lose. Moreover, government can perform a useful function in compelling disclosure or subsidizing the provision of information; because of "free-rider" problems in the market for information (i.e., the ability of people to get the benefit of information without paying anything toward the cost of producing it), a strong case exists for government intervention to stimulate the production of information concerning the quality and cost of health care—information similar to that which Ralph Nader's team recently published concerning doctors in Maryland.

2. *The Problems of Provider Control of Demand and Third-Party Payment*

Consumer ignorance is not the only factor which makes the health care marketplace complex and difficult to order correctly. It has long been recognized that fee-for-service providers have both the opportunity and the incentive to prescribe more care than patients may in fact need. Such provider control of demand originates of course in the consumer's ignorance and his consequent need to delegate decision making to the doctor. While this delegation is not particularly troublesome in itself (since doctors are reasonably trustworthy as a class and patients can enforce fiduciary responsibility by their choice of physician), a very severe problem results once a third-party payer is introduced. The availability of a third-party "deep pocket" relieves the physician of his fiduciary responsibility to his patient for the cost of the care received, and as a result, the physician develops no cost-consciousness but instead opts, often out of ignorance, to do everything which might possibly be of some small benefit to his patient. Given the high costs which it is possible to incur in treating illness, it is socially costly not to have anyone immediately concerned subjected to a meaningful constraint on his willingness to incur costs without regard to the value of the benefit which an additional treatment or diagnostic procedure or a day in the hospital may yield.

It is certainly true that as long as fee-for-service medicine with extensive third-party is the exclusive mode of health care delivery, the market cannot work efficiently. Cost externalization through insurance mechanisms causes waste to creep in and economizing instincts to atrophy. Thus, it has been authoritatively demonstrated that the breathtaking rise in hospital costs in recent years is directly attributable to the artificial increase in "demand" which has attended the spread of health insurance and other forms of third-party payment. Inflation has in turn stimulated consumers to acquire more insurance protection against high costs, thus externalizing more costs and promoting even more inflation. This vicious circle has been viewed by some as proof that the market cannot function effectively in health care.

The widely held view that the market cannot cope with third-party payment is not based on a full appraisal. First of all, the growth of third-party payment is not wholly a market phenomenon, having been accomplished in part by the Medicare and Medicaid legislation and in part by the market response to the liberal tax treatment of employee health benefits since World War II. The prevalence of "shallow" coverage rather than protection against true financial disaster reflects not the preference of consumers but the desire of providers for a convenient bill collection service, a priority which has received expression in Blue Cross and Blue Shield plans, in the tax laws, and ultimately in Medicare and Medicaid. Without government involvement and the Blues' dominance in the insurance industry, the market would have behaved quite differently.

More importantly, although the market has a great capacity for self-correction where problems appear, it has been prevented from responding effectively to the distortion created by ubiquitous third-party payment. Indeed, the only substantial response which has been permitted in the control of cost has been the introduction of co-payments and deductibles and the limitation of coverage in areas where utilization abuses are most likely to occur (*e.g.* outpatient psychiatric care). Besides making efforts to curb demand on the consumer side, however, insurers would also be competitively motivated to control their costs by directly controlling providers' use of resources in various ways. This subcommittee has itself conducted some inquiries into the problems which insurers have faced in attempting to influence the behavior of providers and is generally aware of the techniques which might be used it insurers actively competed in cost control. First, retrospective review of claims allows utilization to be examined and compared to norms, and charges which are out of line can be flagged and questioned. Second, various types of sanctions could be imposed where abuses have occurred, ranging from disallowance of a patient's claims for indemnification, leaving him to pay the provider, to various arrangements wherby the provider would end up bearing the cost; this subcommittee will recall how not too long ago a major insurer undertook to assist its insureds in resisting suits by physicians to recover charges which the insurer had disallowed as unnecessary expenditures. Third, more extreme cost-control measures include requirements for obtaining the insurer's prior approval of certain expenditures for hospitalization, diagnostic tests, or surgery; of course, the medical profession reacts strongly against efforts to control costs in this manner, as was demonstrated when HEW recently attempted to introduce pre-admission certification under Medicare and Medicaid.

One can speculate a great deal about how a market of actively competing insurers would go about introducing controls designed to keep the cost of insured-fee-for-service medicine within bounds. The most likely development would be for each insurer to devise a cost-controlled plan which it would attempt to market to both consumers and providers. Providers would have the option of cooperating or not, but a noncooperating provider would not have its charges covered by the insurance plan—or at least the plan's beneficiaries would run the risk that indemnification would be disallowed in specific cases. What I am visualizing is competition in the development of cost-control mechanisms, an area where a great deal of market experimentation seems to be needed. Moreover, one can imagine plans of different kinds being marketed side by side. Those with strict cost controls would be cheaper to purchase but would offer the beneficiaries more limited access to fee-for-service providers. On the other hand, "Cadillac" plans would provide unlimited access, would involve little or no claims review, but would entail a somewhat higher cost. (It should be noted that, with such competitive developments, each insurer would become, in effect, an HMO, since each would offer only a "closed panel" of doctors—namely those who had agreed to accept its cost-control program; each plan would also probably have to make some explicit assurances to the patient that he would have care available when he needed it.) The next section of this statement examines some of the reasons why this kind of competitive insurance market has not in fact emerged.

Perhaps the most obvious potential market response to the inflationary tendencies of insured-fee-for-service medicine is the health maintenance organization. Because HMOs are paid in advance, rather than retrospectively, they have every incentive to conserve their resources and to seek efficiency in providing needed treatment. Precisely because the prepayment feature of HMOs leads them to conserve resources, their presence in the marketplace would be felt by the fee-for-service sector as a pressure to reduce costs. This subcommittee has already heard testimony regarding the report being issued by the Institute of Medicine of the National Academy of Sciences, entitled *Health Maintenance Organizations: Toward a Fair Market Test.* This statement rather dramatically illuminates the possibility that HMOs will spring up spontaneously in a market where obstacles to their creation have been removed. Precisely to the extent that the fee-for-service system as currently financed and organized contains substantial "fat," a market opportunity for HMOs exists. Given a chance, they should be able to offer consumers an adequate service at a price which substantially undercuts health insurance premiums.

The simplest conceptualization of the HMO's potential market impact is as a "close substitute" for the services sold by the fee-for-service "monopoly." Because of the immense practical difficulty of altering the numerous economic and political conditions which foster the monopoly power of individual fee-for-service providers—namely consumer ignorance, provider control of demand, third-party payment, inhibitions on insurer competition based on cost control, and so forth—, creation of opportunities for independent marketing of a substitute services is probably the best policy alternative currently available. In technical terms, introduction of such a substitute tends to flatten the demand curve for the monopolized service, lowering the monopolist's profit-maximizing price. If consumers find the two services reasonably interchangeable, "cross-elasticity of demand" is high, and the monopoly of one service is of lessened, or no, consequence. *Cf. United States v. E. I. DuPont de Nemours & Co.*, 351 U.S. 377 (1956). The so-called "HMO strategy," as best articulated in the Institute of Medicine report, is designed precisely to make it possible for HMO developers to outflank the fee-for-service system, marketing independently a proven method of health care delivery which should prove an attractive alternative to the existing system Advocacy of a "fair market test" for HMOs means simply that the market should be given a chance to solve the problem. which past restraints on the market's operation have created. While the Institute of Medicine report's agenda of needed policy initiative to make the market viable once again is lengthy, this course toward major improvements in the health care system is much easier to chart than any other that has yet been proposed.

III. Antitrust analysis makes it possible to identify the obstacles which have prevented, are preventing, or may prevent a market response to the health care industry's problems. Such analysis also suggestions how existing trade restraints may be removed by new, or from existing, legislation.

1. Obstacles to Insurer-Initiated Cost Controls

It is interesting to consider why insurers have not competed effectively in cost control in something like the manner which I have described above. The answer is complex. but in large measure the medical profession's massive resistance to independent insurer claims review, and particularly prior authorization, is the source of most of the insurer's hesitancy in these areas. In this connection, I would like to call the subcommittee's attention to the well documented experience in Oregon in the 1940s which occasioned and is reported in the record of the case of *United States v. Oregon State Medical Society*, 343 U.S. 326 (1952). While the government lost that case on the basis of adverse findings of fact in the trial court, the history of the Oregon Blue Shield plan reveals a great deal about the medical profession has prevented insurer claims control from being a significant factor in controlling medical care costs. The Medical Society's brief in the Supreme Court included an appendix detailing the variety of ways in which insurance plans of various kinds in Oregon had been second-guessing doctors' judgments and insisting on justifications in advance for certain medical treatments. The Society presented this evidence to indicate the degree to which lay interference with medical practice had occurred, implying that important ethical values justified the society in opposing closed-panel plans and insurers' cost-control efforts. Even though the trial judge in 1950 was completely won over the doctors' way of thinking about the dangers of lay influence in medical practice, nowadays we might expect that it would be the government's brief rather than the defendants' which would stress the ways in which insurers had attempted to control health care costs in Oregon. The same exhibits would now be regarded as evidence of the Medical Society's monopolistic intent and not as involving a cognizable ethical issue at all.

The Oregon State Medical Society succeeded in stamping out insurers' cost-control efforts by creating a prepayment plan of its own, Oregon Physicians Service (a Blue Shield plan). The government apparently made no issue of the plan's formation and attempted to win its case by proving a boycott of competing insurance plans. This it was unable to do to the trial court's satisfaction, and it did appear that the boycott was far from completely successful. Nevertheless, OPS rapidly gained a market share of 66%, after which it fell back to about 58% and no longer pressed for further expansion. The question of whether this was a legitimate collective action by the Medical Society and its members was never adequately addressed in the government's theory of the case or in the Supreme Court's decision. Yet OPS was clearly a collective enterprise of competitors organized for mutual protection of their individual monopoly power, and it succeeded in restoring "ethical" behavior by the other insurers who remained in the marketplace after the plan's introduction. Examined in detail, the case seems to involve disciplinary pricing, whereby the Society-sponsored plan operated at a loss for a period of time in order to obtain a very substantial market share, supported as well by a partially effective boycott by practitioners urged on by the Medical Society. The competing insurers rapidly learned their lesson and stopped doing those things which the medical profession found objectionable. Thereafter, the Blue Shield plan relaxed its competitive stance, allowed its market share to fall, and thereafter tolerated the coexistence of other insurers who had learned the lesson that cost control invites retaliation. This subcommittee will recognize that disciplinary pricing is a rarely recognized but quite effective device whereby monopolists can keep their potential competitors in line and establish their leadership, reasserting it as the need is presented. The *Oregon State Medical Society* case seems to be a classic instance of this, although neither the government nor the courts detected it as such at the time.

The Oregon experience reveals two things. First, it indicates that an unrestrained competitive market will indeed stimulate insurers in influence physician decision making with a view to controlling costs. Second, the case reveals one of the ways in which providers can resist such cost-control efforts by insurers, namely the interposition of Blue Cross and Blue Shield plans, which, because they occupy a special position with respect to providers, serve to facilitate retaliation against independent insurers who engage aggressively in cost control. An indemnification plans, independent insurers lack the opportunity to deal directly with providers, and they are therefore limited in the sanctions which they can successfully impose. The Blues, on the other hand, enjoy a direct relationship but one which would also be jeopardized if they should be too aggressive in controlling costs at providers' expense. The battles which have been fought recently between Blue Cross and the hospitals in Pennsylvania are extremely revealing in this regard.

Restoration of market opportunities for insurer-initiated cost control efforts would be extremely difficult. It would probably require converting Blue Cross and Blue Shield into health insurers indistinguishable from their commercial competitors, with no ties to the provided establishment. Moreover, antitrust principles would have to be applied aggressively to block concerted provider activities designed to resist insurer cost-control efforts. Obviously, these moves would be extremely difficult to accomplish. Blue Cross and Blue Shield cultivated a public image which makes them nearly sacrosanct, and the provider establishment which created them would assist them in defending their prerogatives. Moreover, these prerogatives are largely matters of state law, and it has been traditional for Congress to leave matters of insurance regulation to the states. Antitrust remedies have already been tried and found unavailing. *See, e.g., Travelers Insurance Co. v. Blue Cross,* 481 F.2d 80 (3d Cir. 1973) Beyond this, the medical profession could launch a persuasive campaign against "lay interference" in the delivery of medical care. It seems reasonably clear that it would not be possible or perhaps even desirable to establish by law conditions similar to those in Oregon prior to OPS.

One way in which the issue might be addressed, however, would be by a law regulating the manner in which insurers might engage in cost control. Such regulation would be quite appropriate not only because of the hazards involved in excessive lay interference with medical decisions but also because insurers will frequently exercise monopsony power, which might be exerted to exploit physicians unfairly. Regulation of insurers' activities in these fields would also serve to legitimize them, and it might therefore be somewhat easier for insurers to take substantial initiatives in cost control. Such regulatory legislation would also clarify Congress's policy to the extent that antitrust courts would no longer shelter professional efforts to curb insurer activity. To the extent that the Blues are becoming more willing to engage in cost-control activities, such legislation would strengthen their hand.

2. Obstacles to HMO Development

An antitrust lawyer would perceive HMOs' problems as entry barriers, and would define the policy objective as one of promoting free entry as a means of creating both actual and potential competition for the fee-for-service sector. Clearly HMOs still face a wide range of difficulties, and these have been canvassed quite effectively in the Institute of Medicine report which I mentioned earlier. The IOM report sets up as its touchstone for policy-making the doing of whatever is necessary to give the HMO a fair chance to make its mark in the medical marketplace. It stresses not only the need to remove obstacles to HMO development but also the need to facilitate HMO growth by affirmative action reducing unwarranted entry barriers in whatever ways are within the power of government. Because the IOM report provides a rather complete agenda for action in this area, I will confine my remarks here to, first, an examination of the HMO Act of 1973 and what I regard as its rather minimal contribution to the implementation of the HMO idea and, second, a number of specific entry barriers which I have been specifically concerned with and which seem to me not to have been fully appreciated by policymakers.

The HMO Act of 1973.—I regard the HMO Act of 1973 as a "white elephant," which Webster defines as "something requiring much care and expense and yielding little profit." I will resist the temptation to extend the metaphor by comparing the law's enactment with the mating of elephants since that joke is told too often in Washington. Nevertheless, the gestation period of this law exceeded even that of elephants, and yet the offspring seems to justify the enthusiasm which went into conceiving the HMO idea. Moreover, I fear that the HMOs which this law will spawn will also be white elephants, beautiful perhaps to look at but oversized and essentially clumsy when it comes to delivering the kind of health care which people want.

The problem seems to me to be that a handful of people on Capitol Hill saw this as an opportunity to write their ideal of a health care system into law. Their idea was to "restructure the system," as the current phrase goes, to organize the delivery of care to a degree never attempted in the past, and thereby to realize the many efficiencies which thy believed could be obtained if their prescriptions were followed. Fearing that the HMO of their dreams would never happen if one counted on private initiatives and investments to produce it, they have dedicated a substantial amount of federal money to subsidize its realization. My first question to them would be why they think subsidiaries are necessary. If their idea is a good one, why wouldn't it happen without subsidies? If the answer is that the health care marketplace is a faulty one, why not correct its faults so that their idea can have a fair test against the competition?

I hope it is clear that I am not being critical of the HMO idea per se. Indeed, I consider myself one of its most enthusiastic champions. What I criticize is the particular embodiment of the HMO idea appearing in the HMO Act. The esssence of an HMO is not the comprehensiveness of the benefits it offers, its particular mode of organization, or its grandiosity in size. It is provider prepayment alone that sets it apart. This financing system changes incentives of providers in important ways, and this change in incentives is alone sufficient to account for the success which some HMOs have experienced over a long period of time. There is no basis for judging size to be an additional plus factor in the HMO equation just because the leading HMOs are large. My judgment is that Congress has made a serious mistake in insisting that HMOs fit a narrowly defined, unproven model and in clearing the way not for all plans featuring provider prepayment, whatever their other characteristics, but only for plans of elephantine proportions.

Economists have found that economies of scale are not particularly important in the provision of outpatient medical care. This is because the rendering of personal services in a business with relatively low fixed costs and a large labor component. While lab and x-ray services can be provided more cheaply with large volume, these economies are obtainable without integrating other aspects of the business. Similarly, doctors' office-sharing arrangements are often sufficient to realize available economies in employing nurses and other office personnel, in record-keeping, and so forth. Furthermore, large group clinics may in fact involve substantial diseconomies of scale for a variety of reasons, not the least of which is the loss of personal attention which lowers perceived quality and may increase the frequency of small foul-ups. Moreover, group practices have not found a really effective way of offsetting the loss of productivity incentives which income-sharing necessarily involves. Whatever else may be said about him, the solo fee-for-service practitioner works hard and sees a direct profit to himself from extra effort exerted. Whether HMOs, relying on group practice or salaried doctors, can achieve through larger size efficiencies which more than offset the productivity losses traceable to these methods of paying the doctor is not yet established.

The draftsmen of the HMO Act of 1973 apparently labored under the common assumption that, because economies of scale exist in many industries, bigger, more highly organized health care systems will also be more efficient. They have therefore undertaken to subsidize them, ignoring the obvious fact that, if efficiencies are really available, they will be attained in the market *without subsidies*, at least as long as costs as reflected in prices continue to have some bearing on consumer choices. It is possible of course that the HMO advocates on Capitol Hill do not *want* price to influence anyone's decisions about health care. I have never been able to tell whether it's because they believe people will economize too much or too little. In any event, they have taken upon themselves an important decision about which health care systems should exist in preference to others, and it is possible that they will be proved dead wrong. The elephantine HMOs which they visualize may topple of their own weight once federal supports are removed.

One way of looking at the HMO Act is as an experiment to see if HMOs really work. It has of course been the AMA's professed view that further experimentation with the concept is needed, and the administration shifted to that view during the 1972 presidential campaign. I consider the treatment of HMOs as an object of experimentation to be a serious mistake, one which flowed from the common assumption in Washington that, if something is good, the government ought to subsidize it. I agree that subsidies are inappropriate in the absence of assurances about the value of what you are buying, but I do not agree that subsidies were the issue when it came to HMOs. Much more important was the need to foster market conditions in which HMOs could make it or not on their own merits. Had Congress had the imagination to see the issue in terms of something besides subsidies, they would not have gotten hung up on experimentation, with all the hesitancy, restrictions, and limited commitment which that view necessarily entails.

What we are witnessing now is of course not an experiment to test the HMO concept itself but merely one version of it. It can in no way enlighten us on the benefits and costs of provider prepayment itself. More important, the notion of experimentation is all wrong as applied to HMOs. It implies that an HMO is like a drug whose safety and efficacy must be proved to a scientific certainty before it can be offered to the public. Not only is this impossible because, unlike chemical substances, each HMO is different and none can be permanently certified as safe, but it is based on a mistaken analogy between public policy-making and medical science. because the marketplace itself provides a kind of on-going experiment, it was only essential to have some basis for confidence that HMO's were not positively harmful before submitting it with other modes of health care delivery to a "vote" of consumers. Certainly there has never been my doubt that HMOs have long since passed their "preclinical" trials with flying colors. All the evidence is that provider prepayment succeeds precisely where third-party payment fails.

Now, what is the evidence to support my view that Congress was carried away by a vision of an ideal health care system and tried to impose that vision by fiat rather than allowing consumers to decide? The first item is the requirement for comprehensiveness of benefits. The minimum benefits which an HMO must offer greatly exceed the benefits of most of the health plans I am aware of. In other words, even with substantial tax incentives, people have not elected to buy voluntarily the package of things which the HMO Act requires to be offered. Moreover, consumers are to be denied the opportunity to be selective about the benefits received. For example, the whole family must sign up. Thus, Mom can't just enroll the kids with the HMO and stay with her own GP and Ob-Gyn man. Neither can she and Dad join, leaving the kids with the neighborhood pediatrician. They must pay the HMO for Johnny's dental care until he's 12. even though they would prefer to have him go to the. same dentist whom the rest of the family has seen and been happy with for years. In addition to multiplying the problems (and cost) of assembling the HMO in the first place and denying the HMO the opportunity to evolve gradually as it wins consumer confidence, requirements for comprehensiveness of benefits also increase the reluctance of consumers to join the HMO by complicating the very decision we should want to make easier. It is interesting to me to observe that antitrust lawyers would characterize all-or-none purchasing requirements such as result from mandating comprehensiveness of benefits as tie-in sales, which violate both the Sherman and Clayton Acts because they contribute to monopoly and deprive customers of free choice. I do not understand why these are not matters of concern here.

Next, consider the requirement that the HMO provide all care through its own doctors rather than by referral to outside physicians. What is the magic in having all the doctors in one building or sharing income in some manner? Why isn't the patient entitled to better care if it's available outside the HMO? And why is'nt the HMO ideally situated to act as an informed purchaser of care in the fee-for-service sector, shopping in repeated dealings with fee-for-service specialists for the best combination of price and quality for its subscribers? Congress again appears to have opted for a large and unwieldy monopoly rather than for a better-functioning marketplace.

There are still further indications that the HMO Act draftsmen saw the HMO as an ideal social institution rather than as a living, breathing human enterprise. One is the requirement for community rating and the attending requirement that enrollees be "broadly representative" of the community. There is thus a prohibition against price competition on the basis of the varying cost of serving the various groups who might enroll. The effect is to lead HMOs to abhor high-risk groups and to seek low-risk ones. To the extent that the requirement for broad representation can be enforced, it amounts to a hidden tax on healthier groups for the benefit of the less healthy. Although I recognize that this is a complex issue, insurance mechanisms should not be perverted into a system of hidden taxation but should continue to provide a means whereby people can pool their risks with others similarly situated. Egalitarian concerns should be handled by explicit taxes.

The limitation on reinsurance in the HMO Act is also troublesome. Primarily it precludes HMOs from serving small populations because of actuarial risks. No HMO would ever want to reinsure risks which it is capable of bearing, and copayments and deductibles would be widely used in such reinsurance to preserve the HMO's cost-consciousness. Moreover, reinsurance can aid in reducing the temptations to overeconomize which worry so many HMO critics. All Congress has achieved by prohibiting reinsurance is a practical denial of the Act's benefits to small-scale HMOs, which might prove more attractive, more efficient, and more competitive than the HMOs which Congress seems determined to foster at taxpayers' expense.

The dual choice provisions of the HMO Act are in my view the most interesting and potentially the most important. However, they also seem to embody the assumption that HMOs will be huge, all-encompassing entities. Thus, the law implies that a single HMO (plus a foundation-type plan) will be sufficient for all the employees of an employer. But, since employees live in all directions from their place of work and are usually spread all over and even beyond a metropolitan area, this will often not be the case even if HMOs are all of the large size which Congress seemed to contemplate. I believe, however, that on this point at least, the law is substantially less pro-monopoly than it seems and that there is some room for DHEW to introduce flexibility in this area even though an initial reading of the law might suggest otherwise.

Section 1310(a) requires employers with over 25 employees to "include in any health benefits plan offered to its employees . . . the option of membership in qualified health maintenance organizations which are engaged in the provision of . . . services in the areas in which such employees reside." At first glance, section 1310(b) appears to provide that no more than two HMO plans need be offered, one being an integrated HMO with its own professional staff or an affiliated medical group and the other being an individual practice association or foundation for medical care. The law thus seems to enact "triple choice," since the original health insurance plan apparently remains available as a third option.

Nevertheless, careful reading of the law seems to impose a greater obligation on employers, because it places particular emphasis on the right of each employee to have an option available *to him* in the area in which he resides.

(Note the use of the plural "areas" in section 1310(a).) Thus, if an HMO does not serve the entire area in which the employer's employees reside, it may be incumbent upon the employer to offer more than one HMO plan in order that all his employees will enjoy the option. If an appropriately high priority is placed on the availability of the HMO option to each individual employee, the risk of HMO monopoly inherent in the HMO Act can be greatly reduced. What must be avoided is allowing a single HMO, claiming to cover an entire metropolitan area, to thereby obtain the benefit of dual choice with respect to all employers in the community and thus exclude all other HMOs except insofar as they could persuade employers to add them as nonmandatory options or to substitute them entirely for the original federally sponsored plan.

Adoption of this approach could of course lead DHEW deeply into problems of defining HMOs' service areas. I see no way around this if we accept the important guiding principle that employers must provide the HMO option to the maximum extent possible at all times. I would recommend that DHEW adopt a rule saying that a fixed minimum number or percentage of the work force living in an HMO's service area triggers the requirement automatically and that in other cases a smaller number of employees can request that an additional option be extended. An employer should be required to make employees' names and addresses available to HMOs or to DHEW if he wishes to claim dispensation from the option requirement on this basis.

To avoid having the service area concept produce a kind of exclusive franchising, with resulting HMO monopoly, several specific policies should be adopted: First, employers should be required to offer all options to all employees—that is, each employee should be free to choose an HMO serving a service area besides the one in which he resides. Second, service areas may overlap, though an employer's obligation to offer a particular HMO would be determined by the residence of his employees in an area not being served by an HMO whose plan was already being offered. Third, existing HMOs should have no right to intervene in the definition of another HMO's service area— to defend their "turf," as it were, or their exclusive status with particular employers. Fourth, a new HMO entrant should be able to assert that it offers a better—that is, a more convenient—option than does an existing HMO in a portion of the incumbent's service area and that employees in that area should be given the new option as well as the old; while the employer, though not the incumbent HMO, could contest this, DHEW would recognize such claims, where established, by narrowing existing service areas with a view to improving the options of some employees. I think that it is clear that the law does not contemplate franchising, protected territories, or exclusive privileges for HMOs, and I believe that regulations along the lines I have outlined are necessary to assure that only the interests of employers, employees, and would-be HMO entrants (and not the interests of established HMOs) are recognized in administering the law. In sum, any HMO which, in DHEW's judgment, is not purely duplicative of an existing one should be made available if a significant number of employees might find access to it desirable.

Let me now point out the implications of the situation which I have just described. If an HMO's vested interest in its "service area" is not legally recognized, it is unlikely that anyone would, in fact, actively contest the delineation of HMO service areas. Employers would usually not have enough at stake to fight the matter and would probably offer as many plans as have a colorable claim to recognition. This does not seem too great a hardship on them, and certainly the creation of a more competitive market and final consumer choice is worth the cost which may be entailed. Moreover, I see no reason why HMOs should not be allowed or even required to pick up some of the employer's extra cost in offering the added option, particularly if a check-off is to be required.

There is another provision of the law that initially seems troublesome but which I think can be accommodated with reality by careful reading and carefully drafted regulations. This is the provision which I discussed earlier and which requires that the services of health professionals be provided through members of the HMO's own staff or through a medical group. The specified exceptions are for those services which the organization determines are "unusual or infrequently used" and for any service provided a member through an outside health professional "because it was medically necessary that the service be provided to the member before he could have it provided by [an in-house doctor]." This requirement seems to attach great importance to the HMO's having its own specialists in-house, but there are clearly cases where this will not be possible or desirable.One case is where the HMO is rather small and the need for a particular specialist's services is not great enough to warrant adding such a specialist to the staff. Although the proposed regulations do not say so explicitly, they leave open the possibility that whether a service is "unusual or infrequently used" would be determined in light of the particular HMO's situation. This would allow the small plans to provide fewer in-house services and to refer out a greater number of patients.

Similarly, a larger HMO may not always have all of its physician slots filled or may regard its specialists as not fully qualified to perform certain tasks usually thought to fall within the specialty. In these cases, it seems to me that the HMO could freely refer the patient to an outside physician on the ground that it was "medically necessary that the service be provided to the member before he could have it provided by such a health professional." Clearly, the HMO should be free to determine on occasion that the patient is better off seeing a non-staff physician. It would be most unfortunate if the statute were construed to prevent HMOs from electing referrals where "medical necessity" seemed to dictate it. If these interpretations are adopted, the effect of section 1301(b)(3) will be merely that the HMO must not function primarily as a middleman but must employ specialists when they are available and when the demands of the group being served are great enough to justify it. My interpretation of this statutory language would also open the way for wider use of reinsurance under the statute.

Even with liberalizing regulations, however, the HMO Act of 1973 is inadequate to implement the HMO idea as it should be implemented. In no sense is it a blow for competition in health services.

Foundations for Medical Care. The so-called foundations for medical care (FMCs) are one of the most interesting recent developments in the health care industry, and they are particularly interesting when viewed from an antitrust perspective. FMCs take several forms, but in their chief manifestation they are prepayment plans sponsored by local medical societies as a sort of second-generation Blue Shield plan, their main feature being that they incorporate controls stricter than those of Blue Chield on the utilization practices and charges of participating fee-for-service doctors. To a significant extent the appearance of FMCs parallels the appearance of OPS in Oregon in the 1940s, both being professionally mounted responses to a competitive threat, in this case the HMO. It is generally conceded that the famous San Joaquin Foundation for Medical Care began specifically to keep the Kaiser plan from invading San Joaquin County. Although the FMC movement is also in some measure a response to the threat of expanded federal intervention in the health care system, its character as a response to HMO competition is what creates the antitrust issue.

I have discussed the antitrust aspects of FMCs in two articles, the first being the previously mentioned one in *Law and Contemporary Problems* and the second, entitled "Speculations on the Market's Future in Health Care," appearing (p. 249) in *Regulating Health Facilities Consrtuction*, a volumn just recently published by the American Enterprise Institute for Public Policy Research. Some of the antitrust arguments in those articles will no longer hold as a matter of substantive law with respect to FMCs meeting the requirements of the HMO Act of 1973, since that law authorizes such plans' existence though presumably none of the monopolistic practices in which they might engage. Nevertheless, the antitrust analysis presented in those articles reveals the hazards which FMCs present. The conclusions of the first article are summarized in the second one (pp. 257-58) as follows:

"I said I thought [FMCs] might easily be found to violate the Sherman Act because they represented a combination of independent economic units—namely, fee-for-service doctors—to keep a competitive form of medical practice—namely, HMOs—out of the market. I said that, in my view, such a combination might be in restraint of trade even if its object was merely to curb universally recognized abuses such as high charges and overutilzation.

"This conclusion follows because such activity by a trade association of competitors is prompted by a desire to lessen the attractiveness of new entry into the marketplace and thus to stifle future competition, which might be more beneficial to consumers in the long run than is the self-regulatory activity. . . .

I suggested that because of the risk of such entry-limiting behavior, FCMs might easily be found to be "per se"—that is, automatic—violations of the Sherman Act. As a less dractic position, I suggested that FMCs might be judged to be illegal unless they were specifically shown [by the defendents under a shifted burden of proof] not to have prevented HMOs from getting established."

The second article develops the analysis of FMCs somewhat further. For one thing, it notes specifically the manner in which the appearance of FMCs confirms my expectation that HMO development will in turn prompt better performance in the fee-for-service sector. In their best manifestation FMCs can be seen as a method whereby the fee-for-service sector can control its own problems, improving its capacity to compete openly and freely with HMOs. Even seen in this light, however, the FMC may still not meet acceptance under the antitrust laws.

My discussion of the appropriate antiturst treatment of FMCs in the AEI volume (pp. 258-59) proceeds as follows:

"FMC's seem capable of moving in either of two directions depending upon the market circumstances in which they find themselves. The FMC which exists to the exclusion of other HMOs will probably limit its enrollment to those groups most likely to sign up with new HMO entrants. These groups will include the poor, the Medicaid population, who might otherwise find their way into HMOs under contracts with cost-conscious state government. Similarly, large employers might be sold the FMC plan as a way of keeping their employees tied to the fee-for-service sector. But FMCs being defensively against HMO entry are unlikely to recruit new members outside these groups, and, insofar as the poor are exclusively served in this manner, a system of second-class care could develope. . . .

"In a competitive market setting with HMOs present, the FMC would probably have a different line of development. Rather than narrowing its coverage, it would probably broaden it. The tendency would be toward taking over the present system of conventional health insurance by providing a program of effective cost controls. Monopolization of insured fee-for-service medicine would be a possible result, particularly since insurers facing excessive costs might actively seek to bring their beneficiaries under the FMC umbrella; but monopoly might be avoided if insurers were not inhibited from initiating cost-control plans of their own.

"Thus, although I think the appearance of FMCs helps to prove my argument that HMO competition will induce responsive change in the entire health care system, I see two reasons to be fearful. The first is that the FMC might monopolize prepaid HMO-type care, excluding independent HMOs much as the San Joaquin foundation appeared to do in California. The second is that the FMC might monopolize fee-for-service care. . . . These two monopolistic dangers are great enough that only unusual circumstances would prevent the FMC from violating antitrust principles. For these reasons, my position on the antitrust issue remains approximately what it was when I wrote the article in *Law and Contemporary Problems*. In the absence of either (1) meaningful competition from the active operation of an independent HMO in the market or (2) some reason to think an HMO could not support itself, FMCs should be held (at least after passage of a reasonable amout of time) to violate both Section I and Section 2 of the Sherman Act. Where such meaningful HMO competition is present, I think an FMC should still be deemed presumptively illegal but should be subject to redemption if it can establish that it is an essential mechanism in the preservation of insured fee-for-service medicine. If this defense can be made out, I would willingly endorse the restraints implicit in the FMC as ancillary to a legitimate and ultimately pro-competitive, over-riding purpose, namely, the preservation of a time-honored kind of medical practice that particularly emphasizes quality and personalized attention to patient needs and provides important incentives for physician productivity. But, since Blue Cross, Blue Shield, and commercial health insurers may ultimately be the better and more competitive vehicles for introducing meaningful cost controls through spontaneous peer review and other mechanisms, an essential item of proof in establishing the antitrust defense of the FMC is a showing that insurers are unable or unwilling to take on this job."

In order to determine if the FMC is indeed an essential mechanism for achieving fee-for-service cost controls in a market featuring active HMO competition, the article then considers in some detail whether health insurers can or will control costs on their own. As indicated in the discussion of insurer-initiated cost controls earlier in this statement, I am far from sure that the FMC device could not be justified on close analysis.

As a way of further summarizing my views of FMCs, I wish to quote below a series of guidelines which I presented in an address to the American Association of Foundations for Medical Care in August 1972. The guidelines proceed on the assumptions that the Sherman Act applies, that the FMC operates in a market where independent HMOs have the opportunity to get a competitive toehold, and that insurers have been found to be a weak and inadequate mechanism for bringing cost and utilization controls to bear on fee-for-service medicine. The guidelines are addressed to FMC organizers:

"Guideline I: Consider carefully the risk involved in starting an FMC to sell prepaid care in an area without any HMOs. Such an FMC runs some risk of being held in restraint of trade even if it takes no actions that are obviously exclusionary. . . .

"Guideline II: Don't count on the FMC to keep HMOs away. If you use it that way, there is a good chance of a triple-damage lawsuit against the medical society by an excluded HMO and a slight chance of a criminal proceeding if the behavior is flagrant enough. Some of the things you should particularly refrain from are (1) special arrangements with hospitals that are more favorable than an HMO could obtain; (2) exclusive arrangements with employers or insurers which prevent group members from being offered the chance to enroll with independent HMOs; (3) confining recruitment to employment and other groups that might be particularly attractive to HMOs, or otherwise revealing a primarily preemptive or anti-HMO intent, and (4) harassment of or encouragement of discrimination against HMO doctors.

"Guideline III: Refrain from actually fixing prices, even maximum prices. For reasons that are not altogether clear, the Supreme Court in the past has treated schemes limiting maximum prices no differently than plans designed to stop competitive price cutting. [See Albrecht v. Herald Co., 3900 U.S. 145 (1968); Kiefer-Stewart Co. v. Joseph E. Seagram & Sons, Inc., 3400 U.S. 211 (1951).] Now I think an FMC's efforts to control maximum prices could probably be distinguished from those activities held automatically illegal in earlier cases, but it would still be necessary for the FMC to behave in the least restrictive way possible in carrying out its claims review function. Moreover, if physician charges seem to gravitate upward toward the maximum allowable, the plan might be subject to attach for its effect on prices generally. Frankly, given the need to avoid price-raising effects, I am not certain that an acceptable scheme for reviewing charges can be designed. One suggestion, however, would be that recommended fees, or fee information likely to encourage fee increases, not be circulated, and, indeed, under the decided cases some substantial questions can be raised concerning the use of society-sponsored Relative Value Studies. Another thing to be avoided is an increase in the uniformity of physician charges, which, without allowance for greater or lesser skill or training, would seem both suspicious and undesirable. Claims review must therefore be as much as possible on an ad hoc basis. Guidelines may be used for administrative convenience, but a substantial percentage of claims should get special attention. To some extent at least, a physician should be entitled to his usual and customary charge, assuming that a competitive market exists in which it can be determined. In the long run you may find that your permissible price-regulating activities will have to be worked out with the Antitrust Division of the Department of Justice.

"Guideline IV: Avoid monopolizing fee-for-service care by preventing or inhibiting the independent cost-control efforts of Blue Cross, Blue Shield, or commercial insurers. Even if the Blues and the insurers should seek the FMC's assistance in implementing cost controls, do not create a single, monolithic review program. I would suggest using separate panels to review the claims of each insurer and preservation of a high degree of independence in decision making on the part of the various insurers.

"Guideline V: Do not engage in boycotts, or in publicity or editorializing likely to result in a boycott, of insurers whose limits on charges or whose supervision of utilization are regarded as too stringent. Do not impose sanctions on physicians who cooperate in cost-control programs you do not like.

Honest advertising to advise consumers of the risks they run under certain programs or of the virtues of free-choice plans is perfectly acceptable, of course."

In general, I believe that FMCs might do more good than harm if they adhere to these rules. Nevertheless, they represent a further acceptance of collective self-help in the medical world, something which has been harmful in the past and which should be regarded with a suspicion adequately informed by antitrust insights.

Professional Standards Review Organizations.—Like FMCs, PSROs are designed to introduce important controls over the cost and utilization of health services. PSROs have an even more extensive legislative charter, and the antitrust laws obviously have only very limited application to them. The issue thus must be addressed as a matter of policy, but the similarity between PSROs and FMCs highlights the cartel-like aspects of the former. As noted earlier in this statement, the PSRO is very much a device for solving the health industry's problems by strengthening an industry cartel.

Acceptance of the PSRO as a device for achieving improvements in fee-for-service medicine might well follow from a conclusion that insurer-initiated cost controls are unlikely to be appreciably effective; the argument is the same as that which would make the restraints of trade implicit in FCMs acceptable as ancillary restraints. But, while the PSRO may make sense as a mechanism for achieving greater control over the fee-for-service setcor and its tendency to overutilize health resources, the PSRO law also provides for PSRO jurisdiction over HMOs. Why this should be deemed appropriate is far from clear, since HMOs have adequate incentives to limit their expenditures to effective treatments and to employ their resources efficiently. Indeed, this strength of the HMO highlights the very weakness of the fee-for-service system which necessitates introducing PSRO cost-control methods in the first place.

The key to PSRO jurisdiction over HMOs is found in the area of quality, which the PSRO is also authorized to regulate. The same incentives which lead HMOs to conserve resources by giving only effective care may also lead them to skimp on quality, denying needed care, and considerable attention has been called to this perverse incentive and to the risk which it imposes on the consumer. While it is certain that this aspect of HMO performance must be carefully watched, it is far from clear that the PSRO is the appropriate mechanism for dealing with the problem. If, as is likely to be the case, PSROs are dominated by fee-for-service physicians, the temptation to make review of HMO care the first priority of the PSRO will be difficult to resist. Viewed from the standpoint of the fee-for-service doctor, the HMO's reduction in hospital utilization and other cost-saving measures may appear to sacrifice quality and to warrant regulation which will increase the HMO's costs and diminish the HMO's ability to compete effectively with the fee-for-service system. The PSRO is thus potentially the most effective anticompetitive device yet put in the hands of the medical profession, which has never had great difficulty in slowing down the growth of prepaid group practice.

Regulation of HMOs in the interests of fee-for-service providers would be a serious blow to hopes for improving the functioning of the health care marketplace. If the threat of HMO competition with the fee-for-service sector is reduced, the local PSRO is less likely to be aggressive in controlling costs since there would be no competing delivery system standing by to pick up patients attracted by the opportunity to obtain adequate health care at a lower price. The absence of a low-cost option (even one which in fact featured slightly lower quality) could thus be costly to all consumers.

Some observers (including Senator Bennett, the author of the PSRO legislation), recognizing the danger of anticompetitive regulation of HMOs, have suggested that HMO representatives should be included on the PSRO governing board. Far from solving the problem, however, this proposed solution simply changes its nature without diminishing its seriousness. The PSRO would then become a forum for negotiating the differences between the fee-for-service sector and the HMOs represented in its councils. The PSRO would then function as a cartel, allocating markets, defining modes of competition, and denying competitive opportunities to new HMO entrants which might be inclined to offer a different cost-quality mix than was convenient from the standpoint of the providers controlling the PSRO. Established HMOs would be equally anxious to preserve their market opportunities against the threat of such competitive entry.

While it seems likely that PSROs would delegate the task of utilization and quality review to some HMOs, subject to PSRO oversight, it is clear that the HMOs achieving this perferred status would be those which had negotiated treaties with the fee-for-service sector and foresworn aggressive competition and price-cutting. New entrants and more vigorous competitors would be subjected to intensive supervision.

I would hope that this subcommittee would take some initiative in warning Congress of this anticompetitive potential of PSROs. On reflection, the subcommittee might determine that the PSRO model of cost-control was not preferable to reliance on insurers to compete more aggressively in cost control. But, even if it determined that further experimentation with the PSRO idea is desirable, the potential for serious restraints of trade, particularly in stamping out major cost-saving initiative, must be borne constantly in mind. I hope that this subcommittee, together with other arms of Congress and the executive branch, will at least exercise vigilance against these particular hazards.

HMOs and Health Planning-cum-Regulation. In my *Virginia Law Review* article, I have examined with some care the case for controlling entry into the health care system. Of specific interest here is the case which I attempted to make in that article for exempting HMOs from such entry controls, whether under state certificate-of-need laws or under federal requirements for prior approval of capital expenditures under section 221 of the Social Security Amendments of 1972. Perhaps the most universal characteristic of regulators in other industries has been the tendency to protect the regulated firms against competition from new entrants and innovative providers of the service. I find powerful reasons to believe that this phenomenon would be repeated under health planning legislation, and I believe that the case for exempting HMOs from such laws is quite strong. For one thing, HMOs do not have the same perverse incentives to grow inappropriately which justify regulation of this kind for fee-for-service providers. Moreover, while I recognize that some planners seem to favor HMO development, I believe that they are likely to fall victim to the same kinds of misconceptions which led to the HMO Act of 1973 and its preference for a single, huge HMO under safe management over a variety of HMOs of different shapes, sizes, and sponsorships.

This subcommittee will recognize that competition is unlikely to exist in a market with only two participants, a single protected HMO and a fee-for-service sector monopolized under an FMC or PSRO. Indeed, the HMO most likely to be favored by the planner-regulators would be one which was sponsored by a local medical school or hospitals and which was therefore beholden in significant respects to the fee-for-service providers in the community. Given the probability that the number of competitors in the health services marketplace will be small in any event, the need to preserve and enhance entry possibilities for HMOs is, I think, undeniable. This subcommittee, initiated as it is in the mysteries of antitrust and the role which freedom of entry can play in preserving potential competititon, is well-situated to enlighten Congress on the importance of removing entry barriers for HMOs.

The Need for Further Legislation.—Removal of entry barriers facing HMOs requires further legislation, at either the federal or the state level. Unfortunately, the HMO Act of 1973 may have compounded the problem of getting clarifying amendments in the states by overriding state laws for a select class of HMOs. It is now possible to say that federal law has removed the important obstacles, ignoring the greater urgency of removing restraints from nonfederally-qualified HMOs. Once again, I would call the subcommittee's attention to the agenda for policy actions appearing in the IOM report. It is my hope that that document will prove to be a more important milestone in the history of HMOs, when it comes to be written, than the HMO Act of 1973. I strongly commend it to the subcommittee's attention.

IV. The antitrust laws are a potentially useful tool for maintaining a competitive market for health services.

The poor past performance of the market for health services is owed to a combination of legal restrictions and collectively imposed restraints of trade. The antitrust laws have played only a very limited part in preserving competitive conditions for a variety of reasons. Although some of these reasons are technical, having to do with jurisdictional limitations and substantive doctrine, the courts' outcomes on these questions as well as others have frequently reflected an ambivalence toward reliance on competitive impulses in the delivery of health care. I believe, Mr. Chairman, that enough evidence has now accumulated to reveal the results of tolerating past restraints and that the time is ripe for a strengthening of the role of antitrust in the industry. Although I believe judges can be educated to this need in due course, the process could be expedited by some demonstration of Congress' commitment to a strengthened competitive regime in this industry. This could take many forms, including a new, pro-competitive HMO law, a law clearing the way for increased competition among insurers, or even a "Little Sherman Act" directed specifically against restraints of trade and monopolization in this industry.

In general, Mr. Chairman, I believe that Sherman Act doctrine is well enough devoloped to handle the issues which are presented by the health services industry and that new substantive rules are not needed. The only exception I would make to this general conclusion is that, not only in this field but in all others, the burden of proof on the "reasonableness' of competitor collaboration of a type not subject to a specific "per se rule should be shifted to the defendants. Inexplicably, the courts have failed to employ the burden of proof in antitrust cases in a way which gives adequate expression to the Sherman Act policy of regarding combinations of competitors suspiciously. *See* Note, "A Suggested Role for Rebuttable Presumptions in Antitrust Restraint of Trade Litigation," 1972 *Duke L. J.* 595.

The landmark case of *American Medical Association* v. *United States*, 317 U.S. 519 (1943), demonstrated the Sherman Act's substantive value in protecting HMOs against certain types of restraints imposed upon them by the medical profession. But Sherman Act principles have potential application to many other practices in the health industry, including the following: (a) the granting and withholding of hospital staff privileges and specialty certification; (b) the fee-setting activities of Blue Shield plans; (c) the promulgation of Relative Value Scales by state and local medical societies; (d) "ethical" restrictions in advertising of objective facts bearing on the cost and quality of care; (e) restrictive accreditation and certification standards; (f) maximum price fixing, market pre-emption, and monopolization by foundations for medical care, including the foundations' usurpation of insurers' claims-review functions; (g) hospital monopolies, including market division accomplished through health planning councils; (h) refusals to deal, both concerted and unilateral, in a wide range of situations; and (i) the competitive advantages of Blue Cross and Blue Shield. Only when traditionally accepted and supposedly innocuous concerted activities of health care providers are characterized in the language of antitrust can one focus on those infirmities of the system which frustrate competitive efforts to control rapidly rising costs. Until these practices are checked, cost consciousness cannot be introduced in the delivery system without a reorganization so vast and so controversial as to be wholly unpredictable in its consequences.

Antitrust provides an established policy base for effectuating a cure for the system's ills. Nevertheless, judicial conservatism has plagued attempts to apply the antitrust laws to their fullest extent, and certain legal obstacles have therefore been created. These obstacls are not so entrenched that the judicial process could not sweep them away, however, if Congressional policy were clearer. The following paragraphs focus on some of these obstacles and briefly describe their scope and the prospects for overcoming them.

In the *AMA* case, the Supreme Court held that a nonprofit prepaid group practice plan was engaged in a "trade" as that term is used in the Sherman Act, and it seems clear that modern HMOs are equally so engaged. On the other hand, the practice of medicine by a solo practitioner may not come within the definition of "trade" but may fall instead within the rather uncertain exemption for the "learned professions." Although such an exemption finds no support in the antitrust statutes and the Supreme Court has generally been reluctant to imply exemptions, the court does seem to have accorded special treatment to the professions. *See FTC v. Raladam*, 282 U.S. 643, 653, (1931). The court also showed some deference to "ethical considerations" within the professions in the *Oregon State Medical Society* case. But, as one federal district court recently observed, economic activities, such as fee setting, are the "least learned part of the profession." *See Goldfarb v. Fairfax County*

Bar Ass'n 355 F. Supp. 491, 494 (E.D.Va. 1973), a decision that seemed to promise a greater willingness to look behind a "profession's professions" to economic reality. Unfortunately, the court of appeals, in a most distressing opinion, has just reviewed that decision and given the "learned professions" exemption more substance than it has had heretofore. 1973 *Trade Cases* ¶75,0043 (4th cir., May 8, 1974). Judge Craven's dissent in that case is much more satisfying to me.

The courts have also seemed to give deference to certain self-regulatory activities of nonprofit organizations. *E.g., Marjorie Webster Jr. College v. Middle States Ass'n of Colleges and Secondary Schools, Inc.*, 432 F.2d 650 (D.C.Cir. 1970). Nevertheless, the characterization of self-regulatory activity as "noncommercial" begs the question, and it is clearly open to courts to discover commercial objectives in the behavior of nonprofit enterprises and professional associations. As indicated above, I believe that those competitors who would justify collaboration should have the burden of establishing both their innocent purpose and the absence of an anticompetitive effect. The judges on their part have a duty to rid themselves of a pro-Establishment bias in these areas.

As to the further jurisdictional requirement of "commerce," an activity, to be subject to federal antitrust proscriptions, need not occur *in* interstate commerce but only have a substantial impact *on* interstate commerce. *Burake v. Ford*, 389 U.S. 320 (1967). It is of course possible to argue that medical practice involves no interstate aspect since the primary ingredient is personal services rather than goods moving across state lines and that the market area in which consumers purchase theese services is localized by factors of convenience and accessibility. *See, e.g., Riggall v. Washington County Medical Society*, 249 F.2d 266, (8th Cir. 1957). But such an argument overlooks the realities of modern medicine, which involves the consumption of drugs and other supplies and which is now primarily financed by the federal government and insurance companies which are engaged in interstate commerce. *Cf. United States v. South-Eastern Underwriters Ass'n* 322 U.S. 533 (1944). Although some courts are still reluctant to view health care as a business fraught with interstate connections, *e.g., Hospital Building Co. v. Rex Hospital*, 1973 *Trade Cas.* para. 74,903 (4th Cir. 1973), an important decision by the U.S. Court of Appeals for the Third Circuit has recently held the antitrust laws applicable to locally imposed restraints on a proprietary hospital. *Doctors, Inc. v. Blue Cross*, 490 F.2d 48 (1973). It would seem that the courts should not require much of a nudge to open up much of this industry to antitrust policing. The test should be whether an intrastate restraint might substantially affect the cost of health insurance or the consumption of drugs and medical supplies.

Although most of the restraints of trade discussed in this statement would seem to meet the test just stated, one area of continuing doubt might be the refusal of staff privileges to a single physician. Even though the situation resembles *Associated Press v. United States*, 326 U.S. 1 (1945), and could be treated handily under *Silver v. New York Stock Exchange*, 373 U.S. 341 (1963), the interstate impact would remain in doubt. Perhaps the persumbtion of "public harm" in *Klor's v. Broadway-Hale Stores, Inc.*, 359 U.S. 207 (1959), would prove helpful here.

The McCarran-Ferguson Act, which was passed in the wake of the *South-Eastern Underwriters* case, *supra* provides that the business of insurance, *Eastern Underwriters* case, *supra*, provides that the business of insurance, that such business is not regulated by State law," except that the Sherman Act would apply to "boycott, coercion, or intimidation." The scope of this exemption is far from clear, especially as it affects hospital and medical "service" plans (Blue Cross and Blue Shield). The recent case of *Travelers Insurance Co. v. Blue Cross*, 481 F.2d 80 (3d Cir. 1973), *cert. denied* 94 S.Ct. 724 (1973), held that a Blue Cross plan, regulated to a substantial degree as an insurer, was entitled to the exemption. Although the issue is still not perfectly clear, the McCarran-Fergusion Act appears to protect provider-sponsored prepayment plans unduly from antitrust proscriptions. If active insurer conmpetition in cost control is to be encouraged, some change in this regime is needed.

Since many of the activities in the health sector which raise antitrust problems are accorded some legitimacy by state law, the state-action exemption creaed in the case of *Parker v. Brown*, 317 U.S. 341 (1943), might also prevent antitrust enforcement. Because the scope of this exemption is unclear, issues would have to be addressed on a case-by-case basis. Presumably, however, the judicially implied power of the states to exempt private activities from the antitrust laws is not as broad as that explicitly granted by Congress in the McCarran-Ferguson Act. But, because the states have traditionally controlled the health care system and because Congress has never revealed a strong commitment to competition in health services, courts will probably be reluctant to use the antitrust laws to upset even uncontrolled delegations of state power to private parties, such as medical societies. The result is that federal abandonment of antitrust priciples may have opened the door for restrictive practices in the states.

A related problem arises where private parties attempt to procure state action which will have an anticompetitive effect. While the Supreme Court has been willing to protect joint lobbying in the legislature and efforts to influence public officials, *e.g., Eastern Railroad Presidents' Conference v. Noerr Motor Freight, Inc.*, 365 U.S. 127 (1961), action by private parties which amounts to an abuse of process will not be so protected. *California Motor Transport Co. v. Trucking Unlimited.* 404 U.S. 508 (1972). Entry regulation under certificate-of-need laws and federal health planning laws provides an opportunity for established health care providers to frustrate new entrants and retard competition. *Cf. Hospital Building Co. v. Rex Hospital*, 1973 Trade Cas. para. 74,428 (E.D.N.C. 1973, *aff'd*, 1974 Trade Cas. para. 74,903 (4th Cir. 1974). There would also appear to be some room for treating political machinations not specifically unlawful in themselves as "exclusionary practices" of a monopoly challenged under Section 2 of the Sherman Act.

In conclusion, Mr. Chairman, let me say that I have not brought with me a legislative blueprint other than a few isolated suggestions and the agenda contained in or suggested by the IOM Report on HMOs. More importantly, I have emphasized the need for Congress to attach a higher level of commitment to competition in health services. Promotion of competition must be an explicit, high-priority objective, and every piece of health legislation should be subjected to careful evaluation in light of this goal. Whatever form national health insurance may take, it should be tailored to maximize competition rather than allowed to foreclose it further.

Because compromises with a policy of competition can be costly, they should not be permitted to occur. Unfortunately, such compromises are occurring all the time in this industry. While paying lip-service to "pluarlism," health planners and legislators are stifling competition in the belief that retention of limited consumer choice is all that is required. The result is a pallid and inadequate substitute for a dynamic competitive market which can adjust quickly to new circumstances and correct its own faults. This subcommittee has a peculiar responsibility as the watchdog of competition in the economy, and I hope it will expressly assume this role with respect to the market for health services and help us to avoid the "pluralism" trap.

EXHIBIT 2.—*Excerpt From Law and Contemporary Problems, Duke University Law School (1970), Re HMO's and Market For Health Services*

HEALTH MAINTENANCE ORGANIZATIONS AND THE MARKET FOR HEALTH SERVICES

CLARK C. HAVIGHURST*

In its health care proposals pending in the Ninety-second Congress, the Nixon administration has specified the so-called "health maintenance organization," or "HMO," as one cornerstone of its solution to the widely noted health care crisis in the United States. First, the pending Medicare amendments, which were included in H.R. 1 along with the President's "Family Assistance Plan" of welfare reform,[1] would incorporate HMOs into the Medicare program as potential providers of care for those program beneficiaries who elect to enroll in them at the federal government's expense. Second, the President's package of health care proposals that was originally announced on February 18, 1971,[2] places heavy emphasis on the restructuring of the health care delivery system by stimulating the organization and growth of HMOs through a series of affirmative measures. The administration hopes that by 1980 HMO enrollment will be available to ninety per cent of the population as an alternative means of procuring health care.[3]

In addition to the administration's proposals, a number of other proposals for meeting the health care crisis are also pending in Congress. Many of these plans incorporate models of health care delivery organizations that are at least subspecies of HMO, indicating the breadth of the consensus that has embraced this mode of rendering health services. Thus, the Kennedy-Griffiths proposal[4] for "national health insurance," widely thought to be the leading contender against the administration's

---

* Professor of Law, Duke University; Director, Committee on Legal Issues in Health Care.

This article was written in conjunction with work performed under contract No. HSM 110-69-214 with the Public Health Service, Department of Health, Education, and Welfare. The research and other assistance of Mrs. Martha D. Ballenger is gratefully acknowledged, as are the comments, on an early draft, of David Mechanic, Guido Calabresi, and Reuben Kessel, members of the Committee on Legal Issues in Health Care.

[1] H.R. 1, 92d Cong., 1st Sess. § 239 (1971). H.R. 1, as reported by the Ways and Means Committee, was passed by the House on June 22. 117 CONG. REC. H5717 (daily ed. June 22, 1971).

[2] MESSAGE FROM THE PRESIDENT OF THE UNITED STATES RELATIVE TO BUILDING A NATIONAL HEALTH STRATEGY, H.R. DOC. No. 92-49, 92d Cong., 1st Sess. (1971) [hereinafter cited as PRESIDENT'S HEALTH MESSAGE]. The final bill embodying the President's proposals was finally submitted to the Congress on April 22, 1971, after this article was substantially completed. S. 1623, 92d Cong., 1st Sess. (1971) (the "National Health Insurance Partnership Act of 1971") [hereinafter cited as S. 1623]. See also H.R. 7741, 92d Cong., 1st Sess. (1971), which is the administration's bill with changes made by Representative Byrnes before introduction. See N.Y. Times, Apr. 28, 1971, at 31, col. 1. Other bills constituting part of the President's program are H.R. 5614 and H.R. 5615, 92d Cong., 1st Sess. (1971). No effort was made to analyze the administration's bills completely in this article, although important points are noted.

[3] Letter to the author from John G. Veneman, Under Secretary of HEW, May 21, 1971.

[4] S. 3; H.R. 22, H.R. 23, 92d Cong., 1st Sess. (1971) (all substantially identical) [hereinafter cited as Kennedy-Griffiths bill].

plan,[5] incorporates the "comprehensive health service organization" as an important feature.

This paper is addressed to the policies needed to obtain the best possible implementation of the HMO concept. The ultimate thrust is toward detailing the policy choices necessary to create a market-oriented system of health care delivery, with HMOs as an essential element. My thesis is that a congeries of legislatively and professionally conceived and executed trade restraints have heretofore prevented the market from functioning with close to its potential effectiveness and that restoration of a market regime offers the best hope for solving the nation's health care problem in all of its numerous dimensions.

Although the paper discusses the role of HMOs in several of the various legislative proposals now before Congress, it does not attempt to give a complete and current picture of any of them. It focuses to the greatest extent on the administration's proposals because I find them to embody an interesting and useful device for effectively implementing the HMO concept in the context of a federally funded insurance scheme covering the poor and the aged. This device, operating against the background of a functioning health care marketplace, would provide simple, non-bureaucratic, but effective protections against excessive costs to government on the one hand and, on the other hand, against turning HMOs into purveyors of "second class" medical care to disadvantaged citizens.

Presupposing adoption of this device and an adequate health insurance plan for the poor, I then proceed to describe the benefits which I think the market, supervised and supplemented by selective regulation, would be able to deliver. This hopeful model is then evaluated in the light of concerns about emphasizing the profit motive in health care and about monopoly tendencies in the health care marketplace. Ultimately I advocate vigorous antitrust enforcement, explicit federal preemption of restrictive state laws, and a number of other policies designed to assist in recreating an unrestrained competitive market for health services. The result is, surprisingly enough to those who think the market is currently being relied upon and has been found wanting, a fairly radical proposal. Although Congress may lack the decisiveness expressly to embrace the notion of a competitive health care marketplace, something approaching it might still be realized if the legislation adopted does not exclude the possibility and if the Antitrust Division of the Department of Justice could be persuaded to take up the cause.

The article is being written in the midst of intense Congressional activity, and the conditions it discusses are subject to sudden change. Nevertheless, some kind of HMO is certain to emerge, with government support, as a permanent feature of the health care scene,[6] and extended discussion of its role and the means available for implementing it must begin before all minds are made up. At the very least, my

---

[5] Altogether eight different plans have been introduced in Congress. N.Y. Times, Apr. 28, 1971, at 31, col. 1.

[6] See, e.g., Am. Med. News, Apr. 5, 1971, at 1.

emphasis on what the market, if given a chance, could be expected to achieve should improve many observers' perspective on the health care "crisis." At best, it might provoke some reconsideration of the desirability of continuing to adopt ever more intrusive governmental policies designed to ameliorate the symptoms of monopoly without considering whether the disease itself might be subject to cure by using traditional remedies.

I

THE NATURE, PROS, AND CONS OF HMOS

A. Terminology

The exigencies of legislative drafting are such that some term will have to be chosen to identify those entities which the government is willing to support in the provision of health care by means of per capita payments rather than on a cost-reimbursement or fee-for-service basis. The most common form of health care delivery featuring such capitation payments is "prepaid group practice," in which this mode of payment by consumers is coupled with the organization of physicians in groups.[7] Because capitation payments may also be accepted by organizations of independent practitioners and by middlemen of various kinds, the term "prepaid group practice" or "group practice prepayment" was too narrow for statutory purposes. The Nixon administration therefore chose "health maintenance organization," and Senator Kennedy and Congresswoman Griffiths selected "comprehensive health service organization," to describe what they had in mind.[8] The distinctive characteristic of the entities encompassed is that the provider of care is also a risk bearer, being paid an actuarially determined premium in return for its largely openended contractual undertaking to provide specified care to the extent of the subscribers' needs.[9] Although the terms selected signify similar concepts, their proposed definitions in the administration and Kennedy-Griffiths bills differ in important respects both from each other and from the traditional model of prepaid group practice.

The term "health maintenance organization" (HMO), which was either coined

---

[7] For an excellent, up-to-date, and exceedingly well-documented discussion of such plans, see Note, *The Role of Prepaid Group Practice in Relieving the Medical Care Crisis*, 84 HARV. L. REV. 887-1001 (1971). In view of the comprehensive documentation provided by this source, I have occasionally felt justified in limiting my own.

[8] Senator Javits' proposals use the designation "comprehensive health service system." S. 836, 92d Cong., 1st Sess. § 407 (1971); S. 837, 92d Cong., 1st Sess. § 2(a) (1971).

[9] An analogy to provider prepayment can be found in service contracts sold by some retailers, such as Sears Roebuck, with major appliances. Warranties providing for free repair are also similar, but when, as with auto warranties, they run from the manufacturer and provide for reimbursement of independent dealers or repairmen, they are more analogous to third-party insurance. The problems that have arisen with respect to auto warranties therefore do not reflect adversely on provider prepayment. They do, however, call attention to the need for uniform disclosure of coverage and the problems of controlling utilization under an insurance scheme, which the auto manufacturers have tried to control, with uneven results, by reducing the profitability of warranty work to dealers.

or popularized by Dr. Paul M. Ellwood, Jr.,[10] and subsequently adopted by the Nixon administration, is something of an overstatement, but it serves a useful descriptive purpose. Thus, under a system where the provider is paid a predetermined premium, it has a direct financial interest in keeping the patient well or in restoring him quickly to health. Fee-for-service medicine, on the other hand, provides no such incentive to practice "preventive medicine."[11] Nevertheless, the expression "health *maintenance* organization" probably promises too much. Medical care is primarily a remedial service, and, while there are some preventive measures (such as prenatal care and some immunizations) that are worthwhile,[12] preventive medicine practiced by providers cannot achieve health benefits even remotely approaching those obtainable from public health measures, over which HMOs will have no direct influence.[13] As a consequence, the "health maintenance" idea, while a sound one, runs the risk of being oversold.

Despite this reservation about the reference to "health maintenance" and despite the gracelessness of the abbreviation, I have still employed the term "HMO" in this paper. "HMO" has not yet been given a statutory meaning, and the definition proposed in the administration's pending Medicare amendments is quite unrestrictive in comparison with the Kennedy-Griffiths bill's definition of "comprehensive health service organization." Moreover, unlike "prepaid group practice," the term is not closely identified with existing plans, and therefore its use will facilitate discussion of those delivery mechanisms that feature prepayment of the provider but differ in some ways from these traditional forms.

For reasons that will appear later on, I wish to exclude the so-called "medical care foundations" from the HMO category. The concept as embodied in the administration's bills would encompass these entities, which are prepayment plans sponsored by medical societies and featuring fee-for-service compensation of the participating doctors. However, being creatures of the medical societies, they are unique in purpose, organization, and function from the independent entities otherwise referred to under the HMO rubric, and any generalizing about HMOs is greatly complicated if the exceptional status of the society-dominated foundations must be constantly noted. It is my view, developed later,[14] that, in a market-oriented system, the foun-

---

[10] *See* P. ELLWOOD, THE HEALTH MAINTENANCE STRATEGY (Institute for Interdisciplinary Studies, 1970). Dr. Ellwood is widely credited with being the architect of the administration's proposals.

[11] On the nature of the incentives provided by the fee-for-service system of payment, see generally W. GLASER, PAYING THE DOCTOR 138-203 (1970).

[12] Many preventive measures, such as periodic physical exams, are of debatable value. *See* Note, *supra* note 7, at 897-99. Particularly in a time of shortage, the opportunity costs of devoting health resources to preventive medicine—that is, the value of other benefits that might be obtained from their use—must be counted and might be substantial.

[13] However, the reversal of incentives would substantially increase the interest of HMO physicians in promoting preventive measures such as pollution control, sanitation, immunization, and better food and drug regulation. Enlistment of the direct interest of a growing segment of the medical profession in these matters might prove the more important contribution of the HMO concept to "health maintenance."

dations are distinctly anti-HMO and that, if the Sherman Act were applied to them, they would be held to violate it.

After excluding the foundation plans, the HMO I am left with differs in outline from familiar group practice prepayment in such matters as its size, the auspices under which it may be formed, and its capacity for rendering care in kind as opposed to providing it through purchase from hospitals or fee-for-service doctors.

B. The Advantages of HMOs

Even more remarkable than the spate of health policy proposals in recent months is the widespread agreement—the medical societies excepted—on the need to steer away from preponderant reliance on fee-for-service medicine toward a system in which consumers, if they wish, may obtain care by prepaying (or having the government prepay) the provider. The enthusiasm for this approach has been prompted in large part by the apparent success over a period of time of the prepaid group practice plans, which, though existing in only some parts of the nation, now serve around eight million people and have generated some impressive statistics on the per capita cost of providing care of a generally high quality.[15]

In addition to the track record of existing prepaid group practice plans, there are important technical arguments, many of them seemingly borne out by the statistics, for supporting the concept of care rendered under a system of provider prepayment.[16] These arguments, stated without documentation or evaluation,[17] are to the effect that HMO-type care does the following things:

(1) reverses the incentives inherent in fee-for-service medicine (especially where health insurance removes the doctor's direct fiduciary obligation to his patient) for physicians and hospitals to provide unnecessary services in order to increase their income;

(2) introduces incentives, particularly absent where third-party insurance is available, for physicians to consider cost effectiveness and to avoid overusing expensive facilities and resources for such purposes as (a) obtaining an incommensurate medical benefit for the patient, (b) adhering uncritically to "routine" practice, (c) minimizing perceived malpractice risks,[18] (d) rendering a certain

---

[14] See text accompanying notes 157-80 infra.

[15] See Note, supra note 7, at 921-24, and references there cited.

[16] In Group Health Cooperative v. King County Medical Soc'y, 39 Wash. 2d 586, 604, 237 P.2d 737, 747 (1951), the court summarized the advantages of a prepaid group practice plan as follows:

"increased opportunities for, and convenience in, effectuating referral of patients to other doctors to take advantage of various specialties; access to more and better equipment and laboratory facilities; improved quality of service because of constant surveillance by other members of the staff; opportunities for consultation, staff conferences, refresher courses, and post-graduate studies; better organization of time as, for example, the rotation of emergency night-call service; greater incentive to give patients proper treatment; security of professional income regardless of daily patient load; and disassociation of the business aspects of the service, so that the doctors may devote themselves entirely to professional matters."

[17] For a fuller statement, documentation, and tentative evaluation, see Note, supra note 7, at 921-33.

[18] This motivation is often alleged to cause excessive x-ray and other diagnostic tests by physicians

service in such a way (for example, on an inpatient basis) as to bring it within the terms of the patient's insurance coverage, or (e) catering to the nonpaying patient's perceived preference that "everything possible" be done whatever the expense;[19]

(3) creates a decision maker with both the knowledge and the incentive to discriminate on the basis of price and value in the purchase of needed goods and services—particularly drugs,[20] hospital services, and specialists' care—, thus strengthening competition and economic performance in markets adjacent to the market for primary care;

(4) strengthens incentives for realizing available efficiencies in the use of manpower and other resources, incentives that are weak where providers are not subject to substantial price competition due to the structure and customs of the marketplace or where cost-reimbursement is more or less assured by government or private health insurance;

(5) creates an organizational structure in which available efficiencies and improvements in performance can be more readily realized in such areas as (a) maintenance of complete, up-to-date, and nonduplicative medical records; (b) manpower and equipment utilization; (c) utilization of specialists' services; (d) continuing education for personnel at all levels; and (e) administration generally, particularly in billing and in freeing physicians of business details;

(6) creates an incentive for providers to keep patients well by such preventive measures as are economic, to detect disease at an early stage, to treat causes rather than symptoms, and generally to effect an early cure;[21]

(7) improves incentives affecting referrals and outside consultations, whereby fee-for-service physicians may only lose income from a patient but prepaid pro-

---

practicing "defensive medicine." This allegation is currently being evaluated in a study being conducted by the *Duke Law Journal*.

[19] This last item differs from (a) only in suggesting how physicians tacitly combine with their patients to form coalitions to take advantage of insurance coverage. These coalitions operate to make health insurance extremely expensive by exploiting the absence of the usual cost constraint on consumers' decisions concerning whether a particular expenditure is worthwhile. Detailed coverage provisions to some extent limit the "luxuries" that may be enjoyed without cost, but since no effort is likely to be made to limit the number of diagnostic x-rays, for example, many x-rays will be done under circumstances where their "value" is less than the sum of the cost plus the discounted hazard from irradiation. It is reasonable to regard the added procedures thus done, or the unwarranted hospitalization expenses incurred in the absence of a cost constraint, as an inefficiency of third-party insurance. In an HMO, on the other hand, the consumer might be denied on purely medical grounds an x-ray or day of hospitalization that he would have elected to purchase if he had been free to do so. The frequent use of outside fee-for-service physicians by prepaid group practice subscribers may be explained in part as the indulgence of such preferences by consumers. It is entirely appropriate for consumers to have and to exercise the right to purchase such additional reassurance, and, without more, their election to do so should not reflect adversely on the HMO concept; indeed, such luxuries *should* be purchased separately with one's own funds.

[20] Advantages connected with drug prescribing are potentially of great importance but are seldom cited in support of HMOs because existing plans do not often cover prescription drugs. The subject is developed at length in another connection in the text accompanying notes 189-99 *infra*.

[21] *But see* note 104 *infra*.

viders may gain protection against the financial costs of a subscriber's worsened condition;

(8) offers the opportunity for organizing care more conveniently for consumers by providing an accessible and continuously available "entry point" into the health care system and responsible guidance for the patient through the system so that he may obtain promptly and centrally such services as he requires;

(9) provides, by encouraging larger organizations of physicians in the place of solo practitioners, a better vehicle for maintaining the quality of care rendered outside the hospital; and

(10) provides stronger incentives for maintaining effective peer review and other quality controls in hospitals than exist in the present system of hospital practice.

The foregoing are persuasive reasons for wishing to see wider use of HMOs. They are especially appealing arguments when the nation is faced with both an existing imbalance between the supply of medical resources and the demand for them and a strong desire for a further stimulation of demand by expanding government's role in health care financing. In this climate, HMOs hold out a politically appealing hope that, by eliminating overutilization and introducing substantial efficiencies, existing resources can be spread further, giving care to more people without sacrifice of essential quality.

C. Some Negative Considerations

A few negative considerations need to be noted here without any attempt at analysis. Several of these matters will be discussed at a later point.

First, despite the governmental boosting that would be put behind HMOs under the various pending proposals, there are still severe impediments to their rapid growth. While several of the proposals would provide financial assistance for HMO formation, the sufficiency of the incentive to private parties to create them and to doctors to accept employment with them remains far from clear. The funds and organizational efforts called for, the difficulty of educating and attracting sufficient enrollees from a public accustomed to fee-for-service medicine, and the problems of attracting physicians into such plans[22] are all likely to be underestimated. It is argued below that these barriers are so substantial that they can be overcome in a reasonable time only by allowing plans to generate profits for the benefit of nonphysician investors of capital and talent in the enterprise.

A more fundamental objection to group practice prepayment centers on the incentive created to deny needed care in some circumstances. Of course, the plan has

---

[22] HMO employment appeals to some physicians as professionally rewarding, and it allows physicians to have greater leisure through better organization of the workload. Greater leisure for individual physicians implies a possible loss in total manhours of physicians' services which might not be offset by improvements in their efficiency, but it is not clear why HMO physicians, like lawyers in large firms, would not take on more paying clients than they could serve in a 40-hour week.

an appropriate stake in quickly restoring health so as to avoid the costs of a worsened condition, but occasionally there would be a temptation to omit an expensive form of treatment solely because of cost considerations. The clearest example would be in the temptation to let a patient die of a cardiac arrest rather than place him in the intensive care unit at a cost of $300 per day. This possibility, while important to consider, is not quite so hair-raising as it sounds, and it is discussed later in connection with the question whether a for-profit HMO is open to particular criticism on this score.

Another area of concern is the fear that HMOs will become a vehicle for delivering care exclusively to low-income or elderly elements in the population and thus, either in appearance or in reality, a "second-class" type of medicine. Again, the possibilities for avoiding this outcome are discussed later on.

Finally, it should be noted that the evidence on prepaid group practice is subject to some dispute, if not as to the existence at least as to the extent of the cost savings realizable from this method of organizing health care delivery. For one thing, plan enrollees are known to purchase substantial amounts of care outside the plan,[23] resulting both in understatement of the costs of serving plan members and in an increase of the services rendered in the fee-for-service sector and counted against that mode of delivery in statistical analyses. Further, the enrolled population of a prepaid group practice plan is probably not comparable to the clientele of the fee-for-service physicians in the community, making statistical comparisons difficult and very possibly misleading.[24] There is also evidence that, while existing plans have been generally well received, they have not been conspicuously successful in delivering care in a personalized and convenient way. Expectations concerning HMO success must take into account the possibility that the advantages of HMOs may have been overstated[25] or that gains in efficiency may be offset by losses in other relevant departments.

Against this background, it can be said that, although enthusiasm for the HMO concept should not be unquestioning, the arguments provide a warrant for affirmative governmental efforts to stimulate HMO formation to the end that consumers and

[23] See Note, supra note 7, at 921-22 n.1; The Kaiser Foundation Medical Care Program, in 2 REPORT OF THE NATIONAL ADVISORY COMM'N ON HEALTH MANPOWER 197, 207 (1967).

[24] M. PAULY, MEDICAL CARE AT PUBLIC EXPENSE 95-96 (1971), suggests that HMOs, because of their tendency to provide less care, may attract only those Medicare beneficiaries with below-average demands for care. This would make HMO's performance seem better in comparison with the fee-for-service sector than it in fact was. Pauly does not indicate whether the apparently lower costs of prepaid group practice plans might be explained by this thesis, but it would seem that they could be in some part.

[25] See, e.g., Klarman, Approaches to Moderating the Increases in Medical Costs, 7 MED. CARE 175, 183 (1969); Densen, et al., Prepaid Medical Care and Hospital Utilization, HOSPITALS, Nov. 16, 1962, at 62: On the other hand, many existing plans have been quite conservative in their use of paramedical personnel and in other respects. See, e.g., The Kaiser Foundation Medical Care Program, supra note 23, at 206. The purposes behind this hesitancy have probably been to avoid accusations and malpractice suits and to reassure their subscribers. Nevertheless, the many potential economies that have not yet been tapped are one basis for the hope that the HMO concept may indeed revolutionize health care. Competitive pressures will be needed, however, to stimulate the search for and implementation of available economies.

providers shall have this mode of transacting for health services available as an option; going any further, such as by forcing any group in the society to accept HMO care, seems unwarranted either by the pro-HMO evidence or by the total performance of the fee-for-service sector. Competition between HMOs and fee-for-service medicine would maximize consumer choice and would determine most democratically—by consumer votes—the role of each system in the delivery of care. Creating the basis for a restructuring of incentives to curtail overuse and to spread resources more widely would seem to be a justifiable goal of public policy at the present time. Moreover, clearing away obstacles to the introduction of larger-scale primary care providers, with greater potentiality for achieving available efficiencies and providing internal quality controls, may also be regarded as a proper function of government.

II

THE ROLE OF HMOs IN RECENT POLICY PROPOSALS

It is beyond the scope of this paper to do full justice to the various pending health policy proposals. The discussion here is primarily for the purpose of highlighting the role contemplated for HMOs in different approaches to health care delivery. The greater portion of the discussion focuses on the administration's proposals, and my main interest here and throughout this discussion is to discover the extent of reliance, if any, on the market and how the various mechanisms proposed would relate to or affect the functioning of market forces.

A. The Administration's Health Care Program

1. The 1971 Proposals

On February 18, 1971, the President announced his program to provide almost universal health insurance coverage for the American people.[26] The program's main thrust was toward financing health care and expanding, extending, and prescribing the scope of health insurance coverage. To these ends, (1) employers would be required to provide specified basic health insurance coverage for their employees on a cost-sharing basis; (2) less extensive insurance coverage would be provided by the federal government for poor families headed by self-employed, intermittently employed, or unemployed persons by means of a "Family Health Insurance Plan" (FHIP) in which the very poor would participate without charge but others would pay increasing premiums, deductibles, and coinsurance payments in accordance with their income; (3) Medicaid would be continued for the aged poor, the blind, and the disabled; (4) Medicare would be continued for persons over sixty-five but without the special monthly charge for part B coverage; and (5) special insurance pools would be established for the self-employed and for high-risk individuals denied other coverage.

---

[26] See PRESIDENT'S HEALTH MESSAGE 14-17. See also note 2 supra.

The President's message expressed the administration's enthusiasm for the HMO concept, reciting the importance of altering incentives in health care delivery to induce efficiencies and reduce overutilization. He indicated his hopes for rapid development of HMOs throughout the country and set forth some strategies for bringing it about. In the way of financial support,[27] he proposed to allocate $23 million for planning grants and to provide $300 million in guarantees of private loans to HMO sponsors. In addition, he proposed $22 million in subsidies for HMOs that would locate in areas where medical resources were in particularly short supply, primarily rural areas and urban ghettoes.

The administration's health insurance bill would require each employer to offer an HMO option to his employees,[28] a step that would open up HMO opportunities to a significant degree since an individual would no longer be locked into the fee-for-service sector by the terms of insurance protection dictated by his employer. Unfortunately, however, the notion of free choice stops here, because the employee is not to be given a choice among available HMOs in the community but would instead be bound by the employer's election of an HMO to which his participation is transferable. It would have been simple enough to allow the employee such a choice and to have the employer pay an appropriate amount to whatever HMO he selected.[29] If this were done, employees would have, in effect, a voucher entitling them to enter the marketplace in search of the kind of HMO care that appealed to them most.[30] Such a strategy would vastly expand the opportunities for competitive HMO development. The administration's bill appears first to assume, and then to guarantee, that the business of rendering HMO-type care will be monopolized.

Under the President's proposal, those poor persons covered by FHIP would have the option of joining an HMO at government expense, and indeed they would have a free choice among those available. The proposed arrangement for exercising this option is similar in many ways to the arrangements for such elections by Medicare beneficiaries that is contained in the administration's pending Medicare proposals.

2. The HMO Defined (The Medicare Proposals)

The administration's proposed Medicare amendments set forth a definition of a "health maintenance organization" for the purpose of confirming in the Secretary of HEW the power to contract with such an agency to provide prepaid health care on a capitation basis to persons whose care has become a federal responsibility

---

[27] PRESIDENT'S HEALTH MESSAGE 6-7. See also H.R. 5615, 92d Cong., 1st Sess. (1971) (the administration's "Health Maintenance Organization Assistance Act of 1971") [hereinafter cited as H.R. 5615].

[28] S. 1623, § 101, proposed § 603(h).

[29] The President referred to the "actuarial value" of the employee's insurance coverage as being transferable, PRESIDENT'S HEALTH MESSAGE 6, but this seems wrong. If "community rating" for persons under 65 is required of HMOs, then the employee should be able to transfer his pro rata share of the employer's total premium. Otherwise only older persons will transfer to HMOs, since only they would not have to make a supplementary payment.

[30] In order to induce cost and value comparisons, an employee transferring his membership to an HMO should be entitled to a cash refund if the HMO membership is cheaper than the insurance coverage, or else he might be given additional benefits by the HMO in lieu of a refund.

under Medicare.[31] Thus, persons covered by the program who would elect to be enrolled in an HMO would become the subject of such a contract, and their federal benefits would then take the form of a periodic fixed-sum payment to the HMO rather than, as formerly, of payments to hospitals or fee-for-service physicians for services actually rendered. Under the FHIP proposal, similar contractual arrangements would be authorized to permit HMO coverage of that program's beneficiaries.[32]

On its face, the administration's Medicare bill (H.R. 1)[33] promised to generate, to the extent HMOs were in fact utilized, an immediate and politically appealing saving in cost over the present method of providing Medicare benefits. Thus, the bill provided that the rate of payment to the HMO "shall be designed to provide payment at a level not to exceed 95 per centum of the amount that the Secretary estimates (with appropriate adjustments to assure actuarial equivalence) would be payable" for Medicare services for the same population if the services were to be furnished by fee-for-service providers.[34] From this it appeared that the draftsman expected that bringing the HMO into the picture would save at least five per cent on the cost of caring for the HMO-enrolled population.

H.R. 1 defined the term "health maintenance organization" at some length. It appeared in most respects to have modeled the HMO on the most familiar type of prepaid group practice plan. As set forth in the version of the bill recently passed by the House of Representatives, an HMO would be a public or private organization which

(1) provides, either directly or through arrangements with others, health services to . . . [enrollees] on a per capita prepayment basis;

(2) provides, either directly or through arrangements with others, . . . (through institutions, entities, and persons meeting the applicable requirements of section 1861), all of the services and benefits covered under parts A and B of this title;

(3) provides physicians' services (A) directly through physicians who are either

---

[31] The immediate occasion for the amendments was the problem that Medicare, providing only for cost reimbursement, did not adequately reward the efficiencies achieved by prepaid group practice plans. The problem has been described by the Senate Finance Committee as follows:

"Under present law, organizations providing comprehensive health services on a per capita prepayment basis cannot be reimbursed by medicare through a single prospective capitation payment such as the organizations normally charge for services covered under both . . . parts of the medicare program. Instead, medicare reimbursement to group practice prepayment plans, whether it is made on a cost or charge basis, must be related, retrospectively, to the costs to the organization of providing specific services to beneficiaries, so that some of the financial incentives which such organizations may have in their regular non-medicare business to keep costs low and to control utilization of services are not fully incorporated directly in their relationship with medicare."

S. REP. No. 91-1431, 91st Cong., 2d Sess. 131-32 (1970) [hereinafter cited as S. REP. No. 91-1431]. *See also* Phelan, Erickson & Fleming, *Group Practice Prepayment: An Approach to Delivering Organized Health Services*, in this symposium, p. 796, 811-12; Note, *supra* note 7, at 988-90.

[32] S. 1623, § 201, proposed § 628(j).

[33] H.R. 1, 92d Cong., 1st Sess. (1971) [hereinafter cited as H.R. 1]. The House-passed version (*see* note 1 *supra*) is hereinafter cited as "H.R. 1 as amended."

[34] H.R. 1 § 239(a), proposed § 1876(a)(2).

employees or partners of such organization, or (B) under arrangements with one or more groups of physicians (organized on a group practice or individual practice basis) under which each such group is reimbursed for its services primarily on the basis of an aggregate fixed sum or on a per capita basis, regardless of whether the individual physician members of any such group are paid on a fee-for-service or other basis;

(4) demonstrates to the satisfaction of the Secretary proof of financial responsibility and proof of capability to provide comprehensive health care services, including institutional services, efficiently, effectively, and economically;

(5) except as provided . . . [elsewhere], has at least half of its enrolled members consisting of individuals under age 65;

(6) assures that the health services required by its members are received promptly and appropriately and that the services that are received measure up to quality standards which it establishes in accordance with regulations; and

(7) has an open enrollment period at least every year under which it accepts up to the limits of its capacity and without restrictions, except as may be authorized in regulations, individuals who are eligible to enroll . . . in the order in which they apply for enrollment (unless to do so would result in failure to meet the requirements of paragraph (5)).[85]

There is of course no uniform mold from which existing prepaid group practice plans have been cast, but certain features associated with the largest plans may have come to be regarded as typical. As defined in H.R. 1, the HMO seems to be distinct from the typical prepaid group practice plan in at least four important respects. First, it appears that the HMO might be permitted to serve some patients on a fee-for-service basis.[86] Thus, any clinic or hospital might form an HMO to serve some of its clientele while continuing to provide traditional care to others. This would greatly facilitate HMO formation by existing providers since an abrupt change in methods of doing business would not be necessary. Moreover, individual physicians could become associated with an HMO without abandoning their former patients, thus simplifying physician recruitment by the HMO. While there is no reason for existing prepaid group practice clinics not to provide fee-for-service care to the general public, this has not been common.[37] The medical care foundations, which fall within the definition of HMO by virtue of a recent clarification of paragraph (3),[38] render all their services through fee-for-service physicians who are paid on a piecework basis for services rendered to foundation enrollees.

Under the H.R. 1 definition, HMOs would be free to be substantially smaller

[85] H.R. 1 as amended, § 226(a), proposed § 1876(b). A similar definition originally appeared in H.R. 17550, 91st Cong., 2d Sess. § 239(a) (1970), and H.R. 1, § 239(a). The administration has since changed its basic definition somewhat. *E.g.*, S. 1623, § 101, proposed § 604(a); *id.* § 201, proposed § 628(b); H.R. 5615, § 2(c), proposed § 1101(1).

[86] The Kennedy-Griffiths bill, § 47(b), would also permit this.

[87] One example is the Palo Alto (California) Clinic, which has 15% prepaid subscribers. Note, *supra* note 7, at 903-04 n.9. It is not clear that all consumers are offered a choice of prepayment or fee-for-service care. *See also id.* at 938.

[38] *Compare* H.R. 1, § 239(a), proposed § 1876(b)(3), *with* H.R. 1 as amended, § 226(a), proposed § 1876(b)(3).

than are the familiar prepaid group practice plans, and this could contribute to the existence of a greater number of HMOs, featuring different prices and varieties of service and contributing to a competitive environment. Other pending definitions of HMO offered by the administration have included a requirement that they have at least 10,000 enrollees.[39] Why so arbitrary an exclusion of would-be providers might be deemed desirable is not clear. Such a requirement would greatly reduce both actual and potential competition and would discourage innovation and free choice. It is notable that H.R. 1 as recently passed by the House, quoted above, does not contain the requirement of 10,000 enrollees.

The third way in which an HMO, as defined in H.R. 1, appears to differ from the familiar type of prepaid group practice plan is in the apparent opportunity for organizing and operating an HMO for the express purpose of earning a profit for someone other than the physicians involved. Most prepaid group practice plans have been organized either by the doctors themselves or by consumer groups, unions, or employers for the benefit for their membership or employees. In the case of consumer-sponsored or employer-sponsored groups, the founding organization normally contracts with a group of doctors to provide the care in return for a per capita payment by or on behalf of the individual participants. The organization itself acts only as a sponsor and takes no profit off the top for its entrepreneurial initiative. The proposed bill would not limit HMO organization to enterprises of the voluntary, nonprofit kind, leaving open the possibility that profit-seeking middlemen might become engaged in HMO formation. The suggestions developed below, which look to potential profits as an important stimulus for HMO formation, depend heavily on the accuracy of this appraisal of the expectations underlying the drafting of H.R. 1. It is notable that the Senate Finance Committee found this a major point of difference with the administration in 1970[40] and that the Kennedy-Griffiths bill contemplates only nonprofit "comprehensive health service organizations."[41]

A final area of difference between HMOs, as defined, and the most familiar variety of prepaid group practice plan lies in the provision of hospital and specialists' services. Many of the major plans of provider prepayment furnish hospital services in hospitals owned either by the plan itself or by the medical group with which the plan contracts.[42] Similarly, physician services are rendered almost exclusively in-house, except where emergency care must be obtained by subscribers away from the plan's facility. No requirement concerning the form in which hospital or physician services are provided would be imposed on the HMO by H.R. 1, leaving it free to provide them by purchase from independent public or private hospitals where its

---

[39] S. 1623, § 101, proposed § 604(a)(5); *id.* § 201, proposed § 628(b)(5).

[40] *See* S. Rep. No. 91-1431, at 131-32, and text accompanying note 90 *infra*.

[41] Kennedy-Griffiths bill § 47(a)(2).

[42] The differences between hospital-based plans and others are discussed in Note, *supra* note 7, at 910-18. Some existing plans do not cover hospital benefits at all, requiring the member to purchase hospitalization coverage elsewhere.

doctors have staff privileges[43] and from fee-for-service specialists by referral of its patients.[44] This freedom would go far towards permitting HMOs to be formed on a relatively small scale compared to the best known prepaid group practice plans and to be constituted without large capital inputs. It would also assure subscribers that specialized hospital and physician care of the highest quality could be obtained when it was needed. Even more important perhaps, HMO purchasing of hospital and physician services could introduce desirable influences into the market for each.

3. A Device for Avoiding "Second-class" Status and Protecting the Public Purse

Because the President's program would provide optional HMO-based care for Medicare beneficiaries and for beneficiaries of the proposed FHIP, there is a risk that it will provide for these disadvantaged persons, the aged and the poor, only a type of "second-class" medicine. Of course, such consumers would be free not to select HMO-type care and to remain in the fee-for-service sector, obtaining care as needed from physicians whom they locate by their own efforts. But the alternatives available to many health care consumers in these groups are so few and so unattractive that this opportunity to reject HMO membership provides only slight protection against forcing the elderly and poor into accepting care from institutions that they might regard as somehow second-class. Some means of guaranteeing that HMOs will not become a vehicle for second-class medicine would be desirable not only as a protection for the poor but also to protect the "image" of HMO-provided care so that the middle-class will not associate it with ghetto dwellers and be induced to reject the HMO for their own purposes.

Another problem is the difficulty of determining the price that government should

---

[43] The Kennedy-Griffiths bill, §§ 47(a)(2)-(3), 87(c), also contemplates the possibility that hospital services may be provided on other than an in-house basis. For the view that hospital services must be at least contracted for rather than purchased randomly, see DIVISION OF MEDICAL PRACTICE, AMERICAN MEDICAL ASS'N, HMO's AS SEEN BY THE AMA—AN ANALYSIS 7-8 (1971). The AMA's argument turned on H.R. 1, § 239(a), proposed § 1876(b)(6), which was altered slightly but significantly in H.R. 1 as amended, § 226(a).

[44] H.R. 1 as amended, § 226(a), proposed § 1876(b)(3), quoted in text at note 35 *supra*, indicates that physicians' services shall be provided "directly through physicians who are either employees or partners" of the HMO or members of a group that has contracted with the HMO to provide the services on a fixed-fee basis. One reading of this language would preclude the possibility of an HMO's purchasing some of the services that it provides from fee-for-service physicians to whom it refers its enrollees from time to time, perhaps for more specialized care than it can render. There is no reason that, having contracted with the patient to provide all the care he needs, the HMO should be precluded from doing so on occasion by employing outside physicians for the purpose, and indeed it would be prejudicial to HMO subscribers to cut off the possibility that specialists' services could be obtained in this manner. Thus, one hopes that the bill will be read as being nonexclusive in its requirement, so that it would be sufficient if the HMO provided only *some* physicians' services, perhaps all primary care, through the specified mechanism. Similarly, although the requirement in *id.*, proposed § 1876(b)(4), of "proof of capability to provide comprehensive health care services" might be read to require either in-house capability or the financial capability to purchase needed additional services in the open market, the regulations should recognize either kind of capability as sufficient. The Comprehensive Health Service Organization of the Kennedy-Griffiths proposal would be permitted to purchase the services of outside physicians. *See* Kennedy-Griffiths bill § 47(a)(2). A proposal in New York would allow only emergency services to be purchased. *See* Note, *supra* note 7, at 979.

pay for the coverage of Medicare and FHIP beneficiaries. The price must be fair to the government and to the HMO and ideally should not involve the government too deeply in supervising the costs and practices of the HMOs with which it deals. The maximum price that the government would pay is, as noted above, ninety-five per cent of the cost of serving the same patient population under a fee-for-service system. Since this is a maximum figure, lower rates might be appropriate, but H.R. 1 provided only an indefinite guide as to how such rates would be fixed, stating that, subject to the ninety-five per cent ceiling, federal payments to HMOs would be determined by "taking into account the health maintenance organization's premiums with respect to its other enrollees (with appropriate actuarial adjustments to reflect the difference in utilization . . .) and such other pertinent factors as the Secretary shall prescribe in regulations . . . ."[45] It was thus contemplated that the primary guide for pricing services received by Medicare and FHIP beneficiaries would be the prices charged by the HMO to private subscribers purchasing HMO services with their own funds.

Tying the government's payments to the prices paid by private subscribers is an attractive idea. It makes each potential private subscriber a sort of proxy who would "shop" for health services not only for himself but also for one or more Medicare, FHIP, or Medicaid clients. For this "proxy-shopping" approach to be effective, however, there would have to be some requirement that each HMO have some minimum proportion of private subscribers. The administration's FHIP bill would require that at least half of the HMO's enrollees not be FHIP or Medicaid beneficiaries,[46] and H.R. 1 would similarly limit HMO enrollment of Medicare beneficiaries to fifty per cent.[47] If the two bills could be coordinated so as to preclude development of plans with half Medicare and half FHIP or Medicaid enrollees and to require specifically that self-supported subscribers constitute at least fifty per cent of the membership, the government should be able safely to rely on such subscribers' willingness to pay for the service as a guide in setting the price it would pay for persons under its sponsorship.

The proxy-shopping device would guarantee that the price the government paid for its clients was one determined, in effect, by a competitive market. It would control costs to the government not by introducing a cumbersome system of quality and cost audits but by relying on the private consumer, who is still the most sensitive indicator of relative values yet discovered. It would maximize free choice and would make the passing of the ultimate market test—the attraction of a relatively sophisticated paying customer—a prerequisite for the HMO's enrollment of each government-sponsored individual. This test would have to be met again and again and would in fact increase the HMO's incentive to attract paying customers since each "sale"

[45] H.R. 1, § 239(a), proposed § 1876(a)(2).

[46] S. 1623, § 201, proposed § 628(b)(5). Exceptions are made for the early years of operation and for special problems precluding compliance. *Id.*, proposed §§ 628(h)-(i).

[47] H.R. 1 as amended, § 226(a), proposed § 1876(b)(5).

would carry with it, as a bonus, the right to sign up a person who, not being price-conscious, must be persuaded only to want the service. The HMO's interest in attracting paying customers would serve to keep the price down, while its interest in attracting customers of both classes would serve to sustain the quality of care (at least as apprehended by the subscribers) and the conditions under which it was rendered. The problem of second-class medicine would be substantially avoided.[48]

The flaw in the proxy-shopping device in the original H.R. 1 lay in the lack of incentive to Medicare and FHIP beneficiaries to accept HMO enrollment rather than more expensive fee-for-service care. If their coverage was the same in either event and the advantage of the HMO's lower cost accrued not to them but to the government, they would be unlikely to surrender the free choice and possibility of greater attention at no extra cost that accompany government-financed fee-for-service care. The administration has evolved an answer to this problem that appears not to sacrifice the advantage of the proxy-shopping device. In the FHIP bill,[49] the cost problem is dealt with by first requiring the HMO to account separately for the costs of serving FHIP beneficiaries and other subscribers. Then there is a requirement that the "retention" rate—that is, profit as a percentage of income—on the FHIP group must not exceed that for the other group, and any such "excessive retentions" are required to be returned to the government unless they are applied either to providing increased benefits or to reducing premiums, coinsurance payments, or deductibles. Thus, as long as such "excessive retentions" are used to make HMO coverage more attractive than coverage under FHIP itself, the government will not require the HMO to refund any of its payments made at the full rate of ninety-five per cent of the anticipated cost of fee-for-service coverage.[50] Although first appearing in the FHIP bill, this approach was recently incorporated by the House Ways and Means Committee in its version of the Medicare amendments, which subsequently passed the House[51] and are now awaiting action by the Senate.

The FHIP bill thus represents a useful modification of the proxy-shopping device, providing in effect a 100 per cent subsidy to the HMO to provide attractive extra benefits to beneficiaries of the government program. The source of the funds for providing this subsidy is the efficiency of the HMO itself, which accounts for the existence and extent of the spread between the HMO's regular charges to private subscribers and the maximum amount the government is willing to commit. The most efficient HMOs will therefore be able to provide the most attractive benefit package to induce enrollment by FHIP beneficiaries.

---

[48] The private-subscriber requirement should of course be imposed with respect to each facility the HMO might operate in order that it could not be met by establishing one branch in the ghetto and one in the suburbs. In addition to avoiding the "separate-but-equal" stigma, this would encourage HMOs to locate themselves so as to be convenient to subscribers of both classes.

[49] S. 1623, § 201, proposed § 628(a)(2)(B).

[50] *Id.*, proposed § 628(a)(2)(A).

[51] H.R. 1 as amended, § 226(a), proposed § 1876(a).

Appropriately, the modified proxy-shopping device also allows the HMO to earn a profit in serving its FHIP enrollees that is proportionate to the profit which it is able to earn in caring for its private subscribers. The profit incentive is thus left intact, and only minimal government supervision is necessitated. The most difficult regulatory problems would probably be accounting ones, particularly in allocating joint costs between the government-sponsored enrollees and others.

Subsequent discussion relies heavily on the modified proxy-shopping technique of accomplishing the dual goals of controlling costs and providing attractive care for the elderly and the poor. Indeed, it forms an important cornerstone of the market-oriented delivery system that I advocate. Of course, a competitive market is essential to the functioning of the modified proxy-shopping device, and most of the rest of the paper explores the prospects in this regard.

B. Some Other Proposals

1. The Proposed Health Security Act (The Kennedy-Griffiths bill)

This bill, sponsored by Senator Edward M. Kennedy and Representative Martha W. Griffiths, would provide federally financed comprehensive health services for virtually all U.S. residents.[52] Financing of the program would be effected through a tax on employers, on employee income, and on self-employment income, with the federal government contributing up to an equal amount of funds, as required, from general revenues. The Health Security Trust Fund established with these contributions would pay for a wide range of services if rendered by a "participating provider," the qualifications for which are specified at length. Independent practitioners could qualify as "participating providers" and could elect to be paid on a fee-for-service basis, although a fee schedule would be imposed for each region, state, or area.

The bill indicates particular support for the delivery of services on a prepaid basis. The independent practitioner would have the option of electing to be compensated by the capitation method, receiving a fixed sum for each person on his list—that is, those to whom he is obligated to render, or arrange for, comprehensive care; a practitioner so compensated would fall just outside my definition of HMO since the capitation payment he receives covers only primary and not comprehensive care. The large-scale HMO is presented as a feasible, and perhaps favored, alternative, though under a different name—Comprehensive Health Service Organization (CHSO). Organizations satisfying specified criteria may be "participating providers" under the proposed scheme and will be eligible to receive the prescribed capitation payment for each person enrolled. An analysis of the bill provided by Congresswoman Griffiths describes the CHSO provisions as follows:[53]

---

[52] See note 4 supra.
[53] M. Griffiths, Section-By-Section Analysis [of the Proposed Health Security Act] 6, 1971.

The section [47] is designed to accommodate forms of organization typical of existing prepaid group practice plans, but also to be flexible enough to permit experimentation with somewhat different forms. In some urban or rural areas, for example, it may be impracticable to bring all of the various services together in one place, and the section has been designed to encompass what has been described as "comprehensive group practice without walls"; the basic essential is the assumption of responsibility for a reasonably comprehensive range of services (including health maintenance) on a continuing and coordinated basis, to a group of persons who have been chosen to receive all or nearly all their health care from the organization.

Other requirements are spelled out in this section: The organization must furnish services through the prepaid group practice of medicine, or as near an approximation to prepaid group practice as is feasible. It must be a nonprofit organization, or if several providers share in the furnishing of services the prime contractor with the Board must be nonprofit. All persons living in or near a specified service area will be eligible to enroll, subject to the capacity of the organization to furnish care and subject to minimal underwriting protections. Services must be reasonably accessible to persons living within the specified service area. Periodic consultation with representatives of enrollees is required. Professional policies and their effectuation, including monitoring the quality of services and their utilization, is to be the responsibility of a committee or committees of physicians. Health education and the use of preventive services must be stressed, and lay persons are to be employed so far as is consistent with good medical practice. Charges for any services not covered by Health Security must be reasonable. Finally, the organization must agree to pay for services furnished by other providers in emergencies, either within the service area of the organization or elsewhere, but may meet this requirement to the extent feasible through reciprocal service arrangements with other organizations of like kind.

This formulation differs from the administration's HMO (1) in requiring the CHSO (a) to be a nonprofit entity, (b) to consult on policies and practices with its enrollees, and (c) to replicate the prepaid group practice model to the extent feasible, and (2) in providing greater specificity about numerous elements that are consistent with the HMO concept in the administration's bill but would not be legally embodied in it, such as utilization of paramedical manpower, maintenance of reasonable charges on services not insured, and maintenance of health education and peer review. The bill seems to contemplate greater supervision of internal affairs than the administration's proposal would impose.

Incentives for the formation and efficient functioning of CHSOs would be afforded by allowing a bonus payment, in addition to the capitation payment, if the organization can establish that, during a fiscal year, (1) the average utilization of hospital and skilled nursing home services was less than the average utilization of such services by comparable population groups not enrolled in such organizations, and (2) the services of such organization have been of high quality and adequate to the needs of its enrollees. The bonus would be equal to seventy-five per cent of the savings achieved and could be used by the organization for "any of its purposes," including the elimination of deductibles and copayments and the provision of additional services not covered under the bill.[54]

In assessing the probable performance of CHSOs, it can be seen that the utilization bonus, if applied to giving additional benefits or to beautifying the clinic's surroundings or to membership recruitment, could lead to increased enrollments. To the extent increased enrollments would permit realization of further efficiencies and hence higher salaries, the physicians involved in formulating CHSO policies might be inclined to invest in such growth, and over-all (though perhaps gradual) growth of the CHSO sector could reasonably be anticipated. The bonus and the benefits of other efficiencies of course represent a "profit" which, in view of the requirement of nonprofit status, may not be distributed to investors but may be reflected in physician and administrator salaries. It does not appear that these would be controlled, although distribution of the utilization bonus directly to the medical staff might be prevented under the vague requirements noted above.

2. "Ameriplan"

This is the designation of a plan approved by the American Hospital Association (AHA) as its proposed solution to the nation's health care needs.[55] The plan would be similar to the administration's in providing for the aged through the Social Security mechanism and for the poor and near-poor through a federal program. Other persons would purchase basic protection—the "standard benefits package"—from prepayment plans or private insurance companies. As a distinctive feature, a two-part package covering "health maintenance and catastrophic illness benefits" would be provided for all persons through a federal program covering the poor and near-poor from general federal revenues and all others through a tax collected though the Social Security system.

Entitlement to the "health maintenance and catastrophic illness benefits package" would be conditioned on a consumer's previous purchase of the "standard benefits package" and registration with a "Health Care Corporation" (HCC). The HCC is the cornerstone of the plan and its nearest counterpart to an HMO. It will be paid on a capitation basis to provide the federally financed "health maintenance" benefits but will be paid for all other services at rates regulated prospectively by state health commissions. Forswearing capitation for these remaining services because of "technical difficulties" and the HCC's undue exposure to financial risk, it nevertheless looks ahead to "the development of total capitation payment."[56] The HCC

---

[54] Kennedy-Griffiths bill §§ 87(d)-(e).

[55] AMERICAN HOSPITAL ASS'N, AMERIPLAN—A PROPOSAL FOR THE DELIVERY AND FINANCING OF HEALTH SERVICES IN THE UNITED STATES (Report of a Special Committee on the Provision of Health Services, 1970) [hereinafter cited as AMERIPLAN]. The plan is said to have been modeled on Health, Inc., of Boston, which is described as a "primary responsibility" organization. Note, *supra* note 7, at 919.

[56] AMERIPLAN, *supra* note 55, at 45. It has been said of Health, Inc. (*See* note 55 *supra*), that "[W]hile it offers fee-for-service on the theory that most people are unfamiliar with anything else, it will encourage consumers to contract with the plan for prepaid comprehensive care." Note, *supra* note 7, at 919.

could make any arrangement it wished with actual providers, employing physicians on a salary, capitation, or fee-for-service basis. The state health commission would license HCCs and establish their primary service areas. Such service areas would be exclusive unless more than one such corporation could establish its capacity to "coordinate needed services effectively" within the area.[57] The HCC would have to demonstrate its ability to care for all persons in its service area who might voluntarily register during regular periods of open registration and would be expected to attempt to recruit an assigned list of potential registrants. It could, however, also accept registrants from outside its primary area to fill its quota.

Each HCC would be directly responsible for the delivery of health care to its registrants, either through its own facility or through contracts with other providers. It would be required to render emergency care to nonregistrants and could provide other services to nonregistrants to the extent that the quality and adequacy of services to registrants would not be jeopardized. The HCC would also be responsible for monitoring the quality of care and for securing the participation of physicians in management and of consumers in policy making. Incentives for rendering preventive care and efficient utilization would be supplied by means of bonuses of the kind described in connection with the Kennedy-Griffiths bill. The HCC would be responsible for the competence of its personnel, and the proposal recommends that the present manpower licensure system be phased out.

By withholding important federal benefits from persons not registered with an HCC, Ameriplan would effectively compel such registration. This requirement would make the Health Care Corporation not merely an available alternative but practically the sole vehicle through which health care could be obtained. Consumers would have no opportunity, or at least no encouragement, to purchase HMO-type care, and individual HCCs would effectively monopolize most markets, with exclusionary regulation apparently contemplated through the system of primary service areas. Each HCC would probably be dominated by physicians dedicated to the preservation of lucrative fee-for-service medicine and would therefore be operated merely as a fiscal agent with that purpose in view. Unless this orientation was reasonably guaranteed, physicians would not accept the plan, since a monopsonistic purchasing agent not under their control might be capable of greatly depressing their incomes.

3. "Medicredit"

The proposed Health Care Insurance Act of 1971, introduced in the Ninety-second Congress as H.R. 1460 and S. 987, is the so-called "Medicredit" proposal of the American Medical Association (AMA). The plan is designed to encourage and facilitate the voluntary purchase of basic and catastrophic health insurance coverage. For persons with no income or income so low as to produce no income tax liability for the base year, the federal government would issue vouchers for full payment for

---

[57] AMERIPLAN, *supra* note 55, at 20.

the coverage specified by the act. Persons with income tax liability would likewise have the portion of the premium attributable to catastrophic coverage paid in full by the government. Tax credits scaled to the amount of tax liability and in some cases part-payment vouchers from the government would be available for application toward the premium for basic coverage.

The principal thrust of the proposal is thus concerned with the financing of insurance protection, although necessary components of the benefit packages are specified and carriers would have to meet qualifications established by state insurance departments pursuant to minimum federal standards. The crucial problem of the system whereby care is actually rendered is not addressed other than by a proscription against federal supervision or control over the practice of medicine, and apparently no federal encouragement of change in delivery methods is contemplated. The AMA's preference for maintaining the many existing barriers against HMO formation is manifest.

III

A MARKET-ORIENTED HEALTH CARE SYSTEM

The administration's proposals stand out among the competing plans in allowing the market a more substantial role in allocating resources, stimulating efficiencies, and controlling utilization of the system. Other proposals, particularly Kennedy-Griffiths, would introduce financial incentives here and there to induce physicians and administrators to do what the proponents think they should do, but otherwise would abjure the market and substitute comprehensive economic regulation in its place. The AMA plan would perpetuate the status quo with respect to the organization of the health care system and, while ostensibly relying on the market, would in fact continue in effect the restraints that have so far precluded a fair test of the HMO's attractiveness to consumers. The AHA Ameriplan, by forcing everyone into large Health Care Corporations, would create monopolistic tendencies in the marketplace so that market forces would have little opportunity to perform their customary functions, necessitating comprehensive regulation.

It is my thesis that a market-oriented system—by which I certainly do not mean laissez-faire or contemplate such drastic measures as termination of physician licensure—would be preferable to the alternatives so far presented. But the market cannot function until existing legislative and professional restraints in health care are lifted, until regulatory efforts are redirected to stimulate and guide, rather than to displace or repress, market forces, and until all the American people are provided with the means of entering the health care marketplace. The administration's proposals, while requiring some substantial modifications and clarifications, have the potential for creating conditions under which market forces could adequately perform their usual allocative and incentive functions and vastly improve the performance of the health care industry.

A. The Possibility of Price Controls to Minimize the Impact of Increased Health Insurance

Prompt government action to make health care available to all Americans is, of course, desirable as a long overdue recognition of a basic civil right and public responsibility. But a sudden influx of previously deprived users into the system would necessarily stimulate the market to ration the limited available resources by attaching still higher prices to them. This result would appeal only to the sellers of these services, and Congress could understandably refuse to appropriate funds to provide care for the poor if, as has happened with Medicare, a large part of the public's investment would be lost in higher prices.[58] Price controls may therefore appear practically imperative if government is not to see providers enriched largely at its expense and care still denied to those whose circumstances, even with a government supplement for health care, would not permit them to bid effectively in the market against the more affluent.

The problem with price controls is that, if prices are not allowed to perform their usual rationing function, some other means of rationing must be found. The system has long used queuing—waiting time—to limit consumption in public clinics, and this could be expected to increase throughout the system. Physicians would be over-burdened and would probably, in keeping with either a sense of professional obligation or much stricter utilization controls, tend to ration their time in accordance with direness of need, turning away the insignificant, self-limiting complaints. Quality of care might be more seriously jeopardized as less ethical physicians, of the kind who profited so handsomely from Medicaid,[59] shortened the time given to treating substantial complaints, without reducing their bills. Whether a black market in health services could get established on a broad scale is perhaps doubtful, but the temptation to resort to bribery would certainly be present.

These possibilities are far from palatable, but the alternatives are perhaps no more attractive. The shortage of resources and the consequent need for a nonprice rationing system would be equally great under the Kennedy-Griffiths national health insurance proposal, which would, however, not provide adequate incentives for attracting private talents and capital into the service of the nation's health, thereby prolonging the shortage and the need for rationing services. The hope, of course, is that rapid HMO growth would introduce new resources, efficiencies, and checks on utilization that would render short-lived any shortage created by new federal programs of health care financing. One cannot of course make reliable predictions in this regard, but the expectation seems not unrealistic.

My preference for a "market-oriented system" of health care delivery does not

[58] One estimate is that approximately half of the additional funds poured into medical care between 1966 and 1969 was swallowed up in price increases. Cooper, *Medical Care Outlays for Aged and Non-aged Persons, 1966-1969*, Soc. Sec. Bull., July 1970, at 3, 11.

[59] *See* Stevens & Stevens, *Medicaid: Anatomy of a Dilemma*, 35 Law & Contemp. Prob. 348, 407-15 (1970).

necessarily exclude price controls designed to minimize the impact of universal health insurance. The question reduces to which rationing system is more appealing, all things considered, and this is ultimately a political decision. One can appreciate Congress's reluctance to repeat the Medicare-Medicaid experience with the unpredictable magnitude of price increases attributable to bidding for scarce resources.[60] Moreover, I have a sense that the disadvantaged would come out worse, at a higher price to taxpayers, if prices are not controlled and that a system of queuing and utilization controls would steer medical resources to their best uses more reliably than an auction system would. Furthermore, Congress may find it politically easier to impose an added burden in finding health care on middle-class voters than to vote the appropriations and the taxes necessary to finance new health services under conditions of shortage. In any event, without venturing a final opinion on the ultimate issue of the need for or desirability of price controls, I can advance several conditions that, under my preference for primary reliance on market forces, should be met by any controls that might be introduced.

First, they should be temporary. There is as yet no reason for making health care the first industry brought by Congress under comprehensive economic regulation since the Depression era. Indeed, the experience with existing schemes of such regulation is anything but reassuring about the ability of regulation to cope with even relatively easy problems, let alone the incredibly complex job of costing individual medical procedures, eliminating price discrimination, valuing the services of individual practitioners, and maintaining the quality of service under a system of "public utility" medicine.[61] The basis for my confidence concerning the market's ability to take over the bulk of the regulatory job once the supply-demand imbalance is roughly restored is set forth at length later on.

Second, price controls should be ceilings only—with lower competitive charges encouraged—and should be in the nature merely of a freeze on all but cost-related increases. In addition to being the simplest and, in the short run, the fairest regulatory mechanism, a price freeze contemplates and lends itself to eventual lifting of the controls and restoration of a market regime. The pending Medicare amendments would use existing prices as a basis for establishing price ceilings,[62] and a temporary freeze might be easily modeled on those provisions.

Third, no direct price controls should be imposed on HMOs except for an across-the-board limit of the kind proposed for government payments to HMOs in the Medicare amendments, namely a premium ceiling of ninety-five per cent of the actuarially determined cost of caring for the HMO's patient population in the fee-for-service sector.[63] Since prices in the latter would be temporarily controlled, the

---

[60] *See* note 58 *supra.* On the estimation problems, see Stevens & Stevens, *supra* note 59, at 378-90. Conceivably the bad experience provided data that would facilitate better estimates in the future.

[61] Some of the problems of introducing comprehensive regulation of hospital charges are indicated in the text accompanying notes 128-39 *infra.* The same arguments would apply a fortiori to physicians' fees and HMO charges.

[62] H.R. 1, § 224. *See* H.R. REP. No. 91-1096, 91st Cong., 2d Sess. 35-38 (1970).

[63] *See* text accompanying note 34 *supra.*

danger of HMO profiteering would be substantially eliminated, and indeed the public would be assured of at least a five per cent saving over the controlled price to the extent it elected HMO-provided care. A particularly attractive by-product of leaving HMOs free to earn profits within this liberal constraint might be substantially increased attractiveness to physicians of HMO employment as providing both a relative haven from government control and a better opportunity for increasing earnings. Such increased incentives for HMO organization under a system of frozen fee-for-service prices would speed the realization of efficiencies and the needed reallocation of resources.

B. Has the Market Already Failed?

My advocacy of a market-oriented system will seem strange to those who believe that the present health care crisis itself reflects a colossal market failure.[64] A word to clarify this point may therefore be in order.

The medical profession's remarkable success in repressing market forces has been amply demonstrated elsewhere.[65] The American Medical Association's domination of the licensure system and particularly of the medical schools since the Flexner Report[66] has limited the number of physicians and raised physician incomes.[67] Emulating the physicians' example, other health professions have likewise obtained exclusionary licensing legislation, which has further raised costs by restricting the supply and mobility of health manpower and the opportunities for achieving efficiencies in the rendering of care.[68] In the name of medical "ethics," prepaid group practice was successfully limited in its impact, often by restrictive state legislation, and generally prevented from competing on an equal footing with fee-for-service providers.[69] A combination of "ethics," customs of the trade, and pressures of varying degrees of subtlety have repressed even the vestiges of price competition in

[64] This belief is widely shared and indeed is a dominant assumption in the debate. *See, e.g.*, Letter to the Editor from William J. Taylor, N.Y. Times, Apr. 16, 1971, at 36, col. 3; Falk, *National Health Insurance: A Review of Policies and Proposals*, in this symposium, p. 669, 693.

[65] *See generally* E. RAYACK, PROFESSIONAL POWER AND AMERICAN MEDICINE (1967); Kessel, *The A.M.A. and the Supply of Physicians*, 35 LAW & CONTEMP. PROB. 267 (1970); Rayack, *Restrictive Practices of Organized Medicine*, 13 ANTITRUST BULL. 659 (1968); Kessel, *Price Discrimination in Medicine*, 1 J. LAW & ECON. 20 (1958). Note, *supra* note 7, at 954-60; Comment, *The American Medical Association: Power, Purpose, and Politics in Organized Medicine*, 63 YALE L.J. 937 (1954).

[66] A. FLEXNER, MEDICAL EDUCATION IN THE UNITED STATES AND CANADA (1910).

[67] *See* Kessel, *The A.M.A. and the Supply of Physicans*, 35 LAW & CONTEMP. PROB. 267 (1970); CARNEGIE COMMISSION ON HIGHER EDUCATION, REPORT ON MEDICAL EDUCATION (1970). There has been much debate as to whether there is truly a physician shortage, some arguing that resources are simply badly distributed. *Compare* R. FEIN, THE DOCTOR SHORTAGE: AN ECONOMIC DIAGNOSIS (1967), *with* E. GINZBERG & M. OSTOW, MEN, MONEY, AND MEDICINE (1969), and McNerney, *Why Does Medical Care Cost So Much?*, 282 N. ENG. J. MED. 1458 (1970). Of course, since there is no easy means of redistributing physicians, the debate seems academic. Improvement of money-making opportunities in areas of shortage would seem to be only one step in luring physicians to those places; educational subsidies to area residents also seem promising.

[68] *See* Forgotson, Bradley & Ballenger, *Health Services for the Poor—The Manpower Problems*, 1970 WISC. L. REV. 756. On licensure generally, see M. FRIEDMAN, CAPITALISM AND FREEDOM ch. 9 (1962); L. Friedman, *Freedom of Contract and Occupational Licensing 1890-1910: A Legal and Social Study*, 53 CALIF. L. REV. 487 (1965).

[69] *See* Note, *supra* note 7, at 954-75; Comment, *supra* note 65, at 976-96.

the delivery of physicians' services.[70] Under these conditions, the market has never had a chance.

It is ironic that ethics and the quality of care have been so successfully advanced as justifications for restrictive legislation and professionally authorized restraints of trade. Whether this was always wholly a pretext on the part of the proponents of restrictive policies is of course doubtful, but the total effect was a raising of the cost of care and the incomes of health professionals. It was apparently not recognized that the allegedly high ethical and quality standards resulting from these exclusionary practices would be heavily paid for, not only in cash by paying patients but also in the suffering and lives of those who were effectively denied care. One regrettable but still recurring theme in medicine is the continuing willingness of many people, most of them prompted only by professional conscientiousness and a real concern for patient welfare, in effect to deny care to large groups in the society on the ground that such care, if provided, might not be good enough by the standards of middle-class medicine. For example, this tendency to ignore the need for expanding quantity, even at the risk of some sacrifice in average quality, is manifested in the frequently encountered hesitation about permitting physicians freely to delegate functions,[71] about scrapping most licensure requirements, and—particularly relevant here—about allowing HMOs and other health care providers to return a profit to their nonphysician organizers. The point is also generally relevant to the objections to reliance on market forces to see that health care gets delivered: the objections are basically quibbles about whether quality might be slightly impaired, while the cost in undelivered care has been and can continue to be high.

The general obeisance to the medical profession's professions of ethical concerns where their economic interests were at least equally affected[72] is matched by this language from the Supreme Court's 1952 decision in *United States v. Oregon State Medical Society*,[73] an antitrust action brought unsuccessfully by the government to vindicate the position of health care prepayment plans in Oregon against certain alleged activities of the medical society:

> We might observe in passing, however, that there are ethical considerations where the historic direct relationship between patient and physician is involved which are quite different than the usual considerations prevailing in ordinary commercial matters. This Court has recognized that forms of competition usual in the business world may be demoralizing to the ethical standards of a profession.[74]

---

[70] Kessel, *Price Discrimination in Medicine*, 1 J. LAW & ECON. 20, 42-51 (1958).

[71] *See* Havighurst, *Licensure and Its Alternatives*, in PROCEEDINGS OF THE 3D ANNUAL DUKE CONFERENCE ON PHYSICIAN'S ASSISTANTS 121, 125-26 (1970).

[72] One citizen who has not been taken in by the profession's ethical pretensions is the typesetter responsible for the following in a recent galley proof: "The American Medical Association's Principles of Medical Ethics are . . . 'not laws but standards by which a physician may determine the proprietary [*sic*] of his conduct . . . .'" *Cf.* Note, *supra* note 7, at 955, *quoting* AMA, PRINCIPLES OF MEDICAL ETHICS.

[73] 343 U.S. 326 (1952). *See also* text accompanying notes 160-63 *infra*.

[74] 343 U.S. at 336. It was noted that the trial judge, in deciding against the government, had engaged in "irrelevant soliloquies on socialized medicine, socialized law, and the like . . . ." *Id.* at 331; *see*

Since this view has had many adherents in the state legislatures and in attorney-general offices as well as in the courts, the medical profession has been largely self-regulated by the medical societies and by the doctor-run state boards of medical examiners, who are legally charged with policing the profession's ethics. Any student of antitrust knows that a self-regulatory regime organized for the prevention of "unethical business practices" is likely to be a device to suppress competition. In most other areas the courts have rejected pleas that a particular industry is a "special case" and have enforced the antitrust laws to restore a competitive regime.[75] With respect to medicine, however, neither courts nor legislatures were so perspicacious, and the market was denied its accustomed role.

The greatest failure of the health care system has of course been in delivering care to the poor. Some of the responsibility here is government's, for failing to recognize the need and to employ its powers of wealth redistribution to make decent health care financially available to all citizens. Government largely surrendered its responsibility to the medical profession, which undertook to provide charity services in return for noninterference. It was thus the profession's failure properly to honor its commitment that produced the crisis, for if the profession had been meeting the needs, there would have been either no need for Medicare and Medicaid or no supply-demand imbalance when they were enacted. Nevertheless, government's abdication of its wealth redistribution function in favor of the medical profession and private charity seems the ultimate cause of the system's failure. The market was implicated only to the extent that it distributes the rewards of the society unequally, a circumstance that is to some extent within the power of government to change. Fortunately, Congress seems about to act to bring about a long over-due rectification of wealth discrepancies with respect to health care.[76]

95 F. Supp. 103, 109-10 (D. Ore. 1950). This juxtaposition of the two professions' interests should indicate that lawyers, who have reasonably effective trade associations of their own, are not conspicuously well qualified to pass, either as legislators or as judges, on the proper role of the market in the delivery of professional services. The judiciary's somewhat more enlightened treatment of the legal profession's analogous activities deserves mention, however. Cf. Brotherhood of R.R. Trainmen v. Virginia ex rel. Virginia State Bar, 377 U.S. 1 (1964).

[76] E g., United States v. National Ass'n of Real Estate Boards, 339 U.S. 485 (1950); Fashion Originators' Guild of America, Inc. v. FTC, 312 U.S. 457 (1941); Sugar Institute, Inc. v. United States, 297 U.S. 553 (1936); Northern Calif. Pharmaceutical Ass'n v. United States, 306 F.2d 379 (9th Cir.), cert. denied, 371 U.S. 862 (1962); United States v. Utah Phamaceutical Ass'n, 201 F. Supp. 29 (D. Utah), aff'd per curiam, 371 U.S. 24 (1962).

[76] The basis for treating health care as a specific subject for wealth redistribution—a "merit good"—is complex. See generally R. MUSGRAVE, THEORY OF PUBLIC FINANCE (1959). To some extent there has always been a societal commitment to render care to persons unable to pay, and the question is in large part merely one of how to finance this service and how better to deliver on a moral commitment long since made but not conspicuously well honored. Further, better health care for the poor may generate externalities benefiting the public generally, primarily by helping to break the poverty cycle and produce more self-supporting citizens. But see Lave & Lave, Medical Care and Its Delivery: An Economic Appraisal, 35 LAW & CONTEMP. PROB. 252, 255 (1970). The harder questions relate to the limits of the commitment and particularly to their implementation. For example, who tells the indigent patient that his benefits are exhausted and that he is asked to leave the hospital? At this point, the burden, which the state escapes by impersonally declaring a dollar limit on the benefits it will pay, falls on the providers of care as a moral matter. While some providers are the beneficiaries of direct public sub-

In the light of the foregoing it cannot be argued that the market's failure accounts for the present state of affairs. In attaching blame, if that is important, it seems unfair to expect the organized medical profession to have acted against its self-interest. Rather, the fault lies with well-meaning policy makers who failed to make the profession's trade-restraining activities unlawful and indeed enacted many trade restraints into positive law. The mystique surrounding medical care and the "physician-patient relation" served to validate the profession's assertions of high ethical and quality standards and led many well-meaning persons into becoming, in Kessel's phrase borrowed from the 1930s, "dupes of the interests."[77] It is thus ironic in a purportedly free-enterprise system that, where radical reforms of the health care delivery system are being proposed on every side, the most radical reform possible might be restoration of a free market. This, coupled with supplementary regulation and a carefully designed system of universal health insurance, could be expected to produce swift and dramatic but orderly change.[78]

C. Some Shortcomings of the Market for Health Services[79]

Even under the best of circumstances, the market for medical care could never function as smoothly as might an unrestrained market for services like those of, say, a barber. For one thing, consumers are not always capable of accurately evaluating the doctor's skill. Moreover, they are not in a position to know what services are and are not needed, and they are consequently forced to delegate numerous economically important decisions to the physician. Finally, these decisions of the physician as well as the consumer's own may often be influenced by the presence of health insurance, which largely removes the cost constraint on the consumption of health services.

We have already seen how HMOs can help to overcome the problem of the consumer's ignorance as to when he is receiving excessive care as well as some of the distorting effects of third-party payment, but, again because of consumer ignorance, HMOs may feature tendencies of the opposite kind, toward denial of needed care as a result of excessive cost-consciousness on the provider's part. The further problem of consumer inability to judge the quality of services received would also still exist to some extent in an HMO-dominated marketplace, and some fee-for-service providers would continue to operate with their bills paid in large part by health insurance carriers, thus perpetuating for consumers choosing that mode of care

---

sidies which enable them to absorb some such costs, the system is anything but rational. Moreover, it seems to defy rationalization that would satisfy both economic and ethical concerns. Clearly there remains a large role for charity even in a health care system dominated by government.

[77] Kessel, *supra* note 67, at 268.

[78] *See* T. Lowi, The End of Liberalism 59 (1969), which, in ranking public and private policies according to their relative likelihood to produce change, includes "Social Security programs based on graduated income tax," "real antitrust," and "competitive business" near the top of the list.

[79] *See generally* H. Klarman, The Economics of Health (1965); Arrow, *Uncertainty and the Welfare Economics of Medical Care*, 53 Am. Econ. Rev. 941 (1963); Fuchs, *The Contribution of Health Services to the American Economy*, 44 Milbank Memorial Fund Q., pt. 2, no. 4, at 65 (1966); Lave & Lave, *supra* note 76, at 252.

some of the market irregularities that have contributed to the present problem. Nevertheless, significant as these departures from the competitive model are, consumers of medical care are probably not much worse off than consumers of many other technical services. For example, I feel about as competent to deal with doctors as I do to instruct an auto mechanic. And in either case my opportunity for repeated dealings and for obtaining confirming opinions from other consumers permits me more secure judgments than I can exercise in choosing a one-time supplier or serviceman from the "yellow pages."

Although many goods and services are bought and sold under substantially less than ideal competitive circumstances, the government has not always intervened. More important, it has often limited its intervention to a strengthening of market forces or to the introduction of some requirement thought to be inadequately enforced either by the market or by apprehensions about potential tort liability or other legal consequences.[80] Therefore, the first question with respect to health care is whether acceptable performance could be expected of the market mechanism if policies were tailored in a conscious attempt to achieve it. If doubt persists, then a regulatory alternative must be considered, but, because regulatory schemes, like economic analysis, are also based on faulty assumptions—about regulators' motivations, resources, and competence and about the tractability of problems—, they should be evaluated with as much skepticism as is the market's behavior. Unfortunately, a comparative inquiry into the relative imperfections of a market-oriented solution to the health care crisis on the one hand and a comprehensive regulatory solution on the other is beyond the scope of this paper. But, while I have confined myself to showing how the market could be expected to function under policies designed to improve its performance, I must say that I have greater confidence in both our ability to predict these matters and the attractiveness of the outcome (even with some deviation from expectations) than I have in our ability to design an appealing regulatory and administrative scheme. I am also impressed by the difficulty of reversing our direction once we are committed to the latter course.

D. How a Market-Oriented System Might Work

Taking the administration's proposals as a starting point, it is possible to speculate about the total performance of a health care market which has been freed of pernicious restraints and which is instead regulated in accordance with wiser policies. It will be appropriate after offering this hopeful description to deal with some specific issues that may be raised and to indicate the policies necessary to realize the hopes expressed and to minimize any fears.

---

[80] For example, the automobile industry is widely thought to be less than highly competitive, due in large part to there being only four domestic manufacturers. Nevertheless, when safety issues were raised, it was thought sufficient to regulate only the industry's safety equipment, since the market and the legal system appeared not to supply sufficient incentives to cause either consumers or producers to value safety highly. *See* National Traffic and Motor Vehicle Safety Act of 1966, Pub. L. No. 89-563, 80 Stat. 718, 15 U.S.C. §§ 1381-1425 (Supp. III, 1968).

In these prognostications I have assumed that HMOs will prove capable of offering significantly lower prices for coverage than do health insurers. The assumption is reasonable, since, whether due to inherent advantages or not, HMOs do appear to feature greater organizational efficiency and effective discouragement of overutilization. Of course, the HMO may gain further advantages by skimping on needed care or by attracting less intensive users of the system—persons less put off by the difficulty of getting the HMO to give attention to minor, self-limiting complaints;[81] if these are real possibilities, the HMO's competitive effectiveness may be somewhat greater than is warranted by the quality of its product, placing fee-for-service medicine at a slightly unfair competitive disadvantage. The corner-cutting issue is discussed at length shortly and is not deemed an insurmountable problem. The further possibility that consumers with low use propensities will be attracted seems not to be a valid basis for criticism since there is room for a system that is less responsive to insignificant complaints; moreover, lower use propensities should entitle subscribers to pay less for coverage than they do under health insurance, where they cannot select themselves out and are consequently exploited by those who overuse the system. In any event, whatever the source of HMOs' advantages, their presence in the marketplace seems likely to enforce efficiency and less discriminatory pricing in the fee-for-service sector with an effectiveness that no other system of social control could easily match.

HMOs could reasonably be expected to spring up in large numbers in a market freed of physician-sponsored restraints. Availability of federal funding would be a factor, though a small one, in such growth. More significant would be the attractiveness to private investors of the potential profits, which could be earned even with rates significantly below health insurance premiums for the same coverage. A requirement that employers make a choice among HMO alternatives available to all employees could open up tremendous competitive opportunities, and consumers, offered a lower-cost alternative and educated by advertising for the first time, could be expected to respond to that inducement as long as other factors did not reduce the attractiveness of HMO-type care. The market opportunities opened up would not be merely short-run phenomena since the federal financing commitment would promise permanent stability. Moreover, the health industry is one in which high rates of return are likely to prevail generally due to consumer willingness to pay for psychic satisfactions and not to make price the main consideration. In economic terms, the possibilities for differentiating "products" and exploiting consumer loyalties would seem to be great, and these factors, coupled with the likely prevalence in health care of large amounts of "consumer surplus"—the excess of each consumer's valuation of his benefits and satisfactions over the price he pays for them—, would allow each seller some pricing freedom. The resulting high profit potential could be counted on quickly to lure resources into the health care industry.

---

[81] See note 24 supra.

Offsetting the high profit potential would be a high degree of risk. Consumers of health services are apt to be volatile, transferring their patronage whenever their confidence in the provider wavers.[82] The marketplace envisioned would offer a sufficient number of both HMO and fee-for-service alternatives and sufficient information concerning each that providers would be faced with fluctuating profits. Once the supply catches up with the demand, high profits would be assured only so long as the provider succeeded in delivering a combination of cost, quality, convenience, and reassurance that a sufficient number of consumers desires.

One possible deterrent to the entry of profit-seeking enterprises would be the presence of nonprofit providers with whom it would be necessary to compete. These enterprises would be accorded certain tax advantages, would enjoy a preference among many consumers, and would have no need to show net earnings at the end of the year, making them formidable competitors. Therefore, rather than competing head-to-head for the customers of an existing nonprofit provider, profit-seeking enterprises would usually prefer to enter those markets, such as the inner city, where consumers were newly supplied with the means for purchasing care and where existing resources were inadequate to meet the new demand.[83] Nevertheless, nonprofit providers may often be so inefficient or may have priced their services so discriminatorily[84] as to invite entry. The competition thus offered by profit-seeking new entrants should be deemed healthy because it would compel efficiency and the elimination of the practice of pricing in accordance with ability to pay.

Greater problems may lie in the lack of managerial talents necessary to create HMOs[85] and in the lack of physicians' interest in accepting employment with them.[86] Nevertheless, no greater stimulus to the creation of the needed expertise could be imagined than the profit potential offered by the market, and businesses interested in diversifying into HMO operation would invest heavily in the necessary training.

---

[82] There is no inconsistency with the earlier reference to consumer loyalty. Volatility would occur at the margin and only when confidence was lost. Otherwise consumers would be disinclined to accept services elsewhere even at lower cost. The incentive to maintain consumer confidence would be very great.

[83] See Steinwald & Neuhauser, *The Role of the Proprietary Hospital*, in this symposium, p. 817.

[84] Discriminatory pricing takes several forms. One is pricing some services below cost and making up the difference through higher prices on other services. See *id*. at 832-34, discussing "cream-skimming," the name given to the proprietary hospital's alleged tendency to provide only the profitable services and to leave the unremunerative services to be provided by voluntary hospitals. Because benefit packages will be prescribed, HMOs will not be able to pick and choose the services they will cover, but in deciding what services to provide in-house they will have an opportunity to practice "cream-skimming" of this kind. The tendency will be to cause hospitals to price their various services more in line with costs.

Another kind of discriminatory pricing is the tendency to price in accordance with willingness and ability to pay. See notes 151 & 159 *infra*. To the extent HMOs offer a flat rate to all subscribers this discrimination would be eliminated. The only troublesome possibility might be a tendency of HMOs to neglect to recruit poor persons, even those supported under a federal insurance system, because of the expectation of unpaid bills for deductibles and coinsurance and for benefits in excess of those contracted for. See text accompanying notes 235-36 *infra*. The burden of caring for these persons would then fall on the voluntary sector, perhaps placing it at a competitive disadvantage.

[85] Note, *supra* note 7, at 953-54.

[86] *Id*. at 946-48.

Physicians, too, would respond to a substantial profit potential held out by the market. Particularly if fees in the fee-for-service sector were controlled to prevent the bidding up of prices for health services, doctors might find the HMO sector more attractive from an earnings standpoint. The potential efficiency gains in HMO operation could be made to redound very largely to the physicians' personal benefit, and they could be expected to move in significant numbers toward those areas where potential gains were greatest.

If a ceiling were imposed on fee-for-service charges, HMOs might soon be established in sufficient numbers to compete effectively with each other and with fee-for-service medicine, perhaps rather quickly driving charges in some areas well below the ceiling. Because competition would develop at different rates in different areas, the greater profit potentials remaining in areas not yet penetrated by HMOs would quickly lead to nationwide HMO establishment. The market would eventually establish the appropriate spread between the HMO's charge and the higher cost of health insurance applicable to the purchase of fee-for-service care; this spread—which could be denominated a "premium" if the word were not already being used in its insurance sense—would probably be substantially greater than the five per cent discount from fee-for-service cost contemplated in the administration's proposed Medicare amendments. Thus, if HMO charges should stabilize in the neighborhood of, say, eighty-five per cent of the current fee-for-service cost of caring for the same population, fee-for-service charges in the market area served by HMOs might fall to, say, ninety-four per cent of their present level if consumers found fee-for-service care only that much more attractive than HMO enrollment. In these circumstances, health insurers, faced with the shrinkage and possible disappearance of the fee-for-service sector, would tend to be stricter about utilization and the level of charges, ultimately driving costs down to levels where fee-for-service care would coexist in some measure with HMOs.

Smaller HMOs, lacking in-house capacity to render hospital and some specialized physician services, would purchase these in the fee-for-service sector, introducing a knowledgeable purchaser who could control utilization and shop with regard to price. Conscientious smaller HMOs, in serving their customers in this important middleman capacity, would hire the best specialists or highest-cost hospitals only for the most difficult cases; in more routine matters they would use less expensive providers, thereby helping the market to perform its important function of allocating scarce health resources to their best uses. (If such informed purchasing became widespread, the incomes of the best specialists might increase while the incomes of mediocre practitioners fell, improving currently weak incentives for achieving and preserving competence.) Patrons of such smaller HMOs, having access to the best specialists in time of greatest need, would possess an advantage denied subscribers to the larger, "closed-panel" plans. In a competitive market, less conscientious HMOs of this smaller variety which skimped too much in search of economies in the purchase of specialist and hospital care would lose subscribers, and serious cases of such overeconomizing would be subject to regulatory control.

The prices charged by different HMOs would vary, of course, even in the same market area. Because HMOs would be of different sizes and would have different reputations for quality and convenience and other things that consumers value, they would be able to price their service differently. Smaller HMOs, for example, would probably be less efficient but might provide more personalized and responsive care, enabling them to survive even at a substantially higher price than was charged by competing HMOs modeled on the Kaiser plans. By the same token, consumers would have a range of choices even in the HMO sector of the marketplace and would be able to shop for the combination of cost, quality, convenience, and amenities that best suited their particular need and pocketbook. As a further example of what the market, responding to consumer wants, might produce, one can visualize a two- or three-man pediatric HMO, providing well-baby and routine sick care in kind and purchasing orthopedic and other specialized attention in the open market; parents subscribing to such a plan might elect either membership in another HMO or insured-fee-for-service care for themselves.

In such a system, the poor and elderly would directly benefit from the efforts of HMOs to attract paying customers from among the self-supporting classes. As described earlier, this result might flow from use of the modified "proxy-shopping" device whereby a certain proportion of private subscribers would have to be attracted and satisfied before the government would pay the HMO to care for its clients. The HMO's efforts to attract such subscribers could be expected to drive down costs and keep up the quality and convenience of the services offered. In such a system, there could never be an accusation that "second-class" care was being provided to those groups who were sponsored by the government so long as the government was willing to pay the higher premiums—up to the ninety-five per cent ceiling—for Medicare, Medicaid, and FHIP beneficiaries who wished to enroll in smaller, higher-priced HMOs.[87] In addition to assuring the poor and elderly access to care of high quality, such a policy would increase the number of smaller HMOs that might exist in the marketplace, thereby preserving not only price competition but also competition in the quality and convenience of the care rendered.

E. The Issues Presented

In trying to picture the results of a properly organized marketplace, I have made some assumptions about market behavior and ignored certain possibilities that must

---

[87] H.R. 1 and the FHIP bill would permit payments up to the 95% amount, thus supporting the higher-priced HMOs. See text accompanying notes 49-51, *supra*. The latter would not be able to offer the inducements of greater coverage to the same extent as the larger HMOs but could compete on other grounds. Because the government would presumptively derive a 5% cost saving on every federal program beneficiary who could be induced to switch from the fee-for-service sector to HMO-type care, it should cultivate HMOs having different characteristics. Concern about relegating the poor and the elderly to the mammoth, superefficient, and impersonal HMOs should argue for the same policy.

now be examined. In the next section, I will take up the possible risks of introducing the profit motive into HMOs and particularly the fear that overeconomizing at the expense of patients' health might be encouraged.

Another controversial question is whether competition and the market can be relied upon to produce acceptable results or whether monopolistic and other anticompetitive forces might subvert the market's functioning. In this connection, the natural monopoly characteristics of the health care market will be considered, together with the risks of medical society exclusionary tactics that might foreclose meaningful HMO development. This discussion leads to a consideration of the antitrust laws as the appropriate means of policing the marketplace against anticompetitive activities. Next, the legislation necessary to overcome the effects of restrictive state laws is suggested, and, finally, a number of supplementary measures to improve market performance are discussed.

If the picture I have drawn of the market's potential performance seems overly hopeful, it is not beyond the range of realistic possibility. To the extent HMO development falls short of my optimistic estimate for reasons unconnected with continued market restraints, nothing would have been lost, and much might have been gained in widening the range of consumer choice and compelling greater efficiencies and utilization controls in the fee-for-service sector. The important thing is to provide the field for a fair market test.

IV

For-Profit HMOs

A truly vexing issue raised by a market-oriented system of health care delivery is whether an HMO should be permitted to earn a "profit"—that is, whether it may distribute to investors other than the participating physicians all or a portion of whatever is left of the premiums after the care contracted for has been rendered. The Nixon administration's proposal makes no distinction between nonprofit and for-profit HMOs, whereas the Kennedy-Griffiths bill would not allow a for-profit CHSO to participate as a provider of primary care.[88] The issue has already provided an occasion for substantial controversy.

In the Ninety-first Congress, the House of Representatives accepted that portion of the administration's proposed Medicare amendments which would have placed no limit on the profitability of HMOs and would have excluded no HMO from

---

[88] In introducing S. 836, *supra* note 8, Senator Javits termed it

"an effort to use the whole private enterprise system for the purpose [of providing access to health care], rather than to establish a new system, to use existing carriers, profit and nonprofit, and to encourage, by financing and other means, the development of group practice and other health maintenance organizations."

117 Cong. Rec. S1472 (daily ed. Feb. 18, 1971). Governor Rockefeller's plan for restructuring medical practice in New York State is reportedly similar to the administration's proposals, but it appears that the plan's equivalent of the HMO will be restricted to nonprofit status. *See* Severo, *Rockefeller Asks a Nonprofit Setup for Health Care*, N.Y. Times, Apr. 16, 1971, at 1, col. 1.

participation in Medicare solely on the ground that it was organized for profit.[89] The Senate Finance Committee, however, took issue with this tolerance of for-profit enterprises in the business of rendering government-financed health care. After noting the administration's strong advocacy of the HMO as a stimulus to cost reduction and quality improvements, the Committee said that it was

> concerned that, to the contrary, the health maintenance organization provision could turn out to be an additional area of potential abuse which might have the effect of increasing health care costs—paying a larger profit than is now or should be, paid to these organizations—and decreasing the quality of service available or rendered.[90]

The Committee proposed some rather complex revisions of the House bill to curb profitability,[91] and its version passed the Senate[92] only to die at adjournment before the differences between the two bills could be resolved. The debate on this issue is likely to be joined again in the Ninety-second Congress.

A. The Consequences of Excluding For-Profit HMOs

Before discussing the validity of the objections that may be raised to for-profit HMOs, it is useful to consider what may be at stake in excluding them since it seems to be more than a matter of principle. HMO formation is a costly and risky business, often involving major construction, extensive delays in reaching break-even operations, difficulty in employing medical staff and experienced managers, and problems in attracting sufficient numbers of consumers. Thus, although the potential for profitably delivering low-cost health care of acceptable quality would seem to be considerable, the risk attending any particular initiative in the formation of an HMO would also be substantial. In these circumstances, it is not clear that the voluntary-nonprofit sector or the governmental sector will be capable of generating either the funds or the entrepreneurial talents necessary to make rapid HMO growth a reality.

Without a profit stimulus, most of the HMOs likely to be formed will be sponsored by labor unions, employers, and substantial consumer groups. These plans will have primarily a middle-class base and may lack interest in caring for the persons now deprived of adequate care.[93] HMOs developed by university medical centers will be community-oriented and dedicated to meeting social needs, but the financial resources of these medical centers are already depleted and are badly needed

---

[89] H.R. 17550, 91st Cong., 2d Sess. § 239 (1970).
[90] S. Rep. No. 91-1431, at 132.
[91] *Id.* at 133-35.
[92] 116 Cong. Rec. S21314-46 (daily ed. Dec. 29, 1970).
[93] A requirement that the plan accept persons on a first-come, first-served basis will not prevent a plan from locating in areas far from the poor and from emphasizing middle-class persons in its recruitment efforts. The first-come, first-served requirement should not be viewed as in itself a substantial protection for the poor. This can come only by giving HMOs an incentive to seek them out and enroll them because it pays to do so.

to expand the capacity of their medical schools. It is therefore unlikely that many broad-based HMO ventures will be commenced except where massive federal support is supplied. President Nixon has proposed a substantial program of such support.[94]

Of course, physicians themselves may be counted upon to start a number of HMOs using their own capital or capital that they borrow on their own account. Their incentive for doing this is, of course, the hope of improving their own level of earnings by providing a service for which consumers will pay. There is no difference in principle between such investments by physicians and investments by private investors not possessing a license to practice medicine, except that the latter would have to retain or employ physicians on some basis to provide care that they or their HMO service corporation had contracted to provide. Thus, an HMO may be organized as a not-for-profit enterprise without its being so in fact, and to this extent it is misleading to attach great importance to the ownership of the sponsoring corporation without reviewing as well the terms of the contract with the physician group and the salaries or other compensation paid by it to its members.[95] No one but the AMA could find a reason for wanting to exclude all but physicians from participating in the profits of this potentially lucrative industry.[96] In any event, physicians, though affluent as a group, cannot be relied upon to supply sufficient funds.

To expect all HMO initiatives to originate with physicians seems clearly unwise. While many doctors are dedicated to social service, there is a limit to what they can do even with lavish federal grants. They are not trained as administrators, and, although the medical schools with which many of them are affiliated could provide administrative skills, the number and location of medical schools impose limits on what can be realistically expected. Doctors have certain preferences about where they want to live and about the kinds of patients they wish to treat. Only exceptional ones are likely to have both the taste and the entrepreneurial skills to initiate an enterprise that would take them into those areas where needs are most acute. Profit-seekers are less fastidious or particular, on the other hand, and could be expected to create opportunities for those physicians who might be attracted into deprived-area practice by the right offer but who otherwise would take the path of least resistance to the suburbs. Finally, physicians are also subject to pressures from their colleagues and, for this reason or because of more subtle influences traceable to their education and professional acculturation, might be more inclined to honor the organized profession's preferences as to the nature, scope, and aggressiveness of any HMO they might organize; nonphysician organizers, less inhibited by the "ethical" im-

---

[94] See text accompanying note 27 supra. The Health Policy Advisory Center (Health-PAC) estimates that the President's proposed $23 million in grants would pay for setting up HMOs serving 1,400,000 people. HEALTH-PAC BULL., Apr. 1971, at 3. In H.R. 5614, 92d Cong., 1st Sess. (1971), the administration proposes aid for medical-school-based HMOs.

[95] See, e.g., Complete Serv. Bureau v. San Diego County Medical Soc'y, 43 Cal. 2d 201, 272 P.2d 497 (1954). The shakiness of the profit-nonprofit distinction is observed in Note, supra note 7, at 962.

[96] See COMMITTEE ON MEDICAL FACILITIES, AMA COUNCIL ON MEDICAL SERVICE, REPORT ON PHYSICIAN-HOSPITAL RELATIONS 4 (1964) (recording opposition to plans in which "a third party . . . derive[s] a profit from payment received for medical services"), quoted in Note, supra note 7, at 956.

plications of competition, would be freer to start HMOs and to realize their true potential. The medical profession's inertia seems too great to be counted on alone for the needed initiatives.

There would therefore seem to be some reason to fear that elimination of the profit potential for nonphysician HMO organizers would significantly retard the growth of the HMO sector.[97] This would mean, quite simply, that needed care would not be rendered and that available efficiencies would not be realized. Even if some arguments against for-profit HMOs seem to have validity, they must be weighed against forfeiture of this potentiality for increased efficiency and for delivering care to people who are now seriously deprived. What may be at stake is whether the HMO will be an occasional experimental curiosity or a serious contender for the role of family doctor for millions of persons at all levels of society in all parts of the country.

Even at best, nonprofit HMOs would probably distribute themselves in such a way that few consumers would have access to more than one, producing a monopolistic situation not conducive to efficiency or to vigorous efforts to please consumers. Moreover, many nonprofit HMOs would be dominated, directly or indirectly, by persons beholden to the organized medical profession and consequently operated responsively to its interests rather than the interests of potential customers. Similarly, university medical centers are often alleged to operate with primary emphasis on their educational and research missions and to fail to hold the interests of their patients foremost. By this token, the performance of university-sponsored HMOs may fall short in important nonscientific respects.

In addition to being slow to develop, nonprofit HMOs are not likely to recruit aggressively both in the middle classes and among the poor. Even under statutory compulsion to engage in such recruitment, there may be a tendency to sign up blue collar employment groups exclusively. The result might be a kind of "public utility" medicine to which, even though the quality of care might be extremely high, the "second-class" image might attach because the conditions under which care was rendered were neglected. Waiting rooms would be crowded, and one could predict an increase in the agitation for consumer control of the delivery of medical care. On the other hand, under the market-oriented system outlined earlier, poor and elderly persons would generally be admitted only to plans that had proved their ability to attract paying patrons in a competitive environment. Health care consumers would indeed have a voice in the care they received, since they would have reasonable alternatives rather than the Hobson's choice of the public utility customer.

Another important dimension of the health care crisis has been the misallocation of capital resources, reflecting excessive or unwise investments undertaken by the

---

[97] The experience of proprietary hospitals, recounted with care by Steinwald & Neuhauser, *supra* note 83, at 818-30, demonstrates the importance of the profit motive in stimulating prompt response to new demand for health services. They show that proprietaries appear primarily in those places where the voluntary sector has failed to generate needed investment.

voluntary-nonprofit and governmental sectors.[98] One consequence of the predominantly nonprofit orientation of the industry has been to free decision makers to maximize just about any value they choose, including in too many cases the gratification of administrators' empire-building impulses or physicians' convenience and income derivable from utilization of plant purchased with government or charitable funds.[99] Thus, a few influential surgeons may be enriched through occasional use of an expensive heart surgery unit which was purchased with charitable funds and is maintained out of monopolistic charges to the hospital's paying patients.[100] The movement toward "comprehensive health planning" can be seen as an attempt to structure decision making in the nonprofit sectors so as to minimize these tendencies and eliminate the impact of conflicts of interests on the part of decision makers.

Of course no one contends any longer that the pursuit of profits inevitably benefits the public or that profitability equates directly with service of the public interest. Nevertheless, decision makers in profit-making enterprises are more closely disciplined—by the market, a constant if not perfect taskmaster—than are decision makers in the nonprofit sector, and their decisions are more likely to accord with public needs than the decisions we have gotten in the past from managers with the other primary goals. Indeed, the competition of profit-making HMOs, by eliminating discriminatory pricing, will deprive many decision makers in the nonprofit sector of substantial amounts of discretionary funds. This should increase accountability by requiring them to appeal more often to legislatures, bureaucrats, and private benefactors, who, with the help of comprehensive health planning, should be able to impose the cost-benefit discipline so lacking in the past. Although comprehensive health planning does promise some improvement in the handling of discretionary funds earned by monopolistic hospitals, curtailment of the opportunity to earn such funds through pricing of services without regard to cost should also be a goal of public policy. Even assuming that discriminatory pricing may once have served a useful function in making care more widely available, the tax system is a better means of redistributing the society's wealth. Indeed, the need for direct public subsidies for capital construction or other purposes may be largely obviated by a truly adequate system of universal health insurance and federal financing for the poor. Once all consumers have or have been given the ability to pay for health care,

[98] See Legislative Findings and Purpose, 1969 Laws of N.Y., ch. 957, § 2, quoted in Annot., N.Y. PUB. HEALTH LAW § 2803 (McKinney Supp. 1970) ("Continued pressure for unnecessary duplication of facilities and heavy standby commitments for under-utilized services in one area contrast with long waiting lists for admission to facilities in other areas."); Randal, *Wasteful Duplication in Our Hospitals*, THE REPORTER, Dec. 15, 1966, at 35; Note, *Unplanned and Uncoordinated Development of Hospital Facilities—A Need for Legislation*, 52 IOWA L. REV. 1187 (1967).

[99] See Cherkasky, *Resources Needed to Meet Effectively Expected Demands for Service*, 42 BULL. N.Y. ACAD. OF MED. 2D SER. 1089, 1091 (1966) (reference to "the haphazard manner by which programs and institutions have grown up in response to a local need, a trustee's pride, an administrator's ambition, a doctor's self-interest").

[100] See id.; H. KLARMAN, *supra* note 79, at 137.

the market should be able to attract and allocate resources satisfactorily, and perhaps only remote rural areas would then require special public investment.

The medical profession could be relied upon vigorously to oppose for-profit HMOs on ethical grounds,[101] and many legislators and policy makers will lend an attentive ear, for an ethical concern is indeed presented.[102] Nevertheless, physicians' preference for reserving the profits of the industry for themselves alone should not be taken too seriously. Denial of profit participation to outsiders in the past has deprived the industry of the benefit of entrepreneurial input and thus of one important ingredient of creative change. With innovational and managerial talents devalued and excluded by the holders of the industry's purse strings, the system failed to develop organizationally, and, partly as a consequence, the current crisis is one of disorganization and misallocation of human and material resources. The ethical importance of the system's breakdown and failure to deliver needed care would seem to outweigh whatever it is that the profession would have in mind in opposing proprietary influences in HMO formation.

Of course many nonphysician observers doubt the wisdom of market-inspired investment and incentives in a field where consumers are thought to be ignorant about true values and consequently prone to select their provider on irrational grounds. There is, however, no obvious reason to fear that mass merchandising will have anything like the effects in the health care field that Galbraith attributes to it in other areas.[108] On the other hand, consumer preferences for such things as convenience, personalized care, and certain amenities are entitled to expression, and indeed irrational factors have an important place in medical care, suggesting that

---

[101] *See* note 96 *supra*. The medical profession might attempt to bring its concerted opposition to for-profit plans under the recent case of Marjorie Webster Junior College, Inc. v. Middle States Ass'n of Colleges and Secondary Schools, Inc., 432 F.2d 650 (D.C. Cir. 1970). In that case, the association refused to accredit the plaintiff college on the sole ground that it was a proprietary institution, without regard to whether it measured up in quality terms. The court of appeals held that the Sherman Act did not apply to activities having "noncommercial" objectives, citing Apex Hosiery Co. v. Leader, 310 U.S. 469 (1940), and further that judicial interference with private groups would be limited by deference to professional judgment where the apprehended harm was not great. The court added, "we do not think it has been shown to be unreasonable for appellant to conclude that the desire for personal profit might influence educational goals in subtle ways difficult to detect but destructive, in the long run, of [an] atmosphere of academic inquiry . . . ." 432 F.2d at 657.

The *Marjorie Webster* case turns primarily on assumptions about the association's motives and objectivity, which the plaintiff had failed adequately to impugn. In the medical care field, where the profession's economic interests are so near the surface, there would be a much firmer basis for skepticism about any effort to exclude for-profit HMOs, and the result should be different. Neither the profession nor any "blue-ribbon" group within it should be given a chance to justify any flat exclusionary rule, with or without the benefit of judicial deference. The judgment on this question should be made finally by Congress, which alone can appraise the total situation and decide whether the health care system needs the shake-up that for-profit HMOs could provide.

[102] The yielding of a profit to one other than a physician could be considered a fee-splitting arrangement. *See* AMA, PRINCIPLES OF MEDICAL ETHICS § 7 (1957). The existence of a third-party profitmaker may also be thought to impose a risk of interference with "the free and complete exercise of [the physician's] medical judgment and skill." *Id.* § 6. More broadly, the risks of corner-cutting in patient care are fundamentally an ethical problem.

[108] *See* J. GALBRAITH, THE NEW INDUSTRIAL STATE 199-210 (1967).

consumers' wishes ought not to be too regularly second-guessed. Moreover, the consumer's highly valued right to take his business elsewhere should not be curtailed without good reason, particularly in a field, unlike telephone service, where personal rapport with and confidence in the provider of the service are so important. Certainly abuses are possible that would require control, but the needed controls can be achieved through regulation of advertising content and through supervision by accrediting agencies and other groups—the HMO offering free tonsillectomies to the children of new subscribers could not long remain in business! In view of the benefits derivable, selective controls on the excesses of the profit seekers should seem sufficient to obviate uneasiness about them.

Whether my high hopes would all be realized is, of course, uncertain. What is clear is that there is a realistic expectation that more health care could be rendered more efficiently and more cheaply to more people sooner if Congress is not too reluctant to allow market forces to function. A high profit potential has traditionally signaled the public's need for new resources, and the question is whether there is sufficient reason to depart from controlled use of the market's allocative function here.

B. The Risks

Recognizing that there is much to gain, we may now consider what risks would be run if for-profit HMOs were tolerated. In the course of this discussion it will be appropriate to consider the ways in which these risks can be minimized, if not eliminated, in order that the substantial benefits anticipated can be achieved without more than minimal danger. What must be avoided here, as elsewhere in the health care system, is the temptation to indulge fastidiousness about quality and other matters to the extent that some members of the public are denied their right to basic health care altogether.

1. Overeconomizing

The most arresting argument against for-profit HMOs is that they will on occasion be tempted to economize at the expense of patients' safety. Generally, of course, it is to the HMO's advantage to cure a patient as quickly as possible in order that his condition not worsen, thereby requiring greater expense to effect a cure. In the vast majority of cases this incentive will work to the combined benefit of the patient and the HMO proprietors, and their interests can be seen as coinciding. The troubling cases are those in which it would be clearly cheaper to let a patient die—death being the ultimate "economy" in these circumstances—rather than undertake expensive efforts to prolong his life, and there would probably also be instances in which the HMO would face the choice of providing a superior treatment that was extremely expensive or a less effective one that was cheaper. The problem in each case is that even with an HMO the incentives are not yet perfectly ordered, and therefore we still cannot rely totally upon the HMO's balancing of costs and benefits to produce optimal results; indeed, we would get closer to the desired incentive system if HMOs also provided life insurance coverage and if employers paid bonuses to the HMO for restoring their employees to good health—both extremely attractive possibilities that should be encouraged and perhaps even required by policy makers. Finally, there may be some reason to fear false economies which HMOs, taking too short-run a view, may occasionally practice.[104]

I think there are many reasons to doubt that HMOs will allow their economizing instincts to jeopardize life unduly or to dictate the choice of treatment. Moreover, I find a variety of substantial controls that already exist or could be introduced to prevent this from occurring.

Whether overeconomizing is a risk associated exclusively with for-profit HMOs is doubtful. If physicians are to respond to the incentives that HMO-type care is supposed to introduce, they must be given a financial stake in the outcomes of particular cases. This is typically done through profit-sharing arrangements and other incentives, and it would seem that the incentive to overeconomize would accompany the implementation of these incentive arrangements whether or not the HMO itself was organized on a for-profit basis. In either case the primary decision maker would be faced with a conflict of interests that could conceivably influence his judgment adversely to a patient in a particular case. There is no evidence that I know of, however, that prepaid group practice plans have been guilty of overeconomizing.

The lay management of a for-profit HMO might exercise limited control over some of the conditions under which care is rendered, influencing, for example, the ratio of staff to patient population or the decision on purchasing life-saving equipment. Those quality matters that are within the control of the HMO management would seem to be rather easily regulated from the outside by quality control teams assigned to visit the installation. Interference by lay management in the actual rendering of care is likely to be strictly prohibited.

Overeconomizing would be subjected to a number of significant sanctions. The first is, of course, the threat of malpractice suits against the HMO.[105] While many

---

[104] The representation that the HMO has an incentive to practice preventive medicine, to detect disease early, and to treat causes rather than symptoms assumes a long-range perspective. Presumably there will sometimes be uncertainties about payoffs and a tendency to short-run conservatism, yielding false economies of the sort referred to.

[105] *See generally* Aspen Systems Corp. (Health Law Center), Group Practice and the Law: A Digest of State Laws Affecting the Group Practice of Medicine 9-11 (1969). Note that malpractice law would fulfill a different quality control function with respect to HMOs than it has performed with respect to fee-for-service medicine, where undertreatment would seem to be a potential problem only when the patient lacks the ability to pay. *Cf.* Cantor, *The Law and Poor People's Access to Health Care*, in this symposium, p. 901, 909-13. (I know offhand of no malpractice case where skimping in the care of a nonpaying patient was charged.) Because of the limited cost-benefit awareness of fee-for-service doctors, courts should avoid being too much influenced by prevailing custom and practice in defining a standard of minimum treatment for HMOs. It is unlikely, however, that HMOs would be allowed by the courts to depart very far from standards in the fee-for-service sector, and therefore they may be compelled to adopt conservative policies in omitting x-rays and other tests and procedures of doubtful medical value. *See* notes 18 and 25, *supra*, and accompanying text. Nevertheless, since

instances of overeconomizing that might occur would escape the notice of potential malpractice plaintiffs, standards in the HMO would probably reflect a healthy respect for the possibility of such litigation, thus drastically cutting down the instances of corner-cutting. Regulatory oversight of quality could be expected to take into particular account those areas where overeconomizing would be likely to occur,[106] and it is certain that any federal legislative move into the health field will provide for substantial increases in external supervision of quality. While there are probably many things related to quality that such medical audits and other investigatory techniques cannot uncover, I would think that most kinds of overeconomizing on any substantial scale could be easily detected. In view of the small return from overeconomizing on any but the largest scale, coupled with the likelihood of detection and the high stakes involved—loss of accreditation, malpractice judgments, and, above all, the loss of consumer confidence—, the HMO's incentive to skimp on patient care would be small indeed.

The HMO's professional staff could be expected to maintain standards, to resist lay interference, and to insist on honoring their Hippocratic Oath. Consumers would be quick to react to any evidence of overeconomizing at their expense, either in the form of malpractice suits, formalized complaints, or word of mouth charges conveyed to other consumers. Anticipating consumer reactions, the HMOs would be extremely concerned about their image and any possible criticism on this score; indeed, I would expect the management to take no chances about matters of this importance. In very few cases will competition ever become so intense as to force HMOs into corner-cutting in search of short-run survival. Occasional cases of this kind might occur, but again there is little reason to think they would be more frequent in for-profit enterprises.

Finally, if one still fears overeconomizing by HMOs, it would be possible to require reinsurance against those risks that seem most likely to produce the temptation. Thus, an HMO might insure its enrollees against the need for such things as treatment in a cardiac care unit or hemodialysis. In any event, reinsurance is likely to be widely used by those HMOs which, because of the smaller patient population enrolled, could not safely rely on actuarial estimates to predict their costs. Reinsurance promises to play an important role in making smaller HMOs feasible and in improving their financial stability. It should also minimize fears about overeconomizing in those HMOs most likely to practice it.

HMOs may find it possible to have malpractice claims arbitrated rather than litigated, Doyle v. Giuliucci, 62 Cal. 2d 606, 401 P.2d 1, 43 Cal. Rptr. 697 (1965), a standard might be evolved in that forum which (1) would allow some freedom to cut back on the numerous minor items having a benefit-cost ratio of less than unity, but (2) would enforce a duty to care for the extremely sick patient without regard to cost, up to the limits of his coverage. Query, however, the HMO's obligation to preserve, at extraordinary cost to itself, the life of a comatose patient whose brain function is permanently impaired.

[106] The administration's proposals include a procedure that would enable consumers to bring their complaints about denial of desired services before an administrator. H.R. 1, § 239(a), proposed § 1876(f); S. 1623, § 101, proposed § 604(c); id. § 201, proposed § 628(f). Query whether these provisions would create a new forum in which to bring a certain class of malpractice cases. Query further whether the forum would be or should be the exclusive one for prosecuting such complaints.

2. Exploitation and Commercialism

A respectable body of judicial authority and tradition stands opposed to for-profit enterprises in the health care field. Much of the sentiment is expressed in the common-law rule against the corporate practice of medicine, which has been applied almost exclusively to for-profit enterprises.[107] The history of medicine discloses many examples of commercialism and exploitation of an unwary public by quacks and profiteering physicians,[108] and most recently distress has been voiced about the advertising, hard-sell tactics, and high prices of the abortion clinics in New York City.[109] Furthermore, proprietary hospitals and proprietary nursing homes have a bad name in some circles and have been the subject of some controversy.[110] All of these factors have contributed to producing a firm conviction on the part of many that the nonprofit tradition must be maintained. But, while these convictions do credit to their harborers, they cannot be honored without regard to cost. Thus, the countervailing considerations noted earlier—the need for incentives to stimulate HMO growth, the potential contribution of proprietary institutions to stimulating economic efficiency, and the need to enlist entrepreneurial talents in the reorganization of health care delivery—must be weighed against the substance of these concerns.

A popular shibboleth is that no one should profit from the illnesses of others. In a free economy, however, reasonable profits signify, at least prima facie, that a needed good or service is being adequately and efficiently supplied, and "excessive" returns betoken a shortage and serve the useful purpose of inducing new efforts to supply the still unsatisfied wants.[111] Of course, some may be tempted to turn the shibboleth around and to insist that health services are so important in the greater scheme of things that the rewards attached to delivering them should be very great. But this is equally wrong, for the price of services must ultimately relate to their cost, including what is needed to induce sufficient numbers of competent people to enter the business of rendering them. In any event, the whole argument has no substance, for physicians and other health personnel—and lawyers, too, for that matter—already "profit" from the misfortunes of others, and there is no way of arranging things otherwise.

Still, "excessive" profits earned in the rendering of health care remain ethically and socially troubling. I have already expressed my willingness to accept a temporary freeze on price increases in health services so that the shortages that would be

---

[107] See Note, supra note 7, at 960-62 and references there cited.

[108] See, e.g., J. Young, The Medical Messiahs (1967); Note, Quackery in California, 11 Stan. L. Rev. 265 (1959).

[109] E.g., Disciplinary Action for Abortion Solicitors Backed, Am. Med. News, Dec. 14, 1970, at 9.

[110] See generally Steinwald & Neuhauser, supra note 83, at 830-37.

[111] While distasteful in the extreme to many, the abortion clinics are providing a service intensely desired by some persons and in seriously short supply. The business is therefore profitable, and advertising makes it more profitable by stimulating demand. If health services of a less controversial kind were involved, their profitability and the effort to make them more widely available might strike us more positively. A New York trial court has recently held abortion referral agencies illegal in large part because of their "commercial" nature. N.Y. Times, May 14, 1971, at 1, col. 6.

created by improved accessibility would not overwhelm government's financing efforts and merely enrich providers. High profits earned temporarily by HMOs under such ceilings would not seem so objectionable since they would flow from achieved cost savings rather than from exploitative price increases.

As to the relevance of some of the experience of the past, some distinguishing elements can be observed. Government's legal powers and administrative capabilities are now somewhat better developed and suited to the job of policing the unethical and dangerous provider. Thus, reasonably effective controls can be exerted over existing operations, and primary reliance need not be placed on exclusion of would-be providers from the marketplace, a costly form of over-kill in an era of shortage. Perhaps more important, the market-oriented system would leave very little room for exploitation of the poor and the elderly, the groups most likely to be imposed upon by unethical providers. This results from the adoption of the modified "proxy-shopping" mechanism, which requires the HMO to demonstrate an ability to attract younger, self-sufficient, and relatively sophisticated consumers before the government would allow it to care for those citizens who are its special responsibility.

The poor reputation enjoyed by proprietary hospitals and proprietary nursing homes—on the justification for which I express no opinion—might suggest to some that tolerance of proprietary HMOs would be an invitation to abuse. But this loses sight of the fact that, whereas HMOs will generally have a direct stake in restoring their patients to health as quickly as possible, proprietary hospitals and nursing homes may not have been adequately penalized by the market for poor performance. The reason for their escape is that, due either to a shortage of facilities or to ignorance, infirmity, or the necessity of the moment, their customers may often not have been able to exercise free and informed choice. Thus, the accusations directed toward proprietary hospitals have been largely confined to their alleged use by their physician-proprietors as a means of facilitating overutilization, which their patients have not the opportunity, the knowledge, or perhaps the interest[112] to detect, and of avoiding the kind of peer supervision that is customary in voluntary hospitals.[113] Similarly, nursing homes may have had insufficient incentive to make their inmates' lives cheerful, since many patients, due to infirmity, disinterested families, and shortage of facilities, effectively lack the opportunity to take their business elsewhere.[114] It would seem that the proprietary HMO could be rather fundamentally distinguished from either of these institutions and that what may be regarded as their poor record ought not to be held as evidence against the proprietary HMO's potential for rendering quality care.

---

[112] *See* note 19 *supra.*

[113] Some think that proprietary hospitals have been to some extent the refuge of poor doctors. *See* Steinwald & Neuhauser, *supra* note 83, at 829. Whether or not this is so, HMOs would certainly not be such a refuge and could be expected to exercise more vigilant peer supervision than do other types of providers.

[114] *See generally Hearings Before the Subcomm. on Long Term Care of the Senate Special Comm. on Aging,* 91st Cong., 1st Sess., pt. 1 (1969).

The decision on for-profit HMOs is not likely to be made by a careful weighing of the merits of the issue but will instead reflect special interests and some emotions. Not only will the health care "establishment" oppose the challenge to their power that rapid HMO promotion by outsiders could produce, but most liberal reformers in the health field will also react negatively. Many of the latter will object viscerally to the proposed comingling of the profit motive with the humanitarian impulses which they wish reform both to reflect and to restore in medical practice. The notion of a market-oriented system also flies in the face of the emerging consensus among reformers in favor of "planning" in health care, and inducing a reconsideration of this preference by these persons, many of whom personally anticipate power and prestige in the new order, is probably impossible. Congress nevertheless has the opportunity to resolve the question as part of the larger decision it must reach on the direction which health care will take. This decision will not necessarily be dictated by health care insiders.

Finally, whatever one's a priori preferences may be on profits from care of the sick, current emoluments—including not only net cash income but also power, prestige, and perquisites—belie most of the health industry's nonprofit pretensions.[115] An explicit recognition of the existing profit orientation thus has the merit of avoiding much hypocrisy. More important, however, it would cause policy makers to focus on the market as the appropriate form of social control and to concentrate on improving and supplementing its functioning. Heretofore their assumption has too often been that the industry is fundamentally humanitarian, ethical, and nonprofit and that more admirable instincts uniformly prevail over crass self-interest. Under the new assumptions, the question becomes the market's ability, with supplemental regulatory assistance, to provide adequate policing of profits and practices. The risk presented by monopolistic and monopolizing tendencies in the marketplace is therefore the next subject for attention.

V

Shaping Policies to Improve the Market's Performance

A. Natural Monopoly

An argument can be made that in some circumstances HMOs will monopolize the market for health services, rendering it unwise to rely on competition and the market to control prices and to maintain the quality of care. If this is a substantial danger, then it may be that more direct regulation than I contemplate would be called for.

A "natural monopoly" is possessed by an enterprise that occupies an entire market by virtue of economies of scale that make it inefficient for more than one competitor to survive. If two competitors were to exist in a natural monopoly market,

---

[115] See generally Health Policy Advisory Center (Health-PAC), The American Health Empire Power, Profits and Politics (1971).

one of them would drive the other out, barring collusion preventing this outcome. One competitor or the other would eventually get a size advantage, and, because its unit costs would then be lower by reason of scale economies, it would be able to set a price with which the other competitor could no longer contend. That hospitals may sometimes enjoy a natural monopoly seems clear. Scale economies are thought to be substantial up to 250 beds,[116] and a hospital of this size is roughly adequate to serve a population of 65,000.[117] Thus, in many population centers a single hospital may exist without significant actual or potential competition due to technological and other efficiencies which are available to only one seller, the incumbent. The implications of this market structure for policy toward HMOs are several.

HMOs themselves are not likely to be the beneficiaries of a natural monopoly except as it derives from that belonging to hospitals with which they are affiliated. Aside from the provision of hospital services, HMOs would probably enjoy some scale economies in the provision of physicians', laboratory, and x-ray services, but these are not likely to be substantial enough to be decisive.[118] HMOs associated with nonmonopolistic hospitals will have additional economies available, but competing hospitals could also be expected to offer HMO care, providing adequate competition. Perhaps most important, consumers are interested in more things than price in purchasing physician services or HMO membership, and some consumers will prefer to patronize a solo fee-for-service practitioner or a small-scale (two- or three-man) HMO, even at a higher cost, because of personalized attention and convenience that a somewhat more efficient HMO could not match; the competitive position of such plans would be further improved by the government's willingness to pay the higher rates (up to the ninety-five per cent ceiling) for Medicare, Medicaid, or FHIP clients electing care though such a plan. Thus, it seems most doubtful that an HMO not affiliated with a monopolistic hospital could ever have a monopoly "thrust upon it."[119] Nevertheless, the number of hospitals with substantial monopoly power is large, and therefore the danger of HMO monopoly derived from a hospital's natural monopoly must be considered in some detail.

An HMO sponsored by a monopolistic hospital will have a potentially decisive competitive advantage over competing, non-hospital-based HMOs and fee-for-service physicians in the community. Depending upon the distance to and competitive environment of the nearby alternative hospitals, independent HMOs would be more or less, but always in some degree, compelled to pay the monopolist's price for hospital services needed by its enrollees; patrons of fee-for-service physicians would likewise

[116] Steinwald & Neuhauser, *supra* note 83, at 836. *But see* Lave & Lave, *Hospital Cost Functions*, 60 AM. ECON. REV. 379, 394 (1970) ("if economies of scale exist in the hospital industry, they are not very strong").

[117] Based on the national ratio of 3.9 beds per 1000 of population.

[118] Group practice by physicians (without prepayment) has shown a tendency to grow but not at a rate suggestive of overwhelming scale economies. *See, e.g.*, Note, *supra* note 7, at 903-04 n.9.

[119] United States v. Aluminum Co. of America, 148 F.2d 416, 429 (2d Cir. 1945).

face these charges, which would in turn influence their health insurance premiums. Under these circumstances the hospital-sponsored HMO would be able to offer comparatively attractive rates by, in effect, subsidizing its HMO operation with the monopoly profits from its hospital services.[120] This subsidization process can also be visualized as the product of discriminatory pricing, whereby the captive HMO is charged lower hospital rates than its competitors and thereby derives a critical cost advantage.[121]

The situation thus presented is not an uncommon one in other contexts involving vertically integrated enterprises.[122] For example, it resembles closely the "price squeeze" described in the famous aluminum monopoly case.[123] In that case, Alcoa, the monopolist of aluminum ingot and one of several sellers of rolled aluminum sheets, was said to have

> consistently sold ingot at so high a price that the "sheet rollers," who were forced to buy from it, could not pay the expenses of "rolling" the "sheet" and make a living profit out of the price at which "Alcoa" itself sold "sheet."[124]

Judge Learned Hand's opinion also indicated the applicable legal rule:

> That it was unlawful to set the price of "sheet" so low and hold the price of ingot so high, seems to us unquestionable, provided, as we have held, that on this record the price of ingot must be regarded as higher than a "fair price."[125]

By making an assumption (to be examined later) that interstate commerce is adequately affected, the *Alcoa* price squeeze principle can be translated to the hospital-

---

[120] It is far from clear that a monopolist would want to spend its money, hard-earned or not, in subsidizing an HMO's competitive ventures. Such an investment would not pay unless the profits from eventual monopolization would more than recoup it, and there are reasons to doubt that the monopoly would be so valuable. *Cf.* Leeman, *The Limitations of Local Price-Cutting as a Barrier to Entry*, 64 J. POL. ECON. 329 (1956). Still, in view of the hospital's control of the supply of a service essential to survival or entry of competitors, the possibility of monopolization, at least of the business of giving HMO-type care, cannot be ignored.

[121] *Cf.* Comment, *Application of the Robinson-Patman Act to Price Discrimination in Intra-Enterprise Transactions*, 53 Nw. U.L. REV. 253 (1958), which discusses the general problems; however, the Robinson-Patman Act, ch. 592, 49 Stat. 1526 (1936), 15 U.S.C. § 13 (1964), would not apply to the pricing of hospital services.

[122] *See generally* C. EDWARDS, MAINTAINING COMPETITION 97-99, 171-75 (1949); C. KAYSEN & D. TURNER, ANTITRUST POLICY 122, 125-27 (1959).

[123] United States v. Aluminum Co. of America, 148 F.2d 416 (2d Cir. 1945). For other examples of the "price squeeze," see United States v. Corn Products Ref. Co., 234 Fed. 964 (S.D.N.Y. 1916); United States v. New York Great Atl. & Pac. Tea Co., 173 F.2d 79 (7th Cir. 1949), *affirming* 67 F. Supp. 626 (E.D. Ill. 1946).

[124] 148 F.2d at 437. *See also* Baush Machine Tool Co. v. Aluminum Co. of America, 72 F.2d 236 (2d Cir. 1934), 79 F.2d 217 (2d Cir. 1935). The best explanation of the "squeeze" is that Alcoa was seeking to compete with sheet steel by lowering prices to auto makers, thus practicing price discrimination in favor of that class of users. *See* Adelman, *Integration and Antitrust Policy*, 63 HARV. L. REV. 27, 45 (1949). Vertical integration facilitates the segregation of markets necessary to permit such price discrimination, and a price squeeze may often be an incidental effect of this practice rather than a predatory tactic. *See* note 126 *infra*.

[125] 148 F.2d at 438. The squeeze potential is itself objectionable even if unexercised, because it discourages entry by those who recognize the risk and because it can be used to discipline aggressive competitors. For these reasons mergers creating a squeeze potential may be held unlawful. *See* U.S. DEP'T OF JUSTICE, MERGER GUIDELINES para. 13 (1968).

sponsored HMO context. The antitrust rule thus derived would be that, although a lawful (natural) hospital monopolist does not violate the law by charging monopoly prices, if it elects to compete with its HMO customers and with fee-for-service physicians by forming an HMO, it may not disadvantage them—that is, "squeeze" them, in the case of competing HMOs—by its pricing policies.[126] The most likely antitrust penalty for so doing would be a treble-damage award to all injured competitors, including fee-for-service doctors. Divestiture and break-up of the HMO would be likely also, and criminal sanctions could be imposed in flagrant cases. Rigorous enforcement of such a rule against unfair competition would be one hope for controlling the problem, but its administration would be difficult because a price advantage of the hospital-based HMO could be as easily attributed to efficiencies from integration of functions as to predatory behavior.[127]

Direct regulation of hospital rates might appear to be another possibility for coping with this problem. This expedient has been adopted in New York, to deal with hospital costs generally,[128] and it is recommended by the apparent congruence of the theory supporting it and the argument for public utility regulation, which is also founded on the natural monopoly characteristics of the market.[129] The public utility analogy is deceptive, however, primarily because it is based on a premise that utility regulation has proved a distinct social success, a pervasive assumption that has nevertheless been effectively disputed.[130] Among other things, utility regulation has proved quite incapable of governing the quality of service and indeed has often foundered on the fact of life that if rates are kept too low, or merely if management prefers short-run profitability, the utility always has available the option of reducing its office staff or plant maintenance or otherwise curtailing the present, or borrowing

---

[126] Classic discussions of vertical integration argue that use of a monopoly position to bring about equivalent domination at a lower level of the market can seldom increase market power, but an exception is noted where domination of a complementary product or service is achieved. See, e.g., Bork, *Vertical Integration and the Sherman Act: The Legal History of an Economic Misconception*, 22 U. CHI. L. REV. 157, 171-72, 196-99 (1954). The instant case of an HMO that might use its hospital monopoly to drive out competing HMOs and fee-for-service physicians falls within this (or a related) exception. Although not all services rendered by independent physicians and HMOs involve hospital care, availability of such care at a reasonable price is necessary to their survival. If a hospital-sponsored HMO squeezed all of its competitors out of the market, it would thereby somewhat increase the sum of its power, thereafter being able to earn monopoly profits on physicians', laboratory, x-ray, and other outpatient services previously rendered competitively.

The situation can also be recast as a "tying" problem by visualizing the hospital's refusal to accept patients except by referral from its own HMO, which refusal would be little different from charging a prohibitive price to patients of the HMO's competitors. Although the usual analysis again recognizes few occasions in which it is possible to increase monopoly power by tying, monopolization of the business of rendering primary care through such a tie-in could expand the hospital's monopoly power. See Bowman, *Tying Arrangements and the Leverage Problem*, 67 YALE L.J. 19, 25-27 (1957).

[127] On the remedies available and the problems with their administration, see KAYSEN & TURNER, *supra* note 122, at 125-27; EDWARDS, *supra* note 122, at 171-75.

[128] N.Y. PUB. HEALTH LAW §§ 2803, 2807 (McKinney Supp. 1970).

[129] See Priest, *Possible Adaptation of Public Utility Concepts in the Health Care Field*, in this symposium, p. 839.

[130] Posner, *Natural Monopoly and Its Regulation*, 21 STAN. L. REV. 548 (1969). See also related articles by Comanor, Swidler, Shepherd, and Posner, in 22 STAN. L. REV. 510 *et seq.* (1970).

against the future, quality of service. This chronic deficiency in regulatory performance is a particularly ill omen in the health field,[131] and it is certainly doubtful that outside accrediting agencies and other supervisory mechanisms would be able to sustain the quality of care in a hospital that is deprived of adequate funds.[132]

Another problem generated by rate regulation is the reduction in the incentive to achieve efficiency.[133] If regulation were able to achieve its theoretical objective and could effectively limit the regulated firm's profits to a predetermined rate of return on invested capital, there would be practically no incentive for the firm to reduce costs. But fortunately, and perhaps ironically, regulation's own inefficiency makes it possible for regulated concerns to enjoy at least temporarily the fruits of improved efficiency. Thus, because of so-called "regulatory lag," reflecting inertia and the time necessary for discovery and negotiation or litigation of a rate reduction, a firm that outperforms predictions of its profitability is not immediately subject to a cutback in rates. This factor, combined with some regulators' willingness to recognize a "zone of reasonableness" in rate of return—that is, to allow some increases in profit rates above the original target rate without intervention—,[134] suggests that efficiency incentives have not been altogether eliminated although they have been reduced. Given the vast inefficiencies known to exist in hospital management, it is fair to ask whether *any* weakening of the incentives to seek and achieve efficiencies would be wise.[135]

Of course, because hospitals are largely nonprofit institutions, many of the normal economic assumptions do not hold. Perhaps my main reason for speaking as if they do is that the natural-monopoly argument for hospital regulation seems likewise to proceed from such assumptions. But monopoly profits earned by a nonprofit institution at consumers' expense are not plainly objectionable from a social

---

[131] One possible answer to the argument that effective rate regulation could not guarantee, and indeed might undermine, the quality of hospital care is that the regulators should be liberal. But that course represents an invitation to "gold-plating" and overinvestment in capital goods, a danger which exists in the regulated sector even when liberality is not an express goal. *See* Averch & Johnson, *Behavior of the Firm Under Regulatory Constraint,* 52 AM. ECON. REV. 1052 (1962); Baumol & Klevorick, *Input Choices and Rate of Return Regulation: An Overview of the Discussion,* 1 BELL J. ECON. & MANAGEMENT SCI. 162 (1970); Posner, *supra* note 130, at 599-601. There is already a widely deplored tendency to excessive and uncoordinated investment in hospitals, attributable in large part to excessive discretion residing in decision makers. *See* notes 98-100 *supra* and accompanying text. Rate-of-return regulation, which also allows excessive room for maximization of managers' welfare at the expense of efficiency, Posner, *supra,* at 601-03, would do little to correct these influences and might play into their hands. Conceivably avoidance of rate-of-return regulation and substitution of comprehensive planning and of rate regulation based on "financial requirements," as tentatively recommended by Professor Priest, *supra* note 129, at 845-47, could avoid some of these particular traps.

[132] *Cf.* Worthington & Silver, *Regulation of Quality of Care in Hospitals: The Need for Change,* 35 LAW & CONTEMP. PROB. 305 (1970).

[133] *See* Posner, *supra* note 130, at 597-606.

[134] The "zone of reasonableness" seems an eminently sensible notion until it is realized that a firm approaching its upper boundary has not merely no incentive to seek but a positive incentive to *avoid* further efficiencies that might push it over the top, prompting a return to the lowest reasonable rate. One can only hope that managers lack the means of exercising such subtle control over profits.

[135] Rate setting on the basis of "financial requirements," looking in large measure to costs, *see* Priest, *supra* note 129, at 845-47, would appear to offer no stronger cost-cutting incentives.

standpoint since they are not redistributed to wealthy investors but are retained in the service of the enterprise, whose purposes are presumptively of general public benefit.[186] Indeed, such wealth-redistributive effects of hospital monopoly as can be identified favor the poor, since it is only the more affluent who are paying more than the cost of the service they receive. Moreover, the public has been dependent on hospital monopolies for a long time to generate the funds needed to provide care for the indigent.[187]

Since enrichment of the monopolist is not likely to be the concern that justifies hospital regulation, it must be that efficiency concerns, stemming from the notion that monopolists—particularly nonprofit ones—are inherently lazy and wasteful, are foremost.[188] I have already expressed my doubts that familiar forms of rate regulation are likely to induce efficiency. Perhaps, however, a loose kind of regulation on the basis of classification of hospitals and comparison of rates within each class might be instituted;[189] receivership of conspicuously inefficient hospitals might then be employed as a sanction against their managements, who, after all, are the people whose self-interest must ultimately be either threatened or appealed to.

Whatever one may think of the foregoing arguments against the regulation of hospital charges, it is easily demonstrable that no kind of regulation can deal adequately with the problem of the hospital-sponsored HMO. The problem is a fairly common one in regulated industries and can be illustrated by a recent rulemaking decision by the Federal Communications Commission.[140] The issue was the right of communications common carriers to offer data processing services to the general public. The difficulty lay, first, in the fact that data processing requires the use of telephone or telegraph lines and, second, in the fears of data firms that communications carriers entering the data processing industry would have an advantage because the regulated end of the business might subsidize the unregulated portion; such subsidization could be accomplished either by providing personnel, facilities, or services at less than cost or by purchasing data services at a favorable price. The danger, of course, was that the monopoly of communications services, even though regulated, could be used to create a monopoly in data processing. The FCC dealt with the problem by ordering "maximum separation," the creation of a rigid barrier between the carrier and its data processing activities. It required that a separate subsidiary be established, that it maintain separate books, offices, and

---

[186] Of course, although I know of no reason to think there have been serious abuses, high salaries and perquisites and payments to enterprises affiliated with trustees or administrators do offer opportunities for diverting profits from public use. Possibly an affiliated HMO would greatly expand opportunities for diverting the nonprofit hospital's earnings into private hands through imaginative bookkeeping, salaries, profit-sharing, and strategic patient referrals.

[187] See note 151 infra.

[188] See Legislative Findings and Purpose, supra note 98.

[189] Cf. Lave & Lave, The Extent of Role Differentiation Among Hospitals, 1970 (working paper, Graduate School of Industrial Administration, Carnegie-Mellon University).

[140] Regulatory and Policy Problems Presented by the Interdependence of Computer and Communication Services and Facilities (Final Decision and Order), No. 16979 (F.C.C., Mar. 18, 1971), in 21 P & F RADIO REG. 2d 1591 (1971).

personnel, and that the carrier not purchase any data services from the subsidiary or engage in any transactions with it other than the sale of communications services at published rates and on a nonpreferential basis. The decision amounted to a confession that no amount of regulatory supervision of bookkeeping or of the nature, purpose, or price of intracorporate transactions could assure that the regulated monopoly was not in some way subsidizing the unregulated portion of the enterprise.

Of course, the FCC might have barred the carriers entirely from entering the data processing business. Its decision not to do so was based on a sense that the data processing field might benefit from the entry of the carriers as a new competitive force with unusual technological capabilities,[141] but the ruling prevents realization of some potential economies which the carriers would have been capable of achieving through integration of functions.[142] The lesson for handling the problem of hospital-connected HMOs seems to be that regulation of one segment does not allay the apprehension that the regulated arm of the enterprise might subsidize the unregulated arm, by allowing customers of the former to bear some hidden expenses of the latter or by other means. Total separation, along the lines ordered by the FCC, seems in no way preferable to a complete prohibition of HMO formation by monopolistic hospitals, and the latter choice, even at the sacrifice of significant economies, would seem a possible solution.[143] This remedy would of course be available whether or not the hospital was regulated, and it would be expedient only in communities where a powerful hospital monopoly existed and, because of the market's characteristics, could not be broken up. In no event could cost accounting be depended upon to protect the public from possible abuse since it could not supply the precision necessary to police transactions and joint-cost allocations between a hospital and its captive HMO.

One possible policy toward the possibility that a "natural" hospital monopoly could be extended into the market for primary health care would be to take no immediate action, on the ground that the problem's dimensions cannot be adequately anticipated at this time. Perhaps, with clarification of the interstate commerce point, the antitrust rule against predatory behavior could be relied upon to protect against serious abuses, and many monopolistic hospitals, being nonprofit enterprises, might abjure aggressive competition and allow other providers to coexist. Those tempted to achieve domination would be faced not only with antitrust risks but with the threat of regulation by their local communities if consumers came to feel that they were being exploited and denied the full benefits of HMO care. The relative ease

---

[141] *Id.* para. 11.

[142] *Id.* paras. 13, 15.

[143] The following opinion on the appropriate antitrust remedy in specific cases is applicable as well to the formulation of a general policy where this class of problem is presented: "There will be at least some cases where horizontal dissolution is not feasible but where vertical dismemberment is, and the superiority of such relief to injunctive remedies—even for the victim—warrants that it be used." KAYSEN & TURNER, *supra* note 122, at 126.

of entry into fee-for-service medicine would impose some restraint, although solo practitioners' higher costs, their reluctance to advertise and to compete on the basis of price, and the HMO's established contractual relationships with its enrollees would dilute this influence. Although somewhat inhibited by vulnerability to the squeeze, potential new entry by an HMO—perhaps stimulated by large employers or consumer groups—would prevent the hospital-affiliated HMO from exploiting its position very far. Finally, the competitive impact of other HMOs on the fringes of the market area would seldom be negligible.

Looked at in another way, however, the problem is somewhat different and substantially more serious than we have yet observed, and it therefore requires a better solution than any of those canvassed above. The source of the additional difficulty lies in the likely domination of community hospitals by the local medical society and physicians dedicated to the preservation of fee-for-service medicine. Traditionally, these hospitals, while nonprofit and often community-owned, are effectively controlled by local physicians and operated largely for their convenience and profit. An HMO established under such domination, far from being an overly aggressive competitor abusing competing HMOs and fee-for-service physicians alike, might instead be enlisted to protect the fee-for-service sector against the encroachment of HMO-type care. In pursuing this objective, it would preempt subscribers, making them unavailable as converts to other HMOs during the term of their contracts, and would serve generally as a "fighting ship," defending against HMO invasion threats by occasional price warfare[144] but otherwise not aggressively developing the potentialities of HMO-type care as a substitute for fee-for-service medicine. The likely pattern would be that local physicians would recommend the hospital-sponsored HMO, would accept referrals only from it, and would use other sanctions of a more or less overt character against physicians and patients associating with new HMO entrants. The hospital-sponsored HMO would probably be designed primarily to serve a low-income clientele, relieving practitioners of their charity burden but leaving unimpaired their opportunities for practicing price-discriminating fee-for-service medicine among the middle and upper classes.

The thrust of our problem is thus abruptly changed. We are no longer worried primarily about HMOs' monopolistic potential but about the indestructibility of the fee-for-service monopoly and its ability to adapt to new environments by invoking

---

[144] The "fighting ship" analogy, drawn from the history of ocean shipping conferences (cartels), can be seen in the following:

"The crudest form of predatory practice was the fighting ship. The conference would select a suitable steamer from among its lines to sail on the same days and between the same ports as the non-member vessel, reducing the regular rates low enough to capture the trade from the outsider. The expenses and losses from the lower rates were shared by the members of the conference. The competitor by this means was caused to exhaust its resources and withdraw from competition."

Federal Maritime Bd. v. Isbrandtsen Co., Inc., 356 U.S. 481, 488 (1958). Shipping conferences, like medical societies, are combinations of competitors interested in the exclusion of noncooperating providers of the service. Monopolists of other kinds have on occasion used "fighting brands" to similar effect.

the profession's control over many of the inputs needed for effective competition and its remarkable ability to police itself. In this new light, the issue becomes joined with that presented by those existing prepayment plans (mostly not hospital-connected) which have been sponsored by medical societies in many communities as a means of reducing the threat of independent entry by prepaid group practice plans. These plans and their legal status are the next subject for discussion, and my final solution to the issue of hospital-sponsored HMOs will be offered as part of an attempt to resolve the larger problem of medical societies' power to inhibit new entry into local markets.

B. The Risk of Subversion by Local Medical Societies

The ability of the medical profession to enforce its preferences as to the organization of the medical care industry has been impressive. The welding of so large a number of economic units into a stable and effective organization to repress competitive tendencies has been accomplished by a variety of customs and devices that could not be easily uprooted or dismantled even if the will to do so could be found.[145] Even assuming that pro-HMO legislation emerges intact from the legislative process without emasculating amendments—such as proscription of for-profit plans—, policy makers must be alert to the danger that realization of the HMO's potential by a fair test in a free market might be somehow prevented by doctors. It is my belief that the antitrust laws, if allowed to operate with accustomed force, could provide much of the needed protection.

The greater threat to realization of the hopes underlying the HMO proposals is presented not by the American Medical Association but instead by state and county medical societies or even by small groups of powerful doctors who occupy strategic positions on hospital boards and in the societies. In *Group Health Cooperative v. King County Medical Society*,[146] decided by the Supreme Court of the State of Washington in 1951, the county medical society claimed to be enforcing "ethical" standards higher than those of the AMA against the Cooperative's prepaid group practice plan, and the court's discussion reflects credit, by comparison at least, on the AMA for its less restrictive policies. Since the AMA was somewhat earlier convicted of antitrust violations in its activities in opposition to Group Health Association, Inc., in Washington, D. C.,[147] the antitrust laws may have contributed something to its moderation of attitude.[148]

---

[145] *See* references cited in note 65 *supra*.

[146] 39 Wash. 2d 586, 237 P.2d 737 (1951).

[147] American Medical Ass'n v. United States, 317 U.S. 519 (1943).

[148] I do not mean to express an opinion as to whether the AMA is complying with the antitrust laws at the present time. My point is rather that the local societies and local professionals often take the initiative in the skirmishing, are so deployed as to be tactically effective, but have lagged behind the AMA in falling back to positions that would be at least arguably defensible in an encounter with the antitrust laws. The AMA's public position on HMOs is a sort of unconvinced tolerance, acceptance of a need for a pluralistic system, and opposition only to government favoritism and subsidies for one delivery mode at the expense of others. *See* DIVISION OF MEDICAL PRACTICE, note 43 *supra*.

Many of the tactics employed by local societies to disadvantage HMO-type care are clearly illegal by federal antitrust standards and would probably be held so if interstate commerce was found to be adequately affected. Some state courts have applied state antimonopoly legislation or other sanctions to restrain such activity. Thus, the practice of refusing medical society membership or hospital staff privileges to HMO-affiliated doctors has been disapproved,[149] and other concerted activities of local professionals undertaken for the purpose of discouraging HMOs would probably be treated similarly by most courts.[150] My concern here is with less overt strategies that the societies might adopt in opposition to HMOs.

Each fee-for-service doctor has a substantial amount of monopoly power over his individual patients as a result of their medical ignorance and dependency and their willingness to pay. Medical societies can thus be viewed as coalitions of monopolists whose purposes in coming together include protection and strengthening of their individual market power. This view explains why the medical societies behave somewhat differently than do classical cartels, not bothering to fix prices or to make overt anticompetitive agreements; not facing intense competition to begin with, they have no need to collude to eliminate it and can be content merely to preserve the status quo. In a sense, of course, the societies engage in market division—a common cartel practice—by enforcement of ethical undertakings not to advertise their services or to criticize their competitors, in effect recognizing each doctor's "sphere of influence" over his particular patients. A further parallel to the activities of other cartels is reflected in the societies' commitment to preservation of a particular, highly discriminatory[151] pricing system—fee-for-service.[152]

The power of a coalition of lawful monopolies may be greater than the sum of its

---

[149] Group Health Cooperative v. King County Medical Soc'y, 39 Wash. 2d 586, 237 P.2d 737 (1951). New York has by statute prohibited the denial of hospital privileges because of participation in a group practice plan. N.Y. Pub. Health Law § 206-a (McKinney Supp. 1970).

[150] Apart from the antitrust implications, courts may be willing to find a denial of equal protection on the basis of an arbitrary classification when the hospital denying privileges to HMO-affiliated physicians receives state funds. Cf. Sams v. Ohio Valley Gen. Hosp. Ass'n, 413 F.2d 826 (4th Cir. 1969).

[151] Price discrimination in medicine involves charging different prices for the same service, usually on the basis of ability to pay. See generally Kessel, supra note 70. See also notes 84 supra & 159 infra. The presence of such discrimination proves the absence of effective competition since competing providers would drive each other to price uniformly in accordance with cost or the physician's supply function. Health insurance and prepaid group practice reduce the discrimination possibilities and have thus been opposed by the profession except as a means of providing for low-income persons, whom they make better able to pay. See Kessel, supra. The popular justification for such price discrimination was that it permitted free care for the indigent and made care available irrespective of wealth. As health insurance covers more people and as government pays more and more of the cost of care for the elderly and the poor, this justification, whatever it was once worth, fades. But see note 84 supra.

[152] Maintenance of a particular pricing system seems often to characterize the stabler form of cartel. For helpful comparisons, see FTC v. Cement Institute, 333 U.S. 683 (1948) ("basing-point" pricing, which produced complete price uniformity, irrespective of freight differentials, from all sellers to each buyer, making shopping and bargaining unproductive); United States v. Paramount Pictures, Inc., 334 U.S. 131 (1948) (motion picture distributors' efforts to preserve a particular system of "runs and clearances"); Securities Exchange Act Release No. 8239 (1968) (describing the New York Stock Exchange's long battle to repress cost-justified quantity discounts and "give-ups" on brokerage services).

parts.[153] Thus a medical society can preserve and strengthen the market power of each physician-monopolist by enforcing mutual recognition of spheres of influence, by collective maintenance of the conditions giving rise to such power—such as consumer ignorance and inability to combine for bargaining effectiveness—, by influencing legislation, by collective opposition to forms of health care financing and delivery that would weaken individual monopolies, and perhaps even by controlling members' exploitation of their individual monopolies so as to reduce the likelihood of government intervention or new entry. Where certain of these purposes appear,[154] the coalition may be open to attack either as monopolization under section 2 of the Sherman Act or as a "combination . . . in restraint of trade" under section 1.[155]

An important defensive tactic employed by the medical profession has been the organization by state and local medical societies of their own prepayment plans. In the 1930s and 1940s, following the example of Blue Cross hospitalization plans, the profession established Blue Shield, a series of state and local physician-dominated service and indemnity plans covering physicians' services primarily.[156] More recently a movement has begun toward creation of society-sponsored "medical care foundations," which are prepaid service organizations whose chief distinguishing characteristic is that they provide intensive peer review of fees and utilization as a means of controlling health insurance costs.[157] Blue Shield reflected the profession's early recognition that avoidance of government intervention in the health care system required, first of all, an available insurance mechanism whereby consumers could obtain financial protection against the risk of illness. It was an attempt to meet that need in the manner least disruptive of the valued relationship between the physician-monopolist and his patients, since independent insurers, representing a vehicle of pro-consumer bargaining, were seen as excessively inclined to police fees

---

[153] In United States v. Grinnell Corp., 384 U.S. 563 (1966), it was held to be monopolization to join together firms controlling 87% of "accredited central station protective service," a business having distinct natural monopoly characteristics at the local level. The Supreme Court's analysis was not satisfying, but the result is easily defensible by observing that the local monopolies were greatly strengthened by eliminating competition along the margin of market areas and the threat of new entry in expanding markets.

[154] The societies' efforts to obtain protective legislation or administrative action cannot be made the subject of antitrust action. Cf. Eastern R.R. Presidents Conference v. Noerr Motor Freight, Inc., 365 U.S. 127 (1961).

[155] 15 U.S.C. §§ 1, 2 (1964).

[156] See, e.g., H. SOMERS & A. SOMERS, DOCTORS, PATIENTS & HEALTH INSURANCE 317-40 (1961).

[157] See Sasuly & Hopkins, A Medical Society-sponsored Comprehensive Medical Care Plan, 5 MED. CARE 234 (1967); Note, supra note 7, at 919-21; Comment, supra note 65, at 992-94; Am. Med. News, Aug. 10, 1970, at 8. The foundations are in fact a species of HMO, but they resemble physician-sponsored health insurance somewhat more than provider prepayment. The society in effect accepts prepaid memberships which entitle enrollees to obtain care from any society member or other participating doctor, who in turn bills the society on a fee-for-service basis. The only departure from ordinary health insurance is the society's oversight of utilization, fees, and quality of care, which is typically more intensive than the review of claims by insurers. Some foundations are underwritten by insurance companies, and some in California have accepted capitation payments from the state for Medicaid beneficiaries. The plans offer no substantial opportunity for reorganizing the delivery system in more efficient ways, and indeed "they are intended to buttress and accommodate the traditional forms of medical practice in a time of change." Sasuly & Hopkins, supra, at 234.

and to second-guess the need for service. The medical care foundations represent, in part at least, a further response to the same fears and conditions, being prompted by the increasingly recognized need for some control—preferably administered in the collective interest of physicians rather than of patients—over those abuses of the insurance system that tend to inflate its cost. More immediately, the foundation plans have often been linked to specific fears about the encroachment of prepaid group practice plans in the medical society's territory.[158]

If society-sponsored prepayment plans could be viewed merely as an attempt to improve the service and performance of the insured-fee-for-service sector,[159] they would present no antitrust problem. Even seen as an attempt to head off consumer coalitions for bargaining, the society plans might be deemed objectionable only if they actively prevented such coalitions from forming, and perhaps a distinction would be drawn between collective action merely removing the abuses inviting consumer coalitions and collective action to create obstacles to coalition formation. In any event, collective efforts preemptive of market opportunities for agencies likely to represent consumer interests, where undertaken with exclusionary intent, would seem promising candidates for a firm antitrust prohibition.

---

[158] A study of the Foundation for Medical Care of San Joaquin County, California, revealed that the impetus behind the formation of that foundation plan was physician concern over "the rapidly rising prices of health care services and the rise of new kinds of health care organization. Viewed as a particularly troublesome problem was the growth in California of the Permanente medical group, providing service for the Kaiser Foundation Health Plan." Sasuly & Hopkins, *supra* note 157, at 235. *See also* Am. Med. News, Aug. 10, 1970, p. 8, 9, col. 1: "At issue, the physicians thought, was the control of the private practice of medicine by physicians. The 'threat' was the proposed establishment of 'closed panel' systems of medicine in hospital-based group practices. Physicians on salary would be a reality." For further evidence of the purpose behind formation of society-sponsored plans, see notes 159 & 163 *infra*.

[159] Where they have been able to get away with it, society-sponsored plans have practiced price discrimination. *See generally* notes 84 & 151 *supra*. This fact and the profession's interest in preserving its ability to price according to ability to pay are revealed in this 1952 statement by a former president of the New York County Medical Society:

"Too many physicians . . . seem still to think that a medical society should be organized solely for scientific purposes and medical education and that it should not consider and act upon the economic and ethical problems that arise . . . [W]ith health insurance plans accepting persons with incomes of $6,500 and over, private practice with free choice of physician is being destroyed . . .

"Blue Shield and similar [doctor-controlled] plans should widen their coverage. The private practitioner must cooperate and be willing to accept lower fees. Medical coverage cost must be made more reasonable for the lower and middle income groups. That this can be done to full satisfaction of patient and physician alike is exemplified by the Windsor plan. The Windsor Medical Services, of Windsor, Ontario, Canada, a voluntary, nonprofit, prepaid medical care plan sponsored by the Essex County Medical Society . . . is a comprehensive insurance plan in which more than 95% of the physicians in [the] Society participate. The physicians are paid on a fixed schedule of fees. The monthly subscription rate varies, according to income, from a single subscriber earning $300 or less to the family subscriber earning $6,500 or less. . . . The successful plan shows what prepaid fee for service could do. That is what Blue Shield should strive for. Compulsory health insurance will then be prevented."

Master, *Impact of Medical Care Plans on the Medical Profession*, 150 J.A.M.A. 766, 770 (1952) (footnotes omitted). *See also* Kessel, *supra* note 70, at 53, which notes that in California, "[i]n an effort to meet this competition [from the Kaiser plan], service-type plans have been offered by orthodox members of the medical profession that are non-discriminatory with respect to income."

In *United States v. Oregon State Medical Society*,[160] the Supreme Court affirmed the lower court's dismissal of the government's charge that a plan of the Blue Shield variety violated the Sherman Act. The plan, the Oregon Physicians' Service, was adopted by the medical society in response to the encroachment of health insurance and other prepayment plans in the state. After noting that before 1941 the society had engaged in a "tooth-and-claw struggle" and "a crusade to stamp . . . out" the prepayment plans, the Court noted that an "abrupt about-face" occurred in that year and that the doctors, "instead of trying to discourage prepaid medical service, decided to render it on a nonprofit basis themselves" through a society-sponsored plan.[161] Because the lower court had found as a fact that the medical society had undergone a change of heart, the Supreme Court had no basis for treating the plan as an exclusionary tactic. Moreover, the Court's description of the two kinds of "contract practice" against which the society-sponsored plan was directed indicated that they were not of the sort that could be successfully excluded from the market by the society's plan.[162] They were merely simple insurance schemes and employers' plans providing care in kind to their employees. Since, unlike an HMO, neither type of plan is dependent on attracting some minimum number of subscribers in a community but can instead depend upon individual physicians devoting some part of their time to treating plan members, the Court did not view the case as one in which the society's plan had any exclusionary or monopolistic effect.[163] If a preemptive or exclusionary purpose or effect of the society-sponsored plans vis-à-vis independent HMOs can be identified, the *Oregon Medical Society* case should not be a barrier to adoption of an antitrust rule condemning them.

I elect not to pursue the antitrust status of Blue Shield plans any further here.[164]

---

[160] 343 U.S. 326 (1952).

[161] *Id.* at 329-30.

[162] *Id.* at 328. There were in fact, according to the trial court's findings, some HMO-type plans in existence in Oregon, including one of the Kaiser-Permanente groups. 95 F. Supp. 103, 114 (D. Ore. 1950). Nevertheless, the government failed to indicate any particular effectiveness of the society-sponsored plan in excluding this variety of prepayment plan.

[163] The record clearly revealed that the society plans were conceived for the purpose of eliminating existing insurance plans. *See* Brief for the United States at 25-29, 36-41. Several plans were driven out of Oregon, but this result may have appeard to flow only from fair competition. The government did not strongly assert that Oregon Physicians' Service was itself illegal, but instead relied on exclusionary practices and an alleged boycott.

[164] Under the federal McCarran-Ferguson Act, the business of insurance is subject to the antitrust laws only "to the extent that such business is not regulated by State law," except that the Sherman Act would apply to "boycott, coercion, or intimidation." 15 U.S.C. §§ 1012(b), 1013(b) (1964). If the society-sponsored prepayment plan were regulated as an insurer, as Blue Shield usually is, it might be entitled to claim this exemption. This is not perfectly clear, however, since the federal rather than the state definition of "the business of insurance" will govern, SEC v. National Securities, Inc., 393 U.S. 453, 458-61 (1969), and group practice prepayment plans have been held by the federal courts not to be insurance for other purposes. Jordan v. Group Health Ass'n, 107 F.2d 239 (D.C. Cir. 1939) (applying the D.C. Code). Moreover, in California, a society-sponsored prepayment plan of the Blue Shield variety was not deemed to be engaged in the insurance business so as to be subject to insurance regulation. California Physicians' Service v. Garrison, 28 Cal. 2d 790, 172 P.2d 4 (1946). Aside from their delegated plenary authority respecting "the business of insurance," the states cannot by regulation or statutory authorization insulate society-sponsored plans from the antitrust laws if federal policy can

For one thing, the *Oregon Medical Society* case indicates that they do not in themselves have a serious exclusionary effect although the surrounding conduct deserves close scrutiny. Moreover, while they do preempt many employer-sponsored groups and thereby help to foreclose HMO entry, they are no worse in this respect than independent insurers, and they must compete for this business on a cost basis with such insurers as well as with HMOs. Introduction of an unrestricted HMO option for all members of employer-sponsored groups would eliminate all market foreclosure effects as to HMOs (a result that might also be accomplished by an antitrust decree if an occasion were presented). Although I do not wish to concede that the antitrust laws are inapplicable to Blue Shield, I am avoiding the issue because I doubt that Blue Shield alone poses a very substantial obstacle to emergence of a satisfactorily competitive health care marketplace.

My reasons for objecting to the medical care foundations more than I do to Blue Shield are the same reasons that one should fear an efficient and subtle monopolist more than a lazy and obvious one: the latter will soon lose its monopoly to new entrants—assuming they are not excluded by law or otherwise—, whereas the former may find sophisticated and highly effective means to ward off new competition. The foundations, properly viewed, are a mechanism for curbing the excesses of some cartel members for the purpose of preserving the cartelists' respective monopolies and profits against government attack and new competition. While they may in fact succeed in lowering health care costs, they will not duplicate the results of maintaining a competitive market. Instead, they will seek an entry-limiting price level which, though responsive in fact to potential HMO competition, will not be a competitive level. Of course, if there is to be no commitment to a market-oriented health care system, then the foundations may have a beneficial impact and should be tolerated or even encouraged,[165] but, under my procompetitive premise, they should be recognized as part of a profit-maximizing strategy of a coalition of monopolists. As such, they may be open to antitrust attack.[166]

A difficult question is presented concerning whether establishment of a foundation might be treated as an "exclusionary practice" for purposes of applying section

---

fairly be said to preempt the field. *Cf.* Sears Roebuck & Co. v. Stiffel Co., 376 U.S. 225 (1964). *But see* the line of cases commencing with Parker v. Brown, 317 U.S. 341 (1943).

[165] The foundations have attracted a good deal of attention and are generating some enthusiasm among reformers. The Nixon administration specifically amended its definition of "HMO" to clarify that foundations could qualify. *Compare* H.R. 1, § 239(a), proposed § 1876(b)(3), *with* S. 1623, § 101, proposed § 604(a)(3); *id.* § 201, proposed § 628(b)(3). The Kennedy-Griffiths bill, § 48, also endorses the foundation concept.

[166] The foundations may be held exempt from federal antitrust law either because they are deemed to be engaged in the "business of insurance" and regulated by the state or because the state has authorized their activities. *See* note 164 *supra.* State laws authorizing *only* society-sponsored or society-approved plans might, for example, be given such an effect. *E.g.*, Ga. Code Ann. tit. 56, § 56-1806 (1960); Iowa Code Ann. § 514.4 (Supp. 1970); Ky. Rev. Stat. § 303.180 (1962); Rev. Codes Mont. 1947, § 15-2304 (repl. vol. 2 (pt. 1), 1967); Nev. Rev. Stat. § 696.100 (1963). By the same token federal legislation revealing a preference for a competitive health care marketplace would improve the chances that antitrust policy would be deemed paramount. *But see* note 165 *supra*, which indicates the foundations may receive an express Congressional blessing.

2 of the Sherman Act, which requires only proof that a monopoly exists and that it has been obtained or protected by such an exclusionary practice. By this doctrine, a monopolist is denied the right to engage in certain kinds of conduct that would be wholly innocuous, or even indeed desirable, if undertaken by a competitive firm. Thus, in the two leading cases on the subject, Alcoa was held to have violated section 2 by the simple act of enlarging its productive capacity to keep ahead of the market's growth,[167] and United Shoe Machinery Corporation was found to have defended its monopoly unlawfully by the nonpredatory tactic of leasing rather than selling its machines.[168] Although it is an interesting question whether a monopolist who simply moderated his pricing policies to discourage new entry would be held to have engaged in an exclusionary practice for the purpose of applying section 2, it is reasonable to assume that he would not. Since a foundation plan does little more than control the abuses that some physicians might perpetrate against the insurance system with respect to utilization and fees, it can be said to be doing nothing more than moderating monopolistic behavior, and this conduct, while exclusionary in fact and restrictive of competition in the long run, may not be enough to make out a section 2 case. Perhaps the real objection lies in the collective nature of the effort being made, and this suggests that it may be more appropriate to pursue the matter as a combination in restraint of trade under section 1.

Taking the society-sponsored foundations briefly through the standard section 1 analysis,[169] I find that a "per se" antitrust rule, requiring no specific showing by the plaintiff of anticompetitive purpose or effect and permitting no justification to be offered in defense, might well be appropriate to condemn them. Looking first to the possible benefits that foundation plans might yield, I expect that the highly desirable controls on fee-for-service physicians[170] could probably be introduced in an equally effective but much less troubling way—namely by independent health insurers, acting ultimately on behalf of consumers but perhaps working in close cooperation with organizations of fee-for-service doctors interested in policing their colleagues for the purpose of reducing health insurance premiums.[171] If this less

---

[167] United States v. Aluminum Co. of America, 148 F.2d 416 (1945).

[168] United States v. United Shoe Mach. Co., 110 F. Supp. 295 (D. Mass. 1953), aff'd per curiam, 347 U.S. 521 (1954).

[169] See P. AREEDA, ANTITRUST ANALYSIS 286-87 (1967).

[170] On the efficacy of these controls see F. GARTSIDE, THE UTILIZATION AND COSTS OF SERVICES IN THE SAN JOAQUIN PREPAYMENT PROJECT (UCLA School of Public Health 1971).

[171] At a later point I discuss the need for fee-for-service doctors to police each other in order to make themselves competitive, i.e., to make health insurance premiums attractive as compared to HMO charges. See text accompanying note 232 infra. Although the foundation plans might seem a good vehicle for accomplishing this needed control over charges and utilization, it is preferable to retain health insurers as intermediaries. For one thing, I would fear the societies' attempts to assert jurisdiction over the charges of all providers, including HMOs, a goal already announced. Am. Med. News, Aug. 10, 1970, p. 8, 15. Furthermore, independent insurance companies would be more likely to dedicate themselves to stimulating some kind of price competition in the fee-for-service sector as a means of reducing premiums and thereby maximizing health insurance sales; a cartel of fee-for-service providers—such as Blue Cross or Blue Shield—would seek price reductions only to that level where monopoly profits would be maximized, resulting in a lower output of fee-for-service medicine. Of course, insurers might find safe and useful ways to enlist the medical societies in the reviewing process.

restrictive alternative is indeed available, a court should not count the obvious benefits very heavily in weighing the plans' validity.

On the potential detriment side of the ledger, the threat to the public interest is considerable. The plans purport to regulate prices to a substantial degree, at least to the extent of setting limits on the fees that can be charged. Although the case law prohibiting the fixing of maximum prices is not terribly convincing on its face,[172] it would almost certainly be binding in these circumstances. Indeed, a much stronger case can be made against the fixing of maximum prices here, not only because the maximum price would almost certainly also become the minimum—as physicians would have no incentive to charge less than the maximum permitted—, but also because the purpose is to set prices not at a competitive level but merely at a level that will reduce the likelihood of entry and therefore restrict competition in the long run. The entry barrier created by the foundation plans' contractual preemption of employer-sponsored groups and other prospective HMO subscribers provides another strong objection to the plan.[173] Finally, although an occasional society plan might be helpful as a counterweight to a monopolistic HMO or as a means of checking the excesses of certain greedy fee-for-service doctors, these benefits would be hard for a court to identify in a given case or to weigh against specific identified harms, since it would seldom be possible to know what would have happened in the plan's absence. In such circumstances, a flat prohibition cutting off an activity with clear anticompetitive tendencies may be appropriate in spite of arguable benefits, and such a prohibition would serve the additional salutary purpose in this instance of not inviting societies to push right up to the line of whatever narrow exception might be carved out. The simplification of enforcement and discouragement of conduct that is at least highly questionable are substantial benefits that would flow from a per se rule.

A per se rule should probably not be adopted without a full judicial inquiry into the nature and functioning of foundation plans,[174] and the outcome of such an inquiry is not easy to predict. Departures from the foregoing analysis are possible at several points. First, the utilization and fee review might be deemed a permissible "ancillary" restraint, a reasonable incident of running a prepayment plan the legitimacy of which might be deemed supported by the *Oregon Medical Society* case, state Blue Shield statutes, and general public policy.[175] Second, the fee review

---

[172] *See* Albrecht v. Herald Co., 390 U.S. 145 (1968); Kiefer-Stewart Co. v. Joseph E. Seagram & Sons, Inc., 340 U.S. 211 (1951). Both cases involved so-called vertical restraints whereby a seller sought to limit the resale prices of his retailer-customers. The illegality of a horizontal restraint on maximum prices would seem to follow a fortiori. The elements of coercion, of assumed extragovernmental power, and restriction on "the freedom of traders," *id.* at 213, are the same in either case.

[173] I suspect that market preemption, rather than real concern with fees and utilization, is the chief object in forming a foundation. In the San Joaquin situation, where a defensive purpose was uppermost, *see* note 158 *supra*, perception of the foundation's defensive effectiveness must have been based on the society's ability immediately to sign up employers who might otherwise welcome or even solicit Kaiser's entry. Intent plays a major role in antitrust outcomes.

[174] *Cf.* White Motor Co. v. United States, 372 U.S. 253 (1963).

[175] *Cf.* Addyston Pipe & Steel Co. v. United States, 85 Fed. 271 (6th Cir. 1898). I find this far

program might be viewed as something other than price fixing,[176] and the adoption of entry-limiting pricing and utilization policies might be somehow viewed as a legitimate collective endeavor, perhaps by analogy to the monopolization argument noted above. Third, the beneficial controls over fee-for-service medicine might be held not to be achievable by other means that did not produce dangers of "lay interference," and, finally, perhaps the plans would be found not to inhibit HMO development in fact.[177] An antitrust court, hearing the enthusiasm of the many eminent physicians and other witnesses that could be produced on behalf of the foundation plans, would in any event have to possess remarkable clarity of vision to see their less appealing side. Perhaps few judges, or other observers for that matter, will be uncompromising enough to share my view that, on the basis of past history, doubts should be resolved against continued domination of health care delivery by organized medicine.

Upon a complete inquiry an antitrust court might reject the per se rule in favor of approaching each society-sponsored plan under what antitrust lawyers denominate the "rule of reason." Under this approach the facts of each case are considered in detail, the courts relying on the ability of enforcement agencies to detect, of evidence to reveal, and of judges to recognize the existence of abuses when they do in fact occur. Many trade association activities of a standard-setting variety have been evaluated and tolerated under such a rule-of-reason approach,[178] and this case might be deemed to fall closest to these precedents. Still, courts have erred egregiously on some occasions,[179] and have so far been inexplicably reluctant to impose the

and away the best argument for upholding the foundations. Properly, it requires an assessment of whether public policy should or should not encourage medical societies' provision of prepayment plans. Since such collective endeavors are fundamentally at odds with a competitive marketplace, they should not be permitted unless an antitrust exemption can be found in federal or state law. *See* notes 164 & 166 *supra*.

[176] Recently some efforts by Blue Cross and others to provide insurance coverage of prescription drugs have run into difficulties with state antitrust laws because of the price fixing involved in obtaining commitments from pharmacists on the amount of their professional service charge ·on each prescription. *E.g.*, Blue Cross v. Virginia *ex rel.* State Corp. Comm'n, 211 Va. 180, 176 S.E.2d 439 (1970) (held to violate Sherman Act as well); B & L Pharmacy, Inc. v. Metropolitan Life Ins. Co., 46 Ill. 2d 1, 262 N.E.2d 462 (1970) (upheld on the basis of special statutory exemptions); Opinion of the Attorney General of Michigan, 1969 Trade Cas. para. 72,801. *See* Comment, 57 VA. L. REV. 315 (1971); Comment, 65 Nw. U.L. REV. 940 (1971). Had the insurance plans been sponsored by an organization of the pharmacists themselves they would have resembled the medical care foundations more closely and been even stronger candidates for illegality. Possibly, however, the foundations could find a way of regulating fees—perhaps merely ascertaining whether they exceed the physician's usual and customary charges—that presents less of an antitrust problem.

[177] Their exclusionary impact would indeed be greatly lessened if market opportunities for HMOs are successfully opened up in other ways—*e.g.*, by requiring employers to make available the option of applying the cost of employer-purchased insurance coverage toward HMO enrollment. *See* text accompanying notes 28-30 *infra*. My estimate of the foundation plans' exclusionary impact is impressionistic, *see* notes 158, 159, 163, 173 *supra*, and subject to correction if HMOs are found capable of entry.

[178] *See* Wachtel, *Products Standards and Certification Programs*, 13 ANTITRUST BULL. 1 (1968); *Legality of Standards—Recent Developments*, 39 MAGAZINE OF STANDARDS 18 (1968).

[179] A trade association's standard-setting scheme caused a firm which truly had a "better mousetrap," a new kind of plywood, to fail, and, in spite of this egregiously anticompetitive effect, the courts could find no antitrust violation. Structural Laminates, Inc. v. Douglas Fir Plywood Ass'n, 261 F. Supp. 154 (D. Ore. 1966), *aff'd*, 399 F.2d 155 (9th Cir. 1968), *cert. denied*, 393 U.S. 1024 (1970).

burden of establishing "reasonableness" on those competitors who would engage in collective activity presenting grave anticompetitive risks though some arguable benefits as well.[180] My preference for a per se rule would be somewhat abated if, as an intermediate solution, the burden of establishing an innocent purpose and absence of an anticompetitive effect could be shifted to the plan's proponents. The treble-damage remedy might then adequately deter excesses.

The foregoing theorizing about society-sponsored prepayment plans can be usefully laid alongside the earlier discussion of the monopolistic potential of an HMO affiliated with a hospital enjoying a high degree of "natural" monopoly power. The fear was there expressed that such hospitals, and thus their HMOs, would often be dominated by the local medical society and that the HMOs would in such circumstances be used primarily as a stalking horse for fee-for-service medicine. Thus it could preempt subscribers, and this foreclosure of market opportunities, together with additional competitive advantages and the "squeeze" potential derived from its hospital connection, would make entry by independent HMOs very difficult. Nevertheless, despite the apparent applicability in these circumstances of the rigid antitrust rule that I approved above, a more selective rule seems to me to be appropriate here. The difference in the two cases is simply that the hospital-based HMO is capable of achieving important efficiencies in the delivery of health care, whereas the society-sponsored prepayment plan is not. This difference could justify applying a more flexible antitrust rule to the former, allowing a private antitrust plaintiff or the Justice Department to succeed only if it could affirmatively establish the purpose or the effect of preempting market opportunties, excluding other HMOs, or protecting the fee-for-service sector of the market from outside competition.

A monopolization or conspiracy-to-monopolize theory under section 2 would seem the soundest doctrinal approach to the problem of the hospital-based HMO dominated by local fee-for-service doctors.[181] The inquiry would be whether the HMO was

---

[180] Cf. United States v. Arnold, Schwinn & Co., 388 U.S. 365, 374 n.5 (1967): "The burden of proof in antitrust cases remains with the plaintiff, deriving such help as may be available in the circumstances from particularized rules articulated by law—such as the *per se* doctrine." Rational allocation of the burden of proof would have prevented the travesty described in note 179 *supra.*

[181] Use of § 1 of the Sherman Act, outlawing contracts, combinations, and conspiracies in restraint of trade, would be appropriate for dealing with the foundation plans since they so clearly involve a combination of competing physicians. The hospital-based HMO, on the other hand, is not a creature of the medical society, and the requisite multiplicity of actors would be harder, though probably not impossible, to identify. The conspiracy-to-monopolize theory would seem to raise a similar problem, but in this context it seems less important that the conspirators be competitors.

There should be no doubt that fee-for-service physicians who by whatever means effectively exclude HMO competition are "monopolizing" (or attempting or conspiring to monopolize) the market for medical care. Their success in eliminating one form of competition strengthens their market power— that is, their ability to discriminate in price, a distinctive feature of monopoly, and to increase returns by artificially creating demand and by repressing both price and quality competition through customary restraints. *See* references cited in note 65 *supra.* One can anticipate some difficulty in persuading courts that a mere strengthening of earning power provides the basis for finding a violation of § 2, since monopolization has traditionally been defined in terms of an overwhelming market share possessed by a single producer. *E.g.,* Aluminum Co. of America v. United States, 148 F.2d 416 (2d Cir. 1945). But no such exacting definition has been insisted on in attempt and conspiracy cases where anticompetitive

being used to perpetuate the local physicians' market power. While taxing the perspicacity of judges, the evidence in such a case should permit discriminating judgments to be made. The following would be relevant subjects for proof: (a) the coexistence of other HMOs; (b) the hospital's pricing policies, particularly any price squeeze attempts; (c) the hospital HMO's aggressiveness in attracting subscribers, with particular reference to whether recruitment efforts are pursued among middle-class patrons of fee-for-service doctors or are confined to low-income groups; (d) the means of securing specialists' services, whether by spreading its business evenly among fee-for-service practitioners while avoiding creation of in-house capability or by practicing selectivity on the basis of skill and price; (e) aggressiveness in exploiting available economies, particularly in the use of paramedical personnel; and (f) the mechanism of control, particularly with respect to the possibility of domination by fee-for-service doctors.[182]

C. Applicability of the Antitrust Laws

The difficulty of introducing a competitive regime into health care delivery should not be underestimated. Traditions are opposed to it, and doctors can be expected to resist what strikes them as unhealthy "commercial" influences. The best means of overcoming this resistance is by vigorous enforcement of the antitrust laws against all concerted efforts to exclude HMOs from the marketplace. Some possible uses of antitrust law have been suggested already.[183]

The Sherman Act is the law most likely to be called into play against professional combinations in restraint of HMO development or collective monopolization of the medical care market by fee-for-service physicians. Two threshold problems that must be faced are raised by the question whether in a particular case the alleged restraint affects "trade or commerce among the several States" within the meaning of the statute. The first question is whether we are dealing with either "trade" or "commerce," and the second is whether, if so, there is sufficient interstate impact.

As to the first question, the Supreme Court held in 1943 in the *AMA* case that Group Health, Inc., of Washington, D.C., a nonprofit prepaid group practice plan whose activities were restrained by organized medicine, was engaged in "trade" and that the Sherman Act applied to the restraints imposed.[184] Any HMO that might be formed would seem to be equally involved in "trade." Even if the case presented should involve a restraint practiced against a single doctor connected with an HMO,

---

intent was clear. *See* Turner, *Antitrust Policy and the Cellophone Case,* 70 HARV. L. REV. 281, 303-08 (1956). To inquire whether the hospital-based HMO has monopolized merely HMO-type care in the community—perhaps a separate economic market despite the availability of fee-for-service care as a substitute—would not sufficiently open up the question of domination by fee-for-service doctors, though it would be appropriate where extension of the hospital monopoly was the only issue.

[183] Active participation by consumer groups in the policy-making function would go far toward dispelling concern.

[183] *See also* notes 185, 220, 221, & 229 *infra.*

[184] American Medical Ass'n v. United States, 317 U.S. 519, 528-29 (1943).

he should have no trouble if he can relate the restraint to a purpose to exclude HMOs from the market or to weaken their competitive position.[185]

The interstate commerce question is harder, in part because the *AMA* case arose under section 3 of the Sherman Act, which is specifically directed to restraints occurring in the District of Columbia. Even though the Supreme Court in that case was not called upon to make a finding of the presence or absence of interstate commerce, some implication of its absence seems to have attached by reason of the Justice Department's selection of the case and its invocation of the more limited jurisdictional nexus. Likewise, in the *Oregon Medical Society* case, the Court did not have to consider whether the restraint alleged in the formation of the Society's own prepayment plan had any interstate impact. The trial court had assumed the existence of interstate commerce in dismissing the case,[186] and the Supreme Court had no occasion to consider the point since the government had failed to establish any violation.[187] Thus, the case law respecting HMO-type providers is indefinite. However, other cases suggest that medical practice generally involves no interstate aspect,[188] reflecting the circumstance that its primary ingredient is personal services rather than goods moving across state lines and that the market area in which consumers purchase these services is localized by factors of convenience and accessibility.

The most likely argument that interstate commerce is involved in HMO operation would be based on the HMO's effect on commerce in prescription drugs. It would probably not be sufficient merely to show that HMOs would engage in pre-

---

[185] Where specialty board membership or hospital staff privileges are to be denied to a physician affiliated with an HMO, stringent procedural requirements may attach because of the anticompetitive risk presented. In Silver v. New York Stock Exchange, 373 U.S. 341 (1963), the Exchange (a "combination" of its members) was held to have violated the Sherman Act by exercising its statutory powers to cut off wire services to the plaintiff without first according him notice of the grounds for the action and an opportunity to rebut the charges. The Court reasoned that the danger of anticompetitive use of the Exchange's self-regulatory powers required that they be exercised in the least restrictive manner compatible with fulfillment of the Exchange's statutory functions. Assuming the requisite impact on interstate commerce, the denial of privileges to an HMO-connected physician is closely analogous: Hospitals and specialty boards have been entrusted by the public with responsibility for quality control in medicine, a power that is subject to grave anticompetitive abuse; procedural protections are therefore appropriate, and failure to provide them, as well as revealed abuses, will be penalized by treble damage awards under the antitrust laws. It is noteworthy that the Joint Commission on Accreditation of Hospitals (JCAH), which includes representatives of several trade groups, including the AMA and the AHA, provides significant procedural protections. *See* JCAH, STANDARDS FOR ACCREDITATION OF HOSPITALS 109-11 (1969). Procedural protections may be required for other reasons as well. *See* Ludlam, *Hospital-Physician Relations: The Role of Staff Privileges*, in this symposium, p. 879.

Another antitrust theory useful to physicians excluded from hospital staff privileges or society membership would be that applied in Associated Press v. United States, 326 U.S. 1 (1945). In that case, an open membership policy was compelled where deprivation carried with it a distinct competitive disadvantage. Presumably the staff's quality-control responsibilities could be reconciled with this principle.

[186] 95 F. Supp. at 105.

[187] The Court did discuss the interstate commerce point with respect to another issue in the case. 343 U.S. at 337-39.

[188] *See, e.g.*, Riggall v. Washington County Medical Soc'y, 249 F.2d 266 (8th Cir. 1957); Spears Free Clinic & Hospital for Poor Children v. Cleere, 197 F.2d 125 (10th Cir. 1952); Polhemus v. American Medical Ass'n, 145 F.2d 357 (10th Cir. 1944).

scribing and occasionally dispensing drugs. Rather the restraint would have to have some likely direct and substantial impact on interstate drug sales.[189] Prescription drugs are a substantial item in the nation's health bill. Out-of-hospital prescriptions cost the public $3.2 billion in 1966, which was 7.6 per cent of national expenditures for health services and supplies in that year.[190] If specific activities of a medical society that are repressive of HMO development could be said to affect this commerce materially, that effect would certainly be substantial enough to warrant application of the antitrust laws. Moreover, this result shoud not appear strained or unreasonable, since the drug industry is already the subject of extensive federal regulatory concern exerted under the commerce power.

If HMOs were required to cover and pay all or a portion of their enrollees' drug bills, there would be an extremely persuasive argument that any restriction on HMOs' ability to penetrate a market area would have substantial effects on interstate commerce and would warrant antitrust action. It is well recognized that fee-for-service physicians are not ideally situated to prescribe drugs in a manner assuring the public the highest value from the drugs they consume. Solo practitioners are thought not to be as well informed about drug therapy as they should be, and the method of merchandizing drugs by brand name and intensive promotion has often been criticized for failing to provide adequate information in a usable form.[191] Physicians are apt to make prescribing decisions without reference to the price that the patient must pay the pharmacist. The result is that the prescription drug market is though to be excessively profitable for the drug companies and generally unresponsive to price competition.[192] Although discussions of provider prepayment plans do not always recognize it, drug prescribing would appear to be an area in which HMO-type care could provide substantial and highly desirable efficiencies.

HMOs providing coverage of their enrollees' drugs would be in a position either to dispense them themselves or to prescribe them. In either case the HMO would be motivated to evaluate efficacy, safety, and price more carefully than do fee-for-service physicians. Judicious prescribing by generic rather than brand name and careful price and quality comparisons among pharmacists would contribute substantially to better performance in the prescription drug market. Furthermore, HMOs would be generally larger-scale providers and would therefore be in a better position to retain a staff pharmacologist or to seek out pharmacological literature and advice

---

[189] *See* Elizabeth Hospital, Inc. v. Richardson, 269 F.2d 167 (8th Cir. 1959).

[190] Task Force on Prescription Drugs, Final Report 1 (1969) [hereinafter cited as Task Force Report].

[191] *See, e.g.,* H. Dowling, Medicines for Man ch. 7 (1970); Ruge, *Regulation of Prescription Drug Advertising: Medical Progress and Private Enterprise,* 32 Law & Contemp. Prob. 650 (1967); Task Force Report, 7-11, 21-24, 36-37.

[192] *See generally Hearings on Competitive Problems in the Drug Industry Before the Monopoly Subcomm. of the Senate Select Comm. on Small Business,* 90th Cong., 1st Sess. (1967); Task Force Report 11-15; Dowling, *supra* note 191, chs. 5 & 6; Baehr, *Drug Costs and the Consumer,* in Drugs in Our Society 179 (H. Talalay ed. 1964).

so as to improve the results of drug therapy. Under these circumstances there would be good reason to think that HMOs would improve the working of market forces in interstate commerce in prescription drugs and could substantially reduce the nation's drug bill while increasing the benefits of drugs to patients.[193] These beneficial results would occur even where a coinsurance or deductible provision was incorporated.[194]

Although the arguments for including coverage of drug costs in HMO coverage are persuasive, the administration's proposals pending in Congress at the present time would not require coverage of out-of-hospital drug costs.[195] This can be explained as an effort to reduce the cost of the insurance provided and to concentrate on those areas where rising costs are the greatest problem.[196] The argument that interstate commerce in drugs would be adversely affected by restraints of trade directed against HMOs would be somewhat weaker if HMO coverage does not typically include drugs. Nevertheless, drugs prescribed while the patient is hospitalized will probably be covered,[197] and HMOs would have the option of making drug insurance available to its enrollees.[198] Furthermore, the larger-scale organization of HMOs would provide opportunities for improved prescribing, and normal competitive urges should lead HMOs to attempt to please consumers by helping them obtain the best drug for the money. One can visualize, for example, an HMO advertising that its prescriptions include generic drugs where appropriate and are written in consultation with a qualified pharmacologist. I would think that the government could procure a sufficient number of medical and economic experts to testify convincingly to the substantiality and desirability of these effects that an antitrust court could be persuaded that interstate commerce was in fact substantially and adversely affected by exclusionary tactics directed against HMOs.

The chances of persuading courts that antitrust enforcement is appropriate in these areas would be increased by a declaration by Congress as part of the legislative history of health care legislation that the antitrust laws are to be relied upon to

---

[193] See McCaffree & Newman, *Prepayment of Drug Costs Under a Group Practice Prepayment Plan*, 58 AM. J. PUB. HEALTH 1212 (1968), which finds a net cost saving to plan subscribers of 28% even after provision for profits earned and taxes payable on drugs purchased outside the cooperative. The substantiality of the potential impact of HMO coverage of prescription drugs is indicated as follows: "If costs similar to the Group Health level could be achieved for most of the population, the nation's drug bill would decline by over $800,000,000 or just about 2 per cent of the nation's total health care expenditures." *Id.* at 1218.

[194] The HMO would seek to minimize drug costs in order to prevent the using up of the deductible or to reduce its coinsurance liability.

[195] Medicare does not cover outpatient drug costs either. See TASK FORCE REPORT 49-69. Under Medicaid most states have exercised the option to cover drugs. See CCH MEDICARE & MEDICAID GUIDE para. 15,504 (1971). Section 25(b) of the Kennedy-Griffiths bill provides for coverage of the costs of *approved* drugs furnished to CHSO enrollees.

[196] Drug costs have remained remarkably stable, particularly as compared to other health costs. See BUREAU OF THE CENSUS, STATISTICAL ABSTRACT OF THE UNITED STATES 62 (1970).

[197] Since these are covered under Medicare, they are likely to be covered in any new scheme. I have not been able to determine how substantial an item this is, but it is not likely to be insignificant.

[198] Several plans, most notably Group Health Cooperative of Puget Sound, have provided drugs with considerable success. See Baehr, *supra* note 192, at 183-86; McCaffree & Newman, *supra* note 193.

maintain HMOs' market opportunities. Further, express recognition of the importance of HMO formation in improving the performance of the drug industry would serve as a helpful guide to a judge faced with appraising the interstate commerce impact. If the Congressional committees should differ with my conclusions on this matter, one can visualize enactment of a "little Sherman Act" specifically applicable to the health care field. If interstate commerce were not thought a sufficient constitutional nexus, the legislation could be seen as being in aid of a legitimate federal purpose under the taxing and spending power as utilized in the Medicare, Medicaid, and proposed FHIP legislation.[199]

Although some of these matters are not as clear as one might wish, it would seem desirable for the Antitrust Division of the Department of Justice to commence some actions to determine the antitrust laws' capacity to recreate a competitive market in health care delivery. If the Nixon administration is sincere in its expressed desire to foster HMO development, it should quickly authorize such litigation, perhaps directed at some of the medical-society-sponsored prepayment plans.[200] There seems to be no reason to await Congressional action on the various health proposals before moving in this constructive way to create opportunities for HMO formation. The Federal Trade Commission might also take an interest in these matters, dealing with exclusionary tactics as "unfair methods of competition."[201]

D. Federal Preemption as a Means of Overcoming Restrictive State Legislation

Many states have statutes, enacted largely at the behest of organized medicine, that in some way inhibit the formation of HMOs.[202] In varying degrees, these laws will have the effect of deterring the formation of HMOs altogether or will tend toward the creation of plans of the kinds supported by medical societies, which, as we have seen, may be nothing but a defensive gambit by fee-for-service medicine. The administration and the national health insurance proponents agree that the presence of these laws would obstruct implementation of any federal policy for dealing with the health care crisis.[203]

---

[199] See notes 211-13 infra and accompanying text.

[200] In recent years the Antitrust Division has performed much useful service in reminding regulators and policy makers of the role that competition can play. It would be appropriate to add health care to the long list of fields, including banking, securities exchanges, transportation, and broadcasting, in which competition had been de-emphasized by policy makers and the Division's influence was exerted to restore it to a higher place. See REPORT OF THE TASK FORCE ON PRODUCTIVITY AND COMPETITION (1969), urging that the Antitrust Division serve "as the effective agent of the Administration in behalf of a policy of competition."

[201] 15 U.S.C. § 45 (1964).

[202] See Note, supra note 7, at 960-75, which concludes that the law is not as restrictive in practice as it appears to be on paper at least as regards nonprofit HMOs; ASPEN SYSTEM: CORP., supra note 105.

[203] See PRESIDENT'S HEALTH MESSAGE 6; S. 1623, § 401(a); Kennedy-Griffiths bill § 56(b). Both S. 1623, § 401(b), and the Kennedy-Griffiths bill § 56(a) would also deal with restrictive state policies toward manpower licensure and utilization.

The following language from the text of the Kennedy-Griffiths proposal suggests both the nature of the laws creating the problem and the remedy proposed:

> If the Board finds that a proposed corporation will meet the requirements . . . for participation as a comprehensive health service organization . . . , but that it cannot be incorporated in the State in which it proposes to furnish services because the State law requires that a medical society approve the incorporation of such an organization, or requires that physicians constitute all or a majority of its governing board, or requires that all physicians in the locality be permitted to participate in the services of the organization, or makes any other requirement which the Board finds incompatible with the purposes of this title, the Board may issue a certificate of incorporation to the organization, and it shall thereupon become a body corporate.[204]

The Kennedy-Griffiths proposal also would permit a nonprofit hospital or CHSO to render care directly through employees without regard to whether state law would regard its activities as prohibited "corporate practice of a profession"; the provision would not, however, permit any employment or arrangement that was "likely to cause lay interference with professional acts or professional judgments."[205]

The Kennedy-Griffiths bill would leave intact any state law requiring the CHSO to be a nonprofit enterprise.[206] Since I consider this an extremely unwise policy, one that is embodied in the Kennedy-Griffiths proposal itself, I would like to see federal law expressly override it. While I recognize that the issue is not free from doubt and that states might have an interest in protecting their citizens in this regard, I am concerned that it will be difficult to get an open-minded re-examination of the question. Moreover, state policy makers may too readily accept the medical societies' version of the issue.

State laws also may purport to regulate HMOs under insurance laws.[207] Federal law regulating HMOs, as under the Kennedy-Griffiths bill, would probably be construed to preempt these efforts.

The Nixon administration's FHIP proposal would deal with laws restrictive of HMO formation by declaring that agreements entered into by the Secretary of HEW with HMOs, under which services would be rendered to FHIP beneficiaries, would make state law inapplicable "to the provision of such services under such an agreement to the extent that such law or regulation is inconsistent with the obligations of the health maintenance organization under the agreement."[208] While effective in dealing with the corporate-practice and insurance regulation problems

---

[204] Kennedy-Griffiths bill § 56(b).

[205] *Id.* § 56(a)(4).

[206] Such a requirement usually flows from interpretation of the rule against corporate practice of a profession. *See* Note, *supra* note 7, at 960-62 and references there cited. A for-profit HMO, Omnicare, is currently trying, without success, to obtain a favorable ruling from the Attorney General of California. *See* letter from R. Stromberg to V. Stein, Nov. 26, 1969 (legal opinion and brief to the effect that Omnicare would not violate the corporate-practice rule).

[207] *See* Note, *supra* note 7, at 969-74.

[208] S. 1623, § 401(a).

insofar as implementation of FHIP is concerned, there may be a question whether this provision would have any effect on state laws as applied to the care of persons not covered by FHIP.[209] If not, the result might be to create federal instrumentalities that are permitted to serve the poor and perhaps the elderly but are prevented by state law from serving other elements of the population. However, in view of the requirement in the FHIP proposal that HMOs must have non-FHIP enrollees to the extent of at least half their enrollment,[210] a state law purporting to limit its right to accept non-FHIP enrollees would be "inconsistent" with the federal scheme.[210a]

The constitutional power of the federal government to override state legislation is of course not plenary. It seems clear, however, that a law like the Kennedy-Griffiths bill, which would be enacted under the same taxing and spending powers of Congress that permitted creation of the Social Security system in furtherance of the "general welfare,"[211] would allow Congress to preempt the field against state laws in aid of achieving its legitimate constitutional purpose.[212] It would be anomalous if a less far-reaching measure, such as the administration's proposals, could not be implemented by a similar express overriding of state authority, but, since the administration plan leaves much of the financing of health care in the private sector, it might be argued that the constitutional basis for preemption—federal spending— does not exist.[213] Nevertheless, federal involvement through Medicare, Medicaid, and FHIP would seem a sufficient basis for specific and total invalidation as to all providers caring for beneficiaries of federal programs. If this were done, a physician with Medicare patients could not be interfered with by state authorities even as to his ability to treat other patients since the federal government could reasonably demand that its clients not be segregated from the general population in obtaining health care. If the taxing and spending power were deemed insufficient, the federal government could act in aid of its power over interstate commerce in prescription

---

[209] The narrowness of the preemption attempted is attributable to the administration's attempt to use the government's contracting power as its basis for moving against state laws. *See* Paul v. United States, 371 U.S. 245 (1963). Subsequent discussion indicates that this is perhaps too narrow an approach to the problem.

[210] S. 1623, § 201, proposed § 628(b)(5).

[210a] The AMA fails to recognize this wider preemptive effect. *See* Division of Medical Practice, *supra* note 43, at 12.

H.R. 1 as amended, § 226(a), proposed § 1876(j), provides, "The [contracting] function vested in the Secretary . . . may be performed without regard to such provisions of law or of other regulations relating to the making, performance, amendment, or modification of contracts of the United States as the Secretary may determine to be inconsistent with the furtherance of the purposes of this title." This language is obscure, but presumably state laws inhibiting performance of HMO contracts, including satisfaction of the membership requirements, would be superseded.

[211] Steward Machine Co. v. Davis, 301 U.S. 548 (1937); Helvering v. Davis, 301 U.S. 619 (1937). *See also* Chapman & Talmadge, *Historical and Political Background of Federal Health Care Legislation,* 35 LAW & CONTEMP. PROB. 334, 342-46 (1970).

[212] Although the regulation of medical practice has traditionally been within the province of the states under their police power to legislate for the protection of the health, safety, and morals of their citizens, Congress may affix conditions to the expenditure of federal tax funds. *See* Oklahoma v. United States Civil Service Comm'n, 330 U.S. 127 (1947).

[213] *See* note 209 *supra.*

drugs and over the interstate health insurance industry. It is hoped that Congress will see the need for clearing away all state legislation likely to inhibit the operation of market forces.

E. Supplementary Measures to Strengthen Market Forces

Numerous factors contribute to the strength or weakness of market forces in any marketplace, and many of these factors are susceptible to legislative and administrative influence to improve the market's over-all performance. A survey of the market for health services suggests some ways of making doubly sure that the market will deliver the things for which we count on it.

1. *Lowering Barriers to Entry*

HMO formation will occur more quickly and more often if the obstacles to their creation are fewer or less difficult to surmount, and it is therefore important that governmental policies be directed to reducing both the number and the negotiability of such obstacles. Only for compelling reasons should policy makers render entry materially more difficult than it has to be. The inquiry here is what entry barriers exist for would-be HMO organizers and what, if anything, can be done about them.

The administration has proposed federal financial aid for HMO formation as a means of reducing entry barriers.[213a] However, subsidies for start-up costs are usually inconsistent with market functioning and can distort competitive outcomes by permanently lowering the costs of the subsidized enterprise (by eliminating the need to earn a return on the full original investment). Nevertheless, the President's aid program may perhaps be justified, at least as to the concept if not as to the precise amount, as a means of compensating for allegedly unnatural and unwarranted barriers to acceptance created in consumers' and physicians' minds by the past activities of government and organized medicine; the proposed planning grants, temporary absorption of operating losses, and loan guarantees are all consistent with a purpose to lower barriers reflecting ignorance and risk attributable in part to these historical factors. More important perhaps, HMO subsidies seem quite appropriate in an industry where charitable and governmental subsidies are already so much a part of the landscape; however, this rationale provides little justification for subsidizing HMOs' provision of primary care, since fee-for-service doctors, their chief competitors in this business, do not enjoy such support.

Government should see that, to the extent possible, HMOs face no requirements for large capital investments. It is therefore significant that in the House-passed Medicare amendments HMOs are not required to render hospital care or to provide all specialists' services but may instead purchase these as needed in the fee-for-service sector. Some financial responsibility requirements will no doubt be imposed, but care should be taken not to be too demanding in this regard, perhaps accepting

---

[213a] *See* text accompanying note 27 *supra.*

bonds from the organizers as a way of protecting plan subscribers. Reinsurance has an important role to play in making small-scale HMOs viable and should be encouraged by policy makers.

Any legal provision mandating large size in an HMO seems inappropriate. It may prove to be the case that certain scale economies will compel many HMOs to be quite large, and indeed these economies are reportedly not exhausted in a hospital-based HMO until it has 25,000 to 30,000 enrollees.[214] Nevertheless, the ability of smaller HMOs to survive, perhaps by dint of characteristics other than rigorous efficiency and low cost, should be tested in the marketplace and not in legislative halls. The Senate Finance Committee, in its version of the proposed 1970 Medicare amendments, would have required an HMO to have at least 10,000 subscribers,[215] and, regrettably, the administration's proposed National Health Insurance Partnership Act of 1971 incorporates this requirement.[216] This would be a most unfortunate and unnecessary blow to the functioning of a health care marketplace.

I wish that it were needless to say that entry by HMOs should not be restricted by government on any grounds but minimal requirements of character, fitness, and financial responsibility. Congress should provide expressly that, even in the currently popular name of "comprehensive health planning," no for-profit HMO should be excluded from the marketplace on the ground that a "need" for it has not been demonstrated or that existing institutions require protection against its competition. Comprehensive health planning, admittedly needed, should not be turned into a system of licensing by "certificate of public convenience and necessity." Instead, it should be seen as a technique for coordinating the health investments of various levels of government and of the voluntary-nonprofit sector and for eliminating all factors besides the public interest in decision making regarding these expenditures.[217] Monopolistic elements created by such governmental intervention

---

[214] Note, *supra* note 7, at 904-05.

[215] S. REP. No. 91-1431, at 136.

[216] *See* S. 1623, § 101, proposed § 604(a)(5); *id.* § 201, proposed § 628(b)(5).

[217] Unfortunately, Congress is on the brink of adopting legislation that would effectively create a system of rigid entry restrictions in the states and would, perhaps inadvertently, remove any realistic hope of recreating a dynamic and workable market for health services. A section of the House-passed version of H.R. 1 as amended, § 221, which seems to this moment to have generated little controversy, would reduce federal Medicare payments to health facilities and HMOs to the extent that they represent recovery of depreciation and other costs connected with capital investments in facilities costing more than $100,000 that are constructed without approval (subject to federal review) of state planning agencies. Thus, the health planners would be ceded the power effectively to control all major new public and private investment in health facilities, including HMOs, and to prevent all new construction for which they are not satisfied that a "need," as they define it, exists. Experience in other regulated industries tells us that "need" is almost always defined with an eye to possible adverse effects on other providers of the service, indicating that legislation of this kind invariably protects existing providers from competition and explaining why it is regularly sponsored by them. This kind of law is depressingly similar to, among other things, the law restricting bank chartering and branching on the basis of "convenience and needs," which developed in the 1930s as an expedient to protect against bank failures but which is now recognized as unnecessarily restrictive of needed and healthy competition. *See, e.g.*, Kreps, *Modernizing Banking Regulation*, 31 LAW & CONTEMP. PROB. 648 (1966).

As discussed earlier (*see* notes 98-100 *supra* and accompanying text), health planning agencies should

have too often redounded to the public detriment and private profit and should be prevented from doing so again.

Ease of entry not only enlarges opportunities for entrepreneurs interested in HMO formation but supplies a beneficial restraining influence on sellers already operating in the market. Thus, a market populated by only a few sellers may yet behave competitively, in part because sellers recognize not only their existing rivals but also the risk that other sellers will appear if prices rise to a level making entry appear attractive. Preservation of such "potential competition"—which might come from HMOs operating in adjoining areas, employers interested in cheaper care for their employees, or indigenous fee-for-service physicians—should be an important policy consideration.

"Entry barriers" and "potential competition" have become largely talismans in antitrust law, used more for conjuring than as analytical tools.[218] Nevertheless, careful antitrust enforcement could perform a useful service wherever certain practices appeared to have an entry-limiting effect. For example, the duration of HMO contracts with subscribers would be subject to control through antitrust rules on exclusive dealing,[219] and tying arrangements, if identifiable, would be subject to antitrust action.[220] Further, the disadvantages of non-hospital-based HMOs in purchasing hospital services might be deemed to flow from entry-limiting devices having conspiratorial aspects.[221] Still, although the antitrust laws might serve, issues of these

---

be scrupulously limited to dealing with the investments of the governmental and nonprofit sectors and should be given no authority over private investment. The expediency arguments advanced for absolute control over entry are that public investments must be protected in order to improve their borrowing prospects and their capacity to serve the poor. But the losses from precluding competition for inefficient, price-discriminating monopolists would surely outweigh any saving in the cost of borrowing, and Congress is likely to improve the ability of the poor to pay for their own care, obviating the need for price discrimination. See note 151 supra. In any event, the arguments for protectionist regulation on behalf of hospitals, weak as they are, are far stronger than the case for restricting HMO entry. The Ways and Means Committee was responsible for extending the coverage of this provision to HMOs. Compare original H.R. 1, § 221. Its work should be undone in the Senate so that at least non-hospital-based HMOs will not become public utilities.

[218] See, e.g., FTC v. Procter & Gamble Co., 386 U.S. 568, 585 (1967) (Harlan, J., concurring); General Foods Corp., [1965-67 Transfer Binder] TRADE REG. REP. 22,743, at 22,746 (1966) (Commissioner Elman dissenting).

[219] See, e.g., FTC v. Motion Picture Advertising Service Co., 344 U.S. 392 (1953).

[220] Consider, for example, whether a hospital-based HMO, such as a Kaiser plan, should be allowed to exclude competing HMOs and fee-for-service physicians and their patients from access to its hospital services. The antitrust issue would seem to turn on whether prepaid health care is a "single product" or whether hospital and outpatient services are deemed to be "tied" together by the HMO, thereby foreclosing competitors from a needed service. Cf. Fortner Enterprises, Inc. v. United States Steel Corp., 394 U.S. 495 (1969). A holding that this was an illegal tying arrangement would be surprising, but it would perhaps be defensible on the theory, often stated with respect to tying, exclusive dealing, and vertical integration, that entry barriers are objectionably raised if, because customers or suppliers are foreclosed, the potential entrant must come in on two levels with commensurately greater capital and know-how, supplying in this case not merely primary care but perhaps hospital services as well.

[221] The difficulties faced by non-hospital-based HMOs are recognized in Note, supra note 7, at 907, 910-18. They take the form, in part at least, of preferential rates given to Blue Cross. Although I choose not to get into the problems of dealing with Blue Cross and Blue Shield under antitrust principles— primarily they are problems of state versus federal power (see note 164 supra)—, it may be that an antitrust attack on Blue Cross-Blue Shield will have to be mounted if HMO entry on equal terms is

kinds seem to me more appropriately committed to administrative oversight when presented in a specific industry context. Congress might wish to adopt this mechanism, specifying that maximization of HMO entry opportunities is to be a primary object.

2. *Facilitating Consumer Choice*

Whatever the precise nature of the insurance scheme adopted, consumers should be in a position to exercise free and informed choice in selecting a mode of coverage and the appropriate provider. The administration's plan would allow employees covered by their employer's health insurance program to elect to apply the cost of that coverage toward the purchase of an HMO membership, but this option should be exercisable with respect to any available HMO, not simply to HMO-type coverage provided by a subsidiary of the health insurer or by the local medical society. HMO subscribers and beneficiaries of health insurance should be entitled to withdraw from either type of plan at fairly short notice in order to transfer their business elsewhere. Administrative requirements should be introduced to define benefit packages on a uniform basis in order to facilitate price comparisons. Thus, some minimum package would be defined by law, and additional benefits could be classed and priced separately.

The medical profession has studiously maintained ethical rules against advertising by physicians.[222] Under these rules the only information which can be conveyed to the public by physicians or groups thereof relates to the type of practice, office location and hours, and similar matters which are not likely to influence greatly the selection of a particular physician. Similarly, the means of communicating even this limited data are restricted. These "ethical" rules cannot be allowed to interfere with HMO developments, and advertising, at least to the extent of permitting consumer education and informed comparisons, seems necessary to facilitate choice between the traditional and innovational systems and among the innovational plans themselves. Administrative attention should be given to some regulatory prescription of disclosure in advertising messages.[223] In addition to standardizing coverage and

---

to be facilitated. If it could be obtained, a legislative or administrative solution would be preferable since it would be both swifter and surer. Probably any attempt to deal with this issue can await a clearer demonstration that there is a problem.

[222] An early version of AMA, PRINCIPLES OF MEDICAL ETHICS § 4 (1953), contained the traditional proscription of advertising by members of the medical profession:

"Solicitation of patients, directly or indirectly by a physician, by groups of physicians or by institutions or organizations is unethical. This principle protects the public from the advertiser and salesman of medical care by establishing an easily discernible and generally recognized distinction between him and the ethical physician . . . ."

Section 5 further elaborated on the proscription. In 1957 a simplified revision of the *Principles* was promulgated in which advertising was prohibited in the following brief sentence: "He should not solicit patients." AMA, PRINCIPLES OF MEDICAL ETHICS § 5 (1957). It was emphasized that the semantic streamlining in this revision did not alter the traditional meaning. *See also* AMA, OPINIONS AND REPORTS OF THE JUDICIAL COUNCIL 25 (1969).

[223] California's Knox-Mills Health Plan Act, CAL. GOV'T CODE §§ 12530-39 (West Supp. 1969), provides regulation of this kind. *See* Note, *supra* note 7, at 977-78.

terminology to facilitate price and quality comparisons, regulators might require disclosure of nonaccreditation or official quality control ratings or demerits. The medical profession's preference for noninformational advertising should be recognized as one more cartel tactic.[224] Although there are of course some legitimate ethical considerations in advertising medical services, they do not extend to advertising of alternative modes of care. Apparently Kaiser-Permanente and other prepaid group practice plans have succeeded in advertising their services.[225]

3. Preventing Competition in Risk Selection

One danger in insurance schemes is that competition will take the form of competing for the better risks while excluding those most in need of insurance protection. Any legislative solution to the health care crisis must provide against this development. The pending proposals all appear to introduce the requirement that HMO-type providers adopt a first-come, first-served policy, and this would appear to be a reasonable approach to the problem. A similar requirement should also be imposed on health insurance companies.

Conceivably, an HMO or health insurer that found its enrolled population to be excessively risk-prone, due to age distribution or a high incidence of chronic ailments, could be allowed to apply for exemption from the first-come, first-served requirement. Such a provision for waiver would seem to be necessary to enable insurers to remain competitive. There are probably other difficulties of this kind that I cannot visualize at this point, but it is perhaps sufficient to call attention to this category of problems and to urge that administrative attention be directed to solving them in the manner most conducive to market competition. It seems almost essential to the achievement of this goal that "community rating" be required, since "experience rating" is probably workable only with a captive population, which would be antithetical to the operation of a competitive market. On the other hand, administratively granted exemptions from the first-come, first-served requirement would allow a plan to re-establish its ability to compete on a community-rating basis.

4. The Role of Private Health Insurers

The Nixon health proposals have been criticized, most notably by Senator Kennedy, as providing a "windfall" to the health insurance industry.[226] Of course, if HMOs become a major provider of primary health care, the role of health insurers would be reduced, though they might find a new function in reinsuring smaller HMOs. Whether the long-term net effect of the administration's plan would be to increase the size or profits of the health insurance industry may not be predictable at this time.

---

[224] The trade association in FTC v. Cement Institute, 333 U.S. 683, 715 (1948), "in the interest of eliminating competition, suppressed information as to the variations in quality that sometimes exist in different cement."

[225] Kessel, supra note 70, at 44.

[226] N.Y. Times, Feb. 19, 1971, p. 1, col. 8, at p. 16, col. 1.

Of course, health insurers might move directly into HMO formation and might profit handsomely in so doing. I see substantial merit, however, in prohibiting health insurers from entering the HMO sector. The obvious reason is to avoid domination of the market by Blue Cross-Blue Shield, which might in some communities come to sell the bulk of the health insurance while also controlling the major HMO and reinsuring the competing HMOs against excessive risks.[227] Since Blue Cross is widely accused of being operated in the interest of the medical establishment,[228] the arguments against Blue Cross's extension into the HMO sector parallel the arguments against medical society sponsorship of prepayment plans: there is good reason to suspect that Blue Cross HMOs would hang back rather than develop the full potential of the HMO concept and that avoidance of the establishment's discomfiture would be their primary *raison d'être*.[229]

A more subtle reason also supports excluding health insurers from HMO sponsorship. Health insurers must have a powerful financial stake in the survival of fee-for-service medicine if their efforts are to be directed, in a way they have never been before, to reducing costs and increasing efficiency in that sector of the market. As long as health insurers have enjoyed a protected position, they have been willing to confine themselves to paying the bills submitted, seldom disputing the amount of fees or the patient's need for the therapy or surgical procedure performed or the hospitalization ordered. The rise in medical costs has not hurt health insurers enough to enlist them in policing the providers, and the easier course has been to seek rate increases from regulatory agencies or experience-based rate adjustments from insured groups. The public has thus lost practically the entire benefit of health insurers' potential economizing influence over providers.[230]

Faced in a free market with vigorous competition from a cheaper and more efficient delivery system, the fee-for-service sector might not survive as more than a vestige if health insurance premiums—which consumers will compare to HMO membership charges—continued to reflect the inefficiencies of the solo practitioner and his overutilization of hospitals and other resources. While some might not mourn the passing of this delivery mode, it seems desirable to maintain fee-for-service medicine as an available alternative for the benefit of those who value highly the

---

[227] Blue Cross has already commenced its move into HMO formation. *See* Am. Med. News, Apr. 5, 1971, p. 12.

[228] *E.g.*, HEALTH-PAC, *supra* note 115, at 158-63; Kotelchuck, *Trying to Shake the Blues*, HEALTH-PAC BULL., Mar. 1971, p. 1.

[229] Whether the antitrust laws could be used to accomplish the exclusion of Blue Cross and Blue Shield from HMO formation is not clear. As long as Blue Cross or Blue Shield performs solely as an indemnitor, it would normally be regulated under state insurance laws and therefore exempt from the antitrust laws under the McCarran-Ferguson Act, 15 U.S.C. § 1012(b) (1964). *See* note 164 *supra*. If, however, it should engage in the provision of services in the manner of an HMO, it would seem no longer to be engaged in "the business of insurance" under the most accepted definition. *See* Jordan v. Group Health Ass'n, 107 F.2d 239 (D.C. Cir. 1939). This would cause the loss of the McCarran-Ferguson Act exemption and might open up remedial possibilities similar to those canvassed with respect to HMOs affiliated with monopolistic hospitals.

[230] *See* generally SOMERS & SOMERS, *supra* note 156, ch. 20.

personalized care and the right of physician selection that it affords. Moreover, HMO enrollees are known to purchase some fee-for-service care, and this alternative source of care should be kept available.[231]

The market alone cannot adequately weed out the inefficiencies of fee-for-service medicine. The reasons are familiar: patients cannot easily recognize excessive treatment and often welcome it for psychological reasons. On the other hand, an insurance company barred from HMO formation would be intensely motivated to keep costs down in order that its premiums not become prohibitive in comparison with HMO charges. While there are substantial limits to what they can achieve without undesirable interference with actual treatment, they are capable of more than they have achieved up to now and could be expected to maximize their efforts only if they are not indifferent whether patients choose health insurance or HMO care. The medical profession should see the benefit to themselves in stimulating insurers' assistance in preserving the best and eliminating the worst aspects of fee-for-service medicine. They should also see the need to strengthen peer review and other utilization controls in the fee-for-service sector.[232] If the great power of the organized profession over its membership is not redirected to this task, fee-for-service medicine may not survive even to the extent to which, on merit, it is entitled.

The health insurance industry will also find an important role in reinsuring HMOs against those risks that the HMOs themselves cannot safely assume. Again, barring unnecessary restrictions, many of the services covered by such reinsurance will be specialist and hospital services purchased in the fee-for-service sector, and insurers will be motivated to control these costs in order that their reinsured HMOs will be better able to compete with larger HMOs which provide these services in-house and require less reinsurance. In this process they will be assisted by the insured HMOs themselves, which will face experience-rated premiums and will therefore seek the best available value in specialist and hospital services. Because insurers and HMOs are more medically aware than other consumers buying care in the fee-for-service sector, their influence will be salutary. With all of these factors operating, it would be reasonable to expect in the future a much better performance from the fee-for-service sector, including its insurance component, than it has delivered in the past.

5. *Implications for Financing Schemes*

The functioning of the market for health care could be destroyed by a financing scheme that failed to preserve the cost-consciousness of at least the greater number of consumers. Medicare and Medicaid have already destroyed the cost-consciousness of many consumers, and these models cannot be extended very much farther. The administration's proposed FHIP would expand the number of federally subsidized consumers, but, since many participants in that plan would be paying their own

---

[231] See notes 19 & 23 supra.

[232] See notes 157-59, 169-80 supra and accompanying text on the form that such efforts should not be permitted to take.

way in part, it has been possible to design the plan to preserve cost-consciousness. The critical feature in making the market-oriented system work even with substantial numbers of federally subsidized consumers is the "proxy-shopping" device explained earlier. Under this system the government in effect accepts a private subscriber's judgment on the value and price of the care rendered by a particular HMO in paying for such care on behalf of one of its clients. Whatever financing system is ultimately adopted—and it will not pay to evaluate specific proposals here—, every detail of it must be evaluated in the light of its effect on consumer cost-consciousness.

The handling of coverage, coinsurance, and deductibles will also require care if the market's ability to function is to be maximized. Complete exclusion from coverage throws consumers back on their own resources, which may be inappropriate from the standpoint of equity to the poor, protection against catastrophe, and loss of the potentiality for improved incentives through HMO development. Outpatient prescription drugs, for example, might be profitably included in coverage, though possibly subjected to a deductible or coinsurance requirement that would reduce program costs while retaining the correct incentives.[233]

While perhaps useful in reducing costs of the program to the government, co-insurance may also serve an important function in discouraging overutilization. A small per-visit charge is commonly recommended for this purpose, and outpatient psychiatric care is sometimes subjected to a large copayment requirement, presumably on the ground that it is largely elective and can be quite costly. Coinsurance does not deter equally in all economic classes, however, and may cause low-income consumers to forgo needed care. Graduated deductibles and coinsurance of the kind provided for in the FHIP proposal could be used to prevent unfairness in this regard.[234]

Another significant set of considerations relates to the benefits of any insurance scheme covering the poor. If coverage is significantly reduced by limits, deductibles, and coinsurance, plans may hesitate to enroll the poor because of the losses to be anticipated from defaults on bills for the services not covered.[235] If enacted in its present form, the administration's proposed FHIP, which imposes more substantial limits on benefits for the poor than for the nonpoor, might disappoint many of the hopes expressed earlier.[236] Because price competition among the plans would substantially eliminate the opportunity for making those overcharges to the affluent which have previously subsidized the poor, inability to pay will be even more significant than it previously was, and the disadvantage to the poor may in this respect be increased. But, since the affluent may ultimately benefit from a lowering of

[233] See notes 189-98 supra and accompanying text.
[234] S. 1623, § 201, proposed § 626(b).
[235] See notes 76 & 84 supra.
[236] Much would depend on whether, as an accounting matter, collection losses could be counted as an expense of caring for the FHIP group in determining "retentions." See text accompanying notes 49-50 supra.

charges over-all, Congress should be less hesitant to employ the income tax system to provide the resources needed to care adequately for the poor and to protect them against discrimination by profit-conscious providers. Parsimony at this stage, by retarding realization of a functioning market-oriented system, would be a false economy.

Conclusion

Enactment of the Nixon administration's health care proposals, even without the changes which I think are needed to create a truly dynamic market and the conditions for optimum HMO development,[237] would somewhat strengthen the basis for relying on the market to improve the health care system's performance. A broadened health insurance plan for the poor, universal health insurance with an HMO option for everyone, and general encouragement of HMO development should expand consumer choice, restore some vigor to price and service competition in health care, and increase cost consciousness. Congress, attracted by the combination of a reasonable likelihood of meaningful change and the essential conservatism of a market-oriented approach, may well find the administration's program to its liking.

The danger that I most apprehend is that Congress, in enacting a program dependent on the market as the primary means of social control, would fail to close

---

[237] Specifically, I would propose the following changes and amendments:

(1) If it is not already so, FHIP coverage should be made adequate to prevent discrimination against program beneficiaries. *See* text accompanying notes 235-36 *supra.* Federal payment of less than 100% of the cost of caring for the poor (after reasonable deductibles and copayments) would be merely a further subsidy to charitable providers but would exclude profit-conscious providers from participating in such care and would bar the poor totally from "mainstream" medical care.

(2) Consideration should be given to whether price controls may be needed to cushion the impact of a truly adequate FHIP. *See* text accompanying notes 58-63 *supra.* The intermediate approach of limiting payments under Medicare and FHIP, while protecting the public treasury, results in the discrimination against the poor objected to in (1) above.

(3) Provisions to put teeth into health planning legislation should exempt HMOs or at least non-hospital-based HMOs. *See* note 217 *supra* and accompanying text. While recognizing the complexity of the question, I also have reservations about enacting protection for existing hospitals.

(4) The legislative history should specify the market as one of the chosen mechanisms of social control and should note the appropriateness of antitrust enforcement to maintain it even in the face of inconsistent state law. *See* text accompanying notes 199-201 *supra.*

(5) To perfect the "proxy-shopping" device, the HMO definition should require that at least 50% of plan subscribers be self-supporting. *See* text accompanying notes 46-47 *supra.*

(6) Employers should be required to give employees a choice of enrolling with any available HMO, not just a selected one. *See* text accompanying notes 28-30 *supra.*

(7) Requirements as to the minimum size of HMOs should be eliminated. *See* text accompanying notes 39 & 214-16 *supra.*

(8) Medical societies and monopolistic hospitals should be barred, by antitrust action if not by statute, from HMO formation if they have the effect of preventing competitive HMO development. *See* text accompanying notes 119-82 *supra.*

(9) Health insurers should be barred from HMO formation. *See* text accompanying notes 226-32 *supra.*

(10) Attention should be given to reducing the incentive to engage in favorable risk selection. *See* p. 788 *supra.*

(11) The provisions preempting the field against the states should be clarified to confirm my understanding of their intended breadth. *See* text accompanying notes 208-13 *supra.*

all of the loopholes that might allow some group—the medical societies, the emerging new elite in university medical centers, or the health planners[238]—to dominate developments and the resulting market to an excessive degree. I have been at pains to show the vulnerability of the health care marketplace to trade restraints and monopoly, often imposed in the euphemistic name of quality assurance, ethics, and, lately, planning, and I have attempted to focus on the precise measures needed to combat monopolistic tendencies wherever they appear. Unfortunately, I see little room for compromise on the need to maximize HMO entry possibilities throughout the system and to foreclose collective action preempting or otherwise restraining independent HMO development. Congress must therefore scrupulously avoid enacting, and indeed must expressly prohibit—or anticipate antitrust action with respect to—, exclusionary measures of all but the most minimal kinds, such as character, fitness, and financial responsibility requirements. It must also prevent the provision of HMO-type care from being dominated, directly or indirectly, by persons—whether in the medical societies or the medical schools—who lack a total commitment to its maximum development, not as a stop-gap to forestall competition or government control or as a social welfare agency but as a competitive alternative attractive to all consumers. Where the need for added quality assurance or for compromise with the health care establishment appears, Congress should offer only strengthened oversight of the care rendered and stricter policing of objectionable practices, not exclusionary measures or exclusive privileges.

The chief obstacle to complete acceptance of the market model for health care delivery is probably an impression that increased reliance on the market and competition will exalt self-interest and commercialism, will dispel what altruism remains in health care, and will further devalue the human element in the relation between provider and patient. The probabilities seem otherwise to me, precisely to the extent that consumers value and, given the opportunity, will shop for attentive and sympathetic care and will express aversion for both the commercialized and the insensitive provider. Furthermore, the HMO's comprehensiveness and direct financial interest in its subscribers' health should make it responsive to the consumer's desire for health security, and salaried doctors in an HMO setting would seem freer to practice medicine altruistically—albeit with regard for economic efficiency—than are fee-for-service doctors. Moreover, the important object of pre-

---

[238] Michaelson, *The Coming Medical War*, N.Y. REV. OF BOOKS, July 1, 1971, p. 32, observes how a three-way split in the ranks of the medical profession is occurring, with the medical societies losing power to "the new medical elite," which resides in the "urban university medical center," *id.* at 34, denigrates the ordinary practitioner and his trade associations, and claims itself fit to be entrusted with all the decisions that must be made. The third group is a new radical fringe, which is about as critical of the new elite as of the old. A book originating with this third group, HEALTH-PAC, *supra* note 115, convincingly demonstrates that too often the values maximized by the decisions of the new elite, which controls vast sums dedicated by government and charity to health needs, are not consistent with the welfare of consumers. *See* notes 98-100 *supra* and accompanying text. The lesson may be that, because of this unresponsiveness to the public's concerns and the opportunities for abuse of power, nonprofit monopolies are no more to be trusted than the other kind.

serving or increasing the physician's respect for his patients, particularly the disadvantaged ones, is more likely to be achieved by giving the latter meaningful alternatives—and assuring that they have the financial means of selecting among them—than by any other scheme that government might foster; only a vigorously competitive marketplace can overcome the monopolist's tendency to take its customers for granted. Unfortunately, the tendency these days is toward fostering monopoly in various forms, often under the protection of exclusionary regulation by comprehensive health planning agencies.[239] This movement seems to pose a much greater threat than does the market to the consumer's freedom to select a provider on the basis of affinity and its responsiveness to his personal needs. The pluralism to which lip service is often paid by health planners and the contrivers of comprehensive "solutions" to the health care crisis is usually a pale substitute for the dynamic diversity that competition could inspire.

If the market model cannot be embraced wholeheartedly, it will probably have to be rejected altogether in the long run. Halfway measures are what we have now, and, lacking a clear perception of the problem, we are already moving clumsily to greater restrictionism. The addition of a monopolistic HMO to each market, which may be all the administration's plan in its present form would be able to achieve, seems to promise only an improvement, not a solution. While consumer choice would be increased slightly, consumers would hardly feel that their sovereignty had been restored, and the doctors' ability to run the health care system in large part for their own rather than consumers' advantage would not be greatly undercut, although power might be subtly shifted away from the medical societies toward what has been called "the new medical elite" in university centers.[240] In these circumstances, the movement for a greater consumer role in decision making would prosper as a continuing exercise in "countervailing power," which is the last resort of a public confronting a powerful and unresponsive monopoly. I personally find such politicization an unsatisfying alternative when compared with what I regard as the market's ability to re-enfranchise consumers by offering them attractive alternatives and, with universal health insurance, meaningful freedom of choice. Even if one pretends, against the evidence, that nonprofit monopolies involve no opportunity for undue private gain, their demonstrated capacity for staggering inefficiency and for ignoring consumer wants should argue for a strong antimonopoly policy and a reinvigorated health care marketplace.

My expectation that independent HMOs can substantially improve the performance of the entire health care system rests, first of all, on their ability to impose, almost for the first time, a needed cost constraint on physicians in caring for their patients. Price and benefit-package competition from aggressive and cost-conscious HMOs

[239] See note 217 supra, describing a federal effort to put teeth in state planning efforts. Parallel legislation in the states poses the same threat. North Carolina, for example, has just passed a bill denying anyone the right to construct health facilities until the "need" for them is certified by a state agency.

[240] See note 238 supra.

would then introduce unprecedented but essential pressure to control costs in the insured-fee-for-service sector, and health insurers would be driven to institute at least a mild form of peer review calculated to reach the most substantial abuses. The extent of HMOs' actual penetration of the market will therefore not directly measure HMOs' over-all value to consumers, and indeed consumers may continue in large numbers to prefer fee-for-service care even at a higher price. Nevertheless, an available lower-cost substitute, even if it is perceived to be somewhat inferior, can impose an effective check on the exercise of monopoly power, resulting in lower prices and greater efficiency than would otherwise prevail. Thus, even if HMO-type care should appear inferior in some respect to fee-for-service medicine, it still has a vitally important market function to perform. No evidence suggests that any loss in essential quality can be anticipated that would outweigh or even approach the substantial benefits that can be expected to flow from infusing HMOs into the health care system.

EXHIBIT 3. — *Excerpt From Virginia Law Review (1973) Re Health Facilities and Certificate of Need*

VIRGINIA LAW REVIEW

VOLUME 59   OCTOBER 1973   NUMBER 7

REGULATION OF HEALTH FACILITIES AND SERVICES BY "CERTIFICATE OF NEED"

By Clark C. Havighurst*

THE high and rising cost of health care, particularly the spiralling of hospital costs at a rate six percent per year above the rate of inflation generally,[1] has prompted numerous proposals to improve the economic performance of the health care system.[2] These proposals would take such diverse approaches to cost control as rejuvenation of the market as a mechanism for controlling the cost and utilization of health services; requiring components of the health care system, perhaps organized on a regional basis, to operate with fixed annual budgets; or direct regulation, perhaps by adapting traditional public utility regulation for hospitals. To date, the chief manifestation of regulatory cost-control techniques has been a pronounced trend toward the enactment of so-called "certificate-of-need" laws in the states.

Flowing in part from experience with community and regional health planning but also incorporating an important element of public utility regulation, certificate-of-need laws place extensive regulatory controls on entry into the health services industry and on new investments in health care facilities. These controls take the form of a requirement for a prior administrative determination that a public need for additional

* Professor of Law, Duke University. A.B., 1955, Princeton University; J.D., 1958, Northwestern University.

This Article reflects work supported by the Health Services Research Center, Inter-Study, Minneapolis. The author also gratefully acknowledges support from the National Center for Health Services Research and Development, U.S. Dep't of Health, Education, and Welfare (contract no. HSM 110-69-214) and the Institute of Medicine, National Academy of Sciences, where he was Scholar-in-Residence during 1972-73.

[1] M. FELDSTEIN, THE RISING COST OF HOSPITAL CARE 10-13 (1971).

[2] Cost inflation is one of two essential dimensions of the so-called health care "crisis." The other is the inaccessibility to some citizens of good quality medical care, due to either geographic or financial barriers. Cost inflation exacerbates the accessibility problem, however, and deters congressional action on national health insurance, the chief means of mitigating financial barriers.

facilities or services exists. Twenty states enacted some kind of certificate-of-need law in the 1971-73 legislative sessions, and, although North Carolina recently repealed its law in the wake of a court decision declaring it unconstitutional,[3] twenty-three states now have such laws.[4] Federal

[3] Ch. 113 [1973] N.C. Sess. Laws, *repealing* N.C. Gen. Stat. §§ 90-289 to -291 (Supp. 1973). In *In re* Certificate of Need for Aston Park Hosp., Inc., 282 N.C. 542, 193 S.E.2d 729 (1973), the North Carolina Supreme Court ruled that the regulatory scheme violated substantive due process guarantees of N.C. Const. art. I, § 19. Following such earlier decisions as Roller v. Allen, 245 N.C. 516, 96 S.E.2d 851 (1957), and State v. Harris, 216 N.C. 746, 6 S.E.2d 854 (1940), and such repudiated federal precedents as New State Ice Co. v. Liebman, 285 U.S. 262 (1932), the court found that the law's potential for public benefit did not justify the deprivation of the certificate-of-need applicant's liberty to engage in a lawful business. Although mentioning the need to spread the "overhead cost" of vacant hospital beds, the court gave no other evidence of understanding that many of the costs of excess hospital capacity are borne publicly rather than privately, as in other industries. *See* text accompanying notes 50-60 *infra*. Thus, the court viewed the legislation as primarily protectionist in character (*see* note 77 *infra*) and therefore also violative of a constitutional provision against monopolies. N.C. Const. art. I, § 34. The court distinguished franchising of public utilities, permitted in North Carolina, on the ground that utility rate regulation protects the public against the evils of monopoly, thus suggesting that it would not be troubled by public utility regulation of hospitals which entailed entry restrictions indistinguishable from the certificate-of-need requirement.

It seems unlikely that courts in other states, even if they apply the same balancing standard, will agree with the North Carolina court on the unconstitutionality of hospital certificate-of-need laws. *See* Attoma v. State Dept. of Social Welfare, 26 App. Div. 2d 12, 18, 270 N.Y.S.2d 167, 171 (1966); Paulsen, *The Persistence of Substantive Due Process in the States*, 34 Minn. L. Rev. 91 (1950); Stuve, *The Less-Restrictive-Alternative Principle and Economic Due Process*, 80 Harv. L. Rev. 1463 (1967). Indeed, even this Article, which is relatively unsympathetic to such laws, makes them out to be no worse than unwise legislative attempts to deal with a substantial public problem. As to the laws' applicability to nonhospital facilities, however, the Article takes a somewhat less tolerant view, with possible constitutional implications. *See* note 96 *infra* and accompanying text, and *compare* text accompanying notes 221-32 *infra*.

Other constitutional arguments against certificate-of-need laws have focused on the delegation of legislative powers, either because of the indefiniteness of standards for the determination of "need" or because the delegation runs to nongovernmental planning agencies. As to the vagueness of the standard, local law will again govern, but such terms as "need" and the "public interest" have usually been accepted as adequate standards in regulatory statutes. *See, e.g.,* Federal Radio Comm'n v. Nelson Bros. Bond & Mortgage Co., 289 U.S. 266 (1933). This Article later advocates greater definiteness as a means of reducing the political dimension of the regulatory program, however, *see* text accompanying notes 125-127 *infra*, and a state court might well conclude that either the legislature or the administering agency does indeed have an obligation to declare clear policies. *See In re* Application of Point Pleasant Hosp., No. A-64-72 (N.J. Super. Ct., App. Div. 1972). *Cf.* People v. Dobbs Ferry Medical Pavillion, Inc., 40 App. Div. 2d 324, 340 N.Y.S.2d 108 (1973). On delegation to nongovernmental agencies, see Simon v. Cameron, 337 F. Supp. 1380 (C.D. Cal. 1970). *See also* note 109 *infra*.

[4] Ariz. Rev. Stat. Ann. §§ 36-401 to -402, -421, -428 (Supp. 1972); Cal. Health &

legislation adopted in late 1972 may foster continuation of the trend to certificate-of-need requirements by underwriting the states' administrative costs.[5]

The enacted certificate-of-need laws[6] are far from uniform, but all except Oklahoma's, which covers only nursing homes, require need certification for new hospital construction. Most also cover construction of new nursing-care facilities[7] and the expansion of the bed capacity[8] and

SAFETY CODE §§ 437.7 to 438.7, 1331-32, (West. Supp. 1973); 66 COLO. REV. STAT. ANN. art. 41 (1973); No. 73-117 [1973] Conn. General Acts (1973 CONN. LEG. SERVICE 151 (1973)); FLA. STAT. ANN. §§ 381.493-.497 (Supp. 1972); KAN. STAT. ANN. §§ 65-2a01 to -2a14 (1972); KY. REV. STAT. ANN. §§ 216.405-.485 (Supp. 1973); MD. ANN. CODE art. 43, § 559 (Supp. 1972); MASS. GEN. LAWS ANN. ch. 111, §§ 25B, 25C (Supp. 1972); MICH. COMP. LAWS §§ 331.451-.462 (Supp. 1973); MINN. STAT. ANN. §§ 145.71-.83 (Supp. 1973); NEV. REV. STAT. §§ 439A.010-.100 (Supp. 1971); N.J. STAT. ANN. §§ 26:2H-1 to -26 (Supp. 1973); N.Y. PUB. HEALTH LAW §§ 2800 to 2801-a, 2801-c to 2802 (McKinney Supp. 1972); N.D. CENT. CODE §§ 23-17.2-01 to -15 (Supp. 1971); OKLA. STAT. tit. 63, §§ 1-851 to -860 (1971); ORE. REV. STAT. §§ 441.090, -.095 (1971); R.I. GEN. LAWS ANN. §§ 23-16-2, -12 (Supp. 1972); S.C. CODE ANN. §§ 32-761 to -786 (Supp. 1971); S. D. COMPILED LAWS ANN. §§ 34-7A-1 to -21 (1972); ch. 257, [1973] Tenn. Pub. Acts; 419 VA. CODE ANN. §§ 32-211.3 to -211.16, (Supp. 1973); WASH. REV. CODE §§ 70.38.010 to .900 (Supp. 1972).

[5] Social Security Amendments of 1972, 42 U.S.C. § 1320A-1 (Supp. 1973).

[6] The 23 statutory references appear in note 4 supra. Notes 7-16 infra refer only to the 23 states without further citation of the laws themselves. Because of ambiguities and wide variations in the laws, generalizations about a group of states may not always be equally accurate for each. Definitive regulations have not yet been available in many cases and could alter the statutes' constructions. Earlier surveys of the laws appear in Curran, National Survey and Analysis of Certification-of-Need Laws: Health Planning and Regulation in State Legislatures, 1972, in AMERICAN ENTERPRISE INSTITUTE, REGULATING HEALTH FACILITIES CONSTRUCTION: PROCEEDINGS OF A CONFERENCE ON HEALTH PLANNING, CERTIFICATES OF NEED, AND MARKET ENTRY (C. Havighurst ed.) (1973 forthcoming) [hereinafter cited as AEI PROCEEDINGS]. Page references to the AEI PROCEEDINGS are not yet available and will be omitted in future citations.

[7] The only exceptions are Michigan, Oregon, and Rhode Island.

[8] Over half the states refer to bed expansion expressly. Colorado, Minnesota, Rhode Island, and Tennessee specify a minimum capital expenditure on new beds before the certification requirement applies, and Colorado also allows up to a 10 percent increase in beds without approval. Massachusetts allows four beds or a 10 percent increase, whichever is less. The Maryland law clearly covers only new or relocated hospitals and nursing homes, but regulations purport to expand coverage to bed expansion and other things. Md. State Dep't of Health and Mental Hygiene, Regulations Governing Determination of Conformance to Comprehensive Health Plan for Hospitals and Non-Profit Related Institutions §§ 10.07.02(F)(3), (4) (1972) [hereinafter cited as Md. Regs.].

physical plant[9] of existing hospitals and nursing-care institutions.[10] Many, of the laws extend as well to all substantial expansions of hospital services[11] and to investments of more than a specified amount in new equipment.[12] About half of the laws cover free-standing outpatient facilities as well as hospitals, with the result that ambulatory surgical facilities

[9] Formulations include references to "capital expenditure," "construction," "expansion," "alteration," "modification," "major modernization," and "change." Colorado, Kentucky, Minnesota, Nevada, Oregon, and Tennessee add that the expansion must also have a certain purpose or effect, and several states allow at least certain types of expenditures up to a fixed amount without approval. E.g., Connecticut ($25,000, with a more elaborate procedure above $100,000); Kansas (the lesser of $350,000 or five percent of annual operating expenses); Massachusetts ($100,000); South Dakota ($50,000). New York's law distinguishes between "establishment" of a new facility and "construction" of added facilities, prescribing different procedures in the two cases. Here again, the narrow Maryland law has been interpreted expansively. See Md. Regs., supra note 8, §§ 10.07.02(F)(5), (6).

[10] Again, the Michigan, Oregon, and Rhode Island laws cover hospitals but not nursing homes, and Oklahoma only covers nursing homes.

[11] All 23 states except Kansas, Michigan (which covers a "change in function" of facilities), New York, Oklahoma, and Washington appear to cover all substantial expansions. However, California (though mentioning "creation or expansion of new areas of service") requires certification only where a service change would change the institution's licensing category. Several states impose, by statute or regulation, a dollar minimum below which expenditures on service changes need not be approved. Only Connecticut, Massachusetts, New Jersey, Oregon, and Tennessee differentiate between the institution of a new hospital service and expansion of existing services, covering only the former. A few states set a certification requirement that combines various criteria. Thus, Colorado requires an expenditure above $100,000 which also produces a change either in service or in licensure category, and Minnesota and Tennessee require certification where a capital expenditure exceeds a certain amount and also expands service offerings or increases the bed count. Maryland's regulations once again overreach the statute. Md. Regs., supra note 8, §§ 10.07.2(F)(2), (5). Florida may also have done so by asserting authority over expansions irrespective of dollar minimum, apparently in reliance on the "legislative intent" section of the law. Florida Bureau of Comprehensive Health Planning, Rules and Regulations Governing the Certificate of Need, ¶ B.l.d. (1973) [hereinafter cited as Fla. Regs.]. In Washington, although the declaration of policy in the preamble of the statute contemplates a certification requirement for new hospital services, the operative provisions do not reach services per se. In New York, service changes require approval and a change in the institution's "operating certificate," but there is no clear statutory authority for withholding such approval on the basis of the public's needs or impact on other facilities. See 10 N.Y.C.R.R. § 701.3 (1973).

[12] In most states, investments in new equipment would be included as service changes, see note 11 supra, or as plant improvements, see note 9 supra. Equipment is expressly mentioned in about half the statutes, and dollar minimums are frequently specified below which approval is not required. Replacement equipment is excluded, expressly or otherwise, in Colorado (if "consistent with . . . planning"), Connecticut, Kentucky, and Massachusetts (up to a $100,000 capital expenditure in each case), and in Arizona, Michigan, South Carolina, and Tennessee.

(surgicenters) and clinics operated by group practices and health main-tenance organizations (HMOs) may require approval,[13] though no law yet extends to the individual practitioner's place of business.[14] Proponents of certification of need usually argue for giving the laws maximum scope so that the health planners' authority will extend to any material altera-tion in available services,[15] and, in this spirit, several laws require approval of major cutbacks in services as well as expansion.[16] Although the laws differ widely in scope and regulatory mechanics,[17] the variations do not obscure the central fact that the regulation imposed differs in kind from customary health and safety regulation in the health care system.

Despite the popularity of certificate-of-need laws, it is appropriate to inquire whether there is a realistic basis for expecting desirable results from introducing such regulatory controls in the market for health services. Moreover, certificate-of-need laws offer an opportunity for assessing generally the view held by some that comprehensive economic regulation following the public utility model can make the health care system function acceptably. An appraisal of the efficacy of certificate-of-need laws and of proposed similar regulatory efforts in health care

[13] See notes 221-32 infra and accompanying text.

[14] But cf. note 56 infra.

[15] E.g., Curran, supra note 6; AMERICAN HOSPITAL ASSOCIATION, GUIDELINES FOR IMPLE-MENTATION OF CERTIFICATION OF NEED FOR HEALTH CARE FACILITIES AND SERVICES (1972) [hereinafter cited as AHA GUIDELINES]; American Hospital Association, Suggested Model Legislation for Implementation of State Certification of Need, Nov. 15, 1972 (mimeo., draft) [hereinafter cited as AHA Model Legislation]. This predilection may pro-duce regulations and practices which exceed statutory authorizations, suggesting that challenges might be successful. See notes 8, 9, and 11 supra and note 16 infra. Mary-land's Comprehensive Health Planning Agency relies on an opinion of an Assistant At-torney General for its broad assertion of authority. Letter from Louis E. Schmidt to Dr. Eugene H. Guthrie, June 9, 1970.

[16] Arizona, Florida, Maryland, South Carolina, and Virginia require certification before contracting the number of hospital beds, nursing-care beds, or hospital services rendered. California and Oregon require certification only when the cutback will result in a change in the institution's licensing category. The Kentucky statute reaches only reductions in bed capacity, not in services. In New York, approval of cutbacks is required as part of changing the institution's operating certificate, 10 N.Y.C.R.R. §§ 701.3(a), (e), and, although need is not explicitly a factor, it is probably considered. See also note 11 supra. Maryland has again acted without statutory authority, Md. Regs., supra note 8, §§ 10.07.02(F)(2)-(5), and the Florida law has been stretched to cover cutbacks on the debatable strength of a declaration of legislative intent regarding "scope" of services. Fla. Regs., supra note 11, at ¶ B.l.d. The Massachusetts provision, on the other hand, covering any "substantial change in service," has been administered to impose no certification requirement for the reduction of bed capacity or service.

[17] See text accompanying notes at 98-133 infra.

can best proceed by considering not only the limited experience to date with need certification but also the strength and implications of the analogy between the health care industry, as regulated under certificate-of-need laws, and other regulated industries. Undertaking such an appraisal, this Article suggests that administrative certification of need is unlikely to be appreciably effective in achieving cost-control objectives because of the practically unavoidable slippage involved in translating a persuasive rationale for regulation into a workable regulatory program. Further, it warns that inflationary pressures may, like a balloon, bulge out at another place even if growth in one direction is effectively prevented. Finally, it argues that the laws' limited benefits may be obtainable only at the cost of repressing useful market forces, particularly those which call forth badly needed innovations and stimulate efficiency. Despite these basically negative conclusions, the Article offers some suggestions for drafting a certificate-of-need law which might produce net benefits in spite of my skepticism. Possibly more important, however, in view of the advanced state of the trend toward enactment of certificate-of-need laws, the discussion should also be helpful in revealing traps to be avoided in administering an existing law.[18]

I. The Background of Certificate-of-Need Laws

A. Origins in Voluntary Health Planning

Certificate-of-need laws have their roots in the methods and institutions of health planning, which began as community efforts to organize philanthropic priorities in the hospital sector.[19] As the federal government began to contribute funds for hospital development, it was logical to adapt the planning mechanisms which had facilitated private philanthropy to the task of allocating public resources. Thus, the federal Hill-Burton legislation of 1946, providing federal subsidies for hospital con-

[18] Unfortunately, space does not permit detailed examination of one important dimension of the argument over certificate-of-need laws, namely the viability of the various alternative means of dealing with the problems which the laws address. Thus, at the risk of seeming less than constructive in largely confining myself to criticism of proposed regulatory ventures, I will suggest only the nature of other measures which might be finally preferred. It may be helpful to disclose, however, that I have not yet despaired, as many purport to have done, of engineering a workable market-oriented solution to the problem of allocating resources to health care. Cf. Havighurst, *Health Maintenance Organizations and the Market for Health Services*, 35 Law & Contemp. Prob. 716 (1970).

[19] See Gottlieb, *A Brief History of Health Planning in the United States*, in AEI Proceedings, *supra* note 6.

struction,[20] contemplated consulting planners in the affected communities, many of them working under nongovernmental auspices, in order to identify needs. Some local planners also found it possible to cooperate with local Blue Cross plans, so that only approved new facilities were deemed eligible for cost reimbursement covering depreciation and interest on capital obligations. While statistical evidence of the utility of such planning has been hard to come by,[21] the prevailing view is that voluntary planning has occasionally succeeded very well, particularly where it was backed by sources of financing. The success achieved was insufficient, however, to forestall pressure for de-emphasizing voluntariness and adding compulsion.

In helping communities to identify their most urgent health needs and to meet them by cooperative and consensual development, health planning agencies have also served to simplify the hospitals' problems by curbing competitive excesses. Indeed, many of the activities undertaken in the name of planning were indistinguishable from such typical cartel practices as output restriction (collective determination of the bed supply) and market division (allocation of areas of responsibility both geographically and by activity).[22] The cartel characterization need not be read pejoratively, however, since agreements among competitors can, in some industry settings, be quite useful in preventing unnecessary duplication of facilities and other wasteful side effects of competition.[23] Even

---

[20] Hospital Survey and Construction Act of 1946, 60 STAT. 1040 (codified in scattered sections of 24, 42 U.S.C.).

[21] See D. Brown, Evaluation of Health Planning, in CENTER FOR HEALTH ADMINISTRATION STUDIES, UNIVERSITY OF CHICAGO SELECTED PAPERS ON HEALTH PLANNING, HEALTH ADMINISTRATION PERSPECTIVES No. A8, at 29 (1969): "Although the planners pointed to many kinds of specific results to illustrate their successes, the achievement considered to be most important is an established ongoing planning process." Id. at 28.

[22] D. Brown, The Process of Areawide Health Planning: Model for the Future?, 11 MED. CARE 1, 3 (1973), describes areawide hospital planning as "a process of blended provider interests," implying its desirability. For a scathing analysis consistent with the cartel characterization, see HEALTH POLICY ADVISORY CENTER (HEALTH-PAC), THE AMERICAN HEALTH EMPIRE: POWER, PROFITS AND POLITICS 191-231 (1971).

[23] P. AREEDA, ANTITRUST ANALYSIS 186-92 (1967). The nonprofit character of most hospitals may make the cartel characterization of their concerted action seem inappropriate. Nevertheless, nonprofit enterprises probably do not differ greatly in their behavior from professionally managed for-profit firms, both seeking growth as the primary source of managerial gratification. Under conditions of reasonable prosperity, management of either type of organization is constrained only partially by the need to show an acceptable relation between costs and revenues. Compare generally W. NISKANEN, BUREAUCRACY AND REPRESENTATIVE GOVERNMENT (1971) (treating nonprofit organizations as "bureaus"), with R. MARRIS, THE ECONOMIC THEORY OF MANAGERIAL CAPI-

though cartels have been outlawed in other industries, special considerations, such as the impact of third-party payment and the prevalence of nonprofit firms, might dictate dispensation for cartel-like behavior in the hospital industry.

Voluntary health planning failed to achieve its promise for the same reason that cartels usually founder—that is, the self-interest of the participants tended to take precedence whenever an opportunity for institutional aggrandizement presented itself.[24] Not only were the hospitals themselves given to self-serving activity despite their eleemosynary status, but certain sponsoring groups, particularly prideful communities and religious, fraternal, and labor organizations, very often chose to go their own way. Even though the Hill-Burton program controlled an important source of funds, hospitals which were denied support could often raise the needed money from other sources.[25] Thus, private philanthropy was often influenced more by institutional and community leadership than by the planners, and broadening health insurance coverage frequently enabled hospitals to accumulate surpluses or assured future revenues to an extent which made borrowing increasingly feasible. Logic appeared to point to the conclusion that, because neither pure voluntarism nor partial control over the various purse strings resulted in adequate effectuation of the planners' directives, "teeth" were essential to make health facilities planning effective. The pattern was similar to that in any cartel, where sanctions against uncooperative members, preferably governmentally imposed, are essential if the plan is not to break down.

TALISM (1964). Nonprofit hospitals sometimes "distribute" profits in the form of perquisites to—or lucrative business contracts with enterprises controlled by—trustees, managers, or controlling physicians. *See, e.g.,* Kessler, *The Hospital Business,* Washington Post, Oct. 29-Nov. 3, 1972, at 1 each day, *reprinted in* 119 CONG. REC. H188-H204 (daily ed. Jan. 11, 1973). *See also* Sonora Community Hosp., 46 T.C. 519 (1966), *aff'd per curiam,* 397 F.2d 814 (9th Cir. 1968). Moreover, it has been shown that, under the demand conditions of a seller's market, hospitals' costs tend to rise so that their prices seem to behave not too differently from those of for-profit firms. Feldstein, *Hospital Cost Inflation: A Study of Nonprofit Price Dynamics,* 61 AM. ECON. REV. 853 (1971). If the excess earnings of nonprofit hospitals are used to supply more or better services and are not wasted in overpayments or invested improperly, there is no reason to object to them, on distributive grounds, as monopoly profits and perhaps no reason to condemn cartel practices which produce them.

[24] *See* Gottlieb, *supra* note 19.

[25] On the sources of funds for hospital construction, see Kotelchuck, *How to Build a Hospital,* HEALTH-PAC BULL. 1 (May 1972). The Hill-Burton program provided only 13 percent of the total funds required for voluntary hospital construction from 1946 to 1967. *Id.* at 1.

The movement for health planning with teeth began in the late 1950s[26] but grew slowly. New York's Metcalf-McCloskey Act of 1964,[27] providing for mandatory need determinations prior to hospital and nursing home construction, was the first substantive development. The next states to adopt the certificate-of-need approach were Maryland, Rhode Island, California, and Connecticut in 1968 and 1969. In 1968, the American Hospital Association (AHA), in response to increasing public concern about rapidly rising hospital costs, first indicated its membership's acceptance of facilities planning using the certificate-of-need model. Since 1968, the AHA has come to assign a higher priority to adoption of this regulatory model,[28] and the recent legislative activity clearly reflects the hospital industry's increased lobbying efforts. The AHA has proposed a draft of a model state law;[29] and its proposal for a national health care policy, embodied in the so-called Ullman bill,[30] reflects its acceptance of an even higher degree of regulation.

B. The Federal Government and Health Planning

Since the Comprehensive Health Planning Act, the federal government has moved gradually toward strengthening reliance on local health planning. Most recently, the Social Security Amendments of 1972 provide that state health facilities planning can be backed up by a denial of Medicare and other federal reimbursement of the capital costs (primarily interest and depreciation) of unapproved facilities.[31] This provision takes the form of authorizing federal contracting with cooperating states for planning services, which would be rendered through existing planning agencies with the federal government paying the full cost. Although some savings in the health care expenditures of the federal government are probably expected, Congress's chief purpose was to assure that federal financing policy was consistent with the policy of encouraging facilities planning in the states.[32]

---

[26] See, e.g., R. Brown, Let the Public Control Through Planning, 33 HOSPITALS 34 (1959).

[27] Metcalf-McCloskey Act of 1964, ch. 730, [1964] N.Y. Laws 1883 (codified in scattered sections of N.Y. PUB. HEALTH LAW, McKinney 1971).

[28] See AHA GUIDELINES, supra note 15.

[29] AHA Model Legislation, supra note 15.

[30] H.R. 1, 93d Cong., 1st Sess. (1973).

[31] 42 U.S.C. § 1320A-1 (Supp. 1973); Proposed Regulations, 38 Fed. Reg. 20994 (1973).

[32] S. REP. No. 92-1230, 92d Cong., 2d Sess. 185 (1972).

The 1972 legislation may provide a further impetus for enactment of certificate-of-need laws, primarily by lowering the state's cost of administration. It is quite possible, however, for states to contract to provide the federal government with the desired planning services without enacting any specific legislation or supplying sanctions other than the federal leverage.[33] Nevertheless, the federal initiative by itself will probably fail to give state or local health planning decisions sufficient impact to obviate more substantial sanctions. The penalty of withholding an interest and depreciation component from payments under Medicare, Medicaid, and maternal and child health programs is a relatively weak sanction, particularly since providers can control the number of federal beneficiaries whom they serve and can bill Medicare beneficiaries for any unpaid excess. On the other hand, if the local Blue Cross plan has also agreed to reflect the planners' decisions in its reimbursement practices, considerable control over hospital facilities will have been achieved.[34]

Of course, the federal government could take more substantial steps.[35] In 1972, for example, the Nixon administration proposed legislation to deny federal payments altogether for services rendered in facilities unapproved by planners.[36] The more comprehensive of the various health policy proposals before Congress also bear on planning, the AHA's pro-

---

[33] See, e.g., Mississippi Division of Comprehensive Health Planning, Federal Certificate of Need Program Review and Recommendation Procedures (April 11, 1973). In many communities, zoning decisions necessary for hospital construction have taken need into account, supplying another form of planning sanction.

[34]   As of November 1972, some 24 Blue Cross Plans had added conformance clauses to either their contract or brochures, stating in effect that reimbursement to member hospitals would be conditional upon evidence of compliance with appropriate local planning agencies. The various clauses . . . range from a simple statement of principle to a more detailed schedule of conditions that would mean a limitation of reimbursement.

      It should also be noted that eight of these states also have an enacted certification-of-need law.

American Hospital Association, AHA Planning Bulletin, April 1973, at 10 (No. 73-1, mimeo.). Continued pressure for certificate-of-need laws in states where both federal and Blue Cross payments are effectively controlled by the planners appears to reflect primarily a desire to curb competitive developments which would substitute ambulatory for inpatient care. See text accompanying notes 221-32 infra.

[35] See Address by Elliot L. Richardson, Secretary of HEW, before the Institute of Medicine, in Washington, D.C., May 10, 1972. This speech is a broad endorsement of health planning.

[36] HOUSE COMM. ON WAYS AND MEANS, AMENDMENTS TO THE ADMINISTRATION'S NATIONAL HEALTH INSURANCE PARTNERSHIP ACT, H. Doc. No. 782-6, 92d Cong., 2d Sess. (1972).

gram being the most far-reaching in its endorsement of planning-cum-regulation at the state level. The Kennedy-Griffiths proposed Health Security Act would embody a requirement that all new or enlarged health facilities be certified as needed by a state or federal agency.[37]

Enthusiasm for health planning may be waning somewhat at the federal level, however, as hospital and other costs apparently remain out of control even in areas where facilities planning has seemed reasonably effective. Pleas from many planners for increased appropriations and power—either direct decision-making responsibility or, as many planners seem to prefer, an influential advisory role[38]—have been met merely by a one-year extension of the Comprehensive Health Planning Act through June 1974.[39] Although Congress may eventually enact a national health insurance program, it seems likely that such action must await a firmer judgment as to whether regulation, the market, or some combination of the two is adequate to contain the inflationary impact of a new infusion of demand.[40]

C. A Possible First Step Toward Public Utility Regulation of Hospitals

Tracing the threads of certificate-of-need laws back through past health planning efforts may imply that they are the culmination of a movement, finally bringing reason to health facilities development by giving the planners needed "teeth." But from another point of view they seem merely a step down the much longer road to comprehensive economic regulation of the hospital industry as a public utility. The signs of a trend in this direction are unmistakable.

Certificate-of-need laws establish entry controls which are similar in intent and impact to the certificate-of-public-convenience-and-necessity device widely employed in public utility and common carrier regulation. Moreover, the utility regulation model has been explicitly adopted by some observers of the hospital scene[41] and is embodied in the AHA-

---

[37] S.3, 93d Cong., 1st Sess. §§ 53, 89 (1973).

[38] See note 186 infra.

[39] Pub. L. No. 93-45, § 106 (June 18, 1973).

[40] At the same time inquiries concerning experience with certificate-of-need laws and comprehensive planning have recently been commissioned by the Department of Health, Education, and Welfare in anticipation of an ultimate decision on the workability of planning-cum-regulation and other variations on the planning model as mechanisms for controlling health care costs.

[41] See, e.g., A. SOMERS, HOSPITAL REGULATION: THE DILEMMA OF PUBLIC POLICY 2-6, 204-08 (1969); R. Brown, supra note 26; Somers, Toward a Rational Community Health Care System: The Hunterdon Model, 54 HOSPITAL PROGRESS 46 (1973); Epstein, Rele-

backed Ullman bill.[42] A number of states have implemented hospital rate regulation,[43] and the federal wage and price control program, which in "Phase III" preserved controls over the health sector while lifting most others,[44] contains the seeds of permanent price regulation. The idea of "franchising" hospitals by assigning them specific area and service responsibilities analogous to the obligations of public utilities and common carriers is also increasingly popular, particularly as the veto power supplied under certificate-of-need laws proves an insufficient tool for affirmatively influencing developments.[45] Various mechanisms for regulating the quality of service have also been proposed. The sum of these various regulatory measures, in being or proposed, would be traditional public utility regulation.[46]

Restrictions on market entry are the type of economic regulation which has been most widely criticized for pernicious effects in other fields.[47] Since certificate-of-need laws prevent a new firm's entry or an existing firm's expansion except upon demonstration of a public "need" for the new service, they are similar to the laws governing admission to a wide range of regulated industries, including banking, for-hire transportation, generation and distribution of electricity, consumer credit, and communications. But in view of what is widely regarded as unsatisfactory experience with economic regulation, it becomes important to

vance of the Public Utility Concept to the Health Care Industry, HOSPITAL FORUM, Sept., 1972, at 12; Priest, Possible Adaptation of Public Utility Concepts in the Health Care Field, 35 LAW & CONTEMP. PROB. 839 (1970).

[42] The AHA appears to be attracted by the argument that the North Carolina statute recently ruled unconstitutional, see note 3 supra, would have been saved had utility-type rate regulation also been provided for. See Attachment to Memorandum from William L. Casady, Director, AHA Division of Planning, Aug. 24, 1973 [hereinafter cited as Casady Memo].

[43] ARIZ. REV. STAT. ANN. §§ 36-346 to -436.03 (Supp. 1973); Conn. Pub. Act No. 73-117 (1973 CONN. LEGIS. SERVICE 151); MD. ANN. CODE art. 43, §§ 568H-X (Supp. 1972); MASS. GEN. LAWS ANN. ch. 7, §§ 30K-P (1973); N.J. STAT. ANN. §§ 26:2H-1 to -26 (Supp. 1973); N. Y. PUB. HEALTH LAW § 807 (McKinney Supp. 1972); ch. 5 [1973] Wash. Laws, 43d Legis., 1st Extraord. Sess. (1973 WASH. LEGIS. SERVICE 404). The Connecticut, Maryland, New Jersey, and Washington laws come closest to embodying the public utility model. For proposals along a similar line, see Pennsylvania Senate Bill No. 863 (May 29, 1973); WISCONSIN GOVERNOR'S HEALTH PLANNING & POLICY TASK FORCE, FINAL REPORT (1972). See also ch. 837 [1973] Ore. Sess. Laws.

[44] See 6 C.F.R. §§ 130.60-.62 (1973).

[45] See, e.g., INTERNATIONAL HEALTH ADVISORY COUNCIL et al., MANAGEMENT MEMORANDUM ON HOSPITAL FRANCHISING (1973) [hereinafter cited as HOSPITAL FRANCHISING].

[46] 1 A. KAHN, THE ECONOMICS OF REGULATION: PRINCIPLES AND INSTITUTIONS 3, 10 (1970).

[47] See note 49 infra.

inquire whether certificate-of-need proponents have carefully examined the ramifications of their proposals.[48]

II. The Rationale for Certificate-of-Need Laws

The arguments offered for certificate-of-need laws are highly persuasive on their face. Indeed, they are considerably stronger in theory than the rationales offered to justify regulatory restrictions on entry and expansion in other industries.[49] They originate in demonstrable market failures attributable to the manner in which health care is paid for, the control which providers exert over demand for health care, and the incentives affecting both consumption and investment decisions. As measures to correct the very real problems of overinvestment in, and overconsumption of, health services, certificate-of-need laws have earned many adherents.

It is important to recognize at the outset, however, that, whatever their merits, certificate-of-need laws are an attempt to deal merely with symptoms rather than root causes. This may be surprising since their origin in health planning, a calling with some scientific pretensions, might suggest a "systems" approach to the total health care crisis and a

[48] The AHA did consult Professor A.J.G. Priest, a well-known expert in public utility law but one who tends to accept the fact of regulation uncritically. *Compare* Priest, *supra* note 41, *with* the approach taken in this Article and in Posner, *Natural Monopoly and Its Regulation*, 21 Stan. L. Rev. 548 (1969), and other references herein.

[49] On the perceived need for entry restriction in so-called natural-monopoly industries (to protect revenues needed for internal subsidization), see note 78 *infra* and accompanying text. In potentially competitive industries, entry controls may be viewed with even greater skepticism because of their necessary effect of depriving consumers of the benefits, and sparing producers the hardships of competition. *See, e.g.,* R. Caves, Air Transport and Its Regulators 169-76, 192-231 (1962); L. Schwartz, Free Enterprise and Economic Organization: Antitrust and Regulatory Controls ch. 4 (4th ed. 1972); Jordan, *Producer Protection, Prior Market Structure and the Effects of Government Regulation*, 15 J. Law & Econ. 151 (1972); Kitch, Isaacson & Kasper, *The Regulation of Taxicabs in Chicago*, 14 J. Law & Econ. 285 (1971); Kreps, *Modernizing Banking Regulation*, 31 Law & Contemp. Prob. 648 (1968); Nelson, *The Effects of Entry Controls in Surface Transport*, in Nat'l Bureau Econ. Research, Transportation Economics 381 (1965). Even the case for controlling entry into broadcasting, which is premised on the technical problems involved in getting maximum use from the electromagnetic spectrum, has been questioned. Coase, *The Federal Communications Commission*, 2 J. Law & Econ. 1 (1959). *See also* Johnson, *Towers of Babel: The Chaos in Radio Spectrum Utilization and Allocation*, 34 Law & Contemp. Prob. 505 (1969). The broadcasting case aside, the case for the entry restrictions in certificate-of-need laws appears to be the strongest by far, being based on objective considerations—third-party payment and provider control of demand—which seem to negate serious hopes for satisfactory market responses.

commitment to solving it in the most fundamental and efficient way. The arguments for certificate-of-need laws—and indeed the foundations of health planning itself—imply the continued predominance of financing mechanisms which encourage inefficiency both by guaranteeing recovery of costs, no matter how great, and by externalizing the costs of doctors' and patients' consumption decisions. Such exclusive reliance on health insurance and other types of third-party payment is not inevitable, nor must its impact necessarily continue to be as pernicious as it has been under existing payment systems. Viewed in the light of possibilities for more fundamental changes in the market for insurance and health services, certificate-of-need laws may appear as conservative measures, designed to preserve the very institutions which create the problems to which they are addressed.

A. Third-Party Payment and Facilities Duplication

The broad consensus on the need for restraining hospital facilities construction flows in large measure from the circumstance that the health care crisis is characterized at least as much by surplus as by shortage. An oversupply of health facilities, particularly hospital beds, exists in many areas,[50] and worrisome shortages occur only where the population is too small or too poor to support the provision of adequate services and where public subsidies have been insufficient. In other industries, overcapacity usually does not qualify as a "crisis" except for the producers themselves, who are seldom able to persuade the government to assert a public interest in their plight.[51] In health care, however, several institutional factors raise the problem of excess capacity to the level of legitimate public concern, by causing the costs of excess health facilities to be borne in large measure by the public rather than by the affected industry itself. Moreover, the excess capacity, rather than remaining idle, may be put

[50] As the argument is developed, oversupply does not take only the form of empty beds, although occupancy rates are declining. MEDICAL WORLD NEWS, June 16, 1972, at 14; AMERICAN HOSPITAL ASSOCIATION, HOSPITAL STATISTICS 1971, 13 (1972) (showing decline from a high of 78.8 percent in 1969 to 76.7 percent in 1971 for nonfederal short-term general and other special hospitals). Excessive hospital utilization by patients who do not require such expensive care is the big problem. See notes 54-60 infra and accompanying text. For a recent and persuasive presentation of the oversupply problem and the conventional wisdom concerning it, see Cohn, Our Unplanned Hospitals, Washington Post, Aug. 26-31, 1973.

[51] Exceptions to this exist, of course, most notably in farming and in industries affected by sudden increases in foreign competition. See also 2 KAHN, supra note 46, at 173-76, on the "ruinous competition" argument.

to inappropriate uses, giving rise to additional, noncapital costs which the public may also bear.

By far the most important factors occasioning entry and construction controls are the frequency of "third-party" payment for medical care—that is, by government, insurers, and Blue Cross-Blue Shield service plans —and the "cost-plus" character of these payments. Government programs and Blue Cross almost invariably pay hospitals on the basis of their costs.[52] Commercial insurers usually pay on the basis of charges rather than cost but often impose a top limit, over which the patient must pay the excess. In reality, because charges are not set under competitive conditions, they never fall below cost as fixed by Medicare and Blue Cross.

Because cost accounting under reimbursement formulas occasions much negotiation, third-party payments for some services frequently include some of the costs of other services, with the result that the public rather than the hospitals may absorb the costs of excess capacity. For example, a hospital can usually expect its revenues from inpatient care to cover its full costs at less than 100 percent occupancy, since third-party payers are willing to pay something toward the maintenance of empty beds in order that the hospital can meet peak demands. Some hypothetical occupancy rate will therefore be adopted for cost-reimbursement purposes and will be negotiable to some degree.[53] Furthermore, negotiations will usually result in at least some costs of unremunerative services being borne by the third-party payers, though increasing cost-consciousness has toughened bargaining in this regard in recent years. Under this payment system, the public pays the full cost of all occupied and many unoccupied hospital beds and of many unremunerative or underutilized services, either through taxation, in the case of public programs, or through health insurance premiums. The hospital, on the other hand, is partially relieved of its concern that the price for its services will fall below cost—as it would in a competitive market characterized by overcapacity. Only when the hospital's vacancy rate or the cost of its underutilized services rises above what it can persuade third-

---

[52] See Sigmond, *How Should Blue Cross Reimburse Hospitals? "Costs!"*, MODERN HOSPITAL, July, 1963, at 91; TeKolste, *How Should Blue Cross Reimburse Hospitals? "Charges!"*, MODERN HOSPITAL, July, 1963, at 90 (reporting on Indiana Blue Cross).

[53] For example, recent changes in Medicare policy allow fixing of maximum acceptable costs for standby facilities, among other things. 42 U.S.C. § 1320a-1 (Supp. 1973). New York assumes at least a 60 percent occupancy rate for maternity units, even though many hospitals have lower rates.

party payers to incorporate in the reimbursement formula are losses from excess capacity borne by the hospital rather than the public.

Why cannot third-party payers be relied upon not to subsidize hospital beds which are truly unnecessary? Putting aside the case of Blue Cross plans, which as creatures of the hospitals in varying degrees may tend to favor provider over consumer interests, insurers and government probably could prevent excess capacity were it not for the control which hospitals can apparently exercise over their own occupancy. By letting it be known that higher occupancy is desired, the hospital can usually cause a loosening of institutional utilization review and can encourage doctors both to opt for hospitalization in close cases and to prolong their patients' stays. Patients have little to say about such decisions[54] and, where insurance is present, may even prefer to consume more hospitalization than is appropriate. Even making allowances for the fact that on marginal cost principles an empty bed can be filled at a relatively low additional cost[55] so that higher utilization rates are economically appropriate, the effect on the total cost of care borne by the public can be considerable. Thus, there is some validity in the widely accepted notion that overbedding breeds overutilization, though this expression overstates the point by implying that the economic decision to fill an empty bed is the same as the decision to build it. The significant point is that the cost of extra beds, including the added variable costs incurred in their use, is borne by the public, and hospitals are therefore insufficiently deterred from unnecessary construction.

Although the supply of health services, and particularly hospital beds,[56] does appear to generate new demand and thus increased utilization and

---

[54] *But see* FELDSTEIN, *supra* note 1, at 28-29 (discussing how "decisions are to an important extent made jointly"); M. Feldstein, Econometric Studies of Health Economics, 8-11, April, 1973 (Discussion Paper No. 291, Harvard Institute of Economic Research) [hereinafter cited as Feldstein, *Econometric Studies*].

[55] It is widely accepted that an empty stand-by bed costs about two-thirds as much as an occupied one. *See, e.g.,* MEDICAL WORLD NEWS, June 16, 1972, at 14. This implies that a bed, *once it is in being*, should be used if the value of hospitalization to the patient is at least one-third the total cost to the hospital.

[56] Although the argument is pushed hardest with respect to hospital beds, it probably applies equally to physicians' services. *See* V. FUCHS & M. KRAMER, DETERMINANTS OF EXPENDITURES FOR PHYSICIANS' SERVICES IN THE UNITED STATES 1948-68 (DHEW Pub. No. (HSM) 73-3013, 1972). There is, for example, good evidence that the amount of surgery done is in large measure determined by the number of surgeons available. Bunker, *Surgical Manpower: A Comparison of Operations and Surgeons in the United States and in England and Wales,* 282 N. ENG. J. MED. 135 (1970). Moreover, if his schedule is light, it is easy for Dr. Smith to tell Ms. Jones to come back every two weeks rather than once a month. *See* Feldstein, *The Rising Price of Physicians' Services,* 52 REV. OF

higher costs—the so-called "Roemer effect" [57]—the nature and strength of this effect may be debated. Some have argued that the new supply may be merely a response to pre-existing but unmet demand, so that new utilization is not really "manufactured." [58] Because most observers have been primarily intent on establishing the existence of the effect, they have given little attention to assessing its limitations.[59] For example, it is clear that hospitals cannot continue to fill new beds indefinitely, and it thus appears that the seriousness of the policy problem presented by the Roemer effect depends on whether it is strong or weak in fact. Although assessment of such an effect is extremely difficult, Martin Feldstein has estimated as "a reasonable first approximation" that about half of the impact of new hospital beds is felt in an outward shift of the demand curve—that is, the creation of new demand—and that the other half of the impact appears in a fall in price.[60] It is probably appropriate to conclude that the Roemer effect, although frequently exaggerated, is nevertheless real.

The foregoing paragraphs state the essence of the main argument for hospital certificate-of-need laws, and it is quite powerful. It says that the mechanism of third-party payment based on cost reimbursement,

---

ECON. & STATISTICS 121 (1970); Monsma, *Marginal Revenue and the Demand for Physicians' Services*, in EMPIRICAL STUDIES IN HEALTH ECONOMICS 145 (H. Klarman ed. 1970) [hereinafter cited as EMPIRICAL STUDIES]. It is striking, therefore, that the nation is embarked on a crash program to educate more doctors while seeking to control facilities development. One distinction is that facilities, unlike physicians, have a fixed location and may be easily compared to local needs. Presumably the increased supply of physicians is expected to spill over into underserved rural areas and urban ghettos, but this is likely to occur only after a great deal of new demand and costs have been generated. If the current educational programs do for physician manpower what the Hill-Burton program has helped to do for hospitals, doctors' services and offices may eventually be subjected to the equivalent of certificate-of-need requirements. Professional groups, which would like to resist expansion of the supply of physicians, are in the awkward position of not wanting to make their most persuasive argument—namely, that doctors influence the demand for their services.

[57] The responsiveness of demand to bed supply was first noted in M. ROEMER & M. SHAIN, HOSPITAL UTILIZATION UNDER INSURANCE (AHA Hospital Monograph Series No. 6, 1959); *see also* Roemer & Shain, *Hospital Costs Relate to the Supply of Beds*, MODERN HOSPITAL, April 1959, at 71. For a review of subsequent literature, see Klarman, *Approaches to Moderating the Increases in Medical Care Costs*, 7 MED. CARE 175, 177-79 (1969). *See also* Feldstein, *Econometric Studies, supra* note 54, at 19-22.

[58] G. ROSENTHAL, HOSPITAL UTILIZATION IN THE UNITED STATES (1964).

[59] *See* Klarman, *Some Technical Problems in Areawide Planning for Hospital Care*, 17 J. CHRONIC DISEASES 735, 742-43 (1964).

[60] Feldstein, *supra* note 23, at 865. One would expect that the ratio between the two impacts would vary depending on how nearly exhausted were the opportunities for demand creation.

when coupled with utilization decisions, results in externalization of much of the business risk involved in creating excess capacity. In other sectors of the economy, a firm would not construct new capacity leading to oversupply and depressed prices unless it had some confidence in its greater efficiency and its ability quickly to eliminate an inefficient competitor. A strong market deterrent to the creation of excess capacity thus appears except where efficiency gains are likely. The analogous deterrent in the hospital industry seems weaker than one would like.

Interest in certificate-of-need laws has increased recently in part because various factors have combined to reduce hospital occupancy rates[61] and make overcapacity more apparent. Although physicians and patients seem to have responded to substantially higher hospital prices as classical market theory says they should—by reducing consumption[62]—newly effective regulatory controls on utilization may better explain the development. Whatever the reason, doctors seem somewhat more aware of costs and of possibilities for reducing hospital stays. In these circumstances, the Roemer effect—and, with it, the case for certificate-of-need laws—may be weakening.

B. *Decision Making in Hospitals*

Incentives in Nonprofit Enterprises

Another dimension of the argument for certificate-of-need laws focuses specifically on nonprofit, including public, hospitals and their lesser responsiveness to market incentives in their investment and other decisions. Such institutions are excessively concerned with institutional size and prestige—reflected in the quantity and technical sophistication of the care rendered—and the concomitant material and other benefits accruing to their managers, trustees, or sponsors. Indeed, a reasonable behavioral premise is that managers of nonprofit firms seek to maximize the size and budgets of their organizations within the constraint that revenues must cover costs,[63] leading in some circumstances to output much greater than

---

[61] *See* note 50 *supra.*

[62] In spite of health insurance, demand for hospital care still responds to price changes. *See* Feldstein, *Econometric Studies, supra* note 54, at 12-19.

[63] *See id.* at 24-30 (emphasizing that a model of the nonprofit firm lacks the 'predictive power" of a model of a profit-maximizing firm); Davis, *Economic Theories of Behavior in Nonprofit Private Hospitals,* Econ. & Bus. Bull. (Winter 1972), at 1; Pauly, *The Behavior of Nonprofit Hospital Monopolies: Alternative Models of the Hospital,* in AEI Proceedings, *supra* note 6.

is socially optimal.[64] Moreover, philanthropy and income in excess of expenses frequently flow into the voluntary hospital without regard to actual need for new investment, and yet these funds cannot be distributed or invested in other than health-related activities. Seldom does the institution demonstrate concern outside its immediate geographic area, and, even if its ostensible allegiance is to the community at large and not to a particular sponsoring religious or fraternal organization, it may be inclined nevertheless to perceive its constituency in socio-economic terms or along racial lines.[65] For these reasons, the nonprofit hospital's choice of investments will often be primarily responsive to neither profit opportunities, which may signal unmet private needs, nor the welfare of the community's neediest residents.

A further factor exacerbating the problem of overcapacity in the hospital industry has been the inability of the market, as currently organized, to induce nonprofit hospitals to close down beds or to go out of business altogether once they have been replaced by more efficient or better located facilities.[66] Those responsible for making such decisions are simply unlikely to vote themselves out of jobs or prestigious positions as long as they can meet the payroll, even at the expense of recoverable capital.[67]

---

[64] A recent theoretical treatment of the economic behavior of nonprofit organizations uses the budget-maximizing postulate and strongly invites application to the hospital context. W. NISKANEN, *supra* note 23, at 81-86, 102-04. The hospital appears to be in some degree both a "discriminating monopolist" and a "bureau with a passive sponsor" (*i.e.*, Blue Cross and other third-party payers) in Niskanen's terminology, and it does in fact sell its services "at a [net] price [to the user] less than the marginal cost." *Id.* at 85. Under certain assumptions, either type of organization in its pure form "will supply a higher output which, given constant marginal costs, is twice that of a competitive industry." *Id.* at 86.

[65] There is some evidence that nonprofit firms may be more inclined than owner-managed for-profit concerns to practice racial, religious, and sex discrimination even if it proves more costly, because the managers indulge their preferences at the organization's expense. *See* Alchian & Kessel, *Competition, Monopoly, and the Pursuit of Money*, in NATIONAL BUREAU OF ECONOMIC RESEARCH, ASPECTS OF LABOR ECONOMICS, SPECIAL CONFERENCE SERIES No. 14, at 157 (1962). Complaints about hospitals' performance in these respects are registered in HEALTH-PAC, *supra* note 22.

[66] *Compare* Carr, *Economic Efficiency in the Allocation of Hospital Resources: Central Planning vs. Evolutionary Development*, in EMPIRICAL STUDIES, *supra* note 56, at 195, 212 ("The . . . results support the hypothesis that the survivorship principle is operative."), *with* Rothenberg, *Comment*, in EMPIRICAL STUDIES, *supra* note 56, at 222.

[67] A for-profit firm will stay in business only as long as it can earn its out of-pocket costs *plus at least a market rate of return on that portion of its capital which it could recover by liquidating;* its other capital investment is "lost" already and does not influence its decisions. Managers of a nonprofit firm might have no concern for capital at all, liquidating only when its cash flow was inadequate to continue. Although a hospital's liquidation value may often be small, the importance of the slow-exit phenomenon

Although some hospitals have reconstituted themselves as nursing homes or have relocated to follow population shifts, such opportunities are not always available, or attractive, to managers. The obsolete nonprofit firm, unnaturally sustained by cost reimbursement, unable either to liquidate for the benefit of its owners or managers or to direct its capital to activities unrelated to health care, and inaccessible to takeover bids,[68] imposes a costly burden on society by its relative permanence. It is far from clear, however, that entry controls which protect such obsolete facilities against new competition are the appropriate social response to this problem.[69]

The Role of Doctors

Competition among hospitals for doctors also explains a great deal of duplicative investment, perhaps not in beds so much as in exotic equipment which duplicates underused facilities at nearby institutions.[70] Hospitals compete more actively for doctors than for patients, since the former have more to say than the latter about hospital use. Since doctors do not pay for the use of the hospital and usually have no reason for concern over their patients' bills, competing hospitals seek to provide services and facilities which make the doctors' practices more lucrative but which are paid for by third-party payers. The resulting equipment duplication resembles that of the airlines industry, where regulated fares have diverted competitive efforts to other areas. Competition among airlines has been vigorous in scheduling, up-to-date equipment, and amenities, but airplanes fly nearly half empty and the cost of service on busy routes is probably half again what it would be if price competition were allowed.[71] Hospitals, too, have a "747" problem arising from the absence

would appear sharply when an HMO, seeking to acquire hospital facilities in a community, finds itself rebuffed by hospitals whose performance seems less than marginal by usual commercial standards. See text accompanying notes 215, 254 infra.

[68] See MARRIS, supra note 23, at 29-30.

[69] See text accompanying note 254 infra.

[70] For example, such competition might lead hospitals to procure such expensive items as radioisotope therapy equipment and open-heart surgery facilities.

[71] W. JORDAN, AIRLINE REGULATION IN AMERICA: EFFECTS AND IMPERFECTIONS ch. 5 (1970), uses intrastate fares in California, which escape CAB regulation, to prove the effect of CAB policies. See also Keeler, Airline Regulation and Market Performance, 3 BELL J. ECON. & MGT. SCI. 399 (1972); Levine, Is Regulation Necessary? California Air Transportation and National Regulatory Policy, 74 YALE L.J. 1416 (1965). On the effect of restrictions on price competition on airline equipment purchases, see JORDAN, supra, at 36-49, 53-56, 230-33; Phillips, Air Transportation in the United States, in TECHNOLOGICAL CHANGE IN REGULATED INDUSTRIES 123, 156-60 (W. Capron ed. 1971).

of price competition—strong competitive pressure to invest excessively in the latest technology even though the market for it is thin.

Even where geographic dispersion or other factors weaken the competitive pressure to attract doctors, the organized medical staff will still exercise considerable influence over trustees' investment decisions.[72] Too often, the doctors will select projects on the basis of convenience or potential fees, and their calculations of net benefits will not include all the institution's costs and may contemplate inappropriate utilization.

C. Quality of Care and Economies of Scale

The tendency of hospitals, under competitive pressure or pressure from their medical staffs, to acquire sophisticated treatment facilities also has an important quality dimension which certificate-of-need laws are thought to address. Where a surgical team performs an operation only rarely, its success rate may be significantly lower than it should be.[73] Similarly, the skills necessary to use certain modern equipment efficiently may not be available or may be maintainable in no more than a few centers. Any effort to maintain additional facilities may spread and underutilize the talent, leading to poorer medical outcomes in each location. Moreover, certain backup equipment may be helpful but too expensive unless the volume of procedures benefitting from it is substantial.

These various considerations reflect the presence of economies of scale in the delivery of certain kinds of specialized care. These economies may sometimes be unattainable by the market if consumers lack the knowledge necessary to penalize providers for poor success ratios. Of course, these problems might be addressed by malpractice suits,[74] by a "no-fault" system of provider-financed compensation for bad results,[75] or by improving the information available to consumers.[76] Nevertheless,

---

[72] See Pauly & Redisch, The Not-for-Profit Hospital as a Physicians' Cooperative, 63 AM. ECON. REV. 87 (1973).

[73] See AEI PROCEEDINGS, supra note 6 (remarks of Calabresi and Stickel).

[74] See generally REPORT OF THE SECRETARY'S COMMISSION ON MEDICAL MALPRACTICE (Dep't of HEW Pub. No. (OS) 73-88, 1973).

[75] See Havighurst & Tancredi, "Medical Adversity Insurance:" A No-Fault Approach to Medical Malpractice and Quality Assurance, 51 MILBANK MEMORIAL FUND Q./HEALTH & SOCIETY 125 (1973); Keeton, Compensation for Medical Accidents, 121 U. PA. L. REV. 590 (1973).

[76] Although it would violate the medical profession's precepts, there is much to recommend disclosure of the presence and value of equipment and experienced manpower and perhaps even the mortality experience of particular providers. But cf. Havighurst & Tancredi, supra note 75, at 131.

certificate-of-need laws may also be employed to permit realization of scale economies. If consumers are unable to assess performance of a service well enough to force producers to strive for the optimal level of quality, regulation may be an appropriate means of permitting quality-related scale economies to materialize.

D. *"Cream-Skimming"*

Another line of argument in support of certificate-of-need laws is not much employed by their proponents in theoretical discussions, though it appears to be commonly used in selling the idea to legislators and hospital administrators.[77] The argument takes a number of forms but usually begins by noting that many new hospitals, particularly proprietaries, are often uncommitted to offering "comprehensive" services but instead offer only those services which are profitable. Similarly, it is argued that expansion is most likely to occur in the profitable lines rather than in those services which cannot support themselves. The specific complaint, often left implicit in the notion that comprehensiveness is desirable for its own sake, is that this new competition deprives existing providers of essential revenues, thereby jeopardizing their ability to offer the arguably needed, though unremunerative, services.

This line of argument is familiar as a popular defense of entry restrictions in other regulated industries, where the so-called "cream-skimming" tendencies of new entrants are objected to because they disrupt the internal subsidization capabilities of existing providers and therefore the useful services which they provide at prices below cost.[78] Internal subsidization is discussed at another point and is found to be troublesome

---

[77] This assertion is based on general conversation, particularly with persons close to the laws' enactment in North Carolina and Virginia. In each case examples of cream-skimming by proprietary hospitals were cited as important in the law's enactment. In North Carolina, improvement of the borrowing capacity of the hospitals—by protecting them from competition—was an explicit purpose. Durham Morning Herald, June 25, 1971, at 1c, col. 1. In the State of Washington, concern was expressed about "promoters coming into the state to build health care facilities on an investment basis—facilities which were often not needed." ABT ASSOC. INC., A CASE STUDY OF COMPREHENSIVE HEALTH PLANNING IN WASHINGTON 34 (1972).

[78] *See* Posner, *Taxation by Regulation,* 2 BELL J. ECON. & MGT. SCI. 22 (1971) and text accompanying notes 163-77 *infra.* Restrictions on entry into most so-called "natural monopoly" markets—that is, those in which economies of scale dictate that having more than one provider would be inefficient—can be justified on practically no ground other than a desire to preserve the regulated firm's capacity for internal subsidization. The only other possible argument might be the social costs involved in a struggle "to the death." *Cf.* Union Leader Corp. v. Newspapers of New England, Inc., 284 F.2d 582 (1st Cir. 1960), *cert. denied,* 365 U.S. 833 (1961).

not only because it necessitates protectionism but also because it is a vehicle for allocative mischief. On these grounds, this rationale for certificate-of-need laws must be counted as generally unpersuasive.

By distinguishing between the long run and the short run, a cream-skimming argument can be developed which, though couched in expediency, might justify a temporary moratorium on competitive developments. Thus, if an existing hospital is currently providing health care for a large number of poor and near-poor, it has a powerful claim to immediate protection against competition which would deprive it of the revenues necessary to continue those services.[79] The argument is of course much weaker if the subsidized service is the obstetric, pediatric, or intensive care unit or some other service which is simply underpriced[80] or if the needed revenues could be obtained from other sources, as in the case of a publicly owned hospital. In any event, the cream-skimming argument has less merit in the long run, when a national health insurance program for the poor may have obviated the social necessity for financing indigent care in this manner.[81]

E. The Laws' Consistency With the Rationales

Coverage in General

The scope of enacted certificate-of-need statutes is not always consistent with their supporting rationales. While the laws are primarily concerned with the hospital bed supply and the danger of excessive dup-

---

[79] The extent of dependence on internal subsidies to support indigent care is not clear. Medicaid leaves many near-poor uncovered and often pays providers less than the cost of the care given. The Department of HEW's "free-care" requirement for hospitals benefitting from the Hill-Burton program regards 3 percent of operating costs as a norm. 42 C.F.R. § 53.111(d) (1972).

[80] To some extent, laboratory, x-ray, and pharmacy profits are earned at everyone's expense, and many of the subsidized services are for everyone's benefit, suggesting that equity issues are not involved. Moreover, insurance tends to spread costs even further and to perpetuate the same allocative concerns which might otherwise be eliminated by doing away with non-cost-related pricing. Also, the hospital may respond to entry threats by underpricing services likely to be competitive while overpricing monopolized services. Cf. United States v. United Shoe Mach. Corp., 110 F. Supp. 295, 325-29 (D. Mass. 1953), aff'd per curiam, 347 U.S. 521 (1954).

[81] Of course, national health insurance may itself be underfinanced, perhaps reflecting a Congressional decision to continue to rely on supplementary revenues produced by the "monopolistic charity" model of the hospital. See Havighurst, Speculations on the Market's Future in Health Care, in AEI Proceedings, supra note 6. In this event, protectionist certificate-of-need laws would make some sense, but their enactment now as a remedy for what appears for the moment to be primarily a short-run problem of financing indigent care might prejudice the long-run prospects for a system permitting freer entry.

lication, a few of them stop short of confronting duplication of services and equipment and the related quality problems.[82]

Although some of the laws bear on all substantial changes in hospital services, the stated rationales fail to explain coverage of cutbacks.[83] Here the explanation is apparently broader than the narrow concern with costs, duplication, and overcapacity. In general, planners sense a need not only to avoid nonessential services but also to assure that essential services are being provided. The power to compel continuation of a service previously rendered is seen as highly desirable, and it is but a short step from this power to mandating the provision of specific services. Thus, the franchising approach from public utility and common carrier regulation appears subtly but unmistakably in the certificate-of-need laws of several states.

The laws do not feature prominently a protectionist, anti-cream-skimming purpose.[84] For one thing, they make no specific issue of proprietary providers or of the hazards which competition poses for providers offering comprehensive services. Moreover, they seem not to contemplate that existing providers will appear in opposition to applications by potential competitors,[85] and decision makers seldom seem to frame the issue expressly in terms of the effect of new competition on existing providers. Nevertheless, the need criterion necessarily incorporates the anticompetitive premise that the need for an aspirant's service should not be determined in the marketplace. If the service is already being provided, the applicant will surely bear a heavy burden.

Although the laws make no distinction between for-profit and nonprofit institutions,[86] somewhat different rationales apply to the two cases. Indeed, there may be a somewhat stronger case, on one level at least, for public control of nonprofit institutions. Even if one had confidence in the prevailing market incentives, nonprofit firms would still be less amenable to market discipline than profit-making firms.[87] On the other

---

[82] Cf. notes 11-12 supra.

[83] Cf. note 16 supra.

[84] But see note 77 supra.

[85] See notes 114-16 and accompanying text.

[86] Maryland's law did for a time cover only nonprofit nursing homes. Law of April 10, 1968, ch. 222, [1968] Md. Laws 274.

[87] For-profit firms with professional (nonowner) managers may also be given to maximizing things other than profits, but shareholders probably provide a more dependable check than anything in the hospital manager's environment. See note 23 supra. See also Hetherington, Fact and Legal Theory: Shareholders, Managers, and Corporate Social Responsibility, 21 STAN. L. REV. 248 (1969).

hand, assuming the continuation of current market conditions, proprietaries are probably more likely to engage in cream-skimming in pursuit of short-run profits. Because the present weakness of market deterrents to overexpansion may affect both for-profit and nonprofit concerns about equally though in different ways, it is probably appropriate to lump the two for regulatory purposes.

The Weaker Arguments for Extending Certificate-of-Need Laws to Nonhospital Facilities

Although twenty of twenty-three states impose certificate-of-need requirements on nursing homes and other institutions providing less sophisticated levels of inpatient care, the argument for doing so is less persuasive than the case for regulating hospital development.[88] To be sure, expansion of the bed supply in such institutions does increase utilization, since many sick or elderly persons seek such care if it is available and if the price is subsidized by public programs or private insurance. Nevertheless, these consumption decisions are somewhat more in the patients' hands than decisions regarding hospital use. Moreover, both utilization and investment decisions are less likely to reflect doctors' judgments. In addition, the predominance of proprietary interests and the strength of competition help relate the incentives for building new capacity more closely to consumer wants. Finally, cost reimbursement is not inevitable as the basis of third-party payment.

 Nor is there compelling evidence of oversupply of nursing-care facilities.[89] Although efficient utilization can be a problem because patients

---

[88] I have seen no careful justification of coverage of nursing homes. Thomas, one of the leading advocates of coverage for such institutions, provides no clear rationale. W. THOMAS, NURSING HOMES AND PUBLIC POLICY: DRIFT AND DECISION IN NEW YORK STATE (1969). Indeed, he describes an experience which suggests rather strongly the value of permitting market responses: rapid growth of the proprietary sector while the voluntary sector was unable to meet the emerging need; uneven quality during the period when demand exceeded supply; and, ultimately, improved quality and efficiency when supply finally allowed competition to be effective in eliminating poorer facilities. One can debate whether stronger quality controls would have been in the public interest during this period or would simply have slowed the supply response, depriving people of care altogether. I expect that the coverage of nursing homes in certificate-of-need legislation usually reflects, as in the State of Washington, nothing more substantive than the "nursing homes' interest in being regulated" and their "very effective legislative pressure." ABT Assoc. INC., *supra* note 77, at 39. *See also* text accompanying note 136 *infra*.

[89] The range is from 9.1 per 1000 in West Virginia to 74.1 per 1000 in Oklahoma, the only state with a certificate-of-need requirement for nursing homes only. NAT'L CENTER FOR HEALTH STATISTICS, HEALTH RESOURCES STATISTICS 1971, 325 (DHEW Pub. No. HSM 72-1509, 1972).

are often placed in institutions which offer more sophisticated care than they require,[90] limiting the number of beds is a less efficient and less fair method of dealing with this problem than utilization review by disinterested doctors. Doctors engaged in such review efforts, perhaps under the auspices of a Professional Standards Review Organization (PSRO)[91] or a foundation for medical care,[92] would probably be less tolerant of overutilization in extended and intermediate care facilities than in hospitals.[93] Furthermore, various other means, including voluntary planning, conditions attached to financing schemes, and licensure requirements, can be used to bring about better coordination and to facilitate patient transfers to more appropriate facilities.

Competition would serve consumers better with respect to nursing care institutions than with respect to hospitals. Most important, a wider range of choice is likely to result, and the poorer homes will readily close their doors if the market does not support them.[94] Decisions are more likely to remain in the hands of patients and their families, who are in a better position than hospital patients to evaluate the total package of services received, particularly the overall quality of life enjoyed by the residents. Given this subjective element and the impossibility of adequately allowing for it in regulation,[95] it must be concluded that one

---

[90] S. REP. No. 91-1230, 92d Cong., 2d Sess. 285 (1972).

[91] PSROs are physician-sponsored mechanisms for reviewing claims for payment under government programs as a means of controlling utilization of resources and quality of care. 42 U.S.C. § 249(f). *See also* note 234 *infra* and accompanying text.

[92] Foundations for medical care are medical-society-sponsored groups which frequently engage in claims review. *See* C. STEINWALD, AN INTRODUCTION TO FOUNDATIONS FOR MEDICAL CARE (1971). *See also* note 234 *infra* and accompanying text.

[93] When patients are paying their own way, concerns about utilization are less warranted. Nevertheless social work, patient advocacy, and ombudsman programs have potential value as protections against families' disinterest and the frequent inability of aged or dependent patients to look out for themselves.

[94] *See* THOMAS, *supra* note 88, at 155-58, 175, 261.

[95] It is coming to be widely recognized that regulation would be more effective if it could be geared to "outcomes" rather than to "inputs" or "processes." *See, e.g., Hearings on Health Maintenance Organizations Before the Subcomm. on Public Health and Environment of the House Comm. on Interstate and Foreign Commerce*, 92d Cong., 2d Sess. 489-531 (1972) (testimony of Dr. Patrick O'Donoghue); Williamson, *Outcomes of Health Care: Key to Health Improvement*, in METHODOLOGY OF IDENTIFYING, MEASURING AND EVALUATING OUTCOMES OF HEALTH SERVICE PROGRAMS 75 (C. Hopkins ed. 1970). Most nursing home regulation is concerned primarily with "inputs," however. *See, e.g.,* 20 C.F.R. §§ 409.1120-.1137 (1973). Moreover, it is difficult to identify the desired outcome of nursing home care, which frequently ends in death and not often in complete recovery. Unlike hospital care, which is generally short-term and geared to achieving a specific improvement in health, nursing homes should be much more concerned with providing a certain "quality of life" for their patients. In the absence of

nursing-care bed is not necessarily interchangeable with another and that market competition is too valuable a protection of patients' vital interests to be sacrificed for possible cost savings.[96]

The appropriateness, under the rationales advanced, for regulating construction or expansion of outpatient facilities may also be questioned. Because ambulatory care is not regularly paid for on a cost-reimbursement basis, is not particularly the province of nonprofit providers, and has not been characterized by overcapacity (other than some maldistribution),[97] its coverage by these laws is not easily justified. Nevertheless, the argument may be made that substitution of cheaper ambulatory care for inpatient care will leave empty hospital beds, which, it is claimed, will attract new patients and raise health care costs over-all. This logic provides special bait for a classic regulatory trap, which is discussed in connection with the consequences of applying certificate-of-need laws to HMOs and other types of outpatient facilities.

III. The Operation of a Certificate-of-Need Program

An evaluation of certificate-of-need laws requires a review of the steps followed in processing an application under a typical program.[98] Individual programs differ in various respects from the general procedural model discussed here,[99] but an overview identifies areas of potential difficulty and provides background for a pragmatic appraisal of certificate-of-need laws.

---

opportunities for regulation geared to inmates' happiness and of suitable proxies for same, a great deal can be said for leaving as much as possible to consumer choice and working to improve opportunities for its informed exercise.

[96] The arguments discussed here would be relevant on the constitutionality of certificate-of-need legislation as applied to nursing-care institutions. It would be possible, for example, to disagree with the North Carolina Supreme Court's reasoning in In re Certificate of Need for Aston Park Hospital, Inc., see note 3 supra, and yet believe that such a holding with respect to coverage of nursing homes would be entirely defensible. But see Attoma v. Dep't of Social Welfare, 26 App. Div. 2d 12, 18, 270 N.Y.S.2d 167, 171 (1966).

[97] See note 56 supra.

[98] The best narrative description of a certificate-of-need program is ABT Assoc. Inc., supra note 77, at 43-54.

[99] Some of the assertions in this subsection are based on interviews in several states and on responses to a comprehensive questionnaire which was sent to the 21 states which enacted certificate-of-need statutes prior to 1973. Questionnaires were returned by the following 14 states: Arizona, California, Florida, Kansas, Kentucky, Maryland, Massachusetts, Minnesota, Nevada, New York, North Dakota, South Carolina, South Dakota, and Washington. The statutes referred to in notes 100-126 infra are those cited in note 4 supra unless otherwise indicated.

The degree of procedural formality in certificate-of-need laws varies widely, but the usual administrative safeguards against arbitrary action are not always provided for.[100] State administrative procedure acts, seldom as demanding or as rigorously applied as the federal Administrative Procedure Act,[101] may compensate for some deficiencies but may not apply to the areawide agencies, which are not, strictly speaking, creatures of the state.[102] In some cases, superimposing regulatory powers on informal health planning may have introduced coercive powers without also imposing the usual responsibility to exercise those powers openly and to accord procedural protections. The absence of these procedural requirements, particularly those requiring the existence, disclosure, and application of objective criteria, may facilitate favoritism and increased political influence in decision making. It is therefore appropriate to suggest desirable procedural safeguards while at the same time providing the groundwork for an estimate of what can reasonably be expected of state agencies charged with certificate-of-need responsibility.

A. Applications

The certificate-of-need application is usually prepared on a prescribed form indicating the information which the agency regards as important in determining need. If not prepared by the applicant itself, the application may be prepared by an architect or a hospital planning consultant, who may also perform supporting surveys and analysis. This contrasts with other regulatory programs, where applications are usually prepared by lawyers specializing in practice before the agency involved. Indeed, the presence or absence of lawyers in the hospital regulation process provides an index of the regulated institutions' perceptions of the process, particularly their view of the friendliness and amenability of the regulators and of the likelihood that obstruction will be offered.[103] Although

---

100 California, Florida, Kansas, Massachusetts, Minnesota, Tennessee, and South Dakota provide the most elaborate procedural protections in their certificate-of-need laws, whereas some other states, including North Dakota, Oklahoma, Virginia, and Washington, incorporate procedural requirements by reference to other laws.

101 5 U.S.C. §§ 551-59, 701-06, 1305, 3344, 7521 (1970).

102 Statutes in most of the states leave procedures in the local agencies largely unspecified.

103 Maryland and New York report that lawyers are "usually" involved where proprietary facilities are concerned, and California indicates that attorney involvement is usual in all types of cases. Most other states indicated that lawyers "rarely" participate in the application process.

planning-cum-regulation may be preferable in some respects to more adversary proceedings, the absence of lawyers in the process may lead to the adoption of procedures which are less well designed to produce a clear articulation of policies and objective standards.

Some of the most revealing cases are apt to be those involving conflicting applications occurring where two hospitals wish to expand in the same area or where several applicants apply for the privilege of building a single new hospital.[104] The result may be a sort of comparative hearing similar to that engaged in by the Federal Communications Commission in dealing with competing applications for a single broadcasting license or by the Civil Aeronautics Board in awarding airline routes. One would expect the action taken on competing applications to be instructive in identifying the priorities and philosophies of the deciding agency, but FCC and CAB experience has shown that criteria or the weight given them have tended to change from case to case, suggesting that the true grounds for decisions are not always the reasons revealed.[105] Brief investigations of the experience of particular certificate-of-need agencies indicate that procedures are generally inadequate to reveal to the parties the reasons for preferring one applicant over another.[106]

---

[104] There would seem to be a danger that the certificate-of-need process may actually stimulate hospital construction by causing applicants to accelerate their plans in order to pre-empt others. The use of population projections facilitates granting of certificates well before the facilities are actually needed, and it is common for applicants to be turned down on the ground that needed beds are already subscribed for though not yet in being—in other words, the application is too late. In one state, a politically influential local hospital authority was given a certificate in 1972 to build a new hospital on the express condition that "first use" not occur before 1976. The effect of this forehandedness was to preclude other applications, possibly more in keeping with the circumstances at the relevant time.

[105] Indeed, the granting of lucrative broadcasting licenses has produced outright corruption in the FCC. See WKAT, Inc. 29 F.C.C. 216, aff'd, 296 F.2d 375 (D.C. Cir. 1960), cert. denied, 368 U.S. 841 (1961). CAB route awards have been largely based on nothing more solid than parcelling out favors among the airlines equally, making up in a later case for hardships imposed in an earlier one, or vice versa. See, e.g., Hilton, The Basic Behavior of Regulatory Commissions, 62 AM. ECON. REV. 47, 49 (1972).

[106] Only two of the 14 responding states (Arizona and Maryland) said that they had specific procedures for dealing with competing applications. But see MASS. GEN. LAWS ANN. ch. 111, § 25C (Supp. 1972), which in providing for "filing periods" recalls the comparative-hearing requirement of Ashbacker Radio Corp. v. FCC, 326 U.S. 327 (1945). Despite the questionnaire response, investigations in Maryland did not reveal anything like the comparative hearing procedures used in federal agencies. See, e.g., Clinton Community Hospital Corp., Md. Comprehensive Health Planning Agency.Application No. 70-16-0012 (Dec. 1970).

B. The Decision Makers

The primary decision maker in a certificate-of-need program is frequently difficult to identify. Usually a state agency, either a separate one or the department of health, appears to have final authority, but influential advice and comments are frequently provided by local planning agencies and state advisory councils. The complex advisory and review processes tend to obscure such matters as whether advice received from various planning and advisory agencies is merely window-dressing or is tantamount to being final and whether appellate review is *de novo* or accords substantial weight to the initial decision.

The relation of the certificate-of-need process to the comprehensive health planning (CHP) process fostered under federal law varies from state to state. Only seven states delegate final decision-making authority to state CHP agencies,[107] but areawide agencies are usually deeply involved.[108] Indeed two states, Arizona and Kansas, give final decision-making authority on need to the areawide agency.[109] Although federal law requires the CHP agencies' planning councils to draw more than half their membership from representatives of "consumers of health services," the imprecision of this requirement has left disadvantaged groups generally underrepresented.[110] The state laws frequently supply

---

[107] California, Colorado, Nevada, Maryland, Oregon, South Carolina, and South Dakota. These are the so called "a" agencies organized pursuant to § 314(a) of the Public Health Service Act, 42 U.S.C. § 246(a) (1970). Areawide CHP agencies are known as "b" agencies after § 314(b), 42 U.S.C. § 246(b) (1970).

[108] Connecticut has by-passed the CHP mechanism almost completely. New Jersey and New York utilize "b" agencies only where the "b" agency and the regional group happen to be one and the same. The Rhode Island, Oklahoma, and Virginia statutes refer to the involvement of "b" agencies in the decision-making process, but the statutory language leaves the extent of involvement largely discretionary.

[109] California also gives substantial decision-making (and appellate) authority to areawide agencies, which are nongovernmental in character, and this latter circumstance prompted a legal challenge on the ground of delegation of legislative power to private interests. The challenge was unsuccessful, partly because a state agency was found to exercise final authority. Simon v. Cameron, 337 F. Supp. 1380 (C.D. Cal. 1970). *Cf.* Self-Help for the Elderly v. Richardson, Civil No. 2016-71 (D.D.C., filed Oct. 6, 1971), *dismissed as moot*, Nov. 20, 1972. The Arizona and Kansas statutes might be subject to possible attack on delegation grounds, a further foundation for which might be found in the historical use of planning agencies to further private interests. *See* notes 22 and 23 *supra*. Nevertheless, the provision for a de novo judicial hearing would probably save the Kansas statute. KAN. STAT. ANN. § 65-2a08 (1972).

[110] 42 U.S.C. § 246(a)(2)(B), (b)(2)(A) (1970). *See* B.C. French, Who Are the Consumers on the State Health Planning Councils?, 1970 (Institute for the Study of Health and Society mimeo.).

similar assurance against provider domination of other agencies which may be involved.[111]

In most states, the areawide health planning agency for the area in which the new facility is to be constructed acts first on the application. The purpose is to provide the opportunity for community reaction and to guarantee local involvement in the decision-making process. Areawide planning councils include both provider and consumer representatives. There is generally a small professional staff, which may or may not undertake significant independent study of the factual circumstances.[112] Sometimes the planners' preferences are embodied in a master plan with which applications may be compared.[113]

C. Hearings, Appeals, and Decisions

While a hearing on the application is frequently held, it may differ in character from hearings in other regulatory settings. In Maryland, for example, the purpose of the hearing is to inform the public about the proposal rather than to afford the applicant an opportunity to make his case before the agency. While opposition to an application may arise in the form of questions and challenges presented by persons appearing at the hearing, there are normally no formal arrangements for recognizing opposition or for intervention.[114] Although most states report that formal opposition is unlikely,[115] a hospital or other institutional provider whose

---

[111] In those states where the final determination is left solely to the state department of health, the number and quality of consumer representation is dependent on the state statute regulating appointment of the commissioner, board of health, etc. Where the certification statute establishes a new agency or advisory board, it usually specifies that (1) the members shall be appointed by the governor or some other public official, (2) there shall be a majority of consumers, (3) expiration of membership should be staggered, and (4) providers should be well represented. The identity of the "providers" is often not specified at all. *Contra,* California, Connecticut, Kentucky, North Dakota, and Tennessee. The nine-member North Dakota State Health Council, the final decision maker, has seven provider representatives, none of them representing nursing homes, which the Director of the Division of Health Planning, in his questionnaire response, says are the more important problem. Kentucky also guarantees a provider majority.

[112] On the financial support of the "b" agencies, *see* note 150 *infra.*

[113] *But see* text accompanying notes 187-90 *infra.*

[114] California, Florida, Kansas, Minnesota, South Dakota, and Tennessee spell out detailed intervention procedures, but Colorado, Massachusetts, and North Dakota also seem to contemplate intervention prior to a ruling.

[115] Six questionnaires reported that existing providers "often" oppose applications, though opposition may not amount to formal intervention but only appearance at the hearing. Only two states indicated that community groups often appear in opposition. Other investigations confirmed that active opposition by competitors occurs regularly

market position is being challenged would be tempted to oppose a proposal by filing a competing application[116] or by arguing that it could meet all future needs itself. The infrequency of formal intervention appears to reflect the perception of the proceeding as nonadversary and nonregulatory in character, but the lack of formal opposition may simply widen the agency's discretion with possible consequences for the quality of decisions.

Certificate-of-need statutes vary widely both as to when a final determination may be appealed and as to who has standing to appeal.[117] In some states the only administrative appeals permitted are those by unsuccessful applicants.[118] Curran argues that, since overcapacity is the main concern of these laws, approvals should also be appealable.[119] Apparently ignoring the possibility that competing institutions may be better equipped and better motivated to raise issues of public concern, Curran would limit appeals to representatives of the "public interest." [120] In other regulated industries, competitors adversely affected by proposed new entry are generally permitted to appeal approvals, not because they are entitled to specific protection but because in asserting their own in-

in Nevada and California. *Cf.* Memorial Hospital of Southern California v. State Health Planning Council, 28 Cal. App. 3d 167, 104 Cal. Rptr. 492 (1972).

[116] In New York, a hospital applied for authority to open an ambulatory care facility in a neighboring town where a new community hospital had been proposed. At the same time, it represented publicly that it was not opposing the pending application.

[117] Connecticut, Kentucky, New Jersey, North Dakota, Oregon, South Dakota, and Tennessee (applicants only) allow appeals only to the courts, whereas Florida contemplates mandamus proceedings, though regulations allow appeal to an advisory council as well. Fla. Regs., *supra* note 11, at ¶ G.1. California allows appeals to the consumer members of another areawide agency before appeal to the state Advisory Health Council. Kansas provides for an appeals panel drawn primarily from other "b" agencies.

[118] Arizona (not on need, but on conformance to the "state plan"), Oklahoma, Rhode Island, and Virginia. In Minnesota, "any person aggrieved" may appeal a denial. The statutes in California, Colorado, Florida, and Michigan provide for administrative appeals from issuance as well as denial of certification, by both the applicant and the planning agencies involved. California clearly allows additional parties to be represented in appeals initiated by others. *Cf.* Memorial Hospital of Southern California v. State Health Planning Council, 28 Cal. App. 3d 167, 104 Cal. Rptr. 492 (1972). Kansas, South Carolina, and Massachusetts allow the widest latitude for initiating administrative appeals. In lieu of an appeal, several states allow a hearing after a tentative decision is reached. *See* note 124 *infra* and accompanying text.

[119] Curran, *supra* note 6. *See also* note 118 *supra*.

[120] The only known formal challenge by a public-interest group occurred in Minnesota, where the case was dismissed for failure to post a bond. *See* Casady Memo, *supra* note 42.

terest, they illuminate the public's stake in the decision.[121] However, formal intervention by competing providers occurs infrequently in certificate-of-need proceedings.[122]

Typically, a decision by the areawide agency is either advisory to, or subject to automatic review by, the statewide agency. In either case the state agency reviews the record and makes the final determination. It is not always stated whether the review merely assures that the initial decision was not clearly erroneous or was supported by substantial evidence or is instead a *de novo* consideration.[123] Some states permit further appeals to the state department of health or to a special review board, and procedures for these appeals vary. New York and several other states allow a hearing only after the state agency has tentatively acted on the application.[124]

The manner of revealing reasons for a decision also varies among the states. New York reveals the detailed grounds for a denial only in the hearing which follows a tentative denial at the state level. Although most agencies claim to make findings of fact, to provide statements of the specific reasons for their decisions, and to make these items public, decisions appear sketchy and unrevealing as to underlying facts or criteria, and files are frequently not freely available. Nor do state procedures in these regards appear to measure up to the high standards prevailing in the federal regulatory agencies.[125] For example, a number of states indicated in questionnaire responses that dissenting views in the deciding agency or advisory body were neither reduced to writing nor otherwise revealed. In other cases, the actions or recommendations of areawide

---

[121] *See* FCC v. Sanders Bros. Radio Station, 309 U.S. 470 (1940); Carroll Broadcasting Co. v. FCC, 258 F.2d 440 (D.C. Cir. 1958).

[122] *See* note 115 *supra.*

[123] The standard for administrative appellate review is seldom stipulated in the statute. Virginia provides for de novo review of denials with a full hearing before the State Board of Health. California (which specifies a substantial evidence standard) and Massachusetts provide primarily for review on the record, with a hearing discretionary. Colorado's appeal is described as a "hearing on the application," suggesting de novo consideration.

[124] Roughly similar procedures are followed in Kentucky, Maryland, Nevada, New Jersey, North Dakota, Oklahoma, Oregon, Rhode Island, South Carolina, and Tennessee. Practices vary as to whether the hearing is before an examiner or the full board or agency responsible for the decision and as to whether anyone besides the applicant can initiate the further proceeding.

[125] Massachusetts is the most explicit in its requirement for written decisions with articulated reasons, and other statutes have reassuring language. Most decisions appear in minutes or memoranda prepared by staff, however, and I know of no agency which issues signed, quasi-judicial opinions of the kind typical of many federal agencies.

agencies could not be effectively contested because the grounds were not clearly specified.[126]

The expectation that administrative agencies explain the basis for their decisions is premised on a belief that it avoids arbitrariness and contributes to consistency and clarity of policy. Of course, written opinions do not necessarily reveal the true reasons for the decisions reached.[127] Even so, it is better to have reasons stated than to have them obscured. The parties may then at least address the ostensible standards, and courts and legislators will have some basis for judgment about the consistency of policies both in application and with the statutory purpose.

D. *Criteria for Assessing Need*

Generally, the statute spells out for the agency the applicable need criteria. These are often articulated further in regulations and in an areawide or state health plan which the agency itself develops.[128] Nevertheless, these criteria may be too numerous, conflicting, and vague to be helpful in resolving particular cases, thus allowing an agency, while ostensibly balancing conflicting values, to pick and choose among various criteria to justify any result it wants.[129] For example, the Oregon certificate-of-need statute provides thirteen paragraphs of criteria for judging need, permitting the state agency to find grounds for granting or denying any application, emphasizing one factor or another and minimizing inconvenient circumstances when they appear.[130]

[126] Questionnaires from only Nevada and New York indicated that reasons for local agency action might not appear, but files from other states including Maryland indicate that this is a more common problem. Moreover, the statutes in Colorado, Connecticut, Massachusetts, Michigan, New Jersey, North Dakota, Oklahoma, South Carolina, Virginia, and Washington suggest that the areawide agency's recommendation may be seen as confidential, although probably some disclosure would occur in practice in some of these states, as indicated in the questionnaires returned by several.

[127] A famous memorandum written to President Eisenhower by Louis Hector upon his resignation as a member of the CAB noted that the agency staff cultivated the ability to write opinions to justify any result in a given case and was careful not to write in such a way as to create precedents which would make future decision writing more difficult. Hector, *Problems of the CAB and the Independent Regulatory Commissions*, 69 YALE L. J. 931, 942 (1960).

[128] Only California, Kansas, Kentucky, Maryland, and New York of the 14 responding states claimed to have master plans as criteria in decision making, and North Dakota referred to its Hill-Burton plan. Maryland was unable to produce any developed plan, however. *See* note 189 *infra* and accompanying text.

[129] *See* H. FRIENDLY, THE FEDERAL ADMINISTRATIVE AGENCIES: THE NEED FOR BETTER DEFINITION OF STANDARDS, ch. 4 (1962).

[130] *Compare* Curran, *supra* note 6, *with* AEI PROCEEDINGS, *supra* note 6 (remarks of Richard A. Posner).

The issue of need for health facilities is so exceedingly complex that, unless the decision maker spells out its policies in advance, the vague criteria of most state programs permit the agency to function with little effective oversight by judicial or other authorities. New York's program, which employs a detailed state plan for hospital beds and a well-defined formula for identifying needs, is an exception. California has legislation pending which would centralize decision-making authority and allow greater use of formulas and explicit plans, an approach which has proved impossible with primary authority lodged in areawide agencies.[181]

Because they act without clear criteria and without the need to reveal the true grounds for actions taken, the certificate-of-need agencies exercise largely discretionary power. Administrative mechanisms for structuring and confining such power should therefore be introduced.[182] Considerable scholarship indicates that informality, dejudicialization, and efficiency in handling a large number of cases can occur without loss of basic fairness and reasonable guarantees of the rights of the parties.[183]

E. Procedural Problems

The procedural aspects of certificate-of-need programs appear to be an inadequate guarantee of good performance. The concern is less that individual applicants have been dealt with unjustly than that the agencies' policies and practices are largely undisclosed, leaving observers to guess whether administration is sound, fraught with favoritism for special interests, or generally ineffective in controlling costs. It is dangerous simply to assume that the logical rationale offered for the laws' enactment in fact represents the policies being implemented or that the policy reflected in the statute has been properly balanced against other policies. Even

---

[181] California Senate Bill No. 413 (March 12, 1973).

[182] See generally K. DAVIS, DISCRETIONARY JUSTICE: A PRELIMINARY INQUIRY, chs. 3-4 (1969); FRIENDLY, supra note 129; Symposium—Administrative Discretion, 37 LAW & CONTEMP. PROB. 1 (1972). See also notes 183-84 infra.

[183] See, e.g., K. DAVIS, ADMINISTRATIVE LAW TREATISE §§ 4.13-.22 (Supp. 1970); Davis, Administrative Procedure in the Regulation of Banking, 31 LAW & CONTEMP. PROB. 713 (1966).

Perhaps the most important mechanism for openly and efficiently developing and articulating policy is the administrative rule-making process. This procedure normally allows interested parties to criticize proposed regulations in writing or at a special hearing. Courts may insist on rulemaking where an agency appears to be acting without stated principles. See K. DAVIS, ADMINISTRATIVE LAW TREATISE ch. 6, §§ 2.00 to 2.00-6 (Supp. 1970); DAVIS, A New Approach to Delegation, 36 U. CHI. L. REV. 713 (1969); Wright, Beyond Discretionary Justice, 81 YALE L. J. 575, 593 (1972).

with good administrative procedures scrupulously observed, opportunities for political influence, favoritism, and misguided policies will still exist. Indeed, no major regulatory program at the federal level, where administrative law is most fully developed, has escaped criticism that the policies pursued usually advance the interests of the regulated industry itself. Nevertheless, adherence to procedural standards seems very close to being a necessary, though it is certainly not a sufficient, condition for successful regulation.

IV. SOME BEHAVIORAL HYPOTHESES ABOUT CERTIFICATE-OF-NEED AGENCIES

Experience with economic regulation in other areas provides a basis for skepticism that regulatory programs consistently advance the broad public interest. Specific failings have been documented in each regulated industry, and some generalizations have begun to appear valid when measured against industry-by-industry experience. While apparently unexamined in the past, the validity of such generalizations as applied to the agencies charged with administering certificate-of-need laws should be helpful in assessing the efficacy of regulation in the hospital industry.[134]

A. The "Producer-Protection" Hypothesis

Economic regulation is widely assumed to be the direct result of legislative concern for the interests of consumers. Those who accept this premise account for the frequent failure in the regulatory process by the regulated industry's alleged subversion—or "capture"—of the regulatory agency through politically inspired appointments, lucrative employment prospects in industry for cooperative regulators, industry's better opportunity to urge its point of view, its ability to outspend the agency, and its influence with the elected officials who control the agency's appropriations and legislative charter.[135] Solutions to the problem are thought to lie in increased political pressure by consumers, better consumer advocacy, better appointments, and increased appropriations.

---

[134] For a general effort to highlight the problems of regulating in the health care industry, see Havighurst, *Government's Increasing Involvement in the Health Care Sector: The Hazards of Regulation and Less Hazardous Alternatives*, in THE CHANGING ROLE OF THE PUBLIC AND PRIVATE SECTORS IN HEALTH CARE 34 (Report of the 1973 Nat'l Health Forum, Nat'l Health Council, Inc., 1973).

[135] *See, e.g.,* M. BERNSTEIN, REGULATING BUSINESS BY INDEPENDENT COMMISSION (1955). My introduction to regulatory performance follows Jordan, *supra* note 49, at 152-54.

Other views of regulation suggest that demonstrable departures from the public interest are so frequent as to make them the rule rather than the exception, requiring a more sophisticated hypothesis about the reasons regulatory controls were adopted in the first place. Noting the frequency with which benefits accrue to the regulated firms, some observers suggest that protection of producers is the primary object of much regulatory legislation and that industries obtain regulation, like other governmental favors, through strategic use of economic and political power.[136] To account for this success in obtaining protective legislation, the concentrated political power of an industry and its sophisticated awareness of its self-interest may be usefully contrasted both with consumers' inability to inform themselves and to aggregate their interests and with their readiness to believe the politicians' representations that regulatory legislation is for their benefit.

The truth about regulatory agencies probably lies somewhere between the notions of legislative sell-out of the public interest and industry subversion of the regulators. On the one hand, many legislators are essentially naive about how regulation works and, in any event, as busy men concerned primarily with re-election, are apt to be interested as much in appearing to act in the consumer's interest as in doing so in fact. On the other hand, while the political appointment process effectively prevents anti-industry zealots from frequently appearing on regulatory commissions, it also precludes a majority of industry stooges. But even if the balance of power in an agency belongs to reasonable men, it is natural for them to develop a belief in the services rendered by the industry and sympathy for its problems, which will usually appear as obstacles to the continued improvement and wider availability of those services. In these circumstances the compromises reached within a multi-member agency will usually be in keeping with industry interests.

A potentially more useful insight—because it stops short of unequivocally condemning all regulation and supplies a basis for predictions about regulatory behavior—is that an agency's policies are the net product of the various incentives inherent in the operation of a politically responsive bureaucracy. These incentives can to some extent be analyzed and, if necessary, restructured by purposive institutional adjustments. Understanding the incentives affecting agency performance requires not only analysis of the rewards which regulators anticipate—either larger agency

---

[136] Jordan, *supra* note 49; Stigler, *A Theory of Economic Regulation*, 2 BELL J. ECON. & MGT. SCI. 3 (1971).

authority and budgets or individual opportunities upon retirement from the agency—but, more importantly in a political world, an estimation of the strength of the various pressures to which the agency is subjected. Fundamentally, regulators operate on a "minimal squawk" principle,[137] and, depending on the array, attentiveness, comprehension, outspokenness, and influence of the various potential squawkers, regulation may be capable of producing results which closely serve the public interest or which significantly depart from it.[138] Appraisal of the tendencies of a particular regulatory program may be inconclusive, however, since the directions and magnitudes of the various pressures can only be estimated. Yet, while the matter may not be reducible to a simple parallelogram of forces, there will be cases where conclusions can be drawn. If the various constituencies of an agency are well balanced in awareness and influence, some confidence in regulatory performance may be justified. But if the effective pressures seem all to push in the same direction, it must be asked whether that is where the public interest lies.

Prisoner of the Hospital Industry?

Although generalization about the past performance of health planning and certificate-of-need agencies is difficult, there seems to be no basis for discounting provider domination as a problem.[139] Moreover, even if some agencies should be deemed to have surmounted this hazard, long-term predictions of independence may be unjustified, since regulatory agencies have historically been more vigorous in their youth than in their maturity.[140] There may, however, be some organizational structures or other arrangements which are less prone to the kind of performance which gives rise to charges of industry "capture." Experience in the state of New York, where a virtual moratorium has been declared on new hos-

---

[137] Hilton, *supra* note 105, at 48, 53.

[138] Lowi criticizes the theory of "interest-group liberalism" for failing to take account of imperfections in pluralistic bargaining, much as proponents of laissez-faire economics down-play inconvenient deficiencies of the market. T. Lowi, THE END OF LIBERALISM 294-97 (1969). The analysis here takes a cue from Lowi's warning against assuming that interested groups, given the proper setting for bargaining, will produce resolutions which benefit the whole society.

[139] *See* HEALTH-PAC, *supra* note 22, at 191-231; HOSPITAL FRANCHISING, *supra* note 45, at 22 (remarks of Lester Breslow, D. Eugene Sibery, and Steven Sieverts); P. O'DON-OGHUE, A. BRYANT, & P. SHAUGHNESSY, A DESCRIPTIVE ANALYSIS OF CHP "B" AGENCIES 79-80 (1973); Douglass, *Effect of Provider Attitudes in Community Health Decision-making*, 11 MED. CARE 135 (1973). *See also* notes 216-18 *infra* and accompanying text.

[140] *See, e.g.*, BERNSTEIN, *supra* note 135, at 79-91.

pital beds under the certificate-of-need law, provides an instructive example.

In New York, the certificate-of-need agency is the Department of Health, which is also directly responsible for setting politically sensitive Medicaid reimbursement rates[141] and for advising the Insurance Department on the setting of highly visible Blue Cross premiums. Since 1970 it has also possessed direct rate-setting authority over individual hospitals,[142] a power which it has exerted so strictly that most of the hospitals in the state are operating at a deficit.[143] Although one can question the fairness of giving a major buyer of care the power virtually to name its own price,[144] combining political responsibility for costs and regulatory power over hospital rates in the same agency does succeed in structuring the regulators' incentives to assure that the public's interest in economy is not sacrificed to the hospitals' interests.

The New York arrangement so completely avoids the imputation of industry capture of the agency that the state hospital association is arguing that New York should create an independent commission to regulate the hospitals.[145] The association's plan adopts the public utility model in a relatively pure form and would free the agency of all responsibility for financing care. Experience with other such "independent" commissions clearly warrants the proponents' obvious expectation that such an agency would be more responsive to industry interests.[146]

---

[141] See Stevens & Stevens, *Medicaid: Anatomy of a Dilemma*, 35 LAW & CONTEMP. PROB. 348, 386-88 (1970).

[142] N.Y. PUB. HEALTH LAW § 2807 (McKinney Supp. 1972).

[143] Hospital Ass'n of New York State, Survey of Fiscal Pressures on Hospitals in New York State, Oct. 12, 1972 (mimeo.), summarized in *Reasons for Concern*, HOSPITAL FORUM, Dec. 1972, at 9.

[144] Constitutional protection against "confiscatory" rates is presumably available under principles similar to those which courts employ in reviewing rates allowed regulated utilities. *See* 1 KAHN, *supra* note 46, at 37-41. *Compare* Sigety v. Ingraham, 29 N.Y.2d 110, 272 N.E.2d 524, 324 N.Y.S.2d 10 (1971). An interesting issue would arise if certain capital investments were held not eligible for depreciation because the facilities invested were not "needed." On the so-called "prudent investment" rule, see Missouri *ex rel.* Southwestern Bell Tel. Co. v. Missouri Pub. Serv. Comm'n, 262 U.S. 276, 289, n.1 (1923) (concurring opinion). On the requirement that property in the "rate base" be "used or useful" in the public service, see F. WELCH, CASES AND TEXT ON PUBLIC UTILITY REGULATION ch.8 (1961).

[145] HOSPITAL FORUM, Dec. 1972, at 2-8.

[146] See also Hospital Ass'n of Pennsylvania, Circular Letter No. 593, Feb. 22, 1973, in which the association announces changing its proposal for an independent Hospital Care Commission to a plan for vesting the same regulatory authority in the state Department of Health.

Most certificate-of-need programs feature neither a measure of financing responsibility, as in the New York model, nor an independent regulatory commission. Rather, they most frequently involve a single decision maker subject to political appointment and removal. Some view this model as increasing agency responsiveness to the executive and therefore political accountability for agency performance, a quality allegedly lacking in the case of the independent commissions.[147] However, such accountability might not provide adequate protection for the public interest if the incumbent governor demonstrated systematic preferences only for those constituents who could influence, with either votes or money, his or his party's future success at the polls.[148] Thus there is a basis for preferring control of regulatory programs by the less monolithic mechanism of the legislature. The efficacy of particular arrangements will of course depend on the power relationships in particular state governments.

Several certificate-of-need programs lodge major decision-making responsibility, either advisory or actual, in nongovernmental planning agencies and advisory councils made up of part-time participants perhaps half of whom are unconnected with provider interests.[149] The nonprovider majorities on such bodies should feel no desire to curry favor with the regulated industry and should evince a weaker dedication than is found in more typical regulatory bodies to expanding the power and dominion of the agency as an end in itself.[150] The defect in this model

---

[147] PRESIDENT'S ADVISORY COUNCIL ON EXECUTIVE ORGANIZATION, A NEW REGULATORY FRAMEWORK: REPORT ON SELECTED INDEPENDENT REGULATORY AGENCIES (1971). For a critique, see R. NOLL, REFORMING REGULATION: AN EVALUATION OF THE ASH COUNCIL PROPOSALS (1971).

[148] How hospitals exercise political influence would be an interesting study. Although political campaign contributions by the hospitals themselves would be unseemly, boards of trustees are likely to include major contributors and persons having other kinds of influence. Moreover, as hospitals are perceived as community enterprises, no one is likely to regard even the most overt pressure as improper.

[149] The New York State Public Health Council and State Hospital Review and Planning Council are examples.

[150] Nongovernmental health planning institutions often derive a portion of their financial support directly from the hospitals or hospital trade associations, creating a dependency whereby "capture" of local planners by local hospitals could occur. A recent study reveals a strong positive correlation between involvement of areawide health planning agencies in facilities regulation and bed control and the extent of financial support drawn from the hospital industry. O'DONOGHUE, BRYANT, & SHAUGHNESSY, supra note 139, at 14-15, 39-40, 46-47, 63-65, 79-80 (1973). Although the average contribution by hospitals to "B" agency budgets is only six percent, id. at 15, the concentration of these funds in those agencies with the most power to influence industry welfare is at least a suspicious circumstance.

is that such decision makers may be unduly dependent for advice and direction on the provider representatives and the agency staff, whom they will regard as experts. Nevertheless, the agency or council members themselves will be largely free, in terms of their personal stakes and prospects, to pursue the public interest as they see it. Moreover, the staff may find it useful to have such a prestigious body, possessing credibility and independence, to shield them from the impact of politically sensitive decisions. This decision-making model has not been much used in other fields and may prove more trustworthy than traditional models.

Organizational factors aside, there remains a potential basis for a convergence of viewpoint between the regulated hospitals and the health planners, the group from which most agency staff members are recruited. Dedicated to developing a more rational and more humanitarian health care system, the planners are likely to contemplate a long list of projects which they believe would contribute to this goal. Their shopping list is apt to be expensive and to contain at least some luxuries.[151] Because many of the desired programs could easily be hospital-based, there is at least a potential ground for agreement between the planners and the regulated industry on the desirability of a larger hospital sector. Similarly, consumer representatives on state boards and advisory councils are quite likely to share in the general enthusiasm for more and better health services so long as duplication is avoided. Although disagreements over the priorities attached to different types of services would inevitably exist, a joint-venture attitude could easily develop if financing problems could be overcome.[152]

Tool of an Industry Cartel?

It is frequently observed, without reference to the theory of agency "capture" as an explanation, that regulatory agencies tend to adopt strategies disturbingly similar to those which an industry-wide cartel or monopoly would pursue if it could.[153] Thus, prices are frequently maintained well above competitive levels, and price discrimination—that is,

---

[151] For a typical shopping list, see Gentry, Veney, Kaluzny, Sprague, and Coulter, Attitudes and Perceptions of Health Service Providers: Implications for Implementation and Delivery of Community Health Services, Oct. 13, 1971 (revised version of a paper presented to the American Public Health Ass'n, Minneapolis, Minnesota).

[152] The prospects for such a development are explored in the text accompanying notes 170-77 *infra*.

[153] *E.g.,* Jordan, *supra* note 49.

pricing which exploits consumers' varying willingness to pay—is facilitated by restrictions which prevent both industry insiders and outsiders from seizing competitive opportunities and thereby driving prices down toward marginal cost.

Does hospital industry support for certificate-of-need laws imply an expectation that the regulators, even if not subject to "capture," will see things the same way that the industry does? Certainly the industry and the regulators appear to agree that capacity must be limited. This confluence of views is explained by Martin Feldstein's demonstration that new bed supply both stimulates new demand and depresses prices[154] since, if the effect of new supply were pure, consensus would not occur. If new supply always generated enough new customers at the original price, the industry would be antagonistic to public intervention, and, if the only impact of new supply was to lower prices in a competitive market, the industry alone would have good reason to see it suppressed.

Although it would be hard to document, a fairly close correlation probably exists between industry attitudes toward certificate-of-need laws and the relative strengths of the two effects of new supply.[155] Thus, the recent decline in occupancy rates of hospital beds, which can only have accentuated the price-depressing effect of new supply, has been accompanied by increased lobbying for regulatory controls.[156] Parity of reasoning suggests that a slackening of industry support for supply restrictions would accompany agency success in moving the industry out of the area where the adverse price effect of new supply is strongest. The pernicious impact of third-party cost reimbursement and provider influence over demand will thus continue to be felt, not only in the eagerness of individual providers to expand but also in industry attitudes toward enforcement of certificate-of-need laws. Indeed, it seems likely that, given the continuation of third-party payment, the hospital industry's strategy will be to restrict supply only to a point considerably higher than the public interest dictates. The problem is therefore not that an agency under strong industry influence would excessively restrict

---

154 *See* note 60 *supra* and accompanying text.

155 For this observation, I rely on my earlier one, *supra* note 60, that the relative strength of the two effects depends upon the extent to which existing demand-creation opportunities are already being exploited. Indeed, real medical need shades gradually into provider-created demand, and neither can be understood except in relation to both marginal and total cost.

156 I have been able to find no correlation between occupancy rate trends and enactment of certificate-of-need laws, however.

supply, as classical cartels have done, but that it might not restrict it enough.

If the hospital industry resists extending supply restrictions beyond its own welfare-maximizing point, who will oppose it and keep the agency attuned to true consumer interests? Consumers will probably fail to present a united front on these issues, but even the most cost-conscious will find it hard to oppose more and better services so long as the most obvious duplication and overcapacity is avoided. In these circumstances, the main constituency influencing the vigor of certificate-of-need enforcement would usually be the hospital industry itself, and its preferences would be influenced by the system's continued reliance on cost-plus pricing and by the phenomenon of supply which seems to generate its own demand. In this event, enforcement would be effective only in reducing egregious overbedding and obvious duplication of facilities.

The cartel hypothesis would not hold under the New York expedient of lodging certification of need and direct responsibility for costs in the same agency. Even in these circumstances, however, the regulators, the overseeing politicians, and most consumer groups as well would lose interest in health care costs as soon as they were brought into line with the cost of living. This would occur because political forces respond primarily to the direction and rate of change and are much less concerned with the correctness of the absolute level of cost or activity achieved by a particular program—hence, the extreme difficulty of raising taxes and the almost total lack of pressure to reduce them. Thus, even if certification of need were made the responsibility of the most cost-conscious state agency, the equilibrium point would be such that hospitals' gross revenues would not be reduced.

Friend of Industry Insiders?

Whether or not unduly responsive to industry interests in general, regulatory agencies are sometimes subject to undue political influence exerted on behalf of particular private interests by legislators and the executive branch. Although it is difficult to generalize about the vulnerability of regulatory programs to such influences, it probably varies with such factors as the agency's esprit and sense of purpose, its dependence for budgetary and other support on legislative and executive favor, the regulators' independence in terms of tenure, and the visibility of the decisions reached. The tendency of regulatory agencies to aggrandize industry insiders is frequently justified on the ground of preferring applicants with good "track records" over unknown quantities. But the result of such a policy over time is to increase the size of industry incumbents and to foreclose new participants. This tendency is most likely to be present where political influence is a significant factor and where award of new privileges is seen as compensation for past cooperation.[157]

That certificate-of-need agencies are subject to a considerable amount of political pressure is clear. Applications to the agency are apt to be of intense local interest, and civic leaders naturally rely heavily on their political representatives in matters of this kind. Moreover, the nonprofit character and/or community identification of most hospitals lead naturally to acceptance on all sides of the propriety of resorting to political influence. Furthermore, since one precept of health planning is that it should allow community judgments to emerge, politicization is viewed as a desirable thing. Nevertheless, reliance on political influence and infighting under circumstances where the public's interest in cost control is weakly asserted is likely to produce regulatory outcomes skewed in favor of influential institutions. Lacking a constituency actively supporting it in an aggressive role, the certificate-of-need agency may be inclined to let many influentially backed projects proceed even though it would really rather stop them.[158]

Limited investigation suggests further that established community hospitals, major medical centers, hospitals associated with religious and similar organizations, and well-entrenched proprietaries seem to be capable of receiving special attention for applications which would be rejected

---

[157] The Civil Aeronautics Board is perhaps the most notorious agency in this regard, preferring its trunkline carrier constituency over all challengers to such an extent that no new trunk carriers have been admitted to the industry in the thirty-five years since the Civil Aeronautics Act was passed. CAVES, *supra* note 49, at 169-76.

[158] The files on applications which were frequently consulted contained letters from legislators and other officials and courteous, noncommittal replies. Agency personnel generally acknowledged such contracts, though they were reluctant to admit any deleterious effects. Some applications were frankly described as being politically touchy, however, and in one agency it was clear—and it is a safe assumption generally—that action on such applications is frequently deferred to avoid disapproval and that accommodations which would permit approval are actively sought.

In another state a file was found to contain the following handwritten note by a subordinate made preparatory to a decision on a particular application to build a new proprietary hospital, which was competing with two other applications:

Environment: [State] Senator [X] pressure; Dr. [Applicant]'s bad mouthing and pressure on [Agency Director]: [Deputy Director] "very impressed" with [Applicant], thinks it politically wise to act soon—immediately—in [Applicant's] favor; [Director] marching orders—"decision by Monday morning"; generally: pressure from all sides to accept [areawide agency's] recom and give [Applicant] go ahead.

out of hand if submitted by less well-connected interests.[159] The long-run consequence of such systematic preferences is that larger hospitals grow while new facilities are discouraged; incumbents enjoy an unwritten presumption in proposing to replace their outmoded facilities; "satellites" of existing hospitals are favored over new entrants; and "chains" and other proprietaries are excluded in favor of existing facilities or community-sponsored organizations. Perhaps economies of scale and quality considerations could in some measure justify these tendencies,[160] but the end result is less consumer choice and more concentrated control in local markets.

The inability of new entrants to obtain certificates of need is not attributable solely to political factors, for the mechanics of this form of regulation alone make displacement of an established provider difficult. Once bed needs have been filled, new facilities can be built only if old beds are shut down, and the agency generally lacks the power to close down existing facilities.[161] Thus, an existing provider, which can offer to replace old facilities even at a different location, has almost a license in perpetuity. Moreover, the lack of incentives for nonprofit firms to sell out even when operating failing enterprises increases the would-be entrant's difficulties in buying up "operating rights."[162]

Many observers will find the entrenchment and aggrandizement of existing providers, whether due to political influence or to the nature of the regulatory scheme adopted largely at the insiders' behest, to be an unattractive feature of certificate-of-need laws. However, the more destructive consequence of a regulatory system in which established providers exercise extensive influence is likely to be the exclusion of desirable innovations which threaten the industry's financial structure. Because this type of producer protection is very nearly the "clincher" in the argument against certificate-of-need laws, its discussion is deferred.

---

[159] *See, e.g.,* text accompanying notes 217-18 *infra.*

[160] The extent of economies of scale in hospitals is the subject of debate. *See* Lave & Lave, *Hospital Cost Functions,* 60 AM. ECON. REV. 379, 394 (1970). *See* Pauly, *supra* note 63. Regulators may be inclined to exaggerate their importance, however, and hence to underestimate opportunities for competition. It is important to distinguish the numerous different services supplied by hospitals in assessing scale economies. *See* text accompanying notes 73-76 *supra.*

[161] Interviews in New York indicated that this situation prevails there.

[162] Although frequently employed in other regulated industries, this term is unlikely, for obvious reasons, to be employed in health care. A few states expressly declare certificates of need to be nontransferable, and only Tennessee expressly permits transfers.

Facilitator of the Industry's Good Works?

Producer protection by regulatory agencies may be more rational and less sinister than the foregoing discussion suggests. Indeed, producers frequently have a strong claim to protection since numerous useful services which are supplied at a loss by the regulated firms would be discontinued if the regulatory agency permitted the firms' revenues to be eroded by competition. The more conspiratorial interpretations of agency behavior may therefore miss the point. One does not have to be corrupt or an industry mouthpiece to endorse the provision of transportation services, electric power, communications services, or other products of the regulated industry which otherwise might not be provided. The next section of the Article, examining the "internal subsidization" phenomenon by which such good works are fostered, leads to some insights about regulation which have considerable bearing on regulatory initiatives in health care. In short, even without the hospital industry's political domination of the regulatory process, regulatory policies are likely to be unduly protective and to foster both inflation and an excessive allocation of resources to the hospital sector. It is simply ironic that such results are the precise opposite of what certificate-of-need proponents promise.

B. The "Taxation-by-Regulation" Hypothesis

Internal Subsidization and Resource Allocation

Programs of economic regulation nearly always require the regulated firm to render various unremunerative services.[163] These services receive financial support from the revenues earned by other services, which are priced well above cost. This "internal subsidization," which could not occur systematically in a competitive market and would not be tolerated by a profit-maximizing monopolist, has been incorporated by Richard Posner into a theory of regulation. He treats regulation as a hitherto unrecognized mechanism of public finance whereby a franchised firm is permitted in effect to impose an excise tax on some of its services on the condition that it apply the excess revenues to providing certain other services, thought to be needed by the public, at less than their cost.[164] Rather than appropriate tax monies, the legislature in effect delegates

---

163 For some examples, see note 166 *infra* and references cited in note 164 *infra*.

164 Posner, *supra* note 78. *See also* Comanor & Mitchell, *The Costs of Planning: The FCC and Cable Television*, 15 J. LAW & ECON. 177 (1972), identifying the same phenomenon as "planning by regulation" and emphasizing the regulators' pursuit of positive goals conceived as being in the public interest. These two articles provide an excellent

the power to tax and spend for public purposes to the regulatory agency
and tolerates the agency's redelegation of these powers to private interests. The title of Posner's article provides a good descriptive name for
this phenomenon—"taxation by regulation."

Internal subsidization can be criticized because it necessitates much of
the protectionism which characterizes all regulation. Market entry and
the expansion of existing firms must be controlled to prevent the high
monopoly price on certain services from inducing new supply of those
services, perhaps offered by firms which, in spite of their lower prices,
are less efficient than the incumbent. In the eyes of the regulators, preservation of the regulated firm and its ability to earn monopoly returns on
some services becomes an essential means of carrying out purposes they
conceive to be desirable. Once this frame of reference is established,
there is practically no room left for using competition as a check on performance or for relying on market signals to guide investment.

Another objection to this mechanism for subsidizing public services
is that the usual governmental process of taxation, authorization, appropriation, and expenditure is bypassed.[165] As a result of their low visibility,
internal subsidies may support unneeded services or may redistribute income from the more affluent to the less affluent.[166] Assessment of the

---

insight into an essential characteristic of regulation, which is described by Hilton, *supra*
note 105, at 50, as a tendency "to generate monopoly gain in one activity, either through
administering a cartel or maintaining a monopoly, and then to dissipate it in uneconomic
activity."

[165] *See* note 172 *infra.*

[166] It is impossible to determine whether subsidies accomplished by this method are
more or less progressive in their net effect than other government programs. The
identification of gainers and losers in the following examples is instructive: Freight
carriers are required to serve outlying areas and small shippers at rates which are below
cost for the particular service; similarly, airlines are expected to use profits from heavily
traveled routes to provide service to smaller towns. Products of particular favored industries are required to be hauled at discriminatorily low rates, while tariffs on other goods
are kept well above cost to make up the difference. Before Amtrak, passenger trains
were compelled to run at losses which the railroads had to make up on freight traffic,
with substantial benefits to suburban commuters. The FCC expects broadcasters to plow
back some portion of their advertising revenues into "public interest" programming, a
category which includes mostly things which appeal only to intellectual and cultural
elites. Utility rates do not return the cost of service in all cases, an example being
Comsat, which must price its Atlantic and Pacific satellite services at the same level in
order to promote the latter at the expense of users of the former. Many transportation
and communication services are compelled because, though presently unremunerative,
they are potentially valuable for "national defense" purposes, though their cost does not
appear in the defense (or any other) budget. *See generally* Breyer, *The Ash Council's
Report on the Independent Regulatory Agencies,* 2 BELL J. ECON. & MGT. SCI. 628, 633-35
(1971); Posner, *supra* note 78, at 23-24, 29-34.

total impact of such subsidies is impossible,[167] but the public has little opportunity to judge the cost or merits of particular subsidies fostered by the regulators. Although reliance on internal subsidies could sometimes be a rational and efficient approach to income redistribution and the provision of public services, it would be unfortunate if policy makers were to favor such secret financing precisely because of its attendant nonaccountability.

Another hazard of internal subsidization is the considerable risk that an excessive amount of society's resources will be allocated to the regulated industry. The agency's power to tax some users and to use the proceeds for what it perceives to be good works is limited only by its ingenuity in finding worthy projects within the industry's competence. The regulators will be supported in their judgments both by the beneficiaries of the subsidies, who may be politically influential, and by the regulated firms themselves, who, assured of a "fair rate of return" on their total investment, will be happy to expand their scope. Believing in the service and being glad to broaden their own authority and influence, the regulators will have no occasion to question whether the money might find better uses elsewhere in the economy. The result, according to Roger G. Noll, is that "regulatory policy might accurately be characterized as maximizing the size of the regulated industry . . . ." [168]

---

[167] *See, e.g.,* Rottenberg, *Misplaced Emphases in Wars on Poverty,* 31 LAW & CONTEMP. PROB. 64 (1966); Stigler, *Director's Law of Public Income Redistribution,* 13 J. LAW & ECON. 1 (1970). Subsidies of this kind are apt to be inefficient, entailing sacrifice of potential welfare gains (consumer surplus) without yielding an equivalent amount of dollars to be used as subsidies. Direct taxation would therefore be preferable. *See* Comanor & Mitchell, *supra* note 164, at 197-98, 204, 206. These authors attempt to calculate the welfare losses imposed by the FCC on would-be cable television subscribers in order to provide other broadcasting services. Internal subsidization seems not to be as inefficient in health care as in other fields, however, because of health insurance. Indeed, if insurance coverage were complete and demand were therefore perfectly price-inelastic—that is, unrelated to price—excess charges on some services would cause no welfare loss from services forgone. Nevertheless, health insurance is itself inefficient, since the internal subsidies which it provides (from one insured to another) induce overconsumption of health resources.

[168] NOLL, *supra* note 147, at 16. *See also* Comanor & Mitchell, *supra* note 164, at 184:
    This concern with television revenues is characteristic of FCC policies and indeed of regulatory commissions generally. Factors which restrict revenues, and thereby the scale of the regulated industries, are immediately suspect, while factors which increase the revenues and size of the sector are to be encouraged. Given a sector-by-sector approach to economic planning, this is to be expected. A larger sector gives rise to greater prospects for regulatory "good works" while a smaller sector does not. Few regulatory authorities would wish to be concerned primarily with a declining sector of the economy, and the view that this might possibly represent a desired reallocation of resources is likely to be anathema to them. *Planning*

Internal Subsidies and Hospitals

Internal subsidization is already an important phenomenon in the hospital industry. Laboratory, x-ray and pharmacy services, and basic per diem charges are ordinarily profitable, while obstetric care, the emergency room, and the intensive care unit are usually subsidized in some degree. Where hospitals have underutilized facilities, revenues from other services usually support them. Perhaps the most defensible use of internal subsidies in hospitals, that which supports care for indigent patients, was recently underscored by the "free-care" requirement imposed by the federal government on all hospitals which have benefitted from the Hill-Burton program.[169] Although pressures from third-party payment programs have begun to narrow the hospitals' freedom to engage in internal subsidization, it is still an important mechanism for financing health care and is tolerated as such by most of the financing programs.

Although the "cream-skimming" issue lurks constantly in the background, certificate-of-need laws are not conceived solely as protectionist measures or to perpetuate internal subsidization. Nevertheless, as long as a need requirement is enforced, discriminatory pricing cannot be eliminated by competition which drives prices down to cost. Moreover, by requiring approval of service cutbacks some states have adopted the franchising model with its dependence on internal subsidies to support obligatory but unremunerative services. In short, some continued dependence on internal subsidies is a necessary by-product of certificate-of-need legislation.

Because certificate-of-need agencies usually lack control over hospital rates and third-party cost-reimbursement formulas, they are unable to impose the "tax" which may be necessary to make certain "needed" services or facilities feasible. If hospitals therefore propose only potentially self-supporting services, the internal subsidization possibilities in hospitals seem unlikely to expand under certificate-of-need requirements. Rather, the prevalence of subsidized services would be largely in the hands of

---

by regulation leads directly to actions which generally distort the allocation of resources between the regulated and the unregulated sectors of the economy.

[169] 42 C.F.R. § 53.111 (1972). It was clear from the vigorous industry opposition to that requirement that many institutions were not dedicating substantial resources to indigent care, but this did not mean that services of other kinds were not being subsidized. The original proposal would have required 5 percent of operating costs to be dedicated to free or below-cost care, 37 Fed. Reg. 7632 (1972); this was reduced three percent in the final regulation. *See Hill-Burton 5 Per Cent: Who Will Pay When Those Who Do Pay Won't Pay Any More?*, MODERN HOSPITAL, June 1972, at 21.

those with ultimate authority over hospital charges—the rate regulators, where they exist, and the third-party payers—either of whom might be unimpressed by an agency's determination of the need for a service which was a candidate for subsidy through the cost-reimbursement formula. Thus, although certificate-of-need laws involve a clear rejection of competition as a force corrective of internal subsidization, they do not necessarily foster internal subsidization in other ways.

To the extent that an agency determination of need for a service effectively guarantees its financial support by third-party payers, the case is analogous to public utility regulation. Under public utility principles, the regulated firm is entitled to a rate schedule which promises recovery of its total costs, plus a fair return on investment, even though some obligatory services must be offered at a loss.[170] Although certificate-of-need laws separate need determinations from financial support, some hospitals and some planners urge more unified control. With many unremunerative services legally mandated or regarded as a duty, the hospitals can legitimately complain when the financing is not forthcoming or, indeed, is eroded by controls imposed by government or other third-party payers who, in the hospitals' view, should share the responsibility.[171] The health planners, on the other hand, sense many unmet needs and desire the power to compel the provision of certain unremunerative services through the franchising of hospitals. But franchising alone would not assure third-party payers' support for services other than those received by their beneficiaries. In these circumstances, the pressure—and indeed the apparent logical case—for public utility regulation is quite strong. Under such regulation, the rates to be paid would be fixed by the same regulators who authorized the services to be rendered.[172]

The case against the public utility model rests fundamentally on considerations of resource allocation, although concerns about inefficiency,

---

170 Baltimore & O.R.R. v. United States, 345 U.S. 146 (1953); United Rys. v. West, 280 U.S. 234 (1930).

171 The proposal by New York hospitals for an independent hospital regulatory commission arises from precisely this set of concerns. See text and accompanying notes 141-46 *supra*.

172 An alternative means of obtaining needed services with greater accountability would be by contract between local governments and providers. See Havighurst, *Franchising Experience From Other Industries and Its Relevance for the Health Field*, in HOSPITAL FRANCHISING, *supra* note 45, at 11, 14. Emergency medical services are sometimes provided in this manner. For a thoughtful endorsement of direct subsidies and rejection of internal subsidies in providing health services to rural residents, see Billings & Paul, *Commercial Airlines Industry: Some Lessons for Health Services Planners*, 11 MED. CARE 145, 151 (1973).

special privileges, repression of innovation, and monopoly also warrant reservations.[173] With 7.6 percent of the gross national product now dedicated to health care and with per capita expenditures on health five times what they were in 1950 and doubling between 1965 and 1972,[174] the adoption of a regulatory system which has uniformly dedicated itself in other settings to, in Noll's words, "maximizing the size of the regulated industry" seems at best a dubious policy. Although all regulated industries have demonstrated allocative inefficiencies, particularly with respect to industry size vis-à-vis the rest of the economy, none of them has offered a potential for growth approaching that of the health care industry. Even without internal subsidies protected by regulatory restrictions, belief in health care as an end in itself, the unlimited commitment to ever-improving quality and accessibility, the continuing scientific and technological explosion, and the further weakening of cost constraints through expanded third-party payment together add up to a considerable potential bill.[175] But when this sum is multiplied by the hidden and virtually inexhaustible revenue source, the planners' enthusiasm for many hospital-based services,[176] and the ever-present necessity for log-rolling in response to numerous clamoring interest groups, the prospect for further inflation in health care costs is staggering.

---

[173] See Havighurst, supra note 172.

[174] Cooper & Worthington, National Health Expenditures 1929-1972, Soc. Sec. Bull., Jan. 1973, at 3, 12, 13. Sweden spends a greater proportion of GNP on health care, England very much less. See generally O. Anderson, Health Care: Can There Be Equity? (1972).

[175] It can be argued that people exaggerate the benefits which can be derived from health care and fail to get value for money. See A. Cochrane, Effectiveness and Efficiency: Random Reflections on Health Services (1972); Neuhauser, The Future of Proprietaries in the Health Care System, in AEI Proceedings, supra note 6. As society assumes responsibility for health care, grave ethical difficulties accompany efforts to limit expenditures, and high costs may be incurred in order to avoid facing these choices. See generally Nat'l Heart and Lung Institute, Report of the Artificial Heart Assessment Panel (1973); Fried, The Value of Life, 82 Harv. L. Rev. 1415 (1969); Schelling, The Life You Save May Be Your Own, in Problems in Public Expenditure Analysis 127 (S. Chase ed. 1968); Zeckhauser, Coverage for Catastrophic Illness, 1972 (Harvard University, Kennedy School of Government, Public Policy Program Discussion Paper No. 12); Calabresi, "Toward a Theory of Tragic Choices," April, 1973 (lectures delivered at the University of Pennsylvania Law School).

[176] Lest it be thought that the hospital sector is already so large as to be incapable of further growth, recall that many of those exerting pressure for franchising and utility-type regulation view it as a means of carrying out an agenda of "needed" projects which hospitals, lacking financial assurances, have heretofore been reluctant to undertake. See text accompanying notes 151-52 supra.

The political environment offers little ground for reassurance. The regulators' small successes in preventing duplication and in vetoing occasional projects would merely obscure their contribution to inflation and, together with the vested interests spawned by the expanded subsidies, make legislative adjustments difficult to accomplish. On the other hand, the regulators might ultimately face political risks if health care costs continue their rapid rise. With this as the only check on the regulators' ability to foster expansion, however, there would be only a slow-down in the rate of inflation and certainly no substantial opportunity to reduce costs below the level eventually attained; as noted previously, political forces are concerned with costs only in proportion to their rate of increase.

In summary, the mechanisms of public utility regulation must seem on balance a distinctly unpromising means of imposing control on the health care system and its already remarkable ability to absorb resources. Indeed, it is a cause for wonder that a mechanism which has been widely criticized precisely because it misallocates resources is today being offered by sincere individuals as a means of obtaining more efficient allocative results in the health care system.

C. The "Brushfire-Wars" Hypothesis

The historical roots of certificate-of-need laws in health planning and the present involvement of CHP agencies in the certificate-of-need process may prompt an expectation that certificate-of-need programs will feature a strong planning orientation and be thereby distinguishable from other regulatory efforts. But if agencies exhaust their energies on problems of the moment—fighting "brushfire wars" [177]—and if health

---

[177] Time has corrected one dearly held illusion. It was thought in the heyday of the New Deal that an operating administrative agency, because of its continuous exposure to the problems of an area, was ideally fitted for progressive planning and programming. We have found that such is not the case. The agency is so deeply, so anxiously involved in solving the problems of the moment that most of its effort goes out in keeping astride of its operating agenda. Furthermore, buffetted by strong, opposing forces it looks for compromise, expediency, and short-term solutions. After its first strenuous years of conflict with those whom it must regulate, it may arrive at a modus vivendi which it looks upon and pronounces to be good. Radical planning under such conditions is not impossible, but it is unlikely. L. JAFFE, JUDICIAL CONTROL OF ADMINISTRATIVE ACTION 51 (1965). See also BERNSTEIN, supra note 135, at 176-79; NOLL, supra note 147, at 93-94; E. WILLIAMS, THE REGULATION OF RAIL-MOTOR RATE COMPETITION 201-15 (1958). Specific planning failures are documented in CAVES, supra note 49 ("The timing and substance of policies on such important

planning therefore turns out to be largely a euphemism for a political bargaining-out of differences among interest groups, it will be fair to conclude that certificate-of-need programs will probably be plagued by the same weaknesses which similar regulatory schemes have consistently revealed.

Planning and Regulation

The adoption of comprehensive regulatory programs for particular industries has usually been accompanied by an expectation that planning and coordination would be facilitated by the use of administrative mechanisms.[178] These hopes have been regularly disappointed, however, as the agencies strive to keep up with immediate problems. Absorbed in deciding inconsequential issues of equity such as which of several applicants shall provide a given service, the agencies are unable to perform the socially more important job of prescribing the industry's structure, determining which services should be offered, and deciding how needed change can be promoted.[179] In many cases, the equitable distribution of the burdens and benefits of regulation and the strengthening of the weaker firms have become primary regulatory goals.[180]

The reason most frequently offered for the inadequacy of regulatory planning efforts is the scarcity of agency resources. Although arguably agencies are funded only at the level necessary to permit them to perform their most pressing functions, it is possible that some kind of Parkinson's

things as the irregular airlines, passenger fares, and the treatment of the local-service carriers are explainable only with reference to the political environment . . . ." *Id.* at 298); Johnson, *supra* note 49. Comanor & Mitchell, *supra* note 164, point out that the "planning" functions most favored by regulators are those which involve the sponsoring of "good works" by internal subsidization.

[178] *See, e.g.,* National Transportation Policy, 49 U.S.C. § 1 (1970) (Note preceding § 1, originally enacted as Act of Sept. 18, 1940, ch. 722, tit. I, 54 Stat. 899).

[179] Cramton, *The Effectiveness of Economic Regulation: A Legal View,* 54 AM. ECON. REV. 182 (1964). *See also* 2 KAHN, *supra* note 46, at 86-92.

[180] The ICC, charged with regulating several modes of surface transport, has adopted policies which are

consistent with a point of view which concerns itself primarily with what must be done in fairness to the carriers which have actually been competing for the particular traffic in issue. It is consistent with keeping everyone in the business. It does not, however, contribute to the development of a more economic division of the traffic, to coordination of the services, or to the development of economy in the handling of the available business.

WILLIAMS, *supra* note 177, at 214. *See also* Hilton, *supra* note 105, at 48-49.

law operates to absorb added agency resources in new brushfire wars, perhaps triggering an expansion of the regulatory domain rather than an increase in planning activities.[181] The commission members themselves may not value planning highly, due to the limited term of their appointments, the lack of pressure to examine and justify policies, and the necessity for tackling the agenda at hand before going on to grander designs. Often the problems which need to be dealt with through planning are so difficult and controversial as to be totally intractable. Even when substantial planning efforts have occurred,[182] they are often short-lived, and their benefit is often dissipated by the press of events and politics, the changing membership of the agency, and the difficulties of implementing major changes.

The difficulty may go much deeper than these explanations suggest. Planning and regulation can be said to differ in that on occasion the former requires major policy decisions which are harmful to the regulated interests.[183] The political environment and the view that the public interest inheres in compromise and accommodation among competing interests have made such decisions impossible under regulation. True to their political orientation, the regulators have defined their function as that of mediating among interest groups rather than defining the public interest objectively and forcing the regulated firms to accept it. As a result, the equilibria achieved are guaranteed to give even an articulate and well represented public only part of a loaf and to be even more biased in favor of the regulated group when, as usually happens, it takes the greatest interest in the matter. Theodore J. Lowi's diagnosis of the shortcomings of "interest-group liberalism" seems well sustained by the performance of the regulatory agencies: "Liberal governments can-

---

[181] See NOLL, *supra* note 147, at 82.

[182] The few substantial planning efforts which have been undertaken from time to time by administrative agencies have been generally applauded. *E.g.*, FPC, NATIONAL POWER SURVEY (1964); SEC, SPECIAL STUDY OF THE SECURITIES MARKETS (1963). *See generally* 2 KAHN, *supra* note 46, at 64-86, emphasizing the gaps in agency power to promote coordination.

[183] Charles Reich faults regulation for being too narrowly conceived and focused and for being dedicated to compromise:

> As the agencies have sought a meaning for the public interest, they have come to this: the public interest is served by agency policies which harmonize as many as possible of the competing interests present in a given situation . . . In all of these cases it is thought that the public interest requires some recognition of the claims of each interest that can be identified.

Reich, *The Law of the Planned Society*, 75 YALE L.J. 1227, 1234 (1966).

not plan. Planning requires the authoritative use of authority. Planning requires law, choice, priorities, moralities. Liberalism replaces planning with bargaining." [184]

Because politicized regulation permits at best only incremental change, it is less appropriate where there is substantial discontent with the status quo. Thus, certificate-of-need laws are favored by those who see them merely as fixing a small defect in an industry which is otherwise performing acceptably. The regulatory approach should be less appealing to those who wish to preserve and expand opportunities for major change in the health care system. [185]

Planning-cum-Regulation in the Certificate-of-Need and Planning Agencies

In spite of their origins in health planning, certificate-of-need laws are essentially regulatory in character. Indeed, some observers perceive a danger that by converting the traditional planning agencies into politicized, quasi-regulatory bodies, certificate-of-need laws will debase health

---

[184] Lowi, *supra* note 138, at 101. Although Reich observes the same tendency to compromise, *see* note 183 *supra*, he and Lowi part company on the remedies. Reich pleads for broader interest-group representation and administrative responsibility to encompass a broader range of interests. Lowi, on the other hand, wants more specific legislative mandates and more administrative rule making, believing that administrators can carry out specific directives but succumb to compromises when told merely to pursue the public interest. The two models probably fit different circumstances, Reich's being possibly appropriate as a means of protecting against "spillover" effects on environmental and "consciousness-III" interests. *See, e.g.,* National Environmental Policy Act, 42 U.S.C. §§ 4321 *et seq.* (1971); C. REICH, THE GREENING OF AMERICA (1970); Breyer, *supra* note 166, at 635-37, and Lowi's being better suited to cases where regulation is directed to a specific market failure. The problems addressed by certificate-of-need laws seem to fit the latter category and Lowi's prescription.

[185] Another helpful characterization of the difference between planning and regulation is Charles Lindblom's distinction between "rational-comprehensive analysis" and "muddling through." Lindblom, *The Science of "Muddling Through,"* 19 PUB. ADMIN. REV. 79 (1959). A study by George Maddox of the handling of the hospital bed supply and other items on the planning agenda of the British National Health Service found that "disjointed incrementalism"—that is, "muddling through"—has been the prevalent means of policy formation and that the regionalized structure of the NHS "maximizes the probability that partisans can and will effectively contest and politicize all decisions of consequence." Maddox, *Muddling Through: Planning for Health Care in England,* 9 MED. CARE 439, 446 (1971). Characterizing incrementalism as "conservative," Maddox attributes to Lindblom the view that "incrementalism is the strategy of choice particularly in stable systems characterized by generally adequate performance vis-à-vis announced objectives." *Id.*

planning.[186] It is difficult to make a reliable assessment of how planning and regulation differ in this context and how they can be expected to interact in practice.

The degree of true health facility planning is suggested by the extent to which actual facility needs have been analyzed and reduced to objective criteria permitting proposals to be evaluated rather than merely bargained over. In one survey of 128 health planning agencies of all kinds, only twenty percent indicated that they were able to project, on the basis of any kind of master plan, a matter so elementary as the facility needs in their area.[187] Other evidence confirms the absence of hard planning.[188] Indeed, the Maryland certificate-of-need agency, operating under a statute which limits it to certifying projects' conformance to a "state plan," carries on even though no master plan exists.[189] This general record of nonplanning follows many years of federally supported

[186] Compare Sieverts, Book Review, 3 HEALTH SERVICES RESEARCH 251 (1968), with May, Planning: Mainstreams and Eddies, 3 HEALTH SERVICES RESEARCH at 327. See also J. MAY, HEALTH PLANNING: ITS PAST AND POTENTIAL (1967); Hearings on H.R. 17550 Before the Senate Comm. on Finance, 91st Cong., 2d Sess. pt. 2, at 714-26 (1970) (testimony of Symond R. Gottlieb); D. Brown, supra note 22; Curran, Health Planning Agencies: A Legal Crisis?, 60 AM. J. PUB. HEALTH 359 (1970). Proponents of preserving a nonregulatory, advisory role for planners stress the agencies' value in education, in increasing contact among groups, in encouraging institutional planning efforts, and in persuading providers to assume more community responsibilities. Although "planning" may be a misnomer for most of the activities engaged in, such agencies have performed useful services in many communities. Their ability to carry on as facilitators of change by persuasion and advice would be harmed, it is said, by giving them regulatory responsibilities which undercut trust, increase political exposure, and reduce the need to maintain credibility and cultivate influence. Whether these strengths could coexist with even an influential advisory role may not be clear.

[187] COMPTROLLER GENERAL OF THE UNITED STATES, REPORT OF THE STUDY OF HEALTH FACILITIES CONSTRUCTION COSTS 880 (Joint Comm. Print 1972) [hereinafter cited as GAO STUDY].

[188] Less than fifty percent of 163 agencies responding to the GAO survey could state that they knew the bed needs in their area for the current year. Id. at 878. See also McCrossin & Simmons, Survey of Planning Agencies Shows Inadequacy of Existing Programs, 50 HOSPITAL TOPICS 21 (1972). Many planners would deny that absence of such master plans is a basis for criticism, however, because in their view planning is a dynamic, political process rather than a numbers game. See note 186 supra.

[189] MD. ANN. CODE art. 43, § 559(a-1) (Repl. Vol. 1971), contemplates certification of conformance to "the comprehensive health plan developed and applicable for the particular area." The statute goes on to say, "Where no comprehensive health plan has been developed for a particular area, the State's comprehensive planning agency shall make the determinations required." No standards whatsoever are provided for indicating the nature of, or making, such "determinations."

planning for Hill-Burton and other purposes, suggesting that the problem extends beyond the newness of the certificate-of-need programs.[190] The universal emphasis on "consumer representation" on health planning bodies suggests that policy makers see community health planning as an exercise in "interest-group liberalism" rather than as an attempt to introduce real planning on the public's behalf.[190a] Moreover, the health planners themselves do not strongly subscribe to master plans and objective criteria but instead see planning primarily as a consensual process. One description, based on a 1967 survey of voluntary planning agencies, reports that

> Areawide hospital planning was fundamentally a process—a process of human involvement and reciprocity. The process was flexible, open to negotiation, and incremental—a rather untidy process that accommodated to the realities of community life. As such, it was based mainly on interpersonal relations and community organization rather than on technical procedures and refined data. Indeed, the essence of the endeavor was not plans or programs but nourishment of the process itself.[191]

This mushy statement reads like a caricature of all that Lowi reprehends. Yet it is these agencies which are being built into the decision-making process under certificates-of-need laws. These various signs establish that most certificate-of-need agencies will act not as planners in any meaningful sense but as mediators and facilitators of the bargaining out of interest-group conflicts. The pro-provider outcomes of the "process" will have been legitimized. Because the public will have had a chance to bargain for its own protection, it must pay the bill, regardless of its size.

[190] The existence of a master plan is not conclusive evidence that the hard decisions essential to real planning have been taken. One would have to evaluate the methodology employed and the results actually produced before a judgment could be made. The ensuing discussion reviews some suggestive evidence on whether health planning methodology is developed to the point of being useful.

[190a] *E.g.*, MINN. STAT. ANN. § 145.71 (Supp. 1973): 'It is the policy of sections 145.71 to 145.84 that decisions regarding the construction or modification of health care facilities should be based on the maximum possible participation on the local level by consumers of health care and elected officials, as well as the providers directly concerned."

[191] D. Brown, *supra* note 22, at 9. *See also* Hall, *The Political Aspects of Health Planning*, in HEALTH PLANNING: QUALITATIVE ASPECTS AND QUANTITATIVE TECHNIQUES 73 (W. Reinke ed. 1972) (including an extensive bibliography).

It may not be inevitable that certificate-of-need agencies will succumb completely to a nonplanning, highly political approach.[192] Health planning does have a methodology for predicting health facility needs and for evaluating arrangements for meeting them.[193] Employed to produce master plans and objective criteria, this methodology could perhaps lend credibility to hard decisions and reduce the impact of political pressures and the equitable claims of established providers. The prospects for real planning would probably be enhanced if the certificate-of-need law included a clear mandate to engage in detailed specification of the bed supply.[194] Further, federal financial support for the planning agencies might allow substantial planning efforts, and indeed the federal bureaucracy might insist upon a minimum level of substantive planning.

Although both the hospitals and the public would profit from lower bed-to-population ratios and more "rational" allocation of specialized services, the apparent coincidence of interests is deceiving. The public would prefer strict controls which would lower the level and distribution of output to approximately that point of optimality which would be found in a hypothetical market featuring, among other ideal conditions, consumers possessing both reasonable ability to pay for hospital services from their own pockets and good information about such services' value.[195] Such severe restrictions would be adverse to provider interests,

---

192 See, e.g., ABT ASSOC. INC., supra note 77, at 47, reporting how one Washington State "B-agency is currently swamped with the demanding task of review but is making headway and will soon have more staff time to concentrate on an overall plan."

193 See, e.g., C. Hopkins et al., Methods of Estimating Hospital Bed Needs, Oct. 1967 (UCLA School of Public Health mimeo.); Klarman, supra note 59; Shonick, Understanding the Nature of the Random Fluctuation of the Hospital Daily Census, 10 MED. CARE 118 (1972) [hereinafter cited as Shonick, Random Fluctuation]; Shonick, Areawide Planning for Hospital Inpatient Resources: A Critical Overview of the Development of Methodology and Concepts (1973) [hereinafter cited as Shonick, Overview].

194 But see note 189 supra and accompanying text.

195 See AEI PROCEEDINGS, supra note 6 (remarks of Mark V. Pauly). It is interesting to compare this concept of optimality with that of an expert in health planning methodology:

Conceptually, proper service volume is that number of patient days which would be incurred if the level of health care available and being delivered to the entire population conformed with standards of good health care presently established by the professional leaders and publications in the various health specialty fields . . . and being taught in the health professional training schools.

Shonick, Overview, supra note 193, at 3-4. The absence of any reference to cost reveals an important shortcoming of the planner's perspective and one reason why planning-cum-regulation will probably not control inflation effectively. Shonick does observe, however, that his stated objective ignores "the question as to what degree 'good' health care, as defined by professional leaders, actually improves health status." Id. at 4. The

however, and it is doubtful whether a law could pass which mandated such rigorous planning. Rather, one is likely to find either vague delegations to the agencies or specification of multiple contradictory criteria of the type found in the existing laws. Such laws merely invite the agency to preside over a bargaining process which, as in other industries, can benefit no one so much as the regulated interests.

Truly efficient use of hospitals would require a drastic reduction in the supply of inpatient services rather than merely a levelling off of growth, the most which might be achieved under a well-administered certificate-of-need law. For example, HMOs have demonstrated an ability to reduce utilization of hospitals dramatically without sacrificing quality of care.[196] Moreover, studies applying the standards of conscientious fee-for-service practitioners have shown that a substantial percentage of all hospitalized persons (the mean seems to be around twenty percent) could be cared for adequately outside the hospital.[197] On the basis of these observations, it is reasonably clear that the public would profit from a major reduction in the supply of hospital beds[198] and (in the absence of changed incentives) the installation of a sound system of bed

formula stated in the text leaves room for second-guessing both providers' judgments and consumers' actual preferences but recognizes the "question" which Shonick by-passes by asserting the relevance of hypothetical choices between consuming either more health services or other "goods." With a supply of beds and services sufficient to produce only the output dictated by either formulation of the objective, it would be necessary—given the predominance of third-party payment—to ration services on the basis of medical "need," which differs fundamentally from "demand." *Id.* at 3-4. Rate regulation would probably also be required, since bed rationing could never be effective enough to eliminate the upward pressure on prices from the excess demand created by insurance.

[196] On the relevance of this experience, see Shonick, *Overview, supra* note 193, at 84-86. Roemer's recent data show that the per capita hospital utilization rates in HMOs—which, incidentally, appeared to cover somewhat higher-risk populations—was less than half the rate for persons covered under Blue Cross plans and also considerably less than the rate for persons covered by commercial insurance. M. ROEMER, *et al.*, HEALTH INSURANCE EFFECTS: SERVICES, EXPENDITURES, AND ATTITUDES UNDER THREE TYPES OF PLAN 21 (1972). The Kaiser Foundation Health Plan has over a long period maintained a supply of hospital beds equal to less than half the number of beds per capita in the nation as a whole.

[197] These are collected in Bureau of Facility Planning, N.Y. State Dep't of Health, Methodology for Determining Inpatient Need Estimates, March 1, 1970 (mimeo.).

[198] A twenty percent reduction would probably not affect health adversely in most places. The supply of general medical and surgical hospital beds by state ranges from 3.9 and 4.0 per 1000 in Maryland and Connecticut, respectively, to 7.6 and 7.3 per 1000 in North Dakota and Rhode Island. NAT'L CENTER FOR HEALTH STATISTICS, *supra* note 89, at 308. Variations in health status have not been correlated with the bed supply. Klarman, *supra* note 57, at 178.

rationing[199] and rate regulation. Nothing in the legislative history of certificate-of-need laws or in their enforcement suggests a dedication to accomplishing anything approaching such a drastic reduction in the bed-to-population ratio. For example, no state has given the regulators the power to close down unneeded beds.[200]

The discipline of health planning itself has never threatened to restrict the supply of hospital beds to the degree warranted by the foregoing evidence. The hospital industry's acceptance of health planning suggests that it is not at all fearful that planners will promote fundamental changes. The cartel-like appearance of health planning efforts of the past strengthens this judgment. Even where consumer and community interests have been well represented, provider interests have tended to prevail. So long as duplication is averted, lay participants have been equally content to see more and better health services made available, without much regard to cost. Noncaptive regulators in other settings have similarly revealed a bias toward expanding or maintaining the size of the industries they regulate, irrespective of the dictates of rationality or mandates to engage in planning.

But perhaps the chief source of discouragement about health planning is the complexity of the task. Among the factors relevant in the planning effort are

> [the] types, sizes, age, condition, and distribution of facilities; use patterns, including service areas within hospitals; population characteristics and size; availability and accessibility of services and facilities; supply of physicians and other health personnel; income levels; levels of medical technology in the community; health insurance coverage; climate; and the habits of people.[201]

---

[199] Bed rationing would be required because the "reverse" Roemer effect, the reduction in demand from a *reduction* of supply, is probably weak. Stevens, *Hospital Market Efficiency: The Anatomy of the Supply Response,* in EMPIRICAL STUDIES *supra* note 56, at 241, 244. Given third-party payment and provider control of demand, the only way to achieve really efficient hospital use is to force rationing by professionals on the basis of medical need. The only really effective utilization review programs in hospitals have occurred in those hospitals which have very high occupancy rates because doctors are willing to accept control as a price of access to a desirable facility. If the bed supply available to the entire population were limited in such a way as to force such rationing over-all, the use of hospital beds might be efficiently controlled. *But see* notes 242-43 *infra* and accompanying text.

[200] New York can close down substandard beds when it wishes.

[201] GAO STUDY, *supra* note 187, at 879.

Even this list fails to convey the difficulty of projecting changes in population, technology, health care financing, delivery systems, and patterns of utilization,[202] all of which are largely beyond the ken of statistics and expert judgment.[203] The complexity is such that the agencies themselves lack confidence in their ability to make hard-and-fast judgments, and the

---

[202] One example may serve to show the primitive state of health planning methodology in practice. The HEW formula for estimating bed needs for Hill-Burton purposes has been quite simple, being based in part on the assumption that past utilization rates will continue into the future even though higher prices and various regulatory and peer-review mechanisms now promise to change utilization patterns substantially. Thus, during a period when excessive hospitalization was widely recognized as a problem, the Hill-Burton program continued to subsidize hospital construction projects the need for which was premised on the continuation of old utilization abuses. GAO Study, *supra* note 187, at 883-84; J. Lave & L. Lave, An Evaluation of the Hill-Burton Program (1973) (forthcoming); Shonick, *Random Fluctuation, supra* note 193. Now that a surplus of hospital beds has been produced, such an example of past "planning" is hardly reassuring.

The 80 percent occupancy rate used for Hill-Burton purposes also arguably contributes to excess capacity. After noting "the tendencies of some features of the present Hill-Burton allocation method to actually aggravate existing imbalances in the distribution of inpatient facilities," Shonick warns that, with certificate-of-need laws, "the consequences of adhering to an inappropriate method for determining bed requirements will become more serious." Shonick, *id.* at 135.

Some planners have begun to make adjustments for obvious overuse in their need calculations. *See, e.g.,* Bureau of Facility Planning, *supra* note 197. The New York State Department of Health's utilization adjustments for nursing homes are described in the Department's Post Hearing Memorandum, In re *Schwartzberg, Lefkowitz & Lefkowitz d/b/a New Rochelle Nursing Home* (no date). Nevertheless, planners still shrink from projections premised on either new methods of financing or stricter bed rationing.

[203] Changes in the methods for estimating need can produce rather dramatic changes in the situation in a local community. One example is reported as follows:

> At the request of a local hospital council, [a new and apparently more accurate] method of estimating bed needs was used by the researchers to assess the validity of a forecast showing that about 1,100 more than the existing 1,550 beds would be needed in 1975 to serve a population of nearly 400,000. The results showed that the estimate could be overstated by as many as 600 beds.

GAO Study, *supra* note 187, at 884-85. The magnitude of the possible error—an overstatement of total need by nearly thirty percent and of unmet need by over 100 percent—must give pause. Similarly, the certificate-of-need agency in New York State has succeeded in dramatically reducing the number of "needed" beds by introducing a utilization adjustment to the Hill-Burton formula and by reclassifying certain marginally substandard facilities as part of the inventory of available beds. It is apparent that small adjustments in methodology can produce substantial results, betraying a high degree of arbitrariness and a high risk of error, neither of which can be avoided. Even methodology which is highly developed may mask decisions based on other, possibly political, factors, such as in the New York instance, where the heavy emphasis on cost control in the Department of Health contributed to the inclusion of substandard beds in the inventory of acceptable facilities.

result is a lack of firm standards for decision making.[204] In such circumstances, the pressures of politics necessarily become dominant.

The prospects for real health planning seem poor enough that they should be given little weight in predicting the behavior of certificate-of-need agencies. Because there is every reason to think that these agencies are expected to serve as political mechanisms and that the areawide planning agencies involved in the process are primarily vehicles for political inputs, the experience of other regulatory agencies, which have also interpreted their mandate in political terms, should serve as a warning signal. It is difficult to find any basis for expecting that the performance of other regulatory agencies can be significantly improved upon in regulating entry into the health services industry.

D. *The Regulatory Response to Innovation and Change*

The *"Producer-Protection"* Hypothesis Revisited

One of the best-supported charges against regulatory agencies is that they actively retard desirable changes harmful to the regulated interests and that they particularly resist the weeding-out of obsolete elements and the erosion of established markets by new technology or organizational innovations.[205] The regulatory techniques employed in defending the regulated interests vary, but restrictions on entry and service offerings are practically essential to prevent the development of competition harmful to the regulated firms. Much regulatory effort is expended on

---

[204] During visits to several areawide health planning agencies in 1970 and 1971, we learned that the agencies were having difficulty in consistently applying any uniform set of criteria to determine need. Lacking any other basis for decision, approvals or disapprovals of proposed projects were given on the basis of the best judgments of agency staff and board officials, who themselves sometimes disagreed. *Id.* at 880. Any expectation that master plans and numbers can make regulation effective should be indulged with Professor Marver Bernstein's warning in mind:

> While exactness and precision are desirable, along with flexibility and adaptability, in the regulatory process, they cannot define away political forces. Regulation is and always will be an intensely political process. Its success depends as heavily upon political leadership and widespread public support as it does upon sound techniques and administrative precision.

BERNSTEIN, *supra* note 135, at 183.

[205] Regulatory agencies pay a great deal of attention to the effect of a potential innovation on the distribution of wealth within an industry. No matter how beneficial an innovation, it has little chance of timely adoption in a regulated industry if it will lead to a substantial redistribution of wealth among the regulated that cannot be compensated through some clever regulatory device.

NOLL, *supra* note 147, at 25. *See also* Hilton, *supra* note 105, at 48-53.

extending the agency's jurisdiction to cover new industries or activities which are threatening to the regulated industry.[206]

The protective attitude adopted by the regulators reflects in part their recognition that the good works subsidized by internally generated funds may be jeopardized if competition is allowed. The agency also often senses that it would somehow be unfair to expose the regulated firms to the full impact of rapid change when their earnings are limited by law and their assets are "dedicated" to the public service. Moreover, regulators tend to view the regulated firms' investments as the agency's special responsibility and to resist any development which would render assets obsolete before they are fully depreciated. This latter attitude has been labelled the "sunk-cost obsession." [207] Finally, the pressure from the affected industry and its allies will always be stronger than any other pressure which the agency feels.

If the hospital industry becomes subject to exogenous threats or pressures, its regulators could be expected to afford it aid and protection. Surprising as it may seem, the hospital industry may in fact be in danger of becoming a "declining industry." Currently, the only overt sign of this possibility is the recent decline in occupancy rates, but a range of new factors present in the hospitals' environment reflect major potential problems.

Because hospitals have permitted their budgets to become grossly inflated during a period of excess demand and ready cost reimbursement, the market offers opportunities for entry by more efficient, less heavily capitalized providers which can render many hospital services cheaply. Cream-skimming proprietary hospitals,[208] HMOs, and a range of other ambulatory substitutes for hospital care are prominent among the threats which are appearing. At the same time, the various third-party payers are becoming more aggressive both in their determinations of hospital

---

[206] The ICC actively assisted the railroads in extending regulation to trucks. W. JONES, CASES AND MATERIALS ON REGULATED INDUSTRIES 484-99 (1967). The FCC's efforts to regulate cable television in the interests of over-the-air broadcasters is a modern example. *See* United States v. Southwestern Cable Co., 392 U.S. 157 (1968); Comanor & Mitchell, *supra* note 164.

[207] NOLL, *supra* note 147, at 25-26.

[208] An executive of a leading chain of for-profit hospitals is of the opinion that planning agencies in a number of communities have discriminated against his firm. Interview with Mark S. Levitan, Senior Vice President, American Medicorp, Inc., Oct. 16, 1973. This regulatory behavior is predictable in view of political factors, incumbents' fear of competition, prevailing prejudices against profit-making enterprises in health care, and the speculative character of the benefits of introducing a competitive stimulus.

costs and in their refusals to underwrite unremunerative services and underused facilities. Government programs in particular are actively supporting mechanisms designed to question and reduce hospital utilization. Moreover, hospitals are exposed to an array of conflicting demands by patients, consumer groups, doctors, labor, public officials, bulk purchasers, and the various regulatory and accrediting authorities. Understandably, hospitals would like to interpose an authoritative decision maker on whom the worst political pressures, as well as the responsibility for the industry's financial condition, would devolve. But while certificate-of-need laws provide some relief, more comprehensive regulation will be necessary if the hospitals are to shift from their role as the focal point of political and other pressures to the more desirable one of being the principal pressure-group constituency of a regulatory agency.

In addition to perhaps curbing growth which is unnaturally induced by third-party payment, certificate-of-need agencies will also obstruct market entry by lower-cost providers. By not stepping aside, they can help existing hospitals to recover their perhaps unwise past investments through depreciation charges and to meet their other inflated costs in full.[209] A central issue is whether certificate-of-need agencies, in assessing "need," will adequately recognize the appropriateness of allowing a choice between expensive and cheap care. Reasons why they might not view competition favorably include the familiar "sunk-cost obsession" and the desire to protect internal subsidization capabilities. In the hospital industry, these justifications for artificially staving off obsolescence are vastly reinforced by belief in the Roemer effect, by which obsolete facilities allegedly generate new demand and thus higher costs to the public through insurance mechanisms. On the face of it, hospital regulators will be strongly tempted to inhibit certain kinds of technological and organizational change.

The actual costs to the public of regulatory curtailment of technical innovation and institutional change may be difficult to identify. Sometimes, of course, the adverse effects of regulatory action may be reason-

---

[209] The hospitals are thus unlikely to suffer substantial deficits as a direct consequence of their past investment excesses. *Cf.* notes 53, 141-45 *supra* and accompanying text. Although one may perhaps expect that the capital recovered through depreciation will, under the guidance of certificate-of-need agencies, be somewhat more wisely invested the next time around, it is interesting to note that certificate-of-need laws, ostensibly designed to prevent future overinvestment, condemn the public to keep the hospitals whole for the same unwise investments which prompted the laws' enactment. The instinct which leads to acceptance of this state of affairs is the same 'sunk-cost obsession'" which has led many regulators into error.

ably apparent, such as where a particular aspirant offering an improved service is turned away, delayed, or required to offer the service on a limited basis.[210] In other cases, however, the true damage done can be assessed only by estimating the value to consumers of innovations which were never developed.[211] In health care, the costs of regulatory inhibition of cost-saving innovations—particularly methods of substituting outpatient for inpatient care—will be largely hidden from public view, and it will therefore be difficult to obtain legislative correction of even a very costly mistake. Indeed, as long as public officials measure the success of health policy only by the rate of cost increases, little attention will be given to missed opportunities for reducing costs. The political process will quite willingly tolerate huge inefficiencies (which in health care could be measured in whole percentage points of GNP) so long as the costs cannot be convincingly laid at government's door.

Impact of Certificate-of-Need Laws on Hospital Construction by HMOs

A strong argument exists for not extending certificate-of-need statutes to hospital construction by a health maintenance organization. For one thing, HMOs do not have the same perverse incentives for overexpansion which characterize fee-for-service hospitals. Indeed, because they are paid in advance, rather than retrospectively on a cost-reimbursement basis, they have every incentive to conserve their resources and to seek

---

[210] Thus, the FCC's restriction of the growth of cable television has been obvious enough to interested observers that estimates of the cost imposed on the public by the FCC's policies have been possible. Comanor & Mitchell, *supra* note 164.

[211] A recent study purports to demonstrate that a net loss of consumer welfare resulted from the 1962 Kefauver-Harris amendments to the Federal Food, Drug, and Cosmetic Act, Pub. L. No. 86-618, §§ 101-103, 201-204, 74 Stat. 397 (codified in scattered sections of 21 U.S.C.), which for the first time required the drug manufacturer to establish the efficacy of his product prior to marketing. Peltzman, The Benefits and Costs of New Drug Regulation, Dec. 4-5, 1972 (paper prepared for the Conference on the Regulation of the Introduction of New Pharmaceuticals, University of Chicago). In this case, it was necessary first to demonstrate by some means that there was in fact a reduced flow of new drug products and then to attempt to attach dollar values to the consumer surplus (excess welfare gain over price paid) which would have accrued from those unidentifiable drugs which were never developed because of the higher cost of obtaining marketing approval. Needless to say, this interesting study proved easy to criticize for failing in the nearly impossible task of proving what might have been under circumstances which were not allowed to occur. *See Hearings on the Present Status of Competition in the Pharmaceutical Industry Before the Subcomm. on Monopoly of the Senate Select Small Business Comm.*, 93d Cong., 1st Sess. (1973); Havighurst, *supra* note 134, at 35-37, 43-44.

efficiency. An HMO's decision to build a hospital therefore reflects a belief that operating through existing hospitals is inefficient. Although a few HMOs have operated with some effectiveness through existing hospitals, good reasons support an HMO's desire to control its own facility.[212] These include the doctors' difficulty in seeing patients at a variety of locations; the burdens which often accompany staff appointments, particularly at teaching hospitals; the loss of the HMO medical group's cohesiveness; and the loss of control over records and other managerial details which may provide much of the HMO's cost and service advantage.[213]

Of course, when existing hospitals are left oversupplied with beds because the HMO has built its own facility, the system's dependence on cost-reimbursement may combine with provider influence over demand to produce added costs to the public. Although regulators will thus be tempted to penalize the HMO because of the distorted incentives prevailing in the fee-for-service sector, they should also recognize that competition from HMOs induces the fee-for-service sector to avert such inflationary effects by better utilization and cost controls.[214] By the same token, enforced affiliation with existing hospitals may generate pressures for HMOs to reach accommodations with local providers and to cease the very competition needed to correct inflationary incentives in the fee-for-service sector. Moreover, as the hospitals come to see new construction by an HMO entrant as a credible threat, the HMO should find it easier to purchase an existing hospital suitable for its purposes, thereby obviating the original concern about the bed supply.[215]

Encounters between HMOs and certificate-of-need agencies over facilities construction have already revealed the potential for difficulty. The

---

[212] See generally A. YEDIDIA, PLANNING AND IMPLEMENTATION OF THE COMMUNITY HEALTH FOUNDATION OF CLEVELAND, OHIO 70-71 (Public Health Service Pub. No. 1664-3, 1968); G. WILLIAMS, KAISER-PERMANENTE HEALTH PLAN—WHY IT WORKS 22-27 (1971); KAISER HEALTH PLAN, INC., 1969 ANNUAL REPORT 15 (1970); Note, The Role of Prepaid Group Practice in Relieving the Medical Care Crisis, 84 HARV. L. REV. 887, 907, 910-15 (1971); Shapiro, Role of Hospitals in the Changing Health Insurance Plan of Greater New York, 47 BULL. OF THE N.Y. ACAD. OF MEDICINE (2d ser.) 374 (1971); Roemer, The Hospital's Relation to Prepaid Group Practice: Review and Analysis, in GROUP HEALTH INSTITUTE PROCEEDINGS 108 (1960); Brewster, Group Health Association's Use of Community Hospitals, id. at 117; Cutting, The Role of the Hospital in the Kaiser Foundation Health Plan, id. at 121. See also American Medical Ass'n v. United States, 317 U.S. 519 (1943).

[213] See also notes 219-20 infra.

[214] See text at notes 246-49 infra.

[215] But see text accompanying notes 66-69 supra.

three West Coast states have special concessions for HMOs built into their certificate-of-need laws, but the interpretation of these clauses, which direct agency recognition of the specific needs of the HMO's enrolled population, remains in doubt.[216] It is unclear, for example, how a new HMO might get permission to build a new facility for a population it has yet to identify. Moreover, both Group Health Cooperative of Puget Sound and the Kaiser Foundation Health Plan, Inc., two of the most substantial and reputable HMOs, have encountered problems in obtaining permission to construct inpatient facilities needed to serve their populations in these states.[217] Although they ultimately obtained the requisite approvals after substantial delays, it is fair to ask whether smaller or newer HMOs or HMOs organized under less impeccable auspices could survive a similar encounter. In the remaining states, where the legislature has made no special provision for HMOs,[218] the opportunity for denying certification of need to HMOs is even greater.

In view of these circumstances, a total exemption from certificate-of-need requirements for HMO hospital facilities is desirable. An alternative would be to allow HMOs to build unless a suitable arrangement were offered by existing hospitals, permitting the HMO to realize the econ-

---

[216] See, e.g., ORE. REV. STAT. § 441.095(k) (1971), requiring that consideration be given to "the needs of members, subscribers and enrollees of institutions and health care plans which operate or support particular hospitals for the purpose of rendering health care to such members, subscribers and enrollees"; references to the needs of a "defined population" may also permit an Oregon HMO to argue the special needs of its subscribers. See also WASH. CODE § 70.38.140(12) (Supp. 1972); ABT ASSOC. INC., supra note 77, at 40-41. The California provisions are not quite so clear. CAL. HEALTH & SAFETY CODE § 437.8(a) (West Supp. 1973) (recognizing "the requirements of the population to be served by the applicant"); 17 CAL. ADMIN. CODE § 40518 (1973) (emphasizing comprehensiveness and coordination of services, the importance of innovation and alternatives, and the "views" of groups of users on the need issue).

[217] Interviews with Kaiser Foundation Health Plan, Inc., officials revealed that construction of a new hospital in Clackamas County, Oregon, was twice approved only by one-vote margins and that the Kaiser Bellflower Hospital in California was approved at one level only in a reversal of an earlier vote. Two votes on a Group Health extended care facility in planning agencies in the State of Washington were likewise decided by one vote, 4-3, one each way.

[218] But see COLO. REV. STAT. §§ 66 41-10(l) to -10(n) (1973), which contains language favorable to HMOs and particularly to the substitution of ambulatory for inpatient care. MICH. STAT. ANN. § 14.1179(54) (1972) confers a discretionary exempting power as follows:

In instances where a state or federal agency contracts with a health maintenance organization to render comprehensive health care services, a certificate of need may be waived for those inpatient and outpatient facilities that are necessary for the health maintenance organizations to achieve maximum effectiveness in rendering comprehensive health care services.

omies of which it is capable[219] and reflecting in lower charges the HMO's greater ability to control utilization.[220] But this approach seems less realistic than a total exemption, particularly since a certificate-of-need agency, operating in a political climate, would always instinctively balance the public's interest in HMO development against the interests of the hospitals.

Impact on Ambulatory Care Facilities

The rationale for extending certificate-of-need laws to cover ambulatory care facilities, whether those of HMOs or other kinds, must rest on a theory similar to that offered for limiting HMO hospital construction. If the substitution of ambulatory care for inpatient care should leave hospital beds in the fee-for-service sector empty, past performance suggests that those beds will now be occupied by patients who do not really require hospitalization. HMOs seem to present this risk rather dramatically, since their most effective cost-control technique has been to reduce hospitalization. Even if an HMO should use existing hospitals exclusively, empty beds might result, and on this basis an argument can be contrived for excluding the HMO altogether.

Another type of ambulatory care facility presenting the same problem is the so-called "surgicenter," which provides outpatient surgical services as a substitute for hospital care.[221] Abortion clinics,[222] dialysis cen-

---

[219] Difficulty in arranging staff privileges, burdensome staff responsibilities (allegedly accounting for 20 percent of physician time in one case), mandatory duplication of previous lab tests, and inability to farm out tests to cheaper or better labs are cited as further obstacles. Schmidt, Lewis, & Rosenberg, Barriers to HMO Development, May 1, 1973 (Group Health Ass'n of America mimeo.). *See also* note 212 *supra* and accompanying text. The possibility that planning agencies might actively assist HMOs to overcome such obstacles is a most attractive one.

[220] ". . . [L]ack of a medical center inflated operating costs because CHF was unable to negotiate the same reduced rates for hospitalization as its more powerful competitor, Blue Cross." KAISER FOUNDATION HEALTH PLAN, INC., 1969 ANNUAL REPORT 15 (1970). I am told that HMOs seeking a special low rate to reflect their better ability to schedule patients and keep beds full are sometimes told that such a preference would violate antitrust principles. I see no grounds for such an assertion and indeed would consider a hospital's refusal to allow an HMO to realize its cost advantage to be substantially more troublesome from an antitrust point of view.

[221] It has been estimated that surgicenter treatment is offered at a savings of 25 percent. *See* Davis & Detmer, *The Ambulatory Surgical Unit*, 175 ANNALS OF SURG. 856 (1972).

[222] *See, e.g.*, People v. Dobbs Ferry Medical Pavillion, Inc., 40 App. Div. 2d 324, 340 N.Y.S.2d 108 (1973); People v. Wickersham Women's Medical Center, 69 Misc. 2d 196, 329 N.Y.S.2d 627 (1972).

ters,[223] midwives, and acupuncturists may also threaten to reduce hospital occupancy rates, and one can imagine diagnostic centers which could perform on an outpatient basis many services which previously required hospitalization.[224] Although these methods of substituting outpatient for inpatient care promise dramatic cost savings, the planners' argument, premised on assumptions about hospitals' right to full cost recovery and the strength of the Roemer effect, would warrant stopping them all until such time as hospital beds could be closed down to compensate for the impact.

It is worth pondering why existing hospitals, who alone possess the power to decide to reduce the number of their beds, would introduce these innovations on their own if they were confident that others could not introduce them.[225] The answer must be that the incentives to innovate in these ways are at best weak and that, to the extent the hospital's bed count and gross revenues dwindle, managers are motivated in the opposite direction. Thus, if exogenous changes are to be foreclosed, the delays in the adoption of even proven cost-saving techniques are likely to be considerable, and interest in seeking out and experimenting with other innovations will be minimal. The costs associated with these delays and missed opportunities may be much higher than any that can be associated with the excess bed supply and the Roemer effect.

---

[223] Proposed Regulation § 81.102(e), 38 Fed. Reg. 20993 (Aug. 3, 1973), covers "kidney disease treatment centers." Entry into this business has also been severely restricted in Medicare regulations. 38 Fed. Reg. 17210 (1973). This cost-control measure could deprive some patients of life-saving treatment and might prevent important cost-saving innovations from materializing.

[224] Nursing homes and other inpatient facilities provide another kind of lower-cost substitute for hospital care. It would be interesting to discover whether hospitals ever intervene in nursing home applications (or take an *ex parte* interest) and whether hospitals' interests are considered in particular cases.

[225] For an instance of certificate-of-need denial raising similar issues, see Review of Proposed Nevada Institute of Medicine and Surgery, Inc., Minutes of the Nevada State Comprehensive Health Planning Advisory Council, April 7, 1972.

The issue is dramatized in another context by Monongahela West Penn Pub. Serv. Co. v. State Road Comm'n, 104 W. Va. 183, 139 S.E. 744 (1927), *appeal dismissed*, 278 U.S. 564 (1928), discussed in SCHWARTZ, *supra* note 49, at 375. Integration of services in multi-modal transportation companies has been proposed as a way around ICC protectionism for interests in established transportation patterns. A. FRIEDLAENDER, THE DILEMMA OF FREIGHT TRANSPORT REGULATION 155-59, 166-68 (1969). If applied in health care, this proposed remedy would mean an expanded role for institutions such as the Health Care Corporations contemplated in the AHA-backed Ullman bill, *see* note 30 *supra,* but the remedy is offered solely as a solution to the waste created by ICC regulation itself and not as an alternative to a system featuring free market entry by lower-cost modes.

Perhaps the case for freeing HMOs from certificate-of-need requirements is slightly stronger than that for relieving other types of outpatient facility. The HMO by its entry into the market would supply precisely the competitive check on excessive hospital utilization which is needed to curb the Roemer effect. Other types of outpatient facility do not carry with them the same inherent ability to check the inflationary forces which they can be said to unleash. A total exemption for HMO development may therefore be easily justified.[226] At present, however, the AHA model bill and the laws of eleven states appear to cover ambulatory care offered by HMOs and other institutional providers,[227] and a

---

[226] This is not to say that HMOs should not be licensed and regulated to assure quality of care. *See, e.g.,* INSTITUTE FOR INTERDISCIPLINARY STUDIES, SPECIFICATIONS FOR A STATE HEALTH MAINTENANCE ORGANIZATION ENABLING ACT (1972). However, a need requirement has implications of a very different kind and should be totally dispensed with. Even though quality- or cost-related entry restrictions are subject to protectionist application, the risk may be somewhat less (and the gain more apparent) than with provisions which are overtly anticompetitive. Nevertheless, high standards set by HMO regulators could produce the outcomes anticipated in the next paragraph in the text even without a need requirement.

A special treatment of the "need" for an HMO is embodied in the Social Security Amendments of 1972. The Secretary of HEW is empowered to ignore a negative decision by the state planning agency and allow Medicare or other federal reimbursement of HMO capital costs if he believes that denial of such reimbursement "would discourage the operation of . . . [any HMO] which has demonstrated to his satisfaction proof of capability to provide comprehensive health care services . . . efficiently, effectively, and economically. . . ." Social Security Act § 1122(d)(2), 42 U.S.C. § 1320a-1(d) (2) (Supp. 1973). Since a provider cannot qualify as an HMO for Medicare purposes without such a demonstration anyway, Social Security Act § 1876(b)(6), 42 U.S.C. § 1320a-1 (Supp. 1973), the provision seems to leave very little room for denying payments attributable to capital expenditures to any HMO. However, it would allow the Secretary to look at a qualified HMO on a facility-by-facility basis and to exclude payments for a new outpatient facility which it built without state approval. Nevertheless, the test of whether the new facility can provide services "efficiently, effectively, and economically" would not allow inquiry into its competitive impact or the adequacy of existing services and would leave only quality, cost, and efficiency issues before the Secretary. *See* Proposed Regulations, 38 Fed. Reg. 20994 (1973). Of course, a state with a certificate-of-need law could effectuate the planning agency's determination by a license denial or an injunction, and therefore the opportunity for special HEW dispensation would exist only in states which do not have such laws. *See* text accompanying notes 32-34 *supra*.

[227] Arizona, Connecticut, Kansas, Kentucky, Massachusetts, New Jersey, New York, Rhode Island, South Carolina, Tennessee, and Virginia. Only Kentucky, New Jersey, and Virginia refer to HMOs by the customary name, whereas Rhode Island uses the term "health care corporation." Possibly a doctor's office or group practice clinic in which HMO patients are served would be exempt in several states, either because of an express exemption for private offices of physicians (Arizona, Kentucky, Tennessee, and Virginia; *but see* S. Car. State Board of Health, Rates and Regulations for Certification of Need for Health Facilities and Services, ¶ E-1 (Dec. 1972)) or because the auspices is not that of a "corporation" (Rhode Island) or an "institution" (New York).

twelfth state, Florida, has a special HMO statute which incorporates a special "need" requirement independent of the state certificate-of-need law.[228]

Although it is currently impossible to document the impact of certificate-of-need laws on HMO development,[229] it is possible to speculate whether certificate-of-need agencies would react to HMO development in the same manner that regulators in other contexts have responded to similar developments. There may be some reason to think that health planners are positively disposed to the HMO concept and might therefore welcome and even encourage HMO development. Nevertheless, many planners appear to value HMO care only for its own sake and not for its possible competitive impact on other providers. For this reason, certificate-of-need laws could eventually lead to determinations that HMOs should be operated by established interests with known "track records," that plans which attract the least opposition should be preferred, and that proprietary newcomers are not needed. Only high-cost HMOs, the safest from a quality standpoint but also the ones least likely to have a major competitive impact on over-all costs, would be admitted. These possible outcomes are consistent both with regulatory experience in other industries and with the need requirement's presupposition that no important price and quality judgments are to be made in the marketplace. The view likely to prevail is that stability is to be preserved once

The Health Insurance Plan of Greater New York, which is largely non-hospital-based, has not sought approval for the practices of its participating doctors. *See also* People v. Dobbs Ferry Medical Pavillion, Inc., 40 App. Div. 324, 340 N.Y.S.2d 108 (1973). Although the North Dakota law expressly covers any "new medical care service," only inpatient facilities are listed in another section as coming within the law's provisions. Similarly, Virginia lists no facilities serving outpatients exclusively. South Dakota covers any "licensed outpatient care facility" but does not as yet license HMOs.

[228] LAWS OF FLORIDA ch. 72-264, § 6(1) (1972); Rules of the Fla. Dep't of Insurance § 4-31.04 (1972). Administratively, HMO need certification is done by the state CHP agency, with advice from "b" agencies, and does not pass through the Hill-Burton agency, which is the decision maker in the usual certificate-of-need machinery. This administrative arrangement plus the promotional mandate in the HMO legislation suggest that there may be little opportunity for protectionist policies to develop in Florida. *But see* LAWS OF FLORIDA ch. 72-264, § 2(5) (1972).

[229] So far as it has been possible to discover, no cases of actual exclusion of a would-be HMO under "need" requirements have yet occurred. Florida had received twelve applications under its liberal HMO statute as of a recent date, but there was no indication that any of these HMOs would be regarded as mutually exclusive or as otherwise unneeded. It is impossible to discover how many HMO developments have been discouraged by the gauntlet of legal restrictions, including certificate-of-need requirements, which fledgling plans must be prepared to run.

1241

a dash of "pluralism" has been supplied. Clearly, curbing HMO development and competitive impact in this manner would entail large but unmeasurable costs.

Certificate-of-need requirements for surgicenters, abortion clinics, and other outpatient facilities also seem poorly conceived. Although some planner-regulators would probably welcome such developments and would grant certificates even without an offsetting curtailment of the bed supply, many others will be willing to sacrifice major efficiencies out of an unshakeable belief in the Roemer effect. The tendency of the hospital interests and the planners to reach out for control over exogenous influences is borne out by the certificate-of-need law enacted in Arizona shortly after an innovative surgicenter had entered a market previously dominated by the hospitals. As a result of the concern generated, the law was expressly drafted to cover ambulatory surgical services requiring general anesthesia,[230] and the clear expectation is that hospital interests will henceforth be consulted before such developments are permitted to occur.[231] Direct evidence of the planners' mentality appears in New York Blue Cross's refusal to pay for care at the Phoenix Surgicenter on the ground of its anticipated impact on hospitals and ultimately on cost, via the Roemer effect.[232]

---

[230] Ariz. Rev. Stat. Ann. § 36-402(3) (Supp. 1972). *See also* Kan. Stat. Ann. §§ 65-2a01(b), 65-425(a), 65-427 (1972).

[231] *See* Am. Med. News, June 4, 1973, at 7:
> The Illinois Hospital Assn. views the proposed [surgicenters] in a skeptical manner, partially because of the competition they could give area hospitals. The IHA hopes that the centers will be subject to licensure and certificate-of-need laws . . . .

[232] Remarks of Dr. Peter Rogatz, Senior Vice President, Associated Hospital Service of New York, Health Staff Seminar, Washington, D.C., May 3, 1973. Rogatz, Ambulatory Care: Digging Out from Under the Bricks and Mortar, Aug. 20, 1973 (Address to the American Health Congress, Chicago, Illinois). Illinois Blue Cross has a similar policy. Am. Med. News, June 4, 1973, at 7. Medicare has adopted a similar policy in the past, but the 1972 amendments now permit reimbursement of surgicenters and similar innovative facilities as "experiments and demonstration projects." 42 U.S.C. at § 1320(B). The trap which will lead to obstruction of change is implied by the stipulation that, even if the centers "offer promise of improved care or more efficient delivery of care," full cost reimbursement will not be allowed unless they also "would not result in cost to the program in excess of what would otherwise be incurred for such services." S. Rep. No. 92-1230, 92d Cong., 2d Sess. at 227 (1972). *Compare* Proposed Rules §§ 81.107(d), .108(b), 38 Fed. Reg. 20997 (1973), which seem to adopt a more positive stance toward ambulatory-care facilities. I have yet to discover a planning agency which has taken (or rejected) a similar view of either surgicenters or HMOs, but the logic will surely seem persuasive. The behavior of Blue Cross and Medicare suggests that, if regulatory authority is assigned to an agency which purchases a substantial amount of care, *see* text accompanying notes 141-146 *supra*, the risk that shortsighted policies will be adopted will be substantially enhanced.

Against this background, it can be seen that regulators in the health sector will have even stronger grounds for resisting exogenous developments than have regulators in other industry settings. Not only will the "sunk-cost obsession" and the fate of valued internal subsidies affect their judgments, but the logical consequences of faith in the Roemer effect will reinforce the tendency to adopt policies excessively protective of the hospital industry and destructive of desirable change.

V. An Assessment of Certificate-of-Need Requirements for Hospitals

Two distinct issues—benefits and costs—must be addressed in making a final assessment of certificate-of-need laws. It seems clear already, however, that certificate-of-need requirements for nursing homes and other extended care facilities and for free-standing ambulatory-care facilities would produce destructive effects exceeding any possible benefits. Moreover, the benefits of a certificate-of-need law for hospitals seem to have been exaggerated, while potential costs have been largely ignored. Although it is impossible to prove conclusively that a net detriment would result from hospital certificate-of-need laws, the case for a closer examination of other possible measures for dealing with hospital costs is certainly strong.

A. Exaggerated Benefits

The Behavior of Certificate-of-Need Agencies

The political environment of most certificate-of-need agencies is likely to be such that they will have no incentive, and in fact no mandate, to do more than bring about conditions roughly equivalent to those which a hospital cartel would maintain if it could. Among the numerous features of the regulatory climate which confirm the expectation of cartel-like behavior are the dominant political influence of the hospital industry; the general belief in the value of more and better health services shared not only by providers and the regulators but also by consumers involved in the regulatory process; the tendency of costs to be submerged in insurance charges and divorced from the services themselves; the importance of internal subsidies in providing services deemed to be in the public interest; the planners' orientation to incremental change based on consensual processes and bargaining rather than "real" planning; and the regulators' naturally protective attitude toward the regulated firms' investments and revenues.

Cartel-like regulation of the hospital industry would foster continued, though reduced, oversupply rather than the undersupply characteristic of cartels generally. This perpetuation of excess capacity would occur precisely because of the continuance of the same underlying conditions—third-party cost reimbursement and provider influence over demand—which produce excessive hospital growth in the first place. Since certificate-of-need laws would not change these conditions, hospitals would continue to prefer to offer more services than are economically justified. These preferences would translate into political pressures inhibiting enforcement which goes much beyond preventing obvious duplication of facilities and services. Avoidance of "duplication" is of course consistent with a cartel's preference for minimizing competition, and Feldstein has shown that, as in other industries, some limitations on growth will have price effects which the industry will regard as desirable.[233]

Given the strong pressures which will act upon it, a certificate-of-need agency may fall short of achieving even a cartel's limited goals for output restriction, much less the public's. For one thing, it seems unlikely that anyone will press the agency to pursue a really tough policy, consumer groups being satisfied if obvious duplication and waste are eliminated and politicians being content with a normalization of the rate of cost increases. On the other hand, particularly potent applicants for certificates of need may tend to win approvals frequently enough to upset the cartel analogy altogether. It would seem that only the best regulatory programs are likely to be effective even to a degree which a provider cartel would approve.

Characterizing agency performance as at best cartel-like should not obscure the possible desirability of whatever reduction they do achieve in the supply of hospital beds and services. However, the dilemma of whether to accept substantially less than total relief is a real one. It is similar to the choice presented by other cartel-like solutions to the health care industry's problems. For example, PSROs and the so-called foundations for medical care may also be analyzed as cartels which, though dedicated to improving existing conditions in real and important ways, will ultimately stop well short of delivering to the public all of the benefits which a well-organized competitive market would yield.[234] Indeed,

---

[233] See note 60 supra and accompanying text.

[234] Both devices have as a goal the reduction of costs by policing physician behavior, but in each case the cartel orientation is clear. Indeed, to ask the question whether physician-dominated agencies such as these will be dedicated primarily to reducing

it is not inaccurate to view the fundamental health policy choice as being between a system controlled directly or indirectly by essentially well-meaning providers who accommodate their public responsibilities with their own self-interest and a system of social control by impersonal market forces allowing consumers a larger impact and assigning government the less intrusive roles of promoter of the competition and referee.

Cartel-like performance in certificate-of-need administration might be avoidable in part by assigning regulatory power to an agency which has major cost-control responsibility—perhaps as regulator of Medicaid rates as in New York State.[235] Given the nature of politics, such an agency would do no more than somewhat retard the rise in health care costs, but this achievement would be better than any result obtainable by regulators lacking direct accountability for costs. Indeed, as population expands, the bed-to-population ratio might gradually fall. Nevertheless, the hospital industry could continue to block the extensive supply restrictions dictated by the public interest.

Effects on Health Care Costs

Even though the rationales for certificate-of-need laws have a great deal of plausibility and intuitive appeal, they need to be evaluated in light of Martin Feldstein's observation that, while new supply does indeed create some new demand—the Roemer effect—, there is a concomitant depressing effect on price.[236] This effect somewhat dilutes hospitals' incentives to grow. Moreover, as a result of the persistence of some of the

---

health care costs to the level dictated by the public interest—*i.e.*, that which an ideal competitive market would yield—is to answer it negatively. The more important issue may be whether the real but relatively minor benefits to be anticipated can be obtained without foreclosing the much more hopeful long-run impact of HMOs. Unfortunately, PSROs have been given direct regulatory power over HMOs, and foundations have both the incentive and the opportunity to preempt HMO market opportunities, suggesting that HMOs' competitive impact may indeed be effectively neutralized. *See* Havighurst, *supra* note 81; Havighurst, *supra* note 18, at 769-76; Havighurst, Foundations for Medical Care: An Antitrust Lawyer's Perspective, Aug. 30, 1972 (address to the American Ass'n of Foundations for Medical Care, Sea Island, Ga. [hereinafter cited as Havighurst, *Foundations*]. *Compare* notes 247 & 252 *infra* on the abuses to which professionally sponsored efforts are subject.

235 It is difficult to assess cost-consciousness in a state agency. Questionnaires from only Florida, Michigan, and New York of the 14 responding agencies acknowledged responsibility for paying for care under Medicaid, but many agencies were subdivisions of departments having such responsibility. On a possibly significant hazard from combining payment responsibility and certificate-of-need administration in the same agency, see note 232 *supra*.

236 *See* note 60 *supra* and accompanying text.

usual impact of supply on price, imposition of a regulatory restraint on the growth of the bed supply will result in somewhat higher prices than would otherwise prevail. This price effect will cancel some of the cost savings which result from the lower utilization produced by controlling supply. Even effective rate regulation would seem incapable of obtaining the price reduction which growth of supply would have generated.

Because certificate-of-need laws look only to certain kinds of hospital costs, they may merely divert inflationary pressures and achieve no control. The mechanism by which prices rise in the hospital sector is complex because of the prevalence of nonprofit firms and financing by cost-reimbursement, which together negate the usual expectation that profits will accrue when demand exceeds supply, as it would under certificate-of-need restrictions. However, Feldstein and others have shown that, instead of the expected profits, new costs emerge rapidly under such market conditions, as managers expand plant and labor force, buy expensive equipment, raise wages, and pay less attention to economizing measures. Consider, for example, how much more likely it is that an unwarranted increase in hospital wages will occur if restriction of the hospital bed supply has increased the hospital's ability to pass the cost on to the public. Although the wage increase might be regarded as socially preferable to the costs associated with uncontrolled growth, the choice between giving extra wages to employees and giving extra hospital care to sick people is not that clear-cut. In any event, other types of cost increases, which are equally likely to occur, will be less appealing.

Against this background, the critical inflationary factor appears to be simply the existence of opportunities for raising prices—that is, the excess demand which is generated by "methods of hospital insurance [which] have encouraged hospitals to raise wage rates and to increase the sophistication and expensiveness of their product more rapidly than the public actually wants." [237] Under such circumstances, regulatory control of less than all the inputs and their prices seems unlikely to produce a very favorable effect on total hospital costs. [238] Certificate-of-need

---

[237] FELDSTEIN, *supra* note 1, at 79.

[238] The second circumstance [contributing to regulatory ineffectiveness] is that the regulatory body is incapable of forcing the utility to operate at a specified combination of output, price, and cost. . . . Since [it] cannot effectively control the daily detail of business operations, it cannot deal with variables whose effect is of the same order of magnitude in their effects on profits as the variables upon which it does have some influence.

Stigler & Friedland, *What Can Regulators Regulate? The Case of Electricity*, 5 J. LAW & ECON. 1, 11 (1962). For example, it is possible that control of capital investment could

laws, or even a second generation of regulatory paraphernalia, can probably never reach such things as wage rates, the size and skill of the hospital labor force, the extent of laboratory and radiographic services ordered, and the myriad small upgradings of "quality" which together spell higher and higher costs even if utilization is somewhat limited by supply restrictions.

In the absence of any affirmative evidence of cost-control benefits from certificate-of-need laws,[239] the possibility that these benefits are no more than minimal must be taken seriously. Indeed, one economist has suggested that the various feedback effects of restricting the bed supply could actually produce a net increase in total expenditures for medical care.[240] Although these observations are inconclusive, it does appear that expectations of major cost-control benefits are unduly optimistic.[241]

shift the input mix in hospitals toward heavier reliance on labor, which in recent years has had the more rapidly inflating price. If so, there is yet another factor cutting away at any cost savings under certificate-of-need laws. See B. Zellner, Inflationary Impact of Certificate-of-Need Laws, January, 1973 (Working note, InterStudy).

[239] One looks in vain for a careful study of New York's experience since 1964. The New York Commissioner of Health claims that the New York program "has disapproved construction of over 51,000 beds, saving approximately $1.6 billion in capital costs and $738 million annually in operating costs." Hollis S. Ingraham, Health Facility Regulation in New York State, an address before a panel of the National Health Forum, Chicago, March 20, 1973. The alleged savings are not broken down between nursing and hospital beds, but, if even a fraction of savings of this magnitude had occurred in the hospital sector, they should be visible in gross hospital expenditures in New York State. But hospital cost inflation seems to have been no less virulent in New York than elsewhere up to 1970, when rate regulation began. Although growth of the bed supply does seem to have been slowed somewhat and occupancy rates improved slightly, against the national trend, the lack of a detectable impact on gross costs, plus the reasons in the text for not expecting any, must argue for not counting on certificate-of-need laws to ameliorate the problem of inflation.

[240] Zellner, supra note 238. Not only do supply restrictions seem likely to cause somewhat higher hospital costs than would prevail in their absence, but substitution of outpatient care for inpatient care, where the latter is more strictly rationed, will have costs associated with it. These costs represent further erosion of the apparent savings produced by limiting the bed supply.

[241] A final assessment of a certificate-of-need agency's actual performance and impact would be very difficult, requiring special analytical skills and considerable manpower and resources. "The test of the economic effect of regulation is essentially independent of the content of the formal regulations. No degree of care in analyzing the regulations, or even their administration, will tell us whether they rubber-stamp or slightly heckle the state of affairs or substantially alter it." Stigler & Friedland, supra note 238, at 2, suggesting the necessity for empirically comparing industry performance in regulated and unregulated markets. New York's early enactment of a certificate-of-need law should provide the data needed for such a comparison. There is an understandable but unfortunate tendency, however, to base judgments on impressions gained in inter-

A final issue which must be confronted is the nature of any cost savings which might be gained. Since some of the savings sought are expected to reflect reduced hospital utilization, it is fair to inquire whether the care forgone is in fact that which is medically unnecessary or not worth the cost. Thus, attention must be directed to the rationing process adopted when facilities are in short supply.[242] Unless the rationing system is in fact rational, any apparent cost savings will be at the expense of patients' health, reflecting the erection of a new barrier to access rather than an improvement in system efficiency. Such an access barrier is likely to affect the disadvantaged patient most directly and to undercut the notion of health care as a right. Certificate-of-need proponents may have assumed too readily that restricting the bed supply would produce more rational use of facilities.[243]

The Extent of the Benefits

The evidence suggests that certificate-of-need laws are likely to give the public substantially less than it is entitled to in the way of restrictions on hospital output and that cost-control benefits will be limited by the tendency of inflationary pressures to reappear in effects on costs which are less easily regulated. However, partial effectiveness alone is not a conclusive argument against such laws, and it seems probable that some potential benefits remain.

---

views and on anecdotes and apparent success in turning away proposals. Counting applications and denials is unreliable because applications may be discouraged (see text accompanying notes 210-11 supra) or stimulated (see note 104 supra) by certificate-of-need laws and projects denied approval might not have gone forward in any event; indeed, some states include in their box score of projects denied those which were clearly pre-empted by approval of a competing application. See note 259 infra.

[242] See Feldstein, Econometric Studies, supra note 54, at 21-22; Klarman, supra note 57, at 188.

[243] See note 199 supra. The common observation that the hospitals with high occupancy rates seem to ration effectively may ignore physicians' use of alternative hospitals and other factors. However, a study by Rafferty, Patterns of Hospital Use: An Analysis of Short-Run Variations, 71 J. POL. ECON. 154 (1971), suggests that rationing is more rational in high-occupancy months than in low-occupancy months in the two hospitals in a single town. Nevertheless, no socioeconomic variable was examined to detect an access barrier, and mere postponements of hospitalization to a low-occupancy month were not distinguished from decisions not to hospitalize at all. Perhaps physicians are more cooperative with respect to postponements. The issue needs both further study and a benchmark for determining whether performance is only slightly improved or approaches optimality. Professional bed-rationing may prove to be either another imperfect cartel solution, see note 234 supra and accompanying text, or an efficient non-market allocative mechanism.

Even if a certificate-of-need law were administered as if the job had been entrusted to a cartel, it would at least go part of the way toward correcting the incorrect incentives for growth in the hospital sector. Hospital administrators would be curbed in their pursuit of growth and in their nonprice competition for doctors, to whom it would be much easier to say "no." Moreover, real social gains may be obtainable by directing new investments away from useless new hospital beds or duplicative facilities and into projects which are in some sense more "needed" even if they are not fully worth their cost—community services or higher wages, for example. Finally, some quality gains could probably be expected from coordination of services among institutions and from discouraging plans which are poorly conceived, which frustrate attainment of scale economies, or which are excessively profit-oriented.

Thus, the projected benefits of regulation appear to lie as much in the areas of assured quality and reduced resource misallocation as in cost control. Even though these benefits are of a somewhat different nature than those projected by certificate-of-need proponents, they may nevertheless be real. For this reason, the extent of any costs which certificate-of-need requirements might impose must be analyzed to determine if they exceed a reasonable estimate of the benefits.

B. *Potential Costs*

Administrative and Compliance Costs

The only obvious costs imposed by certificate-of-need laws are the administrative costs of the regulatory program itself. These include not only the costs of operating the state agencies but also the costs incurred by areawide planning bodies in performing their review and comment functions. Slightly less obvious are the costs of compliance incurred by the applicants themselves. These costs are largely absorbed in providers' overhead and ultimately appear in their charges as costs of "health care." Among the compliance costs are those associated with delay, including those resulting from rises in construction costs while applications are pending.

It is sometimes alleged that the review and comment functions of CHP agencies divert them from other, possibly more useful, activities, suggesting the existence of opportunity costs greater than the actual dollar outlays and recalling the "brushfire-wars" hypothesis explored earlier. A great deal would remain on the health planner's agenda if his mandatory facilities planning functions were curtailed, for the local challenges in dealing with alcoholism, emergency care, drug abuse, community mental health, neighborhood health centers, and a wide range of other matters are immense. Indeed, the planners' past fascination with facilities in the face of other problems of so much greater magnitude argues for a major reordering of priorities.[244]

Hospital Competition

The loss of both actual and potential competition among hospitals, which a need requirement necessarily imposes in some degree, will not seem critical to many observers. Because of limited opportunities for consumer choice, such competition has seldom been a strong force. Where it has appeared, it has not been dependably conducive either to better quality or to lower prices. Instead, it has often produced nonprice competition for doctors, emphasis on amenities and image-building, and cream-skimming at the expense of services to the poor and other socially desirable activities.

Removal of opportunities for hospital competition will nevertheless cause some loss in technical (input-output) efficiency and responsiveness to consumer desires. It may also generate losses from distortions resulting from continued discriminatory pricing and from forgone opportunities for substituting low-cost for high-cost care. Moreover, if competition is restricted, needed changes in the methods of pricing and paying for health care may prove less likely to appear or less effective in improving performance.

Losses in Innovation and Change

Even though it may be difficult to attribute high costs to the loss of hospital competition per se, certificate-of-need legislation also sacrifices significant potential gains from technical innovation and institutional change which competition might induce. Losses from this effect are unmeasurable but would occur if uncertainty surrounding the need requirement reduces the likelihood that innovators will receive economic benefits from their innovations. Thus a lower rate of innovation would result from the prospect that some innovations might be excluded altogether, delayed in introduction, or admitted to the market only on limited terms or only after existing providers had been able to imitate them.

---

[244] This argument probably holds *a fortiori* for nursing homes.

Regulation of entry and premarketing clearance requirements in other industries have had such effects. Moreover, the sympathy which customarily springs up between the regulated and the regulators, as well as the regulators' "sunk-cost obsession" and the perceived need to protect internal subsidies, leads inexorably to policies which inhibit drastic change.

It is unrealistic to rely as heavily as the health world now does on the initiatives of existing providers or on health planners to produce needed change. Protected against sudden competitive developments, the providers have no incentive to innovate in anticipation of them. Some innovations will undoubtedly occur because providers take their public responsibilities seriously, but cost-saving changes have customarily received low priority in comparison to technically sophisticated developments. For these reasons, exogenous influences seem essential to stimulate innovation and organizational flexibility. Commercially inspired efforts, even if sometimes troublesome from a quality standpoint, will usually more than repay their short-term costs in long-term system improvements.

Faith in governmental impetus for change also seems misplaced. Health planners and public administrators have uniformly reported difficulty in effecting major alterations in existing structures, and government in general, reflecting the same environmental factors which influence the performance of regulatory agencies, remains a powerful bulwark of established interests. Even though efforts to work through governmental processes are worthwhile, the likelihood of success is not great enough to warrant foreclosing private initiatives.

The Irrevocability of Choosing Regulation

Of course, the hospital industry is already heavily regulated, not only by governmental agencies but also by accrediting organizations, third-party payers, and professional organizations.[245] Aside from the possibly temporary federal price controls, however, extensive economic regulation is not the universal rule. Yet the pressure for comprehensive regulation, encompassing entry, service responsibilities, rates, and quality of care, is strong. Although the tipping point is hard to identify, the enactment of a certificate-of-need law seems likely to be the first irrevocable step down the road to public utility controls. Seemingly a small step in itself, it may take us past the last decision point at which a choice might

---

[245] See generally A. SOMERS, supra note 41.

still be made for some continued reliance on market forces to organize the health care industry.

It should be assumed for all practical purposes that enactment of a reasonably broad certificate-of-need law is irreversible, even if a considerable amount of evidence accumulates to suggest its failures. Shortcomings such as discouraging innovation and protecting inefficiency will be difficult to establish. Moreover, regulation creates strong vested interests in its continuation, including a bureaucracy with interests of its own, and these interests oppose major policy changes, particularly those strengthening competition or reducing the gross revenues of, or the resources employed in, the industry. Indeed, emendations of regulatory statutes nearly always widen the scope of regulation rather than narrow it, and instances of substantial deregulation of an industry, though widely advocated on the basis of proven social costs, are practically unheard of. Such a serious loss of policy flexibility is another important cost of starting down the road to public utility regulation.

If certificate-of-need laws do in fact disappoint expectations of a favorable impact on health care costs, more extensive hospital regulation is certain to follow. Because the various adverse consequences of comprehensive rate and service regulation do not appear on the face of the legislative package and because the regulatory "solution" purports to address the problems more forthrightly than any other approach, legislators will be tempted to adopt it. As a well-advertised legislative product containing fine sentiments and betokening only the best intentions, it is eminently salable in the legislator's marketplace, and the resulting legislative bias in favor of the regulatory package is reinforced by the preferences of the most prominent interest groups. The difficulty of resisting the pressures for public utility regulation is thus apparent. For this reason, the probable social costs of a system run under these principles must be anticipated in evaluating proposals for certificate-of-need legislation.

VI. Certificate-of-Need Laws Versus the Alternatives

Once the benefits and probable costs are weighed realistically, it is hard to understand how a certificate-of-need law could seem a very attractive device for addressing the rising cost of medical care. Its effect is likely to be very slight, probably undetectable in gross figures, and its potential for destructive impact is considerable. In these circumstances, state legislatures could rationally conclude that excessive hospital growth should be tolerated or dealt with by a variety of other mechanisms which, though also imperfect, may carry a lower degree of risk. Although this is not the place for a detailed examination of the alternatives which might help in this effort, some directions may be pointed.

A. Fundamental Reforms

HMO development is perhaps the most promising nonregulatory strategy for bringing the excessive use of health care resources under effective control.[246] Because the prepayment feature of HMOs leads them to conserve resources, their presence in the marketplace would be felt by the fee-for-service sector as a pressure to reduce costs. There is already evidence that HMOs' competition has stimulated the fee-for-service sector to begin doing privately the cost-control job which many are looking to public agencies to do.[247] Such cost-control efforts have so far concentrated on curbing hospital utilization, thereby reducing hospitals' incentives for inappropriate growth. One could also expect

[246] See, e.g., Ellwood, Anderson, Billings, Carlson, Hoagberg, & McClure, *Health Maintenance Strategy*, 9 MED. CARE 291 (1971); Havighurst, *supra* note 18. The simplest conceptualization of the HMO's potential impact is as a "close substitute" for the services sold by the fee-for-service "monopoly." Because of the immense difficulty of altering the numerous economic and political conditions fostering the monopoly power of individual fee-for-service providers—consumer ignorance, provider control of demand, third-party payment, inhibitions on insurer competition based on cost control, and so forth (*see id.* at 767-69)—creation of opportunities for independent marketing of a substitute service is probably the best policy alternative available. In technical terms, introduction of such a substitute tends to flatten the demand curve for the monopolized service, lowering the monopolist's profit-maximizing price. If consumers find the two services reasonably interchangeable, "cross-elasticity of demand" is high, and the monopoly of one service is of lessened, or no, consequence. *Cf.* United States v. E.I. duPont de Nemours & Co., 351 U.S. 377 (1956). Attention must be directed to maintaining competition between the two modes by facilitating entry, preventing collusion, and barring one mode from being controlled by interests having a stake in the other. *See generally* Havighurst, *supra*, at 759-95; Havighurst, *Foundations*, *supra* note 234.

[247] The activities of those so-called foundations for medical care which follow the "California model" of claims review, pioneered by the San Joaquin Foundation for Medical Care, appear directly motivated by HMO competition, which is much more active in California than elsewhere. *See* Sasuly & Hopkins, *A Medical Society-sponsored Comprehensive Medical Care Plan*, 5 MED. CARE 234 (1967). *See also* STEINWALD, *supra* note 92, at 6-25; Havighurst, *supra* note 18, at 769-77; Havighurst, *Foundations*, *supra* note 234. Similar physician-sponsored plans in Oregon, particularly the Physicians' Association of Clackamas County, were inspired by similar competitive and ethical concerns in the 1930s and 1940s. *See* Brief for the United States at 25-29, 36-41, United States v. Oregon State Medical Society, 343 U.S. 326 (1952). Other mechanisms which the fee-for-service sector can employ in fighting HMO incursions through cost control include PSROs, planning agencies, and third-party-payer claims review and utilization controls. *See* note 234 *supra* and notes 252 & 256 *infra*.

that, under a competitive stimulus, physicians and third-party payers as well as the hospitals themselves would come to scrutinize the investments being made in order that insured-fee-for-service care in the community would be kept competitive with HMO membership. If the institutional arrangements and attitudinal changes necessary for such cooperation in cost control were not forthcoming, competing HMOs would prosper.

It is commonly asserted that HMO impact is both far-off and uncertain and that other cost-control measures are therefore needed. Although this argument has some merit, it is usually overstated, since the benefits of changed incentives in the fee-for-service sector begin to be realized as soon as the environment becomes congenial to HMO development. Effective "potential competition" can be nearly as beneficial as actual competition in stimulating better performance by industry incumbents. Indeed, many of the widely heralded cost-control efforts of foundations for medical care and other provider groups have been inspired in large measure by concerns about HMO entry into the marketing area.[248] For these reasons, facilitation of HMO market entry should be given the highest priority by state legislatures.[249] Clearing the way for a market test of the HMO idea would have a beneficial impact on many of the problems which certificate-of-need laws are meant to address.

Among the other fundamental reforms which might be implemented to address the problems which prompt certificate-of-need proposals are several designed to restore consumer price-awareness in obtaining care. For example, government might abandon insuring on a first-dollar basis and provide universal health insurance having a very high annual deductible, perhaps ten percent of income. Such a plan would restore the consumer to a purchasing role and dethrone cost-reimbursement as the principal method of price determination.[250] A similar result could be obtained by encouraging health insurers to pay per diem indemnities to their insureds rather than actual hospital charges.[251] A further, though highly speculative, possibility is active price competition among health insurers which features, among other things, aggressive cost-control ef-

---

[248] See note 247 supra.

[249] See Havighurst, Foreword—HMOs in Policy Perspective, in HEALTH LAW CENTER, ASPEN SYSTEMS CORP., HMO SOURCEBOOK—1973 EDITION vii (1973).

[250] Feldstein, A New Approach to National Health Insurance, PUBLIC INTEREST, Spring 1971, at 93; see also M. PAULY, NATIONAL HEALTH INSURANCE: AN ANALYSIS 33-48 (1971).

[251] See Newhouse & Taylor, How Shall We Pay for Hospital Care?, PUBLIC INTEREST, Spring 1971, at 78.

forts, perhaps even including requirements for prior authorization of certain procedures.[252]

B. Symptomatic Relief

Remedies for the health care industry's cost problems might be less sweeping than the ones just suggested. One possibility would be a switch from cost reimbursement to some kind of rate regulation, preferably a system of incentive reimbursement. For example, hospitals could be grouped and paid an amount adequate to cover costs of the average hospital in the group.[253] In these circumstances, the more efficient hospitals or those located in areas of high demand would have surpluses and therefore the means and borrowing capacity to modernize and expand, while others would suffer losses and be deprived of the ability to expand. Although such a system would not directly address the problem

---

[252] Insurers demonstrate little inclination to compete in policing the appropriateness of care and the cost thereof, however, mainly because of the medical profession's willingness to boycott insurers who attempt to second-guess medical judgments and charges. See, e.g., Rosenberg, He Challenged Aetna's Hard Line Fee Policy—and Won, MED. ECON., Sept. 11, 1972, at 31, and Letters to the Editor, MED. ECON., Dec. 4, 1972, at 23, 27-29. Although Blue Cross and Blue Shield plans have moved gingerly in the direction of some claims review, there is no basis for expecting that active insurer competition in cost control would be tolerated by doctors. Indeed, when such competition broke out in Oregon in the 1940s, the medical profession's response was to establish a plan of the Blue Shield variety, which eventually brought insurers into line, apparently by means of disciplinary (below-cost) pricing and threats of boycott against insurers who refused to follow Blue Shield's lead. United States v. Oregon State Medical Soc'y, 343 U.S. 326 (1952).

As doctors persuasively allege, insurers may not be trustworthy in interfering in the process of rendering medical care; on prior authorization, for example, see the alleged "horribles" in Brief for the Oregon State Medical Society at 146-53, id. Moreover, in many cases they might wield monopsony power, enabling them to exploit physicians unfairly. Nevertheless, regulation to curb abuses, but otherwise to legitimatize and encourage insurers' cost-control efforts, should be considered. So far as I know, no one has advocated or even studied this approach. Carried to its logical conclusion, this competitive model would yield a variety of insurance plans, most of them offering as a "closed panel" those physicians and hospitals who voluntarily accepted the particular cost-control program. With policies covering only care obtained from these listed providers, insurers would very nearly become, in effect, HMOs. Almost certainly, the prospects for such developments are dim, but real freedom for HMO development would achieve many of the benefits of a system like the one described.

[253] See Lave, Lave & Silverman, A Proposal for Incentive Reimbursement for Hospitals, 11 MED. CARE 79 (1973). See also K. BAUER & P. DENSEN, SOME ISSUES IN THE INCENTIVE REIMBURSEMENT APPROACH TO COST CONTAINMENT: AN OVERVIEW (Harvard Program on Health Care Policy, Discussion Paper No. 7, 1973). For a survey and critique of similar proposals in other regulated industries, see Posner, supra note 48, at 627-32.

of the Roemer effect—which might persist in hospitals threatened with losses and extinction—it might improve the rationality of new hospital investments.

The advantages of rate regulation over certificate-of-need laws include preservation of both entry possibilities and some opportunities for market tests of provider performance. Rate regulation may also be used temporarily, either while the market pressures supplied by HMOs are strengthening or to cushion the inflationary impact of national health insurance. The federal Cost of Living Council appears to be operating in the spirit of returning one day to a market-oriented health care system.

A possibility deserving more attention than it has received is the improvement of the mechanisms whereby a hospital may be encouraged to leave the industry when the need for it has evaporated. Whereas certificate-of-need laws turn off the spigot of fresh supply, it would be preferable if supply were regulated by processes which allowed inadequate or unneeded providers to go "down the drain." Attention to the market exit problem could take two forms. Perhaps state nonprofit corporation acts could be amended to induce or compel a nonprofit corporation to liquidate whenever the salvage value of its assets exceeded its "value" as a "going concern." [254] In the event that the liquidation incentives of trustees and managers of nonprofit hospitals could not be strengthened, regulatory powers to condemn or otherwise eliminate unneeded beds or institutions might be considered. Naturally the politics of any such regulatory program would be explosive, but perhaps the matter could be left to judicial decision under objective criteria, with the right to initiate a liquidation proceeding assigned to public or private agencies which had an interest in cost control.

Other measures for dealing with health care costs are likely to reduce provider control of demand, thereby weakening both the Roemer effect and the case for certificate-of-need laws. Utilization review is being undertaken by foundations for medical care under several state Medicaid programs, and PSROs will soon exercise major controls over costs, utilization, and quality under Medicare and other federal programs. Blue Cross plans have intensified claims review in a number of places, and, particularly in those areas where HMOs are strong, foundations for medical care have become involved in reviewing claims for health insurers and even in providing prepaid HMO-type care directly, with cost and utilization controls over participating physicians. These emerg-

---

[254] See note 67 supra.

ing mechanisms of claims review will surely affect hospital investment decisions and are probably already reflected in declining hospital occupancy rates. However, because these mechanisms of symptomatic relief are largely in the hands of the medical profession, they seem unlikely to achieve their full potential unless incentives are changed by allowing actual or potential HMO competition to materialize.[255]

Rejection of the certificate-of-need approach to controlling health care costs need not constitute a denial of the utility of health planning. Planners without regulatory powers have had a desirable impact in many circumstances, succeeding primarily by educating providers, governmental agencies, philanthropic interests, and others to the existence of needs and to their responsibilities for meeting them. Inefficient as operating without teeth may seem, it may strengthen the planners' incentives to develop the credibility and persuasive arguments needed to prod political organs or providers into action on specific matters. Similarly, the planners' cultivation of influence with third-party payers, including Medicare under the 1972 amendments, can provide quite effective control over egregious facilities duplication. Their impact in this regard could be expected to grow as HMO competition stimulates greater cost-consciousness in the fee-for-service sector.[256]

Quality-of-care concerns also appear in certificate-of-need proposals, and it may be asked whether alternative approaches to this problem are available. Constructive comment on this issue would open up immense complexities, but as a generalization it may be said that regulation expressly based on outcomes of care, now being carefully explored for feasibility, would be much more effective than input regulation under certificate-of-need laws.[257] In addition, incentives for improved quality may be strengthened by disclosure of outcomes and by other mechanisms.[258] More immediately, PSROs are expected to evaluate quality and would seem capable of taking over whatever quality functions are performed by certificate-of-need agencies.

---

[255] See note 234 supra and accompanying text.

[256] See notes 234, 246, 247, & 252 supra. A certificate-of-need agency might also be a useful mechanism in the fee-for-service sector's response to HMO competition. Even functioning as an agent for a cartel, it would be more aggressive in cost control than it would be in the absence of HMOs, though it would leave HMOs a greater share of the market than under competition. Cf. Havighurst, Foundations, supra note 234.

[257] See note 95 supra.

[258] See notes 75-76 supra and accompanying text.

C. A Modified Certificate-of-Need Law

Some observers will probably remain unconvinced that certificate-of-need laws should be dispensed with altogether, since they will still see hospitals as afflicted by perverse incentives to grow in inefficient ways and will not accept the notion that direct action against this manifest problem can be ineffective or destructive.[259] Moreover, the pressures for enactment of certificate-of-need laws will remain intense, originating with the hospital industry, health insurers, the health planning and public health establishment, and particularly the federal government, which is currently offering financial support and other encouragement. In view of these circumstances, it may be useful to offer here some specifications for drafting a modified certificate-of-need law which will produce as many of the expected benefits as possible and minimize the costs. Because many of the existing laws leave the regulators a great deal of discretion, some of these specifications may also prove useful in improving the administration of existing certificate-of-need programs.

My recommendations are as follows:

(1) In order to offset provider influence, certification of need should be lodged in an agency which bears direct political responsibility for the cost of health care as a purchaser of care under Medicaid and state employee health programs.[260] A substantial advisory or appellate role should be assigned to a part-time board having no more than token provider representation.

(2) Coverage of the law should be limited to hospitals only, excluding nursing-care institutions and all ambulatory-care facilities, particularly those of HMOs.

(3) A total exemption from the need requirement should be given to HMO hospital facilities.

(4) Strict standards of openness in policy formulation and implementation should be established, including requirements for public rule-making as to all general policies and for detailed findings of facts and full statements of reasons and dissenting views as to particular decisions.

---

[259] There is a natural tendency to presume regulatory effectiveness on the basis of perceived regulatory activity. "But the innumerable regulatory actions are conclusive proof, not of effective regulation, but of the desire to regulate. And if wishes were horses, one would buy stock in a harness factory." Stigler & Friedland, *supra* note 238, at 1.

[260] However, it should be divorced from any regulation of hospital rates in order that internal subsidy possibilities will be minimized. *See* text accompanying notes 170-77 *supra*. Most rate regulatory programs have preserved this separation.

(5) Reliance on real planning should be mandatory, with decisions based on published quotas and sound (as opposed to historical) utilization practices.[261]

(6) In so far as possible, grounds for departing from published plans should be articulated in advance, and these grounds should reflect an express commitment to increasing the range of consumer choice, strengthening competition, reducing costs, and encouraging innovation.

(7) The need requirement should be defined so as not to shelter non-cost-related pricing or to prevent entry by providers giving less comprehensive care ("cream-skimmers") except where care of indigent patients would unavoidably be jeopardized.

(8) The law should have a fixed expiration date so that it appears more as a moratorium than as a permanent commitment to regulation.

It is still too early to make the ultimate health policy choice between health planning-cum-regulation and a more market-oriented system which relies primarily on decentralized decisions by providers, consumers, and insurers. Both have their adherents in the policy debate, and neither has proved itself as yet, although the imperfections of the market as we know it have been much ventilated. Perhaps in five years it will be possible to assess with greater assurance the impact of such changes as an improved system of national health insurance, HMO development, utilization controls, and various regulatory experiments. If limited regulation producing a moratorium on hospital construction could get us, uncommitted and with better information, to that decision point, it would have provided a valuable service. It may be unrealistic, however, to think that regulation can be employed as a temporizing measure.[262]

This Article has used certificate-of-need laws as the occasion for appraising the imperfections of comprehensive regulatory responses to the health care crisis and has produced a pessimistic judgment. Still, carefully limited regulation having a clear and limited purpose may be use-

---

[261] This requirement may be a mistake for two reasons: (1) facilities planning may hold too little promise to be endorsed in this manner, and (2) the added planning bureaucracy entailed by the requirement may become so influential a vested interest that objective reappraisal of the need for such a law in the future will be impossible. *See* text accompanying note 245 *supra*.

[262] Possibly a better expedient than the one presented would be a moratorium on hospital construction imposed at the federal level, with necessary variances granted or withheld without involving the planning agencies. The very arbitrariness of such a scheme would guarantee its temporary nature and would be consistent with the philosophy behind the wage and price controls.

ful in improving the functioning of the health care marketplace, re-ordering the operative incentives, and checking abuses where they appear. The strong temptation to adopt the "solution" of comprehensive economic regulation, which springs from the frustrations of coping with an unruly market, must be resisted in favor of trying approaches which may succeed in preserving the dynamism of a market-oriented system while minimizing its costs.

EXHIBIT 4.—*Report Prepared for U.S. DHEW Re Iatrogenic Injuries*

THE INCIDENCE OF IATROGENIC INJURIES

Leon S. Pocincki, Sc.D

Stuart J. Dogger, B.S.

Barbara P. Schwartz, R.N.

Summary

In this study of the incidence of iatrogenic injuries, somewhat more than 800 medical records were examined by two medical-legal experts at two hospitals which were chosen to be reasonably representative of American hospitals. The principal random sample of medical records was drawn from adult medicine, surgery, and gynecology cases, which accounted for more than 80 percent of all patients in the hospitals during the period under study. The overall sampling rate was close to 16 percent. Data were abstracted from the medical records, and the reviewers completed a questionnaire for *each case* alleged to be an injury. Statistical analyses, performed to determine the "goodness of sample" on the basis of average length of stay, age distribution, and distribution by hospital service showed that the sample was representative of the population from which it was drawn (i.e., all hospital discharges).

Ninety cases were initially identified by the reviewers as (iatrogenic) injuries. These injury cases were then further examined by the original reviewers plus an additional medical-legal counsultant. Of the 70 injury cases that remained after that meeting, several were still questionable and were further discussed in a final panel meeting which included two additional medical consultants. The final number of cases determined to involve injuries was 62. No effort was made to reexamine the cases that were initially rejected as non-injuries, although subsequent findings indicated that some of these cases may well have been injuries that were overlooked. Hence, the final injury figure can be said to be a lower bound.

In addition to the random sample, a control sample containing records, identified by hospital incident reports or previous claims, was drawn and intermixed with the random sample. The purpose was to establish a measure of the reviewers' "miss" rate in assessing injuries. The reviewers only identified about 60 percent of these records as injury cases.

Data associated with the injury cases were to provide additional information relating to the cause and nature of the injuries. These data included average length of stay, age distribution, service distribution, evidence of injury (charts, reports, etc.), source of injury (personnel), severity of injury, and classification of injury. The results are indicated briefly below. The average stay for injury patients was substantially longer than that for the random sample patients generally. The most frequent initial evidence of injury was in laboratory reports, progress notes, vital sign graphic charts, and operative notes. Attending physicians were by far the largest personnel group specifically associated with injuries by the reviewers. Although most injuries were temporary in nature, eight resulted in death. More than 65 percent of the injuries were due to post-operative complications. Age, service, and length of stay are all strongly related to the injury detection rates, but the underlying causal relationship has not been established.

Those injury cases for which the reviewers ascribed the injury to negligence were subjected to further analysis. Final results indicated an overall patient injury rate at the two sample hospitals of approximately 7.5 percent. This figure, due to the methods used in the study, represents a lower bound on the true injury rate.

Finally, making use of the available data and the above results, projections for both hospitals (combined) were made for the estimated 23,750 patients discharged during 1972. The projections indicate that:

- 1,780 patient injuries occurred
- 517 of the injuries were due to negligence
- 31 claims will be filed against the hospital or medical staff on behalf of patients discharged during the year.

This report was prepared for the Secretary's Commission on Medical Malpractice, U.S. Department of Health, Education, and Welfare, under Contract No HEW-OS-73-22 with Geomet, Inc. Report No. SCMM-ER-GE-11.

The methods developed successfully supported a study of patient injuries in the hospital setting The techniques, modified on the basis of the experience gained, should be applied on a wider scale in the future.

Table of Contents

Section I
Introduction

Heretofore, the principal focus on the malpractice issue has been on claims and associated high awards to plaintiffs, and the resulting high insurance premiums. The Commission felt that it could not concentrate on these facets only; that it was also necessary to examine the basic underlying source of malpractice claims. The major thrust of this study, therefore, was directed toward the *quantification* and analysis of those elements of the health care delivery system that bear directly on how and why injuries that precipitate malpractice claims occur. Additional motivation lies in previous reports that "unfortunate sequelae and accidents attributable to sanctioned and well-intentioned diagnosis and therapy were noted in about five percent of patients admitted to medical wards." (Barr 1955.)

This report describes how the following questions were addressed, and the answers obtained.

- What procedures should be used in medical records review?
- What instruments should be developed (for reviewing medical records)?
- What is the rate of injury detection that can be expected from the medical records check?
- How can the medical-legal experts be utilized with maximum effectiveness (i.e., the method of selecting records to be reviewed)?

The report is essentially a description of a test of one set of answers to these questions and the results thereof. The procedures actually used in the medical records review are described, including the functioning of the medical-legal experts (Section II). The data related to the incidence of reported injuries are presented in Section III.

It was necessary upon initiation of this study to adopt a working definition of iatrogenic disease. The definition adopted was essentially the one proposed by Burgess (1965), i.e., a disease caused by "errors of omission or commission as may be directly or indirectly caused by able physicians acting in accordance with modern medical usage,"; this definition was extended as proposed by Kampmeier (1966) to include the application of methods of diagnosis or treatment to the detriment of the patient's health or even the cause of death. Schimmel (1964) limits the definition to exclude discomforts not considered harmful to the patient but which are necessary in the usual course of current medical diagnosis and therapy. There was considerable discussion, bordering on disagreement, regarding an acceptable definition on the part of the participants in the study during its early stages. Upon review of the results of the study, and on the basis of observing the work of the medical-legal reviewers, these are essentially the definitions that have been applied in the identification of injuries in this study.

Section II
Method

SELECTION OF THE HOSPITALS

Particular care has been taken to maintain strict confidentiality of all information presented in this report. This applies to identification of the participating hospitals, as well as the identity of those patients whose records were examined. The participating hospitals were selected on the basis of six criteria:

- Non-profit
- Community-based general hospital
- In the 250-400 bed range
- Participate in the Professional Activity Study - Medical Audit Program of the Commission on Professional and Hospital Activities (PAS-MAP)
- Operate a training program (at least a residency)
- Operate an organized outpatient department.

These criteria were used to select hospitals that could be considered somewhat representative of the mainstream of American institutional health care.

The two large urban hospitals selected met all six of the criteria; both were short-term general medical/surgical hospitals. Each hospital operates a residency program, but no residents were on their staffs during the period covered by the medical record audit. Without the complete co-operation offered by the administrative staff, and particularly the medical record personnel, this study would have been impossible. The hospitals can be characterized by the data appearing in Table 1. Specific numerical data have been rounded off to prevent identification of the hospitals. The principal approvals and accreditations of each hospital are summarized in Table 2.

TABLE 1

PRINCIPAL CHARACTERISTICS OF PARTICIPATING HOSPITALS

Characteristics	Hospital	
	A	B
Number of Beds	250	290
Number of Admissions (1970)	10,000	12,000
Census (average over 12 months)	190	225
Occupancy Rate	76%	80%
Number of Full-Time Equivalent Personnel	770	860

TABLE 2

APPROVALS OF PARTICIPATING HOSPITALS

Approval	Hospital	
	A	B
Joint Commission on Accreditation of Hospitals	X	X
AMA-approved Residency	X	X
AMA-approved Internship	X	–
Professional Nursing School Reported by National League of Nursing	X	X
Blue Cross	X	X
Medicare Certified	X	X

Although it is not appropriate to attempt to describe two hospitals as totally representative of all hospitals in the United States, it is worthwhile to ask whether they are typical. Of the total of 5,994 short-term general hospitals reported by the American Hospital Association, 3,243 are in the same class as Hospitals A and B with respect to control: "non-governmental not-for-profit." The average occupancy for all hospitals in the same size range was 81 percent. Thus, it is reasonably accurate to characterize the two hospitals selected for the study as not atypical of hospitals in the United States.

SELECTION OF THE RECORDS FOR REVIEW

The medical records selected for review fall into two major groups. A random sample was selected, as well as a set of control cases that had received prior attention for reasons related to possible injury.

Selection of Random Sample

Several approaches to the selection of a set of records for review were considered initially. One approach was to examine only those cases where death occurred in the hospital. Another was to seek records in which the length of patients' hospital stays exceeded the norms. Several other schemes designed to enrich the sample (i.e., provide more than the random occurrence of injuries) were discarded. The wisdom of this choice was not as apparent when originally made as it is now, upon completion of the study. One reason for this is that the adoption of any such scheme would have made extrapolations from the results virtually impossible. The final decision was to simply select a set of records at random, however, only specific services were sampled in the random selection. These services were medicine, surgery, and gynecology. Thus, obstetrics, pediatrics, emergency room, etc., patients were excluded. Relatively low injury rates were predicted for obstetrics and pediatrics. Further, some hospitals do not maintain a pediatric service, so that the three services selected were considered common to all short-term hospitals. Overall, the percentage of discharges from the services included is approximately 82 percent for each hospital.

The mechanics of the random selection were essentially straight-forward. The basic selection of patient medical records was made from the hospital discharge lists for the three alternate months of January, March, and May, 1972. This provided a sample of recent, and thus readily accessible, records, and PAS-MAP summary reports were available for the months selected. The alternate months were chosen to cover a wider span of time than three consecutive months. Each entry on the discharge list is identified by a medical record number or an accounting control number. It was originally estimated that approximately 250 records from each hospital could be reviewed with the resources available. To provide for the possibility that this might be a significant underestimate, approximately 500 records in each hospital were selected initially. The technique was simply to first find every record number ending in the digit "0" on the discharge list that corresponded to a patient in one of the services being sampled. If the resulting number of records drawn was too small, the operation was repeated using all record numbers ending in the digit "5".

Selection of Control Sample

In an attempt to provide an independent test of the reviewers' performance, a set of control records was selected in addition to the random sample. The sample of control records was drawn on the basis of information made available by the hospital administrators. These records belonged to two major subcategories: (1) those records for which a member of the hospital staff had filed an incident report, describing an injury to a patient, and (2) those records for which a claim was made against the hospital or medical staff, including records released by subpoena as an initial or subsequent event in the processing of a claim for an injury. The control records were reviewed by a medical-legal consultant who was not one of the two project record reviewers; in his opinion, every record in the control sample contained evidence of patient injury. It should be noted, however, that in his review of the records, he knew the source of each record. It should also be noted that most of these records were from a period earlier than those in the random sample. For this reason, a limited number of records were selected at random from the period covered by the control sample and included in the random sample to prevent the reviewers from associating injury cases with a particular time period.

SELECTION OF REVIEWERS

The two experts (Reviewers A and B) who did the basic initial review of all records, the random sample and the control cases, were medical-legal specialists. Their usual professional activities involve the review of records and other data in connection with legal actions involving alleged malpractice. A similarly qualified consultant participated in the program as medical-legal consultant to the GEOMET staff. As will be discussed in Section III, two additional consultants served as panel members in a final review of the injury cases. The panel members were board-certified specialists, one in internal medicine, and one in surgery. Both physicians actively see patients and provide care in hospital settings.

DESIGN/CONDUCT OF THE EXPERIMENT

Sequence of Events

An initial planning meeting was held that included GEOMET staff members, the two reviewers, GEOMET's medical-legal consultant, and the Malpractice Commission's Director of Research. At this point, the form to be completed by the reviewers was finalized, and a decision was made to select a random sample of records for review. Neither of the record reviewers was told that his sample would include several records from the administrator's file at each hospital (the "control" records). The original plan was to have each reviewer check half the records in each hospital in an effort to eliminate any correlation between the reviewers' performance and the hospital. For various logistic reasons, this proved to be impossible. Instead, one reviewer checked approximately

425 records in one hospital, consisting of approximately 400 randomly selected records and 25 control records. The second reviewer repeated this procedure in the other hospital.

It was originally planned to have each reviewer examine a sample of the records that had been previously examined by the other reviewer (the "cross-check" sample). Reviewer B did check 50 records previously examined by Reviewer A, but the planned reciprocal operation did not take place because of the illness of Reviewer A.[1]

Conduct of the Review

GEOMET staff members worked with medical records personnel in each hospital to obtain actual records corresponding to the record numbers that had been drawn at random from the discharge lists, as well as the control sample. For each record drawn, a Medical Record Abstract form, shown in Appendix A, was prepared. GEOMET staff members completed the entire form except the portion concerning the identification of the record as an injury case, which was completed by the reviewer. If his answer to the question, "Has an injury occurred?" was "Yes," he was asked to complete the Injury Report form shown in Appendix A. In addition to gathering specific injury data, the Injury Report form was used to record the reviewer's opinion as to whether or not the injury resulted from negligence. The completed forms then became the source of basic data used in the analyses reported here.

Review of Injury Cases

A meeting was held after completing the initial review of approximately 400-425 records in each hospital and the cross-check sample. This meeting (referred to as the "review meeting") included the two reviewers, GEOMET's medical-legal consultant, and GEOMET staff members. At this time, all cases that had been identified as injuries were discussed by the three medical-legal experts. In almost all instances, the discussion centered around the issue of whether or not the case was indeed an injury.

The major outcome of this meeting was that some of the cases initially identified as injuries were eliminated. Essentially, no attempt was made to review the cases that each reviewer had previously decided were non-injuries. In the case of the cross-check records, however, several of the cases that Reviewer A had deemed "no injury" had been identified as injuries by Reviewer B. In four of these cases, Reviewer A indicated that he had made a mistake and that they were indeed injuries. In the analysis presented below, these cases are excluded on the basis that only those injuries that were initially identified by one of the reviewers were counted.

[1] Since the reviewers worked independently, the order in which they examined the cross-check sample of records is irrelevant. The cross-check records thus constitute a reliability measure for the reviewers' work. They do not, however, help us understand how dependent the inter-reviewer reliability is on the individual hospitals, or on the quality of the medical records.

At the meeting, several cases were identified as requiring additional consultation. On the next day, a "panel" meeting was held which included the three medical-legal experts, GEOMET staff members, and the two additional consultants (the board-certified internist and the board-certified surgeon). At this meeting, "problem" cases were reviewed and firm decisions were made as to whether each should be counted as an injury. As in the case of the review meeting, the panel meeting did not consider cases that had previously been deemed non-injuries.

The results of the successive reviews were always in the direction of reducing the number of injury cases. Those cases finally retained in the injury file were those on which a consensus was reached by all five physician panel members.

Section III
Results

This section of the report presents the principal results of the study The first major subsection describes the results associated with the main thrust of the study: the examination of a random sample of hospital records. Injury-rate results are presented, as well as several statistical analyses of the injury data. Subsequent subsections deal with other aspects of the injury detection effort. The final portions of this section of the report contain comparisons of the injured patients with those represented by the sample of randomly selected records, as well as a comparison of the sample of records drawn at random with the population from which it was drawn, i.e., all of the hospital patients.

INJURY RATE

The results of the review of the random sample of medical records are summarized in Table 3. This table shows the number of records in the random sample initially judged to be injury cases, and those that were still so considered as a result of a consensus reached at the review meeting, and the panel meeting, respectively.

The results shown in Table 3 indicate that the final accepted rate of injuries for Hospital A was 6.4 percent, for Hospital B it was 8.8 percent In both cases, the number may be considered an estimate of the lower bound on the injury rate since the review proceedings permitted only the acceptance or rejection of a case previously judged to show evidence of injury. That is, essentially no effort was devoted to dealing with those cases that had initially been classified as non-injury. Thus, the results of the review and panel meetings could only maintain or reduce the original injury rate:

At the review meeting, attended by the two initial reviewers, GEOMET staff members, and GEOMET's medical-legal consultant, every case previously judged to be an injury was reviewed. "Definitional problems" were also discussed, these centered around the question of differentiating between anticipated events during the course of therapy in a hospital setting, and avoidable and unavoidable injuries.

Of the 90 cases first evaluated as injuries by the reviewers, 70, or about three-quarters, were unanimously rated as injuries upon review at this meeting. The other cases were either rated as non-injuries or deferred for additional review at the panel meeting. Cases eliminated included several where the medical record indicated that equivocal circumstances were associated with the patient discharge, but no evidence of any untoward consequence appeared in the record.

Two cases were identified for further study of the medical record by Reviewer B, and the medical records were subsequently reexamined at the hospital. One of these was considered an injury upon the second check of the medical record. Two cases originally evaluated as noninjuries by Reviewer B were classified as injuries during the meeting, but these are not included in the totals reported here.

The 25 cases on which a consensus could not be reached were scheduled for presentation to the additional medical consultants at the panel meeting. These cases included postoperative thrombophlebitis and pulmonary embolism, possible errors of diagnosis in pathology, and indications for oophorectomy or hysterectomy. It may be noted that this meeting was held at one of the hospitals, and the availability of its medical records was an asset during the discussion. This is a point that may be considered worthwhile in conducting further studies of this type.

All 25 cases were discussed and, generally, those still considered injuries following the panel meeting were classified as such on the basis of unanimity among all five physician panel members. One of the cases upon which differences of opinion remained was finally dropped and classified as no injury. Special situations encountered in this review included:

- An injury related to a prior recent hospitalization
- A potential case of injury[2] classified as non-injury due to the absence of information subsequent to hospitalization
- A non-injury classification on the basis of insufficient information during the hospital stay.

ANALYSIS OF FINAL RESULTS

The distribution of diagnoses among the injury cases is such that no statistical analysis of the data appeared worthwhile on this basis. The results can, however, be grouped in several major categories of injury type. The number of cases in each of the major injury categories may be summarized as:

---

[2] Specifically, several discharges under certain circumstances (fever on discharge, potential wound infection, etc.) where the absence of post-discharge data or a short post-operative stay precluded a definite injury assessment.

TABLE 3

NUMBER OF CASES JUDGED TO BE INJURIES IN RANDOM SAMPLE OF
MEDICAL RECORDS AT PARTICIPATING HOSPITALS

Hospital	Size of Random Sample	Number of Injuries			Final Injury Detection Rate
		Initial Review	After Review Meeting	After Panel Meeting	
A	422	40	31	27	6.4%
B	399	50	39	35	8.8%
A & B Combined	821	90	70	62	7.6%

- 40 post operative complications
  - 21 infections
  - 6 pulmonary embolism and thrombophlebitis
  - 13 other complications
- 9 adverse drug reactions
- 5 slip-and-falls
- 4 treatment errors
- 4 others.

Postoperative complications accounted for more than 65 percent of the injuries. The "other" category includes diagnostic errors, complications due to anesthesia, radiography complications, and equipment problems, each of which accounted for one injury case.

The data entered on the forms (Appendix A) by the reviewers were analyzed for all of the injury cases. The analysis was limited to quantitative information provided by the record reviewers, which was not complete in all cases. Each reviewer also dictated extensive notes for each injury case, but it was decided that, in order to maintain complete objectivity, no effort would be made by the study team to translate the comments into actual form entries.

The first question addressed in the statistical analysis was: "Are the injury rate results obtained in the two hospitals significantly different?" A difference of proportions test indicated that the difference in the final injury rates is not statistically significant, and this was further verified by a Chi-Square test. This is accepted as meaning that for many purposes all of the records judged to indicate evidence of medical injury after the panel meeting can be treated as one sample.

Negligence

In those cases in which an injury was judged to have occurred, the reviewers were asked to assess the likelihood that negligence had caused the injury. A further examination was made of all cases in which the reviewers answered "Yes" to the question, "Did negligence cause the injury?" Of the 62 injury cases in the random sample, 18 were judged to have been the result of negligence (9 from each hospital). However, although both reviewers ex-

pressed complete confidence that an injury had occurred in all of these 18 cases (see next section), they were not as confident that their negligence response was correct (an average score of 2 3 on a scale of 1 to 6). Characteristics of these cases are summarized in Table 4.

Although it appears that the average age in the negligence cases is quite high, it should be noted that this result is greatly influenced by the elderly (age 65 and older) patients in Hospital B, where 66 percent of the injury cases were in this age bracket. Seven of the eight deaths among the injuries are in the nine negligence cases in Hospital B. This result may be influenced by the relatively higher average age of the patients in Hospital B. The outcome of legal action as predicted by the reviewer in Hospital B tends to favor the plaintiff. Other parameters are similar to those for all injury cases. Because the number of cases is small, discretion should be used in drawing conclusions.

Reviewer Confidence in Injury Evaluation

The Medical Abstract form (Appendix A) provided a space for each reviewer to indicate whether an injury had occurred. It also asked for an indication of the reviewer's confidence in his answer, on a 6-point scale from "unsure" (1) to "confident" (6). A summary of these results appears in Table 5. Results for both reviewers/both hospitals were sufficiently similar that only the aggregate results are shown. The results indicate that, in more than 93 percent of the final injury cases, the reviewers were above the "unsure-confident" threshold (i.e., a score equal to or greater than 4). Here, only the cases where no entry was made were excluded. The most frequent entry was a score of 6 (confident) by an overwhelming majority.

It is also of some interest to seek a relationship between the reviewers' degree of confidence and the results of the review and panel meetings. For this purpose, the confidence scores were tabulated for all cases originally designated as injuries but later dropped as a result of one or both meetings. These results also appear in Table 5. The degree of confidence in identifying these cases as injuries is

TABLE 4

SUMMARY OF NEGLIGENCE DATA FOR RANDOM SAMPLE INJURY CASES

Hospital	Number of Cases	Average Patient Age (Years)	Average Stay (Days)	Most Common Category of Injury	Most Common Injury Source	Most Common Category of Severity of Injury	Average Predicted Legal Outcome*
A	9	46	13.3	Post-Operative Complications (7 of 9)**	Attending M.D. (3 of 3)**	Major Temporary (6 of 7)**	3.0
B	9	74	9.5	Therapy Error (3 of 9)**	Attending M.D. (5 of 9)**	Death (7 of 9)**	1.8
A & B Combined	18	61	10.5	–	Attending M.D.	–	2.3

*Scale of 1 - 5. 1 = plaintiff, 5 = defense.
**Number of cases reported as shown, out of all cases for which data were available.

also quite high. Of the entries made, approximately 75 percent are above the "unsure-confident" threshold. However, the results do show that the fraction of cases retained as injuries after the review and panel meetings is higher for the high-confidence cases than for the low-confidence cases The fraction of cases retained and the confidence rating are strongly correlated.

TABLE 5

REVIEWERS' CONFIDENCE IN RATING INJURY

Injury Record Sample	Number of Cases							
	No. Response	Confidence Rating*						
		1	2	3	4	5	6
Total Cases	13	1	1	7	8	3	57
Cases Dropped in Review/Panel Meetings	6	1	1	3	5	1	11
Final Injury Cases (Cases Retained)	7	0	0	4	3	2	46
Percent Retained	54	0	0	57	38	67	81

*Scale: 1 = unsure, 6 = confident.

Evidence of Injury

Each reviewer was asked to indicate the source of evidence which led him to evaluate a case as an injury. Al-

though the reviewers were also asked to rank several sources in degree of importance, usually only one check was entered for one source of information. Again, the results for both hospitals are sufficiently consistent that only the aggregate results are presented in Table 6.

More than half the cases for which a source of evidence was noted (55 cases) were rated as injuries on the basis of the Laboratory Report (11 cases), Vital Sign Graphic Charts (8 cases), or Progress Notes (9 cases), in the context of the remainder of the record. These results are of some significance in guiding future studies of the same type. The final decision to rate a case as an injury was not based on any single report in the complete record. The reported sources of evidence should be viewed as an indication of the source that acted as the initial indicator, usually resulting in a reexamination of other portions of the medical record.

Source of Injury

In an attempt to pinpoint the types of personnel associated with the cause of injury, the reviewers were asked to indicate the "source of injury." A tabular summary of the results for both hospitals appears in Table 7. Approximately 70 percent of the entries ascribe the injury to the attending physician.

Severity of Injury

A summary of the ratings of severity of injury based on the scale adopted by the Malpractice Commission is shown in Table 8. Most of the cases were minor temporary injuries, although a total of 8 deaths were reported (all elderly patients in Hospital B). The average age of these patients was 83 for those on the surgical service, and 73 for those on the medicine service.

TABLE 6

REVIEWERS' REPORTED EVIDENCE OF INJURY

Source of Evidence	Number of Cases
Laboratory Report	11
Radiology Report	5
Pathology Report	1
Operative Notes	7
Autopsy	0
Consultant Reports	2
Nurses' Notes	4
Admitting Work-Up	4
Anesthetic Records	1
Vital Sign Graphic Charts	8
Progress Notes	9
Other	3
No Entry	7
Total	62

TABLE 7

REPORTED SOURCE OF INJURY

Source	Number of Cases
Attending Physician	30
Consulting Physician	1
Nurse	6
Aide	1
Pharmacist	0
Radiologist/Radiology Technician	0
Anesthesiologist	1
Pathologist/Laboratory Technician	0
Other/Unknown	3
No Entry	20
Total	62

TABLE 8

REPORTED SEVERITY OF INJURY

Severity of Injury	Number of Cases
Mental Injury Only	0
Temporary	
Insignificant	0
Minor	27
Major	19
Permanent	
Minor	-
Significant	2
Major	1
Grave	0
Death	8
No Entry	4
Total	62

Evaluation of Control Records

As described in Section II, a "control" sample of records was selected in each hospital from records in the administrator's file that were either associated with a hospital-generated incident report, or a legal authorization or subpoena to release the record in connection with a claim for injury against the hospital or medical staff The results of the review of these records by the medical-legal experts are summarized in Table 9. All records initially rated as injuries have been included, since only two cases were later eliminated as the result of the review and panel meetings. In all, both reviewers identified only slightly more than half of the control records. These records were intermixed with the random records throughout the initial phases of the experiment. An independent review of these records reported clear evidence of injury in all of the cases. However, the GEOMET consultant conducting the review selected and knew the source of all records in the control sample; these factors may have influenced his evaluations.

The purpose of selecting the control cases was to establish a measure of the reviewers' "miss" rate in assessing injuries. The results of the initial review of the control cases, as shown in Table 9, indicate that 20 of the cases were "missed." In the absence of a review of these cases by the full panel, which we have essentially adopted as the final scoring device for the random sample, it cannot be stated that all of the missed cases in the control sample are actually injury cases. On the other hand, other results of the study indicate that the reviewers did indeed miss injury cases. Therefore, it can be concluded, although there is considerable risk in assigning quantitative measures, that there are more cases that meet the injury criteria as developed during the study than were detected by the reviewers.

TABLE 9

INITIAL IDENTIFICATION OF INJURIES AMONG
CONTROL SAMPLE RECORDS AT
PARTICIPATING HOSPITALS

Hospital	Source/Status of Record	Number of Records	Percentage of Records Identified as Injuries
A	Claims		
	Administrator's Case File	10	60%
	Subpoena	10	50
	Incident Report*	11	55
	Total	31	55
B	Claims		
	Subpoena	4	75
	Incident Report*	11	55
	Total	15	60
A & B Combined	Claims		
	Administrator's Case File	10	60
	Subpoena	14	57
	Incident Report*	22	55
	Total	46	57

*Documented evidence by member of medical staff.

It was unfortunate that time constraints prevented the thorough review of all cases in the control sample by the panel during the panel meeting, i e., those not considered injuries in the initial review, as well as those initially rated as injuries. It is recommended that in future studies all of the control cases be reviewed by a panel of physicians before the records are examined by the medical-legal record checkers.

Results of the Cross-Check Review

As described earlier, the study plan provided for one reviewer to examine 50 records previously examined by the other reviewer. The 50-record sample contained 40 records from the random sample and 10 from the control sample checked by Reviewer A. Further, the sample was structured to contain 25 records that had been initially evaluated as injuries and 25 that had not. Thus, the composition of the sample for the cross-check was:

- 20 random cases judged non-injury
- 20 random cases judged injury
- 5 control cases judged non-injury
- 5 control cases judged injury.

The 50 records constituting the sample were drawn at random from the records in each of the above categories. The 25 injury cases were reviewed by GEOMET's medical-legal consultant to provide assurance that they were indeed representative of the types of injuries encountered. They were judged to be a representative cross-section of the larger random sample. The 50 records were then drawn from the medical record room, and a cover sheet (the GEOMET Medical Record Abstract form [Appendix A]) was prepared for each one, so that it was identical to the sheet presented to the first reviewer. Reviewer B examined the 50 record sample at Hospital A.

For purposes of the cross-check (i.e., to compare the two reviewers on the same set of records), it was not considered necessary to separate the control cases from the random cases. Actually, the results for the random and control samples were essentially identical. The overall results are shown in Table 10. Of the 25 records previously identified as injury cases by Reviewer A, Reviewer B identified 17 injuries, of the 25 not considered injuries by Reviewer A, 3 were classified as injuries by Reviewer B. Thus, the original sample of 25 injuries and 25 non-injuries (Reviewer A) was classified as 20 injuries and 30 non-injuries by Reviewer B. Overall agreement may be estimated by adding the results of the upper left and lower right boxes in Table 10 (bold outline); thus, the reviewers agreed on 39 out of the 50, or 78 percent of the cases, and disagreed on 22 percent of the cases.

TABLE 10
RESULTS OF EXAMINATION OF
FIFTY RECORDS BY REVIEWERS A AND B

		Initial Evaluation by Reviewer A		Totals - Reviewer B
		Injury	Non-Injury	
Subsequent Evaluation by Reviewer B	Injury	17	3	20
	Non-Injury	8	22	30
Totals - Reviewer A		25	25	50

REPRESENTATIVENESS OF RANDOM SAMPLE

It was considered important to examine the records constituting the random sample to determine whether or not they were representative of patients in the services sampled. The randomness of the sample was established by means of the method by which the records were drawn (see Section II). Although the possibilities for testing representativeness are numerous, a limited number of tests were performed which indicated that the random sample of records is reasonably representative of the total population of patients discharged by each hospital for the services and time period covered. These are reported below.

Distribution of Sample Records Among Services

The first test of representativeness performed was a comparison of the relative numbers of records from each of the three services sampled with the relative number of patients discharged for each of the three services. This examination, as well as the others reported here, was made possible by the availability of the PAS-MAP summaries covering the period from which the sample was drawn. At the time this analysis was initiated, the first quarterly report for 1972 was available for each hospital. When the second quarterly summary was available at a later date, a comparison indicated that the parameters describing the distribution of patients were stable (i.e., their change from quarter to quarter was negligible). For this reason, the first quarter data were used for comparisons with the three-month sample, although one of the months was outside the first quarter (the sample was drawn from January, March, and May of 1972).

Table 11 shows the distribution of patients in each of the three services for the records drawn in the random sample, and for all patients discharged from the three services during the first quarter of 1972 for Hospitals A and B. In the Hospital A sample, the distribution of sample records among the three services matches the distribution of all discharges among the three services quite closely. A Chi-Square test of the two distributions verified this result at the 0.05 level of significance. The records in the sample represent about 18 percent of all discharges for the period. For Hospital B, the sample distribution does not reflect the distribution of all discharges quite as closely as for the other hospital. The Chi-Square test applied to these data indicated that the distributions were significantly different. The difference is indicated by the relatively small percentage of surgery cases in the random sample. The sample cases represent about 14 percent of all cases in the three services for the period sample.

Comparison of Sample Parameters with Hospital Population

It is also appropriate to compare parameters describing several health care attributes of the sample patients with the same parameters for the total patient population. One example is the average length of stay for patients, by service, as shown in Table 12. The average hospital stay for the patients whose records were drawn in the random sample very closely matches the average stay for all patients discharged during the first quarter of 1972, by service. In Hospital B, the sample tended to include surgical patients

TABLE 11

COMPARISON OF NUMBER OF RECORDS IN THREE-MONTH RANDOM SAMPLE
WITH NUMBER OF DISCHARGES BY SERVICE FOR HOSPITALS A AND B

Service	Hospital A			Hospital B		
	Number of Discharges in Quarter	Random Sample		Discharges in Quarter	Random Sample	
		Number of Records	Percent of Discharges		Number of Records	Percent of Discharges
Medicine	735	136	19	916	153	17
Surgery	944	166	17	1571	183	12
Gynecology	425	89	20	242	48	20
Total	2104	391*	18**	2729	384*	14**

*Does not include cases with discharge dates outside three-month sample period, this accounts for discrepancy between this total and size of random sample.
**Overall percentage.

with an average stay somewhat longer than the average for all surgical patients discharged from that hospital during the first quarter of 1972.

TABLE 12
COMPARISON OF AVERAGE HOSPITAL STAY (DAYS) FOR PATIENTS DISCHARGED DURING FIRST QUARTER 1972 WITH PATIENTS IN RANDOM SAMPLE BY SERVICE FOR HOSPITALS A AND B

Service	Hospital A		Hospital B	
	Random Sample	All Patients	Random Sample	All Patients
Medicine	8.1	8.3	8.0	8.0
Surgery	7.8	7.4	8.9	7.3
Gynecology	4.5	4.3	5.3	5.2
Overall Averages	7.2	7.1*	8.1	7.3*

*Only includes services shown, i.e., Pediatrics not included.

Another test is the comparison of the distribution of ages of patients in the random sample with the age distribution for all patients at each hospital. It can be seen in Tables 13 and 14 that the age distribution of the patients whose records were drawn in the sample matches fairly closely the distribution for all patients discharged during

the quarter. The observed differences tend to be where the number of cases is small, thus reducing the significance of the difference. In both hospitals, the highest median patient age is associated with the medical service, the lowest with gynecology. For each service, the Hospital B median patient age is greater than for Hospital A.

Table 15, showing the results of a comparison of the total random sample of medical records with patient age data for discharges from all PAS-MAP hospitals, indicates that the sample had a relatively higher fraction of patients over 65 years of age. Because pediatric patients were excluded from the sample, only data for patients over 20 were examined.

COMPARISON OF INJURY PARAMETERS WITH SAMPLE

One of the issues addressed in the analysis involved a comparison of the distribution of key parameters associated with the patients judged to have been injured with the distribution of the same parameters among the patients in the random sample.

Distribution By Service

First, the distribution of injury cases among the three services was compared with the distribution of the total sample. Note that the injury cases summarized are from discharges drawn for January, March, and May of 1972. The number of injury cases in each hospital is somewhat small for a sophisticated statistical analysis, but the distribution of injury patients over the three services does not strictly match the sample distribution for Hospital A, although the distribution for Hospital B is similar. In

TABLE 13
COMPARISON OF AGE DISTRIBUTION BY SERVICE AT HOSPITAL A FOR PATIENTS DISCHARGED DURING FIRST QUARTER 1972 WITH PATIENTS IN THREE-MONTH RANDOM SAMPLE

Patient Age (Years)	Surgery				Medicine				Gynecology			
	First Quarter Discharges		Three-Month Random Sample		First Quarter Discharges		Three-Month Random Sample		First Quarter Discharges		Three-Month Random Sample	
	Number	Percent	Number	Percent	Number	Percent	Number	Percent	Number	Percent	Number	Percent
0-19	172	18%	10	6%	15	2%	5	4%	37	9%	6	7%
20-34	167	18	38	23	71	10	16	12	248	58	52	59
35-49	188	20	38	23	111	15	21	15	106	25	18	20
50-64	196	21	36	22	202	27	40	29	25	6	11	12
65+	221	23	44	26	336	46	54	40	9	2	2	2
Total	944	100%	166	100%	735	100%	136	100%	425	100%	89	100%

TABLE 14

COMPARISON OF AGE DISTRIBUTION BY SERVICE AT HOSPITAL B FOR PATIENTS
DISCHARGED DURING FIRST QUARTER 1972 WITH PATIENTS
IN THREE-MONTH RANDOM SAMPLE

Patient Age (Years)	Surgery				Medicine				Gynecology			
	First-Quarter Discharges		Three-Month Random Sample		First Quarter Discharges		Three-Month Random Sample		First Quarter Discharges		Three Month Random Sample	
	Number	Percent	Number	Percent	Number	Percent	Number	Percent	Number	Percent	Number	Percent
0-19	89	6%	2	1%	9	1%	1	1%	14	6%	1	2%
20-34	216	14	30	16	76	8	11	7	88	36	22	46
35-49	260	16	34	19	111	12	19	12	94	39	20	42
50-64	358	23	46	25	174	19	32	21	30	12	3	6
65+	648	41	71	39	546	60	90	59	16	7	2	4
Total	1571	100%	183	100%	916	100%	153	100%	242	100%	48	100%

particular, the number of injuries among the patients in medicine in Hospital A is relatively small compared to the fraction of patients in the sample from that service, while the injuries in surgery and gynecology are at higher rates than would be expected from their proportions in the random sample. When the data from both hospitals are combined, the Chi-Square test indicates that the differences in the distributions are not significant at the 5 percent level. The results are confirmed by Table 16, where the injury rates are shown for each service. The Hospital A medicine injury rate is only 1.5 percent, in accordance with the results noted above. The overall results show that the injury rate is highest for surgery patients.

TABLE 15

COMPARISON OF RELATIVE DISTRIBUTION OF
PATIENT AGE IN THREE-MONTH
RANDOM SAMPLE WITH ALL PAS-MAP HOSPITALS*

Patient Age (Years)	All PAS-MAP Hospitals	Random Sample
20-34	20%	20%
35-49	25%	20%
50-64	27%	22%
65+	28%	38%

*Patients over 20 years.

Age Distribution

In examining the age distribution among the injured patients, the numbers were considered too small to break them down by service. Table 17 summarizes the injury rates for different patient age groups. The results indicate a 14 percent injury rate at Hospital B among patients 65 and older. Although this group constituted 42 percent of the sample patients, 66 percent of the injuries were in this age group. Also of note is the 10 percent injury rate among patients 35 to 49 at Hospital A. Tests indicate that the age distribution of injured patients and all patients in the sample are not statistically different for each hospital. It is not clear whether age or service is the principal factor associated with injury. It has been noted, however, that the oldest patients are associated with medicine services, and that the highest injury rate in the Hospital B random sample was among surgery patients.

Length of Stay

The comparison of average length of stay for injured patients with all patients in the sample is shown in Table 18. The results show that injured patients in surgery and gynecology have significantly longer stays than the average patient in the sample; in fact, the stay is about twice as long. This is not true for patients in medicine. Since only two injury cases were reported for medicine at Hospital A, the sample was considered too small for statistically reliable results. Five of the 14 injuries in medicine at Hospital B were deaths. Thus, these results suggest a strong association between over-average hospital stays and injury, except where death terminated the hospital stay. "Association" here does not necessarily imply a cause-and-effect relationship. The longer hospital stay of an injured patient may be due to the additional therapy required to treat the injury,

TABLE 16
INJURY RATES BY SERVICE: THREE-MONTH RANDOM SAMPLE AT HOSPITALS A AND B

Service	Hospital A		Hospital B		Injury Rate Both Hospitals Combined (%)
	Number of Records Three-Month Sample	Injury Rate (%)	Number of Records Three-Month Sample	Injury Rate (%)	
Medicine	136	1.5	153	9.4	6
Surgery	166	7.8	183	10.4	9
Gynecology	89	7.5	48	4.2	7

as opposed to indicating that the injury occurs because the patient is hospitalized longer. The length of stay is also clearly related to the cause of the original hospitalization, which may be the controlling factor.

DATA PROJECTIONS

In order to provide another view of the implications of this study, limited projections from the available data have been made. Although it would appear desirable to provide these projections on as wide a base as possible, statistical limitations make such projections somewhat hazardous. As a compromise, this section gives estimates of the total number of injuries, cases of negligence, and claims that can be expected in both hospitals, associated with patients discharged during 1972.

The number of discharges in 1972 can be stated with reasonable confidence using quarterly figures which appear relatively stable. The total number of discharges from both hospitals is estimated to be approximately 19,000 patients, considering only surgery, medicine, and gynecology patients. The overall final injury rate obtained in the study was 7.5 percent. Although the conduct of the study was such that this rate must be considered low, it can be used as the basis for conservatively estimating that the number of injuries among patients discharged during the year approximates 1,425 cases.

Based on the negligence cases cited above, a "negligence rate" (i.e., the percentage of injuries presumably caused by negligence) can be predicted for the two sample hospitals. The study identified 18 negligence cases among the 62 injuries for a negligence rate of 29 percent. Using this figure in conjunction with the 1972 estimate of injuries, the total estimated number of negligence cases for 1972 would be 413. This procedure, however, must be considered rather tenuous for two reasons: (1) the quantity of data on which the estimate is based is small in the statistical sense, and (2) the reviewers themselves were not highly confident in their rating of the cases in which the injuries were ascribed to negligence.

Data were obtained from each hospital giving the number of claims made against the hospital or medical staff each year, and the year of patient discharge associated with each claim. By means of a regression analysis, the number of claims arising for each year from 1960 to 1971 were used to estimate the total number of claims to be expected from patients discharged during 1972. The estimated number is approximately 31. Since all of the data examined in the study are associated with patients accounting for 80 percent of discharges from the two sample hospitals, this estimate can be adjusted to be compatible with the other results in this section, yielding an estimate of 25 claims.

Estimates of the injury results predicted for medicine, surgery, and gynecology patients discharged from both hospitals (combined) during 1972 are:

- 19,000 patients
- 1,425 injuries
- 413 negligence cases
- 25 claims.

Since the services sampled for this study account for approximately 80 percent of all discharges, these results can be extended to all discharges, if it is assumed that the injury and negligence rates obtained also apply to the services that were not sampled. These estimates for total patients, injuries, negligence cases, and claims are:

- 23,750 patients
- 1,780 injuries
- 517 negligence cases
- 31 claims.

Section IV
Findings and Conclusions

The methods used in this study successfully supported a study of patient injuries in the hospital setting; they included the selection of medical records on a random basis, initial examination of the records by medical-legal

TABLE 17

INJURY RATES BY PATIENT AGE GROUP: THREE-MONTH
RANDOM SAMPLE FOR HOSPITALS A AND B

Patient Age (Years)	Hospital A		Hospital B		Injury Rate Both Hospitals Combined (%)
	Number in Random Sample	Injury Rate (%)	Number in Random Sample	Injury Rate (%)	
0-19	21	0	4	0	0
20-34	106	5	63	5	5
35-49	77	10	73	4	8
50-64	87	5	81	6	5
65+	100	5	163	14	· 11

TABLE 18

COMPARISON OF AVERAGE LENGTH OF STAY (DAYS)
BY SERVICE FOR INJURED PATIENTS AND
RANDOM SAMPLE FOR HOSPITALS A AND B

Service	Hospital A		Hospital B	
	Three-Month Random Sample	Injured Patients	Three-Month Random Sample	Injured Patients
Medicine	8.1	6.5	8.0	9.4
Surgery	7.8	18.7	8.9	14.4
Gynecology	4.5	10.3	5.3	12.0
Overall	7.2	15.0	8.1	12.2

experts, and subsequent review by a medical panel. The techniques modified on the basis of the experience gained in this study can be applied on a wider scale in the future.

The following findings and conclusions are drawn from the results presented in the preceding sections of the report:

- On the basis of a review of a random sample of medical records drawn from medical, surgical, and gynecological services at two general hospitals, it has been found that 7.5 percent of the records show evidence of iatrogenic injury. *Several factors indicate that this number significantly underestimates the true rate.*
- Review of medical records by medical-legal experts is feasible; an average rate of 50 records per day can be achieved, but probably not on a sustained basis.
- Several possibilities exist for screening records to increase the probability of identifying injuries in the

sample; these include seeking records for patients with over-average hospital stays.

Section V
Recommendations for Future Work

On the basis of the results achieved in this preliminary study, it is recommended that additional work of the same type be conducted on a national scale. This study should be structured in such a way as to develop reasonably reliable statistics on a national basis. The scheme should be set up so that a representative sample of hospitals is covered. This sample should be structured to be representative in geographical location, control, approvals, and facilities.

The present study provided some indication that criteria exist by which records can be pre-selected to increase the likelihood of finding injury cases in the sample, as opposed to a purely random sample Specifically, it would appear that hospital stays longer than age- and diagnosis-corrected norms, as well as cases of death in the hospital, may be useful criteria for this purpose. At present, however, such a sample would not allow extrapolation to the general hospital population. Therefore, it is recommended that an initial large-scale study be based on a set of records chosen at random, essentially as was done in the present study. With a reasonably large sample collected on a national basis, reliable statistical relationships can be developed to relate the number of cases found in a biased sample to those found in the random sample. With this information, continuing efforts to monitor the incidence of injuries could then be based on reviews of smaller samples of records, selected on the basis of specific criteria.

The forms (Appendix A) developed for this study could be used in the future with only slight modification. They should be reviewed for purposes of simplifying the transfer of data to digital computer storage. It may be worthwhile in larger studies to consider selecting the sample prior to the time that the PAS-MAP abstract forms are completed, so that duplicates of these forms may be attached to the other data forms used in the study. This would conveniently make available an abstract of the medical record for statistical analysis of the patient data.

It is recommended that close supervision of the record reviewers be maintained during the conduct of the record review. This is not required throughout the entire period of the review, but the information that is desired for the actual cases judged to be injuries should be checked. That is, at periodic intervals during the record review process, those forms completed for the cases identified as injuries should be examined for completeness.

The information developed in successive studies of this type, including a continuous monitoring process, could be designed so as to relate to various other on-going hospital information systems such as the *Illinois Hospital Admission*

Surveillance Program (HASP) for reviewing hospital admissions. Further detailed studies, not possible within the scope of the present effort, should be devoted to relating the injury information for each hospital to its own efforts to ensure quality of care. Efforts should be devoted to relating the criteria discussed above for selecting records for injury examination with criteria used to select records in other hospital admission and utilization review systems.

The injury data that could be obtained from on-going programs of medical chart review could be processed most conveniently by a computerized system. It is recommended that consideration be given to developing an information system that would contain the injury data updated on a continuing basis. This would provide the output needed for overall review of the quality of care provided by each hospital, it would also provide a significant input to the analysis of need for changes in policy relative to malpractice claims.

Steps outlined here that detail how to determine hospital injury rates, combined with quality assurance methods instituted by a hospital, may reduce the incidence of patient injury, and thus constitute a significant measure in reducing the entire malpractice problem, at its source.

Section VI
References

Barr, D. P. 1955. "Hazards of Modern Diagnosis and Therapy: The Price We Pay." *Journal of American Medical Association* 159:452.456.

Burgess, A. M. 1965. "Caring for the Patient—A Thrice Told Tale." *New England Journal of Medicine* 274.1241.1244.

Kampmeier, R. H. 1966. "Diseases of Medical Progress." *Southern Medical Journal*, 59:871.872.

Schimmel, E. M. 1964. "Hazards of Hospitalization." *Annals of Internal Medicine*, 60:100.

Appendix A
DATA FORMS

MEDICAL RECORD ABSTRACT form

DATE OF BIRTH — DAY, MONTH, YEAR — NEWBORN

PATIENT NUMBER

PAS HOSPITAL NUMBER

SEX — MALE / FEMALE

ADMISSION DATE — DAY, MONTH, YEAR — TIME

DIAGNOSES — FINAL DX EXPLAINING ADMISSION — NAME

FINAL DIAGNOSES ·H·ICDA·

OPERATIONS ·H·ICDA· OF SURGEON A MOST IMPORT — NAME — DAY MONTH TIME

OPERATIONS ·H·ICDA· OF SURGEON B

REMARKS·

HAS AN INJURY OCCURED? — NO / YES — IF YES COMPLETE INJURY REPORT

INDICATE DEGREE OF CONFIDENCE IN YOUR ANSWER — UNSURE / CONFIDENT

DATE COMPLETED

(Aug. 24, 1972)

DATA FORMS (Continued)

INJURY REPORT

Describe Injury: _____

Patient No.

[ ][ ][ ][ ][ ]

Time of Occurrence

☐ Before   ☐ During   ☐ After

Hospitalization

☐ During a Procedure

☐ Subsequent to and related to a Procedure

What Procedure: _____

Is there an entry on record indicating recognition of injury?   ☐ YES   ☐ NO

If so, was there a delay in its discovery?   ☐ YES   ☐ NO

If so, how long? _____

What was effect of delay? _____

Evidence of Injury (Number in order of decreasing significance: 1 most significant)

☐ Lab. Report   ☐ Nurses Notes
☐ X–Ray Report   ☐ Admitting Work–up
☐ Path. Report   ☐ Anesthetic Charts
☐ Op. Results from Surgery   ☐ Vital Sign Charts
☐ Progress Notes
☐ Autopsy   ☐ Other _____
☐ Consultation Reports

Source of Injury

☐ Attending M.D.   ☐ Radiologist
☐ House M.D. staff   ☐ Radiology tech.
☐ Consultant M.D.   ☐ Anesthesiologist
☐ Nurse   ☐ Anesthetist
☐ Aide   ☐ Pathologist
☐ Pharmacist   ☐ Laboratory tech.
☐ Other _____   ☐ Unknown

Date Form Completed _____

Severity of Injury

1 ☐ Mental Injury Only

Temporary {
2 ☐ Insignificant
3 ☐ Minor
4 ☐ Major
}

Permanent {
5 ☐ Minor
6 ☐ Significant
7 ☐ Major
8 ☐ Grave
}

9 ☐ Death

Delay in Recovery?   ☐ Yes   ☐ No

Check one or more of following factors associated with case:

☐ Abandonment   ☐ Products Liability
☐ Clinical Research   ☐ Prenatal Injury
☐ Failure to Disclose   ☐ Laboratory Error
☐ Consent   ☐ Diagnosis Error
☐ Defamation   ☐ Pharmacy Error
☐ Other _____

Did negligence cause the injury?   ☐ YES   ☐ NO

Indicate degree of confidence in response

UNSURE [ ][ ][ ][ ][ ] CONFIDENT

Prediction of outcome of legal action:

☐   ☐   ☐   ☐   ☐
FOR PLAINTIFF   UNSURE   FOR DEFENSE

Additional Notes Prepared In this Case?

☐ YES   ☐ NO

If YES show Patient Number on all Continuation Sheets.

(Aug. 24, 1972)

Appendix B
BASIC PATIENT INJURY DATA

Hospital A

Age	Sex	H-ICDA	Diagnosis	Confidence that an Injury Occurred	Evidence of Injury	Source of Injury	Severity of Injury	Description of Injury	Did Negligence Cause the Injury?	Confidence in Answer	Predicted Legal Outcome
31	F	733.5	Dupuytren's Contracture, Foot					Postoperative Infection/Hematoma		5	4
44	F	189.0 998.9	Adenocarcinoma, Kidney Pneumonitis		4	1	5	Neoplasms/Diagnostic Error Pneumonitis		5	4
38	M	724.4 998.9	Knee Surgery Pulmonary Embolism	3	2		4	Pulmonary Embolism		6	5
61	M	550.0 998.9	Recurrent Inguinal Hernia Septic Thrombophlebitis		11		3	Postoperative Thrombophlebitis		6	5
45	F	708.9	Urticaria, Drug-Induced		12	1	4	Antibiotics/Adverse Effects	Y		5
78		440.9 814.0	Arteriosclerosis Fracture, Wrist	6	11	4	4	Slip and Fall/Wrist Injury	Y	4	2
32	F	623.6	Uterine Prolapse		10		4	Hysterectomy/Infection	Y	6	2
22	F	616.0	Abscess, Pelvic	6	10	1	4	Tubal Ligation/Infection	Y	5	2
32	F	998.5	Wound Infection, Surgical	6	1	1	3	Hysterectomy/Infection	Y	6	5
24	F	599.9	Urinary Tract Infection	6	2		3	Hysterectomy/Infection		6	5
66	F	996.6	Osteomyelitis, Tibia	6	2		6	Fracture Fixation/Infection	Y	4	
?	F	623.6	Uterine Prolapse	6				Hysterectomy/Infection	Y		
35	M	998.5	Intra-abdominal Abscess	6	11		4	Colostomy/Infection	Y	3	3
78	F	562.1	Diverticulitis	6	7		4	Colectomy,Infection/Dehiscence		6	5
63	F	725.1	Intervertebral Disc	6	10		3	Slip and Fall/Thoracic Injury		5	4
53	M	820.0	Fracture, Hip		11	5	3	Fracture Fixation/Infection		5	5
26	M	455.0 595.0	Hemorrhoids Cystitis	6			3	Catheterization/Infection		5	5
69	M	600.0	Prostatic Hypertrophy				3	Prostatectomy/Infection		6	5
37	F	640.0 867.0	Abortion, Complete Uterine Perforation	6	4	1	3	Uterine Perforation			3

(Continued)

BASIC PATIENT INJURY-DATA (Continued)

Hospital A (Concluded)

Age	Sex	H-ICDA	Diagnosis	Confidence that an Injury Occurred	Evidence of Injury	Source of Injury	Severity of Injury	Description of Injury	Did Negligence Cause the Injury?	Confidence in Answer	Predicted Legal Outcome
45	F	623.4	Uterine Prolapse	6	10		3	Hysterectomy/Infection		5	5
	M	455.0	Hemorrhoids	6	11	1	4	Hemorrhoidectomy/Complications		5	5
39	F	623.0 620.0	Cystocele Pelvic Infection	6	1	1	3	Hysterectomy/Infection		4	5
39	M	532.1 998.5	Duodenal Ulcer/Hemorrhage Wound Infection	6	11		3	Pyloroplasty/Infection		6	5
89	F	410.9 873.0	Myocardial Infarct Laceration, Scalp	6	11		3	Slip and Fall		4	4
66	M	410.0	Myocardial Infarct	6	11		4	Prostatectomy/Cardiac Arrest/Infection	Y	6	4
28	F	626.6	Menorrhagia	6	4	1		Uterine Perforation	Y	6	5
84	M	820.0	Fracture, Hip		4		4	Fracture Fixation/Complications		5	4

BASIC PATIENT INJURY DATA (Continued)

Hospital B

Age	Sex	H-ICDA	Diagnosis	Confidence that an Injury Occurred	Evidence of Injury	Source of Injury	Severity of Injury	Description of Injury	Did Negligence Cause the Injury?	Confidence In Answer	Predicted Legal Outcome
65	M	436.0 251.0	Cerebral Thrombosis / Hypoglycemia, Drug-Induced	4	1		3	Drug Therapy/Adverse Effects		3	3
88	F	574.9 427.2	Cholecystitis / Cardiac Arrest	6	4	1	9	Cholecystectomy/Cardiac Arrest	Y	3	2
62	M	682.1 787.3	Abscess, Hip / Stress Ulcer/Hemorrhage	6	10	1	9	Infection/Hemorrhage	Y	2	2
75	M	451.0	Thrombophlebitis	6	8	1	3	Prostatectomy/Thrombophlebitis		5	5
65	M	713.0	Arthritis, Hip	6	9	10	4	Anesthesia/Aspiration	Y	1	3
69	F	198.0 450.0	Carcinoma, Breast / Thrombophlebitis	6	11	1	9	Pulmonary Embolism/Therapy	Y	1	3
81	F	433.1 788.7	Cerebral Thrombosis / Hyponatremia	6	1	4	9	Hyponatremia/Fluid Therapy	Y	5	1
41	F	635.0	Hemorrhage/Gastrointestinal	6	12	7	4	Blood Transfusion/Adverse Effects		5	4
41	F	626.6	Menorrhagia	3	10	14	3	Hysterectomy/Infection/Shock Penicillin/Adverse Effects		3	4
85	M	600.0 450.0	Coronary Artery Disease / Pulmonary Embolism	6	10	4	9	Prostatectomy/Aspiration	Y	4	2
60	M	450.0	Pulmonary Embolism	6	2	1	3	Hip Surgery/Pulmonary Embolism		3	4
70	F	531.0 873.0 887.0	Gastric Ulcer / Liver Degeneration / Laceration, Scalp	6	7	4	3	Slip and Fall	Y	4	1
71	F	207.1	Leukemia	6	1	1	4	Drug Therapy/Adverse Effects		3	4
75	M	998.1	Prostatectomy/Hemorrhage	6	8	1	3	Prostatectomy/Hemorrhage		5	5
85	F	820.0	Fracture, Femur	4			4	Hip Surgery/Thrombophlebitis		4	4
24	M	590.2	Renal Abscess	6	1	7	4	Tooth Extraction/Complications		1	3
82	F	154.1 813.4 820.2	Carcinoma, Rectum / Fracture, Wrist / Fracture, Femur	6	2	4	4	Slip and Fall		1	3

(Continued)

BASIC PATIENT INJURY DATA (Continued)

Hospital B (Concluded)

Age	Sex	H-ICDA	Diagnosis	Confidence that an Injury Occurred	Evidence of Injury	Source of Injury	Severity of Injury	Description of Injury	Did Negligence Cause the Injury?	Confidence in Answer	Predicted Legal Outcome
64	F	712.3 531.0 255.9	Rheumatoid Arthritis Peptic Ulcer Adrenal Insufficiency	6	8	1	7	Drug Therapy/Adverse Effects			3
69	M	441.3	False Aneurysm	3	8	1	4	Vascular Surgery/Complications		4	4
72	F	783.0	Epistaxis, Drug-Induced	6	6	1	6	Anticoagulants/Adverse Effects		3	4
45	F	232.2	Cyst, Buttock	3	3	4	3	Injection/Complications		2	4
40	M	357.9	Radiculitis	6	4	1	3	Spine Surgery/Complications			3
69	F	401.0	Hypertension	3	1	1	4	Aortography/Complications			3
71	F	996.6	Wound Infection	6	1	1	3	Fracture Fixation/Infection			3
80	M	173.6 436.0	Lymphoma, Buttock Cerebral Thrombosis	6	7	1	9	Wound Dehiscence/Infection Cerebral Thrombosis		1	3
77	M	551.3	Diaphragmatic Hernia	4	2	1	3	Herniorrhaphy/Complications Esophageal Stricture		4	4
66	M	600.0 450.0	Prostatic Hypertrophy Pulmonary Embolism	6	6	1	3	Prostatectomy/Pulmonary Embolism		6	5
82	M	250.0 390.1	Diabetes Mellitus Cellulitis, Arm	6	1	2	9	Infection/Complications Diabetes Mellitus/Therapy	Y	5	1
74	M	600.0	Prostatic Hypertrophy	5	12	1	4	Prostatectomy/Complications			3
27	F	551.1	Umbilical Hernia	6	4	1	3	Herniorrhaphy/Suture Infection		3	4
69	F	486.0	Pneumonia	6	10	1	9	Pneumonia/Therapy	Y	1	2
69	M	600.0	Prostatic Hypertrophy	5	4	1	3	Prostatectomy/Complications		3	4
29	F	626.9 622.1	Menorrhagia Pelvic Abscess/Hematoma	6	1	1	4	Hysterectomy/Hemorrhage/ Infection		4	4
63	F	427.3 429.0	Arteriosclerosis Cardiac Arrest	6	7	3	3	Pacemaker/Complications		3	4
63	M	574.9 792.0	Cholecystitis Azotemia	6	1	1	3	Tetracycline/Adverse Effects		2	4

Exhibit 5.—*Louisiana State Medical Society Pamphlet Re Confidentiality of Medical Records*

LET'S CONTINUE TO KEEP YOUR MEDICAL RECORDS CONFIDENTIAL

Physicians are taught from their early days in medical school that a patient's record should only be shared by the patient and the doctor. That's the way I still think it should be.

Unfortunately, there's been a disturbing trend in recent years for some organizations and government agencies to collect and exchange medical records as a matter of routine. Patient's records actually have been fed into computers where they are made available to credit agencies, insurance or others who want to pay for this information.

Even more disturbing is a section of a new federal law called Professional Standards Review Organizations that will require millions of Americans to have their medical records fed into computers and exposed to clerks, bureaucrats and others before patients can be reimbursed for their health care expenses. If the computer says you stayed in the hospital too long, or does not agree with the medical treatment rendered or the drugs you received, you may not be paid at all!

I do not practice computer medicine. No two patients are treated alike because no two patients are alike .All of my patients receive what I consider the best care available for their particular ailment. I believe the patient-doctor relationship must be preserved at all costs. I believe this is the type medical care you want too.

HERE'S HOW YOU CAN HELP KEEP YOUR MEDICAL RECORDS CONFIDENTIAL

1. If you are ever asked to authorize release of your medical history, insist that you be told specifically who will have access to the information and why. Specify that you do not want it released to anyone else for any reason.

2. Write your Congressman. Ask him to support H.R. 9375 *to repeal the Professional Standards Review Organizations* (Section 249F) of Public Law 92–603. Let him know that PSRO will add hundreds of millions of dollars to the cost of health care that will have to be paid for by consumers and taxpayers. Let him know that bureaucratic interference will not improve the quality of health care but will destroy the patient-physician relationship. Request that he become a co-sponsor of this bill.

3. Ask questions on this subject. I hope you will feel free to discuss with me how PSRO will affect your health care. You are my patient and I am your doctor because your good health is important to both of us. I invite you to take time to talk about any medical or health matter tha concerns you.

COMPUTERIZED MEDICINE AND PROFESSIONAL STANDARDS REVIEW ORGANIZATIONS

In the closing rush hours of the 92nd Congress, an amendment was tacked on to the Social Security Act of 1972 that will affect the quality and quantity of health care received by millions of Americans. This amendment established Professional Standards Review Organizations (PSROs). Unfortunately most congressmen voted for an amendment that they had not read, studied or understood. Even today many congressmen are not aware of the consequences of PSRO.

By 1976, unless the law is changed, PSROs will control the amount and kind of medical care received by Medicare and Medicaid patients. Already some are making plans to extend PSRO activities to health care provided by private insurance carriers.

How can PSROs do all this? It's all very simple. The law allows PSROs to establish norms, criteria and standards for medical care and put them all in a computer. If your doctor wants to hospitalize you for pneumonia, he will first have to check with the PSRO computer to see if this is sufficient cause for hospitalization. If the computer says "yes," it will then tell your doctor how long you should stay in the hospital and the treatment, based on the PSROs' norms, criteria and standards. If for some reason your progress and recovery do not agree with the PSRO, you may be denied payment for your hospital and doctor's bills.

Have you ever tried to correct an error on a computerized bill or statement? If you have, you know why people say, "To err is human, but to really foul up something use a computer."

Obviously physicians do not like PSROs. Until medicine becomes an exact science, nothing will replace the one to one patient-physician relationship. We believe PSROs are hazardous to your health, your privacy and your finances ... PSROs will cost hundreds of millions in added tax dollars.

HERE'S HOW YOU CAN HELP PREVENT FEDERALIZED, COMPUTERIZED MEDICINE

1. Write your Congressman. Tell him why the PSRO section (249F) of Public Law 92–603 is a bad law.

2. Tell your Congressman that you do not want your doctor to have to treat you according to a federalized, computerized medical cookbook.

3. Tell him you do not want your confidential medical records exposed to clerks, bureaucrats and others.

4. Ask your Congressman to support H.R. 9375 that will repeal PSRO.

Ration Medical Care? That's right! The same Washington politicians and bureaucrats that brought you the energy crisis are now gearing up for the medical care crisis- Like oil, Washington now considers medical care a scarce and expensive commodity. The government's answer to both of these created crises appears to be the same—*rationing.*

How Can the Government Ration Medical Care? By enforcing a little known section of a law already on the books, that's how! Section 249F of Public Law 92–603 provides the machinery for rationing medical care for the millions of Americans entitled to Medicare and Medicaid through Something called Professional Standards Review Organizations.

Why Ration Medical Care? Health care benefits were promised to millions of Americans entitled to Medicare and Medicaid in big, bold headlines. Washington has now found, even by increasing Social Security taxes, that it does not have enough money (your tax dollars) to make good the promises in those big, bold headlines. The politicians answer to the problem, which they created, is *rationing* so a lot of people will get a little bit of what was promised.

How Will Medical Care Rationing Work? First, the government will spend millions ($34,000,000.00 in 1974) not for health care, but for establishing 182 rationing systems called Professional Standards Review Organizations. No telling what the costs of PSROs will be by the time the program becomes fully operational in 1976.

How Can PSROs Ration Medical Care? PSROs will control the amount and kind of medical care received by Medicare and Medicaid patients. Already plans are being made to exceed PSRO control to all medical care. Under the law, PRSOs will have the power to:

1. Tell your doctor *if he can admit you to a hospital.*

2. Tell your doctor *how long you can stay in the hospital.*

3. Tell your doctor *what medications, tests and treatment you should receive.*

How will PSROs be able to tell your Doctor what to do? PSROs will first develop a manual, many doctors call it a "medical cookbook," of norms and standards of care. As long as a doctor follows the PSRO manual, he will be protected by the law. Unfortunately, PSROs make no such guarantee to the patient. Nothing would be easier for your doctor than to look up your ailment and treat you according to "the book."

What can you do about Rationing Medical Care and PSROs?

1. Write your Congressman and Senators. Tell them why the PSRO section (249F) of Public Law 92–603 is a bad law.

2. Tell your legislators that you do not want bureaucrats to ration the medical care you are entitled to and were promised under Medicare and Medicaid. Let them know that you have paid for these benfits through your Social Security tax—and this has not been rationed. The tax has gone up almost annually.

3. Tell them that you want no part of "cookbook" medicine.

4. Ask your Congressman and Senators to support H.R. 9375 and the other bills that have been introduced to reepal PSRO.

EXHIBIT 6.—*Excerpt From Journal of Law and Economics, Vol. 1, October 1958, Entitled "Price Discrimination in Medicine"*

PRICE DISCRIMINATION IN MEĐICINE*

REUBEN A. KESSEL

University of Chicago

M ANY disinguished economists have argued that the medical profession constitutes a monopoly, and some have produced evidence of the size of the monopoly gains that accrue to the members of this profession.[1] Price discrimination by doctors, i.e., scaling fees to the income of patients, has been explained as the behavior of a discriminating monopolist.[2] Indeed this has become the standard textbook example of discriminating monopoly.[3] However this explanation of price discrimination has been incomplete. Economists who have subscribed to this hypothesis have never indicated why competition among doctors failed to establish uniform prices for identical services. For any individual doctor, given the existing pattern of price discrimination, income from professional services would be maximized if rates were lowered for affluent patients and increased for poor patients. However, if many doctors engaged in such price policies, a pattern of prices for medical services would be established that would be independent of the incomes of patients. Yet despite this inconsistency between private interests and the existing pattern or structure of prices based on income differences, this price structure has survived. Is this a contradiction of the law of markets? Why is it possible to observe in a single market the same service sold at different prices?

The primary objective of this paper, which is an essay in positive econom-

---

* The author is indebted to A. A. Alchian, W. Meckling, A. Enthoven, and W. Taylor of the RAND Corporation, W. Gorter, A. Nicols, and J. F. Weston of UCLA, H. G. Lewis and A. Rees of the University of Chicago, and Gary Becker of Columbia University for assistance.

[1] M. Friedman and S. Kuznets, Income from Independent Professional Practice (1945); M. Friedman in Impact of the Trade Union, p. 211, edited by D. M. Wright (1951); Also K. E. Boulding, Conference on the Utilization of Scientific and Professional Manpower, p. 23 (1944).

The results of the Friedman-Kuznets study, at p. 133, using pre-war data, indicate that the costs of producing doctors are seventeen per cent greater than the costs of producing dentists, while the average income of doctors is thirty-two per cent greater.

[2] J. Robinson, Economics of Imperfect Competition, p. 180 (1933). For example, the world famed Mayo Clinic discriminates in pricing. Albert Deutsch, The Mayo Clinic, 22 Consumer Reports 37, 40 (Jan. 1957). A finance department makes inquiries into the patient's economic status and scales the bills accordingly. Fees are not discussed in advance.

[3] E. A. G. Robinson, Monopoly, p. 77 (1941); C. E. Daugherty and M. Daugherty, Principles of Political Economy, p. 591 (1950); T. Scitovsky, Welfare and Competition, p. 408 (1941); K. E. Boulding, Economic Analysis, p. 662 (1955); S. Enke, Intermediate Economic Theory, p. 42 (1950); G. Stigler, The Theory of Price, p. 219 (1952).

ics, is to show by empirical evidence that the standard textbook rationalization of what appears to be a contradiction of the law of markets is correct. It will be argued that the discriminating monopoly model is valid for understanding the pricing of medical services, and that each individual buyer of medical services that are produced jointly with hospital care constitutes a unique, separable market. In the process of presenting evidence supporting this thesis, other closely related phenomena will be considered. These are (1), why the AMA favors medical insurance prepayment plans that provide money to be used to buy medical services, but bitterly opposes comparable plans that provide instead of money, the service itself and (2), why the AMA has opposed free medical care by the Veterans Administration for veterans despite the enormous increase in the quantity of medical services demanded that would result from the reduction to zero of the private costs of medical care for such a large group.

The second half of this paper represents an attempt, by means of an application of the discriminating monopoly model, to further our understanding of many unique characteristics of the medical profession. If the medical profession constitutes a discriminating monopoly, what inferences can be drawn concerning the relationship between this monopoly and other economic, sociological and political aspects of the medical profession? In particular, does the discriminating monoply model shed any light upon, (1) why a higher percentage of doctors belong to professional organizations than is true of other professions, (2) why doctors treat one another and their families free of charge, (3) why doctors, compared with any other professional group, are extremely reluctant to criticize one another before the public, (4) why specialists are over-represented among the hierarchy of organized medicine, (5) why a transfer of membership in good standing from one county society to a second sometimes requires serving a term as a probationary member, (6) why advertising that redounds to the interest of the medical profession as a whole is approved whereas advertising that is designed to benefit particular individuals or groups is strongly opposed, (7) why malpractice insurance is less expensive for members of organized medicine than it is for non-members, and finally (8) why minority groups, particularly Jews, have been discriminated against in admission to medical schools.[4]

The body of this paper is divided into five sections. These are, in order of presentation, a hypothesis alternative to the price discrimination hypothesis, a history of the development of the powers that enable organized medicine to

[4] It is worth noting that there is no inconsistency between the validity of the explanation to be presented and the inability of any or all members of the medical profession, past, present or future, to understand the economic arguments that follow. All that is required of doctors is the ability to engage in adaptive behavior of a very rudimentary character. Consult A. A. Alchian, Uncertainty, Evolution, and Economic Theory, 58 J. Pol. Econ. 211 (1950).

organize effectively a discriminating monopoly, evidence supporting the validity of the discriminating monopoly model for understanding the pricing of medical services, and lastly an application of the discriminating monopoly model to rationalize many characteristics of the medical profession that have been hitherto thought of as either anomalies or behavior that could best be explained as non-economic phenemona.

I. A Hypothesis Alternative to the Discriminating Monopoly Model

The standard position of the medical profession on price discrimination is in conflict with what might be regarded as the standard position of the economics profession. Economists argue that price discrimination by doctors represents the profit maximizing behavior of a discriminating monopolist; the medical profession takes the contrary position that price discrimination exists because doctors represent a collection agency for medical charities.[5] The income of these charities is derived from a loading charge imposed upon well-to-do patients. This income is used to finance the costs of hiring doctors to provide medical care for the poor who are sick. The doctor who is hired by the medical charity and the medical charity itself are typically the same person. Since the loading charge that is imposed upon non-charity patients to support the activities of medical charities is proportional to income or wealth, discriminatory prices result. The following quotation from an unnamed but highly respected surgeon presents the position of the medical profession.

I don't feel that I am robbing the rich because I charge them more when I know they can well afford it; the sliding scale is just as democratic as the income tax. I operated today upon two people for the same surgical condition—one a widow whom I charged $50, the other a banker whom I charged $250. I let the widow set her own fee. I charged the banker an amount which he probably carries around in his wallet to entertain his business friends.[6]

It is relevant to inquire, why have we had the development of charities operated by a substantial fraction of the non-salaried practitioners of a profession in medicine alone? Why hasn't a parallel development occurred for

[5] However, there is not a unanimity of views either among economists or medical men. Means, a retired professor of clinical medicine at Harvard and a former president of the American College of Surgeons, takes the point of view of the economists. He describes this price policy as charging what the traffic will bear. J. H. Means, Doctors, People and Government, p. 66 (1953).

[6] Seham, Who Pays the Doctor?, 135 New Republic 10, 11 (July 9, 1956). Those who favor price discrimination for this reason ought to be in favor of a single price plan with a system of subsidies and taxes. Such a scheme, in principle, could improve the welfare of both the poor and the well-to-do relative to what it was under price discrimination.

The equity of a tax that is imposed upon the sick who are well-to-do as contrasted with a tax upon the well-to-do generally has not troubled the proponents of this method of taxation.

such closely related services as nursing and dental care? Why is it possible to observe discrimination by the Mayo Clinic but not the A and P? Clearly food is as much of a "necessity" as medical care. The intellectual foundation for the existence of price discrimination and the operation of medical charities by doctors appears to rest upon the postulate that medicine is in some sense unlike any other commodity or service. More specifically, the state is willing to provide food, clothing, and shelter for the indigent but not medical care.[7] Since medical care is so important, doctors do not refuse to accept patients if they are unable to pay. As a consequence, discrimination in pricing medical services is almost inevitable if doctors themselves are not to finance the costs of operating medical charities.

The foregoing argument in defense of price discrimination in medicine implies that a competitive market for the sale of medical services is inconsistent with the provision of free services to the indigent. This implication is not supported by what can be observed elsewhere in our economy. Clearly there exist a number of competitive markets in which individual practitioners provide free goods or services and price discrimination is absent. Merchants, in their capacity of merchants, give resources to charities yet do not discriminate in pricing their services. Similarly many businesses give huge sums for educational purposes. Charity is consistent with non-discriminatory pricing because the costs of charity can be and are paid for out of the receipts of the donors without recourse to price discrimination.

However the fact that non-discriminatory pricing is consistent with charity work by doctors doesn't imply that discriminatory pricing of medical services is inconsistent with the charity hypothesis. Clearly what can be done without discrimination can, *a fortiori*, be done with discrimination. Therefore, it is pertinent to ask, is there any evidence that bears directly on the validity of the charity interpretation of price discrimination? The maximizing hypothesis of economics implies that differences in fees can be explained by differences in demand. The charity hypothesis propounded by the medical profession implies that differences in fees result from income differences. The pricing of medical services to those who have medical insurance provides that what might be regarded as a crucial experiment for discriminating between these hypotheses. Whether or not one has medical insurance affects the demand for medical service but does not affect personal income. Consequently if the charity hy-

---

[7] H. Cabot contends that the community is unwilling to provide for the medical care of the indigent. Therefore the system of a sliding scale of fees has evolved; pp. 123, 266 ff. He estimates that the more opulent members of the community pay ". . . from five to thirty times the average fee . . ." p. 270, The Doctors Bill (1935).

Robinson has defended discriminatory pricing of medical services in sparsely populated areas by using an argument based on indivisibilities. A Fundamental Objection to Laissez-Faire, 45 Economic Journal 580 (1935). For a refutation of this position, see Hutt, Discriminating Monopoly and the Consumer, 46 Economic Journal 61, 74 (1936).

pothesis is correct, then there should be no difference in fees, for specified services, for those who do and those who do not have medical insurance. On the other hand, if the maximizing hypothesis of economics is correct, then fees for those who have medical insurance ought to be higher than for those who do not have such insurance. Existing evidence indicates that if income and wealth differences are held constant, people who have medical insurance pay more for the same service than people who do not have such insurance. Union leaders have found that the fees charged have risen as a result of the acquisition of medical insurance by their members; fees, particularly for surgery, are higher than they would otherwise be if the union member were not insured.[8] Members of the insurance industry have found that ". . . the greater the benefit provided the higher the surgical bill. . . ."[9] This suggests that the principle used for the determinations of fees is, as Means pointed out, what the traffic will bear. Obviously fees determined by this principle will be highly correlated with income, although income will have no independent predictive content for fees if the correlation between income and what the traffic will bear is abstracted.[10]

Other departures from the implications of the hypothesis that price discrimination results from the desires of the medical profession to finance the costs of medical care for the indigent exist. These are: (1) Doctors typically do not charge each other for medical care when clearly inter-physician fees ought to be relatively high since doctors have relatively high incomes. (2) The volume of free medical care, particularly in surgery, has declined as a result of the rise in real per capita income in this country in the last twenty years. Yet there has been no change in the extent of price discrimination. As real per capita income rises, price discrimination ought to fade away. There is no evidence that this has been the case.[11] (3) There exists no machinery for matching the receipts and disbursements of medical charities operated by

[8] E. A. Schuler, R. J. Mowitz, and A. J. Mayer, Medical Public Relations (1952), report the attitude of lay leaders of the community towards the medical profession. For the attitudes of union leaders and why they have these attitudes, see p. 97 ff.

[9] Lorber in Hearings Before the House Committee on Interstate and Foreign Commerce on Health Inquiry, 83d Cong. 2d Sess. pt. 7, p. 1954 (1954); Also Joanis, Hospital and Medical Costs, Proceedings of the Fourth Annual Group Meeting of the Health and Accident Underwriters Conference, p. 18 (Feb. 19–20, 1952).

[10] The principle of what the traffic will bear and the indemnity principle of insurance are fundamentally incompatible and in principle make medical care uninsurable. This has been a real problem for the insurance industry and in part accounts for the relative absence from the market of major medical insurance plans. See the unpublished doctoral dissertation of A. Yousri, Prepayment of Medical and Surgical Care in Wisconsin, p. 438, University of Wisconsin Library (1956).

[11] Berger, Are Surgical Fees Too High?, 32 Medical Economics 97, 100 ff. (June 1955).

individual doctors. There are no audits of the receipts and the expenditures of medical charities and well-to-do patients are not informed of the magnitude of the loading charges imposed. Moreover one study of medical care and the family budget reported ". . . no relation in the case of the individual doctor between the free services actually rendered and this recoupment, the whole system is haphazard any way you look at it."[12]

II. History of the Development of the Medical Monòpóly

A necessary condition for maintaining a structure of prices that is inconsistent with the maximization by doctors of individual income is the availability and willingness to use powerful sanctions against potential price cutters. When one examines the problems that have been encountered in maintaining prices that are against the interests of individual members of a cartel composed of less than fifteen members, one cannot help being impressed with the magnitude of the problem confronting a monopoly composed of hundreds of thousands of independent producers. Yet despite the fact that medicine constitutes an industry with an extraordinarily large number of producers, the structure of prices for a large number of medical services nevertheless reflects the existence of discrimination based on income. This implies that very strong sanctions must be available to those empowered to enforce price discipline. Indeed, *a priori* reasoning suggests that these sanctions must be of an order of magnitude more powerful than anything we have hitherto encountered in industrial cartels. What are the nature of these sanctions? How are they employed? In order to appreciate fully the magnitude of the coercive measures available to organized medicine, it is relevant to examine the history of medicine to understand how these sanctions were acquired.

Medicine, like the profession of economics today, was until the founding of the AMA a relatively competitive industry. With very few exceptions, anyone who wanted to practice was free to hang out a shingle and declare himself available. Medical schools were easy to start, easy to get into, and provided, as might be expected in a free market, a varied menu of medical training that covered the complete quality spectrum. Many medical schools of this time were organized as profit making institutions and had stock outstanding. Some schools were owned by the faculty.

In 1847, the American Medical Association was founded and this organization immediately committed itself to two propositions that were to lead to sharp restrictions upon the freedom of would-be doctors to enter the medical profession and the freedom of patients to choose doctors whom the AMA felt were not adequately qualified to practice medicine. These propositions were (1) that medical students should have acquired a "suitable preliminary education" and (2) that a "uniform elevated standard of requirements for the

[12] Deardorff and Clark, op. cit. supra note 9, pt. 6, p. 1646.

degree of M.D. should be adopted by all medical schools in the United States.[13]

These objectives were achieved in two stages. During the first stage, the primary concern of the AMA was licensure. In the second, it was accrediting schools of medicine. During the first stage, which began with the founding of the AMA and lasted until the turn of the century, organized medicine was able by lobbying before state legislatures to persuade legislators to license the practice of medicine. Consequently the various states set up boards of medical examiners to administer examinations to determine whether or not applicants were qualified to practice medicine and to grant licenses to those the State Board deemed qualified to practice. Generally speaking, organized medicine was very successful in its campaign to induce states to license physicians. However, the position of organized medicine was by no means unopposed. William James, in testimony offered before the State House in Boston in 1898 when legislation concerned with licensing of non-medically trained therapists was being considered, adopted a nineteenth century liberal position. To quote from this testimony:

One would suppose that any set of sane persons interested in the growth of medical truth would rejoice if other persons were found willing to push out their experience in the mental healing direction, and to provide a mass of material out of which the conditions and limits of such therapeutic methods may at last become clear. One would suppose that our orthodox medical brethren might so rejoice; but instead of rejoicing they adopt the fiercely partisan attitude of a powerful trade union, they demand legislation against the competition of the "scabs." . . . The mind curers and their public return the scorn of the regular profession with an equal scorn, and will never come up for the examination. Their movement is a religious or quasi-religious movement; personality is one condition of success there, and impressions and intuitions seem to accomplish more than chemical, anatomical or physiological information. . . . Pray, do not fail, Mr. Chairman, to catch my point. You are not to ask yourselves whether these mind-curers do really achieve the successes that are claimed. It is enough for you as legislators to ascertain that a large number of our citizens, persons whose number seems daily to increase, are convinced that they do achieve them, are persuaded that a valuable new department of medical experience is by them opening up. Here is a purely medical question, regarding which our General Court, not being a well-spring and source of medical virtue, not having any private test of therapeutic truth, must remain strictly neutral under penalty of making the confusion worse. . . . Above all things, Mr. Chairman, let us not be infected with the Gallic spirit of regulation and regimentation for their own abstract sakes. Let us not grow hysterical about law-making. Let us not fall in love with enactments and penalties because they are so logical and sound so pretty, and look so nice on paper.[14]

[13] A. Flexner, Medical Education in the U.S. and Canada, Bull. No. 4, Carnegie Foundation for the Advancement of Teaching, p. 10 (1910).

[14] 2 Letters of W. James, 66–72 (edited H. James, 1920). Dollard reports that James took this position at the risk of being drummed out of the ranks of medicine. Dollard, Monopoly

· However, it was not until the second stage that economically effective power over entry was acquired by organized medicine. This stage began with the founding in 1904 of the Council on Medical Education of the AMA. This group dedicated itself to the task of improving the quality of medical education offered by the medical schools of the day. In 1906, this committee undertook an inspection of the 160 medical schools then in existence and fully approved of the training in only 82 schools. Thirty-two were deemed to be completely unacceptable. As might be expected, considerable resentment developed in the medical colleges and elsewhere as a result of this inspection. Consequently the council withheld publication of its findings, although the various colleges were informed of their grades.[15] In order to gain wider acceptance of the results of this study, the Council solicited the aid of the Carnegie Foundation. "If we could obtain the publication and approval of our work by the Carnegie Foundation for the Advancement of Teaching, it would assist materially in securing the results we were attempting to bring about."[16] Subsequently Abraham Flexner, representing the Carnegie Foundation, with the aid of N. P. Colwell, secretary of the Council on Medical Education, repeated the AMA's inspection and grading of medical schools. In 1910, the results of the labors of Flexner and Colwell were published.[17] This report, known as the Flexner report, recommended that a substantial fraction of the existing medical schools be closed, standards be raised in the remainder, and admissions sharply curtailed. Flexner forcefully argued that the country was suffering from an overproduction of doctors and that it was in the public interest to have fewer doctors who were better trained. In effect, Flexner argued that the public should be protected against the consequences of buying medical services from inadequately trained doctors by legislating poor medical schools out of business.[18]

---

and Medicine, speech delivered at Medical Center, UCLA, to be published by the University of California Press as one of a series of papers presented in celebration of Robert Gordon Sproul's 25th anniversary as President of the University of California. The significance of consumers' sovereignty has been recognized by at least one other maverick doctor. Means, op. cit. supra note 5, at p. 72.

[15] Johnson in Fishbein, A History of the American Medical Association, p. 887 ff. (1947).

[16] Bevan, Cooperation in Medical Education and Medical Service, 90 Journal of the American Medical Association 1175 (1928).

[17] Flexner, op. cit. supra note 13.

[18] Flexner, op. cit. supra note 13, at p. 14. Two errors in economic reasoning are crucial in helping Flexner establish his conclusions. One is an erroneous interpretation of Gresham's Law. This law is used to justify legislation to keep low quality doctors out of the medical care market by interpreting it to mean that second-class doctors will drive first-class doctors out of business. The other is that raising the standards of medical education is necessarily in the public interest. Flexner fails to recognize that raising standards implies higher costs of medical care. This argument is on a par with arguing that we should keep all cars of a quality below Cadillacs, Chryslers, and Lincolns off the automobile market.

If impact on public policy is the criterion of importance, the Flexner report must be regarded as one of the most important reports ever written. It convinced legislators that only the graduates of first class medical schools ought to be permitted to practice medicine and led to the delegation to the AMA of the task of determining what was and what was not a first class medical school. As a result, standards of acceptability for winning a license to practice medicine were set by statute or by formal rule or informal policy of state medical examining boards, and these statutes or rules provided that boards consider only graduates of schools approved by the AMA and/or the American Association of Medical Colleges whose lists are identical.[19]

The Flexner report ushered in an era, which lasted until 1944, during which a large number of medical schools were shut down. With its new found power, the AMA vigorously attacked the problem of certification of medical schools. By exercising its power to certify, the AMA reduced the number of medical schools in the United States from 162 in 1906 to 85 in 1920, 76 in 1930 and 69 in 1944.[20] As a result of the regulation of medical schools, the number of medical students in school in the United States today is 28,500, merely 5,200 more than in 1910 when Flexner published his report.[21]

The AMA, by means of its power to certify what is and what is not a class A medical school, has substantial control over both the number of medical schools in the United States and the rate of production of doctors.[22] While the control by the AMA over such first class schools as, say, Johns Hopkins

[19] Hyde and Wolff, The American Medical Association: Power, Purpose, and Politics in Organized Medicine, 63 Yale L. J. 969 (1954).

[20] These figures are from R. M. Allen, Medical Education and the Changing Order, p. 16 (1946). Allen imputes this decline in the number of medical schools to a previous error in estimating the demand for doctors. The decline in the number of schools in existence represented an adjustment to more correctly perceived demand conditions for medical care.

[21] Dollard, op. cit. supra note 14. This result was far from unanticipated. Bevan, the head of the AMA's Council on Medical Education, clearly anticipated a decline in both medical students and schools. "In this rapid elevation of the standard of medical education with the increase in preliminary requirements and greater length of course, and with the reduction of the number of medical schools from 160 to 80, there occurred a marked reduction in the number of medical students and medical graduates. We had anticipated this and felt that this was a desirable thing. We had an over-supply of poor mediocre practitioners." Bevan, op. cit. note 16, at p. 1176. Friedman and Kuznets state, "Initially, this decline in the number of physicians relative to total population was an unplanned by-product of the intensive drive for higher standards of medical education." Op. cit. supra note 4 at pp. 10–11. It may have been a by-product, and there are some grounds for doubts on this count, but it surely was not unanticipated.

[22] Dr. Spahr contends that there is a "... widespread but erroneous belief that the AMA governs the profession directly and determines who may practice medicine." Medicine's Neglected Control Lever, 40 Yale Rev. 25 (1950). She correctly contends that this power belongs to the state but fails to recognize that it has been delegated to the AMA by the state. Mayer on the other hand recognizes both the power in the hands of the AMA and its source. He argues that the AMA has life and death powers over both medical schools and hospitals. 180 Harpers 27 (Dec. 1939).

is relatively weak because it would be ludicrous not to classify this institution a a class A school, nevertheless control over the aggregate production rate of doctors is great because of its more substantial power over the output of less distinguished medical schools.

The delegation by the state legislatures to the AMA of the power to regulate the medical industry in the public interest is on a par with giving the American Iron and Steel Institute the power to determine the output of steel. This delegation of power by the states to the AMA, which was actively sought and solicited, placed this organization in a position of having to serve two masters who in part have conflicting interests. On the one hand, the AMA was given the task of providing an adequate supply of properly qualified doctors. On the other hand, the decision with respect to what is adequate training and an adequate number of doctors affects the pocketbooks of those who do the regulating as well as their closest business and personal associates. It is this power that has been given to the AMA that is the cornerstone of the monopoly power that has been imputed by economists to organized medicine.[23]

III. Evidence Supporting the Discriminating Monopoly Model

The preceding analysis tells us nothing about the mechanism for controlling the price policies of individual doctors; it only implies that the rate of return on capital invested in medical training will be greater than the rate of return on capital invested in other classes of professional training. This difference in returns is imputable as a rent on the power of the AMA to control admissions to the profession by means of control over medical education. Here it will be argued that control over the pricing policies of doctors is directly and immediately related to AMA control of medical education. The relationship is that control over medical education is the primary instrumentality for control over individual price policies. More specifically, control over post-graduate medical training—internship and residency, and control over admission to specialty board examinations—is the source of the power over the members of the·medical profession by organized medicine.

A. THE CONTROL MECHANISM

Part of nearly every doctor's medical education consists of internship and for many also a period of hospital service known as residency. Internship is a necessary condition for licensure in most states. This training is administered by hospitals. However, hospitals must be approved by the AMA for

---

[23] Dollard, op. cit. supra note 21, concedes that medicine is a monopoly but argues that the AMA has used its power, by and large, in the public interest. Therefore, he implies that the monopoly power of the AMA has been unexploited, and the profession has acted against its own self interest.

intern and residency training, and most non-proprietary, i.e., nonprofit, hospitals in this country are in fact approved for at least intern training. Each approved hospital is allocated a quota of positions that can be filled by interns as part of their training. Hospitals value highly participation in internship and residency training programs. These programs are valued highly because at the prevailing wage for intern services, it is possible to produce hospital care more cheaply with interns than without them. Interns to hospitals are like coke to the steel industry: in both cases, it is perfectly possible to produce the final product without these raw materials; in both cases, the final product can be produced more cheaply by using these particular raw materials.

There exist some grounds for suspecting that the wages of interns are maintained at an artificially low level, i.e., that interns receive compensation that is less than the value of their marginal product: (1) Hospitals are reporting that there is a "shortage" of interns and have been known to send representatives to Europe and Asia to invite doctors to serve as interns.[24] (2) University hospitals are more aggressive bidders for intern services than non-university hospitals. The fraction of the available intern positions that are filled by university hospitals is greater than by non-university hospitals.[25] If controls are exercised over what hospitals can offer in wages to interns, university hospitals are apt to be less vulnerable to the threat of loss of their class A hospital ratings than non-university hospitals. This would be true for the same reason that Johns Hopkins would have a freer hand in determining the size of its freshman class. The status of university hospitals is stronger because these hospitals are likely to be among the better hospitals in the country. Therefore, if controls over intern wages exist then it seems reasonable to suspect they would be relatively weaker over the wages of interns in university hospitals. For this reason, one would expect university hospitals to be more aggressive in bidding for interns.

However, whether or not interns are underpaid, the AMA has control over the supply of a vital, in an economic sense, agent of production for producing hospital care. Revocation of a hospital's Class A rating implies the loss of interns. In turn, the loss of interns implies higher costs of production. Higher costs of production result in a deterioration of the competitive position of any given hospital vis-à-vis other hospitals in the medical care market. This control over hospitals by the AMA has been used to induce hospitals to abide by the Mundt Resolution.[26] This resolution advises hospitals that are certified for intern training that their staff ought to be composed solely of members of

[24] Congress to Probe Doctor Shortage, 33 Medical Economics 141 (June 1956).

[25] 162 Journal of the American Medical Association 281 (1956).

[26] "By a long record of authoritative inspection and grading of facilities, organized medicine has placed itself in a position to deny alternatively the services of doctor and hospital to each other." O. Garceau, Political Life of the American Medical Association, p. 109 (1941).

local medical societies.[27] As a result of this AMA control over hospitals, membership in local medical societies is a matter of enormous importance to practicing physicians. Lack of membership implies inability to become a member of a hospital staff.[28]

County medical societies are for all practical purposes private clubs with their own rules concerning eligibility for membership and grounds for expulsion. A system of appeals from the rulings of county medical societies with respect to their members is provided. On the other hand, for non-members attempting to obtain membership in county medical societies, there is no provision for appeal. The highest court in the medical judicial system is the Judicial Council of the AMA. Between this council and the county medical societies are state medical societies. Judicial review is bound by findings of fact made at the local level.[29] For doctors dependent upon hospitals in order to carry out their practice, and presumably this constitutes the bulk of the profession, being cut off from access to hospitals constitutes a partial revocation of their license to practice medicine. Consequently, more doctors belong to their county medical associations than is true of lawyers with respect to local bar associations. More significantly, doctors are subject to very severe losses indeed if they should be expelled from their local county medical associations or be refused admission to membership. It is this weapon, expulsion from county medical associations, that is probably the most formidable sanction employed to keep doctors from maximizing their personal incomes by cutting prices to high income patients. "Unethical" doctors, i.e., price cutters, can be in large part removed as a threat to a structure of prices that discriminates in terms of income by the use of this weapon.[30] For potential unethical physicians, it pays not to cut prices if cutting prices means being cut off from hospitals.

Thus far we have argued that control over the individual price policies of the members of the medical profession has been achieved by the AMA through its control over post-graduate medical education. By means of its power to

[27] Hyde and Wolff, op. cit. supra note 19, at 952. The certification of hospitals for nursing training and the value of nursing training programs to hospitals may be on a par with intern training.

[28] The strike is another instrument for control over hospitals by the AMA. Doctors have refused to work in hospitals that have admitted osteopaths to their staff. Hyde and Wolff, op. cit. supra note 19, at 966; M. M. Belli, Ready for the Plaintiff, p. 115 (1956). The threat of a strike has also been used to induce hospitals to refuse staff membership to "unethical" doctors. Group Health Etc. v. King Co. Med. Soc., 39 Wash. 2d 586, 624, 237 P. 2d 737, 757–758 (1951).

[29] Hyde and Wolff, op. cit. supra note 19, at 949–950.

[30] "Ethics has always been a flexible, developing, notion in medicine, with a strong flavor of economics from the start." Garceau, op. cit. supra note 26, at p. 106. Also consult the Hippocratic Oath.

certify a hospital for intern training, the AMA controls the source of supply of a crucial agent for the production of hospital care. Control over the supply of interns has been used to induce hospitals to admit to their staffs only members of county medical associations. Since membership in the county medical associations is in the control of organized medicine, and membership in a hospital staff is extremely important for the successful practice of most branches of medicine, the individual doctor can be easily manipulated by those who control membership in county medical associations.

Members of the medical profession are also subject to another type of control, derived from AMA control over post-graduate medical education, that is particularly effective over younger members. Membership in a county medical society is a necessary condition for admission to specialty board examinations for a number of specialties, and passing these examinations is a necessary condition for specialty ratings.[31] Non-society members cannot win board membership in these specialties. This is a particularly important form of control over newcomers to the medical profession because newcomers tend to be young doctors who aspire to specialty board ratings.[32] Consequently the AMA has particularly powerful sanctions over those who are most likely to be price cutters. These are young doctors trying to establish a practice.[33]

B. THE EVIDENCE

Just as one would expect an all-out war to reveal a country's most powerful weapons, substantial threats to the continued existence of price discrimination ought to reveal the strongest sanctions available to organized medicine. For this reason, the opposition or lack of opposition to prepaid medical plans that provide medical service directly to the patient ought to be illuminating.

Generally speaking, there exist two classes of medical insurance. One is the cash indemnity variety. Blue Cross and Blue Shield plans fall within this class.[34] Under cash indemnity medical insurance, the doctor and patient are

[31] Hyde and Wolff, op. cit. supra note 19, at p. 952.

[32] A statement of sanctions similar to that noted above appears in Restrictions on Free Enterprise in Medicine, p. 9 (April 1949), pamphlet, Committee on Research in Medical Economics.

[33] "Other things being equal, old well-established concerns tend to be more hostile to price cutting than younger concerns." G. Stocking and M. Watkins, Monopoly and Free Enterprise, p. 117 (1951).

[34] Most of these plans have services provisions; that is, they agree to provide the service required to treat particular ailments only if the subscriber's income is below some pre-assigned level. Of the 78 plans approved by organized medicine, 58 have service provisions. Of these, only 3 provide service to all income classes. The remainder provide a cash indemnity to subscribers whose income exceeds the relevant pre-assigned income levels. Therefore, these plans do not interfere with the discriminatory pricing policies of doctors. Consult Voluntary Prepayment Medical Benefit Plans, American Medical Association (1954).

able to determine fees jointly at the time medical service is sold just as if there were no insurance. Therefore, this class of medical insurance leaves unaffected the power of doctors to discriminate between differences in demand in setting fees. If anything, doctors welcome insurance since it improves the ability of the patient to pay. On the other hand, for non-indemnity type plans, plans that provide medical services directly as contrasted with plans that provide funds to be used to purchase desired services, payments are typically independent of income. Costs of membership in such prepayment plans are a function of family size, age, coverage, quality of service, etc., but are independent of the income of the subscriber. Consequently, such plans represent a means for massive price cutting to high income patients. For this reason, the reception of these plans by organized medicine constitutes an experiment for testing the validity of the discriminating monopoly model. If no opposition to these plans exists, then the implication of the discriminating monopoly model —that some mechanism must exist for maintaining the structure of prices— is invalid. On the other hand, opposition to these plans by organized medicine constitutes observable phenomena that support this implication. If such opposition exists, then it supports the discriminating monoply hypothesis in addition to providing evidence of the specific character of the sanctions available to organized medicine.

A number of independent observers have found that a systematic pattern of opposition to prepaid medical service plans, as contrasted with cash indemnity plans, exists. "In many parts of the county, organized medical bodies have been distinctly hostile to group practice. This is particularly true where the group is engaged in any form of prepaid medical care."[35] "Early groups were disparaged as unethical. But within recent years active steps have been taken only against those groups offering a plan for some type of flat-fee payment."[36] "There is reason to believe that the Oregon, the San Diego, and the District of Columbia cases exemplify a nationwide pattern of behavior by the American Medical Association and its state and county subsidiaries. What has come into the open here is working beneath the surface in other states and counties."[37] This systematic pattern of opposition to single price medical plans has taken two distinct courses. These are (1) using sanctions in an effort to terminate the life of prepaid medical plans already in existence and (2) lobbying for legislation that would abort their birth.

There have been a number of dramatic battles for survival by prepaid nonprice discriminatory medical plans resulting from the efforts of organized medicine to destroy them. These struggles have brought into action the most

[35] Building America's Health, report to the President by the Commission on the Health Needs of the Nation, V. I, p. 34 (1952).

[36] Hyde and Wolff, op. cit. supra note 19, at p. 977.

[37] Op. cit. supra note 32, at p. 14.

powerful sanctions available to organized medicine for use against price cutters. Consequently, the history of these battles provides valuable evidence of
the character of the weapons available to the participants. For this purpose,
the experiences of the following organizations are particularly illuminating:
Farmers Union Hospital Association of Elk City, Oklahoma, the Kaiser Foundation of San Francisco and Oakland, Group Health of Washington, Group
Health Cooperative of Puget Sound, Civic Medical Center of Chicago, Complete Service Bureau of San Diego, and the medical cooperatives in the State
of Oregon. These plans are diverse, from the point of view of location, organization, equipment, sponsorship and objective. However, they all have one
crucial unifying characteristic—fees or service charges are independent of income.[38] Similarly, the experiences of Ross-Loos in Los Angeles and the Palo
Alto Clinic in California are illuminating because these organizations both
operate prepayment single price medical plans and nevertheless continue to
stay within the good graces of organized medicine.

The founder and director of the cooperative Farmers Union Hospital in Elk
City, Oklahoma, Dr. Michael A. Shadid, was harassed for a number of years
by his local county medical association as a consequence of founding and
operating this price cutting organization. He was ingeniously thrown out of
the Beckham County Medical Society; this organization was dissolved and
reconstituted apparently for the sole purpose of not inviting Shadid to become
a member of the "new" organization. Before founding the cooperative, Shadid
had been a member in good standing in his county medical association for over
a decade.

The loss of hospital privileges stemming from non-county society membership was not sufficient for the task of putting Shadid out of business, because
his organization had its own hospital. Therefore, organized medicine turned
to its control over licensure to put the cooperative out of business. Shadid was
equal to this challenge. He was shrewd enough to draw members of the politically potent Farmers Union into his organization. Therefore, in the struggle
to take away Shadid's license to practice medicine, the farmers were pitted

---

[38] The Health Insurance Plan of New York is not included in the foregoing enumeration
because charges are not completely independent of income. For determining premiums, families are divided into two groups, those with incomes above $6,500 are assessed premiums
twenty per cent greater than those applicable to the lower income group. Consult M. M.
Davis, Medical Care for Tomorrow, p. 237 (1955). However, as a threat against the structure of prices for medical services based on income, this plan is almost as potent as those
listed. Consequently, the opposition to it ought to be just about as severe and the weapons
employed just as interesting for gaining insights into the nature of the sanctions over the behavior of individual doctors by organized medicine.

Available evidence suggests that HIP is under attack. See the testimony of G. Baehr, Presi-
dent and Medical Director of HIP in Hearings, op. cit. note 9, at pp. 1604, 1642, and 1663.
Legislation that would outlaw such plans as HIP has been sponsored by organized medicine.
Consult N.Y. Times, p. 15, col. 5 (Feb. 21, 1954).

against the doctors. The doctors came out of this political battle the losers because the state governor at the time, Murray, sided with the farmers.[39] However, the Beckham County Medical Society has been powerful enough to keep doctors who were known to be coming to Oklahoma to join Shadid's organization from getting a license to practice, powerful enough to frighten and cause the departure of a doctor who had been associated with Shadid's organization for a substantial period of time, powerful enough to keep Shadid out of a two-week postgraduate course on bone fractures at the Cook County Graduate School of Medicine (the course was open only to members in good standing of their local county medical societies), and was able to get enough of Shadid's doctors drafted during the war to endanger the life of his organization.[40] In recent years, the tide of battle has turned. The Hospital Association brought suit against the Beckham County Medical Society and its members for conspiracy in restraint of trade. This case was settled out of court. As part of this settlement, the county medical association agreed to accept the staff of the cooperative as members.

The experience of the Kaiser Foundation Plan is parallel to that of the Farmers Union. Both were vigorously opposed by organized medicine. The medical staff in each case could not obtain membership in local county medical societies. In both cases, the plans were able to prosper despite this obstacle, since they operated their own hospitals. In both cases, the doctor draft was used as a tool in an attempt to put these plans out of business.[41]

Control by organized medicine over licensure was used as a weapon in an attempt to kill the Kaiser Plan. Dr. Sidney Garfield, the plan's medical director, was tried by the State Board of Medical Examiners for unprofessional conduct. Garfield's license to practice was suspended for one year and he was placed on probation for five years. However, the suspension was withheld pending good behavior while on probation. This ruling by the State Board of Examiners was not supported in Court. Superior Court Judge Edward P. Murphy ordered the board to rescind all action against Garfield. The judge ruled that the board was arbitrary in denying Garfield a fair trial. Subsequently the appellate court reversed the decision of the trial court on one count but not the second. Nevertheless the judgment of the trial court in

[39] Davis argues that Shadid would have lost his license to practice if he had not had the powerful political support of the farmers. Op. cit. supra note 38 at p. 229.

[40] The story of Shadid and his organization may be found in M. A. Shadid, A Doctor for the People (1939), and Doctors of Today and Tomorrow (1947). In Two Harbors, Minnesota, doctors associated with a medical society disapproved plan could not win admission to their local county medical society and a doctor associated with this plan could not get into the same school from which Shadid had been barred—the Cook County Graduate School of Medicine. 71 Christian Century 173 (Feb. 10, 1954).

[41] For evidence on this point for the Kaiser Plan, see Hearings before a Subcommittee of the Senate Committee on Education and Labor, pt. 1, p. 338 ff., 77th Cong. 2nd Sess. on S. Res. 291 (1942).

rescinding the decision of the board of examiners was upheld. The entire matter was sent back to the board for reconsideration of penalty.[42] Subsequently, Garfield was tried by the county medical association for unethical practices, namely advertising, and found guilty. However, he came away from this trial with only a reprimand and not the loss of his license.[43] By virtue of having its own hospitals and legal intervention by the courts against the rulings of organized medicine, the Kaiser Foundation has been able to resist the onslaughts of its foes. However, the battle is not over yet. Although Kaiser Foundation doctors are now admitted to the Alameda County Society, the San Francisco County Society still excludes them.[44]

Group Health in Washington was not as fortunate as Kaiser or Farmers Union with respect to hospitals. Unlike these other two organizations, Group Health did not have its own hospital and therefore was dependent upon the existing hospitals in the community. Consequently, when Group Health doctors were ejected from the District Medical Society, Group Health was seriously crippled. Nearly all the hospitals in the district were coerced into denying staff privileges to Group Health doctors and bed space to their patients. Moreover, many doctors were deterred from becoming members of the Group Health staff because of fear of punitive action by the District Medical Society. Still other doctors who were members of the Group Health medical staff suddenly discovered attractive employment possibilities elsewhere and resigned their Group Health positions.[45]

It was fortunate for Group Health that it was located in Washington, D.C. and therefore under the jurisdiction of federal laws, in particular the Sherman Act. The tactics of the District Medical Society and the AMA came to the attention of the Justice Department. This led to the successful criminal prosecution of organized medicine under the Sherman Act. The opinion of the Supreme Court delivered by Mr. Justice Roberts pinpoints the primary concern of the petitioners, the District Medical Society and the AMA. "In truth, the petitioners represented physicians who desired that they and all others should practice independently on a fee for service basis, where whatever arrangement for payment each had was a matter that lay between him and his patient in each individual case of service or treatment."[46]

[42] P. DeKruif, Life Among the Doctors, p. 416 (1949). The last two chapters of this book deal with the activities of organized medicine against the Kaiser Plan. For the decision of the appellate court, see Garfield v. Medical Examiners, 99 C. A. 2d 219, 221 P. 2d 705 (1950).

[43] Mayer reports that Dr. Louis Schmidt, the urologist, was expelled from organized medicine for advertising his venereal disease clinic. 180 Harpers 27 (Dec. 1939).

[44] Means, op. cit. supra note 5, at p. 131. Opposition to Kaiser also exists in Los Angeles area where this plan also operates. 83 Bulletin of the Los Angeles County Medical Society 501 (1953) contains a condemnation of the Kaiser Plan and a call-to-arms.

[45] Hyde and Wolff, op. cit. supra note 19, at p. 990.

[46] American Medical Association v. United States, 317 U.S. 519, 536 (1943).

As a result of this victory, consumer sovereignty with respect to Group Health was restored. As might be suspected from the intense opposition of the AMA and the District Medical Society, Group Health has shown unusual survival properties and flourishes in competition with fee-for-service medical care. Since its victory at court, good relations with the District Medical Society have been achieved by the Group Health staff.[47]

In view of the previous cases cited, the experience of the Group Health Cooperative of Puget Sound, Washington, takes on a familiar cast. The King County Medical Association objected to this prepayment plan. They claimed it was "unethical" because under the terms of the plan subscribers could not employ any doctor in the community. Subscribers could use only doctors who were members of the health plan. Staff members of Group Health were expelled from the county medical association and new additions to the Group Health staff were found ineligible for society membership. The local medical society refused to accept transfers of membership from other county medical associations of doctors who expected to join the staff of the cooperative. The Group Health staff was unable to use the existing hospitals of the community, thereby limiting the value of the plan to many members and potential members. Moreover, the staff was cut off from many scientific meetings and was unable to consult with the orthodox members of the profession. However, the cooperative survived despite the hostility of the county medical society.

As a direct consequence of these harassing measures adopted by the King County Medical Society, the cooperative brought action against the county medical society, charging that the defendants had conspired against them in an effort to force the cooperative out of business. This case went to the state supreme court and was won by the cooperative although no damages were allowed.[48] Mr. Justice Hamley said that "The purpose of the Society . . . has been primarily to benefit the members of the Society and its affiliates through the elimination of such competition. The means employed has . . . been oppressive in the extreme. . . ."[49] Subsequently, the justice went on to argue that the activities of the county medical association against Group Health were designed to eliminate competition in the contract medicine field.[50] The court ruled that the defendants should not exclude applicants from membership in the county medical society or hospitals because of their affiliation with Group Health, and should cease discouraging doctors from joining Group Health or consulting with its staff.[51]

[47] Becker, President, Group Health Association, Hearings before Senate Committee on Education and Labor, pt. 5, p. 2528, 79th Cong. 2nd Sess. on S. Res. 1606 (1946).

[48] Group Health Etc. v. King Co. Med. Soc., 39 Wash. 2d 586, 237 P. 2d 737 (1951).

[49] Ibid., at p. 622 and 757.

[50] Ibid., at p. 640 and 766.

[51] Ibid., at p. 664 and 780; Consult Means, op. cit. supra note 5, at pp. 177–181.

In testimony before a Senate Committee, Dr. Lawrence Jacques of the Civic Medical Center in Chicago reported that none of the staff of this medical center (it numbered fifteen at that time) had succeeded in being admitted to the county medical association.[52] Repeated applications for admission had either been ignored or rejected by the Chicago Medical Society. Appeals to the Illinois State Medical Society and the American Medical Association proved to be fruitless. A direct appeal by a committee of patients of the Civic Medical Center to the county medical association on behalf of their doctors was of little avail.

The doctors associated with the Complete Service-Bureau of San Diego could not obtain membership in the county medical society and the patients and doctors associated with the plan were barred from the major hospitals of San Diego County. The county society published paid advertisements in the current editions of the San Diego telephone directory designating the members of the San Diego Medical Society among the physicians listed in the directory. These advertisements contained statements that gave the impression that non-society members were not qualified to practice medicine for professional and moral reasons. As a result of society opposition, the bureau had difficulty in hiring doctors at the going market price for their services.[53]

In Oregon, doctors serving on the staff of medical cooperatives were expelled from county medical societies and hospital facilities were made available only to doctors and the patients of doctors who were members in good standing of their local medical societies. Moreover, society members systematically refused to consult with non-society members and spread false propaganda in an effort to discredit society opposed plans.[54] The government brought action against the Oregon Medical Society under the Sherman Act and lost.[55]

_ The Civic Medical Center in Chicago did not have its own hospital. The members of the center were able to practice in only two hospitals in the entire Chicago area, and in neither of these two hospitals did they have full staff privileges. These limited staff privileges seriously hampered the operations of the group in the two hospitals in which they could practice. For example, in one of the hospitals surgical cases could not be scheduled for more than two days in advance by a physician unless he was a full staff member. In the words of Jacques, "The handicaps of nonmembership in the local medical society are serious and far-reaching and in effect amount to a partial revoca-

---

[52] Hearings, op. cit. supra note 47, at p. 2630 ff.

[53] Op. cit. supra note 32, at p. 11.

[54] Ibid.

[55] For the reasons for this loss, see United States v. Oregon Med. Soc., 343 U.S. 326 (1952) and the discussion of the case in Hyde and Wolff, op. cit. supra note 19, at p. 1020. One gets the impression from reading this case that the practices of the state society that would have led to victory for the government were discontinued in 1941.

tion of licensure to practice medicine."[56] During the war, some of the men in this group were disqualified for service as medical officers in the Navy, but nevertheless draftable as enlisted men, because applications to serve as medical officers were automatically rejected unless accompanied by a letter certifying that the candidate was a member in good standing of his local county medical society.[57] When Jacques was asked why his group was being excluded from the county medical association, his response was: "The evidence at hand suggests . . . that we are being excluded because of our prepayment plan."[58]

Apparently the value of price discrimination is deemed to be so great that the AMA has opposed "free" medical care to veterans by the Veterans Administration.[59] Free VA care for veterans would increase enormously the quantity of medical services demanded by making the marginal costs of these services zero for veterans.[60] Moreover opposing free care to veterans comes at a great cost to organized medicine.[61]

[56] Hearings, op. cit. supra note 47, at p. 2642.

[57] Apparently this rule is no longer in effect. Consult Hyde and Wolff, op. cit. supra note 19, at p. 951 n. 84.

[58] Hearings, op. cit. supra note 47, at p. 2644.

[59] It seems likely that the value of price discrimination has increased in recent years. In the last two decades, there has been a widespread development of consumer credit. This development has made it possible for credit bureaus to collect extensive and reliable data on consumer incomes. Such data are available to subscribers to credit bureau services. Therefore, doctors that belong to credit bureaus are able to price discriminate more precisely than would have been possible if they had to rely on the unsupported testimony of patients for income data. ". . . routine credit check of patient who had always been billed at modest rates—and learned that he was in fact the owner of thirty oil wells!" Mills, Credit Ratings: How You Can Use Them, 33 Medical Economics 171, 172 (May 1956).

[60] AMA opposition to free medical care for veterans constitutes evidence against the hypothesis that the AMA opposes direct service non-indemnity type group plans because they increase the efficiency with which medical resources are employed and therefore effectively increase the supply of doctors.

Still stronger evidence against the rationalization of opposition to direct service prepayment plans as a manifestation of opposition to changes that increase the efficiency with which the existing stock of doctors can be utilized, i.e., increase the supply schedule of physicians services, is the relative lack of opposition to group practices. Therefore, unless one is willing to postulate that it is the method of payment associated with prepayment medical plans that is a source of efficiency, one cannot argue that opposition to prepayment plans is on a par with the destruction by workers of machines that improve workers' efficiency.

"Group practice of medicine on a fee-for-service basis is tolerated and even admired by most doctors. The entire profession also strongly advocates voluntary medical insurance. Yet many physicians and some local medical societies violently disapprove of the combination of group practice with pre-payment and do everything in their power to prevent or destroy it." Baehr, Hearings, op. cit. supra note 9, at p. 1642.

[61] This opposition has won organized medicine a powerful foe. A. J. Connell, an ex-National Commander of the American Legion has attacked organized medicine as à "most powerful and monopolistic medical guild." N.Y. Times, p. 17, col. 3 (Jan. 29, 1954). In opposing "socialized medicine" these two groups were allies.

If price discrimination is in fact highly valued by organized medicine and prepayment direct service medical plans have been opposed in order to maintain a structure of discriminating prices, doesn't the existence of the prepayment plans unopposed by the AMA constitute an anomaly?[62]

How can the Ross-Loos and Palo Alto Clinic cases be explained?[63] The Ross-Loos plan in Los Angeles is a prepaid medical plan that is a profit-seeking organization. It was started in 1929 and by the end of 1952 had 127,-000 members.[64] The Ross-Loos plan does not have hospitals of its own and is therefore forced to rely on the existing hospitals of the community. Consequently, the condemnation of this plan by organized medicine which occurred after it won acceptance from consumers in the medical care market, represented an enormous threat to its continued existence. The Ross-Loos plan doctors were expelled from the Los Angeles County Medical Association. Among the doctors to lose their county society membership was a former President of the Los Angeles County Medical Society. As a result of a number of appeals to higher courts, all within the judicial machinery of organized medicine, the decision that would have crippled if not destroyed this plan was reversed.

An excellent reason for this reversal is suggested by the testimony of Dr. H. Clifford Loos, a co-founder of Ross-Loos. In response to the question, "Are you handicapped to any extent by the fact that you are not able to advertise," Dr. Loos replied:

> As far as that goes, we do not care to be big, or bigger. If I had accepted all of the groups who applied to us, we would need our city hall to house us. We have put the brakes on. We can't accept too many. We feel we can't be too big.[65]

This constitutes strange behavior indeed for a profit-seeking institution that certainly ought to have no fears of Justice Department action for either being too large or monopolizing an industry. One cannot help suspecting that the

[62] Evidence of opposition to price cutting on a more modest scale exists. Individuals who have cut prices have either encountered the sanctions of organized medicine or a threat to employ these sanctions. Consult, Medical Group's Protests Stop Polio Shot Project in Brooklyn, N.Y. Times, p. 33M (Sept. 12, 1956). The Los Angeles Times reports that Dr. Sylvan O. Tatkin filed a complaint in the Superior Court of Los Angeles charging that the local association was engaging in unlawful rate fixing. Tatkin charged that he was refused membership in the local society and therefore dropped from the staff of Behrens Memorial Hospital in Glendale as a result of price cutting. L.A. Times, sec. 2, p. 30, col. 4 (June 29, 1956).
Economic theory implies that there would be no point for a monopolist that has control over supply being concerned with prices directly. For a non-discriminating monopolist, control over supply implies control over prices.

[63] There is evidence that opposition to prepayment plans is not merely local society policy. In Logan County, Arkansas, the entire county society was expelled from the state society by means of charter revocation. The local society was dominated by physicians participating in a disapproved plan. 27 Journal of the Arkansas Medical Society 29 (1930).

[64] Hearings, op. cit. supra note 9, at p. 1451.   [65] Ibid., at p. 1469.

amicable relations with the Los Angeles County Medical Society may have been acquired at the cost of a sharply curtailed rate of expansion.[66]

The Palo Alto Clinic in California provides prepaid medical care that is non-income discriminating to the students, employees, and faculty of Stanford University. This constitutes a small fraction of the clinic's business. Eighty-five per cent of the receipts of the clinic are attributable to conventional fee-for-service practice that lends itself to discriminatory pricing. This clinic continues to stay within the good graces of organized medicine. When questioned about extending the prepaid non-discriminatory service, Dr. Russel V. Lee, Director of the Clinic and Professor of Medicine in the School of Medicine of Stanford University, threw some light upon this apparent anomaly. "Several of the industries in the area have come to us for such service. We have been trying to get our county medical society approval before we go into these things, and we are doing a little job of county medical education because in general the county medical society will not approve of anything that smacks of a closed panel."[67] This suggests that the Palo Alto Clinic is in the position of having to go to its principal competitors for permission to sell its services to new customers. This is comparable to a requirement that a Ford dealer must first obtain the permission of his competing Chevrolet dealer before he can sell Fords to non-Ford owners who have asked for the opportunity to buy them. Probably the county medical society that includes the Palo Alto Clinic does not feel that the present level of sales of prepaid medical services by this clinic is high enough to justify the costs and risks of punitive action.

Organized medicine, i.e., the AMA and its political subdivisions, has opposed prepaid non-price-discriminatory medical plans not only directly by fighting against them but also indirectly by lobbying for legislation that would make such plans illegal. State medical societies have achieved a fair degree of success in sponsoring legislation designed to prevent price cutting in the medical care market caused by prepaid medical plans. As of 1954, "there are at least 20 states that have had such laws passed at the instigation of medical societies, which are designed to prevent prepaid group practice and to keep medical practice on a fee-for-service solo basis."[68] Another source says:

[66] Loos has also served as an expert witness for the San Diego County Society during its struggle with another prepayment plan. Complete Service Bureau v. San Diego County Med. Soc., 43 C. 2d 201, 212, 272, P.2d 497, 504 (1954). Hyde and Wolff, op. cit. supra note 19, at p. 985 impute the tolerance of Ross-Loos by organized medicine to the fact that it is physician sponsored as contrasted with being lay or non-physician sponsored. The theory outlined in this paper implies that this is not a relevant distinction.

[67] Hearings op. cit. supra note 9, at p. 1559.

[68] Baehr, Hearings, op. cit. supra note 9, at p. 1594. Very unorthodox lobbying tactics have been successfully employed by distinguished doctors to achieve the legislative goals of organized medicine. See Osler's forthright description in H. Young, A Surgeons' Autobiography, p. 407 (1940).

"Most of the states now have restrictive statutes permitting only the medical profession to operate or to control prepayment medical care plans."[69] Hansen lists as one of the primary objectives of this legislation "to preserve the fee-for-service system as far as possible by controlling the financial administration of the plans."[70]

IV. IMPLICATIONS OF THE DISCRIMINATING MONOPOLY MODEL

In the preceding section, this paper has been concerned with establishing the validity of the discriminating monopoly model for understanding the pricing of an important class of medical services—those produced by doctors in hospitals. Evidence of the existence of a pattern of relatively direct and obvious controls was presented. Yet it was argued that maintaining a structure of discriminatory prices for this large number of independent producers represents a fantastically difficult control problem. Does the existence of this difficult control problem shed any light upon other aspects of the medical profession? Our concern is largely with the more subtle or less obvious methods of control over the price policies of individual doctors.

The controls previously discussed are analogous to surgery; the controls to be discussed are analogous to preventive medicine. In particular, we explore the possibilities of a relationship between maintaining a structure of prices based on income differences and: the representation of specialists in power positions within organized medicine; discrimination against minority groups in admission to medical schools; the free treatment by doctors of other doctors and their families; the position of organized medicine on advertising; the defense of county medical association members against malpractice suits; the *no-criticism rules* that forbid unfavorable comment by one physician of another physician's work before a member of the lay public.

Specialists have more to gain from price discrimination than non-specialists because their work is more likely to be associated with hospitals. The power to withhold hospital facilities from doctors constitutes the strongest weapon for maintaining price discipline within the medical profession. Therefore, discrimination in pricing ordinary office visits as compared with services rendered in a hospital is much less pronounced. In fact, prices charged for office visits ought to be relatively independent of patient's incomes. Office care can be provided by doctors with no hospital connections whatsoever. Consequently, specialists, particularly those who do most of their work in hospitals, have a

[69] Hansen, Laws Affecting Group Health Plans, 35 Iowa L. Rev. 209, 225 (1950).

[70] Ibid., at p. 209. Yet in his conclusion, Hansen argues that "Farsighted medical societies should find no valid reason for opposing group health enabling legislation. Instead they should welcome experimentation in the field of medical economics with the same spirit they welcome it in the field of medical science." pp. 235–36. It is one of the implications of this paper that the more farsighted medical societies provide the strongest opposition to experimentation in the field of medical economics.

greater interest in maintaining price discrimination than general practitioners. Therefore, the fact that specialists are over-represented, as measured by the ratio of specialists to all doctors, in the AMA hiararchy is no accident.[71] This is precisely the group that has the greatest economic interest in maintaining price discipline and for this reason, are "naturals" for the job.[72]

Newcomers, even if they were formerly presidents of county societies elsewhere, are probationary members when they join some county societies.[73] They achieve full membership only after a successful term as probationary members. Relegating newcomers to a probationary status is a means for segregating from the general membership those who have a relatively high probability of being price cutters.[74] Newcomers represent a group whose members are trying to acquire practices and therefore are more likely to be price cutters than society members who have well established practices. Consequently newcomers require both an extraordinary degree of surveillance and a strong indication of the costs of non-compliance. Probationary membership achieves both of these objectives.[75]

The advertisement of medical services is approved by the medical profession if and only if such advertisements redound to the interest of the profession as a whole. Advertisements in this class are, for example, announcements of the availability for sale of Blue Cross type medical plans. These plans allow their subscribers the choice of any licensed practitioner. Organized medicine consequently takes the position that these advertisements are of benefit to the entire profession. On the other hand, advertisements that primarily redound to the interests of a particular group, for example, advertisements by a closed panel medical group, are frowned upon. Advertisements in this class are, by definition, resorted to only by "unethical" doctors. Why this difference in the

---

[71] Garceau, op. cit. supra note 26, at pp. 55–58. Hyde and Wolff, op. cit. supra note 19, at p. 947.

[72] Some observers have explained the over-representation of specialists in the AMA hierarchy as attributable to their greater incomes. Larger incomes imply that specialists are better able to afford the "luxury" of political activity. This explanation implies that psychiatrists and dermatologists ought to be just as over-represented as surgeons, abstracting from income differences. On the other hand, the argument advanced here implies that surgeons ought to be more strongly represented because membership in the AMA hierarchy can be more useful for advancing the economic interests of surgeons than it can be for those other specialties. This difference stems from the fact that psychiatrists and dermatologists do not use hospitals to the same extent in their practices.

There exists some reason for believing that among specialists, surgeons are over-represented in medical politics. One observer reports, "Our medical societies are not merely specialist-dominated; they are surgeon dominated." Berger, op. cit. supra note 11, p. 272.

[73] Hyde and Wolff, op. cit. supra note 19, at p. 941 n. 20 and p. 951 n. 83.

[74] Stocking and Watkins, op. cit. supra note 33, at p. 117.

[75] Some societies have indoctrination programs for newcomers. Drennen, They Help Young Doctors Get Started Right, 32 Medical Economics 104 (June, 1955). Drennen observes that for the newcomer such a program ". . . helps keep him on the path of righteousness." p. 108.

position of organized medicine with respect to these two classes of advertising? The approved class, insofar as it achieves its objective, tends to increase the aggregate demand for medical care. On the other hand, the disapproved variety will have the effect of reallocating patients from the profession as a whole to those who advertise. Consequently, advertising in this class constitutes competitive behavior and leads to price cutting. It tends to pit one doctor or one group of doctors against the profession as a whole with respect to shares of the medical care market. Active competition for increased shares of the medical care market by doctors would tend to eliminate price discrimination based on income differences.

The significance of advertising as a means for maintaining free entry is revealed by two bits of interrelated evidence. These are the strong opposition of organized medicine to advertising calling the public's attention to the services of a particular group of doctors and the willingness of some prepaid medical plans to incur the wrath of organized medicine by undertaking such advertising. Kaiser, the Civic Medical Center, and the Complete Service Bureau at one time or another advertised.[76] The use of advertising in the face of strong opposition by organized medicine implies that advertising plays a crucial role in enabling these groups to capture part of the medical care market. Consequently the ban on such advertising by organized medicine constitutes a barrier to entry into this market and is a means for keeping doctors from competing with one another and thereby incidentally destroying the structure of prices.

County medical societies play a crucial role in protecting their members against malpractice suits. Physicians charged with malpractice are tried by their associates in the private judicial system of organized medicine. If found innocent, then local society members are available for duty as expert witnesses in the defense of those charged with malpractice. Needless to say, comparable services by society members for plaintiffs in such actions are not equally available. By virtue of this monopoly over the services of expert witnesses and the tacit coalition of the members of a society in the defense of any of their members, the successful prosecution of malpractice suits against society members is extremely difficult.

On the other hand, for doctors who are persona-non-grata with respect to organized medicine, the shoe is on the other foot. Expert witnesses from the ranks of organized medicine are abundantly available for plaintiffs but not for defendants. Therefore the position of a plaintiff in a suit against a non-society member is of an order of magnitude stronger than it is for a suit

---

[76] "For the first ten months of its existence, with a considerable reluctance it continued the policy of institutional advertising, because it was felt that the clinic could not survive unless it was brought actively to the attention of the public." Jacques, Hearings, op. cit. supra note 41, at p. 2634. Complete Service Bureau v. San Diego County Med. Soc., 43 C.2d 201, 214–216, 272 P.2d 497, 504–506 (1954).

against a society member. Consequently it should come as no surprise that the costs of malpractice insurance for non-society members is substantially higher than it is for·society members. Apparently some non-society members have experienced difficulty in obtaining malpractice insurance at any price.[77]

This coalition among the members of the medical profession not to testify against one another, like structured prices, puts some doctors in a position of pursuing a policy that does not maximize personal returns. Therefore more than just professional ethics makes this coalition viable. As might be expected, the ability of organized medicine to expel doctors from hospital staffs plays a crucial role in keeping doctors from testifying against one another. Belli reports that a doctor who acted as an expert witness in a malpractice suit he tried was subsequently barred from the staff of every hospital in California.[78] It is because of sanctions of this character that we can find reports of patients with strong prima facie evidence of negligence and yet unable to hire expert witnesses from·the ranks of the medical profession.[79]

As a result of this coalition among society members for malpractice defense, two effects are achieved. The more direct and obvious consequence is an increase in the monopoly returns to the members of this profession over what they otherwise would be. The other is the welding together of the medical profession as an in-group. In this latter role, the coalition for malpractice defense is a force that has the same effect as a reciprocity, that is, the free treatment by doctors of other doctors·and their families, and the rule that doctors are not to criticize one another in public.[80] The function of reciprocity and *no-criticism* is to induce the members of the medical profession·to behave towards one another as if they were members of an in-group. Doctors are subtly coerced into personal relations with one another. Insofar as these measures bear fruit, doctors view themselves as a large association in which members deal with one another on a personal level. In relation to the general public, i.e., outsiders, the in-group, doctors, are united.

But what does the medical profession achieve by subtly coercing its mem-

[77] Garceau, op. cit. supra note 26, at p. 103 ff; Jacques, Hearings, op. cit. supra note 47, at p. 2642; Hyde and Wolff, op. cit. supra note 19, at p. 951 n. 86; Belli, op. cit. supra note 28, at p. 109.

[78] Belli, op. cit. supra note 28, at p. 98; The California Malpractice Controversy, 9 Stanford L. Rev. 731 (1957).

[79] See the story by Ullman in the Toledo Blade of June 12, 1946, about a surgery patient who was unable to hire an expert witness for demonstrating negligence in a case involving a sponge that a surgeon forgot to remove before sewing up the patient. Belli reports no such problem in hiring expert witnesses for legal malpractice cases. Op. cit. supra note 28, at p. 95.

[80] N. S. Davis, History of Medicine, ch. 14 (1907); Wylie, Conspiracy of Silence, 29 Medical Economics 167 (April 1952); Doctor Fights Expulsion on Slander Charge, 32 Medical Economics 269 (Dec. 1954). This is the story of a doctor expelled from his county medical society for expressing opinions about the professional competence of his colleagues, to patients.

bers into in-group relations with one another? The relationships among members of a family, an in-group par excellence, reveal the importance of these subtle controls. Members of a family are relatively reluctant to criticize one another before outsiders, tend not to charge each other market prices for services extended to one another, and try to avoid being in direct competition. The essence of in-group behavior is personal relationships among its members. On the other hand, the essential property of market place relationships is impersonality. Consequently insofar as a non-market place attitude can be fostered and maintained within the medical profession, such an attitude constitutes a barrier against doctors thinking of one another as competitors in the medical care market. This in itself constitutes a barrier against such market place activities as cutting prices.[81]

To the extent that the culture of members of an in-group is distinct from that of non-members, this difference reduces the probability that non-members can successfully "join" the in-group. Differences in culture and values constitute a natural barrier to integration. This is particularly important for medicine because it is both a social and an economic club and the returns of the economic club are related to the degree of social cohesion that exists within the social club. Consequently, members of culturally distinct minority groups would be more difficult to assimilate into such an in-group and it is likely that many would never feel that they were completely members under the best of circumstances. This implies that members of such minority groups would be more difficult to control by means of the informal controls characteristic of in-groups. Being thrown out of a country club is not much of a loss if one is only the janitor; for informal controls to be effective, they must be exercised over those who belong. Insofar as some minority groups are more difficult to assimilate, there exists an *a priori* basis for discrimination. It is to keep out those who have a higher probability of not being willing to go along with the majority. Minority groups whose culture and values are different from those of the majority could rationally be discriminated against in admission to medical schools because they are more difficult to control by informal controls after they are out in medical practice than is characteristic of the population at large.

The discrimination against Jews in admission to medical schools has been

[81] If the hypothesis presented here is correct, then it should be possible to observe a difference between the variance of surgical and psychiatric fees after abstracting from variations caused by differences in skills, type of operation and difficulty of particular cases. This difference would be imputable to the strong control over the pricing of surgical services by means of control over hospitals. Since reciprocity and *no-criticism* rules are viable because they help maintain structured prices, they should not be observed as rigorously by psychiatrists as surgeons. On this latter point, there exists evidence consistent with the hypothesis presented here. Psychiatrists have been the first, and thus far the only group within the medical profession to abandon reciprocity. Miller, Doctors Should Pay for Medical Care!, 30 Medical Economics 82, 84 (Jan. 1953).

explained, by both Jews and non-Jews alike, as a consequence of irrational prejudice.[82] Yet Jews might be regarded as the prototype of a minority group with cultural properties that, given the special problems of maintaining internal discipline within the medical profession, would make them undesirable candidates for admission to this profession. These cultural attributes evolved as a consequence of centuries of unparalleled persecution. This persecution, which by and large was economic, took the form of laws that barred Jews from particular product and labor markets in many of the most important countries in the history of western civilization. Cartels such as guilds followed similar policies. This exclusion policy channelled Jews into highly competitive markets, markets characterized by free entry, and forced them to develop their commercial skills to a higher level than was characteristic of the population at large in order to survive economically. For Jews, a medieval guild type share-the-market attitude was a non-survival property whereas a policy of vigorously competing was a survival property. The process of adaptation by Jews to laws constraining their economic activities led them to develop considerable ingenuity in minimizing the impact of such laws upon their economic well being. Jews developed into robust competitors with little respect for rules, either government or private, that regulated economic activities and with a substantial body of practical experience in implementing this point of view.[83] These attitudes became a part of Jewish cultural tradition

[82] For direct evidence on discrimination against Jews in admission to medical schools, consult, Hart, Anti-Semitism in Medical Schools, 65 American Mercury 53 (July 1947); Kingdon, Discrimination in Medical Colleges, 60 American Mercury 391 (Oct. 1945); Bloomgarden, Medical School Quotas and National Health, 15 Commentary 29 (Jan. 1953); Goldberg, Jews in the Medical Profession—A National Survey, 1 Jewish Social Studies 327 (1939); Shapiro, Racial Discrimination in Medicine, 10 Jewish Social Studies 103 (1948).

The indirect evidence on this point seems to be more convincing than the direct evidence. Practically all of the Americans who study medicine abroad are Jews. No comparable evidence for the study by American Jews of law, dentistry, accounting, engineering, etc. in foreign countries exists. Therefore, the hypothesis that Jews prefer to study abroad is not tenable. On the other hand, this evidence is consistent with the hypothesis that Jews are strongly discriminated against in this country. Consult Levinger, Jewish Medical Students in America, 2 Medical Leaves 91, 94 (1939) and Goldberg, supra at p. 332.

Some observers have used a Noah's Ark approach to determine whether or not discrimination against Jews in admission to medical schools exists or existed. Because the ratio of Jewish medical students to all medical students exceeds the ratio of all Jews to our total population, some observers have concluded discrimination is absent. D. S. Berkowitz, Inequality of Opportunity in Higher Education. (1948).

[83] The same problem of survival in a hostile world has led a number of observers to argue that the frequency of Jews among alcoholics, dope addicts, and child deserters is low relative to the non-Jewish population. This same argument has been used to conclude that the frequency of Jews among neurotics is higher. Morrison, A Biologic Interpretation of Jewish Survival, 3 Medical Leaves 97 (1940); Meyerson, Neuroses and Alcoholism Among the Jews, 3 Medical Leaves 104 (1940); Liber, The Behavior of the Jewish and the Non-Jewish Patient, 5 Medical Leaves 159 (1943).

There exists evidence that Jews are under-represented among prison inmates. Levinger, A Note on Jewish Prisoners in Ohio, 2 Jewish Social Studies 210 (1940). This is what the sur-

and at least in this respect, distinguished Jews from non-Jews. This was particularly true of Jews that came from Czarist Russia and Poland where discrimination against them was particularly strong.[84]

Because of these special cultural properties, which are vestigial in the United States and therefore are in the process of fading away, the discrimination against Jews in admission to medical schools is far from irrational if one is concerned with maintaining price discrimination in medicine. The *a priori* probability of a Jew being a price cutter because of the special attributes developed in an effort to survive in a hostile environment is greater than that for a non-Jew. The Jewish doctor is more likely to have a commercial market place attitude towards other members of his profession than is the non-Jew. From the point of view of the medical profession, as one doctor expressed it, Jews ". . . spoil everything they go into by turning it into a business."[85]

If, as this analysis implies, admission to medical schools is influenced by the desire to select candidates who will not become price cutters, then it ought to be possible to observe similar policies for postgraduate education. In particular, it should be possible to observe evidence of bias against Jews in surgical relative to non-surgical specialties. Consequently Jews ought to be under-represented in surgery relative to other fields of specialization. Converse results ought to hold for psychiatry. A study of physicians who were diplo-

---

vival hypothesis suggests. It is significant to note, however, that this under-representation is not uniform for all categories of crime. The representation of Jews among prison inmates convicted of crimes of scheming, i.e., fraud, larceny, possession of stolen property, etc., is relatively large. Laws regulating economic affairs, unlike most laws, were directed against Jews. Hence one should expect to find respect by Jews for this category of laws weakest. By this argument a post-war study of prison populations ought to show a relatively large representation of Jews among OPA violators.

[84] J. W. Parkes, The Jewish Problem in the Modern World, (1946) recognizes the unique experiences of Jews in modern history and the impact of these experiences upon Jewish culture in his first chapter, Why Is There a Jewish Question?

[85] Hall, Informal Organization of the Medical Profession, 12 Canadian Journal of Economics and Political Science 38 (1946). This article suggests that young doctors 'buy' positions on hospital staffs by providing free medical care in hospital clinics. The older members of the profession have an interest in maintaining this method of admission to hospital staffs because it helps maintain the acceptability of price discrimination with the public.

Similarly there exist controls over the maximum fees charged, price ceilings in effect, in order to minimize the possibility of fees that the public will regard as outrageous and thereby endanger the existence of structured prices. This function is performed by county medical society review committees that deal with the complaints of excessive fees. For an example of the functioning of such a committee, consult Phillips, Doctor Cancels $1,500 Bill for Hoopers at Medical Group's Urging, N. Y. Times, p. 1, col. 2, (June 23, 1957). For a reflection of public attitudes in this case, consult 70 Time 34 (July 1, 1957). A. Ruppin suggests that Jews developed modern competitive attitudes in commerce before the industrial revolution as a result of their exclusion from medieval guilds, in an effort to survive commercially in this hostile environment. With the onset of the industrial revolution and the weakening of trade barriers, the relative economic position of Jews improved. Jews in the Modern World, p. 110 (1934).

mates in various specialties was made for the year 1946 for Jews and non-Jews for the cities of Brooklyn, Newark, Buffalo, and Hartford-Bridgeport. It was found that thirty-two per cent of the surgeons in Brooklyn were Jews, twenty-five percent in Newark, eight in Buffalo, and six in Hartford. Of the ten specialties considered for Brooklyn, the representation of Jews among the surgeons was lowest. For the other three cities, eleven specialties were considered. For all three of these cities, the representation of Jews among specialists was also lowest in surgery (453 Jewish specialists were considered in Brooklyn, the other three cities added 122). On the other hand, for the category neurology-psychiatry, the representation of Jews among the specialists practicing in this field ranked third for Brooklyn. For the other three cities, the rankings were one tie for fourth place, one first place and one fourth place.[86]

The distinction between psychiatry and surgery is a special case of the general distinction between surgical and non-surgical specialties. Hospital connections are far more important for the practice of surgical than non-surgical specialties. Therefore controls over the members of the medical profession in surgical specialties are stronger. If, as it has been argued, price discrimination is stronger in the surgical specialties, then there should be a significant difference in the frequency of Jews in surgical and non-surgical specialties. Two independent studies provide evidence that is consistent with this implication. For the state of Pennsylvania, one observer found that the frequency of Jews in non-surgical specialties was forty-one percent larger than in surgical specialties. The probability of a sample of this size, 1,175, of which 190 were Jews, being a random sample of a population characterized by an absence of a difference in the frequency of Jews in the surgical and non-surgical specialties is less than one half of one percent.[87] For Brooklyn the frequency of Jews in the non-surgical specialties was thirty percent greater than for the surgical specialties. This difference could occur by chance with a probability of less than one percent if this were a random sample of a population that failed to exhibit this property. Similar results hold for a combination of the other three cities.[88] The hypothesis that there exists a difference between surgical and non-surgical specialties with respect to the admission of

[86] Consult Shapiro, op. cit. supra note 82, at p. 125, table IV.

[87] Weinberg, Jewish Diplomates in Pennsylvania, 4 Medical Leaves 159 (1942). The non-surgical specialties were dermatology and syphilology, pediatrics, psychiatry and neurology, internal medicine, radiology, pathology; the surgical specialties were orthopedic surgery, ophthalmology, otolaryngology, obstetrics and gynecology, surgery, and anesthesiology.

[88] Shapiro, op. cit. supra note 82, at p. 125. One entry for all ophthalmologists in Brooklyn is missing and another entry for all radiologists in Hartford was obviously in error. Therefore Hartford radiologists and Brooklyn ophthalmologists, both Jewish and non-Jewish, were not represented in the foregoing calculations. Personal communication with the author of this article failed to elicit a clarifying response.

Jews is consistent with the qualitative observation found in another report. This source observes that "fair play" exists in the admission of Jews to non-Jewish hospitals for training in the non-surgical specialties but not for training in the surgical specialties.[89] Apparently the Jews who do get into medical schools are "dumped" in the non-surgical specialties.[90]

Another piece of evidence consistent with the price cutting explanation of the discrimination against Jews in medicine is the drop in admissions of Jews to medical schools between 1933 and 1938. During that time, there was a decrease in over-all admissions to medical schools of about five percent and a decrease in admission of Jewish students of about thirty percent.[91] Between 1928 and 1933, the prices of medical services dropped sharply and the real income of doctors as a group decreased. The depression produced a reduction in the size of the pie available to the profession. This smaller pie was contended for quite vigorously by the existing members. The Jews as price cutters were probably relatively successful, and in the process the structure of discriminatory prices was jeopardized. As a result, the threat of Jews to the aggregate income of the profession was brought home in a very forceful way at this time. Therefore the sharp curtailment in admission of Jews to medical schools resulted in an effort to reduce the vulnerability of structured prices to destruction by competitive behavior.[92]

The evidence used to support the proposition that discrimination against certain minority groups results from the desire to maintain price discrimina-

[89] Facilities of Jewish Hospitals for Specialized Training, 3 Jewish Social Studies 375, 378 (1941).

[90] These data are also consistent with at least two other hypotheses worth considering. One is that Jews simply lack the physical dexterity required for success in surgery. This seems to be inconsistent with the frequency of Jews in such fields as dentistry. Levinger, Jews in the Professions in Ohio, 2 Jewish Social Studies 401, 430, table XXXIII (1940). The other is that there exists no more discrimination against Jews in surgical specialties than non-surgical specialties but that there does exist at least an additional barrier that must be surmounted in order to get into the surgical specialties that is absent for the non-surgical specialties. No evidence of the existence of such a barrier has been detected.

[91] Goldberg, op. cit. supra note 82, at p. 332. Another distinguished member of the medical profession who has encountered the disapproval of his colleagues for unorthodox views, recognized the economic motivation for this policy and properly describes it as a trade union tactic. He also recognized the conflict of interest position of organized medicine resulting from its control over admissions to the profession. Cabot, op. cit. supra note 7, at p. 263.

[92] A decrease in the frequency of Jews among medical students could occur for reasons other than an increase in the intensity of discrimination. However only an increase in the intensity of discrimination would (1) increase the frequency of Jews in schools of osteopathy, and (2) increase the frequency of Jews among all Americans studying abroad. Between 1935 and 1946, the frequency of Jews in schools of osteopathy more than doubled (9.1 to 20.3%). A Report of the President's Commission on Higher Education, pt. II, pp. 38 ff. (1947). This report imputes to the blocking of opportunities in medicine the rise in the frequency of Jews in osteopathic schools. The President's Commission concluded that a substantial part of the responsibility for the discriminatory practices of medical schools belongs to professional associations.

tion is also consistent with the implications of simple monopoly theory. If medicine is a monopoly, then it follows that the number of candidates that would like to win entry into the medical profession exceeds the number that in fact are permitted to enter. Therefore unless the number of openings in the profession are sold or auctioned off, a practice that has not been unknown in the American labor movement, non-price rationing is inevitable. This leaves those who have the job of rationing available openings the opportunity to indulge in their tastes for the kind of people that they would like to see in the profession without any effective constraints in the form of costs or positions that must be filled. Under these circumstances, as contrasted with the free entry characteristic of competitive markets, nepotism, discrimination against unpopular cultural groups such as Jews and Negroes, and discrimination against those who hold unpopular ideas such as communists, thrives.[93] Therefore discrimination against Jews and others in admission to medical schools can be rationalized as a manifestation of non-price rationing. Since the surgical specialties are presumed to have more monopoly power than the non-surgical specialties, there is more non-price rationing in the former and as a result, more discrimination.[94] The increase in the tempo of discrimination in the thirties can also be rationalized as a consequence of an increase in the extent of non-price rationing. The demand for medical services is probably highly income elastic and as a result of the depression and admission policies geared to a demand schedule for medical services that existed in the twenties, the monopoly returns in medicine declined during the early depression years. Therefore admissions were subsequently curtailed in order to redress the effects of too liberal admission policies in the past. Consequently the extent of non-price rationing increased.

Conclusion

If different prices for the same service exist, then economic theory implies that there must also exist some means for enjoining producers of this service from acting in their own self interest and thereby establishing uniform prices. Observable phenomena abundantly support this implication. Available evidence suggests that the primary control instrument of organized medicine is the ability to cut off potential price cutters from the use of resources complementary to doctors' services for producing many classes of medical care. How-

[93] On theoretical grounds, there is a sound basis for the belief that generally speaking, the A.F.L. craft unions have more monopoly power than the C.I.O. industrial unions. Wright, op. cit. supra note 1, pp. 207 ff. Observers of discrimination in the American labor movement find that Negroes are discriminated against more frequently by A.F.L. unions than by C.I.O. unions. H. E. Northrop Organized Labor and the Negro, ch. 1. (1944).

[94] If it were found that the surgical specialties had no more monopoly power than the non-surgical specialties, this would be evidence against the simple monopoly hypothesis, but would be consistent with the discriminatory monopoly hypothesis.

ever, techniques other than the withdrawal of staff privileges in hospitals are also employed to maintain discipline in the medical profession. These include *no-criticism rules,* professional courtesy or the free treatment by doctors of other doctors and their families, prohibition of advertising that might reallocate market shares among producers, preventing doctors from testifying against one another in malpractice suits, and the selection of candidates for medical schools and post graduate training in the surgical specialties that have a relatively low probability of being price cutters. All of these sanctions can be rationalized as means for maintaining price discrimination. Therefore the use of these sanctions is consistent with the hypothesis that the medical profession constitutes a discriminating monopoly.

If being cut off from the use of a complementary agent of production, hospital services, is the chief means of disciplining the existing members of the medical profession, then there ought to be a difference in the price discipline maintained in the surgical and non-surgical specialties. Consequently there ought to be a significant difference between the surgical and the non-surgical specialties in the frequency of discriminatory pricing. There are no grounds for believing that there is any difference between the surgical and non-surgical specialties with respect to the effectiveness of the more subtle means of control. Therefore as a result of the relatively weaker impact on the non-surgical specialties of the loss of hospital staff privileges, it should be possible to observe that the non-surgical specialties have not only more price cutters in their midst but also are relatively freer in criticizing other members of the profession, serving as expert witnesses, and violating professional courtesy. Similarly this analysis implies that before the turn of the century, price discrimination in medicine was less pervasive, doctors criticized each other more freely, were more willing to act as expert witnesses against one another, did not as readily provide free medical care to other members of the profession, and did not discriminate against potential price cutters in admission to medical training.[95]

The economic interest of the medical profession in maintaining price discrimination has led to opposition directed against new techniques for marketing medical services that offer promise of utilizing the existing stock of physicians more efficiently than heretofore. Consequently the opposition by organ-

---

[95] Fee splitting, according to the hypothesis presented in this paper, should have been more prevalent at this time. Splitting fees makes for freer entry into the surgical care market. Newcomers can offer large rebates to referring physicians and thereby win patients away from established surgeons. There seems to be evidence that fee splitting was prevalent in medicine around the turn of the century and it was indeed employed by newcomers as a means for winning entry into the surgical care market. Rongy, Half a Century of Jewish Medical Activities in New York City, 1 Medical Leaves 151, 158 (1937). This implies that the older, more established surgeons oppose fee splitting. This is consistent with the evidence. Williams, A. C. S. Closes In On Fee Splitters, 31 Medical Economics 161 (1954).

Berger, op. cit. supra note 17, at p 141 contends that surgeons object to fee splitting for economic reasons.

ized medicine to prepaid service type medical plans probably has resulted in higher economic costs of medical care for the community than would otherwise have been the case. Similarly the incompatibility of the indemnity principle of insurance and the "what the traffic will bear" principle of pricing medical services has inhibited the development of major, medical catastrophe insurance in this country and consequently has limited the ability of individuals to insure themselves against these risks. Insofar as freer criticism by the members of the medical profession of one another before the public is of value to consumers in helping them distinguish between better and poorer practitioners and in raising standards within the profession, the public has obtained a lower quality of medical service than would otherwise have been obtainable at existing costs. And insofar as being a potential price cutter weeds out candidates from medical schools and post graduate training in the surgical specialties who were better potential doctors than those accepted, then the quality of the medical services that could have been achieved at existing costs was reduced.

Economic theory implies that prepaid medical service plans imperil the existence of price discrimination. Consequently theory also implies that in geographical areas where such plans exist, price discrimination ought to be relatively less prevalent. In California, the Kaiser Plan has captured a substantial fraction of the medical care market and is the largest single producer in the state. In an effort to meet this competition, service-type plans have been offered by orthodox members of the medical profession that are non-discriminatory with respect to income. Competition has had the effect of reducing the extent of discriminatory pricing in the area. This has been true in a number of counties in California where the Kaiser Plan is particularly strong.[96] Therefore both economic theory and empirical evidence suggest that if there were more competition among doctors in the sale of medical services, i.e., if doctors were individually freer to pursue their self-interest, there would be less discrimination in the pricing of medical services.

[96] Oakley, They Met the Challenge of Panel Medicine, 32 Medical Economics 122 (Feb. 1955) ; Olds, Usual Fee Plan Put to Test, 31 Medical Economics 131, but especially p. 206 (July, 1954) ; Andrews, How They're Fighting the Kaiser Plan, 31 Medical Economics, 126 (Sept. 1954).

Exhibit 7.—*Letter from Peter M. Milgrom, D.D.S., Re Dentistry and Alleged Anticompetitive Practices With Respect to Dentistry*

MAY 31, 1974.

HON. PHILIP HART,
U.S. Senator,
Senate Office Building,
Washington, D.C.

DEAR SENATOR HART: I am aware of hearings the Senate Anti Trust Sub-committee has been holding regarding actions by professional societies which torpedo projects to improve health care. I would like to share with you several examples of a similar phenomenon in dentistry.

Efforts of the publicily supported schools of dentistry in Michigan, Kentucky, Alabama and the Forsyth Dental Center in Boston to carry-out research on the dental equivalent of the physicians assistant have been hamstrung by political pressure and legal challenges. In some cases, dental school deans have been intimidated by threats of state boards of examiners that recent graduates will be denied licensure. Research grants have been terminated by HEW after meetings with dental association officials.

As you know, dental disease is common. A national survey conducted between 1960 and 1962 found that the average American had at least 20 to 32 teeth missing, filled or decayed. Three of four adults with natural teeth showed evidence of chronic periodical infection. Tooth decay alone is estimated to have caused an already existing backlog of over 800 million unfilled cavities in this country. According to the Health Interview Survey, 59 percent of the population visited the dentist at least once during 1971. However, 10 percent of the population utilized over 60 percent of all dental appointments. Most visits were for symptomatic relief.

The use of dentist-extenders is well known in other countries. New Zealand has had a dental nurse that does simple fillings and preventative care for more than 50 years. The dental health of children there is markedly better than here.

The dental profession is opposed to the use of dental auxiliaries to cutting cavities and other dentist skills. There is a fear of losing autonomy and professional control. At the Forsyth Center, dental hygienists have been trained to drill and fill in only 26 weeks. They perform at a quality level similar to the dentists with whom they have been matched. The hygiene course takes two years at a total cost of $7,700. It takes $62,400 and 8 years to train a dentist. Tremendous savings can be reflected in lower cost services and increased utilization.

I am enclosing a number of articles which provide additional information about the problem. I would be pleased to consult with your staff and offer any assistance to learn more about the problem.

Sincerely,

PETER M. MILGROM, D.D.S.

Enclosures: (4).

Enclosure 1

AUXILIARY UTILIZATION IN DENTISTRY: POSSIBILITIES FOR A DENTAL ASSOCIATE

(By Curtis L. Keith, M.A., Department of Behavioral Science, University of Kentucky College of Dentistry, Lexington, Ky., Peter M. Milgrom, D.D.S., Staff Officer of the Institute of Medicine, National Academy of Sciences, Washington, D.C.)

Abstract: Unlike many health problems, dental diseases and the procedures commonly used to resolve them require direct practioner intervention. Many procedures are routine and well suited for delegation. Surprisingly, the dental profession has been conservative in utilizing auxiliary manpower. The dental assistant, dental hygienist and laboratory technician are officially recognized auxiliary categories. Attempts to expand the duties of the dental assistant have been encouraged by the ADA. Reactions from practicing dentists have been mixed but generally supportive. However, efforts to create a dental auxiliary analogous to the physician's assistant in medicine have received strong resistance from organized dentistry. The need to understand that resistance is emphasized as an important step in the continuing development of a viable dental care delivery system.

Scientific and technological advances as well as increases in dentist productivity markedly improved the quality of oral health for those who were able to receive dental care during the last decade. However, during this same period, many people failed to receive even the most basic dental care. Some within the profession propose the creation of an expanded role for a dental auxiliary as one way of providing increased access to care by a large number of people. The suggested role would be analogous to the physician's assistant in medicine.[1] In exploring the possibility of and need for a dental associate, the nature and distribution of dental disease as well as the current resources available to cope with treatment demands and needs are discussed. Further the current structure of the dental care system is considered. Finally, a description of the traditional types of dental auxiliaries may help predict the likelihood of developing an associate practitioner concept within the American dental care system.

NATURE OF DENTAL DISEASE

Dental disease is ubiquitous, but unlike many common infectious diseases cannot be resolved without professional intervention. A national survey conducted between 1960 and 1962 found that the average American had at least 20 to 32 teeth missing, filled or decayed. Three of four adults with natural teeth showed evidence of chronic periodontal infection. In fact, it has been estimated that only one person in 30 has no dental decay.[2] Much dental cavities can be prevented through fluoridation of communal water supplies but after nearly 25 years of concerted effort toward fluoridation, only one-half of the population drink treated water.[3] In many areas, technology has limited the implementation of fluoridation. Public sentiment has also been mixed. Viable community support for the prevention of acute gingival and chronic periodontal diseases does not exist. Prevention requires direct intervention and assumes a degree of patient motivation and compliance seldom observed. Dental decay in school age children oftentimes begins in the pits and fissures of the biting surface of the tooth. Polymer coatings have been devised to seal off the tooth. However, their application requires a dental visit. Amalgam fillings, crowns, and removable devices as well require direct intevention. To effectively provide care of this nature, large numbers of providers are necessary. Much of the intervention required is therapeutically uncomplicated and routine. It can be given by capable though not necessary highly trained dental personnel. Therefore, it is reasonable that dentistry utilize to the fullest extent the services of auxiliary personnel as a means toward supplying the excessive quantity of routine practitioner intervention required strictly by the nature of dental disease and current therapeutic approaches to correction.

GROWING DEMANDS FOR DENTAL CARE

The demand for dental care is rising. Between 1950 and 1965, demand increased annually by 3.6 percent to a total of 54 percent.[2] However, there still is a marked discrepancy between the need and the demand for dental care in this country. Social, psychological, cultural, economic and technological factors exist which explain a relatively low demand for care in contrast to existing dental care needs. These aspects of the need-demand problem have, for the most part, been poorly analyzed and understood.[4]

On the other hand, increasing evidence points to a narrowing of the gap between health needs and wants. Total demand for care has grown through increases in population as well as relative demand. Income and education have influenced care demand. The doubling of family income between 1950 and 1965 raised the relative dental demand index from 1.19 visits to 1.83 visits or 54 percent. Most projections indicate a growing backlog of patients needing care. By 1980 consumer income is projected to have increased by 120 percent from 1965 levels and this shift toward higher incomes plus more education accounts for a projected rise in the demand index to 2.28 yearly visits per person. Other factors exist to suggest a significant expansion in the public's demand for care. For example, there is a 50 percent annual growth rate in private dental care plans. Support continues to mount for government involvement in dental care programs. By 1980, a full 15 percent of the population is projected to have pre-paid private or government dental benefits.[2]

CURRENT DENTAL CARE SYSTEM

The dental profession's ability to meet both existing and future demands for care is the concern driving this paper. Tooth decay alone is estimated to have caused an already existing backlog of over 800 million unfilled cavities in this country. According to the Health Interview Survey, 59 percent of the population visited the dentist at least once during 1971.[5] However, 10 percent of the population utilized over 60 percent of all dental appointments.[6] In 1971, there were about 92,210 actively practicing non-federal dentists in this country.[7] Each provides care for an average of 1200 patients.[2] Thus, by these measures alone, nearly one-half of the population must receive little or no care. Moreover the distribution of dentists is poorest in rural areas, where caries rates are unfortunately highest. Distribution ranged from 68 active non-federal dentists per 10,000 persons in New York State to 26 in Mississippi.[7]

A force of 113,000 dentists will be available in 1980: this number is set by the long lead time in the development of dental colleges. The highest estimate of dentist productivity increases between 1950 and 1965, an era of rapid technological development, is 42 percent. If this rate of change continues to 1980, the supply of dental services will be short the equivalent of 9,000 dentists just to meet minimal estimated demands. Should a large scale pre-paid government program be developed and demand rise more sharply, dentist productivity will need to rise up to 75 percent to avoid manpower shortages.[2] Even assuming a continued tendency toward less than optimal utilization of dental services by the public, the most conservative prediction of increased demands for care suggest a serious manpower shortage and a growing inability within the dental profession to fulfill its responsibility for providing a care delivery system accessible to all.[8]

AUXILIARIES CAN HELP

There is much evidence now that auxiliaries could ease the predicted shortage of manpower described earlier. A well respected American Dental Association (ADA) report concludes, "The projected shortage of dentists can be alleviated by more effective use of auxiliaries and particularly by those prepared to render selected patient care services now prformed by dntists."[8] Most dentists use auxiliaries: only 10 percent had no employees in 1964, and this proportion will decline further as older dentists retire and are replaced with dentists more specifically trained to utilize auxiliaries.[2] The most common dental paraprofessionals are dental assistants, dental hygienists and laboratory technicians. During the last decade, research and training programs have produced small numbers of expanded duty dental auxiliaries. Auxiliaries have proved valuable in saving the time of the dentist and freeing him to treat more patients. He has also been able to provide a greater proportion of the more complex care for which he has been uniquely trained.

Surprisingly, however. and in contrast to medicine, widespread and optimal utilization of paraprofessionals in dentistry is not highly developed. In 1971, there were a total of 161,950 dental auxiliaries of which 16,800 were hygienists, 114,000 were assistants, and 31,150 were technicians. This represents an average of only 1.6 auxiliaries per dentist.[7] In some states however, one-half the practitioners do not use an assistant. Formal education for auxiliaries is also a problem. In Kentucky, for example, a generally progressive dental care state, the educational system currently graduates more dentists each year than auxiliaries.

DENTAL ASSISTANT

The majority of dental assistants are trained on the job, are young and poorly paid. Dental assistants are neither licensed or registered in most states. A voluntary certification program is often administered by the professional society. The dental assistant's duties generally center on domestic and clerical needs of the dental office. The assistant is sometimes asked to prepare and give to the dentist the materials and instruments used in dental surgery. Further, the chairside assistant retracts the patient's cheek and aspirates fluids from the mouth. Auxiliaries remove and clean the soiled instruments and tidy the operating suite. The more highly skilled assistant is an integral member of the operating team who aids the dentist in providing highly efficient four-handed care. In many traditional offices, however, the assistant doubles as a receptionist and bookkeeper. More recently, innovative dentists have used dental assistants to instruct patients in the skills of oral hygiene. Many assistants expose and develop radiographs. In most states where this is permitted, a test or educational requirement is mandated by law or dental board regulation.[9]

DENTAL HYGIENISTS

The dental hygienist is a graduate of a two-year community college program or is educated in a baccalaureate program through a university health science center. The vast majority of hygienists are women and are licensed by the state after an examination. The military has prepared large numbers of hygienists corpsmen but without additional education they are currently barred from state licensure for private practice. The hygienist, working under the supervision of the dentist, cleans teeth, takes radiographs, applies topical fluoride to children's teeth and assumes the primary responsibility for patient education in the dental office. Few states allow the hygienist to administer local anesthesia and none permit the filling of teeth. Hygiene began early in this century as an institution-based service and that arrangement persists in some schools, hospitals, and community health settings. In 1971, there were 133 schools providing instruction to 8,061 students.[7]

LABORATORY TECHNICIAN

The dental laboratory technician is a surrogate for dentists in the laboratory. Most are trained on the job but 31 institutions do offer technician training in the U.S.[7] Dental education today still prepares the dentist to do much of the fabrication of gold, silver, chrome, and plastic appliances used in the mouth. However, time pressures on the dentist have stimulated the growth of commercial dental laboratories. As technology has become more sophisticated, increasing capital investment and economies of scale possible only in the larger operation have generally restricted laboratory technicians to group rather than solo practices. Technicians in large laboratories are specialists who utilize assembly-line methods in their work. In some parts of this country and in several foreign countries including Canada, technicians fabricate dentures directly for the public. Such a practice is illegal in this country and technicians are strictly forbidden from providing direct intra-oral services. Traditionally, they have not been licensed or effectively regulated. At a recent ADA meeting in Houston ,a resolution was passed encouraging ". . . statutory regulation of dental laboratories and technicians by the state boards of dentistry."[10] A certification program is also maintained by the laboratory association.

EXPANDED DUTY AUXILIARIES

In recent years, the trend toward extending the duties of dental auxiliaries has increased markedly. Current research in the auxiliary area stresses the importance of expanded duties and the concept has been supported at the policy level by the American Dental Association through its Interagency Committee on Dental Auxiliaries. In 1966, the ADA adopted resolution 341 which affirmed the need for ". . . studies, decisions, and the legislative actions which will help meet the manpower needs of the public, including the identification of additional functions which can be delegated to auxiliary personnel . . ."[11] Prior to that charge, research in several settings had already established the feasibility of such a practice by demonstrating increases in care delivery. Most studies examining the expansion of auxiliary duties have utilized the dental assistant. In 1962, the U.S. Naval Dental Corps at Great Lakes trained assistants in rubber dam application, matrix placement, and the insertion and finishing of restorative materials. This study found procedures performed by the dental assistants to be equal in quality to those performed by licensed dentists.[12] The University of Alabama School of Dentistry reported similar results in 1967. This research called upon dental auxiliaries to perform comparable reversible procedures.[13]

The most comprehensive study of the expansion of auxiliaries' duties has been the manpower research project at the Dental Manpower Center in Louisville, Kentucky.[14] This research was initiated under the direction and through support of the Public Health Service in 1960. It considers both the quality of care delivered by expanded duty auxiliaries and increases in productivity when such practices are followed. Results of this ongoing research project have been the basis of the development of the TEAM concept of dentistry now being implemented in several schools throughout the nation. TEAM is an acronym for "training in expanded auxiliary management" and reflects the training modification in dental education required by the extention of duties for dental auxiliaries.

The studies mentioned above have several common characteristics. First, in each study the procedures performed by auxiliaries were limited to reversible tasks. Dentists generally refer to those procedures which may be easily corrected if done improperly as reversible. They define more complex procedures as diagnosis, administration of anesthesia and the cutting of hard or soft tissue as irreversible. Second, the studies all demonstrate the ability of expanded duty auxiliaries to perform high quality care and to contribute significantly to the productivity of the dentist. Finally, though not without some controversy, these experiments and the idea of delegation they represent, have received at least general support from organized dentistry. Since 1968, over 42 states have revised their dental practice acts to permit varying degrees of expanded functions for auxiliaries.[9]

ROLE FOR A DENTAL ASSOCIATE

Within the past three years, much interest and debate has been focused in American dentistry on the training of dental auxiliaries to perform irreversible procedures. Most of this interest has been related to the expansion of duties for dental hygienists whose responsibility in the past has been primarily limited to the cleaning of teeth. Though this procedure is important, it may not justify the extensive training and general education received by the dental hygienist.

The history of dental auxiliaries performing irreversible procedures began in New Zealand where dental nurses have been performing simple restorative procedures, administration of anesthesia, and the extraction of primary teeth for over fifty years.[15] A generally poor state of oral health and an economic structure which could not afford luxury dental care for all were the factors which stimulated the development of the New Zealand dental care system. Among the first in America to advocate a similar approach to oral health was the dental school dean at the University of Minnesota, Alfred Owrie, in the mid-1920's.[16] In 1949, the Forsyth Dental Infirmary in Boston actually experimented with a training program to actualize many of the visionary ideas proposed by Awrie. Both these efforts were soundly discouraged by forces within posed by Owrie. Both these efforts were soundly discouraged by forces within degree of viable change in traditionally accepted approaches to delivering dental care.[17]

In 1965, there was a resurgence of interest within American dentistry toward experimentation with dental auxiliaries performing irreversible procedures. A research project was again initiated by the Forsyth Dental Center in Boston.[18] The Forsyth experiment is still in process and its objectives are three-fold: first, to determine the time and effort required to teach cavity preparation and restoration of teeth to dental hygienists; second, to secure data regarding productivity increases of these auxiliaries as well as their acceptance by the public; and third, to examine the quality of their work. The University of Pennsylvania School of Dental Medicine developed a program in 1969 to assess the ability of dental hygienists to perform periodical surgery. Previously trained hygienists were given additional educational experience in periodical disease, local anesthesia and periodontal surgery. The results of their work was compared with licensed dentists, and evaluators were unable to detect a difference in the quality of surgery performed.[19] The University of Iowa initiated a similar research project in 1972 which included operative dentistry at the less complex restorative level. The research at Iowa will be completed within a five-year period. Howard University is also teaching some operative dentistry and the application of local anesthesia within its existing hygiene curriculum. All hygiene students at Howard are receiving training and participating in the research.

A similar experimental study was begun in 1972 at the University of Kentucky College of Dentistry. It goes beyond earlier projects in two ways. First the hygienists in this experiment specialize in restorative procedures for children. Second, the hygienist is prepared educationally and trained technically to function in a semi-autonomous situation should such a note of practice become desirable. Though currently known as an expanded duty dental hygienist, the person trained in this project could justifiably become a pediatric dental associate with a role analogous to the pediatric associate in medicine. Working under the general supervision of a licensed dentist, such a person would be fully prepared to work in a public school dental clinic where preventive and simple restorative care could be given to children now without access to dental care. The potential value of a pediatric dental associate in rural areas is easily recognized. Existing laws regulating the work of dental auxiliaries prevent the development of this type of ancillary personnel. However, should the legal limits be expanded, the research at Kentucky holds promise as a training model to help resolve the dental health problems of the nation's youth.

Among the more important research questions surrounding these experiments is the question of care quality. Early data from the studies suggest that dental hygienists can be trained adequately and that they are able to perform high quality dental care. Hygienists with this extended training could greatly increase the productivity of the total dental care system. The studies are currently addressing themselves to this important possibility.

REACTION FROM ORGANIZED DENTISTRY

The first real attention given current experimentation with auxiliaries performing irreversible procedures in potentially semi-independent settings followed a speech given by Dr. John Ingle of the University of Southern California Dental School.[6] His speech suggested that American dentistry implement a system similar in focus to the New Zealand dental nurse program. He encouraged the creation of a new paraprofessional for dentistry with major responsibility for the preventative and simple treatment of children. Working in school-based clinics, this new dental auxiliary would be trained to administer local anesthesia, prepare and fill simple cavities, extract baby teeth and perform topical fluoride treatments. In short, he urged the creation of a dental auxiliary who would be the counterpart of the physician's assistant in medicine. The research just reviewed, especially the experiment at Kentucky, is specifically designed to test the philosophy of dental care delivery, suggested in the Ingle proposal.

Resistance to the Ingle speech was immediate and highly charged. Dr. Carl Laughlin, 1972 President of the ADA, firmly stated that dentistry was effectively utilizing three categories of auxiliary personnel already and should not consider even experimentation with new types of auxiliaries performing irreversible procedures. Doctor Laughlin insisted that such a practice would lead to an inferior quality of dental care. He insisted that no parent would want ". . . his children worked on by a second-rate dentist."[20] During his Presidential address to the ADA House of Delegates, Doctor Laughlin warned against ". . . dramatic schemes that purport to solve our problems overnight." He described such schemes as ". . . mediocre in conception and harmful in execution."[21] The House of Delegates then proceeded to pass several resolutions restricting experimentation with new types of dental auxiliaries. Resolution 225, if adhered to, eliminates the possibility of a semi-autonomous dental auxiliary by stating that ". . . all duties involving intraoral patient services . . . shall be performed under direct supervision of the dentist . . ."[22] The House strengthened its position on this issue by limiting all delegation to that performed ". . . under the supervision of a licensed dentist who shall be physically present . . ." when delegated procedures are performed.[22] More resistance to experimentation with a dental associate concept came in the form of Resolution 227 which declared that ". . . development of new categories of dental auxiliaries is not accepted by the American Dental Association and that only the dental assistant, dental hygienist and dental laboratory technician are recognized as dental auxiliaries."[22] Finally, the most restrictive response yet within organized dentistry against further experimentation came at the 1973 ADA House of Delegates meetings. Resolution 82 placed the ADA in opposition to all programs, training or experimental, ". . . which permit dental auxiliary personnel to cut hard or soft tissues in the oral cavity."[23] To encourage compliance with ADA policy on these matters, Resolution 223 states that ". . . experimental training projects for auxiliary personnel shall have the endorsement of the constituent dental society and the state board of dentistry in whose jurisdiction the project is undertaken."[22] In those cases where experimental programs fail to comply with these ADA policies, President Laughlin encouraged the House of Delegates to give the Council on Dental Education the power to withdraw accreditation from any dental school conducting such an experiment.[21]

In summary, the reaction toward current experimentation with expanded duty auxiliaries has been characterized by firm resistance and a considerable degree of opposition throughout organized dentistry. It has stimulated much debate within the profession regarding the general value of dental auxiliaries and the degree to which their duties should be expanded. The official position of the ADA, if adhered to, would discourage and in fact disallow all experimentation leading to the creation of a dental associate.

CONCLUSION

While government at both state and federal levels continues to support allied health education and an extended use of paraprofessionals,[24] the dental profession remains conservative in the utilization of auxiliary personnel and strongly resists the creation of a dental associate concept. Therefore, it is unlikely that a practitioner analogous to the physician's assistant will be developed in dentistry in the near future. Given the nature of dental disease, the excessive need for dental care in this country, and the potential contribution of a dental associate, it is important to seek an understanding of the reasons why the concept is resisted by the profession. The present authors are conducting a study of practitioner attitudes in an effort to better understand the resistance pattern which has developed. Other research projects, discussed earlier, are designed to test issues concerning productivity, cost, quality of care, effects of various types of dental team composition, and patient acceptance when auxiliary functions are expanded. It is important that these research efforts push forward if rational thought is to be the basis upon which an optimal dental care system is developed. Data from such research will help determine the feasibility and likelihood of implementing an associate practitioner concept in American dentistry.

REFERENCES

[1] New members of the Physician's Health Team: Physician's Assistants. Report of the Ad Hoc Panel on New Members of the Physician's Health Team, Board of Medicine, National Academy of Sciences, Washington, D. C., 1970·

[2] Cole RB, Cohen LK: Dental manpower: Estimating resources and requirements. Milbank Mem Fund Q XLIX(3), Part 2:29–62, July, 1971.

[3] According to the 1970 census, 44 percent of Americans drink fluoridated water. One-half of the nation's fifty largest cities are unfluoridated including Boston, Newark, Cincinnati, Houston, New Orleans, and Los Angeles.

[4] Linn EL: The dentist-patient relationship, pps. 195–208. In Social Sciences and Dentistry: A Critical Bibliography. Eds. ND Richards and LK Cohen, The Hague, Netherlands: A. Sijthoff, 1971.

[5] Current Estimates from the Health Interview Survey. Vital and Health Statistics. Series 10, number 79. DHEW (HSM) 73–1505. Table 19. Number and percent distribution of persons by time interval since last dental visit according to sex and age: United States, 1971.

[6] Ingle J: American dental care—1972. A plan designed to deliver preventive and therapeutic dental care to the children of America. Presented at the Conference of Dental Examiners and Dental Educators Chicago, Illinois, February 11–12, 1972.

[7] Health Resources Statistics: Health Manpower and Health Facilities. Chapter 8: Dentistry and allied services. DHEW (HSM) 73–1509, September, 1973.

[8] Dentistry in national health programs. A report with recommendations. J Am Dent Assoc 83:570–600, September, 1971·

[9] Johnson DW, Holz FM: Legal Provisions on Expanded Functions for Dental Hygienists and Assistants. DHEW Publication No. (HRA) 74–6, July, 1973.
[10] ADA House of Delegates Handbook. Board Resolution 121. Legislative and Related Matters. Page 1460, Yellow Sheets, 1973.
[11] Report of the inter-agency committee on dental auxiliaries. J Am Dent Assoc 84: 1029, May, 1972.
[12] Ludwick WE, Schnoebelen ED, Knoedler DJ: Greater Utilization of Dental Technicians: Report of Clinical Tests. Great Lakes, Illinois: US Naval Training Center, May, 1964.
[13] Hammons PE, Jamison HC: Expanded functions for dental auxiliaries. J Am Dent Assoc 75:658–672, September, 1967.
[14] Lotzkar S, Johnson DW, Thompson MB: Experimental program in expanded functions for dental assistants: Phase 1 base line and phase 2 training. J Am Dent Assoc 82:101–122, January, 1971.
[15] Saunders JL: The New Zealand School Dental Service: Its Initiation and Development, 1920–1960. Wellington, New Zealand: R. E. Owen, Government Printer, no date.
[16] Wilson NW: Alfred Owrie: Dentistry's Militant Educator. Minneapolis: The University of Minnesota Press, 1937.
[17] Asgis AJ: The Massachusetts "dental nurse-operator" project of 1949: Reasons for opposing this "sub-level dentistry" project. NY J Dent 20:381–383, October, 1950.
[18] Hein JW: A master plan for dentistry. J. Dent Educ 36:18–24, September, 1972.
[19] Valentine R: Expanded role for dental hygienists. Health Affairs, University of Pennsylvania, pps. 21–23, Summer, 1973.
[20] Nelson H: Dentists take stand against expanded functions by aids. Los Angeles Times. pps. 1, 8, Friday, November 3, 1972.
[21] Laughlin CA: ADA Transactions, 1972–15. Chciago: American Dental Association, 1973.
[22] ADA Transactions, 1972:552. Chicago: American Dental Association, 1973.
[23] ADA House of Delegates Manual, 1973:1262. Chicago: American Dental Association, 1973.
[24] Edwards CC: A candid look at health manpower problems. Presentation to the Association of American Medical Colleges, Washington, D. C., November 5, 1973.

Enclosure 2

Dental Auxiliaries, Universities, and Academic Freedom

(By Peter Milgrom, D.D.S.,* Professional Associate of the Institute of Medicine National Academy of Sciences, Washington, D.C., Chairman-designate of the Department of Community Dentistry, University of Washington, Seattle, Wash.)

Abstract: The practicing profession has lately asked questions regarding the propriety of research programs designed to investigate the use of expanded duty dental auxiliaries. The dental schools see paraprofessional research as socially responsive. Dental societies recognize the usefulness of auxiliaries but feel their responisbilities should be limited. This paper examines the status of dental auxiliaries, universities, and academic freedom.

Who shall decide how dental care is delivered in the future? This paper explores the roles of the university, the dental profession and the society as a whole.

The dental schools and the practicing profession differ in their viewpoints over the growing utilization of expanded duty dental auxiliaries. Many of the schools wish to move rapidly with the training of an extensive paraprofessional work force in dentistry while the practicing profession actively questions the need. This paper will examine the university under challenge.

EVOLUTION OF THE UNIVERSITY

The university is first described in law where the Latin *universitas* was a corporation. J. S. Brubacher, an education researcher, writes, "when professors and students were first drawn together in medieval times they formed a voluntary corporation. To do so, they did not need the permission of civil authorities. They thus became a self-governing body and have continued to be so, more or less throughout their history . . ." [1]

Logan Wilson, retired president of the American Council on Education, disagrees. He points out that "college and university professors have seldom, if ever, managed their own affairs unchecked by any external constraints, and one would be hard put to find a single example in the Middle Ages or later of a completely 'free republic of scholars.' " [2] Other scholars similarly report that the university's development has been tempered throughout history by a healthy respect for political reality. Charles Homer Haskins, the historian, writes, for

*Supported under a fellowship award from the Commonwealth Fund.

example, that while medieval professors were not condemned for preaching free trade or socialism, their philosophies were based on the precepts of the controlling theology. He refers to St. Anselm and his description of the medieval conceptions of truth. Anselm writes, "I believe in order that I may know, I do not order to believe . . . Faith precedes science, fixes its boundaries, and prescribes its conditions."[3] This faith, however, did not settle the matter.

The eminent 18th century Cardinal John Henry Newman helps to explain how the universities evolved. Each time a new role of the university was proposed it was hotly debated and most frequently in the short run rejected, either by society or the professors. Newman excluded research from his university. He wrote that political controversies over the role of the university 'did but afford fuller development and more exact delineation to the principles of which the University was the representative . . ."[4] He answered charges against the "in-utility" or "religious exclusiveness" of liberal studies by this famous retort:

"Knowledge . . . deserves to be sought for its own sake . . . what was so good in itself could not but have a number of external uses, though it did not promise them simply because it was good . . ."[5]

By the Great Depression of the 1930's many leaders in this country insisted that the university enter research on the immediate social problems of the day. The early writers were concerned about this problem of the need for instant relevance. That refrain is repeated by Princeton President James Rowland Angell in 1933. '. . . The universities," he wrote, "have more than once had to safeguard their training for the professions against the tradeschool methods and points of view. To teach the basic scientific principles, and not the mere skills and tricks of a profession, has always been the true university ideal . . ."[6] However, even he, in the depths of the depression, seems to be aware of the political environment of the universities. In fact, the records of the 1933 conference, "The Obligations of the Universities to the Social Order," show there was concern over the cutbacks of public funds to many world renowned universities outside the U.S. during that period of economic downfall. He writes:

"The university is an itegral part of the society it serves and it could not, if it would, be oblivious to the necessities of that social order . . . The university must constantly face, and honestly deal with, the changing obligations which arise from shifting circumstance, and it must be particularly sensitive to those requirements of a given era which are especially urgent" . . .[7]

What is introduced in the recountings of educational history is the notion of the university as a public utility. The university is an integral part of the social problem solving apparatus in this country. What Clark Kerr called the *uses* of the university and Logan Wilson called the *abuses* is one aspect of needed understanding of the role of the university with respect to dental auxiliaries. To give a further picture of the social pressures which the university has encountered, George Soule, in 1933 the editor of *New Republic*, urged that the university apply its scientific, rigorous method to the knowledge needed for economic renewal. He cites the beginnings of the university role in agriculture. In his writings, it is possible to observe many of the pressures which have been again brought to bear on the univeristies in the last two decades. For example,

"It is true that the scholars have no legal right to the formulation of social, economic, and political policies and apparently little direct effect on the decisions of government. Nevertheless, democracy must have meant something by its faith in education and the sacrifices it has made to maintain educational institutions. Perhaps the universities have abdicated a social leadership which was meant to be theirs. Perhaps if they persistently gave a lead, it would in the end be followed."[8]

It is the leadership refrain which is dissonant today in the dental profession. Society has already decided that the university should participate in the solution of health problems. The educators, then, their roles delineated by past political controversies, are figuratively represented by Dean Bohannan who recognizes, "The dental profession is entering a new era of accountability We shall be accountable to a public that will demand more and better health care for more of its citizens than ever before."[9] It is possible to question this role for the university but analysis shows that it has evolved in a pragmatic manner.

THE PROFESSIONAL SOCIETIES

Eliot Freidson is a well-known analyst of medicine as a consulting profes. sion. His theories and evidence are given in the *Profession of Medicine.* Freidson concludes that there are three salient characteristics of the professions of the healing arts.[10]

1. · · · the occupation has gained command of the exclusive competence to determine the proper content and effective method of performing some task.

2. The occupational group . . . must be the prime source of the criteria that qualify a man to work in an acceptable fashion.

3. [The] general public [must believe] in the consulting occupation's competence, in the value of its professed knowledge and skill.

As the technology and science of medicine and dentistry have grown in efficacy and reputability, society's expectations have risen accordingly. Health care, in the hands of the consulting professions, is seen as a "societal" trust.

This key question of trust is amplified in a dichotomy drawn by Freidson. On the one hand, he says that scholarly or scientific professions may obtain and maintain a fairly secure societal status by winning solely the support of the political or social elite. But, he points out, ". . . a consulting profession as medicine must, in order to win a secure status, make itself attractive to the general public which must support its members by consulting them." [11] One concern of this paper is that the dental societies may, as a consequence of basing their goals on the requirements of the present system, miss seeing the social indicators that would be signaling a change in societal expectations. A case in point are the results of University of California professor Stephen Strickland's surveys on public perceptions of the health care system. He reports that most Americans have confidence at present in the health care system but that "they recognize serious problems in the health care system that require basic changes." The problems most often identified by the public are a shortage of manpower and complicated and costly health insurance.[12] The objective of the educators in their research is the production of dental manpower. If Strickland's observations are correct, there is considerable evidence that their goals are correct.[13]

Freidson attempts to explain the distinction between a profession, as an occupation with a special position in the division of labor, and professionalism, as the possession of individual members. He points out that in common usage,

"Whether or not an occupation is a profession is established by the analysis of the relation of occupations to each other in a social structure. Whether or not professionalism exists in an occupation is an entirely different question, answered by the study of the attitudes of individual members of occupations. There is no necessary or substantive relationship between the position of an occupation and the attributes of its members." [14]

Reuben Kessel of the University of Chicago, in a paper published in 1970, gives his historical interpretation of the activities of the American Medical Association.[15] The crux of his thesis is that Abraham Flexner and the public were duped by the profession. Flexner's famous report, *Medical Education in the United States and Canada,* concluded that doctors should be educated according to the Johns Hopkins University model with little or any attempt to evaluate the output of the graduates of the other schools. As a consequence, the graduates of some schools were made ineligible for licensure and the number of "accredited schools" was markedly reduced. Thus, a century of AMA control began, through accreditation and licensure, over the output of physicians. There is no question that the public and medicine have greatly benefitted by this famous review of medical education. Scientific inquiry gained a foothold in medical research and the foundation was set for the conquest of infectious disease. The quality of medical practice improved. Kessel, however, claims that the regulatory responsibility for medical education has been questionably managed by the medical profession by manipulation of the output of physicians according to the economic status of the nation. The recent Newman Task Force [16] on Higher Education considered the control of accrediting agencies and recommended greater flexibility and broader representation. The Council on Dental Education of the American Dental Association has been reorganized in this manner to give it greater autonomy in educational matters.

Organized dentistry has supported more effective use of the existing forms of dental auxiliaries. The report of a task force headed by former American

Dental Association Preisdent Hubert McGuirl supported the selective use of expanded duty personnel.[17] Most dentists use auxiliaries and since 1968, over 42 states have revised their practice acts to permit varying degrees of expanded functions for auxiliaries.[18] The profession supported these changes and model laws were drawn up by the Chicago legal staff and printed in dental and auxiliary journals.

Leaders of the practicing profession have generally opposed the development of new types expanded duty auxiliaries, especially those who would work and be reimbursed for services outside the dental office. A number of such resolutions have been before the House of Delegates. In 1972, ADA President Carl Laughlin asked the House of Delegates to give the Council on Dental Education authority to withdraw accreditation from any dental school with a research program using auxiliaries to cut hard or soft tissues.[18] Under intense pressure from organized dentistry, federal grants supporting controversial research were terminated this year. Health related private foundations have continued their support for the research programs.

Recently, a highly critical report appeared in the literature by a California group who had observed pediatric dental practice in New Zealand. The journal article, *Delivery of Dental Services in New Zealand and California*, contained an uncomplimentary analysis of site visits to dental nurse staffed clinics, yet failed to visit a single California dental office.[19]

Rosemary Stevens of Yale University recognized, in her book *American Medicine and the Public Interest*, the guild-like nature of the professional societies. She argues that the professions have consistently acted to curb specialization in favor of their own economic advantage.[20]

DENTAL SCHOOLS, UNIVERSITIES AND MODERN SOCIETY

It is tempting to reject the conservative views of the dental societies on expanded duties as blatant self-interest. Some evidence points in that direction. In a free society, however, the issues raised merit delineation and analysis. Misuse of the university, if it exists, should be examined.

A public controversy raged over California colleges and student activism during the 1960's that resulted in the firing of University of California President Clark Kerr. In Kerr's famous speeches while president, *The Uses of the University*, he said he was optimistic about the future of the broadly socially conscious "multiversity", and his concerns were first with the *uses* rather than with the *misuses* of the university.[21] Of course, what others considered abuses brought his tumultuous dismissal from the leadership of one of the largest, richest and most distinguished universities in the world.

There is a parallel situation today for determined and creative dental faculties and their deans who are under fire from sometimes hostile and divided dental societies over implementing new practice modes, training dental auxiliaries and positions on compulsory national health insurance. Some innovative deans have resigned preferring escape to an ulcer. Unfortunately, should these controversies be exacerbated further, others will surely quit the profession.

Logan Wilson, in his book *Shaping American Higher Education*, includes the 1940 Statement of Principles on Academic Freedom and Tenure.[22] As a starting point in this discussion, it is possible to extend these principles beyond the individual professor to the institution as a whole. Thus, its pertinent parts would read as follows

"The university is entitled to full freedom in research and in the publication of results;

"The university is entitled to freedom in the community to discuss its work;

"The university is a community of citizens; its house is the sanctuary of the learned professions. Its members must be free to speak or write as citizens, but the institution's special position in society imposes special obligations. At all times, its position should be accurate, it should show respect for the opinions of others."

In a study of this issue one is impressed that the current mood of censure toward the dental schools evolves from a conflicting interpretation of two different parts of these principles. On the one hand, the profession has consistently supported research and the exploration of new knowledge. It has, for example, steadfastly advocated the National Institute for Dental Research. Conversely, some argue that the dental schools are arrogant over the auxiliary issue and refuse to respect the common sense, practitioner's pragmatic view of supply and demand.

Thus, it is possible to see the university as well as the dental society as a vested interest. JB Lon Hefferlin, formerly at the Center for Research and Development in Higher Education in Berkeley, sees this university in such a pecuniary way. In his book, *Dynamics of Academic Reform*, he writes:

". . . The champions of self-regulation, whether in the tobacco industry, automobile manufacturing, the securities market, the medical profession or colleges and universities, hold that these organizations can be expected in their own self-interest to tend adequately toward the public interest."[22]

He goes on to say that he feels that universities do tend to abuse their public responsibilities and thus must be regulated as any other industry. An example frequently cited is the aborted plan of Columbia University to build a gymnasium on park land in Harlem without considering the needs of the community. Another abuse voiced repeatedly by practitioners is that educators attempt to proselytize students into believers of he auxiliary concept. To the extent that this is true, one author at least would consider this poor judgment. Richard Hofstader, the Columbia political scientist, in his celebrated review of academic freedom, contrasts American universities with the German ones from which we draw our notions of freedom. He says:

"The German idea of "convincing" one's students, of winning them over to the personal system and philosopihcal views of the professor, was not condoned by American academic opinion. Rather, as far as classroom actions were concerned, the proper stance for American professors was thought to be one of neutrality on controversial issues."[24]

It is important that the schools address the problem of classroom evangelism and recognize the equivalent argument on the auxiliary issue. At the same time, similar issues in medicine raise questions about the motivation of the critics. Would a surgical team consider operating without highly skilled technicians and paraprofessionals? Do physicians conduct office practice without assistance? Moreover, should the medical schools teach students to work alone? However, an important distinction between the university and the health center needs to be made in the instant case in that expanded duty dental auxiliary training requires students to engage in patient care as an integral function of the curriculum.

Such training programs do abuse patient's rights. Patients are treated by novice students of a dental college. The roots of this problem are found in antiquity. Plato in the *Laws* differentiates the medical treatment of slaves from that received by free men.[25]

1. Slaves were not generally attended by real doctors . . . but by rough empiricists who had learned the superficial routine of the art of healing from a physician, nearly always as his slave.

2. Verbal communication between healer and patient was reduced to a minimum. The medicine practiced on slaves conformed to what was thought about them in classical Greece, and was sort of 'veterinary service for men'.

3. Individualization of treatment was . . . minimal. Patients were submitted indiscriminately to an egalitarian standard . . .

Avedis Donabedian of the University of Michigan has raised valid questions about whether the development of these "crisis" responses to health care needs, such as the dental nurse, will turn health delivery into a dpersonalized "supermarket" model for the masses while private, fee-for-service, solo practice continues to cater to the elite.[26] Certainly, the widely cited New Zealand dental nurse services only dependent children—a dual system. On the other hand, auxiliary programs, by the ADA accreditation guidelines, must offer equivalent dental training where traditional dental skills are involved. Thus, a dental hygienist who is responsible for infiltration anesthesia must complete the same anesthesiology requirements in school as a dentist. In addition, in many states, competition for first year places in hygiene is stiffer than for dental education.

Most practitioners are convinced that the dental auxiliary utilization projects at Louisville, Alabama and Great Lakes did show that the carefully controlled use of expanded duties personnel was successful. It is their full-scale deployment in the field to which the dissenters object.[18] It is possible that the dental schools may be stretching their social tether. The dental societies, however, may not really represent the best interest of the public on this issue.

Many observers today appear to ask the university to take a so-called "Nuremberg defense" to claim that society ordered these programs, and thus, only society can judge them in the end. For example:

"Any university that loses step with current movements, that fails to give consideration to the sweeping changes that are occurring in every part of the world, will soon become archaic and incompetent to educate youth for the exercise of leadership." [27]

The claim of social pressure is not wthout merit. The United Auto Workers union recently won extensive dental benefits in their contract negotiations with the auto industry. Their leaders are publicly concerned about the availability of adequate services—particularly with the adoption of compulsory, universal national health insurance which they support. It is equally clear, however, that dental school programs must stand on their merits, rather than on "orders from higher ups." Public crises have increased medical schools involvement in societal problems. Recent examples are concerns over the health hazards of herbicides after the extensive us of defoliants in the Vietnam war, and radiation induced disease following atomic testing.

The earliest recorded example of this crisis intervention dates to the Middle Ages. Pearl Kibre, a historian, tells us that this public service dates back to October, 1348, in the first year of the Black Death when the medical faculty of the University of Paris responded to King Philip VI's request for an "account of the plague, by giving a written report on the causes, antecedents, effects and salutary measures to be undertaken" for the control of the dread malady. [28]

It is no secret how few citizens receive adequate dental care and the result is plain in the statistics on the number of unfilled cavities, edentulous mouths and undetected oral cancers. There is tremendous pressure on the dental schools to take action. Other educational fields face the same challenges as dentistry. Should law students be allowed give legal aid to indigents? Should legal aides? Should medical students be taught to perform elective abortions? Should nurse-midwives? Should an academic person be involved in making foreign affairs decisions?

A LEGAL ARGUMENT

In some cases, dental societies and examiinng boards have attempted to limit the development of dental auxiliary research through legal action. To date, the courts have unequivocally defended the autonomy of the university. In this section, the legal challenge to the schools is discussed as some dental societies have taken the issue to the dental boards.

"May a state board of dental examiners bar a dental school from conducting an expanded duties research program?"

On the contrary, in most states the university is a separate autonomous state agency charged specifically with the responsibilities of a full-fledged educational institution and not subject to regulation by other state agencies. In Kentucky, for example, the law states, "The government of the Universiy of Kentucky is vested by law in the Board of Trustees . . . The Board of Trustees is a body corporate . . . with the usual privileges, and franchises usually attaching to the governing bodies of educational institutions. [29]

In Iowa, the State Board of Dentistry recently formally recognized the sovereignty of the university. It said:

"The Board recognizes that one of the traditional and proper functions of a University is to conduct controlled and legitimate experimentations which serve to enhance the well-being of mankind" . . . [30]

A judicial precedent, in these cases, is *Sterling* v. *Regents of University of Michigan*. [31] The dispute arose over an order of the state legislature that the university close a homeopathic medical college at its campus in Ann Arbor and move its functions to the City of Detroit. In a now famous decision, the court supported the university's contention that a charter of self government excluded it from regulation by another state agency, namely the legislature. Justice Grant wrote:

"The board of regents and the legislature derive their power from the same supreme authority, namely, the Constitution. Insofar as the powers of each are defined by that instrument, limitations are imposed, and a direct power conferred upon one necessarily excludes it existence in the other hand, in the absence of language showing the contrary intent." [32]

In another case, the Oklahoma Supreme Court ruled that "the Board of Regents of the State University are held to have implied power to do everything necessary to accomplish the objects of the schools not expressly or impliedly prohibited." [33] These cases would apply in the majority of states. The public schools are generally of two types. The first is the constitutionally autonomous state university. The second is a creature of the legislature. In both cases, the university is authorized to have a dental school and its trustees or regents are fully charged with its management. The obtuse case is the university as a subordinate state agency. Alexander cites a case in West Virginia where the state treasurer refused to authorize the sale of bonds for the university. In that state, he had this power but over most land-grant colleges he would not be so directed. The private schools, if they operate under state charter as most do, are considered "public" institutions in such a matter.[36]

Most dental practice acts are similar in that they define the practice of dentistry and prohibit unlicensed practitioners from declaring themselves as dentists. Generally certain exceptions are made for dental auxiliaries and students. For example, in Massachusetts dental hygienists may (1) remove all tartar, deposits, accretions and stains from the exposed services of the teeth and directly beneath the free margin of the gums; (2) polish the teeth and fillings therein; (3) record or report to a registered dentist any oral conditions observed; (4) make topical applications of medicinal agents to the teeth and other oral tissue for prophylatic purposes; (5) assist a registered dentist in any phase of operative and surgical procedures in dentistry and in anaesthesia; (6) use a roentgen or X-ray machine for the purpose of taking dental X-rays or roentgenograms.[37]

Visiting clinicians giving continuing education courses and students "of a reputable dental college . . . granting degrees in dentistry" are also allowed exceptions to the requirement that all those practicing dentistry must be licensed.[38]

In a recent decision, the Massachusetts Attorney General found that the Forsyth Dental Center was violating these sections of the practice act by allowing dental hygienists in their research program to prepare and fill cavities. Specifically, he argued that a dental hygienists may only "assist" the dentist in restorative dentistry.[39][40]

The Attorney General's opinion probably will never be judged in a court since the Forsyth project is nearly completed. Nonetheless, the Massachusetts act is silent on the responsibility of the dental board for research. There is no definition of research. President indicates that the Forsyth trustees are more suited to control the research activities at the center.

A similar question has been raised by Board of Dental Examiners with the use of expanded duty dental assistants in a research program at the University of Alabama in Birmingham.[41] Assistants place and carve restorations, but do not cut tissue or administer anesthetic drugs. The present research grant ends in August, 1974, and the Board has ordered the program terminated at that time.

Several states' legislatures have considered changes in their dental practice acts to specifically allow experiments with auxiliary personnel. For example, an excerpt from Connecticut Public Act 73–183 reads:

"No provision of this section shall be construed to . . . Prevent Controlled Investigations or Innovative Training Programs Related to the Delivery of Dental Health Services" . . .[42]

This is a political method to deal with the problem of unpopular research. The law is probably not necessary to allow the investigations and surely will be challenged in the courts.

CONCLUSION

The universities in this country have traditionally been buffeted by political currents. They exist in a vortex of changing values and struggle to be relevant. Socially desirable research is an accepted responsibility of the schools of the health professions. Governance of dental schools rests with university officials, and the regulation of controversial research appears to be no exception. A number of dental boards have accepted this approach after studying the matter.

Organized dentistry has grown increasingly opposed to research designed to evaluate the use of surrogate practitioners. Political and legal means have been employed to stop active programs. However, the trend toward state recognition of the expanded duty concept in dentistry is unmistakeable. To date, there is no definitive court ruling on a dental care, and even the Massachusetts Attorney General recognized that "it may very well be in the public interest to encourage research programs such as Forsyths' hygienist program."[40]

A compromise is needed. Recent reports show the feasibility and acceptance of the expanded duty concept in the private practice.[43] Congress has actively considered changes in the reimbursement mechanism for public health programs to allow payment for services by paraprofessionals.[44] The American Dental Association, in cooperation with the dental schools, might establish a non-profit public corporation to aid the research and development of selected school clinics using auxiliaries in an acceptable manner. In this way, the dental profession could maintain responsibility for auxiliary utilization and extend dental services to a greater portion of the public.

REFERENCES

[1] Brubacher, J.S. The courts and higher education, San Francisco, Jossey-Bass, Inc., 1969, p. 150.
[2] Wilson, Logan. Shaping American higher education, Washington, D. C., American Council on Education, 1972, pp. 233–34.
[3] Haskins, Charles Homer. The rise of universities, New York, Henry Holt and Co., 1923, p. 72.
[4] Newman, John Henry Cardinal. The idea of a university defined and illustrated, New York, Longmans, Green and Co., 1947, p. 4.
[5] Op. cit., p. 160.
[6] Angell, James Rowland. The university today: its aims and province, in Henry Pratt Fairchild, The obligation of universities to the social order, New York, New York University Press, 1923, p. 9.
[7] Op. cit., p. 12.
[8] Soule, George. The scholar in practical affairs, in Henry Pratt Fairchild, The obligation to universities to the social order, New York, New York University Press, 1933, p. 9.
[9] Bohannan, Harry M. et al. The flexible dental curriculum. JADA 84:112, January 1972.
[10] Freidson, Eliot. Profession of medicine: a study of the sociology of applied knowledge, New York, Dodd, Mead and Co., 1972, pp. 10–11.
[11] Op. cit., p. 188.
[12] Strickland, Stephen P. U.S. health care. What's wrong and what's right, New York, Universe Books, 1972, p. 100.
[13] Cole, Roger B., and Cohen, Lois K. Dental manpower: estimating resources and requirements, in toward a sociology of dentistry, Milbank Memorial Fund Quarterly 49(3):29, July 1971.
[14] Freidson, p. 186.
[15] Kessel, Reubne A. The A.M.A. and the supply of physicians, in Health Care Part I, Law and Contemporary Problems 35(2):267, Spring 1970.
[16] U.S. Office of Education. Report on Higher Education, March 1971. Washington, U.S. Government Printing Office, 1971, p. 66.
[17] Dentistry in national health programs. A report with recommendations. JADA 83:570, September 1971.
[18] Keith, Curtis L. and Milgrom, Peter M. Auxiliary utilization in dentistry: Possibilities for a dental associate. Physician's Associate, (Spring, 1974, in press).
[19] Delivery of Dental Services in New Zealand and California. J South Dental Assoc 41:318, April 1973.
[20] Stevens, Rosemary. American medicine and the public interest, New Haven, Yale University Press, 1971, p. 45.
[21] Kerr, Clark. The uses of the university, New York, Harper and Row, 1963, p. vi.
[22] Wilson, pp. 233–34.
[23] Hefferlin, JB Lon. Dynamics of academic reform, San Francisco, Jossey-Bass, Inc., 1969, p. 150.
[24] Tisdel, Richard P. Academic freedom—its constitutional context. University of Colorado Law Review 40:600, 1968.
[25] Entralgo, P. Lain. Doctor and patient, New York, McGraw Hill Book Co., 1969, pp. 30–31.
[26] Donabedian, A. An examination of some directions in health care policy. Amer J Public Health 63:243, March 1973.
[27] Coffman, Lotus Delta. Civilization through service. The obligation of a state university to the social order, in Henry Pratt Fairchild, The obligation of universities to the social order, New York, New York University Press, 1933, pp. 292–3.
[28] Kibre, Pearl. Scholarly privileges in the middle ages, Cambridge, Mediaeval Academy of America, 1962, p. 261.
[29] Kentucky Revised Statutes 164.130; 164.160.
[30] Action of the Iowa State Board of Dentistry, September 12, 1970.
[31] Sterling v. Regents of University of Michigan 100 Mich. 369, 68 NE 253 (1896).
[32] 30 NW 2d 860.
[33] Rheam et al. v. Board of Regents of University of Oklahoma et al. 18 P 2d 535 (1933).
[34] State ex rel. Black v. State Board of Education et al. 196 P 201 (1921).
[35] Fanning et al. v. University of Minnesota. 236 NW 217 (1931).
[36] Alexander, Kern and Solomon, E.S. College and university law, Charlottesville, The Michie Co., 1972, pp. 26, 40, 43.
[37] Commonwealth of Massachusetts. Dental Laws, Rules and Regulations of the Massachusetts Board of Dental Examiners, Tercentenary Edition, p. 5.
[38] Op. cit., p. 7.
[39] Forsyth found in violation of state law. American Dental Association News, 5(8):5, April 22, 1974.
[40] Letter to Dr. John Horack, Board of Dental Examiners from Kenneth Behar, Assistant Attorney General, Commonwealth of Massachusetts, March 11, 1974.
[41] Personal communication. Dr. Donald W. Legler, May 7, 1974.
[42] Connecticut, Substitute Senate Bill No. 1881. Public Act No. 73–183. An Act Allowing Exception to the Definition of Dentistry.

⁴³ Redig, Dale, Snyder, Mildred, et al. Expanded duty dental auxiliaries in four private dental offices : the first year's experience. JADA 88 :969, May 1974.
⁴⁴ Sadler, Alfred M. Jr., Sadler, Blair, L., et al. The physician's assistant today and tomorrow, New Haven, Yale University Press, 1972, p. 40–43.

Enclosure 3

AMERICAN DENTAL CARE—1972—A PLAN DESIGNED TO DELIVER PREVENTIVE AND THERAPEUTIC DENTAL CARE TO THE CHILDREN OF AMERICA

"Through—shifting times there passed—those little bands of struggling beings who someday would be men. —They survived through plasticity,—through a growing capacity to recognize, in changing times, that today is different from yesterday, and tomorrow from today. Many—most without doubt—were conservative creatures. These died by dry, unanticipated stream beds, or numbed and froze in unanticipated storms. Those, quite obviously, were not your ancestors. It was the others—the witty, sensitive, the flexible, the ones who could recognize a changing environment—these were the ones to assemble— a new and most remarkable genetic package: ourselves." Robert Adrey, The Territorial Imperative.

American dentistry has just passed through a decade of major change. The first half of the 1960's was marked by the impact of third party payment—the financing of dental services through insurance coverage, union clinics and dental service corporations—a movement which originated in the last half of the 1950's.

The early 1960's also witnessed the expansion and improvement in dental instrumentation and manpower utilization triggered by the air rotor handpiece, panographic x-ray, and a more imaginative use of chairside auxiliaries. Prevention of caries by fluoridation was another widespread health measure of the 1960's.

The second half of the 1960's was most affected by major changes emanting from Washington, D.C.—the Medicare and Medicaid laws and the Health Professions Educational Assistance Act. The introduction of mobile equipment and disposable supplies also had a major impact on delivery of dental care.

The decade of the 1970's promises more of the same—more and better equipment, an increase in insurance and dental service group coverage, and an increase in support of dental care and dental education by the federal government. Programs are already financed to expand duties and increase the numbers of dental personnel. More important will be the passage of massive programs guaranteeing full and comprehensive health care to all Americans.

As it is presently constituted, American denistry is not prepared educationally, physically, numerically, or emotionally to enter into the challenge of the 1970's. Dentistry has not truly faced up to the vast responsibilities soon to be forced upon the profession. To date, we have paid only lip service to expanding the duties of dental auxiliaries and we do very little to change state laws to allow this to happen. We speak of refurbishing the dental curriculum but, generally speaking, dental education remains relatively the same. The "establishment" has gone out of its way to discourage formation of group practices. State boards jealously guard their prerogative to determine by less relevant means, the rights of U.S. citizens to practice where they choose.

Dentistry can no longer state their primary objective is a deep concern for the dental health of the American people. Witness a recent statement issued by a group of west coast dental examiners and association officers meeting to discuss regional examinations: "We must first and foremost be concerned with how we are going to protect the Dental Profession in the three states." [1]

When members of the California dental establishment place a higher legislative priority on restricting the statute of limitations for malpractice over enactment of statewide fluoridation, then one must conclude that the dental health of the public is considered secondary to selfaggrandizement.

NOTE.—Presented by Dr. John Ingle, Dean, School of Dentistry, University of Southern California, Los Angeles, at the Conference of Dental Examiners and Dental Educators, February 11–12, 1972, Chicago, Illinois.

DENTAL DISEASE AND CARE

The national statistics on dental disease and dental care are appalling. Half the U.S. population is endentulous by age 65 and two-thirds by age 75 [2].

One out of every five Americans wears a full upper denture by age 35.[2]
Over 56 million teeth were extracted by U.S. dentists in 1969.[3]
There are over 800 million unfilled decayed teeth in the nation.[4]
The average 16 year old is missing 1.3 permanent teeth, has received only 1.6 fillings, and has 10 untreated decayed teeth.[2]
80% of our young adults suffer some form of periodontal disease.[4]
10% of the population account for two-thirds of all dental appointments.[5]
60% of the population did not visit the dentist last year.[5]
One out of every three persons had no dental visits in the preceeding five years.[5]
Non-white Americans averaged only 0.5 dental visits per year compared to white Americans with 1.7 annual visits, and non-white care was more likely to be extractions and dentures than prophylaxes and fillings.[6]
Far and away the most common single disease seen in the Head Start preschoolers was dental caries.[7]
Over half of all the health dollars spent by Operation Head Start go for dental care.[7]

NEED FOR A CHANGE

That an overhauling is needed of the entire health care delivery system, including dental care, is obvious. Many voices, large and small, cry out for change. But change is elusive.

The recent Carnegie Commission Report on Higher Education and the Nation's Health reiterated the position taken by the past three federal administrations—that health care is regarded not only as a necessity but also as a right to which all Americans are entitled. Speaking as Chairman of the Commision, Clark Kerr stated in November 1970, "No matter how many health professionals are educated . . . Americans will not receive adequate health care unless a system developed to deliver services to those who need them—regardless of income, geographich location, age, or race." The Commission then recommended that programs be developed for training physicians' and dentists' "associates" and assistants.

Speaking of the need for change in our health delivery system, Harold Hillenbrand, Emeritus Executive Director of the American Dental Association, has stated :[8]

"There are also those—whom I shall call dental fundamentalists—who look upon the traditional private practice system not as a means to an end, but an end in itself, and to change it so much as a jot or a tittle is to call down the wrath of nature and nature's god. I would suggest that these individuals note that the basic obligation of the dental profession is not to defend a system without regard to its purpose, but to demonstrate the ability of that system to give care to all who need it. As the circumstances of life are modified by history, so too are the methods by which we provide life-giving services."

Bruce Douglas, Professor of Oral Diagnosis at the University of Illinois and member of the Illinois legislature was recently moved to say :[9]

"We need a new philosophy of dental care in this country, and we need it now, or else—or else this great nation will tell us that we have failed in our task and take the initiative out of our hands."

Dr. Joseph T. Brophy, upon taking office as president of the Illinois State Dental Association recently stated, "In the past we have enjoyed the good fortune in meeting problems one at a time. In the seventies' world of lightening change—the problems seem to evolve full blown.—We face a multiplicity of problems which are crying for satisfactory solutions in the immediate future, that is spelled N-O-W."

Dr. Gerald R. Guine, Pittsburgh dental public health expert, addressing the American Dental Association in November 1970 stated:

"The country today is well into a transition from considering that health is largely an individual affair to understanding that health is necessarily a community affair . . .

"It should be perfectly obvious to any moderately careful observer of the health professions that the future holds drastic changes in the delivery of health care. The present system of practice simply cannot meet the present projected needs and demands for services."

And Edward L. Salkin, Chairman of the Dental Care Committee of the Orange County California Dental Society editorialized in January 1971:[10]

"What is the future of dental care: Can we turn back the clock or just stand still? Can we continue to serve our own best intersts and place the public second? Can we be autonomous and self regulatory? The automobile industry in America thought it could and one man named Ralph Nader taught them something about the public's best interests."

Dr. Harvey I. Wolf of Ann Arbor, Michigan, in a recent letter to the American Dental Association NEWS said:

". . . our cottage industry-type of delivery care is not and never will be able to cope with what people deserve to receive—health care as a right for everyone. If it has to take our government to lead the way into new means of delivering that care, then I laud it.Someone should have done it long ago."

The feeling that change is needed and is inevitable in the delivery of dental care is widespread. Where to start? by whom? and how? are the questions not resolved.

RECOMMENDATIONS

The American Dental Association long ago (1967) recommended a children's dental care program to Congress, and during the Johnson years of health legislation the program was passed by Congress but never funded.

While still Executive Director of the ADA, Harold Hillenbrand reinforced the earlier ADA stand when he stated in 1968:[8]

"Organized dentistry believes that the most realistic approach to this mountainous oral health problem must center on children. If we can arrange to bring up a generation of children in a state of good oral health it will be relatively simple to maintain that condition as the child moves through adult life."

As late as January, 1971, the ADA recommended[11] to the Nixon Administration that there could be an improvement "in the nation's dental health if there existed an appropriate national commitment to this end."

The three point attack on the problem, the ADA suggested, is in the areas of: Community and rural school fluoriadtion; Dental care for children; and Increasing dental care services and manpower supply.

In addition to this three point program the ADA House of Delegates had accepted and published by December 1971 the Guidelines for Dentistry's Postiion in a National Health Program presented for their approval by the ADA Task Force on National Health Programs. Again the number one priority was "comprehensive dental services for children."[12]

PROPOSAL

The program which I here propose is based upon the January 1971 ADA recommendations, but goes beyond the Task Force guidelines.

Along with the ADA, I first of all propose that a national fluoridation scheme be voted and funded by Congress with built-in persuasive inducements to states, municipalities and school districts. I suggest that federal funding of any health program such as Medicaid be contingent upon passage of proper state or local laws leading to fluoridation of all communal or school district water supplies. Overnight, with the passage of this legislation, the nation would be well on the road to a 60% reduction in dental caries. Control of periodontal disease and the remaining 40% of caries would in turn be contingent upon establishing a nationwide program in teaching proper oral hygiene.

The second and third parts of this proposal are based upon the ADA recommednations and are dependent upon each other—"a dental care program for children, delivering increased dental services through an increased dental manpower."

I propose a *school-based* program in prevention and therapy which will start with the children of the nation at age three and will continue their care and oversee their dental health through adolescence. At that age their dental needs can be cared for in the private offices and dental clinics of the nation, undoubtedly under one of the national health insurance plans presently forecast.

There is absolutely nothing new in this proposal. I cannot take credit for one original idea. To my knowledge these suggestions were first made by Guy Millberry in the AMERICAN JOURNAL OF PUBLIC HEALTH in April of 1939, nearly one-third of a century ago.[13] Millberry's recommendations were scaracely noticed except for John Oppie McCall who in 1944 spelled out in detail a program which embarrassingly reads today like a combination of the Task Force Report and present day recommendations by the U.S. Public Health Service.[14] One has to ask where we have been for the past quarter century.

I only hope these ancient suggestions, brough again to light, will serve as a catalyst to amalgamate present day thought into action so desperately needed. If we are to be honest as a nation; if we are to maintain our integrity as a health profession, we simply must do somethings about the lost half of the American people—those 50% to 60% who never or rarely see a dentist. We must break the cycle! As Harold Hillenbrand stated the place to start is with a new generation—with the children in school.

What I am proposing is a nationwide dental health program home-based in the nation's elementary schools. Under the supervision of the profession, a totally new category of dental paraprofessionals, who might be called "School Dental Therapists," backed in turn by a corps of assistants, will be responsible for a well organized and aggresive program in prevention and treatment. The School Dental Therapists will be trained specifically and limited to restoring carious teeth, treating initial periodontal conditions, extracting deciduous teeth and guarding the integrity of the dental arches by space maintenance. They will be trained to make their own examinations, diagnosis and treatment plan. They will be thoroughly trained to make their own injections and carry out a full scale preventive program. In all of this they will be *remotely supervised* by the dental profession and will be assisted by the School Dental Therapist Assistants.

All else will be referred out of the school clinic to the profession.

As I have said, there is nothing new in this plan. As a matter of fact, it was fifty years old last year. The School Dental Nurse Program, which began in New Zealand in 1921, has achieved worldwide acclamation and enjoys universal acceptance by the profession and government in that nation.

First of all, let us look at the New Zealand Dental Nurse Plan through a report by Dr. G. H. Leslie, Director of the New Zealand Division of Dental Health:[15]

"In 1921 the first group of 25 young women commenced to train as school dental nurses . . . Concern was understandable, but to its lasting credit the New Zealand Dental Association was prepared to risk an unorthodox approach to dental health if it would benefit children at a time when dental disease was rampant in the youth of New Zealand and many children failed to reach adulthood with their own teeth . . .

"The School Dental Nurse soon earned a permanent place in the health team and is now a normal feature of our way of life. Almost every primary and intermediate school with 100 children has its own clinic and its own nurse, and these facilities are available to other smaller schools in the district. The children, whose ages range from 5 to 13, are regularly examined and treated. The proximity of the dental nurse minimizes interruption of formal lessions, and enables her to give classroom instruction in dental health . . .

"What is there to show for 50 years? As all dentists know, there is more than one yardstick to measure the success of a dental service, and punch cards and computers cannot supply all the answers; the realistic view is that results must be judged in terms of human benefits and the resources available to provide them . . . In 1923 the first group of 29 school dental nurses completed training and were stationed at make-shift clinics with simple and often primitive equipment. In the first year 23,750 fillings and 18,674 extractions were recorded, a ratio of 78.6 extractions for every 100 fillings. By 1933, the 166 dental nurses in the field inserted 397,437 fillings and extracted 69,208 teeth for 78,391 children, a ratio for 17.4 extractions for every 100 fillings, or 88.2 extractions, including 3.0 permanent teeth, per 100 children. In 1968 the 1,334 school dental nurses inserted 2,714,342 fillings and extracted 71,403 unsavable teeth for 568,119 children. This figure, together with 7,427 teeth extracted for School Dental Service by contracting dentists, represented a ratio of 2.9 extractions for every 100 fillings, or 13.9 extractions, including (0.23 permanent teeth) per 100 children . . .

"On the basis of reduced tooth mortality the New Zealand system has been most successful. For the first 10 years the reduction was dramatic; it has been more gradual since, and may not fall much lower. So few permanent teeth now need extracting (23 in 10,000 children) that the three schools for dental nurses no longer teach this subject. If a permanent tooth has to be extracted, the nurse refers the child to a dentist. While the New Zealand scheme might appear as only a repair service (certainly, statistics showing a high output of treatment are a constant reminder of the need for greater preventive effort), nevertheless, the School Dental Service can claim some success . . .

"Since the inception of the Service the enrollment of preschool children has been persistently encouraged. In 1949 only 19% of all children in New Zealand between the ages of 2½ and 5 were enrolled at school dental clinics; the figure is now 59%. Since these crildren are relatively inaccessible, it speaks well for the interest the school dental nurse has created in dental health among parents . . . Improvement has occurred in the dentition of these children. In 1950 the mean number of decayed extracted or filled decisuous teeth at ages 2, 3, 4, and 5 respectively were 1.76, 4.19, 6.41 and 7.45. In 1966 (at the last survey) the figures were 0.77, 2.35, 4.21 and 5.17 (and at this date the national effect of fluoridation of public water supplies was limited). Expressed another way, 13.5% of children commencing school at 5 years of age in 1950 were caries-free; in 1966 the figure has risen to 28% . . .

"What of the results in terms of human experience? More than half the children who commence school each year are already seasoned attenders at the local (school) dental clinic. They have no fear of the dental nurse, or of a dentist; they have learned to accept the dental nurse as a member of the school staff, and the dental clinic is as familiar to them as the classroom. Under such circumstances it is not surprising that fear arising from anxiety and imagination is something now quite foreign to school children in New Zealand . . . Treatment beyonl the scope of the dental nurse is provided by private dental practitioners, and they too find that the children attend them without concern. The value of such results cannot be measured—they are priceless . . . Reprinted with permission from Dental Survey, October 1970."

Sir John Walsh, Dean of the dental profession in New Zealand emphasized the success of the dental nurse program in another way—comparing dental care in New Zealand with the U.S.A.:[16]

"It is . . . interesting to compare today the standard of dental care of the children in the United States of America with New Zealand . . . in New Zealand 93% of school children receive regular dental care. Throughout the school age group an average of 72% of all carious teeth have been treated. In the United States 50% of children have never seen a dentist in their lives and throughout the school age group an average of 23% of decaved teeth are filled. For deciduous teeth, in New Zealand for children aged 6 to 12 years, 91% of decayed teeth are filled; in the United States for the same age group 27% of decayed teeth are filled. Stadt, et al, show that even in families in the top socio-economic group only 50% of the decayed deciduous teeth in children aged 5 years had been filled. Where is the dental care substandard?

"The only countries in the world who can match the standard of dental care of the children in New Zealand are the Scandinavian countries. Countries which rely on the parents seeking and paying for the professional services of the private dentist in order to meet the dental needs of children lag far behind countries which have an organized program of child care based on cooperation between state and professional sources."

And in the same article, Walsh has shown dramatically the embarrassing difference in dental care for children, as indexed by tooth surfaces filled, in ratio to the decayed, missing and filled surfaces for ages 6-12 in each of 5 nations. See fig. 1

These impressive statistics clearly demonstrate to the profession, government and lay public alike, the level of dental care which can be achieved by auxiliaries to the profession, properly trained and supervised. That the United States of America should enjoy something less that this is a national tragedy.

PERSONNEL

If school dental clinics were to be established in the United States, who would staff them? Surely not the dentists, nor the present-day dental hygienists for that matter. There are 85,177 elementary schools in this nation[17] and only 90,000 practicing dentists and 15,000 dental hygienists. Who would man the dental offices of the nation if this national resource all marched off to work in the nation's schools.

To staff a program of this size two entirely new categories of dental auxiliaries would have to be trained and supervised—the School Dental Therapist and his (or her) assistant.

The delineation of duties between these two new auxiliaries, and between them and the profession, must be well spelled-out. Surely they should be well enough trained to work on their own, without the wasteful direct and constant supervision by dentists which is usually suggested. Just as in New Zealand, occasional and comprehensive evaluations would be carried out by dentist supervisors.

"Where would these new people come from and how would they be trained? First, in the case of the School Therapist, I am suggesting that new training centers be established—perferably in the junior colleges and in so far as possible, under the supervision of a school of dentistry. Dental schools themselves should undertake the training of the first School Therapists—the pioneers and future teachers. The program should allow for upward mobility—dental auxiliaries from the armed forces, dental hygienists and dental assistants moving up to new responsibilities. In addition, men and women should also enter the training program from high school or college.

THE RATIO F:DMF PERCENT
(AGE POOLED)

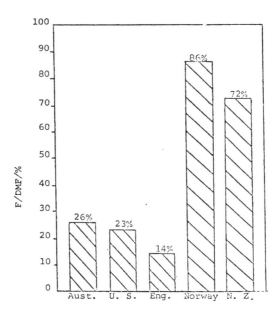

Fig. 1   Comparison of the percentage of decayed teeth which have been filled in Australia, United States, England, Norway, and New Zealand. The illustration shows clearly the effects of cooperation between the profession and the government, as compared with countries where cooperation is less well developed.

The School Dental Therapist should be licensed to practice *only* in school clinics. Under no circumstances should they be allowed to practice in dental offices or group clinics. If they were allowed to practice outside of the schools I visualize them being sidetracked into solo dental offices and huge clinics where they would no longer be caring for the children for whom they have been trained to serve, but working rather as second rate dentists treating the adult population. This has been tried in other countries, notably Germany, and inevitably has led to lower standards and rejection of the program.

These people must be carefully selected, for they will have to relate positively to children and get along well with the assistants under their supervision, as well as the teachers and administrators of the school where they are based. They must also be able to take orders from the district dental supervisor and must be mature enough to handle emotional situations which arise from patients or staff.

The School Dental Therapist must be taught his limitations, and will refer-out to the profession, all treatment beyond his skill or training. I am suggesting for instance, all oral surgery of permanent teeth all orthodontics, all endodontics of permanent teeth, all advanced periodontics, and all prosthodontics be referred.

The Therapist would be either male or female and should be trained in something less than two academic years in the case of the applicant entirely new to dentistry, or one year in the case of a dental hygienist or returning federal service personnel who have been serving as dental assistants, hygienists or technicians and who attended one of the service schools for training. Upward mobility, without a time penalty, must also become available to all Therapists who aspire to continue their education and become a dentist.

In September 1970 I pointed out to the Department of Health, Education and Welfare that 2,600 dental auxiliaries are being separated from the armed services each year and that these people are fairly sophisticated in the dental field—know the nomenclature and instruments, and have been closely associated with dental treatment as auxiliaries. They might well be motivated to continue as School Dental Therapists. Generally speaking the ex-service personnel, particularly the men, cannot get a civilian job as an assistant, and also, in the case of the men, they feel insecure as dental hygienists in the civilian milieu.

In the case of the civilian dental hygienist, there should also be upward mobility possible for emotionally mature women, and in their case, one academic year of training should suffice to produce a skilled School Therapist.

Skilled and trained civilian dental assistants should also be able to achieve admission to the School Dental Corps ranks through additional training. For all previous categories, and for the dental assistant in particular, pretesting should be done to establish the level of knowledge, skill and maturity.

Under no circumstances should rigid rules be established regarding admission requirements or length of education. Logical criteria for completion must be established, and when a candidate reaches this level he should be "graduated." The programs should allow for selpacing. School systems are familiar with the "practice teacher" serving an internship. So too should the neophyte School Therapist be allowed to intern in the school clinics under a more experienced Therapist.

For this new category of professionals, I question the validity of review and examination by the state boards of examiners. A new review "board" should be established and made up of public health personnel, dental educators, public school representatives and faculty from the training programs. Examination should be an on-site experience and since hopefully, the Therapists will not be "graduating" en masse, they can be "examined" in the school clinic environment on many different occasions. Re-examination and "re-certification" is imperative—lifetime "licensing" or certification should be forbidden by law. Moreover, dental supervisory personnel should have the power of instant dismissal (subject to review, of course) in the event abusive or recalcitrant behavior can be documented. Poor work quality should be a reason for instant dismissal.

"In 1949, Massachusetts introduced an experimental dental care program for children. The bill directed the Department of Public Health of the State of Massachusetts to establish a 5-year reasearch program to test the New Zealand system of dental care for children. The bill, 714, was rescinded within one year, the main objection being that substandard dentistry was being offered." [16]

I contend the Massachusetts baby was thrown out with the bath. The participants could hardly have been properly trained in one year; nor should the entire program have been torpedoed. Rather, the "substandard" personnel should have been retained or only the impossible dismissed. One would suspect that a great deal of "dental politics" came to play in putting down this first American experiment.

As New Zealand has shown, the educational offerings in the school dental nurse training program must be carefully planned and programmed. Manuals must be produced for every course, and upon completion, manuals must also be written to cover the evantualities of school clinic practice, including a manual for school teachers explaining the program and their role in it.[13]

In New Zealand, each school dental nurse treats about 450-500 patients depending on whether the local water supply is fluoridated or not.* I contend that in the United States, the School Dental Therapist, backed by a corps of assistants could be responsible for more that twice this number of children.

As previously stated, there are 85,000 elementary schools in the United States. In these schools are 27,500,000 students, or an average of 320 students per school. In actuality, there must be a natural spread in the number of students per school, ranging from a few in some rural elementary schools to over 1,000 in some crowded urban centers. Assignment of the School Therapist to handle 500 school children and a like number of preschoolers would suggest mobility for some Therapisits and fixed assignment for others.

If the program is extended through age 15, there are 58,000,000 children to be treated. Just moving 58,000,000 children from homes and schools to dental offices and clinics is a massive transportation problem rather than a public health problem. Also consider that most children are accompanied by an adult, and 58,000,000 dental visists by children now involves over half of the population of the United states just getting children to dental offices. The problem is staggering—moving 116,000,000 people, just for one dental appointment, let alone multiple appointments.

In any case, each school, with or without a fulltime Therapist should be equipped with adequate facilities to handle the students in attendance and their preschool siblings. Every effort should be made to render dental care and preventive measures without moving the children from their environment. Flexibility in assignment of the Therapist must be counter-balanced by fixed assignment of their assistants.

Each school clinic should be staffed with the necessary number of assistants to establish and maintain proper oral health measures, to control caries and dental plaque and to maintain a continuing dialog with the parents of the students.

If the New Zealand program has any faults it was their early failure to develop a complete preventive dentistry program. They are the first to admit they have been slow to utilize auxiliary help, both for the dentist and the school dental nurse. Even the dental hygienist is relatively new in New Zealand.

Although the school dental nurse has been doing more in preventive education than is done in the United States this is evidently not enough. In spite of reinforcement of toothbrushing methods every six months, the New Zealand caries rate for permanent teeth has changed very little (except in fluoridated areas) over the past 20 years.

To some extent New Zealand school teachers assume part of the dental health responsibility as do the nurse trainees. Admittedly, this has not been entirely satisfactory and dental caries continues unabated to repeatedly challenge the school dental nurse.

An American improvement upon the New Zealand program would be to assign to each School Dental Therapist a number of indigenous paraprofessionals the School Dental Therapists' assistants.

INDIGENOUS PARAPROFESSIONAL

To be successful, particularly in the areas of cities where economically disadvantaged children attend school in great numbers, the School Dental Therapist must be backed by a small corps of assistants who would serve on the

---

*The dental nurse in a fluoridated region places the same number of restorations as the nurse in a nonfluoridated area, but has to see twice as many patients to achieve this goal.

paraprofessional level. These people should be indigenous to the area of the school. ..

Frankenburg, et al, have shown the importance and success in selecting neighborhood girls to conduct medical screening in poverty areas.[19]

"The indigenously poor offer a vast pool of insufficiently used manpower and talent. The challenge is to successfully train these people for careers in which manpower shortages exist now and in the future." Frankenburg also points out the importance of allowing for upward mobility in a program of this type.

DUTIES

The duties of these assistants, as I presently see it, would be manifold. And in this variety of duties will lie the key to success—mobility, self dependence and lack of boredom.

First of all I visualize these people serving as chairside assistants to the School Dental Therapist—handing him (or her) instruments, preparing for treatment, and cleaning up following treatment. They also would be responsible for appointments and record keeping, ordering and stocking supplies.

On a rotational basis, the School Dental Assistant would work on her own at one of the clinic chairs, performing prophylaxis, applying the newly emerging pit and fissure sealants,[20] as well as topical fluorides,[21] There is recent evidence that even in water fluoridated areas, repeated topical fluoride applications reduce dental caries further yet.[22] This had already been demonstrated in nonfluoridated areas.[23] The School Dental Assistant could also be trained to insert carve and polish restorations.

In addition to her rotational clinic duties, the School Dental Assistant and possibly the Therapist, would be responsible for a certain number of classrooms—conducting "brushins" with pastes containing fluorides. She would also be responsible for the dental health in the rooms assigned to "her" and would do the dental screening for those rooms as well as the continually conducted home care and brushing instructions. If ten rooms were assigned to each Assistant, "she" could visit each room every two weeks, conducting individual and group sessions of brushing and home care. Real competition to have the best "homerooms" might motivate these "girls" to "mother over" their responsibilities to be sure they are the best, i.e., lowest caries rate, lowest periodontal indices, etc. Rewards could be worked out to improve morale.

There is no question that proper care of the oral cavity may be learned in infancy. The methods of tooth and gum brushing and dental flossing developed by Bass and long advocated by Arnim, Barkley and others, are now being used to indoctrinate children in proper oral hygiene at a very early age. "Brain washing", if you will, of pre-school children, followed by constant reinforcement throughout the primary years will do more to spell the demise of the dental plaque than any amount of adult education. Plaque removal as an accepted and natural way of life for children, will essentially solve the problems of periodontal disease and dental caries beyond fluoridation.

The final duty of the School Dental Assistant would be to act as a dental health visitor to the homes of her "children". There she would encourage parental cooperation and involvement in plaque control. She would advise the mother about proper diet for her children, show the mother the proper toothbrushing and flossing techniques, check the child's "at home" toothbrush and supply toothbrushes and floss so each child in the family has the proper tools for dental hygiene.

She would also screen the preschool children in the home and encourage the parent to bring these children first into the school dental clinic at ages 2½ to 3. In New Zealand today, 59% of the nation's 2½ to 5 year old preschoolers are attending the school dental clinics.

Serving in the capacity of dental health visitor, the School Assistant should also keep her eyes open for early defects and lesions other than dental. Frankenburg has shown that the Denver indigenous technicians uncovered numerous previously unsuspected health problems while screening 3,000 children.[19]

Frankenburg has also shown that the indigenous nonprofessional, "who shares a common ethnic origin, language, religious and group interest, and is also poor," is ideally suited to bridge the gap between the skilled professional (or paraprofessional) and the poor. He points out further, they "may be in the best position to ward off the suspicion, distrust and obsequiousness which too often characterize the attitude of the poor toward professionals of dissimilar background." [19]

That young women are presently being trained to serve in some of these listed capacities is of interest. Operation Head Start has a pilot training project of this nature in the Virgin Islands. Head Start is also training young women in Mississippi to serve as "dental health visitors." [7]

In Alaska, The Yukon-Kuskokowin Health Corporation, an affiliate of the Alaska Federation of Native, in an even more aggressive program, is "training village people to become health aides." This includes a dental health education program, "which means a complete preventive program." [24]

Where would these people; these assistants, screeners, home-visitor personnel come from" They should be selected in so far as possible from the neighborhoods of the schools, as Frankenburg has proven successfully. This should apply to middle class and suburban neighborhoods as well.

Although a high school degree might be tempting as a prerequisite for training, Frankenburg has shown that more important criteria such as "financial need, socio-ethnic origin, bilingualism, area of residence, age and sex" were very important selection factors. Moreover, the candidates should be thoroughly acquainted with the career for which they are applying.

"Thorough familiarity reduces the loss of personnel due to misunderstanding of what is entatiled in the work." [19]

I would not imagine that youngsters just out of high school or school dropouts would necessarily make the best personnel, although they should not be denied application Being a successful mother might be a good selection criteria. This would allow upward mobility for indigent women now serving as domestic help. They are completely part of their own community yet have been successfully functioning in a middle and upper class milieu. They also are raising their own children which gives them some expertise in this area.

Frankenburg warns, however, that "one error frequently made by persons selecting career applicants among the indigenous poor is the selection of those without firm roots in their community." [19]

The training of these people should be limited in length of time. Again, a lock step program should be avoided. By pretesting and testing, those capable of rapid advancement should be allowed to do so. Six months should be the outside limit of a well structured program.

Vocational training of this type should probably be carried on in vocational training schools. Initially, professionals would do the teaching, but eventually good teachers should emerge from the ranks of those trained, and then they in turn should be allowed the upward mobility of becoming the teachers.

As previously stated, the School Dental Therapist Assistant would be supervised by the Therapist who in turn would be supervised by a dentist supervisor who has a number of schools as his responsibility and who in turn is responsible to the health department. A great deal about establishing hierarchy could be learned from existing programs. To repeat again, at all levels, the supervisors, paraprofessionals and nonparaprofessionals should be repeatedly examined to measure their continued competence.

THE DENTAL PROFESSION

What then would be left for the dental profession, particularly the pedodontist? I would envision that the pedodontist for years to come will be busy caring for the small percentage of the population he now sees from the middle class. Even if a program of this type becomes a reality, enough parents would perfer that their children go to the dentist rather than be stigmatized by treatment in a school clinic.

In addition, if the entire child population is being screened through the school clinic program rather than only 40-50% as now, enough serious dental treatment will be referred from the school clinics to pedodontists, orthodontists, oral surgeons, endodontists, etc., to more than keep them busy. And they will be able to devote themselves to diagnosing and treating really serious problems, rather than being bogged down in the morass of present unmet dental needs.

By breaking the cycle of overwhelming dental caries and periodontal disease, the dentist of the near future, along with his team of expanded duty auxiliaries, will have a chance to managing the onslaught of dental patients who will report for treatment when a national health scheme is passed.

Just by removing a number of patients under 15 years of age from the nation's offices and clinics, the way will be cleared to better care for the adolescents and adults who follow.

Just by having these adolescents report to dental practices with mouths less than "bombed out," as presently seen, will allow the profession for the first time to "get a handle" on dental health.

The economic impact of a program of this type would be hard to measure. The reduction in time loss alone, for dental disease and treatment by dentists, to the adult working population is inestimable. Think of the time lost in the replacement of even a small percentage of these teeth.

One might well ask, "How can the nation possibly afford a program of this type?" The answer should be, "How can we afford *not* to?" But then this answer could be applied to all our current problems—housing, slums, pollution, racism, education, etc.

There should be a way to pay for the operation of the clinical program. It could be financed from benefits from the national health scheme predicted to soon pass Congress. Some of the present plans call for dental care up to age 15 with one year of age added incrementally each year. Fees for the dental work done for children in the school dental clinics could be paid to city or regional school or health departments earmarked to support the school dental health program. If the same fee schedule is allowable as in private practice, enough funds should be generated to support training programs in the junior colleges or occupational schools as well. There should also be sufficient funds available under the national health plan to pay dentists for the therapy on patients referred to them from the school clinics.

Establishment of training programs could be financed under present or emerging federal statutes designed to broaden the types and number of auxiliaries needed in dentistry. Present legislation can fund training programs for Dental Therapists. Both Congress and the Public Health Service have a long history of support for logical and needed health programs.

The great barrier reef to establishing school dental clinics is of course the dental practice act of each state. Enabling legislation would have to be passed in all 50 states unless federal legislation could be written to cover the entire nation.

I am sure a great many members of the dental profession will look upon a program of this type as the death knell for dentistry. I cannot believe this will prove true. It may solve the problem, however, of building more multimillion dollar dental schools to train more and more dentists. There is not a thing I have suggested here in the way of therapy that could not be done by a paraprofessional trained in a fraction of the time it takes to educate professionals. These paraprofessionals, the School Dental Therapist and Assistants alike, should be well paid, but at a level well below the professional who has devoted six to eight years of his life being educated as a professional.*

The dentist as the professional of the near future will undoubtedly serve as chief diagnostician, treatment planner, surgeon, occulsionist, orthodontist, and advanced restorative dentist. Fixed prosthodontics will be a major responsibility. Full denture construction in the future will undoubtedly become the responsibility of technicians serving under supervision by dentists expert in the field.

I also assume that dental hygienists as well as the dentists will be shaken by the suggestions made here. On the contrary, the present-day dental hygienist must herself become upwardly mobile—must become a future dental therapist, so to say, to perform many of the duties now exclusive to dentists. She should become a true member of the dental team, no longer working alone but directly with the dentist. Her new role must be initial information gathering as well as root planning and soft tissue management under local anesthesia she herself administers. Surgical post operative care would also be her responsibility as well as the placement and finishing of restorations in cavities prepared by dentists. If she chooses to serve as a School Dental Therapist, she would take additional training for these expanded duties of cavity preparation, diagnosis,

---

*A profession is an occupation for which the necessary preliminary training is intellectual in character, involving knowledge and, to some extent, *learning* as distinguished from mere skill.

1351

etc. In any event, the presently operating dental hygienist will have to be retrained to become a member of the newly emerging dental team.

It is an occupation which is pursued largely for others, and not merely for one's self. It is an occupation in which the amount of financial return is not the accepted measure of success—Supreme Court Justice Louis D. Brandeis.

I am particularly disturbed by the retraining program presently funded by the NIH and private sources at one of the large eastern dental clinics. If I understand this program correctly, dental hygienists are being restrained to give local anesthetics, prepare cavities and place and carve fillings for all patients, adults and children alike, under the direct supervision of dentists in offices or clinics.

In this I see the emergence of a second class dentist—girls trained in a quarter of the time it takes to train a true professional, but gradually becoming dental Trilbys to professional Svangalis. In contrast, the School Dental Therapist will be very limited in training, in age of patient, in location of clinic solely to schools and in the type of therapy to be rendered.

Group practice is where all of this will happen, not in the present solo offices of the nation. But again, there is nothing original in these predictions. "The end of the solo . . ." said Robert Hutchins in a speech discussing the cooperative effort necessary for any endeavor today; but the end of the solo will hardly evolve for dentistry in the foreseeable future. Plenty of fine solo practices will be around in generations to come. But the profession must steel itself and renew itself through continuing education if it is to meet the massive social changes on the horizon.

REFERENCES

[1] Minutes of Ad-Hoc Committee to Study Regional Examinations for Licensure. Portland, Oregon, August 22, 1970.
[2] U.S. Department of Health, Education and Welfare, Public Health Service, Health Statistics from the U.S. National Health Survey: Loss of Teeth. PHS Publication No. 585–B22, Washington, D. C., U.S. Government Printing Office, 1967.
[3] Dummett, Clifton O., "Year 2000 Community Dentistry," Journal of The American Dental Association, 280–85, February, 1971.
[4] Bohannan, Harry M., et al, "A Concept of the Flexible Dental Curriculum." Read before the 27th Congress on Dental Education and Licensure, Chicago, February, 1971.
[5] U.S. Department of Health, Education and Welfare, Public Health Service, Health Statistics from the U.S. National Health Survey: Dental Care, Interval and Frequency of Visits, United States, July 1957–June 1959 PHS Publication No. 584–B14, Washington, D. C. U.S. Government Printing Office, 1960.
[6] Friedman, Jay W., The Dental Care Program of the Los Angeles Hotel-Restaurant Employer Union Welfare Fund. UCLA Press, 1970.
[7] Hunter, Gertrude, M.D. Director of Health Services, Project Head Start. Personal Communication.
[8] Hillenbrand, H., "Problems of Dental Care in the United States." Harvard Dental Alumni Bulletin Special Supplement: 6–9, November, 1968.
[9] Douglas, Bruce L., "Our Greatest Challenge: A Grave Warning from Washington." New York State Dental Journal, 9:556–7, November, 1969.
[10] Salkin, Edward S., "Review of Dental Care Committee Activities." Bulletin of the Orange County Dental Society, 4–6, January, 1971.
[11] Editorial, "Dental Priorities Detailed for Nixon." ADA News, January 4, 1970.
[12] ADA Guidelines for Dentistry's Position in a National Health Program. Journal of the American Dental Association, 83:1225–33, December, 1971.
[13] Millberry, Guy S., "Possibilities and Means of Improving Dental Conditions in the United States." American Journal of Public Health, 29:321–25, April, 1939.
[14] McCall, John Oppie, "Dental Practice and Dental Education in the Future; With Consideration of Social and Health Aspects." Journal of the American Dental Association, 31:16–30. January 1, 1944.
[15] Leslie, G.H., "Dental Auxiliaries for One-Half A Century," Dental Magazine and Oral Topics, 87:1, February, 1970.
[16] Walsh, John, "International Patterns of Oral Health Care—The Example of New Zealand," New Zealand Dental Journal, 66:143–152, April, 1970.
[17] Statistical Abstract of the United States for 1970. U.S. Department of Commerce, Bureau of the Census, 1970, p. 102.
[18] "Dental Health Education: A Handbook for New Zealand Teachers." Pamphlet No. 132, The Department of Health, New Zealand.
[19] Frankenburg, William K., et al, "Training the Indigenous Nonprofessional: The Screening Technician." Journal of Pediatrics, 77:564–70, October, 1970.
[20] "Epoxylite Fissure Sealant," Technical Bulletin No. 9075, The Epoxylite Corporation, South El Monte, California.
[21] "Epoxylite Fissure Sealant and Topical Fluoride Coating." Supplementary Technical Bulletin No. 9070, December 15, 1970.
[22] Englander, Harold, et al, "Incremental Rates of Dental Caries After Repeated Topical Sodium Fluoride Applications In Children with Lifelong Consumption of Fluoridated Water." Journal of the American Dental Association, 82:354–8, February, 1971.
[23] Englander, Harold, et al, "Clinical Anticaries Effect of Repeated Sodium Applications by Mouth Pieces." Journal of the American Dental Association, 75:638, September, 1967, and Journal of the American Dental Association, 78:783, April, 1969.
[24] Miller, Edward F. Personal communication to Clifton O. Dummett, February 2, 1971.

Enclosure 4

COMMUNITY DENTISTRY—SCHOOL DENTAL THERAPISTS: A CONTROVERSAL PROPOSAL

The health care professions have been challenged to modify the delivery of care to accommodate a changing society. Projections of population growth, need and demand for care and health manpower all suggest increasing difficulty in fulfilling demand for health care in the relatively near future.

Much in the dental literature indicates that the challenge to change is causing major conflict within the profession. Some dentists do not acknowledge the need for change. There is much disagreement over the most desirable kinds of change, as well as the *speed* of change necessary. Often proposed changes bring vitriolic responses from dentists who feel that their cherished values or economic security are threatened by the proposals.

An instructive example of conflict generated by challenges to improve the delivery of dental care is the current controversy over a proposal by John Ingle, Dean, University of Southern California School of Dentistry. As the following material demonstrates, the response of the profession has been prompt and, in some cases, severe.

"Material illustrating the debate over Dean Ingle's proposal has been assembled and presented to the student as in instructional exercise for several reasons:

(1) It indicates the degree of change in the delivery of dental care under consideration by at least a few concerned dentists.

(2) It illustrates some standard arguments which are a routine part of most discussions of expanded duty dental auxiliaries as well as some of the tactics encountered when significant change is proposed.

(3) It suggests the *basic data* which are essential to an informed opinion on the need for change and an intelligent response to specific proposals for change.

As you read the following material keep in mind the following questions: What basic informaion (facts) do I need to: (a) evaluate Dr. Ingle's proposal; (b) evaluate the claims of those who oppose the proposal; (c) propose alternatives to Dr. Ingle's proposal.

In asking and answering the foregoing questions consider yourself a professional person concerned enough to write a letter to the editor of the *Journal of the American Dental Association*, or an editorial in the publication of your local dental society. Such an assignment is probably a relevant educational experience; you will almost surely encounter very similar debates in your professional career.

A BRIEF REPORT OF THE PROPOSAL

The following report appeared in the March-April, 1972 issue of the *Journal of Dentistry for Children*.

'BLOOD PRESSURES RISE AND TEMPERS FLARE AS USC DEAN AND ENDODONTISTS OFFERS PLAN FOR CHILDREN'S DENTAL CARE

"Addressing an audience of 400 at the Conference of Dental Examiners and Dental Educators, Dr. John Ingle criticized American dentistry for not facing up to the vast responsibilities being forced on it. He accused the profession of being unprepared educationally, physically, emotionally, and numerically to accept the challenges of the 70's. He claims that curriculum changes have been minor and state boards have interfered with the right of U.S. citizens to practice where they choose. He provided well known statistics on the dental conditions of the American public to emphasize his call for a change. Many leaders in the dental profession were quoted in support of his statements.

"Dr. Ingle proposed a national fluoridaiton scheme to be voted and funded by the Congress with built-in inducements tot compel states to comply. He continued by recommending a school-based program in prevention and therapy to begin at age three and to continue through adolescence. He reminded his audience that Dr. Guy Millberry and Dr. John Oppie McCall had made the same recommendations more than a quarter of a century ago.

"The speaker proposed a nationwide dental health program based in the elementary schools. Under the supervision of the profession a new category of dental auxiliary, called school dental therapists and backed by a corps of dental assistants, will be responsible for a program of prevention and treatment.

These therapists will be trained and limited to restoring carious teeth, treating early peridontal conditions, extracting primary teeth, and placing space maintainers. They will make mouth examinations, diagnose, and prepare treatment plans. They will be trained, also, to make injections. The speaker stressed that they would be remotely supervised by the dental profession.

"The audience had just listened passively to a report by Dr. Jay W. Friedman on the successes of the School Dental Nurse Program in New Zealand—but, then New Zealand is half way around the world from Chicago."

Question: What are the two major elements of Dr. Ingle's proposal?

Question: To what specific operations would school dental therapists be limited under the proposal?

Question: What does the phrase ". . . remotely supervised by the dental profession" mean?

PROFESSIONAL RESPONSE TO THE PROPOSAL

"The following article appeared in the *ADA News*, June 5, 1972. It suggests the ADA's position on the training and use of auxiliaries. It is possible that the ADA testimony before the subcommittee was to some degree directed toward Dr. Ingle's proposal.

"Dr. Ingle also appeared before the same Senate subcommittee to present his school dental therapist proposal.

"The remainder of the article reports comments by ADA President Carl A. Laughlin on Dr. Ingle's proposal.

"ADA ASKS FOR 5-YEAR EXTENSION OF AUXILIARY TRAINING SUPPORT—SENATORS HEAR INGLE EXPLAIN SCHOOL DENTAL THERAPIST PLAN

WASHINGTON—The American Dental Association has recommended to Congress that it extend for five years legislation supporting the training of a wide range of allied health workers, including the three traditional dental auxiliaries.

Robert I. Kaplan of Cherry Hill, N.J., told the Senate subcommittee on health that 'the dental profession has long recognized the essential role played by its dental auxiliaries' and said that there is 'an appropriate place for federal participation' in operations and construction support of auxiliary training program as well as scholarship and loan assistance to students.

Dr. Kaplan, who was representing both the ADA and the American Association of Dental Schools, was joined in testimony by Mrs. Diane McCain, president of the American Dental Hygienists' Association, and Mrs. Iva Coulter, president of the American Dental Assistants Association.

The legislation to which the dental groups were addressing themselves—the Allied Health Professions Personnel Training Act—is due to expire at the end of the coming fiscal year. Extension of it was being conisdered in open hearing by the Senate health subcommittee, chaired by Sen. Edward M. Kennedy (D.-Mass.).

Dr. Kaplan, a member of the ADA Council on Dental Health, pointed out that two distinct questions needed to be considered in discussing the role of auxiliaries: The number of available auxiliaries and the duties that can be responsibly delegated to them.

With respect to supply, the joint statement noted that 'there are not now and never have been sufficient numbers of hygienists, assistants, or laboratory technicians.' Existing training programs, the joint testimony state, are insufficient to produce the needed numbers.

While private and nonfederal public sources can be expected to continue to contribute to the training of increased numbers of well-trained auxiliaries, the federal government can also be rightfully expected to help, Dr. Kaplan said. In this respect, the dental witnesses submitted to the subcommittee a number of policy statements contained in the ADA's *Guidelines for Dentistry's Position in a National Health Program* that recommend various kinds of federal assistance to dental auxiliary education.

Dr. Kaplan and his associates were critical of the past funding of the allied Health Professions Personnel Training Act and called for a fiscal 1973 appropriation of $103.8 million, rather than the $35.6 million requested by the administration.

With respect to expanded duties of dental auxiliaries, the dental groups took note that 'substantial and fruitful activity has begun in exploring · · · what duties can be reasonably delegated to dental auxiliaries · · · In the past five years, some 40 states have made changes either in their laws or regulations in the direction of greater flexibility' with respect to auxiliary duties.

Dr. Kaplan cautioned, however, that it would not 'serve the present or future needs of the American people to move with undue haste' in making final decisions on auxiliary duties. While emphatically endorsing 'responsible experimentation of expanded function auxiliaries,' Dr. Kaplan said, 'We think . . . that the phrase 'with all deliberate speed' is applicable . . . Deliberate should not be allowed to lapse into lethargy but neither should rapid progress degenerate into haste.'

On the same day of hearing, the Senate health subcommittee also heard from an independent dental witness who called for 'a totally new approach, in this country, to the delivery of dental care' by creation of a new 'category of dental paraprofessionals, who might be called 'school dental therapists'.'

John I. Ingle, Dean of the University of Southern California School of Dentistry, told the subcommittee that the school detnal therapist would be based in the nation's 85,177 elementary schools with the 'primary responsibility' for a 'full program in prevention and dental plaque control.'

'They would be trained specifically, and limited to, restoring carious teeth, treating initial periodontal conditions, extracting deciduous teeth and guarding the integrity of the dental arches by simple space maintenance. In addition, they would be trained to make their own examinations, and treatment plans, as well as their own injections of local anesthetics. In all of this, they would be carefully supervised by the dental profession. . . .'

Dean Ingle appeared at the invitation of the subcommittee. The California educator was appearing independently and was not representing any dental orgnaization. He was accompanied by Jay W. Friedman, a USC dental school faculty member. His statement was not directed to the legislation being considered, nor did it offer any suggested amendments to it.

Dean Ingle previously proffered essentially the same plan in articles and speeches aimed at dental audiences. As he noted in his congressional testimony, the pattern of procedure he suggests is 'hardly new in the world. As a matter of fact, the plan was 50 years old last year. The school dental nurse program, which began in New Zealand in 1921, has achieved worldwide acclaim and enjoys universal acceptance by the profession and the government of that nation.

He emphasized that 'the school dental therapist should be allowed to practice only in school clinics. Under no circumstances should they be allowed to practice in private dental offices or group clinics. If they were allowed to practice outside the schools, I visualize them being sidetracked into dental offices and clinics, no longer caring for children but working rather as second-rate dentists treating the adult population.'

HELP FROM THERAPIST ASSISTANTS

Dean Ingle went on to suggest that the school dental therapist would be helped in this work by school dental therapist assistants 'who should be indigenous to the area served by the school.'

'Their duties would be manifold.' First, they would serve as chairside assistants to the dental therapist on a rotational basis. They would also work on their own at one of the clinic chairs—performing prophylaxes, and applying topical fluoride and pit and fissure sealants.

'They could also be trained to insert restorations in cavities prepared by the therapist if the dental therapist is overwhelmed by a backlog of caries.'

RECRUIT HYGIENISTS AS THERAPISTS

Dean Ingle recommended that 'the school dental therapist be recruited initially from among the nation's 16,000 practicing dental hygienists.'

In comments issued after reviewing Dean Ingle's testimony, ADA President Carl A. Laughlin characterized the overall proposal as a 'much too superficial approach both with respect to the manpower questions involved and, more importantly, to the quality of the care that American children are entitled to receive.'

Dr. Laughlin noted that 'Dean Ingle himself says that his proposed new personnel shouldn't be allowed to treat adults because that would make them 'second-rate dentists,' but seemingly feels that what would be second rate for adults is perfectly acceptable for children.' I doubt that many parents would agree with him.

'I strongly question whether Dr. Ingle is serving the cause of better dental health for all Americans by going before a congressional committee and offering cut-and-dried answers before the serious questions raised by his approach are responsibly and thoroughly investigated.

'As Dr. Kaplan points out, the American Dental Association strongly supports investigation of expanded function auxiliaries and, as Dean Ingle knows, much activity is going on. I very much hope that his rash proposal does no harm to the continuation of such vital investigations.'

Position statements adopted recently by the ADA Council on Dental Education and the Inter-Agency Committee on Dental Auxiliaries express the two groups' belief that the existing dental auxiliary education system offers the greatest potential for training dental auxiliaries for expanded functions under the supervision of a dentist.

MOVE WOULD BE 'UNREALISTIC'

A Council spokesman said the position statements express the belief that 'it would be unrealistic and costly to develop an untested educational system when, in fact, existing programs can be, and are being, restructured to prepare auxiliaries to provide more extensive services.

'In taking this position, however, the Association believes educational institutions should be encouraged to conduct experimental programs designed to determine how auxiliaries can function more effectively.

'Any new plan for delivery of dental care through greater utilization of new or existing auxiliaries should be based on valid research and have the support of the profession and its licensing bodies if it is to be effectively implemented'."

Question: What specific solution is the ADA here requesting for the shortage of dental auxiliaries and training programs?

Question: What portion of ADA testimony may have been at least partially directed toward Dean Ingle's plan? What arguments are presented?

Question: What specific limitations did Dean Ingle emphasize with respect to the *place* in which school dental therapists would be allowed to practice? Note *carefully* the context in which he used the phrase "second-rate dentists."

Question: What are Dr. Laughlin's major criticisms of Dean Ingle's plan?

Questions Dr. Laughlin emphasizes Dean Ingle's use of the phrase "second-rate dentists." Do you think his argument accurately interprets Ingle's intent and message when he used the phrase?

The following letter appeared in the *Journal of the American Dental Association,* July, 1972.

"OPPOSED TO PROGRAMS

(The following letter was sent to Harry W. Bruce, Division of Physicians and Health Professions Education, Bureau of Health Manpower Education, NIH, Bethesda, Md., by Lewis C. Toomey, president, Maryland State Dental Association.)

The Board of Governors of the Maryland State Dental Association met on March 29, 1972, and reviewed a report of the Conference of Dental Examiners and Dental Educators held at the Headquarters Building of the American Dental Association in Chicago, Feb. 11–12, 1972.

The members of the Board were especially distressed to learn that federal funds are being utilized to train dental auxiliaries to perform intraoral functions which legally and traditionally belong to the province of the practicing dentist. The Board of Governors of the Maryland State Dental Association is unalterably opposed to programs similar to the one now, under consideration at the University of Southern California School of Dentistry. This program is apparently patterned after the New Zealand Dental Nurse Program and would have dental therapists with two years of training performing intraoral functions on school children.

In our opinion, the delegation of such a wide range of intraoral functions is not in the best interest of either the public or the profession. The dental profession in the state of Maryland has been most progressive in its willingness to delegate intraoral functions to dental auxiliaries. We have, however, been very careful in requiring that the delegation of such duties be under the direct supervision of a dentist and not go beyond certain limitations. We certainly do not want to be placed in a position of delegating irreversible intraoral procedures to a dental auxiliary which some of the new programs seems to be proposing.

The Maryland State Dental Association would, therefore, like to urge the federal government to exercise extreme caution in funding these programs which might substantially reduce the quality of dental care being made available to certain segments of the American public.

LEWIS C. TOOMEY, D.D.S.,
President, Maryland State Dental Association."

Question: Who (or what agency) is the Maryland State Dental Association attempting to influence? What is being requested?

Question: What concern, or fear, is the explicit basis for the request? Can you think of any implicit, unvoiced concern that might have motivated the request?

The following letter appeared in the August, 1972, issue of the *JADA*.

"ADEQUATE CONTROLS

After reading the 'Report of the Inter-Agency Committee on Dental Auxiliaries' in the May JADA, I most urgently recommended that the delegates seek to assure the membership that adequate controls in experimental programs for dental auxiliaries will be incorporated in any action taken by the House of Delegates.

The 1970 House of Delegates—in my opinion—abrogated its duty and responsibility to the membership when it rescinded Resolution 222 which had been passd in 1961. By rescinding this resolution (*Trans* 1961), the House threw open the floodgates to any irresponsible experimental activities by the very agencies of which the Inter-Agency Committee is composed.

The private practitioner, and particularly the private general practitioner, has neither representation on the committee nor an agency to effectively guard his interests in the design and control of such experimental programs.

The following is a quote from the testimony of John I. Ingle, Dean, USC dental school, before the Senate Health Subcommittee:

'. . . the school dental therapist should be allowed to practice only in school clinics. Under no circumstances should they be allowed to practice in private dental offices or group clinics. If they were allowed to practice outside the schools, I visualize them being sidetracked into dental offices and clinics, no longer caring for children but working rather as second-rate dentists treating the adult population.

It seems logical to me that, if a dental paraprofessional, therapist, and others would be a second-rate dentist when treating adults, such a person would most certainly be at least second-rate—if not a lower category—when treating children. Children represent the future of our country and should be our number one concern.

The above testimony is typical of the sick reasoning offered by those who propose expanding the duties of denal auxiliaries to ease the manpower shortage. Currently, and these people admit it, there are not enough auxiliaries to perform the duties now legally assigned to them. What can be gained by changing dental practice acts to assign more duties, particularly duties that would require the close and continuous supervision of a competent, licensed dentist?

Further testimony by Dean Ingle enlarged upon his theories that would produce an entirely new mode of dental practice for children utilizing partially trained dental hygienists and/or dental assistants. It can happen anywhere. It has already happened in Pennsylvania.

I feel certain that the great majority of dentists do not want any form of two-level dentistry for the citizens of this country. The time to be heard is now—or never.

IVAN D. WILBUR, D.D.S.,
Binghamton, N.Y."

Question: Note that this letter attempts to influence the ADA toward control of experimental programs for dental auxiliaries.

What is the apparent major concern which motivates the request?

Question: Universities have traditionally been centers for research—i.e., the production of new knowledge. Freedom to perform research has been a jealously guarded prerogative in universities.

Should research (experimentation) in health care delivery procedures be included in the freedom of inquiry prerogatives of universities, or is it a special case requiring outside conrol?

Would it be in the public interest to impose control on experimental programs in health care delivery?

The following article appeared in the *ADA News*, August 14, 1972.

'PRESIDENT LAUGHLIN REPLIES TO INGLE'S CHARGE

Editors note:—The following was written by ADA President Carl A. Laughlin in response to a letter to the editor (July 17, *ADA News*) from John I. Ingle, Dean of the University of Southern California School of Dentistry, concerning Senate testimony by Dr. Ingle on the school dental therapist concept.

Dr. Ingle stated in his letter that he believed that I did not take into consideration the remainder of his testimony before the U.S. Senate subcommittee on health when I said: 'Dr. Ingle is going before a congressional committee and offering cut-and-dried answers before the serious questions raised by his approach are responsibly and thoroughly investigated.' Dr. Ingle also said: 'I believe the membership should know that I did not offer cut-and-dried answers.'

Regardless of the words Dr. Ingle used before the subcommittee, his plans for a school dental therapist program have been 'cut-and-dried' for some time. First I would like to quote from an article by Dr. Daniel F. Gordon, president, Southern California Dental Association (JSCDA, Vol. 40, July, 1972) in which Dr. Gordon said: 'On February 12, 1972, Dr. Ingle presented a paper at the Conference of Dental Examiners and Dental Educators in which he spelled out the school dental therapist concept. Nowhere in the paper did he request or indicate that a demonstration or pilot project be conducted first so that the concept could be tested before a commitment is made as to its feasibility in this country.

At a meeting with dental association representatives on May 1, 1972, Dean Ingle stated that he was talking about a school program that would educate about 15 school dental therapist students to establish research facts.

In view of the strong, unequivocal position taken in his original paper, it appears that a cardinal rule of the researcher is being violated. Drawing conclusions regarding the outcome of a research project before it is even begun tends to nullify the credibility of the project.

'If Dean Ingle had stressed from the first that he was interested in a research program involving 15 students in order to test the feasibility of the concept, a project requiring a minimum of three to five years, the response from the profession would have been less vitriolic.'

On January 17, 1972, approximately one month before Dr. Ingle presented his paper at the Conference of Dental Examiners and Educators and prior to his testimony before Congress, he sent a letter to the Hon. Gordon Duffy, Chairman, Assembly Select Committee on Health Manpower, Sacramento, Calif.

In his letter he stated: 'Your committee should also know that this school of dentistry is planning to abandon the present traditional educational program for the dental hygienists and move rather into a program of training the dental therapist as we have defined this position in the attached hierarchical job descriptions.

'We believe that the dental hygienists of the future will be trained in technical schools and junior colleges but the dental therapist should be trained under the auspices of a school of dentistry. We plan to have 100 students involved in the dental therapist program by September, 1972, graduating 50 dental therapists a year thereafter. In order that these young people might provide the dental care for which they have been trained, it is imperative that the State Dental Practice Act be changed to allow them to legally carry out these duties.'

Here are Dr. Ingle's own job descriptions, which he proposes for the school children of this nation:

Dental Therapist.—Under the supervision of a dentist or school dental therapist, may do everything a dental hygienist or dental technician is allowed to do, but in addition may take a history and examine the patient, recording all findings, may inject local anesthetics, perform uncomplicated gingival surgery, and place, contour, and polish plastic (including amalgam) restorations in cavities prepared by the dentist or school dental therapist. Mandatory education—18 months. Examination and licensure necessary.

School Dental Therapist Assistant.—In a practice limited to school clinics, may do everything the dental hygienist is allowed to do, but may in addition place, contour, and polish restorations in cavities prepared by the dentist or school dental therapist. Mandatory education—six months to nine months. Examination and licensure necessary.

School Dental Therapist.—In a practice limited to school clinics, may perform, independent of direct supervision by the dentist, any of the procedures allowable for the dental assistant, technician, hygienist, or therapist. In addition, the school dental therapist may prepare cavities in the children's teeth as well as do minor extractions of deciduous teeth and prepare and place space maintenance devices. He shall be supervised by a traveling supervisory dentist. Mandatory education—1 to 2 years. Examination and licensure necessary.

In his testimony before Congress. Dr. Ingle stated that the dental therapists should not be permitted to practice on adults, as they would be second-rate dentists. One would assume from this statement that he feels that second-rate dentists are good enough for our children but not adults. I doubt if any parent in this nation would agree to this.

Dr. Ingle seems to be speaking from both corners of his mouth when he stated in his letter to the editor that 'once they are educated, we must determine the level of supervision from a dentist that is needed to maintain this quality care.' I ask Dr. Ingle what quality care when they are second-rate dentists? Yet in his job descriptions he stated that the school dental therapist in a practice limited to school clinics may perform, independent of direct supervision by a dentist, all the procedures as stated above, etc.

A takeover of the profession by nonprofessionals, such as the New Zealand dental nurses have attempted to do in Canada, is exactly what Dr. John Ingle is proposing for this nation. Let's not let it happen!

Question: Dr. Laughlin raises the issue of (a) "cut-and-dried answers" lacking adequate investigation and (b) quality of care.

Since, as material previously presented in this paper indicates, Ingle's proposal was modeled after a program operating in New Zealand, could the results of the New Zealand program be considered a major investigation of the system proposed?

Would the results of studies of the quality of care in the New Zealand program be pertinent to the debate?

Question: Note that Dr. Laughlin again uses the phrase "second-rate dentists" against Ingle. Considering the context in which Ingle used the term, do you believe Dr. Laughlin is accurately interpreting the meaning intended by Dr. Ingle?

Question: In the last paragraph Dr. Laughlin raises an issue which he had not previously made explicit. Has anything you have read to this point suggested that Ingle is "proposing" a "takeover" of the profession by nonprofessionals?

The following letter appeared in the September, 1972 issue of *Western Dental Society*.

"DEAR EDITOR: Comments on Dr. John I. Ingle's proposal to train dental technicians and dental therapists.

Dr. Ingle's conviction of the only way which will allow the dental profession to provide care for the entire population of the future by training Dental Technicians and Therapists to work in the mouth after 1 or 1½ years training under the supervision of a dentist, borders on the ridiculous. He appears to be entirely unaware of what advertising and unethical dentists are now doing to the public. I am surprised a man in his position would suggest to make it possible for an unscrupulous dentist to hire unlimited numbers of therapists to mass produce restorations and dentures on a production line. I am sure the cost in dollars would go down for the patient but I cringe at the price paid by that individual to the health of his mouth.

I have been on the Counseling Committee of the Western Dental Society for 5 years and Chairman of this Committee for the past 2 years; and I have examined many mouths that have been restored by dentists under our present 4-year dental school program. The quality of work is in direct proportion to the thoroughness, competence and moral responsibility of the dentist. I can assure you that there is no easy way to perform complex dental restorations in the mouth. If the ethical dentist of today is forced to compete with mediocrity, the quality of dentistry in the United States will drop to an unacceptable level.

I must admit that dentistry is handicapped by being a hand craft art in a machine age, but the answer is not to make a production line out of patients.

Someone in a responsible position should stop this kind of thinking that would lower the quality of dentistry to the public.

PAUL D. WALQUIST, D.D.S."

Question: Dr. Walquist is primarily concerned that Ingle's proposal would permit unscrupulous dentists to ". . . hire unlimited numbers of therapists to mass produce restorations and dentures on a production line." Would Ingle's proposal permit such a practice?

Does Dr. Walquist appear to have understood Dr. Ingle's plan?

Has Dr. Walquist made a constructive contribution to the debate, or has he confused the issue (particularly for dentists who have not studied Ingle's proposal)?

Question: Walquist suggests that ". . . someone in a responsible position should stop this type of thinking [Ingle's] . . .".

Do you think that the interests of the public and the dental profession would be advanced in the long run if "this type of thinking"—i.e., critical, innovative thinking—were stopped by someone in a responsible position?

In the September, 1972 issue of *Western Dental Society* (on the same page as Dr. Walquist's letter, see above) is a letter from Dr. Ingle.

"DEAR EDITOR: The American Dental Association has predicted changes in health care delivery and has called for an increased utilization of auxiliaries. Several states have enacted new legislation permitting auxiliaries' duties to be expanded. In California, with the awareness of the State expanded-duty dental auxiliaries (EDDA). In addition, our state dental associations are advocating expanded duties for dental hygienists and assistants. It seems apparent that we are entering into a new era of dental care delivery.

"Interest in dental auxiliaries has reached Sacramento. During the last year, the California Assembly Select Committee on Health Manpower, chaired by Dr. Gordon Duffy, has been investigating the use of dental auxiliaries. Last fall Dr. Duffy asked a number of people in the State, including me, to comment on proposed expanded duties for dental hygienist and dental assistants.

In my response of January 17, copies of which I sent to the CDA, SCDA and ADA, I suggested to Dr. Duffy what might happen *if* expanded-duty auxiliaries are introduced into the dental health team. I realized that redefining job descriptions for hygienists and assistants, along with possible changes in their educational requirements and licensure, would probably influence *all* dental auxiliaries.

Consequently, I presented to Dr. Duffy's Committee one way to organize all dental personnel—from assistant to dentist—so the relationship of each to the other could be studied. In addition, my intent was to describe a career ladder for the dental profession—one that would give auxiliaries the opportunity for upward mobility and offer educational steps which would lead to the next higher, and more responsible, position.

Beyond this, my major intent was to recommend sound educational and licensure requirements to be established for all auxiliaries to protect the public and the profession in California. It should be emphasized my suggestions were merely—quote from my letter to Dr. Duffy—'a tentative list of job descriptions.' Furthermore, I said, 'there is nothing sacrosanct about the hierarchial job descritpions' I submitted.

Now, let's look at several of these job categories. First, the *dental technician*. I am concerned about the future role of this person. In particular, I foresee the denturist, now legal in Canada, as a terrible threat to dental care, and to dentistry.

Second, the future of our *dental hygienists*, to whom we have an historic educational and moral commitment, deeply concerns me. Currently, the dental hygienist is the most qualified auxiliary we have. However, her position is threatened by the expanded-duty assistant who, without comparable educational or licensure requirements, could become the dentist's primary auxiliary.

Faced with this potential downgrading in the role of the dental hygienist, your school (and many others across the nation) will augment the curriculum of its dental hygiene program beginning this September. As you know, dental hygienists are being educated both in dental school and in junior college programs. I strongly feel that the dental schools can best provide high quality training in expanded duties. Not only are dental faculty available, but the opportunity exists for dental students and hygiene students to work closely together to develop the team skills and attitudes needed in practice. Thus, the expanded curriculum will include training in a number of expanded duties and will place greater emphasis on the prevention and treatment of periodontal disease. Graduates of this program will continue to receive a Bachelor of Science degree in dental hygiene, but in addition will receive a certification of completion in 'dental therapy'.

It is apparent to me now that I used an unfortunate term in describing this new program, which suggested in some minds that we would completely abandon our program in dental hygiene at USC. Nothing could be further from the truth!

We will continue to graduate our fine dental hygienists, but they will have additional skills. Thus, they will be able to meet the demands that may be placed upon them if the CDA-SCDA recommendations are implemented by the legislature.

Third and last, let's briefly examine the role of the *School Dental Therapist*. This new auxiliary would provide school-based preventive and theapeutic dental care to be administered to children.

We have sought research funds for a pilot experiment to study the feasibility of training and utilizing school-based dental auxiliaries. Four other American institutions are already training dental auxiliaries beyond the level planned in our research, so I felt Dr. Duffy's Committee should be made aware of the possibility of the emergence of such a new auxiliary. I have written a paper on the subject, and I expect that it will soon be in print.

Before leaving the subject of dental auxiliary training, I would like to emphasize that in our university educational program we are going to train only the expanded-duty dental hygienist.

Well, where do we stand today? In Sacramento, Dr. Duffy has introduced *Assembly Bill 1953* to appoint a dental committee to make recommendations to the California Legislature concerning possible changes in the Dental Practice Act. *Through this legislation, the profession will gain the right properly to advise the legislature about the use of dental auxiliaries and the future delivery of dental care.* If we as a profession do not formulate workable solutions for the delivery of dental care, then there are those outside the profession who are waiting to arrange our destiny.

Sincerely,

JOHN I. HINGLE, D.D.S.,
Dean."

"Editor's Note: There is no question that Dental Education must progress in the future. Change is inevitable. Let us evaluate programs realitsically, not emotionally, accept the good and reject the others."

Question: Is Dr. Ingle concerned with the regulation by the dental profession of the functions of auxiliaries. How does he propose that this be done?

The October, 1972 issue of the *Washington State Dental Association News* carried two pieces which relate to the debate over Dr. Ingle's plan. The first is an editorial entitled "A Time to Speak Up", a portion of which is reproduced below.

"A TIME TO SPEAK UP

"Dentistry is losing its invisibility because people are no longer accepting the loss of their teeth. What we should benefit from the criticism being offered us is the initiative to strive for long overdue reforms.

1. It is absolutely intolerable in a civilized society that children should be going without dental care. Non-profit charitable foundations may be doing impressive work in some areas, but there are vast numbers of children who do not qualify or whose parents would not accept charity.

2. Peer review must be accomplished at the component society level. It is not being done now mainly because it has never been done before. Somehow, someone must convince dental society leaders that if we do not do it soon, it will be done for us.

3. Courage and imagination are needed to keep pressing for ways to provide more care. Those who speak of 'two-level dentistry' with ridicule should remind themselves that in New Zealand all children receive dental care. In the United States about half do. The days of the anointed dentist must end.

4. Newspapers who criticize dentistry or show interest in other ways should be sincerely requested to join the cause. Any newspaper erally interested in the dental health of the poor should be willing to dvote daily space to things like diet, various methods of plaque removal, curing sugar habits, and how to obtain help. These things have low reader interest, but certainly a newspaper of integrity would not care. Curing the world of ignorance by disseminating free literature is no more difficult than curing tooth decay and pyorrhea with free treatment.

There was a time when dentists were looked upon as a necessary evil. Somewhat like atheists, they seemed harmless enough as long as they kept quiet. Never has there been as propitious a time for men of reason to speak up.

EUGENE F. EIDEN, D.D.S.

Question: When Dr. Eiden refers to "Those who speak of 'two-level dentistry' with ridicule . . ." is he alluding to the quality of care issue repeatedly raised in discussions of Dr. Ingle's proposal?

Below is an excerpt from a news article which appeared on the same page as the foregoing editorial.

"WSDA ASKS ADA HOUSE TO OPPOSE

CONCEPT OF DENTAL THERAPIST

The Washington State Dental Association has submitted two resolutions pertaining to auxiliary personnel to the American Dental Association House of Delegates for action at the ADA annual meeting in San Francisco October 29 to November 2.

One of the resolutions submitted by the WSDA commends the Interagency Committee of the Council on Dental Education for its work in connection with development of guidelines for training auxiliaries in expanded duties.

The other resolution submitted by the WSDA has two 'resolved' clauses, reading as follows:

'Resolved, that the American Dental Association does not accept, promote or recognize any new name, or category of dental personnel such as dental therapist, dental associate or any other nomenclature;

'Be It Further Resolved, that the ADA encourage, with all the means at its disposal, the preservation of the concept that auxiliaries (dental assistants, hygienists and laboratory technicians) shall be directly responsible to and supervised by professionals who have no less than a D.M.D. or D.D.S. degree'."

By October, 1972 opposition to Dean Ingle had become intense in California. The general public was informed of the issue in the following news article in the Los Angeles *Times*.

"DEAN OF USC DENTISTRY SCHOOL UNDER FIRE

(William Trombley, Times Education Writer)

The dean of the USC school of dentistry is under fire for allegedly permitting the school's academic standards to deteriorate and for admitting unqualified minority students.

A special dental advisory committee has been appointed by USC President John Hubbard to investigate wide-ranging charges against John Ingle, who has been dean of the school of dentistry for eight years.

The complaints range from allegations that USC 'is becoming a second- or third-rate institution' and that too many of its students fail the state dental examinations to charges that 'all department chairmen are Jews,' that the school 'has a predominant number of Jews on the faculty and that Ingle himself is a Jew. (He is not.)

There were also allegations that Ingle 'advocates socialistic (even communistic) programs' and that his personality rubs some people the wrong way.'

Hubbard ordered the investigating committee not to consider the charges about the number of Jews on the faculty or in department chairmanships, but the committee is considering a claim that Ingle 'is pro-Jewish when hiring new faculty.'

A university spokesman said this charge was retained because it deals with a question of discrimination in hiring.

Sources of specific allegations could not be learned, but USC officials said the entire list of about 70 came from some leaders of the Century Club, the dental school's fund-raising support group, from some leaders of the USC Dental Alumni Association and from certain individual dentists in Los Angeles and elsewhere.

The executive boards of the Century Club and the alumni group has asked Hubbard to remove Ingle and the Century Club has cut off its $100,000-a-year financial support for the school.

However, Ingle has received strong support from the dental school faculty and students from dental educators across the country.

The dean's opponents charge that the academic quality of the school has slipped under his leadership in part because of vigorous efforts to recruit minority dental students.

For example, one charge states that 'minority students are not held to the same standards as are other students' and another claims 'the presence of minority students lowers the academic standards expected of all students.'

Ingle defended the academic reputation of the school.

'We have been visited twice in the last year by the official accrediting agency of the American Dental Association and have been fully accredited on both occasions,' he said in an interview Thursday.

He also defended the minority recruiting campaign, which produced a freshman class with 10% black and Spanish-speaking students this year.

'It's been our contention all along that there are plenty of bright talented minority students around who would do well in our school if they had the chance to get here,' the dean said. 'Our opponents are saying we went after a bunch of dogs but that's not true.'

MINORITIES' GRADES

According to Ingle, grades of entering black and Spanish-speaking students this year are as high as average grades for all entering freshmen for the past 19 years.

Ingle blamed the Century Club for the flurry of complaints.

'They don't like the students who have come here in recent years,' he said. 'We have alumni who won't recognize that the world has changed. They practice in the white suburbs and don't care about urban problems at all.

'They don't like long hair and radical politics,' he added. 'Their own kids may have long hair, but when they come here I'm supposed to change all that.'

(One of the allegations is that 'dental students' dress in the clinics is improper—dirty clothes and long hair—and is unbecoming of the health profession.')

Ross Huntley, a Sherman Oaks dentist who is president of the Century Club, refused to discuss the matter with *The Times.*

Ingle, a 53-year-old authority on root canal diseases, said his problems with alumni began when he arrived from the University of Washington eight years ago.

But they grew more intense after Ingle made a speech in Chicago last February advocating the 'New Zealand plan' of providing free paraprofessional dental care for all school children.

Ingle said his foes were 'infuriated' by his later appearance before the U.S. Senate subcommittee on health, chaired by Sen. Edward M. Kennedy (D-Mass.).

Gordon Cohn, who directs fund-raising efforts for all USC health sciences, said, 'Late last year, we began to hear many of these things—there seemed to be a wave of negative opinion about John and the school.'

COMPLAINTS INCREASE

At the annual Century Club banquet last winter, Huntley, the club's new president, berated Ingle. Last spring, the club's executive board voted to withhold its annual contribution of about $100,000.

The volume of complaints rose in July, Hubbard appointed the 35-member dental advisory committee to weigh charges against Ingle and the school.

The committee includes dentists who are supporters of Ingle and some who oppose him, some who are USC alumni and some who are not.

Ingle objected to the appointment of the committee.

'Universities are accredited by official accrediting agencies,' he said. 'With this procedure, the president has introduced a second group of people who aren't involved in dental education and I don't think they have the expertise or knowledge.'

However, he added, 'I think we'll get fair treatment from them.'

The full committee will report to Hubbard by Oct. 18."

Question: *Who* is applying pressure to Dr. Ingle?

What are the charges brought against Dr. Ingle?

Do you think the charge that Ingle "advocates socialistic (even communistic) programs" could be related to Ingle's dental therapist proposal?

Question: What influence do you think this news story (particularly the charges against Ingle) might have on the public image of dentistry?

SOME GENERAL DISCUSSION QUESTIONS ON THE INGLE CONTROVERSY

1. In all probability you have now read more on the Ingle controversy than most practicing dentists. This exercise has given you an advantage because you were able to get an overview of the debate in a single sitting, whereas the actual debate has been distributed over time and over a variety of publications. Such distribution makes it extremely difficult for the busy dentist to identify the issues, follow the arguments and detect inaccuracies in the debate. For example, if you had read only one or two of the letters opposing Ingle you would have come away with an inaccurate, distorted understanding of his proposal.

The emotional language in the debate creates another obstacle to clear understanding. It is unlikely that words such as "ridiculous," "takeover," "communist," "socialist," "two-level dentistry," and "unalterably opposed" contribute much to the search for truth.

· A curious aspect of the debate is the almost total absence of reference to pertinent data. You have read appeals to general fears (communism), appeals to specific fears (takeover of the profession by paraprofessionals), name calling ("ridiculous," communistic or socialistic ideas), unsubstantiated warnings (the quality of service provided would be poor), erroneous criticism (unscrupulous dentists could hire school dental therapists and start an assembly line), and debating tactics (taking Ingle's phrase "second-rate dentists" out of context and using it against him). While reading all of this did you simetimes feel that some solid information or data would be welcome and constructive?

Question: Assume that *you* are a concerned professional person—concerned over both public and professional welfare— who wishes to write an editorial or letter on the Ingle plan for publication in a professional dental journal. Assume further that you wish to be scrupulously fair to all parties in the debate. Last, assume that you are writing for an audience which is educated, critical and informed.

Would you feel qualified to proceed with the letter or editorial without the following information:

1. Precisely what did Ingle say to the Conference of Dental Examiners and Dental Educators? Did he provide any data or arguments which should be taken into consideration?

2. If Ingle's proposal was modeled after the New Zealand Dental Nurse Program, then:

   (a) What quality of work has been provided by the nurses? Have there been studies?

   (b) How has the dental profession in New Zealand accepted the dental nurse program?

   (c) What has been the influence of the New Zealand program on the dental health of the population?

   (d) Have New Zealand dental nurses attempted a "takeover" of the dental profession?

3. What is the state of dental health in children in the U.S.A.? Are there any reliable statistics?

4. Are there any reliable statistics on the dental *need* of the entire population of the U.S.A.?

5. Are there any reliable statistics on the current *demand* for dental treatment? Any reliable projections of future demand?

6. What is the state of dental manpower in the U.S.A.? How does available manpower relate to current public need and demand for manpower?

7. Are there any educated projections of the relationship between dental manpowr and public need and demand in the near future?

8. The ADA president expressed concern over the possibility that paraprofessionals might try a "takeover" of the profession. What governmental and professional machinery (e.g., licensure) exists to control professional practice? How does it work?

9. What alternatives to Dr. Ingle's proposal might be proposed? For example, is there a less expensive, less cumbersome, faster way to meet the dental health needs of the country? What solid data are available to support such alternative proposals?

10. How does the American Dental Association determine policy on issues such as the one raised by Dr. Ingle? Who makes such policy decisions? What machinery exists to carry out policy decisions—e.g., controlling the dental practitioner, influencing legislation, and so forth?

Exhibit 8.—*Materials Furnished by Council for the Advancement of the Psychological Professions and Sciences (CAPPS) Re Provisions of Services by Psychologists to Beneficiaries of Health Insurance Contracts Without Mandatory Referral and/or Supervision of Medical Doctors*

[From the Washington Star-News, Aug. 17, 1973]

TRUST SUIT FILED AGAINST BLUE CROSS

(By Miriam Ottenberg)

An antitrust suit against Blue Cross and Blue Shield demanding $70 million in treble damages and $10 million in punitive damages has been filed here on behalf of the hundreds of thousands of government workers enrolled in the Federal Employes Health Benefits Plan and thousands of psychologists.

The class action, filed in U.S. District Court late yesterday, accuses Blue Cross and Blue Shield of unnecessarily inflating health costs and of "featherbedding" by requiring subscribers needing mental health care to be referred to psychologists by physicians, who then must periodically supervise treatment.

The complaint charges that all taxpayers are affected because the government has to pay higher premiums than necessary for health protection for its workers.

The Council for the Advancement of the Psychological Professions and Sciences, Inc., (CAPPS) a non-profit District corporation, brought the suit.

Joining as plaintiffs were the National Association of Government Employees; individual federal employes and psychologists, state Psychological associations of the District, California, Maryland, New Jersey and Louisiana; the Baltimore Association of Consulting Psychologists, and the Division of Licensed Psychologists of the Georgia Psychological Association.

The Civil Service Commission has tried for a number of years to persuade Blue Cross and Blue Shield to cover phychologists' services without physicians' supervision.

Nevertheless, because the Civil Service Commission signed the contract with Blue Cross and Blue Shield for federal workers, the suit names Civil Service Commission Chairman Robert E. Hampton and Commissioners Ludwig J. Andolsek and Jayne Baker Spain as defendants in their official capacities as well as Atty. Gen. Elliot Richardson as the government's chief law officer.

The suit pinpoints a question which various officials have wrestled with for years.

The Civil Service Commission persuaded Aetna Life and Casualty Co., to change its rules on psychological services where it failed with Blue Cross-Blue Shield. Rep, Rep. Jerome R. Waldie, D-Calif., chairman of the House Civil Service subcommittee on retirement and employe benefits, has introduced and recently held hearings on legislation that would allow Federal employes to go directly to licensed psychologists without prior referral by a doctor.

And Mrs. Virginia H. Knauer, special assistant to the President for consumer affairs, has asked Blue Cross and Blue Shield to restudy their position in the light of what other participating insurance carriers such as Aetna have done to make the service of psychologists more directly available to subscribers in need of mental health care.

The suit contends that because of Blue Cross-Blue Shield requirements some 1.6 million federal employes, beneficiaries and annuitants since 1967 have suffered loss of psychological services connected with the diagnosis and treatment of nervous and mental disorders.

The premium payments of the plaintiffs, according to the suit, have been "illegally, excessive and improperly charged and collected' by the Blue Cross and Blue Shield plan in regard to psychological services.

Reimbursement for these services, the suit adds, has been "arbitrarily, capriciously and unfairly denied" by the plan and subscribers have been "illegally, improperly and unfairly denied free access to a health practitioner" of their choice by the plan's requirement for a doctor to make the referral and supervise the psychologist.

This "medical referral and supervision" clause, the suit contends, "improperly and illegally interferes in the relationship between psychologists and their clientele."

The suit points out that the physician who is supposed to supervise the psychologist need not be trained in psychiatry and does not have to follow any special rule or adhere to any standard for his supervision.

In 47 states and the District, the suit notes, mental health care providers are equally licensed with medical providers.

The suit said CAPPS, as a national organization of psychologists interested in promoting the fullest use of psychological knowledge and services in health care delivery, alleges that the "medical referral and supervision" clause is illegal, improper and violates antitrust laws because:

It does not promote better mental health but is restrictive and in restraint of trade.

The required referral and supervision is usually perfunctory and arbitrary.

The supervising physician does not have to be trained in psychiatry or mental health care.

The suit alleges that payments of $25 to $50 to physicians for unnecessary referral and supervision of psychologists has "substantially increased premiums costs to the subscribers and to the United States (which shares the costs of Blue Cross and Blue Shield with the individual federal workers).

In seeking redress for alleged overpayments by subscribers and the government and for alleged damage to psychologists, the suit asks the court to order Blue Cross and Blue Shield to:

Return to subscribers the difference between the premiums that ought to have been paid and what has been paid or $25 million, whatever is lower, and to pay $10 million in punitive damages.

Pay the psychologists treble damages of $45 million for the plan's alleged violation of antitrust laws.

Refund to the Treasury the difference between what should have been paid by the government in premiums and what has been paid since 1967.

The court was asked to direct the Civil Service Commission to launch a study to determine the nature, extent and scope of overpayments" made by the government to the health plan.

Joseph L. Nellis, who recently won the landmark abortion case in the Supreme Court, is in charge of prosecuting the suit as general counsel for CAPPS.

[News Release, Aug. 17, 1973]

LARGEST ANTI-TRUST SUIT AGAINST BLUE CROSS/BLUE SHIELD FILED YESTERDAY

WASHINGTON, D.C., August 17.—A class action anti-trust suit filed in the U.S. District Court yesterday demands $70 million in treble damages plus $10 million in punitive damages on behalf of hundreds of thousands of Federal employees enrolled in the Federal Employees Health Benefits Plan, and thousands of psychologists.

The suit charges Blue Cross—Blue Shield with inflating health care costs unnecessarily and interfering with subscribers' freedom of choice in the selection of mental health care providers.

Also named in the suit as defendants in their official capacities are the U.S. Civil Service Commission, and Commissioners Robert E. Hampton, Ludwig J. Andolsek, Jayne Baker Spain, and U.S. Attorney General Elliot Richardson.

The Council for the Advancement of the Psychological Professions and Sciences (CAPPS) and other Plaintiffs contend Blue Cross—Blue Shield featherbeds charges to subscribers and the Government by requiring medical referral and supervision before reimbursing subscribers for psychological services. The complaint charges this requirement violates anti-trust law by unreasonable interference with the practice of psychology and with the subscriber's freedom to select a health practitioner of his own choice, thus increasing taxes for all citizens because of the higher insurance premiums paid by the Government.

Additional plaintiffs representing many classes of subscribers and health providers are the National Association of Government Employees; individual Federal employees and psychologists; also the following state psychological associations: California, District of Columbia, Maryland, New Jersey, Louisiana; the Baltimore Association of Consulting Psychologists; and the Division of Licensed Psychologists of the Georgia Psychological Association.

CAPPS is a non-profit D.C. corporation formed two years ago to address public-policy issues related to psychology as a science and profession and to promote the development of psychological knowledge and services to the general public.

Dr. Rogers H. Wright of Long Beach, California, is president of CAPPS. A psychologist in private practice, he received his doctorate from Northwestern University in 1955, and specializes in child development psychology. Other members of the CAPPS Executive Committee are Dr. Max Siegel of Brooklyn, New York; Dr. Ernest S. Lawrence of Beverly Hills, California; Dr. Melvin A. Gravitz of Washington, D.C.; Dr. Nicholas A. Cummings of San Francisco, California; and Dr. Jack G. Wiggins of Cleveland, Ohio. General Counsel for CAPPS, who is in charge of prosecuting the suit, is Joseph L. Nellis of the Washington, D.C. bar.

In the United States District Court for the District of Columbia

[Civil Action No. 1623–73]

COUNCIL FOR THE ADVANCEMENT OF THE PSYCHOLOGICAL PROFESSIONS AND SCIENCES, INC., (A VOLUNTARY, NON-PROFIT D.C. CORPORATION), SUITE 606, 1725 EYE STREET, N.W., WASHINGTON, D.C. 20006

Class 1:

BALTIMORE ASSOCIATION OF CONSULTING PSYCHOLOGISTS, (A NON-PROFIT MARYLAND CORPORATION), C/O DR. JAMES OLSSON, MEDICAL SERVICE—SUPREME BENCH, ROOM 309, BALTIMORE CITY COURT HOUSE, ST. PAUL & FAYETTE STREETS, BALTIMORE, MARYLAND 21202

CALIFORNIA STATE PSYCHOLOGICAL ASSOCIATION, (A NON-PROFIT CALIFORNIA CORPORATION), 2365 WESTWOOD BOULEVARD, LOS ANGELES, CALIFORNIA 90064

D.C. PSYCHOLOGICAL ASSOCIATION, (A NON-PROFIT D.C. CORPORATION), C/O DR. HELEN PEIXOTTO), 6451—31ST STREET, N.W., WASHINGTON, D.C. 20015

DIVISION OF LICENSED PSYCHLOGISTS (DIVISION E) OF THE GEORGIA PSYCHOLIGIAL ASSOCIATION, (A VOLUNTARY UNINCORPORATED ASSOCIATION), C/O DR. HERBERT EBER, PSYCHOLOGICAL RESOURCES ASSOCIATION, SUITE 208, 1422 WEST PEACHTREE STREET, N.W., ATLANTA, GEORGIA 30309

MARYLAND PSYCHOLOGICAL ASSOCIATION, INC. (A NON-PROFIT MARYLAND CORPORATION), C/O DR. SHERMAN ROSS, 24 WESSEX ROAD, SILVER SPRING, MARYLAND 20910

NEW JERSEY PSYCHOLOGICAL ASSOCIATION (A NON-PROFIT NEW JERSEY CORPORATION), 422 GEORGE STREET, NEW BRUNSWICK, NEW JERSEY 08901

LOUISIANA PSYCHOLOGICAL ASSOCIATION, INC. (A NON-PROFIT LOUISIANA CORPORATION), C/O DR. CHARLES W. HILL, LSUNO LAKE FRONT, NEW ORLEANS, LOUISIANA 70122

NEW YORK SOCIETY OF CLINICAL PSYCHOLOGISTS, INC. (A NON-PROFIT NEW YORK CORPORATION), 540 EAST 22ND STREET, NEW YORK, NEW YORK 11226

KENTUCKY ASSOCIATION OF PROFESSIONAL PSYCHOLOGISTS, INC. (A NON-PROFIT KENTUCKY CORPORATION), C/O DR. JOSEPH C. FINNEY, 821 CAHABA DRIVE, LEXINGTON, KENTUCKY 40502

MICHIGAN PSYCHOLOGICAL ASSOCIATION, INC. (A NON-PROFIT MICHIGAN CORPORATION), C/O DR. EUGENE SCHOLTEN, 940 EAST 30TH STREET, HOLLAND, MICHIGAN 49423

PSYCHOLOGISTS IN PRIVATE PRACTICE (A VOLUNTARY UNINCORPORATED ASSO-
CIATION), C/O DR. JACOB CHWAST, 20 EAST NINTH STREET, NEW YORK,
NEW YORK 10003
TENNESSEE PSYCHOLOGICAL ASSOCIATION, INC. (A NON-PROFIT TENNESSEE
CORPORATION), C/O DR. CHARLES L. WALTER, 201 DOGWOOD LANE, JOHNSON
CITY, TENNESSEE 37601
OREGON PSYCHOLOGICAL ASSOCIATION, INC. (A NON-PROFIT OREGON CORPORA-
TION), C/O OREGON RESEARCH INSTITUTE, P.O. BOX 3196, EUGENE, OREGON
97403
SAN FRANCISCO BAY AREA PSYCHOLOGICAL ASSOCIATION (A VOLUNTARY UN-
INCORPORATED ASSOCIATION), C/O DR. PAMELA E. BUTLER, THE BEHAVIOR
INSTITUTE, 300 VALLEY STREET, SAUSALITO, CALIFORNIA 94965
DIVISION OF PSYCHOTHERAPY, INC. (A NON-PROFIT D.C. CORPORATION), C/O DR.
JACK D. KRASNER, 388 LYDECKER STREET, ENGLEWOOD, NEW JERSEY 07631

*On behalf of themselves and all other organizations, and associations similarly
situated.*
Class 2:
STANLEY W. CAPLAN, ED. D., 7000 CUTLER AVENUE, N.E., ALBUQUERQUE, NEW
MEXICO 87110
ROSE MARKS ELFMAN, PH. D., 408 PRINCETON BUILDING, WILDMAN ARMS,
SWARTHMORE, PENNSYLVANIA 19081
DAVID B. CHAMBERLAIN, PH. D. 13587 MANGO DRIVE, DEL MAR, CALIFORNIA
92014
RICHARD COVAULT, PH. D., 2793 LOMA VISTA ROAD, VENTURA, CALIFORNIA
93003
WALTER T. MCDONALD, PH. D., MONUMENT SQUARE BUILDING, 524 MAIN STREET,
RACINE, WISCONSIN 53403
CAROLE A. RAYBURN, PH. D., 1200 MORNINGSIDE DRIVE, SILVER SPRING, MARY-
LAND 20904
KENNETH LUOTO, PH. D., 17050 WEST NORTH AVENUE, BROOKFIELD, WISCONSIN
53005
L. J. WARN, PH. D., 802 EAST GRAND AVENUE, ESCONDIDO, CALIFORNIA 92025
LAWRENCE J. SCHNEIDER, PH. D., BOX 7431, NT STATION, DENTON, TEXAS
76203
PAUL BAINBRIDGE, PH. D., 51 FORBUS STREET, POUGHKEEPSIE, NEW YORK 12603
GEORGE P. TAYLOR, JR., PH. D., SUITE 340, EXCHANGE PLACE, ATLANTA,
GEORGIA 30303
DUANE E. SPIERS, PH. D., 2704 SOUTH 87TH AVENUE, OMAHA, NEBRASKA
68124
ARTHUR L. FOSTER, PH. D., 248 BLOSSOM HILL ROAD, LOS GATOS, CALIFORNIA
95030
STEVE LYNCH, PH. D., 141 TOWNE TERRACE, SANTA CRUZ, CALIFORNIA 95060
DANIEL W. PRIMAC, PH. D., SUITE F, 1301 EAST LINCOLN AVENUE, ORANGE,
CALIFORNIA 92665
JAMES E. RUDOLPH, PH. D., 5 MACKY DRIVE, HAUPPUGE, NEW YORK 11787
ALLEN E. WIESSEN, PH. D., ISSAQUAH PROFESSIONAL CENTER, SUITE E, 85 N.W.,
ALDER, ISSAQUAH, WASHINGTON 98027
WILL A. JUSTISS, PH. D., 2819 OAK STREET, JACKSONVILLE, FLORIDA 32205

On behalf of themselves and all other persons similarly situated.
Class 3:
JEROME S. MORSE, 5528 FOURTH STREET, ARLINGTON, VIRGINIA 22201
MICHAEL L. DWORKIN, 33 DRIFTWOOD STREET, APT. 19, MARINA DEL REY,
CALIFORNIA 90291
RALPH E. HAAG, 3113 N. KENSINGTON STREET, ARLINGTON, VIRGINIA 22207
BERNARD J. WALKER, 1511 CHELTEN AVENUE, PHILADELPHIA, PENNSYLVANIA
19126
EDWARD J. LEWANDOWSKI, 3650 ALMOND STREET, PHILADELPHIA, PENNSYL-
VANIA 19134
EDWARD F. YUENGLING, 8204 FRANKFORD AVENUE, PHILADELPHIA, PENNSYL-
VANIA 19136
JOHN BERNARD MCLEOD, 112 HASBROOK AVENUE, CHELTENHAM, PENNSYL-
VANIA 19012

Vincent J. Sabatino, 9408 Kirkwood Road, Philadelphia, Pennsylvania 19114

George Cherenack, 8020 Ditman Street, Philadelphia, Pennsylvania 19136

James E. West, p.o. box 158, Gloucester Pt., Virginia 23062

Gerald E. Smoot, 119 Olin Drive, Newport News, Virginia 23602

John P. Reardon, rt. 1, box 12ee, Hayes, Virginia 23072

Keith A. Oxendine, 1001—7th Street, Newport News, Virginia 23605

Harry B. Stokes, 460 Richneck Road, Newport News, Virginia 23602

Paul J. Shaver, 147 Nicewood Drive, Newport News, Virginia 23602

On behalf of themselves and all others similarly situated.

National Association of Government Employees (a non-profit Delaware corporation), 1241 G Street, N.W., Washington, D.C. 20005, Plaintiffs

v.

Blue Cross Association (a non-profit Illinois corporation), 1700 Pennsylvania Avenue, N.W., Washington, D.C. 20006

National Association of Blue Shield Plans (a non-profit Illinois corporation), 1700 Pennsylvania Avenue, N.W., Washington, D.C. 20006

Health Services, Inc. (an Illinois corporation), c/o Blue Cross Association, 1700 Pennsylvania Avenue, N.W., Washington, D.C. 20006

Medical Indemnity of America, Inc., (an Illinois corporation), c/o National Association of Blue Shield Plans, 1700 Pennsylvania Avenue, N.W., Washington, D.C. 20006

United States Civil Service Commission, 1900 E Street. N.W., Washington, D.C. 20415

Robert E. Hampton, Chairman, U.S. Civil Service Commission, 1900 E Street, N.W., Washington, D.C. 20415

Ludwig J. Andolsek, Commissioner, U.S. Civil Service Commission, 1900 E Street, N.W., Washington, D.C. 20415

Jayne Baker Spain, Commissioner, U.S. Civil Service Commission, 1900 E Street, N.W., Washington, D.C. 20415

Honorable Robert H. Bork, Acting Attorney General of the United States, Department of Justice, Constitution Avenue and Ninth Street, N.W., Washington, D.C. 20224, Defendants

Amended Class Action Complaint Under Amended Rule 23, et. sq. F.R.C.P. Filed Pursuant to Rule 15(a), F.R.C.P.

I. Jurisdiction and Venue

(1) Jurisdiction is founded on Sections 4 and 16 of the Act of Congress of October 15, 1914, c.323, 38 Stat. 730, as amended, said Act being commonly referred to as the "Clayton Anti-Trust Act," in order to recover damages and prevent continued violations by the above-named Defendants, as herinafter alleged, of Sections 1 and 3 of the Act of Congress of July 2, 1890, c.647, 26 Stat. 201, as amended, said Act being commonly referred to as the "Sherman Anti-Trust Act."

(2) Jurisdiction is also founded on the existence of questions arising under the powers of the Federal agency heerin involved to contract with the private Defendant herein involved, under the Act of September 28, 1959, 73 Stat. 712 U.S.C. Title 5, Sec. 8902. The United States Civil Service Commission was authorized by the Federal Employees Health Benefits Act of 1959 to contract on behalf of the United States with insurance carriers for insurance to be provided to employees of the Federal Government. The Federal Government pays a portion of the premium costs under these contracts. Th Government's contribution to the total subscription charge for an enrollee's health benefits plan is presently 40 percent of the average high-option charge of six large representative plans. For the year 1973 the Federal Government's contribution to Defendant Plans was $70,160,635, representing 42.1 percent of all premiums paid to Defendant Plans pursuant to the F.E.H.B.A. contract. Currently pending before Congress is legislation (H.R. 9256) which would further increase the Government's contribution to 55 percent for the year 1973 and would further increase the Government's contribution by an additional 5 percent each year thereafter until 1977 when the Government contribution would reach 75 percent.

(3) Jurisdiction is also based in part on Rule 17(b) of the Federal Rules of Civil Procedure granting an unincorporated association the capacity to sue in its common name in order to enforce rights granted to it under the Constitution or laws of the United States.

(4) Plaintiffs request this Honorable Court to exercise pendent jurisdiction over all non-Federal claims alleged herein on the grounds that all non-Federal claims have a common nucleus of operative facts and the entire action comprises one Constitutional case.

(5) The alleged violations hereinafter described have been and are being executed, carried out and made effctive in substantial part within the District of Columbia and the Defendants transact business within the District of Columbia and are within the jurisdiction of the Court for the purposes of service. The interstate trade and commerce, as hereinafter described, is carried on in part within the District of Columbia and in numerous other states.

II. PLAINTIFFS

(1) Plaintiff Council for the Advancement of the Psychological Professions and Sciences, Inc. is a voluntary, non-profit membership corporation incorporated in the District of Columbia. It was organized for the purpose of promoting and advancing the psychological professions and sciences, including the promotion of the fullest development and utilization of psychological knowledge and services in health care delivery to the general public and for the general purposes of the better assuring the availability and utilization of competent mental health care manpower, including provision of funds for development of psychological reserve manpower.

(2) Plaintiffs identified as Class 1 are organizations whose objectives include advancement of human welfare by promoting the fullest development and utilization of psychological knowledge and services.

(3) Plaintiffs identified as Class 2 are those individuals skilled in the study, development, and application of the principles of behavior, who have met recognized standards of the discipline of psychology in their area of expertise as set forth by law or by their professional or scientific organizations.

(4) Plaintiffs identified as Class 3 Plaintiffs are the individual subscribers to the F.E.H.B.A. Plan (Exhibit A to the Complaint) pursuant to contract between Defendant Plans and the United States Civil Service Commission. Plaintiffs identified as Class 3 Plaintiffs have, since 1967, been forced to pay Defendant Plans illegal and excessive premium payments, with respect to the aforementioned psychological services, reimbursement for which is purported to be provided by Defendant Plans, and their affiliates and subsidiaries, and have been unfairly and illegally denied free access to a health practitioner of his or her choice, by the operation and application of said "Medical referral and supervision" clause. In addition, various of the members of Class 3 have, since 1967, suffered loss of psychological services connected with the diagnosis and treatment of nervous and mental disorders and have had reimbursement for such services arbitrarily, capriciously and unfairly denied by Defendant Plans, and their affiliates and subsidiaries, as part of its continuing conspiracy, as herein described, to minimize access to mental health care, particularly mental health care offered by qualified and competent psychologists licensed or certified according to the laws of the respective states in which they practice.

(5) Plaintiff National Association of Government Employees is the bargaining agent for approximately 90,000 Federal employees. Many of its members are subscribers under F.E.H.B.A. and its has a community of interest with the other plaintiffs named.

III. CLASS ACTION ALLEGATIONS

(1) The above-named representative Plaintiffs in each class bring this action on behalf of themselves and all other members of their respective classes similarly situated, pursuant to Rules 23(b)(1), 23(b)(2) and 23(b)(3) of the Federal Rules of Civil Procedure and Local Rule 1-13 of the Rules of the United States District Court for the District of Columbia.

(2) Plaintiffs in Class I as defined in Section II (2) of this Complaint number approximately 165.

(3) Plaintiffs in Class 2 as defined in Section II (3) of this Complain number approximately 22,000.

(4) Plaintiffs in Class 3 as defined in Section II (4) of this Complaint number approximately 1.35 million.

(5) Each of these classes is so numerous that joinder of all members is impractical.

(6) There are questions of law and fact common to each of these classes.

(A) Among the questions of law and fact common to each member of Class 1 are the existence of the conspiracy alleged herein, its purpose and effects. Other common questions shared by all members of Class 1 are the issues of the disparagement of psychologists and interference with their business (professional) relationships.

(B) Each member of Class 2 shares the necessity of establishing the conspiracy alleged herein, its purposes and effects. Members of Class 2 also share the necessity to establish disparagement of psychologists and interference with their business (professional) relationships.

(C) Each member of Class 3 also shares the necessity of establishing the conspiracy alleged herein, its purpose and effects.

(7) The claims and defenses of the representative parties are typical of the claims and defenses of the class, as the representatives of each party comprise a broad cross section representing the entire class. Each of the representatives thus shares in the necessity of establishing the common questions of law and fact denominated herein.

(8) The representative parties named herein will fairly and adequately protect the interests of each class.

(A) The representatives of Class 1, 15 organizations of psychologists, are among the most influential and prestigious of these organizations. Two of these groups are nationwide in scope, while the remainder are state and local associations representing varying geographic localities and professional and scientific interests, but are all fairly representative of a cross section of American psychology.

(B) The representatives of Class 2, 18 individual psychologists, comprise a broad cross section of licensed and/or certified psychologists engaged in practice and active in mental health care in a variety of professional settings.

(C) The representatives of Class 3, 15 Federal employees, are employed by a number of Federal agencies in various fields. Each of thsee employees has been a Blue Cross-Shield subscriber for sometime past.

(9) The prosecution of separate actions by members of each class would create the risk of establishing incompatible standards of conduct for Defendants and would also create the risk of adjudications that would be dispositive of the rights of other members of the class or would substantially impair or impede their ability to protect their interests.

(10) Defendants engaging in the conspiracy herein alleged and in imposing and administering the "medical referral and supervision" clause have acted on grounds generally applicable to each class, thereby making appropriate the injunctive relief herein sought by each class.

(11) Common questions of law and fact shared by members of each class predominate over any individual questions and the class actions are superior to other means of adjudication of this controversy. In this instance, a class action is not only superior but is, in effect, the only practical manner of effectively resolving this controversy. Establishment of the conspiracy alleged herein predominates over any individual determination of damages that might remain subsequent to the establishment of liability. The interests of the individual members of the class in controlling the litigation are far overshadowed by the inability of any individual Plaintiff to undertake litigation of this nature. To the best of Plaintiffs' and Plaintiffs' counsels' belief, no other litigation has been commenced or is about to be commenced by members of any of the classes represented herein, in order to resolve this controversy. The District of Columbia is uniquely suited to be the forum of this litigation because of the fact that it is the location of the Federal Defendants and the offices of the Blue Cross–Blue Shield Federal Employees Program. In addition, the District of Columbia, and its neighboring jurisdictions, contain the homes and offices of large numbers of Federal employees. Any management problems inherent in this litigation can be mitigated by the strong

community of interest and the common channels of communication possessed by members of each class.

IV. DEFENDANTS

(1) Defendants Blue Cross Association and National Association of Blue Shield Plans are Illinois non-profit corporations (hereinafter referred to as Defendant Plans), which have their principal place of business in a jurisdiction other than the District of Columbia and which are qualified to do business and do business in the District of Columbia. Defendant Plans contract with the United States Civil Service Commission, on behalf of local health insurance organizations, and affiliates and subsidiaries of Defendant Plans, to provide health and hospital insurance for Federal employees, their annuitants and beneficiaries. Defendant Health Services, Inc. is an Illinois Corporation wholly owned by Defendant Blue Cross Association and engaged in providing health insurance. Defendant Medical Indemnity of America, Inc. Is an Illinois Corporation wholly owned by Defendant National Association of Blue Shield Plans and engaged in providing health insurance.

(2) Defendant United States Civil Service Commission, purporting to represent the interests of Federal employees, their beneficiaries and/or annuitants, allegedly negotiates and executes the contract in the public interest and in the interest of all the health and hospital insurance providers and participants.

(3) Defendant Robert E. Hampton is Chairman of the U.S. Civil Service Commission, Defendant Ludwig J, Andolsek is a Commissioner of the U.S. Civil Service Commission. Defendant Jayne Baker Spain is a Commissioner of the U.S. Civil Service Commission. They are sued herein in both their personal and official capacities, as the statutorily designated administrators of the Federal Employees Health Benefits Plan created pursuant to 5 U.S.C. 8900 *et seq.* Acting Attorney General of the United States Robert H. Bork is sued in his official capacity.

V. NATURE OF TRADE AND COMMERCE HERE INVOLVED

(1) Defendant Plans and their affiliates and subsidiaries, are engaged in the business of providing health and hospital insurance either individually or through group plans. To the best of Plaintiffs' information and belief, they operate in all 50 states and the District of Columbia, as well as all territories and possessions of the United States. The Federal Government as an employer has maintained since 1960 a group health and hospital insurance contract with Defendant Plans pursuant to the Federal Employees Health Benefits Act, 5 U.S.C. 8900 *et seq.* in which, to the best of Plaintiffs' information and belief, approximately 1.35 million Federal employees are enrolled. Also covered are approximately 3.95 million annuitants and beneficiaries of such employees.

(2) Defendant Plans are authorized to negotiate and contract for local health insurance organizations, and for affiliates and subsidiaries of Defendant Plans, who are contractually obligated to provide the actual health and hospital care reimbursement to the subscriber. These local organizations extend reciprocal treatment to subscribers enrolled in local plans elsewhere, who are temporarily in their area and incur expenses for covered health and hospital care. Many of these local health plans also provide services to persons living in more than one state.

VI. OFFENSES CHARGED

Count 1

(1) Defendant Plans and Defendant United States Civil Service Commission have annually negotiated since 1960 a contract for health and hospital insurance to be provided to Federal employees, their annuitants and beneficiaries.

None of the plaintiffs in this suit are permitted to, nor do they, participate in any manner in the negotiations as to the import. purpose or meaning of the contract nor may they participate in its execution. although it so substantially affects all of them individually as set out herein.

(2) The Contract (Exhibit "A") is negotiated and executed solely by the Defendant parties named and is presented to the subscribers and the general public as an accomplished fact.

(3) The Contract (Part 3, Article 1, (a) (12)) contains a "medical referral and supervision" clause which is as follows:

"The following services, when billed for by a hospital, a physician, or a member of a mental health team, and when applicable to the diagnosis and treatment of mental health and nervous disorders if provided at the request of and under the supervision and direction of the attending physician:

(A) Day-night care in hospitals, public and other non-profit community mental health centers as defined in the Community Mental Health Centers Act of 1963 (PL 88–164) as amended, and such outpatient psychiatrict facilities as are approved by the Corporations, when such care is provided during the prescribed course of treatment;

(B) Collateral visits with members of the patient's immediate family;

(C) Group therapy; and

(D) Therapy provided by a member of a "mental health team," (i.e., physician-clinical psychologist, psychiatric nurse, psychiatric social worker). The records of the attending physician must show that either he saw the patient or had written or personal contact with the therapist, at least once every 90 days; in any case, the attending physician must see the patient for evaluation at least once every twelve months."

(4) This "medical referral and supervision" clause improperly and illegally interferes in the relationship between psychologists and their clientele in that it purports to insert between the psychologists and his or her client the alleged supervisory role of a physician who need not be trained in psychiatry and whose functions are not governed by any discernible rule, regulation or standard, but whose enforced presence interposes a disparaging element sufficient to cause many subscribers either not to seek the assistance of a competent, licensed and/or certified psychologist, or not to continue utilizing such services. It unnecessarily inconveniences both the beneficiary and the purveyor of psychological services in derogation of the fact that in most states mental health care providers are equally licensed with medical providers. The "referral and supervision" is perfunctory and arbitrary and often performed by persons with only a cursory knowledge of psychiatry.

(5) Plaintiff Council for the Advancement of the Psychological Professions for the purpose of promoting and advancing the psychological professions and and Sciences, Inc. alleges, as a national organization of psychologists organized for the purpose of promoting and advancing the psychological professitns and sciences, including the promotion of the fullest development and utilization of psychological knowledge and services in health care delivery and the promotion of the interests of the public in securing free access to qualified providers of mental health care, that the "medical referral and supervision" clause of the contract is illegal, improper, and a violation of the antitrust laws of the United States in that:

(A) the said requirement does not promote better mental health care for the public; on the contrary, it is restrictive and in restraint of trade.

(B) the "referral" and "supervision" rendered thereunder is in most cases perfunctory and arbitrary.

(C) the physician rendering the alleged service need not be especially trained in psychiatry or mental health care.

(D) the requirement is illegally imposed by Defendant Plains' Boards of Directors, composed predominantly of physicians, as a "featherbedding" requirement pursuant to a combination and conspiracy in violation of Sections 1 and 3 in the Sherman Act, among Defendant Plans, its various subsidiaries and affiliates, physicians, and various other individuals and groups not presently identifiable by Plaintiffs prior to complete discovery by Plaintiffs. This conspiracy has as one of its objects the interference with the free exercise of their profession by members of the discipline of psychology and has gravely distorted the mental health care delivery system and the entire profession and science of psychology, as well as the delivery of health care by other qualified providers. In addition, this conspiracy has as an object limiting the access of Federal employee subscribers of Defendant Plans, and their affiliates and subsidiaries, to mental health care, particularly mental health care offered by psychologists licensed or certified in accordance with the laws of the respective states in which they practice, in order to minimize reimbursements that must be paid out by Defendant Plans, and their affiliates and subsidiaries, and to enhance Defendant Plans' cash flow and net asset position.

(E) psychologists qualified to diagnose and treat nervous and mental disorders are licensed and/or certified in 46 States and the District of Columbia, as of the date of this Complaint, and are, in addition, supervised by the American Psychological Association's professional standards, and by various State certification boards applying accepted standards, at least as strictly applied as those of the several States' statutory medical practice standards.

(F) the requirement illegally disparages the professional and science of psychology by subordinating it to the alleged supervision of another co-equal health provider profession, for no economic, health or other necessary reasonable purpose.

Wherefore, the premises considered, Plaintiff Council for the Advancement of the Psychological Professions and Sciences, Inc. requests this Honorable Court to issue a Preliminary and Permanent Injunction, enjoining Defendants, or anyone acting in concert with them, from in any manner enforcing the provisions of the "medical referral and supervision" clause in the Contract (Exhibit "A", *infra*) ; enjoining Defendant Plans, and their affiliates and subscribers, as a condition precedent to reimbursement for psychological services performed by qualified psychologists freely chosen as providers of psychological services by any F.E.H.B.A. subscriber, beneficiary, or annuitant eligible to receive same, without "referral and supervision," and enjoining any physician from charging or receiving any fee whatever to said subscriber for any alleged "referral" or "supervision," by way of reimbursement from Defendant Plans, and their affiliates and subsidiaries, or otherwise.

Count 2

(1) Plaintiffs in Class 1 reallege and reassert all of the allegations set forth in Count 1 hereof, as though fully set out herein.

(2) Plaintiffs in Class 1 allege that as organizations of psychologists whose objectives include the advancement of human welfare by promoting the fullest development and utilization of psychological knowledge and services and promoting the interests of the public in securing optimum access to providers, the "medical referral and supervision" clause of the contract, imposed in restraint of trade, has had and is continuing to have the following deleterious effects, among others:

(A) Mental health care requirements are not being met, resulting in severe public health problems.

(B) Trained manpower is not being fully utilized despite the need for better and more generally available mental health care.

(C) Defendant Plans' agents, servants and employees in the various States do not apply the present "medical referral and supervision" requirement uniformly and without discrimination ; on the contrary, said agents, employees and servants frequently act arbitrarily, unfairly and unequitably in that they grant or deny claims of subscribers on the basis of extraneous standards, such as the concealment from the subscriber at large of changes, additions to or deletions from the internal alleged rules, regulations and administrative procedures of Defendant Plans, and their affiliates and subsidiaries, which said changes, additions to or deletions are not generally made known to mental health care providers and/or their subscriber clientele, and by such various and diverse arbitrary decisions deny to Plaintiff psychologists and/or their clientele, the equal protection of the laws and the non-discriminatory application of contractual provisions in the Plans affecting hundreds of thousands of subscribers who cannot afford mental health care, although they require it, in part due to and because of the persistent arbitrary refusals by Defendant Plans, and their affiliates and subsidiaries, to reimburse subscribers, or to pay legitimate claims.

(D) The "medical referral and supervision" clause adds immeasurably and unnecessarily to the cost of mental health care since premiums paid by subscribers and by the United States of America, utilizing tax revenues therefor, are and have been increased regularly over the past ten years, and to the extent such increases have reflected payments to physicians for "referral and supervision" since such is totally unnecessary, such premium cost levels are higher than they ought to be and should have been, and Plaintiffs in Class I assert and allege that for the period 1967 through the date of the present suit fees ranging approximately from $25 to $50 paid to physicians per visit for referral and supervision prior to psychotherapy rendered by a qualified member of the organizations represented in Class 1 hereof have substantially increased premium costs to the subscriber and to the United States of America.

Wherefore, the premises considered, Plaintiffs in Class 1 request this Honorable Court to issue a Preliminary and Permanent Injunction, enjoining Defendants, or anyone acting inconcert with them, from in any manner continuing to enforce the "medical referral and supervision" clause in the Contract (Exhibit "A", *infra*); enjoining Defendant United States Civil Service Commission from authorizing, approving or making any contribution towards any payment of premiums under the contract which includes payments for physicians under such clause; declaring said clause null and void, and of no legal effect and directing said Defendant United States Civil Service Commission to forthwith undertake a study, under the supervision of the Court, to determine the nature, extent and scope of overpayments by it to Defendant Plans, the difference between what should have been paid by way of contribution to premiums and what has actually been paid for the period 1967 through 1973 to be ordered refunded to the Treasury of the United States by said Defendant Plans.

Count 3

(1) Plaintiffs in Class 2 reallege and reassert all of the allegations set forth in Counts 1 and 2 hereof, as though fully set out herein.

(2) Plaintiffs in Class 2 allege that they are individuals skilled in the study, development, and application of the principles of behavior, who have met recognized standards of the discipline of psychology in their area of expertise as set forth by law or by their professional or scientific organizations. Said Plaintiffs reside in every State in the Union and have as a result of the "medical referral and supervision" clause suffered serious disparagement to their professional standing by having members of their profession subject to unnecessary "supervision" which places those individual psychologists and the discipline as a whole in a subservient status. Plaintiffs also have suffered serious interference with their relationship with their clients as heretofore set out and have been generally restrained in the free exercise of their trade. In addition, many members of the class have also suffered serious financial losses as a result of the arbitrary and capricious failure by Defendant Plans, and their affiliates and subsidiaries, to reimburse members of said class for services covered under the contract.

Wherefore, the premises considered, Plaintiffs in Class 2 request this Honorable Court to issue a Preliminary and Permanent Injunction, enjoining Defendants or anyone acting in their behalf from in any manner enforcing the provisions of the "medical referral and supervision" clause in the Contract or Plan (Exhibit "A", *infra*); enjoining Defendant Plans, and their affiliates and subsidiaries, from imposing any such requirements upon subscriber-clients of Plaintiffs in Class 2 and other similarly situated as a condition precedent to reimbursement for services performed by Plaintiffs in Class 2 on behalf of any duly registered by Plaintiffs in Class 2 on behalf of any duly registered subscriber to the Plans eligible to receive same without "referral and supervision"; and, in addition, Plaintiffs in Class 2 allege herewith of Defendant Plans, and their affiliates and subsidiaries, the sum of $15,000,000 as damages resulting from Defendants violations of the antitrust laws of the United States, as alleged, and demand of Defendant Plans, and their affiliates and subsidiaries, treble the amount of such damages plus the costs of this action and reasonable attorneys' fees.

Count 4

(1) Plaintiffs in Class 3 reallege and reassert all of the allegations set forth in Counts 1, 2 and 3 hereof, as though fully set out herein.

(2) Plaintiffs in Class 3 sue on behalf of themselves as individual subscribers to Defendant Plans, and their affiliates and subsidiaries, pursuant to the F.E.H.B.A. contract and on behalf of all those similarly situated. Said Plaintiffs in Class 3 reside, to the best of Plaintiffs' knowledge and belief, in every State of the Union and the District of Columbia and have, since 1967, suffered and continue to suffer actual damages as a result of having no control whatever over premiums charged by Defendant Plans, and their affiliates and subsidiaries, and agreed to by Defendant United States Civil Service Commission, have been damaged and continue to be damaged by substantial overcharges (in

the form of higher premiums paid than necessary to be charged) from 1967 to the present; have been denied and continue to be denied freedom of access to a mental health practitioner of the choice of Plaintiffs in Class 3 without taking unnecessary sick leave, chargeable to the subscriber, for obtaining perfunctory "medical reverral and supervision" and have been damaged by interference with their relationship with a psychologist that the intrusion of unnecessary "supervision" by a non-psychiatrist physician causes. Further, various of the members of Class 3 have suffered and continue to suffer refusal of appropriate reimbursement or denial of legitimate claims for covered services rendered by psychologists; have suffered and continue to suffer cancellation of Blue Cross-Blue Shield policies for illegal, arbitrary and capricious reasons; and have suffered and continue to suffer discriminatory application of the "referral and supervision" clause governed by no discernible standards, rules or regulations of Defendant Plans, and their affiliates and subsidiaries, whatever, all of the above being pursuant to the illegal combination and conspiracy as herein described.

Wherefore, the premises considered, Plaintiffs in Class 3 request the same orders of Court and the relief sought by all the other Plaintiffs and on behalf of themselves and all other individuals similarly situated respectfully ask the Court to order same, and, in addition:

(1) Pray for an Order directing the Defendant Plans, and their affiliates and subsidiaries, to disgorge and pay to Plaintiffs in Class 3 a sum equal to three times the difference between that portion of premiums charged since 1967, including the "medical referral and supervision" requirement or $25 million dollars ($25,000,000) whichever is lower.

(2) Pray for an Order directing Defendant Plans, and their affiliates and subsidiaries, to disgorge and pay to Plaintiffs the sum of Ten Million Dollars ($10,000,000) as punitive damages.

Count 5

(1) Plaintiff National Association of Government Employees (NAGE) realleges and reasserts all of the allegatnons set forth in Counts 1, 2, 3, and 4 hereof, as though fully set out herein.

(2) Plaintiff NAGE alleges that as a union of Federal Government employees and an organization concerned with the optimum availability of psychological services both for its own members and for the general public it has a substantial interest in the outcome of this litigation. Said membership has a community of interest with all other Plaintiff organizations, associations and individuals in receiving better mental health care under the contract at the lowest possible premium cost.

Wherefore, the premises considered, Plaintiff NAGE requests the same orders of Court and the relief sought by all other Plaintiffs, and respectfully requests the Court to order same, and such other relief as may seem to the Court just and proper, with respect to said Plaintiff NAGE.

JOSEPH L. NELLIS,
JEFFREY L. NESVET,
1819 H. Street, N.W.,
Washington, D.C. 20006,
Tel. 223-6300
Attorneys for Plaintiffs.

District of Columbia, S.S.

Dr. Melvin A. Gravitz, being duly sworn deposes and says: That he is Secretary of the Council for the Advancement of the Psychological Professions and Sciences, Inc.; one of the Plaintiffs above-named in this proceeding; that he had read the foregoing Complaint and knows the contents thereof; that the same is true to the knowledge of deponent and that all the material allegations of the said. Complaint are within the personal knowledge of deponent.

MELVIN A. GRAVITZ, Ph.D.,
2025 Eye Street, N.W.,
Washington, D.C. 20006
Secretary, Council for the Advancement
of the Psychological Professions
and Sciences, Inc.

District of Columbia, S.S.

I hereby certify that on this _____ day of _____ 1973, before me the subscriber, a notary public in and for the District of Columbia, personally appeared Dr. Melvin A. Gravitz and acknowledged the foregoing statement to be his act.

Witness my hand and notarial seal the day and year last above written.

Notary Public
District of Columbia

My Commission expires: -----------------

In the United States District Court for the District of Columbia

[Civil Action No. 1623–73]

COUNCIL FOR THE ADVANCEMENT OF THE PSYCHOLOGICAL PROFESSION AND SCIENCES, INC., ET AL., PLAINTIFFS,

v.

BLUE CROSS ASSOCIATION, A CORPORATION, 1700 PENNSYLVANIA AVENUE, N. W., WASHINGTON, D. C. 20006,

NATIONAL ASSOCIATION OF BLUE SHIELD, PLANS, A CORPORATION, 1700 PENNSYLVANIA AVENUE, N.W., WASHINGTON, D. C. 20006, AND

UNITED STATES CIVIL SERVICE COMMISSION, 1900 E STREET, N. W., WASHINGTON, D. C. 20451, ET AL., DEFENDANTS.

Reply Memorandum in Support of Defendants' Motion to Dismiss The Complaint

BARRON K. GRIER,
Miller & Chevalier,
1700 Pennsylvania Avenue, N.W.,
Washington, D.C. 20006,
Attorneys for Blue Cross Association
and National Association of Blue Shield Plans.
STANLEY D. ROBINSON,
MICHAEL MALINA,
Kaye, Scholer, Fierman, Hays
& Handler,
425 Park Avenue,
New York, New York 10022,
Attorneys for Blue Cross Association.
FREDERICK M. ROWE,
EDWARD W. WARREN,
Kirkland, Ellis & Rowe,
1776 K Street, N.W.,
Washington, D. C. 20006,
Attorneys for National Association
of Blue Shield Plans.

FEBRUARY 19, 1974.

CERTIFICATE OF SERVICE

I HEREBY CERTIFY that on February 19, 1974, I served, by first-class mail, postage prepaid, the foregoing Reply Memorandum in Support of Defendants' Motion to Dismiss the Complaint to attorney for plaintiffs, Joseph L. Nellis, Esq., 1819 H. Street, N. W., Washington, D. C. 20006, and upon attorney for federal defendants, Thomas G. Corcoran, Jr., Esq., Assistant United States Attorney, U. S. Court House, Room 3423, Washington, D. C.

EDWARD W. WARREN.

In the United States District Court for the District of Columbia

[Civil Action No. 1623–73]

COUNCIL FOR THE ADVANCEMENT OF THE PSYCHOLOGICAL PROFESSIONS AND SCIENCES, INC., ET AL., PLAINTIFFS,

v.

BLUE CROSS ASSOCIATION, A CORPORATION, 1600 PENNSYLVANIA AVENUE, N.W., WASHINGTON, D. C. 20006, AND

NATIONAL ASSOCIATION OF BLUE SHIELD, PLANS, A CORPORATION, 1700 PENNSYL-

VANIA AVENUE, N.W., WASHINGTON, D. C. 20006, AND
UNITED STATES CIVIL SERVICE COMMISSION, 1900 E STREET, N.W., WASHINGTON,
D.C. 20451, ET AL., DEFENDANTS

*Reply Memorandum in Support of Defendants' Motion to Dismiss the Com-
plaint*

PRELIMINARY STATEMENT

In their opening Memorandum, defendants Blue Cross Association ("Blue Cross") and National Association of Blue Shield Plans ("Blue Shield") demonstrated (1) that the medical referral and supervision clause in Blue Cross' and Blue Shield's contract with the United States Civil Service Commission ("the Commission") does not violate the antitrust laws because it neither "restrains" trade nor affects "commercial competition"; and (2) that none of the plaintiffs here other than the individual federal employee subscribers has standing to sue under the antitrust laws.

Plaintiffs' Memorandum, unable to refute our contentions, seeks instead to sidetrack the Court with extraneous discussion of state licensing provisions for psychologists, irrelevant references to "professional and scientific health literature," the membership composition of the American Psychological Association (the chief professional association of psychologists which *significantly is not a plaintiff in this lawsuit*), and plaintiffs' constant refrain that there should be "complete parity" between the *professional status* of psychologists and physicians. (Pltfs.' Mem. at 1–3.)

Although plaintiffs would transform this litigation into a broad legislative inquiry concerning the prestige and status of psychologists,[1] that is not the function of this court in a civil action under the antitrust laws. The plain fact is that plaintiffs' complaint fails to state a claim cognizable under these statutes and hence must be dismissed.

I. FAR FROM VIOLATING THE SHERMAN ACT, THE MEDICAL REFERRAL AND SUPERVISION CLAUSE CONSTITUTES A VALID EXERCISE OF DEFENDANTS' CONCEDED "RIGHT TO DETERMINE WHICH RISKS THEY WILL INSURE," AND ACTUALLY PROMOTES COMPETITION BY PROVIDING EVERY FEDERAL EMPLOYEE WITH THE "CHOICE" OF BENEFIT COVERAGE ADMITTEDLY "MANDATED" BY CONGRESS IN THE FEDERAL EMPLOYEES HEALTH BENEFITS ACT

Our opening Memorandum demonstrated that the medical referral and supervision clause challenged by plaintiffs' complaint does not violate the Sherman Act because it neither "restrains" trade nor affects "commercial competition."

Plaintiffs' response significantly concedes that Blue Cross and Blue Shield have a "right to determine which risks they will insure," and that Congress "mandated a system whereby Federal employees would have a choice among competitng insurance programs offering different levels of coverage and choices of risks"—illustrated here by the Aetna plan (available to every federal employee) which does *not* require medical referral and supervisions. (Pltfs.' Mem. at 20, 23.)

To avoid the inescapable conclusion which follows from these concessions—that the complaint does *not* state a claim under the Sherman Act—plaintiffs lamely argue that, despite defendants' admitted "right to select the risks against which they will insure," Blue Cross and Blue Shield may not lawfully choose to insure only those psychologist services subject to medical referral and supervision. Rather, plaintiffs contend that the determination not to insure the risk of all psychologist services constitutes a group "boycott" and a "conspiracy" among Blue Cross and Blue Shield and unidentified "members of the medical profession." (Pltfs.' Mem. at 20–24.)

Plaintiffs' last-ditch effort to shore up their case is unavailing because:

1. Blue Cross and Blue Shield did not "restrain trade" but simply exercised their admitted "right to determine which risks they will insure" by agreeing

---

[1] Significantly, Congress is currently considering a bill (H.R. 8057) which would amend the Federal Employees Health Benefits Act to grant plaintiffs the very relief which they seek in this lawsuit by providing for reimbursement of psychologists "without supervision or referral by another health practitioner."

Hearings have been held on this proposed amendment with plaintiffs presenting their full case for "complete parity" between physicians and psychologists to the appropriate congressional committee. *Hearings on H.R. 8057 before the Subcommittee on Retirement, Insurance and Health Benefits of the House Post Office and Civil Service Committee,* 93d. Cong., 1st Sess. (1973).

with the Commission to cover psychologist services based on medical referral and supervision.

2. Labeling Blue Cross' and Blue Shield's determination of "which risks they will insure" a "boycott" or "conspiracy" cannot create a "restraint of trade" where none exists.

3. Far from "restraining" competition under the Sherman Act, the Blue Cross and Blue Shield contract actually promotes competition by guaranteeing every federal employee the "choice" of insurance coverage for psychologist services admittedly "mandated" by Congress in the Federal Employees Health Benefits Act.

4. The medical referral and supervision clause does ot affect "commercial competition" in the marketing of goods and services—an essential prerequisite to any Sherman Act violation.

A. THE MEDICAL REFERRAL AND SUPERVISION CLAUSE DOES NOT "RESTRAIN" TRADE BECAUSE, AS PLAINTIFFS CONCEDE, BLUE CROSS AND BLUE SHIELD HAVE A "RIGHT TO DETERMINE WHICH RISKS THEY WILL INSURE"

In contracting with the Civil Service Commission, Blue Cross and Blue Shield are "charged with an obligation to their myriad policyholders" to "get the best deal possible" so that "the savings thus realized" can be passed along to their subscribers. *Ruddy Brook Clothes, Inc.* v. *British & Foreign Marine Ins. Co.*, 195 F.2d 86, 90 (7th Cir.), *cert. denied*, 344 U.S. 816 (1952); *Travelers Ins. Co.* v. *Blue Cross of Western Pennsylvania*, 481 F.2d 80, 84 (3d Cir.), *cert. denied*, 42 U.S.L.W. 3348 (1973).

This cost-control objective can be achieved only if broad risk insurers like Blue Cross and Blue Shield are free "to exercise . . . care in the selection of risks which they assume" without intrusion by third parties such as plaintiffs in this case, seeking "to dictate the terms upon which [Blue Cross and Blue Shield] may offer their benefits to those individuals who need protection against many risks." *Ruddy Brook Clothes, Inc.* v. *British & Foreign Marine Ins. Co., supra; American Family Life Assur. Co.* v. *Blue Cross of Florida, Inc.*, 1973–2 Trade Cas. ¶74,767 at p. 95,341 (5th Cir. 1973).

Because of these considerations, the courts have consistently ruled that no "restraint of trade" within the Sherman Act is present when insurers choose to cover some risks but not others—as Blue Cross and Blue Shield did here when they agreed with the Civil Service Commission to insure psychologist services based on medical referral and supervision. *American Family Life Assur. Co.* v. *Blue Cross of Florida, Inc., supra; Travelers Ins. Co.* v. *Blue Cross of Western Pennsylvania, supra; Ruddy Brook Clothes, Inc.* v. *British & Foreign Marine Ins. Co., supra; American Family Life Assur. Co.* v. *Aetna Life Ins., C.A.* 10582 (N.D. Ga., December 28, 1973); *Nankin Hospital* v. *Michigan Hospital Service*, 1973–2 CCH Trade Cas. ¶74,686 (E.D. Mich. 1973); *Conn. Ass'n of Clinical Laboratories* v. *Conn. Blue Cross*, 1973–2 Trade Cas. ¶74,765 (Sup. Ct. Fairfield Co. 1973).

Faced with this unbroken line of authority, *plaintiffs do not cite a single contrary case*, and instead. expressly *concede* the right of Blue Cross and Blue Shield "to determine which risks they will insure." (Pltfs.' Mem. at 20.)

To salvage their case in the face of this critical concession, plaintiffs offer only the patently specious argument that a restraint of trade is present here because the choice "to insure against costs accruing from treatment for nervous and mental disorders" has already "been made," thus barring any provision allowing psychologists "to provide care only under certain conditions dictated by Defendants." (Pltfs.' Mem. at 20–21.)

This contention does nothing more than reiterate, without supporting authority, the rigid stance taken by both plaintiffs' original and amended complaint—that Blue Cross and Blue Shield cannot contract with the Commission to provide coverage for the services of psychologists *at all* unless reimbursement is provided independent of *any* medical referral and supervision.

Furthermore, plaintiffs' argument that the general rule of "no restraint of trade" does not apply here is factually erroneous, plainly illogical, and contrary to sound policy.

Thus, contrary to plaintiffs' claim, Blue Cross and Blue Shield *never* determined "to insure against costs accruing from treatment for nervous and mental disorders." Rather, they agreed with the Commission to insure only against *some* costs accruing from treatment of nervous and mental disorders *including* the services of psychologists based on medical referral and supervision.

Moreover, since, as plaintiffs concede, Blue Cross and Blue Shield have the right "to determine which risks they will insure," then, by definition, they have the right to withhold coverage for psychologists' services performed without medical referral and supervision. For the choice by Blue Cross and Blue Shield to insure psychologist services with or without medical referral and supervision, like the choice of whether to insure any other risk, requires a balancing, however, imprecise, of the savings to subscribers, including control of runaway benefit costs, against the possible advantages, if any, which might result from dropping the initial medical diagnosis.[2]

Finally, plaintiffs' "all or nothing" stance would inevitably deter insurers from extending *any* coverage for nervous and mental disorders, since risks of a possible Sherman Act violation arise under plaintiffs' perverse approach *only* if the choice is made to provide nervous and mental benefits at all.

Fortunately for federal employees (and even for psychologist plaintiffs, who as a result have received substantial payments), Blue Cross and Blue Shield and the Civil Service Commission have contracted to insure for psychologist services based on medical referral and supervision.

If, as plaintiffs concede, this salutory expression of benefit coverage was not compelled by the antitrust laws, neither should it be condemned as an illegal "restraint of trade."

In sum, plaintiffs' concession of Blue Cross' and Blue Shield's "right to determine which risks they will insure" says no less than what the courts have consistently ruled—no actionable "restraint of trade" occurred when Blue Cross and Blue Shield agreed with the Commission to insure psychologist services based on medical referral and supervision.

B. LABELING BLUE CROSS AND BLUE SHIELD'S DETERMINATION OF "WHICH RISKS THEY WILL INSURE" A "BOYCOTT" OR "CONSPIRACY" CANNOT CREATE A "RESTRAINT OF TRADE" WHERE NONE EXISTS

Plaintiffs cannot concoct a "restraint of trade" where none exists by a simple change of labels. Switching the theory of their case from "disparagement" and "discrimination" against psychologists to a group "boycott" by "one competing group of providers of treatment to exclude another qualified competitng group of providers of health services" does not cure the legal insufficiency of plaintiffs' complaint. (Pltfs.' Mem. at 20.)

Plaintiffs' original complaint conspicuously failed to allege that the medical referral and supervision clause affects "commercial competition," and instead relied on purported "disparagement" of the "profession and science of psychology," interference with "the relationship between psyhhologists and their clientele," and allegations that "perfunctory and arbitrary" medical supervision does not promote "bétter mental health care for the public." (C., VI (5).)

Whatever the remedy for these alleged grievances might be, they have nothing to do with "commercial competition" and hence fail to state any claim cognizable under the antitrust laws.[3]

Straining to keep their moribund case alive, plaintiffs filed a refurbished amended complaint on January 28, 1974, alleging "a combination and conspir-

---

[2] The experience of Aetna, whose costs for psychologist services have increased 71% since 1971 when their medical referral and supervision clause was dropped, suggests that cost control in this area indeed poses a serious problem. *See Statement of Andrew E. Ruddock, Director, Bureau of Retirement, Insurance, and Occupational Health, United States Civil Service Commission, July 24, 1973, Hearings on H.R. 8057 before the Subcommittee on Retirement, Insurance and Health Benefits of the Post Office and Civil Service Committee,* 93d. Cong., 1st Sess. 2–5.

[3] Plaintiffs themselves suggest that state legislation barring medical referral and supervision may be an appropriate remedy for their alleged claim. (Plaintiffs' Memorandum at 1–3.)

Moreover, plaintiffs have previously sought elimination of the medical referral and supervision clause through negotiations between the Commission and Blue Cross and Blue Shield, and also are currently promoting H.R. 8057, a pending bill which would amend the FEHBA to require that all contracts under the Act provide direct reimbursement for the services of psychologists 'without medical supervision or referral by another health practitioner." See fn. 1, *supra.*

acy . . . among Defendant Plans, its various subsidiaries and affiliates, physicians . . . [having] as one of its objects the interference with the free exercise of their profession by members of the discipline of psychology . . . [and a further] object of limiting the access of Federal employee subscribers . . . to mental health care, particularly mental health care offered by psychologists . . . in order to minimize reimbursement that must be paid out by Defendant Plans . . . and to enhance Defendant Plans' cash flow and net asset position." (AC., VI (5) (D).)

Plaintiffs' Memorandum departs one step further from reality by charging a nebulous conspiracy including unidentified "members of the medical profession" "to divert substantial revenues to physicians," and involving a group "boycott" by "one competing group of providers of treatment of exclude another qualified competing group of providers of health services." (Pltfs.' Mem. at 20–21.)

This desperate attempt by plaintiffs to avoid dismissal must fail, because the courts have repeatedly ruled in the context of similar so-called boycott allegations that no illegal "restraint of trade" occurs when insurers, such as Blue Cross and Blue Shield here, exercise their conceded "right to determine which risks they will insure." For conclusory allegations of boycott cannot resurrect an otherwise insufficient complaint.

American Family Life Assur. Co. v. Blue Cross of Florida, supra, is illustrative. There, plaintiffs "*contended* that the application of the Blue Cross-Blue Shield COB [coordination of benefits provision] to their policies in Miami Beach constituted a *boycott* and amounted to a *restraint of trade* within the terms of Section 1 of the Sherman Act." 1973–2 Trade Cas. ¶74,767 at p. 95,340 (emphasis added).

Like plaintiffs here, who seek to meet the "commercial competition" requirement by charging a conspiracy including unidentified "members of the medical profession," plaintiffs in *American Family Life* strongly urged that they were in competition with Blue Cross and Blue Shield even though they sold an entirely different insurance product. *Id.*

The Fifth Circuit ruled, however, that even assuming plaintiffs' allegations of boycott and competition with Blue Cross and Blue Shield, the challenged COB contract provision did *not* constitute an actionable "restraint of trade." In so holding, the Court rested squarely on Blue Cross' and Blue Shield's conceded "right to determine which risks they will insure":

"When they [Blue Cross and Blue Shield] include COB in their policies these companies are simply providing that to a certain extent they shall not make payments received or to be received from some other insurance policy, *thus reducing the cost of their broad risk coverage as well as its cost to the insured.*

*   *   *   *   *   *   *

"We cannot say *under §1 of the Sherman Act* that an insurance company insuring against only one risk *is entitled to dictate the terms upon which broad risk companies* [Blue Cross and Blue Shield] *may offer their benefits to those individuals who need protection* against many risks. *Id.* at p. 95,341 (emphasis added). *See also, Ruddy Brook Clothes, Inc. v. British & Foreign Marine Ins., supra* based on defendant insurer's right of "selection of risks which they would assume").

The principles which prompted the Fifth Circuit in *American Family Life* to hold that the contract provision there did not constitute a "restraint of trade" are strikingly illustrated by two additional cases decided in the last four months, which were not discussed in our opening Memorandum.

First, in *American Family Life Assur. Co. v. Aetna Life Ins. Co., supra*,[4] the Court was faced with essentially the same question previously presented to the Fifth Circuit in *American Family Life Assur. Co. v. Blue Cross of Florida* except that private insurers, not Blue Cross and Blue Shield, were seeking to assert a COB provision against plaintiffs. Like plaintiffs here, plaintiffs there took great pains to couch their complaint in terms of a group boycott.

The Court flatly rejected plaintiff's argument that its "boycott" allegations precluded entry of summary judgment for defendants:

---

[4] A copy of this as yet unreported opinion is submitted herewith for the Court's convenience as Attachment 1.

"In its complaint, of course, and in its brief, plaintiff here does assail defendants' motives and intent at every page, but the . . . circumstances it adduces do no more than recite the advantages and the effects of COB and only convince the court the more that defendants' motives and purposes . . . were simply not anticompetitive." (Slip. Opin. at 5.)

Echoing the Third Circuit in *Travelers Ins. Co.* v. *Blue Cross of Western Pennsylvania, supra*, and the Fifth Circuit in *American Family Life*, the Court dismissed plaintiffs' case because defendants had "done no more than conduct its business as every rational enterprise does, *i.e.*, get the best deal possible." (Slip. Opin. at 7.)

A second case even closer on its facts to the instant situation is *Connecticut Association of Clinical Laboratories* v. *Connecticut Blue Cross, Inc., supra*. There, plaintiffs, three private medical testing laboratories, challenged a contract between Blue Cross and three hospitals providing insurance coverage to Blue Cross subscribers for laboratory tests performed on an outpatient basis. As described by the Court, the effect of this provision on private laboratories was virtually identical to the alleged effect of the medical referral and supervision clause on psychologist plaintiffs in this case:

"This program will allow outpatients whom *any doctor sends to the three defendant hospitals* for laboratory tests to be *covered* by the patients' Blue Cross contract, *but* will *not* provide coverage *for the same tests at a private laboratory.*" 1973-2 Trade Cas. ¶74,765 at p. 95,333 (emphasis added).

On the same theory as the psychologist plaintiffs here, the private laboratories in the *Connecticut Ass'n* case charged a "boycott" by Blue Cross and their alleged hospital competitors:

"Their claim is that coverage of outpatient laboratory tests only at the three hospitals *will persuade or induce Blue Cross subscribers to deal with the hospitals and not with the plaintiffs* . . . and that it is also a primary *boycott* in *that no such contract or pilot program has been agreed to with the private laboratories.*'" *Id.* at p. 95,334 (emphasis added).

Despite this boycott claim, the Court applied the state antitrust law, which "in effect has codified the federal cases interpreting the Sherman Anti-Trust Act," to deny plaintiffs' motion for injunctive relief:

"*Nowhere* does it appear that the agreements with the hospitals were designed to *deprive* anyone including the private laboratories, of *a subscriber's right to go where he wishes* for outpatient tests. The agreement *does not deprive subscribers of their freedom to deal with private laboratories*, albeit they conceivably might go where coverage exists." *Id.* at p. 95,335 (emphasis added).

These controlling cases (which plaintiffs do not even attempt to dispute with a single contrary citation),[5] dictate that the complaint must be dismissed despite the belated conspiracy and boycott charges which plaintiffs have concocted to keep this lawsuit alive.

For, as in the *Connecticut Ass'n* case, the medical referral and supervision clause does *not* deprive "a subscriber [of the] right to where he wishes" or of his "freedom to deal with" plaintiff psychologists. Instead, like the coordination of benefits clause in the *American Family Life* cases, the challenged clause here accords with Blue Cross' and Blue Shield's right to "get the best deal possible" so that "the savings thus realized" can be passed along to their subscribers—indeed, the very "right to determine which risks they will insure" expressly conceded by plaintiffs.

---

[5] Unable to distinguish the pertinent cases dealing with the peculiar circumstances of the insurance business, plaintiffs rely on hornbook decisions involving classic horizontal boycotts. *Fashion Originators Guild of America, Inc.* v. *FTC*, 312 U.S. 456 (1941) (conspiracy among clothing designers not to sell to stores buying from competing fashion "pirates") ; *Klor's Inc.* v. *Broadway-Hale Stores, Inc.*, 359 U.S. 207 (1959) (conspiracy among a retailer of appliances and his suppliers not to sell to a competing appliance retail store) ; *United States* v. *Standard Oil Co.*, 173 Fed. 177, *aff'd*, 221 U.S. 1 (1911) (nothing to do with boycott ; ordered dissolution of the old Standard Oil trust under the Sherman Act "rule of reason").

None of plaintiffs' cases concern the insurers' "right to determine which risks they will insure." *California League of Independent Insurance Producers* v. *Aetna Cas. & Sur. Co.*, 179 F. Supp. 65 (N.D. Calif. 1959) (Pltfs. Mem. at 23) involved a refusal by insurance companies to do business with insurance agents except at a fixed rate, but had nothing to do with the subscriber's choice of insurance benefits or the company's conceded right to determine which risks it would insure.

C. FAR FROM "RESTRAINING" COMPETITION UNDER THE SHERMAN ACT, THE MEDICAL REFERRAL AND SUPERVISION CLAUSE ACTUALLY PROMOTES COMPETITION AND GUARANTEES THE "CHOICE" OF BENEFIT COVERAGE FOR EVERY FEDERAL EMPLOYEE WHICH PLAINTIFFS ADMIT WAS "MANDATED" BY CONGRESS.

The conceded right of Blue Cross and Blue Shield "to determine which risks they will insure" (Pltfs.' Mem. at 20) was adopted and amplified by Congress in the Federal Employees Health Benefits Act of 1959. Both the Act's provisions and its legislative history show that Congress granted the Commission and the health insurance carriers the broadest conceivable authority to conduct arms-length contract negotiations and to resolve all disputes concerning contract benefits. 5 U.S.C. §8902; H.R. Rep. No. 957, 86th Cong., 1st Sess. (1959) ; S. Rep. No. 468, 86th Cong., 1st Sess. 10 (1959).

At the same time, Congress intended that federal employees would have a "free choice among health benefit plans" each offering different benefit coverage. H.R. Rep. No. 957, 86th Cong., 1st Sess. 3 (1959). This "free choice" would not only permit "each employee to exercise independent judgment and obtain the plan which best suits his or her individual needs or family circumstances" but would also "tend to produce lower costs than if only one approach using one carrier or a syndicate of carriers were used to cover all employees." Id., S. Rep. No. 468, 86th Cong., 1st Sess. 8 (1959).

Indeed, because of this indisputable Congressional intent, plaintiffs now concede that the Act "mandated a system whereby Federal employees would have a choice among competing insurance programs offering different levels of coverage and choices of risks." (Pltfs.' Mem. at 20.)

Unquestionably, plaintiffs' lawsuit would destroy this "choice", and would equate Blue Cross' and Blue Shield's coverage of psychologist services with that of their chief competitor Aetna (which does *not* require medical referral and supervision). Plaintiffs, nevertheless, seek a special exception in their case, arguing that nothing in the legislative history "purposes to stand for the proposition that Congress intended to authorize discriminatory treatment of one coequal group of competing providers of health services at the behest of another group of competing providers of health services." Id.

Stripped of its rhetoric, this contention boils down to a patently incorrect charge that Congress intended to withhold from the Commission and the carriers the right to determine when, and under what circumstances, benefit coverages would extend to the services of non-physician health professionals.

The fact is that Congress intended to leave to the Civil Service Commission and the health insurance carriers the decision of whether and on what terms to provide coverage for the services of non-physician professionals including psychologists. The legislative history could not be clearer.

During hearings on the bill which was eventually enacted, Congressman Murray, Chairman of the House Post Office and Civil Service Committee, clarified Congress' position on this very issue during testimony by postal union representatives :

"The CHAIRMAN. Are *optometrists* included in this bill?

Mr. KEATING. I think there is no specific definition on what is included.

The CHAIRMAN. How about *chiropractors* and *foot doctors?*

Mr. KEATING. I think the essential feature of this bill is this. The administrative and controversial details—many are controversial, but many are of such type they have to be settled on the ground—they are *left pretty much to the* [Civil Service] *Commission.*

Mr. REES. Would the [Civil Service] Commission decide whether foot doctors or chiropractors are included?

Mr. KEATING. They would have that authority.

Mr. HALLBECK. It is the contract they would write which would determine that.

Mr. KEATING. If the insurer has a policy of paying certain groups, he would include that in his contract. Whenever you run into this problem in the medical field, you run into a lot of different types of *doctors that the Medical Association does not recognize exactly as being full-fledged doctors that want coverage. The authority in this bill is in the hands of the Commission and in the hands of the companies in making their contracts." Hearings before the Committee on Post Office and Civil Service on S. 2162,* House of Representatives, 86th Cong., 1st Sess. 52–53 (1959) (emphasis added).

No one could seriously suggest that Congress intended to grant psychologists the power to dictate the terms of insurance contracts between the Civil Service Commission and carriers which "optomotrists," "chiropractors" and "foot doctors" are expressly denied. To afford psychologists such a veto power would nullify the right of health insurance carriers "to determine which risks they will insure" and destroy "free choice" for every federal employee, which even plaintiffs admit, lies at the heart of the statutory scheme.

Indeed, the absence of any such veto for psychologists follows *a fortiori* from the recent insurtnce cases cited above, which even in the absence of a statute mandating "free choice" for every federal employee, deny antitrust relief so as to preserve the public's right to "choose" between competing insurance plans.

For instance, in *American Family Life Assur. Co.* v. *Aetna Ins. Co., supra,* the Court rejected plaintiff's antitrust case based on boycott allegations, stressing:

"[A]t stake here is the *right of the public to buy* a policy with or without COB, *as it chooses.*" Slip Opin. at 6 (emphasis added).

Similarly, in *Connecticut Ass'n of Clinical Laboratories* v. *Connecticut Blue Cross, supra,* the Court emphasized that:

"50% of Blue Cross subscribers have the C.M.S. Century contract which presently provides coverage for outpatient laboratory tests. It is interesting to note that C.M.S. does not cover outpatient hospital laboratory tests. Insurance companies' contracts and government programs also provide coverage for outpatient laboratory tests." 1973–2 Trade Cas. ¶74,765 at p. 95,334.

Accordingly, the Court rejected plaintiff private laboratories' effort to deprive the public's right to choose benefit coverage limited to outpatient laboratory tests performed at hospital laboratories:

"Significantly, *Blue Cross has competitors,* in the state, *who insure the ancilliary service involved here* or who could insure it. It has *not* been demonstrtted to this court that the agreements with these three hospitals have a *pernicious effect on competition* and lack redeeming virtue. *Id.* at p. 95,336 (emphasis added).

In sum, just as in *American Family Life,* what is "at stake here is the right of the public to buy a policy with or without" medical referral and supervision "as it chooses." For like Blue Cross" competitors in the *Connecticut Ass'n* case, Blue Cross' and Blue Shield's chief competitor, Aetna, "insure[s] the ancillary service involved here" by providing coverage for psychologist services independent of medical referral and supervision.

Therefore, the "free choice" to every federal employee afforded by this competition between Blue Cross and Blue Shield and Aetna (which even plaintiffs admit was "mandated" by Congress) can be preserved only by dismissing plaintiffs' complaint as contrary to both the antitrust laws and the Federal Employees Health Benefits Act.

D. THE MEDICAL REFERRAL AND SUPERVISION CLAUSE DOES NOT AFFECT "COMMERCIAL COMPETITION" IN THE MARKETING OF GOODS AND SERVICES—AN ESSENTIAL PREREQUISITE TO ANY SHERMAN ACT VIOLATION

As we have shown, the absence of any actionable "restraint of trade" here follows inevitably from plaintiffs' twin concessions of Blue Cross' and Blue Shield's "right to determine which risks they will insure" and the "choice" of benefit coverage for every federal employee "mandated" by Congress—which would be destroyed if Blue Cross and Blue Shield were compelled to equate their benefit coverage for psychologist services with that of their chief competitor, Aetna.

But wholly apart from the absence of any "restraint of trade," plaintiffs cannot establish the requisite restraint on "commercial competition" necessary for a Sherman Act violation. For as plaintiffs recognize, the burden is squarely on them to show both that the medical referral and supervision clause entails "an intent or purpose to affect the commercial aspects of [their] profession" and was "adopted for anticompetitive reasons." *Marjorie Webster Jr. College* v. *Middle States Ass'n of Colleges and Secondary Schools,* 432 F.2d 650, 651 (D.C. Cir. 1970) ; *Nankin Hospital* v. *Michigan Hospital Service, supra,* at p. 95,034 (Pltfs.' Mem. at 25).

Plainly, plaintiffs' complaint fails to satisfy this burden. To be sure, plaintiffs' amended complaint goes to great lengths by vague "conspiracy" allegations, including unidentified "members of the medical profession," to expand the scope of their grievance so as to concoct a tenuous nexus to "commercial competition." (AC., VI(5).)

But, as the *Marjorie Webster* case itself demonstrates, even allegations of "competition" between plaintiffs and defendant insurers and the Commission— which plaintiffs here have not and obviously cannot make—are insufficient to satisfy plaintiffs' burden of showing "an intent or purpose to affect the commercial aspects" of their profession. Thus, in *Marjorie Webster*, the defendant Middle States Association, which denied plaintiff's accreditation, was made up of colleges and secondary schools directly competing with Marjorie Webster for enrollments, donations and financial assistance. 432 F.2d at 652–53.

A fortiori, no "intent or purpose to affect the commercial aspects" of plaintiffs' profession can be shown simply by plaintiffs' vague conspiracy charges involving plaintiffs' purported unidentified competitors in the "medical profession," who are not even parties to this lawsuit.

Nor are plaintiffs helped by conclusionary claims that the challenged clause interferes "with the free exercise of their profession by members of the discipline of psychology," or diverts "substantial revenues to physicians." (AC., VI 5(C)) (Pltfs.' Mem. at 20.)

Indeed, in the face of comparable assertions, the Court in *American Family Life Assur. Co. v. Aetna Life Ins. Co., supra*, entered summary judgment for defendants:

"*In its complaint*, of course, and in its brief, *plaintiff here does assail defendants' motive and intent on every page*, but the . . . circumstances it adduces do no more than recite the advantages and the effects of COB and only convince the court the more that defendants' motives and purposes, already described in some detail, were simply not anticompetitive.

*　　*　　*　　*　　*　　*　　*

As the court views COB, therefore, it is simply a new or at least different product, and *upon analysis, plaintiff's claim of boycott is not based so much on defendants' bad motive or exclusionary intent as upon the naked claim that the mere employment of a COB limitation at all, at any time*, or against any insurance company (including defendants) *amounts to boycott in itself.*" (Slip Opin. at 5–6) (emphasis added).

In short, plaintiffs cannot show that the medical referral and supervision clause was adopted "for anticompetitive reasons." This is so because "upon analysis plaintiffs' claim of boycott" here, like plaintiffs' similar claim in *American Family Life*, "Is not based so much on defendants' bad motive or exclusionary intent as upon the naked claim that the mere employment" of the medical referral and supervision clause "amounts to a boycott in itself." [6]

*　　*　　*　　*　　*　　*　　*

When all is said and done, nothing in plaintiffs' memorandum detracts in the slightest from the indisputable fact that the complaint does not allege a legally sufficient Sherman Act claim. It accordingly must be dismissed.

II. ALL PLAINTIFFS OTHER THAN THE INDIVIDUAL SUBSCRIBERS HAVE NO STANDING TO SUE UNDER THE ANTITRUST LAWS

A. THE ASSOCIATION AND UNION PLAINTIFFS, CONCEDEDLY WITHOUT STANDING TO SUE FOR DAMAGES, HAVE NO GREATER STANDING TO SEEK INJUNCTIVE RELIEF

Faced with the overwhelming authority set forth in our opening Memorandum (pp. 8–11), plaintiffs concede that CAPPS, the psychologist associations and the employees' union have no standing to sue for treble damages under

---

[6] Plaintiffs also challenge the medical referral and supervision clause on an attenuated "disparagement" and "contract interference" theory (Pltfs.' Mem. at 26–27).

If plaintiffs' antitrust case is dismissed, the purportedly "pendant" tort claim must also be dismissed for lack of federal jurisdiction. *See United Mine Workers v. Gibbs*, 383 U.S. 715, 716 (1966) ([I] f the federal claims are dismissed before trial, even though not insubstantial in a jurisdictional sense, the state claims should be dismissed as well").

Moreover, even if jurisdiction over plaintiffs' tort claim were present, their complaint, which alleges neither special damages or actual malice, fails to state a cause of action in tort, 1 F. Harper & F. James, The Law of Torts, § 6.1 at 477 (1956) ; *Robins Dry Dock & Repair Co. v. Flint*, 275 U.S. 303 (1927).

Section 4 of the Clayton Act. (PLTFS.' Mem. at 7). Accordingly, there is no dispute that the damage claims asserted by those plaintiffs (and the purported classes they seek to represent) must be dismissed for failure to state a claim upon which relief may be granted.

Plaintiffs nevertheless seek to maintain the associations and the union as plaintiffs by arguing that the well-settled principles of standing to sue do not apply when injunctive relief is sought under Section 16 of the statute. In support of this proposition, plaintiffs cite two opinions by the Ninth Circuit. *In re Multidistrict Vehicle Air Pollution*, 481 F.2d 122 (9th Cir. 1973), *cert. denied*, 42 U.S.L.W. 3301 (1973) ; *Hawaii v. Standard Oil Co.*, 431 F.2d 1282 (9th Cir. 1970) (dictum), *aff'd on other grounds*, 405 U.S. 251 (1972).[7]

The fact is that these are the *only* cases even suggesting a key difference with respect to the requirements of standing to sue between the two statutory remedies. Rather, the clear intent of Congress in enacting the Clayton Act in 1914 as well as the overwhelming weight of judicial authority establish that injunctive relief may be obtained only by a person threatened with loss or damage to its *commercial interests*. Since the plaintiff associations and the union have no such commercial interests to protect, they have no standing.

1. The legislative history demonstrates beyond question that Congress granted the right to seek injunctive relief under the antitrust laws only to those threatened with pecuniary injury to their commercial interests.

The legislative history of Section 16 establishes beyond question that Congress, in granting private parties the right to seek injunctive relief under the antitrust laws, intended such relief to be available only to persons whose business or property is threatened by an existing or impending antitrust violation.

Prior to the enactment of the Clayton Act in 1914, private parties as distinguished from the federal government—could not obtain equitable relief under the antitrust laws. Although the Sherman Act of 1890 provided (in Section 4, 15 U.S.C. §4) for injunctive relief in equitable suits by the United States and (in Section 7) for treble damages in suits by a private party "injured in his business or property," [8] it made no provision for private party "injured in his and the courts held that no such action could be maintained *E.g., Paine Lumber Co. v. Neal*, 244 U.S. 459 (1917). It was to remedy this omission in the Sherman Act that Section 16 of the Clayton Act was enacted.

The Clayton Act, as passed in 1914, contained two provisions dealing with private remedies, neither of which has ever been amended. The first, Section 4 (15 U.S.C. §15), reiterated the treble-damage remedy already contained in Section 7 of the Sherman Act, but rendered it applicable to injury resulting from violations of all "the antitrust laws," not merely the Sherman Act.[9] The other provision was Section 16 (15 U.S.C. §26), which for the first time granted private parties the right to seek injunctive relief under the antitrust laws.[10]

Although Section 16 speaks of "threatened loss or damage" whereas Section 4 requires injury "to business or property," the statute's legislative history makes it clear that Congress was protecting identical commerical interests in the two provisions and that the difference in language was not designed to create discrepant legal standards. The House Judiciary Committee Report, the House Committee Hearings, and the floor debates in both the House and the Senate reveal that throughout the legislative process, Congress intended Section 16 to be the equitable analogue of Section 4.

---

[7] Plaintiffs also surprisingly cite *N. W. Controls, Inc. v. Outboard Marine Corp.*, 333 F. Supp. 493 (D. Del. 1971). That case states that standing to seek injunctive relief differs from standing to recover damages only in that, in an injunctive case, "the standing requirement is not predicated on a plaintiff's having already suffered actual injury." *Id.* at 509.

The case *holds*, however, that plaintiff had no standing to recover either damages or injunctive relief because it had not suffered *commercial injury* and was not threatened with such injury. *Id.* at 510–11—the very reason why plaintiffs here have no standing to sue for any relief.

[8] In 1955 the treble-damage provision of Section 7 of the Sherman Act was repealed as duplicative of Section 4 of the Clayton Act. *See Monarch Life Ins. Co. v. Loyola Protective Life Ins. Co.*, 326 F.2d 841, 845 (2d Cir. 1973), *cert. denied*, 376 U.S. 952 (1964).

[9] Section 4's text reads, in relevant part, as follows :

"That any person who shall be injured in his business or property by reason of anything forbidden in the antitrust laws may sue therefor . . . and shall recover threefold the damages by him sustained, and the cost of suit, including a reasonable attorney's fee."

[10] Section 16 reads, in relevant part, as follows :

"That any person . . . shall be entitled to sue for and have injunctive relief . . . against threatened loss or damage by a violation of the antitrust laws, . . . when and under the same conditions and principles as injunctive relief against threatened conduct that will cause loss or damage is granted by courts of equity, under the rules governing such

Thus, the House Judiciary Report on the Clayton Bill, H.R. Rep. No. 627, 63d Cong., 2d Sess. (May 6, 1914), in a section entitled "Analysis of the Bill," stated with respect to what is now Section 16:

"Under section 7 of the [Sherman Act], a person injured in his business and property by corporations or combinations acting in violation of the Sherman antitrust law, *may recover loss and damage* for such wrongful act. There is, however, no provision in the existing law authorizing a person, firm, corporation or association *to enjoin threatened loss or damage to his business or property* by the commission of such unlawful acts, and the purpose of this section is to remedy such defect in the law." *Id.* at 21 (emphasis added).

Significantly, the Judiciary Committee, in paraphrasing Section 7 of the Sherman Act (which was virtually identical to the present Section 4 of the Clayton Act), spoke of the recovery of "loss and damage"—language which did not (and does not) appear in the treble-damage section but is the language of Section 16. In other words, to the draftsmen of the Clayton Act, the phrases "injury to business or property" and "threatened loss or damage" were precisely equivalent in meaning.

This explicit statement in the House Report, treating Section 16 as the mirror-image of the treble-damage section and permitting private injunctions only against threatened loss or damage to business or property, reiterated statements by the Judiciary Committee's members during the extensive hearings on the bill. For example, Representative Floyd (later one of the bill's House floor managers), in a colloquy with Felix H. Levy, a New York attorney, explained that Section 16 was designed to permit a person who would be able, under Section 4, to recover damages for injury to his business *after* it was incurred, to obtain injunctive relief *before* the self-same type of injury was actually inflicted upon him:

"Mr. Floyd. It is the intention of the provision [Section 16] to give him a right to prevent the committing of that damage and not have to wait until they have injured him and then try to recover damages.

"Mr. Levy. Theoretically that would be an advantage, but not practically.

"Mr. Floyd. That is the purpose of it, and if there are cases, and I can conceive that there might be, in which the Government would not use this great authority, we ought to give the individual, if he sees proper, *the right to enjoin them from interfering with his business.*" House Judiciary Committee Hearings on Trust Legislation, 63d Cong., 2d Sess. 263 (1914) (emphasis added).

At a later point in the hearings, during the testimony of Samuel Untermyer, Representative Floyd made it even clearer that the right to injunctive relief was limited to those threatened with the very type of commercial injury for which treble damages were available:

"Mr. Floyd. This provision [Section 16] was intended to give an individual that was being injured by one of these unlawful combinations or corporations, *who had a right under section 7 of the [Sherman] act* to recover threefold damages in case he was injured—

"Mr. Untermyer. I understand.

"Mr. Floyd. (continuing) The right *to enjoin them from doing these things to his business,* and, in their general operation, to enjoin them . . . in so far as their unlawful operations affected him individually." *Id.* at 842 (emphasis added).[11]

The views expressed by Representative Floyd at the Committee Hearings were echoed in the floor debates in both houses of Congress. Thus, Representative McGillicuddy, a Judiciary Committee member, stated during the House debate:

"There is no provision under the present law, however, to prevent threatened loss or damage even though it be irreparable. The practical effect of this is that *a man would have to sit by and see his business ruined before he could take advantage of his remedy.* In what condition is such a man to take up a long and costly lawsuit to defend his rights?

"The proposed bill solves this problem for the person, firm or corporation *threatened with loss or damage to property* by providing injunctive relief

---

[11] The point was reiterated during the testimony of Edmond E. Wise:

"Mr. Wise. [T]he absolute power of proving the damage done is one of the most difficult things to prove, unless the individual's business has been totally destroyed. . . . I think that by some action of Congress a court of equity should have that power of relieving the immediate needs of the oppressed victim from further oppression, so that it is unmistakably plain and will be enforced.

"Mr. Floyd. That is the purpose of section [16]." *Id.* at 1140.

against the threatened act that will cause *such loss or damage.* Under this most excellent provision a man does not have to wait until he is ruined *in his business* before he has his remedy." 51 *Cong. Rec.* 9261 (1914) (emphasis added).

In the Senate, Senator Nelson opposed the bill for the precise reason that Section 16's injunctive remedy was limited to threatened loss or damage to business or property:

"Section 16 gives, for the first time, injunctive relief under the antitrust laws to private individuals, but it *is somewhat limited in scope, and there are but a limited number of cases which can come under it. I can not conceive many cases, except cases involving the rights that might be enforced under section 7 of the [Sherman] antitrust law. It is only in those cases where it is available;* and if you will read the section, you will see that its scope is but limited:

'SEC. 16. That any person, firm, corporation, or association shall be entitled to sue for and have injunctive relief, in any court of the United States having jurisdiction over the parties, against threatened loss or damage by a violation of the antitrust laws.'

"In other words, there may be a trust and there may be a monopoly existing, and the complainant is obliged to show not only that there is such a trust and such a monopoly, but he has to show that he is threatened with irreparable special damage. Unless he can make it appear that he is threatened with such damage, he will not be entitled to injunctive relief." 51 *Cong. Rec.* 15944 (1914) (emphasis added).

Despite Senator Nelson's pinpointed objection, Section 16 was enacted in the very language he quoted.

Finally, in summing up the Clayton Act's enforcement provisions in the House debate on the bill as it emerged from the conference committee, Representative Floyd described Section 16 in the "business or property" language of Section 4:

"This provision in section 16 gives any individual company, or corporation, damaged in its *property or business* by the unlawful operation or actions of any corporation or combination the right to go into court and enjoin the doing of these unlawful acts, instead of having to wait until the act is done and the business destroyed and then sue for damages." 51 *Cong. Rec.* 16319 (1914) (emphasis added).

This legislative history makes it crystal clear that, in enacting Section 16, Congress intended to permit private antitrust suits for injunctive relief only by those persons threatened with loss or damage to their business or property—the very type of commercial injury required under Section 4 of the Clayton Act.

The difference between the two standing provisions was that Section 16 permitted intervention to forestall the precise injury which, absent injunctive relief, would produce (or continue to produce) actual damage recoverable under Section 4. Viewed in the light of the unequivocal statement in the House Judiciary Committee Report, the explanations of Representative Floyd during the House Hearings, and the statements on the floor of both the Senate and the House, the verbal difference between Section 4 and Section 16 (*i.e.,* "injured in his business or property" and "threatened loss or damage") has no substantive significance here.[12] For Sections 4 and 16 were intended by Congress to specify the identical commercial requirements of private standing to sue—the former for commercial injury already incurred and the latter for commercial injury threatened in the future.

2. The judicial authorities have construed Section 16 to permit suits for injunctive relief only by persons threatened with injury to business or property.

With the marked exception of the two isolated Ninth Circuit opinions relied upon by plaintiffs, the judicial authorities have uniformly construed Section 16

---

[12] To be sure, Justice Marshall, in *Hawaii* v. *Standard Oil Co.,* 405 U.S. 251, 261 (1972), stated that "the legislative history of the Sherman and Clayton Acts is not very instructive as to why Congress included the 'business or property' requirement in § 4, but not in § 16." But examination of the briefs in *Hawaii* reveals that none of the above-quoted legislative history was cited to the Supreme Court.

The fact is that the 1914 legislative materials are most instructive. As the extensive quotations set forth in the text plainly reveal, Congress used the "loss or damage" language of Section 16 interchangeably with the "business or property" requirement of Section 7 of the Sherman Act (which was adopted in Section 4 of the Clayton Act). The conclusion is thus inescapable that Sections 4 and 16 were intended to deal with the identical type of injury.

in accordance with Congress' manifest intent to permit the issuance of an injunction *only* when injury to a *commercial interest* is threatened.

The cases have consistently held that the "injury to business or property" requirement of Section 4 (as applied to suits for damages) applies equally to the showing of "threatened loss or damage" requisite to the grant of injunctive relief under Section 16. As the court stated in *Revere Camera Co.* v. *Eastman Kodak Co.*, 81 F. Supp. 325, 330 (N.D. Ill. 1948):

"This complaint is brought under Sections 4 and 16 of the Clayton Act, 15 U.S.C.A. §§15, 26, which authorizes [sic] a private person to sue on his own behalf for actual or *threatened injury to his business or property*. . . ." (Emphasis added).

Similarly, in *Tivoli Realty, Inc.* v. *Paramount Pictures, Inc.*, 80 F. Supp. 800, 805 (D. Del. 1948), the Court put the point as follows:

"It is well settled that a person *suing under either of the two cited sections* [*i.e.*, §4 and §16] of the Clayton Act cannot have relief unless he pleads and proves *a pecuniary loss or injury to his business or property*." (Emphasis added).

Judge Rifkind put the point most cogently in *Ring* v. *Spina*, 84 F. Supp. 403, 406 (S.D. N.Y. 1949):

"Plaintiff is entitled to injunctive relief which would protect him against prospective damage. . . . Such damage arises when there is *danger of interference with rights or privileges he now enjoys, not merely as a member of the general public, but as one engaged in the commerce which is being restrained*." (Emphasis added.)

The necessity for a showing of threatened injury to the plaintiff's commercial interests is pointedly illustrated by *Gomberg* v. *Midvale Co.*, 157 F. Supp. 132 (E.D. Pa. 1955), a suit seeking to enjoin the consummation of an allegedly unlawful acquisition. Holding that the plaintiff (the to-be-acquired company) was going out of the business allegedly restrained and thus was not threatened with loss or damage within the meaning of Section 16, the Court stated:

"In sum the injury which the laws envision is the injury *to the economy of the plaintiff*, by virtue of restrictions of trade or something that proximately flows from it, *in the competitive field in which it is engaged when the illegal act is committed*.

"In our case Midvale is going out of the business of producing iron and steel products. It intends to go into the investment business. It therefore can sustain no threatened harm or damages within the meaning of §16. . . ." 157 F. Supp. at 142 (emphasis added).

Peller v. *International Boxing Club, Inc.*, 27 F.2d 593 (7th Cir. 1955), aff'g, 135 F. Supp. 942 (N.D. Ill. 1955), stands for the same proposition. Plaintiff alleged that defendants, in violation of the antitrust laws, "conspired to frustrate plaintiff's attempts to promote certain specific boxing matches and to prevent him from attaining the professional standing and reputation as a promoter of such championship matches which he would have reached in a competitive market." (227 F.2d at 594). The complaint sought both treble damages under Section 4 and an injunction under Section 16. The district court granted summary judgment for the defendants because plaintiff could show neither injury to his business or property nor any threat of such injury. This was because "plaintiff was neither engaged in the business of Boxing Promoter, nor prepared so to engage." (135 F. Supp. at 94). The Seventh Circuit affirmed on the same ground.[13]

Yet another example is *Louisiana Petroleum Retail Dealers, Inc.* v. *Texas Co.*, 148 F. Supp. 334, 337 (W.D. La. 1956), in which the court held:

"[T]he plaintiff . . . has no standing to sue because it has *no property rights* whatever which are being subjected to 'threatened loss or damage' within the purport of Section 16 of the Clayton Act."

These cases thus confirm what is plain from the legislative history. In suits under Section 16, just as in those under Section 4, the plaintiff must establish a commercial interest which is threatened with injury as a proximate result of an antitrust violation.

---

[13] *See also, N.W. Controls, Inc.* v. *Outboard Marine Corp.*, 333 F. Supp. 493, 511 (D. Del. 1971) (no standing to seek injunctive relief against tie-in involving products which plaintiff neither made nor had an intention to make) ; *Broadcasters, Inc.* v. *Morristown Broadcasting Corp.*, 185 F. Supp. 641, 644–45 (D. N.J. 1960) (no standing by applicant for radio station to seek injunctive relief because plaintiff "not engaged in a commercial venture").

1389

The dictum by the Ninth Circuit in *Multidistrict Vehicle Air Pollution* that "standing under section 16 does not require an injury to 'commercial interests' but only an injury cognizable in equity" (481 F.2d at 130) is simply incorrect. The only authority cited by the court to support its unique doctrine is the *per curiam* opinion in *Bratcher* v. *Akron Area Board of Realtors*, 381 F.2d 723 (6th Cir. 1967), which held only that the complaint's allegations of interstate commerce were sufficient and expressly deferred ruling on any other legal questions raised. *See* 381 F.2d at 724. The *Bratcher* decision contains no discussion whatsoever of the standing requirements of Section 16.

Indeed, we are aware of no decision other than *Multidistrict Vehicle Air Pollution* and the Ninth Circuit's similar dictum in *Hawaii* v. *Standard Oil Co.*, 431 F.2d 1282, 1284–85 (9th Cir. 1970), suggesting that threatened injury to a commercial interest is not required in a Section 16 case. The contrary is demonstrably the fact, not only as a matter of legislative history as shown above, but under the judicial authorities as well.

*   *   *   *   *   *   *

It is thus clear, both as a matter of legislative history and judicial decision, that a plaintiff has no standing to seek injunctive relief under Section 16 of the Clayton Act unless it can show that it is threatened with loss or damage to its commercial interest as a result of an antitrust violation.

Plaintiff's admission that the associations and the union have no standing to recover damages in effect concedes that they cannot meet this self-same commercial standard for injunctive relief. What is more, examination of plaintiffs' memorandum reveals that the peculiar type of injury with which these plaintiffs claim they are threatened cannot, by any stretch of the imagination, be brought within the law's requirements.

Thus, plaintiffs assert that CAPPS and the other associations will be injured by defendants' claimed violations because they will be prevented from fulfilling their purposes of promoting the practice of psychology. (Pltfs.' Mem. at 10–12.) Nowhere is it alleged that any of these associations is commercially engaged in such practice or, indeed, that any commercial venture of any association plaintiff will be pecuniarily damaged. The conclusion is inescapable that the associations are not engaged in any commerce allegedly restrained by defendants.

The same is true as to the plaintiff union. Plaintiffs assert that defendants' alleged acts injure "that organization by frustrating the accomplishment of its aims and jeopardizing its ability to continue as an effective representative of its membership." (Pltfs.' Mem. at 13.) Plaintiffs thus admit that it is the union's members—not their representative—which are threatened with the commercial type of injury that the antitrust laws are designed to remedy.

In short, the associations and the union have no personal commercial stake here. They are asserting their members' claims; and the law is crystal clear that neither Section 16 nor Section 4 affords them standing to do so.

B. THE PHYCHOLOGIST PLAINTIFFS, AS SUPPLIERS OF SERVICES TO THE SUBSCRIBER, ARE NEITHER DIRECTLY INJURED BY DEFENDANTS NOR WITHIN THE TARGET AREA OF DEFENDANTS' ALLEGED ILLEGAL ACTS, AND HENCE HAVE NO STANDING TO SUE

In a patent effort to confuse the issue before the Court, plaintiffs assert that there are "two fairly distinct tests" for standing to sue under Section 4 of the Clayton Act—a "direct injury" test and a "target area" standard.

Apparently conceding that the psychologists have no standing to sue under a "direct injury" formulation, plaintiffs argue only that, under a so-called "target area" test, the psychologists do have such standing. (Pltfs.' Mem. at 13–16.) This supposed dichotomy derives from the Ninth Circuit's *Multidistrict Vehicle Air Pollution* decision which, in an attempt to rationalize the legion of standing cases, posits the two "tests" relied upon by plaintiffs. But the fact is that the "direct injury" and "target area" rubrics are but two verbalizations of the same principle.[14] Only those persons at whom a defendant's unlawful conduct is directed and whose injury flows directly from the infraction may sue. This fact is amply illustrated by Judge Gesell's decision in *Stern* v. *Lucy Webb Hayes National Training School*, 1973–2 Trade Cas. ¶74,808 (D. D.C. 1973), where the Court denied standing both because "the losses suffered by

[14] This is demonstrated by plaintiffs' citation of the Second Circuit's ruling in *Calderone* as a "target area" case when that decision reaffirmed the same Court's decision in *Billy Baxter*, relied on by plaintiffs as a leading "direct injury" case. (Pltfs.' Mem. at 15.)

the customers of a directly injured party are remote and indirect, and do not give rise to standing under the antitrust laws" (p. 95,610); and because "plaintiffs' activity . . . was not within the area of the economy in which the elimination of competition occurred, and thus plaintiffs lack standing to sue" (p. 95,611).

Here as well, however phrased, the law precludes the psychologist plaintiffs.

Nothing in plaintiffs' protracted discussion distinguishes the cases discussed at pages 14–17 of our Opening Memorandum which hold that a mere supplier of goods or services to persons directly injured or aimed at has no standing to sue. This principle is not based, as plaintiffs would have it, on notions of privity, but rather derives from the fundamental standing principle that remote injuries suffered by those not aimed at by a violation cannot give rise to treble-damage liability. Extensive quotation from the dissenting opinion in *Billy Baxter* (Pltfs.' Mem. at 19) hardly answers the square holding of the Second Circuit majority. And significantly, plaintiffs fail to mention, much less distinguish, *Volasco, Snow Crest, Knuth* and *Fields*, all of which stand for the same proposition.[15]

The plain fact is, as we explained at pages 16–17 of our Opening Memorandum, that the alleged restraint here affects only subscribers. The psychologist suppliers thus, have no standing to sue.

Nor do the psychologists have standing to seek injunctive relief. With the singular exception of the Ninth Circuit *Multidistrict Vehicle Air Pollution* case, the courts have uniformly held that Section 4's standing requirements are equally applicable to suits under Section 16.

Thus, in *Campo* v. *National Football League*, 334 F. Supp. 1181 (E.D. La. 1971), both the shareholder's of a corporation which operated motels in New Orleans and the corporation itself sued for treble damages and injunctive relief on the ground that the National Football League's decision not to telecast the 1972 Super Bowl in the New Orleans area violated the Sherman Act. The court granted summary judgment for the defendants. The shareholder plaintiffs were held without standing to sue for either damages or an injunction premised on actual or threatened injury to the corporation. As for the corporate plaintiff, it too was unable to meet the standing requirements of Section 4 or Section 16 of the Clayton Act:

"Carriage Inn, Inc. . . . is without standing to sue under the Clayton Act, 15 U.S.C. §§15 and 26, *for either an injunction or far treble damages* far the reason that Carriage Inn, Inc. is not within an area of the economy that could be endangered by a breakdown of competitive conditions in the industry here involved and could not be directly or proximately injured by the lessening of competition therein." 334 F. Supp. at 1185 (emphasis added).

See also, Mid-West Theatres Co. v. *Co-operative Theatres of Michigan*, 43 F. Supp. 216, 220 (E.D. Mich. 1941); *McKeon Construction* v. *McClatchy Newspapers*, 1970 Trade Cas. ¶73,212 at p. 88, 815 (N.D. Calif. 1970) ("the crucial requirement of proximate cause does not diminish when the plaintiff seek injunctive relif rather than treble damages"). As the Court stated in *Gomberg* v. *Midvale Co.*, 157 F. Supp. 132, 142 (E.D. Pa. 1955), a case brought solely for injunctive relief under Section 16:

"In sum the injury which the laws envision is the injury to the economy of the plaintiff, by virtue of restrictions of trade or something that proximately flows from it, *in the competitive field in which it is engaged* when the illegal act is committed." (Emphasis added.)

To sum up the point in the words of Judge McLean in *Bywater* v. *Matshushita Electric Industrial Co.*, 1971 Trade Cas. ¶73,759 at p. 91, 203 (S.D. N.Y. 1971), where employees were held without standing to obtain either damages or injunctive relief for injury allegedly suffered by their employer:

"It is Section [4] which authorizes the institution of a private treble damage action for violation of the Sherman Act. . . . [Section 16 of the Clayton Act] authorizes a suit for injunctive relief. The same principle applies to it."

In short, Section 16 plaintiff in an injunctive case, no less than a damage plaintiff suing under Section 4, must establish standing to sue, *i.e.*, that he is directly injured within the "target area" of the economy affected by the alleged restraint of trade. The psychologist plaintiffs are only suppliers of the subscribers who, if anyone, are the persons directly affected by the alleged restraint. Thus, they have no standing to recover damages, and, likewise, have no standing to seek injunctive relief.

---

[15] Plaintiffs' reliance (p. 16) on *Perkins* v. *Standard Oil Corp.*, 395 U.S. 642 (1969) is misplaced. That case did not involve a claim by a supplier of a target. Rather, as Justice Black makes clear, the plaintiff was "the r[ea]l v[ic]tim of the price discrimi-

CONCLUSION

Stripped to its essentials, plaintiffs' complaint strains to make an antitrust case where none exists. As we have shown, both in our Opening Memorandum and herein, the complaint is legally insufficient and accordingly should be dismissed.

Respectfully submitted,

BARRON K. GRIER,
Miller & Chevalier,
1700 Pennsylvania Avenue, N.W.,
Washington, D.C. 20006,
(202) 223-2626,
Attorneys for Blue Cross Association
and National Association of Blue Shield Plans.
STANLEY D. ROBINSON,
MICHAEL MALINA,
Kaye, Scholer, Fierman, Hays & Handler,
425 Park Avenue,
New York, New York 10022,
(212) 759-8400,
Attorneys for Blue Cross Association.
FREDERICK M. ROWE,
EDWARD W. WARREN,
Kirkland, Ellis & Rowe,
1776 K Street, N.W.,
Washington, D.C. 20006,
(202) 833-8400,
Attorneys for National Association
of Blue Shield Plans.

FEBRUARY 19, 1974.

Attachment 1

United States District Court, Northern District of Georgia, Atlanta Division

[Civil Action No. 10582]

AMERICAN FAMILY LIFE ASSURANCE COMPANY OF COLUMBUS

v.

AETNA LIFE INSURANCE CO., CONTINENTAL INSURANCE CO., EQUITABLE LIFE ASSURANCE SOCIETY OF THE UNITED STATES, GULF LIFE INSURANCE CO., METROPOLITAN LIFE INSURANCE CO., NEW YORK LIFE INSURANCE CO., TRAVELERS INSURANCE CO., AND WASHINGTON NATIONAL INSURANCE CO.

ORDER

A complete recitation of the facts of this case is contained in the reports of its previous appearences in this court and the Circuit Court of Appeals. *See* Order of Sept. 30, 1969, *aff'd.* 446 F.2d 1178 (1971). They will therefore be repeated only to the extent necessary to identify the issues and the subject matter involved.

Plaintiff life insurance company sells a dread disease (cancer) policy which pays, up to specified limits, any expense incurred by the insured for specified medical and hospital care when incurred in connection with cancer. The defendants all sell comprehensive health and accident policies which pay, within their limits, for resulting hospital and medical expense incurred irrespective of the illness or accident from which they arise. Premiums for plaintiff's policies are sold on a "franchise" basis, usually a payroll deduction plan and many of those of defendants are "group" policies paid for, in whole or in part, by employers.

Since the 1950s, at least, one of the chronic complaints in the health and accident insurance field has been the problem of overinsurance; i.e., the situation where an insured, by carrying more than one health insurance policy could thereby recover more than his actual expenses and could in fact make a profit, sometimes even a double recovery for his illness. It is established in the record that this practice was of genuine concern not only to the insurance companies but also to the American Hospital Association, the American Medical Association and others. The feeling being that it contributed to both the overuse and overprice of hospital facilities and medical service as well as contributing to the rising cost thereof.

To combat this tendency the insurance companies in the field began adopting various "antiduplication" provisions, somewhat resembling the "other insurance" clauses in automobile policies, whereby each policy would provide that in case there was other insurance covering the same loss the present policy would be considered "excess" and would cover only the excess of the loss over the other insurance. This led to frequent disputes between the two or more carriers as to their respective coverage and obligation to pay, and in the late 1950s and early 1960s, and in an effort to standardize those provisions and resolve these frequent dilemas, a number of companies in the field, including defendants, acting through two of their trade associations, drafted and recommended to the industry a model Coordination of Benefits provision (hereafter called COB) which, where two policies were involved, spelled out specific rules for ascertaining which insuring companies were liable for cash loss and to what extent. The care provision was and is available to all companies in the field, including plaintiff if it chose to use it. Obviously, and as shown by the record, one of the effects of such a provision is to reduce the cost (premium) of defendants' complete coverage policies to the public.

For reasons sufficient unto itself, however, plaintiff has never used this or any other Coordination of Benefits provision in any of its cancer policies, and as a result when it suffers a loss which is also covered under one of defendants' COB policies, plaintiff, in accordance with the terms of its policy always has to pay in full and the defendant carrier, applying its COB provision only pays the excess, if any.

Each of the defendants sells a full line of health and accident policies covering any disease or accident, from any cause. Plaintiff's policies, however, cover only expenses from one disease—cancer; and as a result many employees, wanting full coverage, buy defendants' policies and forego plaintiff's single disease policy since with a competing COB policy involved the insured could only recover for his loss one time anyway.

In 1967 the plaintiff filed this action against the defendants charging that the collusion of the defendants in employing COB in their policies constituted a boycott of plaintiff and either a monopoly or an attempt to monopolize in violation of the Sherman Antitrust Law, 15 U.S.C. §§ 1 and 2. Following a spate of discovery on both sides plaintiff then moved for a temporary injunction which was denied by this court in 1969, which denial was thereafter affirmed by the Court of Appeals. 446 F.2d 1178, *supra*.

After more voluminous discovery thereafter, the defendants have now filed a motion for summary judgment which has now been briefed and argued and is ripe for decision.

After considering the motion the court concludes that the motion must be granted and the case dismissed for two reasons:

First: The court concludes that under the undisputed facts no boycott of plaintiff by defendants is shown and that the action is therefore barred by the McCarran-Ferguson Act, 15 U.S.C. §§ 1011–1015, which exempts the "business of insurance" from the federal antitrust laws, to the extent regulated by the states, excepting only acts of "coercion, intimidation or boycott."

Second: The court concludes that, even if there were no McCarran-Ferguson Act the conduct complained of is not the kind of competition which is forbidden by the antitrust laws in any event.

Going to the first ground for dismissal, it is undisputed in the record that the employment of COB provisions by the defendant insurance companies in their policies is regulated by the insurance commissioners of all fifty states; and the Supreme Court of the United States has held that the "contract of insurance" [and the type of policy which may be issued] and "its interpretation and enforcement" comprise the very "core" of those matters considered to be the "business of insurance" and which are left to the states by McCarran-Ferguson. *SEC v. National Securities*, 393 U.S. 453, 460 (1969).

This court, of course, is keenly aware of the dangers of summary judgment, particularly in an antitrust setting and where questions of motives, intent and subjective feelings abound. *But see First National Bank of Arizona v. Cities Service Co.*, 391 U.S. 253, 290 (1969), *and Jones v. Borden Co.*, 430 F.2d 569, 574 (5th Cir. 1970).

In its complaint, of course, and in its brief, plaintiff here does assail defendants' motives and intent on every page, but the evidence and circumstances it adduces do no more than recite the advantages and the effects of COB and only convince the court there more that defendants' motives and purposes, already described in some degree, were simply not anticompetitive. In depositions both in this case and in a Florida case, *infra.* plaintiff's president admits that its single disease policy is not a competitor with or substitute for defendants' broad form coverage, that plaintiff's sales do not affect defendants' sales potential, and that defendants' interests are "not advanced in the slightest by the application of COB" to plaintiff's career plan. Under its plan plaintiff has to pay in full either way. Plaintiff's president also admits that in its inception COB was not aimed at plaintiff. Indeed, he could hardly do otherwise since at the time COB was begun plaintiff had not even commenced writing cancer policies. In short, here there simply is no target competitor or class of competitors at whom COB is aimed.[1] COB, where employed, applies against all health policies without coordination of benefits clauses, including a great number of such policies issued by defendants themselves. Finally, plaintiff or any other similar company is at perfect liberty to use COB itself at any time it chooses to do so.

As the court views COB, therefore, it is simply a new or at least a different product, and upon analysis, plaintiff's claim of boycott is not based so much on defendants' bad motive or exclusionary intent as upon the naked claim that the mere employment of a COB limitation at all, at any time, or against any insurance company (including defendants) amounts to boycott in itself.

The court simply cannot believe that the mere offering and sale of a new and different product,[2] available to all and forbidden to none, and which reduces the price to the public of a necessary coverage, either constitutes coercion, intimidation, or boycott or that it constitutes any kind of predatory competition within the meaning of antitrust, irrespective of McCarran-Ferguson.[3] Certainly the mere fact that the COB provision was perfected and standardized by defendants through a trade association does not ipso facto make it a boycott or a violation of antitrust. *United States v. National Malleable & Steel Castings Co.*, 1957 CCS Trade cases ¶68,890 (N.D. Ohio), *aff'd per curiam* 358 U.S. 38 (1957).

We think this is what the Fifth Circuit said and meant when it decided *American Family Life Assurance Co. of Columbus v. Blue Cross of Florida, Inc.* (No. 72–3447, 5th Cir. Nov. 5, 1973), —— F.2d ——, a case involving the present plaintiff and indistinguishable from the one here involved.

There Judge Coleman, speaking for the court, said:

"We think the correct standard for the determination of the issue now before us was enunciated by the Third Circuit in *The Travelers Insurance Company v. Blue Cross of Western Pennsylvania*, [No. 72–1209, slip opinion dated July 10, 1973], —— F.2d ——:

"The antitrust laws, however, protect competition, not competitors; and stiff competition is encouraged, not condemned. "This statement was preceded by the observation that:

In its negotiating with hospitals, Blue Cross has done no more than conduct its business as every national enterprise does, i.e., get the best deal possible * * * Blue Cross passes along the saving thus realized to consumers.

"That is the situation here. American Family Life does not write broad coverage hospital and medical insurance. Blue Cross-Blue Shield do write such coverage. American Family Life sells cancer plan policies. Blue Cross-Blue Shield writes such coverage only as incidental to or as a part of its broad coverage which protects the insured as to many diseases or disabilities. When they include COB in their policies these companies are simply providing that to a certain extent they shall not make the payments received or to be received from some other insurance policy, thus reducing the cost of their broad risk coverage as well as its cost to the insured.

---

[1] This court has never heard of a boycott case where some predatory purpose or intended exclusionary effect was not involved. Else we might still be chained to the outmoded mousetrap, the pony express and the horse and buggy.

[2] Plaintiff's president conceded in this case that plaintiff's single disease policy 'is not the same product as that sold by defendants and, in the Florida case, *infra*, that "we sell only a partial product."

[3] Also at stake here is the right of the public to buy a policy with or without COB, as it chooses.

"This may be tough competition for American Family Life, which chooses to concentrate on only one dread risk, but the test is whether any restraint of trade thus caused is reasonable, *Northern Pacific Railway Company v. United States*, 366 U.S. 1 (1958). In our opinion, there is no logical way in the context of this case by which the COB provisions can be pronounced 'unreasonable'. We cannot say under §1 of the Sherman Act that an insurance company insuring against only one risk is entitled to dictate the terms upon which broad risk companies may offer their benefits to those individuals who need protection against many risks.

"Stated another way, may the Blue Cross-Blue Shield COB provisions be invalidated under the Sherman Act so that American Family Life may write its cancer policies in the form it desires while at the same time denying the same right to Blue Cross-Blue Shield as to broad coverage We think not, and we so hold."

The motion for summary judgment is GRANTED and the case DISMISSED.[4]

IT IS SO ORDERED.

This 28th day of December, 1973.

NEWELL EDERFIELD,
United States District Judge.

In the United States District Court for the District of Columbia

[Civil Action No. 1623–73]

COUNCIL FOR THE ADVANCEMENT OF THE PSYCHOLOGICAL PROFESSIONS AND SCIENCES, INC., ET AL., PLAINTIFFS,

v.

BLUE CROSS ASSOCIATION, NATIONAL ASSOCIATION OF BLUE SHIELD PLANS, UNITED STATES CIVIL SERVICE COMMISSION, ET AL., DEFENDANTS.

PLAINTIFFS' OPPOSITION TO DEFENDANTS' MOTION TO DISMISS THE COMPLAINT

Plaintiffs, by their undersigned attorneys, hereby oppose the Motion to Dismiss the Complaint filed by Defendants Blue Cross Association and National Association of Blue Shield Plans for reasons fully set forth in Plaintiffs' accompanying Memorandum in opposition to this Motion and respectfully move this Honorable Court for an Order denying said Motion in all respects, and with prejudice.

Respectfully submitted,

JOSEPH L. NELLIS,
JEFFREY L. NESVET,
1819 H Street, N.W.,
Washington, D.C. 20006,
Tel. 223-6300,
Attorneys for Plaintiffs,

JANUARY 31, 1974.

In the United States District Court for the District of Columbia

[Civil Action No. 1623–73]

COUNCIL FOR THE ADVANCEMENT OF THE PSYCHOLOGICAL PROFESSIONS AND SCIENCES, INC., ET AL., PLAINTIFFS

v.

BLUE CROSS ASSOCIATION, NATIONAL ASSOCIATION OF BLUE SHIELD PLANS, UNITED STATES CIVIL SERVICE COMMISSION, ET AL., DEFENDANTS

ORDER

Upon consideration of Defendants Blue Cross Association and National Association of Blue Shield Plans Motion to Dismiss the Complaint in the above-captioned litigation and the Plaintiffs' Opposition thereto and for good cause shown, it is hereby

---

[4] The court intends this dismissal to be with prejudice; however, should certiorari be granted by the Supreme Court in the Florida Blue Cross case, we suggest that counsel move the Fourth Circuit to withhold any opinion in this case until that case is disposed of. In this way, additional appeals of the same question may be avoided.

ORDERED that Defendants' Motion to Dismiss the Complaint is hereby denied, with prejudice.

AUBREY E. ROBINSON, Jr.,
United States District Judge.

FEBRUARY   , 1974.

In the United States District Court for the District of Columbia

[Civil Action No. 1623–73]

COUNCIL FOR THE ADVANCEMENT OF THE PSYCHOLOGICAL PROFESSIONS AND
SCIENCES, INC., ET AL., PLAINTIFFS
v.
BLUE CROSS ASSOCIATION, NATIONAL ASSOCIATION OF BLUE SHIELD PLANS,
UNITED STATES CIVIL SERVICE COMMISSION, ET AL., DEFENDANTS

MEMORANDUM IN SUPPORT OF PLAINTIFFS' OPPOSITION TO DEFENDANTS' MOTION
TO DISMISS THE COMPLAINT

JEFFREY L. NESVET,
JOSEPH L. NELLIS,
1819 H Street, N.W.,
Washington, D.C. 20006,
Tel. 223-6300,
Attorneys for Plaintiffs.

JANUARY 31, 1974.

In the United States District Court for the District of Columbia

[Civil Action No. 1623-73]

COUNCIL FOR THE ADVANCEMENT OF THE PSYCHOLOGICAL PROFESSIONS AND
SCIENCES, INC., ET AL., PLAINTIFFS
v.
BLUE CROSS ASSOCIATION, NATIONAL ASSOCIATION OF BLUE SHIELD PLANS,
UNITED STATES CIVIL SERVICE COMMISSION, ET AL., DEFENDANTS

Plaintiffs' Opposition to Defendants' Motion to Dismiss the Complaint

INTRODUCTION

I. The Complaint contains substantive allegations of violations of antitrust and tort law committed by Defendants Blue Cross Association and National Association of Blue Shield Plans.

Preliminary to providing a better understanding of the reasons why the claims asserted against the private Defendants are cognizable under the antitrust laws, it is necessary to set forth some basic facts concerning the role of professional psychologists as providers of health services. Psychologists are now licensed or certified to provide mental health care in 46 states and the District of Columbia. Forty-two jurisdictions now recognize a psychotherapist/patient privilege without distinguishing between medical psychotherapy and psychotherapy provided by a licensed and/or certified psychologist.[1] Thirteen states have amended their insurance codes to provide by law what the Defendants here have refused to provide by contract, namely, the freedom of subscribers to the Defendants' plans to choose among co-equal providers of health services and their freedom of access to psychological services on a par with access to psychiatric services. The professional and scientific health literature abounds with studies by and reference to the role of psychologists and their contributions to improved mental health care and their professional services to the public at large and to vast numbers of Federal employees who are subscribers to Defendants' health plans.

---

[1] The nine jurisdictions not presently recognizing a psychotherapist/patient privilege are Idaho, Massachusetts, Minnesota, North Dakota, Rhode Island, South Carolina, Texas, West Virginia and Wisconsin.

There are three areas within which providers of mental health services function. First, about six percent of the membership of the American Psychological Association (hereinafter "APA") is primarily employed in independent or group practices.[2] Approximately 28 percent perform psychotherapy and counseling on a fee for service basis.[3]

Second, there is the area of professional service provision to the public. About 63 percent of the APA's members are directly engaged in services relating to the resolution of human problems, as distinguished from pure experimental or academic services.[4]

Third, there is the office, clinical and hospital area within the health service function. Those engaged primarily in individual or group practice constitute 30 percent of the psychologists who provide services in major health settings with hospital based and clinic based psychology constituting 38 percent and 32 percent, respectively.[5]

The growing inclusion of coverage for nervous and mental disorder in group health and major medical policies offered by the insurance industry is exerting major pressure on public health care and the expectation of the public that mental health care will be increasingly provided to meet the ever increasing demand. Still, the available coverage is decidedly limited, particularly providing fewer benefits available for non-hospital treatment and care. A recent survey indicates that 55 percent of all psychologists experience some or complete claim denial in their contacts with Defendants.[6] A substantial number also continue to resist having to accept so-called medical sepervision in order to have their claims recognized, supervision that is largely perfunctory and which measurably increases health care costs to the subscribers and the U.S. Treasury.

Yet the statutory policy appears to be far ahead of the policy of such health insurance companies as Defendants. As an example, in the Rehabilitation Act of 1973, Congress recognized psychologists as primary providers and established (in §103) *complete parity between a physician and a licensed psychologist*, licensed (or certified) by the several states when it comes to provision of mental health services.

The profession and science of psychology in the area of human mental disorder treatment is on a par with the profession of science and medicine. Except in some areas of the vital health insurance area, this parity is respected.

II. Motions to Dismiss under Rule 12 are disfavored in these circumstances.

Before proceeding to examine Defendants' arguments in support of their Motion to Dismiss, it is appropriate to examine the standards which govern dismissal under Rule 12, F.R.C.P. in a case of this kind.

Numerous courts have consistently viewed a Motion to Dismiss as a disfavored Motion, which should be granted only in extremely limited circumstances. To overcome this strong majority view, Defendants would be required to produce legal precedents far beyond what is contained in their Memorandum. One of the strongest judicial pronouncements on the reasons why courts are so reluctant to grant Rule 12 Motions was set forth by Mr. Justice Holmes in *Hart* v. *B. F. Keith Vaudeville Exchange*, 262 U.S. 271 (1923) (quoted in *Radovich* v. *National Football League*, 352 U.S. 445, 453 [1957]) : "The test as to sufficiency laid down by Mr. Justice Homes in *Hart* v. *B. F. Keith Vaudeville Exchange*, 262 U.S. 271, 274 (1923) is *'whether the claim is wholly frivolous.'* " (Emphasis supplied.)

The Supreme Court in ruling on a grant of summary judgment in an antitrust case noted that "We believe that summary procedures should be used sparingly in complex antitrust litigation." *Poller* v. *Columbia Broadcasting System, Inc.*, 368 U.S. 464, 473 (1961) ; *Clausen & Sons, Inc.* v. *Theo. Hamm Brewing Co.*, 284 F. Supp. 148 (D. Minn. 1967) ; *Donlan* v. *Carvel*, 209 F. Supp. 829 (D. Md. 1962) ; *South Carolina Council of Milk Producers, Inc.* v. *Newton*, 360 F.2d 414 (4th Cir. 1966) ; *Norfolk Monument Co., Inc.* v. *Woodlawn Memorial Gardens, Inc.*, 394 U.S. 700 (1969).

---

[2] 1972 *Survey of Psychologists in the United States and Canada*, American Psychological Association ; 27,271 (77 percent) of the APA's 35,361 members responded to the survey.
[3] *ibid.*
[4] *ibid.*
[5] *ibid.*
[6] Dorken and Whiting. *Psychologists as Health Service Providers: National Sample Study of Fee for Service Providers*, 1973.

Many other courts have expressed similar reservations about dismissing antitrust cases prematurely. The Fourth Circuit has cautioned that: "Disposition on Motion is not warranted 'unless it appears beyond a doubt that the Plaintiff can prove no set of facts in support of his claim which would entitle him to relief,' *Conley* v. *Gibson*, 355 U.S. 41, 45–6, 78 S. Ct. 99, 102 2 L Ed. 2d 80 (1957) ; *Bolick-Gilman Co.* v. *Continental Baking Co.*, 279 F.2d 649, 650 (9th Cir. 1960) ; *Congress Building Corp.* v. *Loew's*, 246 F.2d 587 (7th Cir. 1957)." *South Carolina Council of Milk Producers, Inc.* v. *Newton*, 360 F.2d 414, 420 (4th Cir. 1966).

The basic reasoning underlying the reluctance of courts to grant Motions to Dismiss is a judicial policy in favor of allowing cases, especially complex antitrust claims, to be decided on their merits. Thus, the Fifth Circuit has held that: "Summary disposition of Litigation, especially antitrust cases, is disfavored and amendments should be liberally granted so that all cases may be decided on their merits. (*Food Basket, Inc.* v. *Albertson's, Inc.*, 383 F.2d 785 [10th Cir. 1967]). Thus, a Motion to Dismiss on the basis of pleadings alone should rarely be granted." (*Cliff Food Stores, Inc.* v. *Kroger, Inc.*, 417 F.2d 203, 205 [5th Cir. 1969]). The Fifth Circuit went on to add that: "A complaint should not be dismissed unless there is no possibility that the Plaintiff can recover under the allegations of his complaint. (*International Steel Erectors, Inc.* v. *Wilhart Steel Erectors & Rental Service*, 400 F.2d 465 [5th Cir. 1968])." Lower federal courts have also expressed great reluctance to deprive Plaintiffs, at a preliminary stage, of an opportunity to present their cases on the merits. Witness a recent comment by the United States District Court for the District of Nebraska. "This Court is not unmindful of the great restraint to be exercised by a court in summarily dismissing an antitrust action." (*Milton G. Waldbaum Company* v. *Roberts Dairy Company*, 325 F. Supp. 772, 775 [D. Neb. 1971]).

In *Brownlee* v. *Malco Theatres*, 99 F. Supp. 312, (W.D. Ark. 1951), a treble damage action, the Court noted that: "In determining the sufficiency of a complaint of this kind, the Plaintiff must be given liberal latitude in the pleadings, since it is inherent in such action that all of the details and specific facts relied upon cannot properly be set forth as part of the pleadings." (*id.* at p. 314.)

The Court considering the case at bar has also considered the question of what standards apply to a Motion to Dismiss in an antitrust action. In *District of Columbia Citizens Publishing Company* v. *Merchants & Manuafacturers Association, Inc.*, 83 F. Supp. 994, 997 (D.C. D.C. 1949), this Court stated that: "It is well settled that in actions of this nature the complaint must be construed with great liberality." In a more recent case, (*Pacific Seafarers, Inc.* v. *Pacific Far East Line*, 48 F.R.D. 347 [D.C. D.C. 1969]), this Court noted that: "The pleadings, particularly in an antitrust action of this kind, should be construed in favor of the Plaintiffs." Since the allegations of the Complaint and Amended Compalint should be construed in Plaintiffs' favor, we have searched in vain for any showing by Defendants in their Motion to Dismiss that would justify this Court's conclusion that Defendants had met their heavy burden of overcoming these powerful presumptions.

What must be considered in any ruling on the sufficiency of a complaint is that the underlying purpose of Rule 8 of the Federal Rules of Civil Procedure, requiring "a short and plain statement of the claim showing that the pleader is entitled to relief," is to give Defendants "fair notice of what the Plaintiff's claim is and the grounds upon which it rests." (*Conley* v. *Gibson*, 355 U.S. 41, 47 [1957]).

Plaintiffs submit that their original and amended complaints have given Defendants fair notice of its claims and the grounds upon which they rest. This is partly demonstrated by Defendants' detailed discussion of Plaintiffs' claims in their instant Motion. Since "liberal latitude" should be given by the Court in a case of this kind "in determining the sufficiency of the complaint." (*Brownlee, supra* and *Citizens Publishing Co., supra*), Plaintiffs contend that they are entitled to a denial of Defendants' Motion on this ground alone, although we will proceed, in the balance of this Memorandum, to meet directly the arguments of Defendants as to Plaintiffs' standing to bring this suit and the restraints of trade, which we contend are extant in the case. Plaintiffs' claims are clearly *prima facie* cognizable by this Court under the antitrust laws applicable.

ARGUMENT

I. Standing

A. Defendants have conceded the standing to sue of Plaintiffs other than the association, union and individual psychologist Plaintiffs.

Defendants have challenged, in their Motion to Dismiss, the standing of all Plaintiffs, except the individual Federal employee subscribers of Blue Cross-Blue Shield, whom they admit have standing to bring this action.

B. The association, union and individual psychologist Plaintiffs have indisputable standing to sue for injunctive relief under §16 of the Clayton Act, 15 U.S.C., §26.

Plaintiffs contend that the Council for the Advancement of the Psychological Professions and Sciences, Inc. (CAPPS), the National Association of Government Employees (NAGE) individually, the professional and scientific organizations of psychologists, and individual psychologists seeking to represent those classes, have clear standing under §16 of the Clayton Act to seek injunctive relief, as demanded in the Complaint and Amended Complaint, and that, in addition, the individual psychologists representing that class have clear standing under §4 of the Clayton Act to seek treble damages, as described in the Complaint and Amended Complaint.

It must first be noted that CAPPS (a District of Columbia non-profit corporation) is suing in its individual capacity and not as a member of a class, as claimed by Defendants.

The scope of §16 is significantly broader than that of §4, reflecting the fact that §16 involves injunctive relief rather than "punitive and potentially disastrous judgments for treble damages." *In Re Multidistrict Vehicle Air Pollution,* 617 Antitrust and Trade Regulation Report F-1 (9th Cir. 1973). *Hawaii* v. *Standard Oil Co.,* 431 F.2d 1282 (9th Cir. 1970), *Aff'd.* 405 U.S. 251 (1972). Thus, Courts have construed the standing requirements under §16 much more liberally than §4 requirements. As noted in *N. W. Controls, Inc.* v. *Outboard Marine Corp.,* 33 F. Supp. 493, 509 (D. Del. 1971), "While the right of a private litigant to sue for treble damages is strictly construed (*Westor Theatres* v. *Warner Bros. Pictures,* 41 F. Supp. 757, 762 (D. N.J. 1941), the test for standing to seek injunctive relief under §16 of the Clayton Act, 15 U.S.C. §26, is less exacting."

The two requisites that must be established in order to obtain injunctive relief, pursuant to §16, are that: (1) Defendants are engaged in a violation of the antitrust laws and (2) Plaintiffs are threatened with loss or damage as a result of that conduct. (*Gomberg* v. *Midvale Co.,* 157 F. Supp. 132 [E.D. Pa. 1955]; *Schwartz* v. *General Electric Co.,* 107 F. Supp. 58 [S.D. N.Y. 1952]). Plaintiffs have met these primary tests.

(1) Plaintiffs assert, in their Complaint and Amended Complaint, a conspiracy between Defendants and certain segments of the medical profession in violation of Sections 1 and 3 of the Sherman Act. (2). To determine whether these violations, as hereinafter described, threaten loss or damage to Plaintiffs sufficient to bring Defendants' actions under the purview of §16 of the Clayton Act, the requisite standard, as exemplified by overwhelming decisional authority, is that Plaintiffs must show injury of a personal nature differing from that suffered by the public at large. (*Revere Camera Co.* v. *Eastman Kodak Co.,* 81 F. Supp. 325 [N.D. Ill. 1948]; *United States v. Borden Co.,* 347 U.S. 519 [1954]). An examination of the interests and activities of the Plaintiffs will clearly show that each has suffered injury and damages, not simply as a member of the public at large, but in a direct, personal way growing out of their daily activities, either as incorporated entities, unincorporated entities or as individuals.

Defendants on their Motion to Dismiss engage in a lengthy discourse (Defendants' Memorandum, pp. 8–11) on the Hornbook principle that a trade association or membership corporation does not have standing to sue under the antitrust laws to enforce the rights of its members. This straw-man principle, undisputed by Plaintiffs, leads Defendants into an inapplicable argument that the association and union Plaintiffs lack standing to sue in the case at bar. This entire argument, however, is inappropriate to the instant litigation because the association and union Plaintiffs have clearly alleged that they have suffered precisely the type of injury Defendants' leading cases hold to be sufficient for standing under the antitrust laws. As noted on page 9 of Defendants' Motion to Dismiss, the Court in *Northern California Monument Dealers' Ass'n.*

v. *Interment Ass'n. of California*, 120 F. Supp. 93 (N.D. Calif. 1954) found plaintiff's complaint deficient because of its failure to allege that "plaintiff has ever sustained damages at the hands of any defendant." (*id.* at 94.) The association and union Plaintiffs in the instant case, however, have ssuffered damages at the hands of Defendants as is fully set out in the Complaint and Amended Complaint and in this Opposition. Defendants also rely heavily on *Nassau County Ass'n., of Insurance Agents, Inc.* v. *Aetna Casualty & Surety Co.*, 345 F. Supp. 645 (S.D. N.Y. 1972). There, also, the deficiency found by the Court was the lack of harm to plaintiff's *own* interests as opposed to the interests of its members, the type of harm indisputably present in the instant situation. Accordingly, the Court will perceive that Defendants' arguments with respect to the legal incapacity of trade associations to sue in antitrust for wrongs committed against their members are really arguments which misapprehend the thrust of Plaintiffs' claims. Plaintiff associations and union have sufficiently alleged *prima facie* injuries to *themselves* as legal entities, entirely apart from injuries sustained by these Plaintiffs' members, which latter injuries are separately alleged and properly pled.

We now turn to a discussion of the standing to sue of the Plaintiff associations and union.

CAPPS is a voluntary non-profit membership corporation, incorporated in the District of Columbia. Its Articles of Incorporation set out the scope of its activities. According to those Articles, "The Corporation is organized for the purpose of promoting and advancing the psychological professions and sciences including, but not limited to, the following:

C. The promotion of the fullest utilization of psychological knowledge and services in health care delivery.

D. The encouragement of the implementation of alternatives to the present health model in public programs." (Art. #II, Certificate dated September 7, 1971.)

Thus, Defendants, by engaging in a conspiracy which has as one of its purposes and effects distorting the mental health care delivery system to hundreds of thousands of Federal employees, annuitants and beneficiaries by forcing many patients, who would otherwise consult licensed and/or certified psychologists, to seek treatment from a limited number of psychiatrists and forcing others to have their professional relationship with psychologists treating them to be subjected to unnecessary and often perfunctory supervision, are damaging CAPPS in the most direct manner imagineable by preventing it from fulfilling its purposes to promote the fullest utilization of psychology mandated by its Articles of Incorporation.

The fact that, in remedying these particular injuries threatening CAPPS, the public at large is to benefit does not in any manner lessen the impact of Defendants' conduct under the antitrust laws. The Congressional purpose underlying our antitrust laws is clearly twofold. Each successful suit by a private party, pursuant to any antitrust provision, obviously serves to remedy some actual or threatened harm to specific plaintiffs. But each such suit also serves the purpose of restoring or maintaining competition, with resultant benefits to the public at large. The fact that the public will substantially benefit from the relief sought in the instant case does not, of course, in and of itself, grant standing to the Plaintiffs, but it certainly should not act as a bar to a finding that Plaintiffs do have standing to proceed. The harm or loss necessary to establish standing under §16 is not strictly limited to injury to "business or property," as is the case with respect to the much narrower §4. There is the lucid difference that "Section 16 lacks mention of 'business or property,' an omission signalling different standing requirements. * * * Unlike standing under Section 4, *standing under Section 16 does not require an injury to 'commercial interests,' but only an injury cognizable in equity.*" (Emphasis supplied.) (*In Re Multidistrict Vehicle Air Pollution, supra* at F–3, 4.)

Turning now to the incorporated and unincorporated organizations of psychologists, each of these organizations has a personal interest (non-public) sufficient to provide standing under §16. Examining the Articles of Incorporation and Bylaws of these Plaintiff organizations, one finds such purposes as "to advance psychology as a science and as a means of promoting human welfare" (District of Columbia Psychological Association, Michigan Psychological Association, California Psychological Association and Maryland Psychological Association) ; "to promote the private practice of psychology and the service to the public which this implies" (Division of Licensed Psychologists of the Georgia Psychological Association) ; "to seek means by which it can provide professional consultation services for the community" (Baltimore Association of Consulting Psychologists) ; and "to foster and maintain high standards of practice in the field of psychology" (Oregon Psychological Association).

The accomplishment of these purposes has been frustrated, hindered or jeopardized by the conspiracy alleged in Plaintiffs' Complaint and Amended Complaint. These are most certainly the type of injuries that Federal Courts were given jurisdiction over "in exercising the traditional equitable powers extended to them by Section 16." (*Zenith Radio Corp.* v. *Hazeltine Research,* 395 U.S. 100, 133 [1969]).

As the challenged practices hinder the practice of psychology and impair its standing as an independent health service provider profession, these organizations are certainly injured in their ability to carry out their purposes and to uphold and improve the standards of the profession and of the mental health care system. Indeed, these practices have severely impeded the stated public policy of 47 jurisdictions (there will soon be 51) which grant licenses for professional psychological services on a par with licenses granted to any other profession.

Individual psychologists also incur serious damages as a result of the imposition and continuance of the "medical referral and supervision" clause, pursuant to Defendants' conspiracy, as alleged herein. There can be no more grievous damage incurred by members of a profession than the present situation in which the ability to enter into unfettered relationships with patients is jeopardized, their professional standing as providers of health services is disparaged and, if the "medical referral and supervision" clause continues to be effective, perhaps permanently destroyed. As noted in *Westor Theatres, Inc.* v. *Warner Bros. Pictures, Inc.,* 41 F. Supp. 757 (D. N.J. 1941), the only relevant question at issue under §16 is whether Plaintiff is threatened with loss or damage as a result of the acts of the Defendant.

A conspiracy which impairs Plaintiffs' ability to practice an acknowledged profession and hinders their ability to compete with other co-equal providers of health services surely threatens Plaintiffs with loss or damage sufficient to allege injury cognizable under §16. The public injury aside, it is a gross interference with practice for one profession to impose an arbitrary standard on another and enforce it by illegal means. Congress passed the Sherman and Clayton Acts in order to provide a remedy for those whose ability to compete has been threatened or damaged. Any construction of the term "injury," in order to artifically limit the rights of litigants under §16, as contended by Defendants, would serve to repudiate that pblicy.

NAGE is a Federal employees union, incorporated separately, whose duties and purposes include insuring the welfare of its members. Thus, the continuation of the "medical referral and supervision" clause, which jeopardizes those goals, injures that organization by frustrating the accomplishment of its aims and jeopardizing its ability to continue as an effective representative of its membership. That must also be viewed as an injury sufficient to bring it within the scope of §16. NAGE's membership consists solely of Federal employees, many of whom are insured by Defendants' health plans.

C. The individual psychologist Plaintiffs have indisputable standing to sue for treble damages under §4 of the Clayton Act, 15 U.S.C., §15.

Unfortunately for Defendants, the law of standing under §4 of the Clayton Act is not nearly as unambiguous as Defendants would have the Court believe and assert in their Motion to Dismiss. There are wide divergences between the various Circuits on this specific issue which the Supreme Court has not yet seen fit to resolve. Until time as the Supreme Court does resolve the varying positions of the Circuits, standing under §4 will have to be determined by application of the underlying policy of the antitrust laws, as expressed by the Court. Two fairly distinct tests have evolved to determine standing under §4, though not all Courts utilize the same labels. One, the "direct injury" test focuses on an attempt to put the parties in classifications or pigeon holes to determine if the plaintiff's injury was "incidental," "remote" or "indirect," thus lacking in standing. This is in the nature of a privity test and is concerned more with the relationship between the parties than whether, in fact, an injury has resulted from some violation of the antitrust laws. The other, the "target area" test focuses on whether plaintiff's injuries are "within that area of the economy which is endangered by a breakdown of competitive conditions." *Karseal Corp.* v. *Richfield Oid Corp.,* 221 F.2d 358 (9th Cir. 1955).

Defendants' extensive arguments (Defendants' Memorandum pp. 12–17) as
to the alleged lack of standing to sue of the individual psychologists who are
Plaintiffs in this action fails totally to distinguish the differences between the
"direct injury" and the "target area" tests, as to which so many impressive
Court decisions have been rendered. Indeed, Defendants indiscrimately cite
precedents supporting the "target area" concept in juxtaposition with cases supporting the direct injury" test. Defendants' failure to perceive the difference
in the two approaches will undoubtedly perplex the Court as much as Plaintiffs' many efforts to decipher Defendants' true position as to which of the
tests of standing under §4 they are urging. With so little light shed on the
legal reasoning of Defendants when they contend that the individual psychologists lack standing under §4, we turn to a discussion of the differences between the two tests of standing as they have been set out by the Courts, leading to our conclusion that the "target area" test is fully met by Plaintiffs and
it should be applied by the Court in this case, as did Judge Gesell in a recent
decision, under similar circumstances (*Stern* v. *Lucy Webb Hayes National
Training School*, 642 Antitrust and Trade Regulation Report A–16 [D.C. D.C.
Dec. 1973]).

Plaintiffs earnestly submit that an examination of the purposes underlying
the antitrust laws, and more specifically §4 of the Clayton Act, leads to the
logical conclusion, applicable here, that, as this Court has recently stated in
Stern v. *Lucy Webb Hayes National Training School*, *supra*: The most realistic view of standing in situations such as that presented here is to apply the
'target area' test." Gesell, J.) *Sanitary Milk Producers* v. *Bergjans Farm
Dairy, Inc.*, 368 F.2d 679 (8th Cir. 1966). (Blackmun, J.) ; *In Re Multidistrict
Vehicle Air Pollution*, 617 Antitrust and Trade Regulation Report F–1 (9th
Cir. 1973) ; *Calderone Enterprises Corp.* v. *United Artists Theatre Circuit, Inc.*,
454 F.2d 1292 (2nd Cir. 1971) ; *South Carolina Council of Milk Producers, Inc.*
v. *Newton*, 360 F.2d 414 (4th Cir. 1966). The concept of a "direct injury" privity limitation was also faulted by the Northern District of Illinois recently
when the Court stated that the language of the statute belies a general privity requirement." *Boshes* v. *General Motors Corp.*, 1973 Trade Cas. 74,483 (D.
N.Ill. 1973).

On a number of occasions, the Supreme Court has indicated the broad sweep
with which it now views the antitrust laws and, more particularly, the Clayton Act. In *Manderville Island Farms, Inc.* v. *American Crystal Sugar Co.*, 334
U.S. 219, 236 (1948), the Court noted that the Act is comprehensive in its
terms and coverage protecting all who are made victims of the forbidden practices by whomever they may be perpetrated." Nine years later the Court reiterated its underlying concern that the right to seek relief and damages from
injuries as a result of the antitrust laws not be unduly foreclosed. The Court
held that petitioners claim need only be 'tested under the Sherman Act's gen-
ing Company v. *United States*, 345 U.S. 594, 614 (1953), and meet the requirement that petitioner has thereby suffered injury. Congress has, by legislative
fiat, determined that such prohibited activities are injurious to the public and
has provided sanctions allowing private enforcement of the antitrust laws by
an aggrieved party. In the face of such a policy, this Court should not add
requirements to burden the private litigant beyond what is specifically set
forth by Congress in those laws." (*Radovich* v. *National Football League*,
supra at 453.) This expansive view of standing under §4, concentrating on
competitive harm rather than the privity between Plaintiff and Defendant,
was bolstered by the opinion of the Supreme Court in *Perkins* v. *Standard Oil
Corp.*, 395 U.S. 642, 648 (1969). Though the Court was there dealing with
price discrimination, as proscribed by §2 of the Clayton Act, the Court's
reasoning that "the competitive harm done * * * is certainly no less because
of the presence of an additional link in this particular chain" argues persuasively for reliance on the "target area" formulation for determining standing. The Supreme Court in *Perkins* also held that certain injuries personally
suffered by Plaintiff Perkins, as opposed to his companies, were cognizable
under §4. Though not specifically mentioning the doctrine by name, the Court
noted the target area quotation from *Karseal* and ruled that Plaintiff had
cognizable claims because "he was the principal victim of the price discrimination." *Perkins, supra* at 660. *Perkins*, therefor,e appears to clarify any am-
biguity in the Supreme Court's failure to fully determine this issue in its
recent decision, *Hawaii* v. *Standard Oil Co.*, 405 U.S. 251 (1972), a view

shared by the Ninth Circuit in *In Re Multidistrict Vehicle Air Pollution, supra*.

Thus, the question becomes whether the class of psychologists is within the "target area" of the conspiracy as alleged by Plaintiffs, as that doctrine has been developed since first put forward by the Ninth Circuit in *Karseal Corp. v. Richfield Oil Corp.*, 221 F.2d 358 (9th Cir. 1955). Karseal manufactured a car wax which was marketed through regional distributors to service stations. Karseal attacked Richfield's exclusive dealing contracts with gasoline station operators, prohibiting them from selling other than Richfield products. Despite the fact that it was Karseal's distributors who were directly affected, the Ninth Circuit held for Karseal because it was "within that area of the economy which is endangered by the breakdown of competitive conditions." (*Karseal, supra* at 55.) The "targe tarea" concept was further developed by the Ninth Circuit in *Twentieth Century Fox Film Corp., v. Goldwyn*, 328 F.2d 190 (9th Cir. 1964), where the Court stated that the "plaintiff must show that, whether or not then known to conspirators, plaintiff's affected operation was actually in the area which it could reasonably be foreseeable would be affected by the conspiracy." Other courts have also noted the foreseeability component of the "target area" test. In *H. F. & S. Co., Inc. v. American Standard, Inc.*, 336 F. Supp. 110 (D. Kan. 1972), the Court concluded its discussion of the alleged violations falling within the area of the economy endangered by the breakdown in competitive conditions by noting that "defendant could reasonably foresee that plaintiff's operation would be affected."

Clearly the conspiracy alleged in Plaintiffs' Complaint and Amended Complaint was "aimed at" psychologists to an extent sufficient to bring them under the scope of §4. Defendants and their co-conspirators know and intended that the operation of the "medical referral and supervision" clause would seriously injure and restrain psychologists in the free exercise of their profession. The fact that they also knew and intended that the conspiracy would also injure the individual subscribers should certainly not operate as a bar to recovery by psychologists. A similar situation was dealt with in *Schulman v. Burlington Industries, Inc.*, 255 F. Supp. 847 (S.D. N.Y. 1966). The Court dealt with the issue by noting that the complaint charges a conspiracy expressly and purposefully aimed at coercing and injuring the plaintiffs as identified targets. It does not matter that defendants, under the allegations, may be conspiring to prduce the restrants hurting plaintiffs only as part of an overall scheme to seek still bigger game. A conspiracy in antitrust law, as elsewhere, may have a variety of objects and victims."

Section 4 and the Congressional purpose underlying it was designed to give private litigants a vehicle to attain compensation for injuries resulting from violations of the antitrust law. In *Mandeville Island Farms, Radovich* and *Perkins*, the Supreme Court clearly underlined this concentration on competitive harm. In *GAF Corp. v. Circle Floor Company, Inc.*, 463 F.2d 752, 755–758 (2nd Cir. 1972), the Second Circuit expressed this principle by stating that "the courts in interpreting §4 of the Clayton Act, have endeavored, although with some inconsistency and conflict, to promote the policy of competition established by the Sherman and Clayton Acts by interpreting §4 as allowing treble damages only to those who have suffered some diminution of their ability to compete." There can be no doubt that Defendants Blue Cross and Blue Shield, guided by members of the medical profession and consistent with the intent of the conspiracy alleged by Plaintiffs, have effected substantially more than 'some diminution" of psychologists' ability to compete in providing health services. Any other conclusion than that Plaintiff psychologists have standing to assert their claims "would do violence to the clear intent of Congress that private antitrust action is an important and effective method of combating unlawful and destructive business practices." (*Flintkote Co. v. Lysfjord*, 246 F.2d 368 [9th Cir. 1957], *cert. den.* 355 U.S. 835.)

Defendants, in their Motion to Dismiss, place great reliance on *Billy Baxter, Inc. v. Coca-Cola Company*, 431 F.2d 183 (2nd Cir. 1970). Plaintiff's comment on that case can best be expressed through the words of Judge Waterman's dissent, therein: "I find it rather strange these days to deny access to a court of law to a plaintiff who alleges facts that show it has suffered compensable damages by reason of the actions of others. Thus, I am constrained to believe that my brother judges have accepted an anachronistic gloss upon the phrase 'by reason of.'" *id* at 190. "Can there be any doubt, again assuming the alleged facts to be provable, that the defendant's aim was to undermine the competitive position enjoyed by Billy Baxter trade name products in the beverage market?" *id* at 194. The foregoing discussion, of course, relates to the question of plaintiff psychologists establishing that their injuries were "by reason of" some violation of the antitrust laws. The other requisite necessary to establish standing is that Plaintiffs have indeed been injured in their business or property. In reaching this determination, the words "business or property" refer to commercial interests or enterprises, *Hawaii* v. *Standard Oil, supra.* "It signifies that which habitually busies or engages time, attention or labor, as a principle serious concern or interest." (*Roseland* v. *Phister Manufacturing Co.,* 125 F.2d 417, 419 [7th Cir. 1942]). That Plaintiff psychologists professional activities are described by this definition cannot be gainsaid.

As to the question of whether these interests were damaged, Plaintiffs' contentions, expressed in its previous discussion of standing under §16, certainly applies as well to standing under §4. The conspiracy alleged herein has resulted in injuries to Plaintiff psychologists position as independent providers of health services and their ability to compete therein has been affected, as has their relationship with their patients. This sort of injury to competitive position is precisely the type which the antitrust laws seek to remedy.

For all these reasons, Plaintiffs submit that Defendants' contentions that Plaintiff organizations and individual psychologists lack standing to present their claims has no merit and must be rejected by this Court.

II. *Restraint of Trade*

A. The "medical referral and supervision" clause in the F.E.H.B.A. contract is a product of an unlawful conspiracy to restrain trade.

Defendants, in their Motion to Dismiss, characterize Plaintiffs' attack as one upon Defendants Blue Cross Association and National Association of Blue Shield Plans' (hereinafter Defendant Plans) right to select the risks against which they will insure their subscribers. This entirely misconstrues the thrust of Plaintiffs' Complaint and Amended Complaint. The gravamen of Plaintiffs' allegations is a conspiracy between Defendant Plans, their affiliates and subsidiaries, and members of the medical profession, whose purpose and effect is: (1) to restrain licensed and/or certified psychologists from freely practicing their profession, (2) to limit the access of Federal employee subscribers of Defendant Plans to mental health services, particularly those mental health services offered by licensed and/or certified psychologists, and (3) to divert substantial revenues to physicians for performing perfunctory and unnecessary "supervision" and "referral." Plaintiffs do not in any respect challenge Defendant Plans' right to determine which risks they will insure. However, once that decision has been made—in this instance to insure against costs accruing from treatment for nervous and mental disorders—Defendants cannot enter into a conspiracy with one competing group of providers of treatment to exclude another qualified competing group of providers of health services completely and allow them to provide care only under certain conditions dictated by Defendants.

Defendants' reliance on *Ruddy Brook Clothes, Inc.* v. *British & Foriegn Marine Ins. Co.,* 195 F.2d 86 (7th Cir.) *cert. den.* 344 U.S. 816 (1952) ; *American Family Life Assurance Co.* v. *Blue Cross of Florida, Inc.,* 1973-2 Trade Cas. 74,767 (5th Cir. 1973) ; and *Travelers Ins. Co.* v. *Blue Cross of Western Pennsylvania,* 481 F.2d 80 (3rd Cir. 1973) *cert. den.* 42 U.S.L.W. 3348 (1973), is entirely misplaced. In no way is the "medical referral or supervision" clause a limitation of coverage for any harm. Rather, it is an attempt by Defendant Plans, pursuant to the herein described conspiracy, to dictate to subscribers the choice between co-equal competing, qualified providers of services for covered risks.

Hornbook law is that "a sused in the Antitrust Act the word 'restraint' is a comprehensive word and covers several kinds thereof described: check; hinder ; repress ; curb ; restrict.' *United States* v. *Reading,* 183 Fed. 427 (1910)." Toulmin's *Antitrust Laws* §13.³. That describes precisely the situation in the instant case.

Over sixty years ago the lower court, in deciding *United States* v. *Standard Oil Co.,* 173 Fed. 177, *aff'd.* 221 U.S. 1 (1911), declared illegal any contract combination or consuiracy "if the necessary effect * * * is to stifle or directly and substantially to restrict free competition." In *Standard Oil,* the Supreme Court first established the rule of reason as determinative of violations of the antitrust laws. Certain types of conduct, however, has been judged inherently so harmful that they are conclusively presumed unreasonable. Examples of such *per se* violations of the antitrust laws include price fixing and market division. But, the reasonableness of the methods utilized to obtain these illegal objectives does not insulate the activities from operation of the antitrust laws.

In *Fashion Originators Guild of America, Inc.* v. *Federal Trade Commission*, 312 U.S. 457 (1941), the Supreme Court added collective boycotts to the list of *per se* offenses. As a result of this decision, joint action taken by competitors to eliminate other competitors could not be justified by the reasonableness of the methods utilized. Thus, Defendants' justification of its conduct is no more material to the issues at bar than the claim that prices were reasonable would be to a charge of price fixing. As noted by the Court, "the touchstone of *per se* illegality has been tthe purpose and effect of the arrangement in question. Where exclusionary or coercive conduct has been present, the arrangements have been viewed as 'naked restraints of trade' and have fallen victim to the *per se* rule." *id* at 187. The coercive effect of the "medical referral and supervision" clause is obvious in that, except for its improper requirements, no psychologist would place himself under the superfluous supervision of a co-equal mental health service provider. Many thousands of individual subscribers of Defendant Plans are either refused reimbursement for treatment of covered risks by licensed and/or certified psychologists or are forced to obtain perfunctory supervision (compensation for which increases their premiums), or are forced to try to obtain treatment from members of the medical profession when they would prefer to obtain treatment from licensed and or certified psychologists, or finally, receive no treatment at all because of Defendants' insistence upon the clause.

A unanimous Supreme Court reiterated the proscription of collective boycotts in *Klor's, Inc.* v. *Broadway-Hale Stores, Inc.*, 359 U.S. 207 (1959), when it upheld the attack by Klor's, a small retailer of appliances, on a combination between one of its competitors and a number of national manufacturers of television and small appliances, to cut off its supplies of those items.

The sanctions against collective boycotts are not, however, limited to complete refusals to deal, as in *Klor's*. Actions taken in order to force the object of the boycott or threatened boycott, only to deal under certain conditions, are also subject to proscription. *Lowe* v. *Lawlor*, 208 U.S. 274 (1908). In *California League of Independent Insurance Producers* v. *Aetna Casualty*, 179 F. Supp. 65 (N.D. Cal. 1959), the Court included, within the definition of boycott, not only a complete refusal of the Defendant insurance company to deal with the Plaintiff independent brokers, but also refusal to deal with them except at a fixed price; a situation remarkably similar to conditions imposed by Defendants, whereby reimbursement for psychologists are only provided pursuant to the prior restraint of medical referral and supervision."

B. The selection of risks, while contemplated by the enabling Federal Statute, 5 U.S.C.§8900, *et seq.*, did not contemplate adoption of blatantly discriminatory standards aimed at competent, qualified providers of health services.

Plaintiffs recognize that Congress, in passing the Federal Employees Health Benefits Act, mandated a system whereby Federal employees would have a choice among competing insurance programs offering different levels of coverage and choices of risks. Defendants' insistence that Plaintiffs somehow seek to impose uniform coverage on all insurance plans is as incorrect as it is irrelevant. Equally out of place is the repeated theme that competition between various insurance carriers answers all questions raised by Plaintiffs' Complaint and Amended Complaint. The Court will not find a scintilla of evidence in Defendants' extended discussion of Congressional history which purports to stand for the proposition that Congress intended to authorize discriminatory treatment of one co-equal group of competing providers of health services at the behest of another group of competing providers of health services. No amount of competition between various insurance carriers, even assuming it exists, can justify or excuse the conspiracy entered into by Defendants, conduct clearly in violation of Sections 1 and 3 of the Sherman Act.

C. A so-called non-profit" corporation may not enter into a conspiracy to restrain trade for the benefit of one competing branch of the health service profession and to the detriment of another competing branch of the health service profession.

Defendants place great reliance on the doctrine enunciated in *Marjorie Webster Jr. College* v. *Middle States Association of Colleges and Secondary Schools*, 432 F.2d 650 (D.C. Cir. 1970), claiming that their activities affected only the "non-commercial aspects of the liberal arts and learned professions" and that any resulting restraint of trade was only incidental. This argument is nothing more than an attempt to triumph form over substance. Admittedly, Defendant Plans are non-profit corporations. This status alone certainly does not entitle them to escape the scrutiny of the antitrust laws. *In Marjorie Webster*, a proprietary junior college alleged that an association of colleges and secondary schools violated the Sherman Act by refusing to accredit the school because of its proprietary character. The Court of Appeals for the District of Columbia overturned a District Court finding for Marjorie Webster on the grounds of the non-commercial nature of the relationship.

The issues raised by Plaintiffs, however, are entirely commercial in nature. Defendants have not foisted upon Plaintiffs a contractual provision restraining trade so as to fulfill some unspecified non-commercial objective. Rather, they have intruded into commercial competition between competing groups of health service providers by conspiring with one group in order to advance the interests of that group at the expense of another competing group and of the individual Federal employee subscribers to Defendant Plans.

It is important to note that, preceding his statement that the Sherman Act was enacted to apply to the business world and not to non-commercial situations, Judge Bazelon, in *Marjorie Webster*, stated "that appellant's objectives, both in the formation and in the development and application of the restriction here at issue, are not commercial, is not in dispute." *id* at 654. This statement, in and of itself, distinguishes the *Marjorie Webster* ruling from the instant situation. Plaintiffs contend that the "medical referral and supervision" clause was imposed pursuant to a conspiracy whose aims and purposes were blatantly commercial in nature. Judge Bazelon recognized the crucial importance of the non-commercial purposes of the restriction when he stated that "it is possible to conceive of restrictions on eligibility for accreditation that could have little other than a commercial motive, and, as such, *antitrust policy would presumably be applicable.*" *id at* 654–4. (Emphasis added.) Precisely such a situation is alleged by Plaintiffs. Moreover, since in considering a Motion to Dismiss, all of Plaintiffs' factual allegations must be taken as true (*Radovich v. National Football League, supra*), the inapplicability of the *Marjorie Webster* doctrine to the instant case is apparent.

Equally inapplicable to the case at bar is *Nankin Hospital v. Michigan Hospital Service*, 1973–2 Trade Cas. 74,686 (E.D. Mich. 1973). That decision fails to support Defendants' contentions because the Court there *expressly* grounded its opinion on Nankin's failure to meet its burden of proving that the standards promulgated by Blue Cross were done for anti-competitive purposes. As noted above, however, Plaintiffs' factual allegations must be taken as true in considering a Motion to Dismiss. Plaintiffs' Complaint and Amended Complaint clearly alleges anti-competitive purposes underlying imposition of the "medical referral and supervision" requirement and, thus, defendants' reliance on *Marjorie Webster* is wholly misplaced.

Roofire Alarm Co. v. Royall Indemnity Co., 202 F. Supp. 166 (E.D. Tenn. 1962), *aff'd.* 313 F.2d 635 (6th Cir. 1963), similarly fails to support Defendants' premises, for the Court there expressly grounded its rejection of plaintiff's allegations on the fact that neither defendant nor other member of the conspiracy were in competition with plaintiff. In the instant situation, however, that missing element is present as Plaintiffs have alleged that competitors of the individual psychologists have conspired with Defendant Plans in order to restrain Plaintiff individual psychologists in the free exercise of their profession.

It is apparent, therefore, that Defendants have failed to sustain their contentions as to the antitrust violations asserted, and that their Motion should be denied for these additional reasons.

III. Plaintiff's Complaint and Amended Complaint Alleges Valid Tort Claims Against Defendant Plans

Plaintiffs' Complaint and Amended Complaint are not confined to allegations of violations of the antitrust laws. It also alleges violations of tort law over which it requests this Court to take pendent jurisdiction. Briefly, these allegations assert that, in the imposition and administration of the "medical referral and supervision" clause, Defendant Plans have disparaged the entire professiona of psychology, its constituent organizations and each individual psychologist. Defendants' conduct also constitutes the tort of interference with Plaintiff individual psychologists' contractual relations with his client.

Plaintiffs' Complaint and Amended Complaint also allege that the conduct of Defendants in imposing and administering the "medical referral and supervision" clause tortiously interferes with the individual psychologist Plaintiffs prospective advantage. The referral clause has persuaded prospective patients, who would otherwise have sought treatment from the individual psychologist Plaintiffs, either to seek treatment elsewhere or not at all because of absence of reimbursement, and because the red tape associated with the referral clause discourages many patients from using the services of psychologists.

IV. Conclusion

In brief summary, therefore, Plaintiffs reassert their contentions that all of the named Plaintiffs in Plaintiffs' Complaint and Amended Complaint are threatened with continuation of the type of injury cognizable under §16 of the Clayton Act and have standing thereunder to sue for injunctive relief. In addition, the individual psychologists and the Federal employee subscribers of Defendant Plans have been injured in their business and property in a manner sufficient to give them standing to sue for treble damages under §4 of the Clayton Act.

In regard to the substantive allegations of restraint of trade, Plaintiffs' contention is that Defendant Plans have entered into a conspiracy with various members of the medical profession, whose purposes and effects include restraining licensed and or certified psychologists in the free exercise of their profession, limiting access of Federal employee subscribers of defendant Plans to mental health services and forcing many such subscribers to consult members of the medical profession, either in addition to or instead of licensed and/or certified psychologists. Plaintiffs contend that this blatant interference with competition between various kinds of health service providers amounts to a *per se* illegal collective boycott which is in no manner immunized from the prohibitions of the Sherman Act by Defendant Plans' status as non-profit corporations. Furthermore, Defendant Plans' activities also constitute tortious invasion of legally protected rights of Plaintiffs. For all these reasons, the Court should deny the pending Motion and direct that Defendant Plans submit an Answer to the Amended Complaint within a reasonable time after the issuance of the Court's order.

Respectfully submitted,

JOSEPH L. NELLIS,
JEFFREY L. NESVET,
1819 H Street, N. W.,
Washington, D. C. 20006,
Tel. 223-6300,
Attorneys for Plaintiffs.

CERTIFICATE OF SERVICE

I hereby certify that on this 31st day of January, 1974, a copy of the foregoing Plaintiffs' Opposition to Defendants' Motion to Dismiss the Complaint was mailed, postage prepaid, to each of the following:

Barron K. Grier, Esq.., Miller & Chevalier, 1700 Pennsylvania Avenue, N.W., Washington, D. C. 20006, Attorneys for Defendants Blue Cross Association and National Association of Blue Shield Plans.

Stanley D. Robinson, Esq., Michael Malina, Esq., Kaye, Scholer, Fierman, Hays æ Handler, 425 Park Avenue, New York, New York 10022, Attorneys for Defendant Blue Cross Association.

Frederick M. Rowe, Esq., Edward W. Warren, Esq., Kirkland, Ellis & Rowe, 1776 K Street, N.W., Washington, D. C. 20006, Attorneys for Defendant National Association of Blue Shield Plans.

Thomas G. Corcoran, Jr., Esq., Assistant United States Attorney, U. S. Court House, Room 3423, Washington, D. C. 20001, Attorney for Federal Defendants.

JOSEPH L. NELLIS.

———

ANONYMOUS LETTERS

To Whom It May Concern:

This will be a brief narrative of my experience with the Blue Cross Blue Shield Government Employees Program relative to psychological services.

Dr. —— my physician (Internal Medicine) referred me to Dr. ——, a psychologist, on November 27, 1973. I first saw Dr. —— in December 1972. My first report to Blue Shield was on January 18, 1973. I continued with psychotherapy each month thereafter through May 1973. Monthly reports were made to Blue Shield along with any pertinent claims for Medicare and medicines.

I saw Dr. —— at four week intervals at least, and Dr. —— made written reports as required by the conditions outlined in the BlueCross/Blue Shield Brochure. Dr. —— was fully aware of the problems I was encountering and felt that I should continue until there was a better physical condition realized. I was making good progress when a crisis in my grandson's life in early June brought about a near breakdown.

In March 29, 1973 I received my first reimbursement from Blue Shield. It was a check without a summary. They stated that the summary would follow. None ever has.

Every month after that I would receive the billing from them that I had submitted from Dr. ——, The same request was always made that I should provide a statement from Dr. —— that treatment was under his supervision. Finally Dr. —— provided me with a cover letter giving consent to the treatment provided. Still billings were returned to me. It was necessary for me to make a trip to Dr. —— office to secure the letter. But more important is the fact that a crucial time I was forced to discontinue pyschotherapy because I could no longer afford to pay Dr. —— with no reimbursement for over six months of billing with no results. I submitted the last billing from Dr. —— in June. Medicare and Medicine billings have been paid *only* during this whole period.

I carry High Option Blue Cross Blue Shield coverage to make sure I get every possible care. I am retired, on a limited income and their handling of this has caused me much financial inconvenience, much anxiety and stress.

Re: CAPPS' Blue Cross-Blue Shield Questionnaire
JOSEPH L. NELLIS,
General Counsel, CAPPS,
Washington, D.C.

DEAR MR. NELLIS: I have gone over the questionnaire which Dr. —— in Dallas sent to me. During my two years of private practice I have had a great many patients who were covered for psychiatric out-patient services by an M.D., but whose policy coverage did not include my services. Most of these people simply did not submit claims because of my past experience in not being able to collect from Blue Shield. I share my office with —— M.D., who is a psychiatrist, and we have been able to qualify as a medical team so that we have no difficulty collecting on patients whom we both see. Most of the time, these patients have to make appointments with Dr. —— just in order to qualify for their insurance coverage and they would not otherwise need to see him in consultation.

I have taken some information from my files regarding Blue Shield refusals which is enclosed. If I come across any other information which might be helpful to you, I will forward it as soon as possible.

JOSEPH L. NELLIS, Esq,
CAPPS General Counsel,
Washington, D.C.

DEAR MR. NELLIS: I am enclosing the exchange of letters with the Federal Employees program and with others in an attempt to complete payment on the case of

As you can see, this has been drawn out over a long period of time and payment is not completed as yet. It appears I will have to go through the whole process of rebilling, and then I am not sure what will happen.

In this case, It was especially unfortunate the patient could not afford treatment unless the insurance was supported and she has been in a severe depression ever since termination.

Sincerely,

Gentlemen: The above captioned has been a patient in this facility since November, 1970, and has been seen various times for an enlargening cyst of the

Careful evaluation of her history and physical examinations led me to think that she needed a little psychological assistance because of her various problems. She was seen in this office on ———— and followed through until last seen ———— and was seen by me 6 times in 1972 and 12 times in 1971, and it was felt that her problems could be greatly assisted by her seeing a psychologist.

She was the type person that made me feel deeply impressed that she should not see a psychiatrist because her problems were more in the psychological realm rather than a deep psychosis.

I have discussed this with Dr. ———— and he saw this young lady and I feel, to great advantage. I shall probably see her again in the near future, and from what I hear, I have every reason to believe that the treatment she received has been very efficacious.

There are times when it does a patient harm to be told that should see a psychiatrist. There are times when the thought of a psychologist elevates them instead of depressing them and her particular emotional problems would respond poorly to psychiatric care.

We feel Dr. ———— is an extremely capable man in his field and that many times his approach is equal or superior to that of a psychiatrist.

If further information is desired, we will be happy to supply the same.

Sincerely yours,

————

BLUE CROSS/BLUE SHIELD,
Claims Dept
Washington, D.C.

GENTLEMEN: Reference attached letters and all other futile attempts to satisfy a nebulous standard of requirements and or procedures to file a supplemental claim for payment of doctor bills covering treatment of mental illness.

It is with this in mind I request the above claim be thoroughly reviewed by the Appeals Section BC/BS as we feel our claim has been unjustly denied, over and over.

For almost a year now BC/BS has apparently been circumventing payment of a legitimate bill from Dr. ———— psychologist, as a team member under supplemental payment benefits. Every attempt made by us to meet expanding requirements has been thwarted . . . . This last letter tops them all (see attached) My husband was at a point of suicide and friends on the scene called the best psychologist in the area to his rescue on an emergency basis. This doctor took professional action. An appointment was made with Dr. ————, M.D., psychiatrist, at the first possible opening. There was *no delay* in taking action. Had anyone advised this information was necessary for filing a claim it would have been gladly furnished. It was just another means of delay, as I see it . . . The fantastic thing about this whole situation is the only information given to begin with (given to me upon seeking assistance at the local BC/BS office at the onset of my husbands illnes (Jan) so that I could furnish correct documentation at time of supplemental claim application) was to have the psychiatrist (attending physician) prepare a statement indicating he referred my husband to ———— as a member of an eventual team. Of course Dr. ———— continued to see my husband and counseled with the psychologist when progress or the lack of it so dictated. (I'm sure had these men known that at a later date written correspondence would have been necessary to meet BC/BS procedures, it would have been done . . . but who is the doctor here? Can you imagine-BC/BS setting down rules for the doctors to follow??? If they don't do it just like BC/BS says they deny the patients claim . . . to me something is wrong with this . . . either the doctor should be able to handle the case as he sees fit and BC/BS accepts his methods or BC/BS furnishes the doctor a form to be completed at the beginning and/of during treatment for patients under this coverage.

It is disgraceful to think of the times this one doctor (————, has been contacted to furnish and re-furnish statement, letters, etc. for just one patient. Multiply this times all psychiatrists and mental patients seeking coverage (I have been assured my husband is only one of many having this same problem with BC/BS) . . the hours lost to patients and or their case handling . . not to mention ancillary personnel . .

However, the main point I want to make is this. .

What do you say to a mental patient when he asks (in this case for almost a year) "Has BC/BS helped us pay on Dr. Crawford's bill, yet? I hope *you*

never have to ask a similar question of your wife . . . 'and be covered by
BC/BS. . . .

Sincerely yours,

[From Psychiatric News, June 21, 1972]

Adapted from Newsletter of Michigan Psychiatric Society

To get to the point quickly, I am concerned about the economics of our profession—the fact that a focal point of the energies of some of our colleagues seems to be psychiatry as a business. It is a distressing situation and one that deserves more examination than has been given previously.

Let us agree that as physicians and even more as trained specialists, we are entitled to compensation that reflects our years of schooling, experience, time, skill, and the great responsibility we carry. If physicians are, as has been indicated. the highest paid profession, then let it be recognized that this must surely represent a deserved achievement that comes from the burden of our daily being instruments of genuine consequence in the lives of our patients. We should not be the objects of scorn or jealousy because of this income.

Yet, we have been criticized on just that account and must be, therefore, in financial matters as in all other aspects of our practices, like Caesar's wife—above suspicion.

Yet I remain concerned that not all of our endeavors in the broad field of psychiatric treatment are generated by therapeutic efforts, and here I do not speak of the small percentage of individuals who in our specialty, just as in all others, fall outside the norm when it comes to ethics and legalities. These are relatively easy to identify and, although they do not enhance our image. They also do not essentially influence the general picture of what a psychiatrist is.

I am referring instead to certain broad trends that seem extent in the midst of many of us.

Some questions arose in my mind when I analyzed a fee survey undertaken last year for the purpose of developing data on psychiatric fees for submission to the relative value scale study committee of the Michigan State Medical Society.

Why did the returns indicate, for example, that group therapy yields a therapeutic fee that is on the average two to three times greater than the average fee charged for individual psychotherapy, when adjusted to a session of the same duration.

The intent of this treatment to offer services to more people at lower costs is admirable, but does this unselfish goal not become clouded when the financial return is so rewarding?

I also wondered why the fees of those of us most recently in practice were on the average higher than those who had been practicing for many more years. Is this consistent with the expressed anti-materialistic idealism of our younger confreres?

Additionally, although not related to the fee survey, I have heard of instances of what I choose to call the "absentee therapist." In these cases the psychiatrist lends his name as consultant to, or member of, a team of allied professionals. He is, however, only distantly and minimally involved in the actual therapeutic process. Yet he shares in the fees. If this is an answer to increasing our capacity to deliver services, it would appear that this social altruism finds its reward not only in the service to society but also in hard coin.

I have chosen these few examples not because they are flagrant violations of customary practices, but because they indicate a malignant potential that could hurt all of us. If we do not, regardless of our type of practice, keep our charges and our income at a level that is reasonable and reasonably standard, we will hasten the day when fee schedules and income limitations will be externally imposed on us.

Most significant of all, if economic incentive becomes our motivating force, professional goals will be compromised. We must, in spite of existing opportunities, resist the temptation to exchange the scholar's cap for the merchant's cloak. I believe that our futures depend on it.

RALPH S. GREEN, M.D.,
President, Michigan Psychiatric Society.

1410

[From the Washington Post, June 1, 1974]

PSYCHIATRY HELD OVERSOLD

PITTSBURGH.—Psychiatry has about as high a success rate among its followers as witchraft and spirit healing have among their believers, according to a Harvard psychiatry professor.

Dr. Leon Eisenberg said Thursday members of his profession have oversold the public on the accomplishments of psychiatrists.

"Any form of treatment seems to work in some cases, and there isn't any one thing that workds better than anything else," he said at the University of Pittsburgh Graduate School of Public Health.

Eisenberg said mental health statistics have been manipulated in the United States to give the impression of a high success rate in treatment. He said that although psychiatrists point to the fact that more patients are being discharged from mental hospitals, they fail to report that 30 to 50 per cent of schizophrenic patients will be readmitted within one year and 60 to 70 per cent within five years.

THE NATIONAL ASSOCIATION FOR MENTAL HEALTH, Inc.

1800 North Kent Street, Rosslyn, Virginia 22209 • (703) 528.6405

NATIONAL HEALTH INSURANCE
For The Mentally Ill

A publication designed to help ensure that national health insurance will not discriminate against people who are mentally ill.

February 1974
(Revised)

A PLAN OF COVERAGE FOR THE MENTALLY ILL IN NATIONAL HEALTH INSURANCE

The National Association for Mental Health, after a year of concentrated study by the Association's Task Force on National Health Insurance, has reached several major conclusions regarding the inclusion of mental illness in National Health Insurance:

1) Mental illness is insurable at a reasonable cost;

2) Any system of National Health Insurance should stimulate the growth and development of community mental health centers;

3) National Health Insurance should promote an integrated and coordinated system of mental health service delivery.

In response to requests by the citizens in our Association and members of Congress, we have developed a proposal that outlines our recommendations regarding specific coverage for mental illness in National Health Insurance. On page 2 is a brief explanation of the information on which we based our conclusions. Our recommendations regarding mental health services to be included in any plan for National Health Insurance follow on page 3.

We are committed to supporting National Health Insurance legislation to the extent that it incorporates our recommendations for services

MENTAL ILLNESS IS INSURABLE AT A REASONABLE COST

Many reasons are given for excluding mentally ill persons from insurance plans, but the most damaging reason is based on the myth that including mental illness causes rates to soar This myth has clearly been refuted by a number of studies. For example, the Health Insurance Plan of Greater New York found that it could provide mental illness coverage to a family of three or more for $2.70 a month, which included outpatient and inpatient psychiatric treatment with no upper limit on the number of services and with no cost to the patient

Mental health care is not only possible at a reasonable cost; such coverage may also re-duce inappropriate utilization of other health services. In a study[1] of the Group Health Association in Washington, D C., it was demonstrated that the provision of mental health services reduced substantially the amount of non-psychiatric medical care provided to a given population.

The myth is just that There is no sound evidence for excluding mental illness from National Health Insurance because of cost. Our organization is pledged to bring this fact before the public and our elected officials so they may judge the cost issue on its merits.

ANY SYSTEM OF NATIONAL HEALTH INSURANCE SHOULD STIMULATE THE GROWTH AND DEVELOPMENT OF COMMUNITY MENTAL HEALTH CENTERS

There are a number of reasons why we support the concept of National Health Insurance promoting the development of community mental health centers It is a fact that the community mental health centers are playing an important role in decreasing the utilization of state mental hospitals. A 1970 survey of 92 community mental health centers indicates that state mental hospitals which are served by well-established (in operation three years or longer) community mental health centers have less than half the admission rate of the national average.

There are additional reasons why we support centers. Centers provide a wide range of treatment alternatives—which are suited to the needs of the patient They provide serv-ice close to home. They are accessible to citizen "watchdog" activities. They hold the major hope for completely reversing the practice of "warehousing" the mentally ill in massive, distant, custodial institutions. Most important, the center, through consultation and education, and through its outreach to the community can help to prevent the onset of mental illness and thereby reduce the number of persons who might otherwise require treatment.

Centers have demonstrated their ability to provide an effective alternative to long-term custodial care and have earned the right to be included in any system of National Health Insurance.

NATIONAL HEALTH INSURANCE SHOULD PROMOTE AN INTEGRATED AND COORDINATED SYSTEM OF MENTAL HEALTH SERVICE DELIVERY

National Health Insurance not only provides an opportunity for delivering more mental health services to people, it can and should influence the delivery system.

Many community mental health centers have already demonstrated that they can provide an integrated coordinated system of mental health service delivery. We think it makes good sense to extend this system by mandating affiliation between centers and state mental hospitals as well as other organized deliverers of mental health care. Therefore, we are requiring, in the following outline of services, that all facilities providing services shall be affiliated with community mental health centers in their geographical area.

[1] Goldberg, I , Krantz, G , Locke, B · "Effect of a Short-Term Outpatient Psychiatric Therapy Benefit on the Utilization of Medical Services in a Prepaid Group Practice Medical Program." *Medical Care.* Sept -Oct 1970, Volume 8, No 5

RECOMMENDATIONS OF THE NATIONAL ASSOCIATION FOR MENTAL HEALTH FOR CATEGORIES OF SERVICE FOR MENTAL HEALTH COVERAGE UNDER NATIONAL HEALTH INSURANCE

CONCEPT

● **Comprehensive Coverage**

The National Association for Mental Health supports comprehensive coverage of mental and emotional disorders under National Health Insurance. Such coverage must provide compensation for active care, including preventive, diagnostic, therapeutic, supportive, or rehabilitative services in all categories of service delivery. There should be no limitations of coverage and no discrimination by providers based upon age, sex, race, creed or economic circumstance. Persons in preventive custody, correctional institutions, juvenile detention centers, and court designated treatment facilities shall not be excluded from the provisions of NHI. Such coverage under NHI should be guaranteed as a matter of right to health.

● **Encouraging Development of Community Mental Health Centers**

The National Association for Mental Health is committed to securing mental health coverage under NHI which encourages and facilitates the continued development and use of community mental health centers (CMHCs). All facilities providing services shall be affiliated with any CMHCs in their geographical area. All treatment facilities must be approved by a state recognized health planning and accrediting board. These facilities may include, but not be limited to, CMHCs, state mental hospitals, private mental hospitals, general hospitals, mental health clinics, comprehensive health service organizations, health maintenance organizations, drug and alcohol treatment centers, and schools and other treatment facilities providing special services to emotionally disturbed children and youth.

SPECIFIC MENTAL HEALTH COVERAGE UNDER NATIONAL HEALTH INSURANCE

I. Services Provided on an Unlimited Basis

A. OUTPATIENT SERVICES (Excluding professional services by private practitioners)

1. There shall be no limit placed on mental health outpatient services. Each client case which has continued for 90 calendar days shall be reviewed by an independent utilization review board. Subsequent reviews shall be made every 90 calendar days

B. PARTIAL HOSPITALIZATION SERVICES

1. There shall be no limit placed on partial hospitalization services. Each client case which has continued for 60 calendar days shall be reviewed by an independent utilization review board. Subsequent reviews shall be made every 60 calendar days

II. Services Provided on a Limited Basis

A. PROFESSIONAL SERVICES BY PRIVATE PRACTITIONERS

1. Consultation by private practitioners shall be limited to twenty (20) consultations per each one-year benefit period. The first seven consultations, per each one-year benefit period, shall be covered in full. Private professional consultations may be provided by private practitioners in categories designated by the Secretary and who hold a valid license or certificate issued by an appropriate governmental agency to provide diagnostic or therapeutic services.

2. Private professional services shall be subject to a periodic review by an independent utilization review board. The review shall be based upon a random sample.

B. INPATIENT SERVICES

1. Inpatient services for adults shall be limited to 45 days of active treatment per each one-year benefit period. No continuous stay of more than 20 days shall be permitted without approval by an independent utilization review board. Coverage of inpatient services shall not be continued after the third day following delivery of notice that continued inpatient services are not therapeutically necessary. Those client cases found by the utilization review board to need treatment for more than 45 days shall be eligible for NHI inpatient coverage under provisions for chronic long-term care.

2. Inpatient services for children 18 years and younger shall be unlimited. Each client case shall be reviewed monthly by an Independent Utilization Review Board.

III. Services Provided on the Same Basis as Chronic Medical Conditions

A. CHRONIC LONG-TERM CARE

1. Coverage under NHI for mental health care in an extended care or intermediate care facility, foster home, or small group home, which has primarily long-term treatment and maintenance objectives should not be less than the most favorable coverage available for long-term treatment and maintenance provided for any other chronic medical condition.

2. Interviews with clients and review of case records should be conducted at least twice annually by an independent utilization review board to determine the nature and necessity for continued treatment and maintenance.

IV. Corollary Considerations and Definitions

A. OTHER SERVICES

1. The cost of covered mental health services shall be reimbursable even though care is provided in non-health care facilities (e.g. schools, day care centers, correctional institutions, etc.)

B. ACTIVE TREATMENT

Active, preventive, diagnostic, therapeutic, supportive, or rehabilitative services shall mean that all treatment modalities consist of a planned and written program of daily activities or services based upon diagnosis and designed to prevent regression, improve adaptive capability, or maximize ability to live independently. Such services may include, but are not limited to: drugs, testing, nursing, psychotherapy, home visits, counseling, group therapy, casework, and other professional and paraprofessional services, which are a part of active care.

C. AFFILIATION

Affiliation shall mean that those facilities delivering service shall be required to have a written contractual agreement binding on both parties and providing for the following:

1. Cross-consultation and exchange of staff resources:

2. Free accessibility of all case and medical information:

3. Planned and coordinated referral and transfer of clients from one service program to another.

D. INDEPENDENT UTILIZATION REVIEW BOARD (IURB)

This Board shall be comprised of mental health professionals and paraprofessionals and informed laypersons. In no instance should members of the IURB be employees or Board members of the organization being reviewed. Access to information upon which judgment can be made and authority to enforce this judgment should be provided by NHI administrative regulations. Such regulations should protect the confidentiality of individual patients' records. The purpose of the utilization review process shall be as follows:

1. To determine the nature and necessity of continued treatment:

2. To safeguard the rights of clients receiving treatment, including the rights of confidentiality;

3. To assure quality care of an active nature.

E. CITIZEN BOARDS

Citizen Boards should be created at the various levels of administration to set standards and evaluate all providers. They shall have ultimate responsibility for governing the program and for assuring an integrated and coordinated system of mental health service delivery, specific to the needs of the geographic area. There should be substantial representation on all Citizen Boards from consumers, minority groups, the poor, and from professionals and laypersons with knowledge of mental health and mental illness. Laypersons not engaged in providing services to the mentally ill should constitute a majority of every Board.

F. OTHER CRITICAL MENTAL HEALTH SERVICES

Education-consultation, manpower training and development, research and evaluation, currently provided for by the Community Mental Health Centers Act of 1963, should be continued and funded separately from NHI through categorical funds or project grants.

APPROVED BY THE NAMH BOARD OF DIRECTORS

FEBRUARY 1, 1974

1416

PUBLIC AFFAIRS COMMITTEE
TASK FORCE ON NATIONAL HEALTH INSURANCE

Hilda H. Robbins

Chairperson
Past-President, Pennsylvania Mental Health
Vice Chairman NAMH Public Affairs Committee

Jerry Cole

Insurance Consultant
Past-President, Kansas Association for Mental Health

Kenneth Gaver, M.D.

*Director, Ohio Department of Mental Health
and Mental Retardation*

Dorothy Knox, M.S.W.

Chairperson, Intervention Concentration
School of Social Welfare
State University of New York at Stony Brook

Member
NAMH Executive Committee

6

[From Psychiatric News, Jan. 3, 1973]

TRUSTEES OK CLOSER TIES WITH NON-MEDICAL WORKERS

APA's Board of Trustees approved a position statement on the relationship of psychiatrists to non-medical personnel that observers say marks a clear change of policy and attitude by the Association, and should contribute significantly toward improvement of relations among the professions. The position, approved in December, argues that "there should no longer be divisive wedges between professions striving toward [a] common goal . . ." and makes a number of specific suggestions for achieving better feelings and working relationships.

Regarding third party payments the Association endorsed paying under medical insurance plans, such as Medicare or Medicaid, non-medical health professionals when their services are rendered as part of a plan of treatment that is supervised or prescribed by a physician.

"However, professionals in these various allied fields often elect to engage independently in health-related practices in a non-medical setting. A person should feel free to select the practitioner of his choice from among qualified professions," the statement reads. "If there is a public demand for health-related services that are not normally regarded as medical, nor offered as part of a total medical treatment program, insurance companies may offer insurance for such health-related services as they currently do for medical treatment. If the federal government wishes to provide publicly supported programs for such services, appropriate legislation will have to be passed."

In outlining psychiatry's responsibility to the public, the statement maintains that psychiatry must recognize the right of the recipients of mental health services to know the competencies and limitations of those offering their services and to "choose which person, professions, or agencies they wish to consult in seeking help."

However, it points out that "psychiatrists are physicians, whereas other mental health professiontls are not" and cites the advantages of seeking help from those professionals. As physicians, it states, psychiatrists are trained to make a "differential diagnois between physical and emotional aspects of disorders which are frequently intertwined" and are capable of choosing the correct treatment modality from the wide spectrum of modalities available such as psychotherapy, medications, other somatic treatment, and at times hospitalization.

"Delay in the use of such other treatment modalities," it warns, "may have serious or even fatal consequences for some patients."

Yet, it declares, psychiatry must recognize the right of every professional group to define its own functions and areas of competence, and to set up its own educational and training programs and to establish its own standard of service. "No profession should attempt to define the functions and responsibilities of any other profession."

It further notes that psychiatrists must recognize that establishing and maintaining codes of ethics are an "internal responsibility of each profession and that complaints against other professionals should be directed to the responsible authorities of the profession concerned."

APA also offers the following other guidelines in reference to the settings and situations in which problems in interprofessional relations often rise:

In medical settings, APA in concurrence with the American Hospita Association, endorses the principle of appointing members of other professions, such as nurses, psychologists, and social workers, to the staff of hospital and other medical facilities "to bring to the treatment of patients their specialized knowledge, skill, and experience." However, in such a setting the physician-psychiatrist would retain the "primary medical responsibility. . . ."

Psychiatrists working as consultants, supervisors, therapist, or administrative staff members in non-medical settings such is some mental retardation centers and correctional institutions, would essentially have the "same relationships to the organization as other professionals have in a medical setting. . . ." The psychiatrist would still "retain ultimate responsibility for the psychiatric and medical care of the patients or clients" he served.

In office practice the psychiatrist would refer people to other professionals for appropriate services based upon the other professional's qualifications.

Finally, when psychiatrists collaborate with other health professionals, including supervision of cases or participation in interdisciplinary teamwork, they are "obliged to know about and be willing to assume the established legal responsibilities involved."

BACKGROUND PAPER: PSYCHOLOGISTS AS AUTONOMOUS PROVIDERS OF SERVICES COVERED BY HEALTH INSURANCE

SUMMARY

Psychology is recognized as a health discipline in licensure/certification statutes in forty-six States and the District of Columbia; nineteen States have enacted "freedom-of-choice" statutes requiring insurance carriers to reimburse their policyholders for the diagnosis and treatment of mental and nervous disorders when services are rendered by a psychologist, with or without medical referral/supervision. Psychologists, representing a significant manpower pool available to meet increasing demands for services, have developed internal controls and accepted external regulation to assure high-quality services. The "medical model" has been perpetuated in the health-insurance industry to the disadvantage of subscribers, who usually are not aware of such differences in their policies.

The medical/referral supervision requirement is an unnecessary and costly burden on the patient, the non-medical providers, and (in cases where government shares in premium cost) to the government. In its contracts covering Federal employees, the Civil Service Commission has urged carriers to drop the medical referral/supervision requirement. The nationwide "Blues" contract covering Federal employees requires medical referral/supervision; the only other Federal employees contract availabl nationwide (Aetna) does not. CAPPS and others are challenging the "Blues" contract in a multi-million dollar class-action suit.

In the 93rd Congress, the House has passed H.R. 9440, eliminating mandatory medical referral supervision from Federal employees' contracts; a companion bill (S. 2619) has been introduced in the Senate; hearings have been held and Committee action is pending.

Many major health insurance carriers and the nationwide CHAMPUS program do not mandate medical referral/supervision.

The official position of the American Psychiatric Association does not mandate medical referral/supervision over psychological services.

Mandatory medical referral/supervision is an unnecessary and costly procedure which does not contribute to maintaining or improving quality care for the beneficiaries of health-insurance contracts. Mandatory medical referral/supervision is not in the public interest.

DISCUSSION

Like other professions, psychology is operating in a complex society where the availability of services is greatly influenced by external forces such as State and federal statutes requiring licensure/certification; the design of health-delivery systems financed and controlled by State and federal governments; policies of third-party payers such as the health-insurance industry; and the overall need of the public who are recipients of the services.

Currently, forty-six states and the District of Columbia require *statutory* licensure or certification of psychologists.

Psychologists pursue a non-medical approach focused on the behavior of the affected individual; psychologists do not prescribe medication. Whenever a psychologist determines that medical consultation and medical care is indicated for his client, the psychologist is ethically bound to refer the client to a medical doctor.

Psychiatrists are medical doctors with experience and often with special credentials, legally authorized to diagnose and treat mental illness and emotional disturbances pursuant to the "medical model" which includes prescribing medication.

Out of a total manpower pool of approximately 26,000 psychiatrists, it is estimated that 10,000 are in private practice and 8,000 are providing services to human beings in other settings; some 8,000 are in other (non-service) activities. With regard to psychologists, the total manpower pool of clinicians is about 14,000. Of these, psychologists in full-time or part-time private practice represent the equivalent of 5,000 full-time practitioners; another 5,000 provide human services in institutional settings. About 4,000 operate in non-service settings.

Psychology has devoted a substantial amount of its organizational resources to the development of internal standards and controls which complement statutory requirements. For example, the American Psychological Association has established a national peer-review structure. It also operates a national accreditation system for psychology training programs and internships. Its national Code of Ethics is included by references in 23 of the State licensure/certification statutes. (All state laws make some reference to unethical or unprofessional conduct as a reason for refusal or revocation. State regulations often cite the APA code: in some States, however, reference in law to a non-governmental organization is not permitted.)

Having established internal controls and having accepted external statutory constraints, it would appear that psychology should be accorded full professional status. Were this the case, psychologists would be readily available to everyone seeking necessary professional service in connection with mental illness and emotional disorders. Regrettably, thousands of individuals have been denied free choice and access to psychologists because Medicine has refused to recognize psychologists (and other qualified providers of service) as independent providers. The health insurance industry, which accommodates the medical model, has established medical doctors (whether psychiatrists or not) as heads of a mental health "team."

This approach requires all services to be rendered under the supervision of a medical doctor and usually only after referral from a medical doctor to another member of the "team."

Thus, an insured individual may be denied direct access to such professionals as psychologists and optometrists unless a medical doctor makes the initial referral and/or is supervising the care. All too often, the insured is unaware of these restrictions in his policy until faced with the need to obtain and pay for services, often learning too late that payment to the provider or reimbursement to the insured will be denied.

The medical referral/supervision requirement is an unnecessary and costly burden on the patient, the non-medical providers, and on the medical profession itself. The referral and supervisory visits to the medical doctor are chargeable expenses borne by the insured and insurer. Whenever the government is involved, the government pays: the cost is borne by federal employees who pay part of the premium and by the U.S. Treasury which pays the remainder.

Parenthetically it should be noted that not all federal employee health insurance contracts with the Civil Service Commission require medical referral and supervision. The nationwide "Blues" contract does require medical referral/supervision. The Aetna contract, available nationwide like the "Blues," does not.

(Seeking relief in the public interest from needless mandatory referral and supervision requirements, the Council for the Advancement of the Psychological Professions and Sciences (CAPPS) is leading a multi-million dollar class-action against the national Blue Cross-Blue Shield and the Civil Service Commission. The suit challenges the medical referral clause of their contract covering several million workers. Complainants in this action include individual federal employees, a leading union of federal employees, individual psychologists, and psychological associations.)

An important development on the national level includes the passage of H.R. 9440 by the House of Representatives on March 5, 1974. This measure is a national "freedom-of-choice" act which will forbid medical referral/supervision requirements in any insurance contract with the Civil Service Commission covering federal employees. An identical proposal (S. 2619) has been introduced in the U.S. Senate. Hearings have been held and Committee action is pending.

Some major national health insurance carriers, recognizing the inequities of mandatory medical referral/supervision, have voluntarily included psychology as a qualified provider of services in many of their contracts. These firms include, but are not limited to: Aetna, Guardian, Liberty Mutual, Massachusetts Mutual, Occidental, Prudential and Travelers.

Similar recognition of psychologists as independent providers was initiated by the Civilian Health and Manpower Program for Uniformed Servicemen

(CHAMPUS) in July 1970. The inclusion of psychological services without medical referral has been well received by retired military personnel and dependents of servicemen covered in the CHAMPUS program.

The autonomy of psychology and other non-medical disciplines has been recognized by the American Psychiatric Association. Its position paper on "Psychiatrists Relationship with Non-medical Mental Health Professionals" states in part:

". . . Every professional group has a right to establish and maintain its identity and independence by defining its own functions and areas of competence, setting up its own educational and training programs, and establishing its own standards of service. As a responsibility to the public, society may recognize the profession and set up such controls as it may deem necessary. No profession should attempt to define the functions and responsibilities of any other profession.

". . . Professionals in various allied fields often elect to engage independently in health-related practices in a non-medical setting. A person should feel free to select the practitioner of his choice from among qualified professionals. If there is a public demand for health-related services that are not normally regarded as medical or offered as part of a total medical treatment program, insurance companies may offer insurance for such health-related services as they currently do for medical treatment. If the federal government wishes to provide publicly supported programs for such services, appropriate legislation will have to be passed."

At the State level, nineteen (19) States have enacted "freedom-of-choice" statutes requiring insurance carriers to reimburse their policyholders for the diagnosis and treatment of mental and nervous disorders whether the services are rendered by a psychologist or not. It should be noted that "freedom-of-choice" laws *do not require insurance carriers to cover the diagnosis and treatment of mental and nervous disorders.* They merely establish that psychologists and psychiatrists and non-psychiatrist physicians shall be treated equally *when they provide covered services.*

The nineteen "freedom-of-choice" States include: California, Colorado, Illinois, Kansas, Kentucky, Maryland, Massachusetts, Michigan, Mississippi, Montana, Nebraska, New Jersey, New York, Ohio, Oklahoma, Tennessee, Utah, Virginia, and Washington.

The population covered in these States far exceeds a majority of the population of the United States.

To our knowledge, "freedom-of-choice" has not resulted in any additional premiums or exceptional increases in utilization. These laws, which have been well received by the public, may very well be responsible for better health care and lower costs. Studies have shown that the availability of mental health care often reduces the utilization of other medical services. "Elimination of referral/supervision requirements eliminates interference by a third-party medical doctor in establishing and maintaining the psychologist-client relationship. It simplifies access to psychologists. It simplifies claim-reimbursement procedures. It maximizes the utilization of available health-service manpower especially in areas with an inadequate supply of psychiatrists. It eliminates unnecessary expenditures of sick-leave by employees for physician visits.

It is common practice for *non-physician* personnel in the office of a supervising medical doctor to complete the "mental health team reports" required by insurers. This frequently amounts to nothing more than "paper work" as indicated in a recent statement by a spokesman for the Civil Service Commission about the reports: ". . . If a patient submits his claim every ninety days, then the mental health team physician's report must be completed every ninety days; if the claim is submitted every thirty days, the physician's report must be completed every thirty days. It does not, however, mean that the physician must see the patient that often. The physician's *office* (emphasis added) can complete the form without seeing the patient except for the required visit every twelve months."

This kind of paper "supervision" is invariably chargeable to the insured and insurer as an office visit at the prevailing rate—estimated to range from $10 to $40!

O

Lightning Source UK Ltd.
Milton Keynes UK
UKHW011000100119
335176UK00007B/261/P